AutoCAD® 2004
Bible

Ellen Finkelstein

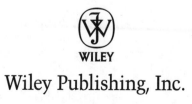

WILEY

Wiley Publishing, Inc.

AutoCAD® 2004 Bible

Published by
Wiley Publishing, Inc.
10475 Crosspoint Boulevard
Indianapolis, IN 46256
www.wiley.com

Library of Congress Control Number: 2003101902

ISBN: 0-7645-3992-2

Manufactured in the United States of America

10 9 8 7 6 5 4 3 2 1

1B/SS/QV/QT/IN

For general information on our other products and services or to obtain technical support, please contact our Customer Care Department within the U.S. at (800) 762-2974, outside the U.S. at (317) 572-3993 or fax (317) 572-4002.

Wiley also publishes its books in a variety of electronic formats. Some content that appears in print may not be available in electronic books.

About the Author

Ellen Finkelstein learned AutoCAD in Israel, where she always got to pore over the manual because it was in English. After returning to the United States, she started consulting and teaching AutoCAD as well as other computer programs, including Microsoft Word, Excel, and PowerPoint. Ellen has written books on Word, Power-Point, and Flash (such as *Flash MX For Dummies,* published by Wiley). Her first book was *AutoCAD For Dummies Quick Reference.* You're holding the fourth edition of this book, which previously appeared for AutoCAD releases 14, 2000, and 2002.

Credits

Acquisitions Editor
Tom Heine

Project Editor
Jade Williams

Technical Editor
Darren Young

Copy Editor
Jerelind Charles

Editorial Manager
Rev Mengle

Vice President & Executive Group Publisher
Richard Swadley

Vice President and Executive Publisher
Bob Ipsen

Vice President and Publisher
Barry Pruett

Project Coordinator
Ryan Steffen

Graphics and Production Specialists
Beth Brooks, Amanda Carter,
Jennifer Click, Sean Decker,
Kristin McMullan, Heather Pope

Quality Control Technicians
Laura Albert, Andy Hollandbeck,
Susan Moritz, Angel Perez,
Carl William Pierce

Permissions Editor
Laura Moss

Media Development Specialist
Gregory Stafford

Proofreading and Indexing
TECHBOOKS Production Services

Cover Image
Anthony Stuart

To MMY for teaching me that there's more to life than meets the eye and that the deeper levels of life are the most powerful.

Foreword

We are delighted to see Wiley's latest update to the very successful AutoCAD Bibles by Ellen Finkelstein. As has oft been noted, if nature didn't make it, someone using Autodesk design software probably did. Autodesk understands better each day that our value proposition is to constantly deliver performance and productivity improvements to you, the users of our products. Delivering on this proposition requires more than great software — such as the recently released AutoCAD 2004 — with the features you need. True productivity improvement also means having available additional resources, services and support. These additional resources make you more productive as you apply Autodesk products to solve your design challenges. The new *AutoCAD 2004 Bible* is a noteworthy addition to this pool of resources you will want at your fingertips.

The creation of Autodesk Professional Services (APS) is a recent example of our commitment to continuously improve your design performance. APS was organized to meet your increasing needs for support, training, and consulting. Almost everything we do assumes a collaborative partnership-based approach. Indeed, "none of us are as smart as all of us" is a principle upon which Autodesk was founded. In 2002 we were able to truly celebrate our 20th anniversary because of this "great group" model and the magic that happens when committed people collaborate with common goals. This includes our increased work with the "virtual" Autodesk enterprise — publishers such as Wiley and experts such as Ellen Finkelstein — to bring you impressive resources that support your Autodesk software. APS is thus able to ensure that you increasingly get the best solutions by assembling just the right combination of features, support, and learning resources.

AutoCAD is a powerful 2D and 3D design and drafting platform that automates your design tasks and provides digital tools so you can focus on the design rather than the software itself. Architects, engineers, drafters, and design-related professionals use AutoCAD to create, view, manage, plot, share, and reuse accurate, information-rich drawings. In addition to software improvements, we are focusing more on supporting the entire process of collaborative design. You'll appreciate the drawing enhancements we've packed into AutoCAD 2004 such as Express Tools which reduce the steps required to perform a task, and the Publish to Web's XML-based i-drop™ publishing capability. New and improved data exchange features include support of multisheet Design Web Format (DWF) files for securely exchanging drawings over the Internet with team members. These new timesaving drawing tools minimize the number of steps you have to take, freeing you and your team to explore more design options — and create even more outstanding designs.

After 20 years we can say, to paraphrase on old marketing line, "This isn't your father's AutoCAD!" Your work today is not just about powering great designs with AutoCAD's productivity and performance tools. AutoCAD enables you to collaborate with others to extend the value of your designs — and maximize the value of your design data across your entire organization. You also need to easily acquire, integrate, deploy, and manage your software assets to increase workflow and affect your bottom line.

However, you can only benefit from what you know and use. Introducing these innovations also poses new challenges, namely learning how to apply these enhancements to the jobs you face. We have done much to address these challenges within AutoCAD, yet the full solution must be more than what Autodesk alone can provide — hence the critical role of the Autodesk virtual community.

We are therefore particularly grateful to Ellen Finkelstein for having written such a comprehensive and reliable guide to AutoCAD, and to the people at Wiley for making it so widely available. Following on the great success of the AutoCAD 2002 Bible, this new version draws upon lessons learned from reader feedback. To get maximum value and performance from AutoCAD, you should have the AutoCAD 2004 Bible right at your fingertips. It will enable you to respond to the unexpected, which is the norm on the job these days. Use it to augment the digital learning resources that come with your software: AutoCAD Learning Assistance, AutoCAD Today, the Help system, and the online resources of Autodesk Point A and Autodesk ProjectPoint which is seamlessly integrated into AutoCAD. You will be even more productive if you use the AutoCAD 2004 Bible to discover the myriad capabilities of AutoCAD you probably weren't aware even existed. However you use it, when you combine the features in AutoCAD with the support of the AutoCAD 2004 Bible, you will discover daily breakthroughs and productivity boosters as you use AutoCAD to power your designs.

Wayne Hodgins

Strategic Futurist
Director of Worldwide Learning Strategies
Autodesk Professional Services
www.autodesk.com & www.discreet.com

Preface

Welcome to the AutoCAD 2004 Bible. AutoCAD 2004 is the most powerful CAD software product available for PCs today. It can perform nearly any drawing task you can give it. This book is designed to be your comprehensive guide to the entire AutoCAD program.

AutoCAD 2004 is the fastest, smoothest AutoCAD yet. Certain features have been added that are not even mentioned in this book because you never see them — you just notice that fewer regenerations occur, drawings load faster, and you spend less time waiting while drawing and editing. Files are automatically and invisibly compressed, so they take up less room on your computer system. In addition to these refinements, of course, are the many new features covered in this book that will make your drawing easier and faster. This book covers every major AutoCAD feature. If you're a beginning AutoCAD user, you'll find everything you need to start out; if you're already using AutoCAD regularly, the book covers advanced material as well. It provides a solid reference base to come back to again and again, as well as short tutorials to get you drawing. Finally, the CD-ROM is chockfull of drawings, a trial version of AutoCAD 2004, and AutoLISP programs. This book should be all you need to make full use of that expensive program called AutoCAD.

Is This Book for You?

The *AutoCAD 2004 Bible* covers all the essential features of AutoCAD and includes clear, real-life examples and tutorials that you can adapt to your needs.

Although I fully cover AutoCAD basics, I have also included material on the many advanced features, such as external database connectivity, AutoLISP, Visual Basic for Applications (VBA), 3D modeling, rendering, and customization. The following categories should help you decide if this book is for you.

If you are a new AutoCAD user

If you are new to AutoCAD, the *AutoCAD 2004 Bible* guides you through all you need to know to start drawing effectively, whatever your field.

If you are upgrading to AutoCAD 2004

This book highlights all the new features of AutoCAD 2004 and helps you make the upgrade transition as seamless as possible.

If you are switching from another CAD program

You already know what CAD is all about. This book clearly explains the AutoCAD way of drawing the models you have already been drawing. In addition, you'll find a great deal of essential information about transferring information from other formats.

How This Book Is Organized

This book is divided into eight parts.

Part I: AutoCAD Basics

Part I provides the background information you need to start drawing. It starts with a "quick tour" that gets you drawing right away, and then covers how to start a drawing, use commands, specify coordinates, and set up a drawing.

Part II: Drawing in Two Dimensions

Part II covers all the commands and procedures for drawing and editing in two dimensions. In addition, I discuss how to control the drawing process with layers, zooming, and panning. Also included in this part is information about dimensioning, plotting, and printing.

Part III: Working with Data

Part III covers many ways to organize and share data, including blocks, attributes, external references, and external databases.

Part IV: Drawing in Three Dimensions

Part IV explains everything you need to know to draw in three dimensions. It also discusses how to present 3D drawings using hiding, shading, and rendering techniques.

Part V: Organizing and Managing Drawings

Part V helps you incorporate AutoCAD into your work world by explaining how to set standards, manage drawings, and work with other applications. It concludes with a chapter on AutoCAD and the Internet. Many of the new features of AutoCAD 2004 are explained in this part.

Part VI: Customizing AutoCAD

Part VI introduces the tools you need to customize commands, toolbars, linetypes, hatch patterns, shapes, fonts, and menus. You'll also find a chapter on script files, which you can use to create macros.

Part VII: Programming AutoCAD

Part VII introduces you to programming AutoCAD. It includes three chapters on AutoLISP and Visual LISP and one chapter on Visual Basic for Applications.

Part VIII: Appendix

Part VIII explains what you'll find on the CD-ROM.

Cross-Reference

The CD-ROM contains a complete copy of this book in PDF format and four appendixes of useful information for AutoCAD users.

How to Use This Book

You can use this book in two ways: as a reference or as a learning tool or tutorial.

As a reference

The *AutoCAD 2004 Bible* is organized as a reference that you can refer to whenever you get stuck or when you try to do something for the first time. Each chapter covers a topic completely, making it easy to find what you're looking for. Each Step-by-Step exercise (with a few exceptions) can be done on its own without doing the other exercises in the chapter. You can easily look up a topic and complete a related exercise without having to go through the entire chapter. A complete index at the back of the book can also help you look up features and topics.

As a tutorial

The overall organization of the book goes from simple to complex, and each chapter has several Step-by-Step sections. This enables you to use the book as a tutorial — from beginning to end. You can then go back and redo any exercise when you need to refresh your memory on a particular feature.

For newcomers to AutoCAD, Parts I and II are essential. After that, you can refer to chapters that interest you. Parts III and V are also useful for beginners. Intermediate users will probably be familiar with most of the material in Part I and will be more likely to skip around looking for the specific topics they need. However, don't forget that many of the new features for AutoCAD 2004 are introduced in Part I. Enough material appears in this book to bring intermediate users up to a fairly advanced level.

I have designed this book to be comprehensive and to include every significant feature of AutoCAD. Therefore, do not be concerned if some of the material seems too advanced. It will be there when you are ready for it.

Doing the Exercises

AutoCAD is a very customizable program. This book assumes that you are working with the default setup. However, a number of changes may have been made to your system that could result in menus, toolbars, and drawings appearing or even functioning differently from those shown in this book. If you installed AutoCAD yourself and made some adjustments, you know what changes you made. However, if you are using a computer that was set up by someone else, it may help to talk to that person first, to see what changes were made.

In addition, as you work through some of the exercises in this book, you will make certain changes in AutoCAD's setup. Most of these are minor changes that any user would make while drawing. For safety, Cautions and Tips accompany all changes that could have serious consequences, such as customizing the menu. For example, when customizing the menu, you will be instructed to copy the menu template file under a new name, and you will then work with the new menu file, not the original one. Nevertheless, if you are working on a network or sharing AutoCAD with someone else, it is proper computer etiquette to consult with others who may be affected by the changes you make.

If you do the exercises, I recommend that you do them from the beginning. Important instructions are given during earlier exercises that may affect your system later. For example, one of the first exercises is to create a new folder to hold your drawings from the exercises. This folder keeps your exercise drawings separate from other drawings created in your office. However, each exercise stands on its own so you can go back and do only the exercise you need.

 Cross-Reference You can create your own AutoCAD configuration that helps ensure that some changes you make will not affect others. Instructions for doing this appear in Appendix A, "Creating Multiple Configurations," on the CD-ROM.

The exercises in the *AutoCAD 2004 Bible* have been carefully checked by a technical editor to ensure accuracy. However, we cannot anticipate all situations, either due to varying hardware/software configurations or customization within AutoCAD. If you have a problem with an exercise, contact me at the e-mail address listed at the end of this Preface so I can correct the problem in the book's next edition.

Conventions Used in This Book

Given all the ways in which you can execute a command in AutoCAD, you'll find it useful to read through this section, which describes this book's typographical conventions. You will find this section helpful for doing the Step-by-Step exercises as well.

AutoCAD commands

AutoCAD uses standard Windows conventions for menus and toolbars. To indicate that you should choose a command from the menu, for example, I say, "Choose View ⇨ Viewports," which means that you should click the View menu with your mouse or puck/stylus and then click the Viewports menu item. A few of AutoCAD's toolbar buttons have flyouts, which are equivalent to submenus. They are called flyouts because they fly out when you click and hold the button on the main toolbar, displaying even more buttons. Therefore, to indicate which button to choose, I may need to tell you to choose (or click) Zoom Extents from the Zoom flyout of the Standard toolbar. Although I haven't found a good alternative, this is not completely satisfactory for two reasons. First, it's a mouthful! Second, the flyout names do not appear, making it hard to know which is the Zoom flyout. However, you can check Appendix B on the CD-ROM. It shows each toolbar and flyout along with its name. Also, in most cases it will be obvious which flyout I'm talking about.

AutoCAD is unique in that every command also has a command name that you can type on the command line, which appears at the bottom of your screen. Command names are shown in capital letters, as in CIRCLE. AutoLISP functions are shown in small capital letters, as in COMMAND.

AutoCAD prompts, your input, and instructions

In the Step-by-Step exercises, most instructions are presented in the same font and style you are reading now. However, when I reproduce the AutoCAD command line, AutoCAD's prompts appear in a nonproportional font and the input you should type in appears in bold. Other instructions (such as "Type in the first coordinate") are shown in italic.

Here's a sample Step-by-Step section. In this exercise, you click the proper toolbar button, type in the X,Y coordinates shown in bold, and press Enter where indicated by the bent arrow (↵) symbol.

1. With your left mouse button (also called the pick button), choose Line from the Draw toolbar. Notice that the command name is repeated on the command line.

```
Command: _line Specify first point: 0,0 ↵ (This arrow means
to press Enter)
Specify next point or [Undo]: 10,0 ↵
Specify next point or [Undo]: 10,7 ↵
Specify next point or [Close/Undo]: 0,7 ↵
Specify next point or [Close/Undo]: 0,0 ↵
Specify next point or [Close/Undo]: ↵
```

Often I make references to specific elements in a drawing. References to these elements appear in the text as numbers in circles, such as ❶, ❷, ❸, and so on. You'll find the corresponding number in the figure to which the text refers.

Mouse and keyboard terms

You can draw in AutoCAD using a mouse or a puck. The mouse is familiar to all users. A puck (or sometimes a stylus) is used with a digitizing tablet. Because most AutoCAD users do not have a digitizing tablet, I do not directly refer to it in this book. If you have one, follow the instructions for using the mouse in the same way, using your puck.

A mouse can have two or more buttons. Many AutoCAD users like using a mouse with at least three buttons because you can customize the buttons to suit your needs. However, because many mice have only two buttons, I assume only two. The left mouse button is used to choose commands and toolbar buttons and to pick points in your drawing. For this reason, it is sometimes called the pick button. The right button usually opens a shortcut menu.

AutoCAD 2004 introduces time-sensitive right-clicking. Because this feature is not on by default, I do not assume that you have turned it on. I use the term *right-click* when you need to access a shortcut menu. If you have time-sensitive right-clicking turned on, you need to hold down the right mouse button more than 250 milliseconds (by default) to display the shortcut menu. See Chapter 3 and Appendix A on the CD-ROM for more details.

If I say one of the following

✦ Choose Tools ➪ Options

✦ Click Line on the Draw toolbar

✦ Select the circle in your drawing

it means to use the left button of your mouse.

When I say to press Enter, it means to press the key that is marked Enter, Return, or ↵ on your keyboard. Often I use the bent arrow symbol (↵) to indicate that you should press Enter.

I also use the mouse terms listed in the following table.

AutoCAD Mouse Terms	
Term	*Description*
Cursor	The shape on your screen that shows you where the mouse is pointed. It can take a number of shapes, such as crosshairs, pickbox, or arrow. Also known as the mouse pointer.
Pickbox	A type of cursor consisting of a small box, used to select drawing objects.
Crosshairs	A type of cursor consisting of intersecting lines.
Pick	Point to a drawing object and click the left mouse button.
Click	Press the left mouse button once and release it.
Double-click	Press the left mouse button twice in rapid succession.
Click and drag	Click the left mouse button and hold it down while you move the mouse, dragging an object on your screen with it.
Choose	Click a menu item, toolbar button, or dialog box item. You can sometimes choose an item using the keyboard as well.
Right-click	Press the right mouse button once and release it. If you have turned on time-sensitive right-clicking, hold the right mouse button at least 250 milliseconds (by default) before releasing it.
Shift and click	While holding down the Shift key, press the left mouse button once and release it.
Shift and right-click	While holding down the Shift key, press the right mouse button once and release it.
Select	Highlight an object in a drawing by picking it or using another object selection method, or highlight text in a dialog box or text document.

What the Icons Mean

The *AutoCAD 2004 Bible* is liberally sprinkled with icons — small symbols in the left margin that call your attention to noteworthy points.

New Feature The New Feature icon means that a feature is new to AutoCAD 2004 or has been significantly changed.

Note A Note icon alerts you to some important point that requires special attention or additional information that may be helpful.

Tip A Tip shows you a way to accomplish a task more efficiently or quickly. You'll find plenty of practical advice here.

Cross-Reference Cross-References refer you to a related topic elsewhere in the book. Because you may not read this book straight through from cover to cover, use cross-references to quickly find just the information you need.

On the CD-ROM The On the CD-ROM icon highlights references to related material on the CD-ROM.

Caution The Caution icon means you should pay special attention to the information or instructions because a possibility exists that you could cause a problem otherwise.

About the CD-ROM

The CD-ROM contains all the drawings you need to do the exercises in this book. These drawings save you time as you learn AutoCAD's features. In addition, the CD-ROM includes the drawings that result after you finish an exercise or tutorial. In this way, you can check what you have done if you want.

The CD-ROM is also chockfull of resource material that I hope you will find useful for many years to come. The Appendix at the back of the book lists the contents of the CD-ROM. I am especially pleased to include a 30-day trial version of AutoCAD 2004 on the CD-ROM as well as this entire book in (nonprintable) PDF format.

Other Information

If you are an advanced AutoCAD user but need tips and secrets for getting the most out of AutoCAD, this book will probably not add too much to your already great store of knowledge.

If you want to learn about Windows, look for a book that focuses on Windows. This book assumes that you know the basics of Windows, although the instructions you'll read here are usually detailed enough to get you through any task. For more information about Windows, try *Windows XP For Dummies*, by Andy Rathbone, or try *Alan Simpson's Windows XP Bible* (both published by Wiley, Inc.). For Windows NT, try *Teach Yourself Windows 2000 Professional VISUALLY*, by Ruth Maran, or *Windows 2000 Professional For Dummies*, by Andy Rathbone and Sharon Crawford (both also published by Wiley).

If you want just the basics, AutoCAD LT might serve your needs better. However, if you do have AutoCAD and want a more basic book, look at *AutoCAD 2004 For Dummies*, by Bud Smith and Mark Middlebrook. The *AutoCAD 2004 Bible* covers AutoCAD 2004. However, most of the information also applies to Release 2002. I have used AutoCAD in Windows XP Professional, but almost everything also applies to Windows NT (4 and 2000), although some of the screens will look different.

Contacting the Author

I would be happy to hear any comments you have about this book. The best way to contact me is by e-mail at ellenfinkl@bigfoot.com. You can also use the United States postal service (aka snail mail) and write to me in care of Wiley. Please note that I can't provide AutoCAD technical support for my readers.

Acknowledgments

I would like to offer special thanks to Tom Heine, my acquisitions editor, who was very supportive throughout the writing of this book.

A huge thank you goes to Jade Williams, whose infinite organizing power kept the book on track. Jade kept up with a seemingly infinite number of versions of text documents and images, coordinating the writing, editing, and production of the entire book.

Kudos to Darren Young, an Autodesk Registered Developer (http://www.mcwi.com), for his extremely knowledgeable and thorough technical editing. Darren's comments improved the book throughout. Darren also updated the customization and programming chapters for this book.

Chapters 34–37 contain contributions by Jerry Coley and the development team at Perceptual Engineering, Inc., an Autodesk Registered Developer, including Stephen S. Green, Estenio R. Gimenez, and William McArthur (www.perceptual-eng.com).

I also thank Jerelind Charles for her precise and careful editing of this very technical book and all the people at Wiley who helped with the production of this book and its CD-ROM.

Thanks to Wayne Hodgins, Strategic Futurist and Director of Worldwide Learning Strategies, for writing the Foreword for this book. I also want to express my great appreciation to the members of Autodesk's beta and product teams who were very supportive throughout the alpha and beta period. For all their hard work and brilliance, they have earned some homemade cookies and a free copy of this book. Shaan Hurley (the great), Traci Van Patten, Misha Belilovskiy, Eric Stover, Bud Shroeder, Kurt Chase, Wayne Fisher, Cynde Hargrave, and anyone else I forgot.

Leonid Nemirovsky created two AutoLISP routines for managing single-line text (on the CD-ROM) at my request. Many people contributed drawings and software for this book. I'd like to thank all of them. They have helped make this book the most comprehensive book on AutoCAD available.

Finally, I would like to thank my husband, Evan, and two kids, Yeshayah and Eliyah, who helped out around the house while I was writing, writing, and writing (and who wanted to see their names in print). Without their support, I could not have completed this book.

Contents at a Glance

Contents

Part II: Drawing in Two Dimensions 107

Chapter 6: Drawing Simple Lines 109

Chapter 7: Drawing Curves and Point Objects 119

Chapter 8: Viewing Your Drawing 137

Part V: Organizing and Managing Drawings 901

Chapter 26: Keeping Control of Your Drawings 903

Part VII: Programming AutoCAD — 1113

AutoCAD Basics

The five chapters in Part I provide all the basics you need to start drawing in AutoCAD. These chapters are essential for the beginner, but even current users can find some new tips and pointers especially related to features that are new for AutoCAD 2004. If you feel you know enough to skip to Part II, skim this part for New Feature icons to bring yourself up-to-date.

Starting to Draw

Learning AutoCAD is a bit like trying to decide which came first — the chicken or the egg. On one hand, you need to know many basics before you can start drawing. On the other hand, it can be very difficult to understand those basics if you haven't had the experience of drawing something. In this chapter, you resolve this problem by drawing a simple rectangle in AutoCAD. The next few chapters then fill you in on basic information you need to move on to more complex drawings. By experiencing the drawing process first, the initial learning curve will be easier and smoother.

Getting Acquainted with AutoCAD

AutoCAD, created by Autodesk, is the most widely used technical drawing program anywhere, with more than 3 million registered users. According to Autodesk, CAD stands for *computer-aided design*, but can also stand for computer-aided drafting or drawing.

The first version of AutoCAD, running under DOS, came out in 1982. AutoCAD was the first significant CAD program to run on a desktop computer. At the time, most other technical drawing programs ran on high-end workstations or even mainframes. AutoCAD's success has been attributed to its famous open architecture — many source code files in plain text (ASCII) files that you can easily customize and programming languages (such as AutoLISP and Visual Basic for Applications) designed especially so that the end user can program AutoCAD.

As a result, AutoCAD is the most flexible drafting program available, applicable to all fields. AutoCAD's support for languages other than English, including those using other alphabets, is unparalleled, making AutoCAD without serious competition abroad. As a result, AutoCAD is used in all disciplines and in more than 150 countries.

Through a high level of technical innovation and expertise, Autodesk has created a program with unequaled features and capabilities, including 3D surface and solid modeling and visualization, access to external databases, intelligent dimensioning, importing and exporting of other file formats, Internet support, and much more.

The major disciplines that use AutoCAD are:

✦ Architectural, Engineering, and Construction (AEC)

✦ Mechanical

✦ Geographic Information Systems (GIS),

✦ Surveying and Civil Engineering

✦ Facilities management

✦ Electrical/electronic

✦ Multimedia

However, AutoCAD has many other lesser-known uses, such as pattern making in the garment industry, sign making, and so on.

In this book, I try to provide examples from many fields. The world of AutoCAD is very broad, and it is worthwhile to see the many approaches that AutoCAD makes possible.

Starting AutoCAD

This section starts the quick tour of AutoCAD, designed to make AutoCAD look easy and simple. The first step is to start AutoCAD.

On the CD-ROM The CD-ROM contains a 30-day trial version of AutoCAD 2004. Look in `\Software\AutoCAD 2004`.

This book covers AutoCAD 2004 running on Windows 2000, Windows NT 4.0, or Windows XP/XP Professional. Every computer is set up somewhat differently, so you may need to adjust the following steps slightly. If you didn't install AutoCAD yourself and are unfamiliar with the folders (once called directories) on your computer, you should get help from someone who is familiar with your computer system.

Cross-Reference If you need help installing AutoCAD, see Appendix A on the CD-ROM.

By default, installing AutoCAD places a shortcut on your desktop, as shown in Figure 1-1. You can double-click this shortcut to launch AutoCAD. Of course, you can also choose Start ➪ Programs ➪ Autodesk ➪ AutoCAD 2004 ➪ AutoCAD 2004.

Figure 1-1: An AutoCAD shortcut on the desktop provides a quick way to open AutoCAD.

Creating a New Drawing

After you launch AutoCAD, you are automatically in a new drawing named Drawing1.dwg. You can see the drawing name on the title bar as shown in Figure 1-2. You can start drawing immediately. In Chapter 2, I explain how to start a drawing based on a template and how to open an existing drawing.

Step-by-Step: Starting AutoCAD

1. Click Start on the task bar at the bottom of your screen.

2. Choose Programs ➪ Autodesk ➪ AutoCAD 2004 ➪ AutoCAD 2004.

You see a blank drawing named Drawing1.dwg.

If you are continuing on with this chapter, keep this drawing open. Exiting from AutoCAD is covered later in this chapter.

Using the AutoCAD Interface

You are probably impatient to start drawing. First, though, it helps to get the lay of the land.

Figure 1-2 shows the screen when you first open AutoCAD. Your screen may look somewhat different — remember that AutoCAD can be customized in many ways — but the general features will be the same.

New Feature
You may see the Tool Palettes window with some sample office furniture and hatches. The palette is a way to access content that you insert into your drawing. I cover the Tools Palette in Chapter 26. For now, you can click the palette's close button to get it out of the way. (If you want it back, choose Tools ➪ Tool Palettes Window.)

The AutoCAD screen consists of four important areas. These are discussed in the next sections.

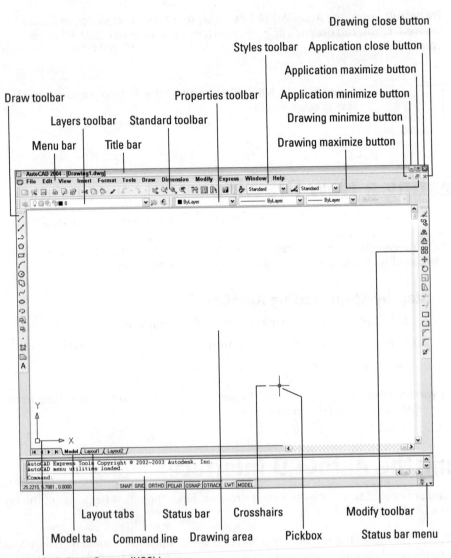

Figure 1-2: The AutoCAD screen

The drawing area

The blank area in the middle of the screen, the *graphics window*, is where you draw. You can think of this as a sheet of drafting paper, except that this piece of paper can be any size—even the size of a huge factory!

At the bottom of the drawing area is a tab labeled Model. You draw on this tab. You use the layout tabs to lay out your drawing for plotting.

When you start to draw, you need to specify where to start drawing. One way is to use coordinates. To specify a coordinate, the universally accepted convention is to put the X coordinate first, then a comma, and then the Y coordinate. Figure 1-3 shows some coordinates on X and Y axes.

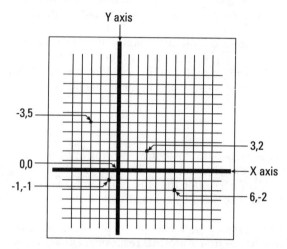

Figure 1-3: Some X,Y coordinates

Chapter 4 is devoted to explaining how to specify coordinates. To create three-dimensional models, you need to add a Z coordinate when specifying a point. Chapter 21 discusses three-dimensional coordinates.

The UCS icon

Notice the symbol with two arrows at the bottom-left corner of the drawing area in Figure 1-2. This symbol is called the User Coordinate System (UCS) icon. The arrows point to the positive directions of the X and Y axes to help you keep your bearings.

You can change the look of this icon. (See Chapter 8.)

The crosshairs

In the drawing area of Figure 1-2, notice the two intersecting lines with a small box at their intersection. The small box is called the *pickbox* because it helps you to pick objects. The lines are called *crosshairs*. They show you the location of the mouse cursor in relation to other objects in your drawing.

As you move your mouse around, the pickbox and crosshairs move with your mouse. At the bottom of your screen, at the left end of the status bar (described later), you can see the X,Y coordinates changing as you move the mouse.

The menus and toolbars

At the top of your screen is the title bar, and directly beneath the title bar is a menu bar. Below that are two rows of toolbars. In addition, your screen has two more toolbars, the Draw and Modify toolbars, which are probably docked at the left and right sides of the screen, as shown in Figure 1-2. Use the menus and toolbars together to give AutoCAD commands to draw, edit, get information, and so on.

Because you can customize the menus and toolbars to suit your needs, your screen may appear somewhat different. AutoCAD provides many more toolbars that you can display when you need them. Some examples of the toolbars are Dimension, Solids, Render, and Zoom. You learn about these and more in this book.

The command line

At the bottom of the screen, you see a separate window showing approximately three lines of text. (You can change it to show as many lines as you like by dragging the top edge of the window up or down.) Notice the word Command:. This is the *command line*. All commands can be executed by typing them on the command line.

Even if you use a menu item or toolbar button to execute a command, you may need to look at the command line to see how AutoCAD responds. Often, AutoCAD provides options that must be typed in from the keyboard. Also, text that you type appears on the command line. For example, when you type in coordinates specifying a point, they appear on the command line. To see more of the command line, press F2 to open the AutoCAD Text window. You can scroll back through previous commands. Press F2 again to close the window.

The status bar

At the very bottom of the screen is the status bar, as shown in Figure 1-2. At the left are the X,Y coordinates. As you move your mouse around, these coordinates change. (If they don't change, click them and move your mouse again.) The status bar also sports several buttons that you read about later.

 New Feature

At the right side of the status bar is a small down arrow. Click it to open the Status bar menu. This menu determines which buttons appear on the status bar. If you don't use a certain button, choose it to remove its checkmark and make it disappear. You can always go back and choose it again to redisplay the button. Also at the right side of the status bar is the new Communication Center icon. See Chapter 26 for details.

Also, you can use the Express Tools FULLSCREEN command to hide the Title bar, menu, and status bar, leaving more room for the drawing area. To return to the regular display, type **fullscreen** on the command line and press Enter. See Appendix A on the CD-ROM for information about installing the Express Tools.

Creating Your First Drawing

You are now almost ready to draw your first lines. It is worthwhile first to take a minute to get accustomed to using the toolbars to give AutoCAD a command.

Toolbars

On the Draw toolbar, move the mouse cursor over the first button. You see a Tooltip that says Line, as shown in Figure 1-4. Also notice the status bar, which tells you that this button creates straight-line segments.

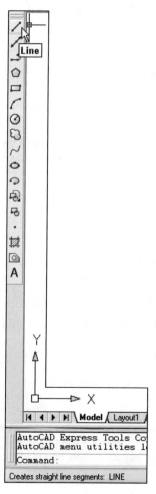

Figure 1-4: Moving the cursor over the Line button displays a Tooltip.

Tip If you inadvertently start a command that you don't want, press Esc. The command-line prompt (`Command:`) returns.

Drawing a rectangle

For this exercise, simply follow the instructions exactly. When you type the X and Y coordinates (shown in bold), type the first number, a comma, and then the second number, with no spaces between them. If you haven't read the Preface, now is a good time to go back and read the part that explains how to follow the exercises. Don't worry if you don't understand everything you are doing. It all becomes clear as you progress through this book.

Follow the prompts shown next. As explained in the Preface, you type what appears in **bold**. Instructions to you in command sections appear in *italics*.

Step-by-Step: Drawing a Rectangle

1. Start AutoCAD.

 AutoCAD displays the new drawing. (If you are prompted for a template, type or choose **acad.dwt**.)

2. With your left mouse button (also called the *pick button*), choose Line from the Draw toolbar. Notice that the command name is repeated on the command line.

   ```
   Command: _line Specify first point: 0,0 ↵ (This arrow means
   to press Enter)
   Specify next point or [Undo]: 10,0 ↵
   Specify next point or [Undo]: 10,7 ↵
   Specify next point or [Close/Undo]: 0,7 ↵
   Specify next point or [Close/Undo]: 0,0 ↵
   Specify next point or [Close/Undo]: ↵
   ```

 The command-line prompt appears again, ready for a new command.

3. To make the rectangle fill up the screen, type the following, shown in bold:

   ```
   Command: zoom ↵
   Specify corner of window, enter a scale factor (nX or nXP),
   or
   [All/Center/Dynamic/Extents/Previous/Scale/Window] <real
   time>: e ↵
   ```

Cross-Reference The rectangle is centered and fills most of the screen, leaving a small space at the edges of the drawing area. The ZOOM command with the Extents (e) option brings the outer extents of the drawing to the edges of your screen. You read more about the ZOOM command in Chapter 8.

4. Keep your drawing open. You save it later in this chapter. It should look like the image shown in Figure 1-5.

Figure 1-5: Your first drawing

You may be wondering what units the coordinates you typed refer to. For now, you can think of them as inches, although they can actually be whatever you want. As a result, you could print out your drawing as a rectangle of 10 inches by 7 inches.

Help! My drawing doesn't look like the figure

If your drawing doesn't look like the image shown in Figure 1-5, there could be several reasons. To fix the problem, try one of the following options:

+ You may have made a mistake. If you think that's the case, choose File ⇨ New to start a second new drawing, choose the acad.dwt template and click Open. Then follow the prompts again.

+ If your drawing still seems wrong, put the CD-ROM that accompanies this book in your CD-ROM drive. Choose File ⇨ Open and use the Open dialog box to find ab-acad.dwg on the CD-ROM. Choose ab-acad.dwg and click Open. Then follow the prompts again.

One of the preceding options should solve your problem. If you began more than one new drawing, you probably have more than one drawing currently open. You can switch from one open drawing to another by choosing any open drawing from the Window menu.

You have learned several things — how to start a command by using the toolbar (the LINE command), how to type in X,Y coordinates on the command line, and how to end the LINE command (by pressing Enter without typing any coordinates). You also used the ZOOM command by typing it on the command line. Most of AutoCAD builds on these basic skills.

Saving a Drawing

Saving a drawing is similar to saving any other file in Windows. You should get in the habit of saving your work every 10 to 15 minutes to avoid losing your work in case your computer system crashes.

For your work with this book, you should create a new folder so that you can save your exercise drawings where they won't get mixed up with other drawings. Although saving is a standard Windows function, I review the steps here because they are so important.

The following directions leave it up to you where to create this new folder. Each computer system is organized differently. If you are unsure what to do, choose the drive (not the folder) where AutoCAD is installed and create a new folder there. I do not recommend creating a subfolder in AutoCAD's folder (which by default is called *AutoCAD 2004*) because it is too easy to make a mistake and delete necessary AutoCAD files.

Step-by-Step: Creating a New Folder

1. Move the mouse cursor down to the task bar at the bottom of your screen and right-click Start. (That means, click the Start button with your right mouse button.)

2. Choose Explore.

3. On the left pane of Windows Explorer, click the drive where you want to create the new folder. If you don't know where to create the folder, choose the drive where AutoCAD is installed. If you are on a network, choose the drive that represents your computer.

4. If you want to make a subfolder (a folder within a folder), choose the folder where you want to create the subfolder.

5. From the Explorer menu, choose File ⇨ New ⇨ Folder.

 A new, highlighted folder, named New Folder, appears in the right pane. You may have to scroll down to see it.

6. Type **AutoCAD Bible** for the folder name and press Enter. (If you did the exercises from a previous edition of this book, such as *AutoCAD 2002 Bible*, and already have a folder named AutoCAD Bible, first rename the original folder to something such as ACAD2002Bible.)

Now you are ready to save your drawing. Saving a drawing for the first time is different from saving it subsequently because you have to name the drawing the first time you save it. The important point is to save the drawing in the right drive and folder. You should save this drawing (and all drawings you create by using this book) in the special folder you created in the exercise just completed.

Caution Creating a folder for your drawings as described in the previous steps is essential before you go on to exercises in the rest of this book.

To save a drawing, click Save on the Standard toolbar. If you are saving a drawing for the first time, the Save Drawing As dialog box appears, as shown in Figure 1-6.

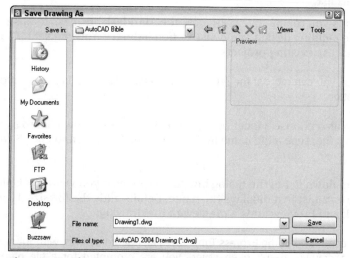

Figure 1-6: The Save Drawing As dialog box

Down the left side of the dialog box are several buttons to help you find a location to save drawings more quickly. Together, these buttons are called the *Places list*. Use the Places list as follows:

✦ **History** lists shortcuts to recently used drawings.

✦ **My Documents** lists drawings and folders in the My Documents folder. Some people store files in this folder. (Your system may call this the Personal folder.)

✦ **Favorites** lists files and folders in the C:\Documents and Settings\[login name]\Favorites folder. (This is the location in Windows XP; it may be different on your computer.) You may have an AutoCAD subfolder; if so, double-click the AutoCAD subfolder to save a drawing there. Usually, this folder

contains only shortcuts to files saved elsewhere. To put a shortcut to an already saved drawing in Favorites, choose File ⇨ Save As and click the Tools drop-down list; then click Add to Favorites. Then you can later open the file from the Favorites folder.

✦ **FTP** sites are locations on the Internet for transferring files. When you choose FTP, you see FTP sites that you added to the list. To add FTP locations, choose Tools ⇨ Add/Modify FTP Locations from the menu of the Save Drawing As dialog box. You need to list the name of the FTP site, choose a logon type (Anonymous or User), and specify your user name and password if you are logging on as a User. You can then save drawings (called uploading) to FTP locations. This feature makes an intranet or any server with FTP capability as accessible as your own computer system.

✦ **Desktop** shows drawings on your desktop. Some of the Windows icons also appear on this list.

✦ **Buzzsaw** sends you to www.buzzsaw.com, the Autodesk business-to-business portal for the building design and construction industry. You can set up a new account or access existing projects.

Tip In a nice touch, you can reorder the buttons in the Places list. Just drag any button to a new location.

Of course, you can also choose a location from the Save In drop-down list to save the file to. To save a file, type a file name in the File Name text box and click Save to save the file.

Use the Views drop-down list of the dialog box to specify how you want to display files in this dialog box. List just displays the name; Details adds the file size, type, and date modified; and Preview adds a preview of the drawing.

New Feature The SAVEALL command of the Express Tools saves all open drawings, without closing them. If a drawing hasn't been saved, you are prompted for a file name. Choose Express ⇨ File tools ⇨ Save All Drawings. For information on installing Express Tools, see Appendix A on the CD-ROM.

Step-by-Step: Saving a Drawing for the First Time

1. The rectangle you created earlier in this chapter should still be on your screen. Click Save on the Standard toolbar.

 The Save Drawing As dialog box opens.

2. Click the Save In drop-down list box. If necessary, choose the drive where you created your AutoCAD Bible folder.

3. Double-click the AutoCAD Bible folder you created for this book.

 You may need to scroll down to display the folder name.

4. In the File Name box, select the file name. Type **ab01-01** and press Enter (or click Save).

AutoCAD saves your drawing under the name ab01-01.dwg. You can use a different name if you like, but this will help you organize your drawings from this book. It just means that this is the first drawing from Chapter 1 of the *AutoCAD 2004 Bible*.

On the CD-ROM The CD-ROM includes a small program, savea.lsp, that automatically backs up your drawing to the floppy drive after you have saved it on your hard drive. If you like to back up to a diskette regularly for safety, this program can be useful. Look in \Software\Chap01\Savea.

Closing a Drawing and Exiting from AutoCAD

You can close your drawing and keep AutoCAD open. The simplest way is to use the drawing Close button just under the application Close button. You can also choose File ➪ Close.

Tip You can choose Window ➪ Close All to close all open drawings. If any have unsaved changes, AutoCAD prompts you to save the changes. If you installed the Express Tools (see Appendix A on the CD-ROM for details), you can choose Express ➪ File tools ➪ Quick Exit, which closes all open drawings (prompting you to save if necessary) and then exits AutoCAD. You can also choose Express ➪ File tools ➪ Close All Drawings to close all drawings without exiting AutoCAD. You are prompted to save any unsaved changes.

To exit AutoCAD, click the Close (X) box at the top-right corner of your screen. You can also exit out of AutoCAD by typing **quit** on the command line and pressing Enter. Another method is to choose File ➪ Exit.

New Feature If you are in the middle of a command, you can now close a drawing without ending the command.

If you have made any changes to your drawing since last saving it, AutoCAD asks you if you want to save your changes. Choose Yes or No as your situation requires. Choosing Cancel returns you to your drawing. If you have more than one drawing open to which you have made changes, AutoCAD asks you about each drawing in turn so that you will not exit AutoCAD without saving all the changes you have made in your open drawings.

Step-by-Step: Closing Your Drawing and Exiting AutoCAD

1. The rectangle of ab01-01.dwg should still be on your screen. Choose File ➪ Close. You now see a gray screen with no drawing. (Repeat this process if you have other drawings open. Save or cancel the changes to these extra open drawings as you like.)

2. Click the Close button in the upper-right corner to exit AutoCAD. AutoCAD closes immediately.

Summary

Chapter 1 explained how to start AutoCAD and a new drawing. I gave you a tour of the AutoCAD screen and explained how save a drawing. This chapter provides the basis for all your work in AutoCAD.

In this chapter, you learned the following:

- ✦ A brief history of AutoCAD
- ✦ Some of the different disciplines that use AutoCAD
- ✦ How to start AutoCAD
- ✦ How to start a new drawing
- ✦ The AutoCAD interface and its various sections, including the drawing area, the UCS icon, the crosshairs, the menus and toolbars, the command line, and the status bar
- ✦ How to start the LINE command from a toolbar
- ✦ How to end the LINE command
- ✦ How to draw a rectangle by specifying X,Y coordinates
- ✦ How to start the ZOOM command by typing it on the command line
- ✦ How to save a drawing for the first time
- ✦ How to close a drawing
- ✦ How to exit AutoCAD

You may have several questions at this point, but "well begun is half done." The next chapter explains all the ways to start a new drawing as well as how to open an existing drawing.

✦　　✦　　✦

Opening a Drawing

AutoCAD offers a number of options for opening new and existing drawings. These options create a great deal of flexibility and save you time as well. You can create complex templates to avoid doing the same basic setup and drawing over and over.

Creating a New Drawing from a Template

A *template* is a special file that contains settings and possibly objects (such as a title block). When you use a template as the basis for a new drawing, the drawing takes on all the settings and objects contained in the template. Use templates to avoid recreating settings and redrawing objects for new drawings. AutoCAD comes with many templates that you can use as is or customize. You can also create your own templates.

Note If you have been using AutoCAD 2002, you may be wondering, "Where did AutoCAD Today go?" AutoCAD Today was a window that opened in front of AutoCAD's main window and contained tools for opening new drawings. It's gone! One feature, the window used by CAD Managers to communicate with AutoCAD users, is in the new Communication Center (covered in Chapter 26). If you have been using an earlier version of AutoCAD, you may have a similar question: "Where is the Startup dialog box?" The Startup dialog box also offered choices for starting a new drawing and is still available. Choose Tools ⇨ Options and click the System tab. In the General Options section, choose Show Startup Dialog Box from the Startup drop-down list. Click OK to close the Options dialog box.

To create a new drawing based on a template, choose File ⇨ New to open the Select Template dialog box. AutoCAD lists all the available templates, as shown in Figure 2-1. Click

any template to see its preview, if any. Double-click a template to create a new drawing based on that template. Because AutoCAD opens with `Drawing1.dwg`, the new drawing is named `Drawing2.dwg`. Subsequent drawings that you open are named `Drawing3.dwg` and so on. After you save and name your drawing, the original template file is unaffected.

New Feature A new command, QNEW, is useful if you always start a new drawing based on the same template. You set a default template and then click QNew on the Standard toolbar to start a new drawing immediately, based on that default template. To set the default template, follow these steps:

1. Choose Tools ➪ Options and click the Files tab.

2. Double-click the Drawing Template Settings item.

3. Double-click the Default Template File Name for QNEW item.

4. Click the listing under the Default Template File Name for QNEW item (which says None by default).

5. Click Browse to choose the template that you want.

6. Click OK to close the Options dialog box.

You can set whether this default template uses metric or imperial measurement by setting the MEASUREINIT system variable. (System variables are discussed further in Chapter 5.) On the command line, type **measureinit**. Enter **0** ↵ for imperial units and **1** ↵ for metric units.

The default template is `acad.dwt`. Another default template is `acad-Named Plot Styles.dwt`, which refers to named plot styles. (See Chapter 17.)

Figure 2-1: Choose a template from the Select template dialog box.

Step-by-Step: Opening a Drawing Based on acad.dwt

1. Start AutoCAD.

2. Choose File ➪ New.

3. From the Select Template dialog box, choose `acad.dwt` from the list.

 You now have a blank drawing named `Drawing2.dwg`, as shown in Figure 2-2.

Figure 2-2: When you create a drawing based on a template, AutoCAD opens a drawing called `Drawing2.dwg`.

Working with Templates

A template contains ready-made settings to get you started drawing quickly. These settings include the size of the drawing (called *limits*), the unit type (such as decimal or feet and inches), and others. An important part of setting standards in an office where people work together on drawings is the creation of a template so that all users work with an identical setup.

A template may contain more than just settings — it often contains a complete title block, for example, and may include boilerplate (standardized) text as well.

Customizing the default template

Most people customize the default template to create one or more templates that suit their particular needs. Once your templates are created, you don't have to worry about most settings; they are already available for you and you can quickly start to draw.

To customize acad.dwt, follow these steps:

1. Open a drawing based on the template as described in the previous section.

2. Make any changes you want.

3. Click Save on the Standard toolbar.

4. In the Save Drawing As dialog box, click the Files of type drop-down list box. Choose AutoCAD Drawing Template (*.dwt). In the list of template files, choose the template that you want to customize. Click Save.

5. When asked if you want to replace it, click Yes.

6. In the Template Description dialog box, revise the description as you like and click OK.

Without templates, you would have to set up your drawing each time you start a drawing—a time-consuming project. The use of templates over time saves hours of work and improves consistency.

Caution

Don't change templates that come with AutoCAD if you are using someone else's computer without first checking with that person. It can be a frustrating experience to start a drawing based on a template and find that all the settings have been changed.

Creating your own templates

You may want several templates to choose from on a regular basis. For example, you may create drawings of several sizes. AutoCAD lets you create as many templates as you want. To create your own templates, either start a drawing based on a template and make the changes you want, or open an existing drawing that already has some of the settings you want and make any further changes you need. Follow these steps:

1. If you start a new drawing based on a template, choose Save from the Standard toolbar. If you open an existing drawing, choose File ➪ Save As from the menu.

2. In the Save Drawing As dialog box, click the Files of type drop-down list box. Choose AutoCAD Drawing Template (*.dwt).

3. In the File name text box, type a name for your template. Click Save.

4. In the Template Description dialog box, enter the description as you want. Click OK.

Tip

Name your templates in a way that clearly differentiates them from regular drawings. You may want drawings set up for each of the standard paper sizes (A through E), with a title block in each. Useful names might be `tb-a.dwt`, `tb-b.dwt` (tb meaning title block), and so on.

Most AutoCAD users take advantage of these techniques as a standard practice. You can usually make profitable use of a template as the basis for a new drawing.

Opening a Drawing with Default Settings

Occasionally, you want to open a drawing without any settings. It is actually impossible for a drawing to have no settings at all, but you can open a drawing with the minimum possible presets. You might want to do this if you are working on someone else's computer and don't want to take the time to get rid of a large number of complex settings that are not helpful for your work.

To open a drawing with the fewest possible settings, choose File ➪ New. Instead of choosing a template, click the arrow to the right of the Open button. (See Figure 2-1.) Choose one of the following options:

✦ Open with no template – Imperial

✦ Open with no template – Metric

Opening an Existing Drawing

Often you need to open an existing drawing, either to complete it or make changes. Opening a drawing in AutoCAD is like opening a file in any Windows program. You can find existing drawings by name or by viewing a thumbnail image of the drawing.

Choose Open from the Standard toolbar. The Select File dialog box appears, shown in Figure 2-3. In the Look in drop-down list box, choose the drive where your drawing resides. In the main box, double-click the folder you need. Then choose your drawing. The Preview box enables you to quickly look at the drawing to see if it's the one you want. Click Open. AutoCAD opens the drawing.

New Feature

If you have Windows XP, you can view thumbnail images of all the drawings in a folder in the Select File dialog box (and other dialog boxes that enable you to choose a file) by clicking the Views button and choosing Thumbnails. In all operating systems, you can view thumbnails in Windows Explorer in the same way — by clicking the Views button and choosing Thumbnails.

Figure 2-3: The Select File dialog box is equivalent to the Open dialog box in most Windows programs.

Note Drawings created and saved in Release 12 or earlier versions of AutoCAD do not show previews. Drawings created in Release 13 and later have previews unless this feature has been disabled.

🔍 To look for a file to open on the Web, click the Search the Web button in the dialog box. You can also use the Places list at the left side of the dialog box to find drawings. The Places list is described in Chapter 1 for the Save As dialog box.

You can also double-click a drawing in Windows Explorer to open it. If AutoCAD is not running, Windows loads AutoCAD and the drawing as well. If AutoCAD is running and a drawing is active, the drawing opens as a second drawing within AutoCAD.

▦ You can also open a drawing from the DesignCenter — a feature for managing both drawing files and many of their components. First, choose DesignCenter from the Standard toolbar. AutoCAD opens the DesignCenter palette, displaying an Explorer-like list of drawings in the left pane. If necessary, choose Desktop from the DesignCenter toolbar. Navigate to the folder containing the drawing and choose the drawing's folder in the left pane. The drawings in the folder are listed in the right pane. Right-click the drawing of your choice and choose Open in Application Window.

Cross-Reference Chapter 26, as well as other chapters throughout this book, covers the DesignCenter in more detail.

You can use several shortcuts when working in dialog boxes that open or save files, as follows:

✦ Double-click the drawing file to open it immediately without clicking Open.

✦ Click the Views drop-down list. Choose List to see a simple list. Choose Details to see file size and the last date and time the file was saved.

✦ Right-click inside the dialog box to open a shortcut menu with more options.

✦ Click the name of a drawing to highlight it and then click it once more to rename it (but don't double-click it—that opens the drawing).

 On the CD-ROM The drawing used in the following Step-by-Step exercise on opening a drawing, ab01-01.dwg, is in the Results folder of the *AutoCAD 2004 Bible* CD-ROM. Place the CD-ROM in your CD-ROM drive.

Step-by-Step: Opening a Drawing

1. If AutoCAD is not open, start AutoCAD.

2. Click Open on the Standard toolbar.

3. In the Select File dialog box, choose the drive for your CD-ROM in the Look in drop-down list box.

4. In the main box, double-click the Results folder.

5. In the main box, click ab01-01.dwg.

6. Click Open. AutoCAD opens the drawing. Keep this drawing open for the next exercise.

Using an Existing Drawing as a Prototype

While a template can be very useful, if you plan to use the objects and settings in a drawing only a few times, you can simply use one drawing as a prototype for other drawings. You often need to draw a series of related drawings—perhaps several related electrical schematics or a group of similar apartments in an apartment complex. When a significant part of the first drawing is applicable to subsequent drawings, don't start over—open an existing drawing, and immediately save it under a new name, as described in the next section. Make the necessary changes and resave the drawing.

Saving a Drawing Under a New Name

Whether you want to use an existing drawing as a prototype or simply make a copy of a drawing, you need to save the drawing under a new name. First open the drawing and then choose File ➪ Save As.

In the Save Drawing As dialog box, type a new name in the File Name text box. Then click Save. You may also want to change the location of the new drawing by changing the folder in the Save in drop-down list box.

On the CD-ROM

In the following exercise, you practice making changes in a drawing as well as saving the drawing under a new name. If you did the previous exercise, you have drawing ab01-01.dwg on your screen. If you didn't do that exercise, open ab01-01.dwg from the Results folder of the CD-ROM.

Step-by-Step: Saving a Drawing Under a New Name

1. Choose File ⇨ Save As. The Save Drawing As dialog box opens.

2. In the File name text box, change the file name to ab02-01.dwg. Choose your AutoCAD Bible folder and click Save.

3. Choose Line from the Draw toolbar. Follow the prompts:

```
Specify first point: 10,.5 ↵
Specify next point or [Undo]: 6,.5 ↵
Specify next point or [Undo]: 6,0 ↵
Specify next point or [Close/Undo]: ↵
```

Your drawing should look like Figure 2-4.

Figure 2-4: A simple title block

4. Click the drawing Close box, which is just below the application Close box.

5. Because you haven't saved the changes to the drawing, AutoCAD asks if you want to save them, as shown in Figure 2-5.

Figure 2-5: If you try to exit AutoCAD without saving the changes you made to a drawing, AutoCAD gives you a chance to save the changes.

6. Click Yes. AutoCAD saves and closes the drawing.

7. Click the application's Close box (X) to close AutoCAD.

Summary

In this chapter, you explored the various ways of opening a drawing. You learned the following:

✦ Starting a new drawing based on a template

✦ Customizing a template

✦ Creating your own templates

✦ Starting a new drawing with no template

✦ Opening an existing drawing

✦ Using an existing drawing as a prototype for a new drawing

✦ Saving a drawing under a new name

In the next chapter, you read about using commands.

✦ ✦ ✦

Using Commands

As a result of AutoCAD's long history, the way you give AutoCAD commands — called the *user interface* — is somewhat unique. You can give the same command in several ways. In this chapter, you read about the various possibilities and start to feel comfortable with all of them.

Commands are important because you can't do anything in AutoCAD without executing a command. In a word processing program, you can simply start typing; in a spreadsheet program, you can begin by entering data; but nothing happens in AutoCAD until you give it a command.

The Windows Interface

Many new commands have been added to AutoCAD over the years. Often, older commands that were no longer necessary were kept to maintain compatibility with earlier versions. In most Windows programs, all commands are included in the menus, but in AutoCAD a number of these older commands, as well as certain rarely used commands, are not found in the menus. Other than this idiosyncrasy, AutoCAD's menus are similar to those of other Windows programs.

Using AutoCAD's menus

A menu item can do three things. As in all Windows programs, the menu provides clues to let you know what is going to occur after you click a menu item. Table 3-1 explains how this works.

Table 3-1	
Menu Symbols and What They Mean	
Symbol	*Menu Action*
No symbol appears	Executes a command after the menu item
. . . (ellipsis)	Opens a dialog box
▶	Displays a submenu

The View menu, shown in Figure 3-1, includes all three types of menu items.

Displays submenu with more options

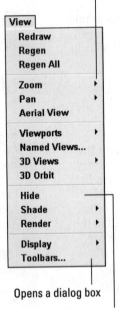

Opens a dialog box

Executes a command

Figure 3-1: The View menu

The screen menu

In early releases, AutoCAD provided a menu on the right side of the screen, called the *screen menu*. If you are still used to the screen menu, I suggest that you adjust to the new interface. You will find its consistency with other Windows programs to be an advantage.

If you must have the screen menu, you can easily display it. Choose Tools ⇨ Options. Click the Display tab. In the Window Elements section, choose Display screen menu. Click OK.

AutoCAD's current default is to not show the screen menu, so I do not use it in this book. Therefore, the word "menu" always means the pull-down menu at the top of the AutoCAD screen.

On the CD-ROM The drawing used in the following Step-by-Step exercise on using a submenu, ab02-01.dwg, is in the Results folder of the *AutoCAD 2004 Bible* CD-ROM.

Step-by-Step: Using a Submenu

1. Open ab02-01.dwg from the Results folder of the CD-ROM.

2. Choose the View menu and point to the Zoom menu item. The submenu opens.

3. Move the mouse pointer over to the submenu. You now have a choice of a list of ZOOM command options.

4. Choose Out from the submenu. The title block gets smaller, as if you have zoomed out using a camera lens.

 Do not save this drawing.

Looking at the command line whenever you click a menu option is worthwhile. The ZOOM command is repeated on the command line, and a list of options appears. Notice that they are mostly the same as those on the submenu, with some minor differences. For example, the Out option that you just used is not available on the command line. This option is actually equivalent to using the Scale option that appears on the command line with a value of 0.5x. AutoCAD's menu sometimes offers preset options of commands to make your work simpler.

Using shortcut menus

AutoCAD's shortcut menus appear when you right-click your mouse. The purpose of shortcut menus is to speed up your work; they can be faster than using the command line because you don't have to take your eyes off the screen. The shortcut

menus try to anticipate the most common tasks you might want to complete. As a result, the menu that appears when you right-click depends on the situation:

✦ If you have neither started a command nor selected any objects, you get the default menu when you right-click in the drawing area. Here you can cut, copy, paste, undo, pan, zoom, and so on.

✦ If you have selected any objects, you see the edit-mode menu, which lists the most common editing commands.

✦ If you have started a command, the command-mode menu opens, letting you choose an option for that command. I explain this in more detail later in this chapter.

✦ When a dialog box is open, you can right-click active sections to see the dialog-mode menu, which varies with the dialog box.

✦ Other menus include the toolbar list you get when you right-click a toolbar and the command-line history you see when you right-click the command line and choose Recent Commands.

These menus are explained as appropriate throughout the book. You also have an opportunity to use many of them in the exercises.

In earlier releases, right-clicking was equivalent to pressing Enter. You can customize how right-clicking works — and that includes changing it back to the way it worked in older releases. Choose Tools ➪ Options and choose the User Preferences tab. Then click "Right-click Customization." For complete details, see Appendix A on the CD-ROM.

New Feature When you set right-click customization, you can turn on time-sensitive right-clicking. Time-sensitive right-click is a great new feature that gives you the best of two worlds — the right mouse button can be used both as equivalent to pressing Enter and to open the shortcut menus.

If you turn on time-sensitive right-clicking, a quick right-click is equivalent to pressing Enter and will repeat the last command, for example, or end the LINE command (and other commands that require Enter to end). A longer right-click (hold your finger on the mouse slightly longer) opens the shortcut menu. You can specify the length of time required for the longer right-click, which is 250 milliseconds by default.

Using dialog boxes

Dialog boxes offer the user a simple way to control AutoCAD without memorizing a lot of technical command and option names. They guide you through a task by clearly laying out all the choices.

If you're familiar with any other Windows program, you're familiar with dialog boxes. AutoCAD, because of its complexity, has some complicated dialog boxes. Nevertheless, you will find that navigating through them is a familiar experience.

As a brief example, look at the Drawing Units dialog box, (Choose Format ⇨ Units), which enables you to define the types of units that AutoCAD uses in your drawing. It has most of the features you see in AutoCAD's dialog boxes and is shown in Figure 3-2.

Figure 3-2: The Drawing Units dialog box is typical of many AutoCAD dialog boxes.

Step-by-Step: Using a Dialog Box

1. Choose File ⇨ New. In the Select Template dialog box, click the down arrow next to the Open button and choose Open with No Template – Imperial to start a new drawing.

2. Choose Format ⇨ Units. The Drawing Units dialog box opens. Notice the two sections called Length and Angle.

3. The default length unit is Decimal. From the Type drop-down list, choose Architectural. Notice how the display of units in the Sample Output box changes.

4. Choose each type of length unit and watch how the Sample Output changes.

5. Choose the Decimal length type again from the drop-down list.

6. Click the Precision drop-down list box in the Length section. The default precision is four decimal places (0.0000). Choose two decimal places (0.00).

7. Now choose various Angle Type options in the Angle section of the dialog box. The angle type determines how angle measurements are shown. Watch the change in the Sample Output box.

8. Choose the default again, Decimal Degrees.

9. In the Precision drop-down list box, choose two decimal places.

10. The Direction button at the bottom of the dialog box has an ellipsis (. . .). This has the same meaning for dialog boxes as it does for menus — it opens another dialog box. Click Direction. The Direction Control dialog box opens. This dialog box enables you to change the standard convention that East is 0 degrees, North is 90 degrees, and so on.

11. Click Cancel because you don't want to change these conventions. You return to the Drawing Units dialog box. Note that you can click Clockwise in the Angle section of the dialog box to change the convention that angles increase counterclockwise.

12. In the Precision drop-down list box for Angles, choose 0 to return this specification to its original setting. You may have to scroll up. (If your setting was different from the default, return it to the way it was when you opened the dialog box.)

13. In the Precision drop-down list box for Length, choose 0.0000 to return this specification to its original setting. (If your setting was different from the default, return it to the way it was when you opened the dialog box.)

14. Click OK. (If you have any doubt that all settings have been returned to the way they were originally, click Cancel.)

Tip If a dialog box has a question mark (?) icon in the top-right corner, click it to change the cursor to a question mark. Then click any item in the dialog box to display a brief explanation of that item.

Using toolbars

Toolbars provide a quick way to execute a command with one click of the mouse. On the other hand, those little pictures on the toolbar buttons are not always self-explanatory. Until you get used to the location of the buttons, you may find yourself wandering (with the mouse cursor) from button to button, reading tooltips. However, once you are familiar with the location of frequently used toolbar buttons, toolbars may become a favorite way to execute commands.

New Feature All the toolbar buttons have been redone for AutoCAD 2004, creating a whole new look. The main toolbars are changed as well, offering a slightly different selection of buttons and adding new toolbars that are displayed by default.

By my count, AutoCAD provides 28 toolbars. Normally, you have the Standard, Styles, Layers, Properties, Draw, and Modify toolbars showing. You can open other toolbars as you need them.

Cross-Reference You can customize toolbars to suit your needs. You can also create your own toolbars from scratch, perhaps containing your favorite command combinations. Toolbar customization is covered in Chapter 29. To see all the toolbars and what their buttons do, see Appendix B on the CD-ROM.

To display a toolbar, right-click any toolbar and choose the toolbar you want to display. Displayed toolbars have a check next to their names. To hide a toolbar, follow the same procedure—choose the toolbar. You can also choose View ➪ Toolbars to open the Toolbars dialog box. Check or clear a toolbar and click OK.

As soon as a toolbar is open, you can close it by clicking the Close button at the upper-right corner, as long as it is not *docked*—that is, parked at one edge of the screen. Toolbars can also float in the drawing area or even outside the AutoCAD window (when it is not maximized). You can move them by dragging them and reshape them by dragging any edge. Docked toolbars have *grab bars* (that look like a double line), which enable you to easily undock and move the toolbars.

New Feature
To close all the toolbars and palettes, press Ctrl + 0. You now have more space to draw. To get back your toolbars and palettes, press Ctrl + 0 again.

In this exercise, you practice manipulating toolbars. This exercise can be done with any drawing on-screen.

Step-by-Step: Manipulating Toolbars

1. Point to the grab bar at the top edge of the Draw toolbar. With the mouse pointer, click, hold down the mouse button, and drag the toolbar until its outline is under the left side of the Layers toolbar (the leftmost toolbar under the Standard toolbar) and it changes to a straight horizontal line. After you release the mouse button, the toolbar docks under the Layers toolbar.

2. Click the Modify toolbar's grab bar and drag it in the same way you did the Draw toolbar until it is docked under the Properties toolbar (which is to the right of the Layers toolbar). Your screen should look something like Figure 3-3. (If your screen resolution is 800×600, the toolbar won't be completely visible. Instead, you can dock it under the Draw toolbar.)

3. To try another configuration, click the grab bar at the left edge of the Draw toolbar. Drag the toolbar to the left side of the screen until the dotted shape shows a one-column vertical toolbar.

Figure 3-3: Docking the Draw and Modify toolbars at the top of the screen

4. In the same way, drag the Modify toolbar to the right of the Draw toolbar. Your screen should look like Figure 3-4. (This configuration is similar to the way toolbars appeared by default in AutoCAD 2002.)

Figure 3-4: Docking the Draw and Modify toolbars at the left side of the screen

5. Right-click any open toolbar. Choose Dimension to display the Dimension toolbar, which provides tools to enable you to show measurements in your drawing. It may be a single line of icons or a rectangular arrangement. If it's docked, click the grab bar and drag it to the drawing area.

6. Point to the fourth button. The tooltip says Radius Dimension. This button enables you to create a dimension showing the measurement of the radius of a circle.

7. With the mouse, point to the bottom edge of the toolbar until the mouse cursor takes the shape of a double-headed arrow.

8. Click and drag upward and/or downward. The toolbar changes shape.

9. Drag the Dimension toolbar by its title bar down to the bottom edge of the drawing area until its outline becomes a dotted horizontal bar. The Dimension toolbar docks at the lower edge of the screen, as shown in Figure 3-5. You don't have as much screen space as before, but the toolbar is off the drawing area.

Figure 3-5: The Dimension toolbar is docked at the bottom of the screen.

10. To close the Dimension toolbar (which you do after you finish placing dimensions in your drawing), drag it by its grab bar onto the drawing area and click the Close button at the right of its title bar.

11. You may leave the Draw and Modify toolbars where they are or return them to their original positions; it's up to you.

As you can see, it's worth the time to learn how to move, dock, display, and hide toolbars. This small effort can greatly increase your comfort level as you draw in AutoCAD.

The Command Line

You have already seen how every command you give AutoCAD is echoed on the command line, although sometimes with slightly different words, syntax, and options. You have also given a command by typing it directly on the command line (the ZOOM command in Chapter 1).

Understanding command names

All commands have a special one-word command name. This may or may not be the same as the wording that appears on the toolbar's tooltip or on the menu. But you can be sure of one thing—every command can be executed by typing its name on the command line. Fast typists often prefer to use the command line because they find it faster than searching for a command on a menu or toolbar. Most users use a combination of command line, menu, and toolbar commands.

Some of the commands are easy to type, such as LINE or ARC. Others are long and harder to remember, such as HATCHEDIT, DDPTYPE, or IMAGEATTACH. Command names such as these can quickly drive you to use a menu or toolbar.

Cross-Reference If you like typing commands, you can create short versions of the command names, called *aliases*. Several are already included with AutoCAD. Aliases are covered in Chapter 29.

You can edit what you have typed on the command line. If you type a long command and make a mistake, you can backspace up to the mistake and retype the last part correctly. Table 3-2 shows how to use the keyboard edit keys to edit the command line.

Table 3-2
Command-Line Editing Keys

Key	Function
Backspace	Backspaces through the text on the command line, erasing each letter as it backspaces.
Left arrow	Moves backward through the text of the command, without erasing.
Right arrow	Moves forward through the text of the command, without erasing.
Home	Moves the command-line cursor to the beginning of the text.
End	Moves the command-line cursor to the end of the text.
Insert	Toggles between Insert/Overwrite mode. Insert mode inserts text. Overwrite mode types over existing text. Note that there is no visual confirmation of which mode you are in.
Delete	Deletes the character to the right of the cursor on the command line.
Ctrl+V	Pastes text from the Windows clipboard.

You can scroll through and reuse previous command-line entries. To repeat the last line you entered, press the up arrow. Press Enter to execute it. To see more of the command-line entries, press F2 on your keyboard to open the text screen. Scroll

until you find the entry you want, highlight it, and then right-click and choose Paste To CmdLine from the shortcut menu. AutoCAD pastes the highlighted text into the current command line. You can also copy selected text from the command-line history or the entire history to the clipboard. Or choose Recent Commands on the shortcut menu and choose one of the commands from the submenu that appears.

Tip

Switching from the mouse to the keyboard and back is time-consuming. In general, if you are picking points by using the mouse (covered in Chapter 4), using menus and toolbars to give commands is faster. If you are typing coordinates as you did in Chapter 1, your hands are already at the keyboard, so typing commands at the keyboard is easier.

Responding to command options

Many commands have a number of options from which you need to choose. The format for command options is as follows:

```
current instruction or [options] <current value>:
```

The current instruction explains what you need to do. For example, if you choose an editing command, AutoCAD usually instructs you to "Select objects." The text in the square brackets lists the various options available for the command. The angled brackets tell you the current or default value for the command, if any.

Choosing an option is easy:

✦ To choose an option on the command line, type the one or two letters that are capitalized in the option name — usually (but not always) the first letter(s) of the option. You can type the letter(s) in lowercase. Press Enter.

✦ To choose a default option or current value on the command line, which appears in angled brackets, as in <Real time>, simply press Enter or provide the point or value required.

✦ To choose an option without going to the command line, right-click in the drawing area and choose one of the options from the shortcut menu. This works best for options that won't need any numerical input on the command line. Choosing options from a shortcut menu on the screen is an example of heads-up drawing, which increases efficiency because you don't need to stop to look down at the keyboard.

At this point, additional options may appear, or you may be prompted to select a point or an object.

In the following exercise, you practice using command options. In Chapter 1, you typed coordinates to specify points. Here you pick points on the screen directly with the mouse.

Step-by-Step: Using Command Options

1. Open a new drawing by using the acad.dwt template.

2. Choose Arc on the Draw toolbar.

3. Look at the command line. You see the following prompt:

 Specify start point of arc or [Center]:

 Specifying the start point is the main instruction, but you have an option to specify the center of the arc. Move the mouse cursor anywhere in the middle of the screen and click to specify the start point. This is called picking a point.

4. Now you see the following prompt:

 Specify second point of arc or [Center/End]:

 Say that you want to specify the end of the arc. Because specifying the second point is the main instruction, right-click to display the shortcut menu, shown in Figure 3-6, and choose End, one of the options. AutoCAD responds with the Specify end point of arc: prompt.

| Enter |
| Cancel |
| Center |
| End |
| Pan |
| Zoom |

Figure 3-6: Using the shortcut menu to choose the End option of the ARC command

5. Pick another point on the screen fairly close to the first one.

6. At the Specify center point of arc or [Angle/Direction/Radius]: prompt, type **r** ↵.

7. At the Specify radius of arc: prompt, type **2** ↵. AutoCAD creates the arc and the command ends. Don't worry at this point if the arc is partly off the screen or doesn't appear as you expect. (It's possible to pick two points for the arc that can't have a radius of 2. If this happens, try again with two different points.)

 Do not save this drawing.

 Note You may have noticed that AutoCAD places an underscore (_) before each command. This mark allows translation to foreign languages and can be ignored.

Sometimes a command has so many options that AutoCAD opens a dialog box. This method offers a more structured way of letting you choose command options.

Command Techniques

To make working with commands easier, AutoCAD offers shortcuts for repeating and canceling commands as well as sophisticated undo and redo options. You can also use certain commands after you have started another command.

You can have more than one command in process concurrently, one in each open drawing. You can switch from one open drawing to another without interrupting your commands. For example, if you are in the middle of drawing a circle in one drawing, you can open a new drawing and start another command to get some information you need for the circle. Then return to the first drawing and complete the circle.

Repeating commands

The most common way to repeat a command you have just used is to press Enter at the Command: prompt. The most recent command appears again.

 You can also press the Spacebar at the Command: prompt to repeat a command you just used. This technique works well if you want to keep one hand on the mouse and use the other hand to press the Spacebar.

 If you create a toolbar button that executes a customized set of actions, right-click to repeat the action of the toolbar button. You cannot press Enter to get this effect.

If you know in advance that you will be using a command several times, you can use another technique — type **multiple** ↵. At the Enter command name to repeat: prompt, type the command name on the command line. The command automatically reappears on the command line until you press the Esc key. For example, you could type **multiple** and then **arc** if you knew you were going to draw several arcs in a row. To stop repeating the command, press Esc.

Canceling commands

Sometimes you start a command and then realize you don't need it. In this situation, you can cancel the command and then choose a different command. Press Esc to cancel a command that you have already started. The Command: prompt reappears.

In the following exercise, you practice the techniques for repeating and canceling commands.

Step-by-Step: Repeating and Canceling Commands

1. Start a new drawing by using the `acad.dwt` template.

2. Choose Circle on the Draw toolbar.

3. At the `Specify center point for circle or [3P/2P/Ttr (tan tan radius)]:` prompt, pick a center point anywhere near the center of the screen.

4. At the `Specify radius of circle or [Diameter]:` prompt, move the mouse cursor and click the pick button when you see a medium-sized circle. AutoCAD draws a circle.

5. Press Enter. The CIRCLE command appears again.

6. Follow the prompts below:

   ```
   Specify center point for circle or [3P/2P/Ttr (tan tan
   radius)]: Right-click and choose 2P from the shortcut menu.
   Specify first end point of circle's diameter: Pick any point
   on the screen.
   Specify second end point of circle's diameter: Press Esc.
   ```

 AutoCAD responds with `*Cancel*` and returns you to the `Command:` prompt without finishing the command that was in progress.

 Do not save this drawing.

Undoing a command

Most Windows applications offer Undo and Redo commands on the Standard toolbar. AutoCAD is no different. Some applications remember a list of your last few actions so that you can undo them one by one. AutoCAD remembers every command you execute starting from the time you open a drawing. You can therefore undo every action and return your drawing to its condition when you opened it.

New Feature The Undo button on the Standard toolbar now lists the commands you have executed so that you can quickly see how many commands you want to undo.

Actually, AutoCAD has a few obvious exceptions. For example, if you print a drawing, you can't unprint it, and you can't unsave a drawing, either. Similarly, commands that provide you with information, such as the coordinates of a point, cannot be undone.

Note Some commands have their own undo options.

Each time you click Undo on the Standard toolbar, AutoCAD undoes one command. If you click the down arrow to the right of the Undo button and choose the bottom-most command, you undo all the commands and get the message:

```
Everything has been undone
```

The UNDO command offers several additional options on the command line. When you start UNDO, you see the following options on the command line:

```
Enter the number of operations to undo or
[Auto/Control/BEgin/End/Mark/Back] <1>:
```

`Enter the number of operations to undo` is the default instruction. If you type a number, such as **3**, AutoCAD undoes your last three commands. This action is equivalent to choosing the third command on the Undo button's drop-down list. Table 3-3 explains the other options:

<div align="center">

Table 3-3
Options of the UNDO Command

</div>

Option	How to Use It
Auto	Can be On or Off. Applies to a menu item that executes more than one command at a time. When Auto is On (the default), the entire menu item is undone in one step. When Auto is Off, UNDO undoes each step one at a time.
Control	Offers three sub-options. All, the default, gives you the full UNDO capability. None disables the UNDO command. One enables you to undo only one step at a time, effectively turning the UNDO command into the U command.
Begin	Works with the End option. This starts a group at the current point of the list of commands. Then, when you use the End option, UNDO undoes all the commands in the group. The U command also undoes everything within a group.
End	Marks the end of all commands in the group created by using the Begin option.
Mark	This option works with the Back option. It is somewhat similar to the Begin option, but you can place several marks as you work.
Back	When you use this option, AutoCAD undoes only to the most recent Mark point. The next Back option you use undoes to the Mark point before that.

Note The word *Group* means that a group of commands is being undone. However, sometimes the word *Group* is used even for a single command. This use of the word *Group* is not significant and can be ignored.

Using the Back option when no Mark has been created undoes everything you have done in a drawing session! Luckily, AutoCAD warns you with a message:

```
This will undo everything. OK? <Y>
```

Type **n** ↵ if you do not want to undo everything.

Tip The Begin/End and Mark/Back options are useful when you are trying something new and want to be able to undo a whole series of commands in one UNDO command in case things don't work out as planned.

Redoing a command

If you undo a command, you might realize that you want to undo the undo. This is called redoing a command. Don't confuse redoing a command with repeating a command. Redoing only applies when you have just undone a command.

 The new MREDO command redoes the effect of the previous UNDO commands.

New Feature AutoCAD 2004 introduces the ability to redo multiple UNDO commands. You can choose recently undone commands from the Redo drop-down list. The old REDO command that only redoes one command still exists, but the Redo button on the Standard toolbar executes the new MREDO command that redoes multiple UNDO commands.

In the following exercise, you practice using the UNDO and MREDO commands.

Step-by-Step: Undoing and Redoing Commands

1. Start a new drawing by using `acad.dwt` as the template.

2. Choose Line on the Draw toolbar.

3. Draw one line and press Enter to end the command.

4. Choose Arc on the Draw toolbar.

5. Using the default options, pick any three points to draw an arc.

6. Choose Circle on the Draw toolbar.

7. Pick one point to be the center of the circle and another nearby point to specify the radius. Your drawing now contains a line, an arc, and a circle, and looks something like Figure 3-7. Of course, your objects will look different because you picked different points.

8. Click the Undo button on the Standard toolbar. The circle disappears.

9. Click the down arrow to the right of the Undo button on the Standard toolbar. Choose Line. The arc and the line disappear.

10. Click the down arrow to the right of the Redo button on the Standard toolbar. Choose Circle. All three objects reappear because they were undone by the previous UNDO commands.

Do not save this drawing. If you are continuing on, keep the drawing on the screen for the next exercise.

Figure 3-7: Your drawing should contain a line, an arc, and a circle.

The OOPS command restores the most recently erased object or set of objects, even if you have used other commands in the meantime. See Chapter 18 for further information.

Using one command within another command

Certain commands can be used within another command. These are called *transparent commands*. After a transparent command is completed, the original command continues its regular operation. Many transparent commands help you display the drawing differently so that you can complete the original command easily. Other transparent commands change settings. In fact, almost any command that doesn't select objects, create new objects, cause regeneration, or end the drawing session can be used transparently. When you start transparent commands from toolbars or menus, they are automatically transparent. If you want to type a transparent command on the command line, you need to type an apostrophe before the command name.

In this exercise, you practice using transparent commands and two commands concurrently.

The drawing used in the following Step-by-Step exercise on using transparent commands and two commands concurrently, ab01-01.dwg, is in the Results folder of the *AutoCAD 2004 Bible* CD-ROM.

Step-by-Step: Using Transparent Commands and Two Commands Concurrently

1. From the previous exercise, you have a line, an arc, and a circle on the screen. If not, begin a new drawing using `acad.dwt` as the template and draw a line and an arc anywhere on the screen. (You don't need the circle.)

2. Choose View ⇨ Zoom ⇨ Out. The drawing zooms out, appearing smaller.

3. Choose Open from the Standard toolbar and open `ab01-01.dwg` from the `Results` folder on the *AutoCAD 2004 Bible* CD-ROM. This is a drawing of a rectangle.

4. Click the Window menu and choose your original drawing.

5. Choose Circle from the Draw toolbar. The following prompt appears:

```
Command: Specify center point for circle or [3P/2P/Ttr (tan
tan radius)]: Pick any point at the center of your screen.
Specify radius of circle or [Diameter]:
```

6. At this point, say that you want to see the drawing closer up to properly decide where to place the radius of the circle. Type **'zoom** ↵. The following appears on the command line. (You may need to press F2 to see the entire prompt.) Follow the prompts.

```
>>Specify corner of window, enter a scale factor (nX or nXP),
or
[All/Center/Dynamic/Extents/Previous/Scale/Window] <real
time>: 2x ↵
Resuming CIRCLE command.
Specify radius of circle or [Diameter]:
```

7. Now suppose that you want the radius to be equal to the height of the rectangle in your other drawing. Choose Window ⇨ `ab01-01.dwg`.

8. Choose Tools ⇨ Inquiry ⇨ List. At the `Select objects:` prompt, pick one of the vertical lines of the rectangle. Press Enter at the second `Select objects:` prompt. AutoCAD opens the Text Window and displays some information about the line you selected. One piece of information is the length, which is 7 units.

9. Click the Window menu and choose your other drawing.

10. Type **7** ↵ to create the circle. If necessary, choose View ⇨ Zoom ⇨ Out to see the entire drawing.

11. Close `ab01-01.dwg`. Do not save the other drawing.

Looking at the prompts for the transparent use of the ZOOM command carefully, note three features:

✦ The ZOOM command is preceded by an apostrophe. This is the sign of a transparent command.

✦ The prompt for the transparent command is preceded by >>. This helps you distinguish between the prompts of the original command and the transparent command that is embedded in it.

✦ When the transparent command is complete, AutoCAD tells you. In this case, you see Resuming CIRCLE command.

Experiment by using transparent commands and you will soon find them indispensable.

Of Mice and Pucks

For the sake of simplicity, this book assumes that you are using a mouse, but many people use a digitizing tablet and a *puck* (or a stylus). A typical digitizing tablet and puck are shown in Figure 3-8. A puck often has more buttons than a mouse and also has crosshairs on a transparent area that you can use for accurately picking points from a paper drawing.

The digitizing tablet is generally configured to include an area that represents the screen you draw on as well as a customizable command area that you use for AutoCAD commands. This command area of the tablet functions as another menu. Figure 3-9 shows the default tablet provided with AutoCAD. This is generally customized to suit individual needs. Each square is equivalent to a toolbar button and executes a command when you click it. The top area is left blank for you to include your own commands. This area is often used to insert parts from a library of standardized parts. Examples would be gaskets and valves in a mechanical drawing environment or doors and windows in an architectural environment.

The square area in the right center represents the drawing area. In this area, the puck functions like a mouse to draw, as well as to access menus and dialog box options. The tablet can also be used for a process called *digitizing*, which means transferring data from paper into AutoCAD. This transference is often done by putting a paper document directly on the tablet and using the entire tablet as a drawing area. Because the puck has crosshairs on a transparent surface, you can pick points on the drawing, which then become endpoints of lines, for example.

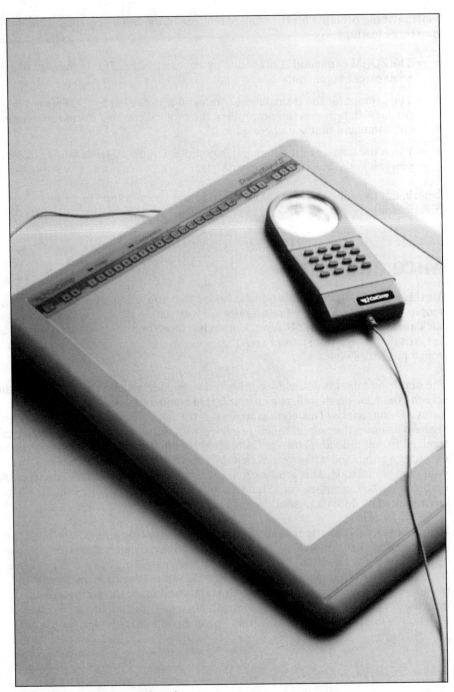

Figure 3-8: A digitizer and puck

Figure 3-9: The standard tablet menu

Getting Help in AutoCAD

AutoCAD has so many commands with so many options that every user needs help at some time. AutoCAD comes with a very complete help system. A complete set of links and tabs makes it easy to navigate through the topics and find related material.

Cross-
Reference

See Appendix D on the CD-ROM for help available on the Internet and other resources.

Getting help on a command

The easiest way to get help on a command is to start the command and press F1. The help screen for that command opens up. Figure 3-10 shows the screen that opens when you type **zoom** ↵ and then press F1.

Note

After you open the Help window one time, when you press F1 it may only cause the button to blink on the Windows task bar. Go to the task bar and click the blink-ing button to open the Help window.

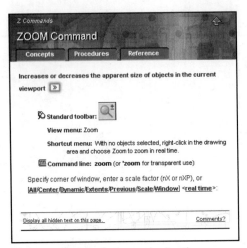

Figure 3-10: The help screen for the ZOOM command

Using the main help system

When you have a question, try AutoCAD's Help system. AutoCAD comes with the most complete Help documentation I have ever seen in a program.

Clicking F1 or choosing Help ⇨ Help opens the User Documentation window, shown in Figure 3-11 with the Contents tab on top. Double-clicking Command Reference on the Contents tab leads you to help on AutoCAD's commands and system variables. Double-click User's Guide for the "how to" manual. You can also click the plus sign to the left to expand the display of topics. If you click any topic on the left, you see it in the right panel.

The help system now has five tabs that offer five different ways of finding the help you need.

The Contents tab

The Contents tabs displays help organized by topic. It's like the table of contents of a book. Click the icon of a book to open that topic and see subtopics. Click a topic to see it displayed in the right panel.

The Index tab

If you have an idea in your head but don't know the command name, you may want to use the index. The index is an alphabetical listing of topics. In the text box, type the first few letters of the word or words for which you want help. As you type, the list jumps to the closest match. When you have found the topic you want, highlight it and click Display (or double-click it). Sometimes subtopics appear from which you can choose.

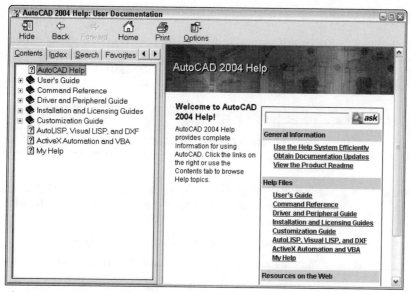

Figure 3-11: The User Documentation window showing the Contents tab and the screen on AutoCAD 2004 Help

The Search tab

The Search tab enables you to find keywords from all the words in the help screens. Type a word in the text box and click List Topics. Choose a topic and click Display (or double-click the topic) to display it on the right.

The Favorites tab

Collect your favorite help topics on the Favorites tab. First, display the topic by using one of the other tabs. Then click the Favorites tab and click Add. To display a help topic from the Favorites list, double-click it.

The Ask Me tab

AutoCAD's Ask Me tab enables you to ask a question in real English and hopefully get the answer you want. Type a question or phrase and press Enter. Then click one of the suggested links to see the topic displayed in the right pane.

Working with help screens

The Help screens have several features that you should know so you can make best use of them. Many of the topics displayed on the right have three tabs:

✦ **Concepts:** The overall description

✦ **Procedures:** How to do it

✦ **Reference:** Related commands

After you arrive at the help screen you want, look for links to related topics.

At the top of most screens are several buttons. The selection of buttons depends on which aspect of help you are accessing. These buttons help you navigate the help system quickly and easily. Table 3-4 explains these buttons and their uses.

Table 3-4	
Help Screen Buttons	
Button	**Action**
Hide/Show	Hides the left pane so that you can work and look at a help screen at the same time. When hidden, the button becomes a Show button that displays the left pane.
Back	Returns you to the previous help screen you viewed.
Print	Prints the topic.
Options	Offers further options such as going to the Home Help page and refreshing the screen.

Using Active Assistance

Active Assistance offers you context-sensitive help as you work. It's great for beginners, but you will eventually find it a nuisance because it pops up in front of your work. To turn on Active Assistance, choose Help ➪ Active Assistance. As you use commands, a brief explanation appears. Figure 3-12 shows the screen that appears when you start the LINE command.

Figure 3-12: Active Assistance displays help for the command that you are using.

You can close the Active Assistance window by clicking its Close box at the top-right corner of the window.

When you turn on Active Assistance, an icon appears in your System Tray at the bottom-right of your screen, on the task bar. Right-click this icon to:

✦ **Display Active Assistance:** Choose Show Active Assistance to display the window at any time.

✦ **Change the settings:** Choose Settings to specify when you want to see Active Assistance and to turn on Hover Help, which displays help for dialog boxes as you pass the mouse cursor over an area of the dialog box.

✦ **Exit:** Choose Exit to turn off Active Assistance. When you close the Active Assistance window, it remains on until you exit it in this way.

Getting more help

AutoCAD's Help menu has some additional options that provide more specialized assistance. When you choose Help from the menu bar, choose one of these four other items:

✦ **Active Assistance:** Turns on Active Assistance, explained in the previous section

✦ **Developer Help:** Opens the Help system for topics relating to programming AutoCAD. See Part VII of this book.

✦ **New Features Workshop:** A combination of explanation and tutorials on AutoCAD 2004's new features.

✦ **Online Resources:** Connects you to various support and training options on Autodesk's web site.

In this exercise, you practice using AutoCAD's help system.

Step-by-Step: Using AutoCAD Help

1. If AutoCAD is not open, start AutoCAD with the `acad.dwt` template. If AutoCAD is already open, this exercise can be done with any drawing on the screen.

2. Choose Circle from the Draw toolbar. At the prompt, press F1 on the keyboard. The Circle help screen opens. (If it doesn't open, click the Help window's button on the Windows taskbar.)

3. Click 2P (Two Points), which appears underlined. The 2P description appears. Read the description of the 2P option.

4. Click the Close button at the top-right corner of the help screen. Press Esc to exit the CIRCLE command.

5. Choose Help ➪ Help.

6. Click the Contents tab if it is not on top. Double-click User's Guide. From the list, double-click The User Interface and then click the plus sign next to Menus, Toolbars and Tool Palettes.

7. Click Shortcut Menus. Read the text in the right pane.

8. Click the Procedures tab. Click "To display a shortcut menu" and read the text.

9. Click the Index tab.

10. In the text box at the top, type **transparent commands** and click Display.

11. From the Topics Found list, double-click Enter Commands on the Command Line.

12. In the right pane, scroll down until you see the heading Interrupt a Command with Another Command or System Variable.

13. Read the text. After you're done, click the Close button of the Help window.

Summary

In this chapter, you read all you need to know about how to use AutoCAD's commands. Specifically, you read about:

✦ Using AutoCAD's menus

✦ Shortcut menus

✦ Using a dialog box

✦ Opening, closing, reshaping, and docking toolbars

✦ Command names

✦ Using and editing the command line

✦ Responding to command options and using the command line and shortcut menus

✦ Repeating commands

✦ Canceling commands

✦ Undoing and redoing commands

✦ Transparent commands

✦ Using a puck and digitizing tablet to enter commands

✦ Getting help

In the next chapter, I explain how to specify coordinates, an essential skill to learn before you start to draw.

✦ ✦ ✦

Specifying Coordinates

S pecifying points on the screen is one of the most funda-mental tasks in AutoCAD. Unless you know how to spec-ify a point, you can't draw anything real, whether a house or a gasket. Most objects you draw have a specific size, and you need to give AutoCAD that information. Drawing lines, arcs, and circles is accomplished by specifying the coordinates of points on the screen. As with most tasks, AutoCAD offers many ways to accomplish this.

Understanding the X,Y Coordinate System

Remember when you studied geometry and trigonometry in high school? You created graphs by drawing X and Y axes. Then you plotted coordinates on graph paper. AutoCAD works the same way.

Look at the User Coordinate System (UCS) icon, as shown in Figure 4-1.

Cross-Reference

The UCS icon can take on different appearances. See Chapter 8 for details.

Figure 4-1: The UCS icon shows the direction of the X and Y axes.

In This Chapter

Working with absolute, relative, and polar coordinates

Using direct distance entry, orthogonal mode, and polar tracking

Using snap settings

Working with object snaps (OSNAPS)

Locating points

The arrow marked X points along the X axis in the positive direction. This means that as you go in the direction of the arrow, the X coordinates increase. The arrow marked Y points along the Y axis in the positive direction.

Using this system, every point on the screen can be specified using X and Y coordinates. This is called a *Cartesian* coordinate system.

As explained in Chapter 1, the universal convention is to place the X coordinate first, then a comma (but no space), and then the Y coordinate. Refer to Figure 1-4 in Chapter 1 for some sample coordinates.

By default, the intersection of the X,Y axes is 0,0. Use negative numbers for points to the left of the X axis or below the Y axis.

Drawing units

What do the coordinates measure? When you draw in AutoCAD, you draw in undefined units. This means that a line from point 3,0 to point 6,0 is three units long. While you are drawing, these units can be anything—a millimeter, a centimeter, a meter, an inch, a foot, or a mile. In reality, you should know exactly what the units represent. After all, you don't want your 36-foot-wide house to end up 36 inches wide!

When you set up a drawing, you specify how units are displayed—for example, whether partial units show as decimal points or fractions. I cover units in Chapter 5. However, you don't actually specify what the units represent until you print or plot your drawing—covered in Chapter 17.

In AutoCAD, you customarily draw full size. If you are drawing a plan for a factory that will be 120 feet long, for example, you create lines with those measurements. On the screen, you can zoom in to see small details or zoom out to see the whole factory, so that you have no reason not to use the actual line lengths. It is only when you need to print those 120-foot-long lines on a real sheet of paper that you have to tell AutoCAD to plot out your drawing at a reduced scale.

Types of measurement notation

Users are typically familiar only with the type of notation used in their own field of specialty, whether scientific, architectural, engineering, or whatever. However, you should be at least somewhat familiar with all the major forms of measurement notation.

If you are using engineering or architectural units, AutoCAD displays parts of inches (fractions) differently than the format you must use to type them in. You must type in coordinates without any spaces because AutoCAD interprets a space

as equivalent to pressing Enter and ends your input. Use a hyphen between whole and partial inches—for example, 3'2-1/2". (You can omit the " after the inches because AutoCAD assumes inches in engineering and architectural units if no symbol follows a number.) However, this appears on the status bar as 3'-2 1/2". This can be confusing because AutoCAD places the hyphen in a different place and uses a space between the whole and partial inches.

Typing Coordinates

One of the most basic ways to specify the location of an object is to type its coordinates using the keyboard. You can enter several types of coordinates. You use the type of coordinates that suit your specific situation.

Absolute Cartesian coordinates

When you type a line and enter the actual coordinates, such as a line from point 3,2 to 6,9, you are using absolute Cartesian coordinates. Absolute coordinates are measured from 0,0. These coordinates are probably familiar to you from high school geometry class.

In this exercise, you practice entering absolute Cartesian coordinates.

Step-by-Step: Entering Absolute Cartesian Coordinates

1. Start a new drawing in AutoCAD using the acad.dwt template.

2. Choose Line from the Draw toolbar. Follow the prompts:

```
Specify first point: -10,-5 ↵
Specify next point or [Undo]: 21,-5 ↵
Specify next point or [Undo]: 21,49 ↵
Specify next point or [Close/Undo]: -10,49 ↵
Specify next point or [Close/Undo]: -10,-5 ↵
Specify next point or [Close/Undo]: ↵ to end the command.
```

Most of the lines are off the screen. By default, a new drawing starts with 0,0 at the lower-left corner of your screen, therefore negative coordinates do not show.

3. Choose Zoom Out from the Zoom flyout on the Standard toolbar. If you still cannot see the entire rectangle, choose Zoom Out again until you can see it. Your picture should look like Figure 4-2.

Note If AutoCAD responds with `Invalid Point` or `Point or option keyword required`, you have entered a coordinate incorrectly. Try typing the coordinate again. Also, don't forget that you can UNDO a command if you make a mistake. (See Chapter 3 for details.)

Figure 4-2: A rectangle drawn by using absolute coordinates

4. Start the LINE command again and follow the prompts:

```
Specify first point: -8,-2 ↵
Specify next point or [Undo]: 19,-2 ↵
Specify next point or [Undo]: 19,21.5 ↵
Specify next point or [Close/Undo]: -8,21.5 ↵
Specify next point or [Close/Undo]: -8,-2 ↵
Specify next point or [Close/Undo]: ↵ to end the command.
```

5. Once more, start the LINE command and follow the prompts:

```
Specify first point: -8,22.5 ↵
Specify next point or [Undo]: 19, 22.5 ↵
Specify next point or [Undo]: 19,46 ↵
Specify next point or [Close/Undo]: -8,46 ↵
Specify next point or [Close/Undo]: -8,22.5 ↵
Specify next point or [Close/Undo]: ↵ to end the command.
```

6. Save this drawing in your `AutoCAD Bible` folder as `ab04-01.dwg`.

You can now see that you have drawn a simple window, as shown in Figure 4-3.

Two questions might have occurred to you during this exercise. First, isn't there a better way of entering absolute coordinates? Typing them in is slow and prone to error. Second, how do you know the absolute coordinates for what you are drawing? Read on for the answers.

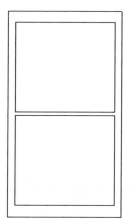

Figure 4-3: A window drawn with absolute coordinates

Relative Cartesian coordinates

In practice, you usually do not know the absolute coordinates of the points you need to specify in order to draw an object. Whether you are drawing an architectural layout, a physical object (as in mechanical drawing), a three-dimensional model, or an electrical schematic, you don't have X,Y coordinates to work from. However, you often do have the *measurements* of what you are drawing. Usually, you start from any suitable point and work from there. In this situation, you know only the length of the lines you are drawing (if you are drawing lines). Real life doesn't have a 0,0 point. Relative coordinates were developed for these situations.

Relative coordinates specify the X and Y distance from a previous point. They are called *relative coordinates* because they only have meaning relative to a point previously specified. Suppose that you need to draw a window. You can start the window from any point. From there, you have the measurements you need. (The measurements may be shown on a piece of paper you're working from, or you may have the actual window sitting next to you so you can measure it.)

You tell AutoCAD that the coordinates are relative by using the @ symbol. For example, if you start a line by picking any point with the mouse, and you know it should be two units long, you can specify the next point as @2,0. AutoCAD creates a line starting with the first point you picked and ending two units to the right, as shown in Figure 4-4. The line is horizontal because the Y coordinate is 0. In a relative coordinate, this means that the Y distance does not change.

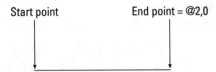

Start point End point = @2,0

Figure 4-4: A line whose start point could be anywhere and whose endpoint is specified with the relative point @2,0 is a horizontal line two units long.

Relative Cartesian coordinates are often used for lines drawn at 90-degree angles, that is, they are either horizontal or vertical. These are called *orthogonal lines*. When you create a diagonal line from point 3,3 to point @2,5 you don't know how long the line is.

When you specify a positive number such as the 2 in @2,0, AutoCAD assumes the positive direction. However, if you want to draw a line in the negative direction of an axis, type a minus sign before the number. Figure 4-5 shows how to draw lines in four directions using relative coordinates.

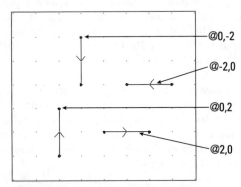

@0,-2

@-2,0

@0,2

@2,0

Figure 4-5: Drawing lines in the four orthogonal directions by using relative coordinates. The arrow on each line shows the direction of the line.

Polar coordinates

Another common situation is to know the distance and angle of a point from either 0,0 or a previous point. In this case, you can use polar coordinates, which can be either absolute or relative. Most commonly, you use relative polar coordinates.

Polar coordinates take the form *distance<angle*. (To type the angle symbol, use the less than symbol on your keyboard.) Relative polar coordinates must have the @ sign before the coordinate.

Cross-Reference Chapter 21 explains more about coordinates in 3D drawings.

By default, angles are measured according to the diagram in Figure 4-6, although AutoCAD enables you to change this system. The positive and negative angles shown next to each other are interchangeable. Use whichever is more meaningful to you.

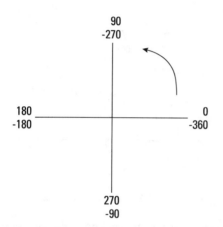

Figure 4-6: The standard angle measurement system

In the following series of steps, you draw part of a portico, the decorative molding above a door or window. Because it is an architectural design, you use architectural units. In this case, only inches are used, which don't need to be specified. You can specify feet by using an apostrophe (also called a *prime*) after any number.

When typing architectural units, partial inches are indicated by fractions in the form 3/4. You need to separate the fraction from the whole inches by a hyphen. This can be a little confusing because the hyphen is also used for negative numbers. For example, to draw a horizontal line of 5¼ inches to the left, you would type **@-5-1/4,0.** (The 0 indicates no change in the Y axis because it is a horizontal line.)

On the CD-ROM The drawing used in this Step-by-Step exercise on using relative and polar coordinates, ab04-a.dwg, is in the Drawings folder of the *AutoCAD 2004 Bible* CD-ROM.

Step-by-Step: Using Relative and Polar Coordinates

1. Open ab04-a.dwg from the CD-ROM. As you move your mouse around, notice that the coordinates displayed on the status bar are in architectural units, that is, in feet and inches. If the coordinates are grayed out, click them or press the F6 key.

2. Choose File ➪ Save As and save the drawing in your AutoCAD Bible folder as ab04-02.dwg.

The next steps involve some complex typing. If you get an error message from AutoCAD, try typing the coordinate again. If you realize you made a mistake after ending the command, click Undo on the Standard toolbar.

3. Start the LINE command. Follow the prompts:

```
Specify first point: Pick any point at the lower-left corner
of your screen.
Specify next point or [Undo]: @0,-3/4 ↵
Specify next point or [Undo]: @75-1/4,0 ↵
Specify next point or [Close/Undo]: @0,3/4 ↵
Specify next point or [Close/Undo]: @-75-1/4,0 ↵
Specify next point or [Close/Undo]: ↵ to end the command.
```

4. Start the LINE command again. Follow the prompts:

```
Specify first point: ↵. This starts the line at the last
endpoint you specified.
Specify next point or [Undo]: @4-3/4,0 ↵
Specify next point or [Undo]: @43<40 ↵
Specify next point or [Close/Undo]: @43<320 ↵
Specify next point or [Close/Undo]: @-2-1/4,0 ↵
Specify next point or [Close/Undo]: @39-7/8<140 ↵
Specify next point or [Close/Undo]: @39-7/8<220 ↵
Specify next point or [Close/Undo]: ↵ to end the command.
```

Note

In this exercise, you draw a line on top of a line, which is not good drawing practice. Later in this chapter and in coming chapters you learn techniques to avoid this.

5. Save your drawing. You have created a portion of a portico, which goes over a window of a house, as shown in Figure 4-7.

Figure 4-7: Part of a portico over a window, drawn using relative Cartesian and polar coordinates in architectural notation

Tip

You can type @ ↵ at the first prompt of any drawing command to indicate the most recent coordinate specified.

Notice that using relative coordinates, both Cartesian and polar, is much more realistic than using absolute coordinates. However, typing in all those coordinates is still awkward. Typing in coordinates is often the only way to get exactly what you want. Nevertheless, several other techniques for specifying coordinates are easier in many circumstances.

Direct distance entry

One shortcut for entering coordinates is direct distance entry. After you specify the start point of a line, at the `Specify next point or [Undo]:` prompt, simply move the mouse cursor in the direction you want the line to go and type in the line's length. It works best in orthogonal mode or with polar tracking, discussed next, which makes it easy to specify exact angles.

Note You can use direct distance entry for any command that requires you to specify a distance and a direction, including both drawing and editing commands.

Orthogonal mode

As mentioned earlier in this chapter, lines drawn at 0, 90, 180, and 270 degrees are called orthogonal lines. When in orthogonal mode — ortho mode as it's called for short — you can only draw orthogonal lines with the mouse. Ortho mode also affects editing. For example, with ortho mode on, you can only move objects vertically or horizontally. Combined with snap and grid, ortho mode makes drawing easier and more efficient. Ortho mode is also great for direct distance entry.

Click ORTHO on the status bar to toggle ortho mode on and off. You cannot have polar tracking on at the same time that ortho mode is on. Polar tracking is discussed next.

Note Orthogonal mode only affects points picked directly on the screen by using your mouse. Any relative or absolute coordinates typed on the command line override orthogonal mode.

Polar tracking

Polar tracking guides you, using a tooltip and vector line, when you want to draw (or edit) at an angle other than the four orthogonal angles, as shown in Figure 4-8. You can use polar tracking for orthogonal angles as well.

Polar tracking makes it easy to use direct distance entry to specify distances for many angles. To use polar tracking, you first set the angles that you want to use.

To set the angles, choose Tools ⇨ Drafting Settings or right-click the POLAR button on the status bar and choose Settings. AutoCAD opens the Drafting Settings dialog box. If necessary, click the Polar Tracking tab, which you can see in Figure 4-9.

Polar tracking vector

Polar: 3'-0 3/8" < 45d — Polar tracking tooltip

Figure 4-8: When polar tracking is on, a tooltip appears when you move the cursor close to one of the polar angles. Here you see a tooltip indicating an angle of 45 degrees.

Figure 4-9: The Polar Tracking tab of the Drafting Settings dialog box

To change the increment angle, click the Increment angle drop-down arrow, where you can pick from angles that range from every 90 degrees to every 5 degrees. You can also type your own incremental angle in the text box. To add additional angles that you think you'll need, check Additional angles, click New, and then type in an angle. You can add up to 10 additional angles. Note that additional angles you add are not incremental angles — if you type 35, AutoCAD will only mark 35 degrees, not 70 degrees or other increments of 35. To delete an additional angle, select it and click Delete.

On the right side of the dialog box, you can choose how polar tracking works with object snap tracking (covered later in this chapter). You can set object snap tracking to use all the polar angle settings or limit it to orthogonal angles only. You can also set whether polar angles are measured absolutely (relative to 0 degrees) or relative to the segment drawn most recently. By default, absolute angles are used.

To customize how polar tracking works, click Options in the Drafting Settings dialog box to open the Options dialog box with the Drafting tab on top. The following settings in the AutoTracking Settings section apply to polar tracking:

✦ **Display polar tracking vector** turns on and off the polar tracking vector, which is the faint dotted line that extends to the end of the screen.

✦ **Display AutoTracking tooltip** turns on and off the tooltip that tells you the distance and angle.

To turn on polar tracking, check Polar Tracking On on the Polar Tracking tab of the Drafting Settings dialog box. If you are not in the dialog box, press F10 or click the POLAR button on the status bar.

To use polar tracking, you need to move the cursor slowly through the angles to give AutoCAD time to calculate and display the vector and tooltip. Say that you are drawing a line. Specify the start point. To specify the second point, move the cursor in the approximate angle of the line you want to draw. When you see the polar tracking vector and tooltip, leave the mouse where it is and type the length of the line. Then press Enter. AutoCAD creates the line with the proper length and angle. You will find this method easier than typing polar coordinates for lines with angles specified in your polar tracking settings.

Tip Turn on NumLock on your keyboard and use the numerical pad for typing in lengths. Use the Enter key on the numerical pad as well.

You can specify a polar angle for just one command. If you're drawing a line, the polar angle applies for one segment only. If you're drawing a line, after specifying the first point, for example, type the angle preceded by the angle symbol (<). AutoCAD then locks the next segment to that angle while you type its length. A polar angle specified in this way is called a polar override angle because it overrides the current polar angles in effect. Of course, a polar override is not faster than simply typing a polar coordinate, but it does let you see the angle of the line segment (if you're drawing a line) before you type its length.

In the following exercise, you practice using direct distance entry with ortho mode and polar tracking. Before beginning, check that Polar Tracking is set for 45 degrees, as described previously.

On the CD-ROM The drawing (ab04-b.dwg) used in the following Step-by-Step exercise on using direct distance with ortho mode and polar tracking is in the Drawings folder of the *AutoCAD 2004 Bible* CD-ROM.

Step-by-Step: Using Direct Distance with Ortho Mode and Polar Tracking

1. Open drawing ab04-b.dwg from the CD-ROM.

2. Choose File ➪ Save As to save the drawing in your AutoCAD Bible folder as ab04-03.dwg. If ORTHO is not on (that is, if the ORTHO button on the status bar doesn't look pushed in), click ORTHO.

3. Start the LINE command and, at the Specify first point: prompt, type **2,2** ↵.

4. Move the mouse horizontally to the right, and then type **.5** ↵.

5. Move the mouse up vertically (in the 90-degree direction) and then type **.5** ↵.

6. Move the mouse horizontally to the right and then type **2** ↵. Your drawing should look like Figure 4-10.

Figure 4-10: Drawing with direct distance entry enables you to specify coordinates by typing in a length after you move the pointer in the desired direction.

7. Move the mouse up in the 90-degree direction and then type **.5** ↵.

8. Move the mouse to the left in the 180-degree direction and then type **2** ↵.

9. Move the mouse up in the 90-degree direction and then type **.5** ↵.

10. Move the mouse to the left in the 180-degree direction and then type **.5** ↵.

11. Move the mouse down in the 270-degree direction and then type **1.5** ↵. Press Enter again to end the command.

12. Click POLAR on the status bar. The ORTHO button pops out.

13. With your cursor in the drawing area, right-click with your mouse and choose Repeat Line from the shortcut menu.

14. Press Enter to start the new line from the most recent point. At the Specify next point or [Undo]: prompt, move the cursor diagonally up and to the left so the line is approximately in the 135-degree direction. When you see the tooltip confirming the angle, let go of the mouse and type **.7071** ↵.

15. Move the cursor up until you see the polar tracking tooltip confirming a 90-degree angle. Type **.5** ↵.

16. Move the cursor diagonally in the 45-degree direction until you see the tooltip. Type **.7071** ↵. Press Enter again to end the LINE command.

17. Save your drawing. It should look like Figure 4-11.

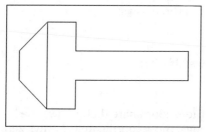

Figure 4-11: The completed drawing
of a bolt

Displaying Coordinates

As you work, you can refer to the coordinate display on the status bar. This display helps you know where your cursor and objects are and is also helpful when editing, such as how far and in what direction you are moving or copying objects.

AutoCAD has three coordinate display modes that you can use:

✦ **Dynamic absolute coordinates (absolute):** Absolute coordinates that change as you move the mouse, as shown in Figure 4-12.

0.7409, 2.1450 , 0.0000 **Figure 4-12:** Dynamic absolute coordinates

✦ **Static absolute coordinates (off):** Absolute coordinates that change only when you specify a point, as shown in Figure 4-13. The coordinate display is dimmed.

0.3485, 3.0654 , 0.0000 **Figure 4-13:** Static absolute coordinates

✦ **Dynamic polar coordinates (relative):** Polar coordinates that change continuously as you move the mouse, as shown in Figure 4-14. They appear after you have already specified a point and are ready to specify a new point, as when you are in the process of drawing a line.

1.4580< 29 , 0.0000 **Figure 4-14:** Dynamic polar coordinates

You can change the coordinate display in three ways:

✦ Press the F6 key.

✦ Click the coordinates area on the status bar.

✦ Press Ctrl+D.

For purposes of this chapter, I ignore the Z coordinate that follows the X and Y coordinates. In two-dimensional drawings, the Z coordinate is always zero.

In the following exercise, you practice using the coordinate display options. This exercise can be done with any new or existing drawing open on the screen.

Step-by-Step: Using Coordinate Display Options

1. Look at the coordinate display on the status bar. It should be shown in black. If the coordinates are shown in gray, press F6 on your keyboard.

2. Move the mouse around in a few directions. Notice how the coordinates constantly change with the mouse movement.

3. Press F6. The coordinate display is grayed out. The command line shows `<Coords off>`.

4. Move the mouse around again. The coordinate display does not change with the movement of the mouse.

5. Start the LINE command and pick any point on the screen.

6. Watch the coordinate display as you pick any point at the `Specify next point or [Undo]:` prompt.

7. Pick several other points and watch as the coordinate display changes only when you pick a point. This is the static coordinate display.

8. Press F6 again without ending the LINE command.

9. Move the mouse to another point that you would like to pick but watch the coordinate display before you pick the point. This time, the length and angle of the new line segment is shown. These are dynamic polar coordinates.

10. Pick a few more points, watching the polar coordinates.

11. Press F6 again to return to dynamic absolute coordinates.

12. Press Enter to end the LINE command. Do not save your drawing.

The next sections introduce three new ways to specify coordinates.

Picking Coordinates on the Screen

The easiest and quickest way to specify coordinates is to pick them directly on the screen with the mouse. AutoCAD offers several techniques to help you do so accurately.

You can adjust the size of the crosshairs that cross the cursor. By default, they are 5 percent of screen size. To change the crosshair size, choose Tools ⇨ Options and click the Display tab. In the Crosshair size text box, you can type a new percentage or drag the bar to increase or decrease the percentage. Choose OK.

Snap settings

The SNAP command is often an alternative to tedious entry of coordinates. This command restricts the cursor to an incremental distance that you choose, such as 0.5 units. You can set the snap size to anything you want. For example, if all your measurements are rounded off to the nearest 0.25 units, you can set your snap to 0.25.

The snap technique is not very useful when you need to draw to three or more decimal places of accuracy. And when you are zoomed out in a large drawing, the snap points may be so close together that you cannot easily find the one you want. But in the right situation, snap is one of the quickest, most accurate drawing techniques available.

AutoCAD 2004 provides two types of snap settings — grid snap and polar snap.

Snapping to a grid

When you snap to a grid, AutoCAD creates an invisible grid (which you can make visible using the GRID command, discussed in the next section). As soon as you turn on snap, the mouse cursor can only move to the snap grid points.

To set the snap size, choose Tools ⇨ Drafting Settings or right-click the SNAP button on the status bar and choose Settings. AutoCAD opens the Drafting Settings dialog box, as shown in Figure 4-15. (If necessary, click the Snap and Grid tab.) In the Snap X spacing text box of the Snap section, type the spacing you want between snap points. Make sure that Grid snap and Rectangular snap are checked in the Snap type & style section of the dialog box. Click OK.

Cross-Reference

Note that you can change the angle of the snap spacing. In Chapter 8, I discuss rotating the angle of the snap and grid. Chapter 8 also discusses Isometric snap, used for isometric drawing.

Figure 4-15: The Drafting Settings dialog box

Usually you want the X spacing (going across) to be the same as the Y spacing (going up and down). You need to specify only the X spacing, and AutoCAD automatically changes the Y spacing to equal the X spacing. X and Y spacing will be different only if you type a different number in the Snap Y spacing box.

You can also turn snap on in this dialog box by clicking the On check box. However, the most common way to turn snap on, after you have set the spacing, is to click SNAP on the status bar (or press the F9 key). Click it again to turn snap off.

Snapping at polar angles

After you set polar tracking settings, discussed earlier in this chapter, you can snap to increments along the polar angles you have set. When polar snap is on, the polar tooltip only shows distances in increments of the snap setting. When you see the distance you want, just click. Polar snap makes it easy to draw accurately without having to type coordinates.

To use polar snap, follow these steps:

1. Right-click the SNAP button on the status bar and click Settings to open the Drafting Settings dialog box with the Snap and Grid tab displayed, as just explained.

2. Check Polar snap in the Snap type & style section of the dialog box. (See Figure 4-15.)

3. Type a number in the Polar distance text box.

4. Click OK to close the dialog box.

5. Click SNAP on the status bar.

Note that polar snap and grid snap are mutually exclusive. If polar snap is on, the cursor will not snap to the grid. Used with polar tracking, polar snap is a powerful tool. Remember that you can polar track along orthogonal as well as other angles.

Tip You can choose either polar snap or grid snap (switch between them) by right-clicking SNAP on the status bar. A shortcut menu lets you choose the type of snap you want, or turn both off.

The grid

Sometimes you may find it helpful to see a grid of dots to help get your bearings while you draw, as shown in Figure 4-16. If the dot grid is not visible, click GRID on the status bar or press the F7 key. Notice how you can quickly judge the approximate width of a windowpane, knowing that the grid dots are half a foot apart. If you turn on snap, the grid helps you visualize the snap points. However, the grid dots do not have to be set to the same spacing as the snap points.

Figure 4-16: A portion of a drawing with the grid turned on and set to 6 inches

Thanks to Henry Dearborn, AIA, Fairfield, Iowa, for this drawing.

The smaller the grid size and the farther out you zoom, the denser the grid and the longer it takes to display. At a certain point, AutoCAD issues a message, Grid too dense to display, and refuses to display the grid.

Some users find the grid annoying, but when you first start to use AutoCAD, you may find it helpful. Even accomplished users can take advantage of the grid, especially when starting a new drawing.

Tip If you are working with a small snap spacing and the dot grid is too dense, set the dot grid to twice the size of the snap spacing. You can even set the dot grid to four or five times the snap spacing.

To set the grid size, choose Tools ⇨ Drafting Settings to open the Drafting Settings dialog box, shown previously in Figure 4-15. If necessary, click the Snap and Grid tab. In the X Spacing text box of the Grid section, type the spacing you want between grid points. Click OK.

As with the snap feature, you usually want the X spacing (going across) to be the same as the Y spacing (going up and down). You need to specify only the X spacing, and AutoCAD automatically changes the Y spacing to be the same. X and Y spacing will only be different if you type a different number in the Y Spacing box.

You can turn Grid on in this dialog box by clicking the On check box, but the most common way to turn the grid on, after you have set the spacing, is to click GRID on the status bar (or press F7).

In the following exercise, you practice using polar and grid snap points as well as grid dots.

On the CD-ROM The drawing used in the following Step-by-Step exercise on using snap points and grid dots, ab04-b.dwg, is in the Drawings folder of the *AutoCAD 2004 Bible* CD-ROM.

Step-by-Step: Using Snap Points and Grid Dots

1. Open ab04-b.dwg from the CD-ROM.

2. Choose File ⇨ Save As to save the drawing in your AutoCAD Bible folder as ab04-04.dwg.

3. Choose Tools ⇨ Drafting Settings. The Drafting Settings dialog box opens. Click the Snap and Grid tab if it is not displayed. In the Snap type & style section, make sure that you check the Grid snap and Rectangular snap.

4. In the Snap section, change the Snap X Spacing to 0.5.

5. Click in the Grid section, in the Grid X spacing text box. Change the Grid X spacing to 0.5. Click OK. AutoCAD automatically sets the Grid Y spacing to match the Grid X spacing of 0.5.

6. On the status bar, click SNAP, GRID, and ORTHO. The grid appears. Make sure that the OSNAP and OTRACK buttons on the status bar are off.

7. Choose View ⇨ Zoom ⇨ All.

8. Move the mouse around and watch the coordinates on the status bar. (Press F6 if they are in static mode.) They show halves of units because you have set the snap to 0.5.

9. Start the LINE command. At the Specify first point: prompt, click when the coordinates on the status bar show 2.000,2.000. (For now, ignore the third Z coordinate, which is always 0.0000 in 2D drawings.)

10. Move the mouse around and watch the coordinates. If you don't see polar coordinates (for example 3.0000<0), press F6 twice until you see them.

11. Move the mouse to the right until the coordinates read 8.5000<0 and click the pick (left) button. You have drawn a horizontal line with a length of 8.5 units.

12. Click the right mouse button and choose Enter to end the LINE command.

13. Move the mouse cursor away from the end of the new line and back to it again, and the absolute coordinates appear. They should be 10.5000,2.0000.

14. Right-click and choose Repeat Line to start the LINE command again. Use the coordinate display to start the line at 1.5000,1.5000. Continue to use the coordinate display to pick points and draw the following line segments:

 .5<0
 3.0<90
 .5<180
 3.0<270

15. End the LINE command.

16. Start the LINE command and use the coordinate display to pick points, drawing the following line segments starting from 10.5,1.5. Then end the LINE command:

 .5<0
 3.0<90
 .5<180
 3.0<270

17. Starting from 2,4 draw an 8.5-unit line at 0 degrees. End the LINE command.

18. Start the LINE command again. At the first prompt, pick 11,2. Right-click SNAP on the status bar and choose Settings. In the Snap type & style section, choose Polar snap. (This is equivalent to choosing the Polar Snap On feature on the SNAP button shortcut menu.) In the Polar Spacing section, change the Polar distance to .5. Choose the Polar Tracking tab and (if necessary) set the Increment angle to 45.0 degrees. Click OK. Click POLAR on the status bar.

19. Move the cursor in a 45-degree direction from 11,2 until you see the tooltip. Move along the polar tracking vector until the tooltip says 3.5000 < 45° and click. End the LINE command.

20. Right-click the SNAP button and choose Grid Snap On. Start the LINE command and, at the `Specify first point:` prompt, choose 11,4.

21. Right-click the SNAP button and choose Polar Snap On. Move the cursor in a 45-degree direction until the tooltip says 3.5000 < 45° and click. End the LINE command.

22. Save your drawing. Your drawing should look like Figure 4-17.

As you no doubt experienced, this is a much easier way to draw compared to typing in coordinates. Note that drawing with snap on works better when you are drawing small objects. However, even when drawing an office building, you spend a great deal of time working on small details that may be easier to draw with snap on.

Figure 4-17: The completed pipe section

Object snaps

Often you need to draw an object in a position relative to a previously drawn object. For example, you may need to start a line from the endpoint or midpoint of an existing line. AutoCAD offers a feature called object snaps (OSNAPS for short) that enables you to specify a point by snapping to a geometrically defined point on an existing object. This is a very precise and efficient way to draw.

You can start an object snap in one of three ways:

✦ Open the Object Snap toolbar and choose the object snap that you want.

✦ Access the object snap shortcut menu by holding down the Shift key and right-clicking. Choose the object snap you want with the left mouse button.

✦ Type the object snap's abbreviation on the command line.

Cross-Reference On multi-button mice, you can customize one of the buttons to show the object snap menu. Displaying the object snap menu with the click of a mouse button is very convenient. Customizing the mouse is discussed in Chapter 33.

Table 4-1 lists the object snaps. Use the abbreviation to type the object snap from the keyboard.

<div align="center">

Table 4-1
AutoCAD's Object Snaps

</div>

Object Snap	Abbreviation	Uses
Endpoint	End	Lines, arcs, and so on.
Midpoint	mid	Lines, arcs, and so on.
Intersection	Int	Intersection of lines, circles, arcs.
Apparent Intersection*	App	The intersection that would be created if two objects were extended until they met.
Extension	Ext	Extends lines, arcs, and so on past their endpoints but in the same direction. After choosing this object snap, pause over the end point of a line or arc until you see a small plus sign. As you move the mouse cursor along the extension path, AutoCAD displays a temporary extension path so that you can draw to or from points on the extension path.
Center	Cen	Circles, arcs, ellipses.
Quadrant	Qua	Nearest quadrant (0, 90, 180, or 270 degree point) of a circle, arc, or ellipse.
Perpendicular	Per	Arc, circles, ellipses, lines, multilines, polylines, rays, splines, or construction lines.
Parallel	Par	Continues a line, polyline, and so on so that it's parallel to an existing line or other straight-line segment. After you choose this object snap, pause over the line you want to draw parallel to until you see a small parallel line symbol. As you move the mouse cursor parallel to the object, AutoCAD displays a temporary parallel path that you can use to create the parallel segment.
Tangent	Tan	Starts or continues a line from or to a point tangent with an arc, circle, or ellipse. See Figure 4-18.
Node	Nod	Point objects (discussed in Chapter 7).
Insertion	Ins	Insertion point of text or a block (inserting text is covered in Chapter 13; blocks are discussed in Chapter 18).
Nearest	Nea	Nearest point on any object.
None	Non	Turns off any object snap modes.

* Apparent Intersection also applies to 3D objects that appear to intersect due to the angle of view.

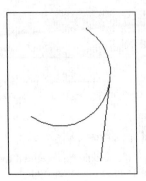

Figure 4-18: A line drawn tangent to an arc

When drawing a line, we think of it as having a starting point and an ending point. After the line is drawn, however, both of these points are considered endpoints in terms of object snaps. When picking the endpoint of a line for the endpoint object snap, pick a point on the line closer to the endpoint that you want. The same applies to arcs. Although the arc prompts read Start point and End, both are considered endpoints for purposes of object snaps.

AutoSnap is a feature that helps you work with object snaps. When you move the cursor near the geometric point you have specified, such as an endpoint, AutoCAD lets you know in three ways:

✦ **Marker:** An object snap shape appears. Each object snap has a differently shaped marker.

✦ **AutoSnap tooltip:** A label that displays the name of the object snap.

✦ **Magnet:** A pull that gently moves the cursor toward the geometric point.

Figure 4-19 shows an endpoint marker and AutoSnap tooltip.

Figure 4-19: AutoSnap shows you the endpoint of the line.

You can customize the AutoSnap feature to suit your needs or make it go away completely if you want. Choose Tools ➪ Options and click the Drafting tab. Here you can individually turn on and off the marker, AutoSnap tooltip, and the magnet.

You can also change the marker size and color. If you want, you can display the aperture box, which Release 13 and prior releases of AutoCAD used in order to let you pick an object snap point. (You probably don't want to display both the marker and the aperture — it can be somewhat confusing.)

In the following exercise, you practice using object snaps.

Step-by-Step: Using Object Snaps

1. Start a new drawing by using the `acad.dwg` template.

2. Save the drawing in your `AutoCAD Bible` folder as `ab04-05.dwg`.

3. Click ORTHO on the status bar to turn on ortho mode. If the OSNAP button is pushed in, click OSNAP on the status bar to turn off running object snaps (covered in the next section).

4. Start the LINE command. Follow the prompts:

```
Specify first point: 2,7 ↵. Move the cursor downward.
Specify next point or [Undo]: 4 ↵. Move the cursor to the
right.
Specify next point or [Undo]: 4 ↵. Move the cursor up.
Specify next point or [Close/Undo]: 4 ↵
Specify next point or [Close/Undo]: Press Enter to end the
command.
```

Your drawing should look like Figure 4-20. The circled numbers are reference points for this exercise.

Figure 4-20: These three lines are the start of a mounting bracket.

5. Choose Arc from the Draw toolbar. Follow the prompts:

Specify start point of arc or [Center]: *Press Shift and right-click. From the shortcut menu, choose Endpoint, as shown in Figure 4-21.*

_endpt of *Move the cursor to* ❶ *in Figure 4-20. When you see the endpoint marker and AutoSnap tooltip, pick it.*

Specify second point of arc or [Center/End]: *Right-click and choose Center.*

Specify center point of arc: *Press Shift and right-click. Choose Midpoint from the shortcut menu.*

_mid of *Move the cursor to* ❷ *and pick.*

Specify end point of arc or [Angle/chord Length]: **end** ↵. *Move the cursor to* ❸ *and pick.*

Figure 4-21: Choosing the Endpoint object snap from the shortcut menu

6. Choose Circle from the Draw menu. Follow the prompts:

Specify center point for circle or [3P/2P/Ttr (tan tan radius)]: *Choose Snap to Center from the Object Snap shortcut menu.*

_cen of *Move the cursor over the arc until you see the Center marker and tooltip, and then click.*
Specify radius of circle or [Diameter]: **.75** ↵

7. Start the LINE command and use any method you want to draw a line from the endpoint at ❸ to the endpoint at ❹. End the LINE command.

Note

When you press Shift and right-click to get the object snap menu, the mouse pointer must be in the drawing area. If it is on a toolbar, you get the Toolbars list. If that happens, press the Esc key, or hold the Shift button and right-click again in the drawing area.

8. Save your drawing. It should look like Figure 4-22.

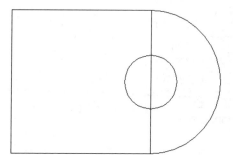

Figure 4-22: The start of a drawing of a mounting bracket (including a construction line that would later be erased). It was created by using the endpoint, midpoint, and center object snaps.

Running object snaps and OSNAP mode

The endpoint object snap is probably the most commonly used of all the object snaps. You might have a drawing project in which you need to use the endpoint object snap often. You can set a running object snap, which keeps one or more object snaps on until you turn them off.

Tip

Many users like to work with three or four running object snaps on at once, such as endpoint, midpoint, center, and intersection. If you can't find the object snap you want because you have several object snaps near each other, press the Tab key to cycle through the object snaps, one by one, until you find the one that you want.

To set running object snaps, choose Tools ➪ Drafting Settings (or right-click the OSNAP button on the status bar and choose Settings) to open the Drafting Settings dialog box, as shown in Figure 4-23. (If necessary, click the Object Snap tab.) Choose the object snaps that you want and click OK. To clear a checked object snap, click it. Click Clear All to clear all running snaps.

Figure 4-23: Use the Object Snap tab of the Drafting Settings dialog box to set running object snaps.

You use the OSNAP button on the status bar to turn on your running object snaps. If you want to turn them off temporarily, just click the OSNAP button. This capability to toggle running object snaps on and off makes it easy to work with running object snaps on almost all the time because you can turn them off at the click of a button. (You can also press F3.)

In the following exercise, you practice using running object snaps with OSNAP mode.

Step-by-Step: Using Running Object Snaps with OSNAP Mode

1. Start a new drawing by using the acad.dwt template. Save the file in your AutoCAD Bible folder as ab04-06.dwg.

2. Choose Tools ➪ Drafting Settings and click the Object Snap tab. Choose Endpoint. Uncheck all other object snaps and click OK.

3. Start the LINE command and start the line at 2,2.

4. Turn on ortho mode by clicking ORTHO on the status bar. If OSNAP is not on, click it on the status bar.

5. Move the mouse in the 0-degree direction and type **6** ↵.

6. Move the mouse up in the 90-degree direction, type **3** ↵, and end the LINE command.

7. Start the ARC command. At the Specify start point of arc or [Center]: prompt, pick the endpoint at ❶, shown in Figure 4-24. (Look for the marker and AutoSnap tooltip.)

Figure 4-24: Drawing a steam boiler with an endpoint running object snap

8. At the `Specify second point of arc or [Center/End]:` prompt, right-click and choose End. Pick the endpoint at ❷, shown in Figure 4-24.

9. At the `Specify center point of arc or [Angle/Direction/Radius]:` prompt, right-click and choose Angle, and then type **180** ↵.

10. Start the LINE command and at the `Specify first point:` prompt, pick the endpoint at ❷ in Figure 4-24.

11. Move the mouse to the left in the 180-degree direction, type **6** ↵, and end the LINE command.

12. Right-click the SNAP button on the status bar and choose Settings. Click Grid snap in the Snap type & style section. Set the Snap X spacing to 0.25. Check the Snap On check box. Click OK.

13. Start the LINE command. At the `Specify first point:` prompt, place the cursor 0.25 units above ❸ in Figure 4-24 (at 2,5.25). You may need to turn off the running OSNAP temporarily. Pick point 2,5.25.

14. At the `Specify next point or [Undo]:` prompt, pick point 2,1.75. (If necessary, press F6 to get absolute coordinates.)

15. Press F6 twice to get polar coordinates. Follow the prompts:

```
Specify next point or [Undo]: Pick .5<180.
Specify next point or [Close/Undo]: Pick 3.5<90.
Specify next point or [Close/Undo]: Pick the endpoint at ❹ in
Figure 4-24.
Specify next point or [Close/Undo]: ↵
```

16. Save your drawing.

Note

Even if you have running object snaps, if you specify an object snap during a command, it overrides the running object snap. For example, having a running endpoint object snap does not mean you cannot use a midpoint object snap for any specific drawing command.

By default, if you type absolute or relative coordinates, they take precedence over any running object snaps. This lets you leave running object snaps on but override them with keyboard entry of typed coordinates whenever you want. In general, the default gives you the most control and flexibility. However, you can change this default to give running object snaps precedence. To change the default, choose Tools ⇨ Options and click the User Preferences tab.

Locating Points

Sometimes you need to locate a point that is not on an existing object. For example, you might need a point a certain distance and angle from an existing object. This section explains three techniques that enable you to locate points that are not on objects — object snap tracking, point filters, and the From feature.

Object snap tracking

The purpose of tracking is to let you specify a point based on the object snaps of existing objects. Temporary tracking lines are drawn from points you specify, and you can use polar snap or direct distance entry to easily specify new points.

Object snap tracking significantly changes the way you draw in AutoCAD, offering increased ease and speed of drawing, because it provides visual confirmation of your tracking points. You will need to use the keyboard less often, and thus you'll be able to do more heads-up drawing. Use the OTRACK button on the status bar to turn object snap tracking on and off.

Object snap tracking can easily handle all of the following tasks and many more:

✦ You are drawing a line and have specified the start point. You want the end-point to be exactly vertical to the endpoint of an existing line.

✦ You are drawing a line and have specified the start point. You want the line to be 3 units long and parallel to an existing line.

✦ You are drawing a circle inside a rectangle (which could be a hole inside a sheet metal plate). You want the center of the circle to be exactly centered inside the rectangle, at the intersection of the midpoints of the rectangle's two sides.

✦ You want to start a line at the point where two existing lines would intersect if they were extended.

To start using object snap tracking, at least one object snap must be active. You can specify an object snap for just that command or turn on a running object snap, as explained in the previous sections. Then click OTRACK on the status bar.

After object snap tracking is on, follow these steps:

1. Start a command that requires you to specify a point.

2. Place the cursor briefly over an object snap, such as the endpoint of a line, to temporarily *acquire* it. You can acquire more than one point. AutoCAD uses these acquired points to calculate the tracking paths. You see a small plus sign (+) over the object snap as confirmation, as shown in Figure 4-25.

Acquired point

Cursor

Figure 4-25: When you pause over an object snap and then move the cursor slightly, you see a plus sign (+) at the acquired point to show that the point has been acquired and can now be used for object snap tracking.

3. Move the cursor away from the object snap toward your desired point. AutoCAD displays temporary alignment paths as you move the cursor over available drawing paths, as shown in Figure 4-26. If ORTHO is on, AutoCAD displays only horizontal and vertical paths. If POLAR is on, AutoCAD displays polar paths based on the polar angle settings, as explained earlier in this chapter.

Acquired endpoint of existing arc

Temporary alignment path

Desired endpoint of new line (at the "X")

Endpoint: 3'-9 15/16" < 270°

Cursor
Start point of new line
Tooltip

Figure 4-26: With the endpoint object snap active and ORTHO on, AutoCAD displays temporary alignment paths based on the acquired point.

4. When you see a tooltip and a small x, click. AutoCAD continues or completes the command, using this point.

After you acquire a point, you can clear it in any one of three ways:

✦ Move the cursor back over the point's plus sign.

✦ Click OTRACK off using the status bar.

✦ Start any new command.

Note Tracking is intended for use in two dimensions only. For 3D point location, use X, Y, and Z point filters, covered later in this chapter.

You can customize the following features of object snap tracking by using the Drafting tab of the Options dialog box (Choose Tools ➪ Options):

✦ Uncheck Display Polar Tracking Vector to eliminate the tracking paths.

✦ Uncheck Display Full Screen Tracking Vector to display the tracking paths only from the cursor to the object snap point.

✦ Uncheck Display AutoTrack Tooltip to eliminate the tooltips.

✦ In the Alignment Point Acquisition section, choose "Shift to acquire" to require you to press Shift to acquire a point when the cursor is over an object snap point.

In the following exercise, you practice locating points with object snap tracking.

On the CD-ROM The drawing used in the following Step-by-Step exercise on locating points with object snap tracking, ab04-c.dwg, is in the Drawings folder of the *AutoCAD 2004 Bible* CD-ROM.

Step-by-Step: Locating Points with Object Snap Tracking

1. Open ab04-c.dwg from the CD-ROM.

2. Save the drawing as ab04-07.dwg in your AutoCAD Bible folder. This drawing is a section of a simple plan layout of an apartment. Set endpoint and midpoint running object snaps only. Make sure that OSNAP and OTRACK are on and that POLAR is off.

3. Start the LINE command. At the Specify first point: prompt, pick the endpoint at ❶ in Figure 4-27. Be sure to pick on the endpoint itself, in order to acquire it.

4. At the Specify next point or [Undo]: prompt, pass the cursor over ❷. Move the cursor down a little, and you see the small plus sign showing that this endpoint has been acquired.

Figure 4-27: The tub, door, and sink to be completed in this plan layout

5. Move the cursor down until it is to the left of ❶ and vertical to ❷. When you see the tooltip (reading Endpoint: < 270°, Endpoint: < 180°) and the small x marking the intersection of the two points, click to end the line segment.

6. At the Specify next point or [Undo]: prompt, click at ❷ and end the LINE command.

7. Start the LINE command again. At the Specify first point: prompt, pick the endpoint of the arc at ❸ in Figure 4-27. If you're not sure that you found the right endpoint, press Tab until the arc is highlighted. Make sure that you have acquired the endpoint by clicking the endpoint itself or passing the crosshairs over it.

8. At the Specify next point or [Undo]: prompt, pass the cursor over ❹ until you see the small plus sign. Move the cursor to the left until you see the tooltip (reading Endpoint: < 90°, Endpoint: < 180°) and click.

9. At the Specify next point or [Undo]: prompt, pick the endpoint at ❹ and end the LINE command.

10. Start the CIRCLE command. At the Specify center point for circle or [3P/2P/Ttr (tan tan radius)]: prompt, pass the cursor over ❺ and then over ❻ to acquire both midpoints.

11. Move the cursor to the middle of the sink, where lines from both midpoints would intersect until you see the tooltip (reading Midpoint: < 90° Midpoint: < 180°) and click.

12. At the `Specify radius of circle or [Diameter]:` prompt, type **7.5** ↵ to complete the sink.

13. Save your drawing. It should look like Figure 4-28.

Figure 4-28: The completed drawing

Point filters

Point filters enable you to specify a coordinate using the X coordinate of one existing object snap and the Y coordinate of another. You construct an X,Y coordinate based on coordinates of existing objects. If this sounds complicated, it is. Object snap tracking should mostly eliminate the need to go back to the old point filter way of doing things. (Point filters have been around for a long time.)

Cross-Reference Point filters are often used in 3D drawings where object snap tracking doesn't work. See Chapter 21 for more details.

Here's how to use point filters:

1. Start a command to draw an object.

2. To specify a coordinate, type **.x** or **.y** on the command line. You can also find point filters on the object snap shortcut menu (Shift+right-click).

3. AutoCAD prompts you for a point. Generally, you specify the point by using an object snap.

4. AutoCAD prompts you for the other coordinate value, which you generally provide by using an object snap. (If you are working in 2D, ignore the request for a Z coordinate.)

5. Continue your command.

Tip

You do not need to use existing coordinates for both the X and Y portions of the coordinate. For example, you can construct an X,Y coordinate by using the Y coordinate of an existing line and picking the X coordinate anywhere on the screen.

In the following exercise, you practice using 2D point filters on the same drawing you used in the previous exercise.

On the CD-ROM

The drawing used in this Step-by-Step exercise on using 2D point filters, ab04-c.dwg, is on the *AutoCAD 2004 Bible* CD-ROM.

Step-by-Step: Using 2D Point Filters

1. Open ab04-c.dwg from the CD-ROM.

2. Save the file as ab04-08.dwg in your AutoCAD Bible folder. Make sure that ORTHO and OSNAP are on and OTRACK is off. Set a running object snap for endpoint and midpoint.

3. Start the LINE command.

4. At the Specify first point: prompt, pick the endpoint at ❶ in Figure 4-29.

Figure 4-29: Using point filters to specify the start of a line

5. At the Specify next point or [Undo]: prompt, type **.x** ↵. At the of prompt, pick the endpoint at ❷ in Figure 4-29.

6. AutoCAD responds with the (need YZ): prompt. (Because you are drawing in 2D, you can ignore the Z.) Choose the endpoint at ❶ in Figure 4-29. AutoCAD draws the line segment to the point defined by the X coordinate of ❷ and the Y coordinate of ❶.

7. At the Specify next point or [Undo]: prompt, pick the endpoint at ❷. End the LINE command.

8. Start the LINE command again. At the Specify first point: prompt, pick the endpoint at ❸. If necessary, press Tab until you see the arc highlighted so that you know you have the endpoint of the arc.

9. At the Specify next point or [Undo]: prompt, type **.y** ⏎. At the of prompt, pick the endpoint at ❹ in Figure 4-29.

10. At the (need XZ): prompt, pick the endpoint at ❸.

11. At the Specify next point or [Undo]: prompt, pick the endpoint at ❹. End the LINE command.

12. Start the CIRCLE command. At the Specify center point for circle or [3P/2P/Ttr (tan tan radius)]: prompt, type **.y** ⏎. At the of prompt, pick the midpoint at ❺. At the (need XZ): prompt, pick the midpoint at ❻. AutoCAD places the center of the circle.

13. At the Specify radius of circle or [Diameter]: prompt, type **7.5** ⏎.

14. Save your drawing.

From feature

The From feature enables you to create a new object starting at a known distance and direction from an existing object. It's like creating one or more invisible lines between the existing object and the new object, helping you start the new object in the proper place. Use From when no object snaps are available to help you determine a new point.

Here's how to use the From feature:

1. Start a command to draw an object, such as LINE.

2. Press Shift, right-click, and choose From on the shortcut menu. You can also type **from** on the command line.

3. AutoCAD prompts you for a base point, which you usually provide by using an object snap, such as endpoint.

4. AutoCAD prompts you for an Offset, which you provide by using relative or polar coordinates.

5. Continue the command you started (in Step 1).

In the following exercise, you practice using the From feature.

The drawing used in the following Step-by-Step exercise on using the From feature, ab04-06.dwg, is in the Results folder of the *AutoCAD 2004 Bible* CD-ROM.

Step-by-Step: Using the From Feature

1. Open ab04-06.dwg, which you created in an earlier exercise. If you did not do the previous exercise, open the drawing from the Results folder of the CD-ROM. Make sure ortho mode is on and SNAP is off. OSNAP should be on. Set a running object snap for endpoint.

2. Save the drawing as ab04-09.dwg in your AutoCAD Bible folder.

3. Start the LINE command.

4. From the Object Snap shortcut menu, choose From.

5. AutoCAD prompts you for a base point. Pick the endpoint near ❶ in Figure 4-30.

Figure 4-30: Using the From feature to complete the steam boiler

6. At the ⟨Offset⟩: prompt, type **@–1,.5**↵.

7. You are now ready to continue the line at the Specify next point or [Undo]: prompt. Move the cursor in the 90-degree direction and type **2** ↵.

8. Move the mouse in the 180-degree direction and type **1** ↵.

9. Move the mouse in the 270-degree direction and type **2** ↵.

10. Move the mouse in the 0-degree direction, find the Endpoint marker of the start point of the first segment of the line, and pick the point. End the LINE command.

11. Save your drawing. It should look like Figure 4-31.

Figure 4-31: The completed steam boiler

Summary

This chapter covered a great deal about specifying coordinates in this chapter. These skills form the basis for all your future work with AutoCAD. You read about:

✦ The X,Y coordinate system

✦ Using absolute Cartesian coordinates

✦ When and how to use relative Cartesian coordinates

✦ Absolute and relative polar coordinates

✦ Direct distance entry

✦ The orthogonal (ORTHO) mode

✦ Using polar tracking

✦ Controlling the display of coordinates on the status bar

✦ Grid and polar snap settings

✦ Using the visible grid

✦ Using object snaps (OSNAPS) to specify geometric points on objects

✦ Running object snaps and turning OSNAP on and off

✦ Using object snap tracking to locate points

✦ Using point filters to locate points

✦ The From feature for locating points not on an object

The next chapter introduces you to the basics of setting up a drawing.

✦ ✦ ✦

Setting Up a Drawing

Often the first step after you start a new drawing is to set its size and unit type. These and other setup options are discussed in this chapter. The entire process of setting up a drawing is essential to accurate results.

Unit Types

One of the first steps in setting up a drawing is to choose the unit type. Units define how objects are measured. You can save the unit type in a template.

The coordinates you use in AutoCAD are measured in units that can represent any real-world measurement, such as inches or millimeters. A surveyor or city planner might even use miles as the base unit. However, different disciplines customarily express units differently, and you should use the unit type appropriate for the type of drawing you are creating. AutoCAD offers five types of units, as shown in Table 5-1. The sample measurement column shows how a line 32.5 inches long would be displayed in the various unit types.

Notice how the engineering and architectural units translate a line of 32.5 units into feet and inches. Engineering and architectural units assume a unit of one inch, unlike the other unit types, which can represent any measurement.

The unit type affects how coordinates are shown on the status bar and how AutoCAD lists information about objects. You generally input coordinates by using the type of units you have chosen, although AutoCAD in some cases accepts coordinates in another unit type.

Table 5-1
Unit Types

Unit Type	Sample Measurement	Description
Decimal	32.50	Number of units, partial units in decimals
Engineering	2'–8.50"	Feet and inches, partial inches in decimals
Architectural	2'–8 1/2"	Feet and inches, partial inches in fractions
Fractional	32 1/2	Number of units, partial units in fractions
Scientific	3.25E+01	Base number + exponent

Note If you are using engineering or architectural units, AutoCAD displays partial inches differently than the format you must use to type them in. You must type coordinates without any spaces because AutoCAD interprets a space as equivalent to pressing the Enter key and ends your input. Use a hyphen between whole and partial inches, for example, 3'2-1/2". (You can omit the " after the inches because AutoCAD assumes inches in engineering and architectural units if no symbol follows a number.) However, this appears on the status line as 3'-2 1/2". This can be confusing because the hyphen is in a different place, and AutoCAD inserts a space between the whole and partial inches.

Setting the drawing units

Once you know the units you want to use, you set them in the Drawing Units dialog box. To set the units, choose Format ➪ Units to open the Drawing Units dialog box, shown in Figure 5-1. The left side of the Drawing Units dialog box enables you to choose which unit type you want to use. In the Precision box in the Length section, click the arrow and a list of precision options drops down. Click the one you want.

Figure 5-1: The Drawing Units dialog box

Look in Chapter 3 for a brief overview of the Drawing Units dialog box in the exercise on using a dialog box. See Chapter 18 for more on inserting drawings into other drawings by using the DesignCenter. See Chapter 26 for full coverage on the DesignCenter.

AutoCAD rounds off measurements to the nearest precision value you choose. Say that you choose a precision of two decimal places, using decimal units. You want to draw a line so that it is 3.25 units long, but when you type the coordinate, by accident you press the 4 key at the end, resulting in a line 3.254 units long. AutoCAD shows this line as 3.25 units long, making it difficult for you to spot the error. Therefore, it is a good idea to set a higher precision than you need to show.

Setting the angle type

As with units, your choice of angle type depends on your profession and work environment. Decimal Degrees is the default. Table 5-2 lists the types of angles.

Table 5-2 Angle Types		
Unit Type	**Sample Measurement**	**Description**
Decimal Degrees	32.5	Degrees, partial degrees in decimals
Deg/Min/Sec	32°30'0"	Degrees, minutes, and seconds
Grads (gradians)	36.1111g	Gradians
Radians	0.5672r	Radians
Surveyor	N 57d30' E	Surveyor (directional) units

A minute is $\frac{1}{60}$ degree and a second is $\frac{1}{60}$ minute. Gradians and radians are simply alternate ways of measuring angles. A gradian is a metric measurement equal to $\frac{1}{100}$ of a right angle. Radians measure an angle by placing a length, equal to the radius, along the circle's circumference. Radians range from 0 to $2 \times \pi$ instead of from 0 to 360 as degrees do. A radian is approximately 57.30 degrees. Surveyor units measure angles in directions, starting with north or south and adding an angle in a degrees, minutes, seconds format that shows how far the angle is from north or south and in which direction (east or west).

To set the angle type, choose the option you want from the Type drop-down list of the Angle section of the Drawing Units dialog box (shown in Figure 5-1).

Changing these angle settings does not automatically change the way your dimensions appear. Use the Dimension Style Manager, which is discussed in Chapter 15, to change dimensions.

Setting the angle measure and direction

When defining angle units, you also need to specify in which direction degrees increase. According to standard convention, you measure angles so that 0 degrees starts to the right, in the East direction. To change this convention, choose the direction that you want for 0 degrees and then click Next.

To set the angle measure in the Drawing Units dialog box, click Direction to open the Direction Control dialog box, shown in Figure 5-2.

Figure 5-2: The Direction Control dialog box

Here you can choose to have 0 degrees start in a direction other than East. You can also type any other angle or click the Pick an Angle button to pick two points on your screen that specify an angle. Choose OK.

Note Changing the angle direction affects what happens when you input angles and what you see in the coordinate display. It does not change the absolute coordinates, which are set according to the UCS (User Coordinate System). Chapter 8 covers using and customizing UCSs.

By standard convention, degrees increase in a counterclockwise direction. To set the angle direction, click Clockwise in the Drawing Units dialog box.

Step-by-Step: Setting Drawing Units

1. Begin a new drawing using the acad.dwt template.

2. Save the drawing as ab05-01.dwg in your AutoCAD Bible folder.

3. Choose Format ⇨ Units to open the Drawing Units dialog box.

4. In the Length section, choose Architectural.

5. Click the arrow to the right of the Precision drop-down list box in the Length section. Choose 0'-0 1/8".

6. In the Angle section, choose Deg/Min/Sec.

7. In the Precision box, choose 0d00'.

8. In the Units to Scale Drag-and-Drop Content drop-down list, set the units to Inches.

9. Click OK.

10. Start the LINE command. Follow the prompts:

```
Specify first point: 2,2 ↵
Specify next point or [Undo]: @1'<0 ↵
Specify next point or [Undo]: @6-3/4<153 ↵
Specify next point or [Close/Undo]: 2,2 ↵
```

11. End the LINE command.

12. Choose View ➪ Zoom ➪ All to zoom to the entire drawing. Save your drawing. If you are continuing through the chapter, keep it open.

Note You would not actually use Deg/Min/Sec for angles in an architectural drawing, but the exercise gives you the opportunity to set the angular units.

Drawing Limits

You can specify the area of your drawing, also called the *limits*. The drawing limits are the outer edges of the drawing, specified in X,Y units. You need to set only the width and length of the drawing. Together, these two measurements create an invisible bounding rectangle for your drawing.

Almost universally, the lower-left limit is 0,0, which is the default. Therefore, the upper-right corner really defines the drawing size. Remember that you typically draw at life size (full scale) in AutoCAD. Therefore, the size of your drawing should be equal to the size of the outer extents of what you are drawing plus a margin for a title block and perhaps for annotation and dimensioning. If you want to show more than one view of an object, as is common in both architectural and mechanical drawings, you need to take this into account.

To decide on the upper-right corner of your drawing *limits* (the width and length of your drawing), you need to consider what the drawing units mean for you. Generally, the smallest commonly used unit is used, often inches or millimeters. Therefore, if you are drawing a plan view of a house that is approximately 40-feet across (in the X direction) by 30-feet deep (in the Y direction), this translates to a top-right corner of 480,360. Adding room for a title block brings you to about 500,380.

Note You can draw outside the drawing limits. However, the drawing limits setting affects the size of the grid if you turn it on. This can help you visualize the size of your drawing if you don't have a title block. The ZOOM command with the All option also uses the drawing limits to resize the display, although it displays the entire drawing if the drawing is outside the limits. Setting the limits makes ZOOM All more useful.

Setting drawing limits

The limits define an artificial and invisible boundary to your drawing. You can draw outside the limits. The limits affect the size of the grid, when displayed. (See Chapter 4 for a discussion of the grid.) The Zoom command with the All option also uses the limits, but only if no objects are outside the limits. (See Chapter 8.)

To set the drawing limits, choose Format ➪ Drawing Limits to start the LIMITS command. Press Enter to accept the lower-left corner default of 0,0 that appears on the command line. Then type the upper-right corner coordinate that you want and press Enter.

On the CD-ROM The drawing used in the following Step-by-Step exercise on setting the drawing limits, ab05-01.dwg, is in the Results folder of the *AutoCAD 2002 Bible* CD-ROM.

Step-by-Step: Setting the Drawing Limits

1. If you did the previous exercise, continue to use ab05-01.dwg. Otherwise, open ab05-01.dwg from the Results folder of the CD-ROM.

2. Save the drawing as ab05-02.dwg in your AutoCAD Bible folder.

3. Choose Format ➪ Drawing Limits.

4. Press Enter to accept the lower-left default of 0,0.

5. Type **16,10** ↵.

6. Start the LINE command. Follow the prompts:

```
Specify first point: 0,0 ↵
Specify next point or [Undo]: 16,0 ↵
Specify next point or [Undo]: 16,10 ↵
Specify next point or [Close/Undo]: 0,10 ↵
Specify next point or [Close/Undo]: 0,0 ↵
```

7. End the LINE command.

8. Choose View ➪ Zoom ➪ All.

9. Save your drawing. If you are continuing through the chapter, keep it open.

Understanding Scales

You need to consider the fact that your drawing will most likely be plotted onto a standard paper (sheet) size. The standard orientation for drafting (and the default for most plotters) is landscape orientation, meaning that as you look at the drawing, the paper is wider than it is tall. Figure 5-3 shows an example. These conventions have carried over from the days of hand drafting. (In a computer program, this is not really necessary, as you can rotate the drawing when you plot it.) To scale a drawing onto a piece of paper in a pleasing manner requires a rectangular shape that somewhat resembles the proportions of standard paper sizes.

Figure 5-3: Drawings are usually oriented horizontally, as in this example.

Thanks to Henry Dearborn, AIA, Fairfield, Iowa, for this drawing, which I have altered somewhat.

In addition, although you specify the scale at plotting time, it helps to be aware of the scale you will use when plotting your drawing at the outset. The scales used for GIS (Geographic Information Systems), where you might be drawing an entire county, will be different from those used when drawing a house. The scales used in mechanical drafting are again totally different. In fact, in mechanical drafting, if you are drawing a very small object, such as a 2-inch screw-plate, you might scale up, that is, enlarge the drawing when plotting.

One important reason for establishing the scale at the beginning is to ensure that text, whether annotations or dimensions, is readable in its final plotted form. Applying a scale makes it possible to ensure that text remains a reasonable size even as the rest of the drawing is scaled up or down. In AutoCAD, scale also affects dotted and dashed lines as well as line widths.

Some drawings are not scaled. Examples are electrical or electronic schematics, piping diagrams, and railroad schematics. These drawings are representations of electrical or electronic connections but do not resemble the actual physical object that will eventually be created from the drawing. These drawings can be any size as long as they are clear and organized.

Cross-Reference You can lay out various views of your drawing on an imaginary piece of paper, called a *paper space layout,* to prepare it for plotting. See Chapter 17 for more on layouts and plotting.

When determining your scale to try to fit a drawing on a sheet of paper, be aware that a plotter cannot print on the entire sheet. A certain amount of the margin around the edge is not available for drawing. Plotters differ in this respect. The plotter's manual can let you know the width of this unprintable margin. On average, you can assume a half-inch margin on each side; thus you should subtract one inch from both the length and width sheet measurements to determine the actual drawing space. Table 5-3 shows standard U.S. sheet sizes.

Table 5-3
Standard Paper Sheet Sizes in the United States (in inches)

Size	Width	Height	Size	Width	Height
A	11	8½	D	34	22
B	17	11	E	44	34
C	22	17			

Table 5-4 lists standard metric sheet sizes.

Table 5-4
Standard Metric Paper Sheet Sizes (in millimeters)

Size	Width	Height	Size	Width	Height
A4	297	210	A1	841	594
A3	420	297	A0	1,189	841
A2	594	420			

Scale formats

A scale is often indicated in the format "plotted size=actual size." Because you draw at actual size in AutoCAD, the actual size is also the drawing size. For example, a scale of ¼"=1' means that ¼ inch on the drawing, when plotted out on a sheet of paper, represents 1 foot in actual life — and in the AutoCAD drawing. This is a typical architectural scale. A windowpane one foot wide would appear ¼-inch wide on paper.

From the scale, you can calculate the scale factor. To do this, the left side of the scale equation must equal 1, and the two numbers must be in the same measurement (for example, both in inches). This requires some simple math. For ¼"=1', you would calculate as follows:

¼" = 1'

1"= 4' Both sides of the equation multiplied by 4

1" = 48" 4' converted to 48"

Therefore, the scale factor is 48. This means that the paper plot is ⅟₄₈ of real size.

In mechanical drawing, you might draw a metal joint that is actually 4 inches long. To fit it on an 8½ × 11 sheet of paper, you could use a 2"=1" scale, which means that 2" on the paper drawing equals 1" in actual life and the AutoCAD drawing. Calculate the scale factor:

2" = 1"

1" = ½"

The scale factor is ½. This means that the paper plot is twice the real size.

Cross-Reference You use the scale factor when you set the size for text in Chapter 13 and for dimensions in Chapter 15.

Most professions use certain standard scales. Therefore, you do not usually have a choice to pick any scale you want, such as 1":27'. Instead, the conventions of your profession, client, or office dictate a choice of only a few scales. Table 5-5 lists some standard architectural scales.

Table 5-5
Typical Architectural Scales

Scale Factor	Plotted Size	Drawing/Actual Size
480	$\frac{1}{40}$"	1'
240	$\frac{1}{20}$"	1'
192	$\frac{1}{16}$"	1'
96	$\frac{1}{8}$"	1'
48	$\frac{1}{4}$"	1'
24	$\frac{1}{2}$"	1'
16	$\frac{3}{4}$"	1'
12	1"	1'
4	3"	1'
2	6"	1'
1	1'	1'

Civil Engineering scales are somewhat different and range to larger sizes — a bridge is bigger than a house — as shown in Table 5-6.

Table 5-6
Typical Civil Engineering Scales

Scale Factor	Plotted Size	Drawing/Actual Size
120	1"	10'
240	1"	20'
360	1"	30'
480	1"	40'
600	1"	50'
720	1"	60'
960	1"	80'
1,200	1"	100'

Table 5-7 shows some typical metric scales that can be used for any purpose. You would most typically work in millimeters, but these could represent any metric measurement.

Table 5-7 Typical Metric Scales		
Scale Factor	**Plotted Size**	**Drawing/Actual Size**
5,000	1	5,000
2,000	1	2,000
1,000	1	1,000
500	1	500
200	1	200
100	1	100
75	1	75
50	1	50
20	1	20
10	1	10
5	1	5
1	1	1

Deciding on a scale and sheet size

As soon as you know the size of your drawing and the scale appropriate for your situation, you need to consider the sheet size of the paper that you will plot on. Again, you often find that certain factors limit your choices. Your plotter or printer may be limited to certain sheet sizes. The conventions used in your discipline or working environment also affect your decision. You may be working on a series of drawings that are all to be plotted on the same size sheet of paper.

As an example, the architectural drawing in Figure 5-3 is 175-feet wide by 120-feet high. The two most typical scales for a drawing of a house are ¼"=1' and ⅛"=1'. On a small plotter, you might have a choice of sheet sizes A, B, or C. The following steps show the calculations you need to do in order to decide on a scale, obtain the scale factor, and determine the appropriate sheet size.

In this exercise, you practice determining the scale and sheet size. You need only a sheet of paper and a pencil. Use Figure 5-3 (shown earlier) as a reference.

Step-by-Step: Determining the Scale and Sheet Size

1. To calculate the plotted size of the drawing at ¼"=1', you can start with the width, which is 175'. Take one-quarter of 175 to get the width of the drawing in inches, which is 43¾".

2. Take one-quarter of the height, 120', to get the height of the drawing in inches, which is 30".

3. A size-C sheet (see Table 5-3) is 22"×17", which is too small for a 43¾"×30" drawing.

4. Recalculate the drawing at ⅛"=1'. Take one-eighth of 175 to get 21⅞. Take one-eighth of 120 to get 15".

5. The actual drawing space (minus the margins the printer requires) on a size-C sheet is about 21"×16". The height of the drawing at this scale is adequate, but the width is ⅞" too long. Therefore, the best bet is to simply make the drawing ⅞" narrower because the drawing has some extra room. This lets you fit the drawing on a size-C sheet.

6. To calculate the scale factor of a ⅛"=1' scale, multiply 1' by 8 to get 8' and convert it to inches, which is 96 (8×12).

Rearranging the views, dimensions, and text on a drawing to fit a standard scale factor and sheet size is a typical task. There is no actual setup step for setting the drawing scale, but you use it when you insert text or dimensions and when you plot the drawing.

Inserting a Title Block

A *title block* is a rectangle that includes spaces for the drawing title, company name, drafter name, and so on. It generally comes with a border that bounds your drawing. Many drawings require title blocks. You can insert an existing title block in two ways:

✦ When creating a new drawing, choose File ➪ New to open the Select Template dialog box. Choose one of the templates that includes a title block. For example, `ANSI A -Named Plot Styles.dwt` includes a title block and border that fit on an A-size sheet. AutoCAD inserts the title block and border on the layout tab. (Chapter 17 covers layouts and named plot styles.)

✦ After you open a drawing, you can insert a drawing of a title block into it. Choose Insert ➪ Block. In the Insert dialog box, type the name of the drawing or block or click Browse to find it. Most of the templates have a corresponding drawing that you can insert into your drawing. You can find them in the `\Template` folder. To insert the file or block at 0,0 with no scaling or rotation, uncheck all the Specify On-screen check boxes. Check Explode if you expect to edit the inserted drawing after it's in your drawing. Click OK.

New Feature

The templates and their corresponding drawings are in a new location. To find this location, choose Tools ⇨ Options and click the Files tab. Double-click Drawing Template Settings and then double-click Drawing Template File Location. You see the path to the new location displayed. The path is very long! This folder may be hidden in Windows Explorer. For instructions on displaying hidden folders, go to Windows Help and enter **hidden folders** in the search box.

Cross-Reference

As explained in Chapter 2, you can create your own title block, make a template from it, and then start a drawing based on that template. Chapter 18 covers blocks.

Common Setup Options

A few other items are generally set up in advance and are included in a template. Other chapters of this book cover the following:

✦ **Layers** (covered in Chapter 11) enable you to organize your drawing into meaningful groups. In an architectural drawing, for example, you might create a layer for walls, another for doors, one for electrical fixtures, and so on.

✦ **Text styles** (covered in Chapter 13) enable you to format the font and other text characteristics.

✦ **Dimension styles** (covered in Chapter 15) format the dimensions that measure your objects.

Setting Snap, Grid, and Ortho

If you know you will be using snap, grid, and ortho a lot in certain drawings and you know the suitable settings for snap and grid, you can set these and save them in a template because these settings are saved with the drawing. In other cases, you might want to leave them off and turn them on only when you need them.

The Windows registry saves many settings, such as running object snaps, the type of snap (grid or polar), and the polar distance when you are using polar snap. As a result, when you open AutoCAD, they are automatically set to the same setting you had when you last closed AutoCAD, regardless of the setting in the drawing. Therefore, you cannot save these settings in a template.

In this final exercise, you practice specifying the drafting settings and creating a template.

On the CD-ROM

The drawing used in the following Step-by-Step exercise on setting drawing aids and creating a template, ab05-02.dwg, is in the Results folder of the *AutoCAD 2002 Bible* CD-ROM.

System variables

When you change settings in AutoCAD, such as the unit type, angle type, drawing limits, blip marks, snap mode (on or off), grid mode, or ortho mode, you are actually changing AutoCAD's *system variables*. These are simply settings that AutoCAD stores in each drawing or in the Windows registry (which stores settings that apply to all drawings). Usually you don't need to pay any direct attention to them, but they are the nuts and bolts behind the dialog boxes you use to change the settings. When you start customizing AutoCAD, you need to learn about them because programming code and script files (AutoCAD macros) cannot access dialog boxes. Also, a few system variables are accessible only by typing them directly on the command line. Appendix C on the CD-ROM provides more information on system variables. Throughout this book, I occasionally mention system variables when it is useful to use them directly. Some system variables store information about a drawing or the drawing environment, such as the drawing name and path. These are *read-only*, meaning that you cannot change them. They exist to provide information and are often used in AutoLISP programs.

You can type system variables on the command line, just like AutoCAD's regular commands.

Information about each system variable, where it is stored, its default, and whether it is read-only is in AutoCAD's help system. Choose Help ⇨ Help and double-click Command Reference on the Contents tab. Then scroll down and double-click System Variables.

Step-by-Step: Setting Drawing Aids and Creating a Template

1. If you did the exercise on drawing limits use that drawing or open ab05-02.dwg from the Results folder of the CD-ROM.

2. Save the drawing as ab05-03.dwg in your AutoCAD Bible folder.

3. Choose Tools ⇨ Drafting Settings.

4. On the Snap and Grid tab, the snap spacing is set to ½". In the Grid section, change the X spacing to 1". Make sure the Snap Type is set to grid snap and rectangular snap. Click OK.

5. Click SNAP and GRID on the status bar to turn them on. Make sure OSNAP is turned off.

6. Choose Format ⇨ Units. Change the Angle Type back to decimal degrees. In the Units to Scale Drag-and-Drop Content section, choose Inches from the drop-down list (if not already set for inches). Click OK.

7. Using the coordinate display as your guide, start the LINE command and draw line segments from 2½, 1½ to ½<270 to 11"<0 to ½<90. End the LINE command.

8. Start the LINE command again. Again use the coordinate display to draw line segments from 2,2 to 1/2<270 to 1'0"<0 to ½<90. End the LINE command.

9. Save your drawing. It should look like Figure 5-4. Notice how the grid and snap settings facilitate the drawing process.

The architectural units create a different drawing experience than decimal units would. Setting up a drawing creates a drawing environment suited to your work needs.

Figure 5-4: The final architectural drawing

10. Choose File ➪ Save As. In the Save Drawing As dialog box, click the Files of Type drop-down list box and choose AutoCAD Drawing Template (*.dwt). Notice that AutoCAD automatically places you in the \Template folder.

11. In the File name text box, change the name to archroof.dwt. Click Save.

12. In the Template Description dialog box, type **Arch units, 16,10 limits, snap & grid** and click OK.

13. Choose File ➪ New. Choose the archroof template and click Open. AutoCAD starts a new drawing by using the template.

Do not save this new drawing.

The MVSETUP Command

The MVSETUP command is used in two different ways — to set up a drawing and to create viewports for paper space layouts.

Cross-Reference Paper space layouts are a way of laying out your drawing in preparation for printing or plotting. Chapter 17, which covers laying out a drawing as well as plotting, discusses paper space layouts.

MVSETUP provides a command-line routine to walk you through some of the basic setup functions discussed in this chapter. You can use MVSETUP when you start to

customize AutoCAD to set up a drawing from a script file or AutoLISP program (topics covered in Parts VI and VII of this book). To use MVSETUP, type **mvsetup** ↵ on the command line. AutoCAD responds with the following prompt:

```
Enable paper space? [No/Yes] <Y>:
```

Type **n** ↵ to use MVSETUP without entering paper space.

The next prompt lets you enter the units type:

```
Enter units type
[Scientific/Decimal/Engineering/Architectural/Metric]:
```

Choose the option you want. Then AutoCAD displays a list of scale factors appropriate to the units option you chose. At the `Enter the scale factor:` prompt, type in a numeric scale factor.

Finally, AutoCAD prompts you to set the drawing limits with the following two prompts:

```
Enter the paper width:
Enter the paper height:
```

After each prompt, enter a number based on the size of the paper you plan to plot on. AutoCAD draws a rectangle of the size you indicated for the drawing limits.

Creating a Customized Template

You can save many of the settings discussed in this chapter in a template so that they are available to you whenever you start a new drawing.

To create a customized template, open any drawing. Make changes as described in this chapter and save the drawing as a template by choosing Drawing Template (*.dwt) from the Save as Type drop-down list box in the Save Drawing As dialog box.

There are two wizards to help you set up a drawing. You need to activate the Startup dialog box to find them:

1. Choose Tools ⇨ Options and click the System tab. In the General Options section, choose Show Startup Dialog Box from the Startup drop-down list. Click OK.

2. Close and open AutoCAD. You see the Startup dialog box.

3. Click the Use a Wizard button. Choose Quick Setup for fewer options or Advanced Setup for more options.

4. Click OK.

Summary

This chapter explained all about setting up a drawing so that it behaves the way you want it to. You read about:

✦ Setting the unit type

✦ Setting the angle type, measure, and direction

✦ Drawing limits

✦ Scales and calculating a scale factor

✦ Setting drawing aids and creating a template that includes the settings that you want

This chapter ends Part I, "AutoCAD Basics." Now that you know the basics, you can go on to Part II, "Drawing in Two Dimensions." The next chapter covers drawing simple lines, polygons, rectangles, and special infinite construction lines.

✦ ✦ ✦

Summary

These chapters... this... image drawing so... techniques, if they're
you want it for, read about.

- Setting the unit type.

- Identifying the multiple types of... and direction

- Dimensions.

- Grids and other drawing assistance.

- Setting the drawing scale and creating templates that hold the settings that
you want.

- This chapter... text...

... image it. Two dimensional... The next chapter covers the vital
snapping... polylines, rectangles, and special building and construction lines.

Drawing in Two Dimensions

Now that you have the basics under your belt, it's time to really draw. In Part II, you learn the techniques for basic drawing and editing in AutoCAD. After chapters on drawing simple lines and curves, I explain the details of how to control the display of your drawings. You can also find chapters on creating text, drawing dimensions, and creating dimension styles. Separate chapters cover getting information from your drawing and drawing complex objects. Part II winds up with a chapter on plotting and printing. This part contains all the basic information you need for two-dimensional drawing and design.

Drawing Simple Lines

L ines are the most commonly drawn object. You will use the LINE command a lot! Other related commands are also used often. Construction lines are not as common, but you should have all these commands in your arsenal. Part I included several exercises in which you drew lines. However, the LINE command has several options and you can still learn a few tricks of the trade by focusing on the LINE command itself.

Using the LINE Command

Learning all the ins and outs of the line command will make your drawing more efficient, because you use the LINE command so often.

To draw a line, choose Line from the Draw toolbar. At the `Specify first point:` prompt, specify any point. Continue to specify points until you are finished. Press Enter to end the command. You can also right-click and choose Enter from the shortcut menu. The LINE command assumes you will continue to use it over and over. For this reason, AutoCAD continues to prompt you until you press Enter.

If you continue to draw line segments, the subsequent prompts are different. Here's how to use them:

✦ AutoCAD displays the `Specify next point or [Undo]:` prompt for the next two segments. Right-click and choose Undo (or type **u** ↵) to undo only the last line segment you created—without exiting the LINE command.

✦ After creating at least two line segments, AutoCAD displays the `Specify next point or [Close/Undo]:` prompt. Right-click and choose Close (or type **c** ↵) to automatically draw a line from the endpoint of the last segment to the original start point, thereby creating a closed figure. You can continue to use the Undo option as well.

If you previously drew a line, press Enter at the `Specify first point:` prompt to start the line at the endpoint of the last line. If you most recently drew an arc, press Enter to start the line at the endpoint of the arc and draw it tangent to the arc.

Step-by-Step: Using the LINE Command

1. Start a new drawing by using the `acad.dwt` template.

2. Save the drawing in your `AutoCAD Bible` folder as `ab06-01.dwg`.

3. Start the LINE command. At the `Specify first point:` prompt, choose any point in the center of your drawing.

4. Click ORTHO on the status bar.

5. Move the cursor to the right in the 0-degree direction and type **.4667** ↵.

6. Type **.7341<129** ↵.

7. Move the cursor to the right in the 0-degree direction and type **.4668** ↵.

8. That was a mistake. Type **u** ↵.

9. The `Specify next point or [Close/Undo]:` prompt reappears. With the cursor still in the 0-degree direction, type **.4667** ↵.

10. Type **c** ↵ to close the figure. This ends the LINE command.

11. Start the LINE command again.

12. At the `Specify first point:` prompt, press Enter. The line starts at the previous endpoint.

13. Type **.8071<270** ↵ and press Enter to end the LINE command.

14. Save your drawing. It should look like Figure 6-1.

Figure 6-1: The completed gate valve symbol

Other aspects of lines are covered elsewhere in the book. Chapter 11 explains how to draw dashed and dotted lines. Chapter 16 explains how to create *polylines*, which combine line segments and curves into one object. Chapter 16 also covers *multilines* — sets of parallel lines that you draw all at once.

`Mend.lsp` is an AutoLISP routine that combines two lines into one. You can find it in `\Software\Ch06\Mend`.

Drawing Rectangles

The RECTANG command draws rectangles. Rectangles are used in all disciplines. The RECTANG command has a number of options that specify how the rectangle appears.

 Use the RECTANG command to create a rectangle by specifying the two diagonal corners. Choose Rectangle from the Draw toolbar.

AutoCAD prompts you for the two corners and creates the rectangle. You can specify the two corners by using any method of specifying coordinates. For example, if you know the rectangle should be 6 inches wide and 3 inches high, you can specify the second point as @6,3.

After you specify the first corner, you can specify the length and the width of the rectangle instead of the second corner. Here are the prompts for specifying the length and width of a rectangle:

```
Specify other corner point or [Dimensions]: Choose the
Dimensions option.
Specify length for rectangles <0.0000>: Type the length and
press Enter.
Specify width for rectangles <0.0000>: Type the width and press
Enter.
Specify other corner point or [Dimensions]:Pick a point to
specify where you want the rectangle.
```

As soon as you specify the length and width, four possible rectangles are possible, as shown in Figure 6-2. As you move your mouse cursor around the first corner you specified, AutoCAD displays these rectangles. Click when you see the one that you want.

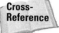

Note After you set the dimensions, they remain as defaults for future rectangles that you draw. As a result, you can use the Dimensions option to quickly draw a number of identical rectangles.

Cross-Reference You can chamfer and fillet the corners as you create the rectangle. Chapter 10 covers chamfering and filleting. You can specify a width for the rectangle's line (see Chapter 16). You can also create a 3D box by using the elevation and thickness options (see Chapter 21). The RECTANG command creates a *polyline*, meaning that all four sides of the rectangle are one object, instead of four separate line objects. Chapter 16 covers polylines.

First corner point

Figure 6-2: When you specify the first corner, a length, and a width, choose which of four possible rectangles you want.

Drawing Polygons

AutoCAD's POLYGON command enables you to draw multisided closed figures with equal side lengths. AutoCAD can draw polygons with anything from 3 to 1,024 sides. To draw a polygon, choose Polygon from the Draw toolbar.

First specify the number of sides. Then choose one of three methods of defining the polygon, as described in Table 6-1.

	Table 6-1
	POLYGON Command Options

Option	Description
Edge	Right-click and choose Edge. Specify the two endpoints of any edge of the polygon. AutoCAD completes the polygon.
Inscribed in circle	After specifying the center, right-click and choose Inscribed in circle. Then specify the radius from the center to a vertex (point). This defines the polygon with reference to an imaginary circle whose circumference touches all the vertices of the polygon.
Circumscribed about circle	After specifying the center, right-click and choose Circumscribed about circle. Then specify the radius from the center to the midpoint of a side. This defines the polygon with reference to an imaginary circle whose circumference touches all the midpoints of the polygon's sides.

If you type a number for the radius, the bottom edge of the polygon is horizontal. However, if you pick a point for the radius with your mouse, you can specify the orientation of the polygon. Rotate the mouse cursor around the center, and you see the polygon rotate. Pick when you like what you see.

Cross-Reference

When you type a number for the radius, the bottom edge actually aligns with the snap rotation angle, which is usually 0. Chapter 8 explains how to change this angle.

The POLYGON command creates a polyline, meaning that the entire polygon is one object, rather than a series of line segments.

In the exercise that follows, I indicate inches with a double-prime (") and feet with a prime ('). It is not necessary to type the double-prime for inches, but you may find it clearer when a measurement has both feet and inches. When you have a measurement that is only in inches, it saves time to leave out the double-prime.

On the CD-ROM

The drawing used in this Step-by-Step exercise on drawing rectangles and polygons, ab06-a.dwg, is in the Drawings folder of the *AutoCAD 2004 Bible* CD-ROM.

Step-by-Step: Drawing Rectangles and Polygons

1. Open ab06-a.dwg from the CD-ROM.

2. Save the drawing in your AutoCAD Bible folder as ab06-02.dwg. Verify that snap and grid are on, set at 1". OSNAP should be off.

3. ⬜ Choose Rectangle from the Draw toolbar.

4. At the Specify first corner point or [Chamfer/Elevation/Fillet/Thickness/Width]: prompt, move the cursor to 0'-1",0'-1" and click. At the Specify other corner point or [Dimensions]: prompt, type 2'1",1'9" ↵.

5. Start the RECTANG command again. At the Specify first corner point or [Chamfer/Elevation/Fillet/Thickness/Width]: prompt, press Shift and click the right mouse button and choose the From object snap. Shift+right-click again and choose the Endpoint object snap. Pick the bottom-left corner of the rectangle. At the <Offset>: prompt, type 2,2 ↵ to start the second rectangle 2 inches up and 2 inches to the right of the first rectangle.

6. At the Specify other corner point or [Dimensions]: prompt, type 1'9",1'3" ↵.

7. Right-click and choose Repeat Rectangle to start the RECTANG command again. At the prompt, find 0'8",1'7" (on a snap point) and click. At the Specify other corner point or [Dimensions]: prompt, type 11,2 ↵. (You don't need to type the double-prime for inches.)

8. Again, start the RECTANG command. At the prompt, find 1'1",1'8" and click. At the Specify other corner point or [Dimensions]: prompt, type **1,–5** ↵.

9. Start the POLYGON command. At the Enter number of sides <4>: prompt, type **5** ↵. At the Specify center of polygon or [Edge]: prompt, type **10,1'8** ↵ to indicate the center.

10. At the Enter an option [Inscribed in circle/Circumscribed about circle] <I>: prompt, press Enter to accept the default. This means you indicate the radius from the center to the vertices. (If your prompt shows <C> as the default, type **i** ↵.)

11. At the Specify radius of circle: prompt, type **.5** ↵. AutoCAD draws the pentagon.

12. Repeat Steps 9–11 using a center of 1'5,1'8.

13. Start the POLYGON command again. At the Enter number of sides <5>: prompt, type **3** ↵.

14. At the Specify center of polygon or [Edge]: prompt, right-click and choose the Edge option.

15. At the Specify first endpoint of edge: prompt, choose the top-left corner of the faucet rectangle (1'1",1'8"), which is on a snap point.

16. At the Specify second endpoint of edge: prompt, choose the top-right corner of the faucet rectangle. AutoCAD completes the triangle.

17. Turn off the grid to get a better look at the drawing. You have completed the sink, which should look like Figure 6-3. Save your drawing.

Figure 6-3: The completed sink, drawn by using rectangles and polygons
Thanks to Bill Wynn of New Windsor, Maryland, for this drawing, which he created in his AutoCAD class as part of a plan drawing of an entire house.

Creating Construction Lines

Sometimes you want to create a line that is used solely for the purpose of reference. For example, you might want to do the following:

✦ Draw two lines from the midpoints of two perpendicular lines so that you can use their intersection as the center for a circle.

✦ Draw a line from one object to another to visually indicate the relationship between the two objects.

✦ Show the relationship between equivalent parts of a model shown in front and right-side views.

✦ Draw a line through the center of an object shown in cross-section so that you can show dimensions from the centerline to the edge of an object.

You could use regular lines for these purposes. However, construction lines (also known as *xlines*) are unique in that they extend infinitely in both directions. This makes them especially useful for seeing the relationships among various objects in your drawing.

Of course, construction lines are not actually infinite. However, they extend to the edge of the drawing area on your screen, and if you zoom out to see more of your drawing, they expand so that they always extend to the edge of the screen. AutoCAD's object snap tracking sometimes eliminates the need for construction lines; nevertheless, sometimes you can work more easily having a line visible for several commands and then erasing it.

If you zoom to show the extents of your drawing, AutoCAD ignores the xlines and shows you just the extents of the regular objects in your drawing. Chapter 8 covers the ZOOM command.

Cross-Reference

Construction lines are especially helpful when working in 3D. See Part IV of this book.

The XLINE command offers several ways to create construction lines. Start the command by choosing Construction Line from the Draw toolbar. You see the following prompt:

```
Specify a point or [Hor/Ver/Ang/Bisect/Offset]:
```

Table 6-2 lists the possible options. AutoCAD continues to prompt you for more points so that you can continue to draw construction lines — much like the LINE command. Press Enter to end the command.

<table>
<tr><td colspan="2" align="center">Table 6-2
XLINE Command Options</td></tr>
<tr><td>**Option**</td><td>**Description**</td></tr>
<tr><td>Specify a point</td><td>This option enables you to define the xline with two points. At the first prompt, specify a point. At the `Specify through point:` prompt, specify another point. The first point becomes the base point for subsequent construction lines that you can draw by specifying other through points.</td></tr>
<tr><td>Hor</td><td>To draw a construction line parallel to the X axis, type **h** ↵ to specify the Horizontal option. AutoCAD responds with the `Specify through point:` prompt. Specify one point. Useful for drawing a series of horizontal construction lines.</td></tr>
<tr><td>Ver</td><td>To draw a construction line parallel to the Y axis, type **v** ↵ to specify the Vertical option. AutoCAD responds with the `Specify through point:` prompt. Specify one point.</td></tr>
<tr><td>Ang</td><td>Type **a** ↵ (for Angle). AutoCAD responds with the `Enter angle of xline (0) or [Reference]:` prompt. If you enter an angle, AutoCAD asks for a through point. Or you can type **r** ↵ and select a line as a reference, and then provide an angle and a through point. AutoCAD then calculates the angle of the construction line from the angle of the reference line. Useful for drawing a series of construction lines at a specified angle.</td></tr>
<tr><td>Bisect</td><td>To draw a construction line that bisects (divides in half) an angle, type **b** ↵. AutoCAD responds with the `Specify angle vertex point:` prompt. Choose any point that you want the construction line to pass through. Then, at the `Specify angle start point:` prompt, choose a point that defines the base of the angle. At the `Specify angle end point:` prompt, choose a point that defines the end of the angle.</td></tr>
<tr><td>Offset</td><td>To draw a construction line parallel to a line, type **o** ↵. You can specify the offset distance by typing in a number or use the Through option to pick a point through which the construction line should pass. Either way, the next step is to select a line. If you specified an offset distance, AutoCAD displays the `Specify side to offset:` prompt. Respond by picking a point on the side of the selected line on which you want the construction line to appear.</td></tr>
</table>

Creating Rays

Rays are similar to construction lines, except that they start at a specific point and extend to infinity in one direction only. If you need a line to extend only in one direction, using a ray may be less confusing.

 Tip You can use most object snaps with construction lines and rays. (You can't use endpoint for construction lines or midpoint for rays.) Construction lines and rays can be edited like any other object.

To draw a ray, choose Draw ⇨ Ray. At the `Specify start point:` prompt, specify the start point for the ray. At the `Specify through point:` prompt, specify another point. AutoCAD continues to ask for through points. Press Enter to end the command.

 On the CD-ROM The drawing used in this Step-by-Step exercise on drawing construction lines and rays, `ab06-b.dwg`, is in the `Drawings` folder of the *AutoCAD 2004 Bible* CD-ROM.

Step-by-Step: Drawing Construction Lines and Rays

1. Open `ab06-b.dwg` from the CD-ROM. A simple cross-section view has been added.

2. Save the drawing as `ab06-03.dwg` in your `AutoCAD Bible` folder.

3. Choose Construction Line from the Draw toolbar.

4. At the `Specify a point or [Hor/Ver/Ang/Bisect/Offset]:` prompt, choose point ❶, shown in Figure 6-4.

5. At the `Specify through point:` prompt, choose point ❷, shown in Figure 6-4.

Figure 6-4: The pipe with cross-section

6. Press Enter to end the command. Notice that the drawing has been set up so that the construction line is drawn in green and with a noncontinuous line-type. This is to distinguish it from the main drawing. (See Chapter 11 for details on how to set up a drawing in this way.)

7. Choose Draw ⇨ Ray.

8. At the `Specify start point:` prompt, choose point ❸, shown in Figure 6-4.

9. At the `Specify through point:` prompt, choose point ❹, shown in Figure 6-4. Press Enter to end the command.

10. Save your drawing.

Summary

This chapter covered the ins and outs of lines. You read about:

✦ Using the LINE command

✦ Drawing rectangles

✦ Drawing polygons

✦ Creating construction lines, including xlines that extend infinitely in both directions and rays that extend infinitely in one direction

The next chapter explains how to draw curves and point objects. Curves include circles, arcs, ellipses, and donuts.

✦ ✦ ✦

Drawing Curves and Point Objects

AutoCAD offers a number of ways to create curved objects. You can draw circles, arcs, ellipses, and donuts (also called doughnuts). In this chapter, I also cover point objects that are neither curves nor lines, but don't deserve their own chapter.

 Cross-Reference Several complex objects involve curves, such as polylines, splines, regions, and boundaries. These are covered in Chapter 16.

Drawing Circles

Circles are common objects in drawings. In mechanical drawings, they often represent holes or wheels. In architectural drawings, they may be used for doorknobs, trash baskets, or trees. In electrical and piping schematics, they are used for various kinds of symbols.

Understanding the circle options

AutoCAD provides five ways to draw a circle. To draw a circle, choose Circle from the Draw toolbar. AutoCAD responds with the `Specify center point for circle or [3P/2P/Ttr (tan tan radius)]:` prompt. Table 7-1 describes how to use these options.

Table 7-1
Five Ways to Draw a Circle

Option	Description
Center Radius	This option is the default. Specify the center and then the radius. You can type the radius as a distance or pick a point on the circumference.
Center Diameter	Specify the center. Type **d** ↵ and type the length of the diameter or pick a point to specify the diameter.
2P	2P stands for 2 point. Type **2p** ↵. Specify one point on the circumference, and then an opposite point on the circumference. These two points define the diameter of the circle.
3P	3P stands for 3 point. Type **3p** ↵. Specify three points on the circumference.
Tangent, Tangent, Radius	Type **t** or **ttr** ↵. AutoCAD prompts Specify point on object for first tangent of circle: and provides an aperture to let you pick a point. Then AutoCAD prompts Specify point on object for second tangent of circle: and you pick a second point. These points can be any points on the object(s) to which you want your circle to be tangent. Finally, type a radius.

Tip You can also create a circle tangent to other objects by using the 2-point (2P) or 3-point (3P) method and picking those points with the Tangent object snap. When you choose Draw ➪ Circle (from the menu), AutoCAD includes a tan tan tan option, enabling you to specify a circle tangent to three objects.

Drawing circles

Drawing circles is fairly straightforward. Often you can use object snaps to define part of the circle. In the following exercise, you practice using the most common methods of creating a circle.

On the CD-ROM The drawing used in the following Step-by-Step exercise on creating a circle, ab07-a.dwg, is in the Drawings folder of the *AutoCAD 2004 Bible* CD-ROM.

Step-by-Step: Creating a Circle

1. Open ab07-a.dwg from the CD-ROM.

2. Save the file as ab07-01.dwg in your AutoCAD Bible folder. This is a drawing of an air compressor from which all the circles have been removed. Make sure that OSNAP is on. Set a running object snap for endpoints only.

3. Choose Circle from the Draw toolbar. Right-click and choose 2P from the shortcut menu. At the `Specify first end point of circle's diameter:` prompt, pick the endpoint at ❶ in Figure 7-1. At the `Specify second end point of circle's diameter:` prompt, pick the endpoint at ❷.

Figure 7-1: The air compressor without its circles

4. Repeat the CIRCLE command by right-clicking and choosing Repeat Circle. Right-click and choose 2P from the shortcut menu. Pick the endpoints at ❸ and ❹ in Figure 7-1.

5. Repeat the CIRCLE command by pressing Enter. At the `Specify center point for circle or [3P/2P/Ttr (tan tan radius)]:` prompt, pick the endpoint at ❺. At the `Specify radius of circle or [Diameter]:` prompt, pick the endpoint at ❻.

6. Repeat the CIRCLE command. At the `Specify center point for circle or [3P/2P/Ttr (tan tan radius)]:` prompt, pick the endpoint at ❼. At the `Specify radius of circle or [Diameter]:` prompt, right-click and choose Diameter; then type **.25** ↵.

7. Repeat the CIRCLE command by right-clicking and choosing Repeat Circle. At the `Specify center point for circle or [3P/2P/Ttr (tan tan radius)]:` prompt, right-click and choose 3P. At the `Specify first point on circle:` prompt, pick the endpoint at ❽ in Figure 7-1. At the `Specify second point on circle:` prompt, pick the endpoint at ❾. At the `Specify third point on circle:` prompt, choose a midpoint object snap and pick the midpoint at ❿.

8. For the last circle on the right, choose any method you want to draw a circle. The circle should be the same size and placement as the second circle from the left.

9. Repeat the CIRCLE command. At the `Specify center point for circle or [3P/2P/Ttr (tan tan radius)]:` prompt, choose the Center object snap ↵ and pick ❼. At the `Specify radius of circle or [Diameter]:` prompt, type **.05** ↵.

10. Repeat Step 9 to create a circle inside the circle whose center is at ❺ and whose radius is 0.05.

11. Repeat the CIRCLE command. At the `Specify center point for circle or [3P/2P/Ttr (tan tan radius)]:` prompt, pick the endpoint at ⑪. At the `Specify radius of circle or [Diameter]:` prompt, pick the endpoint at ⑫.

12. Repeat Step 11, choosing the endpoint at ⑬ for the center of the circle and the endpoint at ⑭ for its radius, as shown in Figure 7-1.

13. Save your drawing. It should look like Figure 7-2.

Figure 7-2: The completed air compressor

Thanks to the U.S. Army Corps of Engineers at Vicksburg, Mississippi, for this drawing. They maintain a Web site of drawings at http://cadlib.wes.army.mil.

It may have occurred to you that this task would have been easier if you could simply have copied one circle to another location instead of creating each circle from scratch. I cover copying in Chapter 9.

Drawing Arcs

An arc is a portion of a circle. Therefore, to define an arc, you have to define not only a circle — for example, by specifying a center and a radius — but also you must define the start and endpoints of the arc. You can do this in many ways. AutoCAD offers several methods of defining an arc. The method you pick depends on the information you have about the arc you want to draw.

Understanding arc options

Arcs have many options. Making sense of them may seem overwhelming, but after you understand the parts of an arc and AutoCAD's terminology, you can choose the options that suit your needs. Figure 7-3 shows the parts of an arc that you can use to draw an arc. Refer to these parts as you read through the arc options.

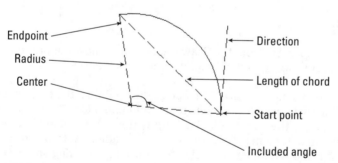

Figure 7-3: The parts of an arc

Figure 7-4 shows the flow of the arc options. When you start the ARC command, you have two options, Start point and Center. Depending on which you choose, more options become available.

You can also press Enter at the first arc prompt to draw a second arc starting from the endpoint of a previous arc, line, polyline, and so on. The new arc continues in the same direction as the end of the first arc. The only other prompt is the endpoint.

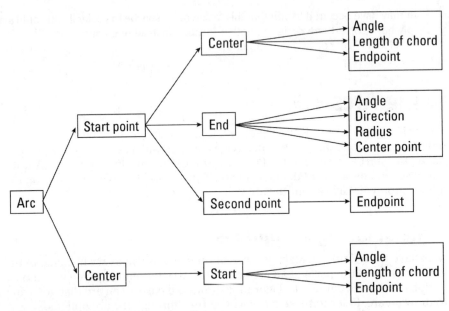

Figure 7-4: The ARC command options

Drawing arcs

To draw an arc, choose Arc from the Draw toolbar and follow the prompts. As with circles, object snaps are often helpful when drawing arcs.

When drawing an arc by using the Start, End, and Radius options, the three specifications actually define two possible arcs, one minor and one major. AutoCAD draws the minor arc by default, in the counterclockwise direction. (A minor arc is less than half a circle.) If you enter a negative number for the radius, AutoCAD draws the major arc (which is more than half a circle). The options requiring an angle also define two possible arcs, one drawn counterclockwise and one drawn clockwise. AutoCAD draws the counterclockwise arc by default. If you type a negative number for the angle, AutoCAD draws the arc clockwise.

On the CD-ROM The drawing used in the following Step-by-Step exercise on drawing arcs, ab07-b.dwg, is in the Drawings folder of the *AutoCAD 2004 Bible* CD-ROM.

Step-by-Step: Drawing Arcs

1. Open ab07-b.dwg from the CD-ROM.

2. Save the file as ab07-02.dwg in your AutoCAD Bible folder. ORTHO is on and units are set to Fractional. Choose Tools ➪ Drafting Settings (clicking the

Object Snap tab, if necessary) and set running object snaps for intersection, center, and endpoint. Make sure OSNAP is on. In this exercise, you draw part of the sealing plate shown in Figure 7-5.

3. Start the LINE command. Start at 2,3 and use Direct Distance Entry to create a 7-unit horizontal line to the right. End the LINE command.

Cross-Reference

See Chapter 4 for a full explanation of how to use Direct Distance Entry.

4. Draw another line starting at 5-1/2,1-5/8 and draw it 2-3/4 units long in the 90-degree direction. These two lines are center lines and would ordinarily appear in a different color and linetype than the object you are drawing.

Cross-Reference

You can read about colors and linetypes in Chapter 11.

5. Draw a circle with its center at the intersection of the two lines (use the Intersection object snap) and a radius of $^{11}\!/_{16}$.

6. Use the Center object snap to draw another circle with the same center as the first circle and a radius of 1.

Figure 7-5: The dimensioned sealing plate for a valve
Thanks to Jerry Bottenfield of Clow Valve Company in Oskaloosa, Iowa, for this drawing.

7. Draw a third circle, using the From object snap (Shift+right-click to open the object snap menu, and then choose From). For the base point, use the Center object snap and pick either of the first two circles you drew. The offset is @-1-15/16,0 (this means 1-15/16 units to the left of the center of the first two circles). Its radius is ⅜.

8. Draw a fourth circle. Use the From object snap again. For the base point, use the Center object snap and pick either of the first two circles. The offset is @1-15/16,0. The radius is ⅜.

9. Choose Arc from the Draw toolbar. Follow the prompts:

   ```
   Specify start point of arc or [Center]: Choose the From
   object snap.
   Base point: Use the Center object snap to pick the center of
   the leftmost circle.
   <Offset>: @-5/8,0 ↵
   Specify second point of arc or [Center/End]: Right-click and
   choose Center. Use the Center object snap to pick the center
   of the leftmost circle.
   Specify end point of arc or [Angle/chord Length]: Right-click
   and choose Angle.
   Specify included angle: 67.23 ↵
   ```

10. Start the LINE command. At the Specify first point: prompt, press Enter to continue the line in the same direction as the end of the arc. At the Length of line: prompt, type **1-13/16** ↵. End the LINE command.

11. Choose Arc from the Draw toolbar. Follow the prompts:

    ```
    Specify start point of arc or [Center]: Use the Endpoint
    object snap to pick the end of the line you just drew.
    Specify second point of arc or [Center/End]: Right-click and
    choose Center. Use the Center object snap and pick any point
    on one of the large central circles.
    Specify end point of arc or [Angle/chord Length]: Use
    Endpoint object snap to pick the lower end of the vertical
    construction line.
    ```

12. Repeat the ARC command. Follow the prompts:

    ```
    Specify start point of arc or [Center]: Right-click and
    choose Center. Use the Center object snap and pick any point
    on one of the large central circles.
    Specify start point of arc: Use the Endpoint object snap to
    pick the endpoint of the arc you just completed.
    Specify end point of arc or [Angle/chord Length]: Right-click
    and choose Angle.
    Specify included angle: 22.77 ↵
    ```

13. Start the LINE command. At the Specify first point: prompt, press Enter to continue the line in the same direction as the end of the arc. At the Length of line: prompt, type **1-13/16** ↵. End the LINE command.

14. Start the ARC command. Follow the prompts:

Specify start point of arc or [Center]: *Use the Endpoint object snap to pick the endpoint of the line you just drew.*
Specify second point of arc or [Center/End]: *Right-click and choose End.*
Specify end point of arc: Choose the From object snap.
_from Base point: *Use the Center object snap to pick the center of the rightmost circle.*
<Offset>: **@5/8,0** ↵
Specify center point of arc or [Angle/Direction/Radius]: **r** ↵
Specify radius of arc: **5/8** ↵

15. Save your drawing. Your drawing should look like Figure 7-6. You can complete this drawing in Chapter 10 by creating a mirror image.

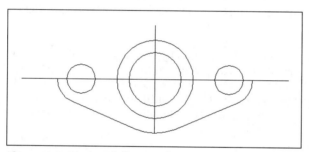

Figure 7-6: The partially completed sealing plate, created by using lines, circles, and arcs

Creating Ellipses and Elliptical Arcs

You can create ellipses (ovals), and you can also create elliptical arcs, which are partial ellipses. Like a circle, an ellipse has a center. The difference, of course, is that an ellipse has a longer radius along its major axis and a shorter radius along its minor axis, as shown in Figure 7-7.

Figure 7-7: The parts of an ellipse

Understanding ellipse options

You can draw ellipses by defining a center first. Another option is to define the axis endpoints first. If you want to draw an elliptical arc, you must specify the start and end angle.

Ellipses

The default option is to specify endpoints 1 and 2 of the first axis. Then you specify the second axis distance, which is the distance from the first axis line to the circumference along the second axis. Instead of specifying a second axis distance, you can choose the rotation option.

The rotation option defines the minor axis by defining an angle from 0 degrees to 90 degrees, which is the ratio of the major axis to the minor axis. (Actually, AutoCAD only accepts up to 89.4 degrees.) When the angle is 0, you get a circle. As the angle increases, the ellipse gets flatter and flatter until you reach 89.4 degrees. A 45-degree angle results in a minor axis whose length is the square root of the major axis length.

Instead of specifying endpoints, you can type **c** to specify the center of the ellipse. Then specify the endpoint of the first axis, which can be either the major or the minor axis. Finally, specify the other axis distance, which is the radius from the center to the circumference along the second axis. Again, instead of specifying the second axis distance, you can define the ellipse by using the rotation option.

Elliptical arcs

To draw an elliptical arc, choose Ellipse Arc from the Draw toolbar. The first prompts are the same as for an ellipse because you must first define the ellipse. Then AutoCAD continues with the Specify start angle or [Parameter]: prompt, offering the following options:

 ✦ **Start angle:** This option is the default. Specify the start angle, which AutoCAD redefines to start along the major axis. AutoCAD responds with the Specify end angle or [Parameter/Included angle]: prompt.

 ✦ **End angle:** Specify the end angle to complete the ellipse arc.

✦ **Included angle:** After specifying the start angle, you can complete the arc by specifying the included angle from the start point to the endpoint, going counterclockwise.

✦ **Parameter:** Choose this option to define the arc portion by the ellipse's area rather than its included angle (which defines the arc portion by its circumference). AutoCAD responds with the `Specify start parameter or [Angle]:` and `Specify end parameter or [Angle/Included angle]:` prompts. By typing in angles, you define the percent of the full ellipse's area that you want to include. (For example, starting at 15 degrees and ending at 105 degrees includes 90 degrees. AutoCAD then draws one quarter of an ellipse.) The options in brackets let you return to regular angle specification.

Drawing ellipses

To draw an ellipse, choose Ellipse from the Draw toolbar. In addition to the information AutoCAD explicitly requests in the prompts, you need to know the angle of the first axis that you define. Not all ellipses are horizontal or vertical. You control this when you stipulate the second point of the first axis. The second axis is automatically perpendicular to the first axis.

To draw an elliptical arc, choose Ellipse Arc from the Draw toolbar. When you draw an elliptical arc, AutoCAD introduces a helpful but sometimes confusing feature: While you are defining the arc angles, AutoCAD redefines 0 degrees along the major axis. This helps you define the included angle in an orientation that relates to the ellipse, rather than the usual orientation where 0 degrees is to the right.

In this exercise, you practice drawing ellipses and elliptical arcs.

On the CD-ROM The drawing used in the following Step-by-Step exercise on drawing ellipses and elliptical arcs, ab07-c.dwg, is in the Drawings folder of the *AutoCAD 2004 Bible* CD-ROM.

Step-by-Step: Drawing Ellipses and Elliptical Arcs

1. Open ab07-c.dwg from the CD-ROM.

2. Save the file as ab07-03.dwg in your AutoCAD Bible folder. The drawing shows an empty conference room. Snap is on, set to 6". Check that OSNAP is on with a running object snap set for endpoint only.

3. Choose Ellipse from the Draw toolbar. At the `Specify axis endpoint of ellipse or [Arc/Center]:` prompt, right-click and choose Center. At the `Specify center of ellipse:` prompt, choose 8',10', which is a snap point. At the `Specify endpoint of axis:` prompt, move the cursor to the right until the coordinates read 3'<0 and click. (If necessary, press F6 until you

see polar coordinates.) At the `Specify distance to other axis or` `[Rotation]:` prompt, move the cursor up until the coordinates read 6'6"<90 and click. This completes the conference table.

4. Choose Ellipse Arc from the Draw toolbar. Follow the prompts:

```
Specify axis endpoint of elliptical arc or [Center]: Right-
click and choose Center.
Specify center of elliptical arc: Pick 8',3', a snap point.
Specify endpoint of axis: Move the cursor to the right until
the coordinates read 1'<0 and pick.
Specify distance to other axis or [Rotation]: Move the cursor
up until the coordinates read 6"<90 and pick.
Specify start angle or [Parameter]: 162 ↵
Specify end angle or [Parameter/Included angle]: 18 ↵
```

5. Turn off ORTHO. Start the LINE command. At the `Specify first point:` prompt, use the Endpoint running object snap and pick the right side of the elliptical arc. At the `Specify next point or [Undo]:` prompt, press F6 to change to dynamic absolute coordinates (if necessary) and pick the snap point 8'6",3'. (You may have to turn off OSNAP in the middle of the command to pick this point and avoid getting an endpoint.) End the LINE command.

6. Start the LINE command. At the `Specify first point:` prompt, choose the Endpoint object snap and pick the left side of the ellipse arc. At the `Specify next point or [Undo]:` prompt, pick the snap point 7'6",3'. End the LINE command.

7. Choose Ellipse Arc again. Follow the prompts:

```
Specify axis endpoint of elliptical arc or [Center]: Use the
Endpoint object snap to pick the free endpoint of the line on
the right.
Specify other endpoint of axis: Use the Endpoint object snap
to pick the free endpoint of the line on the left.
Specify distance to other axis or [Rotation]: @3<90 ↵
Specify start angle or [Parameter]: Use the Endpoint object
snap to pick the free endpoint of the line on the right.
Specify end angle or [Parameter/Included angle]: Use Endpoint
object snap to pick the free endpoint of the line on the
left.
```

8. Choose Ellipse from the Draw toolbar. At the `Specify axis endpoint of ellipse or [Arc/Center]:` prompt, pick point 2',18', a snap point. At the `Specify other endpoint of axis:` prompt, pick point 2',16', also a snap point. At the `Specify distance to other axis or [Rotation]:` prompt, move the cursor to the right until the coordinates read 6"<0. (Press F6 twice if necessary.) This is also a snap point. Click the mouse button to complete the small side table.

9. Save your drawing. It should look like Figure 7-8.

Figure 7-8: The conference room with a conference table, a chair, and a side table

Making Donuts

A donut is a wide polyline that looks like two concentric circles. You define a diameter for the inner and outer circles. AutoCAD accepts both DONUT and DOUGHNUT if you type in the command. Donuts are often used in electrical drawings and to create symbols. If the inner circle's radius is zero, you create a filled-in circle.

The setting of the FILL command determines whether AutoCAD fills in the donut. Type **fill** ↵ and type **on** ↵ or **off** ↵. FILL is on by default. Turning FILL off displays a radial pattern of lines, as shown in Figure 7-9. Type **regen** ↵ or choose View ➪ Regen to update existing donuts to the new FILL setting.

Tip If you have many filled objects in your drawing, AutoCAD may need to take some time to display the drawing. You can save time by turning FILL off while you draw. Then turn FILL on just before you need to print or plot the drawing.

Figure 7-9: The parts of a donut, shown with FILL off

Understanding DONUT options

The DONUT command has the following prompts:

✦ `Specify inside diameter of donut <0.5000>:` Type the diameter of the inside circle or pick two points to specify the inside diameter. The number in brackets is the last inside diameter that you defined or 0.5 if you haven't previously used the DONUT command in this drawing session.

✦ `Specify outside diameter of donut <1.0000>:` Type the diameter of the outside circle or pick two points to specify the outside diameter. The outside diameter must be larger than the inside diameter. The number in brackets is the last outside diameter u that you defined or 1.0 if you haven't previously used the DONUT command in this drawing session.

✦ `Specify second point:` If you define the inside or outside diameter by picking a point, AutoCAD asks for a second point. Use this technique if you are using object snaps to define the diameters.

✦ `Specify center of donut or <exit>:` Specify the center of the donut. Pressing Enter ends the command.

Drawing donuts

Drawing donuts is relatively easy in AutoCAD. Choose Draw ➪ Donut. Then specify the inner and outer diameters and the center. AutoCAD continues to prompt for centers so you can place additional donuts. Press Enter to end the command.

Tip You can use the hatch feature to fill in any object with a solid fill, with a great deal more flexibility in the shape of your objects. (Chapter 16 discusses hatching.) As a result, the DONUT command is not as essential as it once was.

You draw some donuts in the next exercise.

Placing Points

Points are used for reference. It is sometimes helpful to mark a point that you use later as a guide to place an object or to help you return an object to its original position. When it's no longer needed, you may erase the point. This is a typical construction method. In some cases, the From object snap or object snap tracking can be used instead of a point.

Cross-Reference The DIVIDE and MEASURE commands place point objects along an object. Chapter 12 covers these commands.

Changing the point style

Different disciplines have different conventions for drawing point objects. As a result, AutoCAD provides 20 types of point styles that you can use in your drawing. Before you draw a point, you should set the point style. You can save this setting in your template.

Choose Format ➪ Point Style to open the Point Style dialog box, shown in Figure 7-10.

Figure 7-10: Choosing a point style

To set the point style, click the box showing the style that you want. Then set the point size, which has the following options:

✦ **Set Size Relative to Screen:** Use this option if you want the point to always appear the same size, no matter how much you zoom in and out — for example when you are using the point as a reference. The size is set as a percentage of the screen. This option is the default, with the size set to 5 percent of the screen.

✦ **Set Size in Absolute Units:** Use this option if you want the point to have a real size, just like any other object. The size is set in units. Use this option when you want the point to stay the same size relative to other objects in your drawing.

Click OK to close the dialog box.

Note When you change the point style, previously drawn points automatically and immediately change to the new style.

Creating points

After you determine the point style, you are ready to create points. Choose Point from the Draw toolbar.

You see the following on the command line:

```
Current point modes:  PDMODE=0  PDSIZE=0.0000
Specify a point:
```

PDMODE is the system variable for the point style you have chosen. If left in its default value, the PDSIZE system variable remains at zero. Once altered, the PDSIZE is negative if the point size is set relative to the screen. PDSIZE is positive if the point size is set for absolute units. If you set the size in absolute units, the unit size appears here. Specify the point you want, either by picking a point on the screen or by typing coordinates. (You can specify a Z coordinate to create a point in 3D space.) You can use object snaps to specify the point.

AutoCAD automatically repeats the prompt of the POINT command so that you can continue to specify points. To end the command, press Esc.

If BLIPMODE is on and you are using the first point style — a small dot — you cannot see the point until you use the REDRAW command to remove the blips.

Tip If you are using the points for temporary reference, instead of erasing them, you can set the point style to the second style in the Point Style dialog box (no dot) before plotting. Then the points do not appear on your plot.

After you create a point, use the Node object snap to snap to the point.

The drawing used in the following Step-by-Step exercise on drawing donuts and points, ab07-d.dwg, is in the Drawings folder of the *AutoCAD 2004 Bible* CD-ROM.

Step-by-Step: Drawing Donuts and Points

1. Open ab07-d.dwg from the CD-ROM.

2. Save the file as ab07-04.dwg in your AutoCAD Bible folder. The drawing contains a rectangle and connecting wires for an electrical switch. Make sure that OSNAP is on. Set running object snaps for endpoint, quadrant, center, and node.

3. Choose Format ➪ Point Style. The Point Style dialog box opens. Choose the third point type, the plus sign. The radio button Set Size Relative to Screen should be marked. The Point Size should be 5.0000%. Choose OK.

4. ▪ Choose Point from the Draw toolbar. Follow the prompts:

   ```
   Specify a point: Use From object snap. (Shift+right-click to
   open the Object Snap shortcut menu.)
   Base point: Use the Endpoint object snap to pick the top-left
   corner of the rectangle.
   <Offset>: @.08,-.09 ↵
   Specify a point: Press Esc
   ```

 AutoCAD places the point.

5. Choose Draw ➪ Donut. Follow these prompts:

   ```
   Specify inside diameter of donut <0.5000>: .04 ↵
   Specify outside diameter of donut <1.0000>: .06 ↵
   Specify center of donut or <exit>: Use the Node object snap
   to pick the point you drew.
   Specify center of donut or <exit>: @.19,0 ↵
   Specify center of donut or <exit>: ↵
   ```

6. Start the POINT command again. Follow the prompts:

   ```
   Specify a point: .x ↵
   of Use the Center object snap to pick the center of the
   right-hand donut.(You may have to press Tab until you get the
   center object snap, and not a quadrant object snap.)
   (need YZ): Pick a point about halfway between the right donut
   and the bottom of the rectangle, as shown in Figure 7-11.
   Specify a point: Press Esc.
   ```

7. Start the LINE command. Follow the prompts:

   ```
   Specify first point: Use the Quadrant object snap to pick the
   right (0 degrees) quadrant of the left donut. If you don't
   see the Quadrant SnapTip, press Tab until it appears.
   Specify next point or [Undo]: Use the Node object snap to
   pick the point you just drew. End the LINE command.
   ```

8. Save your drawing. It should look like Figure 7-11.

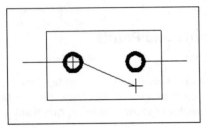

Figure 7-11: The completed electrical switch. The points show as plus signs.

Summary

In this chapter, you learned how to draw curved objects and points in AutoCAD. You discovered:

✦ All the ways to draw circles

✦ Defining and drawing and arc

✦ Defining an ellipse and an elliptical arc

✦ Drawing a donut

✦ Setting the point style and draw points

In the next chapter, you read how to display your drawing for the greatest ease and comfort.

✦ ✦ ✦

Viewing Your Drawing

Often you may wish you could zoom in to see a particular part of a drawing more closely. Several exercises in this book have already used the ZOOM command to zoom in and out. In this chapter, you read about controlling the display of your drawing to meet all your drawing needs and increase productivity.

Understanding How AutoCAD Displays Drawings

AutoCAD is a vector program, which means that it stores information about objects in your drawing in terms of coordinates and equations. This information is stored in your drawing's database. However, your screen displays information in terms of tiny dots called pixels. To display your drawing, AutoCAD converts the vector information in the drawing's database to pixels. When you change the drawing display significantly, AutoCAD has to reconvert the object data to pixels, recalculating the coordinates of every object in the drawing. This is called *regenerating*. Perhaps you have seen the message on AutoCAD's command line: `Regenerating model`.

Regenerating an entire drawing can be time-consuming. To avoid having to regenerate the drawing every time you change the display, AutoCAD keeps a *virtual screen* in your computer's memory. The virtual screen covers an area beyond the current display of your drawing and can be accessed very quickly. When you change the display within the virtual display, AutoCAD doesn't have to regenerate the entire drawing — it only redraws it. Redrawing uses the data stored in the virtual screen to refresh the display. A redraw is much quicker than regeneration.

When should you use REDRAW and when REGEN?

✦ In most cases, you want to redraw rather than regen because it is quicker. Use the REDRAW command to remove blips or to quickly refresh the screen. (The REDRAWALL command redraws the display in all viewports. Viewports are covered later in this chapter.) To redraw the screen, choose View ➪ Redraw (which actually executes the REDRAWALL command).

✦ Use the REGEN command whenever you want AutoCAD to recalculate the entire drawing. AutoCAD users use the word "regen" to refer to the REGEN command and also as shorthand for *regenerate* or *regeneration*. To regenerate the entire drawing, type **regen** ↵ at the command line. (REGENALL regenerates all viewports.)

Certain zooms and pans may require a regeneration, which AutoCAD does automatically.

In recent releases, AutoCAD has significantly improved the mechanics behind the display of your drawing. It is now rarely necessary to regenerate a drawing.

Panning

Often you cannot see the entire drawing on your screen. You therefore need a way to see the parts of your drawing that are not currently visible.

To *pan* means to move the display without changing the magnification. The word refers to the expression of panning a camera across a scene or view. You pan to view a different part of your drawing. You can pan any amount and in any direction by using the PAN command. You can pan vertically and horizontally by using the scroll bars.

Using the PAN command

The PAN command moves the display in the direction and distance you indicate without changing the magnification in any way. Real-time panning moves the drawing as you move the cursor. Real-time panning makes panning quick, intuitive, and easy.

To pan the drawing, choose Pan Realtime from the Standard toolbar. The cursor changes to a hand. Place the cursor anywhere in your drawing, click, and drag in the direction you want the objects to go.

New Feature You can now pan past the edge of the screen (actually the viewport) in Windows XP. This means that when the cursor reaches the edge of the screen you can continue moving your mouse in the same direction to continue the pan.

To leave pan mode, press Esc or Enter or start any command via a menu or toolbar. You can also right-click to open the shortcut menu shown in Figure 8-1. Pan can be used transparently, while you are in the middle of another command. Use the shortcut menu to exit pan mode, switch to real-time zoom or 3D Orbit, or to choose one of the zoom options listed.

Exit
✓ Pan
Zoom
3D Orbit
Zoom Window
Zoom Original
Zoom Extents

Figure 8-1: The pan shortcut menu

Note

AutoCAD 2004 supports Microsoft IntelliMouse pointing devices for panning. To pan, click and hold down the wheel and move your mouse. You see the same panning cursor, the hand, as you do when you pan by clicking the Pan Realtime button on the Standard toolbar. However, you don't need to press Esc or Enter to leave pan mode.

You can use displacement panning (the kind used by Release 13 and earlier versions) by choosing View ➪ Pan ➪ Point. At the `Specify base point or displacement:` prompt, choose any point in your drawing. At the `Specify second point:` prompt, choose another point where you want the first point to appear. The display then moves in the direction and the distance indicated by the difference between the first and second points.

Using the scroll bars

You can use the scroll bars to pan vertically and horizontally as you would with any Windows program. However, you can't easily predict just how much the drawing view will move. Therefore, the scroll bars are less useful than the PAN command.

You can use the scroll bars in three ways:

✦ Drag the scroll box in the desired direction and in the desired amount.

✦ Click the scroll bar between the scroll box and the up or down arrow.

✦ Click the up or down arrow to move the drawing view slightly.

On the CD-ROM

The drawing used in the following Step-by-Step exercise on panning and scrolling, ab08-a.dwg, is in the Drawings folder of the *AutoCAD 2004 Bible* CD-ROM.

Step-by-Step: Panning and Scrolling

1. Open ab08-a.dwg from the CD-ROM. This air compressor was used in an exercise in Chapter 7, but this display is magnified so that you cannot see the entire drawing. The air compressor is shown in Figure 8-2.

Figure 8-2: The air compressor is zoomed in so that you can see only part of the drawing.

2. Choose Pan Realtime from the Standard toolbar. Move the cursor to ❶ in Figure 8-2, click, and drag to ❷. The air compressor moves up and to the right. (Note that by the time you get to ❷, the display of the air compressor has moved — but you should drag to where ❷ was on the screen.) Press Esc.

3. The scroll box of the horizontal scroll bar is all the way to the left. Click anywhere in the scroll bar to the right of the scroll box. The air compressor moves to the left.

4. Click anywhere in the vertical scroll bar between the scroll box and the down arrow at the bottom of the scroll bar. The air compressor moves up as you scroll down.

5. Click the right arrow on the horizontal scroll bar three times. The drawing moves to the left slightly each time. Your drawing should look something like Figure 8-3. You may have a different view if you chose slightly different pan points.

 Do not save this drawing.

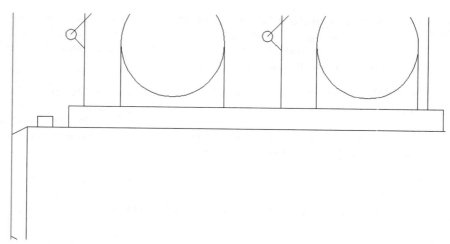

Figure 8-3: The final view. Your view may be somewhat different.

The ZOOM Command

The ZOOM command enables you to zoom in and out of your drawing—like the zoom lens of a camera. When you zoom in, everything is magnified so that you can see it more easily, but you see less of the entire drawing. When you zoom out, objects look smaller, but you can see more of the drawing. The ZOOM command has several options that make it easy to see just what you need at an appropriate size.

Zooming does not affect the actual size of objects, just as zooming with a camera lens does not affect the size of the scene you are viewing. Chapter 9 covers changing the actual size of objects (scaling).

When you use real-time zoom, the drawing zooms in and out as you move the cursor. To use real-time zoom, choose Zoom Realtime from the Standard toolbar. The cursor changes to a magnifying glass with a plus sign on one side and a minus sign on the other side. You determine whether AutoCAD zooms in or out depending on the movement of the cursor.

✦ To zoom in, click and drag up in the direction of the plus sign.

✦ To zoom out, click and drag down in the direction of the minus sign.

A movement from the middle of the screen to the top edge zooms in 100 percent. A movement from the middle of the screen to the bottom edge zooms out 100 percent.

New Feature You can now zoom past the edge of the screen (actually the viewport) in Windows XP. As you move the mouse up or down to zoom, when you reach the edge of the viewport, continue to move the mouse in the same direction to continue the zoom in or out.

AutoCAD supports Microsoft IntelliMouse pointing devices. To do a real-time zoom, rotate the wheel up to zoom in and down to zoom out. AutoCAD does not display the Zoom Realtime cursor. As with panning using the IntelliMouse, you don't need to press Esc or Enter to leave zoom mode. You can also double-click the wheel to do a Zoom to the extents of the drawing.

Right-click to open the shortcut menu to exit zoom mode, switch to real-time pan or 3D Orbit, or to choose one of the zoom options listed. To end real-time zoom, you can also press Esc or Enter or start any command via a menu or toolbar.

Understanding ZOOM options

The Zoom flyout has eight options. The Standard toolbar also has a Zoom Previous button. Table 8-1 outlines these Zoom options.

Table 8-1 Zoom Options		
Button	**Option**	**Description**
🔍	Window	This button lets you define a rectangular window as the boundaries of the new display. AutoCAD prompts you for the two corners of the window. Use Window to zoom in on any area already displayed in your drawing. When you use Zoom Window, AutoCAD displays everything in the window you specify but reshapes the display to fit your screen. As a result, you may see objects that were outside the specified window. You can now continue to move the mouse past the drawing area to define the window past the edge of the screen.
🔍	Dynamic	Enables you to zoom and pan in one operation. This option is covered in the next section of this chapter.
🔍	Scale	Enter a number to scale the display relative to the drawing limits (a kind of absolute scaling). Enter a number followed by x to scale the display relative to the current view (relative scaling). Enter a number followed by **xp** to scale the display relative to paper space units (discussed in Chapter 17). A number less than 1 (such as 0.5) reduces the size of the objects on the screen (such as by half). A number greater than 1 (such as 2) increases the size of the objects on the screen (such as by 2).

Button	Option	Description
	Center	Lets you specify a new center for the display, and then a new magnification/height. The current magnification/height is shown in brackets for your reference. Type a smaller number to increase the magnification, making the objects larger. Type a larger value to decrease the magnification, making the objects smaller.
	In	This button is a shortcut for using the Scale option with a value of 2x. See the Scale option.
	Out	This button is a shortcut for using the Scale option with a value of 0.5x. See the Scale option.
	All	Zooms the display to the greater of the drawing extents or the drawing limits.
	Extents	Zooms to the outer extents of the drawing. You can also double-click the wheel of an IntelliMouse pointing device.
	Previous	Redisplays the most recent display of your drawing. This option has its own button on the Standard toolbar because it is used so often.

ZOOM Dynamic

The Dynamic option of ZOOM enables you to pan and zoom in one operation. The Aerial View (discussed in the next section) offers more sophisticated options, but the simplicity of ZOOM Dynamic is sometimes just what you need.

When you start ZOOM Dynamic, you see the virtual screen area of the drawing in a blue dashed rectangle — the drawing extents or limits, whichever is greater. Your current view is bounded in a green, dashed rectangle. Your mouse cursor changes to a rectangle with a large X inside — the Pan view box. When you click the left mouse button, the X changes to an arrow — the Zoom view box. These are the two modes of ZOOM Dynamic. Each time you click the left mouse button, you switch modes. You can switch back and forth as often as you want. Here's how the two modes work:

✦ **Pan mode:** The box contains an X and can move freely around any displayed area of the drawing.

✦ **Zoom mode:** The box has an arrow. The left side of the box is fixed at the point where you changed to zoom mode. As you move the cursor the box expands or shrinks, letting you zoom to any magnification.

When the view box displays the view that you want, click the right mouse button and choose Enter (or press Enter). AutoCAD pans and zooms to show that view. Figure 8-4 shows the screen during a ZOOM Dynamic operation.

←— Generated area of drawing

View box in Zoom mode

←—Current view

AIR COMPRESSOR

Figure 8-4: Using ZOOM Dynamic

On the CD-ROM

The drawing used in the following Step-by-Step exercise on using ZOOM Dynamic, ab08-b.dwg, is in the Drawings folder of the *AutoCAD 2004 Bible* CD-ROM.

Step-by-Step: Using ZOOM Options

1. Open ab08-b.dwg from the CD-ROM. This is a drawing of a warehouse, as shown in Figure 8-5.

2. To read the text in the lower-right corner, choose Zoom Window from the Zoom flyout of the Standard toolbar.

3. At the Specify first corner: prompt, pick ❶, as shown in Figure 8-5. At the Specify opposite corner: prompt, pick ❷. AutoCAD zooms in to display the window you specified, as shown in Figure 8-6.

4. Choose Zoom All from the Zoom flyout of the Standard toolbar.

5. Choose Zoom Previous from the Standard toolbar. AutoCAD quickly returns you to the previous display.

6. Choose Zoom Extents from the Zoom flyout of the Standard toolbar. The drawing fills the screen. In this drawing, the drawing extents are similar to the drawing limits, so that you see little difference between using Zoom All and Zoom Extents.

Figure 8-5: A drawing of a large warehouse, with shelving and conveyor belts
Thanks to Bryan Kelly of ATI Corporation, Fairfield, Iowa, for this drawing.

7. Choose Zoom Center from the Zoom flyout. At the `Specify center point:` prompt, pick ❸ in Figure 8-5. At the `Enter magnification or height <5315.176>:` prompt, type **500** ↵. AutoCAD zooms in on the office.

8. Choose Zoom Realtime from the Standard toolbar. Place the cursor at the top of the drawing, click, and drag to the bottom of the screen. AutoCAD zooms out the display about 200 percent.

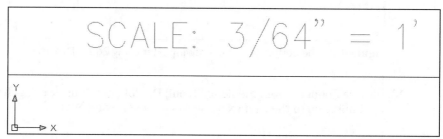

Figure 8-6: Your display should look approximately like this figure after using ZOOM Window.

9. Choose Zoom Scale from the Zoom flyout of the Standard toolbar. Type _2x ↵. AutoCAD zooms in, doubling the scale of the view and returning you approximately to the previous view of the office.

10. Choose Zoom Dynamic from the Zoom flyout. AutoCAD now displays the entire drawing. The current view is shown with a green dashed line. The mouse cursor is a box with an X in it. You are now in Pan mode. To zoom in on the right side of the warehouse, move the Pan box to the lower-right corner of the warehouse and click with the pick (left) button.

11. AutoCAD switches to Zoom mode. The Zoom box contains an arrow. Move the mouse to the left to shrink the Zoom box. Notice that the Zoom box is fixed at its left side. When the Zoom box is about half its original size, left-click again.

12. AutoCAD switches to Pan mode again. Move the Pan box to the bottom-right corner of the warehouse. Right-click and choose Enter. AutoCAD zooms in on this new view. Your display should look approximately like Figure 8-7.

Figure 8-7: The new view of the drawing after using Zoom Dynamic

13. Choose Zoom All from the Zoom flyout. Do not save your drawing. If you are continuing on to the next exercise, leave the drawing open.

Aerial View

In AutoCAD 2004, Aerial View functions like a souped-up version of ZOOM Dynamic. You can use Aerial View to pan and zoom. If you need to pan and zoom often, you can leave the Aerial View window open and use it whenever you need to.

To open Aerial View, choose View ➪ Aerial View. The Aerial View window opens, as shown in Figure 8-8. Like other windows, the Aerial View window can be active or inactive. When active, its title bar is shown in color (usually blue). When inactive, the title bar is gray. Inside the window, you see your entire drawing. To close Aerial View, click the Aerial View window's own Close button. Aerial View has its own toolbar and menu. These are explained in the next few sections.

Figure 8-8: The Aerial View window

Zooming and panning with Aerial View

While you work in your drawing, the drawing window is active and the Aerial View window is inactive. To pan and zoom by using Aerial View:

1. Click anywhere inside the Aerial View window to activate Aerial View. You see a pan/zoom box that looks like the box you see when you use ZOOM Dynamic. It has an X in it, indicating that you can pan.

2. Move the pan/zoom box over the part of the drawing you want to zoom in on. The display in the main screen pans as you move your mouse.

3. Click to switch to zoom mode. You see the arrow in the box, indicating that you can zoom. Move your mouse to resize the window so that it covers the area you want to see. In the main drawing window, you immediately see the new zoomed view.

4. Continue to click to switch between zoom and pan modes as necessary.

5. Right-click or press Esc to fix the new view.

To quickly zoom out in the Aerial View display, click Zoom Out on the Aerial View toolbar. To quickly zoom in, click Zoom In on the toolbar. To see your entire drawing in the Aerial View display only, click Global on the toolbar.

Note When the Aerial View window displays your entire drawing, the Zoom Out button is unavailable. When the current view nearly fills the Aerial View window, the Zoom In button is unavailable. When the drawing extents take up the entire Aerial View window, neither button is available.

You can disable the real-time zoom just described. Choose Options ⇨ Realtime Zoom from the Aerial View menu. Real-time zoom is available when the menu item has a checkmark next to it. You can also right-click in the Aerial View window and choose Realtime Zoom.

Understanding Aerial View options

The Aerial View Options menu contains two options that affect how Aerial View works. Both features are also available by right-clicking the Aerial View window shortcut menu.

✦ Auto Viewport applies only when you have more than one viewport. I discuss viewports later in this chapter. If this option is checked, the view in the Aerial View window changes as you change the active viewport in the main drawing area.

✦ Dynamic Update determines whether the view in the Aerial View window is continually (dynamically) updated as you edit your drawing. As you can imagine, it takes up additional computer resources (mainly memory) to maintain two views of your drawing at once. If you find that Aerial View slows down your computer (but you don't want to close it entirely), choose this option to turn Dynamic Update off. Choose the option again to turn it on.

Using Aerial View

Aerial View is most useful in large maps or floor plans, or any drawing with lots of detail. You can use it transparently.

Don't forget that before you use Aerial Window you need to click in the Aerial View window to activate it. To return to the AutoCAD window, you need to click that window as well.

To close Aerial View, click its Close button in the upper-right corner of the window.

On the CD-ROM The drawing used in the following Step-by-Step exercise on using Aerial View, ab08-b.dwg, is in the Drawings folder of the *AutoCAD 2004 Bible* CD-ROM.

Step-by-Step: Using Aerial View

1. Open `ab08-b.dwg` from the CD-ROM if it is not already open from the previous exercise.

2. Choose View ⇨ Aerial View. The Aerial View window opens. The Aerial View window is not currently active.

3. Click the Aerial View title bar to activate it. At the bottom of the warehouse drawing, somewhat to the left, is a rectangle (representing an office) with some text in it. (If you did the previous exercise, you zoomed into this office by using Zoom Center.)

4. To zoom in to the office, click once in the Aerial View display. To change to zoom mode, click again. Move the cursor down and to the left until the box is not much bigger than the office. Click again to return to pan mode, move the box over the office, and right-click. AutoCAD zooms in on the office. In the Aerial View window, you still see the entire drawing, and the current view is bounded by a thick box, the View box. Your screen should look like Figure 8-9.

Figure 8-9: Your screen after zooming in on the office

5. Click again to activate the pan/zoom box. Move the box just to the left and right-click. AutoCAD pans to show some windows to the left of the office.

6. Click again to start panning and zooming. Using the same technique as you just used in Step 4, pan to the top-left quadrant of the warehouse. Zoom in again if necessary until you can read the text at the top-left corner of the shelving area and right-click. (The red columns represent shelving in the warehouse.) Your screen should look approximately like Figure 8-10.

Figure 8-10: Zooming in on the top-left corner of the warehouse. You can now see the text, which reads "Battery Chargers."

7. Click again and move the pan box to the top-left corner of the drawing. Click to switch to zoom mode and move the cursor to the bottom-right corner of the drawing. AutoCAD simultaneously zooms out to display the entire warehouse.

8. Do not save your drawing. Close the Aerial View window. If you are continuing on to the next exercise, keep the drawing open.

Named Views

After you have done a lot of panning and zooming in a drawing, you may find that you return to the same part of your drawing again and again, especially if the drawing undergoes a lot of changes. In a large drawing, it can take some time to display the part of the drawing that you want, especially if AutoCAD needs to regenerate the drawing. You can speed up the process by saving views.

A *view* is simply a display of a drawing on your screen. It can show any part of your drawing at any magnification. After you have the display, you give the view a name and save it. AutoCAD then lets you retrieve that view at any time, without zooming or panning.

Tip In a very large drawing, you can create views as soon as you create the title block — for example, one for each quadrant of the drawing, and another for the title block lettering. This helps you move quickly from one section of the drawing to another. As you determine the need for more specific views, you can add them.

Saving a view

First display the view that you want to save on the screen. For this purpose, use the ZOOM and PAN commands or Aerial View. Then choose View ➪ Named Views. (You can also choose Named Views from the View toolbar.) This starts the VIEW command. The View dialog box opens, as shown in Figure 8-11.

Figure 8-11: The View dialog box

When you first open this dialog box, it shows only one view, called Current, which is the current display. Click New to open the New View dialog box, shown in Figure 8-12. Type a name for your view in the View name text box.

Figure 8-12: The New View dialog box

View names can be up to 255 characters and can include spaces. You can also save a User Coordinate System (UCS) with a view so that each view can have its own UCS. UCSs are covered later in this chapter.

Choose OK to return to the View dialog box, where you see your new view listed. Click OK to return to your drawing.

You can use the New View dialog box to define several views at once. Here's how:

1. Choose View ➪ Named Views.

2. Click New.

3. Type the name of the first view in the View name text box.

4. Choose the Define Window radio button.

5. Click the Define View Window button. AutoCAD returns you to your drawing.

6. If necessary, adjust the view by zooming and panning. AutoCAD does this transparently.

7. At the `Specify first corner:` prompt, pick one corner of a rectangular window.

8. At the `Specify opposite corner:` prompt, pick the diagonally opposite corner of the window. AutoCAD returns you to the New View dialog box.

9. Click OK. AutoCAD returns you to the View dialog box.

10. Repeat Steps 2–8 for all additional views.

Displaying a view

The View dialog box enables you to easily display any view you have saved. Follow these steps:

1. Choose View ➪ Named Views.

2. Choose the view you want to restore.

3. Click Set Current.

4. Click OK.

Using other view control functions

You can use the View dialog box to manage named views. Choose View ➪ Named Views to open the View dialog box. You can also find these features by right-clicking inside the View dialog box.

✦ To delete a view, choose the view you want to delete and press the Delete key on your keyboard.

✦ To rename a view, click it once and then a second time, but without double-clicking. Type a new name and press Enter.

✦ To get a description of a view, choose the view for which you want to see a description and click Details. The View Details dialog box opens, which provides some statistics about the view. In general, these statistics are more useful for 3D drawings than 2D ones.

On the CD-ROM The drawing used in the following Step-by-Step exercise on working with views, ab08-b.dwg, is in the Drawings folder of the *AutoCAD 2004 Bible* CD-ROM.

Step-by-Step: Working with Views

1. Open ab08-b.dwg from the CD-ROM if it is not already open from the previous exercise.

2. Save the file as ab08-01.dwg in your AutoCAD Bible folder.

3. Choose View ➪ Named Views to open the View dialog box.

4. Click New to open the New View dialog box.

5. In the text box, type **top left**.

6. Click the Define Window radio button and then click the Define View Window button. AutoCAD returns you to your drawing temporarily.

7. At the Specify first corner: prompt, pick the top-left corner of your screen. At the Specify opposite corner: prompt, pick somewhere around the center of the warehouse. AutoCAD returns you to the New View dialog box.

8. Click OK once.

9. Click New. Type **bottom left** in the text box of the New View dialog box.

10. Select Define Window and then click the Define View Window button. At the Specify first corner: prompt, pick the bottom-left corner of your screen. At the Specify Opposite corner: prompt, pick again around the center of the warehouse. Back in the New View dialog box, click OK. The View dialog box should list both of your views, as shown in Figure 8-13. Click OK to close the View dialog box.

Figure 8-13: The View dialog box now lists the views you have saved.

11. Choose View ➪ Named Views. Choose `bottom left` from the View dialog box. Click Set Current and then click OK. AutoCAD displays the view.

12. Save your drawing. The views you created are now part of the drawing database.

Using Named Views to Open a Drawing

Using named views provides two additional advantages. First, you can use named views when you open a drawing so that one of its views is immediately displayed. Second, you can open only the part of a drawing contained in a view.

A drawing with a view

After you have saved views, you can use them to open a drawing so that a view is immediately displayed. Click Open on the Standard toolbar. In the Select File dialog box, choose the file that you want to open and check the Select Initial View check box. Then click Open. In the Select Initial View dialog box, choose the view you want to display and click OK.

Partially opening a drawing

You can also open only the part of a drawing contained in a named view. You would do this for a very large drawing that is slow and cumbersome to work with when it is completely opened. For example, if you have a surveyor's drawing of an entire county, but need to work only with one plat, you could open a named view containing only that plat.

To partially open a drawing from within AutoCAD, follow these steps:

1. Choose File ➪ Open. AutoCAD opens the Select File dialog box.

2. Choose a drawing and then click the Open drop-down box. Choose Partial Open. AutoCAD opens the Partial Open dialog box, shown in Figure 8-14.

3. Choose a view from the list of named views.

4. Choose one or more layers. To include all the layers, click Load All. (If you don't include at least one layer, no objects are loaded. Chapter 11 covers layers.) Click Open.

After you have partially opened a drawing, you can open more of the drawing. Choose File ➪ Partial Load. (This item is only available if the current drawing has been partially opened.) AutoCAD opens the Partial Open dialog box. You can change the view. To display the entire drawing (from whatever is loaded), choose the default view, `*Extents*`. To define a new view on the fly, click the Pick a Window button and define the two diagonal corners of the view you want to see.

Check what layers you want to include or click Load All. Click OK to open the drawing with the new view and layers specifications.

Figure 8-14: Use the Partial Open dialog box to open only the part of a drawing contained in a named view.

Tiled Viewports

Tiled viewports enable you to divide up the screen into rectangular bounding boxes. You can then show a different view of your drawing in each viewport. The purpose of tiled viewports is to make it easier to draw. For example:

✦ You can see the whole drawing in one viewport and a zoomed-in portion of that drawing in another viewport.

✦ You can see widely separated views of a large drawing at one time.

Cross-Reference AutoCAD offers two types of viewports—*tiled* and *floating*. For more information on floating viewports, see the sidebar of that title in this chapter. For a detailed discussion, turn to Chapter 17.

Actually, you are already using a tiled viewport because the regular single view of your drawing that you have been working with represents the default of a one-tile viewport.

Tiled viewports have the following characteristics:

✦ No matter how many viewports you have, they always collectively take up the entire screen. They are not separate entities, but a way of dividing up the screen.

✦ Only one viewport can be active at a time. The active viewport has a bold border.

✦ The crosshairs only appear in the active viewport.

✦ The UCS (User Coordinate System) icon (if set to On) appears in each viewport.

✦ Any change you make to your drawing in one viewport automatically appears in every other viewport (or in each viewport that shows the part of the drawing where you made the change).

✦ AutoCAD enables you to create up to 96 viewports — but you'll never want to create that many!

✦ You can begin a command in one viewport and finish it in another. For example, you can start a line in one viewport, switch to a second viewport, and end the line there.

✦ You can save and restore viewport configurations.

Figure 8-15 shows a drawing divided into three tiled viewports. Each viewport shows a different view of the same drawing.

Figure 8-15: A drawing showing three tiled viewports with a different view in each viewport

Thanks to Jerry Bottenfield of Clow Valve Company, Oskaloosa, Iowa, for this drawing.

Configuring tiled viewports

Creating tiled viewports involves deciding how you want to divide up the screen. A set of tiled viewports is called a configuration. AutoCAD offers a few simple configurations, but you can create your own by further dividing up any of the viewports. You can also join two viewports. Finally, you can always return to the default of one viewport.

Creating tiled viewports

To create additional viewports (that is, more than the one viewport you always see), choose View ⇨ Viewports. This opens a submenu from which you can choose from AutoCAD's preset configurations, as shown in Figure 8-16.

Figure 8-16: The Viewports submenu

You can choose to create up to four tiled viewports from the submenu, at which point you respond to the options that appear on the command line. For example, if you choose 2 Viewports, AutoCAD responds with the `Enter a configuration option [Horizontal/Vertical] <Vertical>:` prompt. Right-click and choose Horizontal or Vertical to create two horizontal or vertical viewports. If you choose 4 Viewports, AutoCAD makes four equal viewports, one in each corner. However, if you choose 3 Viewports, AutoCAD offers several options to let you choose the configuration of the three viewports. These options can be confusing.

An easier way to configure viewports is to choose New Viewports from the submenu. The Viewports dialog box opens with the New Viewports tab on top, as shown in Figure 8-17. Here you choose the configuration that you want. AutoCAD displays a preview of the configuration.

If you have named views in your drawing, you can specify a view for each viewport to display. Click a viewport in the Preview pane and choose a named view from the Change View To drop-down list box at the bottom of the dialog box. If your drawing is in 3D, you can choose 3D from the Setup drop-down list box, and AutoCAD will create standard orthogonal views in the viewports. When you have specified your viewport configuration, click OK to return to your drawing.

Figure 8-17: The Viewports dialog box makes it easy to choose a configuration.

The Viewport dialog box is usually the best place to start creating viewports. However, if the standard configurations do not meet your needs, you can use one of them as a starting point and then use the other options.

Notice the Apply To drop-down list at the bottom-left corner of the Viewports dialog box (New Viewports tab) in Figure 8-17. By default, the tiled viewport configurations apply to the entire display, meaning that they replace your current configuration. You can also choose to apply the configuration to the current viewport. As explained earlier, the active viewport has a bold border and crosshairs. To make a viewport active, click anywhere inside that viewport. Then Choose View ➪ Viewports ➪ New Viewports, choose Current Viewport from the Apply To drop-down list, and choose the configuration you want for that viewport.

Let's say you have four equal viewports, and the top-left viewport is active. If you choose the Four: Equal configuration from the Viewports dialog box while the top-left viewport is active and apply it to the current viewport, AutoCAD divides the top-left viewport into four viewports. Now you have seven viewports in the drawing.

Removing tiled viewports

One way to remove a tiled viewport is to join it to another viewport. To join one viewport to another, choose View ➪ Viewports ➪ Join. At the `Select dominant viewport <current viewport>:` prompt, click the viewport you want to retain or press Enter if you want to retain the current viewport. At the `Select viewport to join:` prompt, click the adjacent viewport that you want to join into the dominant

viewport. You lose the display in this second viewport as AutoCAD joins the two viewports. The adjacent viewports must together form a rectangle.

The only other way to remove all tiled viewports in one step is to return to the single viewport configuration—choose View ➪ Viewports ➪ 1 Viewport. AutoCAD keeps the display in the current viewport and discards the others.

Using tiled viewports

After you have created the viewport configuration that you want, you are ready to use it. The first step is to create the views you need in each viewport.

Creating viewport views

Creating views in each viewport involves two steps:

1. Make a viewport current by clicking anywhere inside it.

2. Zoom and pan until you have the view that you want.

Tip Many users commonly use one viewport to display the entire drawing and the others to display zoomed in views of smaller sections.

Drawing from viewport to viewport

After you have the viewport configuration and views you need, you can start to draw. One of the great advantages of viewports is that you can draw from one viewport to another. In a large drawing, you may need to draw a line from one end of the drawing to another, but when you display the entire drawing you cannot see the detail well enough to specify where to start and end the line. The basic steps to draw from one viewport to another are as follows:

1. Click the viewport where you want to start. This might be a small detail of one corner of your drawing.

2. Start the command and specify any options you need. Specify any necessary coordinates as you usually would.

3. To continue the command in a second viewport, click to activate that viewport. Continue the command, specifying coordinates as necessary.

4. You can continue the command in a third viewport by clicking it. Do this until you have completed the command. If you have a viewport displaying the entire drawing, you immediately see the results in that viewport as well.

Cross-Reference You can also use viewports to edit your drawing. Chapters 9 and 10 cover the commands used to edit your drawing.

All commands except those that change the display—such as zooming, panning, and creating views—can be started in one viewport and continued in another.

Floating viewports

AutoCAD has two types of viewports, *tiled viewports*, which are discussed here, and *floating viewports*, which I cover in Chapter 17. These two types of viewports have many similarities, but they have different purposes. Whereas the purpose of tiled viewports is to help you draw and edit your drawing, floating viewports are generally used to lay out your drawing for plotting.

Floating viewports create layouts, which enable you to treat your screen like a sheet of paper. You create floating viewports and perhaps a title block on this electronic sheet of paper. You can create one or more layouts. Each floating viewport can show a different view of your drawing—just like tiled viewports. But floating viewports then let you plot all those views on one sheet of paper. You can't do that with tiled viewports, which are just devices to let you temporarily display your drawing in a way that helps you draw and edit. However, you can also draw and edit by using floating viewports.

Tiled viewports are covered here because they are appropriate for learning how to draw and edit your drawing. Floating viewports are covered in Chapter 17 because you use them to lay out your drawing for plotting.

Saving and restoring viewport configurations

You can save a tiled viewport configuration. If you find yourself creating a particular configuration over and over, you should save it. Saving a configuration is just a matter of giving it a name. You can then restore it when needed. Viewport configuration names can be up to 255 characters and can include spaces.

Saving a viewport configuration

After you create a viewport configuration that you like, follow these steps to save it:

1. Choose View ➪ Viewports ➪ New Viewports if you are not already in the Viewports dialog box.

2. Type a name in the New name text box.

3. Click OK.

Restoring a viewport configuration

After returning to one viewport or using a different configuration, you can restore a named viewport configuration, as follows:

1. Choose View ➪ Viewports ➪ Named Viewports. AutoCAD opens the Viewports dialog box with the Named Viewports tab on top, shown in Figure 8-18.

Figure 8-18: The Named Viewports tab lists saved viewport configurations.

2. Choose the viewport that you want to restore.

3. Click OK.

On the CD-ROM The drawing used in the following Step-by-Step exercise on creating, naming, and restoring tiled viewport configurations, a08-c.dwg, is in the Drawings folder of the *AutoCAD 2004 Bible* CD-ROM.

Step-by-Step: Creating, Naming, and Restoring Tiled Viewport Configurations

1. Open ab08-c.dwg from the CD-ROM.

2. Save the file as ab08-02.dwg in your AutoCAD Bible folder.

3. Choose View ➪ Viewports ➪ New Viewports to open the Viewports dialog box.

4. In the listing at the left of the dialog box, choose Three: Above. Click OK. AutoCAD creates three tiled viewports.

5. Click the bottom-left viewport. Choose Zoom Window on the Zoom flyout of the Standard toolbar and choose a window around the left portion of the threaded model (the upper part of the drawing).

6. Click the bottom-right viewport. Choose Zoom Window on the Zoom flyout of the Standard toolbar and choose a window around the bottom-left portion of the drawing (not including the title block).

7. Click the top viewport. Choose Zoom Extents from the Zoom flyout of the Standard toolbar. Figure 8-19 shows the results.

8. Choose View ➪ Viewports ➪ New Viewports. In the New name text box, type **3 view O Ring** and click OK.

9. With the top viewport still active, choose View ➪ Viewports ➪ 1 Viewport. AutoCAD displays the view shown in the last active viewport.

10. Choose View ➪ Viewports ➪ Named Viewports.

Figure 8-19: The three tiled viewports now display three different views.

11. Choose 3 view O Ring and click OK. AutoCAD restores the viewport configuration, including the views in each viewport.

12. Save your drawing.

Snap Rotation

Not all 2D drawings are vertical and horizontal. In some drawings a significant portion of your objects are drawn at nonorthogonal angles. One example is an auxiliary view to show the "true size" of an inclined surface. Sometimes it helps to rotate the crosshairs to match the major angles of the drawing.

Consider Figure 8-20. A great deal of this drawing is at an angle. You could handle this in four ways:

✦ Draw as normal, specifying the necessary angles.

✦ Rotate the snap, which also rotates the grid and crosshairs.

✦ Create a new UCS (User Coordinate System).

✦ Draw the entire model vertically and rotate it afterward.

Creating a new UCS is covered later in this chapter.

Figure 8-20: In 2D drawings such as this, you should consider various options, such as rotating the snap or creating a new UCS.

Thanks to Robert Mack of The Dexter Company, Fairfield, Iowa, for this drawing.

If you need to draw several objects at a certain angle, such as 45 degrees, you can rotate the snap to that angle. AutoCAD rotates the grid and crosshairs to follow suit. This technique works best when the decimal point accuracy required lets you draw using snap points. You can also use this technique to guide the cursor at an appropriate angle for direct distance entry, although polar tracking is another way to accomplish the same task.

To change the snap rotation angle, choose Tools ➪ Drafting Settings (or right-click SNAP on the status bar and choose Settings) to open the Drafting Settings dialog box. In the Snap section, type an angle in the Angle text box.

Note that you can also set an X base and a Y base. This simply ensures that the grid goes through a point of your choice, which is very important if you are using snap mode to draw. If you are just starting to draw an object, use the 0,0 base and draw to the existing snap points. However, if you have an existing object and need to add to it, changing the base can be very helpful. Setting X and Y bases does not change the coordinates, which are tied to the UCS. The UCS is discussed in the next section.

Cross-Reference You can use the ID command to get the coordinates of a point. Then use these coordinates as the X and Y bases. Chapter 12 covers the ID command.

Click OK to return to your drawing. Make sure that the grid is on. The crosshairs and grid now reflect the new snap angle. Figure 8-21 shows the same drawing with a snap angle of 45 degrees. Notice how the crosshairs now match the angle of the drawing. The crosshairs have been set to 100 percent of screen size, which is useful when rotating the snap angle. (To reset the crosshairs size, choose Tools ➪ Options and click the Display tab.)

Figure 8-21: The snap angle in this drawing has been changed to 45 degrees. Note that the grid follows the snap.

Tip The grid does not have to be on, but it helps you get your bearings when working with an unusual snap angle.

You can create a new UCS (User Coordinate System) rather than rotate the snap angle. The results are similar, except that when you create a UCS, you also affect the X,Y coordinates. The UCS is much more flexible when you start drawing in three dimensions.

User Coordinate Systems

By default, a drawing is set up by using a *World Coordinate System*. This sets the origin of the X,Y points at 0,0 and the angles using the familiar East (right-facing) equals 0 degrees system. Figure 8-22 shows the UCS icon in its default display.

You can easily create your own UCS and even save it for future use in the drawing. Creating a UCS is essential for 3D drawing but often useful for 2D drawing as well.

Figure 8-22: The UCS icon in its default display

To define a UCS in a 2D drawing, you indicate the angle of the X and Y axes and an origin point. The origin point then becomes the new 0,0 coordinate. AutoCAD offers several options for specifying the UCS.

Understanding UCS options

Understanding the UCS options will help you create a new UCS more easily, based on the information you have available. To create a UCS, choose Tools ⇨ New UCS. A submenu opens offering the options listed in Table 8-2.

Choose Tools ⇨ Move UCS to leave the orientation of the XY axes the same but move the origin. This option is similar to the Origin option. You can specify a new origin or, for a 3D drawing, move the origin along the Z axis by a positive or negative number of units (called the Z depth).

Cross-Reference

Choose Tools ⇨ Orthographic UCS to open a submenu with several preset views. These views are used only in 3D drawings. See Chapter 21 for details on 3D coordinates.

Table 8-2 UCS Options	
Option	**Meaning**
World	Specifies the default UCS, with the X axis horizontal, the Y axis vertical, and the origin at the initial 0,0 location.
Object	Enables you to align the UCS with an object. In general, AutoCAD uses the most obvious object snap as the origin and aligns the X axis with the object. For example, when you choose a line, the endpoint nearest your pick point becomes the origin and the X axis aligns with the angle of the line. When you choose a circle, the X axis points toward the point you pick on the circumference.
Face	Aligns the UCS with the face of a 3D solid.
View	Aligns the X and Y axes with the current view. Used in 3D drawing. AutoCAD arbitrarily sets the origin.

Continued

Table 8-2 *(continued)*

Option	Meaning
Origin	Specifies a new 0,0 point of your choice relative to the current origin.
Z Axis Vector	Specifies which way the Z axis points. This option is not used in 2D drawing.
3 Point	Enables you to specify three points. The first point is the origin, the second point indicates the positive direction of the X axis, and the third point indicates the positive direction of the Y axis.
X	Keeps the current origin and rotates the Y and Z axes around the current X axis. You specify the angle. This is used in 3D drawing.
Y	Keeps the current origin and rotates the X and Z axes around the current Y axis. You specify the angle. This is used in 3D drawing.
Z	Keeps the current origin and rotates the X and Y axes around the current Z axis. You specify the angle. This option can be used in 2D drawing.

Saving and restoring a custom UCS

After you create a UCS, you can save it so that you can easily switch back and forth between the World Coordinate System and your UCS. To save a UCS, follow these steps:

1. Specify the UCS as described in the previous section.

2. Choose Tools ➪ Named UCS. AutoCAD opens the UCS dialog box with the Named UCSs tab on top, as shown in Figure 8-23. If your current UCS is not named, it is listed as Unnamed, and highlighted. Previously named UCSs are also listed. You can also use this dialog box to return to the previous UCS or the World Coordinate System (WCS).

3. Click Unnamed. Type a name for the UCS and press Enter. The name can be up to 255 characters and can include spaces.

4. Click OK.

To restore a saved UCS, choose Tools ➪ Named UCS. Choose the UCS that you want to use and click Set Current. Then click OK.

You can use the same dialog box to return to the previous UCS you used. You can also choose UCS Previous from the UCS toolbar. Using this button, you can quickly switch back and forth between two UCSs.

To delete a saved UCS, select it in the UCS dialog box and press the Del key.

Figure 8-23: Use the UCS dialog box to save and restore a UCS.

Controlling the UCS icon

When you start a new drawing, the UCS icon is at the bottom-left of your drawing at 0,0. By default, the icon remains at 0,0 even if you pan around the drawing. The icon may therefore end up in the middle of your drawing. If 0,0 is not displayed, then the icon reverts to the bottom-left of your drawing.

You can turn off the UCS icon completely. If you are not working with customized UCSs, you often have no reason to see the UCS in a 2D drawing. If you want the UCS icon on, you can also tell AutoCAD to display it only at the bottom-left of your drawing—to keep the icon out of the way so that it does not obstruct your drawing.

If you create a new UCS, keeping the UCS icon at the 0,0 point (the origin) of your new UCS helps you get your bearings. AutoCAD places a plus sign in the icon to indicate the origin. However, if the origin is out of the current display or so close to the edge that the icon won't fit, AutoCAD places the UCS icon at the lower-left corner of your drawing anyway.

To control the UCS icon, choose View ➪ Display ➪ UCS Icon. (Don't confuse this with Tools ➪ New UCS, which creates a custom UCS.) A submenu opens with the following items:

✦ **On:** Toggles the display of the UCS icon on and off.

✦ **Origin:** Toggles the placement of the UCS icon at the origin on and off.

You can customize the look of the UCS icon. To customize the look of the UCS icon, choose View ➪ Display ➪ UCS Icon ➪ Properties (or type **ucsicon** and choose the Properties option) to open the UCS Icon dialog box, shown in Figure 8-24. As you make changes, you can see the result in the preview box.

Figure 8-24: Use the UCS Icon dialog box to customize the look of the UCS icon.

Choose between 2D and 3D styles. The 3D style shows the Z axis, but you won't see it when you are looking at your model from the top (called *plan view*). If you choose the 3D style, you can check the Cone box to display a cone effect for the arrows of the X and Y axes. Either way, the Z axis has no arrow, so that you can distinguish it from the X and Y axes. You can also choose a line width from 1 to 3, 1 being the default.

You can change the size of the icon. Just drag the slider up and down to get the result you like. Finally, you can change the color of the icon both in model space and in paper space layouts. Click OK to close the dialog box.

Using a custom UCS

Although it seems confusing at first, after you try creating your own UCS it's easier to understand how the process works.

In this exercise, you practice drawing with a custom UCS to create the basic framework for the drawing shown previously in Figures 8-20 and 8-21, a bearing housing for a commercial dryer.

On the CD-ROM The drawing used in the following Step-by-Step exercise on drawing with a custom UCS, ab08-d.dwg, is in the Drawings folder of the *AutoCAD 2004 Bible* CD-ROM.

Step-by-Step: Drawing with a Custom UCS

1. Open ab08-d.dwg from the CD-ROM.

2. Save the file as ab08-03.dwg in your AutoCAD Bible folder. ORTHO should be on. If necessary, turn on OSNAP. Set a running object snap for endpoints only.

3. Choose Tools ➪ New UCS ➪ Z. Because no objects exist in the drawing, you cannot easily use the 3 Point or Object options that might otherwise be useful.

4. At the `Specify rotation angle about Z axis <90>:` prompt, type **45** ↵. The UCS icon and crosshairs are displayed at a 45-degree angle.

5. Choose Rectangle from the Draw toolbar. At the prompt, pick a point at the bottom center of your screen. At the `Specify other corner point or [Dimensions]:` prompt, type **@3-15/16,31/32** ↵. AutoCAD creates the rectangle at the proper angle.

6. Start the LINE command. At the `Specify first point:` prompt, choose the From object snap. At the `Base point:` prompt, use the Endpoint object snap to pick point ❶ in Figure 8-25. At the `<Offset>:` prompt, type **@-1/8,0** ↵. At the `Specify next point or [Undo]:` prompt, type **@5-3/16<93.3** ↵. End the LINE command.

7. Start the LINE command again. Follow the prompts:

   ```
   Specify first point: Choose the From object snap.
   Base point: Use the Endpoint object snap to pick point ❷.
   <Offset>: @1/16,0 ↵
   Specify next point or [Undo]: Move the cursor in the 90°
   direction relative to the UCS. 35/64 ↵. (Remember that the
   UCS has been rotated 45 degrees so that 90 degrees looks like
   135 degrees.)
   Press F6 twice for polar coordinates (if necessary) to
   confirm the 90° direction as you move the cursor.
   Specify next point or [Undo]: Move the cursor in the 18°
   direction. 3-9/64 ↵
   Specify next point or [Close/Undo]: Move the cursor in the
   270° direction. 35/64 ↵
   Specify next point or [Close/Undo]: c ↵ (to close the figure)
   ```

8. Start the LINE command. At the `Specify first point:` prompt, choose the From object snap. At the `Base point:` prompt, use the endpoint object snap to pick ❶ in Figure 8-26. At the `<Offset>:` prompt, type **@1/16,0** ↵.

9. At the `Specify next point or [Undo]:` prompt, again choose From. At the `Base point:` prompt, use the endpoint object snap to pick ❷. At the `<Offset>:` prompt, type **@1/8,0** ↵ to complete the model, as shown in Figure 8-26. End the LINE command.

10. Because you would normally continue working on this drawing, you should save the UCS. Choose Tools ➪ Named UCS. In the UCS dialog box, click Unnamed. Type **Rotated 45** and press Enter.

11. Still in the dialog box, choose World, click Set Current, and click OK to return to your drawing. The UCS icon and crosshairs return to their familiar angle.

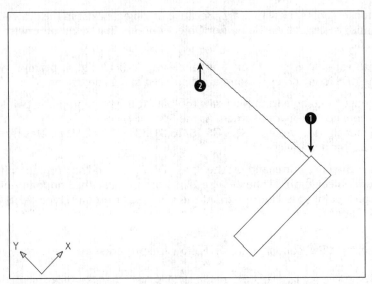

Figure 8-25: Starting to draw the framework for the bearing housing drawn by using a customized UCS

12. To return to the Rotated 45 UCS, choose Tools ➪ Named UCS to open the UCS dialog box. Choose Rotated 45 and click Set Current. Click OK. AutoCAD restores the Rotated 45 UCS.

13. Save your drawing.

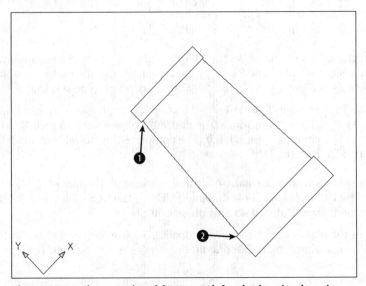

Figure 8-26: The completed framework for the bearing housing

Tip After creating a new, rotated UCS such as the one in the previous exercise, type **plan** (the start the PLAN command) and use the Current UCS option to remove the rotation. Now you aren't working at an angle in your UCS. To return to the World UCS, type **plan** again and choose the World option to return to your drawing's previous state.

Isometric Drawing

An *isometric* drawing is a 2D drawing drawn to look like a 3D drawing. Every child learns how to draw a box that looks three-dimensional. By drawing parallelograms instead of squares, the drawing gives the impression of being in three dimensions. AutoCAD enables you to do the same thing.

Understanding isometric planes

AutoCAD uses the ISOPLANE (short for isometric plane) command to rotate the crosshairs to the special angles required for isometric drawing. You then toggle the ISOPLANE setting from left to right to top to draw on each of the three "planes." As you do so, AutoCAD changes the angles of the crosshairs, snap, and grid to the appropriate angles.

These angles are 30 degrees for the X axis, 90 degrees for the Z axis, and 150 degrees for the Y axis. As you toggle among the planes, you see the crosshairs take on various configurations of these angles. Figure 8-27 shows the standard isometric cube. You can see three sides — left, right, and top. In the figure, the crosshairs are set to the right isometric plane.

Isometric drawing is not often used for precise drawing because it can be difficult to specify the exact points that you need. Also, true 3D drawing has mostly supplanted isometric drawing. It is, however, used for piping work as well as for illustrations.

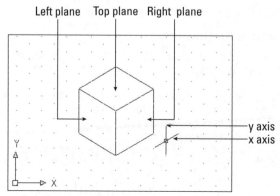

Figure 8-27: The isometric cube

Tip Use snap points and object snaps as much as possible in an isometric drawing. Also, set the cursor to 100 percent of the screen to better visualize the isometric planes. (Choose Tools ➪ Options and click the Display tab.) The grid is also a helpful aid.

Drawing in isometric mode

To start isometric mode, choose Tools ➪ Drafting Settings to open the Drafting Settings dialog box. On the Snap and Grid tab, in the Snap type & style section, choose Grid snap (if not already selected), and then Isometric snap. While you're there, turn on Snap and Grid if you want them on. Click OK. After you are in isometric mode, press F5 to toggle from plane to plane.

Drawing lines in isometric mode is fairly straightforward if the lines are parallel to one of the isometric plane angles. Circles and arcs in isometric mode must be drawn as ellipses and elliptical arcs. When you are in isometric mode the ELLIPSE command has an Isocircle option.

Step-by-Step: Drawing in Isometric Mode

1. Start a new drawing by using the `acad.dwt` template.

2. Save the drawing in your `AutoCAD Bible` folder as `ab08-04.dwg`.

3. Right-click the SNAP button on the status bar and choose Settings. On the Snap and Grid tab, in the Snap type & style section, choose Grid snap (if not already selected), and then Isometric snap.

4. In the Snap section, ensure the Snap Y spacing is set to 0.5 and click Snap On. In the Grid section, ensure the Grid Y spacing is set to 0.5 and click Grid On. Click OK to return to your drawing.

5. Choose Tools ➪ Options and click the Display tab. In the Crosshair size text box, change the cursor size to 100. Click OK.

6. Press F5 until you see the `<Isoplane Left>` prompt.

7. Do a Zoom Window to zoom into the area covered by the grid.

8. Start the LINE command. Follow the prompts:

   ```
   Specify first point: Use the coordinate display to choose
   3.4641,2, which is a snap point. (It may take you a while to
   find the point.)
   Specify next point or [Undo]: Choose 6.4952,0.25. (Press F6
   if necessary to get dynamic absolute coordinates.)
   Specify next point or [Undo]: Choose 6.4952,1.25.
   Specify next point or [Close/Undo]: Choose 3.4641,3.
   Specify next point or [Close/Undo]: Right-click and choose
   Close to close the left side of the model. All these points
   are snap points.
   ```

 The results are shown in Figure 8-28.

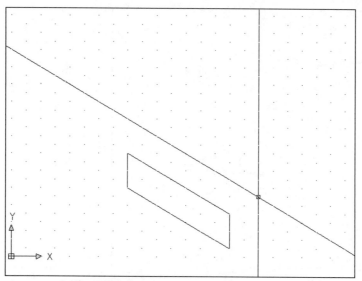

Figure 8-28: The left side of the iron plate. The cursor has been changed to extend to 100 percent of the screen.

9. Press F5 twice until you see `<Isoplane Right>` on the command line.

10. Start the LINE command again. At the `Specify first point:` prompt, pick 6.4952,1.25. Press F6 twice to get dynamic polar coordinates. At the `Specify next point or [Undo]:` prompt, pick when the coordinates show 2.0000<30. At the `Specify next point or [Undo]:` prompt, use the polar coordinate display to draw a line of 1.0000<270. At the `Specify next point or [Close/Undo]:` prompt, draw a line of 2.0000<210. End the LINE command.

11. Press F5 twice until you see `<Isoplane Top>` on the command line.

12. Start the LINE command. Start the line at 8.2270,2.25, which is a snap point. Draw a line of 3.500<150 and continue another line of 2.000<210. End the LINE command. This completes the box.

13. Choose Ellipse from the Draw toolbar. Right-click and choose Isocircle from the shortcut menu. At the `Specify center of isocircle:` prompt, choose 5.1962,3. At the `Specify radius of isocircle or [Diameter]:` prompt, type .5 ↵. AutoCAD draws the ellipse. Your drawing should look like Figure 8-29.

14. Change the cursor size back to 5 (%). Save your drawing.

Tip Polar coordinate display is very helpful while drawing isometrically. The coordinates are easier to understand than the unusual absolute snap point coordinates created by ISOPLANE.

Figure 8-29: The completed iron plate with a hole in it, drawn isometrically

Summary

In this chapter, you read how to control the display of your drawing. You learned about:

✦ The PAN and ZOOM commands, including real-time pan and zoom and the many ZOOM options

✦ Using Aerial View to pan and zoom

✦ Saving several views of your drawing so that you can retrieve them quickly

✦ Creating tiled viewports for drawing and editing, as well as how to name and display useful viewport configurations

✦ Rotating the snap and grid

✦ Creating a User Coordinate System, including how to save a useful UCS and then set it as current at any time

✦ Setting the snap style to isometric to create isometric drawings, which are 2D drawings that give the appearance of three dimensions

In the next chapter, you discover how to start editing your drawings.

✦ ✦ ✦

Editing Your Drawing: Basic Tools

No drawing project is ever completed without changes. You make changes in a drawing for many reasons. Some editing processes are simply part of the drawing process, such as copying an object instead of drawing it a second time from scratch. Other types of editing involve making changes to many objects at once, such as moving an entire section of a drawing to make room for newer added objects. You often need to erase, move, rotate, and resize objects.

Without knowing how to edit, working on a drawing would become repetitive. To avoid drawing the same object a second time, you draw an object once and then copy it to a new location.

Editing a Drawing

Making changes to a drawing is called editing. In order to edit an object, you need to select it. AutoCAD offers numerous techniques for selecting objects. In this chapter, I cover basic editing commands as well as most of the ways to select objects. The rest of the 2D editing commands, as well as additional selection and editing methods — grips, the Object Property Manager, selection filters, and groups — are covered in the next chapter.

Most of the editing commands are on the Modify toolbar. In most cases, you can do one of the following:

 ♦ Start the command first and then select the objects to which the command applies.

 ♦ Select the objects first and then start the command.

The question of which comes first, the command or the object, is fully covered later in this chapter.

Understanding object-selection basics

When you start editing drawings, the main new skill to learn is how to select objects. The selection options are covered later in this chapter.

The simplest selection technique is to place the *pickbox*—the box at the intersection of the crosshairs—over the object and click with the pick button on the mouse. This is known as picking an object. If you start an editing command before selecting an object, AutoCAD responds with the `Select objects:` prompt. When you pick an object, AutoCAD highlights it, usually by making it dashed, as shown in Figure 9-1.

Figure 9-1: The selected line is dashed.

AutoCAD continues to provide `Select objects:` prompts so that you can select other objects. Continue to select objects until you have selected all the objects that you want to edit. Then press Enter or right-click to end the `Select objects:` prompt.

When you select an object first, the selected object becomes dashed and you also see one or more small boxes, called *grips*, as shown in Figure 9-2. The next chapter covers grips. In the next few exercises, you use this picking technique to select objects.

Figure 9-2: The selected line is dashed and also displays grips.

Erasing objects

Somehow, no drawing is ever completed without erasing an object. The ERASE command is very simple—it has no options. To erase an object, select the object and choose Erase on the Modify toolbar or press Del on the keyboard. Alternatively, choose Erase and then select the object.

On the CD-ROM The drawing used in the following Step-by-Step exercise on erasing objects, ab09-a.dwg, is in the Drawings folder of the *AutoCAD 2004 Bible* CD-ROM.

Step-by-Step: Erasing Objects

1. Open ab09-a.dwg from the CD-ROM.

2. Save the file as ab09-01.dwg in your AutoCAD Bible folder. This drawing is a schematic of a gas extraction well, shown in Figure 9-3.

3. To erase the line at point ❶ of Figure 9-3, move the mouse until the pickbox at the intersection of the crosshairs is anywhere over the line and click. Notice that the line is dashed and displays grips.

4. Choose Erase from the Modify toolbar. AutoCAD erases the line.

5. Right-click and choose Repeat Erase.

6. At the Select objects: prompt, pick the line at point ❷ in Figure 9-3.

7. AutoCAD responds with 1 found and repeats the Select objects: prompt. Right-click to end the Select objects: prompt. AutoCAD erases the line.

8. Save your drawing.

Cross-Reference The OOPS command restores the most recently erased object and is covered in Chapter 18.

Moving objects

Use the MOVE command to move objects in your drawing. Moving an object is more complex than erasing one because you need to tell AutoCAD the distance and direction that you want the object to move.

To move an object, select it and choose Move on the Modify toolbar. Alternatively, choose Move and then select the object.

When you choose the MOVE command and after you have selected an object, AutoCAD responds with the following prompt:

 Specify base point or displacement:

You now have two ways of telling AutoCAD how to move the object or objects:

Figure 9-3: The gas-extraction well schematic

Thanks to the Army Corps of Engineers for this drawing. The COE maintains a Web site of drawings at http:// cadlib.wes.army.mil.

✦ **Displacement method:** At the Specify base point or displacement: prompt, state the entire displacement as an X,Y coordinate such as 2,3 or a polar coordinate such as 2<60. Because the word displacement already implies the relative distance from the object, you do not use @. (AutoCAD actually uses 0,0 as the relative point.) AutoCAD responds with the Specify second point of displacement or <use first point as displacement>: prompt. Because you have already given AutoCAD all the information it needs, press Enter. AutoCAD uses the first point you indicated as the displacement (the default) and moves the object.

✦ **Base point/second point method:** At the Specify base point or displacement: prompt, pick a base point. This can be anywhere in your drawing. At the Specify second point of displacement or <use first point as displacement>: prompt, specify the distance and angle of movement either by picking a second point on the screen or by typing a relative coordinate by using @.

The displacement method requires less input and is simpler when you know the exact displacement so that you can type it in. The only disadvantage is that as soon as you type in the displacement, AutoCAD sometimes displays a confusing drag line and copy of your object or objects. Ignore this display, press Enter, and your object or objects move as you specified.

The base point/second point method works best when you want to move an object relative to another object on the screen.

Tip When you move an object, choose an object snap on the object or a nearby-related object as the base point for exact results.

You can use polar snap to move an object. Turn on polar snap and, if necessary, use the Drafting Settings dialog box to set the increment. You can set the polar distance; if the polar distance is 0, AutoCAD uses the Snap X spacing value. Use polar snap with the base point/second point method. At the first prompt, pick a point such as an object snap on the object. At the second prompt, drag the object in the desired direction. Use the tooltip to guide you and then click.

You can use object drag-and-drop to move objects if you are not too particular about where they end up. Here's how it works:

1. Pick an object.

2. Continue to pick as many objects as you want to move. They all show grips.

3. Pick any of the objects, but not on a grip. Keep the mouse button pressed until the cursor changes to an arrow with a small rectangle.

4. Drag the object(s) to any other location in your drawing.

For a little more control over the placement of your objects, use the Windows clipboard. Pick the object(s) that you want to move. Right-click and choose Cut from the shortcut menu. Right-click a second time and choose Paste. AutoCAD asks you for an insertion point, which you can pick with an object snap or by typing coordinates. However, you can't control the base point (AutoCAD uses 0,0) as you can with the MOVE command.

 On the CD-ROM The drawing used in the following Step-by-Step exercise on moving objects, ab09-b.dwg, is in the Drawings folder of the *AutoCAD 2004 Bible* CD-ROM.

Step-by-Step: Moving Objects

1. Open ab09-b.dwg from the CD-ROM.

2. Save the file as ab09-02.dwg in your AutoCAD Bible folder. This drawing shows the plan of a bathroom. Each object is a *block*, a set of objects that you can select as one object. Make sure that OSNAP is turned on. Set a running object snap for intersection only.

3. ✛ Pick anywhere on the tub to select it. Notice the grip and dashed lines. Choose Move on the Modify toolbar. Follow the prompts:

```
Specify base point or displacement: Move the cursor to the
Intersection at ❶ in Figure 9-4 and click.
Specify second point of displacement or <use first point as
displacement>: Move the cursor to the Intersection at ❷ in
Figure 9-4 and click.
```

AutoCAD moves the tub to the bottom-right corner of the bathroom.

4. Choose Move on the Modify toolbar. Follow the prompts:

```
Select objects: Pick the sink.
Select objects: ↵ Specify base point or displacement: 4'<0 ↵
Specify second point of displacement or <use first point as
displacement>: ↵
```

AutoCAD moves the sink 4 feet to the right.

Figure 9-4: The bathroom plan

Thanks to Bill Wynn of New Windsor, Maryland for this drawing.

5. Click SNAP on the status bar to turn it on. Now, right-click SNAP. Choose Polar Snap On (unless it is already on, in which case it is unavailable). Click POLAR on the status bar.

6. Pick the toilet and choose Move on the Modify toolbar. At the `Specify base point or displacement:` prompt, pick the intersection at the bottom-left corner of the toilet tank. At the `Specify second point of displacement or <use first point as displacement>:` prompt, move the toilet to the left until you see `0'-6"<180°` on the tooltip and click. AutoCAD moves the toilet 6 inches to the left. (If you can't get a 180° tooltip, check your polar angle settings.)

7. Save your drawing.

Copying objects

Copying is very similar to moving. In fact, the only difference is that AutoCAD does not remove the object from its original spot so that you end up with two objects instead of one.

To copy an object, select it and choose Copy Object on the Modify toolbar. Alternatively, choose Copy Object and then select the object.

The COPY command has a Multiple option that lets you make any number of copies from the original object or objects.

When you choose the COPY command and after you have selected an object, AutoCAD responds with the following prompt:

```
Specify base point or displacement, or [Multiple]:
```

You now have two ways of telling AutoCAD where to copy the object or objects:

✦ **Displacement method:** At the `Specify base point or displacement, or [Multiple]:` prompt, state the entire displacement as an X,Y coordinate such as 2,3 or a polar coordinate such as 2<60. Because the word "displacement" already implies the relative distance from the object, you do not use @. (AutoCAD actually uses 0,0 as the relative point.) AutoCAD responds with the `Specify second point of displacement or <use first point as displacement>:` prompt. Because you have already given AutoCAD all the information it needs, press Enter. AutoCAD uses the first point you indicated as the displacement (the default) and copies the object.

✦ **Base point/second point method:** At the `Specify base point or displacement, or [Multiple]:` prompt, pick a base point. This can be anywhere in your drawing. At the `Specify second point of displacement or <use first point as displacement>:` prompt, specify the distance and angle of movement either by picking a second point on the screen or by typing in a relative coordinate, using @.

As explained in the previous section on moving objects, you can use polar snap to copy objects.

You can also use drag-and-drop to copy objects. Follow the steps in the previous section, but press and hold the Ctrl key as you drag the object. Notice the plus sign in the cursor's rectangle. In the same way, you can use the clipboard to copy and paste objects from one location in a drawing to another.

On the CD-ROM The drawing used in the following Step-by-Step exercise on copying objects, ab09-c.dwg, is in the Drawings folder of the *AutoCAD 2004 Bible* CD-ROM.

Step-by-Step: Copying Objects

1. Open ab09-c.dwg from the CD-ROM.

2. Save the file as ab09-03.dwg in your AutoCAD Bible folder. This drawing shows part of an electrical schematic. Make sure that OSNAP is turned on. Set a running object snap for endpoint only.

3. Use ZOOM Window to zoom into the area of the drawing marked ❶ in Figure 9-5. This shows a 24-volt transformer.

Figure 9-5: The electrical schematic

Thanks to Robert Mack of the Dexter Company,
Fairfield, Iowa, for this drawing.

4. Note that three of the arcs that make up the right side of the transformer are missing. Pick the arc at ❶ in Figure 9-6. Choose Copy Object from the Modify toolbar. Follow the prompts:

```
Specify base point or displacement, or [Multiple]: Right-
click and choose Multiple from the shortcut menu.
Specify base point: Pick the endpoint at the top of the arc
at ❷ (see Figure 9-6).
Specify second point of displacement or <use first point as
displacement>: Pick the endpoint at the bottom of the first
arc at ❸ (see Figure 9-6).
```

```
Specify second point of displacement or <use first point as
displacement>: Pick the endpoint at the bottom of the second
arc at ❹ (see Figure 9-6).
Specify second point of displacement or <use first point as
displacement>: Pick the endpoint at the bottom of the third
arc at ❺ (see Figure 9-6).
Specify second point of displacement or <use first point as
displacement>: ↵
```

Figure 9-6: Close-up of the transformer

5. Choose ZOOM Previous from the Standard toolbar to return to your previous view.

6. Pick the circle at ❷ in Figure 9-5 (which shows the entire schematic section). Note the grips. You also want to select the text inside the circles, but it's hard to see because of the grips. Press Esc to remove the grips.

7. Choose Copy Object from the Modify toolbar. Now select the circle at ❷ in Figure 9-5 again. This time no grips obscure the text. Separately pick both lines of text inside the circle.

8. Continuing to select objects to copy, select the circle at ❸ in Figure 9-5. Also select the two lines of text inside the circle. Right-click to end the Select objects: prompt.

9. At the Specify base point or displacement, or [Multiple]: prompt, use the Endpoint object snap to pick point ❹ in Figure 9-5. At the Specify second point of displacement or <use first point as displacement>: prompt, use the Endpoint object snap to pick point ❺ in Figure 9-5. AutoCAD copies the two circles with the text.

10. Save your drawing.

Copying and moving objects from one drawing to another

If you use other Windows programs, you usually use the Cut command to move and the Copy command to copy objects. Then you use the Paste command to specify a new location. In AutoCAD these commands are called CUTCLIP, COPYCLIP, and PASTECLIP. (The CLIP refers to the Windows clipboard.) While the MOVE and COPY commands provide more accuracy within one drawing, you can use the clipboard to move and copy objects from one drawing to another.

You can copy objects from one drawing to another by using the drag-and-drop technique. The easiest way is to open both drawings and then choose Window ⇨ Tile Vertically. Select the object(s) that you want to copy, point to one of them, and drag to the second drawing. However, you don't have much control over the exact placement of the new objects. From drawing to drawing, AutoCAD copies the objects, rather than moving them.

For more control over the placement of your objects, use the Windows clipboard. A special feature, Copy with Base Point, gives you control over the placement of your objects. Follow these steps:

1. Pick the object(s) that you want to copy.

2. Right-click and choose Copy with Base Point from the shortcut menu.

3. At the `Specify base point:` prompt, specify a base point. An object snap is a good idea here. AutoCAD copies the object(s) to the clipboard, including the base point.

4. Switch to the second drawing.

5. Right-click in the drawing area and choose Paste (or click Paste on the Standard toolbar). AutoCAD prompts you for an insertion point. Specify the insertion point by picking, using an object snap, or typing coordinates. AutoCAD pastes the object.

To copy the object(s) to the same coordinates as the original drawing, in Step 5 choose Paste to Original Coordinates from the shortcut menu. AutoCAD pastes the object(s) in the second drawing, matching the coordinates. Depending on your drawing, you may need to ZOOM and PAN to see the pasted copy.

You cannot specify a base point for moving (cutting) an object, but AutoCAD does let you specify the insertion point when you paste it. AutoCAD automatically uses the lower-left extent of the selected object(s) as the base point.

Cross-Reference You can drag objects from an AutoCAD drawing into another application, such as a word processing document. For more information on working with AutoCAD and other applications, see Chapter 27.

In the following exercise, you practice copying objects from one drawing to another.

On the CD-ROM

The drawing used in the following Step-by-Step exercise on copying objects from one drawing to another, ab09-c.dwg, is in the Drawings folder of the *AutoCAD 2004 Bible* CD-ROM.

Step-by-Step: Copying Objects from One Drawing to Another

1. Close any open drawings. Open ab09-c.dwg from the CD-ROM. Save the file as ab09-04.dwg in your AutoCAD Bible folder. Then choose Open from the Standard toolbar and open ab09-03.dwg from your AutoCAD Bible folder. If you didn't do the previous exercise, open ab09-03.dwg from the Results folder of the CD-ROM.

2. Choose Window ➪ Tile Vertically. This displays the drawings side by side, as shown in Figure 9-7.

3. In ab09-03.dwg, which should be active, make sure that OSNAP is turned on. Set a running object snap set for endpoint only.

4. Pick the circle at ❶ and the two lines of text inside it.

5. Move the cursor off the selected objects and right-click. Choose Copy with Base Point from the shortcut menu.

6. At the Specify base point: prompt, pick the endpoint at ❷ in Figure 9-7.

7. Click anywhere in ab09-04.dwg to make it the current drawing. Right-click and choose Paste from the shortcut menu. At the Specify insertion point: prompt, pick the endpoint at ❸ in Figure 9-7. AutoCAD pastes the objects.

8. Click in ab09-03.dwg. Press Esc to clear any grips. Pick the circle at ❹ in Figure 9-7. (Don't include the text this time.) Click again and hold the mouse button on the circle, but not on the grips, until you see the pointer arrow with the rectangle. Drag the circle to ❺ in Figure 9-7. As you can see, you have no way to precisely place the circle.

9. Click in ab09-03.dwg again. This time pick both lines of text inside the circle at ❹. Right-click and choose Copy with Base Point. At the Specify base point: prompt, pick the endpoint at the left quadrant of the circle.

10. Click in ab09-04.dwg. Right-click and choose Paste to Original Coordinates. AutoCAD pastes the two lines of text inside the circle (depending on how accurately you dragged the circle).

11. Save ab09-04.dwg. Click in ab09-03.dwg and click its Close box. Don't save changes to ab9-3.dwg.

Figure 9-7: To copy objects from one drawing to another, display them both on the screen together. (The drawings may appear reversed on your screen.)

Rotating objects

AutoCAD enables you to easily rotate an object or objects around a base point that you specify. The base point is usually an object snap point on the object. To indicate the rotation, specify an angle of rotation. As explained in Chapter 5, zero degrees is generally to the right, and degrees increase counterclockwise, although you can change this convention. (To do so, choose Format ➪ Units.) By specifying a negative angle, you can turn objects clockwise.

To rotate an object, choose Rotate from the Modify toolbar and select an object. Alternatively, select an object and then choose Rotate from the Modify toolbar. At the Specify base point: prompt, indicate the point around which you want to rotate. At the Specify rotation angle or [Reference]: prompt, type an angle at the command line.

The Reference option lets you specify an absolute existing rotation angle and the desired angle. At the Specify the reference angle <0>: prompt, you type in an angle or specify an angle by picking two points. These can be object snap points on the object that specify the object's current angle. At the Specify the new angle: prompt, type or pick a new angle. You can also pick an object snap on another object in the drawing to indicate this new angle. You can use the Reference option to align the object with the X or Y axis or with another object in your drawing.

 The drawing used in the following Step-by-Step exercise on rotating objects, ab07-03.dwg, is in the Results folder of the *AutoCAD 2004 Bible* CD-ROM.

Step-by-Step: Rotating Objects

1. Open ab07-03.dwg from the Results folder of the CD-ROM. If you did the Step-by-Step exercise on ellipses in Chapter 7, you can open this drawing from your AutoCAD Bible folder.

2. Save the file as ab09-05.dwg in your AutoCAD Bible folder. This drawing shows a conference room, as shown in Figure 9-8.

3. Click GRID on the status bar to remove the grid.

4. Choose Tools ➪ Drafting Settings. On the Object Snap tab, choose Center, Quadrant, and Perpendicular. Click OK. OSNAP should be on.

5. Pick the small elliptical table at the top-left corner of the conference room. Choose Rotate from the Modify toolbar.

Figure 9-8: The conference room

6. At the Specify base point: prompt, pick the top quadrant of the ellipse. At the Specify rotation angle or [Reference]: prompt, type **90** ↵. AutoCAD rotates the small table 90 degrees around the base point.

7. Click SNAP on the status bar to turn off snap.

8. Start the COPY command. At the `Select objects:` prompt, pick the arc that makes the back of the chair. AutoCAD responds `1 found`. Continue to pick the two lines that make the armrests and the arc that makes the front of the chair, making sure that each time AutoCAD responds `1 found`. Right-click to end the `Select objects:` prompt.

9. At the `Specify base point or displacement, or [Multiple]:` prompt, locate the Center object snap to pick the center of the arc that makes up the back of the chair. (Press Tab to cycle through the object snaps if necessary or move the cursor over the arc itself, or its center.) At the `Specify second point of displacement or <use first point as displacement>:` prompt, pick point ❶ in Figure 9-8. This point doesn't have to be exact.

10. Start the ROTATE command. Follow the prompts:

```
Select objects: Pick all four objects that make up the new
chair you just created and press Enter to end object
selection.
Specify base point: Use the Center object snap to select the
center of the arc that makes up the back of the new chair.
Specify rotation angle or [Reference]: 180 ↵.
```

11. Start the COPY command and select the four objects in the new chair. Right-click to end object selection. Follow the prompts:

```
Specify base point or displacement, or [Multiple]: Right-
click and choose Multiple.
Specify base point: Use the Center object snap to select the
center of the arc that makes up the back of the chair.
Specify second point of displacement or <use first point as
displacement>: Pick a point about a third of the way around
the right side of the conference table.
Specify second point of displacement or <use first point as
displacement>: Pick a point about halfway around the right
side of the conference table.
Specify second point of displacement or <use first point as
displacement>: Pick a point about two-thirds of the way
around the right side of the conference table.
Specify second point of displacement or <use first point as
displacement>: ↵
```

12. Start the ROTATE command and select the four objects in the first of the three chairs (the top one) you just created. Right-click to end object selection. (If Polar Tracking or Object Snap is on, turn them off for better control.) At the `Specify base point:` prompt, pick the center object snap of either arc of the chair. At the `Specify rotation angle or [Reference]:` prompt, move the cursor around, watch the image of the chair rotate, and click when the chair faces the angle of the table.

13. Repeat Step 12 for the second chair.

14. Start the ROTATE command and select the four objects in the last chair you created by using the COPY command. Follow the prompts:

```
Specify base point: Choose the Center object snap of either
of the chair arcs.
Specify rotation angle or [Reference]: Right-click and choose
Reference from the shortcut menu.
Specify the reference angle <0>: Use the Quadrant object snap
to pick the back arc of the chair.
Specify second point: Use the Quadrant object snap to pick
the front arc of the chair.
Specify the new angle: Use the Perpendicular object snap to
choose the conference table next to the chair.
```

15. Save your drawing.

Scaling objects

Scaling, or resizing, objects is another common editing task in AutoCAD. As with rotating objects, you specify a base point, usually an object snap on the object. The base point is the one point on the object that does not move or change as you scale the object. The most common way to resize an object is to specify a scale factor. The current object has a scale factor of 1. Therefore, to increase the size of the object, type in a number greater than 1. For example, a scale factor of 2 doubles the size of the object. To decrease the size of the object, type in a number less than 1. A scale factor of 0.25 creates an object one-quarter of its previous size.

As with the ROTATE command, you can scale by using the Reference option. You specify the reference length, usually the current length of the object, by typing it in or using object snaps on the object. At the `Specify new length:` prompt, you can type a new length or pick a point. AutoCAD measures this point from the base point you specified to determine the new length.

To scale an object, choose Scale from the Modify toolbar and select the object. Alternatively, select the object and choose Scale from the Modify toolbar.

On the CD-ROM The drawing used in the following Step-by-Step exercise on scaling objects, ab09-d.dwg, is in the Drawings folder of the *AutoCAD 2004 Bible* CD-ROM.

Step-by-Step: Scaling Objects

1. Open ab09-d.dwg from the CD-ROM.

2. Save the file as ab09-06.dwg in your AutoCAD Bible folder. This drawing, shown in Figure 9-9, shows part of a valve that is manufactured in several sizes. In this exercise, you scale both views to represent a different-size valve piece. Ensure OSNAP is on. Set running object snaps for quadrant and endpoint.

Figure 9-9: The valve piece in two views

Thanks to Jerry Bottenfield of Clow Valve Company, Oskaloosa, Iowa for this drawing.

3. Choose Scale from the Modify toolbar. At the `Select objects:` prompt, pick both circles in the top view (they are actually arcs because they are broken at the bottom) and the two short lines at the bottom of the circles. Press Enter to end object selection. Follow the prompts:

```
Specify base point: Use the Quadrant object snap to pick the
left quadrant of the inner circle.
Specify scale factor or [Reference]: Right-click and choose
Reference.
Specify reference length <1>: Use the Quadrant object snap to
pick the left quadrant of the inner circle again.
Specify second point: Use the Quadrant object snap to pick
the right quadrant of the inner circle.
Specify new length: 1 ↵
```

Because the distance between the two quadrants you chose is 2.5 units, the SCALE command scales the objects to 40 percent (1 divided by 2.5).

4. Right-click and choose Repeat Scale. Select all eight lines in the bottom view including the green dashed lines. Be sure that AutoCAD says `1 found` each time. If necessary, use ZOOM Window to zoom in. Right-click to end object selection after you finish selecting the lines. Follow the prompts:

```
Specify base point: Use the Endpoint object snap at point ❶
in Figure 9-9.
Specify scale factor or [Reference]: .4 ↵
```

5. Save your drawing. It should look like Figure 9-10.

Figure 9-10: The valve piece has now been scaled down.

Using the CHANGE command

The CHANGE command changes the endpoint of a line and the radius of a circle. This command can also be used to change text and the location of blocks (covered in Chapter 18), but other newer commands do the job better, so that CHANGE is now used mostly for lines and circles. You can also use grips and the Object Property Manager, both covered in the next chapter, to change line endpoints and circle radii (among other object properties).

CHANGE also enables you to change an object's properties—layer, linetype, linetype scale, lineweight, color, elevation (Z coordinate of an object), thickness, and plot style. Layer, linetype, linetype scale, lineweight, and color are covered in Chapter 11. Elevation and thickness are basic 3D concepts that are covered in Chapter 21. Plot styles are explained in Chapter 17.

To change an object, select it and type **change** ↵ on the command line. Alternatively, type **change** ↵ on the command line and select the object.

The CHANGE command works differently depending on whether you select lines or circles. For this reason, it can give unexpected results if you choose lines and circles at the same time. Use the command for either lines or for circles but not for both at once.

Changing lines

If you select one line, the CHANGE command changes the endpoint closest to where you picked the line. AutoCAD prompts you for a change point. When you pick it, AutoCAD brings the endpoint of the line to that change point, as shown in Figure 9-11. You can use an object snap to specify the change point. If ORTHO is on, AutoCAD makes the line orthogonal, bringing the endpoint of the line as close as possible to the change point you specify, as shown in Figure 9-11.

If you select more than one line, CHANGE works differently—it moves the nearest endpoints of all the lines to the change point so that all the lines meet at one point, as shown in Figure 9-12.

Figure 9-11: Using the CHANGE command on one line

Figure 9-12: Using the CHANGE command on several lines. The original lines are shown as continuous. The new lines, after using the CHANGE command, are dashed.

Changing circles

Changing the radius of a circle has the same result as scaling it. When you select a circle, AutoCAD prompts you for a change point. If you pick one, AutoCAD resizes the circle so that it passes through the new point. You can also press Enter. Then AutoCAD prompts you to enter a new radius.

If you select more than one circle, AutoCAD moves from circle to circle, letting you specify a new radius for each, one at a time. You can tell which circle is current because of its drag image, which lets you drag the size of the circle.

If you select more than one circle and try to pick a change point, AutoCAD responds with `Change point ignored`. At that point, one circle becomes active, and you can then pick a change point.

On the CD-ROM The drawing used in the following Step-by-Step exercise on changing circles and lines, ab09-e.dwg, is in the Drawings folder of the *AutoCAD 2004 Bible* CD-ROM.

Step-by-Step: Changing Circles and Lines

1. Open ab09-e.dwg from the CD-ROM.

2. Save the file as ab09-07.dwg in your AutoCAD Bible folder. Ensure OSNAP is on. Set running object snaps for endpoint and perpendicular.

3. Use ZOOM Window to zoom in on the concentric circles at the bottom of the drawing.

4. Type **change** ↵. At the Select objects: prompt, pick the innermost circle. Right-click to end object selection.

5. At the Specify change point or [Properties]: prompt, press Enter (or right-click and choose Enter) so that you can type in a radius. At the Specify new circle radius <no change>: prompt, type **3/16** ↵.

6. Use ZOOM Dynamic to zoom in to the top of the release valve. Your view should look like Figure 9-13.

Figure 9-13: The zoomed-in view of the air and vacuum release valve

Thanks to the Army Corps of Engineers in Vicksburg, Mississippi, for this drawing.

7. Type **change** ↵. At the Select objects: prompt, pick points ❶ and ❷ in Figure 9-13. End object selection. At the Specify change point or [Properties]: prompt, pick the endpoint object snap at ❸ in Figure 9-13. AutoCAD redraws the lines.

8. Pick the line at ❹. Right-click and choose Repeat CHANGE. At the `Specify change point or [Properties]:` prompt, press Shift+right-click and choose the Intersection object snap to pick the new intersection near ❹ in Figure 9-13. AutoCAD trims the line.

Cross-Reference The TRIM command, discussed in Chapter 10, can make the same change that you just performed with the CHANGE command.

9. Do a ZOOM Extents and save your drawing.

Selecting Objects

If you have been following through this chapter's exercises, you have probably thought it tedious to pick several objects one at a time. Imagine trying to individually pick every object in a drawing just to move all the objects one-half unit to the left! Of course, there is a better way. In fact, AutoCAD offers many ways of selecting objects.

Selected objects are also called the *selection set* of objects.

Selecting objects after choosing a command

When you choose an editing command, AutoCAD responds with the `Select objects:` prompt. This prompt has 16 options — all you could ever want for selecting objects — but these options are not shown on the command line. To specify an option, type the option abbreviation. Because the `Select objects:` prompt repeats until you press Enter, you can combine options to select objects for any command.

In the following list of options, the capitalized letters of the option are the abbreviation you type (uppercase or lowercase letters work) at the `Select objects:` prompt.

Window

The Window option lets you pick two diagonal corners that define a window. All objects entirely within the window are selected. Figure 9-14 shows the process of picking the window. Figure 9-15 shows the result — the selected objects are highlighted by appearing with dashed instead of continuous lines.

New Feature You can now drag past the edge of the screen (actually the viewport) to specify a window. Hold down the mouse button and continue to move the mouse in the same direction. The display automatically pans so that you can see objects that were off the screen. When you see all the objects you need to select, pick the second corner of the window.

Last

The Last option selects the last object that you created.

Selection window

Figure 9-14: Selecting objects with a window. AutoCAD selects only objects that lie entirely within the window.

Selected objects

Figure 9-15: The selected objects are highlighted.

Crossing

Crossing enables you to pick two diagonal corners that define a window. All objects entirely or partly within the window are selected. Figure 9-16 shows the process of picking the window. Figure 9-17 shows the result — the selected objects are highlighted.

Crossing window

Figure 9-16: Selecting objects with a crossing window. AutoCAD selects any objects that lie within or partly within the window.

Figure 9-17: The selected objects are highlighted.

New Feature

You can now drag past the edge of the screen (actually the viewport) to specify a crossing window. Hold down the mouse button and continue to move the mouse in the same direction. The display automatically pans so that you can see objects that were off the screen. After you see all the objects you need to select, pick the second corner of the crossing window.

BOX

BOX is a combination of Window and Crossing. If you pick the two window corners from left to right, AutoCAD treats it as the Window option. If you pick the two points from right to left, AutoCAD treats it as the Crossing option. By default, you can select objects this way without specifying the BOX option. See the section on implied windowing later in this chapter.

ALL

The ALL option selects all objects on thawed layers in the drawing. (I discuss layers in Chapter 11.)

Fence

The Fence option enables you to specify a series of temporary lines. AutoCAD selects any object crossing the lines. Figure 9-18 shows the process of defining a selection fence. Figure 9-19 shows the result — the selected objects are highlighted.

Figure 9-18: Using a fence to select objects

Figure 9-19: The selected objects are highlighted.

WPolygon

The Window Polygon option (WPolygon) is like Window except that you create a polygon instead of a rectangular window. AutoCAD selects all objects that lie entirely within the polygon.

CPolygon

The Crossing Polygon option (CPolygon) is like Crossing except that you create a polygon instead of a rectangular window. AutoCAD selects all objects that lie entirely or partly within the window.

Group

The Group option selects a named group of objects. See Chapter 10 for more information on groups.

Remove

The Remove option enables you to deselect objects. After you use this option, all objects you select are deselected and are therefore removed from the selection set. Use the Add option to once again select objects.

Add

Use Add after using Remove to start selecting objects again.

Tip An alternative to using Remove to deselect objects is to press Shift and deselect objects by picking or implied windowing. See the section on implied windowing later in this chapter.

Multiple

The Multiple option turns off highlighting as you select objects. However, you cannot visually determine which objects are in the selection set.

Previous

Previous automatically selects all objects you selected for the previous command. Objects selected and edited by using grips are not remembered for this option. See Chapter 10 for more information on grips.

Undo

Undo deselects the object(s) selected at the last Select objects: prompt. (If you removed objects from the selection set at the last Select objects: prompt, Undo reselects them.)

AUto

AUto combines picking with the BOX option. By default, you can select objects this way without specifying this option. See the section on implied windowing later in this chapter.

Single

When you specify this option, AutoCAD responds with another Select objects: prompt. You select objects by using any option, and then AutoCAD immediately ends the selection process. You don't have to press Enter.

CLass

Allows you to select certain objects that were created in another application. Certain applications, such as Autodesk Map, can add a feature classification to an object. Doing so creates an associated classification (XML) file. If you have such an object and the XML file is present, you can select objects by classification property.

Cycling through objects

It may happen that you have many objects close together in a drawing, making it hard to select the object or point you want. You could always zoom in, but in a complex drawing this can take quite a bit of time. Another trick is to use object cycling. At the Select objects: prompt, hold down Ctrl and pick at the area where more than one object overlaps. AutoCAD displays the <Cycle on> message. One object is highlighted. If it is not the one you want, continue to hold down Ctrl and pick. AutoCAD cycles through the objects. After you have the one you want, release Ctrl. Press Enter to turn object cycling off. You can continue to select other objects or end object selection by pressing Enter.

Selecting objects before choosing a command

If you select objects before choosing a command, your options are more limited than if you choose a command first. Nevertheless, you have enough flexibility for most situations. The reason for the limitation is that the Command: prompt is active and anything you might type at the keyboard to indicate a selection option could be confused with a command. You can pick the object to highlight it, use implied windowing, or use the SELECT command to select objects in advance.

The purpose of the SELECT command is simply to select objects. AutoCAD then saves these objects for use with the Previous selection option. Choose an editing command and type **p** ⏎ at the Select objects: prompt. AutoCAD selects the objects you selected with the SELECT command.

Implied windowing

Implied windowing is equivalent to the Auto selection option listed earlier in this chapter. By default, implied windowing is always active. As a result, implied windowing is useful for selecting objects before or after choosing a command. By carefully choosing which way you create a selection window, you determine how AutoCAD selects objects:

✦ **From right to left:** If the first window corner is to the right of the second one, AutoCAD creates a crossing window. AutoCAD selects all objects that lie entirely or partially within the window.

✦ **From left to right:** If the first window corner is to the left of the second one, AutoCAD creates a regular selection window. AutoCAD selects all objects entirely within the window.

You can now drag past the edge of the screen (actually the viewport) to specify a window. Hold down the mouse button and continue to move the mouse in the same direction. The display automatically pans so that you can see objects that were off the screen. After you see all the objects you need to select, pick the second corner of the window.

The drawing used in the following Step-by-Step exercise on selecting objects, ab09-f.dwg, is in the Drawings folder of the *AutoCAD 2004 Bible* CD-ROM.

Step-by-Step: Selecting Objects

1. Open ab09-f.dwg from the CD-ROM, as shown in Figure 9-20.

2. Save the file as ab09-08.dwg in your AutoCAD Bible folder. Make sure that OSNAP is on. Set running object snaps for endpoint and perpendicular.

3. Draw a line from ❶ to ❷ in Figure 9-20. You will use this later to illustrate the Last selection option.

4. Type **select** ↵.

5. To select the six-burner stovetop, pick a point near ❸, being careful that the pickbox at the intersection of the crosshairs doesn't touch any object. Transparently zoom in and back out if necessary. Then move the mouse to ❹ and pick again. The objects chosen appear dashed to indicate that they have been selected.

Figure 9-20: A kitchen floor plan

6. To select the last object created, the line drawn in Step 1, type **l** ↵. It now appears dashed.

7. Turn off OSNAP. To select the interior lines on the kitchen's island by using a fence, type **f** ↵. Then pick points ❺, ❻, and ❼. Press Enter to end the fence.

8. Type **r** ↵ at the `Select objects:` prompt (the prompt changes to `Remove objects:`) and pick the line at ❽ to remove the external island line picked in Step 7. At this point, all the selected items should be dashed, as shown in Figure 9-21.

Figure 9-21: Kitchen floor plan with all selected items shown dashed

9. Press Enter to complete the command.

10. Turn on OSNAP. Start the MOVE command. At the `Select objects:` prompt, type **p** ↵ and then press Enter again to end object selection. At the `Specify base point or displacement:` prompt, pick the endpoint at ❾ in Figure 9-20. At the `Specify second point of displacement or <use first point as displacement>:` prompt, pick the endpoint at ❿. AutoCAD moves all the objects.

11. Save your drawing.

Customizing the selection process

You can customize the way you select objects. To do so, choose Tools ⇨ Options and click the Selection tab, as shown in Figure 9-22.

Figure 9-22: The Selection tab of the Options dialog box

Noun/verb selection

As you already know, the editing process consists of two parts—using a command, such as COPY or MOVE, and selecting objects. In AutoCAD lingo, *noun* means an object in your drawing. *Verb* refers to a command because a command acts on an object. This option lets you decide whether you want to be able to select objects before starting a command.

AutoCAD originally required you to start the command first and then select the objects. However, in Windows programs, you typically select objects before starting a command. For example, if you are using Microsoft Word and want to erase a sentence, you select the sentence first, and then press Del.

By default, AutoCAD enables noun/verb selection, the first option in the Selection Modes section of the Selection tab, shown in Figure 9-22. With this option enabled, you can select objects first—without giving up the ability to choose commands first. This gives you maximum flexibility.

The advantage of selecting objects first is that when you switch between Windows programs, you don't have to change habitual ways of selecting objects. The disadvantage of selecting objects first is that some AutoCAD commands don't let you select objects first, which can be confusing. Also, when you select objects first, grips appear—sometimes obscuring the objects you need to select.

Use Shift to add to selection

"Use Shift to add to selection" is the second option in the Options dialog box, Selection tab. By default, this option is not checked. In AutoCAD, you often select more than one object at a time for editing. Therefore, AutoCAD simply lets you select object after object — when you select a second object, the first object stays selected — so that you can easily select any number of objects you want.

However, Windows programs typically enable you to select only one object at a time. For example, let's say you choose Drawing from the Standard toolbar in Microsoft Word to open the Drawing toolbar and draw a few shapes. If you select one shape and then select a second shape, selecting the second shape deselects the first shape. However, if you hold down Shift, you can select any number of shapes at a time.

Commands and object selection

Certain commands require you to choose objects in a specific order or require objects that have a certain relationship to each other. For example, the TRIM command (see Chapter 10) requires that you first select an object to trim to (the cutting edge), and then the object to trim. If you select the objects in advance, AutoCAD wouldn't know which object to trim. Only after you start the TRIM command does AutoCAD know to prompt you exactly for the objects it needs to complete the command. Other commands require that you select objects that are related in some way. The FILLET command (also covered in the next chapter) joins objects that meet — or would meet if extended — by drawing an arc to create a rounded corner. Here again, the command would be meaningless if, say, you select three or more objects, so AutoCAD requires that you use the command first and then specifically prompts you to select the first object, and then the second object.

Many comments allow you to select objects first but the following are some of the most common:

ARRAY	DVIEW	MOVE
BLOCK	ERASE	ROTATE
CHANGE	EXPLODE	SCALE
CHPROP	HATCH	STRETCH
COPY	LIST	WBLOCK
	MIRROR	

These commands enable you to select any number of objects without restriction, so that selecting the objects first and the command second works well.

AutoCAD lets you select one object at a time if you want, although it is not the default, probably because selecting more than one object at a time is so common. If you check this option, after selecting one object, you must hold down Shift to select any additional object.

Press and drag

One of the ways to select objects is to create a window that includes a number of objects. You are already familiar with creating a similar window from using ZOOM with the Window option. If the Press and drag option is checked, you need to pick at one corner of the window and, without releasing the pick button, drag the cursor to the diagonally opposite corner. This type of action is typical of Windows programs.

By default, this option is not checked, which means that to create a window you pick at one corner of the window, release the mouse button, and pick again at the diagonally opposite corner.

Note This setting does not affect ZOOM Window, which always requires two separate picks.

Implied windowing

By default, this option is on. Implied windowing means that if you pick any point not on an object, AutoCAD assumes you want to create a selection window. You can then pick the opposite corner to select objects. If you pick the corners from right to left, you get a crossing window. If you pick the corners from left to right, you get a standard selection window. If implied windowing is not on, when you pick a point not on an object, AutoCAD assumes you missed some object and gives you this message on the command line:

```
0 found
```

This option applies only when you have started a command and see the Select objects: prompt. If you turn this option off, you can still enter the Crossing or Window selection options manually (by typing **c** ↵ or **w** ↵). When selecting objects before starting the command, implied windowing is always on.

Object grouping

Creating groups of objects is discussed in the next chapter. Groups are sets of objects that you name. If object grouping is on (the default) when you select one object in a group, all the objects in a group are automatically selected. Object grouping is a global setting; you can also set object grouping on or off for individual groups.

Associative hatch

If checked, selects boundary objects when you select a hatch within the boundary. This option is off by default. Checking this option is equivalent to setting the PICK-STYLE system variable to 2. See Chapter 16 for more information on hatches.

Pickbox size

In Chapter 4, you read about the aperture, which is the little box at the crosshairs that you use to pick object snaps, such as endpoint or intersection. The pickbox is the box that you see at the intersection of the crosshairs when selecting (or picking) objects. The Pickbox Size area lets you set the size of the pickbox.

Note If Noun/verb selection is off and grips are disabled, no pickbox appears at the intersection of the crosshairs until you start an editing command and AutoCAD gives you the `Select objects:` prompt. However, if either Noun/verb selection or grips are on, the pickbox is always at the crosshairs, letting you select objects at any time.

Summary

All drawings need to be edited, either as part of the drawing process or to make corrections. In this chapter, you read about:

✦ Erasing objects

✦ Moving objects

✦ Copying objects

✦ Rotating objects

✦ Scaling objects

✦ Using the CHANGE command on lines and circles

✦ The many ways of selecting objects

✦ Customizing AutoCAD's object-selection features

The next chapter covers the more advanced editing commands and options.

✦ ✦ ✦

Editing Your Drawing: Advanced Tools

This chapter completes the discussion of geometric edit-ing commands — covering the more complex commands used to refine the details of your drawing. Then I discuss grips, which make it easy to move, mirror, rotate, scale, and stretch objects. I explain how to use the Properties palette to edit objects. I end the chapter with a discussion of three ways to control the selection of objects — groups, filters, and the new Quick Select feature.

Copying and Moving Objects

Three commands enable you to copy objects in very specific ways. MIRROR creates a mirror image. ARRAY copies objects in a rectangular or circular pattern. OFFSET creates parallel objects. Although these commands make copies of objects, they produce a result that would be difficult or impossible to produce simply by using the COPY command. The ALIGN command moves objects by aligning them with other objects in the drawing.

Using the MIRROR command

Many drawings have symmetrical elements. Often, especially in mechanical drawing, you can create one-half or one-quarter of a model and complete it simply by mirroring what you have drawn.

 To mirror, select an object or objects and then choose Mirror from the Modify toolbar. Alternatively, choose Mirror from the Modify toolbar and then select an object or objects.

AutoCAD prompts for the first and second points of the mirror line. This is an imaginary line across which AutoCAD creates the mirrored object. The length of the line is irrelevant — only its start point and direction are important.

Tip Most mirror lines are orthogonal. Therefore, after you specify the first mirror point, turn on ORTHO and move the mouse in the direction of the second point. You can then quickly pick the second point. Polar tracking can also easily guide you to specify an orthogonal mirror line.

AutoCAD then asks if you want to delete the source objects. The source objects refer to the objects you have selected to mirror. If you want to keep them, type **n** ↵ or press Enter. You would keep the source objects when you are building a symmetrical model and want the mirror image to be added to the original object(s). Type **y** ↵ when you want to edit an object — change its orientation — so that only the mirror image is retained in the drawing.

 On the CD-ROM The drawing used in the following Step-by-Step exercise on mirroring objects, ab07-02.dwg, is in the Results folder of the *AutoCAD 2004 Bible* CD-ROM.

Step-by-Step: Mirroring Objects

1. Open ab07-02.dwg from the Results folder of your CD-ROM. If you completed the exercise on arcs in Chapter 7, you can open this drawing from your AutoCAD Bible folder.

2. Save the file as ab10-01.dwg in your AutoCAD Bible folder. Make sure OSNAP is on. Set a running object snap for intersections only.

3. Choose Erase on the Modify toolbar. At the Select objects: prompt, pick the line and two arcs to the bottom-right of the two centerlines and then press Enter. The resulting model should look like Figure 10-1.

4. Choose Mirror from the Modify toolbar. At the Select objects: prompt, pick the remaining exterior line and two arcs and press Enter.

5. At the Specify first point of mirror line: prompt, pick the intersection ❶ in Figure 10-1. At the Specify second point of mirror line: prompt, pick the intersection ❷.

6. AutoCAD prompts: Delete source objects? [Yes/No] <N>: **Press Enter** to accept the default, No.

7. Again choose Mirror from the Modify toolbar. At the Select objects: prompt, type **p** ↵ to pick the original lines. Then pick the new exterior line and two arcs and then press Enter.

Figure 10-1: A partially completed mounting plate

8. At the `Specify first point of mirror line:` prompt, pick the intersection ❷. At the `Specify second point of mirror line:` prompt, pick the intersection ❸. Press Enter again at the `Delete source objects?` `[Yes/No] <N>:` prompt.

9. AutoCAD completes the mounting plate. Save your drawing. It should look like Figure 10-2.

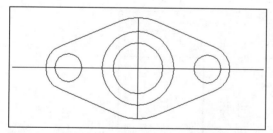

Figure 10-2: The completed mounting plate

Using the ARRAY command

The ARRAY command creates a rectangular or circular (polar) pattern by copying the object(s) you select as many times as you specify. The ARRAY command is a powerful drawing tool. It can quickly create large numbers of objects — saving a huge amount of time and effort.

Rectangular arrays

A rectangular array creates a grid of rows and columns of one or more objects. Figure 10-3 shows an example of a rectangular array. To create a rectangular array, follow these steps:

Figure 10-3: The garage door was drawn with one panel as shown on the left side. A rectangular array created the rest of the door panels as shown on the right.

Thanks to Henry Dearborn, AIA, Fairfield, Iowa for this drawing.

1. ⬜⬜ Select the object or objects and choose Array from the Modify toolbar.
 ⬜⬜ Alternatively, choose Array from the Modify toolbar and select the object or objects. AutoCAD opens the Array dialog box, shown in Figure 10-4.

Figure 10-4: The Array dialog box

2. Click Rectangular Array at the upper-left corner of the dialog box (if it is not already selected).

3. If you have already selected one or more objects, the dialog box indicates the number of selected objects. If you have not selected any object, click Select Objects to return to your drawing and select objects. Press Enter to end object selection and return to the dialog box.

4. Type the number of rows and columns you want in the Rows and Columns text boxes. Press Tab after the last number you type to see the new result in the preview panel.

5. Type the row offset (the distance between the rows). The preview panel doesn't display any change when you change the row or column offsets.

6. Type the column offset (the distance between the columns).

7. If you want to specify the offsets by picking points on your screen, click one of the following buttons:

- Pick Both Offsets

- Pick Row Offset

- Pick Column Offset

8. If you want to change the angle of the array, type an angle. The preview panel displays the results of this value. To specify the angle by picking, click the Pick Angle of Array button.

9. To preview the array, click Preview. Then choose Accept to create the array, Modify to return to the Array dialog box, or Cancel to end the command.

10. To create the array, click OK.

If you change the Snap angle or the UCS (see Chapter 8), AutoCAD creates the rectangular array at the angle of the snap or UCS.

Tip

If you need to create a number of copies of an object along a straight path, use a one-column or one-row array instead of the COPY command. It's faster and easier.

Polar (circular) arrays

A polar array creates copies of one or more objects arrayed in a circle around a center point. An example of a polar array is shown in Figure 10-5.

Figure 10-5: The pulley was drawn with one spoke as shown on the left. A polar array created the additional spokes.

Thanks to Robert Mack of the Dexter Company, Fairfield, Iowa for this drawing.

To create a polar array, follow these steps:

1. ⊞ Select the object or objects and choose Array from the Modify toolbar. Alternatively, choose Array from the Modify toolbar and select the object or objects. AutoCAD opens the Array dialog box.

2. Click Polar Array at the top of the dialog box (if it is not already selected).

3. If you have already selected one or more objects, the dialog box indicates the number of selected objects. If you have not selected any object, click Select Objects to return to your drawing and select objects. Press Enter to end object selection and return to the dialog box.

4. ⊞ Specify the center point by typing X and Y coordinates or click the Pick Center Point button. If you selected an object first, check that the center point displayed is what you want.

5. Select the two items that you want to specify from the Method drop-down box. You can choose any two from the three choices:

 • **Total Number of Items:** Sets the total number of items in the resulting array, including the one you are arraying.

 • **Angle to Fill:** Sets the number of degrees the polar array covers. For example, to array around half a circle, specify 180°.

 • **Angle Between Items:** Specifies the number of degrees between each item in the polar array.

6. Complete the values of the two items you specified. You can click the buttons to pick the angle to fill or the angle between items on the screen.

7. Check the Rotate Items as Copied check box to rotate the objects that you are arraying. Uncheck the box to leave them unrotated.

8. Click Preview to preview the array. Then choose Accept to create the array, Modify to return to the dialog box or Cancel to cancel the command.

9. Click OK to create the array.

You can specify which point on the last object selected AutoCAD uses to array the objects. AutoCAD makes a calculation of the distance from the center point of the array to a base point on the last object selected. Otherwise, AutoCAD uses a default point based on the type of object selected. Table 10-1 lists the default base points. If you are arraying more than one object, you may not get the result you want without specifying the base point. Even for one object, you may want to change the base point used.

To specify the base point, click the More button at the bottom of the dialog box. The dialog box opens up to display the Object Base Point section. Uncheck Set to Object's Default and either type in coordinates or, more likely, click the Pick Base Point button and use an object snap to pick the desired point on an object. The preview box adjusts according to your choice but, because the preview only shows rectangles in the place of your object, the display may not be very helpful.

New Feature You can use the Express Tools COPYM command to enhance your copying options. Choose Express ⇨ Modify ⇨ Multiple Copy. You can create evenly spaced copies between two points, copy objects according to a specified measurement, and create arrays. For information on installing the Express Tools, see Appendix A on the CD-ROM.

Table 10-1
Object Base Points for Arrays

Type of Object	Default Base Point
Arc, circle, or ellipse	Center point
Polygon or rectangle	First corner
Line, polyline (2D or 3D), ray, spline, or donut	Starting point
Text (single-line or paragraph), block	Insertion point
Construction line (xline)	Midpoint
Region	Grip point

On the CD-ROM The drawing used in the following Step-by-Step exercise on arraying objects, ab10-a.dwg, is in the Drawings folder of the *AutoCAD 2004 Bible* CD-ROM.

Step-by-Step: Arraying Objects

1. Open `ab10-a.dwg` from the CD-ROM.

2. Save the file as `ab10-02.dwg` in your `AutoCAD Bible` folder. It looks like Figure 10-6. OSNAP should be on. Set center and intersection running object snaps.

Figure 10-6: A partially completed mounting bracket

3. ⬚⬚ Choose Array on the Modify toolbar. The Array dialog box opens.

4. Click the Select Objects button of the Array dialog box. In the drawing, pick the horizontal centerline ❶ in Figure 10-6 and then press Enter. You return to the dialog box.

5. Make sure that Rectangular Array is selected at the top of the dialog box.

6. In the Rows text box, type **4**. In the Columns text box, type **1**.

7. In the Row Offset text box, type **1**. (You don't need to specify the column offset because you are only creating one column.)

8. Click Preview. You should see a total of four horizontal lines, as shown in Figure 10-7. Click Accept on the small dialog box that appears. (If you don't see the four lines, click Modify and recheck the settings in the Array dialog box.)

9. To add the holes to the pattern, again choose Array from the Modify toolbar.

10. Click the Select Objects button in the Array dialog box. In the drawing, pick the circle ❷ in Figure 10-6 and then press Enter.

11. Back in the Array dialog box, type **4** in the Rows text box and type **2** in the Columns text box.

12. Click the Pick Both Offsets button. In the drawing, pick the center of circle ❷ and the intersection of centerlines near ❸ in Figure 10-6. (You can also pick the intersection of centerlines at the center of circle ❷. If necessary, press Tab until you get the object snap that you want.)

13. Click Preview to preview the array. If the circles look like Figure 10-7, click Accept. Otherwise, click Modify and check you settings. After you're done, AutoCAD arrays the holes to fit the centerlines.

14. To create a six-hole bolt circle, pick the hole ❹ in Figure 10-6.

15. Choose Array from the Modify toolbar.

16. In the Array dialog box, choose Polar Array.

17. Next to the Center Point text boxes, click the Pick Center Point button. In the drawing, pick the center of the large circle at ❺ in Figure 10-6.

18. The Method should read "Total number of items and Angle to fill." In the Total Number of Items text box, type **6**. In the Angle to Fill text box, type **360**.

19. Click Preview to see the array. It should look like Figure 10-7. If it does, click Accept. If not, click Modify and recheck the settings in the Array dialog box.

 AutoCAD completes the mounting bracket.

20. Save your drawing. It should look like Figure 10-7.

Figure 10-7: The completed mounting bracket

Offsetting objects

The OFFSET command creates lines or curves parallel to one existing object. The beauty of this command is apparent when you start to create complex objects, such as polylines (see Chapter 16). Polygons and rectangles are polylines, meaning that they are treated as one object. Using OFFSET, you can create concentric polygons, for example, in one step. Figure 10-8 shows two concentric polygons. The outside polygon was created with the POLYGON command, and the inside polygon was created by using OFFSET.

Figure 10-8: Use OFFSET to create concentric polygons.

 To offset an object, choose Offset from the Modify toolbar. You cannot select objects before choosing the command.

AutoCAD responds with the `Specify offset distance or [Through] <1.0000>:` prompt. AutoCAD offers two slightly different ways to specify the offset:

✦ If you type an offset distance, AutoCAD responds with the `Select object to offset or <exit>:` prompt. You can select one object. Then AutoCAD displays the `Specify point on side to offset:` prompt. Pick a point to indicate on which side of the object AutoCAD should create the offset copy. AutoCAD creates the offset and continues to show the `Select object to offset or <exit>:` prompt so that you can offset other objects by using the same offset distance. Press Enter to exit the command.

✦ If you want to indicate a through point, which is a point that the offset passes through, such as an object snap on another object, type **t** ↵ or right-click and choose Through from the shortcut menu. Then AutoCAD displays the `Select object to offset or <exit>:` prompt. Pick one object. At the `Specify through point:` prompt, pick a point through which you want the offset to go. AutoCAD creates the offset.

 New Feature

Use the Express Tools EXOFFSET command for expanded offset options. You can specify the layer of new objects and create multiple offsets. Choose Express ➪ Modify ➪ Extended Offset. For information on installing Express Tools, see Appendix A on the CD-ROM.

 On the CD-ROM

The drawing used in the following Step-by-Step exercise on using the OFFSET command, `ab10-b.dwg`, is in the `Drawings` folder of the *AutoCAD 2004 Bible* CD-ROM.

Step-by-Step: Using the OFFSET Command

1. Open ab10-b.dwg from the CD-ROM.

2. Save the file as ab10-03.dwg in your AutoCAD Bible folder. It looks like Figure 10-9. Set a running object snap for center and turn on OSNAP.

Figure 10-9: A tension arm for a commercial dryer

3. Choose Offset on the Modify toolbar. Follow the prompts:

```
Specify offset distance or [Through] <Through>: ↵
Select object to offset or <exit>: Pick ❶ in Figure 10-9.
Specify through point: Pick the center of ❷.
Select object to offset or <exit>: ↵
```

AutoCAD copies the centerline through the upper circles.

4. Choose Offset from the Modify toolbar again. At the Specify offset distance or [Through] <Through>: prompt, type **4-19/64** ↵. Pick the centerline ❸ at the Select object to offset or <exit>: prompt, and near ❹ at the Specify point on side to offset: prompt. Press Enter to end the command. AutoCAD copies the vertical centerline 4-19/64 units to the right of the original.

5. Save your drawing. It should look like Figure 10-10.

Figure 10-10: The completed tension arm

Aligning objects

The ALIGN command lets you move and rotate an object or objects in one procedure. It is especially useful in 3D work. By specifying which points on an object move where, you can align the object with other objects in your drawing, as shown in Figure 10-11.

See Chapter 24 for the use of the ALIGN command in 3D editing.

Figure 10-11: Aligning a door with a wall

Aligning requires several steps. Even so, it can save time when you need to both move and rotate at the same time, especially if you don't know the rotation angle that you need. To align an object, choose Modify ⇨ 3D Operation ⇨ Align and select an object or objects. Alternatively, select the object or objects first and then choose Modify ⇨ 3D Operation ⇨ Align. Then follow these steps:

1. AutoCAD asks for the first source point. Specify a point, usually an object snap on the object that you want to move.

2. AutoCAD asks for the first destination point. Specify the point where you want the first source point to end up.

3. AutoCAD asks for the second source point. If you press Enter, AutoCAD simply moves the selected objects. To continue to align, specify another point, usually an object snap on the object that you want to move.

4. AutoCAD asks for the second destination point. Specify the point where you want the second source point to end up.

5. AutoCAD asks for the third source point. You use this for 3D alignment, to specify how you want to rotate the object in the third dimension. For 2D alignment, press Enter to continue the command.

6. AutoCAD displays the `Scale objects based on alignment points? [Yes/No] <N>:` prompt. If the distances between the source and destination points are not the same, type **y** if you want to scale the original object so that the source and destination points match exactly.

On the CD-ROM

The drawing used in the following Step-by-Step exercise on aligning objects in two dimensions, `ab10-c.dwg`, is in the `Drawings` folder of the *AutoCAD 2004 Bible* CD-ROM.

Step-by-Step: Aligning Objects in Two Dimensions

1. Open `ab10-c.dwg` from the CD-ROM.

2. Save the file as `ab10-04.dwg` in your `AutoCAD Bible` folder. It looks like Figure 10-12.

3. Choose Modify ➪ 3D Operation ➪ Align and follow the prompts:

```
Select objects: Select the horizontal angle by using a
window, picking near ❶ then ❷. Press Enter to end object
selection. This angle needs to be aligned with the long,
diagonal support angle.
Specify first source point: Pick the endpoint at ❸ in Figure
10-12.
Specify first destination point: Pick the endpoint at ❹
Specify second source point: Pick the endpoint at ❺.
Specify second destination point: Pick the endpoint at ❻
Specify third source point or <continue>: ⏎
Scale objects based on alignment points? [Yes/No] <N>: ⏎
```

AutoCAD aligns the horizontal angle with the support angle.

4. Save your drawing. It should look like Figure 10-13.

Figure 10-12: A base assembly for a commercial washing machine

Figure 10-13: The washing machine base

Resizing commands

Four additional commands resize objects. The TRIM and EXTEND commands bring the endpoint of an object to another object. LENGTHEN lets you lengthen or shorten a line, polyline, arc, or elliptical arc. STRETCH is used to stretch (larger or shorter) a group of objects, letting you change their direction at the same time.

Trimming objects

As you edit a drawing, you may find that lines or arcs that once perfectly met other objects now hang over. To trim an object, you must first specify the cutting edge, which defines the point at which AutoCAD cuts the object you want to trim. You define the cutting edge by selecting an object. You can select several cutting edges and several objects to trim at one time, as shown in Figure 10-14. When you select an object to trim, you must pick the object on the side that you want trimmed (not on the side that you want to remain). A common use for the TRIM command is to create intersections of walls in architectural floor plans.

Tip　While using the TRIM command, you can switch to extending objects by pressing the Shift key as you select objects to trim.

Before trimming　　　　　　　After trimming

Figure 10-14: Trimming two objects by using two cutting edges

Tip　Generally, you pick the objects to be trimmed individually. You cannot use Windows to select them. However, you can use the Fence object-selection method. AutoCAD trims the side of the object that the fence line crosses. You can also press Enter at the `Select cutting edges:` prompt. Then, when you select the objects you want to trim, AutoCAD automatically uses the cutting edge nearest your pick point. You can use this feature to trim to multiple cutting edges without having to specify each cutting edge.

The object you want to trim does not have to actually intersect the cutting edge. AutoCAD can trim an object to a cutting edge that would intersect the object if extended. This is called *trimming to an implied intersection*, shown in Figure 10-15.

You can trim arcs, circles, ellipses, elliptical arcs, lines, polylines, xlines, rays, and splines. You can use polylines, arcs, circles, ellipses, elliptical arcs, lines, rays, regions, splines, text, or xlines as cutting edges. An object can be used as both a cutting edge and an object to be trimmed in the same trimming process. You can also trim to objects within blocks. (Chapter 18 covers blocks.)

Before trimming After trimming

Figure 10-15: Trimming two arcs to an implied intersection

 To trim an object, choose Trim from the Modify toolbar. You cannot select objects before starting the TRIM command. AutoCAD displays the `Current settings: Projection=UCS, Edge=None Select cutting edges ... Select objects:` prompt. AutoCAD lets you know the values of the two system variables that affect trimming. The Projection setting is used only for 3D models. The Edge setting is used for implied intersections. When Edge is set to Extend, AutoCAD trims to the implied intersection of the cutting edge and the object to be trimmed. At this prompt, pick the object(s) that you want to use as a cutting edge. Press Enter to end object selection.

Tip If the object you want to use for the cutting edge is already selected before you start the TRIM command, AutoCAD deselects it. At the `Select cutting edges ...` prompt, you can type **p** ↵ to reselect that object.

You can trim to an actual or an *implied* intersection (an intersection that would exist if objects were extended):

✦ If you want to trim to an actual intersection, at the `Select object to trim or shift-select to extend or [Project/Edge/Undo]:` prompt, select objects to trim. Be sure to pick each object between the cutting edge and the end you want to trim off. Press Enter to end object selection. AutoCAD trims the object(s).

✦ If you want to trim to an implied intersection, at the `Select object to trim or shift-select to extend or [Project/Edge/Undo]:` prompt, type **e** ↵. AutoCAD responds with the `Enter an implied edge extension mode [Extend/No extend] <No extend>:` prompt. Type **e** ↵. Then select the objects that you want to trim at the `Select object to trim or shift-select to extend or [Project/Edge/Undo]:` prompt. Be sure to pick each object at or near the end that you want to trim. Press Enter to end object selection. AutoCAD trims the object(s).

Use the Undo option if the results of the trim are not what you want. You can then continue to select objects to trim.

On the CD-ROM The drawing used in the following Step-by-Step exercise on trimming objects, ab10-d.dwg, is in the Drawings folder of the *AutoCAD 2004 Bible* CD-ROM.

Step-by-Step: Trimming Objects

1. Open ab10-d.dwg from the CD-ROM.

2. Save the file as ab10-05.dwg in your AutoCAD Bible folder. It looks like Figure 10-16.

3. Start the TRIM command. At the Select objects: prompt, pick lines at ❶ and ❷ in Figure 10-16 and then press Enter.

4. At the Select object to trim or shift-select to extend or [Project/Edge/Undo]: prompt, again pick lines at ❶ and ❷ in Figure 10-16. Be sure to pick them outside the intersection, as shown. Press Enter to end the command.

 AutoCAD trims the lines. Each line is used as the cutting edge for the other line.

Figure 10-16: A schematic of an air compressor

5. Choose Trim on the Modify toolbar again. At the Select objects: prompt, pick the line at ❸ in Figure 10-16 and press Enter.

6. At the `Select object to trim or shift-select to extend or [Project/Edge/Undo]:` prompt, right-click and choose Edge. Then right-click and choose Extend at the Enter an implied edge extension mode [Extend/No extand] <Extend>:: prompt.

7. Pick the line at ❹ in Figure 10-16. AutoCAD trims the line. Press Enter to end the command.

8. Start the TRIM command again. At the `Select objects:` prompt, pick ❺ and press Enter. At the `Select object to trim or shift-select to extend or [Project/Edge/Undo]:` prompt, pick the lines at ❻ and ❼.Press Enter to end the command.

9. Save your drawing. It should look like Figure 10-17.

Figure 10-17: The completed clamp in two views

New Feature

Express Tools contains a command, EXTRIM, available on the command line. EXTRIM can use a polyline, line, circle, arc, ellipse, image, or text as the cutting line. You specify one side of the cutting object, and EXTRIM trims everything on that side. For example, if you choose a closed polyline and pick inside it, every object inside the polyline is trimmed.

Extending objects

The EXTEND command has the same prompts as the TRIM command, but instead of trimming objects to a cutting edge, it extends them to a boundary edge (see Figure 10-18). As with TRIM, when you select an object to extend, you must pick the object on the side that you want extended (not on the side that you want left as is).

The object you want to extend does not have to actually intersect the boundary edge after its extension. AutoCAD can extend an object to a boundary edge that would intersect the extended object if it were longer. This is called extending to an implied intersection, shown in Figure 10-19.

Pick points on lines

Boundary edge →

Figure 10-18: Extending two lines by using an arc as the boundary edge

You can extend arcs, elliptical arcs, lines, open polylines, and rays. You can use polylines, arcs, circles, ellipses, elliptical arcs, lines, rays, regions, splines, text, or xlines as boundary edges. An object can be used as both a boundary edge and an object to be extended in the same extending process.

Tip While using the EXTEND command, you can switch to trimming objects by pressing the Shift key as you select objects to trim.

To extend an object, choose Extend from the Modify toolbar. You cannot select objects before the EXTEND command. AutoCAD displays the Current settings: Projection=UCS, Edge=Extend Select boundary edges ... Select objects: prompt. AutoCAD lets you know the values of the two settings that affect extending. Projection is used only for 3D models. Edge is used for implied intersections. When Edge is set to Extend, AutoCAD extends to the implied intersection of the boundary edge and the object to be extended. At this prompt, pick the object(s) that you want to use as the boundary edge(s). Press Enter to end object selection. You can extend to an actual or implied intersection:

✦ If the extension will result in an actual intersection, at the Select object to extend or shift-select to trim or [Project/Edge/Undo]: prompt, select objects to extend. Be sure to pick each object at the end that you want to extend. Press Enter to end object selection. AutoCAD extends the object(s).

✦ If you want to extend to an implied intersection, at the prompt, right-click and choose Edge. AutoCAD responds with the Enter an implied edge extension mode [Extend/No extend] <Extend>: prompt. Right-click and choose Extend. Then select the objects that you want to extend at the Select object to extend or shift-select to trim or [Project/ Edge/Undo]: prompt. Be sure to pick each object at the end that you want to extend. Press Enter to end object selection. AutoCAD extends the object(s).

Figure 10-19: Extending a line to an implied intersection

Use the Undo option if the results of the extension are not what you want. You can then continue to select objects to extend.

You can use the Fence object selection method to select objects to extend. AutoCAD extends the side of the object that the fence line crosses.

On the CD-ROM The drawing used in the following Step-by-Step exercise on extending objects, ab10-e.dwg, is in the Drawings folder of the *AutoCAD 2004 Bible* CD-ROM.

Step-by-Step: Extending Objects

1. Open ab10-e.dwg from the CD-ROM.

2. Save the file as ab10-06.dwg in your AutoCAD Bible folder. It looks like Figure 10-20.

3. Choose Extend on the Modify toolbar. At the Select objects: prompt, pick the line at ❶ in Figure 10-20 and then press Enter.

Figure 10-20: An electrical schematic

4. At the Select object to extend or shift-select to trim or [Project/Edge/Undo]: prompt, pick the line at ❷ in Figure 10-20. Press Enter to finish selecting objects. AutoCAD extends the line.

5. Repeat the EXTEND command. At the Select objects: prompt, pick the lines at ❸ and ❹ in Figure 10-20 and then press Enter.

6. At the Select object to extend or shift-select to trim or [Project/Edge/Undo]: prompt, right-click and choose Edge. Right-click and choose Extend at the Extend/No extend <No extend>: prompt.

7. Pick lines ❸ and ❹ in Figure 10-20 again at the points shown. AutoCAD extends the lines to meet. Press Enter to end the command.

8. Save your drawing. It should look like Figure 10-21.

Figure 10-21: The completed electrical schematic

Lengthening objects

The LENGTHEN command both lengthens and shortens. It works on open objects, such as lines, arcs, and polylines and also increases or decreases the included angle of arcs. (You can both change the length of an arc and change its included angle by using LENGTHEN.) AutoCAD offers several ways of defining the new length or included angle. Use LENGTHEN when you want to lengthen or shorten an object, but there is no available intersecting edge or boundary to use with TRIM or EXTEND.

In the LENGTHEN command, the length of an arc is measured along its circumference. Don't confuse this with the Length of chord option of the ARC command, which refers to the length of a line stretched from one endpoint of the arc to the other endpoint.

To lengthen (or shorten) an object, choose Modify ➪ Lengthen. You cannot select objects before the LENGTHEN command. AutoCAD responds with the `Select an object or [DElta/Percent/Total/DYnamic]:` prompt. Choose one of the following options:

- ✦ **Select object:** This is the default. However, its purpose is to display the current measurements of the object. This can help you to decide how to define the final length or angle of the object. The current length is displayed at the command line, and the previous prompt is repeated.

- ✦ **DElta:** Right-click and choose DElta. Delta means the change, or difference, between the current and new length or included angle. AutoCAD responds with the `Enter delta length or [Angle] <0.0000>:` prompt. If you want to change an included angle, right-click and choose Angle. Then type the change in the included angle. Otherwise, simply type in the change in the length of the object. A positive number increases the length or included angle. A negative number decreases the length or included angle.

- ✦ **Percent:** Right-click and choose Percent. At the `Enter percentage length <100.0000>:` prompt, type in what percent of the original object you want the final object to be. Amounts over 100 lengthen the object. Amounts under 100 shorten the object. You cannot change an included angle using this option.

- ✦ **Total:** Right-click and choose Total. At the `Specify total length or [Angle] <1.0000)>:` prompt, you can either choose the Angle suboption, as described for the Delta option or use the default total length option. Either way, you enter the total angle or length you want.

- ✦ **DYnamic:** Right-click and choose DYnamic. This option lets you drag the endpoint of the object closest to where you picked it. You can use an object snap to specify the new endpoint.

After you have used an option to specify the length you want, AutoCAD responds with the `Select an object to change or [Undo]:` prompt. Here you select the object you want to change. Be sure to pick the endpoint of the object for which you want to make the change.

AutoCAD then continues the same prompt so that you can pick other objects by using the same length specifications. Choose Undo to undo the last change. Press Enter to end the command.

The drawing used in the following Step-by-Step exercise on lengthening and shortening objects, ab10-f.dwg, is in the Drawings folder of the *AutoCAD 2004 Bible* CD-ROM.

Step-by-Step: Lengthening and Shortening Objects

1. Open ab10-f.dwg from the CD-ROM.

2. Save the file as ab10-07.dwg in your AutoCAD Bible folder. It is a capacitor symbol from an electrical schematic, as shown in Figure 10-22.

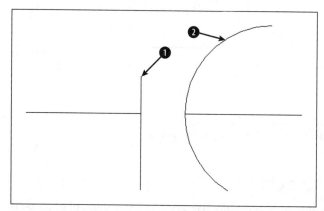

Figure 10-22: A poorly drawn capacitor symbol

3. Choose Modify ⇨ Lengthen and follow the prompts:

```
Select an object or [DElta/Percent/Total/DYnamic]: Pick the
line at ❶ in Figure 10-22.
Current length: 0.200
Select an object or [DElta/Percent/Total/DYnamic]: Right-
click and choose Delta.
Enter delta length or [Angle] <0.000>: .07 ↵
Select an object to change or [Undo]: Pick the line at ❶ in
Figure 10-22.
Select an object to change or [Undo]: ↵
```

AutoCAD lengthens the line.

4. Start the LENGTHEN command again and follow the prompts:

```
Select an object or [DElta/Percent/Total/DYnamic]: Pick the
arc at ❷ in Figure 10-22.
Current length: 0.407, included angle: 150
```

```
Select an object or [DElta/Percent/Total/DYnamic]: Right-
click and choose Total.
Specify total length or [Angle] <1.000)>:)>: Right-click and
choose Angle.
Specify total angle <57>: 120 ↵
Select an object to change or [Undo]: Pick the arc at ❷ in
Figure 10-22.
Select an object to change or [Undo]: ↵
```

AutoCAD shortens the arc.

5. Save your drawing. It should look like Figure 10-23.

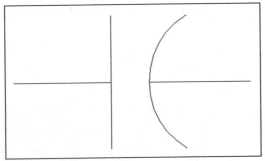

Figure 10-23: The completed capacitor symbol

Stretching objects

The STRETCH command is generally used to stretch groups of objects. It can be used to enlarge a room in a floor plan, for example. You can also shrink objects. You can change not only the length of the objects but the angle as well. You use a crossing window to choose the objects to be stretched. All objects that cross the boundaries of the crossing window are stretched. All objects that lie entirely within the crossing window are merely moved. Successful stretching involves precise placement of the crossing window. Figure 10-24 shows the process of stretching a garage. Note that the walls that cross the boundaries of the crossing window are stretched. However, the dormer, which is entirely within the crossing window, is just moved. This maintains the integrity of the model.

You cannot stretch circles, text, or blocks. You can stretch arcs, although the results may not be what you expect.

The real power of the STRETCH command is in stretching a number of objects at once. However, you can also stretch one line. The results are similar to using the CHANGE command to change the endpoint of a line.

Crossing window

Before stretching After stretching

Figure 10-24: Stretching a garage

 To stretch objects, choose Stretch from the Modify toolbar. AutoCAD responds with the `Select objects to stretch by crossing-window or crossing-polygon...` instruction and then the `Select objects:` prompt. Create the crossing window and select the objects that you want to stretch. (You can also use a crossing polygon.) After completing the crossing window, check to see which objects are highlighted. This helps you avoid unwanted results. You can use the object selection Remove option (type **r** ↵ at the command prompt) to remove objects by picking that you don't want to stretch or move.

New Feature To allow you to use multiple crossing windows or polygons to select the objects that you want to stretch, use the Express Tools MSTRETCH command. Choose Express ➪ Modify ➪ Multiple Entity Stretch. For information on installing Express Tools, see Appendix A on the CD-ROM.

AutoCAD then displays the `Specify base point or displacement:` prompt. This step is just like moving objects. You can respond in two ways.

✦ Pick a base point. At the `Specify second point of displacement or <use first point as displacement>:` prompt, pick a second point. Object snap and polar snap are helpful for picking these points.

✦ Type a displacement, without using the @ sign. For example, to lengthen the objects by 6 feet in the 0-degree direction, type **6'<0** ↵. Then press Enter at the `Specify second point of displacement or <use first point as displacement>:` prompt.

Tip Usually, you want to stretch at an orthogonal angle. If you are going to stretch by picking, turn ORTHO on. Object snaps, polar tracking, and snap mode are other helpful drawing aids for stretching.

When specifying a displacement by typing at the keyboard, you can use both positive and negative distances. For example, 6'<180 is the same as –6'<0. Both would stretch the objects 6 feet to the left.

In this exercise, you practice stretching objects.

On the CD-ROM The drawing used in the following Step-by-Step exercise, ab10-g.dwg, is in the Drawings folder of the *AutoCAD 2004 Bible* CD-ROM.

Step-by-Step: Stretching Objects

1. Open ab10-g.dwg from your CD-ROM.

2. Save the file as ab10-08.dwg in your AutoCAD Bible folder. This drawing is the plan view of a garage, as shown in Figure 10-25. Turn on polar tracking by clicking POLAR on the status bar. Click SNAP on the status bar and then right-click SNAP to make sure Polar Snap is on (the Polar Snap item will be unavailable if it is already on); otherwise, choose Polar Snap. Turn on OSNAP and set a running object snap for endpoints.

3. Choose Stretch from the Modify toolbar. At the Select objects: prompt, pick ❶ in Figure 10-25. At the Specify opposite corner: prompt, pick ❷. AutoCAD notifies you that it found 32 objects. Press Enter to end object selection.

Figure 10-25: A plan view of a garage

4. At the `Specify base point or displacement:` prompt, pick the endpoint at the bottom-right corner of the garage. At the `Specify second point of displacement or <use first point as displacement>:` prompt, move the cursor to the right until you see the polar tracking tooltip. Click when the tooltip says 6'-0"<0. (If you can't find it, type **@6',0** ↵.) AutoCAD stretches the garage by 6 feet.

5. Save your drawing. It should look like Figure 10-26.

Figure 10-26: The longer garage

Using Construction Commands

Three additional commands are commonly used in the process of constructing models. The BREAK command removes sections of objects at points you specify. CHAMFER creates corners, and FILLET creates rounded corners.

Breaking objects

Drawing a long line and then breaking it into two or more shorter lines is often much easier. A common use for BREAK is to break a wall at a door or a window in an architectural floor plan. You specify two points on the object, and AutoCAD erases whatever is between those two points. Typically, you use object snaps to specify the points. Sometimes, you can use TRIM to break an object, but if you have no convenient cutting edge, you may find BREAK more efficient.

You can break lines, polylines, splines, xlines, rays, circles, arcs, elliptical arcs, and ellipses.

To break a line, choose Break from the Modify toolbar. You cannot select the object first. AutoCAD responds with the `Select object:` prompt. (Notice that you can only select one object to break.) At this prompt, you have two choices:

✦ Select the object at one of the break points that you want to create. AutoCAD then responds with the `Specify second break point or [First point]:` prompt. Because you have already specified the first point, you can now specify the second point. AutoCAD breaks the object between the two points.

✦ Select the object by using any method of object selection. AutoCAD then responds with the `Specify second break point or [First point]:` prompt. Right-click and choose First point. At the `Specify first break point:` prompt, pick the first break point. At the `Specify second break point:` prompt, pick the second break point. AutoCAD breaks the object between the two points.

Tip

Sometimes you may want to break an object into two pieces at a point, without erasing any part of the object. Use the Break at Pointbutton on the Modify toolbar to help you easily break an object at a point. After selecting the object, pick where you want to break the object at the `Specify second break point or [First point]:` prompt. The two new objects look the same as before on the screen — until you select one of the objects. To break objects at a point, AutoCAD uses @, which always signifies the last point entered, to specify the second break point. Thus, the first and second break points are the same.

You can use BREAK to shorten an object. Pick one point on the object where you want the new endpoint to be. Pick the other point past its current endpoint. AutoCAD cuts off the object at the point you picked on the object.

On the CD-ROM

The drawing used in the following Step-by-Step exercise on breaking objects, `ab10-h.dwg`, is in the `Drawings` folder of the *AutoCAD 2004 Bible* CD-ROM.

Step-by-Step: Breaking Objects

1. Open `ab10-h.dwg` from your CD-ROM.

2. Save the file as `ab10-09.dwg` in your `AutoCAD Bible` folder. This is a site plan, as shown in Figure 10-27. Turn on OSNAP and set running object snaps for endpoint and intersection.

3. Choose Break from the Modify toolbar. At the `Select object:` prompt, pick the line at ❶. At the `Specify second break point or [First point]:` prompt, pick ❷. AutoCAD shortens the line.

4. Repeat the BREAK command. At the `Select object:` prompt, pick the circle (it's a maple tree) anywhere along its circumference. At the `Specify second break point or [First point]:` prompt, right-click and choose First point. At the `Specify first break point:` prompt, pick the intersection at ❸. At the `Specify second break point:` prompt, pick the intersection at ❹. AutoCAD breaks the circle.

Note

AutoCAD breaks circles counterclockwise. If you had picked ❹, and then ❸, AutoCAD would have left only the smaller arc and erased the rest of the circle.

5. Turn on Object Snap Tracking by clicking OTRACK on the status bar.

Figure 10-27: A site plan

6. Start the BREAK command again. Follow the prompts:

```
Select object: Pick the line at ❺.
Specify second break point or [First point]: Right-click and
choose First point.
Specify first break point: Move the cursor to ❻ to acquire it
as a tracking point. Then move the cursor to the right onto
the line you are breaking. When you see the Endpoint:
Intersection tooltip, click. (You have no visual confirmation
yet that you picked the right point.)

Specify second break point: Move the cursor to ❼ to acquire
it as a tracking point. Then move the cursor onto the line
you are breaking. At the Endpoint: 4'-2 3/4"<0.0000 tooltip,
click.
```

AutoCAD breaks the line.

7. Save your drawing. It should look like Figure 10-28.

Two AutoLISP programs on the CD-ROM can help you with breaking and unbreaking objects. *Pend* puts a break line at the end of a pipe. See \Software\Chap10\Pend. Br draws a line with a break symbol. See \Software\Chap10\Br. The Express Tools contain a command, BREAKLINE, to create a break symbol. Choose Express ➪ Draw ➪ Break-Line Symbol. Another Express Tools command, OVERKILL (available on the command line) deletes objects that are on top of other objects. For information about installing Express Tools, see Appendix A on the CD-ROM.

Figure 10-28: The edited site plan

Creating chamfered corners

The CHAMFER command creates corners from two nonparallel lines. You can also chamfer xlines, rays, and polylines. You can simply extend the lines to meet at an intersection (a square corner), or create a beveled edge. If you create a beveled edge, you define the edge by either two distances or one distance and an angle relative to the first line you are chamfering. Figure 10-29 shows the elements of a chamfered corner.

Figure 10-29: A chamfered corner

Chamfering is a two-step process. First you define how you want to chamfer the corner, specifying either two distances from the corner or a distance and an angle. Then you select the two lines you want to chamfer. AutoCAD chamfers them by using the information you specified.

To chamfer, choose Chamfer from the Modify toolbar. You cannot select objects before the CHAMFER command. AutoCAD responds with the (TRIM mode) Current chamfer Dist1 = 0.0000, Dist2 = 0.0000 Select first line or [Polyline/Distance/Angle/Trim/Method/mUltiple]: prompt. AutoCAD starts by listing the current settings. You can define two distances from a corner or one distance and an angle:

✦ To define two distances from the corner, right-click and choose Distance. At the Specify first chamfer distance <0.0000>: prompt, type the first chamfer distance or press Enter to accept the default (which is the last distance you defined). At the Specify second chamfer distance <0.0000>: prompt, type the second distance. The default for this is always the first chamfer distance because equal chamfer distances are so common.

✦ To define a distance (from the corner) and an angle, right-click and choose Angle. At the Specify chamfer length on the first line <1.0000>: prompt, enter a distance. This is the same as the first chamfer distance. At the Specify chamfer angle from the first line <0>: prompt, type the angle between the first line and the chamfer line.

To extend two nonparallel lines to make a corner, set the chamfer distances to zero and then chamfer the lines. AutoCAD extends them to meet. If they already intersect, AutoCAD trims them to create a corner. The pick points on intersecting lines should be on the part of the lines that you want to keep (not on the part of the lines you want to trim off).

Now that you specified the settings that you want, you're ready to chamfer. Your distances or distance and angle are displayed as you just specified them. AutoCAD repeats the Select first line or [Polyline/Distance/Angle/Trim/Method/mUltiple]: prompt. Select the first line. If you are not creating a chamfer with equal distances, the order in which you select the lines is important. AutoCAD trims the first line selected by the first distance and the second line selected based on either the second distance or the angle. At the Select second line: prompt, select the second line. AutoCAD chamfers the lines.

Choose the Polyline option to chamfer an entire polyline at once. Chapter 16 covers polylines. Chapter 24 discusses chamfering 3D models.

By default, CHAMFER trims the original lines that it chamfers. If you want to keep the full original lines when you add the chamfer line, choose the Trim option and choose No Trim.

Use the mUltiple option to continue the prompts and chamfer several corners in one command.

The drawing used in the following Step-by-Step exercise on chamfering lines, `ab10-i.dwg`, is in the `Drawings` folder of the *AutoCAD 2004 Bible* CD-ROM.

Step-by-Step: Chamfering Lines

1. Open `ab10-i.dwg` from your CD-ROM.

2. Save the file as `ab10-10.dwg` in your `AutoCAD Bible` folder. This drawing is a very small section of a "porcupine" mixer, as shown in Figure 10-30.

Figure 10-30: A mechanical drawing showing a small section of a "porcupine" mixer

3. ⌐ Choose Chamfer from the Modify toolbar. CHAMFER states the current mode and distances. If the distances are not zero, follow the prompts below. If they are already zero, skip to the next step.

   ```
   Select first line or [Polyline/Distance/Angle/Trim/Method/
   mUltiple]: Right-click and choose Distance from the shortcut
   menu.
   Specify first chamfer distance <1/2>: 0 ↵
   Specify second chamfer distance <0>: ↵
   ```

4. At the `Select first line or [Polyline/Distance/Angle/Trim/M ethod/mUltiple]:` prompt, pick ❶ in Figure 10-30. At the `Select second line:` prompt, pick ❷. AutoCAD chamfers the two lines to make a corner. (If this doesn't work, you may have the Trim option set to No Trim. Change the setting to Trim and try again.)

5. Repeat the CHAMFER command. Follow the prompts:

```
Select first line or [Polyline/Distance/Angle/Trim/Method/
mUltiple]: Right-click and choose Angle.
Specify chamfer length on the first line <1>: 9/16 ↵
Specify chamfer angle from the first line <0>: 45 ↵
```

6. At the `Select first line or [Polyline/Distance/Angle/Trim/Method/mUltiple]:` prompt, pick ❸ in Figure 10-30. At the `Select second line:` prompt, pick ❹. AutoCAD chamfers the two lines, as shown in Figure 10-31.

7. Save your drawing.

Figure 10-31: The edited drawing after using the CHAMFER command

Creating rounded corners

The FILLET command creates rounded corners, replacing part of two lines with an arc. Fillets are often used in mechanical drawings. In certain cases, you can use FILLET instead of the ARC command to create arcs. As with CHAMFER, you can fillet lines, xlines, rays, and polylines — they can even be parallel. You can also fillet circles, arcs, elliptical arcs, and ellipses.

The FILLET command defines the fillet arc by its radius, as shown in Figure 10-32.

Like chamfering, filleting is a two-step process. First you define the radius of the fillet arc. Then you select the two lines that you want to fillet. AutoCAD fillets them by using the information you specified. You cannot select objects before the FILLET command.

Figure 10-32: A fillet consisting of two lines and an arc

 To fillet, follow these steps:

1. Choose Fillet from the Modify toolbar. AutoCAD responds with the `Current settings: Mode = TRIM, Radius = 0.0000 Select first object or [Polyline/Radius/Trim/mUltiple]:` prompt.

2. Right-click and choose Radius.

3. At the `Specify fillet radius <0.0000>:` prompt, type the radius you want. The default is either 0.0000 or the last radius you specified.

4. AutoCAD repeats the `Select first object or [Polyline/Radius/Trim/mUltiple]:` prompt. Select the first object you want to fillet.

5. At the `Select second object:` prompt, select the second object you want to fillet. AutoCAD creates the fillet.

By default, FILLET trims the original lines that it fillets, but the FILLET command recalls the last setting you used. If you want to keep the full original lines when you create a fillet, right-click and choose the Trim option, and then choose No Trim.

Cross-Reference Choose the Polyline option to fillet an entire polyline at once. Chapter 16 covers polylines. Chapter 24 discusses filleting 3D models.

Filleting with a zero radius gives the same results as chamfering with distances set to zero. See the previous section on chamfering.

The order in which you select the two objects to be filleted is not important. However, where you pick the objects is quite important. If two objects intersect, AutoCAD keeps the objects on the same side of the intersection as your pick point and fillets them. Those parts of the objects on the far side of the intersection are erased.

When you fillet arcs and lines, if more than one fillet is possible, FILLET connects the endpoints closest to your pick points. Filleting circles and lines can result in unexpected results. Sometimes you need to experiment to find the proper pick points.

New Feature Use the mUltiple option to continue the prompts and fillet several corners in one command.

On the CD-ROM The drawing used in the following Step-by-Step exercise on filleting objects, ab10-i.dwg, is in the Drawings folder of the *AutoCAD 2004 Bible* CD-ROM.

Step-by-Step: Filleting Objects

1. Open ab10-i.dwg from your CD-ROM.

2. Save the file as ab10-11.dwg in your AutoCAD Bible folder. This is the same drawing used in the previous exercise. It is shown in Figure 10-33.

Figure 10-33: A mechanical drawing showing a small section of a porcupine mixer

3. Choose Fillet from the Modify toolbar. At the Select first object or [Polyline/Radius/Trim/mUltiple]: prompt, right-click and choose Radius. At the Specify fillet radius <1/2>: prompt, type **5/8** ↵.

4. At the Select first object or [Polyline/Radius/Trim/mUltiple]: prompt, pick the line at ❶ in Figure 10-33. At the Select second object: prompt, pick the line at ❷. AutoCAD fillets the two lines.

5. Repeat the FILLET command. At the Select first object or [Polyline/Radius/Trim/ mUltiple]: prompt, right-click and choose Radius. At the Enter fillet radius <5/8>: prompt, type **1/4** ↵.

6. At the `Select first object or [Polyline/Radius/Trim/mUltiple]:` prompt, right-click and choose mUltiple. Pick the line at ❸ in Figure 10-33. At the `Select second object:` prompt, pick the line at ❹. AutoCAD fillets the two lines. The prompts continue. This time pick at ❺ and ❻.

7. If you want, you can connect the two loose lines that the fillets created and create some more fillets in the drawing.

8. Save your drawing. It should look like Figure 10-34.

Figure 10-34: The filleted drawing

Creating a Revision Cloud

Some AutoCAD users need to mark areas of their drawings that contain revisions, to draw attention to these revisions. A common method is to draw a *revision cloud* around the revised objects. Figure 10-35 shows a drawing with a revision cloud.

New Feature A new feature of AutoCAD 2004 makes a *revision cloud*, a series of arcs that indicate that an area has been revised.

To create a revision cloud, follow these steps:

1. Choose Revcloud from the Draw toolbar.

2. At the `Specify start point or [Arc length/Object] <Object>:` prompt, you can choose from two options:

 • To change the length of the arc, right-click and choose Arc Length. Then specify a new arc length. You can specify a minimum arc length and a maximum arc length that is up to three times the length of the minimum, for a variable, hand-drawn look.

- To change a closed object into a revision cloud, right-click and choose Object. Then pick a circle, ellipse, closed polyline, or closed spline. You can choose to reverse the direction of the revision cloud. The object is converted to a revision cloud and the command ends.

3. Click where you want the revision cloud to start. You also see an instruction, Guide crosshairs along cloud path. . ., which means that you don't have to pick to create the arcs. You just have to move the crosshairs along the path of the desired cloud.

4. Move the crosshairs counterclockwise to create a circular or elliptical shape. When you approach the start point, the command ends automatically. (You can end the cloud at any time by pressing Enter.)

Note You can pick each arc endpoint to control the size of the arcs, if you want. However, if you move the crosshairs further than the arc length, an arc is created automatically. REVCLOUD multiplies the arc length by the Overall Scale factor (see Chapter 15) to adjust for different scale factors.

Figure 10-35: The revision cloud shows where the drawing has been modified.

Hiding Objects with a Wipeout

A *wipeout* covers up existing objects in order to clear space for some annotation or to indicate that the covered objects will be changed and should therefore be ignored. A wipe out is a polygonal area with a background that matches the background of the drawing area.

New Feature A new command, WIPEOUT, creates a polygon the same color as the screen background.

To create a wipeout, follow these steps:

1. Choose Draw ⇨ Wipeout.

2. At the `Specify first point or [Frames/Polyline] <Polyline>:` prompt, specify the first point of a shape that will cover existing objects. To use a polyline as the shape, right-click and choose Polyline. Then select the polyline and choose whether to erase the polyline or not.

3. At the `Specify next point or [Undo]:` prompt, if you specified a point, specify the next point.

4. At the `Specify next point or [Close/Undo]:` prompt, specify another point or use the Close option to close the wipeout shape. You can also press Enter to end the command and use the shape you specified.

By default, the wipeout has a frame around it, using the current layer's color. You can hide the frames of all wipeouts. Start the WIPEOUT command, choose the Frames option, and choose Off.

Double-Clicking to Edit Objects

You can double-click objects to edit them. What happens after you double-click depends on the type of object. In most cases, double-clicking an object just opens the Properties window where you can change the object's properties. For example, double-clicking a polyline does not start the PEDIT command, a command for editing polylines. For more information about using the Properties palette, see the "Editing with the Properties Palette" section later in this chapter.

When you double-click certain types of objects in a drawing, you see a dialog box (usually) that is specific to these objects:

✦ **Attribute definition:** Opens the Edit Attribute Definition dialog box (the DDEDIT command). See Chapter 18 for more information.

✦ **Attribute within a block:** Opens the Enhanced Attribute Edit dialog box (the EATTEDIT command). See Chapter 18 for more information.

✦ **Block:** Opens the Reference Edit dialog box (the REFEDIT command). See Chapter 18 for more information.

✦ **Hatch:** Opens the Hatch Edit dialog box (the HATCHEDIT command). See Chapter 16 for more information.

✦ **Mline:** Opens the Multiline Edit Tools dialog box (the MLEDIT command). See Chapter 16 for more information.

✦ **Mtext or leader text:** Opens the Multiline Text Editor (the MTEDIT command). See Chapter 13 for more information.

✦ **Text (TEXT or DTEXT commands):** Opens the Edit Text dialog box (the DDEDIT command). See Chapter 13 for more information.

✦ **Xref:** Opens the Reference Edit dialog box (the REFEDIT command). See Chapter 19 for more information.

The DBLCKLEDIT command specifies if double-clicking opens a dialog box in these instances. To turn off double-clicking to edit objects, type **dblclkedit** and choose the Off option.

Grips

Grips offer a way to edit objects without choosing commands. By using grips, you can quickly stretch, move, rotate, scale, copy, and mirror objects.

When you select an object without first choosing a command, the object appears highlighted with *grips* — small boxes at preset object snap points. (If you don't see grips, they may be turned off. See the "Customizing grips" section later in this chapter to read how to turn them back on.)

You can continue to select more objects in this way.

You then activate a grip by clicking it and use it to manipulate the object. When the grip is activated, it turns red (by default). An activated grip is also called a *hot grip*, as shown in Figure 10-36. In some cases, you activate more than one grip at a time. To activate more than one grip, hold down Shift and then click the grips. If you activate a grip in error, click it again to deactivate it. Grips are so called because you can "hold on to" the object by dragging the grips with the mouse.

After you activate a grip, right-click with the mouse to open the Grip shortcut menu listing all the grip options.

You can also press the spacebar or Enter to cycle through five possible commands on the command line. It takes a little time to get used to working with grips, but as soon as you do, they are a quick way to make certain changes. As long as you are familiar with the STRETCH, MOVE, ROTATE, SCALE, and MIRROR commands, you can easily learn how to accomplish the same edits by using grips because the prompts are so similar. After you complete the edit, the object remains highlighted and the grips remain, so that you can further edit the object. If you want to edit another object, press Esc once to remove the grips. Then select another object or objects or choose another command.

Hot grip (red)

Endpoint

Crosshairs

Grip (blue)

Line's original
position

←Line's new
position

Grip (blue)

Figure 10-36: Moving a line. Grips appear
at preset object snaps. A hot grip is used to
manipulate an object.

Stretching with grips

Stretching with grips involves understanding how the grip points relate to the
object. For example, you cannot stretch a line from its midpoint — if you think
about it, there's no way to define in which direction to stretch the line. Also, you
cannot stretch a circle. (You can only scale it.) Aside from these types of limita-
tions, anything goes.

Stretching one line

You can stretch one line. The result is similar to using the CHANGE command to
change a line's endpoint. To stretch a line, select it. Click the grip at the endpoint
you want to stretch. AutoCAD responds with

```
** STRETCH **
Specify stretch point or [Base point/Copy/Undo/eXit]:
```

STRETCH is the first grip editing command on the command line. Simply specify the
new endpoint for the line, using any method of specifying a coordinate. AutoCAD
stretches the line. The other options work as follows:

✦ Base point lets you define a base point — other than the activated grip — and a second point. Right-click to open the Grip shortcut menu and choose Base Point. AutoCAD displays the `Specify base point:` prompt. Define a base point. AutoCAD responds with the original `Specify stretch point or [Base point/Copy/Undo/eXit]:` prompt. Define the second stretch point to stretch the line.

✦ Copy puts you in Multiple mode. Right-click to open the Grip shortcut menu and choose Copy. AutoCAD responds with the original `Specify stretch point or [Base point/Copy/Undo/eXit]:` prompt. AutoCAD keeps the original line and creates a new line stretched as you specify. You can then continue to create new stretched lines.

✦ Undo undoes the last edit. Right-click to open the Grip shortcut menu and choose Undo.

✦ eXit returns you to the Command prompt. Right-click to open the Grip shortcut menu and choose Exit. Esc also returns you to the Command prompt.

Stretching multiple lines

Stretching more than one line at a time is similar to the most common use of the STRETCH command. However, it can also be somewhat confusing.

As explained earlier in this chapter for the STRETCH command, objects that cross the crossing window are stretched while objects entirely within the crossing window are moved. When you stretch multiple lines, you should activate endpoint grips to stretch lines and activate midpoint grips to move lines. Picking all those grips accurately can be difficult and time-consuming. Also, small objects close together create a lot of overlapping grips that are hard to select. For this reason, stretching multiple lines works best with simple models.

To stretch multiple lines, follow these steps:

1. Choose the objects that you want to stretch. The objects are highlighted and display grips. You can use any method of choosing objects — you are not limited to crossing windows.

2. Hold down Shift and pick each grip that you want to stretch. If there are internal objects that you want to move with the stretch, select their grips, too — the midpoints of the lines and arcs, and the centers of the circles.

3. Release Shift and pick a grip to use as a base point. AutoCAD responds:

```
** STRETCH **
Specify stretch point or [Base point/Copy/Undo/eXit]:
```

4. Specify a new stretch point. You can also use any of the other options.

At the end of this section on grips, you have the opportunity to try them out in an exercise.

Moving with grips

Moving objects is easy by using grips. Choose all the objects that you want to move. Click any grip to activate it. This becomes the base point. Right-click to open the Grip shortcut menu and choose Move.

Tip You can also press the spacebar to cycle through the grip editing modes. For example, to move an object, press the spacebar once.

After you choose Move editing mode, AutoCAD responds:

```
** MOVE **
Specify move point or [Base point/Copy/Undo/eXit]:
```

Use any method to specify the second point. Be sure to use @ if you are typing in relative coordinates. AutoCAD moves the selected objects. The other options work as follows:

✦ Base point lets you define a base point — other than the activated grip. Right-click to open the Grip shortcut menu and choose Base Point. AutoCAD displays the `Specify base point:` prompt. Define a base point. AutoCAD responds with the original `Specify move point or [Base point/Copy/Undo/eXit]:` prompt. Define the second move point to move the objects.

✦ Copy puts you in Multiple mode and lets you copy objects. Right-click to open the Grip shortcut menu and choose Copy (or type **c** ⏎). AutoCAD responds with the original `Specify move point or [Base point/Copy/Undo/eXit]:` prompt. AutoCAD keeps the original object and creates a new object where you specify. You can then continue to create new objects.

✦ Undo undoes the last edit. Right-click to open the Grip shortcut menu and choose Undo.

✦ eXit returns you to the Command prompt. Right-click to open the Grip shortcut menu and choose Exit. Esc also returns you to the Command prompt.

Rotating with grips

Rotating with grips is very similar to using the ROTATE command. Choose all the objects that you want to rotate. Click any grip to activate it. This becomes the base point. Right-click to open the Grip shortcut menu and choose Rotate. AutoCAD responds:

```
** ROTATE **
Specify rotation angle or [Base
point/Copy/Undo/Reference/eXit]:
```

Type in a rotation angle or pick a point. AutoCAD rotates the objects. The other options work as follows:

✦ Base point lets you define a base point — other than the activated grip. Right-click to open the Grip shortcut menu and choose Base Point. AutoCAD displays the `Specify base point:` prompt. Define a base point. AutoCAD responds with the original `Specify rotation angle or [Base point/Copy/Undo/Reference/eXit]:` prompt. Define the rotation angle to rotate the objects.

✦ Copy puts you in Multiple mode and lets you copy objects. Right-click to open the Grip shortcut menu and choose Copy. AutoCAD responds with the original `Specify rotation angle or [Base point/Copy/Undo/Reference/eXit]:` prompt. AutoCAD keeps the original object and creates a new rotated object where you specify. You can then continue to create new objects.

✦ Undo undoes the last edit. Right-click to open the Grip shortcut menu and choose Undo.

✦ Reference lets you specify a reference angle and a new angle. Right-click to open the Grip shortcut menu and choose Reference. AutoCAD responds with the `Reference angle <0>:` prompt. Type an angle or pick two points to specify an angle. AutoCAD displays the `Specify new angle or [Base point/Copy/Undo/Reference/eXit]:` prompt. Type an angle or pick a point. This works just like the Reference option for the ROTATE command. (See Chapter 9.)

✦ eXit returns you to the Command prompt. Right-click to open the Grip shortcut menu and choose Exit. Esc also returns you to the Command prompt.

Scaling with grips

Scaling with grips is very similar to using the SCALE command. Choose all the objects that you want to scale. Click any grip to activate it. This becomes the base point. Right-click to open the Grip shortcut menu and choose Scale. AutoCAD responds:

```
** SCALE **
Specify scale factor or [Base point/Copy/Undo/Reference/eXit]:
```

Type a scale factor. AutoCAD scales the objects. The other options work as follows:

✦ Base point lets you define a base point — other than the activated grip. Right-click to open the Grip shortcut menu and choose Base Point. AutoCAD displays the `Specify base point:` prompt. Define a base point. AutoCAD responds with the original `Specify scale factor or [Base point/Copy/Undo/Reference/eXit]:` prompt. Define the scale factor to scale the objects.

✦ Copy puts you in Multiple mode and lets you copy objects. Right-click to open the Grip shortcut menu and choose Copy. AutoCAD responds with the original `Specify scale factor or [Base point/Copy/Undo/Reference/eXit]:` prompt. AutoCAD keeps the original object and creates a new scaled object where you specify. You can then continue to create new scaled objects.

✦ Undo undoes the last edit. Right-click to open the Grip shortcut menu and choose Undo.

✦ Reference lets you specify a reference length and a new scale. Right-click to open the Grip shortcut menu and choose Reference. AutoCAD responds with the `Reference length <0>:` prompt. Type a length or pick two points to specify a length. AutoCAD displays the `Specify new length or [Base point/Copy/Undo/Reference/eXit]:` prompt. Type a length or pick a point. This works just like the Reference option for the SCALE command. (See Chapter 9.)

✦ eXit returns you to the Command prompt. Right-click to open the Grip shortcut menu and choose Exit. Esc also returns you to the Command prompt.

Mirroring with grips

Mirroring with grips is very similar to using the MIRROR command. Choose all the objects that you want to mirror. Click any grip to activate it. This becomes the first point of the mirror line. Right-click to open the Grip shortcut menu. Choose Mirror. AutoCAD responds:

```
** MIRROR **
Specify second point or [Base point/Copy/Undo/eXit]:
```

Specify the second point of the mirror line. AutoCAD mirrors the objects.

Caution By default, AutoCAD erases the original objects. To keep the original objects, you must use the Copy option. This feature is the opposite of the MIRROR command, where the default is to keep the original objects.

The other options work as follows:

✦ Base point lets you define a base point — other than the activated grip — and a second point. Right-click to open the Grip shortcut menu and choose Base Point. AutoCAD displays the `Specify base point:` prompt. Define a base point — that is, the first point of the mirror line. AutoCAD responds with the original `Specify second point or [Base point/Copy/Undo/eXit]:` prompt. Define the second point of the mirror line, and AutoCAD mirrors the objects.

✦ Copy puts you in Multiple mode and lets you keep the original objects. Right-click to open the Grip shortcut menu and choose Copy. AutoCAD responds with the original `Specify second point or [Base point/Copy /Undo/ eXit]:` prompt. AutoCAD keeps the original objects and creates new mirrored objects. You can then continue to create new mirrored objects.

✦ Undo undoes the last edit. Right-click to open the Grip shortcut menu and choose Undo.

✦ eXit returns you to the Command prompt. Right-click to open the Grip shortcut menu and choose Exit. Esc also returns you to the Command prompt.

The drawing used in the following Step-by-Step exercise on editing with grips, `ab10-j.dwg,` is in the `Drawings` folder of the *AutoCAD 2004 Bible* CD-ROM.

Step-by-Step: Editing with Grips

1. Open `ab10-j.dwg` from the CD-ROM.

2. Save the file as `ab10-12.dwg` in your `AutoCAD Bible` folder. This is a small section of a drive block, seen from above, as shown in Figure 10-37. Make sure ORTHO and OSNAP are on.

3. Use a selection window to select the entire model. Now hold down Shift and place a selection window around the small circles and rectangle at the center of the model to deselect them.

4. Pick the grip at ❶ in Figure 10-37 to activate it. AutoCAD responds with the following prompt:

   ```
   ** STRETCH **
   Specify stretch point or [Base point/Copy/Undo/eXit]:
   ```

5. Right-click and choose Mirror from the shortcut menu. AutoCAD responds with the following prompt:

   ```
   ** MIRROR **
   Specify second point or [Base point/Copy/Undo/eXit]:
   ```

6. Right-click and choose Copy so that the original objects that you mirror are not deleted.

7. At the `Specify second point or [Base point/Copy/Undo/eXit]:` prompt, move the cursor to the right. You can see the mirror image of the model. Pick any point to the right (in the 0-degree direction) of the activated grip.

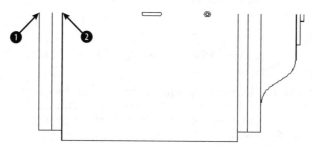

Figure 10-37: This small section of a drive block, seen from above, can easily be edited with grips.

8. Right-click and choose Exit to return to the command line. The original objects are still highlighted.

9. Use a large selection window to select all the new objects including the small rectangle and circles in the middle. Everything (old and new) should be highlighted and display grips.

10. Pick the grip at ➋ in Figure 10-37 to activate it. Right-click and choose Rotate from the shortcut menu. At the `Specify rotation angle or [Base point/Copy/Undo/Reference/eXit]:` prompt, type **90** ↵. AutoCAD rotates the model.

11. Pick the bottom-right grip to activate it. Right-click and choose Scale from the shortcut menu. At the `Specify scale factor or [Base point/Copy/Undo/Reference/eXit]:` prompt, type **.5** ↵. AutoCAD scales the model.

12. Pick the grip at the midpoint of the bottom line. Right-click and choose Move from the shortcut menu. At the `Specify move point or [Base point/Copy/Undo/eXit]:` prompt, type **@0,–3** ↵. The model should look like Figure 10-38.

Figure 10-38: The drive block section, after several grip edits, looks a little like a cookie jar.

13. Press Esc to remove all grips. Define a crossing window by picking first at ➊, and then at ➋ (see Figure 10-38).

14. Hold down Shift and pick all the grips along the bottom three lines. Release Shift and pick the grip at the middle of the bottom line. At the `Specify stretch point or [Base point/Copy/Undo/eXit]:` prompt, type **@0,1** ↵. AutoCAD shrinks the model.

If the stretch does not come out right (it might be hard to see and activate all the grips), choose Undo from the Standard toolbar to undo the stretch and try again.

15. Save your drawing.

Customizing grips

You can turn grips on and off and customize their size and color. Choose Tools ⇨ Options and click the Selection tab to open the dialog box shown in Figure 10-39.

Figure 10-39: Use the Selection tab of the Options dialog box to customize grips.

By default, grips are enabled (that is, turned on). Also by default, grips are turned off for blocks. (Chapter 18 covers blocks.) When grips are off for blocks, you see only one grip when you select a block—its insertion point. When grips are on, you see all the grips you would normally see for objects.

In the Grip Colors section, you can choose the colors you want for unselected and selected (hot) grips. Click the drop-down lists to choose a color.

The Grip Size section lets you drag the slider bar to set the size of the grips. Click OK after you have made the desired changes.

Editing with the Properties Palette

The Properties palette displays the properties of selected objects. You can use the Properties palette to change the properties of objects as well.

To open the Properties palette, click Properties on the Standard toolbar. (You can also choose Tools ➪ Properties or press Ctrl+1.) The Properties palette, shown in Figure 10-40, opens on your screen.

New Feature The Properties palette takes the place of the previous Properties window (or Object Property Manager). If you don't dock the palette, you can set it to collapse down to its title bar when you're not using it.

Figure 10-40: Use the Properties palette to edit objects and their properties.

Managing the Properties palette

The new auto-hide feature of the Properties palette makes it easy to work with the palette open all the time. Whenever the cursor is off the palette, it collapses to just its title bar. To auto-hide the palette, right-click the title bar and choose Auto-hide.

Tip The Properties palette has its own undo function. Right-click the item that you changed in the Properties palette and choose Undo. Multiple levels of undo are available. For more information about palettes, see Chapter 26.

You can dock the Properties palette. Drag the window to the left or right of your screen. You can resize the window by pointing to its edge until you see the double-headed arrow cursor, and then clicking and dragging. You can also resize the two columns by pointing to the column dividing line until you see the double-headed arrow and then clicking and dragging. If the Properties palette has two many rows for its size, you can use the scroll bar to see the undisplayed rows.

Using the Properties palette

The Properties palette can be used to directly edit objects and for editing other object properties as well:

✦ You can change the layer, color, linetype, linetype scale, and lineweight of objects. (See Chapter 11.)

✦ You can edit text and text properties. (See Chapter 13.)

✦ You can edit plot styles. (See Chapter 17.)

✦ You can edit hyperlinks. (See Chapter 28.)

To change values in the Properties palette, do one of the following:

✦ Click a value, select the text, type a new value, and press Enter.

✦ Click a value, click the down arrow at its right, and choose from the drop-down list.

✦ Click a value, click the Pick a Point button, and specify a new point by picking on the screen.

In Figure 10-40, you see the result of opening the Properties window with one line selected. To change either endpoint of the selected line, type new coordinates in the Properties palette and press Enter. Of course, this method of editing a line is only useful when you know the absolute coordinates that you want. When you select a geometric property, such as Start X, the X coordinate of the line's start point, you can also use the Pick a Point button that appears. You can click this button and then pick a new start point directly on your screen. The new point becomes the new start point of the line, changing both the X and Y coordinates of the start point if your pick point requires it.

The information you see in the Properties palette depends on the objects selected:

✦ If no object is selected, you see only properties that apply to the entire drawing, such as UCS, current layer, and viewport data. You can select an object while the window is open to display data on that object.

✦ If one object or one type of object (such as all lines) is selected, you see both general information and geometrical information on that object.

✦ If more than one type of object is selected, you see general information, such as layer, color, and linetype data, but no geometry data.

✦ If more than one object is selected and you choose one type of object from the drop-down list at the top of the window, you see information applying only to that type of object. This drop-down list provides a quick way to filter the type of objects you can edit.

The Properties palette has three buttons at its upper-right corner.

The first button, Quick Select, opens the Quick Select dialog box that's covered in the next section. The Quick Select dialog box lets you create a selection set according to specified criteria—for example, all green lines. You can then change the properties of these green lines.

The second button, Select Objects, enables you to select objects for editing in the Properties palette. After you select the objects you want, you can change their properties. If you're going to pick objects or use implied windowing, the Select Objects button is no advantage. You can just select the objects and apply changes in the Properties palette. However, if you want to use a fence or polygon method of selection, the Select Objects button is helpful. Follow these steps:

1. Click the Select Objects button.

2. On the command line, type the selection method that you want (such as **f** for fence) as you would if a command were active or you had started the SELECT command.

3. Select the objects that you want.

4. Press Enter to end object selection.

5. Use the Properties palette to make the desired changes. (You can also start an editing command to use with the selected objects.)

The third button, Toggle value of PICKADD Sysvar, turns PICKADD on and off. PICKADD changes how you select more than one object. When it's on (set to 1), the default, you can continue to select objects and they are added to the selection set. When it's off (set to 0), you need to press Shift to add objects to the selection set; otherwise, selecting an object deselects previously selected objects.

Here's how to change the PICKADD variable:

✦ When you see the 1, PICKADD is off. Click the button to turn PICKADD on.

✦ When you see the plus, PICKADD is on. Click the button to turn PICKADD off.

Click the Properties palette's close box to close the window. You will return to the Properties palette in the next chapter and in later chapters as appropriate.

Selection Filters

Sometimes you need a more powerful way to select objects. For example, you may want to:

✦ Select all the lines in your drawing to change their color

✦ Check the arc radii of all your fillets

✦ Find short line segments that should be erased

Before selection filters, you had to write an AutoLISP program to accomplish these functions. (Sometimes an AutoLISP program is still the easiest way to go. See Chapters 34 and 35.) Now you can create fairly complex filters that select only the objects you want.

Cross-Reference Don't confuse object selection filters with point filters. Chapter 4 covers point filters.

Using Quick Select to select objects

Quick Select, as its name suggests, is a quick, flexible, and simple way to create object selection filters. Use the FILTER command, covered in the following sections, to create more complex filters and when you want to save filtering criteria for future use.

Start Quick Select in one of these ways:

✦ Choose Tools ⇨ Quick Select.

✦ With no command active, right-click in the drawing area and choose Quick Select.

✦ Choose the Quick Select button in the Object Properties Manager.

✦ Type **qselect** ↵ on the command line.

AutoCAD opens the Quick Select dialog box, shown in Figure 10-41.

To create a filter, start at the top of the dialog box and work your way down. Here's how it works:

✦ **Apply to:** By default the filter applies to the entire drawing, but you can use the Select objects button to return to your drawing and select objects. The rest of the filter will then apply only to selected objects, called Current selection in the drop-down list. If you use this feature at all, you would usually use a window to select an area of your drawing. (The Select objects button is unavailable if `Append to current selection set` is checked at the bottom of the dialog box.)

Figure 10-41: Use the Quick Select dialog box to quickly create a selection set of objects based on specified criteria.

✦ **Object type:** By default, the filter lists Multiple as the object type. Click the drop-down list to choose from the object types available in your drawing (or in your selection set if you created one), such as line, circle, ellipse, polyline, and so on. You can choose only one type of object. To create a filter that includes more than one type of object (but not all types), use the FILTER command.

✦ **Properties:** Here you choose the properties for which you want to filter. (Most of these properties are covered in the next chapter.) All properties that AutoCAD can search for in its database are listed — these depend on the object type you chose. You can choose only one property. The values in the next two sections depend on your choice in the Properties section. If you want to create a filter that specifies criteria for more than one property, use the FILTER command.

✦ **Operator:** After you have chosen a property, you can set it equal to or not equal to a certain value. You can set certain properties as greater than or less than a value. You can use wildcard matching characters (such as * and ?) for editable text. Choose the desired operator from the drop-down list.

✦ **Value:** Here you finally choose the value for your property. For example, you can set the color equal (or not equal) to green or the linetype equal to DASHED. Choose the desired value from the drop-down list or enter a value in the text box.

✦ **How to apply:** As soon as you create a filter, you can use it to create a selection set. To do this, check Include In New Selection Set. You can also use Quick Select to select everything except objects that meet your selection criteria— to do so, choose Exclude From New Selection set.

✦ **Append to current selection set:** Check this box to add objects meeting your criteria to an existing selection set.

To select the objects meeting your criteria and close the dialog box, click OK.

AutoCAD selects the objects that meet your criteria. If you choose "Exclude from new selection set," AutoCAD selects all objects that don't meet your criteria. You can start a command and use the selection set. If the command must be started before selecting objects, you can use the Previous option (type **p** ↵) at the Select objects: prompt to select the objects selected by using Quick Select.

New Feature The Express Tools include two commands to create filtered selection sets. FASTSE-LECT creates a selection set of objects that touch the object you pick. You can create chains of objects to include objects that touch other touching objects. Choose Express ➪ Selection tools ➪ Fast Select. GETSEL creates a selection of objects of the layer and object type that you select. Choose Express ➪ Selection tools ➪ Get Selection Set. For information on installing Express Tools, see Appendix A on the CD-ROM.

Using the FILTER command

The advantage of using the FILTER command over Quick Select is that you can create more complex filters and save them.

To create a filter, type **filter** ↵ on the command line. AutoCAD opens the Object Selection Filters dialog box, as shown in Figure 10-42. If you have already chosen a command, type **'filter** at the Select objects: prompt to create the selection filter transparently. The box at the top of the dialog box lists the filters you specified.

Figure 10-42: The Object Selection Filters dialog box

Note The selection filter only finds colors and linetypes of objects that have been specifically set as such, rather than as part of a layer definition. Chapter 11 covers layers, colors, and linetypes.

Creating a single filter

Use the Select Filter section of the dialog box to specify a filter. The drop-down box lists all the possible filters. Click the arrow to drop the list down. There are several types of items — objects, object properties such as color or layer, object snaps such as arc center or circle radius, and logical operators such as AND, OR, and NOT. These logical operators combine filter specifications in various ways.

The first step is to choose a filter. In Figure 10-43, Line was chosen from the drop-down list. If the item chosen does not need any further clarification, click Add to List. The filter appears in the box at the top of the dialog box. Notice that the filter appears as Object = Line.

Figure 10-43: A filter that chooses all lines

Many filters require a value. You have two ways to enter a value:

✦ If you choose an object that can be listed, the Select button becomes active. Click it and choose the value you want. For example, if you choose Color or Layer, you choose from a list of colors or layers.

✦ If you choose an object that can have any value, the boxes below the drop-down list box become active. They are labeled X, Y, and Z, but this is misleading. These boxes are used for X, Y, and Z coordinates only when you choose a filter requiring coordinates, such as Viewport Center. In most cases, you use the X box to give the filter a value. In this situation, the Y and Z boxes are not used. For example, if you choose Text Height, you type the height in the X box.

However, you don't always want to specify that a filter equals a value. Let's say you want to create a filter that selects all circles with a radius less than 0.75. When you choose Circle Radius, the X box becomes active. Click the arrow to drop down the list of relational operators and choose one. Table 10-2 lists the relational operators.

Table 10-2	
Relational Operators in the Object Selection Filters Dialog Box	
Operator	*Definition*
=	Equal to
!=	Not equal to
<	Less than
<=	Less than or equal to
>	Greater than
>=	Greater than or equal to
*	Equal to any value

Adding a second filter

To add a second filter, you first decide on the relationship between the first and the second filter and then assign a logical operator. Logical operators always come in pairs — when you begin one you must also end it. The logical operators are at the end of the drop-down list of filter objects.

> **Note** When two or more filters are listed without logical operators, AutoCAD calculates them as if they were grouped with the AND operator. This means that AutoCAD only selects objects that meet all the criteria specified.

Table 10-3 explains the four logical operators. (AutoCAD calls them grouping operators because they group filter specifications together.) The Example column explains the results of two filter specifications: Color = 1-Red and Object = Circle.

Click Substitute and choose a saved filter to insert a saved filter into the filter you are currently defining. To add filters based on existing objects, choose Add Selected Object. AutoCAD adds all the properties of the object to the filter definition — which is often more than you want.

Figure 10-44 shows a filter that selects all lines and all polylines. The XOR operator was used because it finds objects that meet one criterion or the other but not both. Obviously, no object can be both a line and a polyline. This is a good example of a filter that you cannot create using Quick Select.

Table 10-3
Logical (or Grouping) Operators Used for Selection Filters

Operator	Explanation	Example
AND	Finds all objects that meet all criteria.	Finds red circles.
OR	Finds objects that meet any of the criteria.	Finds all red objects and all circles.
XOR	Finds objects that meet one criterion or the other but not both. Requires two criteria between Begin XOR and End XOR.	Finds red objects that are not circles and circles that are not red.
NOT	Excludes objects that meet the criteria. May only have one criterion between Begin NOT and End NOT.	If the NOT operator groups the Object = Circle filter, finds all red objects that are not circles.

Figure 10-44: A filter that selects all lines and all polylines

Naming and editing filters

After you have completed the filter, you should save it. Even if you don't think you will use it again, you may make an editing error in the drawing while using it and have to go back to it. To save a filter, type a name in the Save As text box and click Save As.

You edit a listed filter by using three buttons:

✦ **Edit Item:** Choose the line containing the item and click this button to edit the item. AutoCAD places the object name in the drop-down box and lets you specify new values for it.

✦ **Delete:** Choose Delete to delete a chosen item in a filter.

✦ **Clear List:** Choose Clear List to clear all the items in a filter and start over.

To choose a named filter to edit, choose it from the Current drop-down list.

Using filters

You can use filters in two ways. Most often you choose a command first and then realize that you need a filter to select the objects. Follow these prompts:

```
Select objects: 'filter ↵
Define the filter in the Object Selection Filters dialog box.
Click Apply.
Applying filter to selection.
Select objects: Type all ↵ or use a large selection window to
select all the objects you want to consider in the filter.
x found
y were filtered out
Select objects: ↵
Exiting filtered selection. x found
Select objects: ↵
```

AutoCAD continues with the command's usual prompts.

Alternatively, you can start the FILTER command and define the filter. Click Apply. At the `Select objects:` prompt, type **all** or use a selection window. Press Enter to end object selection. Then start the editing command and use the Previous selection option to select the filtered objects.

On the CD-ROM
The drawing used in the following Step-by-Step exercise on using selection filters, ab10-k.dwg, is in the Drawings folder of the *AutoCAD 2004 Bible* CD-ROM.

Step-by-Step: Using Selection Filters

1. Open ab10-k.dwg from the CD-ROM.

2. Save the file as ab10-13.dwg in your AutoCAD Bible folder. Notice that two lines of text appearing in the middle of the drawing plus the text at the bottom of the drawing are black/white rather than blue like all the other text. You want to check the color of all the text and correct it if necessary.

3. Right-click the drawing area and choose Quick Select. In the Quick Select dialog box, click the Object type drop-down list and scroll down until you see Text. Choose it.

4. In the Properties section, color should be selected. If not, select it. In the Operator section, choose Not equal. In the Value section, choose ByLayer. Include In New Selection Set should be chosen. Append to Current Selection Set should not be checked. Click OK. AutoCAD selects three items of black/white text.

5. Press Esc to deselect the objects and remove the grips. Now you'll try the same thing using the FILTER command, but add a level of complexity.

6. Type **filter** ↵. The Object Selection Filters dialog box opens.

7. In the Select Filter drop-down list, choose Text. Click Add to List. At the top, the filter reads `Object = Text`.

8. From the Select Filter drop-down list, choose `**Begin AND` (this is toward the bottom of the list) and click Add to List.

9. From the Select Filter drop-down list, choose Color. In the drop-down list next to X: choose ! = (not equal). Choose Select. In the Select Color dialog box, choose BYLAYER. Click OK. In the Object Selection Filters dialog box, choose Add to List. The BYLAYER color number displays as 256. (Layers and colors are covered in the next chapter.)

10. Say that you want to select only the smaller text, not the heading at the bottom of the drawing, and you know that the larger text's height is greater than .1 but the smaller text's height is smaller than .1. From the Select Filter drop-down list, choose Text Height. From the X: drop-down list choose < (less than). In the text box to the right of X:, type **.1**. Choose Add to List.

11. From the Select Filter drop-down list, choose `**End AND` and click Add to List.

12. In the Save As text box, type **bad text**. Click Save As. The Object Selection Filters dialog box should look like Figure 10-45.

Figure 10-45: A filter that selects all text whose color is not BYLAYER

13. Click Apply.

14. At the `Select objects:` prompt, type **all** ↵. AutoCAD tells you that 469 objects were found, and 467 were filtered out. Press Enter until you get the Command prompt.

15. Choose Color Control from the Object Properties toolbar. Choose ByLayer from the drop-down list. AutoCAD changes the color of the two text objects to BYLAYER—they turn blue like all the other text.

16. Save your drawing.

As you can see, Quick Select is much easier to use than the FILTER command for all but quite complex filters, but the FILTER command offers more control.

Groups

Groups let you save a selection set of objects so that you can easily select them whenever you need to edit them. If you have a certain set of objects that you need to edit as a group, and a busy drawing that makes their selection time-consuming, groups are for you.

Creating and modifying groups

To create or modify a group, type **group** ↵ on the command line to open the Object Grouping dialog box, as shown in Figure 10-46.

Figure 10-46: The Object Grouping dialog box

Creating a new group

To create a new group, follow these steps.

1. Type a name in the Group Name text box. You can use a maximum of 31 characters with no spaces. You can use the hyphen (-) and underscore (_) anywhere in the name.

2. If you want, type a description of up to 448 characters. The description can include spaces.

3. Click New. AutoCAD returns you to your drawing with the Select objects: prompt. Select the objects you want to be in the group. Press Enter to end object selection. AutoCAD returns you to the dialog box.

4. Click OK.

You can now use your group.

> **Note** An object can belong to more than one group.

The Group Identification section of the Object Grouping dialog box also has a Find Name button. Use this to find the name of the group to which an object belongs. AutoCAD lets you select an object and then lists the group's name or names.

The Highlight button highlights a group. First choose a group from the list in the Object Grouping dialog box. Click Highlight and AutoCAD returns to your drawing and highlights all the objects in your group. Click Continue to return to the dialog box. Use this when you are not sure which group you want to work with.

Changing a group

The Change Group section of the Object Grouping dialog box gives you a great deal of flexibility in managing groups. To change a group, click any existing group in the Group Name list at the top of the dialog box. The buttons in the Change Group section all become active. You can do the following:

✦ **Remove:** AutoCAD switches to the drawing area with the Select objects to remove from group... prompt. Select objects to remove and press Enter to end object removal. AutoCAD returns you to the dialog box. Click OK.

✦ **Add:** AutoCAD switches to the drawing area with the Select objects to add to group... prompt. Select objects to add and press Enter to end object selection. AutoCAD returns you to the dialog box. Click OK.

✦ **Rename:** Choose the group you want to rename. Change the name in the Group Name text box. Click Rename. The name changes in the Group Name list at the top of the dialog box. Click OK.

✦ **Re-Order:** Each group in the object has a number, starting from zero. In rare cases, the order may be important to you — for example, if you are running a program that processes the members of a group. Choose the group you want to reorder. Click Re-Order. AutoCAD opens the Order Group dialog box. If you simply want to reverse the order of all the objects, click Reverse Order. Otherwise, click Highlight. AutoCAD opens a small Object Grouping message box with Next and Previous buttons. At the bottom-right corner, the box displays `Object: 0`, and one of the objects in the group is highlighted. Click Next to move from object to object. If you are going to reorder the objects, you probably need to write down the number of each object. Click OK to return to the Order Group dialog box. Complete the following text boxes:

- **Remove from position:** This text box is the position number of the object you want to move.

- **Replace at position:** This text box is the new position number you want for the object.

- **Number of objects:** This text box is the object number or range of numbers you want to reorder.

✦ **Description:** Updates a description for the group. Type a new description in the Group Identification section of the dialog box. Then click Description.

✦ **Explode:** Removes the group entirely. All the objects remain in your drawing, but they are no longer grouped.

✦ **Selectable:** Toggles the selectability of the group. If a group is selectable, then selecting one object of the group selects the entire group. If a group is not selectable, then selecting one object of the group does not select the entire group. This option lets you temporarily work with one object in the group without having to explode the group.

Tip

When you choose Highlight from the Order Group dialog box, the Object Grouping message box opens in the middle of the screen, covering your objects. Drag it to one corner of the screen so that you can see which objects are being highlighted.

Using groups

Using a group is very simple. If a group is selectable, just pick any object in the group to select all the objects in a group. You can then edit the objects in the group as a whole. If you need to temporarily edit one object in a group, change the group's selectable status to No, as described in the previous section. Return the selectable status to Yes to work with the entire group again.

You can change the selectable status of all groups in your drawing by choosing Tools ➪ Options and clicking the Selection tab. Deselect Object Grouping in the Selection Modes section to disable object grouping entirely.

The drawing used in the following Step-by-Step exercise on using groups, `ab10-k.dwg`, is in the `Drawings` folder of the *AutoCAD 2004 Bible* CD-ROM.

Step-by-Step: Using Groups

1. Open `ab10-k.dwg` from your CD-ROM.

2. Save the file as `ab10-14.dwg` in your `AutoCAD Bible` folder. This is a wiring diagram, as shown in Figure 10-47. Set ORTHO and OSNAP on. Set an endpoint running object snap.

3. Type **group** ↵. In the Group Name box of the Object Grouping dialog box, type **switch**. Make sure that the Selectable box is checked. Choose New.

4. At the `Select objects:` prompt, use a window to select the AIR DAMPER switch, picking at ❶ and ❷ in Figure 10-47. Press Enter to end object selection. AutoCAD returns you to the Object Grouping dialog box. Click OK.

5. Choose COPY from the Modify toolbar. At the `Select objects:` prompt, pick anywhere on the switch. The command line informs you of the number of objects selected and that 1 group has been selected. End object selection by pressing Enter. (Grouping must be on in order to select the group.)

Figure 10-47: A wiring diagram

6. At the `Specify base point or displacement, or [Multiple]:` prompt, right-click and choose Multiple. At the `Specify base point:` prompt, use the Endpoint object snap to pick ❸ (at the left quadrant of the small circle). At the `Specify second point of displacement or <use first point as displacement>:` prompt, choose ❹, and then ❺. Press Enter.

7. Save your drawing.

Summary

This chapter covered all the more advanced editing commands. You read about:

✦ Mirroring objects

✦ Creating rectangular and polar arrays

✦ Creating an offset of an object

✦ Aligning objects

✦ Trimming and extending objects

✦ Stretching objects

✦ Lengthening (and shortening) objects

✦ Breaking objects

✦ Creating chamfered corners and fillets for square, beveled, and rounded corners

✦ Using grips to stretch, move, mirror, rotate, and scale objects

✦ Double-clicking objects to edit them

✦ Using the Properties palette, to see the properties of objects and to edit objects

✦ Creating filtered sets of selected objects with the Quick Select feature and the FILTER command

✦ Creating named groups of objects

In the next chapter, I cover layers, colors, linetypes, and lineweights.

✦ ✦ ✦

Organizing Drawings with Layers, Colors, Linetypes, and Lineweights

Until now, you have drawn everything in black or white. Drawing everything in one color is not a very good way to draw—besides, it's boring! If everything is the same color, it is hard to distinguish the various elements of a drawing. If you've followed the exercises throughout this book, you have opened some drawings from the CD-ROM that used various colors and linetypes (such as dashed lines). For example, in some of the architectural drawings, you may have noticed that the walls are a different color than the fixtures (refrigerator, sink, and so on) in the kitchen. When you start to create text and dimensions, covered in Chapters 13, 14, and 15, you will almost always use a color that stands out from the main model you are drawing. You can also create objects with varying widths, called *lineweights*. This use of color, linetype, and lineweight helps to organize your drawings, making them easier to understand.

In AutoCAD, black and white are the same color. If you use the default background of black, the default color is white. If you change the background to white, the same objects appear as black.

Most often, you assign color, linetype, and lineweight to a layer. A layer is simply an organizational tool that lets you organize the display of objects in your drawing. Every object must have a layer, and every layer must have a color, a linetype, and a lineweight. You define layers that meet your

drawing needs. Layers, colors, linetypes, and lineweights are called object properties. You can easily change any object's properties. This chapter explains how to create and change these object properties to organize your drawing.

Working with Layers

The best way to organize your drawing into colors, linetypes, and lineweights is to use layers. Layers offer powerful features that enable you to distinguish all the various elements of your drawing. In an architectural drawing, for example, common layers are walls, doors, windows, plumbing, electrical, fixtures, structural elements, notes (text), dimensions, ceiling, insulation, posts, title block, and so on. Mechanical drawings might use center, hidden, hatch, object, and title block layers. Each discipline has its own conventions, and you might have specific conventions where you work.

Creating layers is an important part of setting up a drawing, in addition to the setup features covered in Chapter 5. Layers should be created and saved in your templates so that they are available to you when you start to draw.

Layers give you many ways to organize your drawing:

- ✦ You can assign different colors, linetypes, and lineweights to layers.

- ✦ You can assign the various colors to different pens in a pen plotter, resulting in a drawing with varying colors or line widths.

- ✦ You can control the visibility of layers. Making a layer invisible lets you focus on just the objects that you need to draw or edit.

- ✦ You can control which objects are plotted.

- ✦ You can lock a layer so that objects on that layer cannot be edited.

Cross-Reference You can also assign a plot style to a layer. A plot style is a group of settings that affects how your drawing is plotted. Chapter 17 covers plot styles.

Understanding layers

Besides having a color, linetype, and lineweight, every layer must have a name. All drawings come with a default layer, called layer 0 (zero). Its color is Black/white, its linetype is Continuous, and its lineweight is Default. (The lineweight for Default is 0.010 inch or 0.25 mm.) All the exercises in this book up to this point have used layer 0. To create a new layer, you must give it a name, a color, a linetype, and a lineweight. You can then start drawing on that layer.

Layers also have four states. These states control visibility, regeneration, editability, and plottability of layers:

✦ **On/Off:** On layers (the default) are visible. Off layers are invisible and are regenerated with the drawing.

✦ **Thawed/Frozen:** Thawed layers (the default) are visible. Frozen layers are invisible and are not regenerated with the drawing. However, when you thaw a frozen layer, it requires a regeneration. If you have floating viewports (covered in Chapter 17), you can also freeze a layer just in the current viewport, or only for new viewports that you create.

✦ **Unlocked/Locked:** Unlocked layers (the default) are visible and editable. Locked layers are visible but cannot be edited.

✦ **Plottable/Not Plottable:** Plottable layers are plotted. Not plottable layers are not plotted. This setting affects only layers that are on or thawed because off and frozen layers are not plotted anyway.

Creating new layers

To create a new layer, choose Layer Properties Manager from the Layers toolbar. AutoCAD opens the Layer Properties Manager, as shown in Figure 11-1.

This dialog box lists all current layers and their properties. You can also create new layers and modify current ones.

Figure 11-1: The Layer Properties Manager after clicking Show Details to open the Details section of the dialog box

Table 11-1 lists the columns in the dialog box and how to use them.

	Table 11-1
	Columns in the Layer Properties Manager Dialog Box

Column Name	How to Change the Setting
Name	Click and type the name of the layer.
On	Click to change the on/off state of a layer.
Freeze in All VP	Click to change the freeze/thaw state of a layer in all viewports.
Lock	Click to change the lock/unlock state of a layer.
Color	Click to change the color of a layer.
Linetype	Click to change the linetype of a layer.
Lineweight	Click to choose a new lineweight.
Plot Style	Click to select a new plot style (Chapter 17 covers plot styles).
Plot	Click to change the plottable/not plottable state of a layer.
Current VP Freeze	Click to change the freeze/thaw state in active floating viewports (only displayed if you have floating viewports and a plot layout is active).
New VP Freeze	Click to change the freeze/thaw state in new floating viewports (only displayed if you have floating viewports and a plot layout is active).

To adjust the display in the Layer Properties Manager, you can do the following:

✦ Change the width of the columns in the Layer Properties Manager dialog box by placing the cursor over the line dividing two column headings and dragging.

✦ Double-click the line dividing two columns to minimize the column width.

✦ Click any column head to sort the layers by that column. Click again to sort in the opposite order.

✦ Resize the entire dialog box by dragging on any side.

Naming the layer

Click New. A new layer appears, named Layer1, as shown in Figure 11-2. The name is highlighted so that you can immediately type in a new name for the layer. Press Enter after you type the name. Notice that AutoCAD has assigned the default color, linetype, and lineweight. If you want the color to be black/white, the linetype to be continuous, and the lineweight to be the default weight, you are finished.

Layer names can be up to 255 characters long and may include spaces. Layer names retain the uppercase/lowercase characters that you type. Layer names may not include the following symbols: < > / \ " ; ? * | , `.

Figure 11-2: The new layer appears as Layer1 and is highlighted so that you can enter the new layer name. AutoCAD assigns the default color, linetype, and lineweight.

Tip To create several new layers at once, click New and type all the layer names you want, separated by commas. If you want a new layer to have the same color and/or linetype as an existing layer — which is very common — choose that existing layer and click New. The new layer will inherit the properties of the selected layer. You can then make any changes you want.

Assigning a color

To change the default color, move the cursor to the color box in the same row as the new layer. Click to open the Select Color dialog box, as shown in Figure 11-3 with the Index Color tab displayed.

Figure 11-3: The Select Color dialog box with the Index Color tab displayed

Click the color that you want. At the bottom of the dialog box, the color's name or number appears along with a sample of the color. Click OK to close the dialog box and return to the Layer Properties Manager dialog box.

Tip If the Details section of the Layer Properties Manager is open, you can click the Color drop-down list and choose one of the standard colors from the list. The Details section is blank when no layer is selected.

Note that the Index Color tab offers you a choice of standard colors, gray shades, and a fuller palette of colors. The standard colors are the original colors AutoCAD offered, and they are the ones most often used, even today. Their advantage is that each color is easily distinguishable from the others. AutoCAD gives these colors both a name and a number, whereas other colors have only a number. The standard colors are yellow, cyan (turquoise), red, green, blue, white, and magenta.

Note AutoCAD gives you a choice of drawing on a black or a white screen. The default screen is black and the default color is white. When you work on a white screen, the default color appears black, but it is still called white. Therefore, if you choose the black color tile in the Select Color dialog box, AutoCAD lists the color as white. To change the screen color, choose Tools ➪ Options ➪ Display ➪ Colors.

For more color choices, click the True Color tab, shown in Figure 11-4.

Figure 11-4: The True Color tab of the Select Color dialog box offers a more precise way to define color.

New Feature The True Color tab is a new feature of AutoCAD 2004. You can define colors more precisely for presentation-quality printouts.

To define a color, first choose the color model from the Color Model drop-down list. You have two choices:

✦ **HSL (Hue, Saturation, Luminance):** Hue is the actual wavelength of light that defines the color. Saturation is the purity or intensity of the color. Luminance is the brightness of the color.

✦ **RGB (Red, Green, Blue):** Defines a color according the intensity of red, green, and blue in the color.

If you choose the HSL color model, specify the color as follows:

1. Specify the hue by dragging the crosshairs horizontally across the colors or type a value from 0 to 360° in the Hue text box.

2. Specify the saturation by dragging the crosshairs vertically over the colors or type a value from 0 to 100% in the Saturation text box.

3. Specify the luminance by dragging the bar on the color slider or type a value from 0 to 100% in the Luminance text box.

 Note When you define a color using the HSL color model, you also see the RGB values displayed in the Select Color dialog box.

If you choose the RGB color model, specify the red color by dragging the color bar or type a value from 1 to 255 in the Red text box. Do the same for the green and blue color values.

You can also choose a color using the Color Books tab, shown in Figure 11-5.

New Feature The Color Books tab is a new feature of AutoCAD 2004.

Figure 11-5: The Color Books tab of the Select Color dialog box

The Color Books tab of the Select Color dialog box displays colors in *color books*. Color books are files that define colors. AutoCAD includes several Pantone color books. Pantone is a commonly used system of matching colors often used for printing on both paper and fabric.

To use a color from a color book, follow these steps:

1. On the Color Books tab of the Select Color dialog box, choose a color book from the Color Book drop-down list.

2. Drag the color slider or use the up and down arrows to choose a "page" of the color book. On the left, you see the colors for that page. A page can hold up to 10 colors.

3. Choose one of the colors on the left side of the dialog box.

4. Click OK.

Assigning a linetype

The default linetype is a continuous line. AutoCAD also provides many other line-types, which are repeating patterns of dashes and/or dots and spaces. Linetypes can also include text and shapes. Linetypes are covered more fully later in this chapter.

To change the default linetype, move the cursor to the linetype in the new layer's row. Click to open the Select Linetype dialog box, as shown in Figure 11-6.

If the linetype that you want appears on the list, click the linetype and choose OK to close the dialog box. If the linetype does not appear, you need to load the linetype. Click Load to open the Load or Reload Linetypes dialog box, shown in Figure 11-7.

Installing Color Books

You can install additional color books. Color book files must have an `.acb` file extension. In addition to Pantone color books, you may be able to find DIC or RAL color specification files.

The default location for color books is in the `Support\Color` subfolder of your `AutoCAD 2004` program folder. If you copy color book files there, you can find them on the Color Books tab of the Select Color dialog box. Another default location is in the `Documents and Settings\username\Application Data\AutoCAD 2004\R16.0\enu\Support\Color` folder. You use this folder for color books that you install. To use color books from another location, follow these steps:

1. Choose Tools ⇨ Options to open the Options dialog box.

2. Choose the Files tab.

3. Double-click the Color Book Locations item.

4. Click Add and then click Browse. Locate the color book file and click OK.

If you have the Select Color dialog box open while you copy a new color book file to a location, close the dialog box and re-open it to access the new colors.

Figure 11-6: The Select Linetype dialog box as it appears before you have loaded any linetypes

Linetypes are stored in text files with the file name extension .lin. AutoCAD's standard linetypes are stored in acad.lin. You can create your own linetypes and store them in acad.lin or another file with the extension .lin. Click File at the top of the dialog box if you want to load a linetype from a file other than acad.lin. Choose the linetype that you want to load and click Open.

Figure 11-7: The Load or Reload Linetypes dialog box

Cross-Reference

See Chapter 31 for a full discussion of creating your own linetypes.

To choose a range of linetypes to load, click the first linetype in the range, press Shift, and click the last linetype in the range. To choose more than one noncontiguous linetype, press Ctrl for each additional linetype you choose. To select all or clear all of the linetypes, right-click in the dialog box and choose the desired option from the shortcut menu.

As soon as you load a linetype and click OK, you return to the Select Linetype dialog box. The loaded linetype now appears on the list. Choose it and click OK. You are now back in the Layer Properties Manager dialog box.

In the Details section of the Layer Properties Manager you can click the Linetype drop-down list and choose from loaded linetypes.

Assigning a lineweight

A lineweight assigns a width to a line. When you give a layer a lineweight, every object on that layer has the same lineweight. A lineweight can help to distinguish various elements of your drawing, both on-screen and on paper. For example, you could use a thicker lineweight to indicate planned construction changes, for dimension lines, or even to represent the true width of an object. The LWT button on the status bar turns on and off the display of lineweights. By default, LWT is off. Lineweights are covered more fully later in this chapter.

To set a lineweight for a layer, click the Lineweight column of that layer to open the Lineweight dialog box, shown in Figure 11-8. Choose a lineweight and click OK.

Figure 11-8: When you click the Lineweight column of the Layer Properties Manager, the Lineweight dialog box opens so that you can choose a lineweight.

Lineweights have the following features:

✦ The default lineweight value for layers and objects is called DEFAULT, which has a value of 0.010 inch or 0.25 mm.

✦ On the Model tab, where you draw, lineweights are displayed in relation to pixels, the unit of measurement for computer screens. A lineweight of 0 is displayed with a width of one pixel. Wider lineweights are calculated proportionally to the actual width of the lineweight. The lineweight display on the Model tab does not change as you zoom in or out.

✦ On Layout tabs (covered in Chapter 17), AutoCAD displays lineweights in real-world units as they will be plotted. Lineweights act like other objects in your drawing and they look bigger or smaller as you zoom in and out.

✦ By default, lineweights are measured in millimeters. You can format lineweights by choosing Format ⇨ Lineweight. AutoCAD opens the Lineweight Settings dialog box, shown in Figure 11-9. The Lineweights section lists available lineweights. Choose a default lineweight from the Default drop-down list. The default is 0.01 inch or 0.25 mm. The Adjust Display Scale slider determines how lineweights are displayed on the Model tab. Adjust this setting if you use several closely related lineweights but can't distinguish them on your screen. The Display Lineweight check box turns the display of lineweights on and off. (See the next bullet for an easier way to do this.)

✦ You can turn the display of lineweights on and off—just click the LWT button on the status bar.

If you don't want to use lineweights, you can just ignore them and let AutoCAD display every object using the default lineweight.

Figure 11-9: The Lineweight Settings dialog box lets you format how lineweights are measured and displayed.

After you have set your new layer's color, linetype, and lineweight, you are ready to use the layer. Click OK to close the Layer Properties Manager.

On the CD-ROM

The drawing used in the following Step-by-Step exercise on creating layers, ab11-a.dwg, is in the Drawings folder of the *AutoCAD 2004 Bible* CD-ROM.

Step-by-Step: Creating a New Layer

1. Open ab11-a.dwg from the CD-ROM.

2. Save the file as ab11-01.dwg in your AutoCAD Bible folder.

3. Choose Layer Properties Manager from the Layers toolbar to open the Layer Properties Manager.

4. Choose New. A new layer named Layer1 appears, highlighted. Type **Walls** ↵ as the name for the new layer.

5. Click the color square in the Color column to open the Select Color dialog box. Choose the blue square from the Standard Colors and click OK.

6. Choose New again to create another new layer. Type **Hidden** ↵.

7. If the Details section of the dialog box is not displayed, click the Show details button. Click the Color drop-down box in the Details section and choose Select Color.

8. In the Select Color dialog box, click the True Color tab. From the Color Model drop-down list, choose RGB. In the Color text box, type **141, 218, 189**. Press Tab. You should see a teal (blue-green) color. Click OK.

9. In the main layer listing, click Continuous in the same row as the Hidden layer to open the Select Linetype dialog box. Click Load to open the Load or Reload Linetypes dialog box. Scroll down until you see the HIDDEN linetype. Choose it and click OK. In the Select Linetype dialog box, choose HIDDEN and click OK. Click OK to close the Layer Properties Manager.

10. Click the Layer Control drop-down box on the Layers toolbar to see the two layers you just created listed there. Click again to close the box.

11. Save your drawing.

Using layers

To use a layer you have just created, click Current in the Layer Properties Manager. Then click OK to return to your drawing. Objects you create now are drawn on that layer and display with their color, linetype, and lineweight. (The lineweight only shows if the LWT button on the status bar is on.)

AutoCAD puts all objects that you draw on the current layer. After you have the layers you need, you need to switch from layer to layer as you draw. You can continue to choose Layers on the Layer Properties Manager dialog box, click the name of a layer, click Current, and then click OK. But there is an easier way — the Layer Control drop-down list on the Layers toolbar, as shown in Figure 11-10.

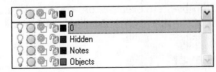

Figure 11-10: The Layer Control drop-down list

The Layer Control drop-down list has two display modes:

✦ If no object is selected, it displays the current layer.

✦ If one or more objects are selected, it displays the layer of the selected object(s).

To check the current layer, make sure no object is selected. If necessary, press Esc to deselect any objects.

Note When objects on varying layers are selected, the Layer Control list goes blank, indicating that more than one layer is included in the selection.

To open the Layer Control drop-down list, click its arrow. You see a list of all your layers, including their states and colors. Pass the mouse over the items, and a tooltip tells you what they mean. The Layer Control drop-down list has three functions:

✦ It switches the current layer so that you can draw on a new layer.

✦ It changes the following states of any specific layer on the list:

• On/Off

• Frozen/Thawed

• Frozen in Current Viewport/Thawed in Current Viewport

• Locked/Unlocked

✦ It changes the layer of a selected object.

Take the time to learn how to use this drop-down list; it can save you a great deal of time. To change other states of a layer (such as plottable/not plottable), click Layers Properties Manager on the Layers toolbar to open the Layer Properties Manager.

Switching the current layer

To switch the current layer, click the Layer Control drop-down list arrow and click the name of the layer that you want to be current. Be careful to click only the name—otherwise, you may change the layer's state. Remember that this only works if no object is currently selected—so you may need to press Esc first to deselect all objects.

After you click a new layer name, the drop-down list automatically closes.

The Layer Previous button on the Layers toolbar switches you to the last layer you used. Click it another time and you are in the layer before that. Use Layer Previous as a shortcut to finding and choosing the last layer you used on the Layer Control drop-down list.

Changing a layer's state

After you create a layer, you can manage that layer—and all the objects on that layer—by changing its states. You can change some layer states through the Layer Control drop-down list; others must be changed in the Layer Properties Manager. The layer states each have different properties and uses:

✦ **On/Off:** Turn layers off when objects on those layers interfere with the drawing process. For example, if you want to edit only objects on your Object layer, but objects exist on other layers nearby, you can turn off the other layers and easily select the objects on the Object layer with a window. Then turn the other layers back on. The on/off state is available on the Layer Control drop-down list.

✦ **Thawed/Frozen:** You can freeze layers for reasons similar to those that lead you to turn off layers. In general, freeze layers when you want to work without those layers for a longer period of time. The thawed/frozen state is available on the Layer Control drop-down list.

✦ **Thawed/Frozen in Current Viewport:** You can freeze or thaw layers in some floating viewports but not in others. For example, you may want to display dimensions in one viewport but not in others; to do so freeze your dimensions layer in all the viewports except one. This state is available on the Layer Control drop-down list if you are working on a layout. You can also check the Freeze in Current Viewport checkbox in the Details section of the Layer Properties Manager.

✦ **Thawed/Frozen in All Viewports:** You can freeze or thaw layers in all viewports if you want to work without seeing those layers at all. This state is available in the Freeze in All VP column of the Layer Properties Manager. It also affects viewports on the Model tab. You can also check the Freeze in All Viewports check box in the Details section of the Layer Properties Manager.

✦ **Thawed/Frozen in New Viewports:** You can also freeze or thaw layers in future viewports that you create. For example, after you display dimensions or text in one viewport, you may want to make sure they will not appear in any new viewports that you create. This state is available in the New VP Freeze column of the Layer Properties Manager or by checking the Freeze in New Viewports check box in the Details section of the Layer Properties Manager, if you are working on a layout.

Cross-Reference See Chapter 17 for an explanation of floating viewports and layouts.

✦ **Unlocked/Locked:** Lock a layer when you want to ensure that objects on that layer are not changed. You can still use objects on locked layers for reference—for example, you can use their object snaps. The unlocked/locked state is available on the Layer Control drop-down list.

✦ **Plottable/Not Plottable:** Make a layer not plottable when you want to create reference text or revision marks on your drawing but don't want to plot them. Another example: If you have a drawing that contains both actual and planned structures, you could plot showing only the actual structures. Being able to change a layer's plottable state makes it possible for you to create variations on your drawing, perhaps for different users, such as electricians, plumbers, and roofers. The plottable/not plottable state is available in the Plot column of the Layer Properties Manager or click the Do Not Plot check box in the Details section.

Tip

Both the off and frozen states make layers invisible. AutoCAD introduced the frozen and thawed layer states to reduce regeneration time—and that's the main difference between On/Off and Thawed/Frozen layer visibility options. However, today's computers are faster, and AutoCAD has since introduced several ways to avoid regeneration while panning and zooming—such as Aerial View, Zoom Dynamic, and real-time zooming and panning. Also, remember that thawing a layer causes a regeneration, whereas turning a layer back on only causes a redraw. As a result, you might actually save a regeneration by using On/Off instead of Thawed/Frozen.

Click any of the state icons to toggle a layer's state. For example, if you want to freeze a layer, click its sun and it switches to a snowflake. Table 11-2 shows the icons for each state.

Table 11-2
Layer State Icons

State	Icon	State	Icon
On		Off	
Thawed (in all viewports)		Frozen (in all viewports)	
Thawed (in current viewport)		Frozen (in current viewport)	
Thawed (in new viewports)		Frozen (in new viewports)	
Unlocked		Locked	
Plottable		Not plottable	

When you change a layer's state, the drop-down list stays open so that you can change the state of more than one layer at a time. Click the top of the list to close it.

Caution

Be careful when editing a drawing with frozen or off layers—it's easy to forget about them. For example, you could move a whole section of your drawing and leave the frozen objects in that section behind.

Saving layer states

Often you work with sets of layer states. For example, you may lock certain layers during part of the editing process so that you don't change objects on those layers inadvertently. You may also set some layers as not plottable just before final plotting but want them plotted for a draft plot. You may also want to temporarily change the properties of certain layers — color, linetype, lineweight, and plot style — and then change them back.

You could spend a lot of time adjusting all these layer states and properties over and over. Instead, you can save and restore sets of layer states — the properties and states of all the layers in a drawing. The save layer states feature automates the process of restoring layer states and properties by saving the set of all layer states and properties. After you save this set, you can restore it at any time. AutoCAD uses the term *layer states* to include the set of all layer states as well as their properties.

You can also export layer state settings to a file. You can then use the layer state settings in another drawing with the same or similar layers.

To save a layer state, follow these steps:

1. Set all of the layer states and properties the way you want them. Usually, you have already done this and should save the state before making changes that you plan to reverse later on.

2. Choose Layer Properties Manager from the Layers toolbar to open the Layer Properties Manager.

3. Click Save State to open the Save Layer States dialog box, shown in Figure 11-11.

Figure 11-11: The Save Layer States dialog box

4. Type a name for your layer state in the New layer state name text box.

5. Choose which of the layer states and properties you want to save.

Caution　States and properties that you do not save are not affected later when you restore the layer state. For example, if you save only the on/off state and then change both a layer's on/off state and its color, when you restore the layer state, only the on/off state is returned to its original setting; the layer retains its new color.

 6. Click OK.

To restore a layer state, open the Layer Properties Manager and click State Manager to open the Layer States Manager, shown in Figure 11-12. Choose the layer state that you want to restore and click Restore. Then click OK to close the Layer Properties Manager.

Figure 11-12: The Layer States Manager

The Layer States Manager enables you to manage layer states in the following ways:

 ✦ **Restore:** Select the layer state you want to restore and click Restore.

 ✦ **Edit:** Opens the Edit Layer State dialog box. You can change which states and properties are saved.

 ✦ **Rename:** Renames the layer state.

 ✦ **Delete:** Deletes the layer state.

 ✦ **Import:** Imports a layer state that has been previously exported as a .las file. Importing a layer state gives you access to layer states that others have saved.

 ✦ **Export:** Saves the settings of a layer state in a .las file. Exporting a layer state gives others access to your layer state settings.

After you finish using the Layer States Manager, click Close to close the dialog box.

The Express Tools contains many layer-related tools that you can add to your arsenal. Many of these layer tools can save you considerable time over the course of creating a drawing. Table 11-3 explains them briefly. See Appendix A on the CD-ROM for information on installing Express Tools.

Table 11-3
Express Tools Layer Commands

Layer Name	Menu	Description
LAYWALK	Express ⇨ Layers ⇨ Layer Walk	A full-featured command that helps you see which objects are on which layers. You can list the number of objects on each layer, count the total number of layers, save layer states, and purge unused layers, using the dialog box and the shortcut menu.
LAYMCH	Express ⇨ Layers ⇨ Layer Match	Changes the layer of selected objects to match that of a selected object.
LAYCUR	Express ⇨ Layers ⇨ Change to Current Layer	Changes the selected object's layer to the current layer.
COPYTOLAYER	Express ⇨ Layers ⇨ Copy Objects to New Layer	Copies objects while changing the copy to the layer you specify.
LAYISO	Express ⇨ Layers ⇨ Layer Isolate	Turns off all layers except the layer of an object you select, so that you can isolate a specific layer.
LAYVPI	Isolate Layer to Current Viewport	Freezes all layers except the layer of an object you select in all viewports except the current one, isolating the selected layer in the current viewport.
LAYOFF	Express ⇨ Layers ⇨ Layer Off	Turns the layer of the selected object(s) off.
LAYON	Express ⇨ Layers ⇨ Turn All Layers On	Turns all layers on.
LAYFRZ	Express ⇨ Layers ⇨ Layer Freeze	Freezes the layer of the selected object(s).
LAYTHW	Express ⇨ Layers ⇨ Thaw All Layers	Thaws all layers.
LAYLCK	Express ⇨ Layers ⇨ Layer Lock	Locks the layer of the selected object(s)
LAYULK	Express ⇨ Layers ⇨ Layer Unlock	Unlocks all layers
LAYMRG	Express ⇨ Layers ⇨ Layer Merge	Changes the layer of all objects on the first layer selected to the second layer selected. The first layer is purged.
LAYDEL	Express ⇨ Layers ⇨ Layer Delete	Deletes objects from the specified layer and purges that layer.

Changing an existing object's layer

Sometimes you need to change the layer of an object or objects you have already drawn. You can do this easily by selecting one or more objects and clicking the layer name that you want for the object in the Layer Control drop-down list. The list automatically closes.

You can also change an object's layer in the Properties palette. Choose Properties on the Standard toolbar. Use the Properties palette if you want to change more than one property of an object at one time.

Caution　　It's easy to inadvertently change an object's layer. Make sure objects are not selected (press Esc) if you are about to use the Layer Control drop-down box just to change the current layer.

Making an object's layer current

If you are adding an object, you usually want to draw on the same layer as an existing object. You could select the object to see what layer it's on, press Esc to deselect the object, and then choose that layer from the Layer Control drop-down list to make it current. However, this process is easier with the Make Object's Layer Current button on the Layers toolbar. Simply select an object and click the button. AutoCAD makes that object's layer current.

On the CD-ROM　　The drawing used in the following Step-by-Step exercise on working with layers, ab11-b.dwg, is in the Drawings folder of the *AutoCAD 2004 Bible* CD-ROM.

Step-by-Step: Working with Layers

1. Open ab11-b.dwg from the CD-ROM.

2. Save the file as ab11-02.dwg in your AutoCAD Bible folder. This drawing is shown in Figure 11-13. The current layer is 0. Make sure OSNAP is on. Set running object snaps for endpoint and quadrant.

3. Click the Layer Control drop-down list and click Pipes to change the current layer to Pipes.

4. Start the LINE command. Draw a line from ❶ to ❷ in Figure 11-13, using the Quadrant running object snap.

5. Click the Layer Control drop-down list and click Object to change the current layer to Object.

6. Click the Layer Control drop-down list and click the On/Off icon (the light bulb) of the Dim layer. Click again at the top of the list to close it.

Figure 11-13: This gas extraction well
plan drawing needs to be completed.

Thanks to the Army Corps of Engineers for this drawing.

7. Start the CIRCLE command. Right-click and choose 2p to use the two point
 option. Draw a circle from the endpoint of ❸ to ❹ in Figure 11-13 using the
 Endpoint running object snap.

8. Without changing the layer, start the CIRCLE command and again use the 2p
 option. Draw a circle between the endpoints at ❺ and ❻ in Figure 11-13.

9. The last circle was drawn on the wrong layer. To change its layer, select the
 circle. Then click the Layer Control drop-down list and choose Pipes. Press
 Esc to remove the grips and see the result. The circle is now on the Pipes
 layer. Notice that the current layer is still Object in the Layer Control display.

10. Pick any red object (the Pipes layer). Choose Make Object's Layer
 Current from the Layers toolbar. The Pipes layer is now the current layer.
 Draw a line from the right quadrant of the circle at ❶ to the left quadrant of
 the circle at ❺ and ❻ in Figure 11-13.

11. You want to draw a line on the Object layer. Because that is the previous
 layer you used, click Layer Previous on the Layers toolbar. The Object
 layer is now the current layer. Draw a line from the endpoint at ❼ to the end-
 point at ❽.

12. Pick any text to see what layer it is on. The Layer Control drop-down box
 changes to show the Text layer. Press Esc to deselect the text. Now choose the
 words GAS EXTRACTION WELL PLAN at the bottom of the drawing. Click the
 Layer Control drop-down box and choose Text. Press Esc to remove the grips.

13. Save your drawing. It should look like Figure 11-14.

Figure 11-14: The completed drawing

Later in this chapter, I explain how to import layers from other drawings and translate layers from one drawing to another.

Modifying layers

Sometimes you need to change the properties of a layer, such as its color or linetype. This is a powerful tool because every object on that layer is automatically regenerated with the new properties. Other layer housekeeping tasks are renaming and deleting layers. You use the Layer Properties Manager for these functions.

Sorting columns

If you have many layers in a drawing, sorting can help you find the layers you need to work on. You can sort the layer listing in a drawing by any column, by clicking once on the column title. Click again to see the list in reverse order. (If sorting by layer name does not appear to be working, increase the value for the MAXSORT system variable, which determines the maximum number of symbols that AutoCAD sorts. Type **maxsort** ↵ on the command line and enter a larger number. Press Enter.) Long layer names display a tooltip with the entire layer name.

Filtering the layer list

Some complex drawings may have dozens of layers. This can make it difficult to find the layer you want to change in the Layer Properties Manager. You can filter the layer list so that you only see the layers you want. This makes it easy to change a group of layers at once. Click the Named Layer Filters drop-down list and pick the filter that you want.

To display all layers except the ones specified by the filter, click Invert filter. If you want the Layer Control listing on the Layers toolbar to be filtered in the same way, check Apply to Layers toolbar.

If AutoCAD's standard filters don't meet your needs, you can create your own filter. Click the ellipsis button to the right of the drop-down arrow to open the Named Layer Filters dialog box, shown in Figure 11-15.

You can set criteria by name, state (on/off, thawed/frozen, thawed/frozen for current and new floating viewports, unlocked/locked, plot/don't plot), color, lineweight, linetype, and plot style. You can use wildcards to specify any of the named properties. The two most common wildcards characters are * (asterisk), which replaces any number of characters, and ?, which replaces any single character. Figure 11-15 shows the layer name filter set to d*. The color is also specified as blue. Therefore, only layers whose names start with the letter d and are blue will be listed.

After you set the criteria for your filter, type a name in the Filter name text box, click Add, and click Close. Next, choose your named filter from the Named Layer Filters drop-down list. AutoCAD filters the layer list. You can invert named filters that you create and apply them to the listing on the Layers toolbar.

Figure 11-15: The Named Layer Filters dialog box

Tip When you work with a large number of layers, think carefully about how you name them. Naming layers in groups is common. For example, if you have several text layers, you could name them Text Title, Text Notes, and Text Schedule. A systematic layer-naming scheme makes it easy to filter the layers you need, which in turn makes it easy to make changes to groups of layers.

Changing a layer's color, linetype, and lineweight

To change a layer's color, choose Layer Properties Manager from the Layers toolbar. AutoCAD opens the Layer Properties Manager. You can change the color in two ways:

✦ Click Show Details if the lower section of the dialog box is not visible. Click the name of the layer that you want to modify. In the Details section, click the Color drop-down list and choose the color that you want. (If you don't want to choose one of the standard colors, choose Other to open the Select Color dialog box, choose a color, and then click OK.) After you have selected the color, click OK to close the Layer Properties Manager dialog box.

✦ Choose the color swatch of the layer that you want to modify. AutoCAD opens the Select Color dialog box. Choose a color and click OK twice to return to your drawing.

For more information about choosing colors, see "Assigning a color" earlier in this chapter.

To change a layer's linetype, follow the same procedure as for changing the color. The only difference is that the Details section doesn't let you load linetypes. If you need to choose a linetype that is not on the list, click the linetype of the layer to open the Select Linetype dialog box. There you can either choose a loaded linetype or load a linetype if necessary.

To change a layer's lineweight, open the Layer Properties Manager and click the lineweight for any layer. Choose a new lineweight from the Lineweight dialog box.

Tip

You can modify more than one layer at a time. In the Layer Properties Manager dialog box, right-click and choose Select All to choose all the layers. Choose Clear All to deselect all layers. You can choose a range of layers by clicking the first in the range, pressing Shift, and clicking the last in the range. Finally, you can choose individual layers by pressing Ctrl for each additional layer. Changes you make to color, linetype, or lineweight affect all the selected layers.

Renaming layers

Thinking out your layer naming scheme in advance is best. Many disciplines and organizations have layer naming standards. However, sometimes you simply need to rename a layer.

To rename a layer, choose Layer Properties Manager from the Layers toolbar to open the Layer Properties Manager. Click the name of the layer, and then click a second time. A border appears, and the name is highlighted. Type the new name and press Enter.

Note

You cannot rename layer 0. Layer 0 is the default layer and always remains the same.

Deleting layers

To delete a layer, choose Layer Properties Manager from the Layers toolbar to open the Layer Properties Manager. Click the name of the layer. Choose Delete and click OK.

Note You cannot delete the current layer or any layer that has objects on it. (Where would those objects go?) You also cannot delete layer 0, which is the default layer. Finally, you cannot delete layers from external references (covered in Chapter 19).

Purging layers and linetypes

Layer and linetype definitions add to the size of your drawing because they are kept in the drawing's database. Therefore, eliminating layers and linetypes that you are not using is worthwhile. You can delete them, but sometimes it is hard to know which layers contain no objects. The PURGE command lets you delete many types of unused definitions, including layers and linetypes.

To purge layers and linetypes, choose File ➪ Drawing Utilities ➪ Purge. AutoCAD displays the Purge dialog box, shown in Figure 11-16.

Figure 11-16: The Purge dialog box

Note The Incremental save percentage option may prevent a purge during a drawing session from removing all unreferenced layers or linetypes from the drawing. To avoid this, you can either set incremental save to zero or save the drawing and reopen it and then immediately use the PURGE command. To set this option, choose Tools ➪ Options ➪ Open and Save tab.

At the top of the dialog box, you can choose to view objects that you can purge or objects that you cannot purge. Why would you want to view objects that you cannot purge? Sometimes it is hard to figure out why you can't purge a certain object and the new dialog box has a handy feature that lets you select an object and view possible reasons why it cannot be purged.

To start purging, choose View items you can purge. A plus sign (+) next to each type of object indicates that it contains purgeable objects. For example, Figure 11-16 indicates that you can purge layers, and shapes. Click the plus sign to display the specific items.

To purge an individual item, select it and click Purge. Check Confirm each item to be purged if you want to see a dialog box asking you to confirm each purge. Click Purge All to purge all possible items. Check Purge nested items to purge items within other named objects. Usually, these are layers, linetypes, and so on inside blocks.

Tip You can select more than one item at a time to purge. To select an additional item, press Ctrl as you click. To select a contiguous group of items, click the first item, press and hold Shift, and select the last item in the group.

After you're done purging, click Close to close the Purge dialog box.

On the CD-ROM The drawing used in the following Step-by-Step exercise on modifying layers, ab11-c.dwg, is in the Drawings folder of the *AutoCAD 2004 Bible* CD-ROM.

Step-by-Step: Modifying Layers

1. Open ab11-c.dwg from the CD-ROM.

2. Save the file as ab11-03.dwg in your AutoCAD Bible folder. This drawing is shown in Figure 11-17.

3. Choose Layer Properties Manager from the Layers toolbar to open the Layer Properties Manager. Next to the Named layer filters drop-down arrow, click the ellipsis button. In the Filter name text box, type **M layers**. In the Layer Name box, type **m*** to list all layers starting with the letter *m*. Click Add, and then click Close. In the Layer Properties Manager, click the drop-down list arrow and choose M layers. The list now looks like Figure 11-18.

4. Click the top layer. Press Shift and click the next-to-last layer. All the layers except for Mydims are selected. In the Details section (click Show Details if this section is not visible), click the Linetype drop-down list arrow and choose Dashed. Notice that all the selected layers now have a dashed linetype. Click OK to return to the drawing. AutoCAD regenerates the drawing with the new dashed linetypes.

5. Choose Layer Properties Manager from the Layers toolbar to open the Layer Properties Manager again. Choose Mydims. Click it a second time so that a black border appears around the layer name. Type **Titles** ⏎. The name of the layer is changed. Click OK.

Figure 11-17: This drawing has 44 layers.

Thanks to Michael J. Lemmons of Winston Products Company in Louisville, Kentucky, for this drawing.

Figure 11-18: The Layer Properties Manager now shows only layers starting with the letter *M*.

6. Start the ERASE command and select any object on the title block (it is all one object) and the three labels FRONT, TOP, and RIGHT SIDE. Press Enter to end the command.

7. Choose Layer Properties Manager from the Layers toolbar to open the Layer Properties Manager dialog box again. Notice that the Titles layer is not on the list because this layer no longer starts with the letter M. Click the Named layer filters drop-down list arrow and choose Show all layers. Scroll down the list of layers and choose Titles. Click Delete. AutoCAD deletes the layer because it no longer has any objects on it. Click OK to close the dialog box.

8. Save your drawing.

Changing Object Color, Linetype, and Lineweight

The properties of layers — color, linetype, lineweight — can also apply directly to objects. You can assign a color, linetype, and lineweight to an object. You can also set a current color, linetype, and lineweight so that all future objects you draw have those properties regardless of the properties assigned to their layer. In most cases, you should avoid assigning properties directly to objects because the organizational value of layers is lost.

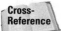

You can also assign plot styles to objects. See Chapter 17 for more information.

Changing an object's color

You can control an object's color by using the Color Control drop-down list on the Properties toolbar, as shown in Figure 11-19. For more information about choosing colors, see "Assigning a color" earlier in this chapter. As with the Layer Control drop-down list, the Color Control drop-down list shows the color of any selected object. When you create a layer, assign it a color, and draw with that layer, AutoCAD displays the color as `ByLayer`, as shown in Figure 11-20.

Figure 11-19: The Color Control drop-down list on the Properties toolbar

The ByLayer color means that the color of the object is taken from the color of the object's layer. At the same time that you see the selected object's color in the Color Control drop-down list, you can look over to the Layer Control drop-down list and confirm the color assignment of the object's layer.

The ByBlock color creates objects by using color 7 (white or black, depending on the screen color), but if the objects are placed in a block, the block takes on the current color when inserted. (For information about blocks, see Chapter 18.)

Figure 11-20: The color of the selected object (some text) is ByLayer

The best way to organize a drawing is to assign colors by layer. It can be confusing if related elements, such as centerlines in a mechanical drawing, appear in different colors. Also, if you see another line with the same color and linetype as most centerlines, you may assume it's a centerline in the wrong place. It is standard practice throughout the AutoCAD world to organize colors by layer.

Colors have a special significance because when you plot, you can assign colors to pens — although you can also use AutoCAD 2004's plot styles (see Chapter 17). If you use a color-based system, color is the basis you use for plotting with various width pens or colors. You may want to temporarily change the color of an object to emphasize it in a plot or for some other reason. However, you should generally refrain from directly changing the color of objects.

If you need to change the color of an object, here are two ways to do it:

✦ To change just an object's color, select the object. Click the Color Control drop-down list and choose the color that you want.

✦ If you want to change other properties at the same time, select the object and choose Properties from the Standard toolbar. AutoCAD opens the Properties palette, shown in Figure 11-21. In this window you can change all the properties of the object. To change the color, choose Color and click the drop-down arrow that appears. Choose the color that you want.

Tip

You can always change an object's color back to ByLayer, using the same Color Control drop-down list.

Figure 11-21: The Properties palette

Changing the current color

When you change the current color, all future objects are drawn using that color, regardless of their layer. In general, you should do this only when you have a special need for two objects to be on one layer but have different colors. An example might be text in a title block. You might want the text to have the same layer so that you can freeze it and thaw it (or turn it on and off) easily without having to remember that the text and title block are on two separate layers. If you also want part of the text to have a different color, change the current color before typing in that part of the text. Remember to change the current color back to ByLayer before drawing anything else.

To change the current color, make sure no object is selected. Then click the Color drop-down list and choose the color you want. To use a color not on the list,

choose Select color to open the Select Color dialog box. (See the section "Assigning a color" earlier in this chapter for more information on assigning colors.) To change the current color back to ByLayer, click the Color drop-down list and choose ByLayer.

You have an opportunity to do an exercise on changing colors later in this chapter.

Changing an object's linetype

Linetypes work according to the same principles as colors. You can change the linetype of an existing object or objects. You can control an object's linetype by using the Linetype Control drop-down list on the Properties toolbar, shown in Figure 11-22. The Linetype Control drop-down list shows the linetype of any selected object. When you create a layer, assign it a linetype, and draw with that layer, AutoCAD displays the linetype as ByLayer.

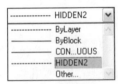

Figure 11-22: The Linetype Control drop-down list on the Properties toolbar

The ByLayer linetype simply means that the linetype of the object is taken from the linetype of the object's layer.

The best way to organize a drawing is to assign linetypes by layer. It can be confusing if related elements, such as plat borders in a surveyor's drawing, appear in different linetypes. Also, if you see another line with the same color and linetype as most plat borders, you may assume it's a plat border in the wrong place. It is common practice throughout the AutoCAD world to organize linetypes by layer.

If you need to change the linetype of an object, you have two options:

✦ To change an object's linetype, select the object. Click the Linetype Control drop-down list and choose the linetype that you want.

✦ Select the object and choose Properties from the Standard toolbar. AutoCAD opens the Properties palette, shown earlier in Figure 11-21. To change an object's linetype, click Linetype, and then click the drop-down arrow that appears. Choose from one of the linetypes.

Tip You can always change an object's linetype back to ByLayer, using the same Linetype Control drop-down list.

As discussed in the section, "Assigning a linetype," earlier in this chapter, you may need to load a linetype before you can use it. To load a linetype, choose Linetype Control from the Properties toolbar. Scroll down to the bottom of the list and choose Other to open the Linetype Manager. Choose Load to open the Load or Reload Linetypes dialog box, choose the linetype file (if not `acad.lin`), and choose the linetype that you want to load. Click OK. Choose the linetype again in the Linetype Manager and click OK to return to your drawing.

To filter the list of Linetypes, choose from the Linetype Filters drop-down list box in the Linetype Manager.

Changing the current linetype

You can also change the current linetype. When you change the current linetype, all future objects you draw have that linetype and are not drawn according to their layer's assigned linetype. In general, you should do this only when you have a special need for two objects to be on one layer but have different linetypes. An example might be a table containing notes in one corner of a drawing. You might want the lines that make up the table to have the same layer so that you can freeze it and thaw it (or turn it on and off) easily without having to remember that the table is on two separate layers. If you also want some of the lines to have a different linetype, change the current linetype before adding those lines. Remember to change the current linetype back to ByLayer before drawing anything else.

To change the current linetype, click the Linetype drop-down list and choose the linetype you want, first making sure no objects are currently selected. To change the current linetype back to ByLayer, click the Linetype drop-down list and choose ByLayer.

Changing an object's lineweight

Lineweights let you represent objects with varying line widths. The widths can represent the width of a pen in a pen plotter that will be used to plot that object. Lineweights can also be used as an organizational tool, to distinguish certain types of objects just as colors and linetypes do. Finally, you can use lineweights to represent the actual properties of objects, such as the width of wires in an electrical schematic.

Lineweights work according to the same principles as colors and linetypes. You can control an object's lineweight by using the Lineweight Control drop-down list on the Properties toolbar, as shown in Figure 11-23. The Lineweight Control drop-down list shows the lineweight of any selected object. When you create a layer, assign it a lineweight, and draw with that layer, AutoCAD displays the lineweight as ByLayer.

Figure 11-23: The Lineweight drop-down list on the Properties toolbar

As with colors and linetypes, the best way to organize a drawing is to assign lineweights by layer. If you need to change the lineweight of an object, here are two ways to do it:

✦ Select the object. Click the Lineweight Control drop-down list and choose the lineweight that you want.

✦ Select the object and choose Properties from the Standard toolbar. AutoCAD opens the Properties palette. To change an object's lineweight, click Lineweight, and then click the drop-down arrow that appears. Choose from one of the lineweights.

Changing the current lineweight

You can also change the current lineweight. When you change the current lineweight, all future objects you draw have that lineweight and are not drawn according to their layer's assigned lineweight.

To change the current lineweight, click the Lineweight drop-down list and choose the lineweight that you want, first making sure no objects are currently selected. To change the current lineweight back to ByLayer, click the Lineweight drop-down list and choose ByLayer.

The drawing used in the following Step-by-Step exercise on changing colors, linetypes, and lineweights, ab11-d.dwg, is in the Drawings folder of the *AutoCAD 2004 Bible* CD-ROM.

Step-by-Step: Changing Colors, Linetypes, and Lineweights

1. Open ab11-d.dwg from the CD-ROM.

2. Save the file as ab11-04.dwg in your AutoCAD Bible folder. This is an elevation view of a lavatory cabinet, shown in Figure 11-24.

Figure 11-24: A lavatory cabinet

Thanks to the Army Corps of Engineers for this drawing.

3. Pick one of the reflection lines in the mirror. Notice that the color is red but the layer's color, as shown in the Layer Control drop-down list, is Magenta. Select all the reflection lines. Click the Color Control drop-down list and choose ByLayer from the top of the list. Press Esc to remove the grips.

4. Select the green dimension at the bottom of the cabinet. (The dimension is all one object.) To make it more visible, click the Color Control drop-down list and choose Red. Press Esc to see the result.

5. Pick the lines at ❶ and ❷ in Figure 11-24. Click the Linetype Control drop-down list and choose the Hidden linetype. Press Esc so that the hidden lines are no longer selected.

6. Select the dashed arc that represents the bottom curvature of the sink. Click the Lineweight Control drop-down list and choose 0.30 mm. Press Esc. Click LWT on the status bar to turn on the display of lineweights and see the result.

7. Click the Color Control drop-down list box and choose Cyan to make it the current color.

8. Start the RECTANG command. Draw a rectangle inside the left cabinet. Use the COPY command to copy the rectangle to the right cabinet. (To copy, use an intersection object snap at point ❸ as the base point and ❹ as the second point of displacement.) The rectangles are drawn in Cyan.

9. Save your drawing. It should look like Figure 11-25.

Figure 11-25: The finished cabinet

Working with Linetype Scales

A noncontinuous linetype is a repeating pattern of dots, dashes, and spaces. (Linetypes can also include repeating text or shapes.) You may find that the linetype patterns in your drawing are too long or short for clarity. The linetype scale may even be so big or so small that the line looks continuous. How often the pattern is repeated is affected by three factors:

✦ The linetype definition

✦ The global linetype scale

✦ The individual object's linetype scale

Changing linetype spacing by using a different linetype

One choice is to change the linetype. There are a number of linetypes that come in short, medium, and long variations, such as Dashedx2, Dashed, and Dashed2, as shown in Figure 11-26.

Figure 11-26: A number of AutoCAD's standard linetypes come in three variations, such as Dashedx2, Dashed, and Dashed2.

AutoCAD's `acad.lin` contains a number of ISO linetypes that meet the specifications of the International Standards Organization. Your organization or field of specialty may require the use of these linetypes. If so, you should know that the ISO linetype pattern definitions are much longer than AutoCAD's other definitions. Figure 11-27 shows the ISO dash linetype and AutoCAD's dashed linetype. You may need to make adjustments to the linetype scale as a result.

Figure 11-27: A comparison of AutoCAD's dashed linetype and ISO dash linetype

Changing linetype spacing by changing the global linetype scale

Another choice is to change the global linetype scale, which affects all noncontinuous linetypes in your drawing. AutoCAD multiplies the linetype definition by the global linetype scale to calculate the length of each repetition of the linetype:

✦ Linetype scales larger than 1 result in longer sections — and fewer repetitions of the linetype definition per unit.

✦ Linetype scales smaller than 1 result in shorter sections — and more repetitions of the linetype definition per unit.

When you change the linetype scale, AutoCAD regenerates the drawing and changes all the linetypes. Figure 11-28 shows three versions of a drawing with linetypes at linetype scales of 0.5, 1, and 2. As you can see, a scale of 2 is too large and a scale of 0.5 is too small. A scale of 1 is just right. (Goldilocks would have been happy with it.)

Linetype scale = 0.5 Linetype scale = 1 Linetype scale = 2

Figure 11-28: Three versions of a drawing, using linetype scales of 0.5, 1, and 2

For purposes of drawing, you simply want to make sure that you can distinguish the linetype both when you can see the entire drawing on the screen and when you zoom in close. The main reason to scale linetypes is for plotting. A linetype scale that works for a drawing of a house on-screen may appear continuous when you plot it at a scale factor of 1=96.

If you want the linetype to appear exactly according to its definition, use the scale factor for the linetype scale. Chapter 5 covers scale factors. If the scale factor doesn't give you the results you want, try a linetype scale of one-quarter to one-half the scale factor—in the 1=96 example, you might use a linetype scale of 24 or 48.

To change the linetype scale, choose Format ➪ Linetype to open the Linetype Manager, shown in Figure 11-29. Click Show Details if the lower portion of the dialog box is not displayed.

In the Global scale factor text box, type the scale factor you want. Click OK. AutoCAD regenerates the drawing, changing the scale of every noncontinuous linetype in the drawing.

Tip The global linetype scale is held in the LTSCALE system variable. You can change the linetype scale by typing LTSCALE at the command line and typing a scale.

Changing linetype spacing by changing the object linetype scale

On occasion, you may want the linetype spacing to be different for one object—or a small group of objects—only. Perhaps the object is too small to show the linetype

pattern or you want to set it off visually. AutoCAD also has a current object linetype scale that works like setting a current color or linetype—all objects drawn after you set the object linetype scale are drawn with the new linetype scale. In most cases, you want to make sure you change the current object linetype scale back to its default of 1 after using it for that one object or group of objects.

Changing the current object linetype scale

To change the linetype scale, choose Format ➪ Linetype to open the Linetype Manager, as shown in Figure 11-29. Click Show Details if the lower portion of the dialog box is not displayed. In the Current Object Scale text box, type the scale factor you want. Click OK. Now all objects that you draw use the current object linetype scale.

Figure 11-29: The Linetype Manager dialog box

The current object linetype scale is held in the CELTSCALE system variable. You can change the current object linetype scale by typing **celtscale** at the command line and typing in a scale.

If you have also set the global linetype scale to a value other than 1, AutoCAD multiplies the two linetype scales to calculate the final result. For example, if you have a global linetype scale of 12 and a current object linetype scale of 0.5, objects you draw will have a resulting linetype scale of 6.

Changing an existing object's linetype scale

It may be more common to draw an object without setting a special object linetype scale and then decide that you want to change its linetype scale. To change an

object's linetype scale, select the object and choose Properties from the Standard toolbar. In the Properties window, click Linetype Scale and then type the new linetype scale. This linetype scale only affects the selected object. It does not affect the global linetype scale.

On the CD-ROM

The drawing used in the following Step-by-Step exercise on changing linetype scales, ab11-e.dwg, is in the Drawings folder of the *AutoCAD 2004 Bible* CD-ROM.

Step-by-Step: Changing Linetype Scales

1. Open ab11-e.dwg from the CD-ROM.

2. Save the file as ab11-05.dwg in your AutoCAD Bible folder. This drawing is of a bushing, as shown in Figure 11-30. Notice that the linetype doesn't show clearly on the short line at ❶ and in the small circle at ❷.

3. Choose Format ⇨ Linetype. Click Show Details to open the Details section of the Linetype Manager, if necessary. Change the Global scale factor to 0.5. Click OK. AutoCAD regenerates the drawing. Note that the circles are better, but the short line at ❶ still looks like a continuous line.

4. Choose the line at ❶. Choose Properties from the Standard toolbar. Click Linetype scale and change it to 0.5. Press Enter. Press Esc to remove the grips and see the result. Notice the difference in the line, which now has a linetype scale of 0.5 (global) times 0.5 (object) = 0.25.

5. Save your drawing. It should look like Figure 11-31.

SECTION A-A

Figure 11-30: This drawing of a bushing has two noncontinuous linetypes.

Thanks to Robert Mack of the Dexter Company, Fairfield, Iowa, for this drawing.

Figure 11-31: The drawing's noncontinuous lines are now more appropriate.

Importing Layers and Linetypes from Other Drawings

The AutoCAD DesignCenter gives you access to drawing content and definitions, such as layers, linetypes, blocks (see Chapter 18), plot layouts (see Chapter 17), and so on that exist in other drawings. I cover the AutoCAD DesignCenter in more detail in Chapter 26, but here I explain how to import layers and linetypes from another drawing. Autodesk calls this "mining your design." In other words, after you have created a layer or a linetype, you can easily use it in any new or existing drawing.

New Feature

The DesignCenter has been redesigned for AutoCAD 2004 to use the new palette interface. For information on working with the palette interface, see "Managing the Properties palette" in Chapter 10. It has a new tab, DC Online, that provides a way to share content for AutoCAD drawings. You can use the DesignCenter not only to access drawing content and definitions but to create tool palettes of block (symbol) libraries. Chapter 26 covers these tool palettes.

Choose DesignCenter from the Standard toolbar to open the DesignCenter, shown in Figure 11-32. The DesignCenter's left pane works like Windows Explorer left pane, letting you navigate throughout your hard drive or your network. (If you don't see the left pane, click the Tree View Toggle button on the DesignCenter's toolbar). If the DesignCenter opens showing only open drawings, click Desktop on the toolbar and navigate to the desired folder. After you click a folder, the drawings in that folder are listed on the right side. Choose Large Icons from the View drop-down list to see a small preview of each item. To access layers

and linetypes, either double-click a drawing icon or click its plus sign. Now you see the various definition categories in the right pane. To see the list of the layers or linetypes, double-click the layers or linetypes icon in either the left or right pane. To import a layer or linetype, double-click the layer or linetype's icon. AutoCAD brings the layer or linetype definition into your drawing. Click the Layer Control drop-down list to check it out!

Figure 11-32: The DesignCenter lets you locate definitions contained in other drawings and import them into your current drawing.

Click the DesignCenter's Close button to close the DesignCenter.

Cross-Reference AutoCAD 2004 enables you to *translate* layers. For example, you can specify that all objects on layer `dashed` be changed to the layer `hidden`. Use this feature to maintain layer standards that you have set up. Chapter 26 fully covers layer translating.

Matching Properties

You may be familiar with the Format Painter button available on the toolbars of many Windows applications. AutoCAD offers something similar that, at the same time, enables you to specify which properties you want to match. AutoCAD calls this process matching properties. It is similar to Excel's Paste Special command, which lets you choose what properties you want to paste from what you copied to the clipboard — everything, or just the formulas, values, formats, and so on.

New Feature You can now match polyline and viewport properties. These properties are matched by default, although you can specify which properties you want to match in the Property Settings dialog box. See Figure 11-33.

An object can have so many properties that this can be a useful tool. To match properties, you need two objects, a source object and a destination object (or objects). Follow these steps to match properties:

1. Choose the object whose properties you want to match (the source object).

2. Choose Match Properties from the Standard toolbar. AutoCAD displays a Format Painter cursor with a pickbox. On the command line, you see the `Select destination object(s) or [Settings]:` prompt.

Note You can choose Match Properties from the Standard toolbar first and then choose the source object.

3. If you want to match all the object's properties, select the object(s) that you want to receive the matching properties, that is, the destination object(s).

4. If you want to match only some of the object's properties, right-click and choose Settings to open the Property Settings dialog box, shown in Figure 11-33. Uncheck all the properties you don't want to match and click OK. AutoCAD returns you to the same prompt as before. Select the object(s) you want to receive the matching properties, that is, the destination objects(s).

Figure 11-33: The Property Settings dialog box

5. Press Enter to end object selection. AutoCAD matches the properties.

 The drawing used in the following Step-by-Step exercise on matching properties, `ab11-f.dwg`, is in the `Drawings` folder of the *AutoCAD 2004 Bible* CD-ROM.

Step-by-Step: Matching Properties

1. Open `ab11-f.dwg` from the CD-ROM.

2. Save the file as `ab11-06.dwg` in your `AutoCAD Bible` folder. This is a drawing of a master bedroom suite plan, as shown in Figure 11-34.

3. Pick the wall at ❶ in Figure 11-34. Click Match Properties from the Standard toolbar. At the `Select destination object(s) or [Settings]:` prompt, use a crossing window to select all the folding closet doors on both sides of the line you just selected. Press Enter to end object selection. AutoCAD matches the properties of the doors to the properties of the wall. (The doors turn from gray to black/white.)

4. Pick the text MASTER SUITE. Choose Match Properties from the Standard toolbar. At the `Select destination object(s) or [Settings]:` prompt, right-click and choose Settings. In the Property Settings dialog box, deselect all the boxes except Text in the Special Properties section. Click OK.

5. At the `Select destination object(s) or [Settings]:` prompt, choose the text CL. in both closets and press Enter to end the command. AutoCAD matches the text properties of the text. Notice that the CL. text becomes bold.

6. Save your drawing.

Figure 11-34: The master bedroom suite plan

Summary

In this chapter, you read all about layers, colors, linetypes, and lineweights. You discovered:

✦ Using layers to help you organize your drawings by assigning the same properties to related objects

✦ Creating a layer by giving it a name, color, linetype, and lineweight

✦ Changing the layer of existing objects, using the Layer Control drop-down list or the Properties palette

✦ All about layer states — On/Off, Thawed/Frozen, Unlocked/ Locked, and Plottable/Not Plottable

✦ Changing the properties of existing layers

✦ Saving sets of layer states and properties and later restoring them

✦ Filtering the layer listing

✦ Purging unused layers and linetypes

✦ Altering the color, linetype, and lineweight of any object

✦ Globally changing the linetype scale, changing the current linetype scale, and changing the object linetype scale of existing objects

✦ Using the DesignCenter to import layers and linetypes from other drawings

✦ Utilizing the Match Properties command to copy properties from one object to one or more destination objects

The next chapter explains how to get detailed information from your drawing.

✦　　✦　　✦

Getting Information from Your Drawing

In This Chapter

Getting drawing-wide information

Getting information about objects

Measuring and segmenting objects

Using AutoCAD's calculator

Your AutoCAD drawing is intelligent in many ways. Several commands can give you the details of each object. In addition, you can get listings that provide information about your drawing as a whole. I have mentioned system variables previously in this book—you can list system variables and their current settings.

You can perform calculations on objects that may assist you in certain drawing tasks. For example, you can divide an object into any number of segments by placing point objects along the object, or you can place point objects at a specified distance along the object. You can use AutoCAD's calculator, which not only does regular numerical calculations but also works with coordinates and geometric points on objects.

Drawing-Level Information

Some information applies to the drawing as a whole or even to your computer system as a whole, rather than to individual objects. This information can be important when there is a problem or when you simply need to find the status of system variables.

Listing the status of your drawing

The STATUS command provides a standard list of information that can be very helpful. To use the STATUS command, choose Tools ⇨ Inquiry ⇨ Status. Figure 12-1 shows a sample status listing.

```
                        X:   8200.00   Y:   6000.00
Model space uses        X:   3906.84   Y:   3284.39
                        X:   6783.63   Y:   4304.04
Display shows           X:   3894.40   Y:   2958.05
                        X:   7027.97   Y:   4630.39
Insertion base is       X:      0.00   Y:      0.00   Z:      0.00
Snap resolution is      X:      1.00   Y:      1.00
Grid spacing is         X:    100.00   Y:    100.00

Current space:          Model space
Current layout:         Model
Current layer:          "0"
Current color:          BYLAYER -- 7 (white)
Current linetype:       BYLAYER -- "CONTINUOUS"
Current lineweight:     BYLAYER
Current elevation:          0.00  thickness:        0.00
Fill on  Grid off  Ortho off  Qtext off  Snap off  Tablet off
Object snap modes:      Center, Endpoint, Intersection, Extension
Free dwg disk (E:) space: 0 KBytes
Free temp disk (C:) space: 454.9 MBytes
Free physical memory: 295.5 Mbytes (out of 511.0M).
Free swap file space: 720.5 Mbytes (out of 866.4M).
```

Figure 12-1: A sample listing from the STATUS command

AutoCAD lists the number of objects in your drawing, and then the limits and extents of the drawing, as well as the extents of the current display on your screen. Other important items are the snap and grid spacing as well as the current layer, color, linetype, and lineweight. You can see that Fill is on but the other drawing aid settings are off. Center, Endpoint, Intersection, and Extension running object snaps are on. Finally, information also appears about free disk space and free memory.

Obviously, much of this information is available without using the STATUS command. The easiest items to find are the current layer, color, linetype, and lineweight, which are readily visible on the Layers and Properties toolbars. However, you would have to use a number of commands to obtain other information such as the snap and grid spacing and the drawing limits. STATUS puts it all together in one listing. Finally, the free disk and memory statistics provide valuable information not easily obtainable otherwise from within your drawing.

The most common use for STATUS is to troubleshoot problems. For example, you could send the listing to a colleague in another office who needs to work on the same drawing. Your colleague can then work more easily by using the same settings you have used.

Listing system variables

In Chapter 5, I explained that AutoCAD stores settings in system variables. In the previous chapter, for example, I mentioned that the global linetype scale is stored in the LTSCALE system variable and the object linetype scale is stored in the CELTSCALE system variable. You may want to know the settings of a group of related system variables. The SETVAR command provides a listing of all the system variables and their settings. It may be quicker to view system variable settings by using the SETVAR command than typing each individual system variable on the command line.

Too many system variables exist to show the entire listing here, but a few can convey the wealth of information available, as shown in Figure 12-2.

```
CLAYER              "0"
CMDACTIVE           1
CMDDIA              1                                        (read only)
CMDECHO             1
CMDNAMES            "SETVAR"                                 (read only)
Press ENTER to continue:
CMLJUST             0
CMLSCALE            1.0000
CMLSTYLE            "STANDARD"
COMPASS             0
COORDS              2
CPLOTSTYLE          "ByLayer"
CPROFILE            "ellen"                                  (read only)
CTAB                "Model"
CURSORSIZE          5
CVPORT              2
DATE                2452632.60235621                        (read only)
DBMOD               4                                        (read only)
DCTCUST             "C:\Documents and Settings\Eliyah Finkelstein\Application
Dat..."
DCTMAIN             "enu"
DEFLPLSTYLE         "Normal"
DEFPLSTYLE          "ByLayer"
DELOBJ              1
DEMANDLOAD          3
DIASTAT             1                                        (read only)
DIMADEC             0
DIMALT              OFF
DIMALTD             2
DIMALTF             25.4000
DIMALTRND           0.00
DIMALTTD            2
DIMALTTZ            12
DIMALTU             2
DIMALTZ             12
DIMAPOST            ""
DIMASO              OFF
DIMASSOC            0
DIMASZ              10.00
DIMATFIT            3
DIMAUNIT            4
DIMAZIN             0
DIMBLK              "A"
DIMBLK1             "A"
DIMBLK2             "A"
```

Figure 12-2: A partial SETVAR listing

Note Read-only system variables are for information only and cannot be changed. An example is LOGINNAME, which shows the current user's name registered on the system. Other system variables can be changed.

While some system variables allow any or a variety of values, many are either on or off. In general, a setting of 1 means on and 0 means off.

On the CD-ROM Appendix C lists useful, new, changed, and deleted system variables, including a brief explanation of each.

Most system variables do not need to be set directly. In Chapter 11, for example, you set the LTSCALE system variable by using the Linetype Manager. However, a few system variables can be accessed only by typing them on the command line.

You can use SETVAR to set system variables (that are not read-only) as well as to list them. To list the system variables, choose Tools ➪ Inquiry ➪ Set Variable. At the Enter variable name or [?]: prompt, type **?** ↵. At the Enter variable(s) to list <*>: prompt, press Enter to list all the system variables or type the name of a variable. (You can use the * and ? wildcards in the name.) AutoCAD either lists all the system variables or just the variable you typed.

If you type a variable, AutoCAD prompts you for a new value so that you can change it. For example, if you type **celtscale**, AutoCAD responds with the Enter new value for CELTSCALE <1.0000>: prompt. You can then change the system variable by typing in a new value. You can simply press Enter to accept the current setting.

Tracking drawing time

You can track the time you spend working on a drawing. This feature is most often used for billing time to clients, or maybe your boss wants to see how much you're getting done.

Cross-Reference Chapter 26 explains how to keep a log file of your drawing activity.

To use the TIME command, choose Tools ➪ Inquiry ➪ Time. A typical listing is shown in Figure 12-3.

```
Command: time

Current time:            Friday, December 27, 2002 at 6:02:19:513 PM
Times for this drawing:
  Created:               Friday, December 27, 2002 at 5:53:28:138 PM
  Last updated:          Friday, December 27, 2002 at 5:54:18:857 PM
  Total editing time:    0 days 00:07:45.328
  Elapsed timer (on):    0 days 00:07:45.047
  Next automatic save in: 0 days 00:04:16.016
```

Figure 12-3: A typical TIME listing

Table 12-1 shows the meaning of the listing that you get from the TIME command.

Table 12-1 TIME Command Information	
Listing	**Comments**
Current time	The current date and time. The time is displayed to the nearest millisecond.
Created	The date and time the drawing was created.
Last updated	The date and time of the last save of the drawing.
Total editing time	Accumulates the time spent in the drawing from session to session, not including plotting time or time you worked on the drawing and quit without saving your changes.
Elapsed timer	Also accumulates time spent in the drawing, but you can turn this on and off and reset it.
Next automatic save in	Shows when AutoCAD will automatically save your drawing. Choose Tools ➪ Options and click the Open and Save tab to set how often AutoCAD automatically saves your drawing.

You can think of total editing time as your car's odometer and elapsed time as a timer (like the trip meter that some cars have that lets you time a specific trip).

At the end of the listing, AutoCAD displays the `Enter option [Display/ON/OFF/Reset]:` prompt. The Display option redisplays the listing with updated times. ON and OFF turn the elapsed time on and off. The Reset option resets the elapsed time to zero.

The drawing used in the following Step-by-Step exercise on obtaining drawing information, `ab12-a.dwg`, is in the `Drawings` folder of the *AutoCAD 2004 Bible* CD-ROM.

Step-by-Step: Obtaining Drawing Information

1. Open `ab12-a.dwg` from the CD-ROM.

2. Choose Tools ⇨ Inquiry ⇨ Status. Look at the listing to see how many objects it contains. Check the limits of the drawing. Look at the grid spacing. Read through any other items of interest to you.

3. Choose Tools ⇨ Inquiry ⇨ Set Variable. At the `Enter variable name or [?]:` prompt, type **?** ↵. At the `Enter variable(s) to list <*>:` prompt, press Enter to accept the default. Look for the BLIPMODE setting. Check the location of the drawing (DWGPREFIX). Look for the global linetype scale (LTSCALE). Press Enter until you see the `Command:` prompt again.

4. Press Enter to start the SETVAR command again. At the `Enter variable name or [?]:` prompt, type **ltscale** ↵. Type **50** ↵ to change the linetype scale. Type **regen** ↵. (Notice that the noncontinuous linetypes now show up more clearly.)

5. Choose Tools ⇨ Inquiry ⇨ Time. Check the current time against your watch. (AutoCAD takes the time from your computer's clock.) Look at the total editing time to see how long you have had the drawing open. Press Enter to end the command.

6. Do not save this drawing. Leave the drawing open if you are going on to the next exercise.

Object-Level Information

Several commands exist solely to provide information about the objects in your drawing.

Listing objects

The LIST command displays information about selected objects. The information displayed depends on the object. For example, the LIST command gives you the radius of a circle and the length of a line.

To list an object, choose Tools ➯ Inquiry ➯ List. Figure 12-4 shows a typical listing for a line.

```
  LINE       Layer: "objects"
             Space: Model space
      Handle = 3AD
  from point, X=0'-4 9/64"  Y=0'-1 3/64"  Z=    0'-0"
    to point, X=0'-5 41/64" Y=0'-1 3/64"  Z=    0'-0"
Length =0'-1 1/2",  Angle in XY Plane =         0
        Delta X =0'-1 1/2", Delta Y =     0'-0", Delta Z =    0'-0"
```

Figure 12-4: A typical listing for a horizontal line

Table 12-2 shows the meaning of the information you receive when you list an object.

	Table 12-2 LIST Command Information
Data	**Comments**
Layer	AutoCAD lists the object's layer. If the color and linetype are not ByLayer or ByBlock, AutoCAD lists these as well.
Space	AutoCAD tells you if the object is in model space or paper space. (Chapter 17 covers paper space.)
Handle	Every object in your drawing has a handle. AutoCAD uses handles to keep track of objects.
from point	Because AutoCAD is listing a line, it shows the start point.
to point	The endpoint of the line.
Length	The line's length.
Angle in XY Plane	The line's angle. This line is horizontal, so its angle is zero.
Delta X	The change in the X coordinate from the start point to the endpoint.
Delta Y	The change in the Y coordinate from the start point to the endpoint.

The Layers and Properties toolbars makes it easy to tell an object's layer, linetype, and color. Remember, when you select an object, its layer, linetype, lineweight, color, and plot style appear in these toolbars. Most of this information is also available from the Properties palette — choose Properties from the Standard toolbar.

Calculating distances

AutoCAD makes it easy to calculate the distance between any two points by using the DIST command. Choose Tools ➯ Inquiry ➯ Distance. AutoCAD prompts you for

two points. You can use any means of specifying a point, although object snaps or snap mode are useful if you want to be sure which point you are specifying. Here is a typical display for a vertical line:

```
Distance = 19'-0", Angle in XY Plane = 270, Angle from XY Plane
= 0
Delta X = 0'-0", Delta Y = -19'-0", Delta Z = 0'-0"
```

You can use this information to check dimensions (covered in Chapter 14) or to make further calculations that you need for drawing.

Finding coordinates

Finding a coordinate is even easier than calculating a distance. Choose Tools ➪ Inquiry ➪ ID Point. AutoCAD prompts you for a point. You can use any means of specifying a point, although object snaps or snap mode are useful. Here is a typical listing:

```
X = 61'-5 1/8" Y = 32'-4 5/8" Z = 0'-0"
```

You can use this information to find or calculate an absolute coordinate.

On the CD-ROM The drawing used in the following Step-by-Step exercise on obtaining object information, ab12-a.dwg, is in the Drawings folder of the *AutoCAD 2004 Bible* CD-ROM.

Step-by-Step: Obtaining Object Information

1. Open ab12-a.dwg from the CD-ROM if it is not already open from the previous exercise. This is a civil engineering drawing showing several plots of land, as shown in Figure 12-5. OSNAP should be on. Set a running object snap for endpoint.

Figure 12-5: A civil engineering drawing of several plots of land

2. Choose Tools ➪ Inquiry ➪ List. At the `Select objects:` prompt, pick ❶ in Figure 12-5. Press Enter to end object selection. The result is shown in Figure 12-6. Note the surveyor's units.

```
        ARC       Layer: "0"
                  Space: Model space
        Handle = 7D3951
center point, X=  7249.24  Y=  3753.29  Z=     0.00
radius   1937.35
  start angle S 89d28'56" W
    end angle S 76d38'19" W
length    434.28
```

Figure 12-6: The result of using the LIST command on an arc

3. Choose Tools ➪ Inquiry ➪ Distance. At the `Specify first point:` prompt, choose the endpoint at ❷ in Figure 12-5, using the Endpoint running object snap. At the `Specify second point:` prompt, choose the endpoint at ❸. Here's the result:

```
Distance = 2740.90, Angle in XY Plane = N 89d23'34" E, Angle
from XY Plane = E
Delta X = 2740.75, Delta Y = 29.05, Delta Z = 0.00
```

4. Choose Tools ➪ Inquiry ➪ ID Point. At the `Specify point:` prompt, pick the endpoint at ❹ in Figure 12-5. Here is the result:

```
X = 6065.67 Y = 3450.58 Z = 0.00
```

5. Do not save this drawing. Leave the drawing open if you are going on to the next exercise.

Caution The precision set in the Units dialog box (Format ➪ Units) affects the results of the LIST, DIST, and ID (Locate Point) commands. See Chapter 5 for more information on the Units dialog box.

Calculating area and perimeter

AutoCAD can also calculate the area and perimeter of any area. To start the AREA command, choose Tools ➪ Inquiry ➪ Area.

You can specify points bounding the area that you want to calculate. The points do not have to be on an object. AutoCAD calculates the area and perimeter as if you had drawn lines between all the points. AutoCAD automatically closes the area if you don't close the area by picking the last point the same as the first point. This option is limited to areas with straight sides.

Instead of picking points, you can use the Object option to calculate the area of objects, which gives you the flexibility to use areas that include curves. Acceptable objects are circles, ellipses, splines, polylines, polygons, regions, and objects created with the 2D SOLID command. (Chapter 16 covers splines, polylines, regions, and solids.) AutoCAD calculates an area but adds a length instead of a perimeter. For a circle, you get a circumference. Although a polyline may have the exact same shape as an arc, you cannot calculate the area of an arc. Polylines and splines can be open. AutoCAD calculates the area as if you had drawn a line from the endpoint to the start point but does not include that last imaginary line when calculating the length.

To calculate the area of irregular shapes, you can keep a running total by using the Add option. Start by specifying the first area. Then use the Add option and specify a second area. AutoCAD adds the two areas. You can continue to add areas. You can also use the Subtract option to subtract areas.

Figure 12-7 shows an example of calculating the open area in an office floor plan by picking points. The point objects show the points that were used to calculate the area and perimeter.

Figure 12-7: Calculating the area and perimeter for an office floor plan

You can also use the BOUNDARY command to create one polyline or region from a complex area. (Chapter 16 covers boundaries and polylines.) You can then use the Object option of the AREA command instead of picking points. However, notice that BOUNDARY included the open doors in the area selected for the office floor plan, as shown in Figure 12-8.

Figure 12-8: Using the BOUNDARY command to create an object for use with the AREA command. The boundary is indicated with a dashed line.

On the CD-ROM The drawing used in the following Step-by-Step exercise on using the AREA command, ab12-a.dwg, is in the Drawings folder of the *AutoCAD 2004 Bible* CD-ROM.

Step-by-Step: Using the AREA Command

1. Open ab12-a.dwg from the CD-ROM if it is not already open from the previous exercise.

2. Use ZOOM Window to zoom in on the parcels of land labeled D and E, as shown in Figure 12-9. OSNAP should be on with a running object snap for endpoint.

3. Choose Tools ⇨ Inquiry ⇨ Area.

4. At the Specify first corner point or [Object/Add/Subtract]: prompt, right-click and choose Add to start Add mode. At the Specify first corner point or [Object/Subtract]: prompt, pick ❶ in Figure 12-9 by using the Endpoint running object snap. At the Specify next corner point or press ENTER for total (ADD mode): prompt, continue to pick ❷, ❸, ❹, and ❺. Press Enter. AutoCAD lists the area and perimeter. (Your figures may be different if you picked different points.)

   ```
   Area = 123575.16, Perimeter = 1480.17
   Total area = 123575.16
   ```

5. At the Specify first corner point or [Object/Subtract]: prompt, pick ❻ in Figure 12-9. At the Specify next corner point or press ENTER

for total (ADD mode): prompt, pick ❼, ❽, and ❾. Press Enter to complete point selection. AutoCAD reports the area and perimeter of the second area and adds the two areas together to give you the total area. Press Enter again to end the command.

```
Area = 183399.88, Perimeter = 1884.62
Total area = 306975.04
```

Figure 12-9: The AREA command can calculate the area of parcels D and E.

6. Do not save the drawing. Keep it open if you are continuing on to the next exercise.

Note

The MASSPROP command is mostly used for 3D drawings, but it can also be used on regions, which are 2D solid surfaces, such as a shape cut from sheet metal. This command provides area and perimeter but also other engineering calculations, such as centroids, moments of inertia, the product of inertia, and so on. Chapter 24 covers this command further.

Getting information from the Properties palette

You can also get information about an object by selecting it and choosing Properties from the Standard toolbar. I discussed this Properties palette in Chapter 11 for changing layer, color, linetype, and lineweight properties. As you can see in Figure 12-10, the window also lists the line's start and end points, delta (change) in X, Y, and Z, length, and angle — much like the LIST command. However, you can change the start and end points directly in this window.

Figure 12-10: The Properties window lists information about a selected object.

Measurement Commands

AutoCAD can make calculations on objects for you. The DIVIDE command divides an object into equally spaced sections. The MEASURE command divides an object into sections of a specified length. These commands are useful in many fields — you might need to space bolt holes evenly around the edge of a bushing, or place fence studs along the edge of a plot every five feet.

Dividing objects

The DIVIDE command divides an object into equally spaced sections. DIVIDE does not break the object — it simply places point objects along the object. You can then use the Node object snap if you want to draw from those points.

To divide an object, choose Draw ⇨ Point ⇨ Divide. Select the object you want to divide. AutoCAD responds with the `Enter the number of segments or [Block]:` prompt. Type in the number of segments that you want to create. AutoCAD places the point objects and ends the command.

Tip
Remember that you can set the point display by choosing Format ⇨ Point Style. An easy-to-see point style is especially useful for the DIVIDE command. Specify the point style *before* using the command.

To create eight segments, for example, AutoCAD places seven point objects. If you have in your mind the number of point objects you want, add one when specifying the number of segments.

You can use the Block option to place a block of your choice along the object instead of a point object. Chapter 18 covers blocks. If you choose the Block option (right-click and choose Block), AutoCAD responds with the Enter name of block to insert: prompt. Type the name of the block. AutoCAD asks, Align block with object? [Yes/No] <Y>. Answer Y or N depending on whether you want to align the block with the object.

Note
Aligning a block is appropriate for curved objects and blocks that are not completely symmetrical.

AutoCAD asks for the number of segments you want, and you type that number, as described earlier. Figure 12-11 shows an electrical schematic. Here you want to divide a line so that you can evenly space wires entering the ignition module. Four wires need to come in so that the line was divided into five segments, using an easy-to-see point object.

Figure 12-11: Dividing a line into five segments by using point objects

Thanks to Robert Muck of the Dexter Company, Fairfield, Iowa for this drawing.

You can practice using the DIVIDE command after the next section.

Measuring objects

The MEASURE command is similar to the DIVIDE command except that you specify the distance between point objects instead of the total number of segments. AutoCAD starts measuring from the endpoint closest to where you pick the object. MEASURE does not break the object — it simply places point objects along the object. You can then use the Node object snap if you want to draw from those points.

To measure an object, choose Draw ⇨ Point ⇨ Measure. Select the object you want to measure. AutoCAD responds with the Specify length of segment or [Block]: prompt. Type the segment length you want. AutoCAD places the point objects and ends the command.

Remember that you can set the point display by choosing Format ⇨ Point Style. An easy-to-see point style is especially useful for the MEASURE command. Specify the point style before using the command.

As with the DIVIDE command, you can place a block along the object using the Block option. AutoCAD prompts you for the name of the block and lets you choose if you want to align the block with the object. AutoCAD asks for the segment length, and you type in the lengths between the points, as described earlier. Figure 12-12 shows a plat drawing with one side of a lot measured into 20-foot segments.

Figure 12-12: Measuring a line into 20-foot segments by using point objects

Thanks to Bill Maidment of Caltech, Inc. Fairfield, Iowa for this drawing.

On the CD-ROM The drawing used in the following Step-by-Step exercise on using the DIVIDE and MEASURE commands, ab12-a.dwg, is in the Drawings folder of the *AutoCAD 2004 Bible* CD-ROM.

Step-by-Step: Using the DIVIDE and MEASURE Commands

1. Open ab12-a.dwg from the CD-ROM if it is not already open from the previous exercise.

2. If you didn't do the previous exercise, use ZOOM Window to zoom in to the parcels labeled D and E, as shown in Figure 12-13.

3. Choose Format ⇨ Point Style and choose the fourth style in the first row. Choose Set Size Relative to Screen and set the size to 5%. Click OK.

4. Choose Draw ⇨ Point ⇨ Divide. At the Select object to divide: prompt, choose ❶ in Figure 12-13. At the Enter the number of segments or [Block]: prompt, type **3** ↵. AutoCAD places two points along the line, dividing it into three segments. (If you want, draw lines from the points perpendicular to the opposite side of the parcel to divide it into three parcels.)

5. Choose Draw ⇨ Point ⇨ Measure. At the Select object to measure: prompt, choose ❷ in Figure 12-13. At the Specify length of segment or [Block]: prompt, type **120** ↵ (10 feet). AutoCAD places two points along the line.

6. Do not save your drawing. Keep it open if you are continuing on to the next exercise.

Figure 12-13: The site plan zoomed in to parcels D and E

AutoCAD's Calculator

AutoCAD's calculator is a geometric calculator that not only can calculate numbers like an ordinary calculator but also can calculate points and vectors. The calculator supports object snaps (except apparent intersection, extension, and parallel) and has its own functions so that it is actually a simple programming language. In fact,

you can even use AutoLISP variables in your expressions. Here I show you the basics of the calculator.

To start the calculator, type **cal** ⏎ on the command line. If you are in the middle of a command, type **'cal** ⏎.

Calculating numbers

Calculating numbers is straightforward and uses standard rules of precedence. The following illustrates this point:

```
Command: cal
.>> Expression: 3*(2+3)/5-1
2.0
```

Because the 2+3 sum is in parentheses, it is calculated first so that the expression multiplies 3 by 5 (which is 15), divides it by 5 (which is 3), and subtracts 1 (which is 2).

Using CAL in this way is just like having a handheld calculator by your computer.

When you use CAL transparently, AutoCAD assumes you want the result to be a response to a prompt. Let's say you want to draw a horizontal line. You know it has to be the total of two other lines whose length you know. Follow the prompts:

```
Turn on ORTHO.
Start the LINE command.
Specify first point: Pick the start point for the line. Move
the cursor to the right to draw at a zero-degree angle and so
you can use Direct Distance Entry.
Specify next point or [Undo]: 'cal ⏎
>> Expression: 3.953+6.8725 ⏎
10.8255
```

End the LINE command. AutoCAD draws a line whose length is the sum of the two numbers.

You can add feet and inches as well. Use the format 6'5" or 6'-5". Don't put any spaces between the feet and inches. With the calculator, all inches must be marked with a double prime ("), unlike regular AutoCAD command-line usage. (See the sidebar "The ins and outs of fractional inches in CAL.")

Using coordinates

You can use coordinates in CAL expressions. Coordinates are enclosed in square brackets. Let's say you want to draw a line that is equal to the length of two other objects in your drawing that you happen to know are 3.953 and 6.8725 units long. You want the line to be at a 20-degree angle. At the `Specify next point or [Undo]:` prompt, start CAL transparently:

```
>> Expression: [@(3.953+6.8725)<20]
```

This creates a relative polar coordinate whose length is the sum of two numbers.

Using object snaps

You can use the object snaps as part of CAL expressions. When you press Enter after completing the expression, AutoCAD prompts you for the objects for each object snap in the expression, one after another.

One of the most common uses for object snaps is to find the midpoint between two points. In Figure 12-14, you want to draw a line starting from the midpoint between the centers of two circles.

To accomplish this, first make sure that OSNAP is off. Then start the LINE command and start CAL transparently at the `Specify first point:` prompt. Follow the prompts:

```
>> Expression: (cen+cen)/2 ↵
>> Select entity for CEN snap: Select the first circle.
>> Select entity for CEN snap: Select the second circle.
 (4.86897 7.73008 0.0)
```

The ins and outs of fractional inches in CAL

Using fractional inches in CAL expressions is tricky. If you type **3'2-1/2"** as a CAL expression, AutoCAD replies `Error: Invalid feet'-inches" format`. AutoCAD expects a hyphen only between feet and inches. Otherwise, it assumes a hyphen is a minus sign. To write out fractional inches, think of them as little division problems being added to the whole inches. Therefore, if you type the following expression

```
(3'2"+1"/2")+(23"+3"/8")
61.875
```

AutoCAD takes 3'2" and adds 1" divided by 2" to get 3'2-1/2". Similarly, in the second expression, AutoCAD adds 23" to 3" divided by 8" to get 23-3/8". Yes, it's slightly awkward. If 3'-2" returns 38.0, as shown below (3' = 36" and 2 more inches is 38"), how do you subtract 2" from 3'?

```
>> Expression: 3'-2"
38.0
```

The trick is to put parentheses around the three feet so that AutoCAD doesn't assume the next expression is part of the same feet-inches expression, as shown here:

```
>> Expression: (3')-2"
34.0
```

Here AutoCAD takes the three feet (36") and subtracts 2" to get 34.

First circle

Midpoint between the circles' centers

Polar: 3 9/64 < 0.00°

Second circle

Figure 12-14: Drawing a line from the midpoint between the centers of the two circles

In this expression, AutoCAD actually calculates the average between the coordinates of the centers of the two circles. If you subtract coordinates, as in the following expression, CAL gives you the change in X and Y, not the length between the two coordinates. In the following expression, two endpoints on a line were chosen:

```
>> Expression: end-end ↵ > Select entity for END snap:
>> Select entity for END snap:
(-57.3212 -20.8632 0.0)
```

Compare this to using the DIST command as shown next. As you can see, the delta X and delta Y numbers match the CAL results:

```
Command: '_dist Specify first point: Specify second point:
Distance = 61.0000, Angle in XY Plane = 20, Angle from XY Plane
= 0
Delta X = 57.3212, Delta Y = 20.8632, Delta Z = 0.0000
```

To calculate the length of the line, use the abs function from the list of mathematical functions in Table 12-3. The following expression shows how this works:

```
>> Expression: abs(end-end) ↵
>> Select entity for END snap:
>> Select entity for END snap:
61.0
```

You can easily use CAL as a substitute for the From object snap. For example, at the Specify first point: prompt you can enter **' cal** ↵ and type **mid+[3,–2.5]** ↵. AutoCAD prompts you for the object for which you want the midpoint and starts the line (3,–2.5) units from there.

Using mathematical functions

CAL supports many mathematical functions typical of a scientific calculator. Table 12-3 lists these functions.

Note

A real number is any positive or negative number. Type large numbers without commas. AutoCAD restricts you to integers between –32768 and +32767 but real numbers (numbers with decimal places) can be larger.

Table 12-3
CAL Mathematical Functions

Function	What It Does
sin(angle)	Calculates the sine of the angle.
cos(angle)	Calculates the cosine of the angle.
tang(angle)	Calculates the tangent of the angle.
asin(real)	Calculates the arc sine of the real number.
acos(real)	Calculates the arc cosine of the real number.
atan(real)	Calculates the arc tangent of the real number.
ln(real)	Calculates the natural log of the real number.
Log(real)	Base-10 log of the number
exp(real)	Calculates the natural exponent of the real number.
exp10(real)	Calculates the base-10 exponent of the real number.
sqr(real)	Calculates the square of the real number.
sqrt(real)	Calculates the square root of the real number.
abs(real)	Calculates the absolute value of the real number (the number not including its + or – sign), also used to calculate lengths.
round(real)	Rounds the number to its nearest integer.
trunc(real)	Truncates any decimal value leaving only the integer.
r2d(angle)	Converts radian angles to degrees.
d2r(angle)	Converts degree angles to radians.
pi	Returns the constant pi.

Using CAL's special functions

CAL has a set of special functions that you can use to find points. Table 12-4 lists most of these functions and what they do. You can find a complete list in the AutoCAD Command Reference.

	Table 12-4
	Special CAL Functions
Function	**What It Does**
rad	Gets the radius of the selected object.
cur	Gets any point that you pick.
@	Gets the last point calculated.
vec(p1,p2)	Calculates the vector from point p1 to point p2.
vec1(p1,p2)	Calculates a one-unit vector from point p1 to point p2.
pld(p1,p2,dist)	Calculates a point on the line from point p1 to point p2 that is dist units from point p1; if dist is 0.327, calculates the point 0.327 units from p1.
plt(p1,p2,t)	Calculates a point on the line from point p1 to point p2 that is t proportion from point p1; if t is 0.45, calculates the point 0.45 of the distance from p1 to p2 (or almost halfway between them).
dist(p1,p2)	Calculates the distance between point p1 and point p2.
dpl(p,p1,p2)	Calculates the distance from point p to the line from point p1 to point p2.
ang(p1,p2)	Calculates the angle between the X axis and the line from point p1 to point p2.
ang(v)	Calculates the angle between the X axis and a vector you define; an example of a vector would be (end-end) where you pick the two endpoints of a line.
ang(apex,p1,p2)	Calculates the angle between the lines from apex to point p1 and apex to point p2; (the apex is the vertex of the angle).
ill(p1,p2,p3,p4)	Calculates the intersection of two lines from p1 to p2 and from p3 to p4.

Note A vector is a direction, which is expressed as delta X, delta Y.

Remember that you can specify these points in many ways, most commonly by object snaps. You can use the `cur` function to pick any point on the screen.

On the CD-ROM The drawing used in the following Step-by-Step exercise on using the CAL command (AutoCAD's calculator), `ab12-a.dwg`, is in the `Drawings` folder of the *AutoCAD 2004 Bible* CD-ROM.

Step-by-Step: Using CAL

1. Open `ab12-a.dwg` from the CD-ROM if you do not have it open from the previous exercise.

2. Save the drawing as `ab12-01.dwg` in your `AutoCAD Bible` folder.

3. If you did not do the previous exercise, use ZOOM Window to zoom in to the parcels labeled D and E, as shown in Figure 12-15.

Figure 12-15: Parcels D and E in the civil engineering drawing

4. In the exercise on calculating area earlier in this chapter, you calculated a total area of 306975.04, in units of inches. To calculate what that is in square feet, type **cal** ↵. At the Expression: prompt, type **306975.04/144** ↵. AutoCAD calculates 2131.77.

5. In the Step-by-Step exercise on the DIVIDE command earlier in this chapter, you divided a line into three segments by placing two points on the line. You can use CAL to calculate the length of those segments. Type **cal** ↵. At the Expression: prompt, type **abs(end-end)/3** ↵. AutoCAD prompts you for the two endpoint snaps. Pick the two ends of the line at ❹ in Figure 12-15. AutoCAD calculates 262.37.

6. Suppose that you want to draw a line starting from the intersection of two intersecting lines going from corner to diagonally opposite corner and ending perpendicular to the top line of the land parcel. Start the LINE command. At the `Specify first point:` prompt, type **'cal** ↵. At the `Expression:` prompt, type **ill(end,end,end,end)** ↵. AutoCAD prompts you for four endpoints. Pick the endpoints (in Figure 12-15) at ❶ and ❷ to define the first line, and then at ❸ and ❹ to define the second line. AutoCAD starts the line at the intersection of the two lines. At the `Specify next point or [Undo]::` prompt, choose the Perpendicular object snap and pick ❺. Figure 12-16 shows the result.

Figure 12-16: Using CAL, you can calculate the intersection of two lines without drawing the lines.

7. Save your drawing.

Summary

AutoCAD stores a great deal of information in each drawing. In this chapter you read about:

✦ Getting a general status listing

✦ Listing system variable settings

✦ Tracking drawing time

✦ Getting information about individual objects by using the LIST, DIST, and ID command

✦ Calculating area and perimeters

✦ Using the Properties palette to display all of an object's properties

✦ Dividing and measuring objects by placing point objects along them

✦ Using AutoCAD's calculator to use calculated results as part of your command input

In the next chapter, I explain how to create and edit text.

✦ ✦ ✦

Creating Text

All drawings include text that labels or explains the objects in the drawing. Such text is called annotation. In each release, AutoCAD has improved the capabilities of its text objects so that you can now easily format and edit text to provide a professional appearance to your drawing. A wide array of font, alignment, and spacing options are available. You can also import text from a word processor. This chapter tells you all you need to know about creating text in AutoCAD.

Creating Single-Line Text

A great deal of text in a drawing consists of short labels or comments. Use single-line text when you want each line of text to be a separate object or when you are creating a small amount of text. Single-line text has fewer options than the multiline text that I explain later in this chapter, but it is easy to create and to place accurately in a drawing.

Creating a single line of text using the defaults for font, height, and so on is very simple. Choose Draw ➪ Text ➪ Single Line Text. This starts the DTEXT command. DTEXT stands for *dynamic text*: You can see the text on the screen as you type it. Follow the prompts:

```
Current text style:  "Standard"  Text height:
0.2000
Specify start point of text or
[Justify/Style]: Pick a start point for the
text.
Specify height <0.2000>: Type a height, or
press Enter to accept the default.
Specify rotation angle of text <0>: Type a
rotation angle, or press Enter to accept the
default.
Enter text: Type one line of text. Press Enter
when you are finished.
Enter text: Press Enter to end the command.
```

Note You must actually press Enter to end the command. You cannot use the Return button of the mouse or the Spacebar.

The next section covers the Justify option. The Style option is discussed later in this chapter.

Single lines of text are very common in drafting. DTEXT continues to prompt you for lines of text so that you can type line after line. Unfortunately, you cannot control the spacing between the lines.

You can use it to fit text into a schedule or other chart in your drawing. Look in \Software\Chap13\ARRT on the CD-ROM. It (for the TEXT command) and Idt (for DTEXT) let you specify the spacing between lines of text as you create them. Look in \Software\Chap13\It.

Thanks to Leonid Nemirovsky, http://home.pacifier.com/~nemi, *for creating* It.lsp *and* Idt.lsp *at my request.*

One advantage of DTEXT is that each line of text is a separate object, making it easy to move or copy individual lines of text.

AutoCAD remembers the location of the previous line of text even if you have used other commands in the meantime. To continue text below the last line of text you created, press Enter at the Specify start point of text or [Justify/Style]: prompt.

You can also create text connected to arrows that point to objects, using the LEADER and QLEADER commands. Chapter 14 covers the QLEADER command.

Justifying single-line text

When you pick a start point for text, the relationship between the start point and the actual letters is determined by the justification. The start point is also called the insertion point. When you want to refer to text by using object snaps, you use the Insert object snap. If you select text without first choosing a command, grips appear at the insertion point as well at the bottom-left corner.

By default, text is left-justified. To change the text's justification, right-click and choose Justify at the Specify start point of text or [Justify/Style]: prompt. AutoCAD responds with this bewildering prompt:

```
Enter an option
[Align/Fit/Center/Middle/Right/TL/TC/TR/ML/MC/MR/BL/BC/BR]:
```

Align and Fit offer two ways to fit text into a specified space. Both respond with the same two prompts:

```
Specify first endpoint of text baseline:
Specify second endpoint of text baseline:
```

Specify the beginning and the end of the text line. Align then prompts you for the text and then squeezes or stretches the text to fit within the text line. The height of the text changes accordingly to maintain the proportions of the font.

Fit adds the `Specify height <0.2000>:` prompt. Type in the height you want and then type the text. Fit also squeezes or stretches the text to fit within the text line but maintains the text height you specified, distorting the font letters to fit the space. Figure 13-1 shows an example of normal, fitted, and aligned single-line text.

Figure 13-1: Normal (left-justified), aligned, and fitted text

The other justification options specify the placement of the text's insertion point in relationship to the text line. They are shown in Table 13-1. Each insertion point is marked with a small *x*.

	Table 13-1 **Text Justification Options**	
Example	**Option**	**Description**
Garage	Left	Because this is the default justification, AutoCAD provides no suboption for left-justification when you choose the Justify option. The insertion point is on the baseline.
Garage	Center	Text is centered around the insertion point. The insertion point is on the baseline.
Garage	Right	Text is right-justified from the insertion point. The insertion point is on the baseline.
Garage	Middle	Text is centered both vertically and horizontally. The vertical center point is measured from the bottom of the lowest to the top of the tallest possible letter.

Continued

Table 13-1 *(continued)*

Example	Option	Description
Garage	Top Left	Text is left-justified and the insertion point is at the top of the highest possible letter. For some fonts the insertion point appears slightly above the highest letter; for others it appears exactly at the top.
Garage	Top Center	Text is centered and the insertion point is at the top of the highest possible letter.
Garage	Top Right	Text is right-justified and the insertion point is at the top of the highest possible letter.
Garage	Middle Left	Text is left-justified and centered vertically. The vertical center point is measured from the bottom of the lowest to the top of the tallest possible letter.
Garage	Middle Center	Text is centered both horizontally and vertically. The vertical center point is measured from the bottom of the lowest to the top of the tallest possible letter.
Garage	Middle Right	Text is right-justified and centered vertically. The vertical center point is measured from the bottom of the lowest to the top of the tallest possible letter.
Garage	Bottom Left	Text is left-justified. The insertion point is below the lowest descending letter. For some fonts the insertion point appears slightly below the lowest letter; for others, it appears exactly at the bottom.
Garage	Bottom Center	Text is centered. The insertion point is below the lowest descending letter.
Garage	Bottom Right	Text is right-justified. The insertion point is below the lowest descending letter.

Tip If you know the option abbreviation of the justification you want, you can use it at the Specify start point of text or [Justify/Style]: prompt. If you choose a justification that centers or right-justifies, the text does not appear with the proper justification until after you press Enter for the second time and return to the command prompt.

Setting the height

Setting the height of text is fairly straightforward. The default is 0.2 units but this is not suitable for all applications. The main point to consider is the scale factor. If you are drawing a house and plan to plot it at 1"=8' (1=96), you need to figure out how big to make the text so that you can still read it when it is scaled down.

For example, if you want the text to be 0.2 units high and your scale factor is 96, your text needs to be 19.2 inches high (0.2 × 96). On the other hand, if you are drawing a very small object, such as a computer chip and your scale is 0.10, your text needs to be 0.02 inches high. The dimension text in Figure 13-2 is five inches high, but at a scale factor of 64, it plots at 5⁄64 inches high.

Figure 13-2: The dimension text in this drawing is 5 inches high.

AutoCAD calculates text height in units. Most word processors calculate text height in points. A point is ¹⁄₇₂ of an inch. Therefore, 12-point text, a standard for most business letters, is about 0.17 inches high. The default of 0.2 units, if you are using inches as your unit, is just over 14 points, which is usually appropriate for annotating a drawing. (You don't usually hold a drawing as closely as you do a letter, so a larger point size is appropriate.)

For information about changing the scale of text, see the section "Editing single-line text" later in this chapter.

Setting the rotation angle

The final prompt in DTEXT is the rotation angle. This angle applies to the entire line of text, not to individual characters. (You can specify slanted text — AutoCAD calls it *obliqued* text — using the STYLE command covered later in this chapter.) Figure 13-3 shows text rotated at 315 degrees.

Figure 13-3: Text rotated at 315 degrees

Adding special characters and formatting

The DTEXT command does not offer the same type of formatting options available for paragraph text (covered later in this chapter). Therefore, you have to use special codes to create special characters and formats. These codes are shown in Table 13-2.

Table 13-2	
Special Character Codes for AutoCAD Text Fonts	
Code	**Results**
%%o	Toggles overscore mode on/off.
%%u	Toggles underscore mode on/off.
%%d	Draws degree symbol (°).
%%p	Draws plus/minus tolerance symbol (±).
%%c	Draws circle diameter dimensioning symbol (Ø).

Figure 13-4 shows text using some of these codes, along with the entries that created them.

On the CD-ROM

The drawing used in the following Step-by-Step exercise on creating text with DTEXT, a13-ab.dwg, is in the Drawings folder of the *AutoCAD 2004 Bible* CD-ROM.

35.3 not 35.8 %%u35.3%%u not 35.8

Ø1.5 %%c1.5

±.002 %%p.002

Figure 13-4: Using special characters and formatting with AutoCAD text fonts

Step-by-Step: Creating Text with DTEXT

1. Open ab13-a.dwg from your CD-ROM.

2. Save the file as ab13-01.dwg in your AutoCAD Bible folder. This is a master bathroom plan drawing, as shown in Figure 13-5. Make sure OSNAP is on. Set running object snaps for endpoint, midpoint, and intersection.

3. Choose Draw ➪ Text ➪ Single Line Text. Follow the prompts:

```
Current text style: "ROMANS" Text height: 0'-4 1/2"
Specify start point of text or [Justify/Style]: Right-click
and choose Justify.
Enter an option [Align/Fit/Center/Middle/Right/TL/TC/TR/ML/
MC/MR/BL/BC/BR]: Right-click and choose BC.
Specify bottom-center point of text: Use the Midpoint running
object snap to pick ❶ in Figure 13-5.
Specify rotation angle of text <0>: Pick the endpoint at ❷.
Enter text: 2-0 ⏎
Enter text: ⏎
```

Figure 13-5: The master bathroom

4. Start the DTEXT command again. Follow the prompts:

```
Specify start point of text or [Justify/Style]: Right-click
and choose Justify.
Enter an option
[Align/Fit/Center/Middle/Right/TL/TC/TR/ML/MC/MR/BL/BC/BR]:
Right-click and choose Middle.
Specify middle point of text: Pick ❸ in Figure 13-5. (This
point doesn't have to be exact.)
Specify rotation angle of text <45>: 0 ↵
Enter text: %%UMASTER BATH ↵
Enter text: ↵
```

5. Save your drawing. It should look like Figure 13-6.

Figure 13-6: The master bathroom plan drawing with added single-line text

Using the TEXT command

The TEXT command was AutoCAD's original command for creating text. DTEXT was an update, showing the characters on your screen as you typed. The relationship between these commands is as follows:

✦ When used in a drawing, the TEXT and DTEXT commands function identically.

✦ You can type **-text** on the command line to get the original TEXT behavior, which ends the command after one line of text.

✦ Only the TEXT commands works in script files, menus, or AutoLISP routines.

Editing single-line text

As with any drawing object, the need often arises to edit your text. You can edit single-line text in two ways.

The most common way to edit single-line text is to use the DDEDIT command. Double-click the text. Remember that each line of text created with DTEXT or TEXT is a separate object. AutoCAD opens the Edit Text dialog box with your text highlighted in an edit box, as shown in Figure 13-7. You can start typing to completely replace the text or click where you want to change part of the text and use standard Windows techniques to edit the text. Click OK or press Enter to make the changes and return to your drawing.

Figure 13-7: The Edit Text dialog box

Tip

If you start the DDEDIT command by choosing Modify ➪ Objects ➪ Text ➪ Edit (or typing DDEDIT on the command line), you are prompted to select an annotation object. Select the object and the Edit Text window opens. When you click OK, you are again prompted to select an object. The command continues to prompt you for objects until you press Enter at the prompt. Use this method when you want to edit several lines of text.

You can also change text using the Properties palette. Select any text object and click Properties on the Standard toolbar to open the Properties window, as shown in Figure 13-8. Here you can edit not only the text content but also every other conceivable property, including layer, linetype, lineweight, color, insertion point, justification, rotation angle, and several other properties that I cover in the next section on text styles.

Scaling text

You can now change the scale of selected text (either one text object or several at once) without moving the text insertion point. The SCALETEXT command scales text without moving the text insertion point. All the text objects stay in their original location.

To use SCALETEXT, follow these steps:

1. Choose Modify ➪ Object ➪ Text ➪ Scale.

2. Select the text objects to scale.

3. At the `Enter a base point option for scaling [Existing/Left/ Center/Middle/Right/Tl/TC/TR/ML/MC/MR/BL/BC/BR] <Existing>:` prompt, press Enter to use the existing insertion point of the selected text or choose a new base point. (Your last choice for this prompt becomes the new default, so if you used another option, type **e** ↵.) These options are the same as the Justify options described earlier in this chapter.

Figure 13-8: The Properties window lets you edit all text properties, including text content, in one place.

4. At the `Specify new height or [Match object/Scale factor] <3/32>:` prompt, right-click and choose Scale factor to specify a scale factor, just as you would for the SCALE command (see Chapter 9.) You can also type a new height or use the Match object option to match the height of the selected text objects to another existing text object. AutoCAD prompts you to select an object with the desired height.

5. If you chose the Scale factor option, type the factor you want at the `Specify scale factor or [Reference] <2>:` prompt.

6. If you want to specify the scale factor with reference to existing text or a value, use the Reference option. At the `Specify reference length <1>:` prompt, type a length or specify two points that measure the reference length. At the `Specify new length:` prompt, type a value or pick two points to indicate the new length.

Justifying text

The JUSTIFYTEXT command lets you change the justification of selected text objects without moving the text. To use JUSTIFYTEXT, Choose Modify ⇨ Object ⇨ Text ⇨ Justify. Then select the text objects you want to modify. At the `Enter a justification option [Left/Align/Fit/Center/Middle/Right/TL/TC/ TR/ML/MC/MR/BL/BC/BR] <Left>:` prompt, right-click and choose the justification you want.

The drawing used in the following Step-by-Step exercise on editing text, `ab13-b. dwg`, is in the `Drawings` folder of the *AutoCAD 2004 Bible* CD-ROM.

Step-by-Step: Editing Text

1. Open `ab13-b.dwg` from your CD-ROM.

2. Save the file as `ab13-02.dwg` in your `AutoCAD Bible` folder. This is an air and vacuum release valve, as shown in Figure 13-9.

3. Double-click the text 1/2" PIPING. The Edit Text dialog box opens. Highlight the text 1/2 and type **3/8**. Click OK. AutoCAD changes the text.

4. Choose Properties from the Standard toolbar. Click Quick Select in the Properties palette. In the Quick Select dialog box, choose Text from the Object type drop-down list. In the Operator drop-down list, choose Select All. Click OK. AutoCAD selects all the text objects in the drawing.

Figure 13-9: An air and vacuum release valve
Thanks to the Army Corps of Engineers for this drawing.

5. Choose Layer. From the Layer drop-down list, choose TEXT. Choose Color. From the Color drop-down list, choose ByLayer. All text is now on the TEXT layer using the ByLayer color. Press Esc to remove the grips and see the result.

6. Select the text at the bottom of the drawing that reads N.T.S. From the grips you can tell that it has a middle left justification. Choose Modify ⇨ Object ⇨ Text ⇨ Justify (or type **justifytext** ↵ on the command line). At the prompt, type **bc** ↵.

 AutoCAD ends the command. If you want, select the text again to see that the insertion point grip is now at the bottom center of the text.

7. Choose Modify ⇨ Object ⇨ Text ⇨ Scale (or type **scaletext** ↵ on the command line). Follow the prompts:

   ```
   Select objects: Select the two lines of text at the bottom of
   the drawing.
   Select objects: ↵
   Enter a base point option for scaling
   [Existing/Left/Center/Middle/Right/TL/TC/TR/ML/MC/MR/BL/BC/BR
   ] <BC>: Type e to use the existing base point.
   Specify new height or [Match object/Scale factor] <1/8">:
   Right-click and choose Scale factor.
   Specify scale factor or [Reference] <2">: Type 1.5 ↵.
   ```

 AutoCAD scales the text without moving it.

8. If you want, click the Properties palette's Close button to close it. Save your drawing.

Understanding Text Styles

You certainly do not always want to use AutoCAD's default font. AutoCAD lets you create text styles that give you full creative control over the font, font style (bold, italic, or both), character width, obliquing angle, and text height. You can even design backward, upside-down, and vertical text. (Vertical text is like the text you occasionally see on the spine of a book. It goes down instead of to the right.)

Text styles are similar to layers, which I discuss in Chapter 11. Like a layer, each text style:

✦ Has a name and several properties.

✦ Is saved with the drawing.

✦ Can be made current when you want to use it.

✦ Can be renamed and deleted.

Creating text styles is part of the typical drawing setup procedure. You should include text styles in your drawing templates.

 AutoCAD comes with two types of fonts—the original .shx fonts, which are created using AutoCAD's shape files, and TrueType fonts—the fonts used by most Windows applications. See Chapter 32 for instructions on creating your own fonts.

Creating a new text style

To create a new text style, choose Format ⇨ Text Style. This starts the STYLE command and opens the Text Style dialog box, shown in Figure 13-10.

Figure 13-10: The Text Style dialog box

Choose New to open the New Text Style dialog box, as shown in Figure 13-11. Type the name of your new text style and click OK. Text style names can be up to 255 characters and can include spaces. AutoCAD returns you to the Text Style dialog box where you define the new text style.

Figure 13-11: The New Text Style dialog box

Font

In the Font section of the Text Style dialog box, you specify the font, font style, and text height. Click the Font Name drop-down list arrow to see the list of fonts. Fonts with the double-T icon are TrueType fonts. The other fonts are AutoCAD's own fonts. AutoCAD fonts are defined in a shape file that has the file name extension .shp and are compiled into a file with the extension .shx for faster access.

Click a font to choose it. You can see a preview of the font in the Preview section of the dialog box. The Preview section also has an edit box. Type some characters and click Preview to see the preview of those characters.

If the font you have chosen supports different styles, such as bold or italic, you can choose one of them in the Font Style drop-down box. None of the AutoCAD fonts supports font styles, but many of the TrueType fonts do.

Type in the height you want for your font. Remember to take into account the scale factor if necessary.

You can leave the height at zero if you want to be able to vary the text height within that one style. If the height is zero, AutoCAD prompts you for a height whenever you use the DTEXT or TEXT command.

Caution If you create a text style using a height other than zero and use that text style when you define a dimension style, the text style height overrides the text height that you specify separately in the dimension style. See Chapter 15 for more information on dimension styles.

Effects

In the Effects section, you specify the orientation, width factor, and oblique angle of the text style.

The default width of characters is set to 1. You can specify a smaller number to compress text and a larger number to expand it, as shown in Figure 13-12.

Width = 1.5 Bearing Housing
Width = .8 Bearing Housing

Figure 13-12: Text using different width factors

The oblique angle refers to the angle of the individual letters. It is generally used to create an effect, such as italic text. Of course, you don't need to use an oblique angle if you are using a TrueType font that supports italic text.

The angle definition used to define oblique text is different from the angle definition used for other objects. Up and down text — that is, normal text — is a zero oblique angle. A positive angle slants the text to the right — typical for italic text. A negative angle slants the text to the left. Figure 13-13 shows text with a positive and negative oblique angle.

Oblique angle = –10 Bearing Housing

Oblique angle = 10 *Bearing Housing*

Figure 13-13: Text using differing oblique angles

You can create text that is backward (like a mirror image) or upside-down. Some fonts let you create vertical text. Figure 13-14 shows an example of each kind of text. Check the appropriate check box to create the effect you want.

Figure 13-14: Vertical, backward, and upside-down vertical text

After you finish defining your text style, click Apply to make it current. Click Close to return to your drawing.

Renaming and deleting text styles

You can rename and delete text styles easily. To rename a text style, start the STYLE command to open the Text Style dialog box. Choose Rename to open the Rename Text Style dialog box, as shown in Figure 13-15. It works just like the New Text Style dialog box.

Figure 13-15: The Rename Text Style dialog box

To delete a text style, choose it from the Style Name drop-down list of the Text Style dialog box and click Delete. AutoCAD asks you to confirm. Click Yes to delete the text style. You cannot delete a text style that is being used.

On the CD-ROM The drawing used in the following Step-by-Step exercise on creating text styles, `ab13-b.dwg`, is in the `Drawings` folder of the *AutoCAD 2004 Bible* CD-ROM.

Step-by-Step: Creating Text Styles

1. Open ab13-b.dwg from your CD-ROM.

2. Save the file as ab13-03.dwg in your AutoCAD Bible folder.

3. Choose Format ➩ Text Style to open the Text Style dialog box. Click New. In the New Text Style dialog box, type **Notes** and click OK.

4. From the Font Name drop-down list, choose romans.shx. In the Height text box, change the height to **1/16"**. In the Width Factor text box, change the width factor to **.95**. In the Oblique Angle text box, type **10**. Click Apply to make the new style current. Click Close.

5. Start the DTEXT command. At the Specify start point of text or [Justify/Style]: prompt, pick a start point at the lower-left corner of the drawing. At the Specify rotation angle of text <0>: prompt, press Enter. At the Enter Text: prompt, type **Note: Not drawn to scale.** ⏎. Press Enter again to end the command.

6. Save your drawing. It should look like Figure 13-16. If you are going on to the next exercise, keep this drawing open.

Figure 13-16: You have added text by using a new text style.

Modifying a text style

To change a style, choose Format ➩ Text Style. From the Style Name drop-down list, choose the text style you want to change. Make changes the same way you did when creating the style. Choose Apply and then Close. AutoCAD regenerates the drawing and changes all text that uses the style you changed. This is a powerful way to control the look of text in your drawing.

Note Unfortunately, only changes to the font and text style affect current text. Other changes, such as width factor, oblique angle, orientation, and height, are ignored. However, new text takes on these other changes.

To change existing text to another text style, choose Properties from Standard toolbar and select the text. In the Properties palette, choose a new text style in the Text Style drop-down list.

Making a style current or changing a text object's style

You can choose the current style when you use one of the text commands. If you use DTEXT or TEXT, AutoCAD displays the Specify start point of text or [Justify/Style]: prompt. Right-click and choose Style. (AutoCAD displays the current style and height before the prompt.) If you know the name of the style you want to use, type it and press Enter. AutoCAD repeats the Specify start point of text or [Justify/Style]: prompt. You can choose the Justify option or pick a start point to continue the command.

New Feature The new Styles toolbar makes is easier to make a style current or change the text style of existing text. To make a style current, choose the style from the Text Style Control drop-down list. To change the text style of existing text, select the text and choose a new style from the list.

If you use MTEXT, the Multiline Editor opens, as explained in the next section. Choose the text style you want from the Style drop-down list.

Importing a text style

As explained in Chapter 11, you can use the DesignCenter to import features from other drawings. To import a text style, follow these steps:

1. Choose DesignCenter from the Standard toolbar to open the DesignCenter.

2. In the left pane, navigate to the drawing that has the text style you want.

3. Double-click the drawing icon or click its plus sign.

4. To see the list of the text styles, double-click the text styles icon in either the left or right pane.

5. Double-click the text style's icon to import it into your drawing.

6. Click the DesignCenter's Close button to close the DesignCenter.

On the CD-ROM The drawing used in the following Step-by-Step exercise on changing text styles, ab13-3.dwg, is in the Results folder of the *AutoCAD 2004 Bible* CD-ROM.

Step-by-Step: Modifying Text Styles

1. If you have ab13-03.dwg open from the previous Step-by-Step exercise, continue to use it for this exercise. Otherwise, open ab13-03.dwg from the Results folder of your CD-ROM.

2. Save the file as `ab13-04.dwg` in your `AutoCAD Bible` folder.

3. The note at the bottom-left corner of the drawing uses the Notes text style. Choose Format ➪ Text Style. In the Text Style dialog box, make sure NOTES is the style name listed, and then choose `italic.shx` from the Font Name drop-down list. Choose Apply and then Close.

4. AutoCAD regenerates the drawing and changes the text's font.

5. Save your drawing.

Creating Multiline Text

Single-line text is awkward when you want to type quite a bit of text. The main disadvantage is that single-line text does not use word wrap, a feature that wraps text to the next line to keep a neat right margin. Multiline text (also called paragraph text and not to be confused with multilines) solves this problem and also offers many more formatting options compared to single-line text. The entire paragraph of multiline text is one object.

New Feature
AutoCAD 2004 introduces a new frameless Multiline Text editor. New features include tabs and indenting. Many of the features that were previously on tabs in the Multiline Text Editor are now available from a shortcut menu that you access by right-clicking anywhere in the text area.

The Multiline Text Editor that you use to create multiline text resembles Windows word processors. You use this box both to create and also to edit text and its properties.

Using the Multiline Text Editor

A To create paragraph text, choose Multiline Text from the Draw toolbar. This starts the MTEXT command. AutoCAD tells you the current style and text height. For example:

```
Current text style: ROMANS. Text height: 4 1/2"
```

AutoCAD continues with the `Specify first corner:` prompt. Specify one corner of a bounding box to specify where to place the text. At the `Specify opposite corner or [Height/Justify/Line spacing/Rotation/Style/Width]:` prompt, specify the diagonally opposite corner of the bounding box. You can also choose one of the other options to specify the text properties before you type in the text. Some of these options are also available in the Multiline Text Editor, which opens after you have specified the bounding box. Figure 13-17 shows the Multiline Text Editor.

New Feature
When you specify the corners of the Mtext box, you see sample text at the cursor to give you an idea of the actual current height of the text. You can change the sample text with the new MTJIGSTRING system variable.

Figure 13-17: The Multiline Text Editor

Type your text in the large edit box. The Multiline Text Editor wraps the text to the next line when AutoCAD senses that the text has met the right side of the bounding box you specified. Although you have created a bounding box with four sides, AutoCAD only limits the text by the paragraph width, that is, the left and right margins. If you type too much text for the bounding box, AutoCAD expands the Text Editor.

Note

When you type, the text may be enlarged or reduced in size. This can be disconcerting, but when you close the editor, the text takes on the correct size. To stop the text from resizing and the MText Editor from floating, set the MTEXTFIXED system variable to 1.

To format selected or new text, use the buttons on the Multiline Editor's toolbar:

✦ **Style:** Choose any text style from the Style drop-down box.

✦ **Font:** Choose any font from the Font from the drop-down list.

✦ **Text Height:** Choose a height from the drop-down list or type a new height in the Text Height box.

✦ **Bold:** If Bold is supported for the font, select text and click Bold.

✦ **Italic:** If Italic is supported for the font, select text and click Italic.

✦ **Underline:** Select text and click Underline.

✦ **Undo:** Undoes recent editing operations.

✦ **Redo:** Redoes recent editing operations.

✦ **Stack/Unstack:** Toggles stacking and unstacking fractions. Use this option to stack characters that are not numerals and not immediately before or after the three AutoStack symbols (slash, pound sign, and carat). Select the text and click Stack/Unstack. See the next section for more details.

✦ **Color:** Choose ByLayer or any color from the Color drop-down box. To choose from additional colors, choose Select Color to open the Select Color dialog box. (See Chapter 11 for details on using this dialog box.)

Tip

To create an exponent (or superscript), type a number and then a carat, as in 2^. Select the number and the carat and click the Stack/Unstack button. To create a subscript, type a carat, and then the number, as in ^2, and stack it.

Right-click in the editor to display the shortcut menu. The shortcut menu contains many important controls that are no longer available elsewhere. You have the following options:

✦ **Undo:** Undoes the last Mtext edit.

✦ **Redo:** Redoes the last undo operation.

✦ **Cut:** Places selected text in the Windows clipboard and removes it from the editor.

✦ **Copy:** Place selected text in the Windows clipboard.

✦ **Paste:** Places text from the Windows clipboard.

✦ **Indents and Tabs:** Opens the Indents and Tabs dialog box, as shown in Figure 13-18. You can set the following:

　• **First line indentation:** Sets the indentation for the first line of the paragraph.

　• **Paragraph indentation:** Sets the indentation for every line of the paragraph except the first line. Use this indentation for creating bulleted and numbered lists.

Tip

To indent an entire paragraph, use both first line and paragraph indentation.

　• **Tabs:** Type the location of each tab.

Tip

It's easier to set indentation and tabs on the Multiline Editor's ruler than in the dialog box. Drag the first line indent marker (the top triangle at the left of the ruler) or the paragraph indent marker (the bottom triangle) to the left or right. To set a tab, click on the ruler where you want the tab. To delete a tab, drag a tab marker off the ruler.

Figure 13-18: Use the new Indents and Tabs dialog box to set indents and tabs for your text.

✦ **Justification:** Choose a justification from the submenu. The justifications are discussed in the "Justifying single-line text" section earlier in this chapter.

✦ **Find and Replace:** Opens the Replace dialog box so that you can find or replace specified text. If you want the search to match the case of the specified text, choose Match Case. If you want the search restricted to whole words that match the specified text, choose Whole Words. To find text, ignore the Replace text box. To both find and replace text, enter text in both boxes. Make sure that the cursor is at the beginning of the text if you want to search the entire Mtext object.

✦ **Select All:** Selects all the text.

✦ **Remove Formatting:** Removes formatting, such as bold and italic. Does not remove color or font changes.

✦ **Combine Paragraphs:** Combines separate paragraphs into one. First select the paragraphs that you want to combine.

✦ **Change Case:** Changes the case of selected text to uppercase or lowercase.

✦ **AutoCAPS:** Automatically changes newly typed and imported text to uppercase, even if the Caps Lock key is not on. (And it's a cute pun on AutoCAD.)

✦ **Symbol:** Inserts the degree, plus/minus, or diameter symbol. You can also insert a non-breaking space. Or choose Other to open the Windows Character Map to choose any of the available symbols. Click a symbol, and then click Select. Click Copy and then click the Close button to close the Windows Character Map. In the Text Editor, press Ctrl+V to paste in the symbol.

✦ **Import Text:** Opens the Select File dialog box, which lets you choose a text (.txt) or Rich Text Format (.rtf) file to import. Find the file, choose it, and click Open. AutoCAD inserts it into the Multiline Text Editor. The maximum file size is 16 kilobytes. Other techniques for importing text are covered later in this chapter.

Note Rich Text Format preserves formatting from application to application. Text-only documents retain no formatting.

After you finish creating multiline text, close the editor in one of three ways:

✦ Click OK on the Text Formatting bar

✦ Click anywhere outside the Multiline Text Editor (but inside the drawing area)

✦ Press Ctrl + Enter

New Feature You can snap to the corners of the Mtext bounding box using the Node Object Snap. (See Chapter 4 for an explanation of object snaps.)

Creating stacked fractions automatically

You can create automatic stacked fractions and tolerances as you type, using a system similar to those described earlier for creating special characters with DTEXT/TEXT.

You can also type unstacked fractions (as in **1/2**), select the fraction text, and then click Stack/Unstack on the Character tab. To create stacked fractions as you type, open the Multiline Text Editor and follow these steps:

1. Type the numerator (or text that you want on top).

2. Type the character that defines the fraction format you want:

- Type a slash (**/**) to create a fraction separated by a horizontal line.
- Type a pound symbol (**#**) to create a fraction separated by a diagonal line.
- Type a carat (**^**) to create a tolerance stack, which is like a fraction separated by a horizontal line except that there is no horizontal line.

3. Type the denominator.

4. Type a space (or other nonnumeric character). AutoCAD opens the AutoStack Properties dialog box.

5. Change any settings you want to change and click OK. AutoCAD creates the stacked fraction.

To use the settings in the AutoStack Properties dialog box:

✦ Uncheck `Enable AutoStacking` to disable the automatic stacked fraction feature.

✦ Uncheck `Remove leading blank` if you want to retain a space between whole numbers and fractions.

✦ Choose whether you want the slash to result in a fraction with a horizontal line or a fraction with a slash. This choice has no effect on how the pound sign and carat work. If you want the slash to result in a fraction with a slash (which would seem to make more sense), you have no automatic way to create a fraction with a horizontal line.

✦ Check `Don't show this dialog again; always use these settings` to stop the dialog box from opening when you create automatic stacked fractions.

✦ Click OK to create the stacked fraction or Cancel to leave the numbers as you typed them.

AutoStack only works with numerals immediately before and after the slash, pound sign, and carat.

You can also set the properties of individual stacked fractions. Right-click the fraction in the Multiline Text Editor and choose Properties from the menu. In the Stack Properties dialog box you can change the following properties:

✦ **Text:** Edit the upper and lower text.

✦ **Style:** Change the fraction style. (See the sidebar figure for the three possible styles.)

✦ **Position:** Position the fraction so that the top, center, or bottom is aligned with other text.

✦ **Size:** Change the size of the numbers that make up the fraction. Fraction numbers are usually smaller than regular numbers.

$\frac{3}{5}$ ⟵ Typed as 3/5

$\frac{3}{5}$ ⟵ Typed as 3#5

$\frac{3}{5}$ ⟵ Typed as 3^5

Specifying and changing line spacing

You can specify the spacing between lines in multiline text. Line spacing is useful for fitting text into a schedule or table in your drawing. To set line spacing:

1. Start the Mtext command.

2. At the `Specify first corner:` prompt, pick the first corner of your Mtext box.

3. At the next prompt, `Specify opposite corner or [Height/Justify/ Line spacing/Rotation/Style/Width]:`, choose Line spacing.

4. At the `Enter line spacing type [At least/Exactly] <Exactly>:` prompt, choose Exactly.

5. At the `Enter line spacing factor or distance <1x>:` prompt, type a number, such as **1** to specify a one unit space between lines of text. (If you type **1x**, you get single line spacing, which varies according to the size of the text.)

6. Then continue with the command.

This setting persists for future Mtext objects. To change existing line spacing, select (but do not double-click) the multiline text. Open the Properties palette and set one or more of the following:

✦ Line space factor: Specifies line spacing as a multiple of lines. Single line spacing is 1.0000; double line spacing is 2.0000.

✦ Line space distance: Specifies line spacing in units. Use this measurement (along with a line space style of Exactly) to fit text into an existing table or schedule.

✦ Line space style: Choose At Least (the default) to adjust line spacing based on the height of the largest charter in the line of text. Choose Exactly to specify line spacing that is the same regardless of differences in character height.

Specifying and changing width and rotation

To change the width of an Mtext object, you can use its grips:

1. Select the Mtext object.

2. Click one of the grips that you want to stretch to make it "hot." (For instructions on using grips to edit objects, see Chapter 10.)

3. At the `Specify stretch point or [Base point/Copy/Undo/eXit]:` prompt, pick a new location for the grip, to make the multiline text wider or narrower.

You can use the Properties palette to change the width and height. You can specify the exact width when creating the Mtext object by using the Width option after you specify the first corner of the Mtext box. Otherwise, you generally specify the width by picking the two corners of the Mtext box.

Tip When the Multiline Text Editor is open, you can change the width of the Mtext object by dragging on the right edge of the ruler. You can also change the width of the editor itself by dragging on the right edge of the editor box.

To rotate an existing Mtext object, use the Properties palette or use the grips:

1. Select the Mtext object.

2. Click one of the grips to make it "hot."

3. Right-click and choose Rotate.

4. At the `Specify rotation angle or [Base point/Copy/Undo/Reference/eXit]:` prompt, pick a new location for the grip or type a rotation angle.

You can also specify the rotation while creating the Mtext object. Use the Rotate option that appears on the command line after you specify the first corner.

Editing paragraph text

To edit paragraph text, double-click the text to open the Multiline Text Editor.

Note If you choose single-line text created with TEXT or DTEXT, AutoCAD opens the Edit Text dialog box (refer to Figure 13-7).

Make your changes in the edit box. The techniques are similar to those in any word processor. Your options are:

✦ Select text and press Del to delete the text or type to replace the selected text.

✦ Click to move the insertion point to where you want to insert text and start typing. (To type over text, press Insert to enter overtype mode.)

✦ Use the toolbar or shortcut menu to change formatting.

To change characters, you must first highlight the characters. This lets you make height or font changes to individual words or even letters. When changing properties that affect the entire paragraph, such as justification, you do not first highlight the characters.

Mmt combines two MText objects into one MText paragraph. Look in \Software\ Ch13\Mmt.

Importing text

As mentioned earlier, you can import text from the Multiline Text Editor. You can import text in three other ways:

✦ You can use drag-and-drop to insert text into a drawing. Open Windows Explorer and locate the file. It should be a text (.txt) or Rich Text Format (.rtf) file. Position the Explorer window so that you can see the file name and your AutoCAD drawing at the same time. Click the file and drag it to your drawing. Close Windows Explorer and move the text to the desired location.

✦ You can copy text from another file to the Windows clipboard. Open the other file, select the text, and choose Copy from the Standard toolbar. Return to your drawing by clicking the AutoCAD button on the Windows Taskbar. Choose Paste from the Standard toolbar. The OLE Properties dialog box opens (by default). Specify the properties of the object and click OK.

✦ If you are in the Multiline Text Editor, you can paste the text directly into the editor. Right-click in the editor and choose Paste (or use Ctrl+V). You can then format the text.

For more information on importing text, see Chapter 27.

The files used in the following Step-by-Step exercise on creating multiline text, ab13-c.dwg and ab13.txt, are in the Drawings folder of the *AutoCAD 2004 Bible* CD-ROM.

Step-by-Step: Creating Multiline Text

1. Open ab13-c.dwg from your CD-ROM.

2. Save the file as ab13-05.dwg in your AutoCAD Bible folder. This is a plat drawing, as shown in Figure 13-19.

Figure 13-19: The plat drawing

Thanks to Bill Maidment of Cantech, Inc., Fairfield, Iowa for this drawing.

3. Choose Multiline Text from the Draw toolbar. At the prompts, pick points ❶ and ❷ in Figure 13-19. The Multiline Text Editor opens. In the Text Height box, change the height to **12.5**. In the main editing box, type the following:

Containing 108.33 acres including 5.97 acres existing R.O.W. and 4.56 acres proposed R.O.W.

4. Highlight the text 108.33 and click Underline. Right-click in the text window and choose Justification ⇨ Middle Left. Click OK AutoCAD places the text.

5. Do a Zoom Window around the table at the lower-right corner of the drawing, so that the table takes up about half the drawing area. Start the MTEXT command. Follow the prompts:

```
Specify first corner: Pick ❹ in Figure 13-19.
Specify opposite corner or [Height/Justify/Line
spacing/Rotation/Style/Width]: Right-click and choose Height.
Specify height <10>: 60 ↵
Specify opposite corner or [Height/Justify/Line
spacing/Rotation/Style/Width]: Right-click and choose Line
spacing.
Enter line spacing type [At least/Exactly] <At least>: Right-
click and choose Exactly.
Enter line spacing factor or distance <1x>: 100 ↵
Specify opposite corner or [Height/Justify/Line
spacing/Rotation/Style/Width]: Pick ❺ in Figure 13-19.
```

The Multiline Editor opens. Depending on your zoom, the text cursor may be larger or smaller than the rows of the table, which is okay.

6. If necessary, drag the right and bottom edges of the editor's text area to approximately match the size of the table. You may also need to drag the right side of the ruler itself to match the width of the table. At the tab line just to the right of the vertical line of the second column, click in the ruler to add a tab. You see a small "L" to indicate a tab at this location.

7. Click at the left of the first line. Type the following table, pressing the Tab key to move from column to column and pressing Enter at the end of each line. Use the Spacebar before the acre figures in the last three rows to line up the numbers.

1	22.93
2	2.85
3	1.51
4	1.38

8. Click anywhere outside the Multiline Text Editor to close the editor and see the results. The text should be lined up in the table. Choose Zoom Previous to see the entire drawing again.

9. Open Windows Explorer (Usually Start ⇨ Programs ⇨ Windows Explorer). Find `ab13.txt` on your CD-ROM. Move the Windows Explorer window so that you can see both `ab13.txt` and your AutoCAD screen. Drag `ab13.txt` from the Windows Explorer window to ❸ in Figure 13-19. If necessary, pick a grip, press the Spacebar once to choose the Move option and click at the proper location.

10. Select the text and open the Properties palette. (Click Properties on the Standard toolbar.) Next to the Width item, type **500** ↵. Next to the Height item, type **12.5** ↵.

11. Use ZOOM Window to zoom in on the new text. You can see how %%d became the degree symbol. This text was originally single-line text in an older AutoCAD drawing. You can see why you wouldn't want to retype it!

12. Choose Zoom Previous on the Standard toolbar to return to your original view. Save your drawing.

Managing Text

Text is a complex object type. Text greatly increases drawing size and adds redraw and regeneration time. The more complex fonts, such as the TrueType fonts, can have a huge impact on how long it takes to open and save a file. The three techniques described in this section help you to manage text and improve performance while editing your drawing. The last section introduces a way to control the mirroring of text objects.

Tip When you draw in three dimensions, you need to figure out how to combine three-dimensional models with two-dimensional text. You can use the HIDETEXT system variable to choose whether you want text to act like a 3D or a 2D object. Use the On setting, the default, if you want text to be hidden behind other objects and to hide other objects when you use the HIDE command, such as other 3D objects. If you use the Off setting, text will not hide other objects, or be hidden, unless it has a thickness. (See Chapter 21 for more on the HIDE command and adding a thickness to objects.)

Using Quicktext

The QTEXT command replaces all text with rectangles that approximate the placement of the original text, as shown in Figure 13-20. All text objects, including dimensions, attributes, and tolerances, are affected. To use QTEXT, type **qtext** ↵ on the command line. Type **on** ↵ to get the rectangles; Type **off** ↵ to return to regular text. Then type **regen** ↵ at the command line. Quicktext takes effect only after a regeneration. It does not apply to OLE objects that you have pasted into a drawing from the Windows clipboard. (See Chapter 27.)

Figure 13-20: A drawing with QTEXT on. Rectangles have replaced all the text.

Thanks to Rod Greer of R. G. Greer Design, Inc., Fergus, Ontario for this drawing.

Using AutoCAD fonts

AutoCAD fonts are simpler than TrueType fonts, and some AutoCAD fonts are simpler than others. The simplest font is txt.shx, the font used by the default Standard text style. You can easily define a text style using an AutoCAD font and

then change the font to something nicer just before plotting. AutoCAD immediately changes the font of all text using that style. Be aware that the text may take up more or less space than before.

When AutoCAD cannot find the specified font, it uses an alternate font. This may happen if you receive a drawing done by someone else that uses a custom or third-party font that you don't have. You can specify the alternate font by choosing Tools ⇨ Options and clicking the plus sign next to Text Editor, Dictionary, and Font File Names on the Files tab. Choose Alternate Font File to specify the alternate font, which is `simplex.shx` by default.

You can further control the fonts used by AutoCAD by customizing the Font Mapping File, `\acad.fmp`. The format is `current_font; font_to_substitute`. You need to use the actual file names of the fonts. To substitute a simpler font for the Arial Black font, you could add the following line:

```
Ariblk.ttf;simplex.shx
```

To find the Windows TrueType fonts, look in the Fonts subfolder of your Windows folder.

Note To find `acad.fmp`, choose Tools ⇨ Options and click the File tab. Double-click Text Editor, Dictionary, and Font File Names. Double-click Font Mapping File. Click the path list to view the location of `acad.fmp`. AutoCAD only reads the font-mapping file when it opens a new drawing, so that any changes you make are effective only after you start a new drawing.

Freezing text layers

Freezing text layers can help regeneration time dramatically — a good reason to give text its own layer. Don't forget to freeze dimension text, too. Dimensions are usually placed on a separate layer (see Chapter 14).

Using MIRRTEXT

When you mirror sections of your drawing that include text, you usually don't want backward text (unless you are Alice going through the looking glass). The MIRRTEXT system variable controls whether text is mirrored or retains its normal orientation.

New Feature The default value for MIRRTEXT is now off, so that mirrored text is not backward. The text is copied to the mirrored location, but reads from left to right (if that is the direction of the language you are using).

If you do want to mirror the text, type **mirrtext** ↵. At the New value for MIRRTEXT <0>: prompt, type **1** ↵ to turn MIRRTEXT on. This system variable is saved with the drawing, so that you may still need to change it when you open older drawings.

On the CD-ROM The drawing used in the following Step-by-Step exercise on managing text, ab13-d. dwg, is in the Drawings folder of the *AutoCAD 2004 Bible* CD-ROM.

Step-by-Step: Managing Text

1. Open ab13-d.dwg from your CD-ROM.

2. Save the file as ab13-06.dwg in your AutoCAD Bible folder. This is a small section of an electrical schematic, as shown in Figure 13-21. Make sure ORTHO and OSNAP are on and set running snaps for endpoint, midpoint, and intersection.

Figure 13-21: A section of an electrical schematic

3. Type **qtext** ↵. At the Enter mode [ON/OFF] <OFF>: prompt, type **on** ↵. Type **regen** ↵. AutoCAD replaces the text with rectangles.

4. Type **qtext** ↵. At the Enter mode [ON/OFF] <ON>: prompt, type **off** ↵. Type **regen** ↵. AutoCAD redraws the original text.

5. Start the MIRROR command. Follow the prompts:

```
Select objects: Start a window by picking ❷ in Figure 13-21.
Specify opposite corner: Pick ❶. Press Enter to end object
selection.
Specify first point of mirror line: Use the Midpoint running
object snap to pick the midpoint at ❸.
Specify second point of mirror line: Pick any point vertical
to the first point.
Delete source objects? [Yes/No] <N>: ↵
```

AutoCAD mirrors the objects and the text. The text is backward.

6. Choose Undo from the Standard toolbar.

7. Type **mirrtext** ↵. At the `Enter new value for MIRRTEXT <1>:` prompt, type **0** ↵.

8. Repeat the mirror operation using the same instructions as in Step 5. This time AutoCAD mirrors the objects, but the text reads properly, as shown in Figure 13-22.

Figure 13-22: The text on the right was mirrored with MIRRTEXT set to 0.

9. Save your drawing.

Express Tools has a number of text routines that you may find very helpful. Table 13-3 lists these tools. See Appendix A on the CD-ROM for information on installing Express Tools.

Table 13-3
Express Tools for Text

Command	Menu	Description
RTEXT	Express ➪ Text ➪ Remote Text	Displays text from an outside file. You can specify the text style, height, and rotation. Use RTEDIT on the command line to edit remote text.
TEXTFIT	Express ➪ Text ➪ Text Fit	Stretches or shrinks Text objects (but not MText) to fit between two points.
TEXTMASK	Express ➪ Text ➪ Text Mask	Creates a wipeout, 3D face, or 2D solid object behind the text with a little extra space around the text. You can use this to make text on top of a hatch more legible.
TEXTUNMASK	Express ➪ Text ➪ Text Unmask	Removes a text mask.
TXTEXP	Express ➪ Text ➪ Explode Text	Transforms Text or Mtext into geometrical shapes.
TXT2MTXT	Express ➪ Text ➪ Convert Text to MText	Converts Text objects to Mtext objects.
ARCTEXT	Express ➪ Text ➪ Arc-Aligned Text	Aligns text along an arc.
TORIENT	Express ➪ Text ➪ Rotate Text	Rotates multiple text, Mtext, and attribute definitions to a specified angle without moving them or aligns them so that they are horizontal or right-side up for easy reading.
TCIRCLE	Express ➪ Text ➪ Enclose Text with Object	Encloses selected Text or Mtext inside a circle, slot (a rectangle but with arcs at each end), or a rectangle.
TCOUNT	Express ➪ Text ➪ Automatic Text Numbering	Numbers lines of text by adding a prefix, suffix, or overwriting the text.
TCASE	Express ➪ Text ➪ Change Text Case	Offers the following ways to change the case of text: uppercase, lowercase, sentence case, title case, and toggle case.

Finding Text in Your Drawing

In a large, complex drawing with a lot of text, you may have difficulty finding specific text that you need to edit. The FIND command lets you find and replace text anywhere in your drawing — not only single-line text and multiline text but also text in block attributes, dimensions, and hyperlinks.

To use the FIND command, choose Edit ⇨ Find to open the Find and Replace dialog box, as shown in Figure 13-23.

Figure 13-23: The Find and Replace dialog box finds text anywhere in your drawing.

Here's how to use the Find and Replace dialog box:

1. Type the text you want to find in the Find text string text box. Use the drop-down list to choose recently used text strings.

2. If you want to replace the text you find with new text, type it in the Replace with text box. This box also includes a drop-down list of recently used text strings.

3. If you want to limit or expand the scope of your search, use the Search in drop-down box. If you selected objects before starting the FIND command, this drop-down list displays Current selection. You can choose Entire Drawing from this list. You can also click the Select objects button to return to your drawing and select objects. The FIND command then limits its search to selected objects.

4. Choose Options to specify the type of text FIND will search. By default it searches all types of text. You can also choose the Match case and Find whole words only options.

5. Click Find (Next) to find the next instance of the text string. The dialog box displays the text in the context of the text around it.

6. Click Replace to replace the text string with the replacement text. Click Replace All to replace all instances of the text string with the replacement text.

7. If the Search in drop-down list is set to Current selection, you can click Select All to return to your drawing with all instances of the text string you have searched for selected. AutoCAD tells you on the command line how many objects it has selected. You can use this to delete all these objects, for example. Also, because the objects have grips, it is easy to locate them in your drawing—this is useful for a drawing large enough so that you can't read the text when you have the entire drawing displayed on your screen.

8. Use the Zoom To button to zoom in to a selection that the FIND command has found. You can then edit the text. As with the Select All button, this feature is useful for large drawings where the text is not legible unless you zoom in.

9. After you are finished, click Close to close the dialog box.

Checking Your Spelling

If you take pride in the accuracy of your drawings, you might as well make sure that the text is spelled correctly. Use the SPELL command to check your spelling. AutoCAD's spelling checker acts just like the one in your word processor.

Choose Tools ➪ Spelling and select some text objects to open the Check Spelling dialog box, as shown in Figure 13-24. You can type **all** ↵ to check the spelling for the entire drawing.

Note Spell checking also checks text inside blocks. See Chapter 18 for the full explanation of blocks.

Figure 13-24: The Check Spelling dialog box

You have the following options:

✦ **Ignore:** Choose Ignore to ignore the current instance of this word only.

✦ **Ignore All:** Choose Ignore All to ignore all instances of this word.

✦ **Change:** Select the suggested word you want and choose Change to change the current instance of the word to one of the suggested words.

✦ **Change All:** Select the suggested word you want and choose Change All to change all instances of the word to one of the suggested words.

✦ **Add:** Choose Add to add the word to the dictionary. The word will not appear again as misspelled.

✦ **Lookup:** Use this if you type a word in the Suggestion text box and want to check its spelling. AutoCAD then lists words similar to the word in the Suggestion text box.

AutoCAD automatically moves from word to word until you see the message `Spelling Check Complete`.

Tip
Strangely enough, if you don't have any misspelled words in your drawing, you cannot open the Check Spelling dialog box. AutoCAD simply issues the Spelling Check Complete message. The trick is to insert a misspelled word and then use the SPELL command. You can erase or correct the word afterward.

Customizing the spelling dictionary

You can change the main and custom spelling dictionaries. To change the spelling dictionaries, choose Change Dictionaries from the Check Spelling dialog box to open the Change Dictionaries dialog box, as shown in Figure 13-25.

Figure 13-25: The Change Dictionaries dialog box

The main dictionary comes with AutoCAD and is not customizable. You can choose from various languages depending on your version of AutoCAD. For example, my list lets me choose from American English, British English (ise), British English (ize), French with unaccented capitals, and French with accented capitals.

The custom spelling dictionary is the dictionary you add to when you click Add in the Check Spelling dialog box. It is a simple text file that includes words that you have added during spelling checks, as well as a list of AutoCAD-related words already included by AutoCAD. To see these words, scroll down the list in the Custom dictionary words section of the Change Dictionaries dialog box.

You can add words to the custom dictionary by typing them in the Custom dictionary words text box and clicking Add. This feature lets you add a number of words at one time.

Tip

Another way to edit the custom dictionary is to open the file directly with a text editor. The AutoCAD custom dictionary is called `sample.cus`. To find `sample.cus`, choose Tools ⇨ Options and click the File tab. Double-click Text Editor, Dictionary, and Font File Names. Double-click Custom Dictionary File. Click the path list to view the location of `sample.cus`.

Figure 13-26 shows `sample.cus` opened in Notepad, the Windows text editor.

Figure 13-26: Opening `sample.cus` in Notepad so that you can edit it directly

You can use a different custom dictionary. It can be useful, for example, to use the same dictionary in AutoCAD as you use in your word processor. For example, here's how to use the Microsoft Word dictionary:

1. Find Word's custom dictionary. If necessary, choose Start ⇨ Find and use the Windows Find dialog box to find the file. It is called `custom.dic`. As with the AutoCAD custom dictionary, you can open it with Notepad and edit it directly.

2. As explained in the previous Tip, find the location of `sample.cus`. Use Windows Explorer to copy the file to that folder. You can hold down Ctrl as you drag it from one folder to another or use the right mouse button to click the file, choose Copy, and then paste it in its new location.

3. Click custom.dic to highlight it. Click it again and change its file name extension to .cus. Press Enter. (Windows asks you if you are sure you want to do this. Click Yes.)

4. Click Change Dictionaries in the Check Spelling dialog box to open the Change Dictionaries dialog box. In the Custom dictionary text box, type in the name of the dictionary file, or choose Browse, find it, and click Open.

5. Click Apply & Close to return to the Check Spelling dialog box and then Cancel to return to your drawing.

Summary

In this chapter, you learned how to create, edit, and manage text. You read about:

✦ Using DTEXT and TEXT to create single-line text

✦ Editing single-line text

✦ Scaling and justifying text without moving it

✦ Creating text styles to control the formatting of your text

✦ Utilizing MTEXT for creating and editing paragraph text, including using the new Multiline Text Editor

✦ Importing text

✦ Managing text for fastest display

✦ Finding and replacing text and how to check spelling in your drawing

In the next chapter, you read how to create dimensions.

✦　　　✦　　　✦

Drawing Dimensions

◆ ◆ ◆ ◆

In This Chapter

Working with AutoCAD's dimensions

Drawing linear and aligned dimensions

Dimensioning arcs, circles, and angles

Creating ordinate dimensions

Drawing leaders

Editing dimensions

◆ ◆ ◆ ◆

Dimensions are an important part of most AutoCAD drawings. Dimensions indicate the measurement of the models you have created and are used in the manufacturing process. AutoCAD's dimensions offer a great deal of flexibility. In this chapter, I cover the process of drawing dimensions. In the next chapter, I explain how to customize the format of your dimensions by using dimension styles.

Working with AutoCAD's Dimensions

Dimensioning is usually done after you complete all or most of a drawing. Dimensioning a drawing all at once lets you create a unified, organized look for your dimensions. Before you can dimension drawing, you need to understand the elements of a dimension and how to prepare for dimensioning.

Cross-Reference In Chapter 17, I explain how to dimension a drawing on a paper space layout.

The elements of a dimension

A dimension is a complex object, containing many parts. Understanding these parts and how they relate to the object you are dimensioning is an important first step. Figure 14-1 shows a typical linear dimension.

Figure 14-1: The parts of a dimension

The parts of a dimension are:

✦ **Extension lines:** These extend from the dimensioned object to the dimension line and arrowheads. A small gap usually separates the dimensioned object and the start of the extension lines. Extension lines visually clarify the extents of the object being dimensioned.

Note In dimensions, the word *extension* (or *extend*) is used in two other ways besides referring to extension lines. First, the extension line itself usually extends not only from the object being dimensioned but past the dimension line. You can specify the amount of this extension. Also, in architectural dimensions, the dimension line extends past the extension lines. You can specify this extension as well.

✦ **Dimension text:** This tells you the actual measurement of the dimensioned object. You can format this text in decimals, fractions, scientific units, and so on.

✦ **Dimension line:** This extends between the extension lines.

✦ **Arrowheads:** These mark the intersection of the dimension line and the extension lines. They can take several forms, such as tick marks, open arrows, or dots.

Dimensions have two interesting properties that you need to understand before you can successfully work with them.

✦ **Dimensions are blocks.** I have mentioned blocks before, and they are fully covered in Chapter 18. Blocks are groups of objects that you can manipulate as one object. As a result, if you pick a dimension, all parts of the dimension are selected.

✦ **Dimensions are associative.** This means that an association connects the dimension and the object it dimensions. If you change the size of the object, AutoCAD automatically adjusts the dimension.

All the parts of a dimension can be formatted individually. You generally format a dimension by creating a dimension style, which is a named set of formats for dimensions — just as a text style is a named set of formats for text. Dimension styles are the topic of the next chapter.

Preparing to dimension

Before starting to create dimensions, you should prepare as follows:

1. Create a layer for your dimensions. It is important that dimensions be easily distinguishable from the rest of your drawing. The color is usually a contrast to that of your models. For example, if your models are black (and you are working on a white screen), you might want your dimensions to be green, magenta, or cyan.

Tip

If you often turn layers on and off (or freeze and thaw them), you may want to create a separate dimension layer for each layer of drawing data. For example, if you dimension an electrical layer that you turn off regularly, you can have a special Dim-elec dimension layer that you can turn off with the electrical layer.

2. If you are dimensioning an existing drawing that was created in a pre-2002 version of AutoCAD, turn on associative dimensioning with the DIMASSOC system variable. Type **dimassoc** on the command line and type **2** ↵ at the prompt. (You can also choose Tools ⇨ Options, click the User Preferences tab, and check the check box in the Associative Dimensioning section of the dialog box. Then click OK.)

3. Create a text style for your dimensions.

Tip

Set the height of the text style to zero. You can then set the text height when you create the dimension style. If you do specify a fixed height in your text style, that height overrides any height you specify in the dimension style.

4. Choose Tools ⇨ Drafting Settings, click the Object Snap tab, and set the running object snaps you want. Endpoint and intersection are a necessity. Add center and quadrant if you need to dimension arcs and circles. Click OSNAP on the status bar to turn it on.

5. Create a dimension style. The next chapter covers dimension styles.

6. Save your dimension layer, dimension text style, and dimension style in your drawing templates.

The Dimension toolbar makes it easy to find the dimension commands quickly. The Dimension menu offers most of the same commands as the toolbar.

To display the Dimension toolbar, right-click any toolbar and check Dimension from the list. The list automatically closes. The Dimension toolbar is shown in Figure 14-2.

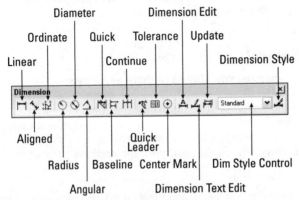

Figure 14-2: The Dimension toolbar

Cross-Reference

The dimensioning command names are generally long. For example, to draw a linear dimension, you would type **dimlinear** ↵. As briefly mentioned in Chapter 3, AutoCAD has shortcuts for many commands, including the dimensioning commands, contained in acad.pgp. Chapter 29 covers these shortcuts and how to create your own.

Drawing Linear Dimensions

Just as the most common objects are lines, the most common dimensions are linear dimensions.

Use linear dimensions for lines, a straight segment of a polyline, or a straight segment in a block. You can also use a linear dimension for arcs and circles — you get the linear length of the arc (not its perimeter length) and the diameter of the circle.

Specifying the dimensioned object

To dimension a line, choose Linear Dimension from the Dimension toolbar. AutoCAD responds with the Specify first extension line origin or <select object>: prompt. You can now either pick two extension line origin points or press Enter (or right-click) and select an object for dimensioning.

<image name="tip_bulb" />

Tip
Make it standard practice to use object snaps for choosing extension line origins. The point you pick specifies the definition point that determines the final measurement. Also, proper association of dimensions with their objects depends on the points you specify. Accurate dimensioning requires accurate drawings and therefore exact specification of the points you want to use for the dimensions.

If you are dimensioning more than one object, such as the distance from the endpoint of one line to the endpoint of another line, pick the first extension line origin. At the `Specify second extension line origin:` prompt, pick the second extension line origin. These two points define the length of the dimension.

If you are dimensioning one object, press Enter (or right-click) at the `Specify first extension line origin or <select object>:` prompt. AutoCAD displays the `Select object to dimension:` prompt. Pick the object.

At the `Specify dimension line location or [Mtext/Text/Angle/ Horizontal/Vertical/Rotated]:` prompt, pick a point for the location of the dimension line. As you move the mouse, you can see the results on your screen, as shown in Figure 14-3. If you want an exact location, you can type in a relative coordinate, such as **0,.5** to specify that the dimension line should be 0.5 units above the object. Snap mode may also work well for you, depending on the drawing environment.

Figure 14-3: Picking a dimension line location for a linear dimension

Object snap tracking makes it a snap to pick points for dimensioning. For example, if you are dimensioning a house, your first extension line origin may be the outside

corner of the house, but the second extension line origin may be an inner wall. At the Specify first extension line origin or <select object>: prompt, move the cursor over the inner wall endpoint to acquire it. Move the cursor back to the line you are dimensioning and click when you see the tooltip showing the snap point you chose. AutoCAD places the dimension just where you need it.

On the CD-ROM

The drawing used in the following Step-by-Step exercise on drawing linear dimensions, ab14-a.dwg, is in the Drawings folder of the *AutoCAD 2004 Bible* CD-ROM.

Step-by-Step: Drawing Linear Dimensions

1. Open ab14-a.dwg from your CD-ROM.

2. Save the file as ab14-01.dwg in your AutoCAD Bible folder. This is a plan of a bedroom, as shown in Figure 14-4. ORTHO and OSNAP should be on. Set running object snaps for endpoint, midpoint, and intersection. The current layer should be set to Dim.

Figure 14-4: A bedroom plan

3. To display the Dimension toolbar, right-click any toolbar. Click Dimension. If you want, drag the toolbar to the top or bottom of your screen until it docks.

4. Choose Linear Dimension from the Dimension toolbar. At the Specify first extension line origin or <select object>: prompt, pick ❶ in Figure 14-4. At the Specify second extension line origin: prompt,

pick ❷. At the `Specify dimension line location or [Mtext/Text/ Angle/Horizontal/Vertical/Rotated]:` prompt, move the cursor to the right until you have sufficient space for the dimension text and click.

5. Repeat the DIMLINEAR command. At the `Specify first extension line origin or <select object>:` prompt, press Enter. At the `Select object to dimension:` prompt, pick ❸ (the window) in Figure 14-4. At the `Specify dimension line location or [Mtext/Text/Angle/Horizontal/ Vertical/ Rotated]:` prompt, move the cursor down until you have sufficient space for the dimension text and click.

6. Save your drawing. It should look like Figure 14-5.

Figure 14-5: The bedroom with two linear dimensions

Using dimension options

You can also use one of the options offered at the command prompt to further control the final dimension. Dimension options control the text and the angle of the dimension.

MText

The MText option lets you replace the dimension text AutoCAD calculates or add a prefix or suffix to it. When you right-click and choose MText at the `Specify dimension line location or [Mtext/Text/Angle/Horizontal/Vertical/ Rotated]:` prompt, AutoCAD opens the Multiline Text Editor, as shown in Figure 14-6.

Figure 14-6: Changing the dimension text with the Multiline Text Editor

The angle brackets represent the dimension text that AutoCAD automatically creates. The best use of the MText option is to add some text before or after the measurement, such as **TYP** (for typical — used when one dimension applies to several objects) or **subject to final approval**. To add text before the measurement, place the cursor before the angle brackets. Similarly, to add text after the measurement, place the cursor after the angle brackets. Add the text and click OK.

If the measurement text itself does not appear the way you want it, you should change the annotation specifications in the dimension style. You can also specify a prefix or suffix (such as *mm*) for all dimensions, as explained in the next chapter.

You can delete the brackets and type your own dimension text, but you lose the ability of the dimension's measurement to automatically adjust to any change in the object's size.

Note Typing your own dimension text is most commonly used where a dimension represents several sizes and refers to a size chart elsewhere in the drawing. For example, the text "Dim A" might be used for this purpose.

Text

The Text option also lets you change dimension text but does not open the Multiline Text Editor. Instead, you can quickly retype the entire dimension text as you want it on the command line.

Angle

The angle of the text (horizontal, vertical, or aligned) is specified in your dimension style. However, you can use this option to change the angle of the dimension text for a particular circumstance. Right-click and choose Angle to get the Specify angle of dimension text: prompt. Type in an angle or pick two points to align the text with an existing object.

Horizontal/Vertical

The DIMLINEAR command assumes that you want a horizontal dimension if you select a horizontal object or two definition points running horizontally — ditto for a

vertical dimension. Also, if you want to draw a vertical dimension of an object at an angle, you can specify this simply by moving the mouse cursor horizontally when specifying the dimension line location, as shown in Figure 14-7. If for some reason you need to force either a horizontal or vertical dimension, you can use the vertical or horizontal options.

Figure 14-7: By dragging the mouse cursor to the right, you can create a vertical dimension for this angled line. The vertical dimension measures the change in the Y coordinates of the line, not the length of the line.

Rotated

Use a rotated linear dimension when the length you want to dimension is not parallel to the extension line origins. Just as the vertical dimension in Figure 14-7 does not measure the length of the line its extension lines extend to, a rotated linear dimension does not measure a specific object but the distance of an imaginary line parallel to the dimension line. Rotated dimensions are not very common, but when you need them they are the only way to get the dimension measurement you need.

To use a rotated dimension, start a linear dimension, pick the two extension line origins and choose the Rotate option. At the `Specify angle of dimension line <0>:` prompt, type the angle (or pick two points). AutoCAD draws the dimension.

Figure 14-8 shows a hexagonal stepping-stone with a rotated linear angle. The extension lines of the dimension extend to a line at 104.5 degrees, but in this case you want to measure a length at an angle of 135 degrees. Note that AutoCAD has really dimensioned an imaginary line parallel to the dimension line, shown in the figure as a dashed line, rather than the side of the hexagon.

Figure 14-8: Drawing a rotated linear dimension for a hexagonal stepping stone

The drawing used in the following Step-by-Step exercise on using linear dimension options, ab14-b.dwg, is in the Drawings folder of the *AutoCAD 2004 Bible* CD-ROM.

Step-by-Step: Using Linear Dimension Options

1. Open ab14-b.dwg from your CD-ROM.

2. Save the file as ab14-02.dwg in your AutoCAD Bible folder. This is part of a plan of a house with an unusual-shaped ceiling, as shown in Figure 14-9. OSNAP should be on. Set running object snaps to endpoint and intersection. If the Dimension toolbar doesn't appear, right-click any toolbar and check Dimension.

Figure 14-9: A house plan with an octagonal ceiling

3. Choose Linear Dimension from the Dimension toolbar. Follow the prompts:

```
Specify first extension line origin or <select object>: ⏎
Select object to dimension: Pick ❶ in Figure 14-9.
Specify dimension line location or
[Mtext/Text/Angle/Horizontal/Vertical/Rotated]: Right-click
and choose Angle.
Specify angle of dimension text: Choose ❷ in Figure 14-9.
Specify second point: Choose ❸ in Figure 14-9.
Specify dimension line location or [Mtext/Text/Angle/
Horizontal/Vertical/Rotated]: Position the dimension line
above the wall you dimensioned.
```

Note You wouldn't actually dimension an architectural drawing in this style.

4. Repeat the DIMLINEAR command. Follow the prompts:

```
Specify first extension line origin or <select object>: ⏎_
Select object to dimension: Pick ❹ in Figure 14-9.
Specify dimension line location or
[Mtext/Text/Angle/Horizontal/Vertical/Rotated]: Right-click
and choose Mtext. In the Multiline Text Editor move the
cursor after the angled brackets and type TYP. Click OK.
Specify dimension line location or [Mtext/Text/Angle/
Horizontal/Vertical/Rotated]: Position the dimension line
above the window you dimensioned.
```

Notice that the text is attached to a leader because it is now too long to fit between the extension lines.

5. Save your drawing. It should look like Figure 14-10.

Figure 14-10: The dimensioned drawing

Drawing Aligned Dimensions

When you want to dimension a linear object that is not orthogonal, use an aligned dimension. The dimension lines of an aligned dimension are always parallel to the object — unlike rotated dimensions. An aligned dimension measures the actual length of the object, not a vertical or horizontal distance that you dimension with a linear dimension. Therefore, your choice of linear, linear rotated, or aligned dimension depends on the distance you want to measure. Figure 14-11 shows several aligned dimensions.

Figure 14-11: Three aligned dimensions

Specifying the dimensioned object

To create an aligned dimension, choose Aligned Dimension from the Dimension toolbar. This starts the DIMALIGNED command. AutoCAD responds with the `Specify first extension line origin or <select object>:` prompt. As with linear dimensions, you can now either pick two extension line origins or press Enter to select an object.

Because Figure 14-11 shows a cross-section view, there is no single object you can select. To create the aligned dimensions shown, you need to pick two extension line origins.

AutoCAD then displays the `Specify dimension line location or [Mtext/ Text/Angle]:` prompt. Pick a point for the location of the dimension line. If you want an exact location, you can type in a relative coordinate, such as **@2<45** to specify that the dimension line should be 2 units in a 45-degree direction from the extension line origins you specified.

Using the options

After you have chosen what you want to dimension, you have three options—
MText, Text, and Angle. The previous section discusses these options in detail.

The drawing used in the following Step-by-Step exercise on drawing aligned
dimensions, ab14-b.dwg, is in the Drawings folder of the *AutoCAD 2004 Bible*
CD-ROM.

Step-by-Step: Drawing Aligned Dimensions

1. Open ab14-b.dwg from your CD-ROM.

2. Save the file as ab14-03.dwg in your AutoCAD Bible folder. This is the same
 drawing used in the previous Step-by-Step exercise, as shown in Figure 14-12.
 OSNAP should be on. Set running object snaps to endpoint and intersection.
 If the Dimension toolbar isn't visible, choose View ➪ Toolbars and check
 Dimension. Click Close.

Figure 14-12: A section of a floor plan
of a house

3. Choose Aligned Dimension from the Dimension toolbar. Follow the
 prompts:

```
Specify first extension line origin or <select object>:
Choose ❶ in Figure 14-12.
Specify second extension line origin: Choose ❷ in Figure
14-12.
Specify dimension line location or
[Mtext/Text/Angle]: Right-click and choose Mtext. In the
Multiline Text Editor, move the cursor to the right of the
angled brackets and type Typ. Click OK.
Specify dimension line location or
[Mtext/Text/Angle]: Pick a location for the dimension line.
```

4. Save your drawing. It should look like Figure 14-13.

Figure 14-13: The house plan with an aligned dimension

Creating Baseline and Continued Dimensions

Often, you want to create a whole series of attached, connected dimensions. AutoCAD offers two ways to accomplish this — baseline and continued dimensions:

✦ Baseline dimensions are a series of dimensions that all start from one point. The first extension line is the same for all the dimensions. The second dimension includes the first dimension plus an additional distance and so on.

✦ Continued dimensions are a series of dimensions that are all attached. The second dimension starts where the first dimension ends and so on. Each dimension measures a different object or distance.

Figure 14-14 shows both baseline and continued linear dimensions. You can also create baseline and continued angular and ordinate dimensions. Quick Dimension, covered later in this chapter, can quickly create baseline and continued linear dimensions. Here I cover the traditional method.

Baseline dimensions Continued dimensions

Figure 14-14: A floor plan of a house using both baseline and continued dimensions

Drawing baseline dimensions

To draw a baseline dimension, first create one linear, angular, or ordinate dimension in the regular way. (Angular and ordinate dimensions are covered later in this chapter.) Then choose Baseline Dimension from the Dimension toolbar. AutoCAD responds with the `Specify a second extension line origin or [Undo/Select] <Select>:` prompt.

If the previous dimension was a linear, angular, or ordinate dimension, AutoCAD uses its first extension line as the base for the new baseline dimension. Specify a new second extension line origin, and AutoCAD creates the baseline dimension with the same first extension origin as the original dimension and the new second extension origin you just specified.

If you don't want to work with the previous dimension in the drawing, press Enter. AutoCAD responds with the `Select base dimension:` prompt. Be careful to pick the dimension closer to the side you want to use as the baseline. AutoCAD then prompts you to specify a second extension line origin. When you do so, AutoCAD creates the dimension.

AutoCAD continues to prompt you for second extension line origins so that you can quickly create a chain of baseline dimensions. At each prompt you can right-click and choose Undo to undo the previous dimension. You can also press Enter at any time and select a different dimension to work from. Press Esc to end the command (or press Enter twice).

Drawing continued dimensions

Continued dimensions work similarly to baseline dimensions. To continue a dimension, first create one linear, angular, or ordinate dimension in the regular way. Then choose Continue Dimension from the Dimension toolbar. AutoCAD responds with the `Specify a second extension line origin or [Undo/Select] <Select>:` prompt.

If the previous dimension was a linear, angular, or ordinate dimension, AutoCAD uses its second extension line as the beginning of the new continued dimension. Specify a new second extension line origin, and AutoCAD creates the continued dimension.

If you don't want to continue from the previous dimension in the drawing, press Enter. AutoCAD responds with the `Select continued dimension:` prompt. Be careful to pick the dimension closer to the side you want to continue from. AutoCAD then prompts you to specify a second extension line origin. When you do so, AutoCAD creates the dimension.

AutoCAD continues to prompt you for second extension line origins so you can quickly create a chain of continued dimensions. At each prompt you can right-click and choose Undo to undo the previous dimension. You can also press Enter at any time and select a different dimension to work from. Press Esc to end the command (or press Enter twice).

On the CD-ROM

The drawing used in the following Step-by-Step exercise on drawing baseline and continued dimensions, `ab14-b.dwg`, is in the `Drawings` folder of the *AutoCAD 2004 Bible* CD-ROM.

Step-by-Step: Drawing Baseline and Continued Dimensions

1. Open `ab14-b.dwg` from your CD-ROM.

2. Save the file as `ab14-04.dwg` in your `AutoCAD Bible` folder. This is the same drawing used in the previous two exercises, as shown in Figure 14-15. OSNAP should be on with running object snaps for endpoint and intersection. If the Dimension toolbar isn't visible, right-click any toolbar and check Dimension.

3. Turn on ORTHO and OTRACK on the status bar.

4. Choose Linear Dimension from the Dimension toolbar. Follow the prompts:

   ```
   Specify first extension line origin or <select object>: Pick
   the endpoint at ❶ in Figure 14-15.
   Specify second extension line origin: Pass the cursor over ❸
   to acquire it for object snap tracking. Move the cursor to
   the right so that it's vertically under ❶ and click when you
   see the 1'-6'<0° tooltip.
   Specify dimension line location or [Mtext/Text/Angle/
   Horizontal/Vertical/Rotated]: Pick a dimension line location
   to the right of the model.
   ```

5. ⊞ Choose Continue Dimension from the Dimension toolbar. At the `Specify a second extension line origin or [Undo/Select] <Select>:` prompt, move the cursor over the endpoint or intersection at ❹ to acquire it for object snap tracking. Move the cursor to the right, vertically below ❶ and click when you see the tooltip. AutoCAD places the continued dimension. Notice that AutoCAD uses a leader to place the text because there is not enough room between the extension lines. (If the leader is placed to the left, select it and pick the grip on the text. Pick a point to the right of the model and click to move the leader to the right.)

Figure 14-15: The house plan with the octagonal ceiling

6. AutoCAD repeats the `Specify a second extension line origin or [Undo/Select] <Select>:` prompt. Pick the endpoint at ❷ in Figure 14-15. AutoCAD places the dimension. Press Enter twice to end the command.

7. Choose Linear Dimension from the Dimension toolbar. Follow the prompts:

```
Specify first extension line origin or <select object>:
Choose the endpoint at ❺ in Figure 14-15.
Specify second extension line origin: Move the cursor over ❼
to acquire it. Move the cursor down so that it's horizontal
to ❺. When you see the 4'0"<270° tooltip, click.
Specify dimension line location or [Mtext/Text/Angle/
Horizontal/Vertical/Rotated]: Pick a dimension line location
fairly close to the line you dimensioned leaving just enough
room for the dimension text.
```

8. ⊟ Choose Baseline Dimension from the Dimension toolbar. At the `Specify a second extension line origin or [Undo/Select] <Select>:` prompt, pick the endpoint or intersection at ❻ in Figure 14-15. Press Enter twice to end the command.

9. Save your drawing. It should look like Figure 14-16.

Figure 14-16: The floor plan with baseline and continued dimensions

Dimensioning Arcs and Circles

When you dimension an arc or a circle, you measure its radius or diameter. It is also common to mark arc and circle centers to clarify what you are measuring. Arc and circle dimensions are most commonly used in mechanical drawings.

Marking arc and circle centers

Circle and arc centers are often marked in mechanical drawings because the center is an important aspect of a circle or arc but is not obvious without a mark. You set the size and type of mark when you create a dimension style, as explained in the next chapter. You can use a center mark (a small cross) or centerlines, as shown in Figure 14-17.

⊕ Choose Center Mark from the Dimension toolbar. At the `Select arc or circle:` prompt, pick the arc or circle you want to mark. AutoCAD draws the mark or lines.

Creating radial dimensions

To dimension the radius of a circle or arc, choose Radius Dimension from the Dimension toolbar. AutoCAD responds with the `Select arc or circle:` prompt. Select an arc or circle. At the `Specify dimension line location or [Mtext/Text/Angle]:` prompt, pick where you want the dimension line to appear. AutoCAD automatically adds an *R* before the measurement to indicate the radius, as shown in Figure 14-18.

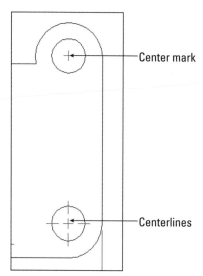

Figure 14-17: Circles — one with a center mark and the other with centerlines

Figure 14-18: This radius dimension uses a leader (a line and arrow pointing to the object) outside the circle because the circle is too small to place the dimension inside it.

You can also choose the MText, Text, or Angle option, as described in the "Drawing Linear Dimensions" section earlier in this chapter.

Creating diameter dimensions

To dimension the diameter of a circle or arc, choose Diameter Dimension from the Dimension toolbar. AutoCAD responds with the `Select arc or circle:` prompt. Select an arc or circle. At the `Specify dimension line location or [Mtext/Text/Angle]:` prompt, pick where you want the dimension line to appear. AutoCAD automatically adds the diameter symbol before the measurement to indicate the dimension, as shown in Figure 14-19.

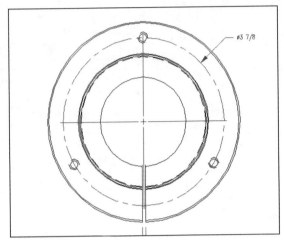

Figure 14-19: A diameter dimension

You can also choose the MText, Text, or Angle option, as described in the section "Drawing Linear Dimensions."

Dimensioning Angles

AutoCAD offers several options for dimensioning angles. You may want to dimension the angular relationship between two lines, but the lines may intersect at their midpoints or may not intersect at all. Therefore, you need to be able to specify the vertex of the angle you want to dimension. Figure 14-20 shows an angular dimension with the points used to define it.

To create an angular dimension, choose Angular Dimension from the Dimension toolbar. AutoCAD displays the Select arc, circle, line, or <specify vertex>: prompt and responds differently depending on what you select:

✦ If you press Enter, AutoCAD asks for the angle vertex, the first angle endpoint, and the second angle endpoint. These three points define the angle.

✦ If you select an arc, AutoCAD dimensions the entire arc, using the arc's center as the angle vertex.

✦ If you select a circle, AutoCAD uses the pick point as the first angle endpoint and the circle's center as the angle vertex. AutoCAD then displays the Specify second angle endpoint: prompt. Pick a point on the circle.

✦ If you select a line, AutoCAD asks for a second line. AutoCAD measures the angle between the two lines. If the lines don't intersect, AutoCAD uses their implied intersection as the angle vertex.

Figure 14-20: An angular dimension

Thanks to Mary Redfern of the Bethlehem Corporation,
Easton, Pennsylvania, for this drawing.

After you define the angle, AutoCAD responds with the Specify dimension arc line location or [Mtext/Text/Angle]: prompt. Pick a point for the dimension arc line — which is the same thing as a dimension line except that AutoCAD uses an arc for angular dimensions.

You can also choose the MText, Text, or Angle option, as covered in the section "Drawing Linear Dimensions."

In the following exercise, you get to practice drawing radial, diameter, and angular dimensions.

On the CD-ROM The drawing used in the following Step-by-Step exercise on drawing radial, diameter, and angular dimensions, ab14-c.dwg, is in the Drawings folder of the *AutoCAD 2004 Bible* CD-ROM.

Step-by-Step: Drawing Radial, Diameter, and Angular Dimensions

1. Open ab14-c.dwg from your CD-ROM.

2. Save the file as ab14-05.dwg in your AutoCAD Bible folder. This is a view of a bearing housing for an industrial washing machine, as shown in Figure 14-21. OSNAP should be on. Set running object snaps to endpoint, intersection, and center. If the Dimension toolbar isn't visible, right-click any toolbar and check Dimension.

Figure 14-21: A bearing housing for an industrial washing machine

Thanks to Robert Mack of the Dexter Company, Fairfield, Iowa, for this drawing.

3. Choose Center Mark from the Dimension toolbar. At the `Select arc or circle:` prompt, pick one of the four small circles at the corners of the model. Repeat the command for the other three circles.

4. Choose Diameter Dimension from the Dimension toolbar. At the `Select arc or circle:` prompt, choose the circle at ❶ in Figure 14-21. At the `Specify dimension line location or [Mtext/Text/Angle]:` prompt, pick a location for the dimension line.

5. Choose Radius Dimension from the Dimension toolbar. At the `Select arc or circle:` prompt, choose ❷ from Figure 14-21. At the Specify dimension line location or [Mtext/Text/Angle]: prompt, pick a location for the dimension line. The line may appear to the left of the angle; try moving the cursor until the dimension appears to its right.

6. Choose Angular Dimension from the Dimension toolbar. Follow the prompts:

```
Select arc, circle, line, or <specify vertex>: ↵
Specify angle vertex: Pick ❸ in Figure 14-21.
Specify first angle endpoint: Pick the endpoint at ❹. (Press
Tab if necessary until you see the endpoint tooltip.)
Specify second angle endpoint: Pick the endpoint at ❺.
Specify dimension arc line location or [Mtext/Text/Angle]:
Choose a location for the dimension line.
```

Dimensioning minor, major, and supplemental angles

When two lines meet at an angle, they create two angles—the *minor angle* and the *major angle*. The angle that is less than 180 degrees is the minor angle. The major angle is always more than 180 degrees. AutoCAD also lets you measure the *supplemental angle*, which is the difference between 180 degrees and the minor angle. These angles are shown here.

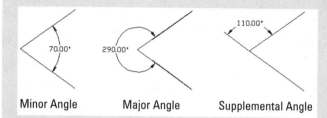

Minor Angle Major Angle Supplemental Angle

Here's how you create each type of dimension. Start the DIMANGULAR command. AutoCAD responds with the `Select arc, circle, line, or <specify vertex>:` prompt.

To dimension the minor angle, select both lines. Then at the `Specify dimension arc line location or [Mtext/Text/Angle]:` prompt, place the dimension arc line inside the angle, as shown in the figure. (You can also press Enter, specify the angle vertex and the two lines, and place the dimension arc line inside the angle.)

To dimension the major angle, press Enter. (Do not select the lines.) At the prompts, specify the angle vertex and the two lines. At the `Specify dimension arc line location or [Mtext/Text/Angle]:` prompt, place the dimension arc line outside the angle, as shown in the figure.

To dimension the supplemental angle, select both lines. At the `Specify dimension arc line location or [Mtext/Text/Angle]:` prompt, place the dimension arc line outside the angle, as shown in the figure.

As you can see, how you specify the angle and where you place the dimension arc line determine which angle you measure.

7. Repeat the DIMANGULAR command. At the `Select arc, circle, line, or <specify vertex>:` prompt, pick the arc at ❻. At the `Specify dimension arc line location or [Mtext/Text/Angle]:` prompt, pick a location for the dimension line.

8. Repeat the DIMANGULAR command. At the `Select arc, circle, line, or press ENTER:` prompt, pick ❼ in Figure 14-21. At the `Second line:` prompt, pick ❽. At the `Dimension arc line location (Mtext/Text/Angle):` prompt, pick a location for the dimension line to the left of the model.

9. Save your drawing. It should look like Figure 14-22.

Figure 14-22: The bearing housing with center marks, radial and diameter dimensions, and angular dimensions

Creating Ordinate Dimensions

Ordinate dimensions are used in mechanical drawing. They dimension an object by labeling X or Y coordinates based on a 0,0 coordinate placed somewhere on the model. Figure 14-23 shows a drawing with some ordinate dimensions.

Figure 14-23: Ordinate dimensions in a mechanical drawing of a tension arm for a commercial dryer

To place the 0,0 coordinate on the model, choose Tools ➪ Move UCS. At the prompt, pick a point on the model, using object snaps for an exact measurement. If you want to check the UCS, choose View ➪ Display ➪ UCS Icon ➪ Origin. Also make sure On is checked. As long as there is room, the UCS icon moves to the new 0,0 coordinate.

To create an ordinate dimension, choose Ordinate Dimension from the Dimension toolbar. At the Specify feature location: prompt, pick the part of the model that you want to dimension. Running object snaps with OSNAP turned on makes this an easy task.

At the Specify leader endpoint or [Xdatum/Ydatum/Mtext/Text/Angle]: prompt, pick the endpoint for the leader. AutoCAD generally decides whether to dimension the X coordinate (Xdatum) or Y coordinate (Ydatum) based on where you pick the leader endpoint. Pick the leader endpoint perpendicular from the coordinate's axis you want to measure. To measure an X coordinate, move up or down from the feature you selected. To measure a Y coordinate, move left or right to pick the leader endpoint.

Usually you work with ORTHO on to create straight lines. If you need to create bent lines to avoid previously drawn dimensions, turn ORTHO off. If you pick a leader endpoint at a nonorthogonal angle from the feature, you may need to force AutoCAD to measure the coordinate you want using either the Xdatum or Ydatum option. Use the MText option to open the Multiline Text Editor and edit the dimension text. Use the Text option to change all the text on the command line.

To perfectly line up the dimensions, when specifying the leader endpoint, use object tracking to track the endpoint of the previous leader. You can also turn on SNAP.

On the CD-ROM The drawing used in the following Step-by-Step exercise on drawing ordinate dimensions, ab14-d.dwg, is in the Drawings folder of the *AutoCAD 2004 Bible* CD-ROM.

Step-by-Step: Drawing Ordinate Dimensions

1. Open ab14-d.dwg from your CD-ROM.

2. Save the file as ab14-06.dwg in your AutoCAD Bible folder. This drawing shows a simple sheet metal template, as shown in Figure 14-24. Snap should be on. Set a snap distance of 0.25 units. Right-click the SNAP button on the status bar and make sure that grid snap is on. If the Dimension toolbar isn't visible, right-click any toolbar and check Dimension.

3. Choose Tools ➪ Move UCS. At the Origin point <0,0,0>: prompt, pick ❶ in Figure 14-24.

4. Choose Ordinate Dimension from the Dimension toolbar. At the Specify feature location: prompt, choose ❶ in Figure 14-24. At the Specify leader endpoint or [Xdatum/Ydatum/Mtext/Text/Angle]: prompt, pick a point 0.5 units to the left of ❶, as shown in Figure 14-25. (Because Snap is on, this is easy. If necessary, press F6 until you get polar coordinates to display in the lower-left area of the drawing screen.)

Figure 14-24: A sheet metal template

Figure 14-25: The dimensioned template

5. Repeat the DIMORDINATE command. At the `Specify feature location:` prompt, choose ❶ in Figure 14-24. At the `Specify leader endpoint or [Xdatum/Ydatum/Mtext/Text/Angle]:` prompt, pick a point 0.5 units below ❶.

6. Continue to dimension the drawing, using Figure 14-25 as a guide. (Tip: Type **multiple** ↵ **dimordinate** ↵ so that AutoCAD automatically repeats the command. Press Esc when you no longer need the command.)

7. Save your drawing.

Drawing Leaders

Leaders are lines pointing to objects. At the end of a leader, you place any text you want. Use leaders to label objects or provide explanatory text. Leaders are not associative; that is, AutoCAD calculates no dimension text. Figure 14-26 shows two leaders.

Figure 14-26: Using leaders to point to objects and add explanatory text

The QLEADER command provides a simple, easy-to-use method of creating leaders. The Leader Settings dialog box lets you specify how you want your leaders to appear. The older LEADER command is still available from the command line.

To create a leader, choose Quick Leader from the Dimension toolbar. At the `Specify first leader point, or [Settings]<Settings>:` prompt, if you want to specify the leader settings, press Enter or right-click and choose Settings to open the Leader Settings dialog box.

Using the Leader Settings dialog box

The Leader Settings dialog box is shown in Figure 14-27 with the Annotation tab displayed. Here you customize how you want your leaders to work so that when you actually create them, they automatically look the way you want. These settings determine what prompts you see after you specify all the points of the leader. You can always change these settings at the first prompt of the QLEADER command.

Figure 14-27: The Annotation tab of the Leader Settings dialog box

The Annotation tab

The annotation tab includes settings about what goes at the end of the leader. In the Annotation Type section of the dialog box, choose the type of annotation:

✦ The default is MText, which creates multiline text.

✦ Choose Copy an Object to have the QLEADER command prompt you to copy an existing object in your drawing—single line text, multiline text, a block, or a tolerance.

✦ If you choose Tolerance, QLEADER opens the Tolerance dialog box so that you can create a tolerance control frame. The next chapter covers control frames.

✦ Choose Block Reference if you want QLEADER to prompt you to select an existing block (a group of objects that are treated as one object) for the annotation. You might have a block consisting of some text and special symbols that are hard to create from scratch each time. Some users put surface, tolerance, or other symbols at the ends of leaders.

✦ Choose None to create a leader with no annotation.

If you chose MText, use the MText options section to specify how MText works. You have three choices:

✦ Choose "Prompt for width" if you want QLEADER to let you specify a bounding box or a width in units. The advantage of this option, which is on by default, is that QLEADER wraps the leader text so that it doesn't get too long if you decide to get verbose.

✦ Choose "Always left justify" if you don't want to set a width and want instead to have QLEADER always left-justify text.

✦ Choose "Frame text" if you want a box around the text.

The Annotation Reuse section enables you to clone your leader annotation. To reuse the text you are about to create, choose Reuse Next. QLEADER automatically uses it for subsequent leaders. (After you use this option, AutoCAD automatically sets this option to Reuse Current.)

The Leader Line & Arrow tab

Use the Leader Line & Arrow tab, shown in Figure 14-28, to specify how you want the lines and arrow of the leader to look.

Figure 14-28: The Leader Line & Arrow tab of the Leader Settings dialog box

In the Leader Line section, choose either Straight line or Spline leader lines. The number of points determines how many times QLEADER displays the `Specify next point:` prompt. By setting a maximum you can streamline the process of creating leaders and avoid ungainly looking leader lines with many segments. However, you can't set the maximum to less than two.

In the Arrowhead section, use the drop-down list to choose an arrowhead style. The picture shown of each type of arrowhead helps you decide.

Use the Angle Constraints section to control the possible angle of the first and second leader lines to conform to standards in your industry or your sense of aesthetics.

The Attachment tab

Use the Attachment tab, shown in Figure 14-29, to specify how MText is attached to the leader line.

Figure 14-29: The Attachment tab of the Leader Settings dialog box

The Attachment tab contains two columns of buttons. The left column sets the attachment for leaders that you draw from right to left. The arrow is to the right and the text is therefore on the left of the leader. By default, the leader line points to the middle of the bottom line of text — that is, to the middle of the last character of the text.

The right column sets the attachment for leaders that you draw from left to right. The arrow is to the left and the text is on the right of the leader. By default, the leader line points to the middle of the top line of that — that is, to the middle of the first character of the text.

Here are your choices for text on both the left and the right:

✦ **Top of top line:** The leader line meets the text at the top of the first line of text. The line will point to the top of an uppercase letter.

✦ **Middle of top line:** The leader line meets the text at the middle of the first line of text, which is halfway between the top and the bottom of an uppercase letter.

✦ **Middle of multi-line text:** The leader line meets the text at the middle of the invisible bounding box containing all the text.

✦ **Middle of bottom line:** The leader line meets the text at the middle of the bottom line of text.

✦ **Bottom of bottom line:** The leader line meets the text at the bottom of the bottom line of text.

Check Underline bottom line to place a line under the bottom line of text. After you have completed the settings in the Leader Settings dialog box, click OK. AutoCAD now continues with the QLEADER command.

New Feature The Express Tools include the QLDETACHSET command, which detaches a leader's annotation from the leader line, to create two separate objects. Choose Express ➪ Dimension ➪ Leader Tools ➪ Detach Leaders from Annotation. QLATTACH attaches leaders and MText objects. Choose Express ➪ Dimension ➪ Leader Tools ➪ Attach Leader to Annotation. For information about installing Express Tools, see Appendix A on the CD-ROM.

Creating a leader

As mentioned earlier, when you choose Quick Leader from the Dimension toolbar, you see the `Specify first leader point, or [Settings]<Settings>:` prompt. You can continue directly to draw the leader or use the Settings option. If you use the Settings option, once you close the Leader Settings dialog box, AutoCAD returns you to the original prompt. Now you can specify your first leader point, usually on or near the object that the leader text labels or explains. The starting point is usually indicated with an arrow.

AutoCAD continues with the `Specify next point:` prompt. You can continue to pick points, up to the limit specified on the Leader Line & Arrow tab of the Leader Settings dialog box. Usually you pick the endpoint of the leader before that limit. Press Enter to stop picking points of the leader.

If the Prompt for Width option has been selected on the Annotation tab of the Leader Settings dialog box, QLEADER displays the `Specify text width <0.0000>:` prompt. You can pick a point and AutoCAD displays a dashed line so that you can visually determine the width. Otherwise, type a width in units.

At the `Enter first line of annotation text <Mtext>:` prompt, you have two choices:

✦ To use the current text style, type the first line of text on the command line. Press Enter at the end of the line. QLEADER displays the `Enter next line of annotation text:` prompt. You can continue to type in new lines of text. Press Enter to end the command.

✦ To open the Multiline Text Editor, press Enter. You then type your annotation text. You have the advantage of being able to format the text as you work. Click OK to close the Text Editor and complete the leader.

On the CD-ROM The drawing used in the following Step-by-Step exercise on drawing leaders, `ab14-e.dwg`, is in the `Drawings` folder of the *AutoCAD 2004 Bible* CD-ROM.

Step-by-Step: Drawing Leaders

1. Open `ab14-e.dwg` from your CD-ROM.

2. Save the file as `ab14-07.dwg` in your `AutoCAD Bible` folder. This is a drawing of a set of pulleys, as shown in Figure 14-30. If the Dimension toolbar isn't visible, right-click any toolbar and check Dimension. OSNAP should be turned off.

Figure 14-30: A set of pulleys

3. Choose Quick Leader from the Dimension toolbar. At the `Specify first leader point, or [Settings]<Settings>:` prompt, right-click and choose Settings. Click the Attachment tab and set both text on the left and on the right to Middle of multiline text. Click OK.

4. Follow the prompts:

   ```
   Specify first leader point, or [Settings]<Settings>: Pick ❶
   in Figure 14-30 (near but not on the drawing object).
   Specify next point: Pick ❷.
   Specify next point: ↵
   Specify text width <0>: 2 ↵
   Enter first line of annotation text <Mtext>: BREAK EDGES ↵
   Enter next line of annotation text: TYP (8) PLACES ↵
   Enter next line of annotation text: ↵
   ```

 AutoCAD places the leader.

5. Repeat the QLEADER command. Pick points ❸ and then ❹ in Figure 14-30. Right-click or press Enter. At the `Specify text width <2>:` prompt, press Enter to use the same width as previously. At the `Enter first line of annotation text <Mtext>:` prompt, type **DRILL 'F' HOLE**. Press Enter twice to end the command and place the leader.

6. Save your drawing. It should look like Figure 14-31.

Figure 14-31: The pulleys with two leaders

Using Quick Dimension

Quick Dimension enables you to dimension several objects at one time. You can use Quick Dimension for baseline, continued, and ordinate dimensions. You can also dimension multiple circles and arcs. Later in this chapter I explain how you can use Quick Dimension to edit dimensions as well. While Quick Dimension may seem like the answer to all your dimension-related prayers, you can't use it in every case. However, it works well in "mass production" situations.

 New Feature Dimensions created with the QDIM command are now fully associative, so that any changes you make to objects automatically update their associated dimensions.

Here's how it works, in three easy steps:

1. Choose Quick Dimension from the Dimension toolbar.

2. At the `Select geometry to dimension:` prompt, select all the objects that you want to dimension. You can't use object snaps; you need to select objects. If you select an object in error, type **r** ⏎ and then pick the object again to remove it. Then type **a** ⏎ to start adding objects again.

3. At the `Specify dimension line position, or [Continuous/ Staggered/ Baseline/Ordinate/Radius/Diameter/datumPoint/Edit/ SeTtings]<Continuous>:` prompt, right-click and choose the type of dimension you want to create. Figure 14-32 shows a set of continuous dimensions. The datum point option sets a new base point for baseline and ordinate dimensions. You can press Enter to use the type of dimension you used just previously because that shows as the default. AutoCAD immediately creates the dimensions for you.

Figure 14-32: A set of continuous dimensions created with Quick Dimension

 On the CD-ROM The drawing used in the following Step-by-Step exercise on using Quick Dimension to create dimensions, `ab14-f.dwg`, is in the `Drawings` folder of the *AutoCAD 2004 Bible* CD-ROM.

Step-by-Step: Using Quick Dimension to Create Dimensions

1. Open ab14-f.dwg from your CD-ROM.

2. Save the file as ab14-08.dwg in your AutoCAD Bible folder. This is the same drawing you used in the previous exercise, except that some of the dimensions have been removed (see Figure 14-33). OSNAP should be turned off. If the Dimension toolbar isn't displayed, right-click any toolbar and choose Dimension.

Figure 14-33: You can use Quick Dimension to dimension the circles and create continuous dimensions.

3. Choose Quick Dimension from the Dimension toolbar. Follow the prompts:

```
Select geometry to dimension: Pick the circle at ❶ in Figure
14-33.
Select geometry to dimension: Pick the circle at ❷ in Figure
14-33.
Select geometry to dimension: ↵
Specify dimension line position, or
[Continuous/Staggered/Baseline/Ordinate/Radius/Diameter/datum
Point/Edit/SeTtings]
<Staggered>: Right-click and choose Radius.

Specify dimension line position, or
[Continuous/Staggered/Baseline/Ordinate/Radius/Diameter/datum
Point/Edit/SeTtings]
<Radius>: Pick a point on the left circle at about 80 degrees
from the right quadrant.
```

Quick Dimension places the radius dimensions.

4. Repeat the QDIM command. Follow the prompts:

```
Select geometry to dimension: Pick the line at ❸ in Figure
14-33.
Select geometry to dimension: Pick the line at ❹ in.

Select geometry to dimension: Pick the vertical centerline
at ❺.
Select geometry to dimension: Pick the vertical centerline
at ❻.
Select geometry to dimension: Pick the line at ❼.

Select geometry to dimension: ↵
Specify dimension line position, or
[Continuous/Staggered/Baseline/Ordinate/Radius/Diameter/datum
Point/Edit/SeTtings]
<Staggered>: Right-click and choose Baseline.

Specify dimension line position, or
[Continuous/Staggered/Baseline/Ordinate/Radius/Diameter/datum
Point/Edit/SeTtings]
<Baseline>: Pick a point below the model.
```

Quick Dimension places the baseline dimensions.

5. Save your drawing. It should look approximately like Figure 14-34.

Figure 14-34: The model with added radius and baseline dimensions

Editing Dimensions

Dimensions have many properties—text size, arrowhead size, text placement, and so on. You change most of these properties by changing the dimension style, either globally changing all dimensions using that style or overriding a dimension style setting for a particular dimension. The next chapter covers dimension styles, but here I cover several other ways to edit dimensions.

Editing associativity

By default, new drawings created in AutoCAD 2004 are associative. However, drawings created in releases prior to 2002 will not have the new associativity.

The DIMASSOC system variable specifies whether dimensions are associative. Here are the settings:

✦ **0** creates exploded dimensions. Each part of the dimension is a separate object and there is no association between the dimension and the object it dimensions.

✦ **1** creates non-associative dimensions. The dimension is all one object but is not updated if the object it dimensions is changed.

✦ **2** creates associative dimensions. The dimension is all one object and is updated if the object it dimensions is changed.

DIMREASSOCIATE

Use the DIMREASSOCIATE command to associate dimensions with their objects. You need to use this command when you open drawings created in releases of AutoCAD 2000i or earlier in Release 2004. You might also need to use this command when dimensions become disassociated from their objects, perhaps through some editing process, or to reassociate dimensions after you have disassociated them for some reason.

To use DIMREASSOCIATE, follow these steps:

1. Choose Dimension ➪ Reassociate Dimensions.

2. At the `Select objects:` prompt, select the dimensions that you want to associate. Press Enter to end object selection.

 You see a prompt that varies according to the type of dimension you have selected. For example, for linear dimensions, you see the `Specify first extension line origin or [Select object] <next>:` prompt. At the same time, you see a marker in the form of an X that corresponds to the prompt, as shown in Figure 14-35. The marker indicates an *association point*—a point that connects an object and all or part of its dimension. If the X has a box around it, the dimension is already associated with the point marked by the X.

Note If you use the wheel of a mouse to pan or zoom, the X disappears. Press Esc and start the command again or type **'redraw** ⏎.

Figure 14-35: When you associate a dimension with an object, AutoCAD displays an association point on the object.

3. Use an object snap to specify the location of the X (whether the same as shown or a different location) or use the Select Object option to select an object (right-click and choose Select Object). To skip to the next prompt, without associating the dimension to the marked point, press Enter.

4. Continue to respond to the prompts in turn. AutoCAD prompts you through all the dimensions you selected.

Caution When specifying object snaps, be careful that you choose the point you want. For example, if you use an Endpoint object snap where two lines meet, you cannot be sure which line's endpoint you have chosen. When you move or stretch the line you expect to be associated with the dimension, you may find that the dimension does not budge. That's because it's actually associated with a different line. Selecting the object itself is often a better solution, because the dimension is associated with the object.

DIMDISASSOCIATE

Occasionally, you may want to edit a dimension in such a way that you need to remove its associativity. Perhaps you need to squeeze it into a tight corner. For these times, use the DIMDISASSOCIATE command by typing it on the command line. At the prompt, select the dimensions that you want to disassociate from their objects.

Note AutoCAD does not disassociate dimensions that are on locked layers. Unlock the layer first and then disassociate the dimension.

DIMREGEN

The DIMREGEN command updates the locations of all associative dimensions. This command is only needed in three unusual situations:

✦ If you pan or zoom with a wheel mouse in a paper space layout while model space is active

✦ If you open a drawing containing dimensioned objects that have been edited with a previous version of AutoCAD

✦ If you open a drawing containing external references that are dimensioned in the current drawing and dimensioned objects in the external reference have been changed

Using the DIMEDIT command

 The DIMEDIT command offers four ways to edit dimensions. The advantage of this command is that you can change more than one dimension at a time. Choose Dimension Edit from the Dimension toolbar. AutoCAD responds with the `Enter type of dimension editing [Home/New/Rotate/Oblique] <Home>:` prompt. Right-click to choose one of the options:

✦ **Home:** Moves dimension text to its default position as defined by the dimension style.

✦ **New:** Lets you type new text to replace the existing text. AutoCAD opens the Multiline Text Editor showing the angle brackets that represent the dimension text. You can use this option to add a suffix, such as *TYP* (typical) to several dimensions.

✦ **Rotate:** Rotates the dimension text. This works like the rotation angle for text.

✦ **Oblique:** Angles the extension lines of the dimension. Use this when you have several dimensions close together that interfere with each other. Specify the final angle of the extension lines, *not* the rotation from the current angle.

Note The Oblique item on the Dimension menu executes the DIMEDIT command with the Oblique option.

As soon as you choose an option, DIMEDIT prompts you to select objects. You can select as many dimensions as you wish.

You have the opportunity to use the DIMEDIT command in an exercise after the next section.

Using the DIMTEDIT command

The DIMTEDIT command repositions dimension text. To start the command, choose Dimension Text Edit from the Dimension toolbar. Although its name gives the impression that you can edit the text content, you can only change its position. You can only edit one dimension at a time. AutoCAD responds with the `Select dimension:` prompt. Select a dimension.

At the `Specify new location for dimension text or [Left/Right/ Center/Home/Angle]:` prompt, you can use the cursor to pick a text location. You can also right-click and choose one of the options:

✦ **Left:** Left-justifies the text of linear, radial, or diameter dimensions.

✦ **Right:** Right-justifies the text of linear, radial, or diameter dimensions.

✦ **Center:** Centers the text of linear, radial, or diameter dimensions.

✦ **Home:** Returns dimension text to its default position and angle.

✦ **Angle:** Rotates dimension text. This option is equivalent to the Rotate option of the DIMEDIT command.

On the CD-ROM

The drawing used in the following Step-by-Step exercise on using DIMEDIT and DIMTEDIT to edit dimensions, `ab14-g.dwg`, is in the `Drawings` folder of the *AutoCAD 2004 Bible* CD-ROM.

Step-by-Step: Using DIMEDIT and DIMTEDIT to Edit Dimensions

1. Open `ab14-g.dwg` from your CD-ROM.

2. Save the file as `ab14-09.dwg` in your `AutoCAD Bible` folder. This is a civil engineering drawing whose dimensions need some editing. It is shown in Figure 14-36. If the Dimension toolbar isn't visible, right-click any toolbar and check Dimension.

3. The dimension at ❶ in Figure 14-36 is not in the proper units because the text was entered explicitly as 14.41. To correct this error, choose Dimension Edit from the Dimension toolbar. At the `Enter type of dimension editing [Home/New/Rotate/Oblique] <Home>:` prompt, right-click and choose New. The Multiline Text Editor opens, showing the angle brackets. Because you want the original text, click OK. At the `Select objects:` prompt, pick ❶. Press Enter to end object selection. (You could correct several dimensions this way.) AutoCAD corrects the dimension, automatically creating the text in the current units.

4. The dimension text at ❷ in Figure 14-36 is too close to the dimension line of the vertical dimension that crosses it. Choose Dimension Text Edit from the Dimension toolbar. At the `Select dimension:` prompt, pick ❷. At the `Specify new location for dimension text or [Left/Right/Center/Home/Angle]:` prompt, right-click and choose Right. AutoCAD moves the text to the right.

5. Save your drawing.

Figure 14-36: A dimensioned civil engineering drawing

New Feature

The Express Tools command, DIMREASSOC does the same thing you accomplished in Step 3 of this exercise, restoring the default measurement value to modified dimension text. Choose Express ➪ Dimension ➪ Reset Dim Text Value. For information about installing Express Tools, see Appendix A on the CD-ROM.

Editing dimension text

You can edit dimension text as you would any other multiline text object. Choose Modify ➪ Object ➪ Text ➪ Edit. At the `Select an annotation object or [Undo]:` prompt, choose the dimension. AutoCAD opens the Multiline Text Editor. Using the Multiline Text Editor for dimension text has already been covered in this chapter under the MText option of the dimensioning commands.

Using the Object Property Manager to edit dimensions

You can edit dimensions by using the Properties palette just as you can edit the properties of any other object. Double-click any dimension to open the Properties palette. You see the properties of the dimensions that you can edit, as shown in Figure 14-37.

Parts of this window make more sense after you learn about dimension styles, which are covered in the next chapter. For example, the listings for Primary Units, Alternate Units, Fit, Lines & Arrows, Text, and so on duplicate the tabs on the New Dimension Style and Modify Dimension Style dialog boxes. Choose Misc to open a line for Dim style where you can switch to another dimension style. (You can also change the dimension style from the drop-down list on the Dimension toolbar.) You can change the color, layer, lineweight, and linetype. To override the automatic dimension text, enter the text in the Text Override field of the Text section of the Properties palette.

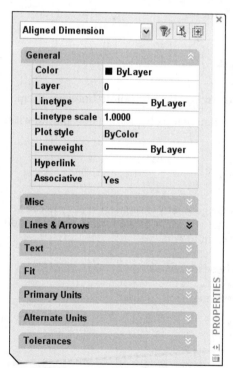

Figure 14-37: The Properties window as it appears with one aligned dimension selected

Using Quick Dimension to edit dimensions

You can also use Quick Dimension to edit dimensions, whether created with QDIM or some other dimensioning command. When you select the geometry and dimensions you want to edit, AutoCAD places an "x" at each eligible edit point, as shown in Figure 14-38.

Figure 14-38: When you edit with QDIM, AutoCAD places an "x" at eligible edit points.

Here's what you can do with QDIM:

✦ You can join two dimensions by removing the edit points between them.

✦ You can split a dimension into two dimensions by adding edit points within the existing dimension.

✦ You can move the dimension line.

✦ You can change the type of dimension.

Caution Editing with QDIM works best when the geometry is simple. Unless you can select only the geometry and dimensions that you want to work with, you will end up changing dimensions that you don't want to edit.

To edit dimensions with QDIM, follow these steps:

1. Choose Quick Dimension from the Dimension toolbar.

2. At the Select geometry to dimension: prompt, select the geometry and the dimensions that you want to edit.

3. At the `Specify dimension line position, or [Continuous/Staggered/ Baseline/Ordinate/Radius/Diameter/datumPoint/Edit/SeTtings] <Continuous>:` prompt, right-click and choose Edit. You see a cross at each eligible edit point.

4. At the `Indicate dimension point to remove, or [Add/eXit] <eXit>:` prompt, you can:

 • Select the points of the dimensions you want to remove. If you see two possible edit points in line with each other that could be creating the dimension you want to remove, select both of them.

 • Right-click and choose Add. Use object snaps to add one or more points.

 • Right-click and choose Exit to continue with the command.

5. At the `Specify dimension line position, or [Continuous/Staggered/ Baseline/Ordinate/Radius/Diameter/datumPoint/Edit/SeTtings] <Continuous>:` prompt, right-click and choose an option if you want to change the type of dimension.

6. The prompt repeats. Pick a location for the new set of dimensions.

7. Press Enter to end the command.

 AutoCAD updates the dimensions.

Using grips to edit dimensions

Grips are ideal for moving dimension lines and text. The grips at the dimension line endpoints and the text insertion point are quite useful for making adjustments in dimensions.

To move a dimension line closer or farther from the dimensioned object, pick the dimension to display the grips. Pick one of the grips at the endpoints of the dimension line to highlight it. The `Specify stretch point or /Base point/Copy/ Undo/eXit:` prompt appears. Drag the dimension line to the desired location. Press Esc to remove the grips.

To move dimension text, pick the dimension to display the grips. Pick the grip on the dimension text to highlight it. Drag the dimension text to its desired location.

Tip For best results, turn ORTHO on while trying to drag the dimension line or the dimension text. Polar tracking also works well.

Figure 14-39 shows the process of dragging a dimension to the right.

Figure 14-39: Using grips to relocate a dimension

Thanks to Bill Maidment of Cantech Inc., Fairfield, Iowa, for this drawing.

Editing objects and dimensions together

Until now, you have not taken advantage of the associativity of AutoCAD's dimensions. This feature enables you to edit objects and have the dimensions automatically adjust to the new object measurements. Stretching the object with the STRETCH command or grips is usually the best way to accomplish this. AutoCAD adjusts both the object and the dimension. Figure 14-40 shows a house plan before and after stretching to move a window six inches to the left. The crossing window included the entire window, so it was simply moved. However, the crossing window crossed the walls on either side of the window and both dimensions so that they were stretched six inches to the left. Notice the change in the dimension text, indicating the new measurements.

On the CD-ROM

The drawing used in the following Step-by-Step exercise on using DDEDIT, QDIM, grips, and STRETCH to edit dimensions, ab14-h.dwg, is in the Drawings folder of the *AutoCAD 2004 Bible* CD-ROM.

Step-by-Step: Using DDEDIT, QDIM, Grips, and STRETCH to Edit Dimensions

1. Open ab14-h.dwg from your CD-ROM.

2. Save the file as ab14-10.dwg in your AutoCAD Bible folder. This is a cross section of a valve part, as shown in Figure 14-41. Open the Dimension toolbar if it is not displayed.

Figure 14-40: When you stretch objects, the dimensions are automatically updated.

Figure 14-41: A dimensioned cross section of a valve part

3. To replace the dimension marked Ht., choose Modify ⇨ Object ⇨ Text ⇨ Edit. At the `Select an annotation object or [Undo]:` prompt, choose the dimension at ❶ in Figure 14-41. The Multiline Text Editor opens with the text displayed. Select the current text and type <>. Click OK. AutoCAD automatically creates the original measured dimension. Press Enter to end the command.

4. Select the two dimensions marked ❷ in Figure 14-41. Also select the cyan center line and the two green hidden lines. Choose Quick Dimension from the Dimension toolbar. At the first prompt, right-click and choose Edit. At the Indicate dimension point to remove, or [Add/eXit] <eXit>: prompt, choose the two edit points (each marked with an "x") on the cyan center line. Right-click and choose Exit. At the Specify dimension line position, or [Continuous/ Staggered/Baseline/Ordinate/Radius/Diameter/ datumPoint/Edit/SeTtings] <Continuous>: prompt, place the dimension line where it was previously. (You can use the outside arrows as a guide.)

5. Pick the dimension at ❶. Click the grip on the text to activate it. Drag it to the left slightly to place it closer to the object it is dimensioning.

6. Choose Stretch from the Modify toolbar. Follow the prompts:

```
Select objects: Pick at ❸.
Specify opposite corner: Pick at ❹.
9 found
Select objects: ↵
Specify base point or displacement: 0,-.25 ↵
Specify second point of displacement: ↵
```

AutoCAD stretches the valve part and adjusts the dimension that measures its height.

7. Save your drawing. It should look like Figure 14-42.

Figure 14-42: The edited valve part

Summary

AutoCAD's dimension features enable you to dimension almost anything. In this chapter, you read about:

✦ Creating linear, radial, dimension, angular, and ordinate dimensions

✦ Formatting and creating leaders

✦ Dimensioning with the Quick Dimension feature

✦ Editing dimensions

In the next chapter, I continue the subject of dimensions by explaining how to gain total control with dimension styles.

✦　　✦　　✦

Creating Dimension Styles and Tolerances

In This Chapter

Understanding dimension styles

Defining a new dimension style

Changing dimension styles

Creating geometric tolerances

In Chapter 14, you drew many dimensions using AutoCAD's default style. However, you have a great deal of control over the way dimensions look. Now that you are familiar with dimensions, you can learn how to bend them to your will.

Understanding Dimension Styles

You should create your dimension styles before dimensioning. Some drawings have several dimension styles, although a drawing can look confusing if it has too many dimension styles. In general, you create a dimension style, save it in your template drawings, and (you hope) rarely have to deal with it again except to override a setting for a unique situation.

The various disciplines each have their own standards and customs regarding dimensions. AutoCAD's dimension styles are flexible enough to accommodate any type of dimensioning practice.

To create a dimension style, choose Dimension Style from the Dimension toolbar to open the Dimension Style Manager, shown in Figure 15-1. The current dimension style is shown as Standard. The Standard dimension style is AutoCAD's default dimension style.

Figure 15-1: The Dimension Style Manager

The Dimension Style Manager is the master control room where you manage dimensions. Here you create new dimension styles and modify existing ones.

The preset Standard dimension style that AutoCAD comes with is most appropriate for mechanical drafting. Whichever type of drafting you do, you will probably find the need to make some changes to the default dimension style. You do this by creating a new dimension style. A preview of the current dimension style is shown at the right side of the dialog box.

To create a new style, click New to open the Create New Dimension Style dialog box, shown in Figure 15-2. Type a new name in the Name text box. In the Start With drop-down box, choose which existing dimension style you want to use as a basis for the new dimension style. If you have more than one to choose from, choose the style that most resembles the new style you want to create.

Figure 15-2: The Create New Dimension Style dialog box

You use the Use for drop-down box to create variant dimension styles for one type of dimension.

The Use for drop-down box, shown expanded in Figure 15-2, lets you decide if you want to use the dimension style for all dimensions or only for a specific type of dimension. Usually, you create a dimension style for all dimension types. Later in this chapter, I explain how to create variants of dimension styles for specific types of dimensions, such as angular dimensions or leaders.

After you are done, click Continue.

You can also use the Dimension Style Manager to rename a dimension style. Click its name to select it. Click it a second time to see an edit box. Type the new name and press Enter.

Defining a New Dimension Style

Dimension styles have many components, so the process of defining a dimension style is complex. Your task is organized for you by the tabs of the dialog box.

When you click Continue in the New Dimension Style dialog box, AutoCAD opens a second New Dimension Style dialog box, as shown in Figure 15-3.

The New Dimension Style dialog box has the following tabs:

- ✦ **Lines and Arrows:** Sets specifications for dimension lines, extension lines, arrowheads, and center marks.

- ✦ **Text:** Determines the appearance, placement, and alignment of dimension text.

- ✦ **Fit:** Sets how text and arrows fit inside narrow dimensions, where text is placed when it doesn't fit in its default position, the scale factor for dimension features, and whether to place a dimension line inside narrow dimensions.

- ✦ **Primary Units:** Determines the format and precision for the primary measuring unit for both linear and angular dimensions.

- ✦ **Alternate Units:** Determines the format and precision for secondary units, if turned on (such as metric measurements if your primary units are English, or vice versa).

- ✦ **Tolerances:** Formats tolerances.

Managing dimension lines and arrows

An important part of defining a dimension style is specifying how the dimension lines and arrows look. You do so on the Lines and Arrows tab of the New Dimension Style dialog box. In Chapter 14, Figure 14-1, I illustrated the parts of a dimension. Refer to that figure if you need a refresher.

The Lines and Arrows tab is divided into four sections: Dimension Lines, Extension Lines, Arrowheads, and Center Marks for Circles.

Dimension lines

To set the color of the dimension line so that it differs from that of the rest of the dimension, click the Color drop-down list and choose a color. Choose Select Color to open the Select Color dialog box if you want to use a nonstandard color. Remember, dimensions are blocks — one object. The default color is ByBlock so that dimensions take on the color of the current layer or color setting. In general, you should have a separate layer for dimensions. Then the entire dimension is the color set for that layer. Use this setting only if you want the dimension lines to be a different color from your dimension layer color. The arrowheads do not have a separate color setting and always follow the dimension line setting.

Figure 15-3: The New Dimension Style dialog box with the Lines and Arrows tab displayed

Cross-Reference See Chapter 11 for a discussion of how to use the Select Color dialog box. See Chapter 18 for coverage of blocks.

To set a lineweight for the dimension line, click the Lineweight drop-down box and choose a lineweight. The default lineweight is ByBlock, which means that the lineweight will follow the lineweight of the dimension's layer. In general, you want your objects to stand out, so dimensions should have the same or a lower lineweight than your objects.

The Extend beyond ticks text box determines how far the dimension lines extend past the extension lines. When you have arrowheads at the ends of the dimension lines, the Extension option is unavailable. However, if you choose Architectural tick, Oblique, Dot Small, Integral, or None in the Arrowheads section of the dialog box, the Extend beyond ticks option becomes available. This type of extension is typical for architectural drafting. Figure 15-4 shows a dimension with an architectural tick and a 0.1-unit extension.

Figure 15-4: A typical architectural dimension showing the text above one dimension line, an architectural tick, and the dimension line slightly extending beyond the extension lines

The Baseline spacing text box determines the distance between successive dimension lines when you create baseline dimensions. AutoCAD uses this specification to create evenly spaced dimension lines.

In some dimension styles, the dimension text splits the dimension line into two parts, as shown in Figure 15-5. This creates two dimension lines. You can suppress — that is, turn off — the first or second dimension line (or both dimension lines) by checking the appropriate box (or boxes). The first line is nearest where you specified the first extension line origin. (If you selected an object instead of specifying two extension line origins, you may not be able to predict which dimension line is the first and which is the second. Experiment.) You would usually suppress dimension lines when they interfere with other dimensions or with objects in your drawing.

Figure 15-5: A typical mechanical dimension with text splitting two dimension lines

Extension lines

As with dimension lines, you can pick a color for the extension lines that differs from that of the rest of the dimension. Click the Color drop-down list and choose a color. Choose Select Color to open the Select Color dialog box if you want a non-standard color. The default color is ByBlock so that extensions take on the color of the current layer or color setting.

Extension lines typically extend slightly past the dimension line, as you can see in some of the figures in this chapter. Use the Extend beyond dim lines text box to specify this extension distance.

Extension lines do not usually touch the object they dimension to make it easier to distinguish the dimension from the object. Use the Offset from Origin text box to define the distance from the specified points on the object to the extension lines.

You manage extension lines similarly to dimension lines. You can suppress the first or second extension line (or both lines) so that either or both are not visible — check the appropriate box (or boxes). (AutoCAD automatically suppresses extension lines when creating baseline and continued dimensions.) Figure 15-6 shows a dimension with the first extension line suppressed.

Figure 15-6: A dimension with the first extension line suppressed

Arrowheads

The Arrowheads section controls the arrowheads that go at the ends of dimension lines. You do not actually have to use arrowheads, as you saw in Figure 15-4. You can also set the first and second arrowheads individually. However, if you change the first arrowhead, the second one follows suit, assuming that you want both ends of the dimension to look the same. To make them different, specify your choice in the first drop-down box, and then in the second drop-down box.

You can create and use your own arrowhead:

1. In any drawing, create the arrowhead you want with a unit size of 1.

2. Make a block out of it. For an arrow-shaped block, pick the point of the arrow for the insertion point and create it pointing to the right. You may have to experiment with the right insertion point. Save the block. (See Chapter 18 for instructions on creating blocks.)

3. In the first and second drop-down lists, choose User Arrow. The Select Custom Arrow Block dialog box opens, displaying the blocks available in the drawing, as shown in Figure 15-7.

4. Choose the block you want.

5. Click OK.

Figure 15-8 shows a dimension with a user arrow.

Figure 15-7: The Select Custom Arrow
Block dialog box

Figure 15-8: A dimension with a user arrow

Tip You can set a different arrow for leaders. Choose the arrow you want from the
Leader drop-down list.

Set the size of the arrowhead in the Arrow size text box. As explained later in this
chapter in the discussion of scale, you should use the final size you want to see
when the drawing is plotted on paper.

Center marks

The Center Marks for Circles section of the New Dimension Style dialog box specifies
how you want to mark the centers of arcs and circles when you choose Center Mark
from the Dimension toolbar (the DIMCENTER command). From the Type drop-down
box, choose Mark to create a small cross, Line to create a cross plus four lines that
cross, or None. Figure 15-9 shows a circle with center lines and an arc with a center
mark.

Specify the size of the center mark or line in the Size text box. For center marks, the
size is the distance from the intersection of the two lines to their endpoints. If you
use center lines, the size also determines the distance from the circle quadrants to
the end of the center lines.

Because the Standard dimension style is closest to mechanical drafting standards,
in the following exercise (and others in this chapter), you start to create an archi-
tectural dimension style using the Standard style as a base. This requires you to
make a maximum number of changes, thereby letting you become as familiar as
possible with the dimension style settings. Here you practice controlling dimension
lines and arrows.

Figure 15-9: A circle with a center line and an arc with a center mark

On the CD-ROM

The drawing used in the following Step-by-Step exercise on controlling dimension lines and arrows, ab15-a.dwg, is in the Drawings folder of the *AutoCAD 2004 Bible* CD-ROM.

Step-by-Step: Controlling Dimension Lines and Arrows

1. Open ab15-a.dwg from your CD-ROM.

2. Save the file as ab15-01.dwg in your AutoCAD Bible folder. This drawing is an elevation of a garage, as shown in Figure 15-10. ORTHO and OSNAP should be on. Set running object snaps for endpoint and intersection. The Dim layer is current. If the Dimension toolbar is not visible, right-click any toolbar and choose Dimension.

3. To see what the Standard dimension style looks like, choose Linear Dimension from the Dimension toolbar. At the Specify first extension line origin or <select object>: prompt, pick ❶ in Figure 15-10. At the Specify second extension line origin: prompt, pick ❷. At the Specify dimension line location or [Mtext/ Text/Angle/Horizontal/Vertical/Rotated]: prompt, pick a location for the dimension line below the line you dimensioned. The arrows and text are so small you cannot even see them.

4. Use a Zoom Window to zoom in on ❶ and the left end of the dimension. Choose Zoom Previous from the Standard toolbar. Do another Zoom Window to zoom in on the center of the dimension to see the text. (You may have to use Zoom Window twice.) Choose Zoom Previous again. As you can see, this dimension needs some modification.

5. Choose Dimension Style from the Dimension toolbar. The current dimension style should be Standard. Click New. In the New Style Name text box, type Arch 48 and click Continue.

6. Click the Lines and Arrows tab if it is not on top. In the Arrowheads section, choose Oblique from the first drop-down list. The size should be 3/16". In the Dimension Lines section, type 3/32 in the Extend beyond Ticks text box. (Due to the units precision setting — set by choosing Format ⇨ Units — AutoCAD rounds this to 1/8" in the display, although the value is still 3/32.) Click OK to return to the Dimension Style Manager.

GARAGE SOUTH ELEV 1/4" = 1'-0"

Figure 15-10: The garage elevation

7. In the Dimension Style Manager, notice that the arrows have been changed to ticks in the preview. Click Set Current. Click Close.

8. Select the dimension you created in Step 3. In the Dim Style Control drop-down list on the Dimension toolbar, choose Arch 48. The dimension now has the geometry settings you just made. To check it out, do a Zoom Window to the left end of the dimension. You can see that the oblique mark has replaced the arrow. Do a Zoom Previous.

9. Save your drawing. Keep this drawing open if you are continuing on to the next exercise.

Managing dimension text

You can format the text of the dimension for readability and to match other text in your drawing. In the New Dimension Style dialog box, the Text tab, shown in Figure 15-11, controls text appearance, placement, and alignment.

Text appearance

You have full control over dimension text appearance, as you do over any other text in your drawing.

Choose a text style from the Text style drop-down list. You may want to create a special text style, such as Dim Text, for dimension text to give you the flexibility to alter dimension text without changing other text in your drawing. Create the dimension text style before creating your dimension style.

Cross-Reference See Chapter 13 for a discussion of text styles.

Figure 15-11: The Text tab of the New Dimension Style dialog box

Choose a color from the Text color drop-down box. You can pick a color for the dimension text that differs from that of the rest of the dimension. Remember, dimensions are blocks. The default color is ByBlock so that dimensions take on the color of the current layer or color setting. In general, you should have a separate layer for dimensions. Then the entire dimension is the color set for that layer. Use this setting only if you want the dimension text to be a different color from your dimension layer color. To choose a nonstandard color, choose Select Color from the drop-down list to open the Select Color dialog box.

Choose the height for your dimension text. Setting the text style height to zero is a good idea, so you can set the height in this box. Otherwise, the text style height takes over. It's much easier to make all your dimension style adjustments in one place than to make changes in the text style as well.

If your unit type uses fractions, use the fraction height scale to set a ratio of fraction text to whole text. This option is only available if your units specify the use of fractions. You may want the fractions to be smaller than whole numbers. A scale of 0.5 makes the fractions half the size of whole numbers; the resulting overall fraction is slightly higher than the whole numbers of the dimension text.

Text placement

The Vertical drop-down box affects how text is justified relative to the dimension line. As you make changes, be sure to look at the preview to see if the results are what you want. Table 15-1 lists the options.

Table 15-1
Vertical Justification Options for Dimensions

Option	Function
Centered	Centers the text in the dimension line, breaking the dimension line into two. This is typical for mechanical drafting. You can see an example in Figure 15-5.
Above	Places text above the dimension line. This is typical for architectural drafting. You can see an example in Figure 15-4.
Outside	Places the text on the side of the dimension line that is farthest from the object you are dimensioning.
JIS	Places dimension text in conformation to the Japanese Industrial Standards rules, which vary the placement according to the angle of the dimension line.

The Horizontal drop-down box affects the placement of dimension text between the extension lines. Here again, AutoCAD provides a handy visual confirmation of your choice. Table 15-2 explains your choices.

Table 15-2
Horizontal Justification Options for Dimensions

Option	*Function*
Centered	This is the default. It centers text between the two extension lines.
At Ext Line 1	Places the text next to the first extension line. The first extension line is always the first point you specified at the `Specify first extension line origin or <select object>:` prompt. The picture and the words Horizontal Justification can be especially confusing for vertical dimensions. If you are not consistent in how you pick your dimensions, you can get some strange results. Figure 15-12 shows two vertical dimensions and two horizontal dimensions using a horizontal justification of the 1st Extension Line. Because the lines were not picked consistently, the results are not satisfactory.
At Ext Line 2	Places the text next to the second extension line. The comments for the previous option apply to this option as well.
Over Ext Line 1	Places the text over the first extension line. The comments for the At Ext Line 1 option apply to this option as well.
Over Ext Line 2	Places the text over the second extension line. The comments for the At Ext Line 1 option apply to this option as well.

Figure 15-12: Using a horizontal justification other than centered can lead to unexpected results if you pick objects inconsistently.

Use the Offset from Dim Line text box to set the gap between the dimension text and the dimension line. If the dimension line is broken, the gap is the space between each side of the dimension text and the two dimension lines. If the dimension line is unbroken and the text is above the line, the gap is the space between the bottom of the text and the dimension line. The gap also controls the space between the box created for Basic tolerance dimensions and the text inside them. Basic tolerances are discussed in the "Formatting tolerances" section later in this chapter.

Tip When trying to fit dimension text, lines, and arrows in a narrow space, AutoCAD also uses the gap to calculate the minimum space required on either side of the dimension text. Reducing the gap can therefore help fit more of the dimension elements between the extension lines.

Text alignment

The Alignment section of the Text tab affects how the text is aligned relative to the dimension line, as follows:

✦ Check Horizontal to keep text between the extension lines horizontal, regardless of the angle of the dimension line (typical of mechanical drawings).

✦ Check `Aligned with dimension line` to keep text at the same angle as the dimension line (typical of architectural drawings).

✦ Check ISO Standard to use the ISO standard that aligns text with the dimension line when text is inside the extension lines, but aligns text horizontally when text is outside the extension lines (because of a tight fit).

AutoCAD provides a useful visual confirmation of your choice.

**On the
CD-ROM** The drawing used in the following Step-by-Step exercise on defining dimension text, ab15-01.dwg, is in the Results folder of the *AutoCAD 2004 Bible* CD-ROM.

Step-by-Step: Defining Dimension Text

1. If ab15-01.dwg is open from the previous exercise, use it for this exercise as well. Otherwise, open ab15-01.dwg from the Results folder of the CD-ROM. ORTHO and OSNAP should be on. Set running object snaps for endpoint and intersection. The Dim layer is current. If the Dimension toolbar is not visible, right-click any toolbar and choose Dimension.

2. Save the file as ab15-02.dwg in your AutoCAD Bible folder.

3. Choose Dimension Style from the Dimension toolbar. The Arch 48 dimension style should be current. Choose Modify to continue working on the Arch 48 dimension style. Click the Text tab.

4. In the Text Appearance section, choose ROMANS as the text style.

5. In the Text Placement section, choose Above from the Vertical drop-down list.

6. In the Text Alignment section, choose Aligned with dimension line. While mechanical dimensions usually require horizontal text, architectural dimensions require that the text be aligned with the dimension line.

7. Click OK and then click Close. AutoCAD automatically updates the dimension to include the changes, although the text is still too tiny to see clearly.

8. Save your drawing. Keep this drawing open if you are continuing on to the next exercise.

Fitting dimensions into tight spaces

When there is not enough room to place the arrowheads, dimension line, and text between the extension lines, AutoCAD needs to place some elements of the dimension outside the extension lines. The Fit tab, as shown in Figure 15-13, lets you specify how you want AutoCAD to handle this situation.

Fit Options

The Fit Options section determines what gets moved outside the extension lines — text, arrows, or both — when they can't fit inside the extension lines. These are among the hardest of the dimension styles options to understand, yet they can greatly affect how your dimensions appear.

Caution The fit options specify what goes *outside* the extension lines. Before Release 2000, they specified what goes inside the extension lines. Be careful — or you will get a result opposite of what you intended.

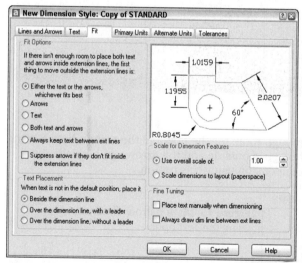

Figure 15-13: The Fit tab of the New Dimension Style dialog box

Here are your choices:

✦ **Either the text or the arrows, whichever fits best:** Puts whatever fits inside the extension lines. The arrowheads might fit inside and the text not, or the other way around. Or if there is not enough room for either, they both go outside the extension lines. Figure 15-14 shows a dimension using this option.

Figure 15-14: A narrow dimension using the Either the text or the arrows, whichever fits best option.

✦ **Arrows:** If there is not enough room for both the text and the arrows between the extension lines, the arrows go outside and the text goes between them. Figure 15-15 shows a dimension using this option. The results of this option happen to look the same as Figure 15-14, but a different setting produced them.

Figure 15-15: A narrow dimension using the Arrows option

✦ **Text:** If there is not enough room for the text and the arrows between the extension lines, the text goes outside and the arrows go between them. Figure 15-16 shows a dimension using this option.

Figure 15-16: A narrow dimension using the Text option

✦ **Both text and arrows:** Keeps the text and arrows together — between the extension lines if there is enough room, outside the extension lines if not. Figure 15-17 shows a dimension using this option.

Figure 15-17: A narrow dimension using the Both text and arrows option.

✦ **Always keep text between ext lines:** As it says, this option always keeps the text between the extension lines, even if they don't fit. Figure 15-18 shows a dimension using this option.

Figure 15-18: A narrow dimension using the Always keep text between ext lines option.

✦ **Suppress arrows if they don't fit inside the extension lines:** Use this check box to suppress the display of arrows completely if they don't fit inside the extension lines (instead of putting them outside). This option is used together with one of the previous options. Figure 15-19 shows a dimension using this option with the Either the text or the arrows, whichever fits best option.

Figure 15-19: A narrow dimension using the Suppress arrows if they don't fit inside the extension lines option along with the Either the text or the arrows whichever fits best option.

Text Placement

The Text Placement section determines where you want the dimension text when it isn't in its default position, due to a tight fit. Your options are:

✦ **Beside the dimension line:** Places the dimension text next to the dimension line, but outside the extension lines. Figure 15-20 shows a dimension using this option as well as the same dimension edited to move the text off the model. You can move the text anywhere to the left or the right of the dimension line, but not above or below it. Editing dimensions is covered later in this chapter.

Figure 15-20: Dimension text is placed beside the dimension line when it doesn't fit inside the extension lines. You can move the text from side to side. On the right, the text has been moved to the right slightly so that it doesn't cross the model.

✦ **Over the dimension line, with a leader:** Places the dimension text over the dimension line, between the extension lines, but above them, with a leader from the dimension line to the text. You can move the text anywhere to suit your needs and dimensioning conventions, as shown in Figure 15-21.

✦ **Over the dimension line, without a leader:** Places the dimension text over the dimension line, between the extension lines, but above them, with no leader, as shown in Figure 15-22. You can move the text anywhere.

Figure 15-21: Dimension text is placed over the dimension line with a leader. On the right, the text has been moved to the right of the model.

Figure 15-22: Dimension text is placed over the dimension line without a leader.

Scale for Dimension Features

The Scale for Dimension Features section lets you specify the scale factor. The scale factor adjusts the size of dimension text (unless a nonzero text style height controls the text), arrowheads, spacing, and so on. It has no effect on the content of dimension text — that is, it does not affect actual measurements. So many size options are possible in a dimension style that you could spend all day trying to multiply each size option by the scale. Then, if you have to change the scale of the drawing, you would need to recalculate all the size specifications. Setting the Overall Scale factor makes your life easier because AutoCAD automatically multiplies every size specification by the scale factor.

Cross-Reference Scale factors are discussed in detail in Chapter 5. See Chapter 17 for a discussion of scaling dimensions in a paper space layout.

In the Fine Tuning section, if you check `Place Text Manually When Dimensioning`, AutoCAD ignores the horizontal text placement settings and uses the point you pick at the `Specify dimension line location or [Mtext/Text/Angle/Horizontal/Vertical/ Rotated]:` prompt. Before you click, as you move the cursor along the dimension line, you can see the text following the cursor.

Check `Always Draw Dim Line Between Ext Lines` to force a dimension line between the extension lines even when there isn't room for text or arrows, as shown in Figure 15-23.

Figure 15-23: A dimension with a dimension line forced

On the CD-ROM The drawing used in the following Step-by-Step exercise on setting dimension fit, ab15-02.dwg, is in the Results folder of the *AutoCAD 2004 Bible* CD-ROM.

Step-by-Step: Setting Dimension Fit

1. If `ab15-02.dwg` is open from the previous exercise, use it for this exercise as well. Otherwise, open `ab15-02.dwg` from the `Results` folder of the CD-ROM. ORTHO and OSNAP should be on. Set running object snaps for endpoint and intersection. The Dim layer is current. If the Dimension toolbar is not visible, right-click any toolbar and choose Dimension.

2. Save the file as `ab15-03.dwg` in your AutoCAD Bible folder.

3. Choose Dimension Style from the Dimension toolbar. Make sure the Arch 48 dimension style is current. Choose Modify to continue working on the Arch 48 dimension style.

4. On the Fit tab, in the Text Placement section, choose Over the Dimension Line, with a Leader.

5. In the Fine Tuning section, check Always Draw Dim Line Between Ext Lines. Architectural dimensions customarily place a line between the extension lines even if the text cannot fit.

6. Because the drawing's scale is ¼"=1', or 1=48, type 48 in the Use overall scale of text box.

7. Click OK. Click Close to return to your drawing.

8. Save your drawing. You can finally see the dimension! It should look like Figure 15-24. Keep this drawing open if you are continuing on to the next exercise.

GARAGE SOUTH ELEV 1/4" = 1'-0"

Figure 15-24: As a result of changing the overall scale, you can finally see the dimension.

Defining primary units

The primary units define the type of units used to display the dimension in your drawing. You need to set primary units separately from the units for the drawing, which affect coordinate display, but not dimensions.

Click the Primary Units tab, as shown in Figure 15-25, to set the format and precision for linear and angular dimensions. You should already be familiar with setting units, which I discussed in Chapter 5. You must separately set your units for dimensions.

Figure 15-25: The Primary Units tab of the New Dimension Style dialog box

Linear Dimensions

The Linear Dimensions section provides settings for linear dimensions:

✦ Choose a format from the Unit format drop-down box. You have the same choices as in the Drawing Units dialog box, namely Scientific, Decimal, Engineering, Architectural, and Fractional, as well as an additional option — Windows desktop.

Note

To see the current Windows desktop units setting, choose Start ➪ Settings ➪ Control Panel ➪ Regional Settings (or Regional Options, depending on your operating system). Click the Number tab. The Windows desktop setting does not give you as complete control over units as AutoCAD. However, if you need consistency with another Windows application, you might find this setting useful.

✦ Choose a precision (the number of decimal points or the fraction denominator) from the Precision drop-down box.

✦ Choose a fraction format from the Fraction format drop-down box. This option is only available if the format you chose uses fractions. Horizontal places a horizontal line between stacked numerators and denominators. Diagonal uses a diagonal slash between the stacked numerator and denominator. Not stacked uses a diagonal line between the numerator and denominator, which are not stacked. You can see the effect of each choice in the preview box.

✦ Choose a decimal separator. This option is only available if the format you chose uses decimals. You can choose from a period, a comma, and a space.

✦ Use the Round off text box to round off linear dimension distances. For example, you can round to the nearest 0.1 unit or ½ inch.

✦ Use the Prefix and Suffix boxes to add a prefix or suffix that you want to place before or after every dimension. For example, you might want to add a suffix of mm after every dimension if you are measuring in millimeters and giving the drawing to a client who usually sees dimensions in inches.

You can use the Scale factor text box to set a scaling factor for linear dimensions, including radial and diameter dimensions, and ordinal dimensions. This factor changes the actual measurement text. For example, if you draw a line 2.5 units long and you specify a linear scale of 0.5, AutoCAD dimensions the object as 1.25 units. You could set this scale to 25.4 to use metric measurements on a drawing you have created with U.S. measurements — perhaps you are sending the same drawing to certain clients in the United States and other clients elsewhere in the world. You can also use this scale in conjunction with alternate units, as explained in the next section.

Check `Apply to Layout Dimension Only` to apply the linear scaling factor only to layout (paper space) dimensions.

Under Zero Suppression, choose if you want to suppress leading and trailing zeros. If you suppress leading zeros, a number such as 0.375 appears as .375. If you suppress trailing zeros, a number such as 3.7500 appears as 3.75.

For architectural units, you can choose to suppress 0 feet and 0 inches. If you suppress 0 feet, a number such as 0'-8" becomes 8". If you suppress 0 inches, a number such as 6'-0" becomes 6'.

Angular Dimensions

✦ The Angular Dimensions section of the Primary Units tab lets you format angular measurements:

✦ Choose from Decimal Degrees, Degrees Minutes Seconds, Gradians, and Radians.

✦ Choose a precision from the Precision drop-down list.

Under Zero Suppression, choose if you want to suppress leading and trailing zeros for angular dimensions. For example, an angle of 37.0° would appear as 37° with the trailing zero suppressed.

Defining alternate units

If you want, you can show an alternate set of units in your dimensions. The most common use of this feature is to show millimeters and inches together. AutoCAD displays the alternate units in square brackets. To show alternate units, click the Alternate Units tab of the New Dimension Style dialog box, as shown in Figure 15-26. Check Display alternate units.

Figure 15-26: The Alternate Units tab

As you can see, this dialog box is very similar to the Primary Units tab, discussed in the previous section. Notice the default scale of 25.40 in the Multiplier for alt units text box. There are 25.4 millimeters to an inch. If your primary units are millimeters, you can set the linear scale to 0.03937, which is the number of inches to a millimeter. Of course, if your units are not inches but meters, miles, or something else, you need to make the appropriate calculations.

Figure 15-27 shows two dimensions with alternate units.

Figure 15-27: Dimensions showing both U.S. and metric measurements
Thanks to Jerry Bottenfield of Clow Valve Company, Oskaloosa, Iowa, for this drawing.

In the Placement section, choose one of the options — to place alternate units after or below the primary units.

On the CD-ROM The drawing used in the following Step-by-Step exercise on defining primary units, ab15-03.dwg, is in the Results folder of the *AutoCAD 2004 Bible* CD-ROM.

Step-by-Step: Defining Primary Units

1. If ab15-03.dwg is open from the previous exercise, use it for this exercise as well. Otherwise, open ab15-03.dwg from the Results folder of the CD-ROM. ORTHO and OSNAP should be on. Set running object snaps for endpoint and intersection. The Dim layer is current. If the Dimension toolbar is not visible, right-click any toolbar and choose Dimension.

2. Save the file as ab15-04.dwg in your AutoCAD Bible folder.

3. Choose Dimension Style from the Dimension toolbar. The Arch 48 dimension style should be current. Choose Modify to continue working on this dimension style. Click the Primary Units tab.

4. In the Unit format drop-down box, choose Architectural.

5. In the Precision drop-down box, change the precision to 0'-0 1/8".

6. In the Fraction format drop-down box, choose Diagonal.

7. In the Zero Suppression section, uncheck the 0 Inches check box because architectural dimensions sometimes show 0 inches.

8. Click the Text tab. In the Fraction Height Scale text box, type **.75**.

9. Click OK. In the Dimension Style Manager, click Set Current and then click Close to return to your drawing. The dimension is automatically updated and now looks appropriate for an architectural drawing.

10. To see how the stacked fractions appear, create a linear dimension from 1 to 2 in Figure 15-28. If necessary, zoom in to see the dimension text clearly.

Figure 15-28: The dimension style is now complete.

11. Return to the previous view if you zoomed in. Save your drawing. It should look like Figure 15-28.

Formatting tolerances

Tolerances are used in mechanical drafting to specify how much deviation is allowed from the exact measurement when the model is manufactured. Format the tolerance notation on the Tolerances tab of the New Dimension Style dialog box. The Tolerances tab is shown in Figure 15-29.

Tolerance Format

Use the Tolerance Format section to specify how you want the tolerances to be displayed. AutoCAD offers four tolerance methods from the Method drop-down list:

✦ **Symmetrical** tolerances have the same upper and lower amounts and are shown with a plus/minus sign, as shown in Figure 15-30. The Upper value text box is active so that you can type in the tolerance amount.

Figure 15-29: The Tolerances tab of the New Dimension Style dialog box

Figure 15-30: Symmetrical tolerances

✦ **Deviation** tolerances can have different upper and lower amounts and are therefore shown after separate plus and minus signs, as shown in Figure 15-31. When you choose a deviation tolerance, the Upper value and Lower value text boxes become active.

✦ **Limits** tolerances include the upper and lower tolerances in the measurement, as shown in Figure 15-32. Use the Upper value and Lower value text boxes to type in the upper and lower tolerance amounts.

Figure 15-31: Deviation tolerances

Figure 15-32: Limits tolerances

✦ A **basic** dimension places the dimension in a box, as shown in Figure 15-33

In the Precision drop-down box, choose a precision. As mentioned earlier, use the Upper value text box to set the tolerance value for symmetrical tolerances. For deviation and limits tolerances, use both the Upper value and Lower value text boxes.

The Scaling for height text box lets you scale the height of the tolerance relative to the dimension text height. Using smaller text for the tolerances is common. A value of 1 creates tolerance text equal to the dimension text height. A setting of 0.5 creates tolerance text that is half the size of regular dimension text.

Figure 15-33: A basic dimension

Use the Vertical position drop-down box to determine how the tolerances are aligned with the main dimension text. This setting has the most effect on Deviation tolerances that display two lines of text for the one dimension text line. You have the following choices:

✦ **Top:** Aligns the tolerance text with the top of the dimension text.

✦ **Middle:** Aligns the tolerance text with the middle of the dimension text.

✦ **Bottom:** Aligns the tolerance text with the bottom of the dimension text.

Note The Vertical position setting also applies to stacked fractions, determining how the fractions are justified with the whole number dimensions.

Use the Zero Suppression section to suppress leading or trailing zeros, or feet and inches. See the preceding explanation of the Primary Units tab for more information.

If you have turned on alternate units, you can separately set the precision and zero suppression for alternate unit tolerances in the Precision text box.

Click OK, and then click Close to return to your drawing. You're ready to start dimensioning!

Changing Dimension Styles

Just as you often need to edit objects in a drawing, you often need to edit dimension styles. You have lots of flexibility to change to another style, change the style, or make exceptions to a style.

You can change dimensions in the following ways:

✦ Choose a new dimension style.

✦ Create a variant of a dimension style for a certain type of dimension.

✦ Modify the characteristics of the dimension style in use.

✦ Override the dimension style with different dimension options for one dimension that you want to be an exception.

The previous chapter covers some dimension editing techniques. This section explains how to make changes related to dimension styles.

Choosing a new current dimension style

To start using another dimension style, click the Dim Style Control drop-down list on the Styles toolbar or the Dimension toolbar and choose the dimension style that you want to use.

New Feature AutoCAD 2004 introduces the Styles toolbar that contains drop-down lists for Text and Dimension styles.

Existing dimensions remain unchanged, but any new dimensions you add from this point forward will use the new current dimension style.

Creating a variant of a dimension style

Create a variant of a dimension style for a specific type of dimension, such as a leader or angular dimension. You might have an architectural dimension style with ticks (rather than arrows) at the end of the dimension lines, but you might want angular dimensions to have open arrows. Here are the steps:

1. Choose Dimension Style from the Dimension toolbar.

2. Click New.

3. From the Use for drop-down list, choose the type of dimension that you want to use with the new variant.

4. Click Continue.

5. Make the changes you want, using the techniques described earlier in this chapter.

6. Click OK to return to the Dimension Style Manager. Here you see the variant listed under its base (parent) dimension style.

7. Click Close.

Dimensions of the type you specified now take on the characteristics of the variant. For example, angular dimensions would have an open arrow.

Modifying a dimension to use a new dimension style

You can change the dimension style used by a dimension. Select the dimension and then choose a new dimension style from the Dim Style Control drop-down list on the Styles or Dimension toolbar.

Another method of changing a dimension's style is to choose Properties on the Standard toolbar and select one or more dimensions. In the Properties palette, click the Dim style item in the Misc section and choose a new dimension style from the drop-down list.

Tip Double-click any dimension to open the Properties palette where you can change the properties of that dimension.

You can choose Match Properties on the Standard toolbar to match the properties of one dimension to those of another. Follow these steps:

1. Choose Match Properties.

2. At the Select source object: prompt, choose the dimension whose properties you want to copy.

3. At the Select destination object(s) or [Settings]: prompt, choose the dimension or dimensions you want to copy the properties to. (Use the Settings option if you only want to copy some of the properties.)

4. Press Enter to end the command.

Modifying dimension styles

You can easily change a dimension style. The advantage of changing a dimension style is that all dimensions using that style are automatically updated. To change a style:

1. Choose Dimension Style from the Dimension toolbar.

2. Choose the dimension style you want to change from the list of styles.

3. Choose Modify.

4. AutoCAD opens the Modify Dimension Style dialog box, which is exactly the same as the New Dimension Style dialog box. Use the settings on all the tabs and make the changes you want. Click OK to close these dialog boxes and return to the Dimension Styles Manager.

5. Click Close.

AutoCAD automatically updates all dimensions using that dimension style.

Tip
You can create a new dimension style from an existing dimension on the fly by using the Properties palette. Double-click a dimension to open the Properties palette. Click the arrow next to the type of change you want to make and make the change. After you're done, right-click in the drawing area and choose Dim Style ⇨ Save as New Style. The New Dimension Style dialog box opens so that you can give the dimension style a name. Click OK.

Overriding a dimension style

Sometimes you want to make an exception to a style for one dimension—for example, when suppressing an extension line in a tight space. It is often not worthwhile to create a new dimension style for such a situation. To override a dimension style, simply change the properties of the dimension by using the Properties palette.

You can also create an override to the current dimension style. The override is like a subset of the dimension style. After you create the override, all new dimensions you create using the dimension style include the override changes. To revert back to the original dimension style, you must delete the override. You also have the option to incorporate the override into the dimension style or save it as a new style.

To create a dimension style override, follow these steps:

1. Choose Dimension Style from the Dimension toolbar.

2. Choose the dimension style for which you want to create an override (if it isn't already selected).

3. In the Dimension Style Manager, click Override.

4. AutoCAD opens the Override dialog box, which is just like the New (or Modify) Dimension Style dialog box. Make the changes you want using any of the tabs. Click OK.

5. In the Dimension Style Manager, you see the style override listed beneath the dimension style you selected. Click Close.

New dimensions that you create using the dimension style you selected now include the override properties.

To stop using the override, open the Dimension Style Manager, right-click the style override to open the shortcut menu, and do one of the following:

✦ Choose Delete to delete the override.

✦ Choose Save to Current Style to incorporate the override properties into the current dimension style.

✦ Choose Rename to create a new dimension style from the override. AutoCAD places a selection box around the name. Type a new dimension style name and press Enter. AutoCAD removes the override and replaces it with the new dimension style.

Removing the override doesn't change dimensions that you have already created with the override.

Updating dimensions

The Dimension toolbar includes an Update button. This command updates selected dimensions so that they use the current dimension style, including any overrides you may have just made. Use this when you realize that you want to include some existing dimensions in the overrides you have made.

Comparing dimension styles

You can compare a dimension style with the current dimension style. To do this, follow these steps:

1. Choose Dimension Style from the Dimension toolbar and choose Compare. AutoCAD opens the Compare Dimension Styles dialog box, shown in Figure 15-34.

2. In the Compare and With drop-down boxes, choose the two dimension styles you want to compare. AutoCAD lists the differences by system variable. For more information about system variables used in dimensions, see the sidebar, "Dimension system variables."

Figure 15-34: The Compare Dimension Styles dialog box enables you to compare the properties of two dimension styles

3. Click Close twice to return to your drawing.

Tip Click the Copy button at the right side of the Compare Dimension Styles dialog box to copy the comparison to the clipboard. You can then paste it into another document. For example, you might want to e-mail the file to a client.

Copying dimension styles from other drawings

With proper planning, dimension styles make dimensioning much easier and produce more uniform results. Although you can save dimension styles in your templates, you may sometimes need to work with someone else's drawing or an old drawing that does not contain the dimension styles you need. As explained in Chapters 11 and 13, you can use the DesignCenter to import features from other drawings. To import a dimension style, follow these steps:

1. Choose DesignCenter from the Standard toolbar to open the DesignCenter.

2. In the left pane, navigate to the drawing that has the dimension style you want.

3. Double-click the drawing icon or click its plus sign.

4. To see the list of the dimension styles, double-click the dimension styles icon in either the left or right pane.

5. Double-click the dimension style's icon to import it into your drawing.

6. If you want, click the DesignCenter's Close button to close the DesignCenter.

New Feature

The Express Tools offer two commands, DIMIM and DIMEX, that enable you to save (export) and retrieve (import) dimension styles. Choose Express ➪ Dimension ➪ Dimstyle Import or Dimstyle Export. For information on installing Express Tools, see Appendix A on the CD-ROM.

On the CD-ROM

The drawing used in the following Step-by-Step exercise on changing dimension styles, ab15-b.dwg, is in the Drawings folder of the *AutoCAD 2004 Bible* CD-ROM.

Step-by-Step: Changing Dimension Styles

1. Open ab15-b.dwg from your CD-ROM.

2. Save the file as ab15-05.dwg in your AutoCAD Bible folder. This is a tension arm for a commercial dryer, as shown in Figure 15-35. ORTHO and OSNAP should be on. Set running object snaps for endpoint, intersection, and center. The Dims layer is current. If the Dimension toolbar is not visible, right-click any toolbar and choose Dimension.

3. The current dimension style is CIR. From the Dim Style Control drop-down list on the Dimension toolbar, choose LIN.

4. Choose Linear Dimension from the Dimension toolbar. At the Specify first extension line origin or <select object>: prompt, choose the endpoint at ❶ in Figure 15-35. (If necessary, press Tab until you see the endpoint tooltip.) At the Specify second extension line origin: prompt, choose the intersection at ❷. At the Specify dimension line location or [Mtext/Text/Angle/Horizontal/Vertical/Rotated]: prompt, choose an appropriate location above the bottom-most dimension.

5. Choose Dimension Style from the Dimension toolbar. Choose Override and click the Tolerances tab. Change the Tolerance Method to None. Click the Lines and Arrows tab. In the Extension Lines section, check Suppress Ext Line 1 to suppress the first extension line. Click OK. In the Dimension Style Manager, click Close.

6. Choose Linear Dimension from the Dimension toolbar. At the `Specify first extension line origin or <select object>:` prompt, choose the intersection at ❷ in Figure 15-35. At the `Specify second extension line origin:` prompt, choose the intersection at ❷. At the `Specify dimension line location or [Mtext/Text/Angle/Horizontal/Vertical/Rotated]:` prompt, pick the endpoint object snap at the right side of the previous dimension's dimension line in order to align the two dimensions.

7. The first dimension (the one you created in Step 4) needs to be updated to remove the tolerance. Choose Dimension Update from the Dimension toolbar. At the `Select objects:` prompt, choose the first dimension. Right-click to end object selection. AutoCAD updates the dimension.

8. To list the overrides, choose Dimension Style from the Dimension toolbar. Choose Compare. In the Compare Dimension Styles dialog box, `<style overrides>` should be displayed in the Compare drop-down box, and `LIN` should be displayed in the With drop-down box. AutoCAD lists the overrides, which are the only differences between the two. Click Close.

Figure 15-35: The tension arm needs some additional dimensions.

9. To remove the overrides (no tolerance and the first extension line suppressed), right-click `<style overrides>` in the Dimension Style Manager and choose Delete. AutoCAD displays the message, `Are you sure you want to delete '<style overrides>'?` Choose Yes. Click Close to return to the drawing.

10. Choose Linear Dimension from the Dimension toolbar. At the `Specify first extension line origin or <select object>:` prompt, choose the intersection at ❹ in Figure 15-35. At the `Specify second extension line origin:` prompt, choose the intersection at ❺. At the `Specify dimension line location or [Mtext/Text/Angle/Horizontal/Vertical/Rotated]:` prompt, pick an appropriate location to the right of the model.

11. To compare the CIR and LIN dimension styles, choose Dimension Style from the Dimension toolbar. Choose Compare. LIN should appear in the Compare drop-down box. Choose CIR from the With drop-down box. AutoCAD lists the differences, as shown in Figure 15-36. Click Close twice to return to your drawing.

12. Save your drawing. It should look like Figure 15-37.

Figure 15-36: This listing compares the two dimension styles in this drawing.

Figure 15-37: The dimensions have been added.

Dimension system variables

All the settings you make in the Dimension Styles dialog box are stored in a large number of system variables devoted to dimensions. AutoCAD stores settings in system variables (See Chapter 5 for more information about system variables).

To get a list of the dimension variables, choose Help ⇨ Help and click the Contents tab. Double-click Command Reference and then double-click System Variables. Double-click D System Variables. All the variables starting with DIM are dimension system variables.

Once upon a time the only way to manage dimensions was by knowing all the dimension system variables and individually setting each one. Today, the Dimension Style Manager makes managing dimensions much easier. However, if you want to create scripts or AutoLISP routines to manage your dimensions, you need to understand how the dimension system variables work because scripts and AutoLISP routines cannot access dialog boxes.

You can use the DIMSTYLE command on the command line to list all the system variable settings for a dimension style. Type **-dimstyle** at the command line. The following figures show a listing for an architectural dimension style, obtained using the STatus option. You can get a great education in dimension system variables by printing out and perusing this list.

```
Command: -dimstyle

Current dimension style:  myarrow
Current dimension overrides:
  DIMBLK     Oblique
  DIMCLRT    6 (magenta)
Enter a dimension style option
[Save/Restore/STatus/Variables/Apply/?] <Restore>: st

DIMASO      Off             Create dimension objects
DIMSTYLE    myarrow         Current dimension style (read-only)

DIMADEC     0               Angular decimal places
DIMALT      Off             Alternate units selected
DIMALTD     2               Alternate unit decimal places
DIMALTF     25.4000         Alternate unit scale factor
DIMALTRND   0"              Alternate units rounding value
DIMALTTD    2               Alternate tolerance decimal places
DIMALTTZ    0               Alternate tolerance zero suppression
DIMALTU     2               Alternate units
DIMALTZ     0               Alternate unit zero suppression
DIMAPOST                    Prefix and suffix for alternate text
DIMASZ      3/16"           Arrow size
DIMATFIT    3               Arrow and text fit
DIMAUNIT    0               Angular unit format
DIMAZIN     0               Angular zero supression
DIMBLK      Oblique         Arrow block name
DIMBLK1     ClosedFilled    First arrow block name
DIMBLK2     ClosedFilled    Second arrow block name
DIMCEN      1/16"           Center mark size
```

Notice that DIMSTYLE states the current dimension style, including the overrides at the start of the listing.

The other DIMSTYLE options are:

✦ **Save:** Saves a dimension style.

✦ **Restore:** Makes a dimension style current.

✦ **Variables:** Lists dimension variables, such as the STatus option, but lets you first choose which dimension style for which you want to list the variables.

✦ **Apply:** Updates dimensions to the current style, including overrides. This is equivalent to choosing Update from the Dimension toolbar.

✦ **?:** Lists all dimension styles in the drawing.

```
DIMCEN        1/16"          Center mark size
DIMCLRD       BYBLOCK        Dimension line and leader color
DIMCLRE       BYBLOCK        Extension line color
DIMCLRT       6 (magenta)    Dimension text color
DIMDEC        4              Decimal places
DIMDLE        1/16"          Dimension line extension
DIMDLI        3/8"           Dimension line spacing
DIMDSEP                      Decimal separator
DIMEXE        3/16"          Extension above dimension line
DIMEXO        1/16"          Extension line origin offset
DIMFRAC       0              Fraction format
DIMGAP        1/16"          Gap from dimension line to text
DIMJUST       0              Justification of text on dimension line
DIMLDRBLK     ClosedFilled   Leader block name
DIMLFAC       1.0000         Linear unit scale factor
DIMLIM        Off            Generate dimension limits
DIMLUNIT      4              Linear unit format
DIMLWD        -2             Dimension line and leader lineweight
DIMLWE        -2             Extension line lineweight
DIMPOST                      Prefix and suffix for dimension text
DIMRND        0"             Rounding value
DIMSAH        Off            Separate arrow blocks
DIMSCALE      48.0000        Overall scale factor
DIMSD1        Off            Suppress the first dimension line
DIMSD2        Off            Suppress the second dimension line
DIMSE1        Off            Suppress the first extension line
DIMSE2        Off            Suppress the second extension line
DIMSOXD       Off            Suppress outside dimension lines
DIMTAD        1              Place text above the dimension line
DIMTDEC       4              Tolerance decimal places
DIMTFAC       0.7500         Tolerance text height scaling factor
DIMTIH        Off            Text inside extensions is horizontal
DIMTIX        Off            Place text inside extensions
DIMTM         0"             Minus tolerance
DIMTMOVE      1              Text movement
DIMTOFL       On             Force line inside extension lines
DIMTOH        Off            Text outside horizontal
DIMTOL        Off            Tolerance dimensioning
DIMTOLJ       1              Tolerance vertical justification
DIMTP         0"             Plus tolerance
DIMTSZ        0"             Tick size
DIMTVP        0.0000         Text vertical position
```

You can also create dimension style overrides by using the DIMOVERRIDE command (Dimension ➪ Override). You need to know the name of the system variable and the setting code you want. AutoCAD offers the `Enter dimension variable name to override (or Clear overrides):` prompt. To create an override, type the system variable and its setting. Then select the dimensions for which you want to override dimension style settings. To clear all dimension style overrides, type c ↵. Then select the dimensions for which you want to remove overrides.

Creating Geometric Tolerances

You can use the TOLERANCE command to create geometric tolerances. (For another way to specify tolerances, see the "Formatting Tolerances" section earlier in this chapter.) AutoCAD offers another way to specify tolerances — geometric tolerances — using the TOLERANCE command. This command creates feature control frames, which define tolerances. This method of denoting tolerances is used to conform to international standards such as ISO (International Standards Organization), ANSI (American National Standards Institute), or JIS (Japanese Industrial Standards). Figure 15-38 shows a drawing using tolerance feature control frames.

Figure 15-38: An example of AutoCAD's tolerance feature control frames

Thanks to Jerry Butterfield of Clow Value Company, Oskaloosa, Iowa, for this drawing.

Starting the tolerance frame

Creating a tolerance frame is a step-by step process that depends on what information you want to include. To start the frame, choose Tolerance from the Dimension toolbar, which opens the Geometric Tolerance dialog box, as shown in Figure 15-39.

Figure 15-39: The Geometric Tolerance dialog box

Use this dialog box to build the frame. The frame enables you to create two rows of two tolerances, three datum references (for up to three dimensions), as well as a projected tolerance zone value and symbol, and a datum identifier. You will rarely, if ever, use all the features in the frame.

Follow these steps to build the frame:

1. Click the first Sym box to open the Symbol dialog box, as shown in Figure 15-40.

Figure 15-40: Use the Symbol dialog box to choose the symbol for the type of geometry for which you want to specify tolerance.

2. Choose the symbol for the geometric characteristic you are tolerancing. (Table 15-3 explains these symbols.) Click OK. If you don't need any symbol, click the blank box.

3. To insert a diameter symbol before the first tolerance, click the Dia box to the left of the text box in the Tolerance 1 section.

4. Type the tolerance value in the Value box.

5. If you want to specify a material condition, click the MC box to the right of the text box. AutoCAD opens the Material Condition dialog box, shown in Figure 15-41. Choose the symbol you want and click OK.

Figure 15-41: The Material Condition dialog box

6. If desired, complete a second tolerance.

7. If desired, type a datum in the Datum box of the Datum 1 section, usually A.

8. If desired, add a material condition, using the same method described in Step 5.

9. If desired, type in datum references in the Datum 2 and Datum 3 sections, usually B and C with material conditions.

10. If you need to specify a projected tolerance zone for a perpendicular part, type in the height. Then click the Projected Tolerance Zone box to insert the Projected Tolerance Zone symbol.

11. Finally, if you want to specify a datum identifier, type the identifier letter in the Datum Identifier box.

12. Click OK to return to your drawing.

If you choose a material condition symbol and then change your mind, click the material condition box again and choose the blank square to delete your symbol.

Table 15-3
Tolerance Symbols

Symbol	Name	Symbol	Name
⊕	Position	▱	Flatness
◎	Concentricity	○	Circularity
÷	Symmetry	—	Straightness
//	Parallelism	⌓	Surface profile
⊥	Perpendicularity	⌒	Line profile
∠	Angularity	↗	Circular runout
⌭	Cylindricity	⌰	Total runout

Inserting the tolerance frame

After you complete the frame, AutoCAD returns you to your drawing and offers the
`Enter tolerance location:` prompt. Specify any point to insert the frame.

Tip You can create a matching Datum reference to place on your model by creating a
tolerance frame with no symbol and only the Datum letter.

Editing a tolerance frame

To edit a geometric tolerance, double-click the tolerance frame. AutoCAD opens the
Geometric Tolerance dialog box, and you can make any changes you need. Click OK
to return to your drawing.

On the CD-ROM The drawing used in the following Step-by-Step exercise on creating geometric
tolerances, `ab15-c.dwg`, is in the `Drawings` folder of the *AutoCAD 2004 Bible*
CD-ROM.

Step-by-Step: Creating Geometric Tolerances

1. Open `ab15-c.dwg` from your CD-ROM.

2. Save the file as `ab15-06.dwg` in your `AutoCAD Bible` folder. This drawing of a gear operator is shown in Figure 15-42. The Dim layer is current. If the Dimension toolbar is not visible, right-click any toolbar and choose Dimension.

Figure 15-42: A mechanical drawing using geometric tolerances

3. Choose Tolerance from the Dimension toolbar. In the Geometric Tolerance dialog box, click the top-left box, labeled Sym.

4. AutoCAD opens the Symbol dialog box. Choose the top-left symbol (for position).

5. In the Tolerance 1 section of the Geometric Tolerance dialog box, click the next black box, the Dia box, to insert the diameter symbol. In the Value box, type **.004**. Click the next black box, the MC box. In the Material Condition dialog box, choose the first image tile (for Maximum material condition).

6. In the Datum 1 section, type **B** in the Datum box. Click OK.

7. At the Enter tolerance location: prompt, pick ❶ in Figure 15-42. AutoCAD places the geometric tolerance.

8. Save your drawing. It should look like Figure 15-43.

Figure 15-43: The drawing with the added geometric tolerance frame

Summary

In this chapter, you gained a thorough understanding of how to use dimension styles to organize your dimensions. You read how to:

✦ Define a dimension's lines and arrows

✦ Define dimension text style and placement

✦ Fit dimensions into small spaces

✦ Define the primary and alternate measuring units

✦ Format tolerances

✦ Create a variant of a dimension style for specific types of dimensions

✦ Change dimension style used by a dimension

✦ Modify a dimension style and update all dimensions that use that style

✦ Override a dimension style for temporary changes

✦ Update existing dimensions

✦ Compare dimension styles

✦ Copy dimension styles from other drawings using the DesignCenter

✦ Create geometric tolerances

In the next chapter, you learn how to draw complex objects.

✦ ✦ ✦

Drawing Complex Objects

AutoCAD offers a number of complex objects that can help you create accurate, professional drawings. Polylines are single objects that can combine line segments and arcs. Splines are mathematically controlled curves based on points you specify. Regions and boundaries create complex shapes from existing objects. Hatches create a solid, gradient, or patterned fill. Multilines are sets of parallel lines. Sketching is a way to create freehand drawings. Digitizing with a tablet is a process that is used to transfer an existing paper drawing into AutoCAD. In this chapter, I introduce you to these complex objects and explain how to use them.

Creating and Editing Polylines

Polylines are single objects that combine line segments and arcs. In certain situations, it is useful to be able to edit an entire set of lines and arcs as one object. Polylines can have a width, which can vary from the start point to the endpoint of each segment. Polylines ensure that all the vertices of a closed area actually meet, which is very helpful if you want to hatch the area. They are also very useful for 3D drawing. In short, polylines are a neat, clean way to draw. (Technically, polylines are called lightweight polylines to distinguish them from the type of polylines used in Release 13 and earlier.)

The RECTANG and POLYGON commands create polylines. Figure 16-1 shows a few examples of polylines.

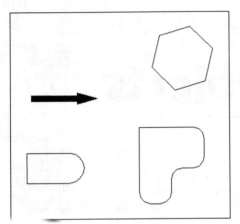

Figure 16-1: Some polylines

Using the PLINE command

To draw a polyline, choose Polyline from the Draw toolbar. This starts the
PLINE command. AutoCAD responds with the `Specify start point:`
prompt. Specify the start point. Then AutoCAD responds with the `Specify next
point or [Arc/Close/Halfwidth/Length/Undo/Width]:` prompt. It offers the
following options:

✦ **Arc:** Draws arcs. This option opens up a set of arc suboptions, which are
 explained next, after this list.

✦ **Close:** Closes a polyline by drawing a line from the endpoint of the last line
 segment to the start point of the polyline. This option appears only after you
 have picked a second point.

✦ **Halfwidth:** Defines half the width of the polyline — the distance from the cen-
 ter of the polyline to its edge. AutoCAD asks you for the starting halfwidth and
 the ending halfwidth, enabling you to create polylines that are tapered.

✦ **Length:** Specifies the length of the next line segment. AutoCAD draws the line
 segment in the same direction as the last line segment or tangent to the last arc.

✦ **Undo:** Undoes the last line segment.

✦ **Width:** Defines the width of the polyline. AutoCAD asks you for the starting
 width and the ending width.

✦ **Specify next point:** Enables you to create a line segment. This is the default
 option.

Like the LINE command, PLINE continues to prompt you for more points, repeating
the entire prompt each time. When you are done, press Enter to end the command.

If you choose Arc, AutoCAD responds with the `Specify endpoint of arc or [Angle/CEnter/CLose/Direction/Halfwidth/Line/Radius/Second pt/ Undo/Width]:` prompt. While this may seem overwhelming, most of the options are similar to the ARC command options. If you need a review, see Chapter 7. The arc options are as follows:

✦ **Angle:** Specifies the included angle.

✦ **CEnter:** Specifies the arc's center.

✦ **CLose:** Closes the polyline by drawing an arc from the endpoint of the last arc to the start point of the polyline.

✦ **Direction:** Specifies the direction of the arc from the start point.

✦ **Halfwidth:** Defines half the width of the polyline—the distance from the center of the polyline to its edge. AutoCAD asks you for the starting halfwidth and the ending halfwidth.

✦ **Line:** Returns you to the main polyline prompt so you can draw line segments.

✦ **Radius:** Specifies the arc's radius.

✦ **Second pt:** Specifies the second point of the arc.

✦ **Undo:** Undoes the last arc.

✦ **Width:** Defines the width of the polyline. AutoCAD asks you for the starting width and the ending width.

✦ **Specify endpoint of arc:** Specifies the endpoint of the arc. This is the default. AutoCAD creates an arc tangent to the previous arc (continuing in the same direction).

PLINE continues to display the arc submenu until you use the Line suboption or end the command by pressing Enter.

Generating linetypes on polylines

When you create a polyline with a noncontinuous linetype, you may find that the linetype does not appear properly along the polyline. One reason is that the segments of the polyline may be too short to fit the entire linetype definition—in this case the polyline appears continuous even though it is defined with a dashed or other linetype. You can tell AutoCAD to generate the linetype continuously along the polyline instead of starting the linetype definition anew at each vertex. This results in a more normal looking linetype along the polyline. To do this, you need to turn on the PLINEGEN system variable. By default it is off (set at 0). To turn on PLINEGEN, type **plinegen** ⏎ and then **1** ⏎.

As explained in the section "Editing polylines with the PEDIT command" later in the chapter, you can also modify the display of linetypes for existing polylines.

On the CD-ROM

The drawing used in the following Step-by-Step exercise on drawing polylines, `ab16-a.dwg`, is in the `Drawings` folder of the *AutoCAD 2004 Bible* CD-ROM.

Step-by-Step: Drawing Polylines

1. Open `ab16-a.dwg` from your CD-ROM.

2. Save the file as `ab16-01.dwg` in your `AutoCAD Bible` folder. It shows a small section of a drive block, as shown in Figure 16-2. In this exercise, you complete part of the drawing. ORTHO and OSNAP should be on. Set running object snaps to endpoint, midpoint, and intersection. Layer 3 should be current.

Figure 16-2: A small section of a drive block

Thanks to Mary Redfern of the Bethlehem Corporation, Easton, Pennsylvania, for this drawing.

3. Choose Polyline from the Draw toolbar. Follow the prompts:

```
Specify start point: Press Shift+right-click and choose the
From object snap.
Base point: Choose ❶ in Figure 16-2.
<Offset>: @-1/2,0 ↵
Specify next point or [Arc/Halfwidth/Length/Undo/Width]:
Move the cursor in the 90-degree direction and type 3/32 ↵.
```

4. Type **a** ↵ to continue with an arc. (Because your hands are already on the keyboard from typing the line length, it's easier to type the option letter than to right-click and choose it from the shortcut menu.) At the `Specify endpoint of arc or [Angle/CEnter/CLose/Direction/Halfwidth/Line/Radius/Second pt/Undo/Width]:` prompt, type **@3/16,3/16** ↵.

5. Type **l** ↵ to continue with a linear polyline segment. At the `Specify next point or [Arc/Close/Halfwidth/Length/Undo/Width]:` prompt, move the cursor in the 0-degree direction and type **11/32** ↵.

6. Type **a** ↵ to continue with an arc. At the prompt, type **@3/16,3/16** ↵.

7. Type **l** ↵ to continue with a linear polyline segment. At the prompt, move the cursor in the 90-degree direction and type **6–3/32** ↵.

8. Type **a** ↵ to continue with an arc. At the prompt, type **@5/16,5/16** ↵.

9. To create the last arc, type **r** ↵. Follow the prompts:

```
Specify radius of arc: 5-5/8 ↵
Specify endpoint of arc or [Angle]: Choose the From object snap.
Base point: Choose point ❷ in Figure 16-2.
<Offset>: @0,7-1/4 ↵
```

10. Press Enter to exit the PLINE command.

11. Save your drawing. It should look like Figure 16-3.

Figure 16-3: The completed polyline

Ar1 creates a label of the area of an enclosed polyline. Look in \Software\ Chap16\ar1. GeomCurves creates several kinds of mathematical curves, including parabolas, hyperbolas, and spirals. Look in \Software\Chap16\GeomCurves.

Editing polylines with the PEDIT command

Because polylines can be quite complex, AutoCAD has a special command to edit them, PEDIT. To edit a polyline, choose Modify ⇨ Object ⇨ Polyline. AutoCAD responds with the `Select polyline or [Multiple]:` prompt. Select a polyline

and AutoCAD responds with the `Enter an option [Close/Join/Width/Edit vertex/Fit/Spline/Decurve/Ltype gen/Undo]:` prompt. The options are:

✦ **Close:** Closes an open polyline. If necessary, it adds a segment to connect the endpoint to the start point. If the polyline is already closed, this prompt becomes Open. Open creates a break between the first and last segments of the polyline.

✦ **Join:** Joins touching lines, arcs, or other polylines to the polyline.

✦ **Width:** Enables you to specify one width for the entire polyline.

✦ **Edit Vertex:** Provides a set of suboptions for editing vertices. These suboptions are explained after this list.

✦ **Fit:** Turns the polyline into a curve that passes through the vertices.

✦ **Spline:** Creates a curve by using the vertices as control points. The curve does not usually actually pass through the vertices. This is not the mathematically exact spline that the SPLINE command produces (covered later in this chapter).

✦ **Decurve:** Returns a Fit or Spline curve to its original vertices.

✦ **Ltype gen:** Turns on continuous linetype generation for the selected polyline.

✦ **Undo:** Undoes the most recent edit.

Tip
You can change any line or arc into a polyline. Start PEDIT and choose a line or arc. AutoCAD responds: `Object selected is not a polyline. Do you want to turn it into one? <Y>`. Press Enter to accept the default. AutoCAD turns the object into a polyline. (You can change the new PEDITACCEPT system variable to 1 to suppress this prompt and automatically turn non-polyline objects that you select for the PEDIT command to polylines.) You can use this technique to turn a series of connected lines and arcs into a polyline. First, turn one of the objects into a polyline as I just explained. Then use the Join option and select the other objects individually or by a selection window. After you finish object selection, AutoCAD tells you how many segments were added to the polyline. In order to create a polyline in this way, the individual lines and arcs must connect exactly end to end. However, if you use the Multiple option, explained following the current list, you can join lines that are not exactly touching.

When you choose the Edit Vertex option, AutoCAD offers a new set of suboptions, with the `Enter a vertex editing option [Next/Previous/Break/Insert/Move/Regen/Straighten/Tangent/Width/eXit] <N>:` prompt. You see an x at one of the vertices. This is the current vertex, which you can edit. The suboptions are as follows:

✦ **Next:** Moves you to the next vertex so you can edit it.

✦ **Previous:** Moves you to the previous vertex.

✦ **Break:** Breaks the polyline. You can choose the Go suboption to break the polyline into two (although you can't see the break). You can move to another vertex using the Next or Previous suboptions and then choose Go. AutoCAD breaks the polyline between the original vertex and the vertex you moved to. Use the eXit suboption to return to the previous prompt. (You can also use the BREAK command.)

✦ **Insert:** Inserts another vertex. AutoCAD prompts you for its location.

✦ **Move:** Moves the vertex. AutoCAD prompts you for its location.

✦ **Regen:** Regenerates the polyline.

✦ **Straighten:** Deletes vertices. This works like the Break option with the same Next, Previous, Go, and eXit suboptions. As soon as you move to a new vertex, AutoCAD draws a straight line between it and the original vertex. If you don't move to a new vertex, this option affects only an arc by changing it to a straight line segment.

✦ **Tangent:** Specifies a direction from the vertex. AutoCAD uses this if you choose the Fit option.

✦ **Width:** Enables you to specify a starting and ending width of the segment starting with the current vertex.

✦ **eXit:** Exits this group of suboptions.

Caution

You can make many changes during the PEDIT session. If you return to the command line and use the U or UNDO command, the entire session is undone. If you want to undo only part of the session, use the Undo options of the PEDIT command.

You can edit polylines with grips as well. A polyline has a grip at each vertex, making it easy to move vertices.

To edit multiple polylines at one time, follow these steps:

1. Start the PEDIT command.

2. Choose the Multiple option (type **m** or right-click and choose Multiple from the shortcut menu) at the first prompt.

3. At the `Select objects:` prompt, select the polylines.

4. You see the `Enter an option [Close/Open/Join/Width/Fit/Spline/ Decurve/Ltype gen/Undo]:` prompt.

5. Choose the option you want. For example, you can change the width of all the selected polylines or apply the Spline option to them.

You can also join two polylines that are not touching—if you use the Multiple option first. Select the polylines and then choose the Join option. You then need to specify two suboptions:

✦ **Fuzz distance:** The maximum distance that the endpoints of the polylines can be from each other. In other words, in order for the join to work, the fuzz distance must be greater than the distance of the endpoints. If you want to join the endpoints no matter what, type in a very large number.

✦ **Jointype:** The method of joining polylines. You can use the Extend method, which extends (or trims) the segments to the nearest endpoints, or the Add method, which adds a straight segment between the two nearest endpoints. You can choose the Both suboption, which tries to extend or trim, but, if it can't, it adds a segment.

Editing polylines using the Properties palette

You can also edit polylines in the Properties palette. Double-click a polyline, and AutoCAD opens the Properties palette for Polylines, shown in Figure 16-4.

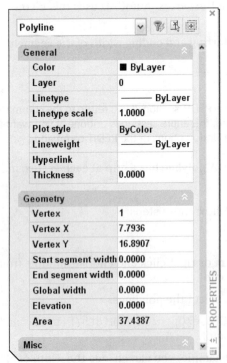

Figure 16-4: The Properties palette with a polyline selected

Notice that you can choose a vertex by clicking Vertex in the Geometry section of the dialog box. An x appears on the polyline to let you know which vertex you have chosen. You can then edit the vertex's coordinates by typing them in, or by clicking

the Pick a Point button that appears and picking a point in the drawing. You can change the start and ending width and specify a global width for the entire polyline.

Notice that you can close and open a polyline in the Misc section. You can also turn on continuous linetype generation for the selected polyline by choosing Linetype generation and choosing Enabled from the drop-down list that appears. Of course, you can change the layer, color, linetype, lineweight, and linetype scale as well.

You can "paint" polyline properties from one polyline to another, using the MATCH-PROP command. Select a polyline, choose Match Properties on the Standard toolbar, and then select the polyline that you want to edit.

The drawing used in the following Step-by-Step exercise on editing polylines, ab16-b.dwg, is in the Drawings folder of the *AutoCAD 2004 Bible* CD-ROM.

Step-by-Step: Editing Polylines

1. Open ab16-b.dwg from your CD-ROM.

2. Save the file as ab16-02.dwg in your AutoCAD Bible folder. This is a topographical drawing as shown in Figure 16-5. The contours are polylines.

3. Choose Modify ➪ Object ➪ Polyline to start the PEDIT command. Select the polyline at ❶ in Figure 16-5.

4. At the Enter an option [Close/Join/Width/Edit vertex/Fit/Spline/ Decurve/Ltype gen/Undo]: prompt, right-click and choose Width. At the Specify new width for all segments: prompt, type **.5** ↵.

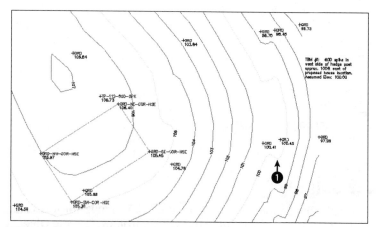

Figure 16-5: The topographical drawing's contours are polylines.
Thanks to Henry Dearborn, AIA, of Fairfield, Iowa, for this drawing.

5. Type **e** ↵ to choose the Edit vertex option. At the `Enter a vertex editing option [Next/Previous/Break/Insert/Move/Regen/Straighten/Tangent/Width/eXit] <N>:` prompt, type **n** ↵ several times until the x mark is at ❶ in Figure 16-5. (There are many vertices — it's not important that you find the exact one.)

6. Type **m** to move the vertex. At the `Specify new location for marked vertex:` prompt, pick a point slightly above the existing vertex. Then, type **x** ↵ to exit the Edit vertex submenu.

7. At the main PEDIT prompt, type **s** ↵. PEDIT smoothes out the polyline.

8. Press Enter to exit the PEDIT command.

9. Save your drawing.

Drawing and Editing Splines

The SPLINE command draws a NURBS, which stands for nonuniform rational B-spline. Not to get too technical, a spline is a smooth curve that is defined by a series of points. The SPLINE command provides a more precise representation of a spline than the Spline option of the PLINE command. By default, the curve passes through each point you define. Figure 16-6 shows a beanbag chair created with two splines. Both the chair and the grips are on all the originally specified points.

Figure 16-6: A beanbag chair created with two splines

Creating splines

To create a spline, choose Spline from the Draw menu. AutoCAD responds with the `Specify first point or [Object]:` prompt. Use the Object option to convert a polyline that you have created with PEDIT's Spline option into a true spline. (It won't look any different, but its internal definition changes.) Otherwise, specify the first point for the spline.

If you choose a point, AutoCAD displays the `Specify next point:` prompt so that you can pick a second point. After you do so, AutoCAD responds with the `Specify next point or [Close/Fit tolerance] <start tangent>:` prompt. Use these options as follows:

✦ **Close:** Closes the spline by connecting the last point with the first in a continuous (tangent) curve. AutoCAD asks for a tangent direction. You can specify a direction by picking a point (watch the spline image change as you move the cursor) or pressing Enter to accept the default tangent direction.

✦ **Fit Tolerance:** Specifies how closely the spline comes to the points you pick. The default, 0, creates a spline that passes through each point. If you want the curve to have a latitude of 0.5 units from the points, set the tolerance to 0.5.

✦ **Specify next point:** The default is to continue to enter points. Press Enter to end point selection.

✦ **Start tangent:** When you press Enter to complete point selection, AutoCAD prompts you for start and ending tangent directions. You can press Enter at both prompts to accept the default tangents based on the curve's current shape. You can see the effect of other tangent points by moving the cursor and watching the image change.

On the CD-ROM The drawing used in the following Step-by-Step exercise on drawing splines, `ab16-c.dwg`, is in the `Drawings` folder of the *AutoCAD 2004 Bible* CD-ROM.

Step-by-Step: Drawing Splines

1. Open `ab16-c.dwg` from your CD-ROM.

2. Save the file as `ab16-03.dwg` in your `AutoCAD Bible` folder. This is a topographical site map, shown in Figure 16-7. OSNAP should be on. Set a running object snap for insertion.

3. Use Zoom Window to zoom in on the area near the start of the north edge of the drive. Choose Spline from the Draw toolbar.

4. At the `Specify first point or [Object]:` prompt, use the Insert object snap to pick the cross at the start of the north edge of the drive, as shown in Figure 16-7. Continue to pick the crosses marked N-EDGE-DR. Choose Pan from the Standard toolbar to do a real-time pan when you reach the edge of the display. Press Esc. Continue picking points until you get to the end of the north edge of the drive, as shown in Figure 16-7. Press Enter to end point selection.

5. At the `Specify start tangent:` and `Specify end tangent:` prompts, press Enter.

Start of south edge of drive Start of north edge of drive

End of north edge of drive

End of south edge of drive

Figure 16-7: A topographical site map. You can complete the gravel road based on surveyor's data.

6. Start the SPLINE command again and pick points for the south edge of the drive, from the start of the south edge of the drive to the end, as shown in Figure 16-7. Pan as necessary. Again, press Enter to accept the default directions for the start and end tangents.

7. If you want, choose Zoom Previous on the Standard toolbar several times until you see the original view of the drawing. Save your drawing.

GeomCurves.lsp is a routine that creates various kinds of geometrical curves, such as spirals and parabolas. You can find it in the \Software\Chap16\GeomCurves folder.

Editing splines

Like polylines, splines have their own editing command. To understand how to edit splines, you need to understand how AutoCAD stores them.

When you pick points to create the spline, AutoCAD stores these points as fit points (or data points). If the tolerance is zero, the curve lies on these fit points. When you select a spline at the command line, grips appear at these fit points. However, when you use the SPLINEDIT command, to see the fit points as grips, you must choose the Fit Data option first. Only then can you edit the fit points.

AutoCAD calculates control points based on the fit points. The spline is then calculated based on the control points, not the fit points. Most of the control points are not on the spline. When you use SPLINEDIT to edit a spline, and use the Move vertex

option described later, AutoCAD displays the control points as grips, and you can move the control points.

Figure 16-8 shows a spline created using point objects as the fit points — these were the points picked when creating the spline. Note that the spline passes through each fit point.

Figure 16-8: The point objects were used as the pick points. These are the fit points of the spline.

Figure 16-9 shows the same spline as in Figure 16-8 as it appears when selected with no command active. Notice that the grips are exactly on the fit points.

Because AutoCAD calculates the spline based on the control points, it doesn't need the fit points to generate the spline. In fact, if you use the Move vertex or Refine options to move or edit a control point, AutoCAD now has to use only the control points to generate the spline and discards the fit point information so that you can no longer edit it. The Fit Data option also disappears from the prompt.

You can edit the fit points using grips, as shown in Figure 16-10.

Figure 16-9: When you select a spline with no command active, you see grips on the fit points.

Figure 16-10: Editing fit points of a spline using grips

To edit a spline, choose Modify ➪ Object ➪ Spline to start the SPLINEDIT command. After you select the spline, AutoCAD responds with the `Enter an option [Fit data/Close/Move vertex/Refine/rEverse/Undo]:` prompt. Here's how to use these options:

✦ **Fit Data:** Fit data means the points you've chosen, their tolerance, and the tangents. Use this option to edit fit data. This option has its own list of sub-options that are explained after this list.

✦ **Close/Open:** If the spline is open, this option closes it by adding a continuous (tangent) curve from the last point to the start point. If the spline is closed, this option appears as Open. If the spline was originally closed, the Open option removes the connection between the last and first points, although the spline looks the same. If the spline was originally open and you closed it, when you use the Open option, AutoCAD erases the curve that it added when you closed it.

✦ **Move Vertex:** This works like the Edit vertex option of PEDIT, except that here AutoCAD displays the points as grips and highlights them. You can use Next and Previous suboptions, select any point to move, and pick a new location for the highlighted vertex.

✦ **Refine:** Enables you to refine the spline in three ways:

• Add control points. This doesn't change the shape of the spline, but AutoCAD adjusts nearby control points slightly.

• Elevate the order of the spline, which adds control points throughout the spline (but once you go up, you can't go down).

• Change the weight of any control point. This is like the gravity the control point exerts on the spline. Watch the spline inch toward the control point as you increase its weight.

✦ **rEverse:** Reverses the direction of the spline so that the start point becomes the endpoint and vice versa.

✦ **Undo:** Undoes the most recent edit operation.

When you use the SPLINEDIT command and select a spline, you see control points, not fit points. In Figure 16-11, the grips indicate the control points.

Fit point

Control point

Figure 16-11: When you choose the SPLINEDIT command and select a spline, the grips indicate the control points, which are not generally on the spline.

If you choose the Fit Data option, AutoCAD responds with the `Enter a fit data option [Add/Close/Delete/Move/Purge/Tangents/toLerance/eXit] <eXit>:` prompt. Descriptions of these options follow:

✦ **Add:** Adds fit data points to the curve. AutoCAD asks you to select a point and then automatically selects the next point as well, shown with highlighted grips. AutoCAD then prompts you for a new point, which must be between the two highlighted points. AutoCAD reshapes the spline accordingly.

✦ **Open/Close:** Opens or closes the spline using the fit points.

✦ **Delete:** Deletes a selected fit point.

✦ **Move:** Moves a fit point. You can use the Next or Previous suboptions or the Select point option to select the point you want to move. Selected points appear as highlighted grips. AutoCAD prompts you for the new fit point location. You can also use grips to edit fit points.

✦ **Purge:** Deletes fit point information.

✦ **Tangents:** Enables you to specify start and end tangents of open splines, or one tangent for closed splines. You can let AutoCAD calculate a default tangent.

✦ **toLerance:** Enables you to specify the tolerance, which determines how closely the spline comes to the fit points.

✦ **eXit:** Exits the suboption menu.

Note You can also use SPLINEDIT to edit 3D splines.

When you use SPLINEDIT and choose the Fit Data option, the grips appear on the fit points so that you can edit them, as shown in Figure 16-12.

Figure 16-12: When you use the Fit Data option of the SPLINEDIT command, the grips appear on the fit points.

You can edit a spline in the Properties palette. It works similarly to editing a polyline. You can choose the fits points or the control points and change them.

On the CD-ROM The drawing used in the following Step-by-Step exercise on editing splines, `ab16.03.dwg`, is in the `Results` folder of the *AutoCAD 2004 Bible* CD-ROM.

Step-by-Step: Editing Splines

1. Open `ab16-03.dwg` from the `Results` folder of your CD-ROM. If you did the previous exercise, you can open it from your `AutoCAD Bible` folder.

2. Save the file as `ab16-04.dwg` in your `AutoCAD Bible` folder.

3. If necessary, use ZOOM Window to zoom in to the area shown in Figure 16-13.

4. Use the MOVE command to move the S-EDGE-DR marker up and to the left slightly. You may find it helpful to turn off OSNAP.

5. Choose Modify ➪ Object ➪ Spline. At the `Select spline:` prompt, choose the spline that makes up the south edge of the drive. Note that the grips appear on the control points, which are different than the original points you selected to create the spline in the previous exercise. Follow the prompts:

```
Enter an option [Fit data/Close/Move vertex/Refine/rEverse/
Undo]: Right-click and choose Fit data to edit the fit
points. The grips move to the fit points.
Enter a fit data option [Add/Close/Delete/Move/Purge/
Tangents/toLerance/eXit] <eXit>: Right-click and choose Move
to move a fit point.
Specify new location or [Next/Previous/Select point/eXit]
<N>: Right-click and choose Select Point to select a point.
Specify control point<exit>: Pick the fit point nearest the
S-EDGE-DR marker you moved. AutoCAD highlights the grip.
Specify new location or [Next/Previous/Select point/eXit]
<N>: Use an insert object snap to pick the S-EDGE-DR marker.
```

6. Type **x** ↵ twice and then press Enter to end the SPLINEDIT command.

7. Save your drawing.

Figure 16-13: The topographical site map with a gravel road created by using the SPLINE command

Creating Regions

Regions are two-dimensional surfaces. They look like closed polylines, but AutoCAD can calculate more information from regions than from polylines, such as the centroid, moments of inertia, and other properties relating to mass. You can also create complex shapes by combining, subtracting, and intersecting regions. While these commands are most often used for 3D drawing, they are often used in 2D drawing as a preparation for 3D drawing. You create a region from other objects. You can use closed polylines, closed splines, circles, ellipses, and combinations of lines, arcs, and elliptical arcs that create a closed shape. The shape cannot intersect itself like a figure 8.

Figure 16-14 shows a complex region. Although it looks like a circle with seven circles inside it, it is actually a circular surface with seven holes in it. When you select it, you can see that it is one object. The real proof of the pudding is when you try to extrude it to create a 3D object out of it. You can then view it at an angle, hide background lines, and clearly see the holes, as shown in Figure 16-15.

To create a region, choose Region from the Draw toolbar. AutoCAD asks you to select objects. Select all the objects and press Enter to end object selection. If all the objects create a closed, nonintersecting shape, AutoCAD tells you:

```
1 loop extracted.
1 Region created.
```

Figure 16-14: A complex region

The original objects are deleted. If your objects aren't perfectly end-to-end, AutoCAD merely states:

```
0 loops extracted.
0 Regions created.
```

Note If you want to keep the original objects, change the DELOBJ system variable to 0 (off) before you use the REGION command.

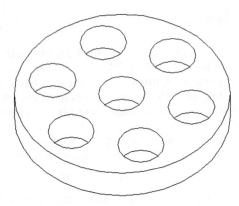

Figure 16-15: A region can be used to create a complex 3D object.

In order to draw your original objects end to end, remember to use Endpoint object snaps. Also, don't forget that you can start a line or arc at the end of the last point drawn by pressing Enter at the first prompt. You can also use TRIM and EXTEND to clean up extraneous endpoints. The BOUNDARY command (see the next section) offers a way to create regions in situations where objects are not neatly drawn end to end.

If you had a hatch inside the objects, you lose hatch associativity. You can rehatch the region if you want. When you create a region that is hatched, AutoCAD has no problem creating the region but doesn't quite know what to say about the hatch. Here's the response:

```
1 closed, degenerate or unsupported object rejected.
```

As mentioned earlier, you can combine, subtract, and intersect regions to create complex objects. The three commands to accomplish these functions are UNION, SUBTRACT, and INTERSECT. These commands are discussed in Chapter 24 because they are most often used in 3D drafting.

The drawing used in the following Step-by-Step exercise on creating regions, ab16-d.dwg, is in the Drawings folder of the *AutoCAD 2004 Bible* CD-ROM.

Step-by-Step: Creating Regions

1. Open `ab16-d.dwg` from your CD-ROM.

2. Save the file as `ab16-05.dwg` in your `AutoCAD Bible` folder.

3. Choose Region from the Draw toolbar. At the `Select Objects:` prompt, use a selection window to select the entire model, shown in Figure 16-16. Press Enter to end object selection. AutoCAD responds with this message:

```
7 loops extracted.
7 Regions created.
```

> **Note** You might experience a slight delay when first using the REGION command while AutoCAD loads the 3D modeling feature.

4. Save your drawing.

Figure 16-16: The outer profile and the six circles can all be turned into regions. The circles could then be subtracted from the outer profile to create a surface with six holes.

Creating Boundaries

The BOUNDARY command creates either polylines or regions from an enclosed area. This command has the capability of analyzing an area and ignoring intersecting lines that give the REGION command so much trouble. However, no spaces between objects are allowed. (Chapter 12 explains how to use the BOUNDARY command to calculate the area of a closed space.) Use the BOUNDARY command whenever you need to create a closed complex area. To create a boundary, choose Draw ➪ Boundary to open the Boundary Creation dialog box, as shown in Figure 16-17. This dialog box is related to the Boundary Hatch and Fill dialog box, covered later in this chapter. Most of the items in the dialog box are not active unless you are creating a hatch.

Figure 16-17: The Boundary Creation dialog box

Follow these steps:

1. The Object Type drop-down list determines the type of object BOUNDARY creates. Choose either Region or Polyline.

2. Choose the boundary set, which is the area AutoCAD analyzes to create the boundary. Usually, you can accept the default of Current Viewport. However, if you have a very complex drawing, choose New to temporarily return to your drawing. Specify a window around the area you want for the boundary set. AutoCAD returns you to the dialog box.

3. To specify the enclosed area for the boundary, choose Pick Points. AutoCAD returns you to your drawing with the Select internal point: prompt.

4. Pick any point inside the closed area you want for your boundary. AutoCAD starts to think as follows:

   ```
   Selecting everything...Selecting everything visible...
   Analyzing the selected data...Analyzing internal islands...
   ```

5. AutoCAD then prompts you for another internal point. If you want to create other boundaries, continue to pick internal points. Press Enter to end point selection.

AutoCAD informs you how many regions or polylines it created and ends the command.

Note By default, island detection is on. BOUNDARY detects enclosed areas that are totally inside the boundary area and creates polylines or regions of those enclosed areas as well.

When BOUNDARY creates a region or polyline, the original objects are not deleted. You end up with a region or polyline on top of your original objects.

On the CD-ROM

The drawing used in the following Step-by-Step exercise on creating boundaries, ab16-e.dwg, is in the Drawings folder of the *AutoCAD 2004 Bible* CD-ROM.

Step-by-Step: Creating Boundaries

1. Open ab16-e.dwg from your CD-ROM.

2. Save the file as ab16-06.dwg in your AutoCAD Bible folder. This is a bushing, shown in Figure 16-18.

Figure 16-18: A bushing

3. Choose Draw ➪ Boundary. In the Boundary Creation dialog box, choose Region as the Object type.

4. Choose Pick Points.

5. At the Select internal point: prompt, choose ❶ in Figure 16-18.

6. Press Enter to end internal point selection. AutoCAD responds:

```
4 loops extracted.
4 Regions created.
BOUNDARY created 4 regions
```

7. To see the new region, start the MOVE command. At the Select objects: prompt, pick ❷. Move the region to the right—the exact distance is not important. You see both the new region and the original objects.

8. Save your drawing.

Creating Hatches with Solid, Gradient, or Patterned Fills

Hatches are patterns that fill in an area. Most types of drafting make use of hatching. In architectural drafting, hatched areas are used to indicate materials, such as insulation or grass. In mechanical drafting, hatching often indicates hidden areas or certain materials. AutoCAD provides a large number of hatch patterns. Hatches are created from repeating patterns of lines. You can also create solid fills in the same way you create hatch patterns.

New Feature AutoCAD 2004 introduces gradient hatch fills that fill any area with a one or two-color gradient. You can choose from a number of gradient styles and angles.

Cross-Reference Chapter 31 explains how to create your own hatch patterns.

Figure 16-19 shows a drawing with a simple hatch pattern. Here the cross section shows solid metal hatched to distinguish it from the holes.

Understanding hatch patterns

Hatch patterns have two qualities that are similar to dimensions:

✦ They are blocks. This means that all the lines that fill in an area are one object. Blocks are covered in Chapter 18.

✦ They are associative. If you edit the object that is hatched, the hatch automatically adjusts to fit the new shape of the object.

Figure 16-19: Hatch patterns help you distinguish between different materials or textures.

Thanks to Jerry Bottenfield of Clow Valve Company, Oskaloosa, Iowa, for this drawing.

You have several ways to specify exactly what area you want to hatch. In order to properly hatch an area, AutoCAD tries to find closed boundaries. Often, the key to successful hatching lies in how you construct the area you want to hatch. You can use the BOUNDARY and REGION commands covered in previous sections of this chapter to create complex closed areas that AutoCAD can easily find and hatch.

AutoCAD stores hatch pattern definitions in the `acad.pat` file. If you create your own hatch patterns, you can put them in another file with the file name extension `.pat`.

Tip Create a separate layer for hatch patterns. You may want to turn off or freeze your hatch layer to reduce visual clutter or assist in selecting objects. Hatches are also typically a different color than the model you are hatching.

Defining a hatch

To hatch an area, choose Hatch from the Draw toolbar. This starts the BHATCH command. AutoCAD opens the Boundary Hatch and Fill dialog box, shown in Figure 16-20.

Figure 16-20: The Boundary Hatch and Fill dialog box with the Hatch tab on top

Use this dialog box to define your hatch. From the Type drop-down box, choose one of the three options:

✦ **Predefined:** Enables you to select one of AutoCAD's hatch patterns.

✦ **User-defined:** Enables you to define your own hatch pattern by specifying the angle and spacing, using the current linetype.

✦ **Custom:** Enables you to choose a pattern you have created in your own `.pat` file.

Click the Pattern drop-down box to choose the hatch patterns from a list. Or click the box marked with an ellipsis to open the Hatch Pattern Palette and choose from the image tiles, as shown in Figure 16-21.

Figure 16-21: The Hatch Pattern Palette, shown with the Other Predefined tab on top

In the palette, click the tabs to see the different types of hatches. Click the image tile to choose a hatch pattern and click OK. The palette is simply another method of choosing the hatch pattern — you can also choose the pattern by using the Pattern drop-down list. The swatch shows you how your chosen hatch will look.

Cross-Reference You can also insert hatches from the tools palette. See Chapter 26 for a description of the tools palette.

The Custom pattern drop-down box is available only if you have chosen Custom as the pattern type. Here you choose the name of your custom hatch pattern.

Use the Angle text box to rotate the angle of the hatch pattern. You can choose from the drop-down list or type an angle. Watch out here — many of the patterns are already defined at an angle. The hatch pattern in Figure 16-22 uses a 0-degree angle because ANSI31 is defined as diagonal lines.

The Scale box determines the scale of the hatch pattern. You can choose from the drop-down list or type a scale. AutoCAD scales the hatch pattern proportionately to its definition. A scale of 1 (the default) creates the hatch as defined. A scale of 0.5 shrinks it by one-half. Figure 16-22 shows two hatch patterns using the ANSI31 pattern. The left one uses a scale of 1, and the right one uses a scale of 0.5.

Figure 16-22: You can scale the hatch pattern to your needs.

The Spacing box and the Double check box are available if you choose a user-defined hatch pattern. A user-defined hatch uses the current linetype and creates a hatch based on the spacing and angle you specify. Figure 16-23 shows a user-defined double hatch with an angle of 45 degrees and 0.1 unit spacing.

Figure 16-23: A user-defined hatch

To define a user-defined hatch pattern:

1. Choose Hatch from the Draw toolbar to open the Boundary Hatch and Fill dialog box.

2. In the Type drop-down box, choose User-defined.

3. In the Angle box, type an angle or choose one from the drop-down list. When creating a user-defined hatch, you need to specify the actual angle that you want to see.

4. In the Spacing box, enter the spacing between the lines. If you type **.5**, AutoCAD creates a hatch pattern with lines 0.5 units apart.

5. If you want to cross-hatch so that the parallel lines are crossed by an equal number of perpendicular lines, check Double.

The ISO pen width box is available only for ISO predefined hatch patterns. AutoCAD adjusts the scale of the pattern according to the pen width you specify. When you choose a pen width from the drop-down box, the scale shown in the Scale box automatically changes to be equal to the pen width. Note that you still have to separately set the width of your plotter pens when you plot your drawing.

In the next section I explain how to place the hatch.

 New Feature The Express Tools SUPERHATCH command creates a hatch pattern from an image, block, xref, or wipeout. Choose Express ➪ Draw ➪ Super Hatch. For information on installing Express Tools, see Appendix A on the CD-ROM.

Determining the hatch boundary

The hardest part of hatching is placing the hatch, not defining it. Hatching an entire object is the simplest way to place a hatch. But often the area you want to hatch is fairly complex, and AutoCAD needs to do some calculations to determine it.

The Boundary Hatch and Fill dialog box offers two ways to specify the hatch boundary—you can pick points inside an area and let AutoCAD try to find an enclosed boundary, or you can select objects. If you want to hatch an entire object:

1. Choose Select Objects. AutoCAD returns you temporarily to your drawing.

2. Select all the objects you want to hatch. You can use all the standard object selection options to select objects. Remove and Add are especially helpful.

3. Press Enter to end object selection and return to the dialog box.

If the area you want to hatch does not neatly fit into one or more objects, choose Pick Points. AutoCAD handles this task in the same way it handles the BOUNDARY command, also covered in this chapter. AutoCAD temporarily returns you to your drawing and displays the following:

```
Select internal point: Selecting everything...
Selecting everything visible...
Analyzing the selected data...
Select internal point:
```

AutoCAD is determining the boundary set, which is simply everything visible on the screen. At the `Select internal point:` prompt, pick a point that is inside the boundary that you want to hatch. You can continue to pick internal points to hatch adjoining areas. AutoCAD helpfully highlights the boundaries it finds. Press Enter to return to the dialog box.

> **Tip**
>
> While you are in your drawing, either before or after picking points or selecting objects, you can right-click to open a very useful shortcut menu.

Choose from the following options on the shortcut menu:

✦ **Enter:** Returns you to the dialog box.

✦ **Undo Last Select/Pick:** Undoes your most recent object selection or point pick.

✦ **Clear All:** Undoes all your picks/object selections.

✦ **Pick Internal Point:** Switches to picking of internal points.

✦ **Select Objects:** Switches to selection of objects.

✦ **Normal Island Detection:** Sets island detection to normal mode.

✦ **Outer Island Detection:** Sets island detection to outer mode.

✦ **Ignore Island Detection:** Sets island detection to ignore mode.

✦ **Preview:** Previews the hatch.

This shortcut menu enables you to manage the hatch boundary without returning to the dialog box. Previewing the hatch before applying it is always a good idea.

> **New Feature**
>
> After previewing a hatch, right-click or press Enter to accept the preview and place the hatch. Press Esc or left-click to return to the Boundary Hatch and Fill dialog box.

Click OK to create the hatch. AutoCAD creates the hatch and closes the dialog box.

The dialog box has several other options:

✦ Click Preview if you want to try it before you apply it.

✦ Click View Selection if you want to temporarily return to your drawing and check which objects you have selected.

✦ Choose Inherit Properties to use the hatch type, pattern, angle, scale, and/or spacing of an existing hatch. AutoCAD returns you to your drawing, and you pick a hatch pattern. You then return to the Boundary Hatch and Fill dialog box.

✦ Click Nonassociative if you want to create a hatch that is not associated with its object.

The Remove Islands option is discussed in the next section.

Islands

Islands are enclosed areas entirely inside a hatch boundary. Islands make hatching more difficult because sometimes you don't want to hatch the inside of the island. Figure 16-24 shows a top view of a 3-inch operating nut, which is a good example of enclosed areas with islands.

Note Text is counted as an island, enabling you to hatch areas that contain text without hatching over the words.

Figure 16-24: A model that includes islands can be more challenging to hatch.

Thanks to Jerry Bottenfield of Clow Valve
Company, Oskaloosa, Iowa, for this drawing.

Managing islands when you select objects to hatch

When you choose the hatching boundary by selecting objects, you must also select the islands. If you can select the entire area by window, you automatically include the internal islands. If you need to pick individual objects, you must also pick the islands individually. If you later erase an island, AutoCAD retains hatch associativity and regenerates the hatch so it covers the entire outer boundary.

The resulting hatch depends on the boundary style. To specify the boundary style, in the Boundary Hatch and Fill dialog box, click the Advanced tab, shown in Figure 16-25.

Figure 16-25: The Advanced tab is used to refine the hatching process.

Three boundary styles affect how islands are hatched:

✦ **Normal:** Hatches alternating areas so that the outer area is hatched, the next inner island is not hatched, the next inner island is hatched, and so on.

✦ **Outer:** Hatches only the outer area and does not hatch any inner islands.

✦ **Ignore:** Ignores islands and hatches everything from the outside in.

Figure 16-26 shows three copies of the nut hatched in the three styles. To hatch this model, I selected the entire model, except the spout at the bottom, with a window.

Normal Outer Ignore

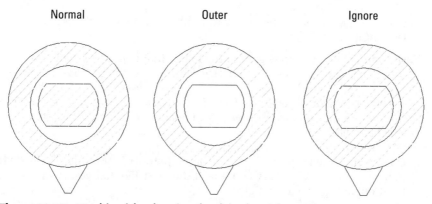

Figure 16-26: Hatching islands using the three boundary styles

Managing islands when you pick points to specify the hatch

When you pick points instead of selecting objects, you do not need to select the islands. AutoCAD detects islands by default. As soon as you pick points, the Remove Islands button becomes available, and you can select the islands to remove them from consideration. For example, if you remove all the islands shown in Figure 16-26, the result is the same as using the Ignore style — everything inside the outside boundary is hatched.

Other advanced options

On the Advanced tab you can also specify a smaller boundary set than the objects visible on-screen. Use this only when you are picking points and have such a complex drawing that AutoCAD takes a long time to analyze the visible objects.

When you pick points to determine the hatch boundary, AutoCAD uses the same mechanism as the BOUNDARY command to temporarily create a boundary for hatching. Check Retain Boundaries on the Advanced tab if you want to draw the boundary as an object and specify if you want it to be a region or a polyline. Otherwise, AutoCAD discards the boundary once it completes the hatch. For more information, see the discussion of the BOUNDARY command earlier in this chapter.

You can choose whether you want to include islands in the boundaries that AutoCAD creates by choosing the Island detection method. The Flood method includes islands as boundary objects. The Ray casting method excludes islands as boundary objects.

Dragging and dropping hatch patterns

You can open a .pat (hatch pattern) file from the DesignCenter, preview its hatch patterns, and drag any hatch pattern into any closed object in your current drawing.

Here's how to drag a hatch pattern from the DesignCenter:

1. Click DesignCenter on the Standard toolbar (or press Ctrl+2) to open the DesignCenter.

2. Use the Tree View to navigate to the folder that contains your acad.pat or other .pat file. If necessary, click the Desktop button and navigate from there.

Note To find the location of your .pat files, choose Tools ⇨ Options and click the File tab. Double-click the Support File Search Path option. One of the paths listed contains your hatch files.

3. Double-click the folder and select a hatch pattern (.pat) file. The main hatch pattern file is acad.pat. (Of course, if the .pat file that you want is in another location, navigate accordingly.)

4. On the right pane of the DesignCenter, drag the hatch pattern that you want onto a closed object in your drawing. If you need more options, right-click the pattern and choose BHATCH to open the Boundary Hatch and Fill dialog box and specify the hatch parameters in the usual way.

Creating gradient fills

Gradient fills are a new feature for AutoCAD 2004. Gradients are fills that gradually change from dark to light or from one color to another. Use gradients to create presentation-quality illustrations without rendering. You can use gradients as a substitute for shading because it offers more flexible options. To create a gradient:

1. Choose Hatch from the Draw toolbar to open the Boundary Hatch and Fill dialog box.

2. Click the Gradient tab, shown in Figure 16-27.

Figure 16-27: Use the Gradient tab of the Boundary Hatch and Fill dialog box to create gradient fills of closed objects.

3. Choose One Color or Two Color.

 • If you choose One Color, click the ellipsis button to the right of the color swatch to open the Select Color dialog box, where you can choose the color you want. (For instructions on using this dialog box, see Chapter 11.) Then use the Shade/Tint slider to choose if you want the gradient to range lighter or darker. You see the result in the gradient swatches below the slider.

 • If you choose Two Colors, you see two color swatches. Click each ellipsis button and choose a color.

4. Choose one of the nine gradient styles.

5. If you want the gradient to be symmetrical, check the Centered check box. To create a gradient that is not symmetrical, uncheck the Centered check box. When you uncheck the Centered check box, the gradient focus moves up and to the left. (You can change this location by changing the angle, as explained in the next step.)

6. From the Angle drop-down list, choose an angle. If your gradient is centered, the gradient rotates around its center and remains symmetrical. If your gradient is not centered, the gradient rotates around the edges. Watch the gradient style tiles to see the results. You can type an angle that is not on the list.

7. Choose Pick Points to pick a location inside a closed area or choose Select Objects to select closed objects, as explained in the section, "Determining the hatch boundary." (The other options are the same as for Hatches.) In your drawing, specify the area you want to hatch and end selection to return to the dialog box.

8. To preview the gradient, click Preview. To return to the dialog box, press Esc.

9. Click OK to finalize the hatch.

See Figure 16-28 for an example of some gradient fills. You could turn off the boundary layer for a more realistic look.

Note When you create a gradient, it appears in front of the line of the object it fills. In some cases, the object's line disappears and all you see is the gradient. To move the object to the front and display its line, select the gradient and choose Tools ➪ Display Order ➪ Send to Back or Send Under Object.

Figure 16-28: These gradients give the illusion of light shining from the left. See Figure 8-29, which shows the original isometric drawing without the gradients.
Thanks to James Wedding for permission to use the drawing on the right from Jones & Boyd, Inc.

Editing hatches

To edit a hatch pattern including a solid or gradient, double-click it. AutoCAD opens the Hatch Edit dialog box, shown in Figure 16-29. You can also choose Modify ➪ Object ➪ Hatch and then select a hatch object.

Figure 16-29: The Hatch Edit dialog box

As you can see, this dialog box is exactly the same as the Boundary Hatch and Fill dialog box, except that not all of the options are available. You can use this dialog box to change any of the hatch properties. You can change the boundary style on the Advanced tab. You can also preview the hatch. After you make your changes, click Apply to return to your drawing.

Because hatches are associative (unless you explode them or chose to create them as nonassociative), when you edit their boundaries, they adjust to fit the new boundary. However, if the new boundary is no longer closed, the hatch may lose its associativity. AutoCAD warns you with the `Hatch boundary associativity removed` message.

To move or stretch a hatched boundary, you can select the hatch along with the boundary. However, perhaps you want to change the boundary's layer. You may find it difficult to select the boundary without the hatch, especially if the hatch is tightly spaced. If you are at a `Select objects:` prompt, use a window to select the boundary and the hatch together, and then use the Remove selection option to pick the hatch. Another option is to turn off the hatch's layer. Finally, you can zoom in enough so that you can pick the boundary without the hatch lines.

New Feature You can also edit a gradient in the Properties palette. Choose Properties on the Standard toolbar and use the items in the Pattern section. You can change the colors, angle, type, and whether or not it is centered.

Note When you create hatches — solid fill or lines — AutoCAD displays them if FILL is on, which it is by default. To turn FILL off, type **fill** ↵ and **off** ↵. You must regenerate the drawing to see the effect.

You may find it difficult to select solid fill hatches. In some locations, you can pick the solid hatch, while at other points you get the Other corner: prompt, meaning that AutoCAD didn't find anything. Try a crossing window. If necessary, try a crossing window at the edge of the hatch. This always selects the solid hatch but also selects the boundary. Hatches have a grip at their center. If you can find the grip and include it in the window, you can easily select the solid hatch.

On the CD-ROM The drawing used in the following Step-by-Step exercise on creating and editing hatches, ab16-f.dwg, is in the Drawings folder of the *AutoCAD 2004 Bible* CD-ROM.

Step-by-Step: Creating and Editing Hatches

1. Open ab16-f.dwg from your CD-ROM.

2. Save the file as ab16-07.dwg in your AutoCAD Bible folder.

3. ⊞ Choose Hatch from the Draw toolbar. On the Hatch tab of the Boundary Hatch and Fill dialog box, choose ANSI35 from the Pattern drop-down list. From the Scale drop-down list, choose 0.5. Click Select Objects.

4. AutoCAD returns you to your drawing. Pick the two large circles in Figure 16-30. Right-click and choose Preview. Press Esc to return to the dialog box. Click OK to create the hatch and end the BHATCH command.

Figure 16-30: The result after editing the two hatches

5. Again choose Hatch from the Draw toolbar. From the Type drop-down list, choose User-defined. Set the angle to 135 and the spacing to 0.05.

6. Choose Pick Points. In your drawing, pick points ❶, ❷, ❸, and ❹ in Figure 16-30. Right-click and choose Preview. Right-click again to create the hatch and end the BHATCH command.

7. Click the circumference of the left large circle. (If necessary, zoom in to avoid selecting the hatching.) Pick the top grip to make it hot. At the `Specify stretch point or [Base Point/Copy/Undo/eXit]:` prompt, type **.35** ↵. Press Esc to remove the grips.

8. Double-click one of the hatches at the top of the model. Notice that AutoCAD selects all of them because they were created with one command. In the Hatch Edit dialog box that opens, change the angle to 90 and the spacing to 0.04. Click OK. Your drawing should look like Figure 16-30.

9. Save your drawing.

Using the SOLID command

AutoCAD also has a command, SOLID, that creates solidly filled areas. (It is not at all related to 3D solids.) In general, BHATCH is much more flexible. However, although the SOLID command is a 2D command, it is sometimes used in 3D drawing. When you create a 2D solid and give it thickness, it creates surfaces with tops and bottoms. See Chapter 24 for a description of how to use the SOLID command to create 3D models.

SOLID is used to create straight-edged shapes. If FILL is on, AutoCAD fills in the shape with a solid fill (that's why it's called SOLID).

To draw a solid, type **solid** ↵. AutoCAD prompts you for first, second, third, and fourth points. You must specify these points in zigzag order, not around the perimeter of the shape. After the fourth point, AutoCAD continues to prompt you for third and fourth points, which you can use to create new adjacent solids. Press Enter to end the command.

Creating and Editing Multilines

Multilines are sets of parallel lines that you draw with one command. You can specify how far apart they are, and each line can have its own color and linetype. Multilines are used for drawing architectural plans where you need to draw an inner and outer wall. To draw a multiline, you first define, save, and load a multiline style. Then you can use the multiline style to draw multilines. There is a separate command for editing multilines that enables you to break multiline intersections, as you would for the doors and windows in a floor plan. Figure 16-31 shows a floor plan for an apartment drawn using multilines.

Figure 16-31: A floor plan of an apartment drawn by using multilines
Thanks to Bill Wynn of New Windsor, Maryland, for this drawing.

Creating a multiline style

The first step in drawing multilines is to design the multiline style. To create a multiline style, choose Format ➪ Multiline Style to open the Multiline Styles dialog box, as shown in Figure 16-32.

Figure 16-32: The Multiline Styles dialog box

Like text styles and dimension styles, multiline styles group a set of properties under one name. AutoCAD provides a default multiline style called Standard that defines two lines 1 unit apart. Multiline styles have two parts: element properties and multiline

properties. The element properties define each individual line element. The multiline properties define properties that apply to the multiline as a whole.

Defining element properties

To start defining the multiline style, type a new name in the Name text box and click Add. Then choose Element Properties to open the Element Properties dialog box, shown in Figure 16-33.

The Elements box lists the current elements of the multiline. Elements are simply the lines that make up the multiline. The offset defines the distance of the line from the start point when you start to draw. An offset of zero places the line on the start point. As you can see, the Standard multiline style has two elements, each 0.5 units from the start point. Figure 16-34 shows the Standard multiline style as it appears in relation to the start point you pick.

Figure 16-33: The Element Properties dialog box

Figure 16-34: The Standard multiline style places two lines on either side of the start point.

Note You can also change the relationship of the start point and the element lines by using the Justification option when you draw the multiline, as explained later, in the "Drawing multilines" section.

To define the element lines of a multiline style, follow these steps:

1. In the Elements box, highlight the first element. Even if you typed a new name for the multiline style, the elements listed are the same as the current multiline style.

Tip

When creating a new multiline style, first set as current the multiline style that is the most similar to the one you want to create.

2. In the Offset box, type the offset you want. The offset should be zero if you want the line to appear on your pick points, a positive number (in units) if you want the line to appear above your pick points, and a negative number (in units) if you want the line to appear below your pick points. (This assumes the default of zero justification, explained later in this chapter.)

Tip

When defining the multiline style elements, think of the multiline as being drawn horizontally to the right to help you visualize what *above* and *below* mean.

3. Choose Color to choose a color for the line element.

4. Choose Linetype to choose a linetype for the line element.

5. Choose Add to add a new element or Delete to delete a listed element.

6. To define the next element, select the second element in the Elements box and repeat Steps 2–4. Continue to define elements until you are done.

7. Click OK to return to the Multiline Styles dialog box.

Note

A multiline style can have up to 16 elements. You can create some very useful and complex multiline styles by using varying linetypes. All 16 elements must be on the same layer.

Defining multiline properties

Choose Multiline Properties in the Multiline Styles dialog box to open the Multiline Properties dialog box, as shown in Figure 16-35.

Use this box to set the overall properties of the multiline. Figure 16-36 shows the effects of all the possible choices in this box.

You can also turn Fill on or off and choose a color to add a solid fill to the multiline. After you make your choices, click OK to return to the Multiline Styles dialog box.

Saving a new multiline style

Before you can use the multiline style, you must save it. AutoCAD saves multiline styles in a file with the file name extension .mln. After you click Save, AutoCAD opens the Save Multiline Style dialog box.

Figure 16-35: The Multiline Properties dialog box

Figure 16-36: The results of choosing the various options in the Multiline Properties dialog box

In general, you can save your multiline styles in the default file, which is acad.mln. Click Save to return to the Multiline Styles dialog box.

Loading a multiline style

Like linetypes, multiline styles must be loaded before you can use them. Choose Load to open the Load Multiline Styles dialog box, shown in Figure 16-37. Choose the style you created from the list and click OK.

Figure 16-37: The Load Multiline
Styles dialog box

AutoCAD returns you to the Multiline Styles dialog box. You are now ready to use the multiline style. Click OK to return to your drawing.

You can also use the Multiline Styles dialog box to rename multiline styles and make another multiline style current.

On the CD-ROM The drawing used in the following Step-by-Step exercise on creating a multiline style, `ab16-g.dwg`, is in the `Drawings` folder of the *AutoCAD 2004 Bible* CD-ROM.

Step-by-Step: Creating a Multiline Style

1. Open `ab16-g.dwg` from your CD-ROM.

2. Save the file as `ab16-08.dwg` in your `AutoCAD Bible` folder. This is a site plan, shown in Figure 16-38.

Figure 16-38: The parallel lines at the bottom of the site plan can be drawn by using a multiline.

3. Choose Format ⇨ Multiline Style to open the Multiline Styles dialog box. In the Name text box, type **siteplan**. Choose Add.

4. Choose Element Properties. With the top element highlighted, change the offset to 0, the color to black (it lists as white), and the linetype to dashdot.

5. Highlight the second element. Change the offset to –132 (11' × 12"), the color to magenta, and the linetype to continuous.

6. Click Add. Change the offset to –180 (15' × 12"), the color to red, and the linetype to center.

7. Click Add. Change the offset to –228 (19' × 12"), the color to magenta, and the linetype to continuous.

8. Click Add. Change the offset to –360 (30' × 12"), the color to black, and the linetype to dashdot.

9. Click Add. Change the offset to –480 (40' × 12"), the color to red, and the linetype to center.

Caution If you are using someone else's computer, check with the owner before saving the linestyle to `acad.mln`. You can't do any damage, but the owner may not want to have your multiline style there. You can change the name in the File Name text box to something else, such as `my_mls.mln`.

10. Click OK. In the Multiline Styles dialog box, click Save.

11. In the Save Multiline Style dialog box, you should see `acad.mln` in the File Name text box. You can also type a new `.mln` file name. Choose Save.

12. Choose Load in the Multiline Styles dialog box. In the Load Multiline Styles dialog box, highlight the SITEPLAN multiline style, and choose OK twice to return to your drawing.

13. Save your drawing. If you are continuing on to the next exercise, keep the drawing open.

Drawing multilines

Defining a multiline style is the hard part. As soon as the style is defined, saved, loaded, and made current, you can draw with it. You may find you need some practice to get the hang of it because you are drawing more than one line at once. To draw a multiline, choose Draw ➪ Multiline to start the MLINE command. AutoCAD responds with the `Specify start point or [Justification/Scale/STyle]:` prompt. AutoCAD also displays the current justification, scale, and style. The default is to pick a point. From there you get the `Specify next point:` prompt. After the first segment, you get the `Specify next point or [Undo]:` prompt, and after the second segment, the `Specify next point or [Close/Undo]:` prompt. Here is how to use the options:

✦ **Justification:** You can choose Zero, Top, or Bottom.

• Zero places the element that has a zero offset in the multiline definition at the pick point. You do not need to have a line at zero offset, as is the

case with the Standard multiline style. The top example in Figure 16-39 shows the Standard multiline style with zero justification.

- Top places the line with the highest positive offset at the pick point. The middle example in Figure 16-39 shows the Standard multiline style with top justification.

- Bottom places the line with the highest negative offset at the pick point. The bottom example in Figure 16-39 shows the Standard multiline style with bottom justification.

✦ **Scale:** Multiplies the offset values in the multiline definition by the scale. The Standard multiline style places two lines 1 unit apart. A scale of 6 would place them 6 units apart.

✦ **Style:** Enables you to specify the current multiline style. Type **?** ↵ to get a list of the available multiline styles.

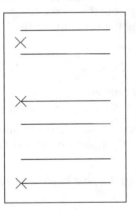

Figure 16-39: Drawing a multiline using the Standard multiline style in zero, top, and bottom justification

As you draw a multiline, whenever you create a corner by changing direction, AutoCAD creates a clean corner with no intersecting lines.

Step-by-Step: Drawing Multilines

1. Continue from the previous exercise. (If you didn't do the previous exercise, you should do it to create the multiline style.) Set a running object snap for intersection.

2. Choose Multiline from the Draw toolbar. AutoCAD displays the following message:

 `Justification = Top, Scale = 1.00, Style = SITEPLAN`

3. At the `Specify start point or [Justification/Scale/STyle]:` prompt, choose the From object snap. At the `Base point:` prompt, choose

❶ in Figure 16-40. (If necessary, press Tab until you get the Intersection object snap.) At the `<Offset>`: prompt, type **@0,–10'** ↵.

4. At the `Specify next point`: prompt, move the cursor to the right and type **255'** ↵. If you want, you can experiment by drawing other line segments. Press Enter to end the command. The drawing should look like Figure 16-40.

5. Save your drawing.

Figure 16-40: The completed multiline

Editing multilines

The entire multiline — no matter how many segments it contains — is one object. Many editing commands simply do not work with multilines. Table 16-1 shows the editing commands and whether they work with multilines.

Table 16-1
Using Editing Commands with Multilines

Command	Usable with Multilines	Command	Usable with Multilines
ARRAY	yes	FILLET	no
BREAK	no	LENGTHEN	no
CHAMFER	no	MIRROR	yes
COPY	yes	MOVE	yes
ERASE	yes	ROTATE	yes
EXPLODE	yes	SCALE	yes
EXTEND	no	STRETCH	yes

You can use grips to stretch, move, copy, mirror, and rotate multilines.

AutoCAD provides a special multiline editing command, MLEDIT. To start MLEDIT, double-click the multiline (or choose Modify ➪ Object ➪ Multiline) to open the Multiline Edit Tools dialog box, shown in Figure 16-41.

Figure 16-41: The Multiline Edit Tools dialog box

This dialog box enables you to edit multiline intersections and corners. You can also add or delete a vertex. Click one of the images, and its name appears at the bottom of the dialog box.

The first column manages crossing intersections. To edit a crossing intersection, choose one of the tiles in the first column and click OK. AutoCAD prompts you to pick a first multiline and then a second multiline. MLEDIT always cuts the first multiline you pick. The second one may be cut if called for by the edit type.

Note Although AutoCAD prompts you to pick two multilines, they can actually be two parts of the same multiline, as shown in Figure 16-42. Figure 16-42 shows the results of using the three crossing intersection edits.

Figure 16-42: Creating a closed cross, an open cross, and a merged cross

The second column manages tee-shaped intersections. To edit a crossing intersection, choose one of the tiles in the second column and click OK. AutoCAD prompts you to pick a first multiline and then a second multiline. MLEDIT always cuts the first multiline you pick. The second one may be cut if called for by the edit type and depending on the shape of the multiline. Figure 16-43 shows the results of using the three tee intersection edits.

Figure 16-43: Creating a closed tee, an open tee, and a merged tee

The third column manages corners and vertices. The top tile creates a corner. Figure 16-44 shows the result of using the corner edit.

Figure 16-44: Creating a corner

The second tile adds a vertex, and the third deletes a vertex. Choose the edit you want and click OK. AutoCAD prompts you to select a multiline. Be careful — the point you pick is the location at which AutoCAD adds or deletes the vertex. To see the current vertices, pick the multiline with no command active to see the grips. Figure 16-45 shows the result of adding and deleting a vertex. The grips show the vertices clearly.

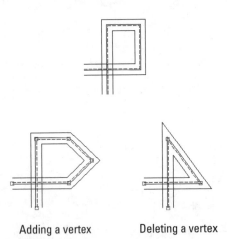

Adding a vertex Deleting a vertex

Figure 16-45: The results of adding and deleting a vertex. The multiline with the added vertex was then stretched by using grips.

The last column of the dialog box makes cuts through multilines and welds them back together again. Here's how to use these options:

✦ Use the top tile to make a cut through one element of a multiline.

✦ Use the middle tile to cut through all the elements of a multiline.

Of In both cases, AutoCAD prompts you to select a multiline and then a second point. Be careful — the point you use to select the multiline is the first point of the cut. For a single cut, the pick point of the multiline also determines which element AutoCAD cuts.

✦ Use the bottom tile to remove the cuts. AutoCAD calls this *welding*.

For all of these editing tools, AutoCAD continues to prompt you for further edits. Press Enter to end selection.

You can also move vertices using grips with the Stretch option.

On the CD-ROM The drawing used in the following Step-by-Step exercise on editing a multiline, ab16-h.dwg, is in the Drawings folder of the *AutoCAD 2004 Bible* CD-ROM.

Step-by-Step: Editing a Multiline

1. Open `ab16-h.dwg` from your CD-ROM.

2. Save the file as `ab16-09.dwg` in your `AutoCAD Bible` folder. This is a simple layout of two rooms using the Standard multiline style, as shown in Figure 16-46.

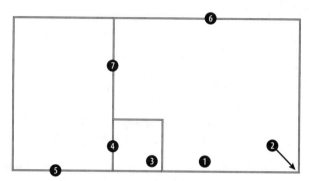

Figure 16-46: A layout of two rooms

3. Choose Modify ⇨ Object ⇨ Multiline. In the Multiline Edit Tools dialog box, choose Delete Vertex and click OK.

4. At the `Select mline:` prompt, choose the multiline at ❶ in Figure 16-46. Press Enter to end multiline selection.

5. Pick the multiline again and click the grip at ❷. At the `Specify stretch point or [Base point/Copy/Undo/eXit]:` prompt, click ORTHO in the status bar and move the cursor in the 90-degree direction and type **4'** ↵.

6. Pick the multiline at ❸ and click the grip at ❸ in Figure 16-46. At the Specify `stretch point or [Base point/Copy/Undo/eXit]:` prompt, move the cursor in the 180-degree direction and type **4'** ↵. Press Esc to see the corner.

7. Choose Modify ⇨ Object ⇨ Multiline. In the Multiline Edit Tools dialog box, choose Corner Joint and click OK. At the prompts, pick the multiline at ❹ and ❺ in Figure 16-46. Press Enter to end multiline selection.

8. Choose Modify ⇨ Object ⇨ Multiline. In the Multiline Edit Tools dialog box, choose Cut All and click OK. At the `Select mline:` prompt, pick the multiline at ❻. (The exact point doesn't matter.) At the `Select second point:` prompt, type **@3',0** ↵. At the `Select mline or [Undo]:` prompt, pick the multiline near ❼ in Figure 16-46. At the `Select second point:` prompt, type **@0,–3'** ↵. Press Enter to end multiline selection.

9. Save your drawing. It should look like Figure 16-47.

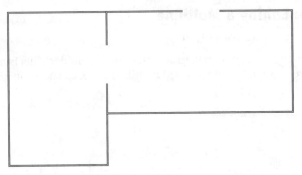

Figure 16-47: The edited multilines

AutoCAD also has an old command, TRACE, that draws lines with width. In general, you can use polylines or multilines instead to create the same effect.

Note Multiline styles are stored with the drawing, so that they can be updated and viewed, even if the multiline style file containing the multiline definition is not available.

Using the SKETCH Command

The SKETCH command enables you to draw freehand in AutoCAD. Freehand drawing is useful for contour lines in architectural or civil engineering drawings, for illustrative effects, and for when you are feeling artistic. Although you may get best results if you have a digitizer and a stylus pen, you can sketch with a mouse or puck as well. Figure 16-48 shows some contour lines created with SKETCH.

Figure 16-48: Contour lines drawn with SKETCH

Sketch can create lines or polylines. Polylines are probably easier to work with if you need to edit the sketch later—you can use the PEDIT command. To specify whether SKETCH creates lines or polylines, set the SKPOLY system variable. A value of zero creates lines, and a value of one creates polylines.

Start the SKETCH command by typing **sketch** ↵. AutoCAD places you in a special sketch mode and displays a special menu on the command line:

```
Record increment <0.1000>: Press Enter or type a new increment.
Sketch.  Pen eXit Quit Record Erase Connect
```

Type the record increment, which is the length of the line or polyline segment you want to create. If the increment is too big, small movements do not create a segment at all and the sketch line appears jagged instead of smooth. However, you need to take into account the scale of your drawing and your zoom factor. You should also turn off ORTHO and SNAP if they are on.

The pick button is equivalent to typing **p** and toggles the pen up and down. Follow these steps to start sketching:

1. Place the cursor where you want to start drawing.
2. Press the pick button. AutoCAD responds with the `<Pen down>` message. You can now draw.
3. Without holding down the pick button, move the mouse or stylus to create the shape you want. SKETCH creates a temporary green line.
4. After you finish, click the pick button again to see the `<Pen up>` message.
5. Move the mouse to the starting point of your next line or polyline. Continue in this manner until you finish sketching.
6. Type **r** to record the sketch. AutoCAD tells you what you created. The sketch changes to the color of the current layer and becomes permanent as shown in this example:

   ```
   4 polylines with 238 edges recorded.
   ```
7. Type **x** to exit Sketch mode.

Here are the other options:

✦ **Quit:** Quits Sketch mode without saving your sketch. The temporary line disappears.

✦ **Erase:** Erases temporary lines.

✦ **Connect:** Enables you to continue drawing from the end of the last sketch. Use this when the pen is up. Type **c** and move to the endpoint of the last temporary sketch.

✦ **. (Period):** Enables you to draw straight line segments from the endpoint of the last sketch. While the pen is up, type a period to add a line segment from the last endpoint to your current cursor position.

On the CD-ROM

The drawing used in the following Step-by-Step exercise on sketching, `ab16-i.dwg`, is in the `Drawings` folder of the *AutoCAD 2004 Bible* CD-ROM.

Step-by-Step: Sketching

1. Open `ab16-i.dwg` from your CD-ROM.

2. Save the file as `ab16-10.dwg` in your `AutoCAD Bible` folder. It shows the front elevation of a house. You will add the sketched path and contours, as shown in Figure 16-49.

3. Type **skpoly** ↵. Set SKPOLY to 1 and press Enter.

4. Type **sketch** ↵. At the `Record increment <0'-0">:` prompt, type **1** ↵ to set the record increment to 1".

5. At the `Sketch. Pen eXit Quit Record Erase Connect.` prompt, move the cursor to ➊ in Figure 16-49. Click the pick button to put the pen down and draw the first line of the path. Click the pick button to put the pen up.

6. Use the same technique to draw the other lines in Figure 16-49. If you make a mistake, type **q** ↵ to quit and then start again.

7. After you are done, type **r** to record the lines.

8. Type **x** to end the SKETCH command.

9. Save your drawing.

Figure 16-49: A sketched path and contours

Digitizing Drawings with AutoCAD's TABLET Command

In Chapter 3, I explained how you can use a digitizer to execute AutoCAD commands. One important use for a digitizer is to copy paper drawings into AutoCAD. Many companies have used this technique to copy old drawings that were drafted by hand so that they could be edited using AutoCAD. Digitizing can also be used to copy artwork and logos into a drawing.

To digitize a paper drawing, you use a special digitizing mode that turns the entire digitizer into a drawing tablet. To start the TABLET command, choose Tools ⇨ Tablet and choose one of the options.

If you have been using the digitizer to execute commands, you need to reconfigure it to eliminate the command areas and enlarge the drawing area. Use the Configure option of the TABLET command and reconfigure the digitizer for 0 tablet menus. Respecify the screen pointing area so that the fixed screen pointing area covers the entire digitizing area.

Attach the paper drawing securely to the digitizer so that it won't move as you work.

To set up the digitizing mode, start the TABLET command and choose the Calibrate option. AutoCAD prompts you to pick two points on the paper drawing and specify which coordinates they represent. To do this you need to mark two points on the paper drawing—take out a ruler and measure their distance. If the drawing has a title block, two corners of the title block are distinctive points to mark and measure. If the drawing is drawn to a scale—and it probably is—the coordinates you type should be the distance in real life, not the measurement. In other words, if the two horizontal points are 1 inch apart and 1 inch represents 48 inches (a scale of 1= 48), you could enter 0,0 for the first point and 48,0 for the second point. However, it is usually useful to choose points over a wider area of your drawing. You can calibrate more than two points if you want.

Note If your drawing is distorted or uses a perspective view that you want to straighten out, you can calibrate additional points and choose either Affine or Projective calibration to account for the distortion. Affine calibration requires at least three points and scales the X and Y axes separately. Projective calibration requires at least four points and stretches the coordinates to adjust for the perspective view. You can provide up to 31 calibration points.

After you finish specifying calibration points and coordinates, press Enter. Now your entire tablet can be used only for picking points. You can press F12 to use a menu or toolbar and press F12 to return to picking points, or type commands on the command line.

Note You can turn Tablet mode on and off by starting the TABLET command and choosing the On and Off options. Tablet calibration settings are lost when you close the drawing session.

Choose the command you need and pick points along the paper drawing. After you are done, turn off Tablet mode and do any editing and cleanup necessary.

In this exercise, you practice digitizing drawings. If you have a digitizer, you can try this exercise. Otherwise, skip it.

Step-by-Step: Digitizing Drawings

1. Start a new drawing using acad.dwt as your template.

2. Save the file as ab16-11.dwg in your AutoCAD Bible folder. This is a sheet metal template as shown in Figure 16-50.

3. Make a photocopy of Figure 16-50 and tape it to the active area of your digitizer.

4. Choose Tools ➪ Tablet ➪ Calibrate. Follow the prompts:

```
Digitize point #1: Pick ❶ in Figure 16-50.
Enter coordinates for point #1: 0,0 ↵
Digitize point #2: Pick ❷ in Figure 16-50.
Enter coordinates for point #2: 7,5 ↵
Digitize point #3 (or RETURN to end): ↵
```

5. Type **tablet** ↵ and **on** ↵.

6. Type **line** ↵.

7. In Figure16-50, pick ❸ with the digitizer, then ❹, and then each line endpoint in turn counterclockwise around the figure.

8. After you reach ❺, do not digitize point ❶ again. Instead, type **c** ↵ to close the figure exactly.

9. Type **tablet** ↵. Type **off** ↵ to return the digitizer to screen pointing mode.

10. Save your drawing.

Figure 16-50: An unfolded sheet metal template

Summary

Several types of complex objects add greatly to AutoCAD's capabilities. In this chapter, you read about:

✦ Using polylines to combine lines, segments, and arcs of any width into one object

✦ Utilizing splines to mathematically calculate curves fit to points that you specify

✦ Regions, which are two-dimensional surfaces

✦ Creating regions or polylines from complex areas by using the BOUNDARY command

✦ Filling in an area with lines, a solid fill, or a gradient with hatches

✦ Drawing complex parallel lines at one time with multilines

✦ Drawing freehand by using the SKETCH command, creating either lines or polylines

✦ Using a digitizer in Tablet mode, when you need to copy a paper drawing into AutoCAD

In the next chapter, I explain how to lay out and plot a drawing.

✦　　✦　　✦

Plotting and Printing Your Drawing

Most drawing jobs are not complete until you see the final result on paper. Traditionally, drawings are plotted on a plotter. However, you can also print a drawing on a regular computer printer. Many printers and plotters can handle a wide range of drawing sizes and paper types. In this chapter, I explain the process of preparing a drawing for plotting, including laying it out in paper space. Finally, I cover the actual process of creating a plot.

Since Release 2000, AutoCAD has used a new term, *layout*, for paper space. You can have more than one layout for a drawing—also called *multiple paper spaces*. You access a layout by clicking one of the layout tabs at the bottom of the drawing area.

Preparing a Drawing for Plotting or Printing

When you complete your drawing, you often have some details to finish. If you did not start with a title block, you may need to insert one. Even if you have a title block, you may need to complete some of its annotation—such as the date you completed the drawing. If the drawing has layers you do not want to appear on paper, you should set their layer state to frozen, off, or not plottable.

Many architectural and mechanical drawings show several views of the model. Now is the time to check that the views are pleasingly laid out with enough space between them for dimensions and annotation.

Doing a draft plot

You may want to do a draft plot, either to check the drawing itself or to be sure it will print out properly. Although you can preview the plot, sometimes the results are not what you want, and it pays to test the plot on inexpensive paper before plotting on expensive vellum. Draft plots for checking purposes can often be done on a printer. Some companies have ink-jet printers or plotters that accept 17×22-inch paper and are used exclusively for check plots. Even if the final plot will be all in black, color printers are a good choice for check plots because you can easily check the layer scheme.

Plotting a drawing from model space

Model space refers to the mode you work in when you draw and edit your model. Throughout this book, you have been working in model space. The Model tab at the bottom of the drawing area visually confirms that you are in model space. Once you have prepared your drawing for plotting, as just discussed, you can plot your drawing. See the discussion later in this chapter on plotting.

Creating a Layout in Paper Space

If you are using several views of your model, you should consider creating a paper space layout. Although paper space was designed for the needs of 3D drawings, it is often used for 2D layout as well. For example, if you want to show views of your model at different scales, paper space is indispensable. Paper space is a tool specifically for laying out several views of a drawing. It is analogous to creating a sheet of paper at the size you will plot on and placing views on the paper. You place the views by means of floating viewports.

 Cross-Reference AutoCAD also has a tiled viewports feature, which is discussed in Chapter 8.

A layout provides a visual environment that lets you know what your plot will look like. By creating more than one layout for a drawing, you can create more than one plot for a single drawing. For example, you can create layouts at different scales for different sheet sizes.

Entering paper space

You draw in model space. Paper space is used to lay out a drawing. When you are in paper space, you can only view your drawing through floating viewports.

To enter a paper space layout, simply click a layout tab. By default, AutoCAD displays the Page Setup dialog box, discussed later in this chapter. If you click OK or cancel the dialog box, you see that AutoCAD has automatically created one floating

viewport through which you can view your model. An example is shown in Figure 17-1. The paper space icon confirms that you are looking at a paper space layout.

Printable area of paper Floating viewpoint

Paper space icon Paper size of currently configured plotter or printer

Figure 17-1: When you click a layout tab, AutoCAD automatically creates a layout with one floating viewport through which you can see your entire drawing.

To switch back to model space, click the Model tab.

Using the Layout Wizard

The Layout Wizard automates the process of laying out a drawing in paper space. While you may eventually want to lay out your drawings on your own, the Layout Wizard is a great way to get started using paper space.

To use the Layout Wizard, follow these steps:

1. Choose Tools ➪ Wizards ➪ Create Layout. You see the wizard screen shown in Figure 17-2, where you name the layout. This name will appears on the layout tab at the bottom of the drawing area.

2. Type a name for the layout and click Next.

3. The second screen asks you to choose a configured plotter. This list also includes printers. For more information on configuring a plotter or printer, see Appendix A on the CD-ROM. Click Next after you're done.

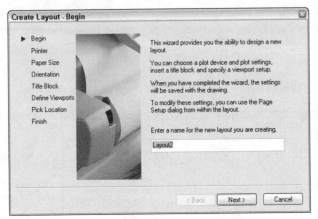

Figure 17-2: The first screen of the Layout Wizard

4. On the third screen, shown in Figure 17-3, specify a paper size and drawing units and then click Next.

5. On the next screen, specify if you want the drawing to plot in portrait or land-scape orientation. The wizard rotates a letter A on a sheet of paper so that you can see which way text, and therefore the rest of your drawing, will plot. Then click Next.

6. On the Title Block screen, shown in Figure 17-4, choose a title block if you want to add one. You can add it as a block (see Chapter 18) or as an external reference (or xref — see Chapter 19).

Tip To add your own title block, create it as a drawing and save it in the \Templates folder. (To find the location of this folder, choose Tools ➪ Options and click the Files tab. Double-click Drawing Template Settings and then Drawing Template File Location.) Notice that most of the templates in that folder have corresponding drawings that are used in the Layout Wizard. If you have a template that you use for a title block, open a new drawing using that template and save it as a drawing in the \Templates folder, using the same name as the template. (It has a .dwg file name extension, however.)

7. On the Define Viewports screen, shown in Figure 17-5, you choose from four viewport configuration options:

 • Choose None if you want to create your own floating viewports.

 • Choose Single to create one viewport.

 • Choose Std. 3D Engineering Views to create a 2×2 array of top, front, side, and isometric views.

 • Choose Array to specify how many views you want, in rows and columns.

 You also set the viewport scale. Then click Next.

Figure 17-3: The Paper Size screen of the Layout Wizard

Figure 17-4: The Title Block screen of the Layout Wizard

Cross-Reference

For more information on scales, see Chapter 5. Also see the discussion of viewport scales later in this chapter.

8. On the Pick Location screen, the wizard prompts you to pick two corners to define the size of the viewport configuration you chose. If you chose more than one viewport, these two corners define the extents of all the viewports combined, not the extents of the individual viewports.

9. Click Finish to close the wizard and return to your drawing.

Figure 17-6 shows the result of completing the wizard with a 2×2 array of viewports. You would still need to scale and pan the model to get the views you want in each viewport.

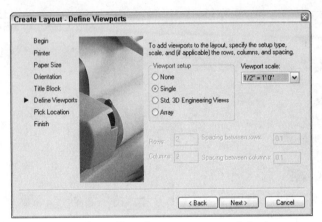

Figure 17-5: The Define Viewports screen of the Layout Wizard

Figure 17-6: After completing the Layout Wizard, you now see your model in the viewport(s) you created.

In the following exercise, you practice using the Layout Wizard to create a paper space layout.

On the CD-ROM The drawing used in the following Step-by-Step exercise on creating a paper space layout with the Layout Wizard, ab17-a.dwg, is in the *Drawings* folder of the *AutoCAD 2004 Bible* CD-ROM.

Step-by-Step: Creating a Paper Space Layout with the Layout Wizard

1. Open `ab17-a.dwg` from your CD-ROM.

2. Save the file as `ab17-01.dwg` in your `AutoCAD Bible` folder.

3. Choose Tools ⇨ Wizards ⇨ Create Layout.

4. On the Begin screen, type **Double** as the name of the layout. Click Next.

5. On the Printer screen, choose the printer or plotter that you want to use. Click Next.

6. On the Paper Size screen, choose a paper size that you have available and that is suitable for the printer or plotter you chose in the previous screen. The drawing units should be inches (but you can use millimeters, if you want). Click Next.

7. On the Orientation screen, choose Landscape. (This is the default.) Click Next.

8. On the Title Block screen, choose `ANSI A title block.dwg`. The type should be set to Block. Click Next.

9. On the Define Viewports screen, choose Array. Set Rows to 1 and Columns to 2. Choose 1:4 from the Viewport Scale drop-down list. Click Next.

10. On the Pick Location screen, click Select Location. In the drawing, choose a point near the top of the border on the left and a second point at the bottom-right of the border, just above the title block. If necessary, turn off OSNAP.

11. Click Finish.

12. Save your drawing. It should look like Figure 17-7.

Figure 17-7: Using the Layout Wizard to create a paper space layout with floating viewports

Laying out a drawing in paper space on your own

Now that you have used the Layout Wizard once, you can try creating layouts on your own. The Layout Wizard only creates the floating viewports, leaving most of the scaling, the panning, and other tasks up to you.

Working with layout tabs

You can have up to 256 layouts, including the model tab. To create a new layout, right-click an existing layout tab to open the shortcut menu shown in Figure 17-8.

Figure 17-8: Use the Layout shortcut menu to manage layouts.

The following shortcut menu options help you manage layouts:

✦ **New layout:** Creates a new layout tab.

✦ **From template:** Opens the Select File dialog box in which you can choose a
.dwg, .dxf, or .dwt file. Click Open. You can then choose the layout or
layouts you want from the Insert Layout(s) dialog box. AutoCAD imports
everything that exists on the paper space layout, including viewports and any
existing text, title block, and so on. (You can then get rid of anything you don't
want, if necessary.)

Cross-Reference

If you import a layout from a drawing, AutoCAD also brings in layers, linetypes, and such. Use the PURGE command to get rid of anything you don't need. See Chapter 11 for information on purging. You can also import a layout using the DesignCenter. See Chapter 26 for details.

✦ **Delete:** Deletes the selected layout. AutoCAD provides a warning. Click OK to
delete the layout.

✦ **Rename:** Opens the Rename Layout dialog box, where you can rename the
layout. Click OK.

✦ **Move or Copy:** Opens the Move or Copy dialog box. To move a layout tab,
you choose the layout tab that you want the selected tab to be to the left of.
You can also choose to move it to the end. Click Create a copy to copy the
selected tab. (You can then rename it.) Click OK after you're done.

✦ **Select All Layouts:** Selects all layouts. You can then delete them. AutoCAD still retains one layout called Layout1.

✦ **Activate Previous Layout/Activate Model Tab:** Moves you to the last layout tab you had displayed or to the Model tab.

✦ **Page Setup:** Opens the Page Setup dialog box, discussed next.

✦ **Plot:** Opens the Plot dialog box, discussed later in this chapter.

New Feature

To move through the tabs (Model and all the layout tabs) from left to right, press Ctrl+Page Down. To move from right to left, press Ctrl+Page Up.

Using the Page Setup dialog box

When you click a new (unused) layout tab, by default the Page Setup dialog box appears, as shown in Figure 17-9. You can uncheck the Display when creating a new layout check box and the Page Setup dialog box will not automatically appear. To display it if it does not appear, right-click the layout tab and choose Page Setup; then recheck the check box. You can also specify if you want the Page Setup dialog box to appear when you click a new layout tab by choosing Tools ⇨ Options and clicking the Display tab. Check or uncheck Show Page Setup dialog box for new layouts.

The Layout Settings tab of the Page Setup dialog box includes most of the Layout Wizard settings explained previously. You can override the settings in the Page Setup dialog box when you plot. The value in using the Page Setup dialog box is that the settings are attached to the layout. If you have more than one layout, each with its own page setup, you can quickly switch the page settings as you move from layout to layout.

Figure 17-9: The Layout Settings tab of the Page Setup dialog box

Here's how to use the Layout Settings tab of the Page Setup dialog box:

✦ **Paper size and paper units:** The plot device is already listed here. Use the Plot Device tab to choose a printer or plotter. Choose a paper size from the drop-down list and set the measurements in either inches or millimeters.

✦ **Plot area:** By default the plot is set to the layout. However, you can set it to display. If you zoom in to a smaller area, only the smaller displayed area will plot.

✦ **Plot scale:** Set the scale from the drop-down list. You can also type a scale in the Custom text boxes. Because you scale your model in your floating viewports, you usually don't have to scale the layout as well. Therefore, you typically plot a layout in paper space at 1:1. If you are using lineweights, you can scale them. This would only be meaningful if you were not plotting at 1:1.

✦ **Plot offset:** If you don't want the lower left corner of the layout to be placed at the lower-left corner of the printable area on the paper, you can offset the plot, using the X and Y text boxes. For example, if you set both X and Y to 2, the plot would be moved up and to the right by two units.

✦ **Drawing orientation:** Choose portrait or landscape. You can also choose to plot upside-down. Use these settings to rotate a drawing as it is plotted.

✦ **Shaded viewport options:** Use this new feature to determine the display of the Model tab. (To set the display of a viewport on a layout tab, select the tab and make the changes in the Properties palette.) Choose one of the four display options (As Displayed, Wireframe, Hidden, or Rendered). You can also choose a quality (resolution). If you choose the Custom quality, you can specify the dots per inch (dpi).

✦ **Plot options:** Clear the Plot with Lineweights option if you used lineweights but don't want the lineweights to be plotted. Clear Plot with Plot Styles if you assigned plot styles to layers or objects but don't want to plot them. (Plot styles are discussed later in this chapter.) Clear the Plot paperspace last option in order to plot objects drawn on the paper space layout first. Check Hide paperspace objects to hide lines of 3D objects that you created *in paper space*. (Later in this chapter, I explain how to hide lines of 3D objects created in model space, a more common situation.)

The Plot Device tab enables you to choose a plotter and a plot style table. You can also choose a plotter and plot style table from the Plot dialog box, which is very similar. See the section "Choosing a plotter/printer" later in this chapter for more information. Choosing a plot style table is covered in the section "Working with Plot Styles," also later in this chapter.

You can plot directly from the Page Setup dialog box. You would probably do so only if you had already created your viewports and then came back to the Page Setup dialog box. If you have just clicked a layout tab and completed your settings in the dialog box, click OK to see the result on the layout.

You can save a page setup so that you can use it on another layout (or on the same layout after changing some of the settings). From the Page Setup dialog box, follow these steps:

1. Create the settings you want.

2. Click Add at the top-right corner of the dialog box. AutoCAD opens the User Defined Page Setups dialog box.

3. In the New page setup name text box, type a name.

4. Click OK.

To import a saved page setup, use the PSETUPIN command on the command line. AutoCAD opens the Select Page Setup From File dialog box where you can choose the drawing that contains the page setup you want. Click to open the Import user defined page setup(s) list. Choose the page setup to apply to the current layout and click OK.

You can also import settings saved in PCP or PC2 files from earlier releases of AutoCAD. PCP and PC2 files contain plot settings similar to those you set in the Page Setup dialog box. Click the layout you want to use and type **pcinwizard** ↵ on the command line. In the Import PCP/PC2 Settings Wizard, locate the PCP or PC2 file and click Import. Click Page Setup to view or change the result in the Page Setup dialog box. (If you do so, click OK to return to the wizard.) Click Finish to close the wizard.

Preparing layers

If necessary, create the layers you need. If you want to insert a title block, create a separate layer for it. The actual viewports should also be on their own layer because it is common to freeze that layer so that the borders do not show. Even if you want to plot the viewports, it is very helpful if they are a different color from your model so you can easily distinguish them.

Inserting a title block

Insert the title block. You can have a file that contains just the title block. You can use a block or external reference. Putting the title block on your layout is common because it defines the edges of your paper and is not a real-life object. These qualities make it appropriate for paper space, which also relates to your paper, rather than the real-life model you have drawn.

Creating floating viewports

Remember that you need a floating viewport to see your model on a paper space layout. By default, AutoCAD creates one floating viewport. Floating viewports have the following properties that are important to understand when you are creating layouts in paper space:

✦ Unlike tiled viewports, floating viewports are actual objects that you can erase, move, and stretch. They can — and should — be on separate layers, so that you can turn off the visibility of the viewport borders when desired. They do not need to take up the entire screen. You can define their size and location freely.

✦ In paper space, the crosshairs are not limited to one floating viewport.

✦ You can separately set the visibility of the UCS icon in each floating viewport.

✦ You can create as many viewports as you want, but it's best to keep the drawing uncluttered.

✦ Whatever you draw in paper space does not affect your models — it exists only in paper space and disappears when you return to the model space tab.

✦ After you create floating viewports, you can switch to model space and work on your models while still on the layout tab — to do so, double-click inside a viewport. You do this mostly to adjust the view of the model in the viewport. In model space, floating viewports are similar to tiled viewports — only one can be active at a time.

To create floating viewports, choose View ➪ Viewports while on a layout tab. You have the following submenu items:

✦ **Named Viewports:** If you have saved a tiled viewport configuration, choose this option to open the Viewports dialog box. On the Named Viewports tab, choose the configuration from the list and click OK. In other words, you can use a tiled viewport configuration for floating viewports.

Cross-Reference See Chapter 8 for a full discussion of saving viewport configurations.

✦ **New Viewports:** Choose this item to open the Viewports dialog box, shown in Figure 17-10. Choose one of the standard configurations. AutoCAD displays it in the Preview box. Click OK to create the viewports.

- **1 Viewport:** AutoCAD displays the `Specify corner of viewport or [ON/OFF/Fit/Shadeplot/Lock/Object/Polygonal/Restore/2/3/4] <Fit>:` prompt on the command line. You can pick two diagonally opposite points or use the Fit suboption to create one viewport that fits the entire screen.

- **2 Viewports:** Creates two floating viewports. You can choose a horizontal or vertical configuration. You can choose Fit to fit them to the entire screen or pick diagonal points. The diagonal points define the combined two viewports, not each viewport.

Figure 17-10: Use the Viewports dialog box to choose one of the standard configurations of floating viewports.

- **3 Viewports:** Creates three floating viewports. You can choose from several configurations. You can choose Fit to fit them to the entire screen or pick diagonal points. The diagonal points define the combined three viewports, not each viewport.

- **4 Viewports:** Creates four floating viewports. You can choose Fit to fit them to the entire screen or pick diagonal points. The diagonal points define the combined four viewports, not each viewport.

✦ **Polygonal Viewport:** Lets you create a viewport using a combination of line segments and arcs, with prompts similar to those you see when creating a polyline:

 1. At the Specify start point: prompt, pick a point.

 2. At the Specify next point or Arc/ Length/Undo]: prompt, continue to specify points or right-click to choose one of the options. If you choose the Arc option, you see suboptions that are just like those you see when drawing an arc in a polyline.

 3. Press Enter to use the Close option (which appears after you have specified two or more points) to complete the viewport.

✦ **Object:** Select an existing object, such as an ellipse, and AutoCAD turns it into a viewport.

You now see your drawing in the new viewport(s). The viewports are created on the current layer.

Returning to model space while on a layout

The next step is to set the view in each viewport. To do this, you need to return to model space while still on the layout tab and make a viewport active. You can do this in two ways:

✦ Click PAPER on the status bar. (The button then says MODEL.) Then click the viewport you want to become active.

✦ Double-click inside the viewport you want to become active.

You can now access your models. Working with floating viewports in model space is quite similar to working with tiled viewports. The active viewport shows a dark border.

Tip To cycle from viewport to viewport while in model space, press Ctrl+R.

Viewport scale

You will probably want to set the zoom for each viewport to exact scale. You can set the zoom in two ways:

✦ From model space, choose Zoom Scale from the Zoom flyout of the Standard toolbar. You need to use the inverse of the scale factor with the xp option of the ZOOM command. If you have an architectural drawing at a scale of 1:48, type **1/48xp** ↵. (The abbreviation *xp* stands for "times paper space.") Each viewport can have its own scale. AutoCAD scales the view of your model in the active viewport.

✦ If you are still in paper space, double-click a viewport on its border. The Properties palette opens. Choose Standard scale and choose one of the standard scales from the drop-down list that appears.

If you remain in model space with a viewport active, and then zoom in or out, you change the displayed scale of the model. After you set the scale, you can lock it to avoid this problem. To lock a viewport, double-click the viewport's border (while in paper space, not model space) to open the Properties palette. Choose Display locked and then choose Yes from the drop-down list. Now, when you zoom in and out, only paper space objects will be affected.

Specifying the viewport view

After you scale each viewport, you need to go back and pan until you see what you want in the viewport. If you can't get it perfectly, don't worry—you can also change the size of the viewport itself.

You can use the MVSETUP command to align views in floating viewports. To pan views so that they are aligned, follow these steps:

1. Type **mvsetup** ↵.

2. Right-click and choose Align.

3. Right-click and choose horizontal, vertical, or angled.

4. At the `Specify basepoint:` prompt, pick a base point that you want to align to in the viewport in which you want the display to remain stationary. (If necessary, click it first to activate it.)

5. At the `Specify point in viewport to be panned:` prompt, pick any point in the viewport in which you want the display to pan, just to indicate which viewport you want, and then pick the point you want to align with the stationary point picked earlier. (For an angled alignment, you specify the distance and angle from the base point.)

 AutoCAD aligns the views.

You can also rotate views using MVSETUP. Choose the Align option and then choose Rotate view. Pick a base point and then specify a rotation angle.

Setting viewport size, placement, and display

To adjust the viewports themselves, return to paper space by clicking MODEL on the status bar or by double-clicking anywhere outside a viewport (but in the drawing area). You cannot access your models anymore but now you can move and resize the viewports if necessary. You can use grips to stretch and move them or use the STRETCH and MOVE commands.

The VPCLIP command enables you to redefine the boundary of an existing viewport. You can delete the boundary of a clipped viewport and change it to a rectangular viewport or create a polygonal boundary just as you do when creating a polygonal viewport.

To redefine the boundary of a viewport, you must be in paper space. Type **vpclip** on the command line. Select a clipped viewport boundary from paper space. At the `Select clipping object or [Polygonal/Delete] <Polygonal>:` prompt, you can select an object to use for the new boundary or press Enter to get the same prompts you see when you create a polygonal viewport. Right-click and choose Delete to delete the boundary of a clipped viewport (one created by choosing an object or using the Polygonal option).

You can also turn viewports on and off. When a viewport is off, it doesn't display your model. Do this when the regeneration process becomes slow as a result of a large number of viewports or a complex drawing. To turn off a viewport, select it (in paper space) and choose Properties from the Standard toolbar. In the Properties palette, choose On and then choose No from the drop-down list.

Tip Another way to turn off a viewport is to select it (by clicking its border while in paper space), and then right-click and choose Display Viewport Objects ⇨ No. Choose Yes to display the viewport objects again.

Setting layer visibility within a viewport

If you want, you can individually set layer visibility in floating viewports. For example, you might have some text or dimensions that appear in more than one floating viewport, but you may not want to show them more than once. Or perhaps you don't want a hatch to appear in one of the viewports. You must be in model space — double-click in any viewport. To freeze a layer in a viewport, click that viewport to make it active. Click the Layer Control drop-down list on the Layers toolbar. Find the layer you want to freeze in that viewport and click the icon in the Freeze or thaw in current viewport column. That layer disappears in the active viewport.

You can also freeze/thaw layers in new viewports — meaning viewports that you have not yet created. Choose Layer Properties Manager from the Layers toolbar to open the Layer Properties Manager. Click the icon for the layer you want in the New VP Freeze column and choose OK to close the dialog box.

Cross-Reference Don't forget that layers have a plottable/not plottable state. You can therefore set certain layers to not plottable if you don't want them to appear on the plot. For more information, see Chapter 11.

Setting hidden and shaded views for viewports

If you have a 3D drawing, you may want to hide back lines for objects in a viewport when you plot (similar to using the HIDE command on the Model tab). This procedure lets you hide lines in one viewport but not in others. You don't see the result until you plot or display a plot preview.

You can also specify shading and rendered views for each viewport, from both model space and paper space layouts. See Figure 17-11.

New Feature Plotting shaded and rendered views is new for AutoCAD 2004. You can use this new feature to create presentation-quality output.

For a paper space layout, you can choose the type of shaded view in two ways. First select any viewport in paper space (so that the selected viewport displays grips):

✦ Right-click anywhere in the drawing area and choose Shade Plot and choose one of the following options:

- **As Displayed:** Plots the objects as they are current displayed
- **Wireframe:** Plots the objects in wireframe display
- **Hidden:** Plots objects with hidden lines removed
- **Rendered:** Plots objects using the default rendering settings. (See Chapter 25 for coverage on rendering.)

✦ Choose Properties on the Standard toolbar to open the Properties palette. From the Shade Plot item choose one of the four options just listed.

Figure 17-11: In this drawing, one viewport displays a wireframe, one a hidden view, and one a rendered view.

In model space, open the Page Setup dialog box (right-click the Model tab and choose Page Setup). You can also specify the settings in the Plot dialog box. In the new Shaded Viewport Options section of the Layout Settings tab of the dialog box, choose one of the four display options (just previously listed). You can also choose a quality:

✦ **Draft:** Plots as wireframe

✦ **Preview:** Plots at 150 dots per inch (dpi)

✦ **Normal:** Plots at 300 dpi

✦ **Presentation:** Plots at 600 dpi

✦ **Maximum:** Plots at the maximum resolution available for the plotter or printer

✦ **Custom:** Use the resolution that you enter in the DPI text box.

New Feature

Express Tools include several commands for working with layouts:

✦ The CHSPACE command (Choose Express ⇨ Layout tools ⇨ Change Space) moves objects from model space to paper space.

✦ The ALIGNSPACE command (Choose Express ⇨ Layout tools ⇨ Align Space) aligns objects in different viewports.

✦ The VPSYNC command (Choose Express ⇨ Layout tools ⇨ Synchronize Viewports) changes the pan and zoom of a second viewport to match that of the first ("master") viewport you select, so that the view of the objects is consistent (synchronized) from viewport to viewport.

✦ The VPSCALE command (Choose Express ⇨ Layout tools ⇨ List Viewport Scale) displays the scale from paper space to model space of the selected viewport.

✦ The LAYOUTMERGE command (Choose Express ⇨ Layout tools ⇨ Merge Layout) moves all objects on one or more layouts that you specify to a single layout.

Adding text on a paper space layout

In general, text that relates directly to the model is created in model space — dimensions, leaders, and so on. However, annotation that applies to the entire drawing, title block text, or whatever, can be, and often is, created on the paper space layout. Change to a text layer and use the DTEXT or MTEXT command as usual.

Dimensions

Dimensioning is usually done in model space, but you can dimension in paper space as well. Since Release 2002, the *trans-spatial dimensioning* feature automatically adjusts dimensions for the scale of the viewport. These paper space dimensions are fully associative. Dimensioning in paper space is now much easier than before. Dimensioning in paper space has several advantages:

✦ You don't have to worry about the size of the dimensions. If you plot from paper space you plot at 1:1 scale.

✦ You can place the dimensions outside the border of the floating viewport, which may make it easier to fit the dimensions.

✦ You can easily dimension just one view of the model. If you dimension in model space, you see the dimensions in all the viewports unless you freeze that layer in some of the viewports.

Tip If you create dimensions in a viewport in paper space and then zoom or pan in that viewport, the objects and the dimension get out of sync. Use the DIMREGEN command on the command line to reset the dimension to match its object.

You still need to scale the size of the dimension itself to your viewport scale, including the text, arrows, and so on:

1. Open the Dimension Style Manager.

2. Choose the dimension style you want to use and click Modify.

3. On the Fit tab, choose Scale dimensions to layout (paper space).

4. Click OK and then click Close.

When you follow this procedure, all the dimensions using the dimension style you chose appear the same size on your final plot.

Note Drawings created in earlier releases (before AutoCAD 2002) do not automatically have the new associative dimensions. If necessary, change the DIMASSOC system variable's value to 2. Also, you usually need to use the DIMREASSOCIATE command to associate existing dimensions to their objects. See Chapter 14 for more information on associative dimensions.

Saving a layout template

After you do all that work to create a layout, you can save it as a template so that you can use it in other drawings. Here's how:

1. Type **layout** ↵ on the command line.

2. At the prompt, right-click and choose Save as.

3. At the `Enter layout to save to template <Layout2>:` prompt, press Enter to save the current layout, the name of which appears in brackets, or type the name of another layout tab.

4. AutoCAD opens the Create Drawing File dialog box, with the `Template` folder active. The Files of type drop-down list shows Drawing Template File (`*.dwt`). Type a name for the drawing template and click Save.

To use the template, in any drawing right-click a layout tab and choose From template, as explained earlier in this chapter.

In the following exercise, you practice laying out a drawing in paper space using the same drawing you used in the previous exercise.

On the CD-ROM The drawings used in the following Step-by-Step exercise on laying out a drawing in paper space, `ab17-a.dwg` and `ab-a-blk.dwg`, are in the `Drawings` folder of the *AutoCAD 2004 Bible* CD-ROM.

Step-by-Step: Laying Out a Drawing in Paper Space

1. Open `ab17-a.dwg` from your CD-ROM.

2. Save the file as `ab17-02.dwg` in your `AutoCAD Bible` folder.

3. Click the Layout1 tab. The Page Setup dialog box opens. (If it doesn't, right-click the layout tab and choose Page Setup.)

4. On the Layout Settings tab, set the paper size to Letter (8.5×11 inches). (This enables you to plot to a printer if you don't have a plotter available.) Click OK.

5. You see one floating viewport with the drawing displayed inside. Click its border and press the Delete key because you want to make your own viewports.

6. Click the Layer drop-down list arrow. Choose the Titleblk layer to make it current.

7. Choose Insert ⇨ Block to open the Insert dialog box. Click Browse. Choose `ab-a-blk.dwg` from the CD-ROM and click Open. In the Insertion Point section of the dialog box, uncheck Specify On-Screen. Click OK. AutoCAD inserts the title block, as shown in Figure 17-12.

8. Click the Layer drop-down list. Choose the np layer to make it current.

9. Choose View ⇨ Viewports ⇨ 1 Viewport. (Turn OSNAP off if it is on.) At the `Specify corner of viewport or [ON/OFF/Fit/Shadeplot/Lock/Object/Polygonal/Restore/2/3/4] <Fit>:` prompt, choose ❶ in Figure 17-12. At the `Specify opposite corner:` prompt, choose ❷.

Figure 17-12: The title block inserted into paper space

10. Click the right mouse button and then choose Repeat 1 Viewport. At the prompt, choose ❸ in Figure 17-12. At the next prompt, choose ❹ in Figure 17-12. Again repeat the command and choose ❺ and ❻ in Figure 17-12. You now see the drawing in the three viewports.

11. Double-click the border of the top-left viewport. The Properties palette opens. Choose Custom scale from the Properties palette. Type **.4** ⏎. Press Esc to deselect the top-left viewport.

12. Select the top-right viewport and set its custom scale to .4. Deselect the top-right viewport.

13. Select the bottom viewport. Choose Standard Scale in the Properties palette. Choose 2:1. This is equivalent to using a ZOOM 2xp, which is a scale factor of 1/2.

14. Double-click each viewport in turn to switch to model space and pan until you see the view shown in Figure 17-13. It doesn't have to match exactly. If you want, you can resize the viewports to fit the models better.

15. Double-click the bottom viewport. From the Layer Control drop-down list on the Layers toolbar, click the icon in the third column (Freeze or Thaw in current viewport) next to the DIM and HATCH layers to freeze those layers in the viewport. Click the name of the DIM-PS layer to make it current. The current dimension style, Style1, is already set to be scaled to paper space.

16. You should now be in paper space. (If necessary, double-click anywhere outside a viewport, but in the drawing area.) Choose Dimension ➪ Linear. Use the Quadrant object snap to create a dimension from the left quadrant to the right quadrant of the ellipse. The ellipse is correctly dimensioned at 1 unit although it is zoomed in to a 1/2 scale.

17. Click the Layer Control drop-down arrow and change the current layer to Text. Click the Layer Control drop-down arrow again. Click the icon in the second column (Freeze or Thaw in ALL viewports) next to the np layer. Click the top of the drop-down box to close it.

18. Choose Draw ➪ Text ➪ Single Line Text. Complete the text in the title block at the default height, as shown in Figure 17-13.

19. Save your drawing.

Figure 17-13: The completed drawing layout is now ready for plotting.

Note

The PSLTSCALE system variable controls linetype scaling in paper space viewports. By default, it is set to 1 so that the paper space scale controls the scale of any non-continuous linetypes. This lets you have viewports of differing scales but display linetypes identically. When you set PSLTSCALE to 0, linetype scales are based on the drawing units where the object was created (in either model space or paper space). Linetypes are still scaled by the LTSCALE factor. When you either change PSLTSCALE or change the zoom scale in a viewport with PSLTSCALE set to 1, you need to do a regen to update the linetype scales in each viewport.

Working with Plot Styles

A *plot style* is an object property, like color, linetype, lineweight, or layer. Just as you can assign a color to an object and also to a layer, you can assign a plot style to an object as well as to a layer. Because a plot style determines how an object is plotted, its function is to override the object's original properties. A plot style is more complex than a color or a linetype, however, because it contains a set of properties, such as color-related properties, linetype, lineweight, and line styles. The use of plot styles is completely optional. Without plot styles, objects are simply plotted according to their properties.

You can use plot styles to create several types of plots for one drawing or layout. Plot styles are also designed to let you use some of the newer printer-like capabilities of plotters, such as screening and dithering.

Plot styles are stored in plot style tables, which are files that you can create and edit. You generally follow these steps to use plot styles in your plots:

1. Create a plot style table.

2. Attach a plot style table to a layout or a viewport.

3. Set the plot style property for a layer or object.

4. Plot.

Setting the plot style mode

Plot styles come in two types — color-dependent and named. Before you work with plot styles you need to choose which type you want to use:

✦ **Color-dependent plot styles**, the default, are saved in color-dependent plot style tables, which are files with a file name extension of .ctb. As with previous releases of AutoCAD, you assign plotting properties based on object color. The disadvantage of color-dependent plot styles is that you cannot assign different properties to two objects that have the same color.

✦ **Named plot styles** are saved in named plot style tables, which are files with a file name extension of .stb. Named plot styles let you assign plotting properties to objects regardless of their color. Therefore, two objects of the same color can be plotted differently.

After you decide which type of plot style you want to use, you set the mode by choosing Tools ➪ Options and clicking the Plotting tab, as shown in Figure 17-14. In the Default plot style behavior for new drawings section, choose either Use color dependent plot styles or Use named plot styles.

In the same location, you can set the default plot style for layer 0 (the default is Normal) and for objects (the default is ByLayer). The default plot style for objects is the current plot style for new objects, similar in concept to the current color, linetype, lineweight, or layer for new objects. After you're done, click OK.

Figure 17-14: Use the Plotting tab of the Options dialog box to choose the plot style mode for new drawings.

It is very important to understand that changing the plot style mode does not affect the current drawing. To use the new setting you must either open a new drawing or open a drawing from a previous release that has not been saved in AutoCAD 2000 or later format.

Caution

If you have color-dependent plot styles for existing pre-AutoCAD 2000 drawings (and want to keep them that way), but decide to use named plot styles for new drawings, you need to avoid opening any of the existing drawings while you are in named plot style mode — because they will be changed to named plot style mode. Remember that pre-AutoCAD 2000 drawings don't have any plot styles and that plot settings had to be according to color. You might consider setting the mode to color-dependent plot styles, creating a script file to open and save all your existing drawings as AutoCAD 2004 drawings, and only then changing the mode to named plot styles. Chapter 30 explains how to create script files.

Creating a plot style table

Each named plot style table comes with a default plot style called Normal. By default, the plot style for each layer is Normal. Figure 17-15 shows the Normal plot style, shown in a plot style table with two other plot styles. The Normal plot style is grayed out because you cannot change it.

The plot style table lists your plot styles side-by-side. Each plot style includes settings for the various definition categories available in a plot style.

Plot style tables are stored in the Plot Styles folder. The default plot style tables are acad.stb (named plot style) and acad.ctb (color-dependent plot style).

Note To find the location of the Plot Styles folder, choose Tools ➪ Options and click the Files tab. Double-click Printer Support File Path and then double-click Plot Style Table Search Path.

You can use plot configuration files (PCP and PC2 files) as well as the Release 14 configuration file (acadr14.cfg) to create plot style tables in order to import your previously created configuration information. You can also create plot style tables from scratch.

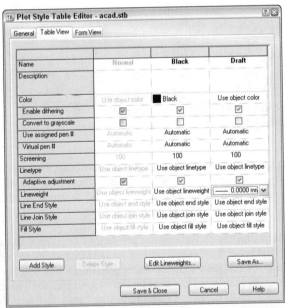

Figure 17-15: The Normal plot style is the default plot style for layers.

Creating a named plot style table

To create a named plot style table, use the Add Plot Style Table Wizard. You can access this wizard in two ways:

✦ Choose File ➪ Plot Style Manager to open the \Plot Styles folder. Then double-click the Add Plot Style Table Wizard icon. From this folder you can also access existing plot style tables for editing.

Note To find the location of the Plot Styles folder, choose Tools ➪ Options and click the Files tab. Double-click Printer Support File Path. Then double-click Plot Style Table Search Path to display the location.

✦ Choose Tools ➪ Wizards ➪ Add Plot Style Table.

The wizard opens with an explanation of plot style tables. Follow these steps:

1. Choose Next.

2. On the Begin screen, shown in Figure 17-16, choose the source you want to use for the plot style table. You can start from scratch or use an existing plot style table. Choose Use My R14 Plotter Configuration (CFG) to use the pen assignments from the `acadr14.cfg` file. If you have a PCP (Release 12/13) or PC2 (Release 14) configuration file, you can use it to import the settings from that file into the plot style table. Then click Next.

Figure 17-16: In the Begin screen of the Add Plot Style Table Wizard, choose the source you want to use for the new plot style table.

3. If you chose to start from scratch or to use R14 Plotter Configuration or PCP/PC2 files, choose whether you want color-dependent or named plot styles. If you chose to use an existing file as a basis for the plot style table, choose the file. If you chose to use a CFG file, also specify the plotter because the CFG file can contain information for more than one plotter. Click Next.

4. On the File Name screen, type a name for the plot style table file. Click Next.

5. On the Finish screen, if the Use this plot style table for new and pre-AutoCAD 2004 drawings option is available, check this option to attach the plot style table to all new drawings by default. You don't have to use the plot styles, but they will be available. Clear the option if you don't want to attach this plot style table to new drawings by default. You can also click Plot Style Table Editor to edit plot styles immediately. You can edit plot styles at any time, as explained next. Click Finish.

Creating a color-dependent plot style table

Prior to AutoCAD 2000, plotting was integrally related to object color. You assigned pens in a pen plotter according to color, for example. If you want to continue to create settings based on color, you can create a color-dependent plot style table. To do this, follow the same steps for creating a named plot style table. On the Pick Plot Style Table screen, choose Color-dependent plot style table and click Next. The rest of the steps are the same. AutoCAD creates a CTB file with 255 styles, one for each AutoCAD color. You cannot add, delete, or rename these styles, but you can edit their properties. For example, you can specify that objects on color 1 should be plotted with no lineweight or a specific linetype. Be aware, however, that color-dependent plot styles result in slower display regeneration.

In this chapter, I focus on named plot styles. Creating color-dependent plot styles is very similar.

Editing a plot style table

After you create a plot style table, you can edit it by adding, naming, and deleting its plot styles (for named plot style tables only) and, of course, creating the settings you want for the plot styles. To open the Plot Style Table Editor, do one of the following:

✦ Choose Plot Style Table Editor from the Finish screen of the Add Plot Style Table Wizard.

✦ Choose File ➪ Plot Style Manager and double-click any existing CTB or STB file.

✦ From the Plot Device tab of the Page Setup dialog box (discussed earlier in this chapter) or the Plot dialog box (discussed later in this chapter), choose the named plot style table you want to edit from the Plot style table drop-down list and click Edit.

✦ From the Select Plot Style dialog box (accessed from the Layer Properties Manager after you click the Plot Style column), choose Editor.

✦ Choose Tools ➪ Options and click the Plotting tab. Choose Add or Edit Plot Style Tables.

The Plot Style Table Editor's Table View tab was shown in Figure 17-15. The Form View tab is shown in Figure 17-17. You can edit styles using either view tab. The Form View tab focuses on one style at a time and provides better visual confirmation of some of the choices. The Table View tab lets you compare your style to existing styles as you work.

To add a style, click Add Style. AutoCAD creates a new style and names it Style1 (or the next style number). Before you go any further, type a more descriptive name for the style.

 Caution You can't rename a plot style that is currently assigned to an object or layer, so that it's best to name it when you create it. You cannot change the names of styles in a color-dependent plot style table.

Each plot style has a description area that you can use to provide a more detailed description of the plot style. For example, you could summarize a plot style as "color black & no lineweight."

Figure 17-17: The Form View tab of the Plot Style Table Editor

Now go down each of the properties and make any changes you want. In table view, you need to click the property in the Plot styles column for a drop-down box to appear. The properties are as follows:

✦ **Color:** You can specify a color other than the default, which is Object Color. For example, you might want to create a plot style that plots everything in black or red. For more options, choose Select Color and define a color in the Select Color dialog box. (See Chapter 11 for an explanation of how to use the Select Color dialog box.)

✦ **Screening:** Specifies the amount of ink used for a color. The range is from 0 (no ink; that is, white) to 100 (full intensity of the color). Some plotters — for example, pen plotters — do not support screening. You could use a 50 percent screen to de-emphasize certain layers, such as those containing proposed changes.

✦ **Dithering:** Dithering is a method of using dot patterns to approximate a greater range of colors. Not all plotters support dithering. Dithering gives the impression of more colors, but can make thin lines and dim colors look unclear.

✦ **Grayscale:** Converts objects to grayscale, if supported by the plotter. You could use grayscale to de-emphasize certain layers.

✦ **Pen # and virtual pen #:** These settings apply to pen plotters only (the Virtual pen # setting applies to non-pen plotters that can simulate pen plotters) and specify which pen to use for the object assigned the plot style.

✦ **Linetype:** You can specify a linetype other than the default, Object Linetype, to override the object's linetype when you plot. You might want to have the option to plot certain objects that are not yet approved in a dashed or dotted linetype, for example.

✦ **Adaptive:** Choose On to adapt the scale of a linetype to complete the linetype pattern on the object. Choose Off if maintaining the proper linetype scale is essential.

✦ **Lineweight:** You can specify a lineweight other than the default, Object Lineweight. For example, if you are using heavy lineweights, you might want to specify a narrower lineweight to save ink on a draft plot.

✦ **Line end style:** When you use lineweights, AutoCAD has to determine how to end lines. You can choose from Butt, Square, Round, and Diamond. The default is Object End Style.

✦ **Line join:** Specifies how objects with lineweights are joined. The choices are miter, bevel, round, and diamond. The default is Object Join Style.

✦ **Line fill style:** You can choose from solid, checkerboard, crosshatch, diamonds, horizontal bars, slant left, slant right, square dots, and vertical bar. The default is Object Fill Style.

To delete a style, select it and click Delete. In table view, click a style's gray column head to select it.

After you are done, click the Save & Close button.

Attaching a plot style table to a layout

As soon as you have your plot style table and the plot styles you want, you can start using the plot styles. The first step is to attach the table to a layout (including the Model tab).

To attach a plot style table to a layout or the Model tab, follow these steps:

1. Choose the Layout or Model tab.

2. Right-click the tab and choose Page Setup.

3. Click the Plot Device tab.

4. Choose a plot style table from the Plot Style Table drop-down list.

5. To see the result of the plot styles in your drawing for a layout tab, click Display plot styles.

6. Click OK.

You can view the effects of plot styles in two ways:

✦ To display plot styles in your drawing all the time, display the layout for which you want to view the plot style. Right-click the layout's tab and choose Page Setup. On the Plot Device tab of the Page Setup dialog box, check Display Plot Styles in the Plot style table section. Click OK. (You may have to use REGENALL to see the result.)

✦ You can also see the effects of plot styles in a full preview of your plot. Choose Plot from the Standard toolbar and click Full Preview.

Setting the plot style property for a layer or object

To use a plot style, you need to assign it to a layer or an object. The plot style is only applied if the plot style is first defined in the plot style table that you have assigned to a layout (or Model tab).

To set the plot style for a layer, follow these steps:

1. Make sure the layout tab you want to use is active.

2. Choose Layer Properties Manager from the Layers toolbar to open the Layer Properties Manager.

3. Choose the layer whose plot style you want to change and click the Plot Style column.

4. Choose the plot style table from the Active plot style table list at the bottom of the dialog box.

5. Choose a plot style from the Select Plot Style dialog box.

6. Click OK.

If you checked Display plot styles in the Page Setup dialog box, as explained in the previous section, you should see the result of the plot style. If not, type **regenall** ↵.

To set the plot style for an object, select the object and choose Properties from the Standard toolbar. Choose the Plot Style item in the Properties palette and choose a plot style from the drop-down list. You can attach a plot style to a viewport (which is an object).

The drawing used in the following Step-by-Step exercise on creating and applying a plot style, `ab17-b.dwg`, is in the `Drawings` folder of the *AutoCAD 2004 Bible* CD-ROM.

Step-by-Step: Creating and Applying a Plot Style

1. With any drawing open, choose Tools ➪ Options and click the Plotting tab. Take note of the current setting under Default Plot Style Behavior for New Drawings. Remember this setting so that you can set it back to its original setting at the end of the exercise.

2. Click Use Named Plot Styles (unless that is the current setting) and click OK.

3. Open `ab17-b.dwg` from your CD-ROM, which is a Release 14 drawing.

4. Save the file as `ab17-03.dwg` in your `AutoCAD Bible` folder.

5. Choose Tools ➪ Wizards ➪ Add Plot Style Table. Click Next.

6. In the Begin screen, choose Start from Scratch and click Next. In the next screen choose Named Plot Style Table (it's probably already selected) and click Next. In the File Name screen, type **ab17-3** and click Next.

7. In the Finish screen, click Finish. (Don't check Use for new and pre-AutoCAD 2004 drawings because this is just an exercise.)

8. Choose File ➪ Plot Style Manager. (You could have opened the new plot style table from the wizard, but this is how you usually do it when you haven't just finished creating a table.) Double-click `ab17-3.stb`.

9. In the description box of the General tab, type **AutoCAD Bible Plot Style Table**.

10. Click the Table View tab. Click Add Style. The name Style1 is highlighted. Type **Black color** and press Enter.

11. Click the Color row under the Black color column and choose Black from the drop-down list. Click Save & Close. Close the `Plot Styles` folder window.

12. Click Layout1. On the Plot Device tab of the Page Setup dialog box, choose `ab17-3.stb` from the Plot style table drop-down list. Check Display plot styles and click OK. This assigns the plot style table to Layout1.

13. Choose Layer Properties Manager from the Layers toolbar. In the Layer Properties Manager, choose A-DETL-PATT (the layer with the magenta color). Click that layer's Plot styles column to open the Select Plot Style dialog box, shown in Figure 17-18. Choose Black color and click OK. The Plot Style for the A-DETL-PATT layer now shows as Black color. Click OK to close the Layer Properties Manager.

14. Type **regenall** ↵. The objects on A-DETL-PATT (the diagonal marks on the mirror) now show as black and will plot as black.

15. Click Properties on the Standard toolbar to open the Properties palette.

16. Click PAPER on the status bar to switch to model space.

17. Select the bottom horizontal line of the sink cabinet.

18. In the Properties palette, click Plot Style. From the drop-down list to the right, choose Black color.

19. Press Esc so that the object is no longer highlighted. The line appears as black.

20. Choose Tools ⇨ Options. On the Plotting tab, change the Default Plot Style Behavior for New Drawings setting to what it was at the beginning of this exercise.

21. Save your drawing.

Figure 17-18: The Select Plot Style dialog box lets you choose a plot style for a layer.

The plot style you created, ab17-3.stb, is in the Results folder of the CD-ROM.

Plotting a Drawing

After you lay out your drawing, you are ready to plot it. Plotting outputs your drawing onto paper (or perhaps vellum or some other medium). While you might go

through several iterations of drawing and editing in electronic form, you eventually plot most drawings.

The first step is to check the plotter or printer — it should be on, connected to your computer, and have the appropriate paper in it. Your drawing should appear on the screen.

Cross-Reference For more information on configuring plotters, see Appendix A on the CD-ROM.

To start plotting, choose Plot from the Standard toolbar to open the Plot dialog box, shown in Figure 17-19 with the Plot Settings tab on top. As you can see, this tab is almost identical to the Layout Settings tab of the Page Setup dialog box.

Figure 17-19: The Plot Settings tab of the Plot dialog box

If you set the Layout Settings in the Page Setup dialog box and clicked OK, those settings were saved with the tab that was current at the time. You can usually just click OK in the Plot dialog box and plot immediately. Plot settings are saved in your drawing.

If you saved a page setup, you can choose it from the Page setup name drop-down list. If you want to make changes for one plot and not save them to the layout, clear the Save Changes to Layout checkbox. Then next time you plot, your earlier settings will be restored. If the box is checked, the settings you make now are saved to the layout. See the discussion of the Page Setup dialog box earlier in this chapter for details on the settings in this dialog box.

Choosing a plotter/printer

Choose the Plot Device tab, as shown in Figure 17-20, to select a plotter or printer.

Choose the plotter/printer you want from the list, and then click OK. A plotter must be either a Windows system printer or a configured plotter. To add a system printer, choose Start ➪ Settings ➪ Printers and double-click Add a Printer. To add a configured plotter, which has a driver especially to optimize the functioning of that plotter, use the Add Plotter Wizard. (Choose Tools ➪ Wizards ➪ Add Plotter.)

Figure 17-20: The Plot Device tab of the Plot dialog box

Tip

To avoid inadvertently plotting to a Windows system printer when you should be plotting to a plotter, you can hide the display of Windows system printers in the Plot and Page Setup dialog boxes. Because these printers won't appear on the list of plotters, you can't plot to them. To hide system printers, choose Tools ➪ Options and click the Plotting tab. At the bottom-left corner of the dialog box, check Hide System Printers and click OK.

If you want to use a plot style table, check that it appears in the Plot Style Table drop-down list.

In the What to plot section, you can choose to plot all layout tabs or selected tabs. By default, you plot the current tab, either the Model tab or one of the layout tabs.

To choose how many copies you want to plot, change the number in the Number of copies text box of the What to plot section.

Where are the plotter configuration settings?

Many of the settings that were once on the Plot dialog box (before Release 2000) are in the Plotter Configuration Editor, shown here.

The thinking is that because you don't configure a plotter very often, it makes sense to remove these settings from the Plot dialog box, which you use all the time. To configure your plotter, choose File ⇨ Plotter Manager to open a window for the \Plotters subfolder of your AutoCAD folder. (To find the location of the Plotters folder, choose Tools ⇨ Options and click the Files tab. Double-click Printer Support File Path. Then double-click Printer Configuration Search Path to display the location.)

Plotter configuration settings are stored in PC3 files. Double-click the PC3 file icon for the plotter you want to configure to open the Plotter Configuration Editor. (You can also open the Plotter Configuration Editor from the Plot dialog box—click Properties in the Plot configuration section of the Plot Device tab.) Click the Device and Document Settings tab. The top section lists the possible types of settings. To open a list with a plus sign to its left, click the plus sign and suboptions appear. As you click each item on the top, the appropriate settings appear in the lower section. For example, if you want to set the color, speed, and width for each pen in a pen plotter, click physical pen characteristics. Then, in the bottom half of the Editor, you can click each pen in the carousel and change its characteristics. Choose Custom Paper Sizes to add custom sheet sizes—these will then appear in the Page Setup and Plot dialog boxes so you can choose them when you plot. In each case, the Editor walks you through the choices you need to make to configure your plotter. See Appendix A on the CD-ROM for further information.

You can filter out unused paper sizes using the Plotter Configuration Editor. However, at the end of the process, you can opt to apply the change only to the current plot. Follow these steps:

1. On the Device and Document Settings tab, choose Filter Paper Sizes.

2. In the list of paper sizes, uncheck sizes you don't want to display.

3. Click OK.

4. In the Changes to a Printer Configuration File dialog box, choose to apply the changes only to the current plot or to the file (that is, permanently or until you edit the printer configuration file again).

5. Click OK.

Check the Plot to file box to create a plot file rather than a paper plot. The File name box becomes active. AutoCAD suggests a file name based on the current drawing's file name. You can change the location by clicking the ellipsis button to the right of the Location box. The File Name and Path box itself is a drop-down list containing recently used folders from which you can choose.

You can merge overlapping objects so that the same area is not printed more than once. To set the merge overlapping property:

1. Click Properties in the Plotter configuration section of the Plot Device tab. (If you want to change the plotting device, first choose it from the drop-down list.)

2. In the Plotter Configuration Editor that opens, display the Device and Document Settings tab. Click the plus sign (+) next to Graphics. If you see Merge Control in the Graphics list that opens, you can use this feature on your printer or plotter. (For more information about the Plotter Configuration Editor, see the sidebar "Where are the plotter configuration settings?")

3. In the Merge Control area that is displayed, choose either Lines Overwrite or Lines Merge and click OK.

4. AutoCAD then gives you the choice of applying the change to the current plot only or making the change permanent by editing the PC3 file that contains the parameters for your plotter or printer. Choose one of the options and click OK.

Previewing your plot

You should preview your drawing before you plot. Choose Full Preview to see exactly how your drawing will plot. Figure 17-21 shows an example of a full preview.

Figure 17-21: A full preview

You can also choose Partial Preview, as shown in Figure 17-22.

Figure 17-22: A partial plot preview

The solid area indicates the area of the paper that the plot will cover. The dashed line indicates the printable area of the paper. While the full preview takes more time, it is much more helpful.

The Print Preview button on the Standard toolbar is just like the one you have in your Windows word processor. When you choose Print Preview, you see a preview of your plot using current plot parameters. Right-click to open the shortcut menu that lets you plot, zoom, pan, or exit the preview.

Note I cover previewing a plot last because it should be the last step before you actually plot. However, it can also be the first step, helping you to determine what settings you need.

Creating the plot

To start the plotting process, simply click OK in the Plot dialog box.

On the CD-ROM

Stmplot stamps a drawing with its name and location, your name, the date, and the time, and starts the PLOT command. Look in \Software\Chap17\Stmplot.

Batch Plotting

Often you need to plot a large group of drawings, perhaps even unattended. Many users plot small draft plots as an archiving technique. Also, a drawing many include many layouts, all of which need to be plotted. The Batch Plot Utility (BPU for short) lets you choose a group of drawings to plot in a batch. You set the plotting parameters and go home!

Cross-Reference

The new PUBLISH command can also batch plot. See Chapter 28 for details.

You must start outside of AutoCAD because the Batch Plot Utility opens AutoCAD for you. To start the BPU, open the folder in which you installed AutoCAD (by default AutoCAD 2004) and double-click batchplt.exe. Wait while the BPU loads AutoCAD and opens the AutoCAD Batch Plot Utility dialog box, shown in Figure 17-23.

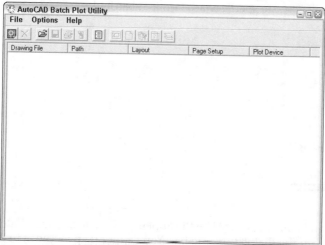

Figure 17-23: The AutoCAD Batch Plot Utility dialog box

Choose Add Drawing on the BPU toolbar to open the Add Drawing File dialog box. Choose any drawing and click Open. Continue to do this until you have chosen all the drawings you want to print. You can choose a contiguous group of drawings by choosing the first, pressing Shift, and choosing the last. You can select noncontiguous drawings by pressing Ctrl as you choose each one.

To save the list of displayed drawings to a batch plot list file (a file with a file name extension of .bp3) for future use, choose Save List from the BPU toolbar. Choose a location and a name. Click OK.

If you have already saved a list, choose Open List to choose the list.

To remove a drawing, choose it and click Remove.

Specifying how to plot

For each drawing, you can specify which layout to use. Select the drawing and click its setting under the Layout column to open the Layouts dialog box, shown in Figure 17-24. Choose either Plot all layouts or Plot selected layouts. If you choose Plot selected layouts, choose one of the standard layout options. Click Show all layouts to display the actual layouts in the drawing—AutoCAD opens the drawing to read the layouts.

Figure 17-24: Use the Layouts dialog box to specify which layout to batch plot.

You can select more than one drawing. The BPU opens the same Layouts dialog box but specifies Multiple on the dialog box title bar. You cannot display the actual layouts when you choose a layout for multiple drawings.

Selecting a page setup

You can specify a page setup to use for each drawing. Select a drawing and click its setting under the Page Setup column to open the Page Setups dialog box, shown in Figure 17-25.

Figure 17-25: Use the Page Setups dialog box to choose a page setup when batch plotting.

From the Page Setups list, choose a saved page setup. Earlier in this chapter, I explained how you can import a page setup from a drawing or template. You can do the same from the Page Setups dialog box. Click the ellipsis button to locate a drawing or template and click Open.

Choosing a plotter or printer

You can specify a plotter or printer to use for each drawing. Select a drawing and click its setting under Plot Device to open the Plot Devices dialog box, shown in Figure 17-26.

You can use a .pc3 (plotter configuration) file. Click Browse to locate the .pc3 file and click Open.

Specifying plot settings

You can also specify plot settings for each drawing by clicking Plot Settings on the BPU toolbar. AutoCAD may display the Page Setup dialog box at this time. Click Cancel to close it. Then the Plot Settings dialog box opens, as shown in Figure 17-27.

Figure 17-26: Use the Plot Devices dialog box to choose a plotter or printer for a drawing during batch plotting.

Figure 17-27: The Plot Settings tab of the Plot Settings dialog box

The Plot Settings tab enables you to specify plot area, plot scale, and plot to file information. These settings are familiar from the Layout Settings tab of the Page Setup dialog box and from the Plot dialog box. If you have selected only one drawing, the Plot Settings tab also has a Layers tab, as shown in Figure 17-28.

Turn a layer off so that it doesn't plot. To turn off a layer, select the layer and click Off. To turn a layer on, select the layer and click On. Then click OK. You can also access the Layer tab by selecting a drawing and clicking Layers on the BPU toolbar.

Figure 17-28: From the Layers tab of the Plot Settings dialog box, you can turn individual layers on and off.

The BPU has two options to help ensure successful batch plotting — plot testing and logging.

Plot testing

Plot testing loads each drawing without plotting. This test checks that all the required components, such as external references, raster images, and fonts are available. Then you can correct the problem so that the batch plot will function without problems. To do a plot test, click Plot Test on the BPU toolbar. At the end of the plot test, the BPU displays the results. You can append the results to the batch plot log or save it as a separate file. Note that the message

```
WARNING: xref file <file name> not accessible, xref checking
ignored
```

does not indicate any problem if the drawing does not contain any xrefs. I also found warnings about fonts in drawings that did not have any text. However, if the plot test does indicate problems, you should try to resolve them before beginning the batch plot.

Plot logging

You can turn on plot-journal logging, error logging, or both. Plot-journal logging records the drawing file's "owner," as registered on your computer, along with the time. Error logging records any errors that come up during batch plotting so you can figure out what went wrong. Because most batch plotting is done unattended, you have no other way to figure out what went wrong at 2:00 a.m. when you return to the office at 8:00 a.m.

To turn on logging, click Logging on the BPU toolbar to open the Logging dialog box, shown in Figure 17-29.

Figure 17-29: Use the Logging dialog box to turn on batch plot logging.

Check Enable journal logging at the top of the dialog box to turn on plot-journal logging. The default file name is listed but you can type a new file name or click Browse to locate one. To overwrite a previously created log of the same name, choose Overwrite. To add the log to the end of an existing log of the same name, choose Append. In the Header and Comment text boxes, you can add text that will appear at the top of the log. If you are appending to an existing log, the header helps you find the beginning of the latest log.

Check Enable error logging in the bottom half of the dialog box to turn on error logging. The default file name is `Bperror.log`. The options are the same except that there is no Comment text box. Click OK after you are done.

Starting the batch plot

You are now ready to start the batch plot. Check that any printers/plotters you need to use are on and ready. Click Plot on the BPU toolbar to start the batch plot. When a drawing has been plotted, the BPU places a checkmark next to the drawing name. If a drawing cannot be plotted, the BPU displays an X next to the drawing's name. After the batch plot is done, click the Close button at the top-right corner of the BPU window to close the BPU. AutoCAD asks you several questions, such as whether you want to quit the BPU and save the current list. Click Yes or No as appropriate.

Note If AutoCAD issues any messages, you may have to move the BPU window to see them, but you'll hear a beep to alert you of the message (but not if you're home sleeping at the time). I found that when I plotted a layout tab, the Page Setup dialog box opened and halted the batch plot until I cancelled the dialog box. You may

want to uncheck the Show page setup dialog for new layouts item on the Display tab of the Options dialog box (Tools ⇨ Options) before batch plotting if you will be plotting from a layout tab.

Creating Plot Stamps

You can place text in the corner of each plot. Typical stamp plots include the name of the drawing and the current date. To create a plot stamp, type **plotstamp** on the command line to open the Plot Stamp dialog box. Check the items you want to appear on the stamp and click OK.

To add custom items, click Add/Edit in the User Defined Fields section. Click Add again to create a new custom item. Click Edit to change an existing custom item.

In the Plot Stamp Parameter File section, you can save your settings as a .pss file. You can also load one of the two existing .pss files that AutoCAD provides, inches.pss or mm.pss.

Caution
If you find that loading inches.pss disables the other settings in the dialog box, locate the file in the AutoCAD\Support folder, right-click it, and choose Properties. Uncheck its Read-only attribute and click OK in the Properties dialog box. Then reload the file.

Click Advanced to set the exact location and appearance of the plot stamp and click OK to return to the Plot Stamp dialog box. After you're done, click OK to return to your drawing.

To turn on plot stamping, check the On check box in the Plot Stamp section of the Plot Device tab of the Plot dialog box. You can also click Settings in the same location to open the Plot Stamp dialog box. Then plot your drawing.

Summary

In this chapter, you read how to lay out and plot a drawing. You discovered:

✦ Laying out a drawing in model space

✦ Using a paper space layout

✦ Creating layouts, including using the Layout Wizard and using the commands individually

✦ Using the Page Setup dialog box to specify layout settings

✦ Creating and using plot styles

✦ How to plot a drawing

✦ All about batch plotting

This chapter ends Part II, Drawing in Two Dimensions. Part III, Working with Data, explains how to integrate your drawing with data about your objects. The next chapter explains how to use blocks and attributes.

✦ ✦ ✦

Working with Data

P art III covers the various ways you work with data in
your drawings. This part brings you to a new level of
sophistication in terms of automation and interfacing with
other drawings and data. Chapter 18 covers blocks and
attributes, which enable you to work repetitively with objects
and text. You can use attribute text to create a simple
database of information related to your objects. Chapter 19
explains how to refer to other drawings with external refer-
ences, also called *xrefs*. Chapter 20 describes how to connect
sophisticated external databases to objects in your drawings.

Working with Blocks and Attributes

As you draw, you'll find that you often need to place the same group of objects several times in a drawing. An architect needs to place windows and doors many times in a plan layout of a house. An electrical engineer places electrical symbols in a drawing again and again. A mechanical model may include nuts, bolts, surface finish symbols, and the like many times in a drawing. *Blocks* are groups of objects that you save and name so that you can insert them in your drawing whenever you need them. A block is one object regardless of the number of individual objects that were used to create it. Because it is one object, you can easily move, copy, scale, or rotate it. However, if necessary, you can *explode* a block to obtain the original individual objects.

One advantage of blocks is that they reduce the size of the drawing file. AutoCAD stores the composition of a block only once, along with a simple reference to the block each time it is inserted, rather than storing each individual object in each block in the drawing database.

As soon as you have a block in a drawing, you can work with it as with any other object. You can snap to object snaps of the individual objects within blocks as well as trim and extend to objects within blocks, even though you can't edit the individual objects. For example, you can draw a line from the midpoint of a line in a block.

Many disciplines use *parts libraries* that may consist of thousands of items. These are saved and inserted using the block feature of AutoCAD. You can save many blocks in a drawing or each as a separate file so that you can insert them in any drawing you wish.

AutoCAD enables you to attach attributes to blocks. Attributes are simply labels that are associated with blocks. Attributes have two main uses — to label objects and to create a simple database.

This chapter explains how to make the most of blocks and attributes.

Combining Objects into Blocks

Any object or set of objects can be saved as a block. Creating a block is easy, but a little planning makes using it much simpler. Before you create a block you need to understand how blocks are inserted and how you want to use the specific block that you are creating.

Understanding base points and insertion points

Figure 18-1 shows the legend for a plat drawing. Each legend symbol is a block that is then inserted in the drawing as needed. The first symbol has been selected, and you can see that it has one grip at the *base point*. The base point is the point you use to insert the block. Every block must have a base point. When you insert the block, the base point is placed at the coordinate you specify for inserting the block — the *insertion point*. All the objects of the block are then inserted in their proper place relative to that insertion point.

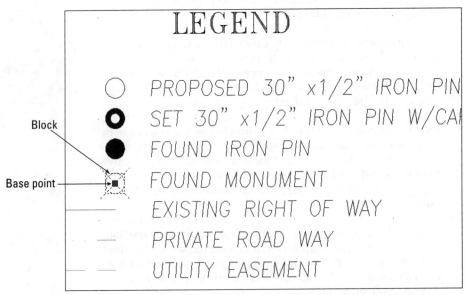

Figure 18-1: Each legend symbol is a block. Every block has a base point.

The base point does not have to be on the object, but it should be in a location that makes it easy to insert the block. Figure 18-2 shows a different sort of block—a title border/block. In this case, the base point is usually inserted at 0,0 of the drawing. By placing the base point at the lower-left corner of the border, you can easily place this block in any drawing. The base point is similar in concept to the justification point on text objects.

Figure 18-2: This title block is a block. Its base point is at the lower-left corner.

Creating a block

To create a block, first create the objects just as you want to save them. You may include other blocks as objects in your block. (A block within a block is called a nested block.)

After you have created the objects for your block, follow these steps:

1. Choose Make Block from the Draw toolbar to start the BLOCK command and open the Block Definition dialog box, shown in Figure 18-3. The dialog box guides you through the process of defining a block.

2. In the Name text box, type a name for the block (up to 255 characters; spaces allowed).

3. Click Select objects. AutoCAD returns you to your drawing temporarily. Use any selection method to select the objects you want in your block. Press Enter to end selection and return to the Block Definition dialog box. (If you select the objects before starting the command, you skip this step. The dialog box notes how many objects are selected.) To filter out the selected objects, choose Quick Select (described in Chapter 10).

Figure 18-3: The Block Definition dialog box

4. Choose a base point. By default, the base point is 0,0 (or 0,0,0 for 3D drawings). To define any other point, such as an object snap on any of the objects in the block, click Pick point. AutoCAD temporarily returns you to your drawing. At the `Specify insertion base point:` prompt, specify a point. AutoCAD returns you to the dialog box.

Caution

For precision, you should always use an object snap when defining the base point. If the base point you need to use is not on any object, you can use the From object snap, tracking, or some other means of specifying a precise coordinate.

5. Choose how you want the objects of the block to be treated:

 • If you want to keep the objects that you selected as individual objects, check Retain.

 • If you created the objects to insert them elsewhere and do not need the original objects, check Delete.

 • To convert the objects to a block, check Convert to block.

6. By default, AutoCAD creates an icon based on the block. If you later use the DesignCenter to insert the block in another drawing, this icon will appear in the preview box to help you decide which block you want to insert. Click Do not include an icon if you don't want one.

7. Choose the insert units you want to use when defining your block. (You can choose anything from microns to parsecs!) Let's say you work in kilometers and save a block with an insert unit of kilometers. When you insert a block, it will be measured in kilometers, rather than millimeters or inches. If the units are not important to you, you can specify the units as Unitless.

8. If you want, enter a description for the block. As with the icon described in Step 6, the description is used by the DesignCenter.

9. Click OK to return to your drawing.

The definition of the block is now stored in the drawing, ready for you to insert as many times as needed. If you checked Delete, your objects disappeared. You can retrieve them by the one AutoCAD command with a sense of humor—OOPS. OOPS un-erases the last object or set of objects you erased—whether by using the ERASE command or by creating a block, even if you used some other command in the meantime. By contrast, UNDO undoes almost all commands but only in the order they were executed.

Tip If you create a number of block definitions that you do not end up using in the drawing, use the PURGE command to delete them. This reduces the size of the drawing file.

Redefining a block

One advantage of deleting the objects is that their disappearance confirms that you selected the right objects. If you make a mistake, or if you want to change the block in some way, you can redefine it. If you just created the block, use UNDO and make any necessary changes. If you created the block earlier, follow these steps:

1. Insert the block and explode it. (Exploding is covered later in this chapter.)

2. Repeat the process of defining the block, using the same name for the block.

3. Click Yes when AutoCAD asks if you want to redefine the block.

If you redefine a block that has been inserted in your drawing, AutoCAD updates all the blocks. This is a powerful technique to control your drawing. If you have repetitive symbols in your drawing, it is worthwhile to make blocks out of them just so that you can make this type of global change if necessary.

On the CD-ROM The drawing that you need for the following Step-by-Step exercise on creating a block, `ab18-a.dwg`, is in the `Drawings` folder of the *AutoCAD 2004 Bible* CD-ROM.

Step-by-Step: Creating a Block

1. Open `ab18-a.dwg` from the CD-ROM.

2. Save the file as `ab18-01.dwg` in your `AutoCAD Bible` folder. This is a small portion of an electrical schematic drawing, as shown in Figure 18-4. OSNAP should be on. Set running object snaps for endpoint, quadrant, and intersection.

Figure 18-4: A portion of an electrical schematic

3. To make a block of the 1.5 amp fuse, choose Make Block from the Draw toolbar.

4. In the Name text box of the Block Definition dialog box, type **1-5 amp fuse**.

5. Click Select objects to return to the drawing temporarily.

6. Select the boxed objects shown in Figure 18-4: the two lines of text, the two circles, and the two arcs. Press Enter to end selection and return to the dialog box. Under the Select objects button, AutoCAD displays `6 objects selected`.

7. Click Pick point in the Base point section of the dialog box.

8. In the drawing, use the Quadrant object snap to pick ❶ in Figure 18-4.

9. In the dialog box, check Delete. Create icon from block geometry should be checked. The Insert units should be Unitless. Leave the Description blank. Click OK to return to your drawing. AutoCAD erases the objects that made up the block.

10. To check that the block has been created, choose Make Block from the Draw toolbar. Click the Name drop-down list arrow to see your block, as shown in Figure 18-5. Click Cancel.

11. Save your drawing.

Saving blocks as files

You can use the DesignCenter to insert blocks from any drawing. Nevertheless, many users need to organize their blocks in their own files so they can be easily stored and located. Parts and symbols libraries are made up of many individual drawing files, one for each part or symbol. Such libraries are a powerful aid to drawing more efficiently.

Cross-Reference

A new feature, the Tools Palette, can store your blocks in an easily accessible palette. To insert the blocks, you drag them from the palette onto your drawing. See Chapter 26 for more information.

Figure 18-5: The Block Definition dialog box lists the blocks you have created.

To save a block as a file, follow these steps:

1. Type **wblock** ⏎. (WBLOCK stands for write block. Writing to a file is another expression for saving to a file.)

2. In the Write Block dialog box, shown in Figure 18-6, choose the location (drive and folder) for the file.

Figure 18-6: Use the Write Block dialog box to save a block as a separate drawing file.

3. In the Source section, choose how you want create the drawing file:

- **Block:** Use this option when you have already created the block and now want to save it as a drawing file. Choose the block from the drop-down list.

- **Entire drawing:** Use this option to make a copy of your drawing.

- **Objects:** Use this option to start defining the block in the same way you define a block within a drawing. The Base point and Objects sections become available.

4. In the File Name and Path text box, type the path and name of the file you want to create. (You can also click the ellipsis button to navigate to a location and then type a file name in the Browse for Drawing File dialog box. Click Save to return to the Write Block dialog box.) If you have already created the block in your drawing, you should generally use the same name as the block to avoid confusion, but you might have special naming conventions for a block library.

5. In the Insert units drop-down box, choose the units you want for your block or choose Unitless for no units.

6. After you're done, click OK to create the drawing file.

Tip When you save a drawing that you plan to insert as a block, use the BASE command to create the insertion point. By default the base point is 0,0,0. By setting the base point to another point in the drawing, such as an object snap on one of the objects, you can control how that drawing is inserted.

Replacing an existing file

If you make a mistake when selecting objects to write to a file with WBLOCK, or want to change the objects in the file, you can replace the file. Start WBLOCK and type the name of the block file you want to change. Be sure to choose the same file location. When you click OK, AutoCAD asks if you want to replace the existing file. Click Yes.

On the CD-ROM The drawing that you need for the following Step-by-Step exercise on saving a block to a file, ab18-b.dwg, is in the Drawings folder of the *AutoCAD 2004 Bible* CD-ROM.

Step-by-Step: Saving a Block to a File

1. Open ab18-b.dwg from the CD-ROM.

2. Save the file as ab18-02.dwg in your AutoCAD Bible folder. This is a large title block as shown in Figure 18-7. OSNAP should be on. Set a running object snap for endpoint.

3. Type **wblock** ↵. In the Source section of the Write Block dialog box, click Entire drawing. Set the File Name and Path box to `AutoCAD Bible\tb-f` by typing the path and the file name. (Alternatively, click the ellipsis (...) button and navigate to your AutoCAD Bible folder. In the File name text box, type **tb-f**. Click Save.) Click OK.

4. Press Enter to repeat the WBLOCK command.

5. In the Source section of the dialog box, choose Objects. In the Objects section, click Select objects.

6. Use Zoom Window to zoom in on the text at the bottom-right corner of the title block. At the `Select objects:` prompt, select all the 90° rotated text at ❶ in Figure 18-7. Press Enter to end selection.

Figure 18-7: A title block can be saved as a file and inserted into any other drawing.

7. In the Base point section, click Pick point. Use the Endpoint object snap to pick the bottom-left corner of the box containing the text you selected. Using this base point lets you easily place the text in the box at any time.

8. In the Object section, choose Delete from drawing.

9. In the File Name and Path text box, type **notes-tol** after the path, which should already be set to your `AutoCAD Bible` folder. Click OK. AutoCAD saves the block as a file.

10. Type **oops** ↵ to bring back the text.

11. Choose Zoom Extents from the Zoom flyout of the Standard toolbar. Save your drawing.

Inserting Blocks and Files into Drawings

Blocks that are defined in a drawing are inserted in the same way as separate drawing files. After you choose the location, AutoCAD lets you change the size and rotation of the block. This capability is ideal for parts libraries. Parts may be created at the size of 1 unit and then scaled or rotated as needed. Figure 18-8 shows a window block inserted at various scales and rotation angles.

Figure 18-8: A block of a window inserted at various rotation angles and scales

Using the Insert dialog box

To insert a block or file, follow these steps:

1. Choose Insert Block from the Draw toolbar to start the INSERT command. AutoCAD opens the Insert dialog box, shown in Figure 18-9.

2. You can insert a block or a file as follows:

 • To insert a block from within your drawing, click the Name drop-down list and choose one of the existing blocks.

 • To insert a file, click Browse. AutoCAD opens the Select Drawing File dialog box. Locate the file's drive and folder and then choose the file. A preview appears to the right. Click Open. The Insert dialog box displays the path of the file.

3. Uncheck Specify On-Screen in the Insertion point, Scale, and Rotation sections if you want to specify the insertion point, scale, and rotation angle in the dialog box. Then provide the requested information in the dialog box.

Figure 18-9: The Insert dialog box

4. Check the Explode check box if you want to insert the block as individual objects instead of as one block object.

5. Click OK to close the Insert dialog box.

6. If any of the Specify On-Screen checkboxes were checked, AutoCAD prompts you for the necessary information:

 - At the `Specify insertion point:` prompt (which varies depending on whether or not you checked the Explode check box in Step 4), specify the insertion point. AutoCAD displays the block with its base point at the cursor so you can see how it looks.

 - At the `Enter X scale factor, specify opposite corner,` or [Corner/XYZ] <1>: prompt, press Enter to accept the default scale factor of 1, or type another scale. The Specify Opposite Corner option lets you define a square box whose side defines the scale factor. A side of 1 unit results in a scale factor of 1. If you specify the X scale factor, AutoCAD now prompts you for the Y scale factor. The default is the same scale as X, but you can specify a different one. For 3D models, use the XYZ option to specify all three scale factors. (If you checked Explode, the prompt is slightly different and you specify the scale factor for all directions at once.)

 - At the `Specify rotation angle <0>:` prompt, type in a rotation angle. You can also pick a point, and AutoCAD uses the angle from the insertion point to the point you picked as the rotation angle. This technique is useful for aligning a block with an existing object.

After you provide all the necessary information, AutoCAD inserts the block or file.

A negative scale factor for any of the axes creates a mirror image of the block or file. When you specify a negative X scale axis, the block is mirrored around the Y axis. When you specify a negative Y scale axis, the block is mirrored around the X axis. Figure 18-10 shows a door block inserted with positive and negative scale

factors. The rotation angle of all of the blocks is 0 degrees. By combining negative and positive scale factors with rotation angles, you can get any door configuration you want. Sometimes it can be difficult to visualize the result of a negative scale combined with a rotation angle. See the sidebar, "Presetting scale and rotation while inserting a block," for a solution.

When you insert a drawing file, paper space objects are not included in the block definition created in your drawing. To insert paper space objects in another drawing, open the original drawing and define the objects as a block. Then use the DesignCenter to insert that block into any other drawing.

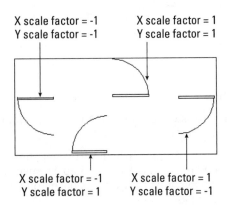

X scale factor = -1
Y scale factor = -1

X scale factor = 1
Y scale factor = 1

X scale factor = -1
Y scale factor = 1

X scale factor = 1
Y scale factor = -1

Figure 18-10: A door block inserted at various positive and negative scale factors, creating mirror images in different directions

Using the DesignCenter

When you want to insert a block from within another drawing, use the DesignCenter. Choose DesignCenter from the Standard toolbar. In the left pane, navigate to the drawing that contains the block you want. Double-click the drawing and choose Blocks from the list that appears. In the right pane you see a list of the blocks in that drawing. Click Preview to see a preview of each block you select. Click Description to see a description of the block. (The description only appears if you saved one when creating the block.) There are two ways to insert the block:

✦ If you double-click the block's icon, AutoCAD opens the Insert dialog box so you can specify exactly how you want to insert the block, just as I described earlier for blocks within a drawing.

✦ If you drag the block's icon onto the drawing area, AutoCAD inserts the block at the point where you release the mouse button, using the default scale and rotation.

You can also use the DesignCenter to insert entire drawings. In the left pane, navigate to the folder containing the drawing. The drawings are then listed in the right pane. Choose a drawing and drag it onto the drawing area. On the command line,

you will see that AutoCAD executes the -INSERT command, the command line version of INSERT. You can simply specify an insertion point, scale, and rotation, or you can use the options described in the sidebar, "Presetting scale and rotation while inserting a block."

Presetting scale and rotation while inserting a block

When you are dragging a block on the screen to specify an insertion point, it may be helpful to see the block at the scale and rotation angle you want. The problem is that the prompts for scale and rotation come after the prompt for the insertion point. If you use the command line version of INSERT, by typing **-insert,** you can preset the scale and rotation angle at the first prompt, using the options shown here. To use one of these options, right-click and choose the option from the shortcut menu at the `Specify insertion point or [Scale/X/Y/Z/Rotate/PScale/PX/PY/PZ/PRotate]:` prompt. All the prompts appear on the command line, including the prompt for the name of the block or file you want to insert.

Option	*Use*
Scale	Specifies the scale factor
X	Specifies the X scale factor
Y	Specifies the Y scale factor
Z	Specifies the Z scale factor
Rotate	Specifies the rotation angle
PScale	Specifies the preliminary scale factor for the display of the block as you drag it and prompts you again for the scale so you can change it
Pxscale	Specifies the preliminary X scale factor for the display of the block as you drag it and prompts you again for the scale so you can change it
Pyscale	Specifies the preliminary Y scale factor for the display of the block as you drag it and prompts you again for the scale so you can change it
PZscale	Specifies the preliminary Z scale factor for the display of the block as you drag it and prompts you again for the scale so you can change it
PRotate	Specifies the preliminary rotation angle for the display of the block as you drag it and prompts you again for the rotation angle so you can change it

On the CD-ROM

The drawings you need for the following Step-by-Step exercise on inserting blocks, `ab14-b.dwg` and `ab18-c.dwg`, are in the `Drawings` folder of the *AutoCAD 2004 Bible* CD-ROM.

Step-by-Step: Inserting Blocks

1. Open `ab18-c.dwg` from the CD-ROM.

2. Save the file as `ab18-03.dwg` in your `AutoCAD Bible` folder. This is the floor plan of the first floor of a house, as shown in Figure 18-11. Many of the doors and a toilet need to be inserted. OSNAP should be on. Set running object snaps for endpoint and midpoint. The current layer is Door.

3. Use Zoom Window to zoom in on the left third of the house.

Figure 18-11: The floor plan of the house needs some doors and a new toilet.

4. Choose Insert Block from the Draw toolbar. In the Name drop-down list of the Insert dialog box, choose DOOR (if it is not already selected). Check all three Specify On-Screen check boxes. Click OK to close the Insert dialog box.

Tip If you make a mistake while inserting a door, press Esc if you are in the middle of the prompts. If you have completed the command, click Undo on the Standard toolbar or erase the door and start over.

5. As you move the cursor, you can see the dragged image of a door. This image shows you the block at an X and Y scale of 1 and a 0-degree rotation angle. Follow the prompts:

```
Specify insertion point or
[Scale/X/Y/Z/Rotate/PScale/PX/PY/PZ/PRotate]: Use the
Endpoint object snap to pick ❶ in Figure 18-11.
Enter X scale factor, specify opposite corner, or
[Corner/XYZ] <1>: -1 ↵
Enter Y scale factor <use X scale factor>: 1 ↵
Specify rotation angle <0>: 270 ↵ (You could also specify -90
degrees.)
```

6. Repeat the INSERT command. The Insert dialog box already shows the DOOR block. Click OK. Follow the prompts. You'll probably want to use Zoom Window to zoom into the area of ❷ in Figure 18-11.

```
Specify insertion point or
[Scale/X/Y/Z/Rotate/PScale/PX/PY/PZ/PRotate]: Pick ❷ in
Figure 18-11.
Enter X scale factor, specify opposite corner, or
[Corner/XYZ] <1>: 2/3 ↵
Enter Y scale factor <use X scale factor>: ↵
Specify rotation angle <0>: 180 ↵
```

7. If you zoomed in for the previous step, return to the previous view using Zoom Previous. Zoom in to the area around ❸ in Figure 18-11. Choose Insert Block from the Draw toolbar. Click OK. Follow the prompts:

```
Specify insertion point or
[Scale/X/Y/Z/Rotate/PScale/PX/PY/PZ/PRotate]: Pick ❸ in
Figure 18-11.
Enter X scale factor or specify opposite corner, or
[Corner/XYZ] <1>: -3/4 ↵
Enter Y scale factor <use X scale factor>: 3/4 ↵
Specify rotation angle <0>: 315 ↵
```

8. Use Zoom Dynamic to zoom in to the area around ❹ and ❺ in Figure 18-11. Choose Insert Block from the Draw toolbar. Click OK. Follow the prompts:

```
Specify insertion point or
[Scale/X/Y/Z/Rotate/PScale/PX/PY/PZ/PRotate]: Pick ❹ in
Figure 18-11.
Enter X scale factor, specify opposite corner, or
[Corner/XYZ] <1>: 1 ↵
Enter Y scale factor <use X scale factor>: ↵
Specify rotation angle <0>: 270 ↵
```

9. Repeat the INSERT command and click OK. Follow the prompts:

```
Specify insertion point or
[Scale/X/Y/Z/Rotate/PScale/PX/PY/PZ/PRotate]: Pick ❺ in
Figure 18-11.
Enter X scale factor, specify opposite corner, or
[Corner/XYZ] <1>: -1 ↵ Enter Y scale factor <use X scale
factor>: 1 ↵
Specify rotation angle <0>: 90 ↵
```

10. Use Zoom Dynamic to zoom in on the area around ❻ and ❼ in Figure 18-11. Start the INSERT command and click OK. Follow the prompts:

```
Specify insertion point or
[Scale/X/Y/Z/Rotate/PScale/PX/PY/PZ/PRotate]: Pick ❻ in
Figure 18-11.
Enter X scale factor, specify opposite corner, or
[Corner/XYZ] <1>: -2/3 ↵
Enter Y scale factor <use X scale factor>: 2/3 ↵
Specify rotation angle: 270 ↵
```

11. Repeat the INSERT command and click OK. Follow the prompts:

```
Specify insertion point or
[Scale/X/Y/Z/Rotate/PScale/PX/PY/PZ/PRotate]: Pick ❼ in
Figure 18-11.
Enter X scale factor, specify opposite corner, or
[Corner/XYZ] <1>: 2/3 ↵
Enter Y scale factor <use X scale factor>: ↵
Specify rotation angle: 90 ↵
```

12. Beneath the doors you just inserted is a water closet with a toilet. Pan down to it. Erase the toilet, which is a block. Change the current layer to FIXTURE.

13. Choose DesignCenter from the Standard toolbar. (If you don't see the two panes, click Tree View Toggle on the DesignCenter toolbar.) In the left pane, navigate to your CD-ROM drive. (You may need to use the horizontal scroll bar if the left side of the list of drives and folders is not in view.) Double-click the CD-ROM drive and then double-click ab14-b.dwg. Click Blocks from the list of named objects. On the right, you see the blocks in the drawing.

14. Double-click TOILET2. You see a preview at the bottom of the DesignCenter. (If not, click Preview on the DesignCenter toolbar.) The Insert dialog box opens. Because you can see the preview, you know the rotation angle is correct and you can assume that the scale is correct because toilets are generally about the same size. The Insertion Point Specify On-Screen check box should be checked. The other Specify On-Screen checkboxes should be unchecked. Click OK.

15. Drag the toilet into the water closet and use a Midpoint object snap to place it at the middle of the bottom wall of the water closet. If you want, choose DesignCenter on the Standard bar to close the DesignCenter (or click its Close button).

16. Do a Zoom Extents and save your drawing.

AutoCAD also has a MINSERT command that lets you insert blocks in a rectangular array. Type **minsert** ↵. MINSERT prompts you for an insertion point, scale factors, and rotation angle using the same prompts as the INSERT command, without the dialog box. It then starts the same prompts as the Rectangular option of the ARRAY command, asking for the number of rows and columns and the distance between them. The value of MINSERT is that it reduces the size of your drawing because AutoCAD saves the array as one block object. The disadvantage is that you cannot edit the individual blocks in the array or the array as a whole in any way. If you need to edit them, erase the entire array of blocks, redefine the single block, if necessary, and start over, this time using DDINSERT and ARRAY separately. You cannot explode a minserted block.

Managing Blocks

Several factors require care when working with blocks. Large libraries of blocks need to be well managed so that you can find the block you need quickly. You also need to consider the issue of which layers you use when you define your blocks, so that you get the desired results when you insert them.

Working with layers

You may want a block to take on the current layer when inserted or to retain its original layer. AutoCAD lets you manage block layers and their color and linetype properties to obtain the desired result. A block can be defined in four ways to determine what layer, color, linetype, and lineweight properties it will use when it is inserted, as shown in Table 18-1. Each method has different results when the block is inserted, although some of the differences are minor.

As you can see, careful planning of the layers you use when creating a block is essential. As Table 18-1 makes clear, two of the methods (setting the objects to ByBlock and creating them on layer 0) create chameleon blocks that take on the properties of the current layer. Use the other two methods when you want the block to retain its properties regardless of the current layer.

Creating blocks on layer 0 is the simplest method. If you want the blocks to have a specific color and linetype, create a layer for them and switch to that layer before inserting the blocks. You can also change the layer of a block, after it is inserted, in the same way that you change the layer of any object.

Table 18-1
Properties of Block Component Objects and Insertion Results

Properties of Component Objects	Insertion Results
On any layer (except layer 0), with color, lineweight, and linetype set to ByLayer	The block keeps properties of that layer. If you insert a block into another drawing without that layer, AutoCAD creates the layer. If you insert the block into another drawing with that layer, but the layer has a different color and linetype properties, the block takes on properties of the layer that are different from those you created it on. If you insert the block on a different layer, the block keeps the properties of the layer on which it was created, but the Properties palette reports the block as being on the layer on which it was inserted because it reports the layer of the insertion point, not the block objects.

Continued

Table 18-1 *(continued)*

Properties of Component Objects	Insertion Results
On any layer (except 0), color, linetype, and lineweight set explicitly	The block keeps the color, linetype, and lineweight with properties that were explicitly set. If you insert the block into another drawing, AutoCAD creates the layer on which original objects were made.
On any layer (except layer 0), with color, linetype, and lineweight set to By	The block takes on the color of the current color Blocksetting. (If the current color is set to ByLayer, the block will take on the current layer's color.) If you insert the block into another drawing, AutoCAD creates the layer on which original objects were made. Note: If the color, linetype, and lineweight are ByBlock when you create objects for a block, the objects are always shown with black/white color, a continuous linetype, and the default lineweight.
On layer 0 (with color, linetype, and lineweight set to ByBlock or ByLayer)	The block takes on the layer and properties of the current layer it is inserted on. If you insert the block into another drawing, no layers are created.

 On the CD-ROM The drawing that you need for the following Step-by-Step exercise on working with blocks and layers, ab18-d.dwg, is in the Drawings folder of the *AutoCAD 2004 Bible* CD-ROM.

Step-by-Step: Working with Blocks and Layers

1. Open ab18-d.dwg from the CD-ROM.

2. Save the file as ab18-04.dwg in your AutoCAD Bible folder. This is a portion of an electrical schematic, as shown in Figure 18-12. OSNAP should be on. Set running object snaps for endpoint, midpoint, quadrant, and intersection.

3. Choose Make Block from the Draw toolbar. In the Name text box of the Block Definition dialog box, type **hl switch**. Choose Select Objects. Use a selection window to select the entire hi-limit switch box (not including the text labels). Right-click to end selection. Choose Pick point in the Base point section of the dialog box. Use the Quadrant object snap to pick the left quadrant of the left circle in the switch, at ❶ in Figure 18-12. Choose Retain in the Objects section. Click OK. The objects in this block were created on the Object layer, which is red with a continuous linetype. The color, linetype, and lineweight are set to ByLayer.

Figure 18-12: The electrical schematic has several symbols that would be useful as blocks.

4. Use a selection window to select the air damper switch. (The objects are currently on the Object layer, which is red with a continuous linetype.) Click the Color Control drop-down list box and choose ByBlock. Do the same with the Linetype Control and the Lineweight Control drop-down boxes. The switch turns black (or white if you are using a black screen). The objects are still selected.

5. Choose Make Block again from the Draw toolbar. In the Name text box, type **ad switch**. The dialog box says `4 objects selected`. Choose Pick point. Use the Quadrant object snap to pick the left quadrant of the left circle in the switch. Click OK.

6. Use a selection window to select the top conduit symbol at ❷ in Figure 18-12 (it is four objects). (It is currently on the Conduit layer, which is black and has a linetype of Hidden2.) Use the Color Control drop-down list box to set the color to green. Use the Linetype Control drop-down list box to set the linetype to Hidden2. Choose Make Block from the Draw toolbar. In the Name text box, type **top conduit**. The dialog box tells you that four objects are selected. Choose Pick point. Use the Intersection object snap to pick ❸. Click OK. The conduit appears green with the Hidden2 linetype.

7. Use a selection window to select the bottom conduit at ❹. (It is currently on the Conduit layer, which is black and has a linetype of Hidden2.) Use the Layer Control drop-down list box to set the layer to 0. Choose Make Block from the Draw toolbar. In the block Name text box, type **bot conduit**. The dialog box tells you that four objects are selected. Choose Pick point. Use the Intersection object snap to pick ❺. Click OK. The conduit appears black with a continuous linetype.

8. Save your drawing. Choose File ➪ New. In the Select Template dialog box, click the down arrow next to the Open button. Choose one of the Open with no Template options. AutoCAD opens a new drawing with only one layer, layer 0. (Click the Layer Control drop-down list to check, if you want.)

9. Choose DesignCenter from the Standard toolbar. In the left pane, locate your `AutoCAD Bible` folder and then locate `ab18-4.dwg`. Double-click the drawing, and then click Blocks. In the right pane, double-click `h1 switch`. In the Insert dialog box, check Specify On-Screen for Insertion point and Scale. Click OK. Follow the prompts to insert the file anywhere in the drawing, using a scale factor of 3. The block, whose objects were created on the Object layer, retained its original color (red), linetype, and lineweight but is listed as being on layer 0. Select the block and look at the Layer Control drop-down list to verify this.

10. Check the Layer Control drop-down list. A new layer, `Object`, is the layer that the original objects were on.

11. In the right pane of the DesignCenter, double-click `top conduit`. In the Insert dialog box, click OK. Follow the prompts to insert the file anywhere in the drawing, using a scale factor of 3. Again, the object retains its explicitly set properties of green color and Hidden2 linetype but is listed as being on layer 0. Click the Layer Control drop-down list to see that the Conduit layer has been added to the drawing.

12. Click the Color Control drop-down list on the Object Properties toolbar and choose Cyan to make it the current color.

13. In the DesignCenter's right pane, double-click `ad switch`. In the Insert dialog box, click OK. Follow the prompts to insert the file anywhere in the drawing, using a scale factor of 3. The block (whose objects were created on the Object layer and whose properties were set to ByBlock) takes on the current color of Cyan and is listed on layer 0.

14. Choose Layer Properties Manager from the Layers toolbar and click New in the Layer Properties Manager. Name the new layer `Green` and set its color to Green. Click Current to make it the current layer and then click OK.

15. Double-click `bot conduit`. In the Insert dialog box, click OK. Follow the prompts to insert the file anywhere in the drawing, using a scale factor of 3. The block, whose original objects were on layer 0, has the properties of layer Green and is listed on layer Green.

16. Click the DesignCenter's Close button to close the DesignCenter. Do not save this new drawing.

Exploding blocks

You can explode blocks into their original objects. You may need to do this to edit a block. If you want, you can then redefine the block as explained earlier in this chapter. To explode a block, choose Explode from the Modify toolbar. (You can select objects before or after choosing the command.) You can also explode polylines, dimensions, hatches, regions, multilines, and certain 3D objects (bodies, 3D meshes, 3D solids, polyface meshes, and polygon meshes) into simpler types of

objects. (Drawing in 3D is covered in Part IV.) When you explode a block with nested blocks, AutoCAD only explodes the top-level block. You need to use EXPLODE again to explode the next level of blocks.

When you explode blocks that were created on layer 0 or with BYBLOCK objects, the objects return to their original status and appear black/white with a continuous linetype and default lineweight again.

If you insert a block with different X and Y scales, AutoCAD does its best to create objects based on their new shapes. For example, if you have a block that includes a circle and insert it with an X scale of 1 and a Y scale of 2, you see an ellipse. Therefore, when you explode the block, AutoCAD creates an ellipse from what used to be a circle.

Using the XPLODE command

The XPLODE command is a version of the EXPLODE command that you can use to control the final layer, color, and linetype of the objects. If you select more than one object, you can set the properties for all the objects you select at once, that is, globally, or for each object individually.

To xplode an object, type **xplode** ↵. (XPLODE is actually an AutoLISP program.) At the Select objects: prompt, select one or more blocks. If you select more than one object, XPLODE displays the XPlode Individually/<Globally>: prompt. Right-click and choose Individually to get prompts for each block individually. Press Enter to accept the Globally default option. If you choose the Individually option, XPLODE highlights each block in turn so you know which block you are working on as you respond to prompts.

At the Enter an option [All/Color/LAyer/LType/LWeight/Inherit from parent block/Explode] <Explode>: prompt, choose whether you want to specify color, layer, linetype, lineweight, or all four. The Color option has been updated to enable you to specify true colors using the RGB system. (See Chapter 11 for more information.) The Inherit from parent block option works only for blocks created on layer 0 whose color and linetype were also set to ByBlock. These ByBlock objects then retain their color and linetype after you explode them.

Xplode cannot explode blocks whose X and Y scale factors have unequal absolute values. That means an X scale of 1 and a Y scale of –1 is okay, but not an X scale of 2 and a Y scale of –3.

On the CD-ROM

The drawing that you need for the following Step-by-Step exercise on exploding and xploding blocks, ab18-e.dwg, is in the Drawings folder of the *AutoCAD 2004 Bible* CD-ROM.

Step-by-Step: Exploding and Xploding Blocks

1. Open `ab18-e.dwg` from the CD-ROM.

2. Save the file as `ab18-05.dwg` in your `AutoCAD Bible` folder. This is the same electrical schematic used in the previous exercise, except that the objects are now blocks that have been inserted. (See Figure 18-13.) OSNAP should be on. Set running object snaps for endpoint, midpoint, quadrant, and intersection. The current layer is Object.

Figure 18-13: The electrical schematic has several blocks that have been inserted.

3. Choose Explode from the Modify toolbar. At the `Select objects:` prompt, choose the air damper switch at ❶ in Figure 18-13. Press Enter to end selection. The switch turns black or white (the opposite of your screen color) because it was created from objects whose color and linetype were set to ByBlock.

4. Choose Undo from the Standard toolbar.

5. Type **xplode** ↵. At the `Select objects:` prompt, choose the air damper switch again. Press Enter to end selection. At the `Enter an option [All/Color/LAyer/LType/LWeight/Inherit from parent block/Explode] <Explode>:` prompt, right-click and choose Layer. At the `Enter new layer name for exploded objects <OBJECT>:` prompt, press Enter to accept the default of OBJECT, the current layer. AutoCAD informs you `Object exploded onto layer OBJECT`.

6. Choose the `hi-limit` switch at ❷. Choose Explode from the Modify toolbar. AutoCAD explodes the block onto the Object layer because these objects were created on that layer with their color and linetype set to ByLayer.

7. Type **xplode** ↵. The top conduit was created from objects set explicitly to green color and hidden2 linetype. The bottom conduit was created from objects set to layer 0. Follow the prompts:

```
Select objects: Choose the conduits at ❸ and ❹. End
selection.
2 objects found.
Xplode Individually/<Globally>: ↵ to accept the default.
Enter an option [All/Color/LAyer/LType/LWeight/Inherit from
parent block/Explode] <Explode>: Right-click and choose All.
New Color [Truecolor/COlorbook]  <BYLAYER>: ↵
Enter new linetype name for exploded objects <BYLAYER>: ↵
Enter new lineweight < BYLAYER >: ↵
Enter new layer name for exploded objects <OBJECT>: conduit ↵
Objects exploded with color of BYLAYER, linetype of BYLAYER,
and layer conduit.
```

8. Save your drawing.

Editing blocks

Blocks can be complex objects. You may need to add, remove, or change a component of a block. Here are a few additional points that can help you work with blocks.

Double-clicking to edit blocks

You can edit a block using the REFEDIT command, which is explained in detail in Chapter 19, because it is often used with external references. Double-click the block to open the Reference Edit dialog box. See Chapter 19 for more details.

Editing blocks with grips

To a certain extent, you can use grip editing with blocks. By default, when you select a block, only one grip — at the base point — is displayed. However, you can show the grips of all the objects by choosing Tools ⇨ Options. On the Selection tab, choose Enable grips within blocks and click OK. Figure 18-14 shows the results of both settings.

As a general rule, you don't want to enable grips for blocks when working with such complex blocks. However, you can turn them on to use grips to mirror, rotate, move, or scale the block if you want to use the grip of a component object as a base point for the edit.

Updating blocks

As I mentioned earlier in the chapter, when you redefine a block, all instances of that block are automatically updated. However, if you inserted a file to use as a block in a drawing and then changed the file, AutoCAD has no way of knowing of the change in that drawing. (Use an external reference instead to solve this problem. See Chapter 19.)

Single grip at base point

Figure 18-14: By default, AutoCAD displays only one grip at the base point for a block. You can also choose to display the grips for all the component objects.

Thanks to Sid Herbage of Mississauga, Ontario, for this drawing of a quadricycle engine.

To update blocks that came from inserting files, you can reinsert the file. Follow these steps:

1. Choose Insert Block.

2. Click Browse.

3. Choose the file you have changed and click Open. (You must locate the actual file rather than choose the block of the same name that already exists in the drawing.)

4. AutoCAD asks if you want to redefine the block because that block already exists in the drawing. Choose Yes.

5. Press Esc to avoid actually inserting a new copy of the block.

AutoCAD updates all the instances of the block with the new file. You can also use the DesignCenter to insert and update blocks.

Substituting blocks

You can also substitute a different file. There are three reasons for doing this:

✦ If you have many instances of complex blocks, you may find that regen times are slow. You can create a simple block, WBLOCK it, and substitute it for the original blocks until plotting time. This is similar to using QTEXT to replace text with rectangles. (See Chapter 13.)

✦ You can create more than one version of a drawing—for example, an office layout with various kinds of desks. You can create the drawing with one type of desk, inserting files of the desks. Substitute a file of another type of desk, and you have a new office layout design.

✦ Another common reason to substitute blocks is when your company switches to a different standard for a part.

To substitute blocks, follow these steps:

1. Type **-insert** ↵ on the command line.

2. Type **blockname=filename** where `blockname` is the name of the block and file name is the name of the file. (If the file is not in AutoCAD's support file search path, type the entire path.) Press Enter.

> **Note**
> To place a folder in AutoCAD's support file search path, choose Tools ⇨ Options and click the File tab. Double-click Support File Search Path. Click Add, and then type the path or browse to it. After you're done, click OK to close the Options dialog box.

3. AutoCAD tells you that the block with this name already exists and asks if you want to redefine it. Type **y** ↵.

4. Press Esc to avoid actually inserting a new copy of the new file.

AutoCAD replaces the current blocks with the file you inserted.

> **New Feature**
> The Express Tools command, BLOCKREPLACE (choose Express ⇨ Blocks ⇨ Replace Block with Another Block) is another way to substitute blocks. Another Express Tools command, NCOPY, (choose Express ⇨ Blocks ⇨ Copy Nested Objects) copies objects nested inside blocks or xrefs. XLIST, (choose Express ⇨ Blocks ⇨ List Xref/Block Properties) lists properties of nested objects within blocks. SHP2BLK (choose Express ⇨ Modify ⇨ Convert Shape to Block) converts a shape definition to a block. (For information on installing Express Tools, see Appendix A on the CD-ROM. For information on shape definitions, see Chapter 32.)

Usually when you insert a file into a drawing, the block name and file name are the same. Likewise, when you WBLOCK a block, you usually name the file with the name of the block. Be aware that when you use block substitution, you have a block in your drawing that is the same as a file of a different name. For example, if you have a block in your drawing called `smalldesk` and substitute a file called `bigdesk`, you now have a block called `smalldesk` that is actually the same as the file `bigdesk`. This can get confusing, so use block substitution with care.

On the CD-ROM

Wb.exe unzips to three programs that create a list of blocks in your drawing and writes them to separate drawing files. Display the list of blocks and open selected drawings from the list; and, after you modify them, update those drawings as blocks in your current drawing. Look in \Software\Chap18\Wb. *MPE-arch* is a library of mechanical, plumbing, and electrical symbols for architectural drawings, mostly lights and outlets. Mpe.dwg contains all the symbols and can be used as a legend. Look in \Software\Chap18\Mpe-arch.

Organizing blocks

Parts or symbols libraries may take two forms — individual files for each part or symbol, or drawings that include many parts or symbols. You have already worked with individual files in this chapter. One technique that works well for some applications is to create 1-unit by 1-unit blocks. You can then easily insert them at any X or Y scale without much calculation.

You can also create files that include many parts or symbols to simplify the number of files you have to keep track of. Each part or symbol should be saved as a block with a preview and perhaps a description. To further simplify matters, you can label the blocks and print out the drawing to use as reference. When you need a part or symbol, follow these steps:

1. Choose DesignCenter from the Standard toolbar.

2. Navigate to the file with your parts or symbols and double-click it.

3. Click Blocks.

4. In the right pane of the DesignCenter, double-click the block you want.

5. Use the Insert dialog box to insert the block.

A simple method to manage blocks is to maintain a block book with each block file or library file printed out and labeled. Insertion points should be marked. You can do this by choosing a visible point style and placing a point on each block using the Node object snap.

New Feature The new Tools Palette is another way to access your blocks. See Chapter 26.

A consistent naming scheme is essential. Choose names that are both meaningful and consistent throughout. Organizing a folder (directory) scheme for block and library files is equally important. Your block book should include the location of each block or library file and an overall diagram of the folder scheme. If you use a separate file for each block, you may have hundreds or even thousands of files to keep track of. Find logical categories so that you can place related blocks together. Finally, make sure you keep the book updated as you add and change blocks and libraries.

Using Windows Features

You can also insert objects by copying them from other drawings and pasting them into your current drawing or using the drag-and-drop feature. You may be able to insert objects in this way without creating blocks.

Manipulating objects with the Windows clipboard

You are probably familiar with cutting or copying data in other Windows applications and then pasting it, either within a file or from file to file. Table 18-2 compares copying, using blocks, and using the clipboard (with the CUTCLIP, COPYCLIP, and PASTECLIP commands) in AutoCAD.

Table 18-2 Comparison of Methods of Moving/Copying Objects	
Method	**Features**
MOVE/COPY	Precise placement of objects; only works within a drawing.
BLOCK/WBLOCK/INSERT	Precise placement of objects; can scale and rotate; creates block definition; can insert many times even after other commands; can insert files (other drawings) that you save permanently. With the DesignCenter or Tool Palette, you can insert blocks from other drawings.
CUTCLIP/COPYCLIP/PASTECLIP	No precise placement of objects (uses bottom-left corner of extents of object(s) you copy); creates anonymous block in file with a name like A$CE314; can scale and rotate; can both move and copy objects; can insert (paste) many times; can copy from drawing to drawing or to other Windows applications.

In general, for one-time moving or copying with a drawing, you should use the MOVE or COPY command. If you want to copy an object several times over a period of time, use a BLOCK command. Use the clipboard when you want to insert objects into another drawing one or more times without saving the objects. Also, the clipboard is indispensable for copying objects to other applications.

To place objects on the clipboard, first select them. To move them, choose Cut to Clipboard on the Standard toolbar. To copy them, choose Copy to Clipboard. If you want to paste them in another drawing, open it. Choose Paste from Clipboard on the Standard toolbar. AutoCAD prompts you for an insertion point.

Cross-
Reference
Chapter 27 covers moving and copying objects to other applications.

Using drag-and-drop

Windows' drag-and-drop feature enables you to drag another drawing file into your drawing. Then AutoCAD prompts you as it would if you inserted the file using the -INSERT command. You need to open either My Computer or Windows Explorer. In the following steps, I use Windows Explorer.

To insert a drawing file using drag-and-drop, follow these steps:

1. Open Windows Explorer (Choose Start ➪ Programs ➪ Windows Explorer).

2. In the Folders window, click the folder containing the drawing file you want to insert.

3. Locate the drawing file.
 • If the AutoCAD window is visible, drag the drawing file into the AutoCAD window.
 • If the AutoCAD window is not visible, drag the drawing file onto the AutoCAD button on the task bar, wait for AutoCAD to open, and then drag the file into the AutoCAD window.

4. Respond to the prompts of the -INSERT command on the command line.

Figure 18-15 shows dragging a drawing from Windows Explorer into an open AutoCAD drawing. When you drag the file into the drawing area, you see a plus sign at the cursor (or a rectangular cursor, depending on your operating system), indicating that you can drop the file.

To open a drawing instead of inserting, drag the file onto the AutoCAD title bar at the very top of the application window.

You can open a drawing file by double-clicking its icon in Internet Explorer.

Tip
If you really don't know where the file is, or are not even sure of its name, use the Windows Find feature. Choose Start ➪ Find/Search ➪ Files or Folders. In the screen that appears, set the criteria for the file. For example, you could find all drawings starting with the letter C by typing **c*.dwg** in the Named text box. From the resulting list, choose the drawing you want and drag it onto your drawing using the same steps listed previously.

Drag-and-drop is easy to use. It is a helpful tool if you aren't sure where the file you want is located because it is easier to navigate with Windows Explorer than from the Select Drawing File dialog box.

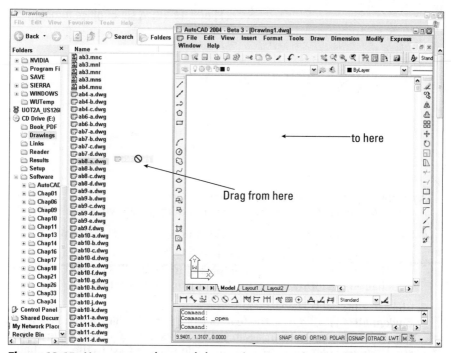

Figure 18-15: You can use drag-and-drop to insert one drawing file into another.

You can also drag an object from one drawing to another. First open both drawings. It helps to be able to see them both at once. Choose Window ➪ Tile Vertically to see them side by side. Select the object or objects you want to copy. Now click the object or objects again—and hold down the mouse button until the cursor displays a small rectangle. Then drag the object(s) to the other drawing.

On the CD-ROM The drawings that you need for the following Step-by-Step exercise on using the Windows clipboard and drag-and-drop, `ab18-f-1.dwg` and `ab18-f-2.dwg`, are in the `Drawings` folder of the *AutoCAD 2004 Bible* CD-ROM.

Step-by-Step: Using the Windows Clipboard and Drag-and-Drop

1. Open `ab18-f-1.dwg` from the CD-ROM. This is a set of office furniture, as shown in Figure 18-16.

2. Pick the chair, which is a block and choose Copy to Clipboard from the Standard toolbar.

Figure 18-16: A set of office furniture

3. Choose Open from the Standard toolbar. Open `ab18-f-2.dwg` from the CD-ROM. This is the plan of an office building, as shown in Figure 18-17.

4. Save the drawing as `ab18-06.dwg` in your `AutoCAD Bible` folder.

5. Choose Paste from Clipboard from the Standard toolbar. At the `Specify insertion point:` prompt, pick ❶ in Figure 18-17. AutoCAD inserts the armchair in the lobby using the default scale and rotation.

6. Choose Window ➪ Tile Vertically. You can now see both drawings at once. Click in `ab-f-1.dwg` to activate it. Select the chair. Click and hold the left mouse button on the chair again until you see the small rectangle at the cursor. Drag the chair into `ab18-06.dwg` and place it next to the first chair.

7. Click the Close button of `ab-f-1.dwg`. (You don't need to save any changes.) Click the Maximize button of `ab18-06.dwg`.

8. From the task bar menu, choose Start ➪ Programs ➪ Windows Explorer. Locate `ab18-f-1.dwg` on the CD-ROM. If necessary, resize the Exploring window so that you can see some of the AutoCAD window.

9. Drag `ab18-f-1.dwg` from its listing in Windows Explorer onto the AutoCAD drawing area and release the mouse button.

10. Use Zoom Window to zoom in to the area around ❷ in Figure 18-17. At the prompt, pick ❷.

11. Press Enter three times to accept the defaults. AutoCAD inserts the entire drawing.

12. Choose Zoom Previous from the Standard toolbar. Save your drawing. It should look like Figure 18-18.

As you can see, copying to the clipboard is ideal when you want to insert part of an existing drawing into another drawing. Drag-and-drop is also a simple way to insert one or more objects or an entire drawing.

Figure 18-17: The office plan

Figure 18-18: The office plan with added chairs and office furniture

Working with Attributes

Your drawings do not exist in a vacuum. The objects in your drawing represent real objects. These objects have characteristics that you cannot visually represent in a drawing, such as cost, manufacturer, date purchased, and so on. *Attributes* are labels that are attached to blocks. Using attributes, you can attach labels with pertinent data to blocks. You can then extract the data and import it into a database program or spreadsheet.

Cross-Reference You can also access and link to outside databases from within AutoCAD. See Chapter 20 for more information on external databases.

Attributes can also be used to place text relative to blocks. A common example is to use attributes for completing title block information, such as the drawing name, drawing number, date, scale, revision number, drafter, and so on. In this case, your plan is not to extract the data at all — you just use the attributes to help you precisely place the text in the title block.

Attributes have several limitations. They can only be attached to blocks. However, you can create a dummy block that contains only attributes. Also, the database features are limited. Nevertheless, attributes are quite useful for simple database needs as well as for placing text.

Defining an attribute essentially creates a template into which you can place values when you insert the block. You define a tag that is equivalent to a field or category in a database. When you insert the block, AutoCAD prompts you for the tag's value. For example, if your tag is COST, the value may be 865.79. This template is called an attribute definition.

Creating attribute definitions

The first procedure when working with attributes is to draw the individual objects that are to make up the block. The exception is when you want to create attributes without creating any other objects in the block. You might do this to extract attributes that apply to the drawing as a whole.

Tip If the block already exists, explode it and then redefine the block, adding the attributes.

After you have the objects, choose Draw ➪ Block ➪ Define Attributes to start the ATTDEF command. AutoCAD opens the Attribute Definition dialog box, shown in Figure 18-19.

Figure 18-19: The Attribute Definition dialog box

Mode section

In the Mode section of the dialog box, you set the attribute's properties, as shown in Table 18-3.

<table>
<tr><td colspan="2" align="center">Table 18-3
Attribute Modes</td></tr>
<tr><td>*Mode*</td><td>*Explanation*</td></tr>
<tr><td>Invisible</td><td>The attribute values you set are not displayed in the drawing. Use this for attributes that you want to extract into a database but do not want to see in the drawing. Examples would be model numbers, purchase dates, cost, and so on. If you are using attributes to place text in a drawing, of course you want them to be visible.</td></tr>
<tr><td>Constant</td><td>Sets a constant value for an attribute. AutoCAD automatically inserts the attribute value you set (in the Attribute section of the dialog box) and does not prompt you for a value. You might use this for the first three digits of employees' telephone numbers that have the same first three digits. You cannot edit constant attribute values.</td></tr>
<tr><td>Verify</td><td>When you insert an attribute, AutoCAD asks you to verify the value. Use this if you have a preset default.</td></tr>
<tr><td>Preset</td><td>AutoCAD automatically inserts a default value that you specify. For example, if the most common manufacturer of a chair is American Interiors, you can specify this as a preset value. As you insert the block, this default is inserted for you, and you have to type a value only if it differs from the default. (You need to insert the attribute with the ATTDIA system variable set to 1 to get a prompt allowing you to change the value. See the explanation of ATTDIA later in this chapter.)</td></tr>
</table>

Attribute section

In the Attribute section of the dialog box, specify the Tag, which is the name of the attribute. You use this tag when you extract the attributes. A tag is equivalent to a field in a database. When you import the data into a spreadsheet, for example, the tags would be the column heads. The tag name cannot include spaces or exclamation marks (!) and is converted to uppercase letters.

The Prompt is simply a plain-English version of the tag. AutoCAD uses the prompt to ask you for the value of the attribute. If the tag is PUR_DATE, you could define the prompt as Date Purchased.

The Value is used for setting a default value. You can use this if the value is usually the same.

Tip You can use the value to clarify a format that should be followed when entering information. For example, you could set the value of a date to dd/mm/yy so that users know how to format the date.

Text Options section

Use the Text Options settings to format the text. Choose a justification and text style from the drop-down text boxes. When you set the height, be sure to take into account the scale factor. You can also set a rotation angle for the text.

Insertion Point section

In the Insertion Point section, choose Pick Point to place the attribute. If you are using the attributes to place text in a schedule or title block, obviously the placement is very important. If you are inserting invisible attributes, simply place them near the block. If you are creating more than one attribute for a block, place the attribute so there is room for the other attributes underneath. When you have placed the attribute and completed the entire dialog box, click OK to end the ATTDEF command. By default, the insertion point is 0,0.

Caution If you are creating an attribute for a table or an electrical symbol, you don't want the insertion point to be 0,0. Instead, you want an insertion point near the block. If you forget to pick a point and click OK to close the dialog box, AutoCAD automatically places the insertion point at 0,0. If 0,0 isn't visible on the screen, you don't see the attribute—it seems to disappear! You can choose Undo from the Standard toolbar and create a new attribute in the right location or move the attribute as explained in the section on editing attributes later in this chapter.

After you define one attribute, the Align Below Previous Attribute Definition check box is active. Click this to line up succeeding attributes under the first one.

Now is the time to check that the attribute definitions are the way you want them. You can edit attribute definitions before they have been placed into a block in two ways:

✦ Choose Properties on the Standard toolbar, select one attribute definition, and edit all its properties, such as the tag, value, prompt, and modes. You can also change properties such as the layer, text style, and so on.

✦ Choose Modify ⇨ Object ⇨ Text ⇨ Edit and change the tag, the prompt, and the default (DDEDIT command).

Tip

If you are creating many blocks with similar attributes, you can copy just the attributes, modify them as just described, place them near other objects, and then create the blocks. This way, you don't have to define all the attributes from scratch.

Creating the block

After you create the objects and their attribute definitions, you generally create a block. Then choose Make Block from the Draw toolbar. Select the objects and the attributes in the block.

Tip

If the order of the attribute prompts is important, don't use a window to select the attributes — select them in the order in which you want the prompts to appear. You can then use a crossing or window box to select the rest of the objects to be included in the block. The order of the attribute prompts will be important if you are taking the data for the attributes from a listing — perhaps a spreadsheet that you have printed out. It will be much easier to insert the attribute values if the prompts follow the order of the printed document you are using.

Name the block and define the block's insertion point as you would normally. Generally, you want to check Delete From Drawing because you have no need for the block with the attribute tags in your drawing.

Don't forget to pay attention to the layer of the attributes just as you would the layer of the block objects. The same layer rules apply to attributes as to blocks.

Note

If you want to insert the objects and the attributes as a file instead of as a block, you don't need to create a block at all. Create a drawing containing just the objects and its attributes. Use the BASE command to change the base point of the drawing (usually 0,0) to the desired insertion point of the block. Then save the drawing. When you insert the drawing, AutoCAD prompts you for the attributes as usual. Use this technique for blocks and attributes that you use for more than one drawing, such as a title block.

After you create the block, you cannot edit the attributes in the Properties palette. I cover other techniques for editing attributes later in this chapter.

On the CD-ROM

The drawing that you need for the following Step-by-Step exercise on creating attributes, ab18-g.dwg, is in the Drawings folder of the *AutoCAD 2004 Bible* CD-ROM.

Step-by-Step: Creating Attributes

1. Open `ab18-g.dwg` from the CD-ROM. This is a plan of an office building zoomed in to one office. A file containing one set of office furniture has been inserted, as shown in Figure 18-20.

Figure 18-20: An office with a set of office furniture

2. Save the drawing as `ab18-07.dwg` in your `AutoCAD Bible` folder.

3. Choose Explode from the Modify toolbar, select the furniture in the office, and press Enter. This block has nested blocks. Choose the chair and explode it again to get its component objects.

4. Choose Draw ➪ Block ➪ Define Attributes. In the Attribute Definition dialog box, check Invisible in the Mode section.

5. In the Attribute section, enter the following:

```
Tag: mfr
Prompt: Manufacturer
Value: American Office Furniture
```

6. Click Pick Point to temporarily return to the drawing. Pick point ❶ in Figure 18-20. Leave the Text Options as they are. Click OK to end the command.

7. Repeat the ATTDEF command. Click Align below previous attribute definition. Enter the following:

```
Tag: pur_date
Prompt: Date purchased
Value: 3/91
```

8. Click OK.

9. Choose Make Block from the Draw toolbar. In the Name text box, type **arm-chair**. Click Select Objects. Select the entire chair plus the two attributes. End selection. In the dialog box, AutoCAD notes that 18 objects are selected. Choose Pick Point. Use the Endpoint object snap to choose ❷ as the base point. Check Delete. Click OK.

10. AutoCAD asks if you want to redefine the block because there is already a block definition with the same name in the drawing. Choose Yes.

11. Save your drawing. If you are continuing on to the next Step-by-Step exercise, leave the drawing open.

Redefining a block updates only block geometry, not attributes. Therefore, if you add attribute definitions to a block, only new blocks that you will insert include the attributes. Existing blocks don't gain these new attribute definitions. To update existing blocks with their current attribute definitions, use the ATTSYNC command.

Inserting blocks with attributes

After you define a block with attributes, you insert it as you would any block. AutoCAD automatically senses the existence of the attributes and prompts you for their values.

You can insert attributes either in a dialog box or on the command line. By default, you insert them on the command line. To use a dialog box, set the system variable ATTDIA to 1. You would use the command line to automate the insertion of attributes using an AutoLISP routine, menu item, or script file. When you use a dialog box, the Verify and Constant modes are not used.

The drawing that you need for the following Step-by-Step exercise on inserting blocks with attributes, ab18-07.dwg, is in your AutoCAD Bible folder if you did the previous exercise. Otherwise, you can find it in the Results folder of the *AutoCAD 2004 Bible* CD-ROM.

Step-by-Step: Inserting Blocks with Attributes

1. Use ab18-07.dwg if you have it open from the previous exercise. Otherwise, open it from the Results folder of the CD-ROM.

2. Save the drawing as ab18-08.dwg in your AutoCAD Bible folder.

3. Type **attdia** ↵. If it is currently set to 0, type **1** ↵.

4. Choose Insert Block from the Draw toolbar. Chose ARMCHAIR from the Name drop-down list. Verify that Specify On-Screen is checked only for Insertion Point and click OK.

5. Pick a point in front of the desk (turn off OSNAP if necessary). AutoCAD inserts the armchair and opens the Enter Attributes dialog box, as shown in Figure 18-21. The values that were entered when the attributes were defined are displayed, but you can change them.

Figure 18-21: The Enter Attributes dialog box

6. The default values exist because most of the furniture was purchased at one time when the office was opened. However, let's assume that this chair was purchased a year later. Change the purchase date to 3/92. Click OK. Because the attributes are invisible, you see only the chair, but the values are there in the drawing database.

7. Save the drawing.

Editing attributes

You can edit the properties of the attribute tags before you create the block, using the Properties palette or DDEDIT (choose Modify ➪ Object ➪ Text ➪ Edit). After you create the block, use the Block Attribute Manager. The Block Attribute Manager manages all the values and properties of block attributes in one place. Use the Block Attribute Manager and its Edit Attribute dialog box to edit any aspect of block attributes.

Editing attribute properties

After you insert a block and given values to its attributes, you can modify the following:

✦ Attribute prompt order

✦ Tag and prompt names

✦ Attribute visibility

✦ Text options

✦ Properties, that is, layer, linetypes, color, lineweight, and plot style

After you make your changes, you can update all the blocks in your drawing to reflect the changes.

Choose Modify ⇨ Object ⇨ Attribute ⇨ Block Attribute Manager to start the new BATTMAN command to open the Block Attribute Manager, shown in Figure 18-22. (You can also find the Block Attribute Manager on the Modify II toolbar.)

Figure 18-22: The Block Attribute Manager

From the Block drop-down list in the Block Attribute Manager, choose the block whose attribute values you want to change. You can also click Select block to select the block in your drawing. Use the Block Attribute Manager to:

✦ **Change the order of the attribute prompts when you insert a block with attributes.** Choose any attribute from the list in the Block Attribute Manager and click Move Down or Move Up. Continue to use this procedure until you have the order you want.

✦ **Delete an attribute.** Choose it and click Remove.

✦ **Change which attribute properties are listed in the Block Attribute Manager.** Click Settings. In the Settings dialog box, click all the properties you want to see listed. For example, you can include columns for layer, style (text style), and color. Click OK.

Tip
When you add properties to the listing in the Block Attribute Manager, resize the dialog box so that you can see all the columns.

✦ **Edit the attributes, including prompt, default, text display, and properties.** Click Edit to open the Edit Attribute dialog box, shown in Figure 18-23.

✦ **Update all the blocks in your drawing to reflect the changes you have made.** Click Sync. Usually you do this after using the Edit Attribute dialog box. Because changes such as attribute order and mode affect only new insertions of the block, this update brings existing blocks into concordance with new blocks.

Figure 18-23: The Edit Attribute dialog box

Use the Edit Attribute dialog box to edit all the properties of individual attributes. This dialog box has three tabs:

✦ **Attribute:** Change the mode and attribute properties. For example, in the Mode section you can change the visibility of attributes. In the Data section, change the tag, prompt, and default.

✦ **Text Options:** Change text style, height, justification, and so on.

✦ **Properties:** Change attribute layer, color, linetype, and so on.

After you finish making changes, click OK in the Edit Attribute dialog box to return to the Block Attribute Manager. Click OK to return to your drawing.

When you create invisible attributes, you can't edit them because you can't select them. The ATTDISP command controls attribute visibility globally, for all attributes in your drawing. Choose View ➪ Display ➪ Attribute Display and choose one of the following options. The currently active option is checked on the menu.

✦ **Normal:** Attributes that were created as visible are visible. Attributes that were created as invisible are invisible. This option is the default.

✦ **On:** All attributes are visible.

✦ **Off:** All attributes are invisible.

AutoCAD regenerates the drawing after you change the current option.

Changing attribute values

You may need to change the values of an attribute. Perhaps you entered the wrong purchase date or a part number changes. Choose Modify ➪ Object ➪ Attribute ➪ Single and select the block containing the attributes you want to change. (You can also type EATTEDIT on the command line or choose Edit Attribute on the Modify II toolbar.) You see the Enhanced Attribute Editor, shown in Figure 8-24.

Figure 18-24: The Enhanced Attribute Editor

As you can see, the Enhanced Attribute Editor is similar to the Edit Attribute dialog box. It has the same three tabs. However, the Attribute tab enables you to change attribute values, something you can't do in the Edit Attribute dialog box. To change an attribute's value, select it and type a new value in the Value text box.

The Text Options and Properties tabs of the Enhanced Attribute Editor are the same as in the Edit Attributes dialog box.

Caution If you explode a block with attribute values, you lose the attribute values.

Another way to change attribute values is to use the ATTEDIT command (on the command line) to open the Edit Attributes dialog box, shown in Figure 18-25.

If a block has a number of attributes and you want to change them all in order, this dialog box makes it easy to go through all the attributes quickly. Press Tab to go to the next attribute.

Note To edit attributes on the command line, type **-attedit**. At the Edit attributes one at a time? [Yes/No] <Y>: prompt, use the Yes option. This command then prompts you for changes in attribute values and properties, such as position, text style, color, and so on.

Figure 18-25: The Edit Attributes dialog box

Making global changes in attributes

You can also use the -ATTEDIT command on the command line to make global changes. If you answer No to the Edit attributes one at a time? [Yes/No] <Y>: prompt, you can make global changes to attribute values — for example, change all instances of A- in your part numbers to B-. You can even change invisible attribute values.

To use -ATTEDIT to make global changes, follow these steps:

1. Choose Modify ⇨ Object ⇨ Attribute ⇨ Global.

2. At the Edit attributes one at a time? [Yes/No] <Y>: prompt, type **n** ⏎.

3. At the Edit only attributes visible on screen? [Yes/No] <Y>: prompt, answer **y** or **n** ⏎, as desired. Answer n to edit invisible attributes, but you must know the attribute text string you want to change because it's invisible.

4. At the Enter block name specification <*>: prompt, you can type a block name to limit the changes to one block or press Enter to include any block.

5. At the Enter attribute tag specification <*>: prompt, you can type a tag to limit the changes to one tag type or press Enter to include any tag.

6. At the Enter attribute value specification <*>: prompt, you can type a value to limit the changes to one value or press Enter to include any value.

7. If you chose to edit only attributes visible on-screen, AutoCAD responds with the Select Attributes: prompt. (If not, skip to Step 8.) Pick each attribute you wish to modify or use a window. Press Enter to end selection. If you include other objects or blocks that do not fit the block name, attribute tag,

or attribute value specifications you made, AutoCAD does not select them. AutoCAD informs you how many attributes were selected.

8. At the `Enter string to change:` prompt, type the text string (any consecutive text) you want to change.

9. At the `Enter new string:` prompt, type the text string that will replace the old string.

If you chose to edit attributes not visible on the screen, AutoCAD regenerates the drawing and lists the changes it made.

Redefining attributes

You can redefine a block with attributes to include different objects and attributes, using the ATTREDEF command. Redefining a block lets you add or delete attributes or redefine a block that contains attributes. Follow these steps:

1. Explode one of the blocks with attributes. If there are nested blocks that you want to change, explode them, too.

2. If you want to add attributes, define and place them. Delete unwanted attributes. Make any other changes you want to the objects.

3. Type **attredef** ↵.

4. At the `Enter name of Block you wish to redefine:` prompt, type the name of the block.

5. At the `Select objects for new Block...:` prompt, select the objects and the attributes you wish to include. Do not include any existing attributes that you want to delete.

6. At the `Specify insertion base point of new Block:` prompt, pick the base point for the block.

Here's how AutoCAD handles the changes:

✦ If you created new attributes, AutoCAD places them for all existing blocks and gives them their default values.

✦ Any attributes that you did not change retain their old values for all existing blocks.

✦ Any attributes that you did not include in the new block definition are deleted from existing blocks.

On the CD-ROM The drawing that you need for the following Step-by-Step exercise on editing attributes, ab18-h.dwg, is in the Drawings folder of the *AutoCAD 2004 Bible* CD-ROM.

Step-by-Step: Editing Attributes

1. Open ab18-h.dwg from the CD-ROM.

2. Save the file as ab18-09.dwg in your AutoCAD Bible folder. This is a portion of an office building plan layout, shown in Figure 18-26.

3. Choose Modify ⇨ Object ⇨ Attribute ⇨ Single. At the Select a block: prompt, pick the chair at ❶ in Figure 18-26. In the Enhanced Attribute Editor, change the date purchased to 4/97. Notice that the manufacturer is American Office Furniture. Because these attributes are invisible, you can't see the result in the drawing. Click OK.

Figure 18-26: An office building plan layout

4. To see the attributes, choose View ⇨ Display ⇨ Attribute Display ⇨ On. You can now see the attributes for the chair as well as nearby attributes for the desk. To turn off the attributes, repeat the process, this time choosing the Normal option.

5. Choose Modify ⇨ Object ⇨ Attribute ⇨ Global. Follow the prompts:

```
Edit attributes one at a time? [Yes/No] <Y>: n ↵
Performing global editing of attribute values.
Edit only attributes visible on screen? [Yes/No] <Y>: n ↵
Drawing must be regenerated afterwards.
Enter block name specification <*>: armchair ↵
Enter attribute tag specification <*>: ↵
Enter attribute value specification <*>: ↵
6 attributes selected.
Enter string to change: American ↵
Enter new string: Acme ↵ (Press F2 to hide the text window if
it opens.)
```

6. Choose Explode from the Modify toolbar and select the chair at ❶ in Figure 18-26. The attributes reappear. Choose Draw ➪ Block ➪ Define Attributes. Create an invisible attribute with a tag and prompt of Color and a value of Dusty Blue. Click Pick Point and pick a point underneath the other two attributes of the armchair. (Exact placement is not important.) Choose OK.

7. Type **attredef** ↵. Follow the prompts:

```
Enter name of Block you wish to redefine: armchair ↵
Select objects for new Block...Select objects: Use a window
to select the chair and the three attributes. Press Enter to
end selection.
Specify insertion base point of new Block: Use an Endpoint
object snap to pick the endpoint at ❷.
```

The armchair block disappears.

8. Choose Insert Block. In the Insert dialog box, choose **armchair** from the Name drop-down list. With Specify On-Screen checked only for Insertion Point, click OK. Insert the chair at ❷. In the Enter Attributes dialog box, click OK to accept the values.

9. To verify that AutoCAD has redefined the block elsewhere, choose Modify ➪ Object ➪ Attribute ➪ Single. Select the block at ❸. Notice that the Color tag has been added with a value of Dusty Blue. Click OK to accept the values.

10. Use Zoom Window to zoom in closely to the telephone at ❹ in Figure 18-26. The telephone has a visible attribute of the phone number. The number is so small that it cannot usually be seen and so does not interfere with the drawing.

11. Choose Modify ➪ Object ➪ Attribute ➪ Block Attribute Manager. From the Block drop-down list, choose Phone. Click Edit.

12. On the Attribute tab of the Edit Attribute dialog box, change the prompt to **Extension.** On the Text Options tab, choose Fit from the Justification drop-down list. On the Properties tab, choose Blue (if you're using a white back-ground) or Cyan (if you're using a black background) from the Color drop-down list. Click OK twice to return to your drawing.

The text of the phone extension is now blue and fills up the entire rectangle on the phone.

13. Choose Zoom Previous from the Standard toolbar. Save the drawing.

New Feature

The Express Tools command BURST (choose Express ➪ Blocks ➪ Explode Attributes to Text) converts attributes to text. ATTOUT and ATTIN (choose Express ➪ Blocks ➪ Export.) Attribute Information and Import Attribute Information work together to enable you to edit attributes in another program. ATTOUT creates a tab-delimited file that you can open in Notepad or Excel, for example. When you use ATTIN, existing blocks are updated with the new attribute information.

Extracting a database from attributes

After you insert all your blocks and attributes, you can extract the data using the Attribute Extraction Wizard, shown in Figure 18-27. To start the wizard, choose Tools ➪ Attribute Extraction.

Figure 18-27: The first screen of the Attribute Extraction Wizard

On the Select Drawing screen of the wizard, choose where you want to extract attributes from. Most often, you want to keep the default of Current Drawing. However, you can select objects (blocks) within the drawing or choose an entirely different drawing. Then click Next.

On the Settings screen of the wizard are two check boxes:

✦ **Include xrefs:** External references (covered in Chapter 19) can also contain attributes. Check this box if you want to extract attributes from external references that are attached to the drawing

✦ **Include nested blocks:** If you want to extract attributes from blocks inside of blocks, check this box.

Click Next to go to the next screen, Use Template. Choose either No Template or Use Template. If you choose Use Template, click the Use Template button to choose a template file. Template files are covered in the next section. After you're done, click Next.

Note Although you can specify the tags and fields you want to extract directly in the Attribute Extraction Wizard and don't need a template file, you can still create a template file to have more control over the results.

In the Select Attributes screen, shown in Figure 18-28, you choose the blocks you want to work with and their attributes. You can also choose from a number of standard data extraction fields, such as the coordinates, scale, and layer of the block. These fields are described in the table in the sidebar "Creating a template file the old-fashioned way."

Figure 18-28: The Select Attributes screen of the Attribute Extraction Wizard

First select the blocks you want to work with. Choose Uncheck All or Check All if you only want to check or uncheck one or two from the list. The attributes you have created are at the bottom of the attributes list. Click Next after you're done.

On the View Output screen, you can view the extracted attributes in two forms:

✦ The horizontal view is like a spreadsheet, with a column for each tag and a row for each incident of the block.

✦ The vertical view lists the attribute values vertically so that each value gets its own row.

Click Alternate view to see each view. Click Copy to Clipboard to copy the data to the clipboard. You can then paste it directly into your drawing or another application. To continue, click Next.

The Save Template screen creates and saves a template file for you. You can then use the template in the future to ensure that you extract attributes with same settings. If you don't want to save a template, just click Next. To save a template, click Save Template to open the Save As dialog box. Here you can specify the name and location of the template. The file name extension is .blk. Click Save. Then click Next.

Note Don't confuse the template file used for extracting attributes with the template file (with a file name extension of .dwt) that you use as a basis for opening an AutoCAD drawing. Also, you cannot use ASCII template files with the Attribute Extraction Wizard, only the .blk templates that you create with the wizard.

In the Export screen, you name the file that will contain the extracted attributes. Click the Ellipsis button to specify the location and file name in a typical file dialog box.

From the File Type drop-down list, choose the type of file you want to create:

✦ **CSV (Comma delimited) (*.csv):** Lists its attribute values with a comma between each value. Most spreadsheets and databases can import this format.

✦ **Tab Delimited File (*.txt):** Like a CSV file, except that there is a tab between each attribute value.

✦ **Microsoft Excel (*.xls):** Creates an Excel spreadsheet.

✦ **Microsoft Access Database (*.mdb):** Creates an Access database file.

To create the file, click Finish. A dialog box asks if you want to write to the file. Click Yes. The wizard closes.

On the CD-ROM The drawing that you need for the following Step-by-Step exercise on extracting attribute data, ab18-i.dwg, is in the Drawings folder of the *AutoCAD 2004 Bible* CD-ROM.

Step-by-Step: Extracting Attribute Data

1. Open ab18-i.dwg from the CD-ROM. This is the same office building plan you used earlier in this chapter, shown in Figure 18-29.

2. Choose Tools ➪ Attribute Extraction to open the Attribute Extraction Wizard.

Figure 18-29: The office building plan includes several blocks of armchairs with invisible attributes.

3. Current Drawing should be selected in the Drawings section of the first screen. Click Next.

4. Leave the Settings screen as is and click Next.

5. On the Use Template screen, choose No Template and click Next.

6. On the Select Attributes screen, click Uncheck All on the Block list and then check Armchair. On the Attributes for Block <ARMCHAIR> list, click Uncheck All and then check the following:

 • X insertion point

 • Y insertion point

 • Orient

 • COLOR

 • PUR_DATE

 • MFR

7. Click Next.

8. You should see a view that shows each attribute in its own column. If you see a list with only four columns, click Alternate View. Click Next.

9. On the Save Template screen, click Save Template. Save the file as ab18-2.blk in your AutoCAD Bible folder. (You don't need to add the .blk extension; AutoCAD does that for you.) Click Next in the wizard.

10. On the Export screen, choose CSV (Comma delimited) (*.csv) from the File Type drop-down list. (If you have Microsoft Excel or Access, you can choose the appropriate file type for one of those applications.)

11. Click the Ellipsis (. . .) button next to the File Name text box and navigate to your AutoCAD Bible folder. In the File Name text box, type **ab18-2** and click Save.

12. Click Finish.

13. To view the output file, from the Windows task bar choose Start ➪ Run. Type **Notepad** and click Run. In Notepad, choose File ➪ Open and locate the ab18-2.csv file in your AutoCAD Bible folder. (You may need to change the Files of type drop-down box to All Files.) Click Open. It should look like Figure 18-30.

You can open this file in any spreadsheet program.

Do not save your drawing.

Tip

If you export attributes in tab delimited format, you can open the Multiline Text Editor and click Import Text to import the output file into your drawing. You can also open the output file, copy it to the clipboard, and paste it into your drawing. The Import Text method enables you to format the text as you would any multiline text but may take some experimenting to align the columns. You cannot format the text you import using the clipboard method, but it is nicely lined up in columns.

Figure 18-30: The output file that results from extracting the attributes in the office building plan

Creating a template file the old-fashioned way

With AutoCAD 2004's Attribute Extraction Wizard, you don't need to create templates "by hand." However, you can still create your own templates on your own, but you must use the ATTEXT command to extract them.

Create the template file in a text editor such as Windows Notepad. The template file contains two columns. The first is the name of the attribute tag. The second is a format code that tells AutoCAD if the data is a character or number, how many spaces to allow for the data, and the decimal precision to use. The format code uses the following syntax:

```
TWWWPPP
```

where T is the data type (either N for numeral or C for character), WWW is the width including commas and decimal points, and PPP is the precision. For integers and all character data, use 000 as the precision.

For example, you would use N006002 for costs that range up to $999.99. The N means the data is numeric, 006 means that you will have up to six spaces including the decimal point, and the 002 means that you have precision of two decimal places.

In addition to information from your attributes, AutoCAD enables you to extract certain standard fields from the drawing's database. The table that follows lists these fields and their formatting.

The block number is a number given to the blocks you select when extracting the data. The block handle is a unique alphanumeric code given to all objects in your drawing—to see a block's handle, use the LIST command and select the block. Handles are used for referring to objects when you write AutoLISP or other programming code. The extrusion data is used for 3D drawing. See Chapter 24 for an explanation of extrusion.

Field	Format	Explanation
BL: LEVEL	NWWW000	Block nesting level
BL: NAME	CWWW000	Block name

Field	Format	Explanation
BL: X	NWWWPPP	X coordinate of block insertion point
BL: Y	NWWWPPP	Y coordinate of block insertion point
BL: Z	NWWWPPP	Z coordinate of block insertion point
BL: NUMBER	NWWW000	Block counter
BL: HANDLE	CWWW000	Block handle
BL: LAYER	CWWW000	Block insertion layer name
BL: ORIENT	NWWWPPP	Block rotation angle
BL: XSCALE	NWWWPPP	X scale factor
BL: YSCALE	NWWWPPP	Y scale factor
BL: ZSCALE	NWWWPPP	Z scale factor
BL: XEXTRUDE	NWWWPPP	X component of Block's extrusion direction
BL: YEXTRUDE	NWWWPPP	Y component of Block's extrusion direction
BL: ZEXTRUDE	NWWWPPP	Z component of Block's extrusion direction

Template files are quite finicky. Here are some of the rules:

✦ You must include at least one attribute tag in your template.

✦ Each row must be unique—don't include the same attribute more than once.

✦ You must use only spaces to line up the two columns—no tabs! (Lining up the two columns just makes it easier to read.)

✦ End each line with a return, including the last line.

✦ Don't put any extra spaces after any line or any extra returns after the last return that is after the last line of text.

Each row in the template file becomes a column in the resulting output file. If you choose space-delimited form for the output file, AutoCAD doesn't automatically put spaces between the columns, resulting in output files that are hard to read. You can place dummy rows in the template file for the purpose of creating spaces in the resulting columns. A typical dummy row looks like this:

```
DUMMY1     C002000
```

Because each row must be unique, if you need another dummy row, call it DUMMY2. This row creates a blank column of two spaces in the output file.

Continued

Continued

The figure shows a typical template file that tracks the company division, as well as the furniture's manufacturer, purchase date, cost, and color.

```
FURNITURE.TXT - Notepad
File  Edit  Format  View
BL:NAME          C001000
BL:X             N007002
DUMMY1           C002000
BY:Y             N007002
DUMMY2           C002000
DIVISION         C015000
MFR              C026000
PUR_DATE         C008000
COST             N007002
COLOR            C015000
|
```

After you're done, save the file with a file name extension of .txt. To use the file, you must use the ATTEXT command, which opens the Attribute Extraction dialog box. In this dialog box, click Template File and choose the file you created. Choose the file format you want to create and name the output file. Then click OK. AutoCAD extracts the attributes.

Summary

In this chapter, I covered all the ways you can use blocks and attributes in your drawings. You read about:

✦ Combining objects into blocks in your drawings so that you can edit them as a unit

✦ Inserting blocks at any scale and rotation

✦ Saving a block as a file

✦ Copying objects by using the Windows clipboard and drag-and-drop

✦ Using the DesignCenter to import blocks from other drawings

✦ Utilizing attributes' two main uses: to place text and to create simple databases

✦ Defining attributes

✦ Inserting blocks with attributes and assign values to the attributes

✦ Extracting attribute data

In the next chapter, I explain how to insert references (xrefs) to other files into your drawings.

✦ ✦ ✦

Referencing Other Drawings

Sometimes you need to refer to another AutoCAD drawing without inserting it. You may want to use part of another drawing as an example for your current drawing or to see how the model in your drawing fits in with models in other drawings. Before AutoCAD offered external references, you had to print the other drawing to refer to it while in a current drawing or perhaps print both drawings and lay one on top of the other to compare them.

Understanding External References

External references (commonly called *xrefs*) enable you to view any drawing as a reference while in your current drawing. The external drawing is not part of your current drawing. The current drawing keeps track of the location and name of an external reference so you can always reference it easily. As with blocks, you can snap to objects in the external reference, thereby using it as a reference for the drawing process. You can also change the visibility settings of the xref's layers.

Xrefs have several advantages over blocks:

✦ Xrefs keep your drawing smaller than blocks. The externally referenced drawing doesn't become part of your drawing. Your drawing maintains only a reference (name and location) to the other drawing.

✦ You always have the most updated version of the xref. Each time AutoCAD loads your drawing, it loads the current copy of the xref. By contrast, you would need to reinsert a file inserted as a block to see the most updated version.

✦ In a team project, several people can use the same drawing as an xref, each having access to the latest changes.

✦ You may not want the xref to be part of your drawing. If you are using only the xref for reference, you may detach it before plotting. Xrefs can be attached and detached easily for maximum flexibility or overlaid for temporary use.

Attaching an external reference

The first step is to attach the external reference, which is just another drawing, to your current (host) drawing. When working with xrefs, you may find it useful to use the Reference toolbar. To open the Reference toolbar, right-click any toolbar and choose Reference.

To attach an xref, follow these steps:

1. Choose External Reference from the Reference toolbar (or choose Insert ➪ Xref Manager) to start the XREF command. AutoCAD opens the Xref Manager, shown in Figure 19-1, your one-stop shopping mall for external references. This dialog box enables you to manage all your xrefs in one place.

 If you don't have any xrefs in use in a drawing, the External Reference dialog box is blank. If you do have xrefs in your drawing, this screen shows your current external references.

2. To attach an external reference, choose Attach in the Xref Manager to open the Select Reference File dialog box. Choose the file you want to attach and click Open. AutoCAD opens the External Reference dialog box, shown in Figure 19-2. The dialog box displays the file you chose along with its path (location).

Figure 19-1: The Xref Manager

Figure 19-2: The External Reference dialog box

3. Choose the type of xref in the Reference Type section:

- **Attachment:** Use an attachment when you want to be sure that the xref will be displayed if someone else xrefs your current drawing., In other words, that person will see your current drawing and your xref will be nested within it.

- **Overlay:** Use an overlay when you are sharing drawings in a networked environment and don't want to change your drawing by attaching an xref. If someone else attaches your drawing while you are working on it, the overlay is not displayed.

4. From the Path Type drop-down list, choose the type of path you want to use:

- **Full path:** Specifies the full path of the xref drawing, including the drive letter (such as c:.)

- **Relative path:** Specifies only part of the xref drawing's path, assuming the current drive or folder. This option enables you to move an xref to a different drive that has the same folder structure.

- **No path:** Uses the current folder of the host drawing. This option enables you to move an xref to another folder with a different hierarchy.

5. Use the bottom half of the dialog box to specify the insertion point; X, Y, and Z scale factors; and rotation angle either in the dialog box or onscreen. These prompts are the same ones you use when inserting a block or file.

6. Click OK.

AutoCAD attaches the xref. If your current view does not show the entire xref, do a ZOOM Extents.

After you have the xref in your drawing, you can start to work. The xref is like a block, but you cannot explode it. However, you can use object snaps on all the objects in an xref, just as you can with blocks. This enables you to use the xref as a basis for your own drawing.

Opening an xref

Sometimes you need to open the xref to work on it directly. You may see an error that you want to correct, for example.

 New Feature The XOPEN command, new for AutoCAD 2004, opens xrefs.

The easiest way use XOPEN is to click the xref to select it in your drawing, right-click, and choose Open Xref. The xref opens in its own window. If you look in the Xref Manager, the xref's status is listed as Open.

You can also select the file in the Xref Manager and click Open. When you click OK to close the Xref Manager, the xref drawing opens.

Viewing xref relationships

To see what type of xrefs you have in your drawing, choose External Reference from the Reference toolbar or Insert ⇨ Xref Manager. The external references are listed in the Xref Manager. You can choose one of two views:

✦ List View lists all the xrefs along with their status, size, type, date and time saved, and the saved path, if any.

✦ Tree View lists all the xrefs in a graphical view that shows their relationships. This view is great for understanding nested xrefs.

 Tip You can change the width of the columns in List View by placing the cursor on a column dividing line until it changes to a two-headed arrow. Then drag in either direction.

Click any xref, and the Xref Found At box displays the location of the xref.

If the AutoCAD cannot find a drawing, it helps to know where it searches for xrefs. AutoCAD searches for xrefs according to a specific order:

✦ **Path specified:** To find the specified path xref

✦ **Current folder:** To find the current folder of the host drawing

✦ **Project path:** To check or change the project path, choose Tools ⇨ Options and click the Files tab. Double-click Project Files Search Path. Click Add and then click Browse to navigate to a folder where you keep drawings that you may want to use as xrefs.

✦ **Support path:** To check or change the project path, choose Tools ➪ Options and click the Files tab. Double-click Support File Search Path. Click Add and then click Browse to navigate to a folder

✦ **Start-in folder:** To find the start in folder, right-click your AutoCAD 2004 desktop shortcut and choose Properties.

The drawings used in the following Step-by-Step exercise on attaching xrefs, ab19-a.dwg and ab19-b.dwg, are in the Drawings folder of the *AutoCAD 2004 Bible* CD-ROM.

Step-by-Step: Attaching Xrefs

1. Open ab19-a.dwg from the CD-ROM. This is the floor plan for a house. If the Reference toolbar is not displayed, right-click any toolbar and choose Reference.

2. Open Windows Explorer (right-click Start on the task bar and choose Explore). Copy ab19-b.dwg from the CD-ROM to your AutoCAD Bible folder.

3. In AutoCAD, choose External Reference Attach from the Reference toolbar. In the Select Reference File dialog box, choose ab19-b.dwg. Choose Open.

4. In the External Reference dialog box, you see the file name displayed. Make sure all Specify On-screen check boxes are unchecked and click OK. AutoCAD displays ab19-b.dwg, which is a title block, in ab19-a.dwg.

5. Save the drawing as ab19-01.dwg in your AutoCAD Bible folder. Click the drawing's Close box to close the drawing.

6. Start a new drawing using the acad.dwt template. Choose Format ➪ Units and choose Architectural. In the Units to Scale Drag-and-Drop Content drop-down list, choose Inches. Choose OK. Save it as ab19-02.dwg in your AutoCAD Bible folder.

7. Choose External Reference Attach from the Reference toolbar. In the Select Reference File dialog box, choose ab19-01.dwg, which you just saved in your AutoCAD Bible folder. Choose Open.

8. In the External Reference dialog box, you see the file name displayed. Leave the other defaults and click OK. Choose Zoom Extents from the Zoom flyout on the Standard toolbar. AutoCAD displays ab19-1.dwg, which includes both the title block and the floor plan of the house in your new drawing. The title block drawing (ab19-b.dwg) is a nested xref in the floor plan (ab19-1.dwg) xref. AutoCAD tells you this with the following message (press F2 to open the AutoCAD Text Window so you can see the message that scrolls by):

```
Attach Xref "ab19-1": C:\AutoCAD Bible\ab19-1.dwg
"ab19-1" loaded.
Attach Xref "ab19-b": C:\AutoCAD Bible\ab19-b.dwg
"ab19-b" loaded.
```

9. To help you visualize the relationships among the three drawings, choose External Reference from the Reference toolbar. The Xref Manager lists both drawings. Click Tree View at the top of the dialog box. AutoCAD now lists the two xrefs in a tree structure, showing their relationship more clearly, as shown in Figure 19-3. Click Cancel.

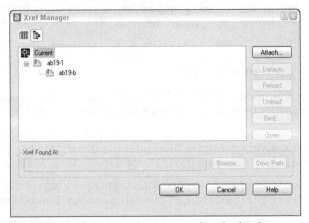

Figure 19-3: Tree view shows nested xrefs clearly.

10. Save your drawing. It should look like Figure 19-4.

Figure 19-4: The current drawing is blank but displays an xref of a house plan that has a nested xref of a title block.

Editing an Xref within Your Drawing

While you are working in a drawing with an external reference you may decide that the external reference needs some modification. The same may apply if you inserted a file as a block. Since AutoCAD 2001i, you can make changes to the xref or block and save those changes back to the original drawing. You can even transfer objects from your drawing to the xref or block and vice versa. AutoCAD calls this *in-place editing.*

The steps to edit an xref or block are as follows:

1. Choose the xref or block in your drawing.

2. Choose from any nested xrefs.

3. Select the objects you want to edit to add them to the working set of objects being edited.

4. Edit the objects.

5. If desired, add or remove objects from the working set to transfer them to or from the xref or block.

6. Save the changes back to the xref or block.

Choosing the xref or block to edit

To start the process of in-place editing, double-click the xref you want to edit. AutoCAD opens the Reference Edit dialog box, shown in Figure 19-5. You can also choose Modify ➪ Xref and Block Editing ➪ Edit Reference In-Place and then select the xref you want to edit.

Figure 19-5: The Reference Edit dialog box enables you to choose which reference you want to edit, including nested references.

As you click each of the available references, its preview appears at the right. You can click Next to cycle through the references.

If the xref has nested objects, choose one of the following options (if not, ignore this section of the dialog box):

✦ **Automatically select all nested objects:** Includes all nested objects in the editing

✦ **Prompt to select nested objects:** Prompts you to select the nested objects you want to edit

For more control, click the Settings tab to set the following options:

✦ **Create unique layer, style, and block names:** Displays layer, style, and block names with a prefix of $#$, to help distinguish them from these named items in your main drawing.

✦ **Display attribute definitions for editing:** Enables you to edit attribute definitions of blocks with attributes. (See Chapter 18 for details on attributes.)

✦ **Lock objects not in working set:** Locks objects in the host drawing so that you can't accidentally modify them

Click OK to close the Reference Edit dialog box.

Note If the references come from an earlier release, AutoCAD warns you that if you save your changes back to the xref, that xref will be updated to an AutoCAD2004 drawing.

If you checked the Prompt to select nested objects item, AutoCAD prompts you to select nested objects. Complete object selection to define the working set — the objects you can edit. Other objects are faded by 50 percent (the default, determined by the XFADECTL system variable).

AutoCAD displays the Refedit toolbar, shown in Figure 19-6, and the message Use REFCLOSE or the Refedit toolbar to end reference editing session. You are now ready to edit the xref or block.

Edit block or Xref

Add object to Refedit working set

Discard changes to reference

Remove objects from the Refedit working set

Save back changes to reference

Figure 19-6: The Refedit toolbar

Editing the xref

There are several types of edits you can make on the working set of objects from the xref or block:

✦ If you change an object's properties, such as its layer, the object will have the new object property.

✦ If you erase an object, the object is deleted from the xref or block.

✦ If you draw a new object, the object is added to the xref or block. An exception is if you create a new object by editing objects outside the working set. For example, if you break a line (not in the working set) into two lines, nothing is added to the working set.

✦ You can transfer an object from the main drawing to the xref or block. Select an object and choose Add objects to working set. Remember that the working set consists of objects from the xref or block, so if you add objects to the working set, they become part of the xref or block.

✦ You can transfer an object from the xref or block to the main drawing. Select an object and choose Remove objects from working set. The working set consists of objects from the xref or block, so if you remove objects from the working set, they are no longer part of the xref or block; instead, they become part of your main drawing.

After you finish editing the working set, if you like what you did, choose Save back changes to reference from the Refedit toolbar. If not, choose Discard changes to reference.

When you save changes to a block, block definitions are redefined and all instances of the block are regenerated according to the new definition. If you gave an xref object properties that don't exist in the xref, such as a layer, AutoCAD copies the new property to the xref so that the object can keep that property.

The drawings used in the following Step-by-Step exercise on editing an xref in place, ab19-a.dwg and ab19-b.dwg, are in the Drawings folder of the *AutoCAD 2004 Bible* CD-ROM.

Step-by-Step: Editing an Xref in Place

1. Open ab19-a.dwg from the CD-ROM. Save it as ab19-03.dwg in your AutoCAD Bible folder.

2. Open ab19-b.dwg from the CD-ROM. Save it as ab19-04.dwg in your AutoCAD Bible folder. Click the Close box of ab19-04.dwg to close the drawing (but not AutoCAD), leaving ab19-03.dwg on your screen.

3. Choose Insert ➪ External Reference and choose ab19-04.dwg from the AutoCAD Bible folder. Click Open. From the External Reference dialog box, uncheck all the Specify On-screen checkboxes and click OK. AutoCAD inserts the xref.

4. Double-click the title block. AutoCAD opens the Reference Edit dialog box. Choose ab19-04.dwg. It is displayed in the preview box. Click OK. AutoCAD opens the Refedit toolbar. You can now edit the xref. Your screen should look like Figure 19-7.

5. Select the title block again and choose Explode.

Figure 19-7: The title block is an xref in the drawing of the floor plan.

6. Choose Draw ➪ Text ➪ Single Line Text. At the `Specify start point of text or [Justify/Style]:` prompt, pick ❶ in Figure 19-7. At the `Specify height <0'-0 3/16">:` prompt, type **10** ↵. Press Enter again for the rotation angle.

7. Type **Davis Floor Plan** and press Enter twice to end the command.

8. Choose the text (the name and address of the architect) at the bottom of the title block and change its color to red to make it stand out.

9. Select the letter N and arrow symbol at ❷ in Figure 19-7. To transfer these objects from the xref to the floor plan drawing, choose `Remove (transfer) objects from working set` from the Refedit toolbar.

10. To save the changes, choose `Save back changes to reference.` Click OK again at the dialog box that informs you that all reference edits will be saved. AutoCAD provides the following information on the command line:

```
The following symbols will be permanently bound to the
current drawing:
Layers: $0$TITLEBLK
Text Styles: $0$STANDARD, $0$ROMANS, $0$ROMAND
Blocks: $0$KNTITL

Enter option [Save/Discard reference changes] <Save>: _sav
Regenerating model.
11 objects added to ab19-04
1 object removed from ab19-04
1 xref instance updated
ab19-04 redefined and reloaded.
```

11. Choose External Reference from the Reference toolbar. In the Xref Manager dialog box, select `ab19-04.dwg` and click Detach. (Detaching xrefs is covered later in this chapter.) Click OK. You can now see that `ab19-03.dwg` includes the North symbol and letter because they were removed from the xref.

12. To see the results of the editing on the xref, open `ab19-04.dwg`. You can see the changes in the title block text and that the North symbol and letter are gone.

13. Close both drawings, saving changes to `ab19-03.dwg`.

Controlling Xref Display

You can control the display of xref layers so that you see only those layers you need. Several features let you control the process of displaying xrefs, making it easier to see only part of an xref and speeding up the display of very large xrefs.

Xrefs and dependent symbols

Dependent symbols are named items in a drawing, such as layers, text styles, dimension styles, and so on. When you attach an xref, these symbols are listed in your current drawing. For example, the Layer Control drop-down list displays the layers of the xref. Xref symbols have the format `xref_name|symbol_name`. This system distinguishes xref symbols from those of your current drawing and ensures that there are no duplicate symbols.

Xrefs and layers

You can turn on and off, or freeze and thaw, xref layers. You can also change an xref layer's properties in the Layer Properties Manager dialog box. By default, these changes are retained. However, you can set the VISRETAIN system variable to 0 to discard these changes. The next time you open the drawing or reload the xref, the original settings are restored.

New Feature The default for VISRETAIN has changed for Release 2004 and is now 1. Previously, this system variable's default was 0, so that layer properties were not retained.

Objects created on layer 0 do not take on the typical xref layer name format, but stay on layer 0. If objects in the xref are on layer 0 with the color and linetype set to ByLayer, they take on the color and linetype properties of the current layer in the current drawing. If color and linetype are set to ByBlock, objects assume the current properties when the xref is attached. If you explicitly set color and linetype, objects retain those settings.

The XBIND command

You can use the XBIND command to import only the symbols you want from the external reference into the current drawing. This makes it easy to work with a consistent set of symbols in the current drawing and the xrefs. For example, you can choose to import the titleblk layer and the dec dimension style. Type **xbind** ↵ on the command line. AutoCAD opens the Xbind dialog box, which lists each xref in the drawing and its symbols in a Windows Explorer-like display, as shown in Figure 19-8.

Click the plus sign next to any symbol type to open a list of symbols. Click the one you want and choose Add to add it to the Definitions to Bind list. Click OK after you are done.

Later in this chapter, I explain how you can use the AutoCAD DesignCenter to move xrefs and other dependent symbols from one drawing to another.

Figure 19-8: Using the XBIND command to import symbols, such as layers, text styles, and so on

Circular references

If drawing *a* includes drawing *b* as an xref and drawing *b* includes drawing *a* as an xref, you have a circular reference. Circular references can exist among three or more xrefs as well when you have nested xrefs. AutoCAD detects circular references and loads as much as it can. If you try to load an xref in such a situation, AutoCAD gives you the following message:

```
Warning: Circular reference from XREF to current drawing.
Circular reference(s) have been found. Continue? <N> Type y to
continue to load the xref.
Breaking circular reference from XREF to current drawing.
```

Clipping xrefs

You may want to see only part of an xref. This option is especially important when you are using very large xref drawings. The XCLIP command enables you to create a border in an xref and hides any part of the xref outside the border.

To clip an xref, choose Modify ➪ Clip ➪ Xref or choose External Reference Clip from the Reference toolbar. AutoCAD prompts you to select objects. Pick the xref you want to clip. Note that any nested xrefs are clipped with the main xref you select.

Table 19-1 explains the options of this command.

Table 19-1
XCLIP Options

Option	How to Use It
ON	Turns the clipping boundary on, displaying only the portion of the xref inside the clipping boundary. By default, the clipping boundary is on. Use this after you have turned it off to see only the clipped portion again.
OFF	Turns the clipping boundary off, displaying the entire xref. The clipping boundary is still retained. This is somewhat like turning off a layer. You may want to see the entire xref for a while, for example, while redefining the boundary. Then you can turn the boundary back on (using the ON option) when you need only the clipped portion again.
Clipdepth	This is used for 3D drawings only. After you set a clipping boundary, you can set front and back planes parallel to the boundary. AutoCAD displays only the portion of the xref within that three-dimensional space. You create the front and back planes by specifying a distance from the clipping boundary. The Remove suboption removes the clipping planes.
Delete	Deletes the clipping boundary. The boundary is no longer retained in the drawing.
Generate polyline	Creates a polyline from the clipping boundary, using the current layer, color, and linetype. If you want to change the clipping boundary, you can edit the polyline by using PEDIT and redefine the boundary with the new polyline.
New boundary	This is the default option. Press Enter to get the suboptions.
Select polyline	Enables you to specify the clipping boundary by selecting an existing polyline. AutoCAD decurves fit-curved or arc portions of the polyline when creating the boundary.
Polygonal	Enables you to specify a polygonal area—such as a polyline with straight edges. AutoCAD creates a rubber-band line as you pick points, keeping the polygon closed. You can use this option to create an irregularly shaped area that includes only the portion of the xref you wish to see.
Rectangular	Enables you to pick two points on diagonally opposite corners of a rectangle, such as creating a selection window.

Tip You can also clip blocks.

To see the clipping boundary (if you haven't used an existing polyline to define it), change the value of the XCLIPFRAME system variable to 1.

Figure 19-9 shows an xref clipped with a polygonal boundary. Compare this to Figure 19-4, which shows the entire xref.

Figure 19-9: An xref clipped with a polygonal boundary

Speeding up the display of large xrefs

In order to reduce the time AutoCAD takes to display large xrefs, such as those used in GIS or 3D drawings, you can use demand loading, which enables AutoCAD to load only the objects necessary to display the xref in your drawing. Demand loading works together with spatial and layer indexes.

✦ The spatial index is created when you save a drawing. AutoCAD uses this index when you have enabled demand loading and attach a clipped xref that was saved with a spatial index. AutoCAD uses the index to determine how much of the xref needs to be read to display it.

✦ The layer index is also created when you save a drawing. AutoCAD uses this index when you have enabled demand loading and attach an xref that was saved with a layer index and has frozen or turned off layers. AutoCAD uses the index to determine how much of the xref needs to be read to display it.

To make it perfectly clear, you need all of the following to use this demand loading:

✦ Demand loading must be enabled in the current drawing.

✦ The xref must have been saved with a spatial or layer index.

✦ The xref must either be clipped (for a spatial index) or have layers that are frozen or turned off (for a layer index).

Demand loading is similar to partial opening and loading of drawings, explained in Chapter 8.

Demand loading

You turn on demand loading in your current drawing. To turn on demand loading, choose Tools ➪ Options and then click the Open and Save tab. In the Demand Load Xrefs drop-down list, choose Enabled. Others on a networked system cannot then edit the original drawing while you are referencing it. To let others edit the original drawing, choose Enabled with copy. AutoCAD then uses a copy of the referenced drawing for your xref. Click OK. You can turn on demand loading just before you attach an xref. It is not necessary to keep demand loading on all the time.

Spatial indexes

You save a spatial index for a drawing that you expect to use as an xref. AutoCAD creates an index of all the objects in the drawing. The saving process takes a little longer, but you save time at the other end when you load a clipped xref or clip an xref for the first time. To create a spatial index, choose File ➪ Save As to open the Save Drawing As dialog box. From the Tools menu at the top right of the dialog box, choose Options to open the Saveas Options dialog box, shown in Figure 19-10 with the DWG Options tab on top.

Figure 19-10: The DWG Options tab of the Saveas Options dialog box

From the Index type drop-down list, choose Spatial or Layer & Spatial. Click OK. Then click Save in the Save Drawing As dialog box.

If you want to create an index for an existing drawing, click OK once to return to the Save Drawing As dialog box. Click Cancel. In other words, you don't have to actually save the drawing to set up the index, which is controlled by the INDEXCTL system variable.

After you create a spatial index, each time you save the drawing AutoCAD displays this message:

```
Updating Indexes for block *MODEL_SPACE
```

To stop saving the index each time you save, choose File ➪ Save As. Choose Tools ➪ Options. In the Saveas Options dialog box, choose None from the Index type drop-down list. Click OK once and then Cancel.

Layer indexes

You save a layer index for a drawing that you expect to use as an xref. AutoCAD creates an index of all the layers in the drawing. As with a spatial index, the saving process takes a little longer, but you save time at the other end when you load an xref with frozen or turned off layers. To create a layer index, choose File ➪ Save As to open the Save Drawing As dialog box. From the Tools menu at the upper-right corner of the dialog box, choose Options to open the Saveas Options dialog box, shown in Figure 19-10.

From the Index type drop-down list, choose Layer or Layer & Spatial. Click OK, and then click Cancel.

After you create a layer index, each time you save the drawing AutoCAD displays this message:

```
Updating Indexes for block *MODEL_SPACE
```

To stop saving the index, choose File ➪ Save As. Choose Options. In the Saveas Options dialog box, choose None from the Index type drop-down list. Click OK once and then Cancel.

The drawings used in the following Step-by-Step exercise on controlling xref display, ab19-a.dwg, ab19-b.dwg, ab19-01.dwg, and ab19-02.dwg, are in the Drawings folder of the *AutoCAD 2004 Bible* CD-ROM.

Step-by-Step: Controlling Xref Display

1. Open ab19-01.dwg from your AutoCAD Bible folder if you did the first exercise in this chapter.

 If you didn't do the previous exercise, first use Windows Explorer to find ab19-b.dwg in the Drawings folder of the CD-ROM and ab19-01.dwg and ab19-02.dwg in the Results folder on the CD-ROM. Copy all three files to your AutoCAD Bible folder. In Windows Explorer, right-click each file and choose Properties. Uncheck the Read-only option and click OK. Then open ab19-01.dwg from your AutoCAD Bible folder. If you get a message that AutoCAD cannot find the xrefs, choose Tools ➪ Options and click Project Files Search Path on the Files tab. Click Add and add your AutoCAD Bible folder. You can click Browse to choose the folder from a dialog box.

2. Choose File ➪ Save As. From the Tools menu of the dialog box, choose Options. In the Index Type drop-down list of the Saveas Options dialog box, choose Layer & Spatial. Click OK. (It may already be set for these indexes.) Click Cancel.

3. Choose Save from the Standard toolbar. Note the message on the command line that AutoCAD is updating the indexes.

4. Close `ab19-01.dwg`.

5. Open `ab19-02.dwg` from your `AutoCAD Bible` folder. This drawing has an attached xref of a house plan and a nested xref of a title block, as shown in Figure 19-11.

Figure 19-11: Picking a polygonal boundary to clip an xref

6. Save it as `ab19-05.dwg` in your `AutoCAD Bible` folder.

7. Choose Tools ➭ Options and click the Open and Save tab. In the Demand Load Xrefs drop-down list, choose Enabled. (It may already be set to Enabled.) Click OK.

8. Click the Layer Control drop-down list. Click the On/Off icon next to the `Ab19-1|notes` layer to turn the layer back on. Click the top of the drop-down list box to close it. AutoCAD displays the notes layer.

9. Choose External Reference Clip from the Reference toolbar or choose Modify ➭ Clip ➭ Xref to start the XCLIP command. Follow the prompts:

```
Select objects: Pick anywhere on the xref in Figure 19-11.
Select objects: ↵
Enter clipping option
[ON/OFF/Clipdepth/Delete/generate Polyline/New boundary]
<New>: ↵
Specify clipping boundary:
[Select polyline/Polygonal/Rectangular] <Rectangular>: Right-
click and choose Polygonal.
```

```
Specify first point: Pick ❶ in Figure 19-11. It might help to
turn off OSNAP if it is on.
Specify next point or [Undo]: Pick ❷.
Specify next point or [Undo]: Pick ❸.
Specify next point or [Undo]: Pick ❹.
Specify next point or [Undo]: Pick ❺.
Specify next point or [Undo]: Pick ❻.
Specify next point or [Undo]: Pick ❼.
Specify next point or [Undo]: Pick ❽.
Specify next point or [Undo]: Pick ❾.
Specify next point or [Undo]: Pick ❿.
Specify next point or [Undo]: ⏎
```

AutoCAD clips the xref.

10. Turn off the `Ab19-1|notes` layer again.

11. Save your drawing. It should look like Figure 19-12. Keep the drawing open if you are continuing on to the next exercise.

Figure 19-12: The clipped xref

Managing Xrefs

If you have many xrefs in a drawing, you need a way to keep track of them and their relationships to your drawing. AutoCAD offers several techniques for managing xrefs. The Xref Manager, DesignCenter, and new xref notification feature are all tools to help you with this task.

> **Tip**
>
> This may be obvious, but the first principle of managing xrefs is to keep them simple. Overly complex nested configurations are hard to manage, no matter what you do.

The Xref Manager

AutoCAD's Xref Manager dialog box is designed to let you manage xrefs from one place. This Xref Manager has the following features, explained in Table 19-2.

Table 19-2
External Reference Dialog Box Features

Feature	What It Does	
Attach	Opens the Attach Xref dialog box and enables you to specify an xref to attach to your drawing, as explained earlier in this chapter.	
Detach	Detaches an xref. The xref is not displayed, and the xref definition is no longer saved in the drawing.	
Reload	Reloads the xref. AutoCAD automatically reloads the xref when you open the drawing or plot. Use this whenever the xref has changed during a session (because someone else on a networked system has edited the xref drawing) or after unloading an xref. AutoCAD then loads the most recent version of the xref.	
Unload	Unloads the xref without detaching it. The xref is not displayed, but the xref definition is still saved in the drawing. You can then use Reload to display the xref again.	
Bind	Changes the xref to a block. Opens the Bind Xrefs dialog box, which enables you to choose to either bind or insert the xref.	
Bind	When creating a block from the xref, this feature changes named layers, text styles, dimension styles, and so on (called symbols) from the format $xref_name	symbol_name$ to $drawing_name\$\#\$symbol_name$, where # is zero (0) if the same name does not exist in the current drawing, 1 if it already exists. In this way, AutoCAD makes sure no symbol names are duplicated. This method enables you to keep track of where the symbols came from.
Insert	When creating a block from the xref, this feature removes the $xref_name	$ portion of symbol names. For example, if a layer of that name already exists in your drawing, objects on that layer take on the properties of that layer as defined in your drawing. The same applies to text styles, dimension styles, and so on. This method removes the complexity that arises with the xref naming of these symbols.
Open	Opens the selected xref in a new drawing window.	
Xref Found At	Specifies where the xref was actually found, which may be different from the saved path. You can then click Save Path to save the current path. If the location of an xref is changed and is not in the Support Files or Project Files search path, AutoCAD lists the status of the xref as Not Found. Use the Browse button to find and open the xref and click Save Path. Click OK and AutoCAD automatically reloads the xref.	

Note You cannot bind or detach nested xrefs without binding the parent xref.

The Xref Manager is now resizable so that you can easily see all the columns.

New Feature Express Tools offer two commands that can help you work with xrefs. XLIST (choose Express ➯ Blocks ➯ List Xref/Block Properties) lists properties of xrefs and blocks such as object type, layer, object, and linetype. BLOCKTOXREF (choose Express ➯ Blocks ➯ Convert Block to Xref) replaces a block with an xref, that is, another drawing file.

Xref notification

If an xref is moved or renamed while you have it displayed in an open drawing, you need to reload it. An xref can change if someone else on your network opens and edits it while you are using it.

New Feature External Reference Notification offers instant notification if an xref changes.

When you open a drawing with an xref, the status bar displays the Manage Xrefs icon. When an xref changes, a "balloon message" appears to notify you, including the name of the drawing and the person who changed it, as shown in Figure 19-13. Click the icon to open the Xref Manager, where you can reload the xref. You may have to browse to find its new location.

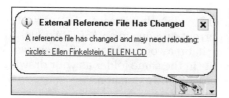

Figure 19-13: If an xref changes, the balloon message appears on the status bar to notify you.

You can control and turn off notification using the XREFNOTIFY system variable.

DesignCenter

As explained in earlier chapters, you can use the DesignCenter to move named objects, including xrefs, from one drawing to another. To insert an xref from another drawing, choose AutoCAD DesignCenter from the Standard toolbar. Navigate to the drawing and double-click it to open the list of named objects. Double-click Xrefs to see a list of xrefs in the right pane as shown in Figure 19-14.

Figure 19-14: You can use the Design Center to insert xrefs into your drawing.

Double-click the xref that you want to insert. AutoCAD opens the External Reference dialog box (refer to Figure 19-2) so that you can insert the xref.

The Xref log file

If you set the XREFCTL system variable to 1 (by default it is set to 0), AutoCAD makes a copy of all xref activity for your current drawing in an ASCII text file. You can read the log to troubleshoot problems that may occur. Figure 19-15 shows part of an xref log file. AutoCAD places the log file in the same folder as your drawing and uses your drawing name with the .xlg file name extension.

Tip	This file can get long. Therefore, once in a while, you should delete all or part of the file.

Cross-Reference The Reference Manager is a stand-alone program that manages xrefs, images, fonts, and plot configurations — outside files that are referenced in your drawing. See Chapter 26 for full coverage of the Reference Manager.

On the CD-ROM The drawing used in the following Step-by-Step exercise on managing xrefs, ab19-05.dwg, is in the Results folder of the *AutoCAD 2004 Bible* CD-ROM.

Figure 19-15: An xref log file

Step-by-Step: Managing Xrefs

1. Use ab19-5.dwg from your AutoCAD Bible folder if you did the previous exercise. Otherwise, open it from the Results folder of the CD-ROM.

2. Save it as ab19-06.dwg in your AutoCAD Bible folder.

3. Choose Modify ➪ Clip ➪ Xref. At the Select objects: prompt, pick the xref anywhere. Press Enter. At the Enter clipping option [ON/OFF/ Clipdepth/Delete/generate Polyline/New boundary] <New>: prompt, right-click and choose Delete. AutoCAD deletes the clip and restores the entire view of both xrefs.

4. Choose External Reference from the Reference toolbar. Click Tree View. Choose ab19-b, the nested xref. Choose Unload and click OK. AutoCAD unloads ab19-b and it disappears.

5. Repeat the XREF command. Choose ab19-b again. Choose Reload and click OK. AutoCAD reloads the xref and it reappears.

6. Repeat the XREF command again. This time choose ab19-1. Choose Bind. In the Bind Xrefs dialog box, choose Insert and click OK twice. AutoCAD inserts both xrefs (ab19-1 and ab19-b) as blocks. (Click the Layer Control drop-down list to see that there are no xref-type layer names.)

7. Save your drawing.

Summary

In this chapter, I covered the techniques you need to know to work with xrefs. You read about:

✦ Attaching and overlaying xrefs

✦ Opening an xref in its own window

✦ Editing xrefs and blocks from within the drawing in which they appear

✦ Clipping xrefs so that only the portion you need to see is displayed

✦ Setting spatial and layer indexes to speed up the display of large xrefs

✦ Deleting, unloading, and reloading xrefs

✦ Binding an xref to make it part of your drawing

In the next chapter, I cover database connectivity, which enables you to access outside databases.

✦ ✦ ✦

Working with External Databases

The AutoCAD database connectivity feature enables you to communicate with an external database from within AutoCAD.

Database connectivity is a powerful way to link drawing objects with data and is more flexible than using block attributes. With database connectivity, you can link data in an external database to any object in a drawing. In this chapter, I show you that database connectivity does not have to be as difficult as it often sounds.

Many AutoCAD users maintain databases separately from their drawings. Now you can work directly with your data by linking the rows of the database tables to objects in your drawings. The drawing objects thus become intelligent and carry these links with them in the drawing. You can also change data, such as a price or a part number, from within AutoCAD and have that change automatically applied and available in all drawing objects that are linked to that database item. Finally, you can create labels in your drawing, based on the data in the database.

Understanding External Database Access

Many organizations maintain extensive databases of objects that are in your AutoCAD drawings. Manufacturers maintain databases of parts, offices maintain databases of furniture, and so on. You need to keep your drawings and the databases synchronized so that the information in the databases and in the drawings are always accurate and up to date.

The linking of databases and AutoCAD drawings is referred to as *external database access*. External database access enables you to:

✦ Create links between AutoCAD drawing objects and the external data

✦ View data in external databases

✦ Edit data in external databases

✦ Display external database data in your drawing

The database connectivity feature works with the following databases:

✦ Microsoft Access

✦ dBASE

✦ Microsoft Excel

✦ Oracle

✦ Paradox

✦ Microsoft Visual FoxPro

✦ SQL Server

After you configure a database, as explained later in this chapter, you can access the data in the database even if you don't have the database program that created the data.

A database is a set of related information, usually maintained by a Database Management System (DBMS) — an application that manages databases. A database is stored in the form of a table that contains rows and columns. A row, also called a *record*, contains one element of data, such as the information for one desk. A column, also called a *field*, contains the attributes of the date, such as the price.

Table 20-1 shows the first three rows of the database used as an example in this chapter.

Table 20-1
A Simple Database Table

Part Number	Description	Dwg Size	Made/Purchased	Units
8665-023-012	Welding Wire — 0.030 StainlessB	B	P	FT
8665-023-013	Weld Rod — 0.045 Dia Stainless Steel	B	P	FT
8665-023-014	Welding — Rod 0.045 Dia S.S.	B	P	FT

A relational database is a type of database that contains a collection of tables. Each table represents a set of data for a defined use.

Structured Query Language (SQL—pronounced *sequel* or *S-Q-L*) was created to provide users with a database language that would be applicable across multiple platforms and database management programs.

Some database systems use environments, catalogs, schemas, and tables to create a hierarchy of database objects. A database object is simply the term used to specify any of the following SQL2 objects: Environment, Catalog, Schema, or Table.

✦ *Environment* means the entire database system—the DBMS, the databases it can access, the users, and the programs that can access those databases.

✦ A *catalog* is a collection of schemas and has the same name as the folder where the database is located.

✦ A *schema* is a set of tables and other database components and has the same name as the catalog subfolder where the database tables reside.

You don't need to work with these concepts if your database system does not require or specify it. AutoCAD can connect to an individual table or to a collection of tables stored in an environment, catalog, or schema.

Preparing for Database Connectivity

Database connectivity involves several components that you need to prepare in advance. Once they are in place, the connection should go smoothly. In this section, I explain the necessary preparation steps.

The basic steps for starting to work with database connectivity are as follows:

1. Make sure you have installed the Database feature of AutoCAD.

2. Make sure you have the ODBC Data Source program from Microsoft.

3. Arrange your database tables into catalogs (folders) and schemas (subfolders) appropriate for your application, if necessary.

4. Configure the appropriate database driver using Microsoft's ODBC (Open Database Connectivity) and OLE DB programs.

5. Configure your data source from within AutoCAD.

6. Start the dbCONNECT command.

7. Establish a user access name and password, if required by the database system.

8. Connect to your data source.

9. Open the Data View window containing your data table.

10. Edit the data, if desired.

11. Link database rows to objects in your drawing.

12. Create labels based on your data in your drawing, if desired.

Installing AutoCAD's database feature

Database connectivity is not part of the Typical AutoCAD installation. To use database connectivity you must either do a Full installation or a Custom installation that includes database connectivity. If you are not sure whether you installed the database feature, open the Tools menu. If you see a dbConnect menu item, you installed it.

If you did not install database connectivity and want to, follow these steps:

1. Choose Start ➪ (Settings) ➪ Control Panel to open the Control Panel. (The steps may vary slightly depending in your version of Windows.)

2. Choose Add or Remove Programs.

3. Select AutoCAD 2004 and click Change.

4. In the AutoCAD 2004 Setup dialog box, choose Add or Remove Features. Click Next.

5. In the next window, click the Database arrow and choose one of the options to install this feature on the hard drive. Click Next

6. Continue to follow the onscreen instructions to install database connectivity.

Organizing the database structure

To connect to a database, you need to know the type of database management system that created the database and the structure of the database itself, along with the folders that contain that structure.

In the following exercise, you create a simple structure for a Microsoft Access database table.

Note In this chapter, you cannot do the later exercises without doing the previous ones. The later exercises depend on the setup and configuration you create in the earlier exercises. You should therefore leave enough time to do all the exercises in this chapter at one sitting — perhaps an hour or two.

On the CD-ROM The file used in the following Step-by-Step exercise on creating the structure for the database, ab20-prt.mdb, is in the Drawings folder of the *AutoCAD 2004 Bible* CD-ROM.

Step-by-Step: Creating the Structure for the Database

1. Right-click Start on the task bar. Choose Explore to open Windows Explorer.

2. If your AutoCAD Bible folder is not displayed in the Folders window, click the plus sign (+) next to the drive containing the AutoCAD Bible folder.

3. Click the AutoCAD Bible folder and choose File ➪ New ➪ Folder from the Explorer menu. A new folder appears in the right window, called New Folder. Type **Databases** ↵ to rename the folder.

4. If necessary, in the Folders window, click the plus sign to open the AutoCAD Bible folder. You should see the new Databases folder. (If not, press F5 to refresh the Explorer view.)

5. From the CD-ROM, copy ab20-prt.mdb to the Databases folder you just created. Be sure to choose the ab20-prt.mdb file, not the ab20-prt.xls file. The .mdb file is a database of parts. Figure 20-1 shows this database as it appears when opened in Microsoft Access 2002.

6. Because this file is coming from a CD-ROM, you may need to change its read-only property. Still in Explorer, right-click ab20-prt.mdb and choose Properties from the menu. Uncheck Read-only and click OK.

7. Click the Close button of Explorer to close it.

Configuring a data source

To start working with external databases, you must tell AutoCAD how to communicate with your database, called a *data source*. AutoCAD uses ODBC and OLE DB for this communication. AutoCAD provides a sample Microsoft Access file, called db_samples.mdb, in AutoCAD's \Sample folder, that you can work with to get started.

First, you must install and configure the ODBC Data Source Administrator. To check if the ODBC Data Source Administrator is installed on your computer, open the Control Panel, by choosing Start ➪ Settings ➪ Control Panel (or as required by your operating system) and look for one of the following items:

✦ ODBC Data Sources (32-bit) or Data Sources (ODBC).

✦ Administrative Tools ➪ Data Sources (ODBC)

Figure 20-1: The Access database

Thanks to Gary Morris of the Dexter Company, Fairfield, Iowa, for this database.

To check if you have the required drivers installed, double-click the ODBC item. In the ODBC Data Source Administrator dialog box you will see a list of database application drivers. Check to see that your database application is listed. A database driver contains information about how to connect to your database.

In most cases, your operating system will include the ODBC Administrator. If you don't have the ODBC 32-bit Administrator, you need to install the Microsoft ODBC Driver Pack. The ODBC Driver Pack 3.0 (or later) is free from the Microsoft Web site at www.Microsoft.com/data/download.htm. The Jet 4.0 Service Pack 3 Update should contain everything that you need.

The instructions to set up the database vary according to the drivers you use. The AutoCAD online help contains help on all supported databases. Look in Help ➪ Help and click the Contents tab. Double-click Driver and Peripheral Guide and then Configure External Databases. Display the Create External Database Configurations topic. Click the Procedures tab and choose the link for your database.

To set up your database using ODBC, follow these steps:

1. From the Windows task bar, choose Start ⇨ Settings ⇨ Control Panel.

2. Double-click the ODBC Data Sources icon. (You may have to double-click Administrative Tools first.) Windows opens the ODBC Data Source Administrator dialog box, shown in Figure 20-2.

3. Click the User DSN tab if it is not already displayed. Choose Add.

4. In the Create New Data Source dialog box, choose the driver appropriate for your database and click Finish.

Figure 20-2: Use the ODBC Data Source Administrator dialog box, accessed from the Windows Control Panel, to choose a database driver to connect to your database.

5. In the ODBC Setup dialog box, which is now titled with the name of the driver you chose (for example, ODBC Microsoft Access Setup), type a name for your data source in the Data Source Name text box. You can also add a description. In general, this name refers to your database program, not the individual database file.

6. Click Select and navigate to the folder containing your database. Choose the database file and click OK.

7. Click OK again in the Setup dialog box.

8. In the ODBC Administrator dialog box, your data source is listed with its appropriate driver. Click OK. Close the Control Panel.

You are now ready to configure your database from within AutoCAD. Follow these steps:

1. Choose Tools ⇨ dbConnect to open the dbConnect palette and display the dbConnect menu.

2. Choose dbConnectin the dbConnect palette, then right-click and choose Configure Data Source. In the Configure a Data Source dialog box, type in a name representing your database file. Click OK.

3. On the Provider tab of the Data Link Properties dialog box, choose Microsoft OLE DB Provider for ODBC drivers. Click Next.

4. From the drop-down list on the Connection tab, choose the name of the data source you used in the ODBC Setup dialog box, as shown in Figure 20-3.

Figure 20-3: Use the Data Link Properties dialog box to configure your data source within AutoCAD.

5. For server-based databases, enter the user name and password.

6. Click Test Connection. You should see a message saying Test Connection Succeeded. (If not, check your settings as well as the spelling and case of the name of the data source.) Click OK.

7. Click OK in the Data Link dialog box.

You are now ready to establish a connection between a database and an AutoCAD drawing.

On the CD-ROM The drawing used in the following Step-by-Step exercise on configuring a Microsoft Access database, ab20-a.dwg, is in the Drawings folder of the *AutoCAD 2004 Bible* CD-ROM. This exercise requires that you have completed the steps in the previous exercise.

Step-by-Step: Configuring a Microsoft Access Database

1. From the task bar, choose Start ➪ Settings ➪ Control Panel. Double-click the ODBC Data Sources icon. (Your item may have a slightly different name.) If you don't have this item, double-click the Administrative Tools icon and look for the ODBC item there.

2. On the User DSN tab of the ODBC Data Source Administrator dialog box, choose Add.

3. In the Create New Data Source dialog box, choose Microsoft Access Driver. Choose Finish.

4. In the Data Source Name text box of the ODBC Microsoft Access Setup dialog box, type **ab20-Access**.

5. Click Select and navigate to your \AutoCAD Bible\Databases folder (which you created in the previous exercise). Choose ab20-prt.mdb and click OK.

6. Click OK twice more to exit the ODBC Data Source Administrator.

7. Close the Control Panel.

8. Open AutoCAD. Open ab20-a.dwg from the CD-ROM. Save it as ab20-01.dwg in your AutoCAD Bible folder.

9. Choose Tools ➪ dbConnect to open the dbConnect palette and display the dbConnect menu. Choose dbConnect in the dbConnect palette, then right-click and choose Configure Data Source. In the Configure a Data Source dialog box, type **ab20-prt**. Click OK.

10. On the Provider tab of the Data Link Properties dialog box (which opens automatically), choose Microsoft OLE DB Provider for ODBC Drivers. Click Next.

11. From the upper drop-down list, choose ab20-Access.

12. Click Test Connection. You see a message saying Test Connection Succeeded. Click OK.

13. Click OK in the Data Link Properties dialog box.

14. Keep ab20-01.dwg open for the next exercise.

Connecting to an Excel spreadsheet

If you have a database in Excel and want to practice working with Excel, you may use the Excel spreadsheet database on the *AutoCAD 2004 Bible* CD-ROM. Here's how:

1. Follow the steps in the exercise "Creating the Structure for the Database." In Step 5, copy the `ab20-prt.xls` file instead of the `.mdb` file. If necessary, uncheck the read-only property as described in Step 6.

2. Double-click the ODBC item in the Control Panel to open the ODBC Data Source Administrator dialog box. (You may have to choose Administrative Tools in the Control Panel and then ODBC Data Source.)

3. On the User DSN tab of the ODBC Data Source Administrator dialog box, choose Add.

4. In the Create New Data Source dialog box, choose the Microsoft Excel driver and choose Finish.

5. In the ODBC Microsoft Excel Setup dialog box, type **ab Excel** as the Data Source Name. (If you want, type a description.)

6. Click Select Workbook. Use the dialog box to choose the `AutoCAD Bible\databases\ab20-prt.xls` worksheet. Click OK three times and close the Control Panel.

7. Open AutoCAD. Open `ab20-a.dwg` from the CD-ROM. Save it as `ab20-01.dwg` in your `AutoCAD Bible` folder. Choose Tools ➪ dbConnect.

8. Choose dbConnect ➪ Data Sources ➪ Configure. In the Configure a Data Source dialog box, type **ab Excel.** Click OK.

9. On the Provider tab of the Data Link Properties dialog box, choose Microsoft OLE DB Provider for ODBC drivers. Click Next.

10. From the upper drop-down list, choose ab Excel.

11. Click Test Connection. At the Test Connection Succeeded message, click OK.

12. Click OK in the Data Link Properties dialog box.

You can continue the rest of the exercises without change.

The equivalent of a table in Excel is a *named range*. You need to open your worksheet, select all the data, and type a range name in the Name box at the left end of the Formula bar. To set up the database, put a field name in the first row of each column.

Connecting to Your Database

After you configure the database connectivity feature, you are ready to connect to your database. Here you actually start making connections between objects in your drawing and rows in your database.

Before connecting to your database, you should think about the relationship between the drawing and the database. For example, you should decide:

✦ If the data is to be in one database with many tables or in several separate databases

✦ Which data you want to link to which drawing objects

✦ If several drawing objects will be linked to one row or only one object will be linked to a row

✦ If you want a drawing object linked to more than one row

✦ Which column(s) will identify unique records

You are now ready to connect your database to your drawing.

Connecting a database to a drawing

You use the dbConnect Manager, shown in Figure 20-4, to perform all the connectivity functions. The dbConnect Manager has its own toolbar, which becomes active when you choose a connected data source. All configured data sources are listed.

Figure 20-4: The dbConnect Manager

You can dock and undock the dbConnect Manager like a toolbar. You can resize it by dragging its right border left or right. After you open the dbConnect Manager, you see a list of open drawings and configured data sources.

New Feature

The dbConnect Manager has been redesigned as a palette, with the same features as the Properties and DesignCenter palettes. You can dock it or move it outside the AutoCAD application window. Right-click the title bar and choose Auto-Hide to collapse the palette automatically when you move the cursor off the palette (and expand it again when you move the cursor onto the title bar).

Follow these steps to connect an external database to a drawing:

1. Open the drawing you want to connect with a database.

2. Choose Tools ⇨ dbConnect to open the dbConnect Manager. You can also press Ctrl+6.

3. Right-click the data source you want to connect to. (The names listed come from the names you entered when you configured the data source in AutoCAD.) Choose Connect.

AutoCAD lists the database tables associated with the data source. The entire database structure is now connected, and you can view and work with the database data within AutoCAD. In order to do the following exercise, you must have completed the previous two exercises.

Step-by-Step: Connecting a Database to a Drawing

1. You should have ab20-01.dwg open from the previous exercise.

2. Choose Tools ⇨ dbConnect to open the dbConnect Manager.

3. Right-click ab20-prt and choose Connect. The dbConnect Manager lists the database table PART NO.

4. Save the drawing. Keep it open. Continue to the next exercise.

Opening a data table

After your database is connected, you choose the database table you want to work with. If necessary, click the plus sign next to the desired database to see the actual database files available. The database file also displays a plus sign. If necessary, click it to display the database tables within the database file. (A database file can contain more than one table.)

You view or edit a table in the Data View window:

✦ View the data when you have no need to edit it. To view your data, right-click the table you want to view and choose View Table.

✦ Edit the data when you need to make changes to your database from within AutoCAD. To edit your data, right-click and choose Edit Table.

To view or edit a table, select the table. Choose View Table or Edit Table from the dbConnect toolbar. You can also right-click the table and choose View Table or Edit Table from the shortcut menu.

Figure 20-5 shows the Data View window when you choose Edit Table. (When you choose View Table, you see the same view but the data cells are gray.)

The Data View window presents your data in a grid, with each piece of data in a cell, like a spreadsheet. You can use the scrollbars to scroll through the data. To the left of the horizontal scrollbar, you can use the arrows to move from record to record. The far left and right arrows with a vertical bar move you to the first and last record, respectively.

When you open the Data View window, a new DataView item appears on the AutoCAD menu.

Figure 20-5: The Data View window displays your data.

You can temporarily change the way the data is displayed. These changes are discarded after you close the Data View window and don't affect the data file in your database. Here are your options:

✦ **Resize a column:** You may find that your data doesn't completely display in a column or that columns don't all appear in the window. Click the grid line to the right of any column header and drag it to the left or right. You can also resize the entire Data View window by dragging on its sides or bottom.

✦ **Move a column:** You can change the order of the columns by moving a column to another location. Click the column's header to select the column. Then click and drag the column to the location you want. A red vertical line indicates where the column will land.

✦ **Hide a column:** You can hide a column you don't need to work with. This is especially helpful if you have many columns and can't fit them easily on the screen. Click the column's header to select the column. Then right-click the column header and choose Hide. To redisplay the column, right-click any column header and choose Unhide All.

✦ **Sort records:** You can sort records in ascending (low to high) or descending (high to low) order. Sorting helps you find the records you want more easily. Right-click any column header and choose Sort to open the Sort dialog box, shown in Figure 20-6. In the Sort By drop-down box, choose the column you want to sort by first. Then choose Ascending or Descending. This column may have duplicate records. If so, you may want to choose a secondary column for sorting in the Then By drop-down box. Choose Ascending or Descending for the secondary column. AutoCAD will then sort first by the first column and then for the secondary column. You can choose up to five columns to sort by.

✦ **Freeze one or more columns:** Freezing one or more contiguous columns moves them to the left column. Select the columns by clicking their column headers. (Press Ctrl to select additional columns. You can also select one column, press Shift, and select another column to select all the columns in-between.) Then right-click a selected column and choose Freeze. To return the column to its original location, right-click and choose Unfreeze All.

✦ **Align text:** You can align text in a column or columns. By default, columns use the Standard alignment, which right-aligns numbers and left-aligns everything else. Select a column or columns by clicking the column header(s), right-click any column header, and choose Align. Then choose Standard, Left, Center, or Right.

✦ **Format text:** You can format the font, font style, font size, effects (strikethrough and underline), and color of the text in the Data View window. Note that, unlike the other changes previously listed, these changes continue to affect the formatting of the Data View window the next time you open a Data View window. Choose Data View ⇨ Format to open the Format dialog box. Choose the formatting you want and click OK.

Figure 20-6: Use the Sort dialog box to temporarily sort your data in the Data View window.

 Tip To get the Data View window out of the way, you can dock it. Right-click in the Data View window's toolbar area and choose Allow Docking. Then drag the window to the right edge of your screen (assuming your dbConnect window is on the left side of your screen).

Although you can scroll through your data's records, if you have many records, this can be time-consuming. You can search for a particular record by specifying a desired value. Follow these steps:

1. Select any cell in the column that contains the record you want to find. If you want to search the entire column, choose the first or last cell in the column.

2. Choose Data View ➪ Find to open the Find dialog box, shown in Figure 20-7. (You can also right-click any cell in the column and choose Find.)

Figure 20-7: The Find dialog box

3. In the Find what box, type a value (text, numbers, or a combination). Choose to search either Up (from the selected cell to the first record) or Down (from the selected cell to the last record). If desired, choose Match case. Then click Find Next to find the next instance of the value. Continue to click Find Next to move to the next matching record.

 Tip If you want, you can copy your formatting, including sorting, to the clipboard and paste it into your DBMS. To do this, select the records you want to export. To export the entire database, click the grid header. Then right-click any cell and choose Copy. Open your DBMS and click Paste from the Standard toolbar.

In the following Step-by-Step exercise, you practice using the Data View window.

Step-by-Step: Working with the Data View Window

1. Ab20-01.dwg should still be open from the previous exercise. If there's a plus sign next to ab20-prt, click it to display the "PART NO" table. The dbConnect window should look similar to Figure 20-8.

Figure 20-8: Displaying a database table in the dbConnect Manager window

2. Right-click the table icon and choose Edit Table. The Data View window opens. (You may have to wait briefly.)

3. From the menu, choose Data View ➪ Format. (A new Data View menu item has appeared.) In the Format dialog box, choose Arial as the font and 10 as the font size. Click OK.

4. The columns are too wide and you can't see all the columns. Drag the grid line to the right of the PART_NO column and drag it to the left so that the width of the column just fits the width of the part numbers. Do the same with the other columns. To access the right grid line of the last column (UNITS), expand the right side of the entire window. Then resize the UNITS column and shrink the Data View window to fit. Your Data View table should look like Figure 20-9.

5. Right-click the PART_NO column's header and choose Align ➪ Right to right-align the first column.

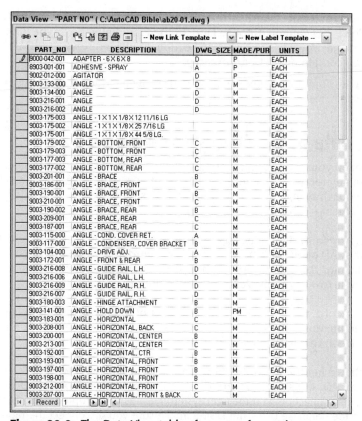

Figure 20-9: The Data View table after some formatting

6. To practice moving around the table, click the right-most arrow at the bottom of the Data View window (to the left of the horizontal scrollbar) to move to the last record. Use the vertical scrollbar to scroll through the database and get an idea of its contents. Click any cell. Click a row header to select an entire row. Click a column header to select an entire column.

7. To sort the records by description and help you find all the angles, right-click the DESCRIPTION column header and choose Sort. In the Sort dialog box, choose DESCRIPTION from the Sort By drop-down box and then click Ascending (if it's not already selected). Because there are a number of duplicate records in the DESCRIPTION column, choose PART_NO in the Then By drop-down box, which should also be sorted in ascending order. Click OK. AutoCAD sorts the data by description, and then by part number.

8. Say that you want to find part number 9003-242-001. Right-click the top cell in the PART_NO column. Choose Find. In the Find dialog box, type **9003-242-001** and choose Down in the Direction section. Click Find Next. AutoCAD highlights the cell containing that part number.

9. Close the Find dialog box and save your drawing. Keep it open for the next exercise.

Editing data in the Data View window

After you open your data in edit mode, you can easily edit the data. You can change the value of any record. You can add or delete records to reflect new or deleted objects in your drawing. Changing a record is as simple as selecting a cell and typing a new value.

To add a new record, right-click any record (row) header and choose Add New Record. AutoCAD opens up a space for a new record at the end of the list of records. Type the data for the new record, tabbing from column to column. (You can also use the right-arrow key to move to the next column.)

To delete a record, right-click the record header of the record that you want to delete, selecting the entire record. Choose Delete record. You need to confirm the deletion twice in the dialog boxes that pop up.

Caution You should not use the DBMS to edit a database separately while it is connected to AutoCAD. If you do edit the database table outside of AutoCAD during an AutoCAD connection, you may get system crashes or corrupted data. If you need to edit the database using the DBMS, make sure you disconnect the table first in the dbConnect window.

AutoCAD doesn't save your changes until you commit them. To save your changes, right-click the grid header — the cell at the top-left corner of the Data Table window — and choose Commit. To discard your changes, choose Restore, which restores the original values of the database when you opened the Data Table window.

Step-by-Step: Editing Data

1. With `ab20-01.dwg` and the Data Table window still open from the previous exercise, the part number you found in the previous exercise (9003-242-001) should still be highlighted. If not, find it following the instructions in Step 8 of the previous exercise.

2. Note that the MADE/PUR column indicates that this horizontal angle is purchased. Say that the company has decided to make this angle. Click the P in the MADE/PUR column of the 9003-242-001 record and type **M**.

3. To add a record, right-click any record (row) header and choose Add New Record. AutoCAD moves you to the end of the records with a space for a new record. Type the following, tabbing between each column:

```
8665-023-018    WELDING ROD - .05 DIA S.S.    B    P    FT
```

4. I don't recommend saving the changes to the database so that you can do this exercise again in the future if you want. So right-click the grid header (upper-left corner of database) and choose Restore. AutoCAD closes the Data Table.

5. Keep the drawing open for the next exercise.

Linking Data to Drawing Objects

The main purpose of using data connectivity is to link data to objects in your drawing. A row of data contains information about the real-life object that objects in your drawing represent. By connecting a row of data to an object or objects in your drawing, you can:

✦ View information about the real-life object while in your drawing, such as price, source, next service date, and so on.

✦ Update a drawing based on changes in the database or vice versa, to keep your drawings and your database synchronized.

✦ Display a label containing data information next to a drawing object.

Creating a link template

When AutoCAD creates a link, it associates an object or objects with a row in your database. To do so, AutoCAD needs to know which field (column) to look in to identify the row. For example, let's say you want to link price information to some objects. However, several rows may contain the same price information. If you provide a field that contains no duplicate data, AutoCAD can always locate the required row. If AutoCAD finds two rows with the same data, it accesses the first row. It makes sense, therefore, to be careful to choose a column that contains no duplicate values. If your data doesn't contain such a column, most DBMSs can create an index field that ensures that each row is unique.

A link template identifies which fields are associated with a link between the data and a drawing object. A link template also identifies your database. After you create a link template, you can open your data directly from the template, which is listed in the dbConnect window.

If you want to associate data from more than one database table to a single object, you may need to create more than one link template for an object.

To create a link template, follow these steps:

1. Choose dbConnect ➪ Templates ➪ New Link Template.

2. If you haven't already opened a data table, AutoCAD opens the Select Data Object dialog box. Choose a table and click Continue.

3. In the New link template name text box of the New Link Template dialog box, shown in Figure 20-10, type a name for the link template. AutoCAD assigns an automatic name using the name of the data source and Link1, Link2, and so on. You can use that name or type your own. If you have a previous link template that you want to use as a basis for the new template, choose it from the Start with template drop-down list. Click Continue.

Figure 20-10: The New Link Template dialog box

4. In the Link Template dialog box, check a key field. If the key field you choose contains any duplicate rows, you should choose a second key field.

5. Click OK. AutoCAD creates the link template, which is added to the dbConnect window beneath the current drawing.

You are now ready to link data with drawing objects.

If the structure of your database changes dramatically, you may need to edit a link template. For example, a field that contained no duplicate entries might now contain some. Other changes requiring a change in the template would be a change in the name or length of a field. To edit a link template:

1. Connect to the desired database table.

2. Choose dbConnect ➪ Templates ➪ Edit Link Template.

3. In the Select a Database Object dialog box, choose a link template.

4. Click Continue.

5. Check one (or more) of the key fields and click OK.

You can also delete a link template by choosing dbConnect ➪ Templates ➪ Delete Link Template.

This exercise requires that you have completed the previous exercises in this chapter.

Step-by-Step: Creating a Link Template

1. Continue with ab20-01.dwg from the previous exercise. In the dbConnect window, right-click "PART NO" and choose Edit Table to open the Data Table window.

2. Choose dbConnect ➪ Templates ➪ New Link Template.

3. Select the PART_NO table and click Continue.

4. In the New Link Template dialog box, use AutoCAD's suggested name, PART_NO_Link1. Click Continue.

5. In the Link Template dialog box, check PART_NO. This column contains no duplicate rows.

6. Click OK to return to the drawing. You see the new link template with a chain-link icon in the dbConnect window just under the name of the open drawing.

7. Save your drawing. Leave it open to continue with the next exercise.

You are now ready to link drawing objects to your database.

Creating a link

You can link a drawing object to as many records in a database as you want, and you can link one database record to several drawing objects. For example, you may want to link a record containing part number information to the part in the drawing. However, that part may be made up of a number of objects, such as lines, arcs, and circles. You can link the record to all those objects in your drawing that make up the part. On the other hand, if you have a database of office equipment, you may attach a row representing telephone numbers and telephones to an object in your drawing representing a phone. But if someone has a two-line phone, you may need to attach two rows to that one telephone object in your drawing.

Here's how to create a link:

1. Open a Data View window that has a defined link template and choose a link template from the Select a Link Template drop-down list at the top of the window.

2. Select one or more records you want to link to your drawing.

3. Choose Data View ➪ Link and Label Settings ➪ Create Links.

4. Choose Data View ➪ Link! (You can also choose Link in the Data View Table window.)

5. AutoCAD returns you to your drawing. Select one or more objects and press Enter to end object selection.

AutoCAD provides a message on the command line, for example: 1 Record(s) linked with 1 Object(s). You now have a link between your data and your drawing.

Caution If you create a link between a drawing object and a row and in a later session of AutoCAD edit that object without connecting to the database table, the link information may become corrupted.

You can delete a link by selecting a linked object and right-clicking in the drawing area. From the shortcut menu, choose Link ➪ Delete Link.

Viewing linked objects and rows

After you create a link, you need to be able to see which rows are linked to which objects before you can make decisions regarding either the data or the drawing objects. You can view the link from either side. That is, you can select an object and see which row or rows it is linked to or you can select a row and have AutoCAD select the object or objects it is linked to. In both cases, you need to have a Data View table displayed.

✦ To find out which row an object is linked to, select one or more objects. Then choose Data View ➪ View Linked Records. AutoCAD highlights the row or rows that are linked to the selection set of objects. Later in this section I explain how to customize the display of a row or rows.

✦ To find out which object a row is linked to, select one or more records. Choose Data View ➪ View Linked Objects. AutoCAD pans, zooms (or does both so you can see the objects in the center of the screen), and selects them. Later in this section, I explain how to customize the panning and zooming.

You will find that the Data View window obscures your drawing. You can drag it to the bottom of your screen, resize it, or dock it.

When you use View Linked Objects, the selected objects form a selection set. You can then use the results with other commands that allow prior selection of objects. For commands that you must execute before selecting objects, type **p** ↵ at the Select objects: prompt to use the Previous option and get the selection set.

If you want to move from object to object or row to row to view your links one after another, you should use Auto-View. The Auto-View feature automatically highlights either object when you choose a row in the Data View window or rows when you choose objects in your drawing. However, you can work from only one side of the equation — either rows or objects — at a time. Here's how it works:

✦ To automatically select linked objects when you select a row, choose Data View ➪ AutoView Linked Objects (or use the AutoView Linked Objects in Drawing button in the Data View window). Then select a record (or records) by clicking the row header(s) in the Data View window. AutoCAD highlights the linked objects. You can continue to select different records to highlight their linked objects. Choose Auto-View Linked Objects (or click the button) again to turn off Auto-View.

✦ To automatically select linked rows when you select an object, choose Data View ➪ AutoView Linked Records (or use the AutoView Linked Records in Data View button in the Data View window). Then select an object (or objects). AutoCAD highlights the linked rows. You can continue to select different objects to highlight their linked rows. Choose Auto-View Linked Records (or click the button) again to turn off Auto-View.

When you are in Auto-View, you can't select records. If you click another record's row header to create a link, AutoCAD just tells you 0 Object(s) found matching 0 selected Record(s). So be sure to turn off Auto-View when you go on to another task.

You can customize how AutoCAD displays linked rows and how AutoCAD pans (AutoPan) and zooms (AutoZoom) to display selected objects. Choose Data View ➪ Options. In the Record Indication Settings section of the Data View and Query Options dialog box, choose either Show Only Indicated Records or Show All Records - Select Indicated Records (the default). You can also choose the highlight color. To set AutoPan and AutoZoom, use the AutoPan and Zoom section of the same dialog box. Uncheck Automatically Pan Drawing and Automatically Zoom Drawing if you don't want this feature. When Automatically Zoom Drawing is checked, you can also choose a zoom percentage. You can choose from 20 to 90 percent. The default, 50 percent, means that the height (or width, if less) of the extents of the zoomed area is 50 percent of the drawing area. Click OK after you finish using the dialog box.

Editing links

After you create links in your drawing, you need to be careful how you edit your database from within AutoCAD. For example, you don't want to inadvertently delete a record that is linked to an object.

You may need to edit the key value assigned to a linked object. For example, your company may change the part-numbering scheme or you may have simply assigned the wrong part number to an object. The Link Manager enables you to edit key values for linked objects. Follow these steps:

1. Choose dbConnect ➪ Links ➪ Link Manager to open the Link Manager, shown in Figure 20-11. You can also select a linked object, right-click in the drawing area and choose Link ➪ Link Manager.

2. At the `Select an object:` prompt, select an object.

3. In the Link Manager, choose the Link Template that you want to work with from the drop-down list.

Figure 20-11: The Link Manager enables you to edit key value data for its linke object.

4. In the Value column, type a new value, such as a new part number.

5. Click OK.

AutoCAD updates the link.

You can also click the Delete button to delete the object's link.

Exporting link information

You can export a list of links and the handle of the associated links' objects. A handle is a unique name that AutoCAD gives to each object in the drawing. (To view an object's handle, select it and choose Tools ➪ Inquiry ➪ List.) You can export the reports in the same format as your database (called the native format) or in space- or comma-delimited formats. You might use these reports to keep track of how

many objects are linked to a row because the exported information tells you how many instances a drawing contains of a record in a database. For example, if your database lists configurations of desktop computers and you have linked each person's computer to the appropriate row in the database, the list will let you know how many people have each configuration.

Follow these steps to export links:

1. Choose dbConnect ⇨ Links ⇨ Export Links.

2. At the `Select objects:` prompt, choose the objects whose links you want to export. When you complete object selection, AutoCAD opens the Export Links dialog box, shown in Figure 20-12.

Figure 20-12: The Export Links dialog box

Tip You can select the entire drawing (type **all** ↵ at the `Select Objects:` prompt, and AutoCAD finds just the linked objects.

3. In the Include Fields section, select the fields you want to include.

4. In the Save in drop-down list, navigate to the folder where you want to save the file.

5. In the Save as type drop-down box, choose one of the three options: comma-delimited format, space-delimited format, or native database format.

6. In the File name text box, type a name for the file.

7. Click Save.

 AutoCAD creates the file.

You can use this file to create a schedule of objects with links — but it takes some work. The comma-delimited format seems to work better than the space-delimited format. You'll probably want to edit the file first to remove the object handles. You can open the Multiline Text Editor and click Import Text to import the output file into your drawing. You can also open the output file, copy it to the clipboard, and

paste it into your drawing. The Import Text method enables you to format the text as you would any multiline text but takes some experimenting to set up in the proper columns. You can also import the file into a spreadsheet and format it before importing it into your drawing. If you used the native format, you can open it in your DBMS, format it, and import it into your drawing. (See Chapter 27 for more information on importing files.)

Step-by-Step: Creating and Viewing Links

1. You should have `ab20-01.dwg` open from the previous exercise. The Data View window is open with the database visible. The PART_NO_Link1 link template is current. You can see the entire drawing in Figure 20-13.

Figure 20-13: This drawing of a base assembly for a commercial washing machine has objects that can be linked to the database of parts.

Thanks to Robert Mack of The Dexter Company, Fairfield, Iowa, for this drawing.

2. To locate the record you need, in the Data View window click the leftmost arrow next to the horizontal scrollbar to move the first record. Choose Data View ➪ Find. In the Find dialog box, type **9003-242-001**. The direction should be down. Click Find Next. AutoCAD finds the record. Close the Find dialog box by clicking its Close button.

3. Click the row's header to select the entire row.

4. Choose Data View ➪ Link and Label Settings ➪ Create Links. The Create Links menu item may already be checked.

5. Choose Data View ➪ Link!

6. AutoCAD returns you to your drawing. Use Zoom Window to zoom into the area marked ❶ in Figure 20-13.

7. Select all the objects that make up the angle bracket indicated by ❶ in Figure 20-13 (and which the drawing itself labels as 2), as shown in Figure 20-14. Include the two cyan hidden lines representing the hole, but not the yellow centerline. Don't select the vertical line on the right of the angle, which belongs to another part. Press Enter to end selection. AutoCAD returns you to the Data View table and displays 1 Record(s) linked with 8 Object(s) on the command line.

8. The linked row is still highlighted in yellow. Make sure the arrow cursor in the row header points to the highlighted row. (AutoCAD moves it down one so that you can work on the next row.) To view the objects connected to the row, choose Data View ⇨ View Linked Objects. Drag the Data View window to the bottom of the screen so you can see the drawing (or dock it). The objects you selected in Step 7 are selected.

Figure 20-14: The horizontal angle

9. In the drawing, press Esc to deselect the objects and remove the grips. To check the link, click any other row in the Data View window to move the cursor. (Try to position the Data View window so that you can see both the row you were working with and the objects you linked it to at the same time.) Choose Data View ⇨ View Linked Records. At the Select objects: prompt, select one of the objects in the angle and press Enter. AutoCAD displays the correct row in the database.

10. Save your drawing and keep it open for the next exercise.

Creating Labels

A *label* is multiline text that appears in your drawing, displaying data from a row in your database. You can choose which fields from the row are displayed. There are two types of labels:

✦ *Attached labels* are attached to objects and are displayed with a leader pointing to the object. If you move the object, the label moves as well. Use an attached label when the row in the database applies to one or more specific objects in your drawing.

✦ *Freestanding labels* are independent of any object. You would use freestanding labels when your database applies to the drawing as a whole.

Creating label templates

Before creating a label, you need to create a label template. A label template specifies which fields will be included in the label as well as text formatting. Here's how to create a label template:

1. Choose dbConnect ➪ Templates ➪ New Label Template.

2. In the Select a Database Object dialog box, choose a link template to use with the label template. Click Continue.

3. In the New Label Template dialog box, shown in Figure 20-15, type a template name in the New label template name text box. AutoCAD suggests a default name. If you have an existing label template you would like to use as a basis for the new label template, choose it from the Start with template drop-down box. Click Continue.

Figure 20-15: The New Label Template dialog box

4. AutoCAD opens the Label Template dialog box, shown in Figure 20-16, with the Label Fields tab displayed. Use the Character and Properties tabs to format the text. (Note that this dialog box looks like the pre-2004 Multiline Text Editor.)

5. On the Label Fields tab, choose a field that you want to appear on the label from the Field drop-down list. Then click Add. Continue to add fields as desired. You can add text to this field. For example, you could type **Part No:** before the PART_NO field.

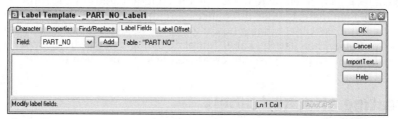

Figure 20-16: Use the Label Template dialog box to format and define label templates.

Note

If you add text before or after the field, don't forget to add a space between the text and the field so that the result is Part No: 9003-242-001 rather than Part No:9003-242-001, for example.

6. Click the Label Offset tab, shown in Figure 20-17. This tab defines the placement of the label and the leader that connects the label with the object. In the Start drop-down list, choose a justification. This defines where on the object AutoCAD places the tip of the leader.

Figure 20-17: The Label Offset tab of the Label Template dialog box

7. In the Leader offset text boxes, type an X and Y offset (in units). This offset represents the X and Y distances between the point of the leader arrow and the insertion point of the text. (If this distance is too small to fit an arrow, the arrow is suppressed.)

8. In the Tip offset text boxes, type an X and Y offset (in units). This offset represents the distance between the point of the leader arrow and the object it points to. By default, this is set to 0,0 so that the point of the leader arrow touches its object.

9. Click OK to close the Label Template dialog box and place the label.

After you create the label template, you can create attached and freestanding labels. The settings on the Label Offset tab apply only to attached labels.

You can edit a label template to change the included fields or the formatting. To edit a label template, choose dbConnect ⇨ Templates ⇨ Edit Label Template. In the Select a Database Object dialog box, choose the label template you want to edit and click Continue. Then use the Label Template dialog box to edit the label template using the same steps you used to create it. Click OK after you're done.

Creating attached labels

You create a link between a row and an object and an associated attached label at the same time. You need to have a table open and to have defined both a link and a label template. If you have defined more than one link or label template, choose the desired template(s) from the drop-down list at the top of the Data View window. Follow these steps:

1. Select the record you want to link by clicking its row header in the Data View window.

2. Choose Data View ⇨ Link and Label Settings ⇨ Create Attached Labels. This puts you in Creating Attached Labels mode, which means that from now on any links you create also create labels.

3. Choose Data View ⇨ Link!

4. At the `Select objects:` prompt, choose the object(s) you want to attach to the label. End object selection.

5. AutoCAD automatically places the label based on the label template. If you selected more than one object, labels are placed on all the objects (which can get confusing).

Of course, you can then move the labels and leaders to a more suitable location.

If you have already created a link to an object, follow the same procedure. The link is re-created along with the attached label.

Creating freestanding labels

To create a freestanding label, you need to have a table open with at least a link and a label template. If you have more than one template defined, choose the one you want to use in the drop-down list at the top of the Data View window. Follow these steps:

1. Select the record that you want to link to the freestanding label.

2. Choose Data View ➪ Link and Label Settings ➪ Create Freestanding Labels.

3. Choose Data View ➪ Link!

4. At the `Specify point for label:` prompt, pick a point in your drawing. AutoCAD places the freestanding label and displays this message on the command line: `1 Record(s) linked with 1 Label(s)`.

When you create a freestanding label, the row and the label are linked. If you select a row linked to a freestanding label and choose Data View ➪ View Linked Objects, AutoCAD selects the label.

If the data in the database is changed from within the DBMS, the labels in your drawing may become outdated. To ensure that your labels are always accurate, you should periodically update them. To update labels, choose dbConnect ➪ Labels ➪ Reload Labels. In the Select a Database Object dialog box, choose the label template you want to use and click OK.

Step-by-Step: Creating a Label Template and a Label

1. Continue with `ab20-01.dwg` from the previous exercise. The Data View window should still be open. Press Esc to make sure no objects are still selected.

2. Choose dbConnect ➪ Templates ➪ New Label Template.

3. In the Select a Database Object dialog box, click Continue.

4. In the New Label Template dialog box, click Continue to use the default name.

5. In the Label Template dialog box, click the Label Fields tab. Choose PART_NO from the Field drop-down list. Click Add.

6. Choose DESCRIPTION from the Field drop-down list and click Add.

7. Click the Label Offset tab. In the Start drop-down list, choose Top Left. Set the Leader offset X and Y values to 2.

8. Click the Character tab. Select all the text and change the height to 5/16.

9. Click OK.

10. Choose Data View ➪ Link and Label Settings ➪ Create Attached Labels.

11. Choose Data View ➪ Link!

12. At the `Select objects:` prompt, choose the horizontal line marked at the top of the angle that you linked in previous exercise. Press Enter to end object selection. AutoCAD automatically places the label.

13. The label covers existing objects. Pick the text of the label and then click its grip. Move the text to the left and pick a better location. The leader automatically changes direction and ends at the left side.

14. Save your drawing. Leave it open for the next Step-by-Step exercise.

Querying with the Query Editor

You can use SQL (Structured Query Language) statements to gather more information about the elements in the drawing and database files. SQL (pronounced *sequel* or by its letters) is the language used by almost all database management systems for refining the information you get from a database.

AutoCAD uses the Query Editor to enable you to design queries. For example, you can do the following:

✦ Query the contents of a database to view a specified subset of the data

✦ View a subset of records that falls into a certain range of values

✦ Access all the tables in one data source with a series of SQL commands

In addition, the Link Select dialog box enables you to create a selection set of objects by combining SQL queries and direct selection of objects in your drawing.

To open the Query Editor, follow these steps:

1. Choose dbConnect ➪ Queries ➪ New Query on a Link Template. (You can also right-click the table in the dbConnect Manager and choose New Query.)

2. In the Select a Database Object dialog box, choose the link template you want to use and click Continue.

3. In the New Query dialog box (shown in Figure 20-18), type a name for the new query or accept the name AutoCAD supplies. To base a query on an existing query, choose an existing query from the drop-down list. Click Continue.

AutoCAD opens the Query Editor, shown in Figure 20-19. The Query Editor is designed to provide something for everyone—whether you're just starting out or are an expert at SQL.

Figure 20-18: The New Query dialog box

Figure 20-19: The Query Editor's four tabs enable you to build queries to refine how you view your database.

To restore the original view in the Data View window, do one of the following:

✦ Close the Data View window and then reopen it from the dbConnect window.

✦ Click the Query Builder tab and right-click any used cell. Choose Clear Grid. Click Yes at the warning message. Then click Execute.

Using the Quick Query tab

Use the Quick Query tab to create simple queries based on one field, an operator, and a single value. For example, you can create a query that finds all records from the current table where the field DWG_SIZE equals E. You can also find all records where DWG_SIZE does not equal E.

The advantage to using Quick Query over the Find dialog box, described earlier in this chapter, is that Quick Query displays all the records matching the query and hides the rest. You don't have to click Find Next to move from record to record.

From the Field box, choose a field. In the Operator drop-down box, choose an operator, such as equal (=) or greater than (>). In the Value box, type a value for the field. If you're not sure what values are available, click Look Up Values. (This can be slow in a large database or when you are working with a database across a busy network.)

Caution Queries are case sensitive. A value of "B" is not the same as "b." You need to be aware of the case used in your database. Some databases are all uppercase, making it easy to specify values. Just turn on CAPS LOCK and type away.

Choose Indicate Records in Data View and/or Indicate Objects in Drawing. By default, both are checked. To save the query for future use, click Store. Click Execute to see the results.

To return to the Query Editor, choose Return to Query on the Data View window toolbar.

Table 20-2 lists the available operators.

<table>
<tr><td colspan="2">Table 20-2
Query Operators</td></tr>
<tr><td>*Operator*</td><td>*Description*</td></tr>
<tr><td>Equal (=)</td><td>Records that match the value exactly.</td></tr>
<tr><td>Not equal (<>)</td><td>All records except those that match the value exactly.</td></tr>
<tr><td>Greater than (>)</td><td>Records greater than the value. Includes text. For example, D is greater than B.</td></tr>
<tr><td>Less than (<)</td><td>Records less than the value.</td></tr>
<tr><td>Greater than or equal (>=)</td><td>Records that are greater than or match exactly the value.</td></tr>
<tr><td>Less than or equal (<=)</td><td>Records that are less than or match exactly the value.</td></tr>
<tr><td>Like</td><td>Records that contain the value. You must use the % wildcard (which is like the * wildcard used in Windows).</td></tr>
<tr><td>In</td><td>Records that match the values you specify. You list the values, separated by a comma. For example, you could find records for which the field DWG_SIZE is B or D by typing B,D in the value box.</td></tr>
<tr><td>Is null</td><td>Records that have no value. The value box is unavailable. You can use this to find missing data.</td></tr>
<tr><td>Is not null</td><td>Records that have a value. You can use this to remove from view all records with missing data.</td></tr>
</table>

Using the Range Query tab

The Range Query tab, shown in Figure 20-20, finds records based on one field and a range of values. For example, you can find all records where the field DWG_SIZE ranges from B to D. The range can be either textual or numeric.

To construct a range query, choose a field from the Fields list. Then type the beginning value of the range in the From box and the ending value of the range in the Through box. In both cases, you can click Look up values to choose from a list.

Click Store to save the query. Click Execute to execute the query.

Figure 20-20: Use the Range Query tab to find records that match a range of values.

Using the Query Building tab

The Query Builder enables you to create multiple criteria. For example, you can create a query that finds records where the field DWG_SIZE ranges from B to D and the field PART_NO is greater than 9029-072-001. In order to build the criteria, you use Boolean operators and parenthetical grouping. This tab also enables you to specify which fields will appear in the Data View window and to sort the records. Using all these options offers a great deal of flexibility to create a complex query without knowing SQL. Here's how it works:

✦ **And operator:** Displays the records that meet both the criteria before and after the And operator.

✦ **Or operator:** Displays records that meet either of the criteria before and after the Or operator.

✦ **Parenthetical grouping:** Enables you to group sets of criteria. For example, you can group two criteria that use an And operator and a second group of two criteria that use an And operator. Then you can put an Or operator between the two groups.

Figure 20-21 shows an example of a query using all three elements.

Figure 20-21: Use the Query Builder tab to design a query with multiple criteria.

Building a query with multiple criteria

To create a query using multiple criteria, follow these steps:

1. On the first line, choose a field from the Field column. (When you click the first cell in the Field column, a drop-down arrow appears.)

2. Choose an Operator from the Operator column.

3. Type a value in the Value cell. (An ellipsis button appears, and you can choose from all the values in the database.)

4. Click in the Logical cell to insert the And operator. Clicking again changes the operator to Or.

5. Move to the second line and create the next row of criteria. Continue until you have specified all the criteria you want.

6. Add parenthetical grouping. Click to the left of the Field column of a row to insert a left parenthesis and between the Value and Logical columns to insert a right parenthesis. Continue to insert all the parentheses you need. You can't insert parentheses until you have enough rows defined for a parenthesis to make sense.

7. Click Store to save the query. Click Execute to execute the Query.

Specifying fields and sorting

You can also limit which fields appear in the Data View table. First define the query in the top half of the tab. The query does not need to be complex. Then select the first field from the Fields in table list. Click Add above the Show Fields list. Continue

until you have all the fields you want. By default all of the fields are shown. To start from scratch, right-click in the Show fields box and choose Clear All. To remove one field, right-click it and choose Clear Field Name.

To sort the data, choose the first field that you want to sort by from the Show Fields list. (You can only sort by fields that you are showing.) Click Add above the Sort By list. By default, AutoCAD sorts by ascending order. To sort by descending order, click the Ascending/Descending button. You can click it again to change the order back to ascending. You can repeat the process for additional fields.

Click Store to save the query. Click Execute to execute the Query.

Using the SQL Query tab

Here's where the fun is. Try creating a query in one of the first three tabs and then click the SQL Query tab. Lo and behold, there is your query in SQL language. It's a great way to learn SQL. (I'm still waiting for a macro recorder that does the same thing in VBA, such as the one contained in Microsoft Office.) Figure 20-22 shows the SQL Query tab for the same query shown in Figure 20-21.

Note AutoCAD 2004 uses the SQL 92 standard. Not all DBMSs are fully compliant with SQL 92 so check your system's documentation to see what SQL commands and syntax are valid for your database.

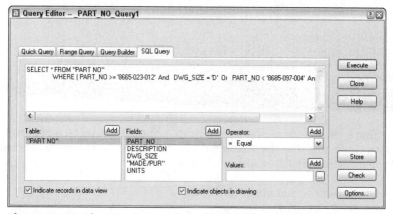

Figure 20-22: The SQL Query tab enables you to create free-form SQL queries and displays queries created on the other tabs in SQL.

The SQL Query tab is the only tab you can use to create a query to search more than one database table. Choose a table in the Table section and click Add. You can build the query by specifying fields, an operator, and values. As you work, you see the results in the top box, in SQL language.

The Check button enables you to check the SQL query before executing it. Click Store to save the query. Click Execute to execute the Query.

While a full coverage of SQL syntax is beyond the scope of this book, you may find a few rules helpful:

✦ Text data must be enclosed in single quotation marks ('B').

✦ Column names are not case-sensitive, but column values are.

✦ There are certain SQL keywords that are used in the program. You cannot use these as table or column names. Examples include CHAR, GROUP, SQL, TABLE, USER, and CURRENT.

✦ In most standard SQL syntax, you need to end each statement with a semi-colon (;) — however, this is not necessary in AutoCAD.

✦ You cannot use AutoCAD or DOS wildcard characters, such as ? or * in column values or names.

✦ To name more than one specification, separate each one by commas.

The SELECT statement is probably the most common SQL statement. The SELECT statement can retrieve a subset of the rows in one or more tables, retrieve a subset of the columns in one or more tables, or link rows in two or more tables to retrieve common data to both tables.

The following shows the syntax of the SQL SELECT statement, including modifying statements that instruct the DBMS exactly which rows to select.

```
SELECT <select list>
FROM <table name> [{,<table name>}...]
[WHERE <search condition>]
[GROUP BY <column spec>[{,<column spec>}...]
[HAVING <search condition>]
[ORDER BY <sort spec> [{,<sort spec>}...]
```

In the preceding syntax, square brackets indicate optional elements, an ellipsis (three periods) indicates that the statement may be repeated, and curly brackets mean that the elements are listed in sequence.

Here is the meaning of the statement functions:

✦ The SELECT statement specifies the columns to retrieve.

✦ The FROM clause specifies the tables containing the specified columns.

✦ The WHERE clause specifies the rows you want to retrieve in the tables.

✦ The GROUP BY clause divides a table into groups. Groups are designated by a column name or by the results of computed numeric data type columns.

✦ The ORDER BY clause sorts results into one or more columns in either ascending (ASC) or descending (DESC) order.

Step-by-Step: Creating a Query

1. You should still have `ab20-01.dwg` and the PART_NO Data View window open. Choose dbConnect ➪ Queries ➪ New Query on a Link Template.

2. In the Select a Database Object dialog box, click Continue.

3. In the New Query dialog box, click Continue to open the Query Editor.

4. Your goal is to locate the part number of a trip arm that appears in a size B drawing you have open because the part number has been smudged on the paper drawing. You know that arms all have a part number starting with 9001. Because you need to specify a range of part numbers, click the Range Query tab.

5. PART_NO is already selected in the Field box. In the From range, type **9001-000-000**. In the Through range, type **9001-999-999**. This will include all part numbers that start with 9001.

6. You also need to specify the drawing size. To add to the query, click the Query Builder tab. Your range query is already there. You could have built it on the Query Builder tab, but using the Range Query tab was much easier.

7. Click in the second row of the Logical column, at the end of the last existing line of the query. AutoCAD places an `And` operator there.

8. Click in the third row of the Field column to open the drop-down list. Choose `DWG_SIZE`.

9. Click in the third row of the Operator column. By default, AutoCAD places the Equal operator, which is what you want.

10. Click in the third row of the Value column. Type **B**. (Make sure to make it uppercase.)

11. Click Execute. You now have only four items in the Data View table and can easily find the trip arm's part number.

12. Save your drawing.

Creating selection sets with Link Select

Link Select enables you to create combined selection sets of objects. You can define the selection sets either by using the Query Editor or by selecting objects directly in your drawing, or you can use a combination of these two methods. You first define a selection set, called A. Then you define a selection set, called B. Then you combine the two selection sets using logical operators.

You need to have your links already set up so that AutoCAD knows the relationship between your records and objects in the drawing.

As you work, the status area at the bottom of the dialog box displays the results of the running link select operation, both in terms of the number of linked objects and the number of records that currently meet your specifications.

Table 20-3 shows how the logical operators work.

Table 20-3
Logical Operators for Selection Sets in Link Select

Operator	Function
Union	Combines both selection sets.
Subtract A-B	Subtracts the second selection set of objects from the first.
Subtract B-A	Subtracts the first set selection of objects from the second.
Intersect	Selects only objects that are contained in both selection sets.

The Link Select dialog box contains its own version of the Query Editor so that you can build queries without leaving the dialog box.

To use Link Select, follow these steps:

1. Choose dbConnect ⇨ Links ⇨ Link Select, to open the Link Select dialog box, shown in Figure 20-23.

2. At the top center of the dialog box, choose either Use Query or Select in Drawing.

 • If you choose Use Query, use the Query tabs to specify a query.

 • If you choose Select in Drawing, click Select (the Execute button changes to the Select button) to return to your drawing and choose objects in the drawing at the `Select objects:` prompt. End object selection to return to the Link Select dialog box.

3. Click Execute to add the query or selection of objects in your drawing to the Link Select operation.

4. Create a second selection set using the same process.

5. From the Do drop-down list, choose one of the logical operators. You now have one selection set from the combined selection sets you specified.

6. If you want, you can now create an additional selection set and use an operator to combine it with the previous selection set created in Step 5.

7. Choose Finish to complete the process.

Figure 20-23: Use the Link Select dialog box to create combined selection sets of objects from queries and/or direct selection in your drawing.

Working with Query Files

You can store, edit, rename, and delete queries. You can also import and export them for use by others. To use ASE links created in Releases 13 and 14, you need to convert them to AutoCAD 2004 format.

Storing queries

As I discussed previously, you can store a query by clicking Store on any tab. Stored queries are displayed under the drawing in the dbConnect window. To execute a stored query, choose dbConnect ➪ Queries ➪ Execute Query. Choose the query you want to execute and click OK. It helps if the queries have names that meaningfully relate to the query.

You can also edit a query. Choose dbConnect ➪ Queries ➪ Edit Query. Choose the query and click Continue. In the query Editor, make the desired changes and choose Store.

To rename a query, click it in the dbConnect window. Click it again to display an edit box. You can now edit the query's name. Remember that you have to name the query up front. If you're not sure what the query will consist of, use the default name, construct your query, and then rename it to something more meaningful afterward.

To delete a query, choose dbConnect ⇨ Queries ⇨ Delete Query. Choose the query or queries and click OK.

Importing and exporting queries

To export a query that has been saved (by clicking Store in the Query Editor), choose dbConnect ⇨ Queries ⇨ Export Query Set. In the Export Query Set dialog box, navigate to the desired folder and choose a name. Click Save. Queries have a .dbq file name extension.

Note To find the location of your queries, choose Tools ⇨ Options and click the Files tab. Double-click Data Sources Location to see the path.

To import a query that has been exported and named, choose dbConnect ⇨ Queries ⇨ Import Query Set. You need to know the name and location of the .dbq file. In the Import Query Set dialog box, locate the file and click Open. If your drawing already contains a query with the same name, AutoCAD 2004 adds a number to the name of the query so it has a unique name. This can easily occur because AutoCAD 2004 assigns default names to queries.

Converting prior release links to AutoCAD 2004 format

The link format changed with AutoCAD 2000; therefore, if you are upgrading from Release 14 or earlier, you need to convert your old links before you can use them.

You will need to collect the necessary information first. Read through the steps to see what you will need. Figure 20-24 shows the dialog box as it appears when you choose to convert R13/R14 links.

Follow these steps:

1. Choose dbConnect ⇨ Link Conversion.

2. Choose either R13/R14 or R12 Link Format.

3. Complete the entire top section of the dialog box. For R13/R14, you need the environment, catalog, schema, table, and link path name. For R12, you need the DBMS, the database, and the table.

4. Complete the entire New Link Format section — the Data Source, Catalog, Schema, Table, and Link Template. This section offers drop-down lists so you can choose from a list.

5. Click OK.

6. In AutoCAD 2004, open the drawing that contains the links you want to convert and save it.

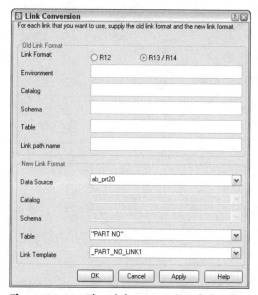

Figure 20-24: The Link Conversion dialog box

Summary

Using external databases to store data about drawing objects can reduce the size of drawings, simplify reporting, make data accessible to all users on a network, and enable you to edit a database from inside AutoCAD. In this chapter you read about:

✦ Configuring a data source

✦ Connecting a database table with your drawing

✦ Creating a link template

✦ Creating links between drawing objects and rows in the database

✦ Creating labels containing information from the database

✦ Defining SQL queries to select and sort the data you view

✦ Selecting objects based on queries

✦ Storing and saving queries

✦ Converting links from Releases 12 through 14.

This chapter ends Part III, "Working with Data." In Part IV, you start to draw in three dimensions. In the next chapter, I discuss how to specify 3D coordinates.

✦ ✦ ✦

Drawing in Three Dimensions

Part IV introduces you to three-dimensional drawing. AutoCAD creates three types of 3D objects, also called models — wireframes, surfaces, and solids. Wireframes, as the name implies, look like models created with wire. They do not have real surfaces or solidity. However, they are useful for creating shapes that you can turn into surfaces or solids. Surfaces, unlike wireframes, can hide objects behind them. They are especially useful for creating unusually shaped objects. Solids are defined as the entire volume of space they enclose. You can add and subtract solids from each other, creating realistic objects.

In Chapter 21, I explain the basics of 3D drawing, including specifying 3D coordinates, using the User Coordinate System for 3D drawing, and creating objects with elevation and thickness. Chapter 22 explains the techniques for viewing 3D objects. Chapter 23 covers surface models. Chapter 24 explains how to create true solids and covers editing in three dimensions. Chapter 25 explains how to create photorealistic views of your 3D drawings using AutoCAD's rendering feature.

Specifying 3D Coordinates

Until now, you have worked with two axes, X and Y. When you work in three dimensions, you add the Z axis. After you have a drawing with 3D objects, you can view it from any angle. The view you have been using in 2D drawings is like looking at a house from the top. Just as an architect calls this a plan view or a floor plan, AutoCAD calls this *plan view*. From this view, even a 3D drawing looks two-dimensional. But when you look at a 3D drawing from an angle, you can see that there's more to it than meets the eye. Figure 21-1 shows the plan view of an office building. Figure 21-2 shows the same drawing viewed in a perspective view from the front.

Figure 21-1: An office building in plan view
Thanks to Roger Cusson of Interface Architectural Software, Montreal, Quebec, for this drawing.

Figure 21-2: The same office building viewed from the front

Although this drawing is quite complex, you can easily get started by working on simpler models. Three-dimensional drawing is not as difficult as it seems at first. In this chapter, I first explain how to work with 3D coordinates. I also cover wireframe models and 3D surfaces created with thickness and elevation. These are essentially 2D objects placed in 3D space and are therefore a good place to start when learning about drawing in 3D.

Working with 3D Coordinates

All the 2D methods of specifying coordinates have their 3D counterparts. Just as you can draw a line by specifying a start point of 3,4 and an endpoint of 5,7, you can draw a 3D line by specifying a start point of 3,4,2 and an endpoint of 5,7,6. Absolute coordinates are the same in 3D—you just add a Z coordinate. In the same way, you can specify relative coordinates. In 3D drawings, you can use two new types of coordinates that are 3D counterparts of polar coordinates—cylindrical and spherical. Figure 21-3 shows the three axes X, Y, and Z. The arrows show the positive direction of the axes. Note that the UCS is set to display at the origin.

Working with the User Coordinate System (UCS) is essential in 3D work. If you are not familiar with the User Coordinate System, review the discussion in the section "User Coordinate Systems" in Chapter 8.

Most 2D commands, however, accept 3D coordinates (that is, a coordinate that includes a Z value) only on the first point. After that you must omit the Z coordinate because AutoCAD requires that it be the same as that of the first point. For example, if you draw a rectangle, you can specify its first corner as 2,3,8 but the second corner must be specified without the Z value, as in 6,7. The Z value for the opposite corner is automatically 8.

Figure 21-3: The three axes in 3D drawing

The LINE command is an exception. It is a true 3D command, so you can specify X, Y, and Z values at all points.

Absolute and relative Cartesian coordinates in 3D

You don't use absolute coordinates more in 3D than you do in 2D—maybe less. But understanding absolute coordinates is important to understanding the Cartesian coordinate system that AutoCAD uses to define every point in your drawing. Figure 21-4 shows a wireframe model of a square and a triangle drawn with absolute coordinates, viewed from above (plan view) and from the southeast view (above, to the right, and in front). The square is drawn in 2D—which means that the Z coordinates are all zero—to be a reference point for visualizing the 3D points of the triangle.

You can use relative coordinates in the same way by including the change in coordinates. For example, to draw the line from (3,2,1) to (6,4,3), shown in Figure 21-4, you can start with the absolute coordinate (3,2,1) and then specify @3,2,2 because that's the difference between (3,2,1) and (6,4,3).

Cylindrical and spherical coordinates

Just as polar coordinates are often more useful than Cartesian coordinates in 2D, cylindrical and spherical coordinates can be more useful in 3D. Here's how they work.

Cylindrical coordinates have the format (@)distance<angle,distance:

✦ The first distance is the number of units in the XY plane from the origin (for absolute coordinates) or your last point (for relative coordinates).

✦ The angle is the number of degrees from the X axis in the XY plane.

✦ The second distance is the number of units along the Z axis.

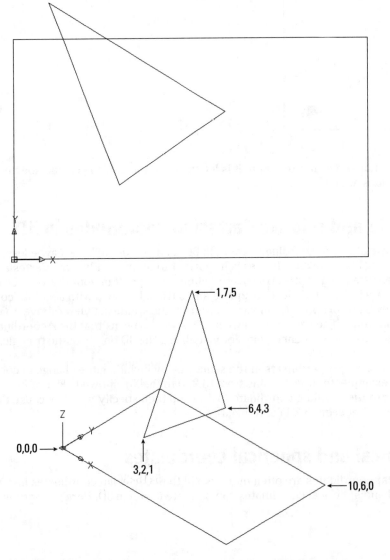

Figure 21-4: A rectangle and triangle viewed from plan view and southeast view

Cylindrical coordinates can be absolute or relative. Add the @ for relative coordinates. When you draw a line using cylindrical coordinates, neither distance you specify is the length of the line. In essence, you are defining the lengths of two sides of a triangle to draw the hypotenuse. Figure 21-5 shows an example of a line drawn with cylindrical coordinates. The line was drawn from 0,0,0 to @5<30,3, which results in a line 5.8310 units long. (The @ wasn't necessary because the line was drawn from 0,0,0.)

The two sides of the triangle are 5 and 3 units long. To calculate the length of the hypotenuse, use the Pythagorean theorem, which says that $a^2 + b^2 = c^2$ where a and b are the two sides of the triangle and c is the hypotenuse. Therefore, the hypotenuse is the square root of 25+9 or 34, which is 5.8310. Of course, you can use the DIST or LIST command to check it out.

Figure 21-5: A line drawn using cylindrical coordinates

Spherical coordinates have the format (@)distance<angle<angle:

+ The first distance is the total number of units from the origin (for absolute coordinates) or your last point (for relative coordinates).
+ The first angle is the number of degrees from the X axis in the XY plane.
+ The second angle is the number of degrees from the XY plane in the Z direction.

Spherical coordinates can be absolute or relative. Add the @ for relative coordinates. When you draw a line using spherical coordinates, the first distance is the actual length of the line. Figure 21-6 shows an example of a line drawn with spherical coordinates. The line was drawn from 0,0,0 to @5<15<30,

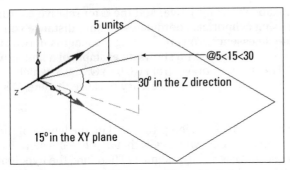

Figure 21-6: A line drawing using spherical coordinates

Using editing commands with 3D wireframes

Certain 2D editing commands work well in 3D. Others have special 3D versions. Because wireframes are simply 2D objects placed in 3D space, you can generally use the familiar editing commands. For example, to move an object 3 units in the positive Z axis direction, type **0,0,3** at the Specify base point or displacement: prompt and press Enter twice.

You need to be careful when selecting objects for editing. For example, if you draw two identically sized rectangles at different Z coordinates, you see only one rectangle when you look at them from plan view. How do you know which rectangle you are selecting? By changing the angle from which you view your drawing (fully covered in the next chapter), you can see all the parts of the drawing and can select objects easily.

Multiple tiled viewports in which you view your drawing from different viewpoints can be very helpful in 3D drawing. For example, you can have a plan view in one viewport and a southeast view in another. Tiled viewports are covered in Chapter 8, "Viewing Your Drawing."

In the following exercise, you draw a simple wireframe piano bench and practice using 3D coordinates for both drawing and editing commands. You also view the drawing from two different angles.

The drawing used in the following Step-by-Step exercise on using 3D coordinates, ab21-a.dwg, is in the Drawings folder of the *AutoCAD 2004 Bible* CD-ROM.

Step-by-Step: Using 3D Coordinates

1. Open ab21-a.dwg from the CD-ROM.

2. Save it as ab21-01.dwg in your AutoCAD Bible folder.

3. Choose Rectangle from the Draw toolbar. At the Specify first corner point or [Chamfer/Elevation/Fillet/Thickness/Width]: prompt,

type **0,0,19** ↵. At the Specify other corner point or [Dimensions]: prompt, type **39,15** ↵. This creates a rectangle 39 units long by 15 units wide that is 19 units above the plane created by the X and Y axes. Notice that you omit the Z coordinate for the second corner.

4. Start the COPY command. To copy the rectangle 2 units above the original rectangle, follow the prompts:

```
Select objects: Pick the rectangle.
Select objects: ↵
Specify base point or displacement, or [Multiple]: 0,0,2 ↵
Specify second point of displacement or <use first point as displacement>: ↵
```

You now have two rectangles, but because you are looking from the top, you see only one.

5. Choose View ➪ 3D Views ➪ SE Isometric. Now you can see the two rectangles, as shown in Figure 21-7.

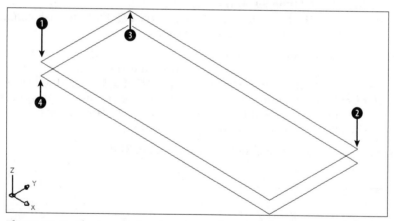

Figure 21-7: The two rectangles, shown from Southeast Isometric view

6. If OSNAP is not on, click it on the status bar. Set a running object snap for endpoints.

7. Start the LINE command. Follow the prompts:

```
Specify first point: Pick the endpoint at ❶ in Figure 21-7.
Specify next point or [Undo]: 0,0,0 ↵
Specify next point or [Undo]: 1,0,0 ↵
Specify next point or [Close/Undo]: 1,0,21 ↵
Specify next point or [Close/Undo]: ↵
```

8. Start the COPY command. At the Select objects: prompt, select the three lines you just drew. End object selection. At the Specify base point or displacement, or [Multiple]: prompt, type **38,0,0** ↵. At the Specify second point of displacement or <use first point

as displacement>: prompt, press Enter. AutoCAD copies the three lines. Because the bench is 39 units long and the legs are 1 unit wide, copying the leg 38 units in the X direction places the copy in the right location.

9. Do a Zoom Extents so that you can see the entire drawing.

10. Repeat the COPY command. Use two separate crossing windows to select the first leg, then the second leg. AutoCAD should find three objects each time. End object selection. At the Specify base point or displacement, or [Multiple]: prompt, type **0,15,0** ↵ to copy the legs 15 units in the Y direction. Press Enter at the Specify second point of displacement or <use first point as displacement>: prompt. AutoCAD copies the legs to the back of the bench.

11. To draw an open cover for the piano bench, start the LINE command. Start it at the endpoint at ❷ in Figure 21-7. At the Specify next point or [Undo]: prompt, type **@15<90<45** ↵. You know the length of the line because the cover is the same as the width of the piano bench. At the Specify next point or [Undo]: prompt, turn on ORTHO, move the cursor parallel to the length of the bench, and type **39**. At the Specify next point or [Close/Undo]: prompt, use the Endpoint object snap to pick ❸. End the LINE command. Zoom out and pan so you can see the entire bench.

12. To draw some bracing inside the bench, start the LINE command again. At the Specify first point: prompt, choose the endpoint at ❹. At the Specify next point or [Undo]: prompt, type **@15<90,2** ↵. End the LINE command. Here, cylindrical coordinates are ideal because you don't know the length of the line but you know the change in the X and Z coordinates (the width and the height of the bench's body, respectively).

13. Save your drawing. It should look like Figure 21-8.

Figure 21-8: The completed wireframe piano bench

Using point filters, object snaps, and grips in 3D

As mentioned earlier, it is often hard to tell which point you are picking in 3D. On a flat screen, you can only be sure of two dimensions. The other dimension is, so to speak, going in or out of the screen—it could be X, Y, or Z depending on the angle you are using to look at the drawing. That dimension is the one that is hard to pick on the screen. In AutoCAD you use point filters, object snaps, and grips to be sure you have the right point in 3D drawing.

Point filters

In Chapter 4, "Specifying Coordinates," I discuss point filters for 2D objects. They work the same way in 3D. You usually use point filters together with object snaps. For example, for the X coordinate you might pick the endpoint of a line. Often point filters are the only way to define a 3D point that is not on an existing object. The point filters for 3D drawings are .xy, .xz, and .yz. For example, if you want to pick a point 3 units in the Z direction from the endpoint of an existing line, you can use the .xy point filter to choose the endpoint of the line. AutoCAD then asks you for the Z coordinate, which you can specify as a number or using an object snap. You can also use point filters to specify each coordinate (X, Y, and Z) separately.

Object snaps

Object snaps are essential for 3D work. Turn on OSNAP and set running object snaps. Object snaps ensure that you are specifying the point you want. However, don't forget that in 3D drawings, you can have two lines, one on top of the other. Use a view that enables you to see the two lines separately so that you can pick the object snap you want. The Apparent Intersection object snap is especially useful for 3D work. You can use it to specify points that look as if they intersect from your viewpoint, even though in true 3D they would not intersect.

Grips

You can use grips to edit many 3D objects as well. Again, it is important to choose a view that makes the editing easy. Chapter 24 discusses editing in 3D in more detail.

New Feature

Grips are now shown parallel to the plane of the current User Coordinate System. When you change your viewpoint, the grips change their shape slightly to look as if they are lying on the XY plane.

On the CD-ROM

The drawing used in the following Step-by-Step exercise on using point filters and object snaps with 3D wireframe objects, ab21-b.dwg, is in the Drawings folder of the *AutoCAD 2004 Bible* CD-ROM.

Step-by-Step: Using Point Filters and Object Snaps with 3D Wireframe Objects

1. Open `ab21-b.dwg` from the CD-ROM.

2. Save it as `ab21-02.dwg` in your `AutoCAD Bible` folder. OSNAP should be on. Set a running object snap for endpoint and midpoint. This is the same piano bench drawn in the previous Step-by-Step exercise, but without the cover. In this exercise, you use the bench to create a chair.

3. Choose Stretch from the Modify toolbar. Use a crossing window to select the right side of the bench. AutoCAD should find eight objects. End object selection. At the `Specify base point or displacement:` prompt, use the Endpoint object snap to pick ❶ in Figure 21-9. At the `Specify second point of displacement:` prompt, type **@–15,0** ↵.

4. Use Pan Realtime to pan the chair to the bottom of your screen.

Figure 21-9: The piano bench after being shrunk with the STRETCH command

5. Start the LINE command. Follow the prompts:

   ```
   Specify first point: Choose ❷ in Figure 21-9.
   Specify next point or [Undo]: .xy ↵
   of Pick ❷.
   (need Z): 45 ↵
   Specify next point or [Undo]: .yz ↵
   of Pick the top endpoint of the line you just drew.
   (need X): Pick ❸.
   Specify next point or [Close/Undo]: Pick ❸.
   Specify next point or [Close/Undo]: ↵
   ```

6. Repeat the LINE command. Draw a line from the midpoint of the left side of the back of the chair back to the midpoint of the right side.

7. Choose Fillet from the Modify toolbar. At the `Select first object or [Polyline/Radius/Trim/mUltiple]:` prompt, right-click and choose Radius. At the `Specify fillet radius <0.5000>:` prompt, type **1** ↵.

8. At the `Select first object or [Polyline/Radius/Trim/mUltiple]:` prompt, pick ❶ in Figure 21-10. At the `Select second object:` prompt, pick ❷.

9. Repeat the FILLET command and pick ❷ and ❸ for the two lines.

10. Save the drawing of the chair. It should look like Figure 21-10.

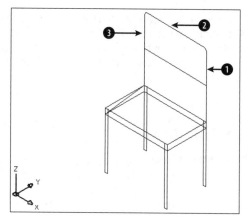

Figure 21-10: A wireframe model of a chair

Creating 3D polylines

You have already created 3D lines by specifying 3D coordinates for the endpoints. The LINE command is a true 3D command because it accepts 3D coordinates. However, many commands cannot accept 3D coordinates. For example, you cannot place the center of a circle on one Z coordinate and the circumference on another. The whole circle must be on the same XY plane. Later in this chapter, I explain how to change the UCS to get around this restriction.

This doesn't mean that you don't use circles in 3D work. You can always create a circle in one XY plane and then use that circle as a base for a cylinder, for example. The point is that the CIRCLE command itself is only a 2D command.

One command that has a 3D counterpart is PLINE. The 3D command is called 3DPOLY. The 3DPOLY command is like the PLINE command with a few differences:

✦ You cannot draw arcs.

✦ You cannot give the polyline a width.

✦ You cannot use a noncontinuous linetype.

The 3DPOLY command can accept all 3D coordinates. You can also edit it with the PEDIT command, although there are fewer options.

> **Tip** If you want to create curved shapes in 3D space, you can create 2D polylines with
> a width and then add a thickness and an elevation. Elevation and thickness are
> both explained in the next section.

Using Elevation and Thickness

Wireframes have a number of limitations. In Figure 21-10, the chair you drew in the
previous exercise, you can see the back leg through the seat of the chair. Also, cre-
ating the detail of a real chair would be tedious if you were to use individual lines
or 3D polylines. Finally, wireframes don't have any surface or solid properties. You
can't display them in any realistic fashion or calculate properties, such as area,
mass, and so on.

Creating surfaces with thickness

You can create simple surfaces by adding thickness to 2D objects. When you add
thickness to a 2D object, AutoCAD pushes it out into the third dimension. For exam-
ple, a circle becomes a cylinder and a rectangle becomes a box. Remember that you
won't see the thickness if you're looking at the object from the top. Figure 21-11
shows some objects created using thickness.

Figure 21-11: 3D surfaces created by adding
thickness to 2D objects

Surfaces created by adding thickness are sometimes called 2½D objects. Although
they have three dimensions, the third dimension can only be a straight side perpen-
dicular to the 2D object at the base.

The parallel lines on the cylinder are called tessellation lines. AutoCAD uses them to help you visualize curved surfaces. They are not actually part of the cylinder — you cannot use object snaps on them, for example.

To add thickness to an existing 2D object, choose Properties on the Standard toolbar and select the object. (You can also select the object first.) In the Properties palette, click the Thickness property and change the number in the Thickness text box. Press Enter.

You can also change the current thickness. The current thickness affects new objects as you draw them, but not existing objects. There are two ways to change the current thickness:

✦ Choose Properties on the Standard toolbar with no object selected. Click the Thickness property and type a value in the text box. Press Enter.

✦ Use the ELEV command (which also changes the current elevation, discussed in the next section) by typing it on the command line. The ELEV command prompts you for the current elevation and the current thickness. To change the current thickness, type a number and press Enter.

In most cases, you use a positive number, which extrudes objects in the positive direction of the Z axis. However, you can use a negative number to extrude objects in the negative direction of the Z axis. As soon as you change the current thickness, all objects you draw have that thickness.

Tip Because it is easy to forget the current thickness, unless you are drawing a number of objects with the same thickness, it is usually safer to draw objects with no thickness and then change the thickness. If you do change the current thickness, don't forget to change it back to zero when you are finished creating the 3D objects.

Using the HIDE command

Because objects with thickness are surfaces, not wireframes, you can use the HIDE command to hide lines that would normally be hidden from view in real life. AutoCAD calculates which lines are behind surfaces from the current viewpoint you are using and hides them. Figure 21-12 shows the same objects as Figure 21-11 after using the HIDE command. You may notice that the cylinder has a top but the triangular prism and the box don't. For a further explanation, see the sidebar, "Do objects with thickness have tops and bottoms?"

To return to the wireframe display, use the REGEN command.

New
Feature Two new system variables, INTERSECTIONDISPLAY and INTERSECTIONCOLOR, control the display of polylines at the face intersections of solid and surface objects. A new command, HLSETTINGS, opens a dialog box so that you can set these system variables, as well as the others listed in this section that affect the display of hidden lines.

Figure 21-12: 3D surfaces after using the HIDE command

Several system variables affect the 3D display only when you use the HIDE command or the Hidden option of the SHADEMODE command. Like the HIDE command, they work on both solids and surfaces. Type **hlsettings** on the command line to open the Hidden Line Settings dialog box, shown in Figure 21-13.

Figure 21-13: The Hidden Line Settings dialog box

Here's how to use the Hidden Line Settings dialog box:

Use the Obscured lines section to choose a linetype and color for displaying hidden lines. (This sets the OBSCUREDLTYPE system variable.) When you choose a linetype, hidden lines are shown in the linetype you choose. These linetypes are not affected as you zoom in or out. Choose from these linetypes:

 ✦ Off

 ✦ Solid

 ✦ Dashed

✦ Dotted

✦ Short Dash

✦ Medium Dash

✦ Long Dash

✦ Double Short Dash

✦ Double Medium Dash

✦ Double Long Dash

✦ Medium Long Dash

✦ Sparse Dot

If you choose a linetype, then choose a color from the Color drop-down list (the OBSCUREDCOLOR system variable). You can choose from one of the standard AutoCAD color index numbers (from 1–255) Use the Off setting (the default) to fully hide back lines.

Use the Halo Gap Percentage section to create a gap that shortens lines at the point that they would be hidden by the HIDE command, in order to set off the lines from the unhidden portion of the model. By default, this percentage (the HALOGAP system variable) is set to 0, which creates no gap. Set the gap as a percentage of an inch — the gap doesn't change as you zoom in or out.

Use the Display Intersections check box in the Face Intersections section to turn on the display of polylines at the intersections of 3D model faces. Then use the Color drop-down list to choose a color for the polylines.

Do objects with thickness have tops and bottoms?

If you look carefully at Figure 21-12, you see that the cylinder has a top but the triangular prism and the box don't. AutoCAD puts top and bottom surfaces on some objects with thickness, but not on others.

When you add a thickness to objects created with the SOLID command (a 2D command), circles, and wide polylines, AutoCAD treats them as surfaces with tops and bottoms.

However, if you draw a closed polyline, for example with the RECTANG or POLYGON command, and give it a thickness, AutoCAD does not give it a top or a bottom surface. The same is true for a closed figure you draw with the LINE command.

Therefore, if you want a top and bottom, use the SOLID command, draw a polyline with a width greater than zero, or draw a circle. (Hatching a closed figure with a solid fill does not have the same effect as the SOLID command.) These objects create opaque horizontal surfaces. You can see the difference when you use the HIDE command.

Use the Hide Precision section of the Hidden Line Settings dialog box if you want a more exact calculation of the HIDE command results.

Check Include Text in HIDE Operations (the HIDETEXT system variable) to hide text behind other objects and for text to hide other objects. When this item is unchecked, text will not hide other objects, or be hidden, unless it has a thickness.

Figure 21-14 shows a model using a HALOGAP value of 15, a green, dashed line to display hidden lines, and face intersections displayed in red.

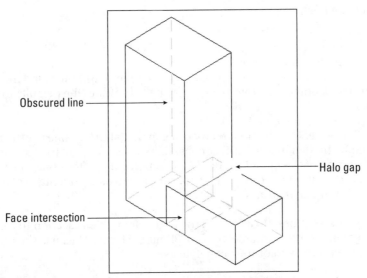

Figure 21-14: This model uses HALOGAP, OBSCUREDLTYPE, and OBSCUREDCOLOR to display hidden lines.

Note

> The word *wireframe* is used in two ways in AutoCAD. First, it means 3D objects that are created using only lines and 3D polylines. These objects have no surfaces or solidity. Second, it means surfaces and solids that are displayed as if they are created with lines and 3D polylines, such as the models in Figure 21-11. This can get confusing. In this book, I usually distinguish between wireframes and wireframe display. If the subject is surfaces and solids, the term *wireframe* generally means wireframe display.

Adding elevation to objects

Until now, all of your 3D objects were based on 2D objects that were on the XY plane. In other words, their Z coordinate was zero. Although you generally don't want objects to float in the air, you certainly may want to place one object on top of

another. To do this, you need to start the object above the XY plane—you can also place objects below the XY plane—and give an object elevation, which is its Z coordinate.

To give elevation to an existing object, you can use one of two methods:

✦ Select the object and choose Properties on the Standard toolbar. Click the Elevation property and type a new elevation in the text box and press Enter.

✦ Move the object(s) with the MOVE command in the Z direction.

For new objects, change the current elevation with the ELEV command as described earlier in this chapter in the discussion on thickness.

Note

For some objects, you can use the Properties palette to change the Z coordinate. This works for circles, lines, arcs, and ellipses, but not for polylines. To elevate an entire line, you need to change the Z coordinate of both the start point and the endpoint. Choose Properties on the Standard toolbar to open the Properties palette.

When you change the current elevation, all objects you create are drawn on that elevation. Remember to change the elevation back to zero when you want to draw on the XY plane again.

Caution

If you specify an object snap of an object on a different elevation (with a different Z coordinate) than your current elevation, AutoCAD uses the elevation of the object snap, not the current elevation. However, if you specify the first point of a 2D command, such as PLINE (to create a polyline), on the current elevation, you can use object snaps at a different elevation for subsequent points. Because the entire polyline must be on the same elevation, subsequent points follow the elevation of the first point.

Step-by-Step: Working with Elevation, Thickness, and the HIDE Command

1. Start a new drawing using the `acad.dwt` template.

2. Save it as `ab21-03.dwg` in your `AutoCAD Bible` folder.

3. Start the CIRCLE command. Specify the center as 6,6 and the radius as 18.

4. Do a Zoom Extents.

5. Choose Properties on the Standard toolbar. Select the circle. Click the thickness property. In the Thickness text box, type **3** ↵. Choose Properties again to close the Properties palette.

6. Type **elev** ↵. At the `Specify new default elevation <0.0000>:` prompt, type **3** ↵. Because you just changed the existing circle's thickness to 3, you set the elevation to 3 to place an object on top of the circle. At the `Specify new default thickness <0.0000>:` prompt, type **24** ↵.

7. Start the CIRCLE command again. Press Shift+right-click and choose Center from the Object Snap shortcut menu to pick the center of the existing circle as the center of the new circle. Set the radius to 3.

8. Type **elev** ↵. At the `Specify new default elevation <3.0000>:` prompt, type **27**. At the `Specify new default thickness <24.0000>:` prompt, type **3** ↵. This places any new object on top of the two circles you just drew.

9. Start the CIRCLE command. Specify the center as 6,6 and the radius as 18. Because you don't specify a Z coordinate, AutoCAD uses the current elevation.

10. Choose View ⇨ 3D Views ⇨ SE Isometric. You can now see the three circles.

11. Type **hide** ↵. You can now see the cable spool clearly.

12. Save your drawing. It should look like Figure 21-15.

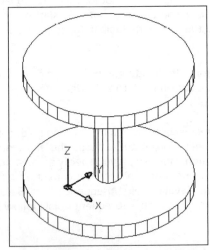

Figure 21-15: A cable spool created by drawing 2D circles with thickness and elevation

On the CD-ROM The 3dspiral routine creates 2D and 3D spirals. You can find it in `\Software\ Chap21\3dspiral`.

Working with the User Coordinate System

Except for certain true solids, much of 3D work starts with a 2D shape. However, the 2D drawing commands can be drawn only on, or parallel to, the XY plane. The spool in Figure 21-15, for example, consists of three circles, all parallel to the XY plane. How do you draw a circle, or any other 2D object for that matter, that is not parallel to the XY plane?

The answer is to change the User Coordinate System (UCS), thereby changing the definition of the XY plane. You can move the UCS to any location to define the XY plane any way you want. After you do so, you can draw a 2D object at any angle. This section offers a brief review of UCS features that are particularly useful for 3D drawing. (See Chapter 8 for complete coverage of the UCS feature.)

Using the UCS icon

Although you may have found the UCS icon an annoyance in 2D work, you should display it when working in 3D. Otherwise, it is easy to lose track of which direction is which. Remember that you can also choose the Origin option, which displays the UCS icon, if possible, at the origin. Choose View ➪ Display ➪ UCS Icon ➪ Origin.

Cross-Reference You can customize the look of the UCS icon. The 3D style is helpful when you're working in 3D. See Chapter 8 for the details on customizing the UCS icon display.

UCSs and viewpoints

A plan view of the World UCS (the default) is different from the plan view of a UCS you have created by rotating the UCS around the X axis, for example. The UCS defines the orientation and origin of the X, Y, and Z axes. On the other hand, the viewpoint shows your drawing from different angles without changing the orientation or origin of the axes. Understanding the difference between the UCS and viewpoints is important.

The broken pencil

When you choose a viewpoint that shows your drawing from the front, back, or one side instead of the top or an angle, you are looking straight across the XY plane. This is like looking at a table (which represents the XY plane) by kneeling down so your eyes are exactly at the same height as the surface of the table. From this vantage point, you cannot easily pick objects on the XY plane. A circle looks like a line. In such a situation, if you have created a new UCS (not the World UCS) and if you are using the 2D display of the UCS icon, AutoCAD replaces the UCS icon with a broken pencil to warn you that you are looking at the XY plane of the current UCS edge on.

Figure 21-16 shows the same drawing from three viewpoints: plan view, the SE Isometric view (one of AutoCAD's preset viewpoints), and the front view. From the front view, AutoCAD displays the broken pencil icon. Notice that the plan (top) view displays even fewer details of the drawing and would also make it difficult to select objects. The middle version uses the SE Isometric preset view, which displays the drawing from above and one corner. This view displays the drawing most clearly.

New Feature Express Tools has a command, RTUCS, that enables you to rotate the UCS icon by dragging with the mouse. You can set an incremental angle for rotation and specify an active axis around which you rotate the UCS. Choose Express ➪ Tools ➪ Real-Time UCS. For information on installing the Express Tools, see Appendix A on the CD-ROM.

Figure 21-16: Looking at a drawing from different viewpoints in a custom UCS. When you are looking at the XY plane edge on and are using the 2D UCS icon display, AutoCAD displays the broken-pencil icon.

UCS options

To change the UCS, choose one of the UCS menu items on the Tools menu. The following UCS options on the Tools ⇨ New UCS submenu are useful for 3D drawing.

Object

You can align the UCS with any existing object. Because AutoCAD orients the UCS differently for different objects, this option can sometimes be confusing. However, to modify some objects you must be on its XY plane—a good time to use the Object option. The overall principle is that AutoCAD leaves the UCS's XY plane parallel to the previous UCS, except for 3Dface objects. Table 21-1 explains how AutoCAD aligns the UCS for various kinds of objects.

Table 21-1	
UCS Orientation with the Object Option	
Object	*UCS Orientation*
Line	The endpoint nearest your pick point is the origin. The line lies on the X axis.
2D Polyline	The endpoint of the polyline nearest your pick point is the origin. The first segment of the polyline lies on the X axis.
Dimension	AutoCAD places the origin at the midpoint of the dimension text. The X axis is parallel to the X axis that you used when you created the dimension.
Text	AutoCAD places the origin at the insertion point and aligns the X axis with the rotation angle of the text. The same applies to attributes.
Block	AutoCAD places the origin at the insertion point and aligns the X axis with the rotation angle of the block.
Circle	The origin is at the circle's center. The X axis is aligned with your pick point.
Arc	The origin is at the arc's center. The X axis is aligned with the endpoint closest to your pick point.
Point	The origin is at the point. The X axis may be difficult to determine in advance.
Solid	AutoCAD uses the first point you specified for the origin and the first and second points to align the X axis.
3Dface	AutoCAD uses the first point for the origin. The X axis is aligned with the first two points. The Y axis is aligned with the first and fourth points. The new UCS may not be parallel to the prior UCS.

Face

The Face option aligns the UCS on a face of a solid object. At the `Select face of solid object:` prompt, click within the boundary of a face or on its edge. AutoCAD highlights the face and aligns the X axis of the UCS with the closest edge of the first face it finds.

At the `Enter an option [Next/Xflip/Yflip] <accept>:` prompt, you can now refine the UCS. Right-click and choose Next to move the UCS to the adjacent face or the back face of the selected edge. Right-click and choose Xflip to rotate the UCS 180 degrees around the X axis. Right-click and choose Yflip to rotate the UCS 180 degrees around the Y axis. When you have the UCS you want, press Enter to accept the current location of the UCS.

View

The View option aligns the X and Y axes with the current view. AutoCAD retains the current origin. The View option is most often used for creating text that you want to appear flat from your viewpoint of a 3D view of the drawing.

Origin

The Origin option creates a UCS parallel to the current UCS but with a new origin that you specify. You can use the Origin option for working at a new elevation, instead of changing the current elevation.

Z Axis Vector

The Z Axis Vector option enables you to define an origin and then a point on the positive side of the Z axis. You can keep the previous origin to twist the UCS around its origin.

3Point

The first point you specify is the origin, the second point indicates the positive direction of the X axis, and the third point indicates the positive direction of the Y axis.

X

The X option maintains the current origin and rotates the Y and Z axes around the current X axis at the rotation angle you specify. The most common rotation is 90 degrees or a multiple of 90 degrees, but you can specify any angle.

Y

The Y option keeps the current origin and rotates the X and Z axes around the current Y axis. You specify the angle.

Z

The Z option keeps the current origin and rotates the X and Y axes around the current Z axis. You specify the angle.

On the CD-ROM The drawing used in the following Step-by-Step exercise on creating UCSs, ab21-c. dwg, is in the Drawings folder of the *AutoCAD 2004 Bible* CD-ROM.

Step-by-Step: Creating UCSs

1. Open ab21-c.dwg from the CD-ROM.

2. Save it as ab21-04.dwg in your AutoCAD Bible folder. This drawing contains some center lines based on measurements of a chair. OSNAP should be on. Set running object snaps for endpoint, midpoint, center, and quadrant. The UCS icon is set at the origin.

3. Choose Circle from the Draw toolbar. Use the From object snap to specify the center at @2,0 from ❶ in Figure 21-17. Set the radius to 0.5.

Figure 21-17: These center lines are the basis for drawing a chair.

4. Choose Properties on the Standard toolbar and select the circle you just drew. Change the thickness to 16. Press Enter. Close the Properties palette (or right-click its title bar and choose Auto-Hide).

5. Click ORTHO on the status bar to turn it on. Choose Mirror from the Modify toolbar. The circle should still be selected. (If it isn't, select it.) Specify the endpoint at ❷ for the first point of the mirror line. Specify any point vertical to ❷ for the second point of the mirror line. Choose not to delete the source object (the circle).

6. Repeat the MIRROR command. Select the two circles. Pick the midpoint of the line at ❸ for the first point of the mirror line. Pick any point horizontal to the first point for the second point of the mirror line. Press Enter. There are now four legs. Turn ORTHO off.

7. Type **elev** ↵. Change the elevation to 16 and the thickness to 1.

8. Choose View ⇨ 3D Views ⇨ SE Isometric. You can now see the four chair legs.

9. Choose Polyline from the Draw toolbar. At the `Specify start point:` prompt, choose the From object snap. Use the Center object snap of the top of the circle near ❶ in Figure 21-16 for the base point and an offset of @–2,0. (You may have to tab to get the Center object snap.) Continue to pick points ❹ through ❿. Notice that AutoCAD displays the Endpoint object snap symbol at the height of the first point. Then right-click and choose Close to close the polyline.

10. Choose Modify ⇨ Object ⇨ Polyline (or type **pedit** ↵). Select the polyline. At the prompt, right-click and choose Fit to fit the polyline. Press Enter to end the command.

11. To see the result, type **hide** ↵. Remember that the polyline has no top or bottom surface. Imagine your model as a glass-bottomed chair. It should look like Figure 21-18.

Figure 21-18: Part of a 3D chair

12. Choose Tools ⇨ Inquiry ⇨ List. Select the front left leg at ❶ in Figure 21-18. Press Enter. The center (of the circle at the bottom of the leg) is X= 3.5000; Y= –7.0000; Z= 0.0000.

13. To see the effect of a different UCS option, choose Tools ⇨ New UCS ⇨ X. To rotate the UCS around the X axis, type **90** ↵. Again, choose Tools ⇨ Inquiry ⇨ List and select the same leg of the chair. Now the center is X = 3.5000, Y = 0.0000, Z = 7.0000. Look at the UCS icon (which is at 0,0,0) and try to visualize why the coordinates are as AutoCAD lists them.

14. Because you know the center of the circle of the front leg, you can move the UCS there. Choose Tools ⇨ New UCS ⇨ Origin. At the `Origin point <0,0,0>`: prompt, type **3.5,0,7** ↵. This places the X axis through the center of the circle.

15. Choose Tools ⇨ New UCS ⇨ View. AutoCAD places the UCS parallel to your current view. Choose Draw ⇨ Text ⇨ Single-Line Text. Start the text at ❷ in Figure 21-18. Set the height to 1.0 and the rotation to 0. Type **A glass-bottomed chair**. Press Enter twice to end the command.

16. Choose Tools ⇨ New UCS ⇨ Object. Pick the line at ❸. Choose Tools ⇨ New UCS ⇨ Origin. Type **0, 0,17** as the origin to place the UCS at the top of the seat.

17. Choose Tools ⇨ New UCS ⇨ X. Type **–10** ↵ to rotate the UCS around the X axis by –10 degrees. This enables you to create the back of the chair at a 10-degree angle. Type **plan** and press Enter again to accept the default. (This command is covered in the next chapter.) It enables you to view your drawing from plan view, in this case relative to the current UCS.

Tip Although it's not necessary for this exercise, this would be a good UCS to save (choose Tools ⇨ Named UCS and rename the Unnamed current UCS to Chair Back). After you have gone through all these steps, it would be a shame to have to re-create the UCS again.

18. With no objects selected, choose Properties on the Standard toolbar. Set the thickness to 16. (The elevation is irrelevant because you will use OSNAPS in the next step.) Close the Properties palette.

19. Start the CIRCLE command. Choose the center of the lower circle of the top-left leg (it's inside the chair's seat) for the center. Accept the default radius of 0.5. Use the same technique to draw a circle at the corresponding right circle. Choose View ⇨ 3D Views ⇨ SE Isometric to see the results. Then choose Zoom Previous on the Standard toolbar to return to your previous display.

20. Change the thickness to –5. Type **hide** ↵ so that you can see the circles you just created more clearly.

21. Start the ARC command. The start point should be at the left quadrant of the left circle you just drew. The second point is the intersection of the vertical center line and the top horizontal center line. (There is an Endpoint object snap there.) The endpoint is the right quadrant of the right circle.

22. Choose Tools ➪ New UCS ➪ World. Choose View ➪ 3D Views ➪ SE Isometric. Then type **hide** ⏎ to see the final result.

23. Save your drawing. The chair should look like Figure 21-19.

Figure 21-19: The completed glass-bottomed chair

A glass-bottomed chair

Summary

This chapter introduced you to 3D drawing. You read about:

✦ Understanding all the types of 3D coordinates and how to use them

✦ Using editing commands in 3D

✦ Using point filters, object snaps, and grips in 3D drawings

✦ Utilizing elevation and thickness

✦ Understanding the HIDE command and the system variables that affect the hidden display

✦ Working with User Coordinate Systems in 3D

In the next chapter, I explain all the ways to view 3D drawings.

✦　　✦　　✦

Viewing 3D Drawings

As soon as you start to work in three dimensions, you
need to be able to see the drawing from different
angles. By combining various User Coordinate Systems (UCSs)
and different viewpoints, you can draw any object in 3D.

Your basic point of reference is plan view in the World
Coordinate System (WCS). This is the way you draw in 2D, so
it is familiar. Plan view is the view from the top. For a building,
the top is obvious. However, for a bushing, which view is the
top? Figure 22-1 shows a 2D drawing of a bushing. Figure 22-2
shows the 3D version. The left view of Figure 22-1 is the plan
view looking down from the top. (Although AutoCAD calls this
the plan view, engineering practice might call this the front
view.) The drawing was created this way because it is easier
to extrude a circle than to turn a polygon into a circular
model.

When working in 3D, you can use many of the familiar 2D tech-
niques for viewing your drawing:

 ◆ Use ZOOM Previous to display the previous viewpoint.

 ◆ Save views so that you can easily return to them.

 ◆ Use real-time zoom and pan as well as all the other zoom
 options.

 ◆ Creating tiled viewports to display more than one view
 at a time.

Figure 22-1: The left view is the plan view, looking down from the top.

Thanks to Robert Mack, the Dexter Company, Fairfield, Iowa, for this drawing.

Figure 22-2: A 3D view of the bushing after using the HIDE command

Working with the Standard Viewpoints

AutoCAD offers ten standard viewpoints on the View toolbar. (Right-click any toolbar and choose View to display the View toolbar.) These viewpoints are useful and easy to use because they are the most commonly used viewpoints. You can do a lot of your work just using these viewpoints. The standard viewpoints show viewpoints relative only to the WCS, not the current UCS. Therefore they are most useful when you are using the WCS.

To use a preset viewpoint you can choose it from the View toolbar. You can also choose View ➪ 3D Views and choose the viewpoint you want from the submenu. Each of the preset viewpoints automatically does a Zoom Extents.

Using the VPOINT command

The VPOINT command was the original, command-line method of setting viewpoints. Now it is generally used for scripts and AutoLISP routines when you need a way to set a viewpoint from the command line.

The VPOINT command defines a viewpoint using X, Y, and Z vectors. The vectors for the standard viewpoints are based on a maximum of 1 unit. Imagine a model of the three axes floating out in space. You are Superman and can fly around the model from any angle. When you are over the Z axis, you can define the Z vector from 0,0,0 to your position as 1. The other vectors are zero (0) because you are right over them so that 0,0,1 defines the top, or plan, view. The next section shows the vector equivalents for the standard viewpoints to give you a feel for the vector system.

The VPOINT command also has a Rotate option that is the command-line equivalent of the DDVPOINT command's Viewpoint Presets dialog box. Using this option, you define a viewpoint by the angle from the X axis in the XY plane and then the angle from the XY plane.

Looking at a drawing from the standard viewpoints

It is easier to show than to describe the viewpoints. Here I show a simple 3D house from all ten standard viewpoints.

Note A system variable, UCSORTHO, automatically changes the UCS to match the viewpoint when you switch to one of the orthographic (top, bottom, left, right, front, and back) viewpoints. In order to distinguish between the viewpoints and UCSs, I have turned UCSORTHO off for the following section.

Top view

 The top view is the plan view. You are looking at the model from a bird's eye perspective, suspended over the model. The VPOINT equivalent is 0,0,1. Figure 22-3 shows a house from the top.

You can also get this view by typing PLAN on the command line. Note that the PLAN command does not change the UCS even though you choose to see the plan view of a different UCS. This actually makes it very flexible — you can see what your drawing looks like from a different UCS without actually changing the UCS. The PLAN command is explained later in this chapter.

Figure 22-3: The top viewpoint of a 3D house

Bottom view

The bottom view is the plan view for groundhogs. It's not very useful for buildings, but may be very useful for 3D mechanical drawings. The VPOINT equivalent is 0,0,–1. Figure 22-4 shows the house from the bottom. Notice the direction of the UCS icon. Also the square is missing on the icon, indicating you are viewing from the negative Z direction, or from "underneath."

Figure 22-4: The bottom viewpoint of the 3D house

Left view

The left view shows you your model from the side — the left side, of course. In architecture it would be one of the elevation views. The VPOINT equivalent is –1,0,0. Figure 22-5 shows the house from the left view. Notice the backward text. The text was drawn from the right view.

Figure 22-5: The left view of the 3D house

Right view

The right view shows you your model from the right side. Like left view, right view is an elevation view. The VPOINT equivalent is 1,0,0. Figure 22-6 shows the house from the right view. Notice that the text now appears correctly because it was drawn from this view.

Front view

The front view, another elevation view, shows your model from the front. The VPOINT equivalent is 0,–1,0. Figure 22-7 shows the house from the front. The text, stating that the front faces the east, doesn't represent any rule in AutoCAD. It simply helps you see the differences in the sides of the house.

Back view

The back view, another elevation view, shows your model from the back, as shown in Figure 22-8. Here you see the text of the front of the house, shown backward. The VPOINT equivalent is 0,1,0.

Figure 22-6: The right view of the 3D house

Figure 22-7: The front view of the 3D house

SW isometric view

The SW (southwest) isometric view shows you your model from a diagonal viewpoint in all three dimensions (see Figure 22-9). Notice how one corner of the house is closest to you (the corner between the left and front views), and you are also looking at the house from a view halfway between a side view and the top view. The isometric views are excellent for viewing all the 3D objects in a drawing. As you can see, many more objects are visible than with the top view or any of the side views. The VPOINT equivalent is –1,–1,1.

Figure 22-8: The back view of the 3D house

Figure 22-9: The SW isometric view of the 3D house

Don't get confused with the house's direction — the front facing east. From AutoCAD's point of view, east is 0 degrees when looking from the top view, and 0 degrees faces to the right.

SE isometric view

The SE (southeast) isometric view also shows your model from a diagonal viewpoint in all three dimensions. Here you are looking at the house at the corner between the right and front views, as well as halfway between a side view and

the top view. You see the same objects as you do in SW isometric view. However, in a drawing not as symmetrical as the house, one view may bring certain objects to the front so that you can select them. The VPOINT equivalent is 1,–1,1. Figure 22-10 shows the house from the SE isometric view.

NE isometric view

The NE isometric view shows your model from the corner between the right and the back views, as well as halfway between a side view and the top view. The VPOINT equivalent is 1,1,1. Figure 22-11 shows the house from the NE isometric view.

Figure 22-10: The SE isometric view of the 3D house

Figure 22-11: The NE isometric view of the 3D house

NW isometric view

The NW isometric view shows your model from the corner between the left and the back views, as well as halfway between a side view and the top view. The VPOINT equivalent is –1,1,1. Figure 22-12 shows the house from the NW isometric view.

Figure 22-12: The NW isometric view of the 3D house

Using DDVPOINT

If the standard views are not sufficient for your needs, DDVPOINT can give you both flexibility and precision. To use this command, choose View ➪ 3D Views ➪ Viewpoint Presets to open the Viewpoint Presets dialog box, shown in Figure 22-13. This dialog box enables you to set the view to a great degree of accuracy.

The left side of the dialog box determines the angle from the X axis in the XY plane. These angles work as follows:

270	Front view
0	Right view
90	Back view
180	Left view

Other angles result in viewpoints between these views. For example, an angle of 315 degrees enables you to look at your drawing from a view between front and right. If you're thinking that this is similar to the SE isometric view, you are correct.

Figure 22-13: The Viewpoint Presets dialog box

The right side of the dialog box determines the angle from the XY plane, in the Z direction. A 0-degree angle enables you to look at your drawing from the front, back, or one side (elevation views) — depending on the setting on the left part of the dialog box. Often you want to look at your drawing from above. A 90-degree angle shows you the plan view. An angle between 0 and 90 gives you a slanted view from the top — such as one of the isometric standard views. (Actually, the isometric views set the angle from the XY plane to 35.3 degrees.)

Tip There's an art to using the two dials to set the view angle that you want. If you click the inside border of either one, close to the indicator needle, AutoCAD sets the angle based on exactly where you clicked. This results in uneven degrees, such as 47.6. However, if you click the outside border of either image, or the numbers themselves, AutoCAD rounds the angle to the value in the segment.

When you open the dialog box, the black needles indicate the angles for the current view. When you change the angles, the black (or white) needles move to the new angle but the original needle remains to indicate the current angle. This enables you to constantly see the current angles for reference.

Beneath the dials are text boxes that reflect your choices. You can simply type the angles you want in the text boxes.

A very handy Set to Plan View button is at the bottom of the dialog box. This enables you to quickly return to plan view when you get a little dizzy from flying around your model.

You can set the viewing angles either based on the WCS or relative to a different UCS that you are using. It can get confusing if you have several different UCSs and start viewing them from several different viewpoints. As a result, the default is to view the drawing based on the WCS. However, sometimes you need to see your drawing relative to a UCS you have created. To do so, click Relative to UCS.

Tip Keep the number of UCSs to the minimum necessary and save them. When possible, use a new viewpoint instead of creating a new UCS.

Click OK after you complete making your changes.

The drawing used in the following Step-by-Step exercise on using standard viewpoints and DDVPOINT, ab22-a.dwg, is in the Drawings folder of the *AutoCAD 2004 Bible* CD-ROM.

Step-by-Step: Using Standard Viewpoints and DDVPOINT

1. Open ab22-a.dwg from the CD-ROM.

2. Save it as ab22-01.dwg in your AutoCAD Bible folder. It shows the same house used in the earlier figures in this chapter from the SE isometric view.

3. Type **ucsortho** ↵ **0** ↵ to turn off the UCSORTHO system variable. Turning off UCSORTHO prevents the UCS from changing whenever you switch to one of the six orthogonal viewpoints.

4. Right-click any toolbar and choose View to open the View toolbar. Choose Top View from the Viewpoint toolbar.

5. Choose Bottom View from the Viewpoint toolbar. Notice that the small circle at the intersection of the X and Y axes disappears.

6. Choose Front View from the Viewpoint toolbar. You see the front of the house with the two strange bushes.

7. Choose Right View from the Viewpoint toolbar. You see the text "North side."

8. Choose NW Isometric View from the Viewpoint toolbar. You are looking at the back of the house.

9. Choose SW Isometric View from the Viewpoint toolbar. You are looking at the front of the house. If you want, try the rest of the standard viewpoints

10. Choose View ➪ 3D Viewpoint ➪ Viewpoint Presets to open the Viewpoint Presets dialog box. Set the left dial (angle from X axis) to 315 degrees by clicking the number 315. Set the right dial (angle from XY plane) to 60 degrees by clicking the second from the top segment pointed to by the number 60. Click OK. You see a view somewhat like the SE isometric view, but from much higher up.

11. Repeat the DDVPOINT command. In the X Axis text box, type **240**. In the XY Plane text box, type **5**. Click OK. You get a view from slightly off the ground, much as you might see it if you were walking up to the house.

12. Type **hide** ↵. Notice that you can see the windows on the far side through the windows on your side of the house.

13. Choose View ➪ Named Views on the Named Views tab and click New. In the New View dialog box, type the name of the view, **walk up**. Click OK. Click OK again to return to your drawing. It should look like Figure 22-14.

Figure 22-14: The final view of the house

14. If you are working on someone else's computer or want UCSORTHO on, type **ucsortho** ↵ **1** ↵ to turn it back on.

15. Save the drawing.

Note You cannot save the display that you see when you use the HIDE command. When you restore the view, you see it as a wireframe display. You can, however, make a slide of the view. Chapter 30 covers slides. You can also use SHADEMODE to continue to work with the hidden view. Choose View ➪ Shade ➪ Hidden.

Working with the Tripod and Compass

You can choose another method of defining views, using the VPOINT command. To start this command, choose View ➪ 3D Views ➪ Viewpoint. AutoCAD displays the tripod and compass, as shown in Figure 22-15.

Figure 22-15: The VPOINT tripod and compass are used to define viewpoints in 3D.

If you type the VPOINT command, or press Enter to repeat the command, press Enter at the Current view direction: VIEWDIR=-1.0000,-1.0000,1.0000 Specify a view point or [Rotate] <display compass and tripod>: prompt to see the compass and tripod. (The numbers show the current viewpoint.)

Move the cursor about, and two things happen. The cursor moves within the compass, and the axes dynamically shift position.

Imagine that you take a tangerine and make a large cross-shaped cut at the very bottom. Then you open out the bottom and remove the peel from the tangerine. Flatten the peel on the table. This is the concept of the compass, except that the outer edge is round. (The tangerine peel would have the shape of the cuts on its outer edge.) The very center of the compass — or the peel — is like the North Pole. When you are over the North Pole, you are looking straight down at your model — or the tangerine. This produces a plan view. The inner circle of the compass is where the middle of the tangerine was — at the equator. From the equator, you are looking sideways (from the front, back, or side) at your model. The outer circle of the compass represents the South Pole. From over the South Pole, you are looking at the bottom of your model — or the tangerine.

All of this is equivalent to the right image in the Viewpoint Presets dialog box that you use with the DDVPOINT command — it determines your view relative to the XY plane:

✦ At the center of the compass, you are right on top, looking down. This is a plan view.

✦ At the inner circle, you are on the side, looking at the XY plane on its edge.

✦ At the outer circle, you are beneath the XY plane, looking up.

The cross that goes through the compass represents the X and Y axes. If you place the cursor on the positive (right) side of the X axis, you are looking at the tangerine from its right side — this is equivalent to a right view. The position of the cursor relative to the X and Y axes is equivalent to the left image in the Viewpoint Presets dialog box that you use with the DDVPOINT command — it determines your view relative to the X axis in the XY plane. To summarize, going clockwise:

- ✦ The positive X axis gives you a right view.
- ✦ The negative Y axis is equivalent to a front view.
- ✦ The negative X axis gives you a left view.
- ✦ The positive Y axis gives you a back view.

When you have the cursor at the desired location, simply click. AutoCAD displays your drawing with the viewpoint you specified.

You cannot get an exact viewpoint this way. However, some people find this method of defining a viewpoint more intuitive. You can also look at the tripod as the axes move about. But be careful — sometimes it's difficult to see if an axis is coming toward you or going away from you.

Along with the tripod and compass, AutoCAD includes the current UCS icon based on the current UCS to help you get your bearings. Figure 22-16 shows a cursor location that results in the viewpoint shown in Figure 22-17. This is very close to the SE isometric view.

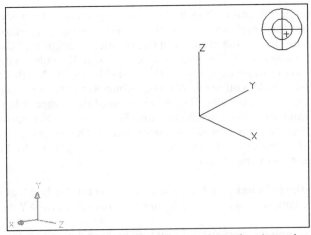

Figure 22-16: This cursor location results in the viewpoint shown in Figure 22-17.

Figure 22-17: This viewpoint results from the cursor location on the compass shown in Figure 22-16.

Getting a Quick Plan View

The PLAN command is a quick way to return to plan view. Type **plan** ↵. This command has three options:

✦ **<Current UCS>:** This is the default. You get the plan view of the current UCS.

✦ **UCS:** The UCS option enables you to choose a named UCS. Type **?** ↵ to get a list of the named UCSs. Otherwise, type the name of a UCS.

✦ **World:** This option gives you the plan view of the WCS. If your current UCS is the WCS, there is no difference between this option and the Current UCS option.

Figure 22-18 shows a sample UCS listing. Note that the units are architectural.

```
Enter UCS name(s) to list <*>:

Current ucs name: *NO NAME*

Saved coordinate systems:

"EASTELEV"
    Origin = <0'-0",0'-0",0'-0">, X Axis = <0'-0",0'-0",0'-1">
    Y Axis = <0'-0",0'-1",0'-0">, Z Axis = <-0'-1",0'-0",0'-0">
"FRONTROOF"
    Origin = <0'-0",10'-0",0'-0">, X Axis = <0'-0",0'-0",0'-1">
    Y Axis = <0'-0 7/8",0'-0 7/16",0'-0">, Z Axis = <-0'-0 7/16",0'-0
7/8",0'-0">
"NORTHSIDE"
    Origin = <0'-0",0'-0",40'-0">, X Axis = <0'-1",0'-0",0'-0">
    Y Axis = <0'-0",0'-1",0'-0">, Z Axis = <0'-0",0'-0",0'-1">
```

Figure 22-18: A listing of saved UCSs

Returning to plan view when you change the UCS

If you like plan views, you'll love UCSFOLLOW. UCSFOLLOW is a system variable that tells AutoCAD to return to plan view whenever you change the UCS. It's for those of you who like to get your bearings in plan view first before going on to change the viewpoint in another UCS.

Most 2D objects you use in 3D drawings can only be drawn and edited in plan view because they don't interpret the Z coordinate. Therefore, returning to plan view is helpful in many situations.

The default value is zero (off), which means that AutoCAD does not return to plan view. In other words, your display remains unchanged when you change the UCS. Type **ucsfollow** and change the value to 1 to turn UCSFOLLOW on. From then on, AutoCAD automatically displays the plan view when you change the UCS.

New Feature
The Express Tools' extended PLAN command, EXPLAN, prompts you to select objects so that you can see the plan view zoomed in on those objects. Choose Express ⇨ Tools ⇨ Extended Plan. For information about installing Express Tools, see Appendix A on the CD-ROM.

On the CD-ROM
The drawing used in the following Step-by-Step exercise on using the compass and tripod and the PLAN command, ab22-b.dwg, is in the Drawings folder of the *AutoCAD 2004 Bible* CD-ROM.

Step-by-Step: Using the Compass and Tripod and the PLAN Command

1. Open ab22-b.dwg from the CD-ROM. This is the same house used in the previous Step-by-Step exercise.

2. Choose View ⇨ 3D Views ⇨ Viewpoint. Pick the point shown at ❶ in Figure 22-19. You see the result in Figure 22-20.

Figure 22-19: Picking a front viewpoint on the compass

Figure 22-20: The front viewpoint. Notice that it is not exact.

3. Press Enter twice to repeat the VPOINT command and display the tripod and compass. Pick the point shown by the cross in Figure 22-21. Use the HIDE command to clearly see the results, as shown in Figure 22-22.

Figure 22-21: Picking a back left viewpoint from beneath the house

Figure 22-22: The resulting viewpoint. Notice that the house doesn't have a floor!

4. Type **vpoint** ↵. Press Enter again. Pick the point shown in Figure 22-23. Do a hide to see the results. This time you get an above-ground view from the front-left corner.

Figure 22-23: The pick point for Step 4

5. Type **plan** ↵. Type **w** ↵ for the World UCS. AutoCAD displays the plan view of the house.

6. Do not save this drawing.

Shading Your Drawing

Shading is a simple version of rendering. You can use shading to get a quick visualization of your drawing. Shading is based on one default light source that AutoCAD automatically places behind the viewer and that shines on the model.

You can edit your objects in shaded mode. When you select shaded objects, the wireframe display and grips appear over the shading to help you work. Objects remain shaded until you choose to unshade them, even if you regenerate or close and reopen the drawing. You can display different shading in different viewports. Because shading can now stay on as you edit, it has been transformed from a simple form of rendering into a means of viewing your drawing while you work.

Objects in color shade better than those objects in black and white. As explained in the section "Using materials" later in this chapter, you can set your 3D graphics system display properties to show attached materials when you shade objects. (Chapter 25 covers materials.)

Using the shading options

To shade, choose View ➪ Shade or type **shademode** ↵. Here are the options:

✦ **2D Wireframe:** Displays objects in the familiar wireframe display, with no shading. Choose this option to return to "normal."

✦ **3D Wireframe:** Displays objects in wireframe along with a shaded UCS icon. Raster (bitmap) and OLE (embedded) objects, linetypes, and lineweights are not visible.

- ✦ **Hidden:** Equivalent to using the HIDE command.

- ✦ **Flat Shaded:** Creates flat blocks of color between each polygon face. There is no smoothing from face to face.

- ✦ **Gouraud Shaded:** Creates smoothed shading from face to face, resulting in a more realistic appearance, especially for curved surfaces.

- ✦ **Flat Shaded, Edges On:** Combines flat shading and wireframe display. Useful for editing objects while they are shaded.

- ✦ **Gouraud Shaded, Edges On:** Combines Gouraud shading and wireframe display. Useful for editing objects while they are shaded.

Note

The FACETRATIO system variable affects the mesh density created for cylindrical and conic solids. By default, it is set to zero (0), which creates the normal mesh density. Set it to 1 to increase the mesh density. This should improve the quality of rendered and shaded cylindrical and conic solids.

Using materials

Materials are used in rendering, which is covered in Chapter 25. You can set your 3D graphics system display properties to display materials that you have attached to objects. Then, shaded objects display these materials. You can also display lights and textures. The difference in the quality of your image is striking. You can see the effect in 3D orbit as well.

Lights in 3D orbit and SHADEMODE do not display shadows, have no attenuation, and use a default light intensity instead of the light intensity specified with the LIGHT command. Materials in 3D orbit and SHADEMODE display the color/pattern material component only. 3D textures are not shown; neither are bump maps, opacity maps, refraction, and reflection. For more information, see Chapter 25.

Here's how to set your display:

1. Choose Tools ⇨ Options and choose the System tab.

2. In Current 3D Graphics Display, choose your graphics system (it's probably already selected) and click Properties.

3. In the 3D Graphics System Configuration dialog box, check Render Options.

4. Check the types of effects you want to display. You can choose to display lights, materials, and textures.

5. Choose one of the transparency options: high, medium, or low quality.

6. Click Apply & Close.

7. Click OK to close the Options dialog box.

For information about how to attach a material to an object, see Chapter 25. Figure 22-24 shows a model with the Brassy Valley material attached, viewed with Gouraud shading.

Figure 22-24: A model with Gouraud shading and the Brassy Valley material attached. (It looks better in color!)

The drawing used in the following Step-by-Step exercise on shading a drawing, ab22-c.dwg, is in the Drawings folder of the *AutoCAD 2004 Bible* CD-ROM.

Step-by-Step: Shading a Drawing

1. Open ab22-c.dwg from the CD-ROM.

2. Save it as ab22-02.dwg in your AutoCAD Bible folder.

3. Choose Tools ⇨ Options and choose the System tab.

4. In Current 3D Graphics Display, choose your graphics system (it's probably already selected) and click Properties.

5. Check Render Options and then click Enable Materials. (If you're not using the Heidi graphics display system that comes with AutoCAD, your options may be different.)

6. Click Apply & Close. Click OK to close the Options dialog box.

7. Choose View ⇨ Shade ⇨ Flat Shaded. This model has a brass-like material attached to it.

8. Choose View ⇨ Shade ⇨ Gouraud Shaded.

9. Choose View ⇨ Shade ⇨ Gouraud Shaded, Edges On.

10. Save your drawing. It should look like Figure 22-25.

Figure 22-25: The model shaded with the Gouraud Shaded, Edges On option

Using 3D Orbit

3D orbit enables you to view a 3D model by freely changing your view in real-time. Using 3D orbit is like orbiting the earth to view any continent or ocean below. When you enter 3D orbit mode, you cannot use other commands. In this regard, 3D orbit is like Realtime Pan and Realtime Zoom. Similarly, you press Esc or Enter to exit 3D orbit mode.

Because you cannot use other commands while in 3D orbit, you access the 3D orbit options by right-clicking in the drawing area to display the 3D Orbit shortcut menu. You might find the 3D Orbit toolbar helpful when working with 3D orbit. The toolbar contains many of the options available on the 3D Orbit shortcut menu. Right-click any toolbar and choose 3D Orbit to display the toolbar.

Tip 3D orbit can be used as a substitute for DVIEW, which is covered later in this chapter.

Starting 3D orbit

To start 3D orbit, choose View ➪ 3D Orbit. AutoCAD places you in 3D orbit mode and displays the arcball around the objects in your view, as shown in Figure 22-26.

Tip You can use 3D orbit transparently, that is, in the middle of another command. Just start a command, type **'3dorbit** ↵, rotate your model as you want, and press Esc or Enter to close 3D orbit. AutoCAD then continues the command in progress.

Arcball

Figure 22-26: 3D orbit mode

Tip For faster performance, select only the objects you want to view with 3D orbit before starting the command. Objects you did not select disappear while you are in 3D orbit mode. Of course, they reappear as soon as you leave 3D orbit mode.

3D orbit has four cursors that affect how your model rotates. Each cursor is location-based. As you move your cursor to a new location, the cursor shape automatically changes and the type of rotation changes.

Rolling with the circular arrow cursor

When you place your cursor outside the arcball, it takes the shape of a circular arrow. As you click and drag around the outside of the arcball, your model turns around an imaginary axis that extends from the center of the arcball outward, perpendicular to the screen — that is, pointing at you. AutoCAD calls this type of rotation a roll. Figure 22-27 shows a model with the circular arrow cursor at 0°, 90°, 180°, and 270°. The model uses a hidden view for clarity — using hidden and shaded views with 3D orbit is covered later in this chapter. After you get to the view you want, release the mouse button and AutoCAD redraws your model on the screen in the new position.

Figure 22-27: Using the circular arrow cursor to rotate your model around an axis

Rotating freely with the sphere and lines cursor

As soon as you move your cursor within the arcball, it takes a shape that AutoCAD calls "a small sphere encircled by two lines." As you click and drag within the arcball, your model moves around the center of the arcball in the direction you drag. Imagine that your model is encased in a transparent sphere, like one of those gerbil or hamster balls. As you drag the cursor, you are rotating the sphere around its center point. If you drag from one edge of the arcball to its opposite edge, you can release the mouse, move back to your starting point, and then click and drag again in the same direction. When you do this a few times, you rotate your model 360 degrees. You get best results dragging in a line of any direction, rather than round and round. Figure 22-28 shows a model rotated using the sphere and lines cursor. For each pane of the figure, the cursor is dragged from just inside the right arcball circle to just inside the left arcball circle, that is, horizontally.

Figure 22-28: Using the sphere and lines cursor to rotate your model around its center

Rotating around the vertical axis with the horizontal ellipse cursor

When you move your cursor over either the left or right quadrant circle on the arcball, it becomes a horizontal ellipse. As you click and drag from either quadrant, your model rotates around the arcball's vertical axis, which extends from the top quadrant to the bottom quadrant. Although your cursor enters the arcball, it retains its horizontal ellipse form until you release the mouse button. You can drag from one quadrant to its opposite quadrant, release the mouse button, move back to your starting point, and then click and drag again in the same direction. When you do this a couple of times, you rotate your model 360 degrees. Figure 22-29 shows a model rotated using the horizontal ellipse cursor.

Figure 22-29: Using the horizontal ellipse cursor to rotate your model around the arcball's vertical axis

Rotating around the horizontal axis with the vertical ellipse cursor

When you move your cursor over either the top or bottom quadrant circle on the arcball, it becomes a vertical ellipse. As you click and drag from either quadrant, your model rotates around the arcball's horizontal axis, which extends from the left quadrant to the right quadrant. You can drag from one quadrant to its opposite quadrant, release the mouse button, move back to your starting point, and then click and drag again in the same direction. When you do this a couple of times, you rotate your model 360 degrees. Figure 22-30 shows a model rotated using the vertical ellipse cursor.

Figure 22-30: Using the vertical ellipse cursor to rotate your model around the arcball's horizontal axis

Using the 3D orbit visual aids

3D orbit includes three visual aids that can help you get your bearings:

✦ **Compass:** Displays a sphere within the arcball made up of three dashed lines labeled as the X, Y, and Z axes. The lines make your arcball look like a baseball. To display the compass, right-click and choose Visual Aids ➭ Compass from the shortcut menu.

✦ **Grid:** Displays a grid of lines representing the XY plane. The Z coordinate of the grid is equal to the value of the ELEVATION system variable, which is set to zero (0) by default. Up to ten horizontal and vertical lines are drawn between the major lines, whose distance from each other is equal to the value of the GRIDUNIT system variable. You can set this value by choosing Tools ➭ Drafting Settings before you use this visual aid.

✦ **3D UCS icon:** Displays the 3D UCS icon, a shaded, three-dimensional UCS icon. The X axis is red, the Y axis is green, and the Z axis is blue.

Figure 22-31 shows a model with the grid and one with the compass. Both display the 3D UCS icon. You would rarely want to use all three. The compass and grid can both interfere with viewing your model and should be used temporarily when needed.

Figure 22-31: 3D orbit's visual aids — the 3D UCS icon, the grid, and the compass

To display the visual aids, right-click while in 3D orbit mode and choose Visual Aids from the shortcut menu. Then choose the aid you want from the submenu. To turn off the visual aids, follow the same procedure — the submenu items toggle the visual aids on and off when you click them.

Note If you choose a shading mode (other than the default 2D wireframe), the visual aids remain active after you exit 3D orbit. You can switch to 2D wireframe shading mode, as explained earlier in this chapter, or you can re-enter 3D orbit and turn off the visual aids.

Creating a continuous orbit

Absolutely the coolest feature of 3D orbit — and one of the coolest features of AutoCAD 2004 as a whole — is continuous orbit. Continuous orbit enables you to choose a direction of rotation and let go. 3D orbit automatically continues the rotation in the same direction and continues it until you change or stop it. With continuous orbit, who needs screensavers any more? Here's how it works:

1. With 3D orbit active, right-click and choose More ➪ Continuous Orbit.

2. Click and drag in the direction of rotation that you want to create.

3. Release your mouse button. Your model continues to rotate in the same direction. All you do is watch.

Continuous orbit is an ideal way to view your model. As your model rotates, you can pick out any errors and stop continuous orbit then. You can change the direction of your continuous orbit at any time by clicking and dragging in a new direction and then releasing the mouse button.

To stop continuous orbit, choose Pan, Zoom, or Orbit from the shortcut menu. Zoom Previous exits 3D orbit and restores the view to the way it was before the orbit began.

Resetting the view

You can end up with some strange views of your model with 3D orbit. With that in mind, AutoCAD 2004 provides a way to reset your view to the view that was current when you first started 3D orbit. With 3D orbit active, right-click and choose Reset View from the shortcut menu.

Refining your 3D orbit view

3D orbit offers many options for refining your view so that you get just the view you want. You can pan and zoom, adjust the camera distance, change the camera and target locations, create parallel and perspective views, set clipping planes, use a preset view, use shading options, and use materials that you have attached to objects. (See Chapter 25 for more about materials.)

Because you cannot use other commands while in 3D orbit mode, you access most of these options by right-clicking in the drawing area to access the 3D Orbit shortcut menu. You can also use the 3D Orbit toolbar for some of these options.

Panning in 3D orbit

To pan in 3D orbit, right-click and choose Pan from the 3D orbit shortcut menu. You see the familiar hand cursor. Click and drag to pan, in the same way you normally pan in real-time. To stop panning, right-click and choose Orbit or Zoom from the shortcut menu.

You can pan with visual aids, shading modes, and projection options active.

Zooming in 3D orbit

To zoom in 3D orbit, right-click and choose Zoom from the 3D orbit shortcut menu. You see the familiar magnifying glass cursor with a plus (+) and a minus (–) sign. Click and drag in the direction of the plus sign (toward the top of your screen) to zoom in; click and drag in the direction of the minus sign (toward the bottom of your screen) to zoom out, just as you do when you normally use zoom real-time. To stop zooming, right-click and choose Orbit or Pan from the shortcut menu. You can zoom with visual aids, shading modes, and projection options active.

Zooming to a window and to extents in 3D orbit

To zoom to a window in 3D orbit, right-click and choose More ⇨ Zoom Window from the shortcut menu. Your cursor displays a small rectangle. Click and drag, and then release the mouse button to define the two corners of the window.

To zoom to drawing extents in 3D orbit, right-click and choose More ⇨ Zoom Extents from the shortcut menu.

Keeping the Z axis orientation steady

Controlling the orbiting with 3D orbit can be difficult. You may find that as you drag horizontally in the arcball, your model tumbles upside down. Orbit Maintains Z keeps the Z axis in its current direction when you drag horizontally within the arcball or horizontally from the left or right ellipse of the arcball. Use this option to prevent your object from rolling around. The idea is that you don't want to see certain objects, such as houses, upside down.

To turn on this feature, right-click in 3D orbit and choose More ⇨ Orbit Maintains Z. Repeat the process to turn off the feature — it's a toggle. AutoCAD saves this setting in your user profile so that it carries over to other drawings.

Adjusting the camera distance

You can adjust the distance between the viewer, called the camera, and the target, which by default is set to the center of the 3D view (which may be different from the center of your model). Changing this camera distance is equivalent to zooming in and out.

To adjust the camera distance in 3D orbit, right-click and choose More ⇨ Adjust Distance from the shortcut menu. The cursor changes to a horizontal line with a double-headed arrow pointing up and down. Click and drag toward the top of your screen to move the camera closer to your objects — similar to zooming in. Click and drag toward the bottom of your screen to move the camera away from your objects — similar to zooming out.

Changing the camera and target locations

You may also want to change the focus of your view. 3D orbit uses a default focus that is the center of the 3D view. You can change both the camera and target locations, but you must do so before you start 3D orbit.

To change the camera and the target locations, type **camera** ↵ on the command line.

At the `Specify new camera position <-41.0494,129.5726,56.6437>:` prompt, use any method to specify new coordinates for the camera position. The numbers in the brackets are the current settings. At the `Specify new camera target <20.8937,67.6295,-5.2993>:` prompt, use any method to specify new coordinates for the target position.

Tip Specifying the proper coordinates can be difficult in 3D. You may find it helpful to place a point object at the two desired locations before starting the command. You can then use the Node object snap to pick the camera and target positions you want.

Controlling view width and height

When you use 3D orbit, the Properties palette displays special properties that relate to 3D orbit features.

✦ **View Height** is a way to specify the distance of the imaginary camera. In other words, you can use this property to zoom in and out on your model. A larger number makes your model look smaller because the distance (or height) of the camera from the model increases.

✦ **View Width** is another way to zoom in and out. Here you specify the width of the view of the imaginary camera. A larger number makes your model look smaller because the view encompasses a larger area (and your model is a smaller part of that area).

To change these properties, click their row in the Properties palette. Type a new value and press Enter.

Creating parallel and perspective views

By default, 3D orbit (and all three-dimensional viewpoints) displays a parallel view. In a parallel view, parallel lines never converge. The value of a parallel view is that the shapes in your drawing do not appear distorted as you zoom in. In a perspective view, parallel lines converge. You may have had an assignment in art class (long ago) to draw railroad tracks that converge to give the impression of distance. Perspective view is more realistic because railroad tracks really do seem to converge in the distance. However, when you zoom in, these objects appear distorted. Use a perspective view when you want to convey a realistic sense of depth. In general, perspective view is most useful in architectural settings.

To create a perspective view in 3D orbit, right-click and choose Projection ⇨ Perspective. To return to parallel view, choose Projection ⇨ Parallel. For more information on perspective views, see the section "Defining a Perspective View" later in this chapter.

Caution If you leave 3D orbit in perspective view, you cannot edit, pick points, zoom, or pan. To return to your normal parallel view, re-enter 3D orbit, right-click, and choose Projection ⇨ Parallel. Then exit 3D orbit again.

Using a preset view

After using 3D orbit a few times, you might find your model all askew, with no idea how to get it back to a viewpoint you can comprehend. You can switch to any of the

preset views discussed at the beginning of this chapter. From 3D orbit, right-click and choose Preset Views from the shortcut menu. Then choose one of the standard viewpoints on the submenu list.

Setting clipping planes

You can create two invisible planes, a front clipping plane and a back clipping plane, that block your view of any objects outside the planes. Setting clipping planes is a good way to discard objects that you don't want to see because they are too close or too far away. For example, you might have a 3D house with trees in the background and a street sign in the foreground. Using clipping planes, you can block out the view of the trees and the street sign and view only the house.

The Adjust Clipping Planes window enables you to visually move the front and back clipping planes in real-time and immediately see the results.

Because the clipping planes are parallel to your screen, you need to start by creating a view that is straight enough so that your clipping planes will cut across your model at the desired angle. I suggest using one of the preset views, as I just previously explained. For example, if you are looking at a house and want to clip off the front and back porches, use the Front preset view to view your house from the front. You will then be able to create the desired front and back clipping planes. After you set your view, follow these steps:

1. From 3D orbit, right-click and choose More ➪ Adjust Clipping Planes. AutoCAD displays the Adjust Clipping Planes window, shown in Figure 22-32.

2. In the Adjust Clipping Planes window you can do the following:

 - **Adjust Front Clipping:** Click this button on the toolbar to move the front clipping plane. Use the Adjust Clipping Planes cursor to click and drag the line that represents the front clipping plane.

 - **Adjust Back Clipping:** Click this button on the toolbar to move the back clipping plane. Use the Adjust Clipping Planes cursor to click and drag the line that represents the back clipping plane.

 - **Create Slice:** After you adjust both the front and back clipping planes, use this button to move both clipping planes together, either up or down. Their distance from each other remains constant.

 - **Front Clipping On/Off:** Click this button to toggle the front clipping plane on or off.

 - **Back Clipping On/Off:** Click this button to toggle the back clipping plane on or off.

3. If you can't see the back clipping plane, click Adjust Back Clipping and continue to drag down until the line representing the back clipping plane appears. If you can't see the front clipping plane, click Adjust Front Clipping and continue to drag up until the line representing the front clipping plane appears.

4. After you set the clipping planes to your satisfaction, click the window's Close box. You can now rotate you model in any direction and 3D orbit continually hides any portion of the model outside the clipping planes. However, as you rotate your model, the parts of the model outside the clipping planes change so that you see different portions of the model.

Figure 22-32: The Adjust Clipping Planes window, shown with the model on the drawing area

To turn off either or both clipping planes, right-click and choose More ➪ Front Clipping On or More ➪ Back Clipping On. Both these items show a checkmark when their clipping plane is on. Choosing the item again turns the clipping plane off.

Figure 22-33 shows how the house shown in Figure 22-32 looks after setting clipping planes and changing the rotation slightly. The front and back walls have been clipped off.

Figure 22-33: A house after setting clipping planes and using the Hide shading option

Using shading options

You can use the shading options explained earlier in this chapter in 3D orbit. To choose a shading option, right-click in 3D orbit and choose Shading Modes, and then choose one of the options from the shortcut submenu. These shading modes persist after you exit 3D orbit. To remove a shading mode from 3D orbit, right-click and choose Shading Modes ⇨ Wireframe. You can also remove a shading mode after leaving 3D orbit mode by choosing View ⇨ Shade, as explained earlier.

On the CD-ROM

The drawing used in the following Step-by-Step exercise on working in 3D orbit, ab22-d.dwg, is in the Drawings folder of the *AutoCAD 2004 Bible* CD-ROM.

Step-by-Step: Working in 3D Orbit

1. Open ab22-d.dwg from the CD-ROM. This is a 3D chair shown from a Northwest isometric view.

2. Choose View ⇨ 3D Orbit. AutoCAD displays the arcball.

3. Place the mouse cursor outside the arcball so that you see the circular arrow cursor. Click and drag the cursor 360 degrees around the outside of the arcball so that the chair ends up in its original position.

4. Place the cursor inside the right small circle on the arcball so that you see the horizontal ellipse cursor. Click and drag the cursor to the left small circle. Release the mouse button. Again, click and drag the cursor from the right circle to the left circle so that the chair is approximately in its original position.

5. Place the cursor inside the arcball so that you see the small sphere/two lines cursor. Click and drag the cursor around in several directions until you get a feel for how the movement of the cursor moves the chair. See if you can get the chair back to its original position.

6. Right-click and choose Shading Modes ➪ Hidden.

7. Right-click and choose More ➪ Continuous Orbit. Click and drag with the cursor, making a small movement from right to left, and then release the mouse button. You may need to try this a couple of times to get a continuous orbit that you like. Try clicking and dragging in a different direction to change the direction of the continuous orbit, and then release the mouse button.

8. Right-click and choose Orbit to stop the continuous orbit.

9. Right-click and choose Reset View to re-display the chair in exactly its original view.

10. Right-click and choose Pan. Pan the chair to the right a little.

11. Right-click and choose Zoom. Zoom the chair in slightly.

12. Right-click and choose Projection ➪ Perspective. You can see how the chair looks slightly distorted. Right-click and choose Projection ➪ Parallel.

13. Right-click and choose Preset Views ➪ NW Isometric.

14. Press Esc to exit 3D orbit mode.

Don't save your drawing.

Using Tiled Viewports

As you learned in Chapter 8, you can create multiple viewports to view your drawing at different zooms and pans. Tiled viewports are very helpful in 3D drawings as well. Although you can, and should, save UCSs and views, if you find yourself switching back and forth between two to four viewpoints, try creating two to four viewports with the different viewpoints and UCSs in them. The only disadvantage is that you have less screen real estate for each viewpoint.

Defining a Perspective View

AutoCAD's original command for defining views with perspective from any angle and distance was DVIEW. The new 3D orbit now outclasses DVIEW, but you may still find it helpful for its precise ways of defining a view.

Like 3D orbit, DVIEW uses the metaphor of a camera. There is a camera point—where you are standing—and a target point—what you are looking at. By defining these two points, you can create either close-up or distance views, much as you would with the zoom or panoramic lens of a camera.

The DVIEW command creates both parallel and perspective views. Figure 22-34 shows a parallel view. Notice the side brackets. Figure 22-35 shows a perspective view of the same model. The side brackets appear to approach each other as they become more distant.

Figure 22-34: A parallel view created with DVIEW
Thanks to Robert Mack of the Dexter Company, Fairfield, Iowa, for this drawing, a base housing for an industrial washing machine.

Figure 22-35: A perspective view of the same model

Using DVIEW

To create a perspective view, type **dview** ↵ on the command line. At the `Select objects or <use DVIEWBLOCK>:` prompt, select the objects you want to include in the process of defining the perspective view.

You should select as few objects as you need to visualize the final result if you have a complex drawing. If you want to select the entire drawing, type **all** ↵ even if the current view doesn't display the entire drawing.

Press Enter if you don't want to choose any objects. AutoCAD substitutes a block called dviewblock, which is a simple house. You can use the house to set your perspective view.

Tip If you want, you can create your own block and name it dviewblock. Create it with X, Y, and Z dimensions of 1. When you press Enter at the `Select objects or <use DVIEWBLOCK>:` prompt, AutoCAD looks for dviewblock and uses it to display the results of the perspective view settings.

Understanding the DVIEW options

DVIEW comes with a bewildering array of options that you use to specify the angle and distance of the view. To use these options, start the DVIEW command and select the objects you want to view or press Enter. You see the following prompt:

```
Enter option
[CAmera/TArget/Distance/POints/PAn/Zoom/TWist/CLip/Hide/Off/
Undo]:
```

You use these options to define the perspective view, as explained in the following sections.

CAmera

Use the Camera option to specify the angle of the camera, which represents where you are standing. You need to specify the angle from the X axis in the XY plane and the angle from the XY plane. This is very similar to the way you specify a view using the DDVPOINT command, explained earlier in this chapter.

When you choose this option, by right-clicking and choosing Camera, you see the following prompt:

```
Specify camera location, or enter angle from XY plane, or
[Toggle (angle in)] <35.2644>:
```

The default angle is based on the current view when you start DVIEW. If you know the angle from the XY plane, you can just type it in. You can also move the cursor vertically to dynamically see the results. The view constantly changes as you move the cursor, moving up over your objects as you move the cursor up, and down as you move the cursor down. Move the cursor in one direction and then keep it still for a second to see the full effect.

However, moving the cursor horizontally changes the angle from the X axis in the XY plane. It can be confusing to change both angles at once so AutoCAD enables you to limit the effect of your cursor movement to one angle. You do this with the Toggle suboption.

Right-click and choose Toggle (angle in) to see the next prompt of the Camera option:

```
Specify camera location, or enter angle in XY plane from X
axis, or [Toggle (angle from)]
<66.12857>:
```

Now, your cursor affects only the angle from the X axis. Move the cursor horizontally to see your objects rotate around you at a constant altitude. Press Enter when you like what you see, or you can type in an angle.

Tip If you want to set the angle in the XY plane first and limit the effect of cursor movement to that change, you need to use the Toggle suboption to get to the `Enter angle in XY plane from X axis:` prompt. After you set the angle in the XY plane, the suboption ends. Start the Camera option again to set the angle from the XY plane.

TArget

The Target option (right-click and choose Target) works exactly like the Camera option except that it defines the angles for the target of your viewpoint — what you would see through the camera lens. However, the angles are relative to the camera position. If you have already set the camera angles, the target angles default to those created by drawing a straight line from the camera angle through 0,0,0. As with the Camera option, use the Toggle suboption to switch between the two angles you need to specify.

Distance

The Distance option is very important because using it turns on perspective mode. Before you use this option, the views you see are parallel views. When you use the Distance option, you see a slider bar at the top of the screen, as shown in Figure 22-36. After you choose a distance, AutoCAD replaces the UCS icon with the perspective mode icon if your UCS display is set to 2D. (Choose View ➪ Display ➪ UCS Icon ➪ Properties.)

Figure 22-36: Using the Distance option turns on perspective mode and displays a slider bar.

AutoCAD displays the `Specify new camera-target distance <3.0000>:` prompt. You can type a distance from the camera to the target or use the slider bar. Move the cursor to the right to zoom out. Moving the cursor to 4x is equivalent to using the ZOOM command and typing **4x** ↵. Move the cursor to the left of 1x to zoom in. The zoom factor is relative to the current display so that 1x leaves the zoom unchanged.

You can also type a distance in drawing units.

POints

You can use the Points option (right-click and choose Points) to define the camera and target. AutoCAD displays the `Specify target point <0.3776, -0.1618, 1.0088>:` prompt. The default target point, which is different for each drawing, is the center of the current view. AutoCAD places a rubber-band line from the target point, which you can use to get your bearings when choosing a new target point. You can also type a coordinate. At the `Specify camera point <-1.5628, 0.9420, 2.2787>:` prompt, pick or type a point. AutoCAD keeps the rubber-band line from the target so that you can visualize the camera and target points.

Because it is difficult to know what 3D points you are picking, you should use an object snap or XYZ point filters to pick points.

Tip While it is common to choose a target point on one of the objects in your drawing, often you want the camera point to be off the objects so that you are looking at the objects from a certain distance and angle. To pick the camera point, choose Format ⇨ Point Style (before starting DVIEW) and choose an easily visible point style. Decide what elevation you want, type **elev** ↵ and set a new elevation. From plan view, choose Point from the Draw toolbar and pick a point. The point is created on the current elevation. Then use the Node object snap to snap to the point when specifying the camera point in the Points option.

Even though the Points option sets both distance and angle for the camera and target points, you still need to use the Distance option to turn on perspective mode.

PAn

You cannot use the regular PAN or ZOOM commands within DVIEW, so DVIEW has its own Pan and Zoom options. At the `Specify displacement base point:` prompt, pick any point. At the `Specify second point:` prompt, pick the point to which you want the first point to pan. The model moves the distance and direction indicated by an imaginary line from the base point to the second point.

Zoom

The Zoom option displays the same slider bar you see with the Distance option, explained previously. If perspective mode is not on, you see the `Specify zoom scale factor <1>:` prompt, which works like the Distance option slider bar. If perspective mode is on, you see the `Specify lens length <50.000mm>:` prompt. A shorter lens length, such as 35mm, zooms you out, giving a wider angle view. A longer lens length, such as 70mm, zooms you in, giving a narrower angle view.

Note Although the prompt shows a default in the form 50.000mm, you can only type in a number. Omit the mm.

TWist

The Twist option turns your objects around in a circle parallel to the current view you have defined. The default is zero (0) degrees, which is no twist. Assuming your current view looks at the objects right side up, 180 degrees turns the objects upside down, as if you had turned the camera in your hands upside down. AutoCAD displays a rubber-band line from the center of the view, which you can use to pick a twist point, or you can type in an angle.

CLip

The Clip option enables you to create front and back planes that clip off the view. Objects in front of the front clipping plane or behind the back clipping plane are not displayed. You can use the front clipping plane to clip off a wall in front of the camera, letting you see through the wall to the objects beyond — a kind of AutoCAD X-ray vision. Use the back clipping plane when you want to exclude objects in the

distance from your perspective view. The clipping planes are always perpendicular to the line of sight, so you only need to set their distance from the target point.

Compare Figure 22-37 to Figure 22-35. In Figure 22-37, the front posts and brackets have been clipped so that they no longer obscure the rest of the model.

Figure 22-37: This model has a front clipping plane that hides the front of the model. Compare it to Figure 22-35.

When you choose the Clip option, you see the Enter clipping option [Back/Front/Off] <Off>: prompt. Specify Back or Front to set the back or front clipping planes. Specify Off to turn off all previously defined clipping planes.

Note When you use the Distance option to create a perspective view, AutoCAD automatically turns on a front clipping plane at the camera point.

When you specify the Front suboption, AutoCAD responds with the Specify distance from target or [set to Eye(camera)/ON/OFF] <2.5682>: prompt. Specify Eye to set the clipping plane at the camera point. You can define the clipping plane by typing in a distance or using the slider bar that appears at the top of your screen. As you move the cursor on the slider bar, stop to let the drawing redraw so you can see the result.

When you specify the Back suboption, AutoCAD displays the Specify distance from target or [ON/OFF] <-5.5826>: prompt. Specify On or Off to turn the clipping plane on or off, or specify the distance as for the front clipping plane.

Hide

The Hide option performs a hide, just like the HIDE command, letting you clearly see the results of the view you have created.

Off

The Off option turns off perspective mode and returns you to a parallel view. Otherwise, when you leave DVIEW after going into perspective mode, AutoCAD retains the perspective view until you change the view — for example, with VPOINT. Until then, you cannot pick points on the screen or use object snaps, which can be very frustrating. This option enables you to exit from DVIEW in the normal viewing mode.

Undo

The Undo option undoes the effect of the last DVIEW option. You can undo through all the changes you have made in DVIEW.

The drawing used in the following Step-by-Step exercise on creating perspective views, ab22-e.dwg, is in the Drawings folder of the *AutoCAD 2004 Bible* CD-ROM.

Step-by-Step: Creating Perspective Views

1. Open ab22-e.dwg from the CD-ROM.

2. Save it as ab22-03.dwg in your AutoCAD Bible folder. This is a portion of a 3D house in plan view, as shown in Figure 22-38. Make sure that OSNAP is on. Set a running object snap set for endpoint and turn off any other object snaps.

3. You want to create a perspective view from approximately ❶ to ❷ in Figure 22-38. You can see right away that the wall near ❶ will need clipping. To get the distance of the clipping plane from the target, choose Tools ⇨ Inquiry ⇨ Distance and pick ❸ and ❹. The pertinent information is Distance = 12'-5 9/16". You may get a slightly different distance. To see the distance information, press F2 to open the AutoCAD Text window.

4. Choose View ⇨ 3D Views ⇨ NE Isometric. The result is as shown in Figure 22-39. This is a quick approximation and helps you plan your camera and target points. To test for endpoints, start the LINE command. Place the cursor at ❶ in Figure 22-39. The Endpoint SnapTip and marker appear. Place the cursor at ❷, the top of the table leg. You should see the Endpoint SnapTip and marker. Press Esc to cancel the LINE command without drawing a line.

5. Type **dview** ↵. At the Select objects or <use DVIEWBLOCK>: prompt, type **all** ↵. Press Enter to end object selection.

6. At the main DVIEW prompt, right-click and choose Points. At the Specify target point <14'-5 15/16", 21'-9 3/8", 6'-1 1/4">: prompt, pick the endpoint at ❷ in Figure 22-39. At the Specify camera point <14'-6 15/16", 21'-10 3/8", 6'-2 1/4">: prompt, pick the endpoint at ❶.

Figure 22-38: A 3D house in plan view

Thanks to Andrew Wilcox of Virtual Homes, Inc.,
Hammonds Plains, Nova Scotia, Canada, for this drawing.
I have used only a small portion of it.

Figure 22-39: The NE isometric view of the house

7. Right-click and choose Distance. At the `Specify new camera-target dis-tance <20'-10 15/16">:` prompt, move the cursor to 4x on the slider bar. Take your hand off the mouse to let the drawing redraw until you can see the result. Pick at the 4x mark. Notice the perspective view icon.

8. To move the camera point, right-click and choose Camera. At the `Specify camera location, or enter angle from XY plane, or [Toggle (angle in)] <11.7252>:` prompt, type **8** ↵ to lower the camera point

slightly. At the `Specify camera location, or enter angle in XY plane from X axis, or [Toggle (angle from)] <11.72523>:` prompt, move the cursor close to ❸ in Figure 22-39 *relative to the screen, not the model* and click.

9. Right-click and choose Zoom. At the `Specify lens length <35.000mm>:` prompt, type **60** to zoom in slightly.

10. Right-click and choose Clip. Right-click and choose Front to set the front clipping plane. At the `Specify distance from target or [set to Eye(camera)] <83'-7 1/2">:` prompt, type **13'** ↵. AutoCAD hides the front walls that are blocking the view.

11. Right-click and choose Pan. At the `Specify displacement base point:` prompt, pick ❹ in Figure 22-39 relative to the screen, not the drawing. At the `Specify second point:` prompt, pick ❺ relative to the screen. The display moves down.

12. Right-click and choose Hide to hide the drawing. Your drawing should look approximately like Figure 22-40.

13. Press Enter to end the DVIEW command.

14. After all that work, you should save the view. Choose View ➪ Named Views. On the Named Views tab, click New. In the New View dialog box, type **Perspective 1** in the View Name text box. Click OK. Click OK to return to your drawing.

15. Save your drawing.

Figure 22-40: The final perspective view

Laying Out 3D Drawings

Laying out a 3D drawing on a layout tab is an important aspect of viewing a 3D drawing, because the layout determines the final output of the drawing. AutoCAD offers three commands that help you lay out your 3D drawing in paper space layouts — SOLVIEW, SOLDRAW, and SOLPROF. You can find them on the Solids toolbar. (Chapter 17 explains layouts.)

On the CD-ROM Flatten converts 3D polylines to 2D and flattens everything except blocks. Look in `\Software\Chap22\Flatten`.

Using SOLVIEW to lay out paper space viewports

SOLVIEW automates the process of creating floating viewports and orthogonal views — views at right angles from each other.

 To start SOLVIEW, choose Setup View from the Solids toolbar. SOLVIEW has five options:

✦ **UCS** enables you to choose the UCS to work from as well as set the scale, center, and clipping corners of a floating viewport. Use this option first. After you choose a UCS, type in a scale. You can change this later if you want. Then SOLVIEW prompts you for the center of the view. Pick a point and wait until the 3D model regenerates. SOLVIEW continues to prompt you for a view center, letting you pick points until you like what you see. Press Enter to continue the prompts. The clipping corners are the corners of the viewport. At the `Enter view name:` prompt, type a name. SOLVIEW creates the first viewport.

Choose a view name that describes the view, such as Top, Side, or East Elevation. This helps you when you start creating orthogonal views.

✦ **Ortho** creates orthogonal views. At the `Specify side of viewport to project:` prompt, pick one of the edges of the first viewport. Again, choose a view center and clip the corners to create the viewport. Type a name for this new view.

If you don't see the model properly when you pick the view center, continue with the prompts, picking clipping corners where you want them. Then pick the viewport (in model space with tile off) and do a Zoom Extents. You can then pan and zoom as you want. This problem can happen when you have several separate 3D objects in your drawing.

✦ **Auxiliary** creates inclined views. At the `Specify first point of inclined plane:` prompt, pick a point in one of the viewports. At the `Specify second point of inclined plane:` prompt, pick another point in the same viewport. The two points are usually at an angle to create the inclined view. At the `Specify side to view from:` prompt, pick a point. You then pick a view center and clipping corners, and specify a view name.

✦ **Section** creates cross sections. At the `Specify first point of cutting plane:` prompt, pick a point in a viewport. At the `Specify second point of cutting plane:` prompt, pick a point on the opposite side of the model to create a cross section. You then pick a side to view from, and enter the view scale, a view center, clipping corners, and a view name.

✦ **eXit** exits the command. (This option is not visible in the command prompt.) You can exit the command after using an option and restart the command to use another option, or you can use all the options and then exit the command at the end.

Figure 22-41 shows an example with a top view, an orthogonal view from one side, an auxiliary view, and a section.

Figure 22-41: An example of using SOLVIEW

Using SOLDRAW to create hidden lines and hatching

SOLDRAW uses the views created by SOLVIEW and creates 2D profiles that include solid and hidden lines to represent the profiles and hatching for sectional views. You must use SOLVIEW before using SOLDRAW.

To use SOLDRAW, choose Setup Drawing from the Solids toolbar. SOLDRAW puts you into a paper space layout and prompts you to select objects, which means floating viewports. You can select all of them if you want. SOLDRAW then proceeds to automatically create the profile views. Figure 22-42 shows an example of the hatching created for a sectional view.

Figure 22-42: The result of using SOLDRAW on a sectional view

SOLDRAW uses hatch pattern defaults to define the hatch. You may have to change these settings using HATCHEDIT.

Note SOLVIEW creates a whole set of new layers in your drawing. SOLDRAW freezes your original layers, leaving visible only the layers needed to display the profile in that paper space viewport. SOLVIEW creates a special layer that you can use for dimensioning — one for each view that you create. For a view named front, the layer is named front-dim. You can use these dimensioning layers to create dimensions in paper space.

Using SOLPROF to create profiles

The SOLPROF command creates profiles like SOLDRAW, but you don't need to use SOLVIEW first. In addition, SOLPROF is more interactive than SOLDRAW. To start the command, choose Setup Profile from the Solids toolbar. SOLPROF prompts you to select objects.

Note When you start SOLPROF, you must have already created a floating viewport, and you must be in model space.

At the Display hidden profile lines on separate layer? [Yes/No] <Y>: prompt, type **Y** or **N**. By specifying Yes, you give yourself the capability of freezing or turning off the layer containing hidden parts of the model. You can also hide other 3D objects behind the one you are profiling.

At the Project profile lines onto a plane? [Yes/No] <Y>: prompt, type **Y** or **N**. If you choose Yes, SOLPROF creates 2D objects. If you choose No, SOLPROF creates 3D objects.

At the Delete tangential edges? [Yes/No] <Y>: prompt, type **Y** or **N**. A tangential edge is the meeting of two contiguous faces. Most drafting applications do not require you to show tangential edges.

Figure 22-43 shows the result of SOLPROF after freezing the layer containing the original object — SOLPROF creates its own layers for the profile.

Figure 22-43: A profile created with SOLPROF

Figure 22-44 shows the result of SOLPROF after also freezing the layer that SOL-PROF created containing the hidden parts of the model. In this case, the layer was named PH-159. Look for the h, which stands for hidden. The last part of the layer name is the handle of the object you are profiling and so differs for each object.

Figure 22-44: A profile created with SOLPROF after freezing the layer containing the hidden parts of the model

You can combine viewports created with SOLPROF and viewports created with SOLVIEW and SOLDRAW. For example, you can create two orthogonal views with SOLVIEW and SOLDRAW and then add a viewport and use SOLPROF to create another view.

Tip As soon as you have a separate layer for the hidden portion of the model, you can modify that layer's color and/or linetype to show the hidden lines in a contrasting color or linetype.

Summary

In this chapter, I covered all the ways to view your 3D drawing. You read about:

- ✦ Using the standard viewpoints on the Viewpoint flyout for a quick look
- ✦ Utilizing the DDVPOINT command to specify exact angles
- ✦ Using the tripod and compass for flexibility
- ✦ Using the PLAN command to quickly return you to plan view
- ✦ Shading your drawing in one of several modes — these shading modes persist until you turn them off.
- ✦ Applying 3D orbit to view your model from any position. You can zoom and pan, create parallel and perspective views, and set clipping planes. You can also create a continuously moving orbit.
- ✦ Using the DVIEW command to let you create parallel and perspective views. You set the camera and target where you can create front and back clipping planes.
- ✦ Employing the three commands — SOLVIEW, SOLDRAW, and SOLPROF — that help you lay out views of a 3D drawing for plotting

In the next chapter, I explain how to create 3D surfaces.

✦ ✦ ✦

Creating 3D Surfaces

In this chapter, you learn to create all types of surfaces, also called *meshes*. Surfaces have a great advantage over 3D wireframe models because you can hide back surfaces and create shaded images for easier visualization of your models. Surfaces also enable you to create unusual shapes, such as for topological maps or free-form objects. Figure 23-1 shows a lamp created by using surfaces.

Figure 23-1: A lamp created with surfaces

You cannot obtain information about physical properties, such as mass, center of gravity, and so on, from surfaces. Such information can be obtained only from 3D solids, which are covered in the next chapter.

AutoCAD approximates curved surfaces by creating a mesh of planes at varying angles. You see the planes because AutoCAD displays them using a web of intersecting lines. AutoCAD defines the mesh by its vertices — where the lines intersect. Figure 23-2 shows a mesh with its vertices.

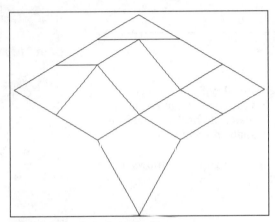

Figure 23-2: A surface mesh

When working with surfaces you may want to display the Surfaces toolbar, shown in Figure 23-3. Right-click any toolbar and choose Surfaces.

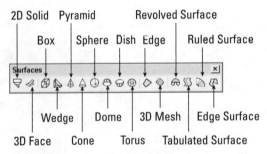

Figure 23-3: The Surfaces toolbar

Drawing Surfaces with 3DFACE

Two-dimensional objects are often used to create three-dimensional models. In Chapter 21, I discuss how you can use 2D solids (the SOLID command), wide polylines, and circles to make horizontal surfaces when you add a thickness to them. In fact, the SOLID command is so useful in 3D that you can find its icon on the Surfaces toolbar.

You can also use regions in 3D drawings. While regions are 2D objects and cannot be given a thickness, when you use the HIDE command, AutoCAD displays the region as a surface. When the drawing is regenerated to a wireframe display, the region is displayed as a wireframe again, losing its surface properties.

Another option is to use 3DFACE, which is a true 3D command. 3DFACE creates three or four-sided surfaces that can be in any plane. You can place surfaces together to make a many-sided surface. While AutoCAD draws lines between these surfaces, you can make the lines invisible to create the effect of a seamless surface. You define the surface by specifying the points that create the corners of the surface. As a result, a 3D face cannot have any curves. 3DFACE only creates surfaces — you cannot give a thickness to a 3D face. However, you can create a 3D solid from a 3D face using the EXTRUDE command. 3D solids are covered in the next chapter.

Using the 3DFACE command

 To create a 3D face, choose 3D Face from the Surfaces toolbar. AutoCAD prompts you for first, second, third, and fourth points. You must specify points clockwise or counterclockwise, not in the zigzag fashion required by the 2D SOLID command. When creating a 3D face:

✦ Press Enter at the `Specify fourth point or [Invisible] <create three-sided face>:` prompt to create a three-sided surface. Then press Enter again to end the command.

✦ To create a four-sided surface, specify a fourth point. AutoCAD repeats the `Specify third point or [Invisible] <exit>:` prompt. Press Enter to end the command.

✦ To create surfaces of more than four sides, continue to specify points. AutoCAD repeats the third and fourth point prompts until you press Enter — twice after a third point or once after a fourth point.

As you continue to add faces, the last edge created by the third and fourth points becomes the first edge of the new face so that adding a face requires only two additional points.

Tip It often helps to prepare for a complex 3D face by creating 2D objects for some or all of the faces. You can then use Endpoint object snaps to pick the points of the 3D face. Place these 2D objects on a unique layer, such as Frames or Const.

Making 3D face edges invisible

Making edges invisible makes a series of 3D faces look like one 3D face. Figure 23-4 shows three 3D faces with and without internal seams.

You can control the visibility of 3D face edges in several ways.

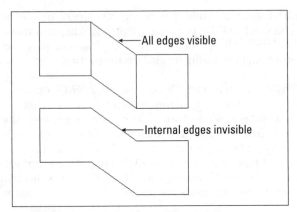

Figure 23-4: You can make internal edges of a 3D face invisible.

Controlling visibility during 3D face creation

While you are drawing the 3D face, you can right-click and choose Invisible before each edge. Then specify the next point. However, it is sometimes difficult to predict exactly where to indicate the invisible edge.

Using the EDGE command

After creating the entire 3D face, you can use the EDGE command. The sole purpose of the EDGE command is to make 3D face edges visible and invisible — this is probably the easiest way to control the visibility of 3D face edges.

Choose Edge from the Surfaces toolbar. At the Specify edge of 3dface to toggle visibility or [Display]: prompt, select a visible edge that you want to make invisible. AutoCAD repeats the prompt so that you can select additional edges. Press Enter to make the edges invisible. Although a visible edge might actually be two edges belonging to two adjacent 3D faces, EDGE makes them both invisible.

To make invisible edges visible, right-click and choose the Display option. AutoCAD displays all the edges in dashed lines and shows the Enter selection method for display of hidden edges [Select/All] <All>: prompt. Press Enter to display all the edges or use the Select option to select 3D faces (you can use windows for selection). Either way, you see the edges of the 3D face you want to edit. AutoCAD then repeats the Specify edge of 3dface to toggle visibility or [Display]: prompt. You can now select the edge you want to make visible. Press Enter to end the command and make the edge visible.

Using the Properties palette

After creating one or more 3D faces, you can also open the Properties palette (choose Properties on the Standard toolbar) and select one 3D face. (See Figure 23-5.) You can choose more than one, but the results are difficult to predict.

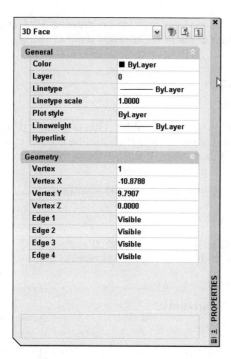

Figure 23-5: You can use the Properties palette to change the visibility of 3D face edges.

Using this palette to edit 3D face edge visibility presents two difficulties. First, you have no easy way to know which edge is which. The dialog box only labels them Edge 1, 2, 3, and 4. Second, while the EDGE command makes both edges of adjacent 3D faces visible or invisible, the Properties palette does not. You need to use it for each adjacent face. The best method is to use the EDGE command to control visibility of 3D face edges.

Using the SPLFRAME system variable

Setting the SPLFRAME system variable to 1 and then regenerating the drawing makes all 3D face edges visible. (The SPLFRAME system variable also affects the display of spline-fit polylines, hence its name.) To return edges to their original setting, set SPLFRAME to 0 and do a REGEN.

On the CD-ROM The drawing used in the following Step-by-Step exercise on drawing 3D faces, ab23-a.dwg, is in the Drawings folder of the *AutoCAD 2004 Bible* CD-ROM.

Step-by-Step: Drawing 3D Faces

1. Open ab23-a.dwg from the CD-ROM.

2. Save it as ab23-01.dwg in your AutoCAD Bible folder. This is a blank drawing with architectural units. Turn on ORTHO. OSNAP should be on. Set running object snaps for endpoints and midpoints. If the Surfaces toolbar is not displayed, right-click any toolbar, and check Surfaces.

3. Choose 3D Face from the Surfaces toolbar. Follow the prompts:

```
Specify first point or [Invisible]: 6,6 ↵
Specify second point or [Invisible]: @20,0 ↵
Specify third point or [Invisible] <exit>: @0,2' ↵
Specify fourth point or [Invisible] <create three-sided
face>: @-20,0 ↵
Specify third point or [Invisible] <exit>: ↵
```

4. Start the COPY command. Follow the prompts:

```
Select objects: Select the 3D face.
Select objects: ↵
Specify base point or displacement, or [Multiple]: Right-
click and choose Multiple.
Specify base point: Pick any point.
Specify second point of displacement or <use first point as
displacement>: @0,0,1.5' ↵
Specify second point of displacement or <use first point as
displacement>: @0,0,3' ↵
Specify second point of displacement or <use first point as
displacement>: ↵
```

You don't see any difference because you are looking at the three 3D faces in plan view and they are on top of each other.

5. Choose View ➪ 3D Views ➪ SE Isometric. Your drawing should look like Figure 23-6. You now have the top, bottom, and the middle shelf of the cabinet.

6. Start the 3DFACE command again. Follow the prompts:

```
Specify first point or [Invisible]: Pick the endpoint at ❶ in
Figure 23-6.
Specify second point or [Invisible]: Pick the endpoint at ❷.
```

```
Specify third point or [Invisible] <exit>: Pick the endpoint
at ❸.
Specify fourth point or [Invisible] <create three-sided
face>: Pick the endpoint at ❹.
Specify third point or [Invisible] <exit>: Pick the endpoint
at ❺.
Specify fourth point or [Invisible] <create three-sided
face>: Pick the endpoint at ❻.
Specify third point or [Invisible] <exit>: Pick the endpoint
at ❼.
Specify fourth point or [Invisible] <create three-sided
face>: Pick the endpoint at ❽.
Specify third point or [Invisible] <exit>: ↵
```

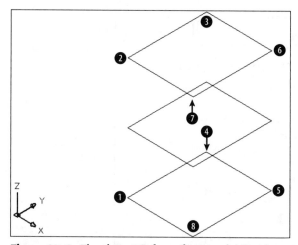

Figure 23-6: The three 3D faces from an isometric viewpoint

7. To draw the door of the cabinet, change the current layer to CONST. Start the LINE command and draw a line from ❷ in Figure 23-6 to @18<225. End the LINE command. Now start the COPY command and copy the line from ❷ to ❶. These two construction lines frame the door.

8. To make it easier to work on the door, choose Tools ⇨ New UCS ⇨ 3 Point. Follow the prompts:

```
Specify new origin point <0,0,0>: Pick the left endpoint of
the bottom construction line.
Specify point on positive portion of X-axis <-0'-5 3/4",-0'-6
3/4",0'-0">: Pick ❶ in Figure 23-6.
Specify point on positive-Y portion of the UCS XY plane
<-0'-7 7/16",-0'-6",0'-">: Pick the left endpoint of the top
construction line.
```

9. Start the LINE command again. Follow the prompts:

```
Specify first point: Choose the From object snap.
Base point: Pick the left endpoint of the top construction
line.
<Offset>: @3,-3 ↵
Specify next point or [Undo]: Move the cursor to the right
and type 12 ↵.
Specify next point or [Undo]: Move the cursor down and type
30 ↵.
Specify next point or [Close/Undo]: Move the cursor to the
left and type 12 ↵.
Specify next point or [Close/Undo]: c ↵
```

Your drawing should look like Figure 23-7.

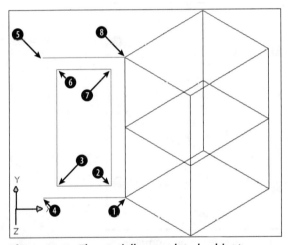

Figure 23-7: The partially completed cabinet

10. Change the current layer to 0. Choose 3D Face from the Surfaces toolbar.
Follow the prompts:

```
Specify first point or [Invisible]: Pick the endpoint at ❶ in
Figure 23-7.
Specify second point or [Invisible]: Pick the endpoint at ❷
in Figure 23-7.
Specify third point or [Invisible] <exit>: Pick the endpoint
at ❸.
Specify fourth point or [Invisible] <create three-sided
face>: Pick the endpoint at ❹ in Figure 23-7. Notice the edge
lines between ❶ and ❷ and between ❸ and ❹.
Specify third point or [Invisible] <exit>: Right-click and
choose Invisible. Pick the endpoint at ❺ in Figure 23-7.
```

```
Specify fourth point or [Invisible] <create three-sided
face>: Pick the endpoint at ❻.
Specify third point or [Invisible] <exit>: Right-click and
choose Invisible. Pick the endpoint at ❼.
Specify fourth point or [Invisible] <create three-sided
face>: Pick the endpoint at ❽.
Specify third point or [Invisible] <exit>: Pick the endpoint
at ❶ in Figure 23-7.
Specify fourth point or [Invisible] <create three-sided
face>: Pick the endpoint at ❾.
Specify third point or [Invisible] <exit>: ⏎
```

11. ◇ Choose Edge from the Surfaces toolbar. At the `Specify edge of 3dface to toggle visibility or [Display]:` prompt, pick the edge between ❶ and ❷ and then the edge between ❸ and ❹. (A midpoint marker and SnapTip appear.) Press Enter. The edges disappear.

12. Choose Tools ⇨ New UCS ⇨ World.

13. Choose View ⇨ 3D Views ⇨ Viewpoint Presets to open the Viewpoint Presets dialog box. Set the From: X Axis angle to 200 degrees. Set the XY Plane angle to 35 degrees. Choose OK.

14. Choose View ⇨ Hide to see the result. You can clearly see through the cabinet door's window.

15. Save your drawing. It should look like Figure 23-8.

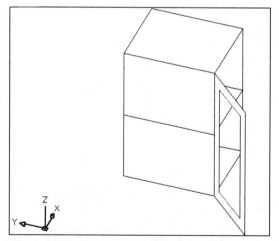

Figure 23-8: The completed kitchen cabinet, including a window in the door

Drawing Surfaces with PFACE

PFACE draws surfaces called polyface meshes, which are a type of polyline. However, you cannot edit them with PEDIT. The best way to edit them is with grips. AutoCAD designed PFACE for the creation of surfaces using AutoLISP routines or other automated methods. Consequently, the input for polyface meshes is somewhat awkward. However, polyface meshes have the following advantages:

✦ You can draw surfaces with any number of sides, unlike 3D faces, which can only have three or four sides.

✦ The entire surface is one object.

✦ Sections that are on one plane do not show edges so that you don't have to bother with making edges invisible.

✦ You can explode polyface meshes into 3D faces.

✦ If you create a polyface mesh on more than one plane, each plane can be on a different layer or have a different color. This can be useful for assigning materials for rendering or other complex selection processes.

On the other hand, polyface meshes are difficult to create and edit. Figure 23-9 shows two polyface meshes — one on one plane and the other on three planes.

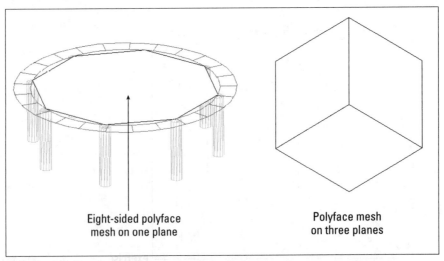

Eight-sided polyface
mesh on one plane

Polyface mesh
on three planes

Figure 23-9: You can create many-sided polyface meshes on one plane, or on several different planes. After you use the HIDE command, the polyface mesh hides objects behind it.

The prompts for PFACE are divided into two phases. The first phase simply asks for vertices. The second phase asks you to specify which vertex makes up which face (or plane). The second phase is fairly meaningless for polyface meshes on one plane, but you have to specify the vertices anyway. Here's how to do it:

1. Type **pface** ↵.

2. At the `Specify location for vertex 1:` prompt, specify the first vertex.

3. Continue to specify vertices at the `Specify location for vertex 2 or <define faces>:` or `Specify location for vertex 3 or <define faces>:` prompts (and so on). Press Enter when you have finished.

4. At the `Face 1, vertex 1: Enter a vertex number or [Color/Layer]:` prompt, type which vertex starts the first face of the polyface mesh. It is usually vertex 1, so you type **1** ↵.

5. At the `Face 1, vertex 2: Enter a vertex number or [Color/Layer] <next face>:` prompt, type which vertex comes next on the first face. Continue to specify the vertices for the first face.

If you are drawing a polyface mesh on one plane, continue to specify all the vertices in order and press Enter twice when you are done to end the command.

If you are drawing a polyface mesh on more than one plane, continue to specify the vertices on the first face (that is, plane) and press Enter. At the `Face 2, vertex 1: Enter a vertex number or [Color/Layer]:` prompt, type the first vertex of the second face (plane) and continue to specify vertices for the second face. Press Enter. Continue to specify vertices for all the faces. Press Enter twice to end the command.

Tip In order to easily draw a polyface mesh with PFACE, draw 2D objects as a guide for picking vertices. Then you can use object snaps to pick the vertices. Also, for polyface meshes on more than one plane, draw a diagram that numbers the vertices. This helps you specify which vertices make up which face.

During the second phase of the prompts, when PFACE asks you to define the faces, you can right-click and choose Layer or Color and specify the layer or color. Then specify the vertices that are to be on that layer or color.

In the following Step-by-Step exercise, you draw a hexagonal night table with polyface meshes.

On the CD-ROM The drawing used in the following Step-by-Step exercise on drawing polyface meshes, ab23-b.dwg, is in the Drawings folder of the *AutoCAD 2004 Bible* CD-ROM.

Step-by-Step: Drawing Polyface Meshes

1. Open ab23-b.dwg from the CD-ROM.

2. Save it as ab23-02.dwg in your AutoCAD Bible folder. Two hexagons have been drawn, one 24 inches above the other, on the Const layer, as shown in Figure 23-10.

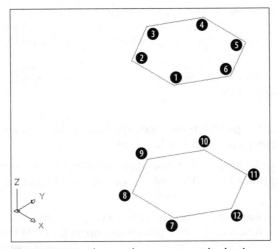

Figure 23-10: The two hexagons are the basis for a night table.

3. Type **pface** ↵. Follow the prompts. First you specify all the vertices. Then you specify the top hexagon, then the five sides (the front is open), and finally the bottom hexagon. Unfortunately, if you make a mistake, you must start over.

```
Specify location for vertex 1: Pick ❶ in Figure 23-10.
Specify location for vertex 2 or <define faces>: Pick ❷ in
Figure 23-10.
Specify location for vertex 3 or <define faces>: Pick ❸.
Specify location for vertex 4 or <define faces>: Pick ❹.
Specify location for vertex 5 or <define faces>: Pick ❺.
Specify location for vertex 6 or <define faces>: Pick ❻.
Specify location for vertex 7 or <define faces>: Pick ❼.
Specify location for vertex 8 or <define faces>: Pick ❽.
Specify location for vertex 9 or <define faces>: Pick ❾.
Specify location for vertex 10 or <define faces>: Pick ❿.
Specify location for vertex 11 or <define faces>: Pick ⓫.
Specify location for vertex 12 or <define faces>: Pick ⓬.
Specify location for vertex 13 or <define faces>: ↵
Face 1, vertex 1: Enter a vertex number or [Color/Layer]: 1 ↵
Face 1, vertex 2: Enter a vertex number or [Color/Layer]
<next face>: 2 ↵
Face 1, vertex 3: Enter a vertex number or [Color/Layer]
<next face>: 3 ↵
```

```
Face 1, vertex 4: Enter a vertex number or [Color/Layer]
<next face>: 4 ↵
Face 1, vertex 5: Enter a vertex number or [Color/Layer]
<next face>: 5 ↵
Face 1, vertex 6: Enter a vertex number or [Color/Layer]
<next face>: 6 ↵
Face 1, vertex 7: Enter a vertex number or [Color/Layer]
<next face>: ↵
Face 2, vertex 1: Enter a vertex number or [Color/Layer]:
12 ↵
Face 2, vertex 2: Enter a vertex number or [Color/Layer]
<next face>: 6 ↵
Face 2, vertex 3: Enter a vertex number or [Color/Layer]
<next face>: 5 ↵
Face 2, vertex 4: Enter a vertex number or [Color/Layer]
<next face>: 11 ↵
Face 2, vertex 5: Enter a vertex number or [Color/Layer]
<next face>: ↵
Face 3, vertex 1: Enter a vertex number or [Color/Layer]:
5 ↵
Face 3, vertex 2: Enter a vertex number or [Color/Layer]
<next face>: 11 ↵
Face 3, vertex 3: Enter a vertex number or [Color/Layer]
<next face>: 10 ↵
Face 3, vertex 4: Enter a vertex number or [Color/Layer]
<next face>: 4 ↵
Face 3, vertex 5: Enter a vertex number or [Color/Layer]
<next face>: ↵
Face 4, vertex 1: Enter a vertex number or [Color/Layer]:
10 ↵
Face 4, vertex 2: Enter a vertex number or [Color/Layer]
<next face>: 4 ↵
Face 4, vertex 3: Enter a vertex number or [Color/Layer]
<next face>: 3 ↵
Face 4, vertex 4: Enter a vertex number or [Color/Layer]
<next face>: 9 ↵
Face 4, vertex 5: Enter a vertex number or [Color/Layer]
<next face>: ↵
Face 5, vertex 1: Enter a vertex number or [Color/Layer]:
3 ↵
Face 5, vertex 2: Enter a vertex number or [Color/Layer]
<next face>: 9 ↵
Face 5, vertex 3: Enter a vertex number or [Color/Layer]
<next face>: 8 ↵
Face 5, vertex 4: Enter a vertex number or [Color/Layer]
<next face>: 2 ↵
Face 5, vertex 5: Enter a vertex number or [Color/Layer]
<next face>: ↵
Face 6, vertex 1: Enter a vertex number or [Color/Layer]:
8 ↵
Face 6, vertex 2: Enter a vertex number or [Color/Layer]
<next face>: 2 ↵
Face 6, vertex 3: Enter a vertex number or [Color/Layer]
<next face>: 1 ↵
```

```
Face 6, vertex 4: Enter a vertex number or [Color/Layer]
<next face>: 7 ↵
Face 6, vertex 5: Enter a vertex number or [Color/Layer]
<next face>: ↵
Face 7, vertex 1: Enter a vertex number or [Color/Layer]: 7 ↵
Face 7, vertex 2: Enter a vertex number or [Color/Layer]
<next face>: 8 ↵
Face 7, vertex 3: Enter a vertex number or [Color/Layer]
<next face>: 9 ↵
Face 7, vertex 4: Enter a vertex number or [Color/Layer]
<next face>: 10 ↵
Face 7, vertex 5: Enter a vertex number or [Color/Layer]
<next face>: 11 ↵
Face 7, vertex 6: Enter a vertex number or [Color/Layer]
<next face>: 12 ↵
Face 7, vertex 7: Enter a vertex number or [Color/Layer]
<next face>: ↵
Face 8, vertex 1: Enter a vertex number or [Color/Layer]: ↵
```

4. Choose View ➪ Hide to see the final result.

5. Save your drawing. It should look like Figure 23-11.

Figure 23-11: The completed hexagonal night table

Creating Polygon Meshes with 3DMESH

The 3DMESH command creates polygon meshes (not to be confused with the poly-face meshes created by PFACE). The 3DMESH command is used for creating irregular surfaces, vertex by vertex. The great advantage of polygon meshes is that AutoCAD considers them to be polylines and they can therefore be edited with the

PEDIT command—although in a limited manner. Figure 23-12 shows two surfaces created with 3DMESH. The surface on the right has been smoothed using PEDIT.

To use 3DMESH, choose 3D Mesh from the Surfaces toolbar. AutoCAD then asks you for the Mesh M size and Mesh N size. M is the number of vertices going in the first direction. N is the number of vertices going in the other direction. Figure 23-13 shows a 3D Mesh with an M size of 5 and an N size of 3.

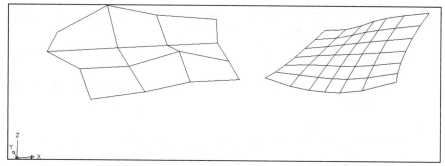

Figure 23-12: Two surfaces created with 3DMESH. The surface on the right has been smoothed using the Smooth option of PEDIT.

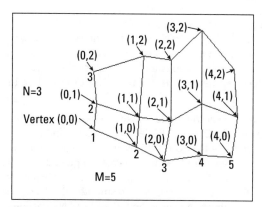

Figure 23-13: A 3D Mesh with an M size of 5 and an N size of 3, showing the vertex designations

After you set the size of the 3D Mesh, you need to specify each vertex. For example, the 3D Mesh in Figure 23-13 has 15 vertices that you need to specify. AutoCAD prompts you for each vertex in order, starting with (0,0). Vertex (0,1) is the second vertex in the first column. Vertex (1,0) is the first vertex in the second column, starting from the bottom. It's a little confusing because AutoCAD starts the counting from zero (0), not 1. For the 3D Mesh in Figure 23-13, the last vertex is (4,2).

Note In Figure 23-13, the 3D Mesh is five vertices wide and three vertices high as you look at it in plan view. However, you do not have to specify the vertices in the same direction. For the 3D mesh in the figure, I started at the bottom left, continued to move up for (0,1) and (0,2), then moved to the right. However, you could start at the bottom left and move to the right for (0,1) and (0,2), and then go back to the left either above or below (0,0) — resulting in a 3D mesh that is three vertices wide and five vertices high as you look at it in plan view. In other words, M and N can be in any direction.

3D meshes are especially suitable for AutoLISP routines; in fact, AutoCAD supplies several. These are discussed in the next section.

To smooth a polygon mesh, start the PEDIT command and select the polygon mesh. AutoCAD responds with the `Enter an option [Edit vertex/Smooth surface/Desmooth/Mclose/Nclose/Undo]:` prompt. Table 23-1 explains how to use these options.

Table 23-1
PEDIT Options for 3D Polygon Meshes

Option	Description
Edit vertex	Displays the `Current vertex (0,0). Enter an option - [Next/Previous/Left/Right/Up/Down/Move/REgen/eXit] <N>:` prompt. Use the Next, Previous, Left, Right, Up, and Down suboptions to move the X marker that displays the current vertex. When you are at the vertex you want to move, use the Move suboption. REgen regenerates the 3D mesh. Use eXit to return to the original prompt.
Smooth surface	Smoothes the surface according to one of three possible sets of equations — Quadratic, Cubic, or Bézier. Bézier results in the smoothest surface. Use the SURFTYPE system variable to set the type of smoothing. Set SURFTYPE to 5 to create a quadratic b-spline surface, 6 to create a cubic b-spline surface, or 7 to create a Bézier surface. Cubic (6) is the default setting. To smooth a 3D Mesh, there must be more than three vertices in both the M and N directions.
Desmooth	Removes the smoothing on the 3D mesh surface.
Mclose	Closes the surface in the M direction by connecting the last edge to the first edge.
Nclose	Closes the surface in the N direction by connecting the last edge to the first edge.
Undo	Undoes the last option.

You can use 3DMESH to create 3D topological surfaces. You may have a surveyor's drawing marking measurement points. Open a new drawing, using the surveyor's drawing as an xref. In plan view, create a polygon mesh. For the vertices, pick the surveyor's measurement points. (You'll need to count them first to determine a regular grid for the M and N sizes.) Then select the polygon mesh to display its grip points. Select each grip in turn, and at the prompt, type (for example) **@0,0,100.78** ⏎ where the last coordinate is the measured height. When you are done, look at the surface in any nonplanar viewpoint to see the result.

Drawing Standard 3D Shapes

AutoCAD includes several AutoLISP routines that use the 3DMESH command to create some standard shapes. These shapes all have icons on the Surfaces toolbar. You can also choose Draw ➪ Surfaces ➪ 3D Surfaces to open the 3D Objects dialog box, as shown in Figure 23-14.

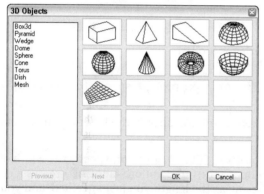

Figure 23-14: The 3D Objects dialog box

On the command line, you can type **3d** ⏎ and choose the shape you want to draw from the command options. You can also type **ai_** followed by the name of the shape, such as **ai_box**.

Box

Figure 23-15 shows a box from the SE isometric viewpoint after using the HIDE command.

Figure 23-15: A box from an isometric viewpoint after using the HIDE command

Here's how to draw a box:

1. Choose Box from the Surfaces toolbar.

2. At the `Specify corner point of box:` prompt, specify the lower-left corner of the base of the box.

3. At the `Specify length of box:` prompt, specify the length of the box along the X axis.

4. At the `Specify width of box or [Cube]:` prompt, specify the width of the box along the Y axis. If you choose the Cube option, AutoCAD creates a cube with a width and height the same as the length you just specified, and you don't see the height prompt.

5. At the `Specify height of box:` prompt, specify the height of the box along the Z axis.

6. At the `Specify rotation angle of box about the Z axis or [Reference]:` prompt, specify an angle. AutoCAD rotates the box in the XY plane. There is no default of zero (0) degrees, so you must type **0** ↵ even if you do not want to rotate the box. You can also use the Reference suboption, which works like the Reference option of the ROTATE command.

As you define the box, AutoCAD draws a temporary image in yellow to show you the result of your specifications.

Wedge

Figure 23-16 shows a wedge. The prompts are the same as for the box, except that there is no Cube option. A wedge is half of a box.

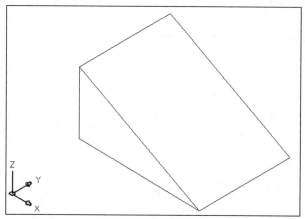

Figure 23-16: A wedge from an isometric viewpoint after the HIDE command

Here's how to draw a wedge:

1. Choose Wedge from the Surfaces toolbar.

2. At the `Specify corner point of wedge:` prompt, specify the lower-left corner of the base of the wedge.

3. At the `Specify length of wedge:` prompt, specify the length of the wedge along the X axis.

4. At the `Specify width of wedge:` prompt, specify the width of the wedge along the Y axis.

5. At the `Specify height of wedge:` prompt, specify the height of the wedge along the Z axis.

6. At the `Specify rotation angle of wedge about the Z axis:` prompt, specify an angle. AutoCAD rotates the wedge in the XY plane. There is no default of zero (0) degrees, so you must type **0** ↵ even if you do not want to rotate the wedge.

Pyramid

You can draw pyramids with three- and four-sided bases. A pyramid with a three-sided base creates a four-sided object called a tetrahedron. You can top the pyramid with a point, a flat top, or for four-sided bases, a ridge. Figure 23-17 shows the various types of pyramids you can draw.

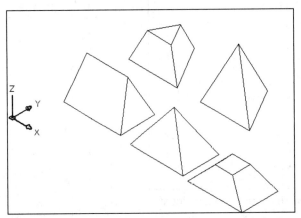

Figure 23-17: You can draw all these pyramidal shapes.

Here's how to draw the pyramids:

1. Choose Pyramid from the Surfaces toolbar.

2. At the `Specify first corner point for base of pyramid:` **prompt,** specify the first point (any point) on the base.

3. At the `Specify second corner point for base of pyramid:` **prompt,** specify the second point on the base.

4. At the `Specify third corner point for base of pyramid:` **prompt,** specify the third point on the base.

5. At the `Specify fourth corner point for base of pyramid or [Tetrahedron]:` prompt, specify the fourth point on the base or choose the Tetrahedron option (creates a pyramid with a base of three points).

 • If you chose the Tetrahedron option, at the `Specify apex point of tetrahedron or [Top]:` prompt specify the apex (top point) or choose the Top option. AutoCAD prompts you for three top points.

 • If you specified a fourth base point, at the `Specify apex point of pyramid or [Ridge/Top]:` prompt specify the apex (top point) or choose the Ridge or Top options. If you choose the Ridge option, specify the two points for the ridge. If you choose the Top option, specify the four top points.

Specifying the apex or ridge can be tricky unless you know the absolute coordinates you want. You can't change viewpoints during the command. However, you can easily change the points later using grips. Another trick is to start any drawing command, such as LINE, before starting the pyramid. At the `Specify first point:` prompt, pick the point you want to use for the first base point of the pyramid. Then press Esc to cancel the command. This leaves that point as the last point specified. Now define the base of the pyramid, using the same point as the first base point. When you need to specify the apex or ridge, you can use relative coordinates from the first base point. For example, to create an apex two units directly over the first base point, specify @0,0,2 for the apex. When you use the Top option, AutoCAD provides a rubber-band line from each of the base corners in turn, letting you use relative coordinates from the base corners. You can also create a temporary 2D object before starting the pyramid to frame a ridge or top.

Cone

You can create full or partial cones. Figure 23-18 shows both types, as displayed after using the HIDE command.

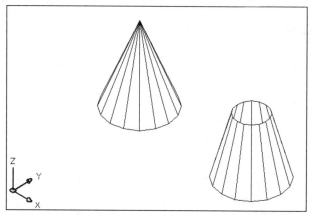

Figure 23-18: You can draw full or partial cones.

Follow these steps to create cones:

1. Choose Cone from the Surfaces toolbar.

2. At the `Specify center point for base of cone:` prompt, pick the center for the circle that makes the base of the cone.

3. At the `Specify radius for base of cone or [Diameter]:` prompt, specify the radius for the circle at the base or choose the Diameter option to specify the diameter.

4. At the `Specify radius for top of cone or [Diameter] <0>:` prompt, specify the radius of the top or choose the Diameter option and specify the diameter. If you accept the default of zero, you get a complete cone. If you specify a radius or diameter, you get a truncated cone.

Note You can specify the base's size to be larger than the top's size, resulting in an inverted cone.

5. At the `Specify height of cone:` prompt, specify the height.

6. At the `Enter number of segments for surface of cone <16>:` prompt, specify the number of mesh segments. A higher number results in a smoother-looking cone.

Sphere

Drawing a sphere is quite easy — you just specify the center and radius, and then the number of segments to display in each direction. Figure 23-19 shows a sphere after using the HIDE command.

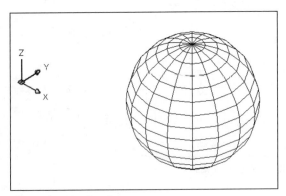

Figure 23-19: A sphere

Here's how to draw a sphere:

1. Choose Sphere from the Surfaces toolbar.

2. At the `Specify center point of sphere:` prompt, specify a point.

3. At the `Specify radius of sphere or [Diameter]:` prompt, specify the radius, or choose the Diameter option to specify the diameter.

4. At the `Enter number of longitudinal segments for surface of sphere <16>:` prompt, type the number of north-south lines you want. A higher number results in a smoother-looking sphere.

5. At the `Enter number of latitudinal segments for surface of sphere <16>:` prompt, type the number of east-west lines you want. A higher number results in a smoother-looking sphere.

The only tricky point with spheres is remembering that the center point is the center in all three dimensions. If you want to draw a ball on a table, it's easy to specify the center on the plane of the tabletop — but you end up with a ball that's half beneath the table. So plan ahead.

Dome

A dome is the top half of a sphere, as shown in Figure 23-20. The prompts are very similar to those for a sphere.

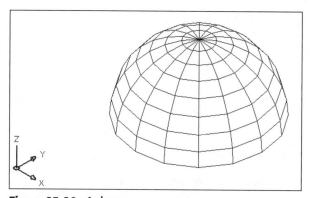

Figure 23-20: A dome

Follow these steps to draw a dome:

1. Choose Dome from the Surfaces toolbar.

2. At the `Specify center point of dome:` prompt, specify the center point of the circle that makes up the base of the dome.

3. At the `Specify radius of dome or [Diameter]:` prompt, specify the radius or use the Diameter option to specify the diameter.

4. At the `Enter number of longitudinal segments for surface of dome <16>:` prompt, type the number of north-south lines you want. A higher number results in a smoother-looking dome.

5. At the `Enter number of latitudinal segments for surface of dome <8>:` prompt, type the number of east-west lines you want. A higher number results in a smoother-looking dome. Notice that the default is 8 instead of 16 for the sphere because you are drawing only half a sphere.

Dish

A dish is the bottom half of a sphere, as shown in Figure 23-21. Actually, a bowl would be a better name for it.

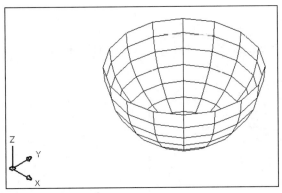

Figure 23-21: A dish

Follow these steps to draw a dish:

1. Choose Dish from the Surfaces toolbar.

2. At the `Specify center point of dish:` prompt, specify the center point of the circle that makes up the base of the dish.

3. At the `Specify radius of dish or [Diameter]:` prompt, specify the radius or use the Diameter option to specify the diameter.

4. At the `Enter number of longitudinal segments for surface of dish <16>:` prompt, type the number of north-south lines you want. A higher number results in a smoother looking dish.

5. At the `Enter number of latitudinal segments for surface of dome <8>:` prompt, type the number of east-west lines you want. A higher number

results in a smoother-looking dish. As with the dish, the default is 8 because you are drawing only half a sphere.

As with spheres, remember that the center point is the center of the top of the dish, not its base.

Torus

A torus is a 3D donut, as shown in Figure 23-22.

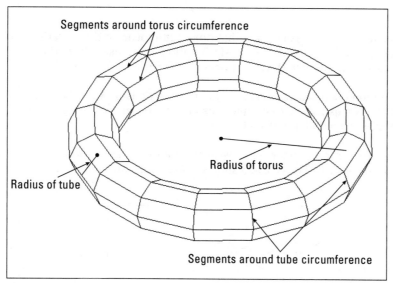

Segments around torus circumference

Radius of torus

Radius of tube

Segments around tube circumference

Figure 23-22: A torus

Follow these steps to create a torus:

1. Choose Torus from the Surfaces toolbar.

2. At the `Specify center point of torus:` prompt, specify the center of the torus.

3. At the `Specify radius of torus or [Diameter]:` prompt, specify the radius of the torus, as shown in Figure 23-22 or use the Diameter option to define the diameter.

4. At the `Specify radius of tube or [Diameter]:` prompt, specify the radius of the tube, as shown in Figure 23-22, or use the Diameter option to define the diameter.

5. At the Enter number of segments around tube circumference <16>: prompt, specify the number of segments around the tube, as shown in Figure 23-22.

6. At the Enter number of segments around torus circumference <16>: prompt, specify the number of segments around the torus, as shown in Figure 23-22.

As with a sphere, a torus is half above and half below the center point in the Z direction.

Mesh

The 3D command has a Mesh option that does not appear on the Surfaces toolbar, but you can type **3d** ↵ and choose the Mesh option or choose it from the 3D Objects dialog box. (Choose Draw ⇨ Surfaces ⇨ 3D Surfaces.)

The Mesh option creates a 3D mesh. All you have to do is pick the four corners and the M and N mesh sizes. Of course, this option does not give you the flexibility of the 3DMESH command, but it's a lot easier!

Specify the four corner points in clockwise or counterclockwise order. Then specify the M and N mesh sizes. Figure 23-23 shows a mesh with M=8 and N=4.

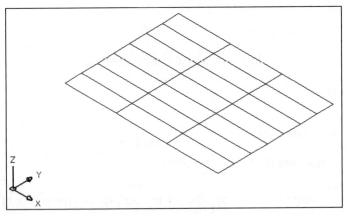

Figure 23-23: A mesh with M=8 and N=4

On the CD-ROM The drawing used in the following Step-by-Step exercise on drawing 3D polygon meshes, ab23-c.dwg, is in the Drawings folder of the *AutoCAD 2004 Bible* CD-ROM.

Step-by-Step: Drawing 3D Polygon Meshes

1. Open ab23-c.dwg from the CD-ROM.

2. Save it as ab23-03.dwg in your AutoCAD Bible folder. The drawing is in architectural units. OSNAP should be on. Set running object snaps for end-point and midpoint. If the Surfaces toolbar isn't displayed, right-click any toolbar and choose Surfaces.

3. Choose Box from the Surfaces toolbar. Follow the prompts to make the tabletop:

```
Specify corner point of box: 1,1,30 ↵
Specify length of box: 4' ↵
Specify width of box or [Cube]: 3' ↵
Specify height of box: 1 ↵
Specify rotation angle of box about the Z axis or
[Reference]: 0 ↵
```

4. Do a Zoom Extents to see the entire box. You are in plan view, so it looks like a rectangle.

5. Choose Box from the Surfaces toolbar again. Follow the prompts to make a leg:

```
Specify corner point of box: 1,1 ↵
Specify length of box: 1 ↵
Specify width of box or [Cube]: 1 ↵
Specify height of box: 30 ↵
Specify rotation angle of box about the Z axis or
[Reference]: 0 ↵
```

6. Mirror the leg, which appears as a small square at the lower-left corner of the large rectangle, from the midpoint of one side of the table to the midpoint of the opposite side. Then mirror the two legs in the other direction (from the other two midpoints) so that you have four legs.

7. Choose Dish from the Surfaces toolbar. Follow the prompts to create a bowl on the table:

```
Specify center point of dish: 2',2',35-1/2 ↵
Specify radius of dish or [Diameter]: d ↵
Specify diameter of dish: 9 ↵
Enter number of longitudinal segments for surface of dish
<16>: ↵
Enter number of latitudinal segments for surface of dish
<8>: ↵
```

The dish's diameter is 9, so its height is half that, or 4½. The center of the dish is at height 35½ because the tabletop is at 31 (31+4½=35½).

8. Type **elev** ↵. Change the elevation to 31. Leave the thickness at zero (0).

9. Choose Cone from the Surfaces toolbar. Follow the prompts to create a salt shaker:

```
Specify center point for base of cone: 2',1'6 ↵
Specify radius for base of cone or [Diameter]: 1 ↵
Specify radius for top of cone or [Diameter] <0>: .5 ↵
Specify height of cone: 4 ↵
Enter number of segments for surface of cone <16>: 8 ↵
```

10. Choose Sphere from the Surfaces toolbar. Follow the prompts to draw an orange in the bowl:

```
Specify center point of sphere: 2',2',32-1/2 ↵
Specify radius of sphere or [Diameter]: d ↵
Specify diameter of sphere: 3 ↵
Enter number of longitudinal segments for surface of sphere
<16>: 8 ↵
Enter number of latitudinal segments for surface of sphere
<16>: 8 ↵
```

11. Choose Cone from the Surfaces toolbar. Follow the prompts to make a plate.

(It may not seem logical to use a cone to make a flat plate. It works because you can create a truncated cone upside down and very shallow. It's an unusual but interesting use for the CONE command.)

```
Specify center point for base of cone: 1',1' ↵
Specify radius for base of cone or [Diameter]: 2 ↵
Specify radius for top of cone or [Diameter] <0>: 5 ↵
Specify height of cone: 1/2 ↵
Enter number of segments for surface of cone <16>: ↵
```

12. Choose View ➪ 3D Views ➪ SE Isometric to get a view of what you have already drawn.

13. Choose Wedge from the Surfaces toolbar. Follow the prompts to make a wedge of cheese on the plate:

```
Specify corner point of wedge: 10,10 ↵
Specify length of wedge: 5 ↵
Specify width of wedge: 2 ↵
Specify height of wedge: 2 ↵
Specify rotation angle of wedge about the Z axis: 30 ↵
```

14. Choose Pyramid from the Surfaces toolbar. Follow the prompts to draw a pyramidal pepper shaker:

```
Specify first corner point for base of pyramid: 2'6,2'6 ↵
Specify second corner point for base of pyramid: @1,0 ↵
Specify third corner point for base of pyramid: @0,1 ↵
Specify fourth corner point for base of pyramid or
[Tetrahedron]: @-1,0 ↵
```

```
Specify apex point of pyramid or [Ridge/Top]: t ↵
Specify first corner point for top of pyramid: @1/4,1/4,3 ↵
Specify second corner point for top of pyramid: @-1/4,1/4,3 ↵
Specify third corner point for top of pyramid: @-1/4,-1/4,3 ↵
Specify fourth corner point for top of pyramid: @1/4,-1/4,3 ↵
```

15. Choose View ➪ Hide. You can now visualize the drawing better.

16. Save your drawing. It should look like Figure 23-24. If you look carefully, you'll see that the edge of the cheese wedge goes through the plate slightly.

Figure 23-24: The table with a plate, wedge of cheese, bowl, orange, and nonmatching salt and pepper shakers

Drawing a Revolved Surface

A common way to define a surface is to revolve an outline around an axis. You can create some very complex surfaces in this way. The REVSURF command takes an object that defines an outline or profile—AutoCAD also calls it a *path curve*—and revolves it around an axis, creating a 3D polygon mesh. Figure 23-25 shows two examples of revolved surfaces.

The path curve must be one object—a line, arc, circle, polyline, ellipse, or elliptical arc. It can be open, like the path curves shown in Figure 23-25, or closed. A closed path curve creates a model that is closed in the N direction.

Figure 23-25: Two revolved surfaces

 Tip If you have several adjoining objects that you would like to use as one path curve, remember that you can use PEDIT to change lines and arcs to polylines and join them together. For more information, see Chapter 16.

Determining the angle of rotation

You can start the angle of rotation at any angle; it doesn't have to start on the plane of the path curve. You can rotate the path curve to any angle. Of course, rotating the path curve 360 degrees closes the model (in the M direction of the mesh).

When you rotate the path curve less than 360 degrees, you need to know which way to rotate. You can specify a positive (counterclockwise) or negative (clockwise) angle.

The point at which you pick the axis of rotation object affects the positive direction of rotation. Then you use the right-hand rule to determine which way the path curve will rotate around the axis. To do this, point your right thumb along the axis in the opposite direction from the endpoint closest to where you pick the axis. The direction in which your other fingers curl is the positive direction of rotation. Figure 23-26 shows the same model revolved in different directions. In the left model, the line of the axis was picked near the bottom endpoint. In the right model, the line of the axis was picked near the top endpoint.

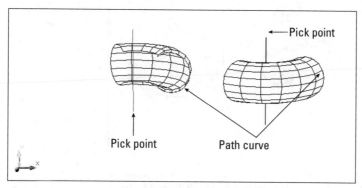

Figure 23-26: From the viewer's point of view, the left revolved surface was rotated back 125 degrees, and the right revolved surface was rotated forward 125 degrees.

Setting the number of segments

You use the SURFTAB1 and SURFTAB2 system variables to determine how AutoCAD displays the mesh. AutoCAD calls this the *wireframe density*.

✦ SURFTAB1 affects how the M direction—the direction of revolution—is displayed.

✦ SURFTAB2 affects how the N direction—the path curve—is displayed.

The higher the setting, the more lines AutoCAD uses to display the model. However, if the path curve is a polyline with straight segments, AutoCAD just displays one line at each segment vertex.

In Figure 23-26, SURFTAB1 is 6 and SURFTAB2 is 12. Figure 23-27 shows the same model with SURFTAB1 at 20 and SURFTAB2 at 5 to show the contrast between the two.

Note While you count M and N mesh sizes by vertices, you specify SURFTAB1 and SURFTAB2 by the number of surface areas you want to see.

To set these system variables, type them on the command line and specify the new value you want.

Figure 23-27: The same model re-created with SURFTAB1=20 and SURFTAB2=5

Using the REVSURF command

To create a revolved surface, follow these steps:

1. First create the path curve, which must be one object.

2. Then draw the axis of revolution, usually a line.

3. Choose Revolved Surface from the Surfaces toolbar.

4. At the `Select object to revolve:` prompt, select the path curve object.

5. At the `Select object that defines the axis of revolution:` prompt, select the axis of revolution object.

6. At the `Specify start angle <0>:` prompt, press Enter to accept the default of zero (0) or type in a start angle.

7. At the `Specify included angle (+=ccw, -=cw) <360>:` prompt, press Enter to revolve the surface 360 degrees or type in a positive or negative angle.

You may need to create the path curve and the axis in a different plane than the one you use when revolving them. You can draw the path curve and axis in one UCS and use REVSURF in another. If the object doesn't come out in the right direction, you can rotate the entire object when completed. Rotating objects in 3D is covered in the next chapter.

REVSURF retains the original path curve and axis objects. It helps to draw them in a different layer and color so you can easily erase them afterward. Otherwise, they are hard to distinguish from the revolved surface. Having them on a separate layer also helps if you need to redo the revolved surface — you can more easily avoid erasing them when you erase the revolved surface.

The drawing used in the following Step-by-Step exercise on drawing revolved surfaces, ab23-d.dwg, is in the Drawings folder of the *AutoCAD 2004 Bible* CD-ROM.

Step-by-Step: Drawing Revolved Surfaces

1. Open ab23-d.dwg from the CD-ROM.

2. Save it as ab23-04.dwg in your AutoCAD Bible folder. The path curve and axis are already drawn in a UCS revolved around the X axis of the World Coordinate System (WCS) by 90 degrees.

3. 🔧 Choose Revolved Surface from the Surfaces toolbar.

4. At the Select object to revolve: prompt, select the polyline to the right.

5. At the Select object that defines the axis of revolution: prompt, select the line.

6. At the Specify start angle <0>: prompt, press Enter. At the Specify included angle (+=ccw, -=cw) <360>: prompt, press Enter to revolve the path curve in a full circle.

7. Choose Tools ➪ New UCS ➪ World to return to the WCS.

8. Choose Top View from the View flyout of the Standard toolbar to return to plan view of the WCS.

9. Choose View ➪ 3D Views ➪ SE Isometric.

10. Choose View ➪ Hide to see the shape more clearly.

11. Save your drawing. It should look like Figure 23-28.

Figure 23-28: The revolved surface

Drawing an Extruded Surface

A simple way to create a 3D object is to start with a 2D object and give it thickness. Giving a 2D object thickness is sometimes called *extruding*. To extrude means to thrust out. In AutoCAD, it refers to creating a 3D object from a 2D object. The TABSURF command takes an outline, or profile, which AutoCAD calls a *path curve*, and extrudes it along a vector that defines the direction and distance of the extrusion. TABSURF creates a 3D polyline mesh. The type of surface created is called a *tabulated surface*. Figure 23-29 shows two examples of extruded surfaces.

Figure 23-29: Two extruded surfaces created using TABSURF

For the I-beam, you could have simply given the 2D polyline profile a thickness and achieved a similar result. However, the extruded surface on the left could only have been created with TABSURF because the extrusion is not perpendicular to the XY plane that contains the 2D polyline profile. TABSURF can extrude a shape in any direction.

When you select the vector object, your pick point determines the direction of the extrusion. AutoCAD starts the extrusion from the end of the vector closest to the pick point.

You use SURFTAB1 to control the number of lines AutoCAD uses to display the curve. If the curve is made up of polyline segments, AutoCAD displays one line at each segment vertex.

Caution Note the I-beam in Figure 23-29. If you create an object by mirroring, stretching, and so on, you will see extra tabulation lines at the separate segments in the polyline definition. If you want a clean look, you need to draw clean. You might need to use the original shape as a guide to draw a new polyline on top of the old one, and then erase the original.

You should use a nonplanar view when using TABSURF to check that you have accurately defined the extrusion vector into the third dimension. Any of the preset isometric views will be helpful.

To draw an extruded surface, follow these steps:

1. Draw the object to extrude—a line, arc, circle, polyline, ellipse, or elliptical arc. This is the path curve.

2. Draw the vector, usually a line. If you use a 2D or 3D polyline, AutoCAD uses an imaginary line from the start point to the endpoint to determine the vector.

3. Choose Tabulated Surface from the Surfaces toolbar.

4. At the `Select object for path curve:` prompt, select the path curve object.

5. At the `Select object for direction vector:` prompt, select the line you are using for the vector.

On the CD-ROM

The drawing used in the following Step-by-Step exercise on drawing tabulated surfaces, `ab23-e.dwg`, is in the `Drawings` folder of the *AutoCAD 2004 Bible* CD-ROM.

Step-by-Step: Drawing Tabulated Surfaces

1. Open `ab23-e.dwg` from the CD-ROM.

2. Save it as `ab23-05.dwg` in your `AutoCAD Bible` folder. You see a tabletop drawn at a Z height of 30. The current elevation is 30. You are looking at the table from the SE isometric view. OSNAP should be on. Set running object snaps for endpoint, midpoint, and center. The current layer is Const. The drawing is shown in Figure 23-30.

3. Start the CIRCLE command. Follow the prompts:

   ```
   Specify center point for circle or [3P/2P/Ttr (tan tan
   radius)]: Choose the From object snap.
   _from Base point: Pick the endpoint at ❶ in Figure 23-30.
   <Offset>: @-1,3 ↵
   Specify radius of circle or [Diameter]: .75 ↵
   ```

4. Start the LINE command. At the `Specify first point:` prompt, choose the Center object snap of the circle you just drew. At the `Specify next point or [Undo]:` prompt, type **@3,–3,–30** ↵ to draw a line flaring out from the circle and going down to the floor. End the LINE command.

5. Choose Tabulated Surface from the Surfaces toolbar. At the `Select object for path curve:` prompt, select the circle. At the `Select object for direction vector:` prompt, select the line. (You can see only the top part of the line, but that's the part you need to pick.) AutoCAD creates the tabulated surface.

Figure 23-30: The tabletop

6. Start the MIRROR command. Select the entire leg. Choose the midpoint of the bottom edge of both long sides of the table for the two points of the mirror line.

7. Repeat the MIRROR line and select both legs. Mirror them using the midpoints of the bottom edge of the short sides of the table for the two points of the mirror line.

8. Do a ZOOM Extents to see the entire table.

9. Save your drawing. It should look like Figure 23-31.

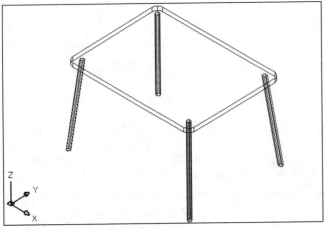

Figure 23-31: The completed table

Drawing Ruled Surfaces

If you have two existing objects, you may want to define the surface that would extend between these objects. Use the RULESURF command to create a surface that extends between two objects. The objects can be lines, polylines (2D or 3D), circles, ellipses, elliptical arcs, splines, or points. The two objects must either be both open or both closed. Only one of the two can be a point.

Use the SURFTAB1 system variable to control the number of lines AutoCAD uses to display the surface. Figure 23-32 shows some ruled surfaces.

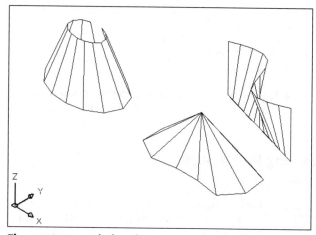

Figure 23-32: Ruled surfaces

The pick points of the two objects affect the resulting curve. If you pick them both on the same side, you get the type of curves shown in Figure 23-32. If you pick them on opposite sides, the curve intersects itself, as shown in Figure 23-33.

Follow these steps to draw a ruled surface:

1. Draw the two objects for the ruled surface.

2. Choose Ruled Surface from the Surfaces toolbar.

3. At the Select first defining curve: prompt, choose the first object.

4. At the Select second defining curve: prompt, choose the second object.

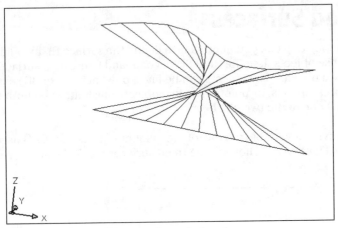

Figure 23-33: A self-intersecting ruled surface

The drawing used in the following Step-by-Step exercise on drawing ruled sur-
faces, ab23-f.dwg, is in the Drawings folder of the *AutoCAD 2004 Bible*
CD-ROM.

Step-by-Step: Drawing Ruled Surfaces

1. Open ab23-f.dwg from the CD-ROM.

2. Save it as ab23-06.dwg in your AutoCAD Bible folder. You see a spline, as
 shown in Figure 23-34. In this exercise, you use the spline to draw some
 drapes.

3. Mirror the spline. For the mirror line, turn on ORTHO and use ❶ and ❷ as
 shown in Figure 23-34. Don't delete the original spline.

Figure 23-34: A spline

4. Start the COPY command and select both splines. At the `Specify base point or displacement, or [Multiple]:` prompt, type **0,0,73** ⏎ to copy the splines 73 units in the positive Z direction. Press Enter at the `Specify second point of displacement or <use first point as displacement>:` prompt.

5. Choose View ➪ 3D Views ➪ SE Isometric.

6. Choose Ruled Surface from the Surfaces toolbar. At the `Select first defining curve:` prompt, choose the top-right spline near its right endpoint. At the `Select second defining curve:` prompt, choose the bottom-right spline near its right endpoint.

7. Repeat the RULESURF command. At the `Select first defining curve:` prompt, choose the top-left spline near its left endpoint. At the `Select second defining curve:` prompt, choose the bottom-left spline near its left endpoint.

8. Save your drawing. It should look like Figure 23-35.

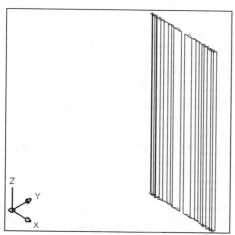

Figure 23-35: The completed drapes

Drawing Edge Surfaces

You may have several edges and want to create a surface that extends between them. You can use the EDGESURF command to create unusual surfaces bound by four touching objects. The objects can be lines, arcs, splines, or polylines (2D or 3D). EDGESURF creates a polygon mesh that approximates a Coon's surface patch mesh — a surface defined by four edges. Figure 23-36 shows an edge surface.

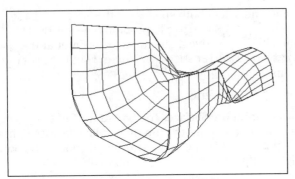

Figure 23-36: An edge surface created with the EDGESURF command

Use the SURFTAB1 and SURFTAB2 system variables to vary the displayed lines in each direction.

Follow these steps to create an edge surface:

1. Draw the four objects to create a boundary for the surface. They must touch, so use Endpoint object snaps to create them or to move them into place.

2. Choose Edge Surface from the Surfaces toolbar.

3. AutoCAD prompts you to select edges 1 through 4. You can select them in any order.

Creating the four edges involves moving from UCS to UCS because they are all in 3D. It helps to create a bounding box for your object using the AI_BOX command. You can then use the corners of the box to define your UCSs.

On the CD-ROM The drawing used in the following Step-by-Step exercise on drawing edge surfaces, ab23-g.dwg, is in the Drawings folder of the *AutoCAD 2004 Bible* CD-ROM.

Step-by-Step: Drawing Edge Surfaces

1. Open ab23-g.dwg from the CD-ROM.

2. Save it as ab23-07.dwg in your AutoCAD Bible folder. You see four curves in a bounding box, as shown in Figure 23-37. In this exercise, you use the curves to draw a dustpan.

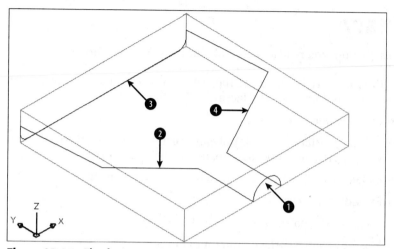

Figure 23-37: The four curves are the basis for creating an edge surface.

3. Freeze the Const layer.

4. Choose Edge Surface from the Surfaces toolbar. At the prompts, select ❶, ❷, ❸, and ❹ in Figure 23-37.

5. Choose View ➪ Hide to see the result.

6. Save your drawing. It should look like Figure 23-38. It's either a dustpan or a starship — your choice.

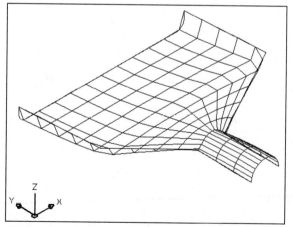

Figure 23-38: The completed dustpan — or starship

Summary

In this chapter, you read all about 3D surfaces. You read about:

✦ Creating surfaces by using the 3DFACE command and controlling the visibility of the lines between the faces

✦ Creating polyface meshes

✦ Creating surfaces with 3D polygon meshes, including the basic shapes — box, wedge, pyramid, cone, sphere, dome, dish, and torus

✦ Making a surface by revolving a profile around an axis

✦ Extruding a curve

✦ Creating a ruled surface between two curves

✦ Making an edge surface from four curves

In the next chapter, you discover how to create true solids (well, true electronic ones at least) as well as how to edit in 3D.

✦　✦　✦

Creating Solids and Editing in 3D

Although you can create great-looking models with surfaces, if you want truly realistic models, you need to create solids. After all, in real life, objects have solidity. Even a thin object such as a wastepaper basket or a drape has some thickness. Solids enable you to create more realistic models than surfaces. You can also combine or subtract solids and get information about their physical properties. Figure 24-1 shows a complex model created using solids.

Figure 24-1: You can create complex and realistic models using solids.

Thanks to Hans-Joachim Fach, Bremen, Germany, for this drawing.

To work with solids, display the Solids toolbar by right-clicking any toolbar and choosing Solids from the Toolbars dialog box. You can also access all the solids commands by choosing Draw ➪ Solids and then choosing the specific command from the submenu that opens.

Controlling the display of solids

Curved surfaces are drawn using segments. When you draw a surface sphere, AutoCAD prompts you for the number of lines to draw. The wireframe display of all curved solids in a drawing is controlled by the ISOLINES system variable. The default, 4, provides a bare minimum of curved lines to let you view the outlines of the curve and results in the quickest display. Increasing the ISOLINES value improves the visual result but slows down the drawing display. Generally, you can find a happy medium based on the size of your drawing, the speed of your computer, and your personal preferences. The ISOLINES variable affects only wireframe display — it has no effect when you use the HIDE or SHADEMODE commands. Figure 24-3 shows the effect of varying the ISOLINES setting. When you change the ISOLINES value, use the REGEN command to see the result on existing objects. The FACETRES system variable is the 3D version of VIEWRES, and it determines the display of curved surfaces and solids when using the HIDE, SHADEMODE, or RENDER commands. You can set FACETRES from 0.01 to 10.0. Here you see a hidden sphere at FACETRES settings of 0.05 (left) and 5.0 (right). The default is 0.5, which is generally a happy medium.

The DISPSILH system variable determines whether AutoCAD creates a silhouette of a model based on the current viewpoint. The effect is most noticeable after a hide. The left-hand model here shows the result of setting DISPSILH to 0 (the default) after a hide. The right-hand model shows the results of setting DISPSILH to 1 (on) after a hide. You can see that the right-hand model provides a very uncluttered display. When you set DISPSILH to 1 in wireframe display, AutoCAD adds silhouette lines. For complex objects, you may find that DISPSILH slows down your display. This is a complicated matter for AutoCAD to compute. So, you may want to set DISPSILH back to zero (0) after doing a hide, depending on the models you are working with.

Drawing Standard Shapes

As with surfaces, AutoCAD makes it easy to create most standard geometrical shapes. The prompts are similar to the surface commands, but there are some slight differences.

Drawing a box

Figure 24-2 shows a solid box after a hide. Visually, it looks the same as a surface box.

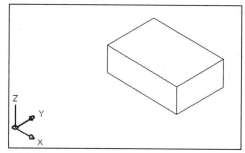

Figure 24-2: A solid box

To draw a box, follow these steps:

1. Choose Box from the Solids toolbar.

2. At the `Specify corner of box or [CEnter] <0,0,0>:` prompt, specify any corner of the box or right-click and choose Center to specify the 3D center of the box.

3. If you specify the corner (the default), you then see the `Specify corner or [Cube/Length]:` prompt.

 The default is to pick the opposite corner in the XY plane. AutoCAD then asks you for the height in the Z direction. This completes the box.

 If you specify the Length in the XY plane, AutoCAD asks you for a width and a height.

 If you use the Cube option, AutoCAD asks for one length and completes the box.

4. If you specify the center, you see the `Specify center of box <0,0,0>:` prompt. Specify the center of the box. Then the `Specify corner or [Cube/Length]:` prompt appears.

 If you pick the corner of the box, AutoCAD completes the box by calculating the length, width, and height from the two points — the center and the corner.

If you specify the length, AutoCAD then asks for a width and a height.

If you use the Cube option, AutoCAD asks for a length and completes the box.

You can specify a negative length, width, or height to build the box in the negative direction. If you specify the center of the cube, don't forget that the center's Z coordinate is different from the corner's Z coordinate. AutoCAD always creates the box parallel to the XY plane.

Drawing a sphere

Figure 24-3 shows two solid spheres. The left sphere uses the default ISOLINE value of 4. The right sphere uses an ISOLINE value of 8.

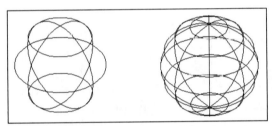

Figure 24-3: Two solid spheres, with ISOLINES set at 4 (left) and 8 (right)

To draw a sphere, follow these steps:

1. Choose Sphere from the Solids toolbar.

2. At the `Specify center of sphere <0,0,0>:` prompt, specify the center of the sphere. If you want the sphere to lie on the XY plane, the Z coordinate of the center should be equal to the radius of the sphere.

3. At the `Specify radius of sphere or [Diameter]:` prompt, type the radius or right-click and choose Diameter to specify the diameter.

Drawing a cylinder

Figure 24-4 shows four solid cylinders. The grid helps you visualize the XY plane. You can draw cylinders with circular or elliptical bases. By specifying the center of the top of the cylinder separately, you can draw them at an angle.

Follow these steps to draw a cylinder:

1. Choose Cylinder from the Solids toolbar.

Figure 24-4: Some solid cylinders

2. At the `Specify center point for base of cylinder or [Elliptical] <0,0,0>:` prompt, specify the center point for a circular cylinder or choose the Elliptical option to define an ellipse as a base.

 If you specified a center point, at the `Specify radius for base of cylinder or [Diameter]:` prompt, specify a radius or use the Diameter option to specify the diameter.

 If you chose the Elliptical option, use the prompts to define the elliptical base.

3. At the `Specify height of cylinder or [Center of other end]:` prompt, specify the height or use the Center of other end option to specify the center of the top of the cylinder.

Drawing a cone

You can draw cones with circular or elliptical bases. By specifying a negative height, you can create an inverted cone (like an ice cream cone). By specifying the apex, you can draw cones on an angle from the XY plane. Figure 24-5 shows some cones.

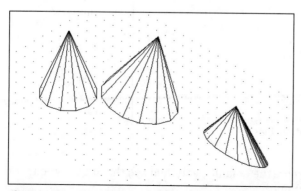

Figure 24-5: Cones with varying heights and bases

Follow these steps to draw a cone:

1. Choose Cone from the Solids toolbar.

2. At the `Specify center point for base of cone or [Elliptical] <0,0,0>:` prompt, specify the center of the base if you want a circular cone. Otherwise, use the Elliptical option to define an elliptical base.

 If you specified a center point, at the `Specify radius for base of cone or [Diameter]:` prompt, specify a radius or use the Diameter option to specify the diameter.

 If you chose the Elliptical option, use the prompts to define the elliptical base.

3. At the `Specify height of cone or [Apex]:` prompt, specify the height or use the Apex option to specify the coordinate of the apex. A temporary line marks the center of the base so you can use relative coordinates for the apex.

Drawing a wedge

A wedge is a box sliced in half. The prompts are virtually the same as the Box command. Figure 24-6 shows two wedges.

To create a wedge, follow these steps:

1. Choose Wedge from the Solids toolbar.

2. At the `Specify first corner of wedge or [CEnter] <0,0,0>:` prompt, specify any corner of the wedge or type **c** ↵ and use the Center option to specify the 3D center of the wedge.

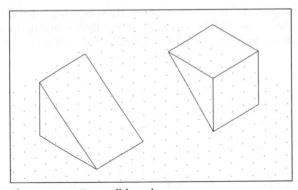

Figure 24-6: Two solid wedges

3. If you specify the corner (the default), you then see the `Specify corner or [Cube/Length]:` prompt.

The default is to pick the opposite corner in the XY plane. AutoCAD then asks you for the height in the Z direction. This completes the wedge.

If you specify the Length in the XY plane, AutoCAD asks you for a width and a height.

If you use the Cube option, AutoCAD asks for one length and completes the wedge. For positive lengths, the wedge slopes in the X direction.

4. If you specify the center, you see the Specify center of wedge <0,0,0>: prompt. Specify the center point. Then the `Specify opposite corner or [Cube/ Length]:` prompt displays.

If you pick the corner of the wedge, AutoCAD completes the wedge by calculating the length, width, and height from the two points — the center and the corner.

If you specify the length, AutoCAD then asks for a width and a height.

If you use the Cube option, AutoCAD asks for a length and completes the wedge.

Drawing a torus

A *torus* is a solid 3D donut. Figure 24-7 shows some examples. You can make some unusual shapes by varying the torus and tube radii. If the torus radius is negative and the tube radius is larger than the absolute value of the torus radius (for example, –2 and 3), you get the lemon (or football) shape. If the tube radius is larger than the torus radius, you get the puckered ball (or apple) shape. (You cannot get such unusual shapes using the Torus shape on the Surfaces toolbar.)

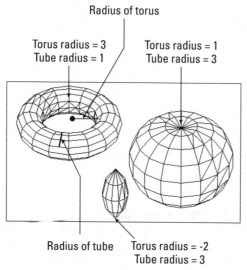

Figure 24-7: Torus examples

To create a torus, follow these steps:

1. Choose Torus from the Solids toolbar.

2. At the `Specify center of torus <0,0,0>:` prompt, specify the center of the torus (the center of the hole).

3. At the `Specify radius of torus or [Diameter]:` prompt, specify the radius of the entire torus or use the Diameter option to specify the diameter.

4. At the `Specify radius of tube or [Diameter]:` prompt, specify the radius of just the tube or use the Diameter option to specify the diameter.

Step-by-Step: Drawing Standard 3D Solids

1. Start a new drawing using the `acad.dwt` template.

2. Save the file as `ab24-01.dwg` in your `AutoCAD Bible` folder. If the Solids toolbar is not displayed, right-click any toolbar, and choose Solids. Turn on OSNAP and OTRACK. Set running object snaps for endpoint, midpoint, and center.

3. Choose Box from the Solids toolbar. Follow the prompts:

```
Specify corner of box or [CEnter] <0,0,0>: 3,3 ↵
Specify corner or [Cube/Length]: Right-click and choose
Length.
Specify length: 3 ↵
Specify width: 2 ↵
Specify height: 1 ↵
```

4. Choose Cylinder from the Solids toolbar. Follow the prompts:

```
Specify center point for base of cylinder or [Elliptical]
<0,0,0>: Pass the cursor over the midpoint of the right side
of the box to acquire it. Move the cursor to the midpoint of
the bottom side of the box to acquire it. Move the cursor to
the middle of the box's top until you see the tooltip listing
both midpoints, and click.
Specify radius for base of cylinder or [Diameter]: .5 ↵
Specify height of cylinder or [Center of other end]: 1 ↵
```

5. To see the result, choose View ➪ 3D Views ➪ SE Isometric. Then choose Zoom Out from the Zoom flyout.

6. Choose Cone from the Solids toolbar. At the `Specify center point for base of cone or [Elliptical] <0,0,0>:` prompt, type **7,5** ↵. At the `Specify radius for base of cone or [Diameter]:` prompt, type **1** ↵. At the `Specify height of cone or [Apex]:` prompt, type **–4** ↵.

7. Choose Sphere from the Solids toolbar. At the `Specify center of sphere <0,0,0>:` prompt, use the Center object snap to pick the center of the cone's base. At the `Specify radius of sphere or [Diameter]:` prompt, type **1** ↵.

8. Type **isolines** ↵. Set the new value to 8. Do a regen to see the result.

9. Choose Zoom Extents from the Zoom flyout of the Standard toolbar.

10. Do a hide. Notice the objects appear realistic, regardless of the ISOLINES setting.

11. Save your drawing. It should look like Figure 24-8.

Figure 24-8: The four solids

Creating Extruded Solids

The EXTRUDE command creates solids from closed 2D objects. The result is similar to adding thickness to a 2D object (discussed in Chapter 21) or using the TABSURF command (see Chapter 23) except that you get a solid instead of a surface.

You can extrude closed 2D polylines, circles, ellipses, closed splines, donuts, and regions. You can use the REGION command to create one object from several objects for this purpose. You can select several objects and extrude them at one time. Figure 24-9 shows several extruded solids.

Figure 24-9: Some extruded solids

Tip The DELOBJ system variable determines whether objects used by EXTRUDE to make other objects are retained. By default, they are deleted. Therefore, when you use a 2D object to make a solid, the 2D object is deleted. If you make a mistake during extrusion and notice it later—after it's impractical to undo several commands you want to keep—when you erase the solid, you have no 2D object to use to re-create the solid. (You can put such objects on a layer that can be turned off, in case you need them again.) Set DELOBJ to zero (0) to keep objects used to create other objects. On the other hand, if you are sure about what you are doing, keeping DELOBJ at 1 avoids having to erase unwanted 2D objects in your drawing.

When you extrude an object, by default you extrude it perpendicular to the object. However, you can also taper the extrusion, as in the extruded rectangle in Figure 24-9. The angle is measured so that a positive angle tapers the object inward. A negative angle tapers the object outward so it gets wider as it extrudes.

Note Don't taper the object too much. If the taper angle results in the object coming to a point before its full height, AutoCAD cannot create the solid.

You can extrude the object along a path. A path can be a line, circle, arc, ellipse, elliptical arc, polyline, or a spline. The path object must be in a different plane than the original object. Figure 24-10 shows a circle extruded along an arc.

Not all paths are suitable for extruding objects. In the following situations, the extrusion may not work. The path should not be:

✦ Too close to the original object's plane

✦ Too complex

✦ Too tightly curved or bent for the size of the original object

Original circle Arc used as path for extrusion

Figure 24-10: A circle extruded along an arc

Here are the steps for creating an extruded solid:

1. Draw the object you want to extrude. If you want to extrude along a path, draw the path object.

2. Choose Extrude from the Solids toolbar.

3. Select the object or objects to extrude.

4. At the `Specify height of extrusion or [Path]:` prompt, specify the height of extrusion or use the Path option to extrude along a path object.

 If you specified a height, at the `Specify angle of taper for extrusion <0>:` prompt, press Enter to extrude with no taper angle or specify a taper angle.

 If you chose the Path option, at the `Select extrusion path or [Taper angle]:` prompt, select the path object.

On the CD-ROM
The drawing used in the following Step-by-Step exercise on creating extruded solids, ab24-a.dwg, is in the Drawings folder of the *AutoCAD 2004 Bible* CD-ROM.

Step-by-Step: Creating Extruded Solids

1. Open ab24-a.dwg from the CD-ROM.

2. Save the file as ab24-02.dwg in your AutoCAD Bible folder. If the Solids toolbar is not displayed, right-click any toolbar and choose Solids. Make sure OSNAP is on. Set running object snaps for endpoint and midpoint. This is a small mounting angle, shown in an edge view.

3. The angle is made up of lines and arcs. To extrude it, you need to change it into a polyline or region. To change it into a polyline, choose Modify ⇨ Object ⇨ Polyline. Follow the prompts:

```
Select polyline or [Multiple]: Select any object on the
angle.
Object selected is not a polyline
Do you want to turn it into one? <Y> Right-click.
Enter an option [Close/Join/Width/Edit
vertex/Fit/Spline/Decurve/Ltype gen/Undo]: Right-click and
choose Join.
Select objects: Use a window to select all the objects in the
angle.
Select objects: Right-click.
6 segments added to polyline
Enter an option [Open/Join/Width/Edit
vertex/Fit/Spline/Decurve/Ltype gen/Undo]: Right-click and
choose Enter.
```

4. Choose Extrude from the Solids toolbar. Select the mounting angle, and then right-click to end object selection. At the `Specify height of extrusion or [Path]:` prompt, type **3** ↵. At the `Specify angle of taper for extrusion <0>:` prompt, press Enter to accept the default.

5. Choose View ⇨ 3D Views ⇨ SE Isometric.

6. Do a hide using the HIDE command.

7. Save your drawing. It should look like Figure 24-11.

Figure 24-11: The completed mounting angle

The mounting angle should have two holes in it. You would create the holes using the SUBTRACT command, which is covered later in this chapter.

Drawing Revolved Solids

The REVOLVE command creates solids from closed profiles. (By contrast, the REVSURF command, which creates surfaces, revolves an open profile around an axis.) You can revolve closed 2D polylines, circles, ellipses, closed splines, and regions.

The DELOBJ system variable affects whether the original objects are deleted. The default setting is 1 (delete objects). Set DELOBJ to zero (0) to retain the original objects.

Figure 24-12 shows a solid created by revolving a rectangle around a line. You can also create this solid by drawing two circles and extruding them and then subtracting the smaller circle from the larger one — it just depends on which technique you're more comfortable.

Figure 24-12: A solid created by revolving a rectangle around a line

To create a revolved solid, follow these steps:

1. Choose Revolve from the Solids toolbar.

2. At the Select objects: prompt, select one or more closed objects.

3. At the Specify start point for axis of revolution or define axis by [Object/X (axis)/Y (axis)]: prompt, you can pick two points to create an axis of revolution. You can also select an object as an axis by using a line or one segment of a polyline. Use the X or Y options to revolve the object around the X or Y axes.

4. At the Specify angle of revolution <360>: prompt, press Enter to revolve the object 360 degrees or type an angle, either positive or negative.

As with the REVSURF command, you need to determine the positive direction of rotation if you are revolving less than 360 degrees. (Of course, it may be quicker to try one way and just do it the other way if it doesn't turn out right.) Here's how to figure it out:

1. First determine the positive direction of the axis. If you specify start and end points, the positive axis direction goes from the start point to the endpoint. If you pick an object, the positive axis direction goes from the pick point to the other endpoint. If you choose the X or Y axis, the positive direction is obvious.

2. Point your right thumb in the positive direction of the axis.

3. Look at the curl of your fingers on that hand. That's the positive direction of rotation.

Creating Complex Solids

To create realistic objects, you usually need to edit the simple shapes I discussed in this chapter. You can create complex solids by adding them, subtracting them, or intersecting them. These processes are called Boolean operations, which in this context means using logical functions, such as addition or subtraction on objects.

Adding solids

You use the UNION command to add two solids together, making one solid. If the solids are touching, you get a new, unified solid. If the solids are not touching, but rather completely separate, using UNION is similar to grouping, because you select them as one object.

Tip You can also use the UNION command with 2D regions, either for 2D drawings or as a basis for a 3D model.

Figure 24-13 shows the union of two solids after a hide.

 To start the UNION command, choose Modify ➪ Solids Editing ➪ Union. (You can also open the Solids Editing toolbar and choose Union.) At the Select objects: prompt, select the objects you want to unite.

Caution When you create complex solids, the original solids are not retained. Setting the DELOBJ system variable to zero (0) doesn't work because the original solids have been changed. If you want, you can copy the original objects to another location in the drawing in case you need to use them again. You can also use UNDO if the result is not what you expected.

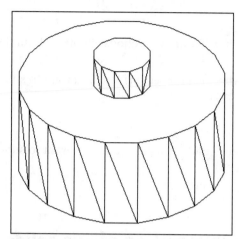

Figure 24-13: The results of UNION on two solids—shown after a hide

Subtracting solids

You use the SUBTRACT command to subtract one solid from another. This command is most commonly used to create holes. Figure 24-14 shows the result of subtracting a small cylinder from a larger one and performing a hide.

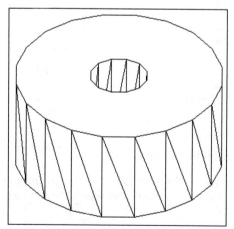

Figure 24-14: You can create holes using the SUBTRACT command.

To subtract solids, follow these steps:

1. 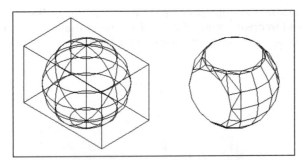 Choose Modify ⇨ Solids Editing ⇨ Subtract or choose Subtract from the Solids Editing toolbar.

2. At the following prompt, choose the solid (or region) that you want to subtract from (the one you want to keep):

   ```
   Select solids and regions to subtract from...
   Select objects:
   ```

3. At the following prompt, choose the solid (or region) that you want to subtract (the one you want to get rid of):

   ```
   Select solids and regions to subtract...
   Select objects:
   ```

Creating a solid from the intersection of two solids

You can also create a solid from the volume that two solids have in common. This volume is called their intersection. Figure 24-15 shows two solids before and after using the INTERSECT command. The solid on the right is shown after a hide.

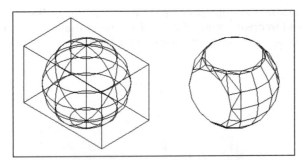

Figure 24-15: A box and a sphere before and after using the INTERSECT command

As you can see, you can create some very unusual models this way.

To use the INTERSECT command, choose Modify ⇨ Solids Editing ⇨ Intersect or choose Intersect from the Solids Editing toolbar. Just select the objects in any order. AutoCAD creates the new solid.

Creating a new solid using INTERFERE

INTERFERE is similar to INTERSECT except that the original solids remain. AutoCAD creates a third solid from the volume that the two solids have in common. The INTERFERE command can also be used to highlight the common volume of several pairs of solids. Figure 24-16 shows a solid that was created using INTERFERE, after it was moved away from its original location. As you can see, the original solids remain intact.

Figure 24-16: When you use INTERFERE, the original solids remain intact.

INTERFERE is useful when you have a number of interfering solids. This command enables you to divide the selection set of solids into two sets so that you can compare one against the other. For example, you can compare a box with three other solids by putting the box in one set and the other three solids in the other set. INTERFERE highlights each pair of interfering solids in turn so that you can easily visualize your drawing.

Tip

You can use INTERFERE for troubleshooting and visualizing a complex drawing. For example, you can use INTERFERE to determine which solids need to be subtracted from other solids. The new objects are created on the current layer. You can change the current layer before using INTERFERE to help you more clearly distinguish the new solid you create.

To use INTERFERE, follow these steps:

1. Choose Interfere from the Solids toolbar.

2. At the `Select first set of solids:` prompt, select objects. If you want to compare only two objects, you can put them both in the first set. Otherwise, select solids for the first set and press Enter to end object selection.

3. At the `Select second set of solids:` prompt, select the second set of objects and press Enter to end object selection. If you don't want a second set, press Enter. AutoCAD displays the number of solids and sets and how many interfering pairs it finds.

4. At the `Create interference solids? [Yes/No] <N>:` prompt, press Enter if you don't want to create a new solid. Right-click and choose Yes if you do.

5. If you are testing more than two solids, you see the `Highlight pairs of interfering solids? [Yes/No] <N>:` prompt. Press Enter if you don't need to see each pair of interfering solids highlighted. Right-click and choose Yes if you want AutoCAD to highlight the pairs. If you choose Yes, AutoCAD highlights the first pair of solids that interfere.

6. At the `Enter an option [Next pair/eXit] <Next>:` prompt—which appears only if there is more than one pair—press Enter to see the next pair highlighted. Continue to press Enter to cycle through the interfering pairs. Right-click and choose Exit to exit the command.

On the CD-ROM

The drawing used in the following Step-by-Step exercise on creating complex solids, `ab24-b.dwg`, is in the `Drawings` folder of the *AutoCAD 2004 Bible* CD-ROM.

Step-by-Step: Creating Complex Solids

1. Open `ab-24-b.dwg` from the CD-ROM.

2. Save the file as `ab24-03.dwg` in your `AutoCAD Bible` folder. Make sure OSNAP is on. Set running object snaps for endpoint, midpoint, and center. This drawing is measured in millimeters. The solids have been created by drawing circles, using EXTRUDE, and moving the solids to the proper Z coordinate. The result is shown in Figure 24-17.

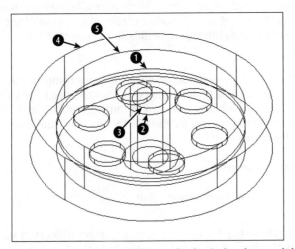

Figure 24-17: These solids are the basis for the model.

3. Display the Solids Editing toolbar by right-clicking any toolbar and choosing Solids Editing.

4. To create the six holes arrayed around the center plate, choose Subtract from the Solids Editing toolbar. Follow the prompts:

```
Select solids and regions to subtract from...
Select objects: Select the central plate at ❶ in Figure
24-17.
Select objects: Right-click.
Select solids and regions to subtract...
Select objects: Select the six circles arrayed around the
plate. Right-click to end selection.
```

5. To create the central tube, choose Subtract from the Solids Editing toolbar. Follow the prompts:

```
Select solids and regions to subtract from...
Select objects: Select the outer tube at ❷.
Select objects: Right-click.
Select solids and regions to subtract...
Select objects: Select the inner tube at ❸. Right-click to
end selection.
```

6. To "carve out" the central disk, choose Subtract from the Solids Editing toolbar. Follow the prompts:

```
Select solids and regions to subtract from...
Select objects: Select the outer circle at ❹.
Select objects: Right-click.
Select solids and regions to subtract...
Select objects: Select the inner circle at ❺. Right-click to
end selection.
```

7. Use the HIDE command to see the result. This enables you to check the effects of the subtraction operations. Your drawing should look like Figure 24-18.

Figure 24-18: The result of three subtraction operations

8. Choose Union from the Solids Editing toolbar. Select the three solids at ❶, ❷, and ❸ in Figure 24-18 and right-click to end selection.

9. Use the HIDE command again to see the result.

10. Save your drawing. It should look like Figure 24-19. If you are continuing on to the next exercise, leave it open.

Figure 24-19: The final model after using the UNION command to create one object from three

Sectioning and Slicing Solids

In many mechanical drawings, you need to show a cross section of your models. A cross section displays the inside of a 3D object. The SECTION and SLICE commands are both used to create cross-section views of your 3D models.

Using the SECTION command

The SECTION command creates a 2D region from a cross-section of a 3D model along a plane you specify. The original objects are left untouched. Figure 24-20 shows a region created using the SECTION command.

Tip The SECTION command creates the region on the current layer. Make the current layer color different from the object layer color so that the region is clearly visible.

To use the SECTION command, choose Section from the Solids toolbar. Select the object you want to section. AutoCAD displays the `Specify first point on Section plane by [Object/Zaxis/View/XY/YZ/ZX/3points] <3points>:` prompt. Use these options to define the plane of the cross section. Table 24-1 explains how to use the options.

Region created using SECTION

Figure 24-20: The region created using SECTION is shown with a dashed line.

Table 24-1
SECTION Options

Option	Description
Object	Enables you to choose a circle, ellipse, arc, spline, or 2D polyline.
Zaxis	Defines the plane by defining a Z axis. The sectioning plane is then the XY plane perpendicular to the Z axis you defined. You define the Z axis by first specifying a point on the sectioning plane. This point is the 0,0,0 point (for purposes of this command only) where the sectioning plane and the Z axis meet. Then you pick a point on the Z axis.
View	Defines the section plane parallel to the current view at the intersection of a point you specify.
XY	Defines the section plane parallel to the XY plane at the intersection of a point you specify.
YZ	Defines the section plane parallel to the YZ plane at the intersection of a point you specify.
ZX	Defines the section plane parallel to the ZX plane at the intersection of a point you specify.
3points	This is the default. Specify three points to define the section plane. Using object snaps is a good idea.

You can move the region you create and view it separately to spot errors in your models.

Using the SLICE command

The SLICE command slices a solid into two parts along a plane. The original solids are modified but can be reunited with UNION. You can delete either part or keep both. Figure 24-21 shows the result of slicing a model, after one-half of the model has been deleted. This can help to identify problems in the construction of the model. For example, this slice reveals a fault with the model—the flat disk continues through the central tube—not the desired result.

Figure 24-21: The result of slicing a solid and retaining one of the resulting pieces

To use the SLICE command, choose Slice from the Solids toolbar. Select the object you want to slice. AutoCAD displays the `Specify first point on slicing plane by [Object/Zaxis/View/XY/YZ/ZX/3points] <3points>:` prompt. Use these options to define the plane of the cross section. The options are the same as for the SECTION command and are explained in Table 24-1.

On the CD-ROM
The drawing used in the following Step-by-Step exercise on slicing solids, `ab24-3.dwg`, is in the `Results` folder of the *AutoCAD 2004 Bible* CD-ROM.

Step-by-Step: Slicing Solids

1. If you have `ab24-03.dwg` open from the previous exercise, use it. Do a regen to remove the hidden view. If you don't have it open, open it from your `AutoCAD Bible` folder or from the `Results` folder of the *AutoCAD 2004 Bible* CD-ROM. Make sure that OSNAP is on. Set running object snaps for endpoint, midpoint, center, and quadrant. Make sure you have both the Solids and the Solids Editing toolbars open. The drawing is shown in Figure 24-22.

2. Save your drawing as `ab24-04.dwg` in your `AutoCAD Bible` folder.

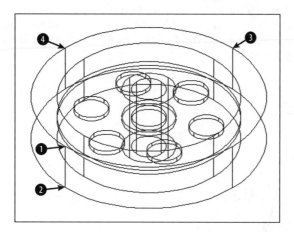

Figure 24-22: The 3D model for slicing

3. Choose Slice from the Solids toolbar. Follow the prompts:

```
    Select objects: Select the solid model.
Select objects: Right-click.
Specify first point on slicing plane by
[Object/Zaxis/View/XY/YZ/ZX/3points]
<3points>: Pick the quadrant at ❶ in Figure 24-22.
Specify second point on plane: Pick the quadrant at ❷.
Specify third point on plane: Pick the quadrant at ❸.
Specify a point on desired side of the plane or [keep Both
sides]: Pick the model at ❹.
```

4. As mentioned earlier, the slicing reveals an error — the disk cuts through the central tube, as shown in Figure 24-23. To fix the error now, choose Zoom Realtime from the Standard toolbar and zoom in so the model takes up the entire screen.

5. Start the CIRCLE command. At the `Specify center point for circle or [3P/2P/Ttr (tan tan radius)]:` prompt, pick the midpoint at ❶ in Figure 24-23. At the `Specify radius of circle or [Diameter]:` prompt, pick the endpoint at ❷.

6. Choose Extrude from the Solids toolbar. Select the new circle. Set the height of extrusion to 16 and accept the default taper angle of zero (0).

7. Choose Subtract from the Solids Editing toolbar. At the `Select solids and regions to subtract from... Select objects:` prompt, select the large solid and right-click to end object selection. At the `Select solids and regions to subtract... Select objects:` prompt, select the new extruded circle you just drew and right-click. AutoCAD subtracts the extruded circle from the larger model.

Figure 24-23: The solid after slicing and deleting one-half of it

8. Use the HIDE command to hide the model. Your drawing should look like Figure 24-24.

Figure 24-24: The solid after subtracting the extruded circle and doing a hide

9. Save your drawing. If you are continuing on to the next Step-by-Step exercise, keep the drawing open.

Note The error explained in the preceding Step 4 could have been avoided by subtracting the inner tube from the outer tube as the last step, instead of doing it earlier. If you wanted to correct the entire model, you could subtract out the circle as you just did in the exercise, mirror the entire model, and use UNION to make the two halves whole. Mirroring in 3D is covered in the next section. You could also undo the slice as soon as you saw the error and make the correction on the entire model.

Using Editing Commands in 3D

When you draw in 3D, you need to edit your models either to make corrections or as part of the construction process. A number of editing commands are exclusively for 3D or have special 3D options. In this section, you explore these special commands and options.

Table 24-2 lists most of the regular editing commands and how they are used in 3D drawings.

You can use grips on 3D objects, although it is sometimes difficult to visualize in which plane you are moving or stretching an object. You cannot stretch solids, but you can stretch surfaces and wireframes. (If you try to stretch a solid, AutoCAD just moves it.)

Mirroring in 3D

If the mirror line is on the XY plane, you can mirror any 3D object with the regular MIRROR command. If you want to mirror in any other plane, use MIRROR3D.

To use MIRROR3D, follow these steps:

1. Choose Modify ➪ 3D Operation ➪ Mirror 3D.

2. Select the object or objects you want to mirror.

3. At the `Specify first point of mirror plane (3 points) or [Object/Last/Zaxis/View/XY/YZ/ZX/3points] <3points>:` prompt, choose one of the options to define the mirroring plane. These are the same options described in Table 24-1 for the SECTION command. The only additional option is Last, which uses the last defined mirroring plane.

4. At the `Delete source objects? [Yes/No] <N>:` prompt, press Enter to keep the original objects or right-click and choose Yes to delete them.

Table 24-2
Editing Commands in 3D

Command	Use in 3D Drawings
ERASE	Same as for 2D.
COPY	Same as for 2D.
MIRROR	Can be used on 3D objects as long as the mirror line is in the XY plane. Otherwise, use MIRROR3D.
OFFSET	Can be used in 3D space but only on 2D objects.
ARRAY	Can be used on 3D objects in the XY plane. Otherwise, use 3DARRAY.
MOVE	Same as for 2D.
ROTATE	Can be used on 3D objects in the XY plane. Otherwise, use ROTATE3D.
SCALE	Can be used on 3D objects. Scales all three dimensions.
STRETCH	Can be used in 3D space but only on 2D objects, wireframes, and surfaces. The results may not be what you expect because it is hard to visualize the direction of the stretch.
LENGTHEN	Can be used in 3D space but only on 2D objects.
TRIM	Has special options for 3D but only works on 2D objects, such as lines.
EXTEND	Has special options for 3D but only works on 2D objects, such as lines.
BREAK	Can be used in 3D space but only on 2D objects.
CHAMFER	Has special options for 3D.
FILLET	Has special options for 3D.
EXPLODE	Works on 3D objects—solids explode to surfaces, and surfaces explode to wireframes. You can also explode blocks containing 3D objects.
ALIGN	Works on 3D objects.

On the CD-ROM

The drawing used in the following Step-by-Step exercise on mirroring in 3D, ab24-4.dwg, is in the Results folder of the *AutoCAD 2004 Bible* CD-ROM.

Step-by-Step: Mirroring in 3D

1. If you have ab24-04.dwg open from the previous exercise, use it. Do a regen to remove the hidden view. If you don't have it open, open it from your AutoCAD Bible folder or from the Results folder of the *AutoCAD 2004 Bible* CD-ROM. Make sure OSNAP is on and set a running object snap for endpoint. If you don't have the Solids Editing toolbar open, right-click any toolbar and choose Solids Editing from the toolbar list. The drawing is shown in Figure 24-25.

Figure 24-25: This 3D model was sliced and can now be mirrored.

2. Save your drawing as `ab24-05.dwg` in your `AutoCAD Bible` folder.

3. Choose Modify ➪ 3D Operation ➪ Mirror 3D. Follow the prompts:

```
Select objects: Select the solid. Right-click to end object
selection.
Specify first point of mirror plane (3 points) or
[Object/Last/Zaxis/View/XY/YZ/ZX/3points] <3points>: Pick ❶
in Figure 24-25.
Specify second point on mirror plane: Pick ❷.
Specify third point on mirror plane: Pick ❸.
Delete source objects? [Yes/No] <N>: Right-click and choose
Enter.
```

4. Choose Union on the Solids Editing toolbar. Select both solids. Right-click to end object selection. AutoCAD unites them.

5. Save your drawing.

Arraying in 3D

You can array any 3D object using the ARRAY command as long as you define the array in the current XY plane. The 3DARRAY command enables you to create a rectangular array with the normal rows and columns but adding levels in the Z direction. For a 3D polar array, you define an axis of rotation instead of the 2D point used in the ARRAY command.

Creating 3D rectangular arrays

To create a 3D rectangular array, follow these steps:

1. Choose Modify ➪ 3D Operation ➪ 3D Array to start the 3DARRAY command.

2. Select the objects you want to array.

3. At the `Enter the type of array [Rectangular/Polar] <R>:` prompt, right-click and choose Rectangular.

4. At the `Enter the number of rows (---) <1>:` prompt, type the total number of rows you want. Rows are parallel to the X axis.

5. At the `Enter the number of columns (|||) <1>:` prompt, type the total number of columns you want. Columns are parallel to the Y axis.

6. At the `Enter the number of levels (...) <1>:` prompt, type the total number of levels you want. Levels are parallel to the Z axis.

7. At the `Specify the distance between rows (---):` prompt, type a unit distance or pick two points.

8. At the `Specify the distance between columns (|||):` prompt, type a unit distance or pick two points.

9. At the `Specify the distance between levels (...):` prompt, type a unit distance or pick two points.

On the CD-ROM

The drawing used in the following Step-by-Step exercise on creating a rectangular array in 3D, ab24-c.dwg, is in the Drawings folder of the *AutoCAD 2004 Bible* CD-ROM.

Step-by-Step: Creating a Rectangular Array in 3D

1. Open ab24-c.dwg from the CD-ROM.

2. Save the file as ab24-06.dwg in your AutoCAD Bible folder. This is a drawing showing a sphere, a bead-like shape sometimes used for table legs. In this exercise, you create a 3D rectangular array to create four table legs.

3. Choose Modify ➪ 3D Operation ➪ 3D Array. Follow the prompts:

```
Select objects: Select the bead. Right-click to end object
selection.
Enter the type of array [Rectangular/Polar] <R>: Right-click
and choose Rectangular.
Enter the number of rows (---) <1>: 2 ↵
Enter the number of columns (|||) <1>: 2 ↵
Enter the number of levels (...) <1>: 20 ↵ (The bead is 1.5
inches high and the leg should be 30 inches high.)
Specify the distance between rows (---): 26 ↵ (This is the
narrower distance between the legs.)
Specify the distance between columns (|||): 36 ↵ (This is the
wider distance between the legs.)
Specify the distance between levels (...): 1.5 ↵ (You want
the beads to touch along the leg.)
```

4. Do a Zoom Extents to see the result. (Now you would create the tabletop.)

5. Save your drawing. It should look like Figure 24-26.

Figure 24-26: The four legs of a table, created by using a 3D rectangular array

Creating 3D polar arrays

To create a 3D polar array, follow these steps:

1. Choose Modify ⇨ 3D Operation ⇨ 3D Array to start the 3DARRAY command.

2. Select the objects you want to array.

3. At the `Enter the type of array [Rectangular/Polar] <R>:` prompt, right-click and choose Polar.

4. At the `Enter the number of items in the array:` prompt, type the total number of items you want.

5. At the `Specify the angle to fill (+=ccw, -=cw) <360>:` prompt, press Enter to array around a full circle or type any lesser angle.

6. At the `Rotate arrayed objects? [Yes/No] <Y>:` prompt, press Enter to accept the default or type **n** ↵ if you don't want to rotate the objects as they are arrayed.

7. At the `Specify center point of array:` prompt, specify the center point of the array. This is also the first point of the axis of rotation.

8. At the `Specify second point on axis of rotation:` prompt, specify any other point on the axis of rotation.

If you rotate less than a full circle, you need to determine the positive angle of rotation. The positive direction of the axis goes from the first point you specify (the center point) to the second point. Point your right thumb in the positive direction and follow the curl of the fingers of that hand to determine the positive angle of rotation.

On the CD-ROM The drawing used in the following Step-by-Step exercise on creating 3D polar arrays, ab24-d.dwg, is in the Drawings folder of the *AutoCAD 2004 Bible* CD-ROM.

Step-by-Step: Creating 3D Polar Arrays

1. Open ab24-d.dwg from the CD-ROM.

2. Save the file as ab24-07.dwg in your AutoCAD Bible folder. You see part of a lamp, as shown in Figure 24-27. Make sure OSNAP is on. Set a running object snap for endpoint.

Figure 24-27: A partially completed lamp

3. To array the bracket that supports the lampshade, choose Modify ➪ 3D Operation ➪ 3D Array. Follow the prompts:

```
Select objects: Select the support at ❶ in Figure 24-27.
Select objects: Right-click.
Enter the type of array [Rectangular/Polar] <R>: Right-click
and choose Polar.
Enter the number of items in the array: 3 ↵
Specify the angle to fill (+=ccw, -=cw) <360>: ↵
Rotate arrayed objects? [Yes/No] <Y>: ↵
Specify center point of array: Pick the endpoint at ❷.
Specify second point on axis of rotation: Pick the endpoint
at ❸.
```

4. One of the three supports cannot be seen in this view. To see all three, choose View ⇨ 3D Orbit. From inside the arcball, click and drag down a bit until you can see all three supports.

5. Choose View ⇨ 3D Views ⇨ Top to return to plan view and save your drawing.

Rotating in 3D

You can rotate 3D objects in the XY plane with the ROTATE command. Use ROTATE3D when you need to rotate objects in any other plane. The ROTATE3D options are shown in Table 24-3.

| Table 24-3 | |
| **ROTATE3D Options** | |
Option	**Description**
Object	Enables you to choose a line, circle, arc, , or 2D polyline. If you choose a circle or arc, AutoCAD rotates around a line that starts at the object's center and extends perpendicular to the object's plane.
Last	Uses the last defined axis of rotation.
View	Defines the axis of rotation parallel to the current view at the intersection of a point you specify.
Xaxis	The axis of rotation is parallel to the X axis and passes through a point you specify.
Yaxis	The axis of rotation is parallel to the Y axis and passes through a point you specify.
Zaxis	The axis of rotation is parallel to the Z axis and passes through a point you specify.
2points	This is the default. Specify two points to define the axis. It's a good idea to use object snaps.

Tip Sometimes creating an object in the XY plane and then rotating it afterward is easier. In other words, you may create an object in the wrong plane on purpose and use ROTATE3D later to properly place it.

To use ROTATE3D, follow these steps:

1. Choose Modify ⇨ 3D Operation ⇨ Rotate 3D.

2. Select the object or objects you want to rotate.

3. At the Specify first point on axis or define axis by [Object/Last/View/Xaxis/Yaxis/Zaxis/2points]: prompt, select one of the options explained in Table 24-3, and define the axis according to the option prompts.

4. At the Specify rotation angle or [Reference]: prompt, specify a positive or negative rotation angle or choose the Reference option. (The reference option works like the Reference option for ROTATE. See Chapter 9.)

You need to determine the positive direction of rotation. Point your right thumb in the positive direction of the axis and follow the curl of your fingers. If you pick two points, the positive direction of the axis goes from the first pick point to the second pick point.

On the CD-ROM The drawing used in the following Step-by-Step exercise on rotating in 3D, ab24-e.dwg, is in the Drawings folder of the *AutoCAD 2004 Bible* CD-ROM.

Step-by-Step: Rotating in 3D

1. Open ab24-e.dwg from the CD-ROM.

2. Save the file as ab24-08.dwg in your AutoCAD Bible folder. You see the same lamp used in the previous Step-by-Step exercise, but it has now been completed, as shown in Figure 24-28.

Figure 24-28: The completed lamp

3. To insert the lamp in a plan view drawing of a house, you need to see it in plan view from the WCS. In other words, you should be looking down at the lamp. To do this, you need to rotate the lamp around the X axis. To visualize this, look at the UCS icon and imagine rotating the top of the lamp toward you around the horizontal (X) axis. To rotate the lamp, choose Modify ⇨ 3D Operation ⇨ Rotate 3D. Follow the prompts:

```
Select objects: Start a crossing window to select the entire
lamp.
Other corner: Pick the other corner.
Select objects: Right-click.
Specify first point on axis or define axis by
[Object/Last/View/Xaxis/Yaxis/Zaxis/2points]: Right-click and
choose Xaxis.
Specify a point on the X axis <0,0,0>: Right-click.
Specify rotation angle or [Reference]: 90 ↵
```

4. Choose Zoom Extents from the Zoom flyout of the Standard toolbar to see the entire lamp. The lamp is now rotated 90 degrees around the X axis in relation to the UCS, and you are looking at it from the top.

5. To get a better view, choose View ⇨ 3D Views ⇨ SE Isometric. Use the HIDE command to hide the drawing. It should look like Figure 24-29. Of course, looking at the lamp from a different viewpoint does not change the orientation of the lamp relative to the UCS.

Figure 24-29: The lamp is now ready to place in a 3D drawing of a house.

6. Save your drawing.

Aligning in 3D

I have already covered the ALIGN command in Chapter 10. When you work in 3D, you can use the ALIGN command to move, rotate in the XY plane, and rotate in the Z direction—all in one command.

On the CD-ROM The drawing used in the following Step-by-Step exercise on aligning in 3D, `ab24-f.dwg`, is in the `Drawings` folder of the *AutoCAD 2004 Bible* CD-ROM.

Step-by-Step: Aligning in 3D

1. Open `ab24-f.dwg` from the CD-ROM.

2. Save the file as `ab24-09.dwg` in your `AutoCAD Bible` folder. You see part of the base assembly for an industrial washer, as shown in Figure 24-30. One sidebar needs to be moved and rotated into place. Make sure OSNAP is on. Set a running object snap for endpoint.

Figure 24-30: Part of a base assembly for an industrial washer with a sidebar that needs to be moved and rotated into place

Thanks to Robert Mack of the Dexter Company, Fairfield, Iowa, for this drawing.

3. Notice that it's hard to tell which way the sidebar is facing because it is displayed in wireframe. Use the HIDE command to do a hide. This tells you that ❶ in Figure 24-30 is facing away from you. Use the REGEN command to get back to wireframe display.

4. Choose Modify ➪ 3D Operation ➪ Align. Follow the prompts.

```
Select objects: Select the sidebar.
Select objects: Right-click.
Specify first source point: Pick ❶ in Figure 24-30.
Specify first destination point: Pick ❸.
Specify second source point: Pick ❹.
Specify second destination point: Pick ❺.
Specify third source point or <continue>: Pick ❷.
Specify third destination point: Pick any point further back
than ❸ on the plate. The smaller bars (shown in red in the
drawing) provide several endpoints that you can easily
locate.
```

5. AutoCAD aligns the sidebar. Save your drawing. It should look like Figure 24-31.

Figure 24-31: The sidebar has been aligned with the rest of the model.

Tip The trick when aligning in 3D is to properly visualize the parts. It helps to hide the drawing first, as you did in the exercise. Also, take the time to find the UCS and a viewpoint that make the points you are specifying easy to see and pick.

Trimming and extending in 3D

Chapter 10 covers the TRIM and EXTEND commands. Review that discussion if necessary. Here I explain how to use them in 3D.

You can use the TRIM and EXTEND commands to trim or extend 2D objects in 3D space. AutoCAD provides the Project option for working in 3D space. The Project option has three suboptions:

✦ **None:** AutoCAD only trims or extends objects that actually intersect or can intersect in 3D space.

✦ **UCS:** This is the default. AutoCAD projects objects onto the XY plane of the current UCS. Therefore, if two lines are on different Z coordinates, you can trim and extend one of them with reference to the other, even though they do not and cannot actually meet in 3D space.

✦ **View:** This projects objects parallel to the current view. Objects are trimmed or extended based on the way they look on the screen. They need not (and probably won't) actually meet in 3D space.

You can also use the Extend option to trim or extend to implied intersections, as explained in Chapter 10. In the next exercise, you practice extending objects in 3Dand trimming works the same way.

The drawing used in the following Step-by-Step exercise on extending objects in 3D, ab24-g.dwg, is in the Drawings folder of the *AutoCAD 2004 Bible* CD-ROM.

Step-by-Step: Extending Objects in 3D

1. Open ab24-g.dwg from the CD-ROM.

2. Save the file as ab24-10.dwg in your AutoCAD Bible folder. You see a bushing, in 2D and 3D, as shown in Figure 24-32. The 3D bushing has been exploded into simple geometry — otherwise you wouldn't be able to use it to extend the 2D lines.

Figure 24-32: A bushing in 2D and 3D. The 3D bushing has been exploded but still looks the same. It can now be used to extend lines.

3. To turn the UCSORTHO system variable off, type **ucsortho** ↵ **0** ↵. (If its current value is 0, just press Enter at the `Enter new value for UCSORTHO <0>:` prompt.)

4. Choose Extend from the Modify toolbar. Follow the prompts.

```
Select boundary edges ...
Select objects: Pick the 3D bushing at ❶ in Figure 24-32.
Select objects: Right-click.
Select object to extend or shift-select to trim or
[Project/Edge/Undo]: Right-click and choose Project.
Enter a projection option [None/Ucs/View] <Ucs>: Right-click
and choose View.
Select object to extend or shift-select to trim or
[Project/Edge/Undo]: Pick the 2D bushing at ❷.
Select object to extend or shift-select to trim or
[Project/Edge/Undo]: Right-click and choose Enter.
```

5. Choose View ⇨ 3D Views ⇨ Top. You can now see that the 2D line doesn't actually meet the 3D bushing. By using the View option, you only extended the line in that view.

6. Choose Zoom Previous from the Standard toolbar.

7. Again, choose Extend from the Modify toolbar. Follow the prompts:

```
Select boundary edges...Select objects: Pick the bottom edge
of the 3D bushing at ❸.
Select objects: Right-click.
Select object to extend or shift-select to trim or
[Project/Edge/Undo]: Right-click and choose Project.
Enter a projection option [None/Ucs/View] <View>: Right-click
and choose None.
Select object to extend or shift-select to trim or
[Project/Edge/Undo]: Pick the same line you picked in Step 3,
but this time pick it closer to the 3D bushing, on the new
length you created by extending it.
Select object to extend or shift-select to trim or
[Project/Edge/Undo]: Right-click and choose Enter.
```

8. Choose View ⇨ 3D Views ⇨ Top. You can now see that the 2D line now actually meets the 3D bushing.

9. Click Undo on the Standard toolbar twice to undo the viewpoint change and the extend operation.

10. Choose Move from the Modify toolbar. Select the entire 3D bushing. At the `Specify base point or displacement:` prompt, type **0,0,2** ↵. Press Enter again to end the command. If you miss any of the objects, pick them and move them, too. This moves the entire 3D bushing 2 units in the Z direction.

11. Choose Extend from the Modify toolbar. Follow the prompts:

```
Select boundary edges...
Select objects: Pick the 3D bushing at ❸ (the bottom ring).
Select objects: Right-click.
Select object to extend or shift-select to trim or
[Project/Edge/Undo]: Right-click and choose Project.
Enter a projection option [None/Ucs/View] <View>: Right-click
and choose Ucs.
Select object to extend or shift-select to trim or
[Project/Edge/Undo]: Pick the same line you extended before,
closer to its left endpoint.
Select object to extend or shift-select to trim or
[Project/Edge/Undo]: Right-click and choose Enter.
```

12. Choose View ⇨ 3D Views ⇨ Top. It looks as if the 2D line now actually meets the 3D bushing.

13. Choose View ⇨ 3D Views ⇨ Front. (Because UCSORTHO is off, the UCS does not change.) Now you can see that the 2D line doesn't meet the 3D bushing.

14. Type **ucsortho** ⏎ 1 ⏎ to return UCSORTHO to its previous setting, if you changed it in Step 3.

15. Save your drawing. It should look like Figure 24-33.

Figure 24-33: When you use the UCS option, the lines seem to touch the boundary edge when you look at it from the top, but they can have different Z coordinates.

Filleting in 3D

You can fillet solids but not surfaces. If you create a 3D object from lines, you can fillet the lines. Figure 24-34 shows a 3D mechanical drawing with several filleted edges.

Figure 24-34: Filleted edges are common in 3D mechanical drawings.

To use the FILLET command for solids, follow these steps:

1. Choose Fillet from the Modify toolbar.

2. At the Select first object or [Polyline/Radius/Trim/ mUltiple]: prompt, select the edge of the solid that you want to fillet. You cannot deselect this edge, so you must select the solid at the proper edge. Ignore the other options.

3. AutoCAD senses that you have selected a solid and responds with the Enter fillet radius <0.5000>: prompt. Press Enter to accept the default of 0.5 or type a new radius.

4. At the Select an edge or [Chain/Radius]: prompt, press Enter if you only want to fillet the one edge you have already selected. You can also select other edges of the same solid. Press Enter to end selection of edges. AutoCAD fillets the edge or edges you selected. You can also change the Radius at this prompt.

5. Use the Chain option to fillet a set of attached edges. AutoCAD responds with the Select an edge chain or [Edge/Radius]: prompt. Continue to pick edges that are attached to the previous edge you picked. Press Enter to end selection of edges. AutoCAD fillets the entire chain of edges.

You can select different radii for different edges. At the first Enter radius <0.5000>: prompt, specify the radius for the edge you just selected. After that, use the Radius option to set the desired radius before you select the edge.

The drawing used in the following Step-by-Step exercise on filleting solids, ab24-h.dwg, is in the Drawings folder of the *AutoCAD 2004 Bible* CD-ROM.

Step-by-Step: Filleting Solids

1. Open ab24-h.dwg from the CD-ROM.

2. Save the file as ab24-11.dwg in your AutoCAD Bible folder. This is a solid model of a mounting angle, as shown in Figure 24-35. It needs to be filleted.

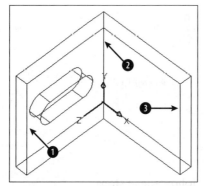

Figure 24-35: The mounting angle needs filleting.

3. Choose Fillet from the Modify toolbar.

4. At the Select first object or [Polyline/Radius/Trim/mUltiple]: prompt, pick the edge at ❶ in Figure 24-35.

5. At the Enter fillet radius <0.5000>: prompt, type **.25** ↵.

6. At the Select an edge or [Chain/Radius]: prompt, pick ❷.

7. At the Select an edge or [Chain/Radius]: prompt, pick ❸. Press Enter to end the command. AutoCAD fillets all three edges.

8. Save your drawing. It should look like Figure 24-36.

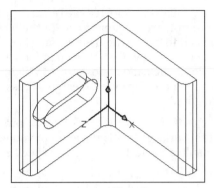

Figure 24-36: The filleted mounting angle

Chamfering in 3D

You can chamfer solids but not surfaces. If you create a 3D object from lines, you can chamfer the lines. Figure 24-37 shows a solid with chamfered edges. (You can see this solid as part of the wheel shown at the beginning of this chapter in Figure 24-1.)

Figure 24-37: A solid with chamfered edges

To chamfer a solid, follow these steps:

1. Choose Chamfer from the Modify toolbar.

2. At the `Select first line or [Polyline/Distance/Angle/Trim/ Method/mUltiple]:` prompt, select the edge you want to chamfer. The edge is displayed as a line between two surfaces. AutoCAD highlights one of the surfaces that touches the edge you selected.

3. At the `Base surface selection...Enter surface selection option [Next/OK (current)] <OK>:` prompt, press Enter to accept the highlighted surface as the base surface. You need to define the base surface in case the two chamfering distances are not equal or if you want to chamfer a loop, which is the entire base surface. Right-click and choose Next to highlight the next surface. (Only two surfaces touch the edge you selected.) Press Enter when the desired surface is highlighted.

4. At the `Specify base surface chamfer distance <0.5000>:` prompt, type the chamfering distance for the first surface. This is the amount you want to cut off from that surface. (The default is the last distance you specified.)

5. At the `Specify other surface chamfer distance <0.5000>:` prompt, type the chamfering distance for the other surface. (The default is the last distance you specified.)

6. At the `Select an edge or [Loop]:` prompt, select the edge you want to chamfer. You can also use the Loop option. AutoCAD then prompts you to select the edge loop. Select the surface, and AutoCAD chamfers all the edges of that surface.

7. AutoCAD continues to prompt you to select edges or edge loops. Press Enter to end selection when you are finished.

On the CD-ROM

The drawing used in the following Step-by-Step exercise on chamfering solids, ab24-i.dwg, is in the Drawings folder of the *AutoCAD 2004 Bible* CD-ROM.

Step-by-Step: Chamfering Solids

1. Open ab24-i.dwg from the CD-ROM.

2. Save the file as ab24-12.dwg in your AutoCAD Bible folder. This is a simple box with dimensions of 233×102×12 millimeters, as shown in Figure 24-38.

3. Choose Chamfer from the Modify toolbar. Follow the prompts:

```
Select first line or
[Polyline/Distance/Angle/Trim/Method/mUltiple]: Pick the edge
at ❶ in Figure 24-38.
Base surface selection...
Enter surface selection option [Next/OK (current)] <OK>: ↵
Specify base surface chamfer distance <0.5000>: 30 ↵
Specify other surface chamfer distance <0.5000>: 30 ↵
Select an edge or [Loop]: Pick ❶.
Select an edge or [Loop]: ↵
```

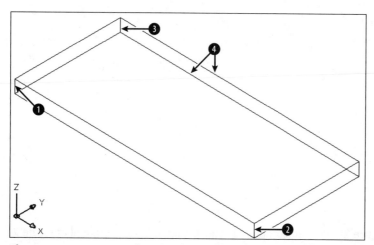

Figure 24-38: You can chamfer this solid box to create a new shape.

You can't see the chamfer because of the viewpoint. You change the viewpoint at the end of the exercise.

4. Repeat the CHAMFER command. Do the exact same operation as in Step 3, but pick ❷.

5. Repeat the CHAMFER command. Follow the prompts:

```
Select first line or
[Polyline/Distance/Angle/Trim/Method/mUltiple]: Pick the edge
at ❸.

Base surface selection...
Enter surface selection option [Next/OK (current)] <OK>: ↵
Make sure the surface indicated by ❹ is highlighted. If not,
type n ↵. Then press Enter again.
Specify base surface chamfer distance <30.0000>: 233 ↵
Specify other surface chamfer distance <30.0000>: 40 ↵
Select an edge or [Loop]: Pick ❸.
Select an edge or [Loop]: ↵
```

6. Choose View ➪ 3D Views ➪ Top. This shows you the shape in profile.

7. Save your drawing. It should look like Figure 24-39.

Figure 24-39: The completed solid. Compare it to the model in Figure 24-1.

Exploding 3D objects

The EXPLODE command has a particular effect that varies according to the type of 3D object. Table 24-4 lists the effects of exploding 3D objects.

Table 24-4 Using EXPLODE on 3D Objects	
Object	**Result**
Solids	Flat surfaces become regions. Curved surfaces become bodies.
Bodies	Curved surfaces become single-surface bodies. Flat bodies become regions or curves.
Polyface meshes	3D faces.
Polygon meshes	3D faces.
Polylines with thickness	Lines.

Note A body is a free-form solid. You cannot directly create a body. AutoCAD uses bodies when 3D models do not fit into any other object type.

ACIS and stereolithography (.stl) are two file formats especially applicable to 3D models. Chapter 27 explains how to export drawings in these formats.

Editing Solids

Prior to AutoCAD 2000, direct editing of solids was very limited. You could chamfer, fillet, slice, or explode a solid. You could also use UNION, SUBTRACT, and INTERSECT. Other editing commands did not actually modify the solids. AutoCAD 2000 introduced SOLIDEDIT to directly edit solids. This command has so many options that it might as well be several commands.

SOLIDEDIT offers three major types of solid editing:

✦ **Faces:** A number of options enable you to edit the faces of solids. You can extrude, move, rotate, offset, taper, delete, copy, and color (assign a color to) faces.

✦ **Edges:** You can color and copy edges.

✦ **Bodies:** The body options apply to solids as a whole. You can imprint, separate, shell, clean, and check solids. These options are more easily done than said.

The easiest way to use SOLIDEDIT is to open the Solids Editing toolbar, shown in Figure 24-40.

Union
Subtract
Intersect
Extrude Faces
Move Faces
Offset Faces
Delete Faces
Rotate Faces
Taper Faces
Copy Faces
Color Faces
Copy Edges
Color Edges
Imprint
Clean
Separate
Shell
Check

Figure 24-40: Use the Solids Editing toolbar to edit solids and forget the labyrinthine command line.

The next three sections explain how to edit faces, edges, and bodies.

Editing faces

A face is a surface on a solid. A face can be either flat or curved. For example, a hole in a block is a face and many of the face editing operations work well to modify holes. Of course, you can edit an outer face of a surface as well.

The SOLIDEDIT command supports several methods of selecting a face or faces. You are accustomed (by now) to selecting a solid by picking one of its edges. However, an edge borders on two faces, and when you pick an edge AutoCAD highlights both its adjoining faces, as shown in Figure 24-41.

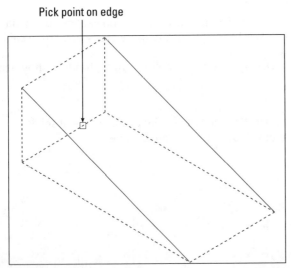

Pick point on edge

Figure 24-41: When you pick an edge in the SOLIDEDIT command, AutoCAD selects its two adjoining faces.

Sometimes, picking a face on an edge works — for example, when you want to pick the entire face represented by a hole.

For other situations, to enable you to pick only one face, you can use the *boundary* set method, by picking within the closed boundary of a face. Generally, AutoCAD selects the front-most face. You can also use a crossing window, crossing polygon, or fence to select a face. For these three latter selection methods, you need to type **c**, **cp**, or **f**, respectively, and then press Enter.

Because selecting the right face can be difficult on a first try, especially for a complex solid, SOLIDEDIT offers plenty of opportunity for correction. After choosing

the type of solid editing you want, AutoCAD displays the `Select faces or [Undo/Remove]:` prompt. Right-click and choose Undo to undo your last selection operation. Right-click and choose Remove to select a face to remove from the selection set. The prompt then includes an Add option that you can use to start adding faces again. You may have to remove and add faces more than once to get the result you want. Then press Enter to end face selection.

You may want to perform more than one operation on a face. After you complete an operation, you can right-click to open the shortcut menu and choose another operation. To exit the command, right-click and choose Exit twice.

Extruding faces

Extruding a face is like extruding a 2D object. If you are familiar with the EXTRUDE command, you will feel comfortable extruding faces. To extrude a face, follow these steps:

1. Choose Extrude Faces on the Solids Editing toolbar. AutoCAD starts the SOLIDEDIT command and automatically enters the first two prompts of the command for you.

2. At the `Select faces or [Undo/Remove]:` prompt, select the face or faces you want to extrude, using the selection method(s) explained previously. After your first selection, the prompt adds the ALL option. When you're done, press Enter to end face selection.

3. At the `Specify height of extrusion or [Path]:` prompt, type a height or right-click and choose Path to specify a path for the extrusion.

4. If you specify a height, at the `Specify angle of taper for extrusion <0>:` prompt, specify an angle. (As with the EXTRUDE command, a positive angle tapers inward.) If you choose the Path option, at the `Select extrusion path:` prompt, select an object, usually a line or arc, to extrude along.

5. To extricate yourself from the command, right-click and choose Enter twice.

 You can also use the eXit option that appears on the command line.

AutoCAD extrudes the face. As you exit, AutoCAD performs a validation of the solid to make sure the solid is a valid solid if the SOLIDCHECK system variable is on. By default, SOLIDCHECK is on (set to 1) and automatically checks solids when you edit them.

Moving faces

You can move a face when a solid is complex enough to have at least two separate elements—for example, a plate with a hole in it. You can then move the hole around wherever you want. Look at the mounting bracket in Figure 24-36, earlier in this chapter. You could move the hole from the left face to the right face using SOLIDEDIT. To move a face, follow these steps:

1. Choose Move Faces on the Solids Editing toolbar. AutoCAD starts the SOLIDEDIT command and automatically enters the first two prompts of the command for you.

2. Select the face or faces you want to move, using the selection method(s) described earlier. Press Enter to end face selection.

3. At the `Specify a base point or displacement:` prompt, specify a base point if you want to pick two points, or specify a displacement, as you would with the MOVE command.

4. At the `Specify a second point of displacement:` prompt, specify a second point of displacement if you specified a base point. Otherwise, press Enter.

5. Right-click and choose Enter twice to exit the command.

If you choose a face that cannot be moved, AutoCAD displays the `Modeling Operation Error: No solution for an edge` message.

Offsetting faces

You can offset a face when a solid has two separate elements, such as a wall with a window cut out of it. You can then resize the window by offsetting it. Offsetting a face increases all parts of the face equally by a distance you specify.

Use a positive offset value to increase the volume of the solid. If your face is a solid axle in the middle of a disk, for example, and you offset the axle with a positive value, the axle gets bigger. However, if your face is a hole in the middle of a disk, a positive offset value makes the hole smaller because that makes the resulting solid bigger.

Use a negative offset value to decrease the volume of the solid. Using the same example, a negative offset value would make the axle smaller, but it would make the hole bigger.

To offset a face, follow these steps:

1. Choose Offset Faces from the Solids Editing toolbar. AutoCAD starts the SOLIDEDIT command and automatically enters the first two prompts of the command for you.

2. Select the face or faces you want to offset and press Enter to end face selection.

3. At the `Specify the offset distance:` prompt, type a positive or negative distance. You can also pick two points to specify a positive offset.

4. Right-click and choose Enter twice to exit the command.

AutoCAD offsets the face. If there is no room for the offset, AutoCAD displays the message `Modeling Operation Error` on the command line.

Deleting faces

You can delete a face of a solid. This is a great way to instantly get rid of a hole, axle, or window within a solid. You can delete faces to undo the effects of both the UNION and SUBTRACT commands. You can also remove filleted and chamfered faces. AutoCAD won't delete every face; for example, you can't turn a box into a tetrahedron by deleting the box's top face. However, the capability to delete faces is a very powerful tool for editing your solids.

To delete a face or faces, choose Delete Faces from the Solids Editing toolbar. Select the face or faces and press Enter. AutoCAD deletes the face or faces you selected. If your face(s) can't be deleted, you see the message Modeling Operation Error on the command line.

Rotating faces

You can rotate a face when a solid is complex enough to have at least two separate elements: for example, a box with a hole in it. The prompts for rotating are very similar to those for ROTATE3D, covered earlier in this chapter. To rotate a face, follow these steps:

1. Choose Rotate Faces on the Solids Editing toolbar. AutoCAD starts the SOLIDEDIT command and automatically enters the first two prompts of the command for you.

2. Select the face or faces you want to rotate, using the selection method(s) described earlier. Press Enter to end face selection.

3. At the Specify an axis point or [Axis by object/View/Xaxis/ Yaxis/Zaxis] <2points>: prompt, specify the first point of a rotation axis or use one of the options to define an axis of rotation.

4. If you specified a first point, at the Specify the second point on the rotation axis: prompt, specify the second point.

5. At the Specify a rotation angle or [Reference]: prompt, specify a rotation angle (the right-hand rule applies in determining the direction of rotation) or use the Reference option to specify a reference (starting) angle, and then an ending angle.

6. Right-click and choose Enter twice to exit the command.

AutoCAD rotates the face. If you choose a face that cannot be rotated, or if there isn't room on the solid for the rotation, AutoCAD lets you know with the message Modeling Operation Error on the command line.

Tapering faces

You can taper an entire simple solid, such as a box, or you can taper a face that is an element within a complex solid, such as a hole or an axle. Tapering angles the sides of the face. To determine the direction of the taper, that is, which end gets tapered, you specify a base point and a second point. The base point side of the

solid is not tapered, and AutoCAD tapers the face in the direction from the base point toward the second point. You also specify the angle of the taper. A positive taper angle tapers the face inward; a hole is tapered outward. A negative taper angle tapers the face outward; a hold is tapered inward. Figure 24-42 shows a box before and after tapering at a 15-degree angle, as well as the base point and second points that were used. All the faces except the bottom were selected.

In general, use small tapering angles. If the face would taper to a point before it reaches its existing height, AutoCAD cannot complete the taper.

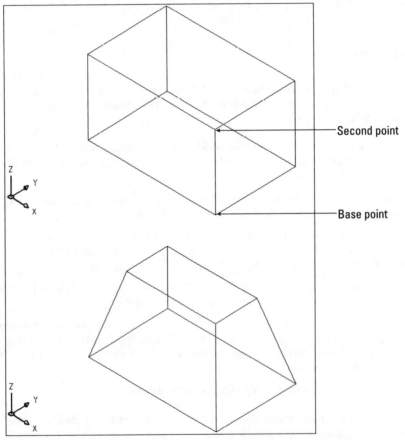

Figure 24-42: A box before and after tapering at a 15-degree angle

To taper a face, follow these steps:

1. Choose Taper Faces on the Solids Editing toolbar. AutoCAD starts the SOLIDEDIT command and automatically enters the first two prompts of the command for you.

2. Select the face(s) you want to taper. Press Enter to end face selection.

3. At the `Specify the base point:` prompt, pick the base point for the taper direction. Object snaps are a good idea.

4. At the `Specify another point along the axis of tapering:` prompt, specify a second point to indicate the direction of the taper. Again, use an object snap.

5. At the `Specify the taper angle:` prompt, specify an angle between –90° and +90°.

6. Right-click and choose Enter twice to exit the command.

AutoCAD tapers the face. If AutoCAD can't taper the face, you see the message `Modeling Operation Error` on the command line.

Copying faces

You can copy any face, including a hole. AutoCAD creates regions or bodies out of the face. You can then use the EXTRUDE command to extrude one region. However, if you copy a complex face, such as a hole that may consist of several regions, you can't turn it back into a solid again.

To copy a face, follow these steps:

1. Choose Copy Faces from the Solids Editing toolbar. AutoCAD starts the SOLIDEDIT command and automatically enters the first two prompts of the command for you.

2. Select the face(s) you want to copy. Press Enter to end face selection.

3. At the `Specify a base point or displacement:` prompt, specify a base point. Object snaps are helpful.

4. At the `Specify a second point of displacement:` prompt, specify a second point to indicate the direction and distance for the copy.

5. Right-click and choose Enter twice to exit the command.

AutoCAD copies the face.

Coloring faces

You can assign a color to a face of an object. You might want to color a face to make it easier to see. You can also color a face so that you can assign a material to it (you can assign materials by color) for the purpose of rendering. The color overrides the color setting for the solid's layer.

Note When an object is assigned more than one material, priority goes to attachment by object, then by color, and finally by layer. If you attach a material to a solid by layer, and then attach a material to one of its faces (that you have colored) by color, both the solid and the face display their materials. For more information, see Chapter 25.

To color a face, follow these steps:

1. Choose Color Faces from the Solids Editing toolbar. AutoCAD starts the SOLIDEDIT command and automatically enters the first two prompts of the command for you.

2. Select the face or faces you want to color. Press Enter to end face selection.

3. AutoCAD opens the Select Color dialog box. Choose a color and click OK.

4. Right-click and choose Enter twice to exit the command.

AutoCAD colors the face.

On the CD-ROM The drawing used in the following Step-by-Step exercise on editing solid faces, ab24-11.dwg, is in the Results folder of the *AutoCAD 2004 Bible* CD-ROM.

Step-by-Step: Editing Solid Faces

1. Open ab24-11.dwg from the Results folder of the CD-ROM. If you did the exercise on filleting solids, you can open it from your AutoCAD Bible folder.

2. Save the file as ab24-13.dwg in your AutoCAD Bible folder.

3. If the Solids Editing toolbar is not displayed, right-click any toolbar and choose Solids Editing. This is a mounting bracket, shown in Figure 24-43. Note the UCS icon, which is at 0,0,0.

4. Make sure OSNAP is on. Set a running object snaps for midpoint.

5. Choose Offset Faces from the Solids Editing toolbar.

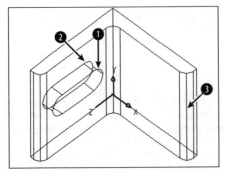
Figure 24-43: The mounting bracket

6. At the `Select faces or [Undo/Remove]:` prompt, select the slot in the mounting angle. Selecting the slot may require a few picks to make sure that all the parts of the slot are highlighted and to remove from selection the unwanted faces of the mounting bracket that become highlighted. (Hint: Try picking on the cross-lines that connect the front and back of the slot.) To remove a face, right-click and choose Remove. Then pick on a face's edge. To add faces again, right-click and choose Add. After you're done, press Enter (or right-click and choose Enter) to end face selection.

7. At the `Specify the offset distance:` prompt, type **.1** ↵. AutoCAD makes the slot smaller.

8. You are still in the SOLIDEDIT command. Right-click and choose Taper. At the next prompt, select the slot and press Enter after you're done selecting.

9. At the `Specify the base point:` prompt, pick the midpoint at ❶.

10. At the `Specify another point along the axis of tapering:` prompt, pick the midpoint at ❷.

11. At the `Specify the taper angle:` prompt, type **10** ↵. AutoCAD tapers the slot.

12. Right-click and choose Delete. At the next prompt, select the filleted face at ❸. Right-click and choose Enter. AutoCAD removes the fillet.

13. Right-click and choose Extrude. At the next prompt, select the face at ❸ by picking inside the face. Right-click and choose Enter.

14. At the `Specify height of extrusion or [Path]:` prompt, type **.2** ↵.

15. At the `Specify angle of taper for extrusion <0>:` prompt, type **10** ↵. AutoCAD extrudes the face.

16. Right-click and choose Enter twice to exit the command.

17. Save your drawing. It should look like Figure 24-44.

Figure 24-44: The editing mounting angle

Editing edges

The two-dimensional place where two faces meet is an edge. You can perform only two editing operations on edges — you can copy them and color them.

Copying edges

When you copy an edge, you get a line, arc, circle, ellipse, or spline, depending on the shape of the solid's edge. To copy an edge, follow these steps:

1. Choose Copy Edges from the Solids Editing toolbar. AutoCAD starts the SOLIDEDIT command and automatically enters the first two prompts of the command for you.

2. Select the edge or edges you want to copy.

3. At the Specify a base point or displacement: prompt, specify a base point, preferably using an object snap or a displacement.

4. At the Specify a second point of displacement: prompt, specify a second point or press Enter if you specified a displacement in Step 2.

5. Right-click and choose Enter twice to exit the command.

AutoCAD copies the edge or edges.

Coloring edges

You can color an edge to make it more visible. The color overrides the color setting for the solid's layer. To color an edge, follow these steps:

1. Choose Color Edges from the Solids Editing toolbar. AutoCAD starts the SOLIDEDIT command and automatically enters the first two prompts of the command for you.

2. Select the edge or edges you want to color. Press Enter to end edge selection.

3. AutoCAD opens the Select Color dialog box. Choose the color you want and click OK.

4. Right-click and choose Enter twice to exit the command.

AutoCAD colors the edge.

Editing bodies

Several of the SOLIDEDIT options apply to solids as a whole. The operations available are imprinting, separating, shelling, cleaning, and checking. Each operation is discussed in the following sections.

Imprinting solids

You can imprint an arc, circle, line, 2D polyline or 3D polyline, ellipse, spline, region, body, or 3D solid on a solid. The object you are imprinting must intersect a face on the solid. The shape made by the intersection of the object is left on the solid, as if you put ink on the edges of the object and stamped it on the solid. Figure 24-45 shows an example of imprinting.

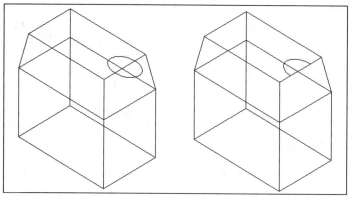

Figure 24-45: The ellipse was drawn on the top of the solid. After imprinting and deleting the ellipse, the shape of half the ellipse remains on the solid.

To imprint a solid, follow these steps:

1. First create one of the stampable objects previously listed so that it intersects with a solid. If you draw in top view, check in an isometric view to make sure the intersection is where you want it.

2. Choose Imprint from the Solids Editing toolbar. AutoCAD starts the SOLIDEDIT command and automatically enters the first two prompts of the command for you.

3. At the `Select a 3D solid:` prompt, select a solid. You can select only one.

4. At the `Select an object to imprint:` prompt, select the object you want to imprint.

5. At the `Delete the source object [Yes/No] <N>:` prompt, type **y** ⏎ or press Enter to indicate No.

6. AutoCAD repeats the `Select an object to imprint:` prompt. You can continue the command in the same way or press Enter if you're done.

7. Right-click and choose Enter twice to exit the command.

AutoCAD imprints the solid. If you didn't delete the source object, you'll need to move it to see the result.

Cleaning solids

After all the editing, you can end up with some pretty strange solids. Cleaning solids removes imprints as well as adjacent faces that share the same surface.

 To clean a solid, choose Clean from the Solids Editing toolbar. At the `Select a 3D solid:` prompt, select a solid. AutoCAD cleans it.

Separating solids

You can separate a solid that is made up of more than one completely separate section. You would generally create such a solid from separate, nontouching solids, using the UNION command. The Separate option undoes the effect of the UNION command so that the solids become separate again. You can compare this operation to grouping and ungrouping objects. (See Chapter 18.)

To separate a solid, choose Separate from the Solids Editing toolbar. At the `Select a 3D solid:` prompt, select the solid by picking any of its sections. AutoCAD separates the solids.

If your solid sections are even touching, you get one of the funnier AutoCAD messages: `The selected solid does not have multiple lumps.`

Shelling solids

When you shell a solid, you hollow out its inside, leaving a thin wall. Think of making a drinking glass from a truncated cone (or tapered cylinder) or a room from a solid box. Shelling is a common process in high-end 3D modeling programs. To shell a solid, follow these steps:

1. Choose Shell from the Solids Editing toolbar. AutoCAD starts the SOLIDEDIT command and automatically enters the first two prompts of the command for you.

2. Select a solid.

3. At the `Remove faces or [Undo/Add/ALL]:` prompt, remove any face or faces that you don't want to shell. For example, if you are making a drinking glass from a truncated cone, you want to remove the larger circular face (the one you would drink out of) so that it will remain open. Otherwise, you end up with an enclosed solid that has a hollow interior. After you finish removing faces, press Enter. (The command line confirms `1 face found, 1 removed,` but there is no obvious confirmation that AutoCAD has removed the correct face.)

4. At the `Enter the shell offset distance:` prompt, type the width of the wall you want to create. A positive value creates a shell to the inside of the current solid. A negative value creates a shell to the outside of the current solid.

5. Right-click and choose Enter twice to exit the command.

AutoCAD shells the solid.

Checking solids

Checking ensures that your solid is a valid 3D solid object so that you can edit it without getting ACIS failure error messages. This might be a useful feature to put into an AutoLISP or VBA program, to make sure that it doesn't fail because of invalid solids.

To check a solid, choose Check from the Solids Editing toolbar. At the `Select a 3D solid:` prompt, select a solid. Usually, AutoCAD replies with the message: `This object is a valid ShapeManager solid.`

On the CD-ROM
The drawing used in the following Step-by-Step exercise on editing solid bodies, `ab24-j.dwg`, is in the `Drawings` folder of the *AutoCAD 2004 Bible* CD-ROM.

Step-by-Step: Editing Solid Bodies

1. Open `ab24-j.dwg` from the CD-ROM.

2. Save the file as `ab24-14.dwg` in your `AutoCAD Bible` folder. This is a simple solid box with an ellipse drawn on part of its top face.

3. Choose Imprint from the Solids Editing toolbar. Follow the prompts:

   ```
   Select a 3D solid: Select the box.
   Select an object to imprint: Select the ellipse.
   Delete the source object [Yes/No] <N>: y ⏎.
   Select an object to imprint: Right-click.
   ```

4. Right-click and choose Clean. At the `Select a 3D solid:` prompt, select the box.

5. Right-click and choose Shell. Follow the prompts:

   ```
   Select a 3D Solid: Select the box.
   Remove faces or [Undo/Add/ALL]: Pick anywhere inside the top
   face.
   Remove faces or [Undo/Add/ALL]: Right-click and choose Enter.
   Enter the shell offset distance: .1 ⏎
   ```

6. Press Enter twice to exit the command.

7. Choose View ➪ Hide. You can now see the result of the shell operation.

8. Save your drawing. It should look like Figure 24-46.

Figure 24-46: The shelled box

Listing Solid Properties

The MASSPROP command provides information about regions and solids that is useful for engineering applications. The bounding box, for example, is an imaginary box that contains the solid. The calculations are based on the relationship of the solid to the UCS. If you rotate the solid or change the UCS, you get different results. For example, after running MASSPROP to find the center of gravity (centroid) and axes of your model, move the UCS to the centroid and then run MASSPROP again to identify the moments of inertia.

For 2D regions, the area moment of inertia that MASSPROP generates can be used to calculate bending and twisting stresses. You could generate a 2D region of a solid model using the SECTION command and then use the UCS command with the OBJECT option to set the UCS coplanar to the region. The MASSPROP command would then report the area moment of inertia.

AutoCAD assumes a density of 1 for all solids. You can then apply material density multipliers on the values that get reported. Figure 24-47 shows the results of MASSPROP on a solid.

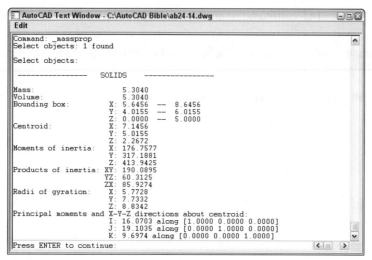

Figure 24-47: The results of the MASSPROP command

To list a solid's properties, choose Tools ➪ Inquiry ➪ Region/Mass Properties. Select the object you want to list. AutoCAD opens the Text window to display the calculations. At the `Write analysis to a file? [Yes/No] <N>:` prompt, press Enter to accept the No default or right-click and choose Yes. AutoCAD prompts you for a file name and copies the data to that file.

Summary

In this chapter, you learned how to create and edit solids. You read about:

✦ Drawing standard shapes

✦ Creating extruded and revolved solids from 2D profiles

✦ Using UNION, SUBTRACT, and INTERSECT to create more complex shapes

✦ Using the INTERFERE command to see the volume of interference between solids

✦ Utilizing the SECTION and SLICE commands to help visualize solids

✦ The special 3D editing commands MIRROR3D, 3DARRAY, and ROTATE3D

✦ Using the TRIM, EXTEND, FILLET, and CHAMFER commands for 3D editing

✦ Exploding into surfaces and surfaces into 2D objects

✦ Using the SOLIDEDIT command to edit faces, edges, and bodies — solids as a whole

✦ Calculating a number of engineering functions on solids by using the MASSPROP command

In the next chapter, I cover rendering 3D models.

✦ ✦ ✦

Rendering in 3D

While 3D drawings are more realistic than those rendered in 2D, they look very artificial—they lack realistic color, shading, and lighting, for example. Rendering enables you to display a 3D drawing more realistically. Some of the more advanced features let you create shadows, make objects transparent, add backgrounds, and map 2D images onto the surface of 3D models. You can shade and render 3D surfaces and solid models. Figure 25-1 shows a whimsical rendering that uses shadows and a background.

Figure 25-1: This cog has been rendered with shadows and a background of clouds.

Understanding Rendering

Rendering is a much more sophisticated means of visualizing a drawing than shading. AutoCAD offers three kinds of rendering—Render, Photo Real, and Photo Raytrace.

✦ **Render** is AutoCAD's original rendering tool. It provides the fewest options but the fastest results.

✦ **Photo Real** creates images line by line, displays bitmaps, creates transparent materials, and makes volumetric and mapped shadows.

✦ **Photo Raytrace** traces rays of light to generate reflections, refraction, and precise ray-traced shadows.

Learning the steps

Rendering is a multi-step process. It generally requires a good deal of trial and error to get the exact results you want. Here are the steps to render a drawing:

1. Start with trial rendering using the default settings. The results let you know what settings need to be changed.

2. Create lights. AutoCAD has four types of lights: ambient, distant, point, and spotlight. These are explained in the section on lights later in this chapter.

3. Create scenes. Scenes are views with lights.

4. Load materials from the materials library. You can create your own materials. Materials are surface characteristics and include color and/or pattern, ambient light, reflection, roughness, transparency, refraction, and bump map. These characteristics are explained later in this chapter in the section on materials.

5. Attach materials to the objects in your drawing. You can attach materials by object, color, or layer.

6. Add a background or fog effect.

7. Set your rendering preferences, if desired.

8. Render the drawing.

The order of the steps is flexible. For example, you can create scenes after you have attached materials. Also, after you render, you will probably see some room for improvement, so you may go back and change the lights, scenes, and/or materials.

Doing a default rendering

Doing a default rendering often helps. The results help you decide what materials and lights need to be created and reveal any problems with the models themselves. When you render, you should open the Render toolbar, which contains most of the tools you need. Right-click any toolbar and choose Render. Figure 25-2 shows the Render toolbar.

 To render a drawing using the default settings, choose Render from the Render toolbar to open the Render dialog box, shown in Figure 25-3.

I cover the Render dialog box completely later in the chapter, but there are a couple of things you can do when you are trying to get a quick rendering.

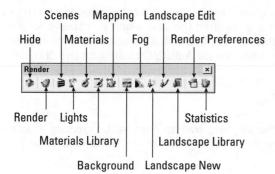

Figure 25-2: The Render toolbar

Figure 25-3: The Render dialog box

You can save time by rendering only some of the objects in the view. To do this, use the Rendering Procedure section of the dialog box.

✦ Check `Query for Selections` to tell AutoCAD to display the `Select objects:` prompt before rendering. AutoCAD renders only the objects you selected, instead of the entire drawing, saving time.

✦ Check `Crop Window` to tell AutoCAD to prompt you to specify a window before rendering. By rendering only a section of the drawing, you can save time.

✦ In the Rendering Options section, check `Render Cache` if you plan to render the same scene several times, as is often the case when you are working on a rendering. AutoCAD saves the rendering data in a file and uses it for subsequent renderings — saving the time needed for AutoCAD to analyze the drawing each time.

Click Render to render the drawing.

On the CD-ROM The drawing used in the following Step-by-Step exercise on creating a default rendering, ab25-a.dwg, is in the `Drawings` folder of the *AutoCAD 2004 Bible* CD-ROM.

Step-by-Step: Creating a Default Rendering

1. Open ab25-a.dwg from the CD-ROM.

2. Save the file as ab25-01.dwg in your `AutoCAD Bible` folder. If the Render toolbar is not displayed, right-click any toolbar and choose Render.

3. Choose Render from the Render toolbar. In the Rendering Procedures section of the Render dialog box, check Crop Window. In the Rendering Options section, check Render Cache.

4. Click Render.

5. At the `Pick crop window to render:` prompt, pick a window similar to that shown in Figure 25-4. Wait until AutoCAD renders the drawing.

6. Save your drawing. It should look like Figure 25-4. As you can see, the rendering is too dark and the objects need realistic materials.

Figure 25-4: An initial rendering using default options and a crop window

Creating Lights

When you render using the default options, AutoCAD uses one light source from behind the viewer, which falls on the objects in the view. However, that is rarely enough — nor is it realistic. AutoCAD offers four types of lights to give you a great deal of flexibility in creating a realistic scene. If you plan to cast shadows in your rendering, the proper placement of lights is most important.

To create lights, choose Lights from the Render toolbar to open the Lights dialog box, shown in Figure 25-5.

Figure 25-5: The Lights dialog box

Assigning color to a light

The process of assigning a color to a light applies to all types of lights. Light colors are somewhat different from pigment colors, which are more familiar. You know that there are three primary colors — red, yellow, and blue — and you know what colors you get when you mix them. The three primary light colors are red, green, and blue. Their mixtures are different as well — for example, red and green make yellow. White light is the sum of all colors of light together. Black is the absence of any colors of light.

In addition to the RGB light color system there is the HLS (hue, lightness, saturation) system. Instead of mixing primary colors, you choose the color from a range of hues and then vary its lightness (brightness) and saturation (intensity).

You have three options for choosing a color for a light:

✦ **RGB:** The RGB (red-green-blue) system enables you to define colors by the amount of each primary light color. You can use the slider bars or type in a number from 0 to 1. When all three are set to 1, you get white light, the default.

✦ **True Color:** Choose Select Color to open the Select Color dialog box with the True Color tab on top, which lets you select colors either by an RGB or an HLS system. An HLS system determines color by hue, lightness, and saturation settings. Hue is the color. Lightness — or brightness — is the amount of white the color contains. Saturation is the amount of black the color contains. You can also click the Color Book tab to use a color from a color book. (See Chapter 11 for a full discussion of using true color and color books.)

✦ **ACI:** Choose Select Indexed to use the AutoCAD Color Index system. AutoCAD opens the Select Color dialog box with the Index Color tab on top so that you can choose a color.

Tip In most cases, white light is fine. You can get some unexpected results when using colored lights on colored objects.

Setting the North location

Click North Location to set which direction is north. Setting the North location is important if you want to use the Sun Angle Calculator to create a distant light and if you will create shadows. By default, north is the positive Y direction in the World Coordinate System. To change the default, type a new angle in the Angle box, use the slider bar, or click the "clock face" to specify the new angle. The positive Y axis is at 0 degrees, the positive X axis is at 90 degrees, and so on clockwise.

If you have saved a UCS, you can choose it from the list on the right side. AutoCAD uses the Y axis in that UCS as the default North direction.

Setting the ambient light

Ambient light is background light that has no source or target. It illuminates all surfaces in your drawing equally. It can, however, have a color. By default, ambient light is set at 0.30. Use the Intensity slide bar to change the setting or type a number from 0 to 1. Making ambient light too high results in a rendering that looks like an overexposed image. Use a lower setting for night scenes.

Creating a point light

A point light is equivalent to a typical light bulb or a candle. It comes from a specific location and radiates in all directions. A point light attenuates, meaning that the intensity lessens as the distance away from the light's source increases.

To create a new point light, choose Point Light from the drop-down list next to the New button. Then click New to open the New Point Light dialog box, shown in Figure 25-6.

Name

In the Light Name text box, type a name for the light, no more than eight characters long.

Tip Use a name that makes it clear that the light is a point light. Keep the name short. A simple sequence of P1, P2 is often sufficient. However, you could also use P-overhd and P-door or something similar.

Figure 25-6: The New Point Light dialog box

Attenuation

Set the attenuation, which is the manner in which the light loses intensity as the distance from its source increases. You have three choices:

✦ **None:** The light doesn't lose intensity.

✦ **Inverse Linear:** The light loses intensity in a linear manner, so that at 2 units from its source the light is half as intense and at 4 units away the light is one-quarter as intense. This is the default.

✦ **Inverse Square:** The light loses intensity at the square of the distance, so that at 2 units from its source the light is one-quarter as intense and at 4 units away the light is one-sixteenth as intense. Setting the attenuation to inverse square means that the intensity of the light drops off very quickly.

Intensity

Set the intensity, or brightness, of the light in the Intensity text box or use the slider bar. AutoCAD sets the maximum brightness based on the attenuation and the drawing extents.

✦ If you chose inverse linear attenuation, the maximum intensity is twice the distance from the lower-left corner to the upper-right corner of the extents of the drawing. The default is half of the maximum.

✦ If you chose inverse square attenuation, the maximum intensity is twice the square of the extents (the distance from the lower-left corner to the upper-right corner of the drawing).

✦ If you chose no attenuation, the maximum intensity is 1.

Tip Set the intensity to zero (0) to turn a light off. You can use this technique to switch a scene from a day view to a night view or to experiment with different lights without having to delete them.

Position

The position of the light is quite important, especially if you decide to create shadows. If you set the XY coordinates in plan view, be sure to set the proper Z coordinate as well. In an architectural drawing, you don't want your lights to be coming from the floor! However, in a mechanical drawing, it might be appropriate to light your model from any angle.

Note You can also set the transparency of materials. Use transparency for windows, for example. If you create an opaque lampshade and place a light inside it, light will get out only through the top and bottom.

Choose Show to see the current position and target of the light. Choose Modify to temporarily return to your drawing to pick a position.

Use object snaps or point filters to specify the position of your lights. If there are no objects available, work out the position in advance and place easily visible point objects there. You can then snap to the point objects using the Node object snap. You can also type the absolute coordinates. You can also use the From object snap to specify a coordinate based on a point on the model.

Color

Set the color of the light. Setting light color is discussed in the previously section "Assigning color to a light."

Shadows

I cover shadows in a separate section at the end of the discussion on lights. Check Shadow On if you want to create shadows. Choose Shadow Options to set the type of shadows you want, and set Shadow Map Size and Softness. Creating shadows adds significantly to rendering time.

When you are done creating the point light, click OK.

Creating a spotlight

A spotlight differs from a point light in that it has a direction. As a result, you not only specify its location but also its target — two coordinates instead of one. In addition, a spotlight has a brighter center called the hotspot. Outside the bright center is a ring of lesser brightness called the falloff. Figure 25-7 shows the same scene used previously in this chapter, but with one overhead spotlight.

Figure 25-7: A rendering with one spotlight overhead

To create a new spotlight, choose Spotlight from the drop-down list next to the New button in the Lights dialog box. Then click New to open the New Spotlight dialog box, shown in Figure 25-8.

Figure 25-8: The New Spotlight dialog box

Name

In the Light Name text box, type a name for the light. As mentioned earlier for point lights, use a name that makes it clear that the light is a spotlight. Keep the name short. A simple sequence of S1, S2 is often sufficient. However, you could also use S-roof and S-door or something similar, but the name cannot be more than eight characters long.

Hotspot and falloff

Set the hotspot and falloff angles. These angles emanate from the spotlight in the direction of the light's target. The maximum angle for both is 160 degrees. If the hotspot and falloff angles are the same, there is no falloff—the entire spotlight is bright. The defaults are 44 degrees for the hotspot and 45 degrees for the falloff. This does not leave very much falloff area. You may need to experiment to get the desired result.

To set the hotspot and falloff angles, type the angles in the text boxes or use the slider bars.

The rest of the options for a spotlight are the same as for a point light. Set the attenuation, intensity, position, color, and shadows. When you are done creating the spotlight, click OK.

Creating a distant light

A distant light is equivalent to the sun. Its rays come from so far away that for all practical purposes they are parallel. A distant light does not attenuate (unless you're drawing a model on Pluto).

To create a new distant light, choose Distant Light from the drop-down list next to the New button in the Lights dialog box. Then click New to open the New Distant Light dialog box, shown in Figure 25-9.

Name

In the Light Name text box, type a name for the light. As mentioned earlier for point lights and spotlights, use a name that makes it clear that the light is a distant light. Keep the name short.

Intensity

Set the intensity, or brightness, of the light in the Intensity text box or use the slider bar. The intensity can range from 0 to 1.

Tip

To turn the distant light off, set the intensity to zero (0). You can use this technique to switch a scene from a day view to a night view or to experiment with different lights.

Position

The position of the light is quite important, especially if you decide to create shadows. If you set the XY coordinates in plan view, be sure to set the proper Z coordinate as well. Generally, you position a distant light at the extents of your drawing.

You have three ways to specify the position of a distant light, as described in the following sections.

Figure 25-9: The New Distant Light dialog box

Azimuth and altitude

The *azimuth* is the angle in the XY plane—North is located at 0 degrees. Use a positive angle to move clockwise from North and a negative angle to move counterclockwise from North. Values can range from –180 to 180. (Both –180 and 180 would represent South.) The altitude is the angle from the XY plane. The slider bar lets you enter angles from 0 to 90, or you can type in angles from –90 to 90. (An altitude of –90 would mean the light was coming from beneath the model.)

Light source vector

Click Modify to return temporarily to your drawing. AutoCAD prompts you to enter the light direction to and from. This only sets the direction of the light. AutoCAD places the light outside the model.

Sun Angle Calculator

Click Sun Angle Calculator to open the Sun Angle Calculator dialog box, shown in Figure 25-10.

Use the Sun Angle Calculator when you are using a distant light to simulate the sun. The calculator locates the sun based on the latitude and longitude of the model's location and the time of day. Naturally, you would use this for architectural or surveying drawings. It's fun, too.

Figure 25-10: The Sun Angle Calculator dialog box

Use the left side of the dialog box to specify the information that Render needs to calculate the position of the sun. Follow these steps to complete the dialog box:

1. Type the date or use the slider bar.

2. Type the time using 24-hour format or use the slider bar.

3. Choose the time zone from the drop-down list. Check Daylight Savings if applicable.

4. Specify the latitude and longitude by typing them in or using the slider bars. Latitude goes from 0 degrees (the equator) to 90 degrees (the North or South Pole). Longitude goes from 0 degrees in Greenwich, England, to 180 degrees at the opposite side of the globe.

5. Specify the hemispheres — North or South and East or West.

6. If you don't know the latitude and/or longitude, click Geographic Location to open the Geographic Location dialog box, shown in Figure 25-11.

 Choose the continent from the drop-down list above the map. The appropriate map appears. (Try choosing various continents — it's a great way to travel.)

 Check Nearest Big City if your model is in a big city. Then click the map. The blue crosshairs jump to the nearest big city. You can also choose from the City list, and the blue crosshairs move to the proper location on the map.

 When you are done, click OK.

7. In the Sun Angle Calculator dialog box, click OK to return to the New Distant Light dialog box.

Note If you forgot to set the North location, choose North Location now. None of the sun calculations works properly if North is not properly defined. See "Setting the North location," earlier in this chapter.

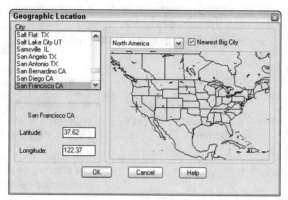

Figure 25-11: Use the Geographic Location dialog box to determine latitude and longitude for specific locations.

Color

Set the color of the light. Setting light color is discussed previously in the section "Assigning color to a light."

Shadows

Check Shadow On if you want to create shadows. Choose Shadow Options to set the type of shadows you want, and set Shadow Map Size and Softness. I cover shadows in the next section.

After you finish defining the distant light, click OK to return to the Lights dialog box.

Creating shadows

Shadows add greatly to the realism of your rendered image. They also add greatly to the rendering time.

Tip

For your practice renderings while you are creating lights and materials, turn shadows off in the Render dialog box. Shadows significantly add to rendering time, and you'll do a lot of waiting. When you are satisfied with the other settings, turn shadows on.

Types of shadows

AutoCAD creates three different types of shadows. Table 25-1 compares these types of shadows.

Table 25-1
Shadow Characteristics

Type	Which Renderer to Use	Description	Characteristics
Volumetric	Photo Real or Photo Raytrace	Based on volume of space cast by object's shadow	Hard edges, outlines are approximate, affected by color of transparent objects
Maps	Photo Real or Photo Raytrace	Based on the map size that you set	Soft edges you can adjust, not affected by the color of transparent objects
Raytraced	Photo Raytrace	Calculated by tracing the path of rays from a light	Hard edges, accurate outlines, affected by color of transparent objects

Base your choice of the type of shadows you want on the shadow characteristics and your needs.

Shadow settings

To create shadows, you need to turn on shadows in two places. When you create a new light, you check Shadow On in the dialog box you use to create the new light. In addition, you need to check Shadows in the Rendering Options section of the Render dialog box. This shadows option is available only if you choose Photo Real or Photo Raytrace as the type of rendering in the Render dialog box.

You set shadow settings when you create or modify a light source. Click Shadow Options to open the Shadow Options dialog box, shown in Figure 25-12.

Check Shadow Volumes/Raytrace Shadows to create volumetric shadows with Photo Real rendering and raytraced shadows with Photo Raytrace rendering. The shadow map settings are disabled.

Figure 25-12: The Shadow Options dialog box

If you uncheck Shadow Volumes/Raytrace Shadows, you can create a shadow map. You can set the shadow map size from 64 to 4,096 pixels. Larger map sizes are more accurate but take longer to render.

Set the shadow softness from 1 to 10 pixels. This determines the number of pixels at the edge of the shadow that are blended into the rest of the image, creating the soft effect. AutoCAD recommends using a setting from 2 to 4.

Choose Shadow Bounding Objects to temporarily return to the drawing to select objects for creating a bounding box that AutoCAD uses to clip the shadow maps.

On the CD-ROM

The drawing used in the following Step-by-Step exercise on creating lights and shadows, ab25-a.dwg, is in the Drawings folder of the *AutoCAD 2004 Bible* CD-ROM.

Step-by-Step: Creating Lights and Shadows

1. Open ab25-a.dwg from the CD-ROM. OSNAP should be on. Set a running object snap for endpoint.

2. Save the file as ab25-02.dwg in your AutoCAD Bible folder. If the Render toolbar is not open, right-click any toolbar and choose Render.

3. ✦ Choose Lights from the Render toolbar. Choose Point Light from the drop-down list next to the New button. Click New to open the New Point Light dialog box.

4. Type **P1** in the Light Name text box. Click Modify. AutoCAD returns you to your drawing. Click Pan Realtime and pan to the right a couple of times until you see the floor lamp, as shown in Figure 25-13. Press Esc to exit Pan mode. At the Enter light location <current>: prompt, pick the endpoint shown in Figure 25-13. AutoCAD returns you to the New Point Light dialog box.

5. Set the Intensity to 250. In the Color section, click Select Indexed and choose the yellow box. Notice that AutoCAD adjusts the RGB settings. Click OK.

6. Click Shadow On. Click OK to return to the Lights dialog box.

7. Choose Spotlight from the drop-down box and click New. Type **S1** in the Light Name text box. Set the Intensity to 250. Click Modify. At the Enter light target <current>: prompt, pick an endpoint at the top of the bowl on the table. At the Enter light location <current>: prompt, type **@0,0,5'** ↵ to place the light directly over the table as a light hanging from the ceiling.

8. Set the falloff to 55.00 and click Shadow On. Click OK to return to the Lights dialog box.

9. Choose Distant Light from the drop-down box and click New. Type **D1** in the Light Name text box. Click Shadow On.

Figure 25-13: Picking the point light location

10. Click Sun Angle Calculator. Set the date to 9/1. Set the time to 8:00 in the morning. (You're having breakfast.) Set the time zone to CST. Click Daylight Savings. Set the latitude to 41.00 and the longitude to 91.57. The two drop-down list boxes below should read North and West. Click Geographic Locator to see where you ended up. (If you typed in the right latitude and longitude, the blue cross should be in southeast Iowa.) Click OK until you return to the Lights dialog box.

11. In the Lights dialog box, click North location. Type **90** degrees in the text box. Click OK twice to return to your drawing.

12. Choose View ⇨ Named Views. Choose Render1, click Set Current, and click OK.

13. Choose Render from the Render toolbar. Crop Window should be unchecked. Change the Light Icon Scale to 24 so you can see the icons that AutoCAD creates at the location of each light you have created. (You should use the drawing scale factor.) In the Rendering Type drop-down list, choose Photo Real. Shadows should be unchecked. Click Render. The rendering should take less than a minute. It should look like Figure 25-14. There is more than enough light this time — but remember you wouldn't normally eat breakfast with all the lights on. Notice the effect of the yellow point light.

14. Choose Render again. Check Shadows in the Rendering Options section. Click Render. Notice that the rendering takes much longer. Wow! Lots of shadows. This rendering also makes it clear that no light is coming through the windows. See the "Creating Scenes" section to learn how to make materials transparent. The rendering should look like Figure 25-15.

15. Save your drawing. If you are continuing on to the next Step-by-Step exercise, keep this drawing open.

Figure 25-14: A rendering with lights but no shadows

Figure 25-15: The same rendering with shadows

Creating Scenes

Scenes help you manage lights and views. For example, you can create two scenes — the first with only a distant light to mimic the effect of exclusively natural light, and another with no distant light but with point lights and spotlights to create a night-time effect. You can also change the view so that you can look at the objects from different vantage points.

To create a scene, choose Scenes from the Render toolbar to open the Scenes dialog box, shown in Figure 25-16. This dialog box lists your scenes and enables you to create, modify, and delete scenes.

Figure 25-16: The Scenes dialog box

To create a new scene, follow these steps:

1. Click New to open the New Scene dialog box, shown in Figure 25-17. The New Scene dialog box lists all the saved views and all the lights you have created.

2. Type a name in the Scene Name text box, no more than eight characters long.

3. Choose a view. You can choose only one.

4. Choose the lights you want. Press Ctrl to choose more than one light. Press Shift to choose a range of lights. You can also choose *ALL* to quickly choose all the lights for the scene.

5. Click OK.

Figure 25-17: The New Scene dialog box

Your scene is now listed in the Scenes dialog box. Click OK again to return to your drawing. When you render the drawing, you can choose this scene from the Render dialog box.

The drawing used in the following Step-by-Step exercise on creating a scene, ab25-2.dwg, is in the Results folder of the *AutoCAD 2004 Bible* CD-ROM.

Step-by-Step: Creating a Scene

1. If you have ab25-02.dwg open, use it. Otherwise, open it from your AutoCAD Bible folder or the Results folder of the CD-ROM.

2. Save the file as ab25-03.dwg in your AutoCAD Bible folder. If the Render toolbar is not open, right-click any toolbar and choose Render.

3. Choose Scenes from the Render toolbar. Click New in the Scenes dialog box to open the New Scene dialog box.

4. Type **morning** in the Scene Name text box.

5. Choose RENDER1 from the Views list.

6. Choose D1 and P1 from the Lights list, pressing the Ctrl key while you select the second light.

7. Click OK twice to return to the drawing.

8. Save the drawing. If you are continuing on to the next Step-by-Step exercise, keep it open.

Working with Materials

Working with materials involves two steps — adding them to the drawing and attaching them to objects. Designing appropriate materials is an important part of the rendering process and greatly affects the results. Materials interact with lights. For example, shiny materials reflect light differently than dull materials because shiny materials create highlights. The object's color affects how light appears on it as well.

Adding materials

AutoCAD comes with a large selection of materials. You can modify these to create your own materials. To add materials to the drawing, choose Materials Library from the Render toolbar to open the Materials Library dialog box, shown in Figure 25-18.

Figure 25-18: The Materials Library dialog box

Working with lists of materials

Materials are saved in a file with the extension .mli (materials library). The default materials library is render.mli. The left side of the Materials Library dialog box represents materials in the current drawing. The right side of the dialog box represents the entire list of materials provided by AutoCAD.

In the Current Drawing section, you can:

✦ Click Save As to save the list of materials in the current drawing in an .mli file.

✦ Click Purge to delete all the materials in the list from the drawing.

In the Current Library section, you can:

✦ Click Save to save changes to the entire library list in the MLI file in the current folder.

✦ Click Save As to save the entire current library list in a new MLI file in any location.

✦ Click Open to open a different library list and use its materials.

Importing and previewing materials

To add existing materials to your drawing, follow these steps:

1. Choose a material from the Current Library list on the right side of the dialog box.

2. Click Import.

3. Choose the material from the Current Drawing list.

4. From the Preview drop-down list, choose the preview type of either Cube or Sphere, based on whether the object you want to use the material for is flat or curved.

5. Click Preview to see a sample of the material.

6. Repeat Steps 1 through 5 until you have all the materials you want.

7. Click OK.

Tip

If you don't find the exact material you want, import the closest one you can find. You can then create a new material based on that material. The next section explains how to edit existing materials.

You can choose a range of materials by holding down Shift and clicking the first and last materials in the range. You can choose any nonconsecutive materials by holding down Ctrl and clicking the materials you want.

If you don't like a material that you have imported, highlight it and click Delete. Use the Export option to save materials you have created in the drawing to the materials library file. When you click OK to close the Materials Library dialog box, AutoCAD asks you if you want to save the changes you have made to the materials library file. Saving the changes updates the file.

On the CD-ROM

The drawing used in the following Step-by-Step exercise on importing materials, `ab25-3.dwg`, is in the `Results` folder of the *AutoCAD 2004 Bible* CD-ROM.

Step-by-Step: Importing Materials

1. If you have `ab25-03.dwg` open from the previous exercise, use it. Otherwise, open it from your AutoCAD Bible folder (if you did the exercise) or the `Results` folder of the CD-ROM.

2. Save the file as `ab25-04.dwg` in your `AutoCAD Bible` folder. If the Render toolbar is not open, right-click any toolbar and choose Render.

3. Choose Materials Library from the Render toolbar. Hold down Ctrl, and scroll as necessary to choose Beige Plastic, Green Glass, Light Wood Tile, Pink Marble, Stitched Pattern, White Matte, Wood Med. Ash, Wood White Ash, and Yellow Plastic. Click Import.

4. From the left list, choose Pink Marble. Choose Cube from the Preview drop-down list and click Preview to see the result. Do the same with Stitched Pattern.

5. Preview Green Glass with the Sphere.

6. Click OK. Save your drawing. If you are continuing to the next Step-by-Step exercise, keep the drawing open.

Creating your own materials

After you import materials from the materials library, you can modify them to create your own materials. Choose Materials from the Render toolbar to open the Materials dialog box, shown in Figure 25-19.

Notice that you can click Materials Library in this dialog box to open the Materials Library dialog box. You can therefore use the Materials dialog box to manage the entire process of importing, creating, and attaching materials. You can preview imported materials in this dialog box as well.

Figure 25-19: The Materials dialog box

When you create a new material, you have three choices:

✦ You can modify an existing material.

✦ You can duplicate an existing material and then make modifications to the copy, leaving the original material intact.

✦ You can start from scratch and create an entirely new material.

The dialog box that AutoCAD opens when you choose one of the preceding options depends on what you choose from the drop-down list below the New button. You have four choices: standard, marble, granite, and wood.

✦ Standard creates a standard material.

✦ Marble creates a material that mimics marble. In this dialog box you specify turbulence and sharpness of the veins as well as the scale of the veins to the entire object of marble.

✦ Granite creates a material that mimics granite. In this dialog box you can specify up to four colors and their sharpness (distinctness) as well as the scale of the texture relative to the entire granite object.

✦ Wood creates a material that mimics wood. In this dialog box you specify the light/dark ratio of the grain, the ring density and width, and the scale of the rings relative to the entire wood object.

When you choose a method of creating a new material, whether by modifying, duplicating, or creating from scratch, AutoCAD opens the dialog box appropriate to the material you have chosen. Figure 25-20 shows the New Standard Material dialog box.

Figure 25-20: The New Standard Material dialog box

Unless you are modifying an existing material, you first give the material a name in the Material Name text box.

You use this dialog box by choosing the attributes listed on the left side one by one and then specifying the values for each attribute from the choices on the right.

Color/Pattern

The color is the basic color of the object. The reflection of light off the object (called diffuse reflection) is determined by this color. You set the color in the Color section of the dialog box, using one of four methods:

✦ Choose By ACI (AutoCAD Color Index). This option enables you to set the color to the color of the object in the drawing. You must uncheck this to choose one of the three other methods.

✦ Choose RGB from the Color System drop-down list to specify the color using the red-green-blue system. These are the three primary light colors. For each color you can type in a value from 0 to 1 or use the slider bars. When all three are set to 1, you get white light.

✦ Choose HLS from the Color System drop-down list to specify the color using the hue, lightness, and saturation system. Hue is the color; lightness — or brightness — is the amount of white the color contains; saturation is the amount of black the color contains.

✦ Click the color swatch to open the Windows Color dialog box, letting you specify a color using either the RGB or the HLS system.

In addition to setting the color, you set the value. The value affects the surface finish and interacts with the reflection value. For example, AutoCAD recommends using a color value of 0.7 and a reflection value of 0.3 for a dull finish and reversing the values for a shiny finish. You can type a value or use the slider bar. If you choose a bitmap (raster) file, the color becomes a pattern. See the sidebar on "Mapping" for more information.

Ambient

The Ambient color and value affect the color reflected by ambient light. Remember that you set the amount of ambient light when you created lights. You can click the Lock check box in the Color section of the dialog box to lock the ambient and reflection colors to the main color. (You cannot use Lock if you checked By ACI as the color.)

Reflection

The reflection setting affects highlights created by light that shines on the object. To create a shiny object, you can use a reflection value of 0.7 with a color value of 0.3. Shiny objects often create a white highlight — for this effect, set the color to white by setting red, green, and blue to 1. You can also choose a bitmap file to create a reflection map. See the sidebar on "Mapping" for more information.

Roughness

Roughness has no color setting — you only set a value. A rough surface produces smaller highlights. Use a lower value to create smaller highlights. If you chose a zero value for reflection, the roughness setting is not used.

Transparency

The transparency setting enables you to create transparent or translucent materials. You set the value from 0 to 1. Higher values mean greater transparency. Using transparency increases rendering time. You can choose a bitmap to create an opacity map. See the sidebar on "Mapping" for more information.

Mapping

AutoCAD lets you project a 2D image onto the surface of a 3D object. This is called *mapping*. You must use the Photo Real or Photo Raytrace rendering types to render with mappings. The 2D images are bitmap (raster) files that can be in several file formats, such as TGA, BMP, TIF, and JPEG. AutoCAD provides a large number of TGA files. To locate them, choose Tools ⇨ Options and click the Files tab. Double-click `Texture Maps Search Path`. (You need to do a full or custom installation of AutoCAD to get all the texture maps.) You can actually place up to four bitmaps onto an object. When you create a material, you can add bitmaps to the Color/Pattern, Reflection, Transparency, and Bump Map characteristics of a material.

Four kinds of maps correspond to the four characteristics:

✦ Texture maps place a pattern of colors onto the object. When you include a bitmap in the Color/Pattern definition, you turn a plain color into a pattern.

✦ Reflection maps place a scene on the surface of a reflective object, in the same way that you can see yourself reflected in a pool of water. Add a bitmap to the Reflection definition.

✦ Opacity maps mimic areas of opacity and transparency. Add a bitmap to the Transparency definition.

✦ Bump maps create the effect of varying heights. Choose Bump Maps and choose a bitmap file.

AutoCAD comes with a number of materials that include maps. In the Materials Library dialog box, check out the Bumpywhite stone and Checker textures, for example. As their names make clear, the first material is a bump map and the second a texture map. Import and preview them to see how they look. Using these materials saves you the task of specifying a bitmap file.

Bitmap Blend determines how much the bitmap is used. The values range from zero (0) to 1. For example, a 1.0 value for a bump map gives you the full value of the bumps. A lower value creates lower bumps.

Choose Adjust Bitmap to open the Adjust Material Bitmap Placement dialog box. Here you set the offset of the origin of the bitmap and the scale. The scale is the number of times the bitmap fits onto the object. If you are unfamiliar with the bitmap, you'll need to experiment. You can try various options and click Preview to see the results. Bitmapping uses U and V axes, which are like X and Y axes but can have any direction and origin. Click Maintain Aspect Ratio to keep the U and V scales equal.

By default, bitmaps are tiled, which means that if the scale is less than 1, AutoCAD repeats the pattern to cover the entire object. You can also crop, which creates a decal effect—the pattern is placed just once on the object.

Refraction

Refraction only applies to Photo Raytrace rendering when you have a transparent (or translucent) material. Refraction is the bending of a light wave when it passes through an object to an object of another density. A higher value increases the refraction.

Bump Map

Bump maps create the effect of varying heights on the surface of the object — in other words, bumps. You use the bottom part of the dialog box to choose the bump map and for bump map settings. See the sidebar "Mapping" for more information about bump maps.

As you complete the dialog box, you can press Preview and see the result as a sphere or cube at any time. When you like the results you see with Preview, click OK.

On the CD-ROM The drawing used in the following Step-by-Step exercise on creating materials, ab25-4.dwg, is in the Results folder of the *AutoCAD 2004 Bible* CD-ROM.

Step-by-Step: Creating Materials

1. If you have ab25-04.dwg open from the previous exercise, use it. Otherwise, open it from your AutoCAD Bible folder (if you did the exercise) or the Results folder of the CD-ROM.

2. Save the file as ab25-05.dwg in your AutoCAD Bible folder. If the Render toolbar is not open, right-click any toolbar and choose Render.

3. Choose Materials from the Render toolbar. The materials that were imported in the previous Step-by-Step exercise are listed on the left. Choose Yellow Plastic and click Duplicate.

4. In the Material Name text box of the New Standard Material dialog box, type **Yellow Cheese**.

5. With Color/Pattern selected from the Attributes section of the dialog box, click the color swatch to the right of the Color System drop-down list. In the Color dialog box, click the Index Color tab and pick the yellow box. Click OK.

6. Choose Ambient from the Attributes section. Click Lock in the Color section. The color changes to the same yellow as the Color/Pattern swatch.

7. Choose Reflection. Change the value to 0.10 because cheese isn't very shiny. Click Lock here as well.

8. Choose Roughness. Change the value to 0.75.

 You can omit transparency because its default value is zero (0). Refraction is irrelevant without a transparency setting.

9. Omit this step and Step 10 if you don't have a full installation or a custom installation that includes textures. Preview the yellow cheese on a cube. Choose Bump Map from the Attributes section. Choose Find File at the bottom right of the dialog box. In the Bitmap File dialog box, the `Textures` folder should be current. (If not, find the `Textures` folder inside the main AutoCAD folder and double-click.) Change the Files of Type drop-down list to `*.tga`. Choose `bmps.tga` and click Open. Change the Bitmap Blend to 30. Click Preview again to see the difference. Note that the bumps are too big.

10. Click Adjust Bitmap. In the Adjust Bitmap Material Placement dialog box, check Maintain Aspect Ratio. Change the scale to 2 and click Preview using the cube. The bumps are smaller now. Click OK three times to return to your drawing.

11. Save your drawing.

Attaching materials

After you import, create, and modify the materials you need, you can attach them to objects. AutoCAD lets you attach materials by object, layer, or color. To attach any material, follow these steps:

1. Choose Materials from the Render toolbar.

2. Choose the material from the list of materials.

3. Use one of these methods to attach the material:

 • Click Attach to attach a material by selecting the object or objects. AutoCAD temporarily returns you to your drawing and prompts you to select objects.

 • Click By ACI (AutoCAD Color Index) to attach a material by its color in the drawing. AutoCAD opens the Attach by AutoCAD Color Index dialog box, which lets you choose a color, or colors, by their numbers.

 • Click By Layer to attach a material by layer. AutoCAD opens the Attach by Layer dialog box, which lets you choose a layer or layers.

Tip

Attaching materials by layer can be a very efficient method. It requires some planning in advance. For example, if you have a block that is a chair, and if you create it so that the legs are on one layer and the seat and back are on a second layer, then you can easily attach a wood-like material to the legs and a decorative pattern to the seat and back.

You can assign a material to an object, to its layer, and to its color, which would mean that the object has three materials. AutoCAD gives priority to direct attachments by object, then to attachments by color, and finally to attachments by layer.

The drawing used in the following Step-by-Step exercise on attaching materials, ab20-b.dwg, is in the Drawings folder of the *AutoCAD 2004 Bible* CD-ROM.

Step-by-Step: Attaching Materials

1. Open ab25-b.dwg from the CD-ROM.

2. Save the file as ab25-06.dwg in your AutoCAD Bible folder. If the Render toolbar is not open, right-click any toolbar and choose Render. This is the same drawing used earlier in the chapter, but all the materials have been imported and modified, and some materials have been attached to objects. Also, the table and chairs have been separated into appropriate layers.

3. Choose Materials from the Render toolbar. Click By Layer. In the Attach by Layer dialog box, choose PINK MARBLE from the Select a Material list. Choose TABLE_TOP from the Select Layer list. Click Attach. The PINK MARBLE material appears next to the TABLE_TOP layer.

4. Choose STITCHED PATTERN from the left list and CUSHIONS from the right list and click Attach. In the same way, attach WOOD-WHITE ASH to the LEGS layer. Click OK.

5. In the Materials dialog box, choose GREEN GLASS and click Attach. AutoCAD finds the bowl, which has already been attached to the GREEN GLASS material and displays the Gathering objects...1 found. Select objects to attach "GREEN GLASS" to: prompt. Select the plate on the table and press Enter to return to the dialog box.

6. Click OK to return to your drawing.

7. Save your drawing. Keep it open if you are continuing to the next Step-by-Step exercise.

Using Backgrounds

AutoCAD offers some sophisticated features for adding backgrounds to your rendering. For example, you can place a picture of the sky in the background. You can also add landscape features such as trees and bushes. This section covers the basics of backgrounds. You have a choice of four types of backgrounds:

✦ **Solid** places a solid color in the background. You might use solid black for a night scene.

✦ **Gradient** creates a background of up to three colors in a graded blend.

✦ **Image** places an image in the background (for example, an image of the sky).

✦ **Merge** lets you combine your rendering with the image you currently have on your screen.

To create a background, choose Background from the Render toolbar to open the Background dialog box, shown in Figure 25-21.

If you choose Solid, you can use the current AutoCAD background (usually white or black) or define a color using the same color controls you use for lights and materials, explained earlier in this chapter. If you choose Gradient, you set separate top, middle, and bottom colors. Click the color swatch of the color you want to work with to set its color. Then use the horizon setting to determine the center of the gradient. The height determines, in percentage form, where the second color starts. For example, 33 percent would create three equal levels of color. If you want only two colors, set the height to zero (0). Use Rotation to rotate the gradient.

Figure 25-21: The Background dialog box

If you choose Image, use the Image section to specify a file. If you did a full installation (or a custom installation including textures), you have a number of .tga files to choose from in the \Textures subfolder of AutoCAD. Of course, you can use your own files. You can use the following file types:

BMP JPG TGA PNG

GIF PCX TIF

Merge uses the current AutoCAD background (usually solid white or black) as the background for the rendering. It doesn't require any settings.

You can choose an additional file in the Environment section (at the bottom of the dialog box) to create reflection and refraction effects. You can use the same types of files for environment as for images. AutoCAD maps the image onto a sphere surrounding the scene.

Foggy landscapes

The landscape commands enable you to create and edit landscapes. AutoCAD comes with a small library of trees, bushes, people, and a DO NOT ENTER road sign. Choose Landscape New from the Render toolbar, choose an item, and preview it. When you find one that you like, set the geometry. Single Face results in quicker rendering than Crossing Faces but is less realistic. Choose View Aligned if you want the object to always face the viewer, like a tree. You might uncheck this for the road sign—you don't want the sign to face the viewer from both directions. Set the height (usually in inches) and click Position to place it in your drawing.

Note: When you place the landscape object, it appears as a triangle or a rectangle. You don't see the object until you render the view. Choose Landscape Edit to edit the characteristics of an existing landscape object. Choose Landscape Library to edit, delete, and add landscape objects.

Choose Fog from the Render toolbar to open the Fog/Depth Cue dialog box. Fog is used to give a sense of distance because objects in the distance often do not appear to be as clear as those close up. Choose Enable Fog to turn fog on. You set the color, near and far distances (where the fog starts and ends), and near and far percentages of fog (how much fog there should be at the near and far distances).

On the CD-ROM The drawing used in the following Step-by-Step exercise on adding a background, ab25-6.dwg, is in the Results folder of the *AutoCAD 2004 Bible* CD-ROM. The graphic file, sky.gif, which you may or may not need, is in the Drawings folder of the CD-ROM. See the instructions in the exercise.

Step-by-Step: Adding a Background

1. If you have ab25-06.dwg open, use it. Otherwise, open it from your AutoCAD Bible folder if you did the previous exercise or from the Results folder of the CD-ROM.

2. Save the file as ab25-07.dwg in your AutoCAD Bible folder.

3. If you did a full AutoCAD installation or a custom installation including the textures, choose Background from the Render toolbar. If not, find sky.gif on the CD-ROM and copy it to AutoCAD's \Support subfolder. Then choose Background from the Render toolbar.

4. Choose Image at the top of the Background dialog box.

5. In the Image section, choose Find File.

6. Open the Textures folder (to locate this folder, choose Tools ➪ Options, click the Files tab, and double-click the Texture Maps Search Path) and choose sky. tga (make sure the Files of Type drop-down list box says *.tga) or choose sky.gif from AutoCAD's \Support subfolder. Click Open.

7. Click Preview. AutoCAD displays the file.

8. Click OK. You won't see the result until you render the drawing.

9. Save your drawing. If you are continuing to the next Step-by-Step exercise, keep the drawing open.

Doing the Final Render

You are finally ready to render. Preparing to render can be a long process. If you want, you can choose Render Preferences from the Render toolbar first to open the Rendering Preferences dialog box. This dialog box is an exact copy of the Render dialog box and lets you preset the rendering settings. However, you can also make all these settings in the Render dialog box.

To render, choose Render from the Render toolbar. This opens the Render dialog box, shown in Figure 25-22.

Figure 25-22: The Render dialog box

This dialog box has the following components:

✦ From the Rendering Type drop-down list, choose the type of rendering you want.

✦ In the Scene to Render box, choose a scene.

✦ In the Rendering Procedure section, check one of the options if you want. Query for Selections means that AutoCAD asks you to select objects. Use this to test a rendering on one or more objects. Choose Crop Window to choose a window to render. Choose Skip Render Dialog to render immediately without even opening the dialog box (the next time) — choose Render Preferences on the Render toolbar to change this option when you want the Render dialog box back again.

✦ Set the light icon scale. Use the drawing scale factor for this.

✦ Set the smoothing angle. The smoothing angle determines the angle at which AutoCAD assumes an edge as opposed to a smooth curve. The default is 45 degrees. A lower angle would result in more edges.

✦ In the Rendering Options section, check Smooth Shade to smooth out a multi-edged object. AutoCAD blends colors across adjacent faces.

✦ Check Apply Materials to use the materials you imported and attached.

✦ Check Shadows to generate shadows. You can only create shadows with the Photo Real and Photo Raytrace rendering types.

✦ Check Render Cache to save rendering information in a file. AutoCAD can reuse this information for subsequent renderings, saving time.

✦ Click More Options to open a dialog box that varies with the type of rendering. Usually, you can use the defaults, but you can click Help to get an explanation of each item.

✦ In the Destination section, choose where you want the rendering to appear. The default is Viewport. If you have one viewport, the rendering covers the entire drawing area. If you are using several viewports, the rendering appears in the active viewport. You can also render to the render window. The render window is a regular Microsoft Windows window that lets you copy the rendering to the clipboard or save the rendering as a bitmap (.bmp) file. Finally, you can save the rendering directly to a file.

✦ Use the Sub Sampling drop-down box to set the sampling of pixels that AutoCAD renders. The default is 1:1, which means all the pixels are rendered. You can speed up the rendering by choosing another ratio.

✦ The Render dialog box has buttons to take you to the Background and Fog/Depth Cue dialog boxes if you decide at the last minute that you want to use these features.

When you have finished the settings, click Render to render the drawing.

On the CD-ROM

The drawing used in the following Step-by-Step exercise on creating a final rendering, ab25-7.dwg, is in the Results folder of the *AutoCAD 2004 Bible* CD-ROM.

Step-by-Step: Creating a Final Rendering

1. If you have `ab25-07.dwg` open, use it. Otherwise, open it from your `AutoCAD Bible` folder if you did the previous exercise or from the `Results` folder of the CD-ROM.

2. Save the file as `ab25-08.dwg` in your `AutoCAD Bible` folder.

3. Choose Lights from the Render toolbar. In the Lights box, choose P1 and click Modify. Change the intensity to 200 and click OK twice to return to your drawing. This is the type of adjustment you often make when doing the final rendering.

4. Choose Render from the Render toolbar.

5. Make sure that Rendering Type is set to Photo Real.

6. Set Scene to Render to MORNING. Check Shadows.

7. Click Render. Wait until AutoCAD finishes the rendering. Look at those shadows! Look at the transparent green bowl with the orange in it. Note the sky image outside the window. Okay, so the pink marble is a bit gaudy.

8. To get rid of the ugly UCS icon, choose View ⇨ Display ⇨ UCS Icon ⇨ On.

9. The rendering should look like Figure 25-23, only a lot better because you see it in color on your screen. Save your drawing.

Figure 25-23: The final rendering with shadows, transparent objects, and a background

Thanks to Autodesk for the `sky.gif` *file. This material has been reprinted with permission from and under the copyright of Autodesk, Inc.*

Remember that rendering is a trial-and-error process. Don't expect to get it right the first time. You can probably see several areas for improvement. At this point, you would go back and tweak the lights, materials, and so on until you were satisfied.

On the CD-ROM AccuRender is a rendering program that offers additional rendering capabilities. Look for it in \Software\Chap25\AccuRender.

Statistics

Choose Statistics on the Render toolbar to open a window that lists statistics relating to your rendering. You can save these to a file. This information is very helpful if you can't remember which rendering type you used or if you want to compare the time it takes to render a scene using different options. Figure 25-24 shows an example.

Figure 25-24: A statistics listing of a rendering

Saving rendered images

You can save your rendered images and redisplay them at another time. You can also use saved rendered images in other applications and print them from those applications. After rendering to a viewport, choose Tools ➪ Display Image ➪ Save. In the Save Image dialog box, choose the file type .bmp, .tga, or .tif.

You can change the size and placement (offset) of the image or accept the defaults. Click OK. AutoCAD opens the Image File dialog box so that you can specify a file name. After selecting a file, click OK again.

After rendering to a render window, choose File ⇨ Save from that window's menu and enter a file name. Click OK. AutoCAD saves the image as a .bmp (bitmap) file.

To redisplay a rendered image, choose Tools ⇨ Display Image ⇨ View. Choose the file and click Open in the Replay dialog box. You have the opportunity to crop the image or you can accept the original size. AutoCAD displays the image. Do a regen to return to your regular drawing display.

You can import these saved rendered images back into your drawing. Figure 25-25 shows three floating viewports. One of the views shows the rendered image.

 Cross-Reference See Chapter 27 for detailed instructions on importing images. In AutoCAD 2004, you can now plot rendered viewports. See Chapter 17.

Figure 25-25: You can include your rendered images in your drawings.

Unloading Render

When you render, a Render window may open, minimized.

 New Feature You can now close the Render window by clicking its Close box.

Closing the Render window when you are finished rendering frees up memory for other tasks.

Summary

In this chapter, I cover the process of rendering. You read the following:

✦ Creating lights

✦ Creating scenes

✦ Importing and creating materials

✦ Attaching materials

✦ Using backgrounds

✦ Rendering a drawing

This chapter ends Part IV, "Drawing in Three Dimensions." Part V, "Organizing and Managing Drawings," explains how to manage drawings, work with other applications and file types, and use AutoCAD on the Internet.

✦ ✦ ✦

Organizing and Managing Drawings

◆ ◆ ◆ ◆

◆ ◆ ◆ ◆

Part V is all about how to manage drawings. In Chapter 26, I discuss keeping control of your drawings by using the DesignCenter, the new Tool palettes, and the new Communication Center, while also setting and maintaining standards, keeping track of your drawings, handling errors and crashes, and working with prior AutoCAD releases. Chapter 27 explains how to interface with other applications and file formats, including raster (bitmap) images. Finally, Chapter 28 covers getting your drawings onto the Internet.

Keeping Control of Your Drawings

When you create a drawing in AutoCAD, you not only create objects, you create a complex structure to support those objects. You create named blocks, layers, layouts, text styles, dimension styles, and linetypes to help define those objects. You spend a lot of time creating them, too! All of these named drawing components can be reused and organized for greater efficiency.

Having standards for named drawing components, such as layers and text styles is important for consistency and readability. AutoCAD offers a comprehensive system for maintaining CAD standards. Security is also important and AutoCAD 2004 offers new features to help.

You also need to keep track of your drawings and make sure that they are accessible. Archiving and repair procedures are important in any CAD environment.

Accessing Drawing Components with the DesignCenter

I mention the DesignCenter many times in this book—for example, in Chapter 11 on layers and Chapter 18 on blocks. In this chapter, I cover the DesignCenter in detail. You can use the DesignCenter to easily drag named drawing components from one drawing to another. You can access this *drawing content* from drawings on your hard drive, on a network drive, or over the Internet. You never need to re-create them again. Autodesk calls this *mining your design*. You can even drag raster images directly into your drawing.

You can do the following with the DesignCenter:

✦ Browse and insert named drawing components, including blocks, xrefs, layers, text styles, dimension styles, linetypes, and layouts. You can also access custom objects created by third-party applications that work with AutoCAD.

✦ Create shortcuts to drawings and locations that you use most.

✦ Search for drawings and named drawing components.

✦ Open drawings by dragging them into the drawing area.

✦ View and insert raster image files by dragging them into the drawing area.

Navigating with the DesignCenter

To open the DesignCenter, choose DesignCenter from the Standard toolbar or choose Tools ➪ DesignCenter. As a shortcut, press Ctrl+2. The DesignCenter appears as shown in Figure 26-1.

New Feature

The DesignCenter has been updated to use the new palette interface — the same one you see in the Properties palette. Four tabs provide access to folders, open drawings, history, and the new DC Online, where you can find content provided by Autodesk, manufacturers and other users.

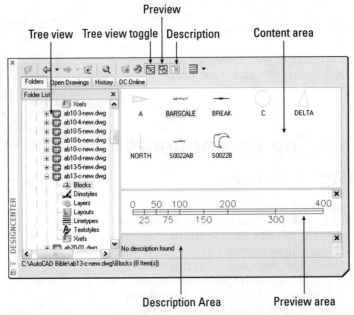

Figure 26-1: The DesignCenter with the Folders tab displayed

The Folders tab displays a tree view of any location—your hard drive, network, or the Internet—that you can access. This tree view is very similar to Windows Explorer. Click the plus sign next to a drive or folder to display its contents. Use the vertical scrollbar to display any location.

A selected drawing displays its named components in the content area on the right side of the palette. You can also click the plus sign next to a drawing to see (in the tree view side) the named components it contains. Then click a component type, such as blocks, to see a list of the blocks in the drawing, as shown in Figure 26-1. Click Preview on the DesignCenter toolbar to see a preview in the preview pane of blocks, drawings, and raster images. Click Description to display a description, if one is saved.

After you narrow your search, you may want to click Tree View Toggle to toggle off the tree view, hiding the navigation pane. By default, the navigation pane displays your desktop, meaning the files and folders on your hard drive and network. To narrow down your search, you can click two other tabs from the DesignCenter:

✦ Open Drawings displays currently open drawings.

✦ History displays the most recently opened drawings.

Finding named components and drawings

What do you do if you don't know the location of the drawing you want? Suppose you know the name of the layer, but not which drawing it is in. The DesignCenter includes a Search feature to help you out.

Choose Search from the DesignCenter toolbar to open the Search window, shown in Figure 26-2. (You can also right-click in the Content area and choose Search.)

Here's how to use the Search window:

✦ Click the Look for drop-down list to choose what you are looking for. You can look for blocks, dimension styles, drawings, drawings and blocks, hatch pattern files, hatch patterns, layers, layouts, linetypes, text styles, and xrefs.

✦ Click the In drop-down list to specify the drive you want to look in. By default the Search subfolders check box is checked so that AutoCAD searches all folders and subfolders within the drive.

✦ Use the tabbed area to specify the name of the components you are looking for. The tab's name and content changes depending on what you chose in the Look for drop-down box. For example, if you chose Layers, the tab is called Layers and asks you for the name of the layer. If you are looking for drawings, you have three tabs to work with:

- The **Drawings** tab enables you to choose to look for a drawing by file name (the default), title, subject, author, or keywords. Choose one of these options in the In the field(s) drop-down list. Then type the text you want to look for in the Search for the Word(s) text box. You can use the wildcards * (to substitute for any number of characters) and ? (to substitute for any one character). Specifying a drawing's title, subject, and keywords is discussed later in this chapter.

- The **Date Modified** tab enables you to search by the last date the file was saved or modified. You can specify a range of dates or look in the last *x* days or months.

- The **Advanced** tab enables you to search for text in drawing descriptions, block names, attribute tags, and attribute values. You can also search here by drawing size.

✦ When you have created your specifications, click Search Now.

Figure 26-2: Use the Search window to locate drawings and drawing components.

Cross-Reference See Chapter 18 for information on creating block descriptions when you create a block. The main reason for creating a block description is to display it in the DesignCenter and to be able to use it in a search on the Advanced tab, as just described.

Using the Favorites folder

The Favorites folder is a Windows convention that helps you to find files that you use often. This folder contains shortcuts to actual files. The files remain in their original locations. Choosing a file from the Favorites folder has the same effect as choosing the file from its source location.

AutoCAD 2004 creates an Autodesk subfolder within the Favorites folder, where you can store shortcuts to drawings and other files that you use often. You can then easily open the Favorites folder and find these files. Favorites is one possible place to keep drawings that contain block libraries.

To add a shortcut to Favorites, right-click the drawing (or other file) in the DesignCenter and choose Add to Favorites.

 Caution If you right-click in the content pane and choose Add to Favorites, AutoCAD adds a shortcut to the entire content of the folder. This is great for adding all the items in a folder at once, but if you do it inadvertently, you could end up with lots of junk in Favorites. To add one item, remember to select it first.

To access the drawings in Favorites, click Favorites on the DesignCenter toolbar. You can also right-click the content pane and choose Favorites. AutoCAD displays the Favorites folder in the content pane.

To move, copy, or delete shortcuts from Favorites, right-click the Content pane and choose Organize Favorites.

Accessing named drawing components

As soon as you have the item you need in the content area, you need to insert it into your drawing. If you used the Search window to locate a file, you can also insert directly from results you get. You can either drag the item onto the drawing area or right-click it and choose an option. Sometimes these two methods provide slightly different results. In this section, I explain how to insert drawing components into your drawing.

Inserting drawings

You can insert an entire drawing into your drawing. Choose the drawing's folder in the navigation pane so that the drawing appears in the content area. Drag the drawing's icon onto the drawing area. AutoCAD prompts you for an insertion point, scale, and rotation angle, using the -INSERT command, which prompts you on the command line.

If you right-click the drawing, you can choose to insert the drawing as a block or attach it as an xref.

Opening drawings

You can open a drawing using the DesignCenter. Display the drawing in the content pane, right-click it, and choose Open in Application Window. AutoCAD opens the drawing, keeping your current drawing open as well.

Inserting blocks

In Chapter 5, I explain that you can use the Units dialog box (choose Format ➪ Units) to set a unit, such as inches, for automatically scaling drawings when they are inserted from the DesignCenter.

You can insert blocks in two ways:

✦ If you drag the block's icon onto the drawing area, AutoCAD uses Autoscaling, which compares the current drawing's units with those of the block and scales the block appropriately, using the value set in the Units dialog box. AutoCAD uses default scale and rotation.

✦ If you double-click the block's icon or right-click it and choose Insert Block, AutoCAD opens the Insert dialog box where you can specify the insertion point, scale, and rotation.

Inserting raster images

A raster image is a bitmap graphic file. You can insert raster images directly into your drawing—they don't have to be within an AutoCAD drawing.

Cross-Reference
See Chapter 27 for more information on raster images, including determining which type of files you can import, attaching images, clipping images, and controlling how they are displayed.

To attach a raster image, drag its icon onto the drawing area. AutoCAD prompts you for an insertion point, scale, and rotation angle on the command line.

Tip
Knowing the appropriate scale of an image before inserting it is often hard. When you move the cursor at the `Specify scale factor or [Unit] <1>:` prompt, you can see a bounding box that will help you visualize the resulting size of the image.

Attaching an xref

To attach or overlay an xref, right-click its icon and choose Attach Xref to open the External Reference dialog box. Choose either Attachment or Overlay in the Reference Type section. Specify an insertion point, scale, and rotation (or choose to specify them on-screen) and click OK.

If you drag the xref onto the drawing area, AutoCAD provides prompts on the command line similar to those of the -INSERT command.

Inserting layers

To insert a layer into a drawing, drag its icon onto the drawing area. You can drag multiple layers at one time. To select a contiguous group, click the first layer, press and hold Shift, and click the last layer. To select individual multiple layers, click the first layer, press and hold Ctrl, and click any other layer you want to insert. You can also double-click a layer to insert it.

AutoCAD does not check for duplicate layer names. If you try to insert a layer with the same name as a layer in your current drawing, you see a message: Layer(s) added. Duplicate definitions will be ignored. You should check for duplicate layer names before trying to insert layers from the DesignCenter.

Inserting content from DC Online

The new DC Online tab provides access to online resources, including standard parts and manufacturers' information. Figure 26-3 shows the outline of the DC Online content. To insert any content, select it and drag it into your drawing. Follow the prompts for insertion point and so on.

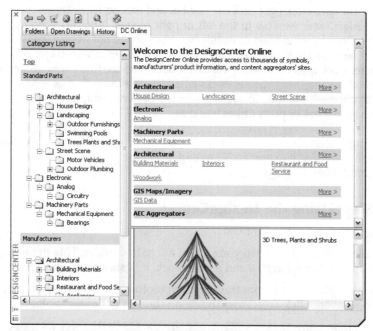

Figure 26-3: The DC Online tab of the DesignCenter offers a large selection of content that you can drag into your drawing.

Controlling the DesignCenter display

The DesignCenter provides several controls that help you manage its display.

A great feature of the DesignCenter is the preview pane. Click Preview on the DesignCenter toolbar to open this pane. Then select the item in the content pane. You may or may not see a preview of a block. (The new Block Definition dialog box specifically lets you create a preview icon.) Usually, you will see a preview of drawings and raster images. No previews exist for layers, linetypes, text styles, and so on.

 If you saved a description with a block, select the block in the content pane and click Description on the DesignCenter toolbar to see the description.

 To set the view, choose Views from the DesignCenter toolbar. The drop-down arrow lets you choose from four types of displays: large icons, small icons, list, and details. You can only see details for drawings and other files — AutoCAD displays their size and type.

If you make changes in the structure of a folder while the DesignCenter is open, for example by deleting a drawing using Windows Explorer, right-click the navigation or content pane and choose Refresh. AutoCAD re-reads the data and refreshes the list.

Tip

To dock the DesignCenter, right-click the title bar and choose Allow Docking. Then drag the DesignCenter window to the left or right of your AutoCAD window. To collapse the DesignCenter down to its title bar when you're not using it, right-click the title bar and choose Auto-hide; whenever you move the mouse cursor off the DesignCenter it collapses. Just move the cursor back onto the title bar to expand it again. Sometimes the DesignCenter docks when you are trying to drag it past the AutoCAD application window. To avoid unwanted docking, either uncheck Allow Docking on its title bar or press Ctrl as you drag.

On the CD-ROM

The drawings used in the following Step-by-Step exercise on using the DesignCenter, ab26-a.dwg and ab26-b.dwg, are in the Drawings folder of the *AutoCAD 2004 Bible* CD-ROM.

Step-by-Step: Using the DesignCenter

1. Open ab26a-dwg from the CD-ROM.

2. Save the file as ab26-01.dwg in your AutoCAD Bible folder. This drawing needs an updated set of layers and a title block. It is shown in Figure 26-4.

3. Choose DesignCenter from the Standard toolbar. If the navigation pane is not displayed, click Tree View Toggle on the DesignCenter toolbar.

4. In the navigation pane, locate ab26-b.dwg on the CD-ROM. Click its plus sign.

5. Choose Blocks. The ansi_d block appears in the content pane. Double-click ansi_d. Uncheck any Specify Onscreen check boxes and click OK.

6. Do a Zoom Extents.

7. In the navigation pane, click Layers for ab26-b.dwg.

8. In the content pane, click the first layer, press and hold Shift, and click the last layer to select all the layers. Drag them onto the drawing area. AutoCAD imports the layers.

9. Save your drawing.

Figure 26-4: This drawing needs updated layers and a title block.

Thanks to Vladimir Sevastyanov of Ukraine for this drawing of a gyrating swivel that feeds oil to an uncoiling machine used in the cold rolling of metal.

Accessing Drawing Content with Tool Palettes

The Tool Palette is a tabbed window that contains drawings, blocks or hatches. AutoCAD provides three tabs with sample content. Each tab is considered a separate tool palette within the Tool Palettes window. Figure 26-5 shows the Tool Palettes window that comes with AutoCAD. To open the Tool Palette, choose Tool Palettes on the Standard toolbar or press Ctrl+3.

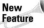

New Feature The Tool Palettes window is a new feature in AutoCAD 2004, designed to make inserting often-used blocks and hatches easier and quicker.

Tools palettes are meant to be customized with your own content. You can easily create new tabs with your own blocks. After you create the tab, you can drag the blocks into your drawing. Each block (or hatch) is called a tool.

The three types of tool palettes are:

✦ **Drawing:** Contains drawings that are inserted as blocks. You cannot change the name of the block.

✦ **Block:** Contains blocks. You can change the name of the block.

✦ **Hatch:** Contains hatch patterns.

Figure 26-5: The standard Tool Palettes has three tabs.

Creating a new tool palette

When you create a new tool palette, you add a tab to the Tool Palette window. The easiest way to create a new tool palette is from the DesignCenter, discussed in the previous section of this chapter. When you use this method, you simultaneously create not only the tool palette, but also its contents. To create a new tool palette:

1. Open the DesignCenter (choose DesignCenter from the Standard toolbar).

2. In the tree view or content area, navigate to a folder, drawing file, block icon, or hatch icon.

3. Right-click the item and choose Create Tool Palette.

 • If you select a folder, choose Create Tool Palette of Blocks.

 • If you select a hatch file (*.pat), choose Create Tool Palette of Hatch Patterns.

AutoCAD works for a few seconds and then creates the new tool palette tab, displaying each drawing, block, or hatch on the tab:

✦ If you chose a folder, the tab includes all drawing files in the folder

✦ If you chose a drawing file, the tab includes all blocks in the drawing

✦ If you chose a block icon, the tab includes the block

✦ If you chose a hatch icon, the tab includes all hatches in the .pat file. (See Chapter 31 for more information about creating hatch patterns in .pat files.)

To create an empty tool palette, right-click in the Tool Palette window and choose New Tool Palette. A label appears so that you can name the tool palette. Type the name and press Enter.

Cross-Reference You can also create a new, empty tool palette by using the Customize dialog box. See Chapter 29 for details.

Adding content to a tool palette

After you create a tool palette, you can add drawings, blocks, or hatches to it, depending on the type of tool palette you have created. The most common method is to use the DesignCenter:

1. Open the DesignCenter (choose DesignCenter from the Standard toolbar).

2. In the tree view or content area, navigate to a drawing, block, or hatch.

3. Drag the item onto the tool palette, as shown in Figure 26-6.

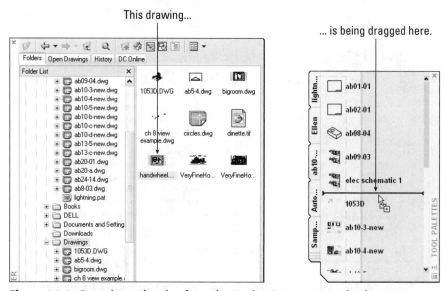

Figure 26-6: Dragging a drawing from the DesignCenter to a tool palette

You can also move or copy a tool (drawing, block, or hatch) from one tool palette to another. Follow these steps:

1. Display the tool palette (tab) that contains the item you want to move.

2. Right-click the item and choose Cut (to move it) or Copy (to copy it).

3. Display the tool palette (tab) where you want to place the item.

4. Right-click any blank area on the tab and choose Paste.

You can use this method to consolidate tabs or re-organize the tools on a tab.

Setting tool properties

Each tool on a tool palette has properties that you can set. The properties vary slightly depending on whether the tool is a hatch, drawing, or block. The properties specify how that tool is inserted into a drawing. By using properties, you can ensure that any drawing, block, or hatch is inserted with the proper scale, color, and so on. To set the properties of a tool, right-click it and choose Properties to open the Tool Properties dialog box. Figure 26-7 shows the Tool Properties dialog box for a block tool and a hatch tool.

Figure 26-7: The Tool Properties dialog box for a block and a hatch pattern

The top of the Tool Properties dialog box displays the name of the drawing, block, or hatch and a description, if one has been saved. The middle section of the dialog box contains Insert or Pattern properties and the bottom of the dialog box displays General properties:

✦ **Insert properties:** Defines how a block or drawing is inserted — scale, rotation, and whether or not the item is exploded when inserted. (For information about inserting blocks, see Chapter 18.)

✦ **Pattern properties:** Defines how a hatch pattern is inserted — angle, scale, spacing, ISO pen width, and whether or not the hatch pattern is doubled. (For information about inserting hatch patterns, see Chapter 16.)

✦ **General properties:** Defines drawing properties that are used for the item — layer, color, linetype, lineweight, and plot style. These properties are applied to the item, overriding the current drawing settings.

The General properties all default to Use Current. Change the General properties when you want an item to always have a particular color or layer, for example.

To specify any property, click the right column for that property. Either type a new value or choose from the drop-down list. After you're done, click OK to close the Tool Properties dialog box.

Moving, deleting, and renaming tools and tool palettes

You can change the order of both tool palettes (tabs) in the Tool Palette window and of tools on a palette.

✦ To move a tool on a palette, drag the tool. A horizontal cursor appears to show you where the tool will go.

✦ To move a palette, right-click the tab itself and choose Move Up or Move Down.

To delete a tool palette, right-click the palette and choose Delete Tool Palette. A warning message is displayed, explaining that you cannot recover the deleted tool palette unless you export it to a file. To delete a tool on a tool palette, right-click the tool and choose Delete Tool. Here, too, you need to confirm the deletion when a warning message appears.

To export a tool palette, you save it to a file. You can then share tool palettes with others. You import and export tool palettes on the Tool Palettes tab on the Customize dialog box. See Chapter 29 for details.

To rename a tool palette, right-click the palette and choose Rename Tool Palette. To rename a tool, right-click the tool and choose Rename. In both situations, type a new name and press Enter.

Updating tools

If a drawing, block, or hatch changes, its icon does not automatically change to match. In this situation, the icon will not accurately represent its tool. To update an icon, use one of the following methods:

✦ Right-click the tool and choose Properties. Click the Source File (or Pattern Name) item and use the Ellipsis button to choose any other file, block, or hatch pattern, and then immediately choose the correct item again. This updates the icon for the tool.

✦ Delete the tool and re-insert it using the DesignCenter.

If you move the source file for a tool, you need to update the tool with the new location:

1. Right-click the tool and choose Properties.

2. In the Tool Properties dialog box, use the Ellipsis button to choose the file again.

3. Click OK.

Setting tool palette options

To work most comfortably with the Tool Palette window, you can adjust its display options. Right-click any empty area on the tool palette (except the tab itself) and choose from the following options:

✦ **Allow Docking:** Enables you to dock the tool palette on the left or right side of the AutoCAD drawing area.

✦ **Auto-hide:** Collapses the tool palette to just its title bar when the mouse cursor is off the Tool Palette window. Pass the mouse cursor back over the title bar to expand the tool palette again. You can store the collapsed tool palette outside the AutoCAD application window (if it is not fully maximized).

✦ **Transparency:** Opens the Transparency dialog box, shown in Figure 26-8. When the tool palette is transparent, you can see the drawing through it. You can specify the amount of transparency or turn it off.

Figure 26-8: The Transparency dialog box

Note Transparency is only available when hardware acceleration is off (which it is by default). Hardware acceleration is governed by your computer's video card and helps to speed up the display. If you want to use the transparency feature, you can use software acceleration instead (and see if it affects your display speed). Choose Tools ⇨ Options and click the System tab. In the Current 3D Graphics Display section, click Properties. In the Acceleration section, choose Software. Click Apply & Close and then click OK to close the Options dialog box. Also, transparency is only available when the palette is not docked and is not available if you are using Windows NT.

✦ **View Options:** Opens the View Options dialog box, shown in Figure 26-9. You can change the size and layout of the tool icons on a tool palette. Use the slider to change the size of the icons. Choose from the following display styles:

 • **Icon only:** You see the icon displaying the drawing, block, or hatch, but no text.

 • **Icon with text:** Text is displayed beneath each icon and the icons are arranged in columns.

 • **List view:** You see one column of icons, with the text to the right of each icon.

✦ You can choose to apply the changes to the current tool palette or to all tool palettes.

Figure 26-9: The View Options dialog box

Tip If you have docking enabled, but want to drag the Tool Palettes window without docking it, press Ctrl as you drag.

Using a tool palette

Inserting a tool from a tool palette is as simple as dragging the tool onto the drawing area. Drag hatch patterns inside any enclosed shape. The tool is inserted using the properties specified in the Tool Properties dialog box (discussed previously in this section).

If you want the flexibility to insert a block or hatch with more than one setting, you can insert more than one copy of the item onto a tool palette. For example, you can

place two copies of a hatch pattern on a tool palette and set their properties to different spacing. You would then rename the tools to make the differences clear, for example, lightning1 and lightning 2.

The drawings used in the following Step-by-Step exercise on creating and using a tool palette, ab26-c.dwg and ab26-d.dwg, are in the Drawings folder of the *AutoCAD 2004 Bible* CD-ROM.

Step-by-Step: Creating and Using a Tool Palette

1. Open ab26-c-dwg from the CD-ROM.

2. Save the file as ab26-02.dwg in your AutoCAD Bible folder. This drawing needs some blocks and a hatch pattern inserted. It is shown in Figure 26-10.

3. Choose Tools ➪ Tool Palettes Window.

4. Choose DesignCenter from the Standard toolbar. In the DesignCenter's Folder List, navigate to the Drawing folder of your CD-ROM and click the plus sign to the left of ab26-d.dwg. Click the Blocks item to display the two blocks (post and post-structural) in the content area on the right side of the DesignCenter.

Figure 26-10: This back porch needs some columns, which are blocks, as well as some hatching.

5. Right-click any empty area of the tool palette and choose New Tool Palette. A label appears. Type **2d arch** and press Enter. You now have a new tool palette named 2d arch.

Note

If the tool palette is collapsed when the mouse cursor is not over it, right-click its title bar and choose Auto-hide to uncheck this item.

6. From the content area of the DesignCenter, drag each of the blocks to the new tool palette. An icon appears on the tool palette for each block.

7. In the Folder List of the DesignCenter, navigate to `acad.pat`, which contains hatch patterns. Click `acad.pat` to display the hatch patterns in the content area.

Note

> By default, `acad.pat` is in `\Documents and Settings\[user name]\ Application Data\Autodesk\AutoCAD 2004\R16.0\enu\Support`. However, your location may be different, depending on your operating system and customization. To find the location of `acad.pat`, choose Tools ⇨ Options and click the Files tab. Double-click the first item, Support File Search Path, to display the location of the support files.

8. Drag User Defined, one of the hatch patterns near the end of the list, to the tool palette. (This hatch pattern is equivalent to choosing User Defined as the Hatch Type in the Boundary Hatch and Fill dialog box. See Chapter 16 for details.) The tool palette now has three items on it.

9. Right-click the User Defined hatch icon and choose Properties to open the Tool Properties dialog box. You want to specify settings so that this hatch pattern will look like scored concrete for the porch floor.

10. In the Tool Properties dialog box, make the following changes and then click OK:

 • For the Angle, type **45**.

 • For the Spacing, type **2'** (or **24**).

 • Click the Double item and then the arrow at the right side of the row. Choose Yes from the drop-down list.

 • Click the Layer item and choose FLOOR from the drop-down list. (You may have to drag the bottom edge of the dialog box down to see the layer item.)

11. Drag the `User Defined` hatch icon to ❶ in Figure 26-10. Then do the same for ❷ and ❸. These areas are hatched, as shown in Figure 26-11.

12. Choose Zoom Window from the Zoom flyout on the Standard toolbar and zoom into the central area of the drawing so that you can still see the double doors at the bottom and the steps at the top.

13. Click the `post` icon. At the `Specify insertion point:` prompt, pick ❹ in Figure 26-10. Click the `post-structural` icon. At the prompt, pick the upper-right corner of the post block, as shown in Figure 26-11.

14. Click the `post` icon. At the prompt, pick ❺ in Figure 26-10. Use the same technique to place the `post-structural` icon at the upper-right corner of the post block. (The posts would then need to be spaced and mirrored to the other side of the porch, but these tasks are not necessary for this exercise.)

15. Right-click the tool palette's title bar. If Allow Docking is checked, click Allow Docking to uncheck this item. If Auto-hide is not checked, click Auto-hide to enable this feature. Move the mouse off the tool palette. It collapses to its title bar. Move the tool palette to the right side of your screen.

16. If you are working on someone else's computer, you should delete the tool palette. Move the cursor over the palette to display it. Right-click any blank area and choose Delete Tool Palette. Click Yes to confirm the deletion.

17. Save your drawing. It should look like Figure 26-11.

Figure 26-11: The drawing now has hatches and blocks inserted from the tool palette.

Setting Standards for Drawings

One person rarely has complete control over a drawing. You may xref in other drawings, or others may xref in your drawings. Several people may work on one drawing. You may send a drawing to a client who may work on it as well. More and more, working in AutoCAD is becoming a collaborative effort — and it can get out of control.

One way to get in control is to set standards for drawings — and issue those standards so that everyone involved has access to them. If you don't have agreed-upon standards, you not only waste time changing layers, text styles, and so on, but your drawings get very complicated. You should set standards for the following:

✦ Drawing names and property summaries

✦ Blocks, including names, layers, and insertion points

✦ Layers, including uses, names, colors, linetypes, and lineweights

✦ Text styles, including uses, names, and properties

✦ Dimension styles and tolerances, if any

✦ Multiline styles

✦ Units settings

✦ Layouts

In some cases, your standards are set by outside conventions. For example, the American Institute of Architects (AIA) and the Construction Standards Institute (CSI) publish layering standards for members.

If you use coded names, such as 97GR134.dwg, you may want to keep a list of the drawing names with a description of the drawing next to it. A key that explains the coding system helps as well.

Using symbol libraries

One aspect of setting and maintaining standards is the use of a symbol (block) library. A symbol library is simply a drawing file containing blocks. AutoCAD 2004 comes with several sample symbol libraries that you can drag into your current drawing using the Tool Palettes window. Of course, as explained earlier in this chapter, you will want to create your own.

Cross-Reference

See Chapter 18 for information on using the DesignCenter specifically for blocks and for a discussion of creating your own symbol libraries.

Using the CAD Standards tools

The CAD Standards tools facilitate the process of checking drawings against standards. You can check the following in a drawing:

✦ Layers

✦ Text styles

✦ Linetypes

✦ Dimension styles

New Feature

AutoCAD 2004 updates these tools. New features include selecting the type of standard you want checked and real-time notification of standards violations.

AutoCAD checks for both names, such as layer names, and properties, such as layer color or linetype.

Here's the general procedure for setting and maintaining standards with the CAD manager's tools:

1. Create a standards file (*.dws).

2. Associate the standards file with a drawing.

3. Test the drawing against its standards file.

You can test drawings against a standards file one-by-one (interactively) or as a group (batch auditing).

Creating a standards file

You use a standards file to set standards for drawings. A standards file has a file name extension of .dws. Unlike many of the support files used in AutoCAD, a standards file is not a text file; rather, it is similar to a drawing file. You create a standards file by creating a drawing that contains the standards — layers, linetypes, text styles, and dimension styles — that you want.

To create a standards file from scratch, follow these steps:

1. Choose File ➪ New.

2. Choose a template or click the Open button's down arrow and choose one of the Open with No Template options.

3. Create the layers, linetypes, dimension styles, and text styles that you want to place in the standards file.

4. Choose File ➪ Save As. In the File Name text box, type a name for the standards file.

5. In the Files of Type list, select AutoCAD Drawing Standards (*.dws).

6. In the Save In drop-down list, choose a location for the file.

7. Click Save.

AutoCAD saves the drawing standards file.

You can use an existing drawing for your standards file. But be careful to purge all layers, linetypes, dimension styles, and text styles that you don't want.

Associating a standards file with a drawing

As soon as you have your standards file, you associate it with a drawing that you want to check, using the new STANDARDS command. To associate a standards file with the current drawing, follow these steps:

1. On the CAD Standards toolbar, click Configure Standards. (You can also choose Tools ➪ CAD Standards ➪ Configure or type **standards** ⏎.)

2. On the Standards tab of the Configure Standards dialog box, shown in Figure 26-12, choose the + button.

3. In the Select Standards File dialog box, choose the standards file you want to use and click Open. You can associate more than one standards files with the drawing. Just continue to click the + button and choose more standards files.

New Feature The check boxes on the Plug-ins tab are a new feature of 2004 and enable you to select only those standards that you want to check.

Figure 26-12: Use the Configure Standards dialog box to associate a standards file with a drawing.

4. Click the Plug-ins tab and click any standards you don't want to check. (All four, Dimension Styles, Layers, Linetypes, and Text Styles are initially set to be checked. Afterwards, the choices you make persist for future standard checks until you change them.)

5. Click OK to close the Configure Standards dialog box and return to your drawing.

Checking a drawing against standards

To check a drawing against a standards file, you must first associate the standards file with the drawing, as just previously explained. Then choose Check Standards from the CAD Standards toolbar to start the CHECKSTANDARDS command (or choose Tools ➪ CAD Standards ➪ Check) and open the Check Standards dialog box, shown in Figure 26-13.

Figure 26-13: The Check Standards dialog box guides you through the process of checking a drawing against a standards file.

Tip If you just finished associating a standards file with a drawing, you can click Check Standards in the Configure Standards dialog box.

The Check Standards dialog box lists all the problems — items in the drawing that don't match the standards file — that it finds, one by one. Here's the procedure for using this dialog box:

1. You see the first problem in the problem section of the dialog box.

2. Use the Replace with section to choose a replacement for the non-standard item. This section contains all eligible replacements according to the standards file.

3. Look at the Preview of Changes section to see how the replacement will affect your drawing.

4. [Fix] To make the replacement and standardize your drawing, click the Fix button.

 [Next] To ignore the problem and go on to the next one, click the Next button.

AutoCAD continues to display problems that you can fix or ignore. After you are done, you see the Checking is complete message in the Problem area, along with a short report explaining how all the problems were handled, as shown in Figure 26-14. You can click the Next button again to recheck the drawing.

Figure 26-14: The completed standards check report

5. Click Close to return to your drawing.

For information on checking standards for many drawings at once, *batch checking,* see the sidebar, "Checking standards for multiple drawings."

When you fix nonstandard objects — for example layers or linetypes with nonstandard names — AutoCAD purges these objects from the drawing. For example, after you change the layer Layer1 to the layer Notes, objects on Layer1 are changed to the layer Notes and Layer1 is purged.

Specifying CAD standards settings

You can specify how the CAD standards feature functions to provide real-time notification and automatic repair. To specify CAD standards settings, open the Check Standards dialog box (choose Tools ⇨ CAD Standards ⇨ Configure), as shown in Figure 26-15. Click the Settings button. (You can also click Settings from the Check Standards dialog box.)

 New Feature Real-time notification and automatic repair are new features of AutoCAD 2004. The new STANDARDSVIOLATION system variable stores the notification settings.

Figure 26-15: Use the CAD Standards Settings dialog box to specify how you want CAD standards checking to work.

In the top section, Notification Settings, choose one of the following:

✦ **Disable standards notifications:** No real-time notification of standards viola-
tions. You can still check standards using the Check Standards dialog box at
any time.

✦ **Display alert upon standards violation:** Displays a message if your drawing is
associated with a standards file and you make a change that puts the drawing
in non-compliance with the standards file, as shown in Figure 26-16.

✦ **Display standards status bar alert icon:** Displays an icon on the AutoCAD sta-
tus bar, as shown in Figure 26-17. The icon has an exclamation point if there is
a non-standard object in the drawing. A balloon appears to notify you that a
standards violation has occurred. Click the Run Check Standards text or the
icon to open the Check Standards dialog box so that you can fix the problems.

Figure 26-16: The Standards Violation Alert
message

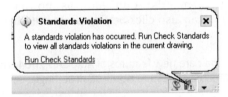

Figure 26-17: The status bar alert of a
standards violation

In the bottom section, Check Standards Settings, check Automatically Fix Non-
standard Properties to fix non-compliant drawings automatically. Automatic fixing
only applies to a situation where a drawing object has a name that matches a stan-
dard but has different properties. For example, if a standards file contains a layer
named OBJ that has a blue color and the current drawing has an object on the OBJ
layer that is red, the object will be changed to blue, to match the color of the OBJ
layer in the standards file.

Check Show Ignored Problems to display any problems that were not fixed in the
standards check report.

From the Preferred Standards File to Use for Replacements drop-down list, choose a
standards file to use by default in the Replace With section of the Check Standards
dialog box. This standards file is only used if you choose to automatically fix non-
standard properties and the associated standards file for the drawing does not pro-
vide a suitable replacement.

Translating layers

If you receive drawings from clients or colleagues, you might find that their layer system doesn't suit yours. Translating one set of layers to another to fit your layer standards could be a tedious job — until now. The LAYTRANS command changes the layers of objects by specifying sets of "from" and "to" layers. For example, you can change all objects on layer1 to the layer "objects." Use this feature to maintain layer standards.

Setting up the layer mapping

 To translate one layer to another, choose Layer Translate from the CAD Standards toolbar (or choose Tools ➪ CAD Standards ➪ Layer Translator). The Layer Translator, shown in Figure 26-18, opens.

Figure 26-18: The Layer Translator

On the Translate From side of the dialog box, you see the layers in the drawing. (Layers with a white icon to their left are not being used. You can right-click them and choose Purge Layers to purge them from the drawing.) Select layers by clicking them. You can select multiple layers. You can type a selection filter in the Selection Filter text box to select certain layers.

Cross-Reference See Chapter 11 for more information about filtering layer lists.

To load existing layers, choose Load. In the Select Drawing File dialog box, you can choose a drawing, a drawing template, or a drawing standards file. Click Open. The layers from that file now appear in the Translate To list. Select the layer to which you want to translate.

Checking standards for multiple drawings

What do you do if you want to check standards for hundreds of drawings at once? For this scenario, AutoCAD has created Batch Standards Checking, shown here. Here's how to use the Batch Standards Checker:

1. From the Windows taskbar, choose Start ➪ Programs ➪ Autodesk ➪ AutoCAD 2004 ➪ Batch Standards Checker.

2. On the Drawings tab, click the + button and select the drawings you want to include. Click Open. You can select a range of drawings by clicking the first drawing, pressing Shift, and selecting the last drawing. You can select individual drawings by pressing Ctrl for each additional drawing. After you click Open, you can click the + button again and add drawings from a different folder. Use the Delete button to delete drawings and the Move Up and Move Down buttons to change the order of the drawings. If you also want to check external references, check the Check External References of Listed Drawings check box.

3. On the Standards tab, choose to check each drawing against its associated standards file if you have associated standards files for all your drawings. Otherwise, choose to check the drawings against the standards file(s) that you select. To select a standards file, click the + button, choose a standards file (.dws), and click Open.

4. On the Plug-ins tab, choose the standards that you want to check. This tab is the same as the Plug-ins tab of the Configure Standards dialog box, discussed earlier in this section.

5. Click Save on the Batch Standards Checker toolbar. In the Batch Standards Checker - File Save dialog box, save the standards check file. A standards check file (.chx) contains information about which drawings and standards files you are using for the

batch standards check. AutoCAD gives the file a default name, but you can change the name if you wish.

6. To start checking the drawings, click Start Check on the Batch Standards Checker toolbar. (You can click Stop Check to stop the check any time during its progress.) The Batch Standards Checker starts checking your drawings. Click the Progress tab to see what is happening, if you want. When the checking is done, your Standards Audit Report is displayed. An example is shown here. Standards Audit Reports appear in your Internet browser.

STANDARDS AUDIT REPORT

C:\AutoCAD Bible\elect1.chx

Show:
- ⦿ Overview
- ○ Plug-ins
- ○ Standards
- ○ Problems
- ○ Ignored Problems
- ○ All

For:
- ☑ All Drawings

- ☑ ab01-01.dwg
- ☑ ab02-01.dwg
- ☑ ab08-04.dwg
- ☑ ab09-03.dwg
- ☑ ab09-04.dwg
- ☑ ab10-3-new.dwg
- ☑ ab10-4-new.dwg
- ☑ ab10-5-new.dwg
- ☑ ab10-b-new.dwg
- ☑ ab10-c-new.dwg
- ☑ ab10-d-new.dwg

Overview

Created by:
Ellen Finkelstein

Created on:
Sunday, December 29, 2002

Notes:
Check of all files to be sent to the electrician.

Summary:

Drawing	Problems	Ignored problems
ab26d-new.dwg	3	0
ab01-01.dwg	0	0
ab02-01.dwg	0	0
ab8-03.dwg	17	0
ab08-04.dwg	0	0
ab09-03.dwg	8	0
ab09-04.dwg	9	0
ab10-3-new.dwg	27	0
ab10-4-new.dwg	39	0

Here are some other features of the Batch Standards Checker:

✦ To open an existing standards check file, click Open on the Batch Standards Checker toolbar. Choose the check file and click Open.

✦ To view an existing batch audit report, open an existing standards check file and click the View Report button on the toolbar.

✦ Use the Notes tab of the Batch Standards Checker to add notes that will appear on the batch audit report.

✦ A new feature of AutoCAD 2004 enables you to export the Standards Audit Report to HTML format. Click Export Report on the Batch Standards Checker toolbar. You can then easily email the report to others. You can also copy and paste the table portion of the report into a spreadsheet program.

To define a new layer, choose New. In the New Layer dialog box, type a name for the new layer and specify its color, linetype, lineweight, and plot style. Click OK.

To specify how layers are translated, *map* layers in the current drawing (listed in the Translate From list) to the layers you want to convert to (listed in the Translate To list). Select a layer in the Translate From list, select a layer in the Translate To list, and click Map. The mapping appears below in the Layer Translation Mappings list. Finally, you're ready to translate your layers. Click Translate, and AutoCAD takes care of the rest. All objects on the Translate From layers are now on the Translate To layers. The translation process also purges unused layers from the drawing.

Tip You can select more than one layer from the Translate From list by pressing Ctrl for each additional layer. You can select a contiguous group of layers by clicking the first layer in the group, holding Shift and selecting the last layer in the group. Then select the layer from the Translate To list that you want to map that group of layers to and click Map. You can also quickly map all layers with the same name by choosing Map Same.

In Figure 26-19, you see an example of a mapping where the CEN, HAT, and HID layers will be mapped to new layers.

Figure 26-19: The three layers CEN, HAT, and HID are mapped to new layers.

Managing layer translations

After you create your mappings, you can edit, remove, or save them:

✦ To edit a mapping, select it and click Edit. In the Edit Layer dialog box, you can choose a new layer, color, linetype, lineweight, or plot style.

✦ To remove a mapping, select it and click Remove.

✦ To save a mapping, click Save. You can choose to save a mapping as a drawing standards file (.dws) or as an actual drawing file (.dwg). Type a file name, choose a location, and click Save. (If you don't save your layer mapping, AutoCAD prompts you to do so.)

✦ Click Settings to customize the translation process. Here are your options:

- The first two options in the Settings dialog box force objects to take on their layer's assigned color and linetype. Check these two settings to enforce consistency in your layer properties.

- The `Translate objects in blocks` item determines whether layer mappings are applied to objects within blocks. See Chapter 18 for more about blocks.

- Check Write transaction log to create a .log file in the same folder as the drawing you are translating (the current drawing). The log file lists the details of the translation and can help you troubleshoot problems later.

- Check Show layer contents when selected to help you figure out which objects are on which layers. If you check this item and then select a layer translation in the Translate From or Layer Translation Mappings list, only objects on that layer are shown.

After you finish specifying the translation settings, click OK to close the Settings dialog box.

On the CD-ROM

The drawings used in the following Step-by-Step exercise on managing CAD standards, ab26-e.dwg and ab26-e.dws, are in the Drawings folder of the *AutoCAD 2004 Bible* CD-ROM.

Step-by-Step: Managing CAD Standards

1. Open ab26-e.dwg from the CD-ROM.

2. Save the file as ab26-03.dwg in your AutoCAD Bible folder.

3. Click the Linetype Control drop-down list on the Object Properties toolbar. Notice the Borderx2, Centerx2, Hiddenx2, and Phantom2 linetypes.

4. Right-click any toolbar and choose CAD Standards to open the CAD Standards toolbar. Choose Configure Standards from the toolbar.

5. In the Configure Standards dialog box, click the + button. Find and choose ab26-e.dws, a drawing standards file, on the CD-ROM. Click Open to associate ab26-e.dws with ab26-03.dwg.

6. In the same dialog box, click Check Standards to open the Check Standards dialog box.

7. [Next] The first standards problem, Layer 'AME_FRZ' Name is non-standard, is listed in the Problem box. Click Next to ignore this problem.

8. [Fix] The next problem is Layer 'CEN' Properties are non-standard. Choose CEN from the Replace With list and click the Fix button.

9. Continue to make the following changes, clicking the Fix button after each one:

 LINETYPE BORDERX2 BORDER

 LINETYPE CENTERX2 CENTER

 LINETYPE HIDDENX2 HIDDEN

 LINETYPE PHANTOM2 PHANTOM

 TEXT STYLE ZONE ROMAND

10. The Checking Complete dialog box appears with a summary of the standards check. Click OK.

11. Click Close.

12. Open the Linetype Control drop-down list again. All the "x2" linetypes have been purged.

13. Click Layer Translate on the CAD Standards toolbar.

14. On the right side of the Layer Translator dialog box, click Load. Choose ab26-c.dws, the same standards file you used previously in this exercise and click Open.

15. In the Translate From box, click CEN. Hold down the Ctrl key and click HAT.

16. In the Translate To box, click HID.

17. Click Map. This will map the layers CEN and HAT to the HID layer.

18. Click Translate to translate the mappings.

19. At the message asking if you want to save mapping information, click No. All objects on the CEN and HAT layers are now on the HID layer.

20. Save your drawing.

The Communication Center

The Communication Center feature notifies you about AutoCAD updates, product support, tips, articles, and so on. An icon at the right end of the AutoCAD status bar connects you to the Communication Center.

New
Feature

The Communication Center is new for AutoCAD 2004. It incorporates live updates, which were previously part of AutoCAD Today.

When new information or updates are available, a bubble appears from the status bar to notify you, as shown in Figure 26-20.

Figure 26-20: The Communication Center notification appears to let you know that new information or updates are available.

To access the information, click the icon or the Click Here text to open the Communication Center window, shown in Figure 26-21. From this window, you can click any link to access its source on the Internet.

Figure 26-21: Click any item to access it on the Autodesk Web site.

You can configure how the Communication Center works. Right-click the Communication Center icon or choose settings from the Communication Center window to open the Configuration Settings dialog box, with two tabs:

✦ **Settings:** Use this tab to specify your country, how often you want to check for updates, and whether or not you want to see the bubble notification.

✦ **Channels:** Choose the types of updates you want to see.

Cross-Reference You can disable the Communication Center. For more information, see Appendix A on the CD-ROM, where I discuss the Network Setup Wizard and the CAD Manager Control Utility.

Renaming named objects

AutoCAD drawings contain many named objects, such as layers, text styles, dimension styles, and so on. Sometimes you need to rename these objects in order to maintain CAD standards and consistency. To rename objects, type **rename** on the command line and press Enter, to open the Rename dialog box, shown in Figure 26-22.

Figure 26-22: The Rename dialog box

To rename objects, follow these steps:

1. Choose the type of object you want to rename from the Named Objects list.

2. Choose the item you want to rename from the Items list. This item appears in the Old Name text box.

3. In the Rename to text box, type the new name for the item.

 • If you want to change only one item, click OK to close the dialog box.

 • If you want to change more than one item, click Rename To. The dialog box remains open so that you can make other changes. Click OK after you are finished.

Organizing Your Drawings

Some offices keep track of thousands of drawings. You must not only track your drawings' names and other properties but also make sure you don't lose them! Archiving and finding drawings are important procedures in any CAD environment.

Archiving drawings

You should use AutoCAD's Autosave feature to save a backup of the drawing to the hard drive regularly. The default time has finally been changed to 10 minutes, but automatic backups can still be useful. Choose Tools ➪ Options ➪ Open and Save tab and change the Automatic Save setting. Click OK. Of course, you shouldn't rely on AutoSave; instead, save your drawing frequently by clicking the Save button.

Backing up to the hard drive doesn't provide sufficient security. Hard drives can fail. Every time you exit AutoCAD, you should back up every drawing you worked on to some type of external storage medium. Backing up drawings for storage is called *archiving*.

On the CD-ROM, I include an AutoLISP program, savea.lsp, that backs up to the a: drive without leaving your drawing. This enables you to back up while working on a drawing. See the Software\Chap01\Savea folder of the CD-ROM.

Some drawings are too large to fit on a floppy disk, and the number of disks you need to store all your drawings may make easy storage impossible. You will probably want to invest in one of the many types of removable backup systems. These come in four main types:

✦ **Tape drives** (internal or external) are cheap and good for entire hard drive backups.

✦ **Disk cartridge drives** offer the convenience of a floppy disk but with more capacity.

✦ **Read/write CD-ROM drives** enable you to write to a CD-ROM.

✦ **Optical drives** have the longest life (at least 30 years) and resist accidental erasure.

If your drawings are *really* important to you, back them up twice and store one backup set off-site. This way, if your office burns down, you haven't lost everything. Remote backup services provide this type of archiving for you, and you can access your files via modem or the Internet.

A new option is to store drawings online. Online storage and management is discussed in the next section.

The secret to backing up is to create a schedule and then stick to it. For example, you may do a complete hard drive backup once a week, and do drawing backups at the end of each day. Each situation is different, but take the time to think about your needs, create a system, and let everybody know about it. Then do it.

Finding drawings

Let's say your client calls and says, "I want to see the apartment building on Fourth Street that you did three years ago." How do you find the drawing?

One low-tech way is to keep a book of 8½×11 plots. Using the Batch Plot Utility, you can plot out a week's drawings overnight and put them in a book. Amazingly, it doesn't take that long to leaf through even a few hundred pages. (You usually have *some* idea of when you did the drawing.)

Tip Place the drawing name and date written in large text on a separate layer in the drawing. Set the Plot property of the layer to Not Plottable while you work and for Regular Plotting. Set it to Plottable for your batch plots. Then, even reduced, you'll know the drawing name when you look at the drawing in the book.

A number of third-party drawing management programs are available. Some of these enable you to view and manage drawings created in other CAD programs as well. Some also manage workflow by letting you route drawings to team members.

Here's a short selection of the many drawing management programs available:

✦ **AutoEDMS:** www.acssoftware.com

✦ **Altris eB:** www.altris.com

✦ **Cyco AutoManager Workflow EDM:** www.cyco.com

✦ **Columbus:** www.oasys-software.com/product/downloads

A fairly new option is to store and manage drawings online. Web-based services, such as buzzsaw.com (www.buzzsaw.com) let you store drawings online, view and mark them up, organize and track them, and access them from within AutoCAD.

Before backing up drawings, purge any unused layers, blocks, text styles, and so on to reduce file size.

Finding drawings from within AutoCAD

If you know a drawing is on the hard drive, you can use the Find function. Click Open on the Standard toolbar. In the Select File dialog box, choose Tools ➪ Find to open the Find dialog box, shown in Figure 26-23. Use the Name & Location tab to set criteria according the file name, file type, and location. Use the Date Modified tab to set criteria by the date the file was saved.

Figure 26-23: You can use the Find dialog box to set criteria for finding drawings.

Specifying drawing properties

You can specify drawing properties, similar to those found in Microsoft Office. You can use these properties not only in the DesignCenter, but in Windows Explorer. These properties are therefore available to people who can access your drawings but who don't have AutoCAD.

You can specify a title, subject, author, and keywords. You can also write comments. At the bottom of the dialog box, you can specify a base for relative hyperlinks in the drawing. For example, you could use www.companyname.com as the base. AutoCAD would then attach this base to the beginning of links in the drawing.

To specify drawing properties, choose File ⇨ Drawing Properties to open the Properties dialog box, shown in Figure 26-24.

In general, you will find the Summary tab the most useful. However, you can also use the Custom tab to create custom properties and give them values. This lets you create a simple database of your drawings that you can search using the DesignCenter's Find dialog box.

To access a drawing's properties in Windows Explorer, navigate to the drawing and right-click it. Choose Properties from the shortcut menu.

New Feature The Express Tools contain a command, PROPULATE (choose Express ⇨ File tools ⇨ Update Drawing Property Data) that automatically creates or updates Property data for one or more drawings.

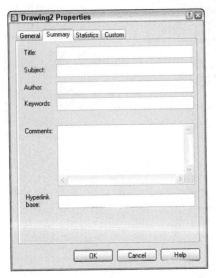

Figure 26-24: The Summary tab of the Properties dialog box

Maintaining Security

In these days of collaboration and interconnectivity, maintaining security is an important issue. AutoCAD 2004 offers two new features to help you keep your designs secure.

Password protection

Password protection ensures that unauthorized people don't open your drawings. To create a password for a drawing, do one of the following:

✦ Choose Tools ➪ Options, click the Open and Save tab, and click Security Options.

✦ When you first save a drawing (choose File ➪ Save), which opens the Save Drawing As dialog box, choose Tools ➪ Security Options.

✦ Type **securityoptions** ↵ on the command line.

The Security Options dialog box opens, shown in Figure 26-25.

Caution Before adding a password, save the drawing under another name or in a different location so that you have a copy. If you lose or forget the password, you will not be able to open the drawing. You can turn password protection off for network installations of AutoCAD.

Figure 26-25: The Security Options dialog box with the Password tab on top

To password protect a drawing:

1. Type a password.

2. If you also want to encrypt drawing properties that identify the drawing, such as the title, author, subject, and keywords, check the Encrypt Drawing Properties check box.

3. Click OK.

4. The Confirm Password dialog box appears. Retype the password.

5. Click OK.

You can also change or remove a password:

1. Open the Security Options dialog box.

2. Type a new password or delete the current password. Click OK.

3. If you type a new password, reconfirm the password and click OK.

The dialog box displays the current encryption type. To specify a different encryption, click Advanced Options. Choose a new encryption type from the list and a key length, and then click OK.

When a password protected drawing is opened, the Password dialog box appears. To open the drawing, type the password and click OK.

Digital signatures

A digital signature uses software that confirms who signed the drawing, that it has not been changed, and non-repudiation (so that signers cannot claim they never signed the drawing). To use a digital signature, you need to purchase a digital ID.

Generally, you would use a digital signature when you send a drawing to someone else. That person can then verify that the drawing is from you and has not been changed. If the person sends the drawing back to you, you can verify that the person has not changed the drawing, because changing the drawing invalidates the digital signature.

Note The Digital Signatures tab of the Security Options dialog box contains a link to VeriSign, a company that sells digital certificates. You can obtain a 60-day free trial or purchase a digital ID at one of several levels of security. If you don't have a digital signature and want to use VeriSign, choose Tools ⇨ Options and click the Open and Save tab. Click Security Options and then the Digital Signatures tab. A message displays explaining that you don't have a valid digital ID. Click Get a Digital ID to go to VeriSign's Web site. Follow the instructions at the site to sign up for and install the digital ID. While the initial Web page is specific to Autodesk, the final instructions assume that you want to use the digital ID for e-mail. You can ignore those instructions.

To attach a digital signature to a drawing, follow these steps:

1. Choose Tools ⇨ Options and click the Open and Save tab. Click Security Options and then the Digital Signatures tab, shown in Figure 26-26.

Figure 26-26: The Digital Signatures tab of the Security Options dialog box

2. Choose a digital signature and check the `Attach digital signature after saving drawing` check box.

3. To place a time stamp on the drawing, choose one of the options from the Get Time Stamp From drop-down list.

4. To add a comment (that appears when the drawing is opened), type the text in the Comment text box.

5. Click OK.

When a digitally signed drawing is opened, the Digital Signature Contents dialog box appears, verifying the digital signature and the fact that the drawing has not been changed since it was signed. See Figure 26-27. Click Close to close the dialog box.

Figure 26-27: The Digital Signature Contents dialog box appears when you open a digitally signed drawing, confirming the original and unchanged state of the drawing.

Note that making any changes to the drawing invalidates the digital ID. If you make changes or try to save a drawing with an attached digital signature, a message appears asking you if you want to continue. When you re-open the drawing, the Digital Signature Contents dialog box appears, displaying the fact that the digital signature is invalid.

A drawing with a valid digital signature has a check mark attached to its icon in Windows Explorer. The drawing itself also sports an icon in the AutoCAD status bar, as shown in Figure 26-28.

 Figure 26-28: A drawing with a valid digital signature, shown in Windows Explorer and on its status bar.

> **Note**
>
> Users who don't have the Digital Signature feature can download the Digital Signature Verifier, a free application to verify digital signatures on signed drawings. The Digital Signature Verifier is available from the Autodesk Web site at `http://usa.autodesk.com/adsk/item/0,,877495-123112-587113,00.html`. (You can also go to `www.autodesk.com` and do a search on Digital Signature Verifier.)

Keeping Track of Referenced Files

A drawing references several types of outside files and you often need to keep track of these files, especially when you send a drawing to someone else or move it to another computer. Also, the referenced files may be moved, even if the drawing stays in the same place. Without these outside files, the drawing is not complete. Outside files include:

✦ Other drawings (xrefs)

✦ Text fonts

✦ Images

✦ Plot configurations

The Autodesk Reference Manager not only lists referenced files but enables you to change saved reference paths so that the drawing can find the needed files. You don't even need to open the AutoCAD drawing, because the Reference Manager is a stand-alone application.

To open the Reference Manager, choose Start ⇨ Programs ⇨ Autodesk ⇨ AutoCAD 2004 ⇨ Reference Manager, shown in Figure 26-29.

Figure 26-29: The Reference Manager

To add drawings to the Reference Manager, click Add Drawings and select the drawings. If a drawing has xrefs, you see a message asking if you want to add the xrefs. To add them, click Yes.

The left pane of the Reference Manager contains a tree view of the drawings you have added and external references, if any. The right pane is a Reference list and displays the specific external files associated with the added files. You can choose View ➪ Options in the Reference Manager to customize how the Reference Manager displays files.

Note Reference Manager does not find text fonts not used in a text style, TrueType fonts not saved in the Windows `Fonts` folder, OLE links, hyperlinks, database file links, PMP files, and external references to URLs on the Web.

To modify the path of an external reference so that a drawing can find it, follow these steps:

1. Close any drawings or files that you might need to access.

2. Choose a drawing in the left pane.

3. Right-click the external reference in the Reference list that you want to change and choose Edit Selected Paths. (You can also choose Edit Selected Paths from the Reference Manager's toolbar.)

Tip You can also choose Find and Replace Selected Paths to change all references that use a certain saved path and replace them with a new path. Use this feature when you have a large number of drawings that need paths to changed referenced files.

4. Type in a new path or use the Ellipsis button to browse to the location. Click OK.

5. From the Reference Manager's toolbar, choose Apply Changes. A summary message appears to confirm that the drawing has been updated.

To create a list of references, choose Export Report. In the Export Report dialog box, choose the file type you want to create from the Files of Type drop-down list. You can create the following file types:

✦ Comma-separated values report file (`*.csv`)

✦ Extensible Markup Language report file (`*.xml`)

✦ Microsoft Excel Workbook (`*.xls`)

Choose a name and a location for the file and then click Save.

New Feature The Express Tools contain a command, REDIR (choose Express ➪ File tools ➪ Redefine Path) redefines paths for xrefs, images, shapes, and fonts.

Handling Errors and Crashes

Although AutoCAD 2004 is stable, and the latest versions of Windows and especially Windows NT are more stable than previous versions, nothing can eliminate the occasional crash. Knowing how to reopen a drawing after a crash can save hours of work.

Taking care of temporary files

When AutoCAD is loaded it opens one or more temporary files as part of its normal functioning. Note the following two points regarding these files:

✦ You need to leave room on your hard drive for these files — 50MB is a good starting point.

✦ Never erase current temporary files if you are on a network because someone else might be using them.

Caution Never erase temporary files (they have an extension of .ac$) while AutoCAD is open. Normally, they are erased when you close a drawing. Others are erased when you close AutoCAD.

However, if AutoCAD or your entire computer crashes, you will probably be left with one or more .ac$ files. A good guideline for erasing .ac$ files is to only erase those from yesterday or earlier. Leave today's alone.

Tip If you don't see the date and time of the files in Explorer, choose View ➪ Details.

You can also specify where AutoCAD places these temporary files. You might want to place them on a hard drive with more room. If you are on a network, you might want to place them on your local drive so that there is less traffic back and forth on the network. If you don't specify the temporary file location, AutoCAD places temporary files in the Windows temporary folder (probably c:\windows\temp). Here's how to change the location:

1. In AutoCAD, choose Tools ➪ Options. The Files tab should be displayed.

2. Click the plus sign next to Temporary Drawing File Location to open the current location, as shown in Figure 26-30.

3. Click the current location and click Browse.

4. In the Browse for Folder list, find and choose the desired folder and click OK.

5. Click OK to close the Options dialog box.

Figure 26-30: The Files tab of the Options dialog box

Repairing corrupted drawing files

The most common cause for a corrupted drawing file is an AutoCAD crash, but power surges and system crashes can also be causes. If AutoCAD detects an error in a file during loading, it attempts to fix the problem automatically. In many cases, it is successful.

When it is not, you can try AutoCAD's AUDIT or RECOVER commands. These commands search the database for errors and try to fix them. If they cannot fix an error, they simply move on, letting you recover at least part of the file.

If you have a drawing open and get an error message that AutoCAD can't read the file or part of it, follow these steps:

1. Choose File ➪ Drawing Utilities ➪ Audit.

2. At the ⌐ix any errors detected? [Yes/No] <N>: prompt, type **y** ⏎ to tell AutoCAD to fix any errors it finds.

3. Watch the screen as it displays messages for errors.

Use RECOVER when you can't even load the drawing. Follow these steps:

1. Open a new drawing.

2. Choose File ➪ Recover.

3. In the Select File dialog box, choose the corrupted drawing file and click Open. AutoCAD begins recovery and displays the results in the text window.

Here are some other tips for opening a recalcitrant drawing:

✦ Open a new drawing and choose Insert ➪ Block. Click Browse and insert the problem drawing as a block. (See Chapter 18 for more information on blocks.) Then use the AUDIT command.

✦ Open a new drawing and choose Insert ➪ External Reference. Locate and attach the problem drawing as an external reference. (See Chapter 19 for more information on external references.) Then use the AUDIT command.

✦ If the drawing crashes just when it looks as if AutoCAD is about done loading it, try again; but this time, press Esc repeatedly until the loading is complete. This procedure aborts the regeneration of the drawing, which may be causing the crash due to corrupt objects. Then use the AUDIT command.

✦ If you can open the drawing but objects are not displayed, try the following:

 • File ➪ Save As and save it as a new drawing.

 • Use the WBLOCK command to save the drawing as a new file.

 • Save the drawing as a DXF file. (See Chapter 27 for more on the DXF file format.)

 • Use File ➪ Save As or save as a DXF format, but to an earlier version of AutoCAD.

Thanks to Darren Young of Minnesota CADWorks, Inc. (www.mcwi.com) for these suggestions.

Using backup drawings

If you can't repair a drawing, perhaps you have an archived copy you can use. If not, AutoCAD automatically creates backup drawings that have the same name as your drawings but with a .bak extension. You can change the extension to .dwg and open it. You may also find one of the .ac$ drawings. You can also try changing the extension of this file to .dwg.

If you want to troubleshoot a persistent crash, try turning on the log file. Choose Tools ➪ Options and choose the Open and Save tab. Check Maintain a log file. This log file lists all your activity and can be used to try to determine what actions caused a crash. You can also customize the log file's location using the Files tab of the Options dialog box.

New Feature The Express Tools contain a command, MOVEBAK (choose Express ➪ Files tools ➪ Move Backup Files) that moves backup files (*.bak) to a folder that you specify and thereafter saves the backup files in that folder every time you save your drawing.

Taking care of your hard disk after a crash

After your hard disk crashes, you should run ScanDisk. In Windows 98, choose Start ➪ Programs ➪ Accessories ➪ ScanDisk. This deletes lost chains and clusters, which are orphaned bits of data that are not in a file.

Defragmenting your hard drive regularly is also a good idea. Files become *fragmented*, meaning that they are stored in noncontiguous locations on your hard drive. This slows down disk access. In Windows XP, choose Start ➪ All Programs ➪ Accessories ➪ System Tools ➪ Disk Defragmenter.

Managing Drawings from Prior AutoCAD Releases

When you upgrade to a new release of AutoCAD, you need to understand how to work with drawings from earlier releases. Also, you may need to send drawings to clients or colleagues who have an earlier release. AutoCAD 2004 uses a new drawing format so that AutoCAD 2002 cannot read AutoCAD 2004 drawings. AutoCAD 2004 reads all earlier drawings.

You can save your AutoCAD 2004 drawings in the following earlier drawing formats:

✦ AutoCAD 2000/LT 2000 Drawing (*.dwg). Because 2002 and 2000 used the same drawing format, this format is also openable in AutoCAD 2002.

✦ AutoCAD 2000/LT 2000 DXF (*.dxf)

✦ AutoCAD R12/LT 2 DXF (*.dxf)

See the next chapter for more about DXF format. Choose File ➪ Save As and choose the file type in the Save as type drop-down list. Then click Save.

Summary

In this chapter, I covered various methods for managing drawings. You read the following:

✦ Using the DesignCenter to access drawing components

✦ Using the new tool palettes to access drawings, blocks, and hatches

✦ Maintaining CAD standards, including checking a drawing against a standards drawing and translating layers

✦ Understanding the new Communication Center

✦ Renaming named objects

✦ Organizing your drawings, including archiving drawings, finding them, and setting properties for them

✦ Maintaining security of your drawings with a password and digital signatures

✦ Using the Reference Manager to keep track of external files referenced in a drawing

✦ Handling errors and crashes

✦ Managing drawings from prior releases

In the next chapter, I cover how to use AutoCAD with other applications.

✦ ✦ ✦

Working with Other Applications

In This Chapter

Coordinating
AutoCAD and
other data

Importing and
exporting other
file formats

Working with
raster images

Pasting, linking, and
embedding objects

AutoCAD is not a world unto itself. Many times you need to work with files or data from other applications. Here are some possibilities:

✦ Working for a client who uses another CAD program

✦ Placing a logo into your title block

✦ Inserting an AutoCAD drawing into a report

✦ Inserting a spreadsheet into your AutoCAD drawing

✦ Using a satellite photo as a basis to create a map

You have several ways of working with other applications:

✦ You can import another file format so that the entire file is brought into AutoCAD.

✦ You can export to another file format so that the entire drawing can be imported into another application.

✦ You can import a *raster* image (bitmap) without changing any file format. A raster image is made up of dots, called *pixels*, as opposed to vectors. AutoCAD is a vector program.

✦ You can import, or export to, a DXF file, which is a way of interchanging drawings between AutoCAD and other CAD programs.

As you can imagine, the possibilities are endless. This chapter explains how to work with other applications.

Importing and Exporting Other File Formats

AutoCAD can export to several other file formats, thereby, enabling you to save the file in another format. You can also import several formats. This section explains how to do both.

Exporting AutoCAD drawings

Table 27-1 shows the file formats AutoCAD can create. Except as noted, you are prompted to select objects to export.

Table 27-1 Export File Formats	
Format	**Description**
WMF	Windows Metafile Format — a Windows vector format.
ACIS	A solid modeling file format stored as `.sat` files, in text (ASCII) form.
STL	Exports a single solid only in a format usable with stereolithography.
BMP	Windows bitmap — a raster format.
EPS	Encapsulated PostScript — a format used by certain printers to create high-quality text and images. Exports all objects.
DXX Extract	A text file containing only block attributes. A variation of DXF format that is used to extract attributes.
3DS	The format used by Autodesk's 3D Studio.
DXF	Drawing Interchange Format — a text format for CAD drawings that most CAD programs accept. You can choose from Releases 2000, 14, 13, and 12 DXF file formats. Exports the entire drawing.
DXB	Another format for transferring CAD drawings, but in binary format (not text) and used less often than the DXF format.
DWF	Drawing Web Format — a format for placing a drawing on a Web site.
JPG	Joint Photographic Expert Group — a raster (bitmap) format commonly used on the Web. It can be compressed, but will lose some detail. Often used for photographs because it supports many colors.
TIF	Tagged Image File Format Format — a raster (bitmap) format often used for scanned images. Provides good quality.
PNG	Portable Network Graphics — a raster (bitmap) format that supports many colors and also compresses well without losing detail. It also supports transparency.

Cross-Reference For more information on the XML and DWF file formats, see the next chapter.

Exporting to DXF format

Figure 27-1 shows the part of a DXF file that defines a line. Not only are objects defined, but all layers, linetypes, and other settings are defined as well. The file lists codes that specify a certain type of data (for example, the X coordinate of a line's endpoint), followed by the values for the codes (for example, 7.55). Because most CAD programs accept this format, you can export to DXF and send the file to someone else who can import it into another CAD program.

```
    8
   0
  100
 AcDbBlockEnd
   0
 ENDSEC
   0
 SECTION
   2
 ENTITIES
   0
 LINE ←──────────────── Object
   5
 4C
 100
 AcDbEntity
   8
 0
 100
 AcDbLine
  10
 2.502408 ←──────────── X coordinate of start point
  20
 4.5 ←────────────────── Y coordinate of start point
  30
 0.0
  11
 7.551711 ←──────────── X coordinate of endpoint
  21
 3.033333 ←──────────── Y coordinate of endpoint
  31
 0.0
```

Figure 27-1: Most CAD programs accept the DXF file format.

To create a DXF file, choose File ⇨ Save As. Choose one of the DXF formats in the Files of type drop-down list. You can save in DXF formats for Releases 14, 2000, and 2004. Click Save.

Note The only way to save an AutoCAD 2004 drawing in Release 14 format is to save it in DXF 14 format. AutoCAD 2004 does not save to Release 14 format directly.

Exporting to other file formats

To export a drawing to another format (except for DWF, JPG, PNG, and TIF), follow these steps:

1. Choose File ⇨ Export to open the Export Data dialog box, shown in Figure 27-2.

2. Choose the file format you want in the Files of type drop-down list.

3. Find the desired folder using the Save in drop-down list and the Folder box.

4. Click Save.

Figure 27-2: The Export Data dialog box

New Feature The JPGOUT, PNGOUT, and TIFOUT commands export to JPG, PNG, and TIF formats respectively.

To export to JPG, PNG, or TIF formats, use the JPGOUT, PNGOUT, or TIFOUT command on the command line. Then, choose a folder, click Save, and select objects at the prompt.

Controlling the display of exported WMF files

The WMFBKGND system variable controls the background of WMF files that you export, whether using the Export dialog box, copying and pasting, or dragging and dropping. When the value of this system variable is Off (the default), the background color of the file is transparent, so that it doesn't interfere with the background on which it is pasted. You can set it to On, so that the background is the same as that of the AutoCAD background. (AutoCAD 2004 changed that default of this system variable from On to Off.)

The WMFFOREGND system variable works in tandem with the WMFBKGND system variable. It controls the foreground (line) color of AutoCAD objects when you export WMF files. WMFFOREGND takes effect only when you set WMFBKGND to 0, which makes the background color transparent. A value of 0, the default, swaps foreground and background colors, if necessary, to make the foreground color (the objects) darker than the background color. A value of 1 does the opposite — the foreground color is lighter than the background color.

On the CD-ROM The drawing used in the following Step-by-Step exercise on exporting a WMF file, ab27-a.dwg, is in the Drawings folder of the *AutoCAD 2004 Bible* CD-ROM.

Step-by-Step: Exporting a WMF File

1. Open ab27-a.dwg from the CD-ROM.

2. Save the file as ab27-01.dwg in your AutoCAD Bible folder. You can see it in Figure 27-3.

Figure 27-3: The Easy Cotton Mills logo

3. Choose File ➪ Export. The Files of type drop-down list should say Metafile (*.wmf). The file name automatically reads ab27-01.wmf.

4. If necessary, locate your AutoCAD Bible folder. Click Save.

5. At the Select objects: prompt, make a window around the red rectangle to include all three objects. End object selection to end the command.

You have created a WMF file.

Importing files

For most file formats, choose Insert from the menu and then the file type you want to import. Find the file in the dialog box and click Open. In most cases, AutoCAD then prompts you for an insertion point, X and Y scale factors, and a rotation angle, just as for block insertion.

Inserting a DXF file

You can import a DXF file in two ways:

✦ To import a DXF file into a new drawing, use the OPEN command to open a new drawing, choose DXF in the Files of type drop-down list, choose the DXF file, and click Open.

✦ To insert a DXF file into an existing drawing, choose Insert ➪ Block. In the Insert dialog box, click Browse. Then choose DXF in the Files of type drop-down list, choose the DXF file, and click Open.

On the
CD-ROM

The file used in the following Step-by-Step exercise on importing a WMF file, ab27-01.wmf, is in the Results folder of the *AutoCAD 2004 Bible* CD-ROM. If you did the previous exercise, you can also find the file in your AutoCAD Bible folder.

Step-by-Step: Importing a WMF File

1. Open a new drawing using the acad.dwt template.

2. Save the file as ab27-02.dwg in your AutoCAD Bible folder.

3. Choose Insert ➪ Windows Metafile.

4. If you did the previous exercise, locate your AutoCAD Bible folder in the Import WMF dialog box. Choose ab27-01.wmf. If you didn't do the previous exercise, find ab27-01.wmf in the Results folder of the CD-ROM. In the Import WMF dialog box, choose Tools ➪ Options. Check Wire Frame (No Fills), uncheck Wide Lines if necessary, and click OK. Click Open.

5. At the Specify insertion point or [Scale/X/Y/Z/Pscale/PX/PY/ PZ/Protate]: prompt, pick any point near the top of your screen. Notice that the insertion point is at the top-left corner of the image.

6. Press Enter to accept the defaults for X and Y scales and rotation angle. Notice that you've lost the solid fill in the logo. The red rectangle came in fine. Also, you may see an added a rectangle around the extents of the image where the extents of the screen were when the WMF file was created.

7. Pick the image. Notice that AutoCAD selects everything with one grip at the insertion point. Choose Explode from the Modify toolbar.

8. Choose Tools ➪ Inquiry ➪ List and pick any part of the logo. Press Enter. Notice from the listing that AutoCAD has converted it to polylines. Repeat the LIST command with the text. It has been converted to a TEXT object. (If the text was based on an AutoCAD SHX font, it would be converted to polylines.) Because AutoCAD converts WMF files to AutoCAD objects, you can edit them, but they may require a good deal of cleanup to attain a pleasing result.

9. Choose Insert ➪ Windows Metafile. Choose `ab27-1.wmf`. Click Options to open the Import Options (WMF In) dialog box, as shown in Figure 27-4. This time check Wide Lines, uncheck Wire Frame, and click OK. In the Import WMF dialog box, click Open to import the file. Pick in a different location in your drawing, and accept the defaults.

10. Explode the inserted image. (You may have to pick it at its edge.) Erase the rectangle and the line at the right that remains. Now you have an image that is very close to the original. The text comes in with the Bookman Old Style font (or the font you used — the same font as the original), although the spacing is not exact. Also, the logo now has its solid fill. It should look like Figure 27-4.

11. Save your drawing.

Figure 27-4: An imported WMF file

Later in this chapter, I show how you can create a WMF file from almost any image by copying it to the clipboard. Because AutoCAD converts these files to AutoCAD objects, you have almost limitless possibilities when importing images into AutoCAD.

Working with Raster Images

You can easily import scanned images and digital photographs into your drawings. Although raster images are generally much larger files than vector drawings, AutoCAD lets you quickly zoom and pan throughout your drawing. You can usually plot these raster images as well. Table 27-2 shows the raster formats that AutoCAD 2004 supports.

File Type	File Extension	Comments
Table 27-2		
Raster Formats Supported by AutoCAD 2004		
BMP	`.bmp, .dib, .rle`	Windows and OS/2 bitmap
CALS-1	`.gp4, .mil, .rst, .cg4, .cal`	Mil-R-Raster 1
GIF	`.gif`	CompuServe Graphics Exchange Format
GeoSPOT	`.bil`	GeoSPOT (used in GIS applications); HDR and PAL files with correlation data must be in the same folder)
JFIF or JPEG	`.jpg, .jpeg`	Joint Photographic Expert Group
FLIC	`.flc, .fli`	Autodesk Animator FLIC
IG4	`.ig4`	Image Systems Group 4
IGS	`.igs`	Image Systems Graysacle
PCX	`.pcx`	Paintbrush
PICT	`.pct`	Macintosh picture
PNG	`.png`	Portable Network Graphic
RLC	`.rlc`	Run-Length Compressed
TARGA	`.tga`	True Vision Raster-Based Data Format
TIF	`.tif, .tiff`	Tagged Image File Format

Inserting images

To insert an image, choose Insert ➪ Raster Image to open the Select Image File dialog box, as shown in Figure 27-5.

Figure 27-5: The Select Image File dialog box

Locate the image you want to insert and choose Open. AutoCAD now opens the Image dialog box, shown in Figure 27-6, which lets you specify how to insert the image. You can specify the insertion point, scale, and rotation in the dialog box or on-screen. This dialog box is very similar to the Insert dialog box that you use when inserting drawings and blocks.

Figure 27-6: The Image dialog box

Note The insertion point is at the bottom-left corner of the image. Check Retain Path if you don't plan to move the image file's location and if the file is not in AutoCAD's Support file or Project file search path. The support and project search paths can be customized by choosing Tools ➪ Options and using the Files tab.

Click Details to open the bottom of the dialog box, shown in Figure 27-7.

Figure 27-7: The Image Information section of the Attach Image dialog box

Here AutoCAD lists the resolution (number of pixels) per drawing unit and the size in pixels, as well as the size in drawing units. The Current AutoCAD Unit is based on the specification in the Units dialog box. (See Chapter 5 for more information.) This information is very helpful in deciding how to scale an image.

Note Raster images usually don't scale up very well. If you enlarge them too much, the dots get too far apart and the image looks grainy. However, the higher the resolution, the better the image will look when enlarged.

Click OK to insert the image.

You can also use the DesignCenter to insert raster images, as described in Chapter 26.

New Feature The Express Tools contain a command, IMAGEEDIT (choose Express ➪ File tools ➪ Edit Image) that opens a selected image in a specified image-editing application.

Managing images

Choose Insert ➪ Image Manager to open the Image Manager (as shown in Figure 27-8), which enables you to manage the images in your drawing. You can insert images from this dialog box as well.

Figure 27-8: The Image Manager

You can use the List view and Tree view buttons at the top of the dialog box to view your images in a flat list or a hierarchical (tree) format. Here are the other options:

- ✦ **Attach** inserts an image, opening the Image dialog box, shown previously in Figure 27-6.

- ✦ **Detach** erases the image from your drawing and deletes all reference to it in the drawing database.

- ✦ **Reload** redisplays an image after you have unloaded it.

- ✦ **Unload** removes the display of the image but retains the reference to it. Later, you can reload the image to redisplay it.

- ✦ **Details** provides you with a preview, as well as information about the image, its path, and its size.

✦ The **Image Found At** box shows you the location of the image. If you didn't save a path when attaching the image, you can do so by clicking Save Path. You can also find an image whose Status shows Not Found by choosing Browse. This would happen if you moved the image after attaching it.

Tip

You can attach rendered images that you have saved as TIF, TGA, or BMP files. A great way to do this is to create a floating viewport in paper space for the rendered image, letting your clients see not only the regular drawing but the rendered result on one sheet of paper. Figure 25-25 in Chapter 25 was created this way. Remember that you can now plot shaded and rendered images. See Chapter 17 for details.

Clipping images

A powerful feature of AutoCAD lets you clip images just as you clip external references. Large images can slow down your drawing display. You may also simply find it distracting to see parts of an image that you don't need for your work. For example, if you attach an aerial photograph of a city block but want only one house, it is a great advantage to be able to clip around the house and not display the rest of the image.

To clip an image, follow these steps:

1. Insert an image.

2. Choose Modify ➪ Clip ➪ Image.

3. At the `Select image to clip:` prompt, select the image. Pick the image at its border.

4. At the prompt, press Enter to accept the default of creating a new clipping boundary.

5. At the `Enter clipping type [Polygonal/Rectangular] <Rectangular>:` prompt, press Enter to create a rectangular clip or right-click and choose Polygonal to create a multisided boundary.

 • For a rectangular boundary, pick a first point and the opposite corner to create the boundary.

 • For a polygonal boundary, specify the first point and then use the `Specify next point or [Undo]:` prompt to pick points until you have completed the boundary. You can use the Undo option to undo the last pick or the Close option (which appears after you pick three points) to close the final boundary. AutoCAD creates a rubber-band boundary as you pick points so you can see the result. Press Enter when you are done.

At the `Enter image clipping option [ON/OFF/Delete/New boundary]` `<New>`: prompt, you can also use the following options:

✦ Choose ON to turn on a boundary that you previously turned off.

✦ Choose OFF to turn off a boundary and redisplay the entire image.

✦ Choose Delete to delete the clipping boundary.

Note
Images are 2D objects. The clipping boundary must be parallel to the plane of the image. For information on placing images on 3D objects, see the sidebar, "Mapping," in Chapter 25.

Controlling image display

You can control several aspects of image display using the commands detailed in this section.

Image display

Choose Modify ➪ Object ➪ Image ➪ Adjust to start the IMAGEADJUST command and open the Image Adjust dialog box, as shown in Figure 27-9.

Figure 27-9: The Image Adjust dialog box

This dialog box enables you to dynamically change the brightness, contrast, and fade of the image, using the slider bars or text boxes. You immediately see the results in the preview box. Choose Reset to return the image to its original status.

Image quality

Choose Modify ➪ Object ➪ Image ➪ Quality to start the IMAGEQUALITY command. AutoCAD displays the `Enter image quality setting [High/Draft] <High>`: prompt. Choose either High or Draft. This command affects the display of all the images in a drawing. Use it when a high-quality image slows down performance. A regen is not necessary after you change this setting. Plotting is always done at high quality.

Image transparency

If the image format you are using supports transparent pixels, you can use the TRANSPARENCY command to create a transparent background for your image. This works for bitonal or grayscale images. (*Bitonal* images have only a foreground and a background color.) By default, transparency is off.

To turn transparency on, choose Modify ➪ Object ➪ Image ➪ Transparency and select the image(s) you want to change. At the `Enter transparency mode [ON/OFF] <OFF>:` prompt, type **on** ⏎ and do a regen. Other objects in your drawing will now be visible through the background of your image.

Image frame

The IMAGEFRAME command turns off the frame that surrounds all images in a drawing. Choose Modify ➪ Object ➪ Image ➪ Frame. Turning off the frame often improves the way the image looks. However, you select an image by clicking its frame. Therefore, an Off setting means you cannot select the image, except when using commands specific to images, such as TRANSPARENCY, IMAGEADJUST, and IMAGECLIP.

Tip

Don't turn the frame off until you have finished editing the image. You can also select raster images using Quick Select. Because raster images are considered to be on the layer that is active when they are inserted, you can use Quick Select to select them by layer.

When an image has a border, the border displays the properties of the layer that was current when the image was inserted.

On the CD-ROM

The drawing used in the following Step-by-Step exercise on working with raster images, ab27-b.dwg, and the images ab27-b.tif and ab27-b1.bmp, are in the Drawings folder of the *AutoCAD 2004 Bible* CD-ROM.

Step-by-Step: Working with Raster Images

1. Open ab27-b.dwg from the CD-ROM.

2. Save the file as ab27-03.dwg in your AutoCAD Bible folder.

3. Choose View ➪ 3D Views ➪ Top.

4. Choose Insert ➪ Raster Image.

5. In the Select Image File dialog box, choose ab27-b.tif from the CD-ROM. Click Open. Click Details. Notice that the image is 1×0.61 units. Compared to the house, it is tiny.

6. In the Image dialog box, uncheck Specify on-screen for the Scale factor and change the scale factor to 5. Click OK.

7. At the `Specify insertion point <0,0>:` prompt, pick any point on the left side of the screen. The image is still tiny, but that's okay. Choose Zoom Window from the Zoom flyout of the Standard toolbar to zoom closely into the image.

8. Choose Modify ⇨ Object ⇨ Image ⇨ Adjust. At the `Select image(s):` prompt, select the image by picking its frame. Press Enter. In the Image Adjust dialog box, change the Contrast to 60 and the Brightness to 40. Choose OK.

9. Choose Modify ⇨ Clip ⇨ Image. At the `Select image to clip:` prompt, select the image again, which is shown in Figure 27-11. Follow the prompts:

```
Enter image clipping option [ON/OFF/Delete/New boundary]
<New>: ↵
Enter clipping type [Polygonal/Rectangular] <Rectangular>: ↵
Specify first corner point: If OSNAP is on, turn it off. Pick
❶ in Figure 27-10.
Specify opposite corner point: Pick ❷.
```

Figure 27-10: Clipping the raster image

10. Use Zoom Realtime to zoom out so that you have room to insert another image. Choose Insert ⇨ Raster Image and attach `ab27-b1.bmp` (located on the CD-ROM) with a scale factor of 5. Insert it below the first image.

11. Click the Layout1 tab to enter paper space, which has three floating viewports. Click PAPER to enter model space. Click the bottom-left viewport. Choose View ⇨ 3D Views ⇨ Top. You should now see the images as a small dot to the left of the house. Use Zoom Window to zoom into the rendered table. Your drawing should now look like Figure 27-11.

12. Click the right viewport. If necessary, pan the house to the right until you can see the two images you attached. Move the Cottonmill Houses image to ❶ in Figure 27-11. Scale it, using a base point at its lower-left corner and a scale factor of 25. Move it until it fits nicely in the upper-right corner of the floor plan. Pan again to center the house in the viewport. (If it disappears, do a Zoom Extents.)

13. Choose Modify ⇨ Object ⇨ Image ⇨ Frame. Right-click and choose Off. AutoCAD removes the frames from the two images.

14. Save your drawing.

Figure 27-11: The drawing with a rendered view in one viewport

Tip

The DRAWORDER command changes the display order of objects, including raster and OLE objects. (OLE is discussed later in this chapter.) This command is very helpful when working with raster and OLE objects, where you may or may not want to hide the other objects in your drawing. You can move an object to the top or bottom or change its order in relation to another object—above or below it. To change an object's display order, choose Tools ⇨ Display Order and choose one of the submenu options. AutoCAD then prompts you to select objects. Draw order settings are now saved with the drawing.

Pasting, Linking, and Embedding Objects

To maximize the data you have in your AutoCAD drawing and other documents, you can insert objects from other applications into your drawing. For example, you may have a description of your drawing in a word processing application or a table in a spreadsheet. You can use the Windows clipboard to share data between applications.

Cross-Reference

In Chapter 18, I explain how to use the Windows clipboard to copy and move material from one drawing to another. Chapter 13 includes a discussion of several techniques for importing text into your drawing.

You can insert data (text or images) created with other applications into an AutoCAD drawing in three ways:

✦ **Embed** the object if you want to have the capability of returning to the source application to edit the object. When you double-click the object, the source application opens so that you can edit the object.

✦ **Paste** the object when you don't need any connection with the source application — perhaps you want to be able to edit it using AutoCAD or you just want to display it.

✦ **Link** the object when you want to retain a permanent link to the source file so that when the source file is changed the change is updated in your AutoCAD file.

You can use the clipboard to move material from one application to another and take advantage of the special options for pasting, linking, and embedding data. Linking and embedding are often referred to as *OLE* — Object Linking and Embedding. You can also use drag-and-drop between applications.

The instructions that follow assume that the source application — the application that contains the data you want to insert — is also a Windows or Windows NT application.

Embedding objects into AutoCAD

You have three ways to embed data from other applications. Each method has its advantages and disadvantages.

Here's the first way:

1. From AutoCAD, choose Insert ➪ OLE Object to open the Insert Object dialog box, shown in Figure 27-12. This starts the INSERTOBJ command. (The entries listed in this dialog box depend on the applications you have installed on your computer.)

2. If you want to create a new file in the other application, choose Create New. Choose the application you want to use from the Object Type list, and click OK. The other application opens, so you can create the new data. When you are done, choose File ➪ Update from the other application's menu. (This menu item can vary, depending on the application.) Click the Close button at the top-right corner of the application to close it and return to AutoCAD. If the OLE Properties dialog box appears, specify how you want the object to appear and click OK. The new file is inserted.

Figure 27-12: The Insert Object dialog box

3. If you want to choose an existing file, choose Create From File. Click Browse to find the file. Click Open. You return to the Insert Object file where you can choose Link to link the data (described in the next section of this chapter). Choose OK. AutoCAD places the file at the top-left corner of your screen with handles that you can use to move and/or resize the object.

Here's the second way:

1. Open the source application, select the data, and copy it to the clipboard. (Click Copy on the Standard toolbar or choose Edit ➪ Copy.) Leave the source application open.

2. If AutoCAD is open, switch to it by choosing its button on the task bar. Otherwise, open it.

3. In your drawing, choose Edit ➪ Paste Special.

4. In the Paste Special dialog box, choose the first option, which lets you embed the object as an object of the source application. Click OK.

5. You can now close the other application.

The third way to insert data is to use drag-and-drop:

1. If AutoCAD is not open, open it. Open the drawing where you want to embed the data.

2. Open the source application and select the data.

3. Press Ctrl and click the selected data again, holding down the mouse button.

4. Drag the data to the AutoCAD button on the Windows task bar and continue to hold down the mouse button until the AutoCAD screen comes up.

5. Drag the data to the desired location in your drawing.

Using INSERTOBJ gives you the option of creating a new file on the spot in the other application. You don't have to keep the other application open when you return to AutoCAD. Note that you cannot create a link if you are creating a new file.

Using the clipboard enables you to insert part of a file — for example, part of a spreadsheet — which can be a great advantage. You need to keep the other application open until you paste the object into AutoCAD.

OLE objects have a few limitations in AutoCAD:

✦ If they are contained in a block or an external reference, they may not be displayed or plotted.

✦ In certain cases, OLE objects can be printed out only on Windows system printers. You can usually configure your plotter to be the system printer.

✦ OLE objects don't rotate with your drawing when you use a PLOT rotation. Instead, you could use the system printer's Landscape setting.

Tip If you don't mind a few steps, you can sometimes get good results importing large Excel spreadsheets by way of Microsoft Word, as follows: In Excel, use Save As to save the spreadsheet in Text (Tab delimited) format. Insert the file into Word (choose Text Files from the Open dialog box's Files of type drop-down list). Select the entire file and choose Table ➪ Convert ➪ Text to Table. Change the Page Setup to accommodate the large size of the table, using a custom paper size. Format the table if you want. Copy it to the clipboard. In AutoCAD, choose Paste on the Standard toolbar.

When you insert an OLE object, AutoCAD opens the OLE Properties dialog box, as shown in Figure 27-13.

Use this dialog box to specify the height or scale of the OLE object. If the OLE object is a text document, you can specify the text size in points or AutoCAD units.

In the OLE plot quality, choose the type of file you are inserting. You can choose from Line Art (such as a spreadsheet), Text, Graphics (such as a chart), Photograph, and High-Quality Photograph. Click OK to insert the OLE object.

Tip If you try to use HIDE on a 3D model that contains OLE objects, the OLE objects disappear! The solution is to insert them in paper space. You can then hide the 3D model in one floating viewport and display the OLE object in another.

Using Paste Special

When you copy data to the clipboard, it is stored in several formats, depending on the type of data. You can then choose which format you want to use when you paste it into your drawing, using the PASTESPEC command. Choosing the right format can make a big difference, enabling you to edit the data in your drawing as you wish.

Figure 27-13: The OLE Properties dialog box

Pasting data into AutoCAD

To paste data using PASTESPEC, open the source application, select the data, and copy it to the clipboard. (Click Copy on the Standard toolbar or choose Edit ⇨ Copy.) Leave the source application open.

If AutoCAD is open, choose its button on the task bar. If not, open it.

In your drawing, choose Edit ⇨ Paste Special. This opens the Paste Special dialog box, shown in Figure 27-14. In this figure, you see the options available when you paste in a range of cells from a spreadsheet.

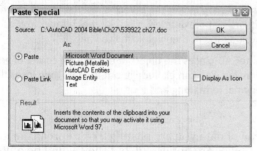

Figure 27-14: The Paste Special dialog box after copying spreadsheet data to the clipboard

The choices you see in the As box of the Paste Special dialog box depend on the type of data you copied. In most cases, you can paste as an object of the source application, as a picture (metafile), as a bitmap, and as text. Table 27-3 describes the characteristics of the choices available in the example in Figure 27-14.

	Table 27-3
	Paste Special Data Types
Data Type	**Characteristics**
Object of source application	AutoCAD places the object at the top-left corner of your drawing. You cannot explode the object, but you can select it and then resize it or move it using its handles. This is an embedded object—if you double-click it, the source application opens, letting you edit the object using the source application's tools.
Picture (Metafile or Enhanced Metafile)	AutoCAD places the object at the top-left corner of your drawing. You cannot explode the object, but you can select it and then resize it or move it using its handles. You cannot edit the object using the source application (or using AutoCAD). It maintains good quality when scaled up.
Bitmap	AutoCAD places the object at the top-left corner of your drawing. You cannot explode the object, but you can select it and then resize it or move it using its handles. You cannot edit the object using the source application (or using AutoCAD).
AutoCAD Entities	AutoCAD prompts for an insertion point, scale factor, and rotation angle. You can explode the object into AutoCAD objects. (Objects were once called *entities* in AutoCAD.) Text objects maintain their original font and formatting.
Image Entity	AutoCAD prompts for an insertion point, scale factor, and rotation angle. The object is inserted as a 1×1 unit square—approximately. It is a kind of bitmap. You can explode it, but then you lose the image!
Text	AutoCAD places the object at the top-left corner of your drawing. You can explode it, but the text then loses the original formatting and font.

The best choice depends on the type of data you are pasting. For a spreadsheet, the Picture, Bitmap, and Image Entity choices are not useful, but they would be quite appropriate if you were pasting in an image.

Converting objects

Some pasted objects can be converted to other types of objects. Try right-clicking anywhere on the object that was pasted. If you get a menu, choose an object type and then Convert Picture Object (the menu item varies with the type of object) to open the Convert dialog box, as shown in Figure 27-15. Sometimes no choices are available other than the current image type.

Figure 27-15: Sometimes you can convert one object type into another with the Convert dialog box. Here you can convert a Paintbrush object to a Picture object.

Pasting AutoCAD objects into another application

You can also copy AutoCAD objects to the clipboard and paste them into another application, such as a word processing document, a spreadsheet, or a presentation program. Figure 27-16 shows a PowerPoint slide that includes a model from an AutoCAD drawing. To paste AutoCAD objects into another application, select the objects you want to copy. Click Copy on the Standard toolbar. Load the other application (in this case PowerPoint), create a document or file (in this case a slide), and click Paste from the application's Standard toolbar.

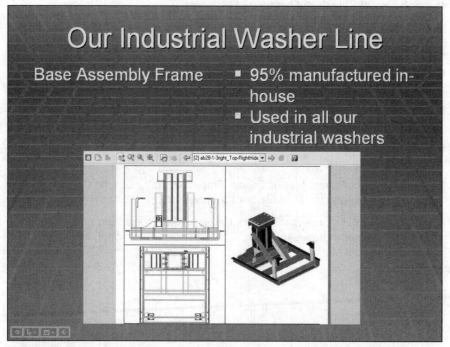

Figure 27-16: Placing part of an AutoCAD drawing on a PowerPoint slide

Tip

You can hide a 3D view and copy and paste the view into another application. However, you cannot copy and paste a rendered view. To bring a rendered view into another application, save it as an image and import it. Chapter 25 covers saving rendered images. You can freeze any layers that you don't want to include, such as dimension and text layers.

Inserting AutoCAD as an ActiveX component into PowerPoint

When you insert or paste AutoCAD objects into another document, such as a Word document or PowerPoint presentation, the objects are static images. What if you could display your AutoCAD drawing dynamically, with zooming and panning? You could then show your intended audience all the detail you want.

It turns out that you can. You can use the DWF format (covered in more detail in Chapter 28) and insert it into any version Word, Excel, or PowerPoint that supports ActiveX components. Viewers need the free Autodesk Express Viewer, which they can download at `http://usa.autodesk.com/adsk/section/0,,2396677-123112,00.html`.

Here are instructions for PowerPoint.

1. Create the DWF file. (See Chapter 28.)

2. In PowerPoint, choose a slide layout that gives you room for the DWF file.

3. Choose Insert ⇨ Object.

4. Click Create New and then choose Autodesk Express Viewer Control. Click OK. You see a box with handles on your slide.

5. If you want, resize or move the box. (If you deselect the box, it disappears. Click inside the box to select it again.)

6. Right-click the box and choose Autodesk Express Viewer Control Objects ⇨ Properties.

7. In the Autodesk Express Viewer Control Properties dialog box, on the SourcePath tab, type the path to the DWF file or click browse to browse to the file.

8. In your PowerPoint presentation, click the Slide Show View button to enter Slide Show view. You can now pan, zoom, turn layers on and off, print, and so on from within your presentation.

Linking data

You can insert data from a spreadsheet or text document and maintain a link to the original file, so that if the original file changes the inserted data is updated as well, very similar to xrefs. You could use this feature to place a schedule of doors and windows in an architectural drawing or a bill of materials in a mechanical drawing, for example. You have two ways to link data. You can link data using INSERTOBJ as described earlier in this chapter. You can also use the clipboard, using these steps:

1. Open the source application, select the data, and copy it to the clipboard. (Click Copy on the Standard toolbar or choose Edit ➪ Copy.)

2. If AutoCAD is open, choose its button on the task bar. If not, open it.

3. In your drawing, choose Edit ➪ Paste Special.

4. In the Paste Special dialog box, choose Paste Link. Click OK.

When you create a link, you don't have all the format options you do when you simply paste. You can only create a link in the source application's format.

When you open an AutoCAD drawing containing a link, AutoCAD displays a message asking if you want to update the links. In this way, you can update the links

whenever you open the drawing. You can manage links by choosing Edit ➪ OLE Links, to open the Links dialog box, shown in Figure 27-17.

The Links dialog box enables you to manually update the links at any time by choosing Update Now. You may want to do this if you know that someone has changed the source of the link during your drawing session. You can also break the link, open the source, or change the source in this dialog box.

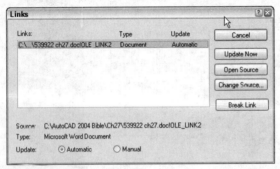

Figure 27-17: Use the Links dialog box to manage your links.

Remember that if you give a drawing to someone else, you also need to include any attached images or embedded objects. If the person does not have the source application for an embedded object, you can paste it in as an image.

On the CD-ROM
The drawing, ab27-c.dwg, and the file, ab27-c.xls, used in the following Step-by-Step exercise on pasting, linking, and embedding objects are in the Drawings folder of the *AutoCAD 2004 Bible* CD-ROM.

To do the following exercise, you need a spreadsheet application. I use Microsoft Excel in this exercise, but you can use Lotus 1-2-3 as well.

Step-by-Step: Pasting, Linking, and Embedding Objects

1. Open ab27-c.dwg from the CD-ROM.

2. Save the file as ab27-04.dwg in your AutoCAD Bible folder.

3. Choose Insert ➪ OLE Object. Choose Create New and choose your worksheet application from the list. Click OK. Your worksheet program opens.

4. Create the worksheet shown in Figure 27-18. Adjust the width of the columns to fit the data.

5. In the spreadsheet application, choose File ➪ Update and then choose File ➪ Exit. The worksheet appears in the AutoCAD drawing, as shown in Figure 27-19.

	A	B	C	D
1	Tag	Part No.	Description	
2	11	9075-052-002	Collar-Shaft	
3	17	9029-072-001	Bracket-Tube Assembly	
4	19	9081-114-001	Channel Motor Mtg. Rod	

Figure 27-18: Create this worksheet to insert into your AutoCAD drawing.

Figure 27-19: The spreadsheet inserted into the drawing

6. In the OLE Properties dialog box, change the OLE Plot Quality drop-down list to Line Art and click OK.

7. Place the cursor in the spreadsheet object and drag it so that it is just above the model in the drawing. Press Esc to remove the handles.

8. Open your spreadsheet application and open ab27-c.xls from the CD-ROM. Select the last three columns, as shown in Figure 27-20. Click Copy on the spreadsheet's Standard toolbar.

	A	B	C	D	E	F	G
1	Qty.	Tag	Part No.	Description	Dwg. Size	Pur/Made	Units
2	2	19	9081-114-001	CHANNEL-MOTOR MTG ROD	B	P	EACH
3	2	17	9029-072-001	BRACKET-TUBE ASSY	D	M	EACH
4	2	11	9076-052-002	COLLAR-SHAFT	B	M	EACH

Figure 27-20: Selecting part of a file to insert into AutoCAD

9. Leave your spreadsheet open and click the AutoCAD button on the Windows task bar. Choose Edit ➪ Paste Special. While you would probably insert this as an Excel Worksheet (or object from your spreadsheet application), to try another method, choose AutoCAD Entities and click OK. Pick an insertion point near the top-right corner of the existing OLE object.

10. Choose Tools ➪ Inquiry ➪ List and select any of the new text objects. A sample is shown in Figure 27-21. Notice that AutoCAD has created a new text style that closely matches the original text in the spreadsheet.

11. Return to your spreadsheet and choose Edit ➪ Copy again. Return to AutoCAD and choose Edit ➪ Paste Special. Choose Paste Link. Now you can only paste in your spreadsheet's format. Click OK. AutoCAD inserts the spreadsheet at the top-left corner of your screen.

```
Select objects: 1 found, 1 total

Select objects:

                    TEXT      Layer: "0"
                              Space: Model space
                    Color: 7 (white)    Linetype: "BYLAYER"
                    LineWeight: 0.00 mm
                    Handle = 4F1
            Style = "WMF-Arial3"
            Typeface = Arial
            start point, X=  51.2493  Y=  17.9381  Z=   0.0000
        height    0.5999
         text Dwg. Size
     rotation angle         0
        width scale factor      1.0000
   obliquing angle         0
  generation normal
```

Figure 27-21: A listing of one of the new text objects

12. Return to your spreadsheet and change the cell F2 (which now says P) to M and press Enter. Go back to AutoCAD and watch the P change to an M. Any changes made to the spreadsheet are updated in your AutoCAD drawing.

13. Save your drawing. Close your spreadsheet program without saving the change you made.

Summary

In this chapter, you read the following:

✦ Importing and exporting other file formats, including both vector and bitmap (raster) formats

✦ Working with DXF files

✦ Managing images and controlling their display

✦ Pasting, linking, and embedding objects into AutoCAD

The next chapter discusses how to integrate AutoCAD with the Internet.

✦ ✦ ✦

Getting on the Internet

AutoCAD 2004 offers many ways to integrate your drawings with the Internet. You can open AutoCAD drawings from a Web site, hyperlink objects to anywhere on the Web, and publish drawings on a Web site. When you access a Web site (perhaps your company's intranet), you can find blocks or other data and drag them into your drawing. This chapter covers all the ways to connect AutoCAD and the Internet.

Sending Drawings

You can send your AutoCAD drawings to others on your team or to your clients instantly — by either faxing or e-mailing them, just as you fax and e-mail other documents. Fax a drawing if the recipient doesn't have AutoCAD and wants to quickly see the drawing on paper. (Later in this chapter, I explain how someone without AutoCAD can use Autodesk Express Viewer to view AutoCAD drawings.)

Use e-mail if the recipient has AutoCAD and may need to edit the drawing. You can also send a drawing to an FTP site.

Faxing a drawing from within AutoCAD

If you have fax software installed that you use to fax files from your computer, you can fax a drawing by following these steps:

1. Open the drawing you want to fax.

2. Choose File ➪ Plot. On the Plot Device tab of the Plot dialog box, choose the printer driver included with your fax software. Use the Scaled to Fit option on the Plot Settings tab so your drawing fits on the recipient's 8½×11 sheet of fax paper. Choose OK.

3. Your fax software opens a dialog box to let you specify the recipient, whether or not to send a cover page, and so on. Choose Send or Send Fax in the dialog box to send the fax.

FTPing a drawing

FTP stands for File Transfer Protocol and is a method of uploading or downloading drawings from a computer via the Internet or an intranet. You can set up FTP locations by choosing Tools ⇨ Add/Modify FTP Locations from the menu of any dialog box that lets you select drawings (such as Select File or Save Drawing As). You need to list the name of the FTP site, choose a log on type (Anonymous or User), and specify your user name and password if you are logging on as a User. You can then open drawings from, and save them to, FTP locations.

To FTP a drawing, choose File ⇨ Save As. Choose FTP, which is the last item on the Places list on the left side of the dialog box. (You may have to scroll down to see it.) Here you see FTP sites that you have added to the list. Select the FTP site and click Save.

E-mailing a drawing

You can e-mail a drawing from your e-mail program. In most cases, when you e-mail a drawing, you write an e-mail message and include the drawing file as an attachment. Your recipient opens the attachment, automatically launching AutoCAD. You may want to use compression software, such as PKZIP or WinZip to compress the drawing to reduce sending and receiving time.

The eTransmit feature is essentially the same as Pack and Go in Microsoft Office, packing together all associated files with your drawing so that you can e-mail it to colleagues, clients, customers, and so on.

To start a transmission, choose File ⇨ eTransmit. AutoCAD opens the Create Transmittal dialog box, shown in Figure 28-1 with the General tab on top.

In the Notes section, write a note to the recipient. The content of the Notes section becomes part of the transmittal report, a separate file included in the EXE or ZIP file. If you send an e-mail message, the note becomes the body of the message.

In the Type section, use the drop-down list to choose one of the following types of transmittals:

Figure 28-1: The Create Transmittal dialog box enables you to create a transmittal file that you can attach to an e-mail message. The transmittal file contains a drawing along with all its associated files.

✦ **Folder (set of files):** Creates a folder that includes all the files in the transmittal. The files are not compressed.

✦ **Self-extracting executable (*.exe):** Creates a compressed EXE file. Recipients can double-click the file to decompress and extract the files. (Some people won't open .exe files for fear of computer viruses so you might need to notify your recipient in advance that you are sending the .exe file. Also, some e-mail programs block .exe attachments.)

✦ **Zip (*.zip):** Creates a compressed ZIP file. Recipients need WinZip, PKZIP, or a similar decompression application.

For added security, click Password to specify a password that will be required to open the drawing. Be sure to tell your recipient the password.

By default, AutoCAD creates the transmittal file in the same location as the open drawing. You can use the Location section to specify a different location by clicking Browse.

Tip Because you don't need the transmittal file after you have sent it (you already have all the files), you can put it in the `Windows\Temp` file or another location where you place files that you will delete.

At the bottom of the dialog box are several check boxes:

✦ Check **Convert Drawing To** if you want to convert the drawing to AutoCAD 2000 format before sending. Choose the version from the drop-down list.

✦ Check **Preserve Directory Structure** to keep the same structure of directories (folders) during decompression. For example, the transmittal file includes font files, which normally do not go in the same folder as a drawing. Preserving Directory Structure makes it easier to install the font and other files in their proper locations. You'll probably need to explain this to your recipient.

✦ **Remove Paths from Xrefs and Images** removes references to folder locations of xrefs and images. If you have xrefs or images and don't check this box, when your recipients open the drawing, the drawing will search for the xrefs or images in a folder that most likely won't exist.

✦ **Send E-mail with Transmittal** opens your e-mail program and creates a new message with the files as attachments and the notes as the body of the message. Using this feature makes sending your drawings extremely easy.

✦ **Make Web Page Files** creates a Web page with a link to the transmittal files. You can post this Web page on an intranet or tell recipients the Web page URL so they can download the files from the Web page. See Figure 28-2 for an example of the Web page this feature creates.

Click the Files tab to see the files that AutoCAD is planning on including in your transmittal. The normal files are `acad.fmp` (the font map that specifies font substitutions), SHX files (usually compiled fonts), and any xrefs, raster images, or standards files attached to the drawing. However, eTransmit does *not* include files referred to by hyperlinks. Therefore, if you want hyperlinks to work, you need to add the referenced files.

To add files, click Add File, navigate to the desired file, select it, and click Open.

You can view the files as a list or in a branching tree format by clicking either the List View or Tree View button.

You can exclude fonts by unchecking the Include Fonts check box at the bottom of the dialog box. If your drawing only uses fonts included in a normal installation of AutoCAD, you can probably assume that your recipients have them. TrueType fonts are not included because they are proprietary.

To see the Transmittal Report, click the Report tab. The report includes your Notes (from the General tab) and instructions to the recipient for using the associated files. For example, there are instructions for where to place SHX files and xrefs. Choose Save As to create an additional copy of the report for your own records.

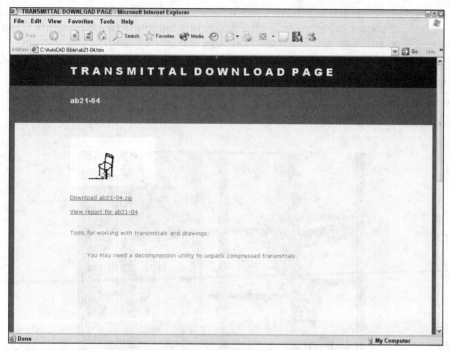

Figure 28-2: The Web page created by eTransmit

When you're done, click OK. If you checked Send E-mail, AutoCAD opens your e-mail program, and you can send an e-mail message and the files. Either way, AutoCAD creates the type of transmittal files you requested. If you checked Make Web Page Files, don't forget to upload not only the HTM file, but the transmittal file or files as well. AutoCAD also creates a bitmap file to display as a thumbnail of the drawing.

Opening Drawings from the Web

You can access drawings, blocks, and so on from the Internet in the same way you currently access them on your hard drive or network. Sharing drawings around the world can be as easy as opening a drawing on your hard drive. AutoCAD 2004 now has two methods for bringing objects from the Internet into your drawings.

Using the Browse the Web – Open dialog box

 You can directly open a drawing from the Web from the Select File dialog box (choose File ➪ Open) using the Search the Web button. As long as you have an

active connection to the Internet, AutoCAD opens the Browse the Web – Open dialog box, as shown in Figure 28-3. This dialog box functions as a Web-aware Open dialog box, enabling you to access drawings and other files over the Internet.

Figure 28-3: The Browse the Web – Open dialog box

Note If you have Microsoft Internet Explorer, version 4.0 or higher, you will be able to open drawings from the Web.

In the Browse the Web – Open dialog box, use the Look in text box just like the Address box of your Web browser. (The Look in box defaults to the Autodesk Web site.) You can click the down arrow at the right and see the same list of recently used Web addresses (URLs) that you see in your browser. You may need to enter a user name and password, depending on the requirements of the Web site. When you get to the Web page you need, you can click the drawing or its link to place the drawing name in the File name text box at the bottom of the dialog box. You can also directly type the URL and name of a drawing, such as `http://www.rainbow.com/ffairport/hangar-a.dwg`. (This is not an existing URL—it is an example only.)

As soon as you find the drawing you want, click Open. AutoCAD opens the drawing file.

You can do the same with raster images and xrefs. With proper authorization, you can save drawings to a Web URL.

Using i-drop to drag objects into a drawing

 An i-drop enabled Web site displays the i-drop cursor when you pass the cursor over an image, as shown in Figure 28-4. This cursor indicates that you can drag the object represented by the image into your drawing. For more information on creating i-drop-enabled Web sites, go to `http://idrop.autodesk.com`. The Publish to Web feature, covered later in this chapter, also contains i-drop capability.

Figure 28-4: Dragging an object from an i-drop-enabled Web site

Thanks to Eric Stover of Autodesk for permission to display this i-drop example from the Autodesk i-drop Web site.

New Feature Since AutoCAD 2002, i-drop has been expanded to add a feature that prompts you to save associated blocks or data when you drag with the right mouse button. Also, inserted blocks automatically include a hyperlink to the source of the content. A history log has also been added.

Creating Object Hyperlinks

You can insert hyperlinks between objects in your drawing and files or Web sites that may be located anywhere on the Internet, a network, or your own hard drive. A hyperlink creates a permanent connection between your drawing and other files that may provide supporting documentation or additional information.

When you follow a hyperlink, the appropriate application is opened with the specified file. For example, a Web site will be opened with your Web browser, and a word processing document will be opened with your word processing application.

Creating a hyperlink

Before you create your hyperlink, consider the environment in which it will be used. The file or Web page you are linking to must be available for the hyperlink to work. If you send an AutoCAD drawing with hyperlinks to a colleague, for example, be sure to include the files that the hyperlinks refer to. If you are posting the drawing on a Web site as a DWF file, you need to upload the files the hyperlinks refer to along with the DWF file.

Here's how you create a hyperlink:

1. Select one or more objects in your drawing. The hyperlink will be attached to these objects.

2. Choose Insert ⇨ Hyperlink (or Ctrl+K) to open the Insert Hyperlink dialog box, shown in Figure 28-5. (If you choose Insert Hyperlink first, select objects at the prompt.)

Figure 28-5: The Insert Hyperlink dialog box attaches hyperlinks to objects in your drawing.

3. Use the Link to list to choose the type of hyperlink you want to create. The central portion of the dialog box changes depending on which of these options you choose to use to specify the appropriate file, Web page, view, or e-mail address.

- **Existing File or Web Page:** Creates a hyperlink to another file (on your own computer, network, intranet, or the Internet) or a Web page. You can choose from Recent Files, Browsed Pages, or Inserted Links.

- **View of This Drawing:** Creates a hyperlink to a named view in the open drawing. You can use this to help viewers navigate to detail views or schedules (tables of data) in the drawing.

- **E-mail Address:** Opens the viewer's e-mail program and starts a new message to the address specified.

4. To help you specify the file or Web page, click either the File button or the Web Page button at the right side of the dialog box. To specify a named view in a drawing, click the Target button. In the Select Place in Document dialog box, click the plus sign next to the layout and select a view. Click OK.

5. In the Text to Display text box, type a short description of the hyperlink. If you don't create a description, when you pass the cursor over the hyperlink, the tooltip lists the URL or file name. If the URL or file name may be confusing, use a description instead. The description is displayed as the tooltip.

6. Uncheck Use Relative Path for Hyperlink if you want to use the entire path you placed in the Link to file or URL text box. A relative path uses a base as a given, requiring you to only specify the part of the path after the base. Use relative paths when you are working from a company intranet, for example, and all the URLs have the same base.

7. Click OK. AutoCAD creates the hyperlink.

Note You set the base path using the HYPERLINKBASE system variable. By default, the base is the folder of the current drawing and is listed in the Base text box of the Insert Hyperlink dialog box.

Check the hyperlink by passing the cursor over the object to which you attached the hyperlink. You see the Web cursor, shown in Figure 28-6.

Figure 28-6: The Web cursor appears when you pass the cursor over a hyperlinked object.

Using a hyperlink

After you create a hyperlink, you can use it at any time to open the associated file or move to the associated location within the drawing. If you use a dial-up connection to the Internet and open a drawing with hyperlinks to the Internet while not connected, AutoCAD prompts you to connect so that it can find URLs on the Internet.

To open a file associated with a hyperlink, select any object with an attached hyperlink. Then right-click anywhere in the drawing area and choose Hyperlink ⇨ Open from the shortcut menu. Remember that you can't just click a hyperlink as you do on a Web site because that just selects the object in your drawing.

Tip You can use the Web toolbar, shown in Figure 28-7, to navigate back and forth between previously visited Web sites, drawings, and other locations.

Go Forward Stop Navigation

Go Back Browse the Web

Figure 28-7: The Web toolbar

Editing a hyperlink

To edit any feature of a hyperlink, select the hyperlinked object and choose Insert ⇨ Hyperlink. You can also right-click and choose Hyperlink ⇨ EditHyperlink. AutoCAD opens the Edit Hyperlink dialog box. This dialog box is the same as the Insert Hyperlink dialog box and lets you edit the hyperlink. Click OK when you are done.

On the CD-ROM The files used in the following Step-by-Step exercise on creating hyperlinks, ab28-a.dwg, ab28-a.txt, and ab28-b.dwf, are in the Drawings folder of the *AutoCAD 2004 Bible* CD-ROM.

Step-by-Step: Creating Hyperlinks

1. Open ab28-a.dwg from the CD-ROM.

2. Save the file as ab28-01.dwg in your AutoCAD Bible folder. This is a 3D drawing of a base assembly frame for an industrial washer, shown in Figure 28-8.

Figure 28-8: The base assembly frame
Thanks to Robert Mack of the Dexter Company, Fairfield, Iowa, for this drawing.

3. Copy `ab28-a.txt` and `ab28-b.dwf` from the CD-ROM to your `AutoCAD Bible` folder. (You can use Windows Explorer to drag the files.)

4. Choose Insert ➪ Hyperlink. At the `Select objects:` prompt, pick ❶ and ❷ in Figure 28-8. AutoCAD opens the Insert Hyperlink dialog box.

5. Click File. Choose `ab28-a.txt` in your `AutoCAD Bible` folder. Click Open. Click OK in the Edit Hyperlink dialog box.

6. Repeat the HYPERLINK command. This time attach ❸ and ❹ in Figure 28-8 to `ab28-b.dwf` in your `AutoCAD Bible` folder. Click OK to close the dialog box.

7. Pass the cursor over all four objects to check the hyperlinks.

8. Save your drawing. Keep it open if you are going on to the next Step-by-Step exercise.

New Feature

The Express Tools contain three commands to help you find and change URLs that you create with hyperlinks. SHOWURLS (choose Express ➪ Web tools ➪ Show URLs) lists all the hyperlinks in your drawing, can show you to which objects they are linked and enables you to edit them. CHURLS (choose Express ➪ Web tools ➪ Change URLs) prompts you to select a hyperlinked object so that you can change the hyperlink. REPURLS (choose Express ➪ Web tools ➪ Find and Replace URLs) replaces the existing hyperlink URL of a selected hyperlinked object.

Publishing Drawings on the World Wide Web

AutoCAD 2004 lets you save drawings as DWF (Design Web Format) files. You can place a DWF drawing on a Web site so that others can view the drawing. They can zoom, pan, and print the drawing. You can place links in your drawing so that viewers can jump to supporting data, to other DWF drawings, or to other Web sites.

Understanding DWF files

Most graphics that you view on the Web are bitmaps, often in GIF or JPEG format. This is not very useful for technical drawings because you want viewers to be able to zoom in to see the details. Zooming in closely on a bitmap format just displays dots.

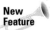
New Feature The updated DWF format allows for multiple pages. You can include as many drawings as you want, plus as many layouts as you have created for each drawing.

The DWF format has several advantages:

✦ It is a vector format. Viewers can zoom in closely and see the details clearly.

✦ DWF files are 2D representations, similar to a plot. The actual objects are not available to the viewer. They cannot edit the drawing or access object information such as layers, object coordinates, and so on. This feature maintains security for the creator of the drawing.

✦ DWF files are compressed while being transmitted to reduce the time it takes to download and view them.

✦ DWF files support URL links to other drawings, data, or files, so you can provide the viewer with supporting schedules, and so on.

Creating DWF files

To create a DWF file for a set of drawings, you use the new PUBLISH command to do the following:

✦ Create the drawing set, that is, the list of drawings and layouts to include in the DWF file

✦ Specify a Page Setup for each drawing

✦ Save the list of drawings or load an existing list

The PUBLISH command is new for AutoCAD 2004. The PUBLISH command creates the new multi-page DWF format. The PUBLISHTOWEB command, which creates DWF files (but can also create JPEG or PNG files) is different — it uses a wizard and a template to format a Web page containing images of your drawings. The PUBLISHTOWEB command is covered later in this chapter. Before using the PUBLISH command, save your drawing. If you have made changes that aren't saved, you see a message saying that your drawing must be saved before it can be published.

Starting the PUBLISH Command

Start the PUBLISH command by typing **publish** ↵ on the command line. The Publish Drawing Sheets dialog box opens, as shown in Figure 28-9. You see all the layouts of the current drawing displayed.

Figure 28-9: The PUBLISH command opens the Publish Drawing Sheets dialog box, listing the layouts of the current drawing.

Tip You can resize the Publish Drawing Sheets dialog box by dragging on its lower-right corner.

Adding Drawings to the Drawing Set

The next step is to add any other drawings and layouts that you want to include in the drawing set. The PUBLISH command streamlines the process of defining scale and plot area for each drawing by assuming that you have defined layouts. Because layouts include this information, you can quickly create drawings sets for many drawings without individually deciding how to plot each drawing. You can specify a saved setup for individual drawings for more control. (For more information on setups and layouts, see Chapter 18.)

You can add new drawings and layouts to the drawing set using any of the following methods:

✦ Drag drawings directly from Windows Explorer. You can add large numbers of drawings this way — in any folder, click the first drawing, press Shift and click the last drawing.

✦ Click Add Sheets and choose drawings from the familiar Select Drawings dialog box.

✦ Click Load List and choose a saved drawing set.

You can save any drawing set list and use it again later. To save a drawing set list, click Save List. The Save List As dialog box opens. Change the name if you want, choose a location, and click Save. Drawing Set Lists have a .dsd extension. (DSD stands for Drawing Set Description.)

> **Note** You can use the +PUBLISH command, a variant of the PUBLISH command that lets you start with a saved DSD file instead of with the current drawing. The Select List of Sheets dialog box opens. Choose a DSD file and click Select. You can use the –PUBLISH command with a saved DSD file to publish DWF files from a script file. In the script file, set the FILEDIA system variable to 0 to suppress the display of the Select List of Sheets dialog box. You are then prompted for the DSD file. The process automatically generates a log file (with the name of the drawing sheet list and an extension of .csv) that you can look at in case there are errors.

Removing Model Space from the Drawing Set List

By default, the model tab and layouts tabs for each drawing are all included in the drawing list. If you don't want to see the model tab for drawings, right-click in the main area of the Publish Drawing Sheets dialog box and click Include Model Layout When Adding Sheets, to uncheck it, as shown in Figure 28-10. After you change this setting, new drawings that you add to the drawing set will not include the model space tab.

```
Add Sheets...
Load List...
Save List...

Remove
Remove All

Move Up
Move Down

Rename Sheet
Change Page Setup
Copy selected sheets
✓  Display Drawing File Path Names

✓  Include Layouts When Adding Sheets
✓  Include Model When Adding Sheets
```

Figure 28-10: When you right-click in the Publish Drawing Sheets dialog box, you get a shortcut menu that offers most of the same options available in the dialog box, plus a couple of additional options.

Editing the Drawing Set List

After you have the drawings and layouts you want, you can modify the list in several ways:

✦ **Change the sheet name:** The sheet names are generated automatically from the drawing and layout names, but you might want to use a different name. Click the drawing's row and then click the sheet name one time. Enter a new name.

Tip

If you are not in the habit of renaming your layout tabs, you might find that your sheet names are rather unhelpful. Handwheel-Layout1 doesn't explain very much. To rename a layout tab, right-click it and choose Rename. In the Rename Layout dialog box, enter a new name and click OK.

✦ **List/don't list path to drawing:** The second column of the Publish Drawing Sheets dialog box, Drawing Name, lists the path to the drawing by default. If you don't want to list the path, right-click and choose Display Drawing File Path Names from the shortcut menu to remove the check next to the menu item.

✦ **Specify page setup:** If you have specified a page setup, you can assign it to any drawing. (You can apply model page setups to model listings and layout page setups to layout listings.) Right-click the drawing on the drawing list and choose Change Page Setup to open the Change Page Setup dialog box, as shown in Figure 28-11. Choose a page setup from the selected drawing (the drawing you right-clicked) or from another drawing. If you choose from another drawing, click Browse to get there and then choose the page setup. Click OK when you're done.

Figure 28-11: Use the Change Page Setup dialog box to choose a page setup to apply to a drawing.

✦ **Change drawing order:** The drawing order defines how the drawings in the DWF file will be listed in the viewer. The easiest way to change the order of any drawing is to click and drag the drawing to where you want it. You can also choose a drawing and use the Move Up and Move Down buttons.

✦ **Remove drawings:** To remove a drawing (or a layout of a drawing) from the list, click it and click Remove. You can also click Remove All to start from scratch.

Defining the Output

Your list is done. Now you decide on the output. From the Publish To section of the Publish Drawing Sheets dialog box, you can choose two types of output:

✦ **Multi-sheet DWF File:** When you want to create DWF files for viewing, choose this option. By default, the name of the file is the same as the name of the drawing (and in the same location), but with a .dwf extension. To password protect the DWF file, enter a password. Don't forget this password!

✦ **Plotters Named in Page Setups:** Choose this option to plot all the layouts in the list. This is essentially a batch plot. Each item in the drawing set is plotted to the plotter named in its page setup, including the default page setup. The folder setting is used if you have saved a plotter configuration file that plots drawings to a file.

Publishing

When you have created your drawing set list and defined your output, you're ready to publish. Click the Publish button. When the publishing process is completed, you should see the following message, shown in Figure 28-12.

Figure 28-12: When you publish, you see a Publishing Complete dialog box.

If the Publishing Complete dialog box contains an `Errors Found` message, you should definitely save the log file. Click Save Logfile, specify a name and location, and click Save. You see a small Logfile Saved message — just click OK. Log files are in CSV (comma delimited) format and you can easily open them in any spreadsheet program or Notepad. The Status column of the Publish Drawing Sheets dialog box also indicates the problem. Here are the three errors I came across:

✦ **Layout unitialized:** You may see this error for model tab items. If there is a previously saved model tab page setup, right-click on the item and choose Change Page Setup. Choose a page setup and click OK. If there is no previously saved model tab page setup, you need to create one in the drawing, save the drawing, and then close it. Re-open the drawing and then the PUBLISH command will find the new page setup. You can then assign it to the model tab item. You may also see this error for Layout tabs that you have never displayed in the drawing.

✦ **Drawing failed to load:** This error may occur if there is some problem with the drawing or its location.

✦ **None device:** If you open an old drawing that was saved to plot to a device that no longer exists, the plot device is set to None. Open the Page Setup dialog box (right-click any tab and choose Page Setup) and choose the plotter or printer you want to use. You may need to close and re-open the drawing before PUBLISH recognizes the new plot device.

To view the DWF file immediately, click View DWF File. Autodesk Express Viewer opens, displaying the DWF file. Later in this chapter, I explain how to use Autodesk Express Viewer. Otherwise, click OK.

You can customize several settings for DWF files, such as the resolution, background color (for example black or white), and whether or not to allow viewers to turn layers on and off. You can also create your own ePlot plotting configuration file. For more information, see the sidebar, "Customizing DWF settings."

On the CD-ROM

The drawing used in the following Step-by-Step exercise on creating a DWF File, `ab28-1.dwg`, is in the `Results` folder of the *AutoCAD 2004 Bible* CD-ROM. If you did the previous exercise, you also have this file in your `AutoCAD Bible` folder.

Step-by-Step: Creating a DWF File

1. If you did the previous exercise, use ab28-01.dwg. If not, open it from the Results folder of the *AutoCAD 2004 Bible* CD-ROM and save it to your AutoCAD Bible folder.

2. Type **publish** ⏎ on the command line.

3. Choose ab28-1-Model and click Remove.

4. Make sure that Multi-Sheet DWF File is chosen in the Publish To section of the Publish Drawing Sheets dialog box.

5. Click Publish. AutoCAD goes through a plotting process and creates the DWF file.

6. Click Close. A List of Sheets Changes dialog box opens and asks if you want to save the current list of sheets. Click No. If you are continuing on to the next Step-by-Step exercise, keep this drawing open.

Customizing DWF settings

You can modify the PC3 file that defines the DWF file to specify certain settings that you might want, including compression, resolution, and whether or not to include layer information. The new DWF file format follows the specification of the DWF6 ePlot.pc3 file. For safety, it is good to make a back up of the PC3 file before modifying it. To find the PC3 file, choose File ➪ Plotter Manager. Double-click DWF6 ePlot.pc3. Right-click the file and choose Copy. Right-click in the file listing and choose Paste. Rename the copy (perhaps DWF6 ePlot-original.pc3). If you don't like the results of your editing, delete the DWF6 ePlot.pc3 file and remove -original from the name of the copy.

To modify the PC3 file, follow these steps:

1. Choose File ➪ Plotter Manager.

2. Double-click DWF6 ePlot.pc3.

3. Click the Device and Document Settings tab and choose Custom Properties. In the middle of the dialog box, click the Custom Properties button to open the DWF6 ePlot Properties dialog box.

You can specify the following settings:

✦ **Resolution (dpi):** Defines the resolution for vector and raster (bitmap) graphics. Of course, a higher resolution results in a larger file size. You can choose from the drop-down lists or enter a custom resolution. For plotting, you can use a resolution that matches the output of your plotter or printer. Use high resolutions for viewing highly detailed drawings.

✦ **Format:** Specifies the compression format. Compressed Binary is the recommended format and the default. The Uncompressed Binary option doesn't seem to be available at all. The Zipped ASCII Encoded 2D Stream (advanced) option is an ASCI (text) format that can be uncompressed using WinZip or a similar program.

✦ **Font Handling:** Specifies how many fonts can be included in the file. Use this setting to reduce file size by limiting the number of possible fonts.

• Use Capture None (all viewer supplied) if you are sure that the viewer's computer has all the fonts that the DWF file needs to display.

• Use Capture Some to specify which fonts the DWF file includes. Then click Edit List and deselect all the fonts that you don't need. The fonts still selected will display properly even if they are not on the viewer's computer.

• Use Capture All if you want to include all fonts from the drawing in the DWF file. When you choose this option, the All as Geometry (largest file size) option becomes available. This includes fonts as geometry (objects) in your drawing and requires plotting the drawing at 1:1 or better to get good quality output.

Continued

Continued

✦ **Background Color:** Specifies the background color shown in the viewer. Click the Color drop-down list. You can use custom colors if you want. If you change the background from black to white, make sure that the objects are still easily visible. (Yellow doesn't show up very well on white.) If viewers will be plotting from Autodesk Express Viewer, change the background color to white or their plots come out with a black background! If the AutoCAD background color is set to black, color 7 objects are plotted in white. For all other background colors, color 7 objects are plotted in black.

✦ **Virtual Pen Set Patterns:** If and only if, in the Plotter Configuration File dialog box, for Vector Graphics, you chose 255 Virtual Pens in the Color Depth drop-down list, you will see an option to edit virtual pen set patterns. You can set the color, width, and other properties of virtual pens.

✦ **Include Layer Information:** Includes layer information so that viewers can turn layers on and off. This option is off by default.

✦ **Show Paper Boundaries:** This displays a paper boundary such as the one you see on a layout tab. It is on by default and not editable.

✦ **Save Preview in DWF:** This option is only for use on buzzsaw.com, because a small preview is always saved with the DWF file.

When you finish specifying the DWF format, click OK. You then see a message asking if you want to apply the changes for the current plot only (which creates an override of the configuration file but doesn't change it) or to save the changes to the file (which creates a permanent change — you can always change it back).

Using the Publish to Web Wizard

The Publish to Web feature creates HTML pages that display your drawings in DWF, JPEG, or PNG format. Through the use of templates, you can upload drawings without getting involved in Web design issues.

To publish drawings to the Web, first prepare your drawings and decide how many you want to publish. Then choose File ➪ Publish to Web to open the Begin page of the Publish to Web Wizard. Follow these steps:

1. Choose to create a new Web page or edit an existing one. Then click Next.

2. On the Create Web Page screen, shown in Figure 28-13, type a file name for the Web page. (AutoCAD creates a folder with this name and places all the files for the Web page in the folder.) Then click the ellipsis button (. . .) to navigate to where you want to create this file. If you already store Web page files on your system, you can use the same location. Finally, add a description that will appear on the Web page. Click Next.

Figure 28-13: On the Create Web Page screen, specify where you want to create your Web page on your own computer system and create a description of the page.

3. On the Select Image Type screen, choose the type of image you want to create—DWF, JPEG, or PNG. As you choose each type from the drop-down list, a description appears on the screen. For JPEG and PNG, also click an image size, as it will appear on the Web page. Click Next.

4. On the Select Template screen, choose a template that structures your Web page and click Next. You have four choices:

 • **Array of Thumbnails:** Creates a set of thumbnail images. Clicking any image displays a larger image.

 • **Array plus Summary:** Creates a set of thumbnail images. Adds information from the Summary tab of the Drawing Properties dialog box, displayed when the mouse cursor is over a thumbnail. (Choose File ⇨ Drawing Properties to create summary information.)

 • **List of Drawings:** Creates a list of drawings and a frame displaying a drawing image. Users select a drawing from the list to update the image in the frame.

 • **List plus Summary:** Creates a list of drawings, an image frame, and summary information from the Summary tab of the Drawing Properties dialog box, displayed when the mouse cursor is over a thumbnail. (Choose File ⇨ Drawing Properties to create summary information.)

5. On the Apply Theme screen, choose one of the preset themes that control colors and fonts on your Web page. You see an example in the preview pane. Click Next.

6. On the Enable i-drop screen, choose whether or not you want to create an i-drop Web page so that users can drag actual drawings from the Web page into a drawing.

7. On the Select Drawings screen, shown in Figure 28-14, choose the drawings that you want to publish. If the drawing is open, you can select it from the Drawing drop-down list. Select each drawing, choose a layout (or model) from the Layout drop-down list, type a label, and type a description to appear on the Web page. Then click Add. (If the drawing is not open, click the ellipsis button, navigate to the drawing, and click Open. Then click Add.) Click Next.

Figure 28-14: On the Select Drawings screen, add each drawing you want to include on the Web page and specify a layout, label, and description for each.

8. On the Generate Images screen, choose to regenerate either all images or only those that have changes. (There is no difference if you are creating a new Web page.) Click Next and wait while AutoCAD plots and formats your drawings to files.

9. On the Preview and Post screen, click Preview to preview what the Web page will look like. AutoCAD opens your Web browser and displays a fully functional Web page, including links, if any. Figure 28-15 shows an example.

10. Click Post to post your new Web page. AutoCAD opens the Posting Web dialog box, which is like the Save As dialog box. In the Save In drop-down list, choose the desired location. To use FTP to post directly to a server, choose FTP locations or choose FTP from the Places list. (If you're saving to an intranet, you'll choose a location designated by your network administrator.) Double-click the FTP location and wait until you see the folder structure of your Web site. If you want, double-click one of the folders to save there. Click Save. You should see a File Upload dialog box showing the progress of the file transfer. If everything goes well, you'll see the success message shown in Figure 28-16.

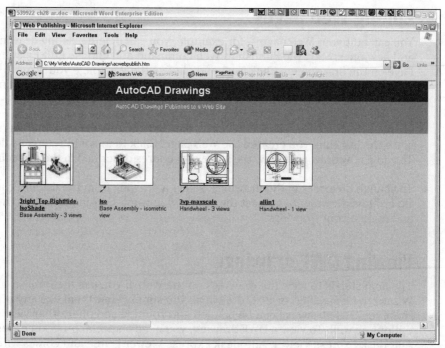

Figure 28-15: A preview of some drawings using the Array of Thumbnails template and DWF files. You can click on any thumbnail to see the full-size DWF file. Note the i-drop icons.

Figure 28-16: Success with the file transfer!

11. If you want, click Send Email to notify people of the URL to the new Web page.

12. To find your new page, look for a file named `acwebpublish.htm`. For example, if your Web site is `www.ellenfinkelstein.com` and you placed all the files in the root, look for `www.ellenfinkelstein.com/acwebpublish.htm`. Don't forget to add a link to this new page on other pages of your Web site or at least to tell people about the new page's URL.

You can always upload the files by yourself, using your own FTP program or whatever other means you use to post to the Web site.

Editing Web pages

You can edit your Web page—for example, you can delete existing drawings and add new ones. Start the Publish to Web command and choose Edit Existing Web Page on the first screen. Click Next and choose the Web page you want to edit by choosing a .ptw (Publish to Web) file. Click Next again. From this point on, you can change any existing information.

On the Select Drawings screen, click Update to update a drawing that has changed since the last time you created the Web page. Click Remove to remove a drawing. To add a new drawing, follow the same procedures described in the previous section.

To change the order of the drawings, select a drawing from the list and click Move Up or Move Down until you get the results you want. Continue through the wizard and re-post your drawings.

Viewing DWF drawings

The final step is to view the drawings on the Web. If you use the Publish to Web Wizard to create JPEG or PNG drawings, you simply view them like any other image. However, DWF drawings can be panned and zoomed and offer other viewing options as well. To view a DWF drawing, you need a special program called Autodesk Express Viewer. Autodesk Express Viewer is free and comes with AutoCAD 2004. It is also available as a free download from the Autodesk Web site at www.autodesk.com/expressviewer. Autodesk Express Viewer replaces Volo View Express, used with earlier versions of DWF files.

Note You still need Volo View Express or Volo View to view DWG files.

You view the new DWF files using the new drawing reader, Autodesk Express Viewer. Autodesk Express Viewer can function in two ways:

✦ As a stand-alone reader, it opens like any program. (You can usually find it by choosing Start ➪ Programs ➪ Autodesk ➪ Autodesk Express Viewer.) Choose File ➪ Open to open a DWF file. You can also double-click the DWF file in Windows Explorer. Use the reader this way when you are sending DWF files to people without AutoCAD or with a version of AutoCAD that doesn't support the multi-page DWF files.

✦ As an ActiveX component, Autodesk Express Viewer functions within Microsoft Internet Explorer, as shown in Figure 28-17. Use the reader within Internet Explorer when you have posted DWF files on a Web site. Enter the URL in the browser and the DWF file appears.

If you send DWF files to clients or colleagues, you can send them the Install file for Autodesk Express Viewer as well. This file is less than 2MB so including the file in an e-mail or as a download on a Web page is easy.

If you have given a DWF file a password, a dialog box opens requesting the password before the DWF file is displayed.

Using View Options

As shown in Figure 28-17, to view any sheet in the DWF file, choose it from the drop-down list. The Next and Previous buttons on either side of the drop-down list let a viewer systematically view each sheet in order. Other options are available either on the toolbar or by right-clicking and choosing from the menu.

By default, layer information is not included in the DWF format. As explained earlier in the "Customizing DWF Settings" sidebar, you can include layer information if you want. If the DWF file includes layer information, viewers can use the Layers button to open the Layers window. A viewer can choose any layer and click the Off or On button to turn that layer off or on.

Figure 28-17: Here is Autodesk Express Viewer used in Internet Explorer. From the drop-down list on the toolbar, you can see the three sheets in the drawing set.

Use the Views button to display any named views that were saved with the drawing. You can use saved views to help a customer focus on certain details and provide information about the views you saved.

Viewers have complete freedom to pan and zoom however they want. Note that if you are sending a DWF file to a client that doesn't use AutoCAD, the controls may not be obvious.

✦ Click the Fit to Window button to do a Zoom Extents. The button looks like the Zoom Extents button in AutoCAD.

✦ Click the Zoom Rectangle button to do a Zoom Window.

✦ Click the Zoom button to zoom. Drag up to zoom in and drag down to zoom out.

✦ Click the Pan button to pan. Drag in any direction to pan in that direction.

✦ A mouse with an IntelliMouse wheel works just like in AutoCAD. Zoom in by scrolling forward and zoom out by scrolling backward. Press the wheel and drag to pan.

If the DWF file has hyperlinks, when your cursor passes over a URL area, the cursor changes to a hand, as shown in Figure 28-18. A tag appears telling you to press Ctrl+click to follow the link.

Figure 28-18: Passing over a URL in a DWF drawing

Printing and Plotting

You can print/plot drawings from Autodesk Express Viewer without having AutoCAD. The print options are somewhat like those in Microsoft Word because they take into account the fact that the DWF file can have many pages. Click the Print button to open the Print dialog box, as shown in Figure 28-19.

The Print dialog box offers the following features:

✦ **Printer:** In the Printer section, choose the printer or plotter you want to use. Click Properties to specify how the printer/plotter functions. The features depend on the device you choose.

✦ **Print What:** In the Print What section, you can choose to print the full page or the current view. Check Force All Geometry to Black to print in black only. This feature doesn't affect the color of raster images.

✦ **Page Size & Orientation:** Choose the page size from the drop-down list and choose Portrait or Landscape. The paper sizes that are available vary depending on your printer or plotter.

✦ **Reduce/Enlarge Drawing:** Check Fit to Paper Size to scale the drawing to the chosen paper size. To scale the drawing, uncheck Fit to Paper Size and enter a scale percentage. If the drawing will be larger than the paper, you can check Show Tiles in Page View to display dashed lines that indicate how the drawing will be divided up into sheets of paper.

✦ **Print Range:** You can print the current page, all the pages, or specify which pages you want to print.

 Tip

On the toolbar's drop-down list of sheets in the drawing set, each layout is numbered. You can use these numbers to specify which pages you want to print.

✦ **Copies:** You can specify how many copies you want of each drawing, reverse their order so you don't have to shuffle through all the pages yourself, and collate them.

There is no print preview.

Click OK to print. If you choose a size that doesn't fit on one sheet of paper, you see a message saying that the drawing may print across several pages.

In the following exercise, I use the capability of Internet browsers to browse your hard drive as well as the Internet. This enables you to complete the exercise even if you don't have an Internet connection available. You need only the files on the *AutoCAD 2004 Bible* CD-ROM, your Internet browser, and Autodesk Express Viewer.

Figure 28-19: The Print dialog box helps you print or plot drawings from Autodesk Express Viewer.

The files used in the following Step-by-Step exercise on viewing a DWF drawing, \Results\ab28-1.dwf, \Drawings\ab28-a.txt, and \Drawings\ab28-b.dwf, are on the *AutoCAD 2004 Bible* CD-ROM. If you didn't do the previous Step-by-Step exercise, copy all three files from the CD-ROM to your AutoCAD Bible folder.

Step-by-Step: Viewing a DWF Drawing

1. Open Windows Explorer and navigate to ab28-1.dwf in your AutoCAD Bible folder. Double-click the file top open it in Autodesk Express Viewer.

If the DWF file were on a Web site, you would view it by typing the URL (Web address) in Internet Explorer.

2. Autodesk Express Viewer opens automatically and displays the DWF file created in the previous Step-by-Step exercise. From the drop-down list on the Autodesk Express Viewer toolbar, choose the second sheet, labeled (2)ab28-1-Iso (11x8.5 in), as shown in Figure 28-20.

3. Press Ctrl and click ❶ in Figure 28-20. The text shown in Figure 28-21 opens in a new Internet Explorer window. (You may have to minimize Autodesk Express Viewer to see the text.) This comes from an Excel spreadsheet saved in text format.

4. Right-click in the drawing to open the shortcut menu. Choose Zoom Rectangle. Drag a window to zoom in. Choose Pan from the menu and pan to the left. Choose Fit in Window to return to the previous view. (If you want, choose Print to print the drawing to the system printer.)

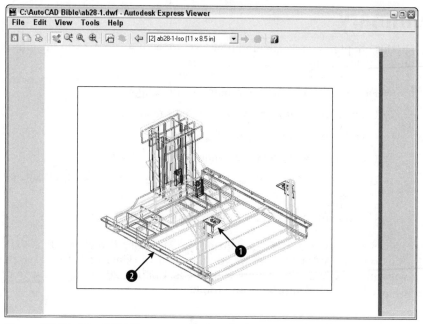

Figure 28-20: The DWF file as seen in Autodesk Express Viewer

5. Press Ctrl and click ❷ in Figure 28-20. You see the horizontal angle in a new Internet Explorer window.

6. Close Autodesk Express Viewer and the Internet Explorer windows.

```
QTY   TAG NO  PART_NO DESCRIPTION      DWG_SIZE      MADE/PUR    UNITS
1     21      9538-171-002  SPACER-SUPPORT  B      P      EACH
AR    20      8665-023-016  WELDING ROD     B      P      FT
2     19      9081-114-001  CHANNEL-MOTOR MTG ROD  B    P      EACH
AR    18      8665-023-012  WELDING WIRE - .030 STAINLESS  B   P      FT
2     17      9029-072-001  BRACKET-TUBE ASSY     D      M      EACH
1     16      9003-237-001  ANGLE-REAR      B      M      EACH
4     15      9452-628-001  "PLATE-SUPPORT, SML (UPR)"   D      M      EACH
2     14      9452-627-001  "PLATE-SUPPORT, LRG (UPR)"   D      M      EACH
1     13      9452-629-001  "PLATE-MTG, BFR HSG"  D      M      EACH
4     12      9003-236-002  "ANGLE-SUPPORT, VERT"  B     M      EACH
2     11      9076-052-002  COLLAR-SHAFT    B      M      EACH
1     10      9003-232-003  "ANGLE-HORIZ, SUPPORT"  B    M      EACH
2     9       9003-232-002  "ANGLE-HORIZ, MID, & REAR"   B      M      EACH
2     8       9003-236-003  "ANGLE-SUPPORT,DIAGONAL"  B   M      EACH
1     7       9548-277-001  "SUPPORT-PLATE, MTG (BRG HSG)"  B   M      EACH
4     6       9003-236-004  "ANGLE-SUPPORT, SPREADER"  B   M      EACH
2     5       9003-233-001  "ANGLE-MTG, RING ASSY"  B    M      EACH
2     4       9548-278-001  "SUPPORT-CORNER, FRONT" B    M      EACH
2     3       9452-646-001  "PLATE-BASE, SUPPORT"  B     M      EACH
2     2       9003-242-001  "ANGLE-HORIZ, RH & LH" B     M      EACH
1     1       9003-232-001  "ANGLE-HORIZ, FRT"  B        M      EACH
```

Figure 28-21: The text database for the drawing

Summary

In this chapter, you discovered how to work with AutoCAD and the Internet. You read the following:

✦ Faxing, e-mailing, and eTransmiting drawings

✦ Opening drawings from anywhere on the Internet

✦ Creating hyperlinks in your drawings

✦ Using the new PUBLISH command to create DWF files

✦ Using the Publish to Web Wizard to create Web pages with DWF, JPEG, or PNG images

✦ Utilizing Autodesk Express Viewer to view DWF files

This chapter ends Part V, "Organizing and Managing Drawings." Part VI, "Customizing AutoCAD," shows you the inner workings of AutoCAD so that you can work in the way that best suits your needs. Chapter 29 explains how to create customized command shortcuts and toolbars.

✦ ✦ ✦

Customizing AutoCAD

◆ ◆ ◆ ◆

In Part VI, you discover how to make AutoCAD work the way you want. Customizing AutoCAD can speed up your work, make it easier, create standards for all drawings where you work, and automate often-used or repetitive tasks. You can customize the process of issuing commands, customize toolbars and tool palettes (Chapter 29), create macros and slide shows with script files (Chapter 30), create your own linetypes and hatch patterns (Chapter 31), create your own fonts and other shapes (Chapter 32), and customize AutoCAD's menus (Chapter 33).

◆ ◆ ◆ ◆

Customizing Commands, Toolbars, and Tool Palettes

Customizing AutoCAD can increase your efficiency and productivity. The time spent in preparation will be paid back many times. Before you start customizing, you need to know some basics that apply to almost all AutoCAD customization. After you understand these basics, the process becomes much easier.

Working with Customizable Files

The capability to customize AutoCAD is based on the fact that most of AutoCAD's support files are text files that you can edit yourself. Table 29-1 lists the most important files and their functions. Some customization can be done using dialog boxes.

Figure 29-1 shows a portion of one of these files, `acad.pgp`, which lists command shortcuts, or aliases.

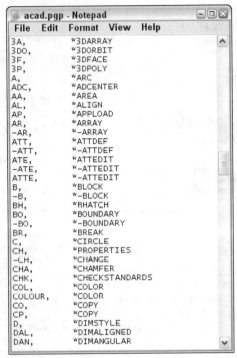

Figure 29-1: `Acad.pgp`, one of AutoCAD's customizable files

Table 29-1	
Customizable Files	
File Name	**Function**
`*.cus`	Custom dictionary files. You can add words to a custom dictionary for use with the SPELL command.
`acad.pgp`	AutoCAD's program parameters file. This file is generally used to create keyboard shortcuts (called aliases) for commands.
`acad.mnu`	AutoCAD's template menu file. You can also create your own menu template files.
`acad.mnl`	AutoLISP routines used by AutoCAD's main menu. If you create your own menus, you can have an `.mnl` file with the same name as your menu for AutoLISP routines.
`acad.mns`	AutoCAD's menu source file generated from the template `.mnu` file. You can also create your own menu source files from custom template files.

File Name	Function
Acad2004.cfg	AutoCAD configuration file for storing digitizer and other settings. Usually, you should use the Options dialog box to make these selections rather than manually editing this file. See Appendix A on the CD-ROM for more information about this file.
acad.dcl	AutoCAD's Dialog Control Language (DCL) file. This file describes the AutoCAD standard dialog boxes. You usually don't edit this file, but you can create your own DCL files to create dialog boxes for your AutoLISP routines.
acad.lin	AutoCAD's linetype definition file. You can also create your own linetype definition (*.lin) files or add your own definitions to acad.lin.
acad.lsp	AutoCAD's AutoLISP file. You can create this file from scratch. If it exists, you can edit or add to this file to automatically load AutoLISP routines. Other customizable .lsp files are discussed in Chapter 35.
acad.mln	AutoCAD's multiline library file.
acad.pat	AutoCAD's hatch pattern file. You can also create your own.
*.pc3	AutoCAD's plot configuration files. You can also create your own. A PC3 file contains all configuration settings for a plotter. This is not a text file; you customize it using a dialog box. For more information, see Chapter 17 and Appendix A on the CD-ROM. You can use these files with the Batch Plotting Utility.
acad.fmp	AutoCAD font mapping file. Use this file to specify substitute fonts, whether or not the original fonts are available on your system.
acad.psf	The AutoCAD PostScript support file. It is used for the PSOUT and PSFILL commands.
acad.slb	The AutoCAD slide library file, used for hatch pattern examples in menus. You can use this file or create your own slide libraries. This is not a text file; see Chapter 30 for an explanation of how to create a slide library.
*.scr	A script file that you create and name. Script files are macros of commands and options that run automatically.
*.shp	A shape file that you create and name. Shape files usually hold fonts but can hold other shapes as well. A shape file is then compiled into a file with a .shx extension for more efficient use.
acad.rx	A list of ARX (an interface for programming AutoCAD) applications that load automatically.
mtextmap.ini	Font mapping for the appearance of text in the MTEXT editor.
acad.unt	A file that defines every conceivable type of unit.

Editing customizable files

To customize AutoCAD, you usually have to edit the appropriate customizable file. These files are often in text-only (ASCII) format. To edit them, you need a text editor, which is like a word processor but does not place any codes in the file. Files that are not in ASCII format generally have an interface in AutoCAD for editing them. For most of the ASCII files, you can use Notepad, which comes with Windows. All major word processors let you save documents as Text Documents — just remember not to click that Save button until you have specified the right file format.

Backing up customizable files

Before editing any pre-existing AutoCAD files, back them up. Some of these files, especially the menu files, are critical to AutoCAD's functioning. You should back up in three stages:

✦ Back up the original file as it came out of the box. Keep a disk with all the customizable files that you might ever edit in their original form.

✦ After you edit the file, back it up before each editing session. This way you always have your most recent version of the file. If you make a mistake, it's easy to copy that file on top of the one with the mistake and put everything back to normal.

✦ After you edit a file, back it up again so that you have it in case your hard drive crashes or you need to re-install AutoCAD.

In some cases, it is safer to create your own files than to edit AutoCAD's original file. For example, when customizing AutoCAD's menus, you can copy `acad.mnu` to a file named `mymenu.mnu`, edit `mymenu.mnu`, and then load your new menu instead of AutoCAD's standard menu.

This means you should have two disks, one with the original customizable files, and one with your most recent versions of them. At the very least, these disks should contain the following files:

✦ `acad.lin` ✦ `acad.mns`

✦ `acad.lsp` ✦ `acad.mnu`

✦ `acad.mln` ✦ `acad.pat`

✦ `acad.mnl` ✦ `acad.pgp`

You may also want to back up templates that you have created.

You will use these disks not only when you make a mistake, but also whenever you need to reinstall AutoCAD whether due to hard disk failure, a virus on your system, the replacement of your old computer with a new one, and so on. Also, when you upgrade AutoCAD to the next release, you can continue to work with your familiar, customized files (usually).

Using the command-line form of commands

For many customization tasks, you need to work with commands. When you create a script file, which is a series of commands, or when you edit the menu file, you need to type out the commands you want to execute. In these cases, AutoCAD's customizable files can only contain the command-line form of the commands. You have no way to enter values in a dialog box from within a script or menu file. As a result, you need to learn a whole new way of working in AutoCAD — the old-fashioned way — by typing commands on the command line.

Tip　If you're not sure of the command name but know the menu or toolbar item, execute the command on the menu or toolbar and then press Esc. AutoCAD displays the command name on the command line.

A number of commands have a non-dialog-box version. Several commands can also be run in their command-line version by placing a hyphen (-) before the command name. For some commands that have no command-line equivalent, you can use system variables to create the same effect. Table 29-2 lists these commands.

<table>
<tr><th colspan="2">Table 29-2
Command-Line Forms of Commands</th></tr>
<tr><th>*Command*</th><th>*Command-Line Form*</th></tr>
<tr><td>ARRAY</td><td>-ARRAY</td></tr>
<tr><td>ATTDEF</td><td>-ATTDEF</td></tr>
<tr><td>ATTEDIT</td><td>-ATTEDIT</td></tr>
<tr><td>ATTEXT</td><td>-ATTEXT</td></tr>
<tr><td>BHATCH</td><td>-BHATCH</td></tr>
<tr><td>BLOCK</td><td>-BLOCK</td></tr>
<tr><td>BOUNDARY</td><td>-BOUNDARY</td></tr>
<tr><td>DDPTYPE</td><td>PDMODE, PDSIZE</td></tr>
<tr><td>DDVPOINT</td><td>VPOINT</td></tr>
<tr><td>DSETTINGS</td><td>ORTHO, SNAP, GRID, ISOPLANE, AUTOSNAP, SNAPTYPE</td></tr>
<tr><td>EXPORT</td><td>DXFOUT, STLOUT, BMPOUT, PSOUT, ACISOUT, 3DSOUT, WMFOUT</td></tr>
<tr><td>GROUP</td><td>-GROUP</td></tr>
<tr><td>HATCHEDIT</td><td>HATCHEDIT</td></tr>
<tr><td>IMAGE</td><td>-IMAGE</td></tr>
<tr><td>INSERT</td><td>-INSERT</td></tr>
</table>

Continued

Table 29-2 *(continued)*

Command	Command-Line Form
LAYER	-LAYER
LAYOUT	-LAYOUT
LINETYPE	-LINETYPE
MTEXT	-MTEXT
OSNAP	-OSNAP
PAN	-PAN
PARTIALOPEN	-PARTIALOPEN
PLOT	-PLOT
PLOTSTAMP	-PLOTSTAMP
PROPERTIES	CHANGE, CHPROP, -COLOR, -LAYER, -LINETYPE, -LTSCALE, CELTYPE, CELTSCALE, ELEV, THICKNESS
PURGE	-PURGE
RENAME	-RENAME
STYLE	-STYLE
TOOLBAR	-TOOLBAR
UNITS	-UNITS
VIEW	-VIEW
WBLOCK	-WBLOCK
XBIND	-XBIND
XREF	-XREF

In addition, you can use the dimension variables to format dimensions in place of using the DIMSTYLE command, which opens the Dimension Style Manager dialog box. See the discussion of the -DIMSTYLE command in Chapter 15.

The FILEDIA system variable determines whether AutoCAD displays a dialog box for commands, such as SAVEAS and OPEN, that request file names. When FILEDIA is set to 1, the default, AutoCAD displays dialog boxes.

Note Since AutoCAD 2000, even if FILEDIA is set to 1, if a script or AutoLISP/ObjectARX program is active, AutoCAD displays a command prompt instead of a dialog box. You can still set the FILEDIA system variable to 0, but be sure to change it back again at the end of your script or program.

Documenting your files

Placing comments in customized files to explain how you customized them is standard practice. While your customizations may seem obvious at the time, if you go back to a file later, you may not understand what you were trying to accomplish. Also, other people may need some explanation.

You can place comments in many of the customizable files by placing a semicolon (;) before any line of text. AutoCAD ignores these lines. In menus, you create comments by placing a / or // before any line of text.

Now that you know the basics of customizing AutoCAD files, you can move on to creating keyboard shortcuts and customizing toolbars.

Creating Keyboard Shortcuts for Commands

You can create keyboard shortcuts for commands, thereby enabling you to enter commands on the command line without remembering and typing the full command name. Shortcuts are stored in the acad.pgp file. You can use the acad.pgp file for two purposes:

✦ To create shortcuts to Windows programs

✦ To create keyboard shortcuts for AutoCAD commands

You can also use acad.pgp to create shortcuts to DOS commands.

 You can also create keyboard shortcuts, such as Ctrl+G or F11 for commands. These shortcuts are saved in the AutoCAD menu. See Chapter 33 for more information. The shortcuts in acad.pgp use only letters and numbers.

Creating shortcuts to Windows programs

The acad.pgp file includes the following three shortcuts to Windows programs:

```
EXPLORER,   START EXPLORER, 1,,
NOTEPAD,    START NOTEPAD,  1,*File to edit: ,
PBRUSH,     START PBRUSH,   1,,
```

The first column is the command name you type at the AutoCAD command line. The second column is the command you want Windows to execute. The number 1 tells AutoCAD to start the application but not to wait until you have finished using it. This lets you return to AutoCAD at any time. After the 1, you can finish with two commas. However, notice that the Notepad entry has *File to edit: before the last comma. This is a prompt that you see on the AutoCAD command line. Type the

name of the file to edit, and Windows opens it in Notepad. (You need to type in the complete path of the file.) To open Notepad without a file, press Enter at the *File to edit: prompt.

Creating keyboard shortcuts to commands

Most of the acad.pgp file contains aliases, or keyboard shortcuts, for common AutoCAD commands. You can change these or add your own. After you get used to them, it's often faster to type shortcuts at the command line than to click the toolbar button or menu item, especially if your hands are already on the keyboard. You cannot include a command option in the acad.pgp file. To do that, you need to create a menu item, toolbar button, or AutoLISP routine.

New Feature The Express Tools contain an Alias Editor that enables you to edit the acad.pgp file through a dialog box interface. Choose Express ➪ Tools ➪ Command Alias Editor.

The format for creating an alias is as follows:

```
Shortcut,*Full command name
```

Refer back to Figure 29-1 for some examples of shortcuts. Note that the space between the columns is not necessary — it simply improves readability.

You can use aliases transparently if the command itself can be used transparently. Aliases cannot be used in script files or menus. Note that you cannot use control or function keys in command aliases in the .pgp file.

Tip You can print out acad.pgp and tape it up on the wall where you work.

Caution If you are working on someone else's computer, do not do the following Step-by-Step exercise without that person's permission. It is not good computer etiquette to modify other people's AutoCAD files without asking first.

Step-by-Step: Customizing the acad.pgp File

1. Start AutoCAD.

2. Place a blank disk in your floppy disk drive. Type **explorer** ↵. After opening a preliminary window, AutoCAD opens Windows Explorer using the acad.pgp shortcut.

 Note By default, `acad.pgp` is in `\Documents` and `Settings\[user name]\ Application Data\Autodesk\AutoCAD 2004\R16.0\enu\Support`. However, your location may be different, depending on your operating system and customization. To find the location of `acad.pgp`, choose Tools ⇨ Options and click the Files tab. Double-click the first item, Support File Search Path, to display the location of the support files.

3. Find `acad.pgp`, click it, and drag it to the drive (in the Folders window) that contains your floppy disk. Windows copies `acad.pgp` to the disk. If you haven't already backed up your other customizable files, copy `acad.lin`, `acad.lsp`, `acad.mln`, `acad.mnl`, `acad.mnu`, and `acad.pat` to the disk as well. (If they don't fit, you may need to use two disks or a CD-ROM.) Remove the disk and label it "AutoCAD customizable files — original form."

4. While Explorer is open, double-click `acad.pgp`. Windows opens the file in Notepad. (If Windows opens the Open With dialog box, choose Notepad from the list. Check the Always Use This Program To Open This File option and click OK. From then on, Windows will automatically open your `acad.pgp` file with Notepad. (Another method is to right-click and then choose Open With to choose the application you want to use.)

5. Scroll down roughly two screens until you see the three Windows commands, as shown in Figure 29-2. Place the cursor at the end of the PBRUSH line and press Enter.

```
; Examples of external commands for windows
; See also the (STARTAPP) AutoLISP function for
an alternative method.

EXPLORER,   START EXPLORER,  1,,
NOTEPAD,    START NOTEPAD,   1,*File to edit: ,
PBRUSH,     START PBRUSH,    1,,
```

Figure 29-2: The Windows commands in the `acad.pgp` file

6. Type the following and press Enter (the uppercasing and spaces are used to match the format of the rest of the file):

```
WORDPAD,    START WORDPAD,  1,,
```

7. Look at the next section of `acad.pgp`. Read AutoCAD's guidelines for creating new aliases.

8. Scroll down until you see the following two lines:

```
CH,         *PROPERTIES
-CH,        *CHANGE
```

The alias for the CHANGE command follows the guideline of using a hyphen to distinguish command-line versions of commands. Suppose you have trouble finding that hyphen quickly (you end up typing =ch instead). You want to change the alias to `cg` (with no hyphen).

9. To be extra careful, add a new alias rather than changing the current alias (which someone may be in the habit of using). Place the cursor after the word *CHANGE and press Enter. Type the following and press Enter (don't worry about the spaces—I've matched the spacing of the acad.pgp file):

```
CG,        *CHANGE
```

10. Choose File ⇨ Save. This section of acad.pgp that you worked on should look like Figure 29-3.

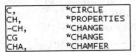

Figure 29-3: A section of the edited acad.pgp file

11. Close Notepad. Generally, AutoCAD only reads acad.pgp when loading a new or existing drawing. However, you can use the REINIT command to reload the file at any time. Type **reinit** ↵. AutoCAD opens the Re-initialization dialog box, as shown in Figure 29-4.

Figure 29-4: The Re-initialization dialog box

12. Check PGP File and click OK. In your drawing, draw any line.

13. Type **cg** ↵. AutoCAD starts the CHANGE command. Select the line, right-click to end selection, and pick a new endpoint location. AutoCAD changes the endpoint of the line.

14. Do not save your drawing.

On the CD-ROM The edited acad.pgp file is on the CD-ROM in the Results folder. Although you made only two changes, if you want, you can copy the acad.pgp file from the CD-ROM over your original acad.pgp file. Of course, you can make additional changes to suit your needs.

Customizing Toolbars

In the Windows environment, you frequently find yourself using toolbar buttons for many of your tasks. Nevertheless, how many times have you found yourself typing a command because you couldn't quickly find an equivalent button on a toolbar, or because it was on a flyout that was too annoying to deal with? In addition, think how often you start a command with a toolbar button, only to return to the keyboard to type in a simple option.

You can customize AutoCAD's toolbars to make your work easier and faster. You can create new toolbars from scratch, or edit existing ones. You can even create your own toolbar buttons. When you create a toolbar button, you can attach any sequence of commands to it — a complex macro or even an AutoLISP expression.

Using the Customize dialog box

The Toolbars tab of the Customize dialog box (choose View ➪ Toolbars), shown in Figure 29-5, combines all the tools you need to manage toolbars.

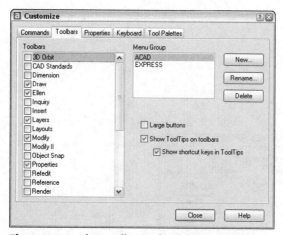

Figure 29-5: The Toolbars tab of the Customize dialog box

To display a toolbar, you don't need to use the Toolbars dialog box. You can right-click any toolbar and choose from the list on the shortcut menu. However, you can also display toolbars from the Toolbars tab of the Customize dialog box by checking the toolbar you want to see. Both lists include flyouts. It is therefore very easy to turn a flyout into a toolbar if you want — click the flyout — for example, Zoom — and it appears as a regular toolbar.

You also use the Toolbars tab of the Customize dialog box to create new toolbars, delete toolbars, and customize existing toolbars. If you create your own menus, they can have toolbars as well. You can then choose toolbars from your menus using the Menu Group drop-down list.

Creating a new toolbar

To create a new toolbar, choose New in the Toolbars dialog box. In the New Toolbar dialog box, shown in Figure 29-6, name your toolbar (and the Menu Group if you have created one) and then click OK. Your toolbar now appears in the Toolbars list of the Toolbars dialog box, and a small, new toolbar appears on the screen, as shown in Figure 29-7.

Cross-Reference　You use menu groups when you start to create your own menus. For more on Menu Groups, see Chapter 33, which covers customizing menus.

Figure 29-6: The New Toolbar dialog box

Figure 29-7: The new toolbar shown in the Toolbar list and on the screen

The new toolbar is just a baby, but as you add buttons to it, it grows automatically.

Tip An important part of managing toolbars is finding a place to dock them so that they don't take up valuable real estate on the screen. You can make several small toolbars and fit them in the blank spaces next to existing toolbars. The AutoCAD 2004 Standard toolbar is shorter than the previous one and gives you more room for your own toolbars.

Removing buttons

You can customize any toolbar by removing buttons that you rarely use. To remove buttons from a toolbar, follow these steps:

1. Display the toolbar.

2. Choose View ➪ Toolbars to display the Customize dialog box. If necessary, move it out of the way so you can access the toolbar that needs a button removed.

3. Drag the unwanted button off the toolbar and onto the screen area and release the mouse button.

Note It's easy to forget that you need to have the Customize dialog box open to remove buttons because there's no direct connection between dragging buttons off the toolbar and the dialog box — but you can't drag buttons off a toolbar unless the dialog box is open. Inadvertently dragging a button off the Customize Toolbars dialog box is also easy — if you do, you create a new toolbar.

Adding buttons

If you have created a new toolbar, you need to add buttons to it. You have several ways to do this:

✦ **Add a button from the Commands tab of the Customize dialog box.** Display the Commands tab of the Customize dialog box and choose a category. AutoCAD provides a number of preset buttons in each category (including many of the flyout buttons from Release 13). You can also choose All Commands in the Category pane and then choose any command from the alphabetical Commands list. Click a button to see its description at the bottom of the dialog box. When you have found the button you want, drag it to your new toolbar.

✦ **Move a button from another toolbar.** With the Customize Toolbars dialog box open, drag a button from one open toolbar to your new toolbar. This moves the button, deleting it from the original toolbar.

✦ **Copy a button from another toolbar.** If you want to leave the original toolbar intact, use the same technique as for moving a button, but hold down the Ctrl key as you drag a button from one open toolbar to your new toolbar. This procedure copies the button.

Creating your own button definition

You can also create your own button definition from scratch. Follow these steps:

1. With the Commands tab of the Customize dialog box displayed, choose User Defined from the Categories list. The Commands pane lists a User Defined Button and User Defined Flyout.

2. Drag the button you want onto your toolbar. Because the buttons have no borders, they are indistinguishable from the background until you click them.

3. Click the Properties tab of the Customize dialog box and then click the blank button to display the Button Properties tab of the Customize dialog box, as shown in Figure 29-8.

Figure 29-8: The Button Properties tab of the Customize dialog box

4. Type a name for the button. This name appears as a tooltip, so don't make it too long.

5. Type a help description in the Help text box. This text appears on the status line to further explain the function of the button.

6. Write the macro. AutoCAD places ^C^C there for you. This cancels any other command that may be active when you use the button. You can place any valid menu command string as it would be typed on the command line or even an AutoLISP expression.

Cross-Reference

You should use menu syntax for the macro. I explain the details of creating command strings in Chapter 33, where I cover customizing menus.

7. Choose a button icon from the list of button icons or choose Edit to create your own button, as explained in the next section.

8. Click Apply and click the Close button of the Customize dialog box to close it. Close any other open dialog boxes.

AutoCAD updates the menus, showing its progress on the status bar.

Using the Button Editor

The Button Editor, shown in Figure 29-9, enables you to make your own button icons. Open the Button Editor by clicking Edit on the Button Properties tab of the Customize dialog box. You can choose one of the provided buttons and edit it — which I recommend — or start from scratch if you have artistic tendencies.

Figure 29-9: The Button Editor

The center of the editing area shows an enlarged view of the button. You see the button's actual size at the top-left corner of the dialog box. Check Grid to show a grid of pixels — this is just for your reference. Choose a color from the color palette and then choose one of the four tools at the top of the dialog box:

✦ The Pencil tool draws any shape. To draw, drag it across the editing area.

✦ Click and drag the Line tool to draw a straight line.

✦ The Circle tool draws circles and ellipses. You click the center and drag out to the circumference to indicate the radius.

✦ The Erase tool erases. You can click to erase pixel by pixel or drag to erase a series of pixels.

Here are the other features of the Button Editor:

✦ Choose Clear to clear the editing area and start from scratch.

✦ Choose Open to open an existing button for editing. Button icons are stored as .bmp files.

✦ Choose Undo to undo your most recent action.

✦ Choose Save to save the button icon as a .bmp file. The default file name is ICON.bmp.

✦ Choose Save As to save an existing .bmp file under a new name.

✦ Choose Close to close the Button Editor.

✦ Choose More to select a standard index color or true color.

New Feature

With the introduction of true color support in AutoCAD 2004, you can now create your toolbar icons with a wider variety of colors. Choose More in the Button Editor dialog box (shown in Figure 29-9) to access this colorful new feature.

Creating flyouts

You can also create your own flyouts, or you can use one of the existing flyouts. To use an existing flyout, open the Commands tab of the Customize dialog box and choose Flyouts. You can simply drag one of these to a toolbar.

To create your own flyout, follow these steps:

1. Create a toolbar with the buttons that you want on the flyout, as explained in the previous section.

2. Open the Customize dialog box and display the Commands tab.

3. Choose User Defined from the Categories list and drag User Defined Flyout from the Commands list onto an existing toolbar. You see a blank flyout on the toolbar.

4. Click the Properties tab of the Customize dialog box and then click the blank flyout button to display the Flyout Properties tab, shown in Figure 29-10.

4. You see a message telling you to associate a toolbar with the flyout.

5. From the list of toolbars, choose the new toolbar that you created. This toolbar will be the flyout from the flyout button you just added.

6. Click Apply and then click Close.

7. Your new toolbar is now a flyout on a toolbar. You can close the new toolbar you created because you can access it from its parent toolbar.

Figure 29-10: The Flyout Properties tab of the Customize dialog box

The following exercise changes your menu files. After the exercise, I explain how to undo the changes if you want. If you are working on someone else's computer, do not do this exercise without that person's permission. As I mentioned before, it is not good computer etiquette to modify other people's AutoCAD files without asking first.

Step-by-Step: Customizing Toolbars

1. Open Windows Explorer and copy `acad.mnu`, `acad.mnc`, and `acad.mns` from the `AutoCAD 2004\Support` folder to a floppy disk. Label and date the disk.

Note

By default, `acad.mnu`, `acad.mnc`, and `acad.mns` are in `\Documents` and `Settings\[user name]\Application Data\Autodesk\AutoCAD 2004\ R16.0\enu\Support`. However, your location may be different, depending on your operating system and customization. To find the location of `acad.mnu`, `acad.mnc`, and `acad.mns`, choose Tools ➪ Options and click the Files tab. Double-click the first item, Support File Search Path, to display the location of the support files.

2. Start a new drawing using any template. Save the file as `ab29-01.dwg` in your `AutoCAD Bible` folder.

3. Choose View ➪ Toolbars to open the Customize dialog box. From the Toolbars list, scroll down to find the Zoom toolbar and check it. When it appears, drag it away from the Toolbars dialog box, if necessary.

4. Drag the Zoom Center and Zoom All buttons off the toolbar (or choose the two buttons that you use least and drag them off), confirming the deletion each time. A small space appears between the last (Zoom Extents) button and the rest of the buttons. Drag the Zoom Extents button to the left slightly to eliminate the space.

5. Drag the toolbar to the space at the right of the Standard toolbar and dock it there. (The space you have depends on the size of your screen and your screen resolution. If it doesn't fit, drag one more button off the toolbar or dock it on the right side of the screen.)

6. Choose New on the Toolbars tab. In the New Toolbar dialog box, type **Special** in the Toolbar Name text box and click OK. A small toolbar appears on your screen.

7. Click the Commands tab. From the Categories list, choose Draw. Find the Donut button and drag it to your new toolbar. The I-beam cursor on the toolbar indicates the button placement.

8. Choose the Modify category and find Edit Polyline. Drag it to your new toolbar.

9. Choose the View category and drag Hidden to the toolbar.

10. Choose the User Defined category and drag User Defined Button to the new toolbar. Click the blank button to display the Button Properties tab.

11. Complete the dialog box, as shown in Figure 29-11. Type the macro as follows after the ^C^C, which is already there, being careful to include the spaces as well:

```
pedit \w .1 ;
```

12. Choose the Polyline Edit button from the Button Icon list, as shown in Figure 29-11. Choose Edit to open the Button Editor.

Figure 29-11: The completed Button Properties dialog box

13. You want to change the button so that it looks as if a zero-width polyline is being changed to a wider polyline because that's what the macro does. Click the red color. Choose the pencil tool (by default, it is already chosen). Click Grid to help you work. Click (or drag) the point of the pencil tool in each box, using Figure 29-12 as a guide. (Figure 29-12 shows the button in black and white.) When you're done, choose Save and then Close.

Figure 29-12: The new button

Tip

If you make a mistake, it's easy to correct it. If you place a red pixel over an existing black pixel, choose black and redraw the black pixel. If you place a red pixel in a wrong spot, choose the Erase tool and click the pixel.

14. On the Button Properties tab, click Apply. The new button appears in your toolbar. Click the Close button to close the dialog box. AutoCAD saves the changes to your menu source file (`.mns`).

15. Drag the new toolbar under the Zoom toolbar you modified. (If it doesn't fit, dock it on the right side of the screen.)

16. Choose Polyline from the Draw toolbar and draw any series of polyline segments. Choose the Plines .1 wide button from the new toolbar. At the `Select polyline:` prompt, pick the polyline. AutoCAD changes its width to 0.1. (If it doesn't work, check the macro. Right-click the Plines .1 wide button, choose Customize, and click the Plines .1 wide button to open the Button Properties tab.)

17. Save your drawing.

Caution

If you later customize the ACAD menu by editing `acad.mnu`, your toolbar modifications will be erased! In Chapter 33, where I discuss customizing AutoCAD's menus, I explain how to avoid this problem.

Undoing toolbar changes

To undo your toolbar changes, you need to reload the template menu, `acad.mnu`. This overwrites the compiled and source menu files that include your toolbar changes. The following steps explain the process. But first, be sure to have a backup of your `acad.mnu`, `acad.mnc`, and `acad.mns` files. (To find the location of the menu files, choose Tools ⇨ Options and click the Files tab. Double-click the first item, Support File Search Path, to display the location of the support files.)

1. Choose Tools ⇨ Customize ⇨ Menus. The Menu Groups tab should be on top. In the Menu Groups box, ACAD should be highlighted, as shown here.

2. In the bottom section of the dialog box, check Replace All so that AutoCAD loads all your menu files on the menu bar. In the File Name box, type **acad.mnu** and click Load. When you load the `acad.mnu` file, AutoCAD warns you that you will lose any toolbar customization changes you have made, as shown in the following figure. Click Yes because you do want to overwrite all your toolbar customization changes.

3. AutoCAD loads the menu and displays the message `Menu loaded successfully.` `MENUGROUP: ACAD.` Click Close. Your new toolbars and buttons disappear.

Reloading `acad.mnu` would remove any partial menus that you may have loaded. For more information, see my coverage of menu files in more detail in Chapter 33.

Here's how the `pedit` macro you used in the previous Step-by-Step exercise works:

```
pedit \w .1 ;
```

1. `Pedit` issues the PEDIT command. The space after `pedit` is equivalent to pressing Enter after you have typed the command on the command line. PEDIT then displays the `Select polyline:` prompt.

2. The backslash (\) is a special character that pauses the macro for your input. When you select the polyline, the macro continues, displaying the `Enter an option [Close/Join/Width/Edit vertex/Fit/Spline/Decurve/Ltype gen/Undo]:` prompt.

3. The `w` then specifies the Width option. The space following it is like pressing Enter. PEDIT then displays the `Specify new width for all segments:` prompt.

4. The macro then specifies 0.1. The space after it is like pressing Enter again. PEDIT then issues the `Enter an option [Close/Join/Width/Edit vertex/Fit/Spline/Decurve/Ltype gen/Undo]:` prompt.

5. The macro then uses a semicolon, which is used to specify pressing Enter at the end of a menu macro. This ends the command.

Customizing Tool Palettes

Tool palettes give you quick access to blocks and hatches. I cover tool palettes in Chapter 26. Some customization can be accomplished on the tool palettes themselves. Here I explain the procedure for customizing the tool palettes using the Customize dialog box.

To customize tool palettes, choose Tools ➪ Customize ➪ Tool Palettes to display the Tool Palettes tab of the Customize dialog box, shown in Figure 29-13. The current tool palettes are listed. Remember that each tab on the Tool Palette window is considered a separate tool palette.

Use the Customize dialog box to customize tool palettes as follows:

✦ **Change the order of the tool palette tabs:** Select one of the tabs in the Tool Palettes list and click Up or Down. This action moves the tab up or down one and also changes the tab's order in the dialog box listing. Continue to click Up or Down until the tab is in the desired position. You can also move the tabs directly on the Tool Palette by right-clicking the tab name and choosing Move Up or Move Down.

✦ **Create a new tool palette:** Click New. In the New Tool Palette dialog box, enter a name and click OK. To create a new tool palette on the palette itself, right-click anywhere on the palette and choose Create New Tool Palette.

✦ **Rename a tool palette:** Click Rename. In the Rename Tool Palette dialog box, enter a new name and click OK. To rename a tool palette on the palette itself, right-click on the tab's name and choose Rename Tool Palette.

✦ **Delete a tool palette:** Click Delete. In the Confirm Tool Palette Deletion dialog box, which warns you that deletion is permanent unless you first export the tool palette, click OK to delete the tool palette. You can also right-click any tool palette and choose Delete Tool Palette.

✦ **Import a tool palette:** Click Import. In the Import Tool Palette dialog box, locate the `.xtp` file and click Open.

✦ **Export a tool palette:** Click Export. In the Export Tool Palette dialog box, choose the location for the file. You can change the name if you want. The tool palette is saved as an `.xtp` file. Click Save.

Figure 29-13: The Tool Palettes tab of the Customize dialog box

Summary

In this chapter, I covered the basics of customizing AutoCAD. You started to customize AutoCAD by:

✦ Creating command shortcuts (aliases) in the `acad.pgp` file

✦ Creating your own toolbars that can contain any command sequence you need.

✦ Working with tool palettes, a new feature of AutoCAD 2004, including changing their order, renaming and deleting them, and also saving them as a file so that you can share them with others.

In the next, chapter you read how to create macros with script files.

✦ ✦ ✦

Creating Macros and Slide Shows with Script Files

◆　◆　◆　◆

In This Chapter

Automating
commands with
script files

Creating slide shows

Creating slide
libraries for menu
customization

◆　◆　◆　◆

Script files are like macros that you create in your word processor or spreadsheet. They execute a series of commands automatically. You can use script files to automate plotting, set up a drawing, clean up a drawing, create a slide show, or do any repetitive task.

Creating Macros with Script Files

To create a script file, you need to think out the commands that you want to execute and their options and prompts. Then you create the text for the script file. Script files have the following characteristics:

+ They must use the `.scr` file name extension.

+ They are text-only (ASCII) files.

+ They must use command-line syntax only.

Note One of the most common uses for script files before Release 14 was to automate plotting of several drawings at once. The Batch Plot Utility, introduced with Release 14, can do many multiple plotting tasks for you.

Creating the script file

You can create the script file using a text editor, such as Notepad. For early practice with script files, type each command on its own line. A blank space is equivalent to pressing Enter. End each line by pressing Enter (also called Return), without extra blank spaces. If you need two returns one after another at the end of a line, use a blank line for the second

return. Every space is meaningful—getting those spaces and blank lines right is probably the hardest part of creating a script file. One technique is to start your script files in a word processing program that can display with nonprinting characters (blank spaces and returns). You can either save the script file in text format or copy it into Notepad. Following are some tips to help you create successful script files with the least aggravation:

✦ Go through the steps once using the command line only before creating the script file.

✦ If you will use any dialog boxes that ask for files, set the system variable FILE-DIA to zero (off) before experimenting with the commands you will use in the script file. This lets you practice the keystrokes without opening dialog boxes. Or you can practice using the version of the command with the hyphen in front of it (such as -layer); in most cases, you don't need the hyphen in the script file itself.

Note AutoCAD automatically runs script files as if FILEDIA were off, even if it is set to 1 (on).

✦ For commands that require inputting text such as layer or file names, enclose the names in quotation marks and for the next use of Enter, press Enter and go to the next line in the script instead of using a space. Otherwise, AutoCAD may misinterpret a space as a space in the layer or file name, rather than an Enter.

✦ Place comments in your script file to explain what you are doing. A comment is any line that starts with a semicolon.

✦ Keep Notepad open as you work. When you have completed a set of keystrokes that you want, open the AutoCAD Text Window (press F2), select the command string you want, right-click, choose Copy, switch back to Notepad, and paste. Then cut out all the prompts, leaving only the keyboard entry. You will probably have to readjust the spaces between the words.

✦ You can press End to check for blank spaces at the end of a line. Pressing Ctrl+End moves the cursor to the end of the document—useful for checking for extra spaces and lines at the end of a script.

Remember, you can open Notepad from within AutoCAD by typing **Notepad** at the command line. At the File to edit: prompt, press Enter to open a new file. The acad.pgp file includes this Windows command by default. See Chapter 29 for details on the acad.pgp file.

Another option is to simply write down what you type at the command line. As you write, use an underscore to represent each space. It's very hard to remember that you left three spaces between two words unless you see three underscores. Of course, when you create the script file, you must use spaces, not underscores.

As soon as you complete the script file, save it with any name that is meaningful to you plus an extension of .scr.

Here's an example of a script file that draws a series of circles:

```
circle 2,2 1.5
circle 6,2 1.5
circle 10,2 1.5
circle 14,2 1.5
```

This script file starts the CIRCLE command, specifies a center point, and specifies a radius four times. The results are shown in Figure 30-1.

Figure 30-1: Running a script file created this drawing

Running script files

You can run a script file from within a drawing. Use this technique when you want the script to apply only to that drawing. However, you can also start a script within a drawing, then close the drawing and continue on to open and process other drawings.

You can also run a script file when loading AutoCAD. You would do this when you want the script file to apply to more than one drawing. For example, you could use script files in the following situations:

✦ You want to use a script file to set up every drawing you open. Although the script file applies to only one drawing at a time, you use it on a different drawing each time.

✦ You want to use a script file to clean up a list of drawings in one batch — such as thawing all layers on all the drawings in a folder.

Running a script file from within a drawing

To run a script from within a drawing, follow these steps:

1. Choose Tools ➪ Run Script. This opens the Select Script File dialog box, as shown in Figure 30-2.

Figure 30-2: The Select Script File dialog box

2. Choose the script file you want.

3. Click Open. AutoCAD runs the script file.

Running a script when loading AutoCAD

Run a script when loading AutoCAD by changing the target expression that Windows uses to open AutoCAD. The easiest way to do this is to use the shortcut to AutoCAD on your desktop and modify the target there. Right-click the AutoCAD shortcut and choose Properties. Click the Shortcut tab, shown in Figure 30-3.

Figure 30-3: The Shortcut tab of the AutoCAD 2004 Properties dialog box

The Target text box displays the command expression that Windows uses to open AutoCAD. Don't make any change to the current expression — just add to it. The format for starting a script file is:

```
drive:\path\acad.exe drive:\path\drawingname.dwg /b script_file
```

For example, if your current target reads `C:\Program Files\AutoCAD 2004\acad.exe` and you want to open a drawing named `ba-349.dwg` in `c:\drawings` and run a script file named `pre-plot.scr`, your target should read:

```
"C:\Program Files\AutoCAD 2004\acad.exe" c:\drawings\ba-349.dwg
/b pre-plot
```

You don't need to add the `.scr` extension after the script file name. Long file names that contain spaces must be enclosed in quotation marks — both in the target and in the script file itself. You need to include the full path of the drawing. If the script file is not in AutoCAD's support file search path, include the entire path. For example:

```
"C:\Program Files\AutoCAD 2004\acad.exe" "c:\aec\drc\Dobbs
Ferry Apts.dwg" /b c:\aec\drc\cleanup
```

If you want to start a new drawing, you might want to specify a template. In the preceding format, replace the AutoCAD drawing file name with:

```
/t template_name
```

When you have finished typing your additions in the Target text box, click OK. Now, when you start AutoCAD, the drawing or template opens, and the script starts.

From within a script file, you can open (and close) other drawings. In this way you can run a script file on as many drawings as you want. Figure 30-4 shows a script file, `multi-cleanup.scr`, which is used when loading AutoCAD. The target is set so that AutoCAD opens `Apt 1A.dwg`.

```
chprop all  c bylayer

-layer f no-plot

qsave
close
open "f:\aec\Apt 1B"
chprop all  c bylayer

-layer f no-plot

qsave
close
open "f:\aec\Apt 1C"
chprop all  c bylayer

-layer f no-plot
qsave
```

Figure 30-4: A script file that cleans up three drawings

Note Don't forget that you can open multiple drawings within the same session of AutoCAD. You may need to set the SDI (single document interface) system variable to 1, if you plan to use older script files. Otherwise, use the new CLOSE command to close each drawing after your script file has finished working on it. Without one of these methods, you may end up with 100 drawings open at once—and probably a major computer crash as well!

Here's how `multi-cleanup.scr` works:

1. The CHPROP command selects all objects and sets their color to BYLAYER.

2. The LAYER command freezes the layer named no-plot.

3. The script file saves the drawing.

4. The script file closes the drawing and opens the next drawing.

5. This process is repeated until the last drawing is edited and saved. The last drawing is left open.

Tip It's nice to leave the last drawing open so that when you return to see the results, you can see that the last drawing has been properly edited. You then feel pretty sure that all the previous drawings were similarly edited.

Notice the quotation marks around the file names in the script file. These are necessary because the drawing file names include spaces.

In the following exercise you practice creating and using a script file similar to the multi-cleanup script file used in the previous example, but for only one drawing.

On the CD-ROM The drawing used in the following Step-by-Step exercise on creating and using a script file, `ab30-a.dwg`, is in the `Drawings` folder of the *AutoCAD 2004 Bible* CD-ROM.

Step-by-Step: Creating and Using a Script File

1. Open `ab30-a.dwg` from the CD-ROM.

2. Save the file as `ab30-01.dwg` in your `AutoCAD Bible` folder.

3. Type **notepad** ↵. At the `File to edit:` prompt, press Enter to open a new file.

4. Type the following, replacing the underscores with spaces. Note that there should be two spaces between `all` and `c` in the second line. Press Enter after the `qsave` line.

    ```
    chprop_all__c_bylayer

    -layer_f_no-plot

    qsave
    ```

5. Save the file as `cleanup.scr` in your `AutoCAD Bible` folder. Close Notepad.

The script file changes the color property of all objects to ByLayer and freezes the no-plot layer. Notice that the drawing has some text that has been set to a blue color (maybe to make it more readable). The title block is on the no-plot layer.

6. Choose Tools ➪ Run Script.

7. In the Select Script File dialog box, find `cleanup.scr` in your `AutoCAD Bible` folder and click Open. AutoCAD runs the script, changing the text's color to ByLayer (green) and freezing the no-plot layer. It also saves the drawing.

If the script file doesn't work, press F2 to open the Text Window and see where it got hung up. This will help you see where to correct the script file. Reopen it (on the Windows task bar choose Start ➪ Documents or Start ➪ My Recent Documents (depending on your version of Windows) and choose `cleanup.scr`) and make the correction. Save the file, close it, and try again.

8. Save your drawing.

Taking script files to the max

What if you want to execute that multi-cleanup script file on 200 drawings? Typing in all those file names would take so long you would wonder if you were saving any time.

You *can* save time. First, you need to find a text editor or word processor that can create vertical blocks of text. This means that you can select columns of text rather than lines of text. You can do this in Microsoft Word by holding down Alt and dragging down the text. (Using a fixed-width font, such as "Courier New" makes selecting columns of text easier.) Then, you need to format the script file so that the entire set of commands is in one row, as in the figure shown here. In Microsoft Word, you can use Page Setup to set the paper to landscape and make it as wide as you need so that the text doesn't wrap. (Of course, you type the script once, and then copy the line and paste it as many times as you need.) You do this so that all the file names will be in one column. Here you see the path but no file name at the end of each line. The file name will be inserted before the quotation mark at the end of each line.

```
chprop all  c bylayer  -layer f no-plot  qsave close open "f:\aec\ "
chprop all  c bylayer  -layer f no-plot  qsave close open "f:\aec\ "
chprop all  c bylayer  -layer f no-plot  qsave
```

Now, open a DOS window. (From the Windows task bar, choose Start ➪ ProgramsAccessories ➪ Command Prompt.) Use the DOS `cd` command to navigate to the folder where all your drawings are. (They should all be in one folder.) Type **dir *.dwg /b >dwglst.txt** and press Enter. This creates a listing of all the files in that folder and places it in a text file named `dwglst.txt`. The `/b` parameter creates a file that contains only the names of the drawings.

Open the file in a text editor or word processor that can create vertical blocks. Create a vertical block over the drawing names and copy it to the clipboard.

Continued

Continued

Open the script file in the same text editor or word processor, place the cursor at the top-left corner of the vertical block, and paste. You should get all the drawing names inserted in the right place, as shown here with two drawings. If you're in a word processor, don't forget to save the file as a Text Only document.

```
chprop all  c bylayer  -layer f no-plot  qsave close open "f:\aec\ Apt 1B"
chprop all  c bylayer  -layer f no-plot  qsave close open "f:\aec\ Apt 1C"
chprop all  c bylayer  -layer f no-plot  qsave
```

Used in this way, script files can be an extremely powerful tool for editing large numbers of drawings in one batch.

Creating Slide Shows

One common use for script files is to create a slide show. AutoCAD enables you to save a view of a drawing as a slide. You can then create a slide library from the slides and show the slides one after another automatically.

Tip You can save any drawing as an image file and import it into a presentation program that creates slide shows, such as Microsoft PowerPoint, Lotus Freelance Graphics, or Corel Presentations. You can add text, special effects, and more to create a professional slide show. For more information, see "Saving rendered images" in Chapter 25 and "Exporting to other file formats" in Chapter 27.

Creating slides

Creating a slide is like capturing the screen of your drawing. AutoCAD makes a simplified vector file from the current viewport in model space, or from all viewports in paper space layouts. You can also create a slide of a *wireframe*, or hidden display. Unfortunately, you cannot make slides of shaded or rendered displays.

To create a slide, follow these steps:

1. Display the view of the drawing that you want to save as a slide.

2. Type **mslide** ↵.

3. In the Create Slide File dialog box, choose a location and name for the slide. Its extension will automatically be .sld.

4. Choose Save.

Viewing slides

To view a slide, follow these steps:

1. Type **vslide** ↵.

2. In the Select Slide File dialog box, choose the slide you want to view.

3. Choose Open. AutoCAD displays the slide.

Do a Redraw to return to your drawing. You cannot draw in or edit a slide.

On the CD-ROM The drawing used in the following Step-by-Step exercise on creating and using a script file, ab30-b.dwg, is in the Drawings folder of the *AutoCAD 2004 Bible* CD-ROM.

Step-by-Step: Creating and Viewing Slides

1. Open ab30-b.dwg from the CD-ROM.

2. Save the file as ab30-02.dwg in your AutoCAD Bible folder.

3. Type **hide** ↵. AutoCAD hides the drawing.

4. Type **mslide** ↵. In the Create Slide File dialog box, click the Save in drop-down box and select your AutoCAD Bible folder, if it isn't already selected. In the File name text box, change the name from its default of ab30-02.sld to ab30-02a.sld. Click Save.

5. Choose View ⇨ 3D Orbit from the Standard toolbar. Click and drag the right quadrant circle of the arcball slightly to the left. Press Esc.

6. Issue the MSLIDE command again. This time save the slide as ab30-02b.sld.

7. Choose 3D Orbit from the Standard toolbar. Again, click and drag the right quadrant circle of the arcball slightly to the left. Press Esc.

8. Issue the MSLIDE command again and save the slide as ab30-02c.sld.

9. Click Zoom Previous on the Standard toolbar until you see the message No previous view saved.

10. Type **vslide** ↵. In the Select Slide File dialog box, choose the first slide, ab30-02a.sld. Click Open. AutoCAD displays the slide.

11. Repeat the VSLIDE command and display ab30-2b.sld. Do the same with ab30-02c.sld.

12. Click Redraw All on the Standard toolbar.

13. Save your drawing.

Using scripts to create slide shows

You can create a script file that displays slides one after another, resulting in a slide show. AutoCAD provides two special script file commands for this purpose:

✦ DELAY *nnnn* pauses the script for the number of milliseconds you specify. For example, DELAY 3000 pauses the script for three seconds.

✦ RSCRIPT repeats the script from the beginning. Use this command to create a continuously running script. To stop the script (whether repeating or not), press Esc or backspace, or drop down any menu.

✦ RESUME restarts a script file after you have stopped it.

The VSLIDE command, which displays a slide, can also be used to preload the next slide into memory. You use this command to preload a slide while viewers are looking at the previous slide. This reduces the waiting time between slides. To use this feature, put an asterisk (*) before the file name in the VSLIDE command. The next VSLIDE command detects that a slide has been preloaded and displays it without asking for the slide name. Here's how it works:

```
vslide ab30-2a
vslide *ab30-2b
delay 3000
vslide
vslide *ab30-2c
delay 3000
vslide
rscript
```

This script file does the following:

1. It displays ab30-02a.sld.

2. It preloads ab30-02b.sld.

3. It waits three seconds, displaying ab30-02a.sld.

4. It displays ab30-02b.sld.

5. It preloads ab30-02c.sld.

6. It waits three seconds, displaying ab30-02b.sld.

7. It displays ab30-02c.sld.

8. It repeats the script from the beginning.

Step-by-Step: Creating a Slide Show

1. Open Notepad and type the following script:

```
vslide ab30-02a
vslide *ab30-02b
delay 3000
```

```
vslide
vslide *ab30-02c
delay 3000
vslide
delay 3000
rscript
```

2. Remember to press Enter at the end of the last line. Save the file as
 `ab30-02.scr` in your `AutoCAD Bible` folder. Close Notepad.

3. So that AutoCAD can find the slide files, place your `AutoCAD Bible` folder in
 AutoCAD's support file search path. To do this, click Tools ➪ Options ➪ Files
 tab. Click Support File Search Path and click Add. Click Browse and find your
 `AutoCAD Bible` folder. Click OK twice.

4. In any AutoCAD drawing, choose Tools ➪ Run Script. Locate `ab30-02.scr` in
 your `AutoCAD Bible` folder and click Open. AutoCAD runs the slide show.
 Notice that the last slide still takes a while to display.

5. Let the slide show run through twice. The last slide displays a little more
 quickly the second time. Press Esc to stop the slide show.

6. Do not save your drawing.

Tip When running a slide show, you might want to maximize the screen area by reduc-
ing menu and command-line space. You can unload your menu, thus quickly dis-
missing toolbars from the screen. Use Tools ➪ Options ➪ Display to reduce the
number of lines of text to show on the command line to 1. Remember that when
you unload the menu, you have no menus available. You can reload the menu by
following the instructions for unloading and loading menus in Chapter 33.

Creating Slide Libraries

You can organize your slides into slide libraries. Slide libraries have an extension of
`.slb`. One reason for creating slide libraries is to create image tiles when you are
customizing your menu. To see an example of an image tile menu, choose Draw ➪
Surfaces ➪ 3D Surfaces. These image tiles are created with slides organized into
libraries.

To view slides in a library, use the following format:

```
library(slidename)
```

Say that you placed the three slides used in the preceding Step-by-Step exercise in a
slide library called `3dmodel.slb`. You would then use the following command in
the script file to preload the second slide (the second line of the script file):

```
vslide *3dmodel(ab30-02b)
```

To create a slide library, you need to use the DOS prompt. AutoCAD provides the SLIDELIB utility in its `AutoCAD 2004` folder to create slide libraries.

To get to the DOS prompt, choose Start ➪ Programs ➪ Accessories ➪ Command Prompt.

Follow these steps to create a slide library:

1. Create a text file (you can use Notepad) containing the names of the slide files. Include the paths of the slide files if they are not in AutoCAD's support file search path. Place each slide file name on a new line.

Tip SLIDELIB can read a listing created using DOS's `dir` command with the `/b` parameter, which creates a simple listing of just the file names. Therefore, you can place all the slide files in a folder and redirect the `dir` listing to a file. For example, you can create a list named `ab30sld.lst` by typing the following at the DOS prompt:

```
dir *.sld /b >ab30sld.lst
```

This creates the list in the same folder as the slide files.

2. Assuming that you are still in the same folder where you created the slide file list and you want to create a library called `ab30sld.slb` in the same folder, type the following at the DOS prompt:

```
"c:\program files\acad2004\slidelib" ab30sld < ab30sld.lst
```

Note SLIDELIB cannot accept file names with spaces but it can handle long file names, provided you use a character, such as an underscore where you might normally have a blank space.

Summary

This chapter explained how to create script files to automate repetitive commands. You read the following:

✦ Creating script files that contain commands, options, and values in command-line format

✦ Running script files from within a drawing or when loading AutoCAD

✦ Creating slides from the display in your viewport and creating a script file that displays several slides one after another, resulting in a slide show

✦ Organizing your slides into slide libraries

In the next chapter, you read how to create your own linetypes and hatch patterns.

✦ ✦ ✦

Creating Your Own Linetypes and Hatch Patterns

As you know, AutoCAD comes with a large number of linetypes. However, sometimes these may not serve your particular needs. You can therefore create your own linetypes and use them in your drawings in the same way you use the linetypes that AutoCAD provides. Linetypes are useful whenever you don't want a continuous linetype. They apply not only to lines, but also to polylines, arcs, ellipses, wireframes, and solids — in fact, to most AutoCAD objects.

Creating Linetypes

There are two types of linetypes: simple and complex. Simple linetypes consist of dashes and dots only. Complex linetypes usually have dashes and/or dots also but contain text and/or shapes as well.

The default linetype file is `acad.lin`. You can add your own linetype definitions to this file or create your own linetype files. Linetype files are text files and must have an extension of `.lin`. Of course, be sure to make a backup copy of `acad.lin` before you edit it.

Creating simple linetypes

In the syntax for creating simple linetypes, each linetype is defined using two lines of text. The first line contains the linetype name and an optional description, formatted as follows:

```
*linetype name[, description]
```

Here are the points to note:

✦ Always start the definition with an asterisk.

✦ The description is limited to 47 characters.

✦ If you include a description, precede it with a comma.

The second line of the linetype syntax is its definition. With simple linetypes, you are limited to dashes, dots, and spaces, measured in units and shown as follows:

✦ A dash is indicated by a positive number.

✦ A dot is indicated by a zero.

✦ A space is indicated by a negative number.

✦ Each item is separated by a comma, there are no spaces, and the maximum line length is 80 characters.

✦ Each line must start with the letter A.

The following definition creates a line with two dashes of 0.25 units, followed by two dots, all separated by spaces of 0.1 units.

```
*seeingdouble, Future hedge line
A,.25,-.1,.25,-.1,0,-.1,0,-.1
```

The result is shown in Figure 31-1.

Figure 31-1: The seeingdouble linetype

If you feel quite confident, you can even create linetypes on the fly, using the command-line form of the LINETYPE command. Type **-linetype** ↵ and use the Create option. Follow the prompts and type the linetype definition on the command line. If you make a mistake, you still have to open the linetype file in a text editor to make corrections.

Tip　　If your linetype definition will include both dashes and dots, you'll get best results if you start a linetype definition with the dash. Starting the definition with a dash is a matter of aesthetics, perhaps, but such a line connects better to other lines.

Step-by-Step: Creating a Simple Linetype

1. Open a drawing using the `acad.dwt` template.

2. Save your drawing as `ab31-01.dwg` in your `AutoCAD Bible` folder.

3. Type **notepad** and press Enter at the `File to edit:` prompt to open a new file in Notepad.

4. Type the following:

```
*3dotsandadash, temporary fencing
A,.5,-.25,0,-.1,0,-.1,0,-.25
```

5. Press Enter after the last line. Save the file as ab31-01.lin in your AutoCAD Bible folder and close Notepad.

6. In your drawing, choose Layer Properties Manager on the Layers toolbar and then click New. Name the new layer tfence. Set its color to red.

7. Click Continuous in the Linetype column to open the Select Linetype dialog box. Click Load.

8. In the Load or Reload Linetypes dialog box, click File. In the Select Linetype File dialog box, find ab31-01.lin in your AutoCAD Bible folder, choose it, and click Open.

9. Back in the Load or Reload Linetypes dialog box, choose 3dotsandadash and click OK.

10. Again, in the Select Linetype dialog box, choose 3dotsandadash and click OK. The layer tfence now shows the correct linetype. Click Current and then OK.

11. Start the LINE command and turn on ORTHO. Draw any line to see the linetype. Save your drawing. The linetype should look like Figure 31-2.

Figure 31-2: The 3dotsandadash linetype

Creating complex linetypes

A complex linetype includes either shapes or text in the linetype definition. Figure 31-3 shows an example of each.

Complex linetype definitions are similar to those for simple linetypes, except that they add a definition for a shape or text.

Figure 31-3: Complex linetypes include shapes or text.

Shapes are covered in the next chapter — for now you only need to know that they are contained in files with the extension .shx.

The first line of the linetype definition is the same as for simple linetypes. The second line of the definition can contain all the same features as those for a simple linetype. However, you add the special shape or text definition in square brackets:

✦ **Syntax for shapes:** [shapename,shxfilename,details]

✦ **Syntax for text:** ["text string",textstyle,details]

"Details" refers to an optional series of rotation, scale, and offset specifications that you can add to the definition. Table 31-1 describes these specifications.

The following complex linetype definition uses a shape and has no details:

```
*TEMPFENCE, FENCE SHAPE AND DASH
A,.5,-.25,[FENCE,"C:\AUTOCAD BIBLE\FENCE.SHX"],-.5
```

Note that the specification for the shape is simply part of the rest of the definition that includes a dash and spaces before and after the shape. The shape is enclosed in both commas and square brackets. The first part of the shape definition is the name of the shape (which is defined in the shape's definition file), and the second part is the name of the shape file. In this case the shape file is not in AutoCAD's support file search path so the entire path needs to be specified. Don't forget to use quotation marks around the shape file name if the folder name or file name contains embedded spaces.

Tip Note that the space after the shape (created with the –.5 code) is larger than the space before it (created with the –.25). You need to allow for the space that the shape takes up. This is largely a matter of trial and error, but if you know the shape definition well, you can make a good estimate. When you go back and change the linetype definition (if your first trial was an error), don't forget to reload the linetype (by using the Load option).

The following complex linetype definition uses text and has no details:

```
*TFENCE, DASH & TEXT
A,.5,-.25,["TEMP FENCE",FENCE],-1.5
```

Again, the specification for the text is placed within a linetype definition that includes a dash and spaces. The first part of the text definition is the text string, which is always in quotation marks. The second part of the definition is the text style. Again, the space after the text is larger than the space before, to leave room for the text.

You must define the text style in the drawing before you load the linetype.

Table 31-1 lists the details that you can add to both the shape and text portion of complex linetype definitions.

		Table 31-1 Optional Details for Shapes and Text in Complex Linetype Definitions		

Detail	Syntax	Description
Relative rotation	R=##	Rotates the shape or text relative to the angle of the line you draw. This number is in degrees unless you put a g (for grads) or r (for radians) after it.
Absolute rotation	A=##	Rotates the shape or text based on the World Coordinate System, regardless of the angle of the line. Because the default is a relative rotation of zero, you can use absolute rotation to keep text facing upright, no matter what the direction of the line. This number is in degrees unless you put a g (for grads) or r (for radians) after it.
Scale	S=##	Scales the text or shape. This scale is multiplied by any scale contained in a shape definition or height in a text style. If you use a text style with a height of zero, this scale number defines the text's height.
X offset	X=##	A positive number moves the shape or text toward the endpoint of the line. A negative number moves the shape or text toward the start point of the line. You can use an X offset to place a shape or text along a continuous linetype. You can also use an X offset to adjust the spacing of a shape or text between dashes, instead of changing the spaces before or after the dashes.
Y offset	Y=##	Moves the shape or text perpendicular to the direction of the line. A positive number moves the shape or text up if the line is drawn from left to right. Use a Y offset to center text and shapes along a linetype.

*Although using an absolute rotation of zero might sound like a good idea for complex linetypes with text, if you use the linetype at varying angles or on curves, you may find that the text shifts to an undesirable location due to the text's justification point.

Here is a definition that includes a shape with a scale and a Y offset:

```
*TEMPFENCE, FENCE SHAPE AND DASH
A,.5,-.25,[FENCE,"C:\AUTOCAD BIBLE\FENCE.SHX",S=.025,Y=-.07],-.5
```

This shape definition scales the shape to 0.025 of its original size. This results in the linetype shown in Figure 31-4. Of course, in order to scale the shape, you need to know its original size. You can use the SHAPE command to insert a shape and get an idea of what it looks like. In this case, the shape's original definition is much too large for a linetype and needs to be scaled down.

Figure 31-4: The TEMPFENCE linetype

The shape definition also moves the shape in the minus Y direction by 0.07 units. This nicely centers the shape within the linetype.

Caution When you create drawings by using shapes or custom fonts, as in the case of complex linetypes, you need to include the shape files or font files when you distribute the drawings to others.

By including more involved shapes in a complex linetype and not much else, you can create a linetype that is, for all practical purposes, a series of shapes displayed one after the other. You can create some interesting effects in this way.

AutoCAD comes with several complex linetypes that are at the end of the \support\ acad.lin linetype definition file. Look at their definitions and try them out to get ideas for your own complex linetypes. Express Tools have a command, MKLTYPE (choose Express ➪ Tools ➪ Make Linetype) that automatically creates linetypes, even complex ones.

Note By default, acad.lin is in \Documents and Settings\[user name]\ Application Data\Autodesk\AutoCAD 2004\R16.0\enu\Support. However, your location may be different, depending on your operating system and customization. To find the location of acad.lin, choose Tools ➪ Options and click the Files tab. Double-click the first item, Support File Search Path, to display the location of the support files.

On the CD-ROM The drawing used in the following Step-by-Step exercise on creating a complex linetype, ab31-a.dwg, is in the Drawings folder of the *AutoCAD 2004 Bible* CD-ROM.

Step-by-Step: Creating a Complex Linetype

1. Open ab31-a.dwg from the CD-ROM.

2. Save the file as ab31-02.dwg in your AutoCAD Bible folder. This drawing is a simple plan for a trailer park.

3. Choose Format ➪ Text Style. Click New and type **TVCABLE** for the Style name. Click OK. In the Font name drop-down list, choose Arial. Click Apply and then Close.

4. Type **notepad** ↵ and press Enter at the File to edit: prompt. AutoCAD opens Notepad. Type the following:

```
*TV, Buried television cable
A,.5,-.5,["TV",TVCABLE,S=.3,X=-.1,Y=-.15],-.75
```

5. Choose File ➪ Save and save it in your AutoCAD Bible folder as ab31-02.lin.

6. Choose Layer Properties Manager from the Layers toolbar. Choose `Buried_cable` and click its Continuous linetype in the Linetype column. In the Select Linetype dialog box, choose Load. Click File. Find `ab31-02.lin` in your `AutoCAD Bible` folder, choose it, and click Open.

7. In the Load or Reload Linetypes dialog box, choose TV and click OK. Do the same in the Select Linetypes dialog box. Click Current. Click OK.

8. Click Linetype Control from the Layers toolbar and choose Other. In the Linetype Manager, click Show Details to display the Details section. Change the Global Scale Factor to 192. Click OK.

9. Draw some lines or polylines. Zoom in to see the linetype more clearly. Figure 31-5 shows the resulting linetype.

10. Save your drawing.

Figure 31-5: The TV linetype

Creating Hatch Patterns

Hatch patterns are sets of parallel line patterns that are used to fill an enclosed area. Although the part of the hatch pattern definition that defines each line has some similarities to a linetype definition, for hatch patterns you also need to specify the angle and spacing of the lines. You cannot include text or shapes in hatch patterns.

Hatch patterns are stored in files with an extension of `.pat`. AutoCAD includes a large number of hatch patterns in `acad.pat`. You can add to or edit this file or create your own `.pat` file. As always, don't forget to make a copy of `acad.pat` before you edit it. When creating your own `.pat` file, remember the following:

✦ If you are not adding patterns to `acad.pat`, you can only put one hatch pattern in a custom `.pat` file. The file name and pattern name must be the same.

✦ You can insert comments in your `.pat` file after a semicolon.

✦ You must press Enter after the end of the last line of the hatch definition.

Note By default, acad.pat is in \Documents and Settings\[user name]\ Application Data\Autodesk\AutoCAD 2004\R16.0\enu\Support. However, your location may be different, depending on your operating system and customization. To find the location of acad.pat, choose Tools ➪ Options and click the Files tab. Double-click the first item, Support File Search Path, to display the location of the support files.

Here is the syntax for hatch patterns:

```
*pattern-name[, description]
angle, x-origin,y-origin, delta-x,delta-y [, dash1, dash2, ...]
```

Here are some general points for hatch pattern definitions:

✦ The pattern name cannot have spaces.

✦ The description is optional.

✦ Add the dash specifications only for noncontinuous lines.

✦ You can have more than one definition line (the second line in the preceding syntax), creating sets of hatch definitions that combine to create the hatch pattern.

✦ Each definition line can be no more than 80 characters.

✦ You can include a maximum of six dash specifications (which include spaces and dots).

✦ You can add spaces in the definition lines for readability.

Table 31-2 describes the features of a hatch pattern definition.

Table 31-2
Hatch Pattern Definitions

Specification	Explanation
Angle	Defines the angle of the lines in the hatch pattern. If you also specify an angle in the Boundary Hatch dialog box, the two angles are added. For example, if a hatch pattern defines lines at 105 degrees and you specify a hatch angle of 30 degrees, you end up with lines running at 135 degrees.
X-origin	Specifies the X coordinate of the base point of the hatch pattern. Although your hatch probably won't go through 0,0, AutoCAD uses this point to line up sets of lines in hatch patterns as well as to align hatch patterns in different areas. Because all hatch patterns are calculated from the base point, they are always aligned, no matter where they actually appear in the drawing.
Y-origin	Specifies the Y coordinate of the base point of the hatch pattern.

Specification	Explanation
Delta-x	Specifies the offset of successive lines. This only applies to dashed lines and is measured along the direction of the lines. Specifying a delta-x staggers each successive line by the amount you specify so that the dashes do not line up.
Delta-y	Specifies the distance between lines, measured perpendicular to the direction of the lines. This applies to both continuous and dashed lines.
Dash	Defines a noncontinuous line using the same system as linetype definitions: positive for a dash, negative for a space, and zero for a dot.

The hatch pattern shown in Figure 31-6 is the simplest form of hatch pattern.

Figure 31-6: The ftrailer hatch pattern with continuous lines

Although you could specify this simple hatch pattern in the Boundary Hatch dialog box by specifying a user-defined hatch with an angle and spacing, the example that follows shows the syntax clearly. The lines are at an angle of 105 degrees, the hatch pattern starts at 0,0, and the spacing between the lines is 0.5 units. The lines are continuous.

```
*ftrailer, proposed future trailers
105, 0,0, 0,0.5
```

Adding one level of complexity, you can make the lines in the hatch pattern noncontinuous, as follows:

```
*ftrailer, proposed future trailers
105, 0,0, 0,0.5, .5,-.25,0,-.1,0,-.25
```

Note that this definition uses the maximum of six dash specifications (the dash, space, dot, space, dot, and space).

A close-up of this hatch pattern is shown in Figure 31-7.

Figure 31-7: The ftrailer hatch pattern with a dash and two dots

If you add a delta-x of 0.25, the lines in the pattern are staggered by 0.25 units, along the direction of the lines, as shown in this code and in Figure 31-8:

```
*ftrailer, proposed future trailers
105, 0,0, 0.25,0.5, .5,-.25,0,-.1,0,-.25
```

Figure 31-8: The ftrailer hatch pattern with an added delta-x

You might wonder why the pattern staggers downward when you added a positive delta-x. The answer is that the direction of the lines (in this case, 105 degrees) becomes the X axis for this calculation. Figure 31-9 shows a zoomed-in display of the hatch pattern around 0,0, which is the base point. The hatch pattern is being generated up and to the left. The first line starts at 0,0, and the second line starts to the left by 0.5 units (the delta-y) and up by 0.25 units (the delta-x), as shown by the dimensions.

Figure 31-9: Calculating how the delta-x and delta-y affect a hatch pattern

Finally, you can add additional definition lines. One of the definition lines should start at 0,0, but the others may start anywhere. Here is the definition for the pattern in Figure 31-10. It actually creates the shape of the trailers. Although you see the rectangular shape, the hatch pattern is created from four separate lines, two at 0 degrees and two at 90 degrees. Note that the two 0-degree lines are the same except that they start at different base points. The same is true for the two 90-degree lines.

```
*trail, whole trailers-proposed
0, 0,0, 0,2, .5,-1
90, 0,0, 0,1.5, .5,-.25,0,-.25,.5,-.5
90, .5,0, 0,1.5, .5,-.25,0,-.25,.5,-.5
0, 0,1.5, 0,2, .5,-1
```

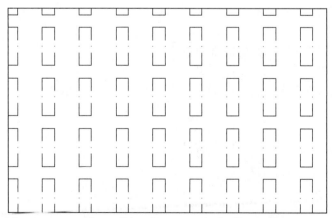

Figure 31-10: The trail hatch pattern looks like trailers.

Step-by-Step: Creating and Using a Hatch Pattern

1. Open a drawing using any template.

2. Save the file as ab31-03.dwg in your AutoCAD Bible folder.

3. Type **notepad** ↵ and press Enter at the File to edit: prompt.

4. Type the following:

```
*lightning, interwoven lightning
90, 0,0, 0,.5, .5,-.25
0, -.25,.5, 0,.75, .25,-.25
90, -.25,.5, 0,.5, .5,-.25
```

5. Press Enter after the last line. Save the file as lightning.pat in your AutoCAD Bible folder. Close Notepad.

6. If you haven't already done so, you need to add your AutoCAD Bible folder to AutoCAD's support file search path. Choose Tools ⇨ Options ⇨ Files tab. Click the plus sign to the left of Support File Search Path. Choose Add. Choose Browse. Find your AutoCAD Bible folder and click OK. Click OK again to close the Options dialog box.

7. Choose Rectangle from the Draw toolbar. At the first prompt, type **0,0** ↵. At the Specify other corner point or [Dimensions]: prompt, type **10,6** ↵.

8. Choose Hatch from the Draw toolbar. In the Type drop-down list, choose Custom.

9. Click the ellipsis to the right of the Custom Pattern text box. Choose the lightning.pat file you just created. Click OK.

10. Choose Select Objects and pick the rectangle in your drawing. Press Enter. Click OK. AutoCAD fills the rectangle with the lightning hatch, as shown in Figure 31-11.

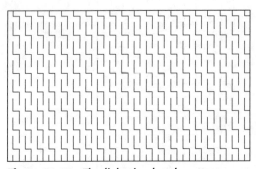

Figure 31-11: The lightning hatch pattern

11. Save your drawing.

Check out AutoCAD's acad.pat file for some ideas on how to create your own hatch pattern definitions.

Summary

In this chapter, you discovered how to create your own linetypes and hatch patterns. You read the following:

✦ Creating simple linetypes containing only dashes, dots, and spaces

✦ Making complex linetypes that include shapes and text

✦ Constructing your own hatch patterns that are made up of a set of parallel lines

In the next chapter, you read how to create shapes and fonts.

✦　　✦　　✦

Creating Shapes and Fonts

Shapes are similar to blocks. You create them, store them, and insert them. There are several differences, however:

✦ Shapes are much harder to create.

✦ Shapes are compiled into a format that conserves storage space, memory, and regeneration time.

✦ You can use shapes to create fonts.

✦ Font and shape files are support files — if you distribute a drawing, be sure to include any font or shape files that the drawing uses.

You can use shapes for simple forms that you need to insert many times quickly. Examples are shapes inserted into complex linetypes and font characters.

Creating Shapes

Shape files are used for both shapes and fonts. You create them with a text editor and save them with the extension .shp. You then use the COMPILE command (by typing it on the command line), which opens the Select Shape or Font File dialog box, shown in Figure 32-1.

Choose the .shp file and click Open. AutoCAD automatically compiles the file into a new file with the same name but with an extension of .shx, and displays a message on the command line that compilation succeeded.

Figure 32-1: The Select Shape or Font File dialog box

Using shape files

After you have a compiled shape file, you must load it, using the LOAD command, before you can place it in a drawing. AutoCAD opens the Select Shape File dialog box. Choose the .shx file and click Open. Font files do not have to be loaded because they are automatically referenced by text styles that use the font files.

To insert a shape, use the SHAPE command prompts as follows:

1. `Enter shape name or [?]:` Type the name of the shape or type **?** ↵ to get a list of loaded shapes.

2. `Specify insertion point:` Pick a point on the screen. AutoCAD drags the shape as you move the cursor.

3. `Specify height <1.0000>:` This functions like a scale factor. For example, type **.5** ↵ to insert the shape at one-half its original size.

4. `Specify rotation angle <0>:` Type a rotation angle.

Creating shape files

Shape files and font files are essentially the same. In this section, I explain how to create shapes. At the end of the chapter, I explain the few distinctions necessary to create a font file.

As with most customizable files, use a text editor to create shape files. You can add comments following a semicolon. A shape definition has the following syntax:

```
*shapenumber,#ofspecs,SHAPENAME
spec1,spec2,...,0
```

The definition must start with an asterisk. Each line cannot contain more than 128 characters. Table 32-1 explains the parts of this shape definition.

Table 32-1
The Parts of a Shape Definition

Item	Explanation
shapenumber	You can use any number from 1 to 255. Each shape in a file must have a unique number.
#ofspecs	This is the number of specifications in the second line of the definition, including the mandatory zero at the end.
SHAPENAME	You must use uppercase for the shape name. This is the name you use with the SHAPE command.
spec1...	This is a code that defines the actual shape. Each specification code defines a part of the shape, such as a line segment or an arc. Together, all the specifications draw the shape.
0	The definition must end with a zero.

Length and direction codes

You can use two sets of codes to define a shape. The first set, the length and direction codes, only lets you draw straight line segments. You use this system to create specifications in the three-character hexadecimal format.

✦ The first character is 0, which tells AutoCAD that the next two characters are hexadecimal values.

✦ The second character is a length in units. The maximum is 15 units. The number values can range from 0 to 9. For values from 10 to 15, use A to F. However, the length is measured along the nearest X or Y distance. Therefore, diagonal lengths are not true lengths.

✦ The third character is a direction code. Figure 32-2 shows how this code works. Use the code that represents the desired direction of the line from the start point.

Figure 32-2: The direction codes

Here is the code for the shape shown in Figure 32-3:

```
*2,4,PENNANT
044,02F,029,0
```

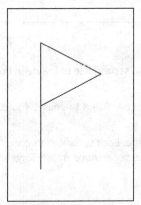

Figure 32-3: The
PENNANT shape

Here's how this shape works:

- ✦ 2 is the shape's unique number.
- ✦ 4 is the number of bytes (specifications) on the second line of the definition.
- ✦ PENNANT is the shape's name.
- ✦ 044 draws the pole, a line that is 4 units in the vertical direction.
- ✦ 02F draws the top line of the pennant, a line that is approximately 2 units in the F direction. (See note below.)
- ✦ 029 draws the bottom line of the pennant, a line that is approximately 2 units in the 9 direction. (See note below.)

Note Although the length of the two diagonal lines was specified as 2, they are actually about 2.22 units long because the line endpoints snapped to the nearest imaginary grid point.

Supplemental codes

The length and direction codes have a number of limitations:

✦ You can draw in only 16 directions.

✦ The maximum length of a line is 15 units.

✦ You can only draw straight line segments.

✦ The shape has to be continuous — you cannot lift the "pen" up and start in a new place.

The second set of codes, the supplemental codes, brings additional flexibility (and complexity) to your shapes. Table 32-2 lists these codes, which can be in either hexadecimal or decimal format.

Table 32-2
Supplemental Shape Codes

Hexadecimal Code	Decimal Code	Explanation
000	0	Specifies the end of the shape definition.
001	1	Starts draw mode (puts the "pen" down).
002	2	Ends draw mode (lifts the "pen" up) so that you can move to a new location.
003	3	Divides the vector lengths by the specification that follows, as in 3,5 to divide the lengths by five. This scales down the shape. You should reverse this at the end of the shape by using the 4 code.
004	4	Multiplies the vector lengths by the specification that follows, as in 4,2 to multiply the lengths by two. This scales up the shape. You should reverse this at the end of the shape by using the 3 code.
005	5	Saves the current position so that you can return to it later in the shape definition. You must use (restore) every position you save (a maximum of four).
006	6	Restores the last saved position.

Continued

Table 32-2 *(continued)*

Hexadecimal Code	Decimal Code	Explanation
007	7	Draws another shape defined within the same shape file, whose number follows. For example, use 7,230 to draw shape 230. When the other shape is complete, AutoCAD returns to the current shape definition.
008	8	Draws a line specified by X and Y displacements that follow the code. For example, 8,(8,–12) draws a line whose endpoint is 8 units to the right and 12 units down from the current coordinate. (You can add parentheses to your shape codes for readability.)
009	9	Draws multiple X,Y displacements. You end this code with a displacement of 0,0. For example, 9,(8,–12),(1,0),(0,12), (–8,0),(0,0) draws four X,Y displacements. (You can add parentheses to your shape codes for readability.)
00A	10	Draws an octant arc specified by its radius (ranging from 1 to 255), and a second code in the syntax (–)0SC where the minus optionally indicates a clockwise arc, the zero is mandatory, S specifies the starting octant, and C specifies the number of octants that the arc covers. An octant is an eighth of a circle. Figure 32-4 shows the octant codes you must use for the starting octant. For example, 10,(2,014) indicates an arc with a radius of 2 that is drawn counterclockwise from octant 1 and covers 4 octants (ending at octant 5). This is a semicircle.
00B	11	Draws a fractional arc not limited by octants specified by the five following codes in the syntax: start_offset, end_offset,high_radius,radius,(-)0SC. The start offset specifies how far past an octant the arc begins and is calculated as follows: (starting degrees – degrees of the last octant passed) * 256/45. The end offset specifies how far past an octant the arc ends and is calculated as follows: (ending degrees – degrees of the last octant passed) * 256/45. For both the start and the end of the arc, the last octant passed is specified in degrees, not the numbers in Figure 32-4, and is always a multiple of 45. The high radius is 0 unless the radius is more than 255. If your radius is larger, the high radius is the maximum number of 256 multiples in the value of the radius (for example, 2 if your radius is 600). The difference (the radius minus 256 times the high radius value, or 88 if your radius is 600) is placed in the radius specification. The radius is just the radius of the arc. The (–)0SC part of the code is the same as for code 10 (00A) except that S is the octant the arc starts in and C is the number of octants the arc covers.

Hexadecimal Code	Decimal Code	Explanation
00C	12	Draws an arc using a system of X,Y displacement and bulge specified in the following three codes using the syntax X-displacement, Y-displacement, bulge. These three codes can range from −127 to +127. The X and Y displacements just specify the endpoint of the arc. The bulge equals ((2 * H/D) * 127) where D is the chord length (the distance from the start point to the endpoint) and H is the height measured from the midpoint of the chord to the circumference of the arc. The bulge should be negative if the arc is drawn clockwise.
00D	13	Draws multiple arcs using the X,Y displacement and bulge system. End the arcs with (0,0). You can use 0 for a bulge to place a line segment in the midst of several arcs.
00E	14	This code is used only for text fonts that can be used in the vertical orientation (each letter is drawn under the previous letter). When the vertical orientation is chosen, the specifications after this code are used. Use this code to move the starting and ending point of letters to a point appropriate for vertical orientation, that is, on top of and below the letter. See the section "Creating Fonts" later in this chapter for more information.

Figure 32-4: The codes for octant arcs

All these codes can seem pretty overwhelming. The most common use for shapes is for fonts. Here are a few examples:

```
*3,22,ALEF
010,07E,010,2,8,(-6,5),1,8,(-2,-4),01C,2,8,(5,2),1,8,(2,4),014,
0
```

This is a squared-off alef, the first letter of the Hebrew alphabet, as shown in Figure 32-5. Displaying non-Roman fonts is a common use for shapes.

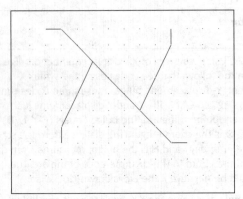

Figure 32-5: A squared-off alef

Planning in advance is almost essential by drawing the shape in a drawing on a grid set to 1-unit spacing. You can use only integers in your shape codes, so you must often scale the shape up so the smallest line segment is 1 unit.

Here's how the code for the alef works:

✦ The shape starts at the top left. The code 010 is a hexadecimal length and direction code and specifies a line with a length of 1 unit and a direction of 0 degrees.

✦ The second code, 07E, is also a hexadecimal length and direction code. It specifies a line with a length of 7 units in the E direction (315 degrees). The line is not actually 7 units long, but its X (and in this case Y) distance is 7.

✦ The third code, 010, is the same as the first code and ends the first set of line segments.

✦ The fourth code, 2, lifts up the pen so that you can move to the start of the next line.

✦ The fifth code, 8, indicates that the following two codes will be an X,Y displacement.

✦ The sixth and seventh codes (-6,5) are placed in parentheses for readability. They move the pen (while it is up) -6 in the X direction and +5 in the Y direction from the end of the last line to the start of the next line. (Count the grid dots to find it.)

✦ The eighth code, 1, puts the pen down so that you can draw.

✦ The ninth code, 8, is the same as the fifth code.

✦ The 10th and 11th codes (-2,-4) draw the first segment of the second line so that the endpoint is –2 units in the X direction and –4 units in the Y direction from the start point.

✦ The 12th code, 01C, is a hexadecimal code and finishes the second line with a 1-unit line segment in the C direction (270 degrees).

✦ The 13th code, 2, lifts up the pen again.

✦ The 14th code, 8, is the same as the fifth code.

✦ The 15th and 16th codes (5,2) move the pen (which is up) +5 in the X direction and +2 in the Y direction.

✦ The 17th code, 1, puts the pen down again.

✦ The 18th code, 8, is the same as the fifth code.

✦ The 19th and 20th codes (2,4) draw a line whose endpoint is 2 units in the X direction and 4 units in the Y direction from its start point.

✦ The 21st code, 014, is a hexadecimal length and vector code and draws a 1-unit line in the 4 (90-degree) direction.

✦ The 22nd code, 0, ends the shape definition.

Here's another example, in this case a script alef, shown in Figure 32-6:

```
*4,10,S-ALEF
06C,2,8,(6,5),1,10,(3,016),0
```

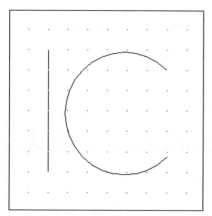

Figure 32-6: A script alef

Here's the explanation of the code for the script alef:

✦ The first code, 06C, creates the line on the left, starting at the top and making it 6 units long.

✦ The second code, 2, lifts up the pen.

✦ The third code, 8, specifies an X,Y displacement, with the pen up.

✦ The fourth and fifth codes (6,5) move the pen 6 units to the right and 5 units up, to the start of the arc.

✦ The sixth code, 10, introduces an octant arc.

♦ The seventh and eighth codes (3,016) specify an arc with a radius of 3 that starts at octant 1 and covers 6 octants (to octant 7). (See Figure 32-4 to review the octant codes.)

♦ The last code, 0, ends the definition.

New Feature The Express Tools contain a command, MKSHAPE (choose Express ➪ Tools ➪ Make Shape) that makes shapes for you. You just draw the objects.

On the CD-ROM The drawing used in the following Step-by-Step exercise on creating a shape, ab32-a.dwg, is in the Drawings folder of the *AutoCAD 2004 Bible* CD-ROM.

Step-by-Step: Creating a Shape

1. Open ab32-a.dwg from the CD-ROM.

2. Save the file as ab32-01.dwg in your AutoCAD Bible folder. This drawing shows an uppercase P, with dashed lines to indicate space before and after the letter, as shown in Figure 32-7. This is the type of drawing that you use as a basis for creating a shape definition.

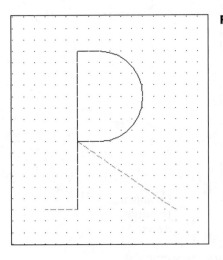

Figure 32-7: An uppercase P

3. Type **notepad** ↵ on the command line and press Enter at the File to edit: prompt to open a new file.

4. Type the following in Notepad:
```
*80,15,UCP
2,030,1,0E4,020,12,(0,-8,-127),028,2,8,(9,-6),0
```

5. Press Enter at the end of the last line. Choose File ➪ Save in Notepad and save the file in your AutoCAD Bible folder as ab32-01.shp. Close Notepad.

6. In AutoCAD, type **compile** ↵. Double-click ab32-01.shp. AutoCAD compiles the .shp file. AutoCAD confirms on the command line that the compilation succeeded. (Press F2 to open the Text window if necessary.)

7. Type **load** ↵ and choose ab32-01.shx. Click Open. Type **shape** ↵. To insert the shape, follow the prompts:

```
Enter shape name or [?]: ucp ↵
Specify insertion point: Pick any point.
Specify height <1.0000>: ↵
Specify rotation angle <0>: ↵
```

8. Save your drawing. It should look like Figure 32-8.

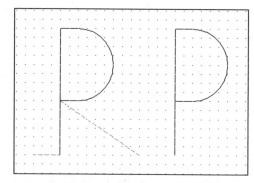

Figure 32-8: The picture and shape of the letter P

Editing shape files

You don't often get a shape right the first time. You don't see the result until after you have compiled, loaded, and inserted the shape. Editing shape files involves the following steps:

1. Erase all copies of the shape.

2. Purge the .shx file by using the PURGE command and choosing Shapes in the dialog box. (You may sometimes need to purge more than once.) If you forget this step, when you try to insert the corrected shape, AutoCAD uses the old definition!

3. Edit the .shp file. Don't forget to change the #ofspecs value in the first line if necessary. Save the file.

4. Recompile the .shp file.

5. Reload the .shx file.

6. Reinsert the shape using the SHAPE command.

Creating Fonts

AutoCAD's support for TrueType fonts makes so many fonts available that the need to create your own is certainly less than with earlier versions. However, you might want to add special symbols to some existing fonts, especially if you often use these symbols within text.

Font files use the same codes to define the characters as shape files. They have the following unique characteristics:

✦ The shapenumber part of the definition must correspond to the ASCII code value for the character you are defining. Appendix A of the "AutoCAD Customization Guide" (choose Help ➪ Help ➪ Contents ➪ Customization Guide ➪ ASCII Codes) contains all the ASCII codes in octal, hexadecimal, and decimal formats. Fonts generally use either hexadecimal or decimal format.

✦ The shapename part of the definition is lowercase and is usually used to label the character — for example, ucp for uppercase p and lcr for lowercase r.

✦ The file must include a special shape number 0 that defines the entire font, using the following syntax:

```
*0,4,font-name
above,below,modes,0
```

The above value specifies how far above the baseline uppercase letters extend. The below value specifies how far below the baseline lowercase letters, such as p or q extend. Together, these two values define the size of the characters. AutoCAD uses these values to scale letters when you define a text height for the font. Modes should be 0 for a horizontal font and 2 for a font that supports both horizontal and vertical orientations. For example, a header for a font named arch with capital letters 21 units high and lowercase letters that extend 7 units below the line could be:

```
*0,4,arch
21,7,0,0
```

✦ You must define the line feed (LF), which drops down one line without drawing so that lines of text can be placed beneath each other. The line feed is ASCII code 10.

✦ You need to create a start point and endpoint with the pen up to create spacing between letters. See the previous Step-by-Step exercise for an example.

As with all shapes, you probably want to use AutoCAD to draw all the characters on a grid with a spacing of 1. Decide on the height of the letters and be consistent.

Big fonts and Unicode fonts

The Japanese and Chinese written languages use fonts with thousands of characters because each character represents a word. AutoCAD uses big fonts to support these languages. It is beyond the scope of this book to go into detail about how to create these fonts, but a short explanation is useful. Big font files use special codes to allow for the larger number of shapes. Big fonts allow up to 65,535 shape numbers. Unicode fonts support the ISO10646 standard, which uses 16-bit encoding to support many languages in one font file. If you open one of the .shp files, you will see characters for all the letters that may have accents in French, Spanish, and so on. All the fonts in AutoCAD are now compliant with this standard.

The advantage of Unicode fonts is that characters that you type appear the same in all systems and countries. This is important if you exchange drawings with clients or colleagues in other countries. Unicode fonts use a special header that includes two extra codes.

Unicode special characters can be inserted by typing **\u+** and the hexadecimal Unicode value in the font file. (For this reason, Unicode font files use hexadecimal shape numbers.) For example, the hexadecimal code for the plus/minus sign is 00B1. If you type **\u+00b1** and press Enter (using DTEXT in this example), you get the plus/minus sign. (It works with multiline text, too.)

If you don't need the additional capabilities of big fonts or Unicode fonts, you can create fonts without them.

Summary

In this chapter, you read how to create files. You discovered:

- ✦ Using shape files when you need to insert a shape many times using as little storage space as possible
- ✦ Creating fonts using shape files with a few special codes that define both the font as a whole and each character

✦ ✦ ✦

Customizing Menus

You probably use AutoCAD's menus all the time. (If you don't, you can skip this chapter.) AutoCAD's menus are designed to be useful for most people, but the whole point of customization is that everyone has different needs. You can draw a lot easier and faster by customizing the menus to suit your own individual requirements. Not only can you add commands to a menu, but you can also add menu items consisting of a series of commands that run just like a macro. You can even add AutoLISP routines to your menus. You can edit the menu that comes with AutoCAD or create your own menu. You may want to create specialized menus that are used only for one drawing — for example, a menu to help clients view a drawing. The only limit is your imagination — and the time you can devote to customization.

Working with Menu Files

Menu files were once simple (a long time ago). Now, under Windows, menu files are a complex subject indeed. However, you need to understand the menu files and how they interact with each other before starting to change them.

Caution Don't even think about customizing a menu until you have backed up at least `acad.mnu`. Better yet, back up all the menu files (see Table 33-1 for a listing of menu files).

Understanding the menu files

Table 33-1 lists all the menu file types and their functions.

Table 33-1
Menu Files and Functions

File	Function
.mnu	The template menu file. AutoCAD comes with `acad.mnu`. This is an ASCII file that you can edit.
.mns	The source menu file generated by AutoCAD based on the .mnu file. It is also an ASCII file. When you customize your toolbars as described in Chapter 29, AutoCAD places the changes in this file. You can edit this file instead of using the .mnu file to retain your toolbar customizations.
.mnc	The compiled, binary file that AutoCAD actually uses when you choose an item on a menu. AutoCAD compiles menu files for faster access. When you start AutoCAD, if you have made changes in the .mns menu file, AutoCAD recompiles, creating a new .mnc file.
.mnr	A binary file that contains bitmaps used by the menu.
.mnl	An ASCII file that contains AutoLISP routines used by the menu. When AutoCAD loads a menu file, it automatically loads this file if it has the same file name. AutoCAD contains a number of commands that are actually AutoLISP routines—these are found in `acad.mnl`.

These file types constitute a family of menu files. For example, AutoCAD comes with `acad.mnu`, `acad.mns`, `acad.mnc`, `acad.mnr`, and `acad.mnl`. If you create your own menu, you create a file called, let's say, `custom.mnu`. From that file AutoCAD creates `custom.mns` and `custom.mnr` as a minimum. You can also place AutoLISP routines in a file called `custom.mnl`, which will be loaded automatically whenever `custom.mnc` is loaded. If your menu has bitmaps, AutoCAD also creates `custom.mnr`. You can place your custom menus in any folder in the support file search path.

Note Remember that you can add to the support file search path by choosing Tools ⇨ Options ⇨ Files tab, choosing Support File Search Path, and clicking Add. The same item shows you the current location of your menu files.

Loading and unloading menu files

AutoCAD supports two types of menus—complete and partial. A partial menu usually has only one or two pull-down menus (or toolbars). You can then load this partial menu into your regular base menu. If your menu customization consists of simply adding a few menu items, you can create a partial menu and add it to your current menu.

However, you may also want to have alternate complete menus. Perhaps two different people work on one computer and have different menu needs. Or you may find it useful to have one menu for architectural drawings, another for mechanical

drawings, and a third for electrical schematics. Of course, you can customize your one full menu to better suit your needs.

Loading a complete menu

To load a complete menu, use the MENU command at the command line. AutoCAD opens the Select Menu File dialog box, as shown in Figure 33-1.

Figure 33-1: The Select Menu File dialog box

AutoCAD assumes that you want to load either an .mnc or .mns menu file. However, you can use the Files of type drop-down list to choose an .mnu template file. You do this when you are customizing a menu and want to recompile all the menu files that arise from the .mnu file. If you are simply loading a different menu to use, you should load either the .mnc or .mns file. Select the file and click Open to load the menu.

Caution Loading a full menu unloads any partial menus that you might have loaded.

When you start AutoCAD, the last menu you used, which is stored in the Windows registry, is loaded. AutoCAD does not reload menus between drawings. If you want to use a new menu while in AutoCAD, you must load it.

Caution When you load an .mnu file, AutoCAD warns you that loading the file will overwrite any changes you have made to your toolbars. To avoid this problem, either customize the .mns menu file or follow the procedure explained here.

If you have customized a menu using the .mnu file, here's how you save the changes you have made to your toolbars while you are customizing a menu:

1. Make the changes to the toolbars.

2. Open the .mns file of the menu you are using. You can use NotePad to do this.

3. Select the entire toolbar section. It starts with ***TOOLBARS. Copy it to the clipboard.

4. Close the .mns file.

5. Open the .mnu file of the same menu. (It has the same file name.)

6. Select the entire toolbar section.

7. Choose Paste from the Standard toolbar. NotePad (or your text editor) replaces the entire toolbar section with the new one from the .mns file.

8. Save the .mnu file and close it.

Now your customized toolbars are incorporated into your template .mnu menu file. You can customize this file as much as you like and ignore any messages about overwriting your toolbar changes.

Of course, if you make a mistake, you have backed up your .mnu, .mns, and, .mnc menu files, so you can simply copy them back over the ones on your hard disk.

Loading or unloading a partial menu

To load a partial menu, choose Tools ➪ Customize ➪ Menus to start the MENULOAD command. AutoCAD opens the Menu Customization dialog box, as shown in Figure 33-2.

Figure 33-2: The Menu Customization dialog box

Every menu, both complete and partial, has a menu group name. The menu group name of the menu that AutoCAD comes with is ACAD. When you create your own menus, you give them a menu group name, often (but not necessarily) the name of the file. For example, the files for the ACAD menu group are acad.mnu, acad.mns, acad.mnc, and so on.

Use the Menu Groups tab to load and unload partial menus:

✦ To load a partial menu, type the name of the file in the File Name text box or choose Browse to locate the file. Then click Load. AutoCAD immediately loads the menu.

✦ To unload a loaded partial menu, choose the menu you want and click Unload. If you modify a menu, you must unload it first and then reload it.

Note You can load a full menu in the Menu Customization dialog box by checking the Replace all checkbox. However, if you want to load a partial menu only, be sure that this box is not checked.

Use the Menu Bar tab, as shown in Figure 33-3, to display, hide, or reorder pull-down menus. First choose the menu group you want from the Menu Group drop-down list. The Menus box on the left lists all the available pull-down menus. The Menu Bar list on the right displays the current order of the menu bar, from left to right.

Figure 33-3: The Menu Bar tab of the Menu Customization dialog box

To remove a pull-down menu, choose it from the Menu Bar list and click Remove. Click Remove All to remove all the pull-down menus.

To insert a pull-down menu, follow these steps:

1. Choose the menu from the Menu Bar list that you want your menu to be to the left of. For example, to insert the Modify menu to the left of the Dimension menu, choose Dimension.

2. Then choose the menu that you want to insert—for example, the Modify menu.

3. Click Insert.

You can move menus by first removing them and then reinserting them in a new location. Click Close after you finish using the dialog box.

Customizing a Menu

Menu files are long and complex. However, you often do not need to deal with every part of the menu file. And even simple changes can be very useful. Start simple and take it from there.

Menu files have eight major types of sections, each defining a different menu section:

✦ Button menus control the buttons on your mouse or puck.

✦ POP menus are the pull-down menus at the top of your screen. You can also create shortcut menus in this section. Shortcut menus appear when you click the right mouse button. (See Chapter 3 for more information on right-clicking.)

✦ Toolbar menus create toolbars.

✦ Image menus create dialog boxes with images, such as the one you see when you choose Draw ➪ Surfaces ➪ 3D Surfaces.

✦ The screen menu is AutoCAD's original menu that used to appear at the right side of your screen. By default, it is not displayed, but it still exists in the menu file. You can display it by choosing Tools ➪ Options, clicking the Display tab, and checking the Display Screen Menu check box.

✦ Tablet menus control the menu that can be overlaid on a digitizing tablet.

✦ Helpstrings create the short descriptions of each command that appear on the status bar when you place the mouse cursor over a toolbar or a menu item.

✦ Accelerators are keyboard shortcuts. An example is Ctrl+C for the COPYCLIP command.

The AutoCAD menu files `acad.mnu` and `acad.mns` contain sections for all these types of menus. Each section starts with three asterisks—for example, `***TOOL-BARS`. Most sections also have subsections that start with two asterisks. You do not

need to customize all the types of menus. You may want to customize only the pull-down menus. If you use a digitizer, you will want to customize the tablet menus.

Looking at acad.mns

The best way to start customizing a menu is to look at AutoCAD's `acad.mns` file and use it as a guide. Each type of menu has its own unique features, but certain features apply to most, if not all, menu types.

Note

When you create a new, complete menu file based on `acad.mnu` or `acad.mns`, don't forget that AutoCAD uses the AutoLISP routines in `acad.mnl` for many commands. You should, therefore, make a copy of `acad.mnl` with the same name as your new menu. For example, if you created a menu called `mech.mnu` from `acad.mnu`, make a copy of `acad.mnl` and name the copy `mech.mnl`.

Here you see the beginning of the pull-down Format menu:

```
***POP5
**FORMAT
ID_MnFormat     [F&ormat]
ID_Layer        [&Layer...]'_layer
ID_Ddcolor      [&Color...]'_color
ID_Linetype     [Li&netype...]'_linetype
ID_Linewt       [Line&weight...]'_lweight
                [--]
ID_Style        [Text &Style...]'_style
ID_Ddim         [&Dimension Style...]'_dimstyle
ID_PlotStyle    [$(if,$(eq,$(getvar,pstylemode),1),~,)Plot
St&yle...]^C^C_plotstyle
ID_Ddptype      [&Point Style...]'_ddptype
ID_Mlstyle      [&Multiline Style...]^C^C_mlstyle
                [--]
ID_Units        [&Units...]'_units
ID_Thickness    [&Thickness]'_thickness
ID_Limits       [Dr&awing Limits]'_limits
                [--]
ID_Ddrename     [&Rename...]^C^C_rename
```

Notice that each menu item has three parts:

✦ The first part is a name tag. Each name tag must be unique. The most common use for the name tag is to link pull-down menu items and toolbar buttons to their status bar help. You can also use the name tag to link a keyboard shortcut to a menu item. Name tags are only used in the POP (pull-down) and Toolbar sections of the menu. However, they are not mandatory even in these sections. They must not be more than 12 characters and cannot have spaces — or they are ignored.

✦ The second part, in square brackets, is the label. This is what you actually see on the menu. The ellipses (. . .) after menu items provide a visual cue on the menu that these items open dialog boxes. The ampersand (&) places an underscore under the following letter. You can then type the letter to execute the menu item (instead of clicking the menu item with your mouse). The Buttons, Aux, and Tablet menus do not display or require any label, but you can use the label for your own notes. Shortcut menus don't display the label either, but the label is required.

✦ The third part is the actual command, called a *menu macro*. This can be a simple command, any group of commands, or an AutoLISP expression. The following conventions are recommended practice:

- Add an apostrophe (') before commands that can be used transparently. (Otherwise, the commands won't work transparently when chosen from the menu macro.)

- All other commands start with ^C^C, which is equivalent to pressing Esc twice. This cancels any other command that may be active. One Esc is generally enough, but occasionally two are necessary.

- The underscore is used before each command. This tells AutoCAD to translate the command into whatever language version of AutoCAD is being used. Your menus would automatically be translated into French in France!

Figure 33-4 shows the Format menu. Compare it to the text of the menu file.

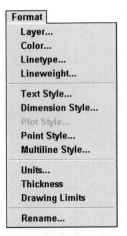

Figure 33-4: The Format menu displays the labels shown in the menu file.

Writing menu macros

The menu macro is the heart of the menu. You need to know a number of special characters and conventions in order to write menu macros. Table 33-2 lists some of the most common ones.

Table 33-2 Special Characters for Menu Macros	
Character	**Description**
;	Equivalent to pressing Enter. The end of a line in a menu macro is also equivalent to pressing Enter. Use the semicolon when you need two returns at the end of a line. Some commands, such as DTEXT/TEXT, also require a return to complete. You can also use ^M.
Space	Similar to pressing Enter, except when entering text that contains spaces (such as between words). Use between the command and its options. Note that you can use a space even on the command line for most commands.
\	Pauses for user input, such as picking a point or typing a value.
+	Used at the end of a line to continue the macro on the next line.
*	Placed at the beginning of a macro (before the ^C^C), repeats the macro until you end it by pressing Esc or choosing another menu item.
^P	Turns on and off (toggles) the display of the menu macro, including menu prompts, on the command line.

Note Because the backslash pauses for user input, you cannot use it to specify a path, as in C:\Program Files\AutoCAD 2004\Support. Use the regular slash (/) instead.

Here is one line from AutoCAD's Draw pull-down menu that uses the backslash and the space:

```
ID_ArcStCeAn    [S&tart, Center, Angle]^C^C_arc \_c \_a
```

Here's how this command works:

> ^C^C Cancels any previous command.
>
> _arc Starts the ARC command, enabling translation to another language version of AutoCAD.

Space	Equivalent to pressing the spacebar, which acts like pressing Enter after typing **arc** on the command line. AutoCAD displays the `Specify start point of arc or [Center]:` prompt.
\	The backslash lets you specify a start point.
_c	Chooses the Center option, enabling translation to another language.
Space	Equivalent to pressing the spacebar, which acts like pressing Enter after typing c on the command line (for the Center option). AutoCAD displays the `Specify center point of arc:` prompt.
\	The backslash lets you specify a center point.
_a	Chooses the Angle option. Because this is at the end of the command, you don't need to specify a pause. The user specifies an angle and presses Enter, ending the command. AutoCAD draws the arc.

The backslash allows for only one input, except when used with the SELECT command. Therefore, you can use the SELECT command in menu macros to collect a selection set and use another command with the Previous option to act on the entire selection set. For example:

```
ID_MoveRight [Move .1 Right]^C^Cselect \move previous ;.1,0 ;
```

This macro cancels any existing command, starts the SELECT command, and lets you select as many objects as you want. You end object selection by pressing Enter. Then the macro automatically moves those objects to the right by 0.1 unit.

Here are a few more examples of macros from earlier chapters.

You could place this macro on a pull-down menu to make a selected polyline 0.1 unit wide:

```
^C^Cpedit \w .1 ;
```

You would use the following macro to automatically draw four circles with the specified centers and radius. It uses a plus sign near the end because the macro is too long to fit on one line.

```
^C^Ccircle 2,2 1.5 circle 6,2 1.5 circle 10,2 1.5 circle +
14,2 1.5
```

You could use this macro to clean up a drawing. It uses CHPROP to select all the objects in a drawing, and the Color option to change their color to ByLayer. Then it uses the LAYER command to freeze the layer named "no-plot" and saves the drawing.

```
^C^Cchprop all  c bylayer  -layer f no-plot  qsave
```

Note that using the All selection option is another way to select more than one object in a menu macro.

Swapping menus

Here is AutoCAD's Buttons2 menu. These menus are explained in the next section.

```
***BUTTONS2
// Shift + button
$P0=SNAP $p0=*
```

This menu introduces some new special characters that are used in AutoCAD's menus. Sometimes you want a menu item to switch to another menu item. This is called *menu swapping*. Because you cannot customize the pick button, the first button listed is the second button. In this case, pressing Shift and the second button (the right button on a two-button mouse) opens the Object Snap menu (as you probably know). The Object Snap menu, however, is elsewhere in the menu. In fact, it is contained in the POP0 pull-down menu. This menu item therefore switches you to the POP0 pull-down menu and displays that menu.

The special syntax is as follows:

```
$section=menugroup.menuname $section=menugroup.*
```

If the menu group is the same as that of the menu where you are placing the macro, you can leave it out. The different sections or menu types have their own special abbreviations for menu swapping, as shown in Table 33-3.

Table 33-3
Menu Section Abbreviations for Menu Swapping

Abbreviation	Menu Section
A1–A4	The AUX menus 1 through 4
B1–B4	The BUTTONS menus 1 through 4
P0–P999	The POP (pull-down) menus (1–499 are for pull-down menus; 0 and 500–999 are for shortcut menus)
I	The IMAGE menu
S	The SCREEN menu
T1–T4	The TABLET menus 1 through 4

Here's another example from the Draw pull-down menu. The first line shows the Surfaces item on the Draw menu. The next three items are items on the Surfaces submenu. The last item swaps to and displays the subsection of the IMAGE section called image_3dobjects.

```
ID_MnSurface    [->Sur&faces]
ID_Solid        [&2D Solid]^C^C_solid
ID_3dface       [3D &Face]^C^C_3dface
ID_3dsurface    [&3D Surfaces...] $I=ACAD.image_3dobjects $I=ACAD.*
```

In Figure 33-12, later in this chapter, I show the image tile portion of the menu that this 3D Surfaces menu item displays.

In other words, when you choose Draw ⇨ Surfaces ⇨ 3D Surfaces, you get a dialog box displaying all the 3D surface objects you can draw.

Tip You could use this technique to create a menu that swaps to an image menu that inserts commonly used blocks. However, the new Tool Palettes are another way to accomplish a similar effect.

Working on menu sections

Table 33-4 lists the sections in acad.mnu and acad.mns. There may be several sections for a type of menu; for example, there are a number of button menu sections. You can also add sections. For example, users can, and often do, add a pull-down menu.

Table 33-4 Acad Menu Sections	
Section	**Function**
***BUTTONS1	This menu defines what happens when you press a button on a digitizing puck or other input device (but not the system mouse). The first button (pick) cannot be customized, and one button is usually reserved to open shortcut menus, so you generally only customize this button menu if you have three or more buttons on your pointing device.
***BUTTONS2	This menu defines what happens when you hold down Shift and press a button on a digitizing puck or other input device (but not the system mouse).
***BUTTONS3	This menu defines what happens when you hold down Control and press a button on a digitizing puck or other input device (but not the system mouse).
***BUTTONS4	This menu defines what happens when you hold down both Control and Shift and press a button on a digitizing puck or other input device (but not the system mouse).
***AUX1	This is an auxiliary button menu that defines what happens when you press a button on your system mouse. The first button (pick) cannot be customized, and one button is usually reserved to open shortcut menus, so that you generally only customize an Aux menu if you have three or more buttons on your system mouse.

Section	Function
***AUX2	This is an auxiliary button menu that defines what happens when you hold down Shift and press a button on your system mouse.
***AUX3	This is an auxiliary button menu that defines what happens when you hold down Ctrl and press a button on your system mouse.
***AUX4	This is an auxiliary button menu that defines what happens when you hold down Ctrl and Shift and press a button on your system mouse.
***POP0	This is the first pull-down menu. Although you can display it on the menu, it is meant to be used for the shortcut menu and usually displays the object snaps.
***POP1	This is the second pull-down menu. It usually displays the File menu commands.
***POP2	This is the third pull-down menu. It usually displays the Edit menu commands.
***POP3	This is the fourth pull-down menu. It displays the View menu commands.
***POP4	This is the fifth pull-down menu. It displays the Insert menu commands.
***POP5	This is the sixth pull-down menu. It displays the Format menu commands.
***POP6	This is the seventh pull-down menu. It displays the Tools menu commands.
***POP7	This is the eighth pull-down menu. It displays the Draw menu commands.
***POP8	This is the ninth pull-down menu. It displays the Dimension menu commands.
***POP9	This is the tenth pull-down menu. It displays the Modify menu commands.
***POP10	This is the eleventh pull-down menu. It displays the Window menu commands.
***POP11	This is the twelfth pull-down menu. It displays the Help menu commands.
***POP500	This is the shortcut menu that displays the Grips menu commands that appear at the cursor when there is a hot grip and you right-click.
***POP501	This is the default shortcut menu that appears when you right-click in the drawing area.
***POP502	This is the default shortcut menu that appears when an object is selected and you right-click in the drawing area.

Continued

Table 33-4 *(continued)*

Section	Function
***POP503	This is the shortcut menu that appears when you are in the middle of a command and you right-click in the drawing area.
***POP504	This is the shortcut menu that appears when you select a dimension object and right-click in the drawing area.
***POP505	This is the shortcut menu that appears when you select a floating viewport object and right-click in the drawing area.
**POP506	This is the shortcut menu that appears when you select multiple xrefs and right-click in the drawing area.
***POP507	This is the shortcut menu that appears when you select an MText object and right-click in the drawing area.
***POP508	This is the shortcut menu that appears when you select a Text object and right-click in the drawing area.
***POP509	This is the shortcut menu that appears when you select a hatch object and right-click in the drawing area.
***POP510	This is the shortcut menu that appears when you select a lwpolyline and right-click in the drawing area.
***POP511	This is the shortcut menu that appears when you select a spline and right-click in the drawing area.
***POP512	This is the shortcut menu that appears when you select a polyline and right-click in the drawing area.
***POP513	This is the shortcut menu that appears when you select a single xref and right-click in the drawing area.
***POP514	This is the shortcut menu that appears when you select a block reference that has no attributes and right-click in the drawing area.
***POP515	This is the shortcut menu that appears when you select a block reference that has attributes and right-click in the drawing area.
***POP516	This is the shortcut menu that appears when you select multiple floating viewport objects and right-click in the drawing area.
***TOOLBARS	This section defines all the toolbars. You can add as many as you like. You can define toolbars using acad.mns or your own menu, but it is easier to do so in AutoCAD, as described in Chapter 29.
***IMAGE	This section defines image tiles that occasionally appear in dialog boxes.
***SCREEN	This section creates the screen menu.

Section	Function
***TABLET1	The Tablet menu is divided into four parts. Each part represents a section of the menu area on your digitizing tablet. The parts are divided into small squares, each of which can contain a menu item. This first part is left blank for you to configure. Figure 33-5 shows AutoCAD's tablet and its four parts.
***TABLET2	This is the second part of the Tablet menu.
***TABLET3	This is the third part of the Tablet menu.
***TABLET4	This is the fourth part of the Tablet menu.
***HELPSTRINGS	This section creates status line descriptions of menu and toolbar items that appear when you highlight a menu item or place your cursor over a toolbar button.
***ACCELERATORS	The Accelerators section lets you create keyboard shortcuts. These include several standard Windows shortcuts, which you should not change, such as Ctrl+C, Ctrl+V, and Ctrl+X.

You don't need to have all of these sections in your menu. After backing up your menu files, you can delete the button sections (if you only use a system mouse), the screen menu, and the Tablet menus (if you don't have a digitizing tablet).

Figure 33-5: AutoCAD's standard digitizer Tablet menu and its four parts, which correspond to four sections in the menu file

The Buttons and Aux menus

The first item on the Buttons menu, BUTTONS1, is the second button because you cannot customize the pick button. You can add as many menu items as your input device has buttons. Here is AutoCAD's BUTTONS1 menu. The AUX1 menu is identical.

Note You can customize the Button and Aux sections for full menus only, not for partial menus.

```
***BUTTONS1
$M=$(if,$(eq,$(substr,$(getvar,cmdnames),1,5),GRIP_),$PO=ACAD.
GRIPS $PO=*);
$PO=SNAP $pO=*
^C^C
^B
^O
^G
^D
^E
^T
```

Here's what the remaining buttons do:

✦ The second button usually functions as a return (the semicolon at the end of the line represents the return). The first part of the macro includes an expression in a programming language called DIESEL, which is beyond the scope of this book. However, its purpose is to display the Grips shortcut menu. The Grips shortcut menu only appears if you have a hot grip in your drawing.

✦ The third button, if you have one, displays the Object Snap menu. You can change this to whatever you want.

✦ The fourth button, ^C^C, is equivalent to pressing Esc twice.

✦ The fifth button, ^B, is equivalent to pressing Ctrl+B, which turns Snap on and off.

✦ The sixth button, ^O, is equivalent to pressing Ctrl+L, which turns Ortho on and off. (Once upon a time, before Windows, Ctrl+O toggled Ortho on and off.)

✦ The seventh button, ^G, is equivalent to pressing Ctrl+G, which turns the grid on and off.

✦ The eighth button, ^D, is equivalent to pressing Ctrl+D, which toggles the coordinate display mode.

✦ The ninth button, ^E, is equivalent to pressing Ctrl+E, which switches to the next isometric plane.

✦ The tenth button, ^T, is equivalent to pressing Ctrl+T, which turns the tablet on and off.

If you have a number of buttons on your pointing device, you can leave these macros as they are or change them to suit your needs.

Tip

AutoCAD supports panning and zooming with the IntelliMouse. The MBUTTON-PAN system variable controls the third button or wheel on your pointing device. By default, it is set to 1, which supports panning and zooming. Set it to 0 to support definition in the `.mnu` menu file.

The following Step-by-Step exercise shows you how you can customize even a two-button device. Because you may be working on someone else's computer, the exercise undoes the customization at the end.

Step-by-Step: Customizing the Buttons Menu

1. Copy `acad.mnu`, `acad.mns`, `acad.mnc`, `acad.mnr`, and `acad.mnl` to one ore more floppy disks or some other safe location.

Caution

Do not continue this exercise until you have completed Step 1. If you are working on someone else's computer, ask permission before doing this exercise.

2. To make a duplicate of `acad.mns`, right-click `acad.mns` in Windows Explorer and choose Copy from the shortcut menu. Right-click again and choose Paste. Windows places a copy of `acad.mns`, called `Copy of acad.mns` in the same folder as `acad.mns`.

Note

By default, `acad.mnu`, `acad.mns`, `acad.mnc`, `acad.mnr`, and `acad.mnl` are in `\Documents and Settings\[user name]\Application Data\Autodesk\ AutoCAD 2004\R16.0\enu\Support`. However, your location may be different, depending on your operating system, language, and customization. To find the location of `acad.mnu`, `acad.mns`, `acad.mnc`, `acad.mnr`, and `acad.mnl`, choose Tools ⇨ Options and click the Files tab. Double-click the first item, Support File Search Path, to display the location of the support files.

3. Click the copied menu file and rename it `ab1.mns` (that's the number one, not the letter "L"). Press Enter.

4. Do the same with `acad.mnl`, making a copy and renaming the copy `ab1.mnl`.

5. Open NotePad. (Choose Start ⇨ Run. Type **NotePad** and click OK.) Open `ab1.mns`. (To find it, you need to change the Files of type drop-down list to All Files.)

6. Look for `***MENUGROUP=ACAD`. Change `ACAD` to `AB1`.

7. If you use a digitizing tablet or other nonsystem input device, scroll down to the ***BUTTONS3 and ***BUTTONS4 sections. If you use a system mouse, scroll down to the ***AUX3 and ***AUX4 sections. Change the current macros, if any, so that they read as follows:

```
***BUTTONS3
// Control + button
^B
***BUTTONS4
// Control + shift + button
^F

***AUX3
// Control + button
^B
***AUX4
// Control + shift + button
^F
```

This lets you turn Snap on and off using Ctrl plus the right button on your pointing device and lets you turn OSNAP on and off using Ctrl+Shift+right-click.

8. Save the file as a text document and close NotePad.

9. Start AutoCAD if it is not already open. Open a new drawing using the acad.dwt template.

10. Type **menu** ↵. Choose ab1.mns and click Open. AutoCAD responds with the Menu loaded successfully. MENUGROUP: AB1 message on the command line.

11. Hold Ctrl and click the right button. The SNAP button on the status bar looks pushed in. Move your cursor around to verify that Snap is on. (If the cursor doesn't snap to points, then polar snap is on. Right-click SNAP on the status bar and choose Grid Snap On.)

> **Note** You may find that the shortcut menu is also displayed. This appears to be a bug.

12. Hold Ctrl+Shift and click the right button. OSNAP turns on if it's currently off or turns off if it's currently on.

13. Hold Ctrl+Shift and click the right button again to toggle OSNAP again.

14. To return to your original menu, type **menu** ↵. Notice AutoCAD has added the compiled menu ab1.mnc. Choose acad.mnc and click Open. AutoCAD loads acad.mnc.

15. Again try using Ctrl plus the right button and Ctrl+Shift+right-click. The button no longer works as before. Instead, it opens the OSNAP shortcut menu.

16. Do not save your drawing.

The POP menus

The POP menus control the pull-down and shortcut menus. The pull-down menus are the menus along the top of your screen. The shortcut menus appear at the cursor. In addition to the Snap menu, which appears when you press Shift and the right mouse button, and the Grips menu, which appears when there is a hot grip and you right-click, AutoCAD 2004 has several context-sensitive shortcut menus.

Pull-down menus

The use of the ampersand (&) in the menu label is unique to the pull-down menus. As explained earlier, this places an underscore under the following letter to let you choose the menu item using the keyboard instead of the mouse. You also see [–] in several places. This adds a dividing line in a pull-down menu and is used only to organize the menu into sections.

Here is the beginning of AutoCAD's POP2 menu:

```
***POP2
**EDIT
ID_MnEdit    [&Edit]
ID_U         [&Undo\tCtrl+Z]_u
ID_Redo      [&Redo\tCtrl+Y]^C^C_mredo 1
             [--]
ID_Cutclip   [Cu&t\tCtrl+X]^C^C_cutclip
ID_Copyclip  [&Copy\tCtrl+C]^C^C_copyclip
ID_Copybase  [Copy with &Base Point\tCtrl+Shift+C]^C^C_copybase
ID_Copylink  [Copy &Link]^C^C_copylink
ID_Pasteclip [&Paste\tCtrl+V]^C^C_pasteclip
ID_Pastebloc [Paste as Bloc&k \tCtrl+Shift+V]^C^C_pasteblock
ID_Pastehlnk [Paste as &Hyperlink]^C^C_pasteashyperlink
ID_Pasteorig [Paste to Original Coor&dinates]^C^C_pasteorig
ID_Pastesp   [Paste &Special...]^C^C_pastespec
             [--]
ID_Erase     [Cle&ar\tDel]^C^C_erase
ID_SelAll    [Se&lect All\tCtrl+A]^C^C_ai_selall
             [--]
ID_Links     [&OLE Links...]^C^C_olelinks
             [--]
ID_TextFind  [&Find...]^C^C_find
```

Figure 33-6 shows how the Edit menu appears in AutoCAD.

The POP menus can have submenus. Use the following codes to start and end submenus:

->	Starts a submenu
<-	Ends a submenu
<-<-	Ends a submenu of a submenu

Note that several of the items include \t and then text that describes a keyboard shortcut, such as Ctrl+A. In the label portion of a POP menu item, text after \t is moved to the right side of menu. See Figure 33-6 for several examples of this technique.

Edit	
Undo	Ctrl+Z
Redo	Ctrl+Y
Cut	Ctrl+X
Copy	Ctrl+C
Copy with Base Point	Ctrl+Shift+C
Copy Link	
Paste	Ctrl+V
Paste as Block	Ctrl+Shift+V
Paste as Hyperlink	
Paste to Original Coordinates	
Paste Special...	
Clear	Del
Select All	Ctrl+A
OLE Links...	
Find...	

Figure 33-6: The Edit menu. Compare it to the menu code and look for the dividing lines and the underscored letters.

Here is an example from the end of the Draw menu. Notice that both the Surfaces and Solids items have submenus. At the end of the Solids submenu, the Setup item has a second-level submenu. Therefore, the Profile menu item is preceded by <-<-.

```
ID_MnSurface    [->Sur&faces]
ID_Solid        [&2D Solid]^C^C_solid
ID_3dface       [3D &Face]^C^C_3dface
ID_3dsurface    [&3D Surfaces...]$I=ACAD.image_3dobjects
$I=ACAD.*
                [--]
ID_Edge         [&Edge]^C^C_edge
ID_3dmesh       [3D &Mesh]^C^C_3dmesh
                [--]
ID_Revsurf      [Revolved &Surface]^C^C_revsurf
ID_Tabsurf      [&Tabulated Surface]^C^C_tabsurf
ID_Rulesurf     [&Ruled Surface]^C^C_rulesurf
ID_Edgesurf     [<-E&dge Surface]^C^C_edgesurf
ID_MnSolids     [->Sol&ids]
ID_Box          [&Box]^C^C_box
ID_Sphere       [&Sphere]^C^C_sphere
ID_Cylinder     [&Cylinder]^C^C_cylinder
ID_Cone         [C&one]^C^C_cone
```

```
ID_Wedge        [&Wedge]^C^C_wedge
ID_Torus        [&Torus]^C^C_torus
                [--]
ID_Extrude      [E&xtrude]^C^C_extrude
ID_Revolve      [&Revolve]^C^C_revolve
                [--]
ID_Slice        [S&lice]^C^C_slice
ID_Section      [S&ection]^C^C_section
ID_Interfere    [&Interference]^C^C_interfere
                [--]
ID_MnSetup      [->Set&up]
ID_Soldraw      [&Drawing]^C^C_soldraw
ID_Solview      [&View]^C^C_solview
ID_Solprof      [<-<-&Profile]^C^C_solprof
```

Figure 33-7 shows how this code looks on the AutoCAD Draw menu.

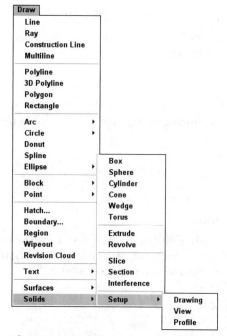

Figure 33-7: The Draw menu with the Solids and Setup submenus

Tip The titles of pull-down POP menus appear as the menu title. Keep these fairly short to keep the menu titles from running into each other. Don't place spaces in menu title names — it becomes hard to distinguish where one menu ends and the next one starts.

Step-by-Step: Creating a Pull-Down Partial Menu

1. If you haven't already done so, back up `acad.mnu`, `acad.mns`, `acad.mnc`, `acad.mnr`, and `acad.mnl`.

Caution Do not continue with this exercise until you have completed Step 1. If you are working on someone else's computer, ask permission before doing this exercise.

Note By default, `acad.mnu`, `acad.mns`, `acad.mnc`, `acad.mnr`, and `acad.mnl` are in `\Documents and Settings\[user name]\Application Data\Autodesk\ AutoCAD 2004\R16.0\enu\Support`. However, your location may be different, depending on your operating system and customization. To find the location of `acad.mnu`, `acad.mns`, `acad.mnc`, `acad.mnr`, and `acad.mnl`, choose Tools ➪ Options and click the Files tab. Double-click the first item, Support File Search Path, to display the location of the support files.

2. Open Notepad. (Choose Start ➪ Run. Type **notepad** and click OK.)

3. To create the menu group name, the pull-down menu, and the menu name (which will appear on the menu bar), type the following:

```
***MENUGROUP=AB2
***POP1
[&AB2]
```

4. To create the first menu item with a submenu, type the following on the next few lines:

```
ID_SpecEdits    [->&Special Edits]
ID_MoveRight    [&Move .1 Right]^C^C_select
\_move;_previous;;.1,0 ;
ID_Plinewdth    [<-&Pedit .1]^C^C_pedit \_w .1 ;
```

Be careful to put in the spaces as shown.

5. To create the next few menu items, starting with a dividing line, type the following. I added the ALIGN command because AutoCAD places it at the bottom of a submenu — you can place it here to make it more accessible.

```
[--]
ID_4circles  [&4 circles]_circle 2,2 1.5 _circle 6,2 +
1.5 _circle 10,2 1.5 _circle 14,2 1.5
ID_Cleanup   [&Clean up]^C^C_chprop _all ;_c _bylayer ;+
-layer _f no-plot ;_qsave
ID_Align     [&Align]^C^C_align
```

6. End the menu file with a return. Proofread your typing and save the file as `ab2.mnu` in AutoCAD's support folder or any other folder that you have placed in the support file search path. Close Notepad.

7. Open `ab33-a.dwg` from the CD-ROM. Save it as `ab33-1.dwg` in your `AutoCAD Bible` folder.

8. Choose Tools ➪ Customize ➪ Menus. On the Menu Groups tab of the Menu Customization dialog box, make sure that the Replace All check box is not checked and choose Browse. Select Menu Template (`*.mnu`) from the Files of type drop-down list. Find and choose `ab2.mnu` and click Open. Click Load. Click Yes to the AutoCAD message that warns you about overwriting toolbar changes (because this little menu doesn't have any toolbars).

9. Choose the Menu Bar tab. Choose AB2 from the Menu Group drop-down list. In the Menu Bar list, choose Window so that your menu will be inserted just before the Window menu. Choose Insert. AutoCAD inserts the menu. Choose Close. The menu should look like Figure 33-8. Notice the submenu and the dividing line.

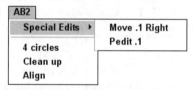

Figure 33-8: The AB2 menu, including the submenu

10. To try out the menu, choose AB2 ➪ Special Edits ➪ Move .1 Right. At the `Select objects:` prompt, pick the vertical red line and right-click to end object selection. The menu macro moves the line 0.1 units to the right.

11. Choose AB2 ➪ Special Edits ➪ Pedit .1. At the `Select polyline or [Multiple]:` prompt, choose the green polyline. AutoCAD makes it 0.1 unit wide.

12. Choose AB2 ➪ Clean up. AutoCAD changes the color of all the objects to ByLayer and freezes the no-plot layer.

13. Choose Tools ➪ Customize Menus and unload AB2.

14. Save your drawing.

Note If you made a mistake and some of the items don't work properly, re-edit and save `ab2.mnu`. Then choose Tools ➪ Customize ➪ Menus, unload AB2, reload it, and insert it again.

Replacing your partial menus

When you are customizing a partial menu, the process of unloading, loading, and inserting a partial menu can get pretty tedious. Here's a routine that you can put on your partial menu. You can't use it the first time (because the partial menu isn't on your menu bar yet), but after that, you can use it to quickly replace your old partial menu with the new one. This routine turns off the FILEDIA system variable so that you can load and unload the partial menu on the command line, and then it unloads and loads the menu. It then uses a simple AutoLISP expression to place the menu where you want it.

```
ID_MenuLoad  [&Reload ab2 menu]_filedia 0 +
_menuunload ab2 menuload ab2.mnu (menucmd +
"P10=+ab2.pop1") _filedia 1
```

The first part is the name tag, which can be anything you want. The second part is the label that you see on the menu. It can also be anything you want. Then comes the menu macro. Here I have used the menu group name ab2 and the menu file name ab2.mnu. Replace these with your menu group and menu file names. The AutoLISP expression syntax is

```
(menucmd "Pn=+menugroup.section")
```

where n is the number of the POP menu to the right of where you want to insert your partial menu (P10 is usually the Help menu), menugroup is the menugroup name, and section is the section name (usually POP1 if your partial menu has one pull-down menu).

If your partial menu has more than one pull-down menu, you must place each POP section using the same syntax.

Shortcut menus

You access a shortcut menu by using the buttons on your mouse or puck. The shortcut menus are therefore accessed from the Buttons menu by swapping, as described earlier in this chapter.

Here you see the POP0 menu, which is the menu that appears when you press Shift and right-click.

```
***POP0
**SNAP
                    [&Object Snap Cursor Menu]
ID_Tracking         [Temporary trac&k point]_tt
ID_From             [&From]_from
ID_MnPointFi        [->Poin&t Filters]
ID_PointFilx        [.X].X
ID_PointFily        [.Y].Y
ID_PointFilz        [.Z].Z
                    [--]
ID_PointFixy        [.XY].XY
ID_PointFixz        [.XZ].XZ
```

```
ID_PointFiyz      [<-.YZ].YZ
                  [--]
ID_OsnapEndp      [&Endpoint]_endp
ID_OsnapMidp      [&Midpoint]_mid
ID_OsnapInte      [&Intersection]_int
ID_OsnapAppa      [&Apparent Intersect]_appint
ID_OsnapExte      [E&xtension]_ext
                  [--]
ID_OsnapCent      [&Center]_cen
ID_OsnapQuad      [&Quadrant]_qua
ID_OsnapTang      [Tan&gent]_tan
                  [--]
ID_OsnapPerp      [&Perpendicular]_per
ID_OsnapPara      [Para&llel]_par
ID_OsnapNode      [No&de]_nod
ID_OsnapInse      [In&sert]_ins
ID_OsnapNear      [Nea&rest]_nea
ID_OsnapNone      [&None]_non
                  [--]
ID_Osnap          [&Osnap Settings...]'_+dsettings 2
```

Note that, unlike a regular pull-down menu, the title — in this case, Snap — doesn't appear at the top of a shortcut menu. However, a title is required anyway.

Note You can customize shortcut menus that are specific to a command or to a selected object. For example, if you right-click when a polyline is selected, the shortcut menu includes a Polyline Edit item. However, if you right-click when a spline is selected, the shortcut menu includes a Spline Edit item instead. Shortcut menus can also be called context menus because they are context-sensitive. You can create your own context menus.

To create a shortcut menu, you use sections ***POP500 through ***POP999. Sections ***POP500 through ***POP516 define the existing context-sensitive shortcut menus in acad.mns.

Tip Although the examples shown here use both the initial underline to allow for translation and the ampersand to allow for keyboard entry, you don't need to use these if you don't want to. When was the last time you used the keyboard to choose a menu item on a shortcut menu?

You can create two kinds of context-sensitive menus — object menus and command menus. The context-sensitive menus work only for full menus.

Note If you have turned on time-sensitive right-clicking, remember to hold down the right mouse button long enough to open the shortcut menu. See Chapter 3 for details.

Object menus

The Edit mode shortcut menu appears when you right-click in the drawing area when one or more objects are selected but no command is active, as shown in Figure 33-9.

You can create *object menus* that are specific to a type of object. You might want to add certain commands that you use often with that type of object. The commands that you add to an object menu are appended to the Edit mode shortcut menu so that the result is a menu that contains the Edit mode shortcut menu plus any additional commands that you have added for that type of object.

Repeat Circle
Cut
Copy
Copy with Base Point
Paste
Paste as Block
Paste to Original Coordinates
Erase
Move
Copy Selection
Scale
Rotate
Deselect All
Quick Select...
Find...
Properties

Figure 33-9: The Edit mode shortcut menu

To create an object menu, you must name the menu either OBJECT_objectname, used when one object of a type is selected, or OBJECTS_objectname, used when more than one object of a type is selected. The object name is the DXF name of the object. (Three exceptions exist — use BLOCKREF for a block insertion with no attributes, ATTBLOCKREF for a block insertion with attributes and XREF for an xref.) To find out the object name of an object, type the following on the command line:

```
(cdr (assoc 0 (entget (car (entsel))))) ↵
```

That's five closing parentheses at the end. AutoCAD then prompts you to select an object. As soon as you do, you see the object's name on the command line.

Cross-Reference See Chapters 34 and 35, which cover AutoLISP and Visual LISP, for an explanation of the parts of this AutoLISP expression. These two chapters explain all the functions used in this expression.

For example, to create an object menu that appears when one or more circles are selected, create an object menu named OBJECTS_circle. Look at `acad.mns` for examples to help you create your own menus. Here you see ***POP509, which is the hatch object menu:

```
***POP509
**OBJECT_HATCH
              [Context menu for HATCH object]
ID_Hatchedit   [&Hatch Edit...]^C^C_hatchedit
```

Figure 33-10 shows how this menu appears when you select a hatch object. As you can see, the menu adds only one item, which executes the HATCHEDIT command.

Figure 33-10: The hatch object shortcut menu

Command menus

The Command mode shortcut menu appears when you right-click in the drawing area while a command is active. You can create command menus that are specific to a command. The contents of the menu are appended to the Command mode shortcut menu so that the result is a menu that contains the Command mode shortcut menu plus any additional commands that you have added for that command. AutoCAD does not come with any existing command menus. To create a command menu, you must name the menu COMMAND_commandname, where commandname is any valid AutoCAD command, including any custom or third-party commands. After you name the menu, you can add commands to it that you would like to have available in the middle of the command just by right-clicking. Here are a couple of possibilities:

✦ For the LINE command, you might want to add the PLINE command to the shortcut menu, so that you can change your mind mid-command and create a polyline instead of a line. Of course, you can execute the PLINE command with one pick from the Draw toolbar, but the shortcut menu is closer.

✦ For the COPY command, you might want to add some OSNAP changes that you can use transparently in the middle of the command. For example, you could turn OSNAP off or set an Endpoint object snap.

Figure 33-11 shows a possible command menu, which turns the running OSNAP off and sets OSNAP to endpoint, using the OSMODE system variable.

Enter
Cancel
Multiple
Pan
Zoom
OSNAP Off
OSNAP Endpoint

Figure 33-11: A custom command menu that appears when you right-click during the COPY command

Here's the code for the menu file:

```
***POP517
**COMMAND_COPY
                [Context menu for COPY command]
ID_Osmode       [OSNAP Off]'osmode 0
ID_OsmodeEnd    [OSNAP Endpoint]'osmode 1
```

Note that you cannot create a similar menu for the MOVE command because the MOVE command doesn't have any options. Therefore, you can't right-click to open a shortcut menu.

Step-by-Step: Creating a Context-Sensitive Object Menu

1. If you did the exercise on customizing the Buttons menu, start WordPad by choosing Start ➪ Run, typing **wordpad**, and clicking OK. Open ab1.mns from AutoCAD's support folder. Choose File ➪ Save As and save it as ab3.mns. Use Windows Explorer to find ab1.mnl in AutoCAD's support folder. Click it and rename it ab3.mnl. Then go to Step 3.

Caution Don't continue with this exercise without first completing Step 1. If you are working on someone else's computer, ask permission before doing this exercise.

2. If you didn't do the exercise on customizing the Buttons menu, back up acad.mnu, acad.mns, acad.mnc, acad.mnr, and acad.mnl. Then right-click acad.mns in Windows Explorer and choose Copy from the shortcut menu.

Right-click again and choose Paste. Windows places a copy of `acad.mns`, called `Copy of acad.mns` in the same folder. Click the copied menu file and type **ab3.mns** ↵. Find `acad.mnl` and rename it `ab3.mnl`. Start WordPad (choose Start ➪ Run, type **wordpad**, and click OK). Open `ab3.mns`.

> **Note**
>
> By default, `acad.mnu`, `acad.mns`, `acad.mnc`, `acad.mnr`, and `acad.mnl` are in `\Documents and Settings\[user name]\Application Data\Autodesk\ AutoCAD 2004\R16.0\enu\Support`. However, your location may be different, depending on your operating system and customization. To find the location of `acad.mnu`, `acad.mns`, `acad.mnc`, `acad.mnr`, and `acad.mnl`, choose Tools ➪ Options and click the Files tab. Double-click the first item, Support File Search Path, to display the location of the support files.

3. Look for `***MENUGROUP=`. Change the word after the equal sign to **AB3**.

4. Press PageDown until you see `***POP516` and then `**OBJECT_VIEWPORT`. Place the cursor after the `POP515` menu but before the `***TOOLBARS` section and press Enter a couple of times. Place your cursor so that there is a blank line after the previous menu and before the next section. Type the following:

```
***POP517
**OBJECT_3DSOLID
                  [Context menu for 3DSOLID object]
ID_Hide           [&Hide]^C^C_hide
ID_VPointSE       [SE &Viewpoint]^C^C_vpoint 1,-1,1
ID_VPointTop      [Top Vie&wpoint]^C^C_vpoint 0,0,1
```

5. Choose File ➪ Save. Save `ab3.mns` as a Text Document and close WordPad.

6. Start AutoCAD if it is not already running. Open a new drawing using any template.

7. Choose Draw ➪ Solids ➪ Box and follow the prompts to draw a solid box of any size.

8. Type **menu** ↵. Choose `ab3.mns` and click Open. AutoCAD compiles the menu. You see the message `Menu loaded successfully. MENUGROUP: AB3` on the command line. (If it scrolls up, you may need to press F2 to open the AutoCAD Text Window.)

9. Select the box. Right-click and choose SE Viewpoint from the shortcut menu. AutoCAD changes the viewpoint.

10. Select the box again. Right-click and choose Hide from the shortcut menu. AutoCAD hides the box.

11. Select the box again. Right-click and choose Top Viewpoint. AutoCAD changes the viewpoint.

12. To return to your original menu, type **menu** ↵. Choose `acad.mnc` and click Open. AutoCAD loads `acad.mnc`.

13. Select the box and right-click. You no longer have your custom options. Press Esc. Do not save your drawing.

Creating toggles on pull-down menus

By examining `acad.mnu`, you can accomplish some interesting things with your menus, even if you don't understand the code. You may have noticed that when the UCS icon is displayed, the View ⇨ Display ⇨ UCS Icon ⇨ On menu item shows a checkmark. If you choose this item again, not only does the UCS icon disappear, but the checkmark does too. This is called a *toggle* and is created using the DIESEL programming language, a language that enables you to customize the command line and works only with text strings. However, you can use it for your own menus, even if you don't know any DIESEL — simply by examining the code and making a few educated guesses. Here is the code:

```
ID_UcsiconOn [$(if,$(and,$(getvar,ucsicon),1),!.)&On]+
$M=$(if,$(and,$(getvar,ucsicon),1),^C^C_ucsicon +
off,^C^C_ucsicon _on)
```

You see the UCSICON system variable mentioned in the expression `(getvar,ucsicon)` first. Then you see the expression `&On`. By now you know that this is the menu label. Finally, you see the two commands at the end that issue the UCSICON system variable and turn it off and on.

Perhaps you could use a similar example in your own menu. For example, when customizing AutoCAD, you often have to turn the FILEDIA system variable on and off. Perhaps you always forget if it is FILEDIA or DIAFILE and then have to look it up, so you'd like to put it on your menu. Here's what you would do:

```
ID_Filedia   [$(if,$(and,$(getvar,filedia),1),!.)+
&File Dialogs On]$M=$(if,$(and,$(getvar,filedia),1),+
^C^C_filedia 0,^C^C_filedia 1)
```

All you've done is substitute FILEDIA for UCSICON in two places, `&File Dialogs On` for `&On`, and the new commands at the end (you use 0 and 1 for FILEDIA instead of off and on). It's okay if you don't understand the code; the point is that it works!

Customizing the toolbars from the menu file

Although it is much easier to customize toolbars directly, as explained in Chapter 29, you can also customize them from the menu file. Here is a section of the Standard toolbar code from `acad.mnu`:

```
**TB_STANDARD
ID_TbStandar  [_Toolbar("Standard Toolbar", _Top, _Show, 0, 0,
1)]
ID_QNew       [_Button("QNew", "RCDATA_16_NEW",
"RCDATA_16_NEW")]^C^C_qnew
ID_Open       [_Button("Open", "RCDATA_16_OPEN",
"RCDATA_16_OPEN")]^C^C_open
ID_Save       [_Button("Save", "RCDATA_16_SAVE",
"RCDATA_16_SAVE")]^C^C_qsave
              [--]
```

```
ID_Print        [_Button("Plot", "RCDATA_16_PRINT",
"RCDATA_16_PRINT")]^C^C_plot
ID_Preview      [_Button("Plot Preview", "RCDATA_16_PREVIEW",
"RCDATA_16_PREVIEW")]^C^C_preview
ID_Pub          [_Button("Publish", RCDATA_16_PUBL,
RCDATA_16_PUBL)]^C^C_publish
                [--]
ID_Cutclip      [_Button("Cut to Clipboard", "RCDATA_16_CUT",
"RCDATA_16_CUT")]^C^C_cutclip
ID_Copyclip     [_Button("Copy to Clipboard", "RCDATA_16_COPY",
"RCDATA_16_COPY")]^C^C_copyclip
ID_Pasteclip    [_Button("Paste from Clipboard",
"RCDATA_16_PASTE", "RCDATA_16_PASTE")]^C^C_pasteclip
ID_Matchprop    [_Button("Match Properties", "RCDATA_16_MATCH",
"RCDATA_16_MATCH")]'_matchprop
                [--]
ID_CtrlUndo     [_Control(_Undo)]
ID_CtrlRedo     [_Control(_Redo)]
                [--]
ID_Pan          [_Button("Pan Realtime", RCDATA_16_RTPAN,
RCDATA_16_RTPAN)]'_pan
ID_ZoomRealt [_Button("Zoom Realtime", RCDATA_16_RTZOOM,
RCDATA_16_RTZOOM)]'_zoom ;
ID_TbZoom       [_Flyout("Zoom", RCDATA_16_ZOOM, RCDATA_16_ZOOM,
_OtherIcon, ACAD.TB_ZOOM)]
ID_ZoomPrevi [_Button("Zoom Previous", RCDATA_16_ZOOPRE,
RCDATA_16_ZOOPRE)]'_zoom _p
                [--]
ID_Ai_propch [_Button("Properties", RCDATA_16_MODIFY,
RCDATA_16_MODIFY)]$M=$(if,$(and,$(>,$(getvar,opmstate),0)),^C^C
_propertiesclose,^C^C_properties)
ID_Content    [_Button("DesignCenter", RCDATA_16_OPTCONTENTX,
RCDATA_16_OPTCONTENTX)]$M=$(if,$(and,$(getvar,adcstate),1),'_ad
cclose,'_adcenter)
ID_TPalette    [_Button("Tool Palettes", RCDATA_16_TPALETTE,
RCDATA_16_TPALETTE)]$M=$(if,$(and,$(getvar,tpstate),1),'_ToolPa
lettesClose,'_ToolPalettes)
                [--]
ID_Help         [_Button("Help", RCDATA_16_HELP,
RCDATA_16_HELP)]'_help
```

The first line below the heading defines the entire toolbar. The codes refer to the toolbar's display status (show/hide), shape, whether it is floating or docked, and so on. Because you routinely change these items directly in AutoCAD, they are not crucial.

Note Remember that AutoCAD saves toolbar changes that you make directly in AutoCAD in the .mns file.

The next several lines define buttons. The first section of each line is the name tag. In brackets, you specify the actual bitmap that creates the button. Then specify the macro.

Note that the format of the Undo and Redo buttons is different from a standard button. Instead of defining a tool button, these items use specially predefined button controls that are built into AutoCAD. These predefined button controls vary in function and are specific to their command. In the case of the Undo and Redo controls, when you pick on the button, they call up a special window that displays the various commands you can undo or redo. The other custom button controls are the Dimstyle, Color, Linetype, Lineweight, Plotstyle, Layer, Txtstyle, View, Refblkname (for the REFEDIT command), UCSmanager, and Viewportscale controls. Because these button controls are built specially for particular commands, only the control's name is specified.

Also, notice the toolbutton entry for Zoom. This item also doesn't define a toolbutton but instead defines a toolbar flyout. The OtherIcon code means that whichever button is used last remains on top. You can specify OwnIcon to keep the icon specified here, where the flyout is defined, always on top. The last part refers to the toolbar section that creates the flyout. No macros are listed here because they are in the referenced toolbar section.

Because Windows lets you display toolbar buttons in both large and small formats, each button actually has two bitmaps.

On the CD-ROM

Keypad creates a toolbar that contains a keypad for numbers and other often-used symbols, such as @ and <. Look in \Software\Chap33\Keypad.

Image tile menus

Image tile menus are created with slides. The image tile displays the contents of the slides.

The first line after the section or subsection heading appears at the top of the image tile menu. (See an example following Table 33-3 earlier in the chapter.)

Image tile menus have both a list box and an image tile for each item. The menu labels use a special format that provides the slide library name, the slide, and a label for the list box. You have the following options:

- ✦ [slidename] puts the slide name in the list box and displays the slide in the image tile.
- ✦ [slidelibrary(slidename)] does the same as the first option, but specifies the slide library that contains the slide.
- ✦ [slidename,labeltext] puts the label text in the list box and displays the slide in the image tile.
- ✦ [slidelibrary(slidename,labeltext)] does the same as the third option but specifies the slide library that contains the slide.

Chapter 30 discusses slides and slide libraries.

Image tile menus cannot contain name tags. Here's the image_3Dobjects subsection of the IMAGE section of acad.mnu:

```
***IMAGE
**image_3DObjects
[3D Objects]
[acad(Box3d,Box3d)]^C^C_ai_box
[acad(Pyramid,Pyramid)]^C^C_ai_pyramid
[acad(Wedge,Wedge)]^C^C_ai_wedge
[acad(Dome,Dome)]^C^C_ai_dome
[acad(Sphere,Sphere)]^C^C_ai_sphere
[acad(Cone,Cone)]^C^C_ai_cone
[acad(Torus,Torus)]^C^C_ai_torus
[acad(Dish,Dish)]^C^C_ai_dish
[acad(Mesh,Mesh)]^C^C_ai_mesh
```

Figure 33-12 shows the resulting dialog box.

As explained in the earlier section on menu swapping, you display an image tile menu from another menu. For example, to display the 3D Objects menu, AutoCAD uses the following code in the Draw pull-down menu:

```
ID_3dsurface    [&3D Surfaces...]$I=ACAD.image_3dobjects
$I=ACAD.*
```

This swaps to the 3D Objects image tile menu and displays it.

AutoCAD automatically creates the dialog box. If it has more than 20 items, AutoCAD creates Previous and Next boxes as well.

Figure 33-12: A subsection of the Image menu creates the 3D Objects dialog box.

To create your own image tile menus, you need to create the slides. So that they fit into the image tiles properly, you should create a floating viewport 3 units wide by 2 units high, center the drawing so that it takes up most of the viewport, and create the slide.

The files used in the following Step-by-Step exercise on creating an image tile menu, `ab33-b.dwg`, `ab4.mnu`, `ab33-b01.dwg` through `ab33-b17.dwg`, and `ab33-b01.sld` through `ab33-b17.sld`, are in the Drawings folder of the *AutoCAD 2004 Bible* CD-ROM.

Step-by-Step: Creating an Image Tile Menu

1. If you haven't already done so, back up `acad.mnu`, `acad.mns`, `acad.mnc`, `acad.mnr`, and `acad.mnl`.

By default, `acad.mnu`, `acad.mns`, `acad.mnc`, `acad.mnr`, and `acad.mnl` are in `\Documents and Settings\[user name]\Application Data\Autodesk\ AutoCAD 2004\R16.0\enu\Support`. However, your location may be different, depending on your operating system and customization. To find the location of `acad.mns`, `acad.mns`, `acad.mnc`, `acad.mnr`, and `acad.mnl`, choose Tools ➪ Options and click the Files tab. Double-click the first item, Support File Search Path, to display the location of the support files.

Do not continue with this exercise until you have completed Step 1. If you are working on someone else's computer, ask permission before doing this exercise.

2. Use Notepad to open `ab4.mnu` from the CD-ROM. This includes the AB2 menu from a previous Step-by-Step exercise, an Image menu, and a new item in the POP1 menu that calls the Image menu, as shown in Figure 33-13. Note that the macros in the Image menu simply use the -INSERT command (the command-line version of INSERT) to insert the files. Read over `ab4.mnu` so you understand how the new image tile feature is created. Close `ab4.mnu`.

3. For this exercise to work, you need to copy `ab4.mnu` and all the slides and drawings used in `ab4.mnu` from the CD-ROM to a folder in AutoCAD's support file search path. You can copy them to your AutoCAD support directory, but because there are so many files (the menu file plus 17 drawings and 17 slides), it is probably better to create a new folder and add the folder to AutoCAD's support file search path. You can copy them to your `AutoCAD Bible` folder and add that folder to AutoCAD's support file search path. Then copy `ab4.mnu`, `ab33-b01.dwg` through `ab33-b17.dwg`, and `ab33-b01.sld` through `ab33-b17.sld` to that folder.

Remember that you can add any folder to the support file search path by choosing Tools ➪ Options ➪ Files, expanding Support File Search Path, and choosing Add.

4. Open `ab33-b.dwg` from the CD-ROM. This drawing shows a rectangle 40 feet long by 30 feet wide, which could represent any building.

```
***MENUGROUP=AB4
***POP1
[AB4]
ID_SpecEdits    [->&Special Edits]
ID_MoveRight    [&Move .1 Right]^C^C_select \_move _previous .1,0 ;
ID_Plinewdth    [<-&Pedit .1]^C^C_pedit \_w .1 ;
[--]
ID_4circles     [&4 circles]^C^C_circle 2,2 1.5 _circle 6,2 +
1.5 _circle 10,2 1.5 _circle 14.2 1.5
ID_Cleanup      [&Clean up]^C^C_chprop _all _c _bylayer ;+
-layer _f no-plot _qsave
ID_Align        [&Align]^C^C_align
[--]
ID_AEC_sym   [Architectural &Elect Symbols]$I=AB4.AEC_sym +
$I=AB4.*

***IMAGE
**AEC_sym
[Architectural Electrical Symbols]
[ab33-b01,Duplex Receptacle Outlet]^C^C_insert ab33-b01;\ ;
[ab33-b02,Dryer Outlet]^C^C_insert ab33-b02;\ ;
[ab33-b03,Surface Mounted Light]^C^C_insert ab33-b03;\ ;
[ab33-b04,Recessed Light]^C^C_insert ab33-b04;\ ;
[ab33-b05,Wall Washer Light]^C^C_insert ab33-b05;\ ;
[ab33-b06,Recessed Eye Ball Light]^C^C_insert ab33-b06;\ ;
[ab33-b07,Pendant Light]^C^C_insert ab33-b07;\ ;
[ab33-b08,Wall Mounted Light]^C^C_insert ab33-b08;\ ;
[ab33-b09,Sconce]^C^C_insert ab33-b09;\ ;
[ab33-b10,Flood Lights]^C^C_insert ab33-b10;\ ;
[ab33-b11,Thermostat]^C^C_insert ab33-b11;\ ;
[ab33-b12,Single Pole Switch]^C^C_insert ab33-b12;\ ;
[ab33-b13,Three-Way Switch]^C^C_insert ab33-b13;\ ;
[ab33-b14,Master Switch]^C^C_insert ab33-b14;\ ;
[ab33-b15,Exhaust Fan]^C^C_insert ab33-b15;\ ;
[ab33-b16,Smoke Detector]^C^C_insert ab33-b16;\ ;
[ab33-b17,Whole House Fan]^C^C_insert ab33-b17;\ ;
```

Figure 33-13: The AB4 menu. The Image menu label format is `[slidename,labeltext]`.

5. Save it as `ab33-2.dwg` in your `AutoCAD Bible` folder.

6. Choose Tools ⇨ Customize ⇨ Menus. On the Menu Groups tab, in the File name text box, type **ab4.mnu.** Make sure Replace All is not checked and click Load. As long as the menu file is in AutoCAD's support file search path, AutoCAD will find the menu. Click Yes in the message dialog box that warns you about overwriting toolbar changes.

7. Choose the Menu Bar tab. AB4 should be listed as the Menu Group. Choose Window from the Menu Bar list and click Insert. AutoCAD inserts AB4 before the Window menu. Click Close.

8. Click the AB4 menu. It now has a new item, Architectural Elect Symbols. Choose this item. The Architectural Electrical Symbols dialog box opens, created by the Image Tile section, as shown in Figure 33-14.

9. Look at the list box on the left and compare it to the `**AEC_sym` subsection shown in Figure 33-13. You can see that all the labels in the list box were created using the `labeltext` part of the slide definition. The image tiles are created by the slides.

10. Choose any image tile. The corresponding item in the list is also selected. Click OK. At the prompt, pick any point in the rectangle. The macro of the image tile section inserts the drawing.

Figure 33-14: The AB4 menu's Image Tile section creates the Architectural Electrical Symbols dialog box.

11. Again choose AB4 ⇨ Architectural Elect Symbols. Choose any item from the list. The corresponding image tile is also selected. Click OK. Pick any point to insert the drawing. Continue to insert as many symbols as you wish.

12. Choose Tools ⇨ Customize ⇨ Menus and unload AB4. Save your drawing.

Tablet menus

Tablet menus are fairly straightforward. You can print out AutoCAD's standard tablet drawing, `AutoCAD 2004\Sample\Tablet.dwg`, and compare it to the `TABLET` section of `acad.mnu`. The entire first section is left blank for you to configure. This menu section is preset to contain 9 rows and 25 columns. If you configure this menu area (using the TABLET command) to contain 9 rows and 25 columns, you can place your own macro in each of these boxes.

Cross-Reference For information on digitizing drawings and calibrating a tablet, see Chapter 16.

Here is the beginning of the `TABLET1` section from `acad.mnu`:

```
***TABLET1
**TABLET1STD
[A-1]\
[A-2]\
[A-3]\
[A-4]\
[A-5]\
[A-6]\
[A-7]\
[A-8]\
[A-9]\
[A-10]\
```

This section continues through [I-25].

The TABLET2 sections starts this way:

```
//      TABLET2 menu.
//      Rows: J to R (9)
//      Columns: 11
//
***TABLET2
**TABLET2STD
// Row J View
^C^C_regen
 '_zoom _e
'_zoom _a
'_zoom _w
'_zoom _p
[Draw]\
^C^C_box
^C^C_mtext
^C^C_circle
^C^C_line
^C^C
```

As you can see, the menu includes instructions to help you configure the tablet. When you configure the tablet you need to specify the number of rows and columns, so the menu tells you here that the TABLET2 section has 9 rows and 11 columns. The syntax of the Tablet menu is very simple; you don't need name tags or labels, just the menu macro itself.

Note If you customize the Tablet menu, don't forget to also open Tablet.dwg provided by AutoCAD in the AutoCAD 2004\Sample\ folder, make the corresponding changes, and print it out to overlay on your digitizer so that the drawing you place on your tablet reflects the menu properly.

Working with the Screen menu

I don't spend much time on the Screen menu here because it is no longer used very much. If you are interested in customizing it, read the comments just above the ***SCREEN section of acad.mnu.

Tip The Screen section is very long. If you don't use the Screen menu, you can delete it from acad.mns or the menu file you are using. Don't forget to back up acad.mns, or your own menu, first.

Creating status line help messages

The ***HELPSTRINGS section of a menu file creates help messages on the status line for pull-down and toolbar menu items. This section uses the name tag of the menu item. Here is part of the HELPSTRINGS section of acad.mns:

```
ID_VPOINTTOP_0 [Sets the view point to top:  VIEW]
ID_3DDISTANC   [Starts the 3DORBIT command and makes objects
appear closer or farther away:  3DDISTANCE]
ID_3dcorbit    [Starts the 3DORBIT command with continuous orbit
active in the 3D view:  3DCORBIT]
ID_3ddistanc [Starts the 3DORBIT command and makes
objects appear closer or farther away:  3DDISTANCE]
ID_3dface      [Creates a three-dimensional face:  3DFACE]
ID_3dmesh      [Creates a free-form polygon mesh:  3DMESH]
ID_3dorbit     [Controls the interactive viewing of objects
in 3D:  3DORBIT]
ID_3dpan       [Starts the 3DORBIT command and enables you
to drag the view horizontally and vertically:  3DPAN]
ID_3dpoly      [Creates a polyline of line segments in 3D space:
3DPOLY]
ID_3dsin       [Imports a 3D Studio file:  3DSIN]
ID_3dsurface [Creates three-dimensional surface objects
using a dialog box]
ID_3dswivel    [Starts the 3DORBIT command and simulates the
effect of turning the camera:  3DSWIVEL]
ID_3dviews     [Sets the view to a predefined or named view]
```

In `acad.mns`, the help string gives the actual text that appears on the status line followed by a colon, two spaces, and the name of the command. You can follow this convention for the sake of consistency — however, some of your macros may use more than one command, so it is not always appropriate. The space between the name tag and the help string is for readability only.

The file used in the following Step-by-Step exercise on creating help strings, `ab4.mnu`, is in the `Drawings` folder of the *AutoCAD 2004 Bible* CD-ROM.

Step-by-Step: Creating Help Strings

1. If you haven't already done so, back up `acad.mnu`, `acad.mns`, `acad.mnc`, `acad.mnr`, and `acad.mnl`.

By default, `acad.mnu`, `acad.mns`, `acad.mnc`, `acad.mnr`, and `acad.mnl` are in `\Documents and Settings\[user name]\Application Data\Autodesk\ AutoCAD 2004\R16.0\enu\Support`. However, your location may be different, depending on your operating system and customization. To find the location of `acad.mns`, `acad.mns`, `acad.mnc`, `acad.mnr`, and `acad.mnl`, choose Tools ➪ Options and click the Files tab. Double-click the first item, Support File Search Path, to display the location of the support files.

Do not continue with this exercise until you have completed Step 1. If you are working on someone else's computer, ask permission before doing this exercise.

2. Use Notepad to open `ab4.mnu` from the CD-ROM. If you did the previous exercise and copied `ab4.mnu` to your hard disk, open it from there.

3. Add the following lines to the end of the file and then press Enter. The name tags come from the first section of ab4.mnu but don't include the first item, which only opens a submenu. (Each helpstring should be on one line; do not wrap to the next line in Notepad.)

```
***HELPSTRINGS
ID_MoveRight    [Moves selected objects .1 unit to the right]
ID_Plinewdth    [Makes the width of one polyline .1]
ID_4circles     [Draws 4 circles in one row with radius 1.5]
ID_Cleanup      [Changes color of all objects to BYLAYER,
freezes no-plot layer, and saves]
ID_Align        [Moves and rotates objects to align with
other objects: align]
ID_AEC_sym      [Inserts AEC electrical symbols using a
dialog box]
```

4. If you did the previous exercise, save the file as ab5.mnu in the same location as ab4.mnu. If you opened ab4.mnu from the CD-ROM, save it as ab5.mnu in your AutoCAD support folder or another folder in AutoCAD's support file search path. Note that the file is still Menu Group AB4. Minimize Notepad.

5. Start AutoCAD with any drawing. Choose Tools ➪ Customize ➪ Menus. On the Menu Groups tab, in the File Name text box, type **ab5.mnu.** Making sure that Replace All is not checked, click Load. Click Yes at the message warning you about overwriting toolbar changes. AutoCAD loads the menu file.

6. Choose the Menu Bar tab. Choose Window on the Menu Bar list and click Insert. AutoCAD inserts the partial menu to the left of the Window menu. Click Close.

7. Open the AB4 menu and place the cursor over each item, including the submenu items. The help strings appear on the status bar.

8. Unload AB4. Do not save your drawing.

Creating keyboard shortcuts

The ***ACCELERATORS section creates keyboard shortcuts. Here is the Accelerators section of acad.mns:

```
***ACCELERATORS
ID_Hyperlink    [CONTROL+"K"]
[CONTROL+"L"]^O
[CONTROL+"R"]^V
ID_SelAll       [CONTROL+"A"]
ID_Copyclip     [CONTROL+TOOLBAR+"C"]
ID_New          [CONTROL+"N"]
ID_Open         [CONTROL+TOOLBAR+"O"]
ID_Print        [CONTROL+TOOLBAR+"P"]
ID_Save         [CONTROL+TOOLBAR+"S"]
ID_Saveas       [CONTROL+SHIFT+"S"]
ID_APP_EXIT     [CONTROL+INTERNAL+"Q"]
ID_Pasteclip    [CONTROL+TOOLBAR+"V"]
ID_Copybase     [CONTROL+SHIFT+"C"]
```

```
ID_Pastebloc   [CONTROL+SHIFT+"V"]
ID_Cutclip     [CONTROL+TOOLBAR+"X"]
ID_Redo        [CONTROL+"Y"]
ID_U           [CONTROL+"Z"]
ID_Ai_propch   [CONTROL+TOOLBAR+"1"]
ID_CleanScreen [CONTROL+"0"]
ID_Content     [CONTROL+TOOLBAR+"2"]
ID_TPalette    [CONTROL+"3"]
ID_dbConnect   [CONTROL+"6"]
ID_VBARun      [ALT+"F8"]
ID_VBAIDE      [ALT+"F11"]
[CONTROL+"H"]'_setvar;pickstyle;$M=$(if,$(eq,$(getvar,pickstyle
),0),1,$(if,$(eq,$(getvar,pickstyle),1),0,$(if,$(eq,$(getvar,pi
ckstyle),2),3,2)))
```

Note Some of the Control shortcut codes are different in the menu than on the keyboard. For example, CONTROL+L on the keyboard is mapped to ^O in the menu (which toggles Ortho), and CONTROL+R is mapped to ^V (which moves you from one floating viewport to the next). These inconsistencies came about when Windows took over some of AutoCAD's original keyboard shortcuts.

When you customize the menu, you can create keyboard shortcuts in two ways:

✦ You can use a name tag, such as ID_Spell, followed by a label in brackets containing the keyboard shortcut. When you execute the shortcut, AutoCAD looks for the name tag in the rest of the menu file and executes the command attached to that name tag.

✦ You can start with the label containing the shortcut, such as [CONTROL+"L"], and follow it with the menu macro you want the shortcut to execute. Use this method to create shortcuts for macros that do not exist elsewhere in the menu.

Table 33-5 lists the expressions you need to use for all the keys you can use to create shortcuts. When you include CONTROL+ before a key, you need to hold down the Ctrl key as you press the key. You can also use SHIFT+ for the Shift key. You can also use both: CONTROL+SHIFT+.

Caution In general, you should not reassign the commonly used Windows shortcuts, such as Ctrl+C (to copy data to the clipboard), Ctrl+V (to paste data from the clipboard), and so on.

New Feature Since Release 2000i, you can also create keyboard shortcuts in a dialog box.

Choose Tools ⇨ Customize ⇨ Keyboard to open the Customize dialog box with the Keyboard tab on top, shown in Figure 33-15. When you use the dialog box to create keyboard shortcuts, you can use only the function keys, Ctrl+, Ctrl+Shift+, and Ctrl+Alt+ combinations.

Table 33-5 Expressions for Keys in the Accelerators Section of the Menu File	
Key	**Expression**
F1–F12	"F1," "F2," and so on
Insert	"INSERT"
Delete	"DELETE"
Arrow keys	"UP," "DOWN," "LEFT," "RIGHT" — must be used with the Ctrl key
Numeric keypad	"NUMPAD0," "NUMPAD1," and so on through "NUMPAD9"

Figure 33-15: Use the Keyboard tab of the Customize dialog box to easily create keyboard shortcuts without having to open the menu file.

To specify a keyboard shortcut for a command or toolbar button, follow these steps:

1. From the Categories drop-down list, choose a menu or toolbar. You can also choose AutoCAD Commands at the bottom of the list to display an alphabetical list of all AutoCAD commands. The choice you make determines your options; for example, the Draw menu includes many Circle and Arc options that are not available if you choose the Draw toolbar.

2. From the Commands drop-down list, choose the command you want to use.

3. Click the Press New Shortcut Key text box. Then use the keyboard to press the keyboard shortcut you want. For example, press F12 or Ctrl+3.

4. Click Assign.

5. If you want, continue to assign keyboard shortcuts to other commands.

6. When you're done, click Close to close the dialog box.

Your changes are saved to the `.mns file` with the Menu Group specified in the Menu Group text box. In order for your shortcuts to work, the Windows Standard Accelerator Keys check box on the User Preferences tab of the Options dialog box (choose Tools ➪ Options) must be checked; however, it is checked by default.

To remove a keyboard shortcut, click the shortcut in the Current Keys section of the Customize dialog box and click Remove. To view all your shortcuts, click Show All.

On the CD-ROM The drawing used in the following Step-by-Step exercise on creating keyboard shortcuts, `ab5.mnu`, is in the `Results` folder of the *AutoCAD 2004 Bible* CD-ROM.

Step-by-Step: Creating Keyboard Shortcuts

1. If you haven't already done so, copy `acad.mnu`, `acad.mns`, `acad.mnc`, `acad.mnr`, and `acad.mnl` to one or more floppy disks.

Note By default, acad.mnu, acad.mns, acad.mnc, acad.mnr, and acad.mnl are in \Documents and Settings\[user name]\Application Data\Autodesk\AutoCAD 2004\R16.0\enu\Support. However, your location may be different, depending on your operating system and customization. To find the location of acad.mns, acad.mns, acad.mnc, acad.mnr, and acad.mnl, choose Tools ➪ Options and click the Files tab. Double-click the first item, Support File Search Path, to display the location of the support files.

Caution Do not continue with this exercise until you have completed Step 1. If you are working on someone else's computer, ask permission before doing this exercise.

2. Use Notepad to open `ab5.mnu` from the `Results` folder of the CD-ROM. If you did the previous exercise and copied `ab5.mnu` to your hard disk, open it from there.

3. Type the following at the end of the file and then press Enter:

```
***ACCELERATORS
[CONTROL+"E"]'osmode 1
[CONTROL+"7"]'osmode 7
[CONTROL "up"]'snap 1
[CONTROL "down"]'snap .25
```

The code `osmode 1` sets an endpoint object snap; `osmode 7` sets object snaps for endpoint, midpoint, and center.

4. If you did the previous exercise, save the file as `ab6.mnu` in the same location as `ab5.mnu`. If you opened `ab5.mnu` from the CD-ROM, save it as `ab6.mnu` in your AutoCAD support folder or another folder in AutoCAD's support file search path. Note that the file is still `Menu Group AB4`. Minimize Notepad.

5. Open a new drawing using the `acad.dwt` template. Choose Tools ➪ Customize ➪ Menus. Make sure that the Replace All check box is not checked. On the Menu Groups tab, in the File Name text box, type **ab6.mnu** and click Load. Click Yes at the message warning you about overwriting toolbar changes. AutoCAD loads the menu file.

6. Choose the Menu Bar tab. Choose Window on the Menu Bar list and click Insert. AutoCAD inserts the partial menu to the left of the Window menu. Click Close.

7. Choose Tools ➪ Customize ➪ Keyboard. From the Menu Group list, choose ACAD. From the Categories drop-down list, choose the Render toolbar. From the Commands drop-down list, choose Hide.

8. Click the Press New Shortcut Key text box. Press F12. Click Assign and then click Close to close the dialog box.

9. Press Ctrl+up arrow (the up arrow on your keyboard). AutoCAD sets the snap to 1. Press Ctrl+down arrow. AutoCAD sets the snap to 0.25. (If the cursor doesn't snap to the setting, you have polar snap on. Right-click SNAP on the status bar and choose Grid Snap On.)

10. Right-click OSNAP and choose Settings. In the Drafting Settings dialog box, uncheck all object snap modes and click OK.

11. Draw a line and a circle. Start the LINE command. At the `Specify first point:` prompt, press Ctrl+E. Pick either endpoint of the line. At the `Specify next point or [Undo]:` prompt, point to the circle and verify that you can't find its Center object snap.

12. Press Ctrl+7 (on the keyboard). Now pick the circle's Center object snap and end the LINE command.

13. Start the BOX command and create a box of any dimensions. From the View flyout on the Standard toolbar, choose SE Isometric View. Press F12. AutoCAD uses the HIDE command to hide the view.

14. Choose Tools ➪ Customize ➪ Menus to unload the AB4 menu group. Don't save your drawing.

Summary

In this chapter, you read how to customize the menu to suit your situation and speed up your everyday work. Menu customization is very powerful. When you start customizing your menus, you suddenly find yourself thinking of new ways to use this option. The result will be a major improvement in the way AutoCAD serves your needs.

This chapter ends Part VI, "Customizing AutoCAD." Part VII challenges you to go further in your customization of AutoCAD by starting to program with AutoLISP and Visual Basic for Applications.

✦ ✦ ✦

Programming AutoCAD

◆ ◆ ◆ ◆

In This Part

◆ ◆ ◆ ◆

Part VII invites you to go the distance and start programming AutoCAD with AutoLISP, Visual LISP, and Visual Basic for Applications (VBA). AutoLISP is a powerful programming language that lets you quickly create your own commands and routines tailored to your needs. Visual LISP adds an easy-to-use interface to AutoLISP programming.

VBA is a programming language that is supported by many Windows applications. You can create programs and dialog boxes for AutoCAD with VBA. Using ActiveX, which lets you access other Windows applications, you can write programs that integrate AutoCAD with other applications.

Understanding AutoLISP and Visual LISP Basics

AutoLISP is a programming language that can substantially enhance your productivity by automating often-used or repetitive tasks. AutoLISP provides a glimpse into the inner workings of AutoCAD and can serve as an excellent stepping stone to learning more advanced automation methods, such as ObjectARX and VBA. An AutoLISP routine gives you complete control of its interaction with the user and what it does once it is loaded.

AutoLISP expressions can be typed at the command line in response to prompts or can be saved to a file to be loaded and used when needed. AutoLISP offers wide and varied possibilities for shortcuts. Best of all, AutoLISP can be customized to any level of complexity.

AutoLISP intimidates many AutoCAD users, but this fear is unwarranted. The many benefits of AutoLISP well justify the initial time you invest to learn this rich and full-featured programming language.

The number of AutoLISP routines available to the user is tremendous. Every office with more than a trivial number of AutoCAD workstations has probably created at least one AutoLISP routine to expedite some common task.

Many of the commands you already use in AutoCAD are in AutoLISP routines, including 3DARRAY, MVSETUP, AI_BOX, and others. Users of AutoLISP often get examples of how to handle complex problems by reviewing these applications.

LISP stands for *LISt Processing*, and as you will see in the next chapter, the understanding of lists is crucial to using AutoLISP.

Most AutoLISP routines define a command name, which you then type at the command line to run the routine. Some routines include a dialog box to help you choose options and specifications.

Introducing Visual LISP

Visual LISP (VLISP) is an integrated development environment (IDE) that provides an easy-to-use interface to help you create code, debug errors, and test programs.

Some useful Visual LISP features include:

✦ Syntax checker and highlighting to help correct syntax errors

✦ File compilation for security and faster execution

✦ Debugger, with support for stepping through source code to find errors

✦ Helpful Inspect and Watch windows for querying a value or examining a variable during execution

✦ Context-sensitive help

✦ Management of multiple file applications from a project window

✦ Compiled multiple projects, as well as other files, using the application wizard

✦ Console history, which makes it possible to recall previously entered information

Opening Visual LISP

To start Visual LISP, you can either type **Vlide** ↵ at the AutoCAD command prompt, or choose Tools ➪ AutoLISP ➪ Visual LISP Editor. At any time, you can switch to Visual LISP using either of these methods. Figure 34-1 shows your screen after you open Visual LISP.

AutoLISP and Visual LISP are discussed throughout Chapters 34, 35, and 36. While this book does not provide complete coverage of either AutoLISP or Visual LISP, many of the major features are explained within these three chapters.

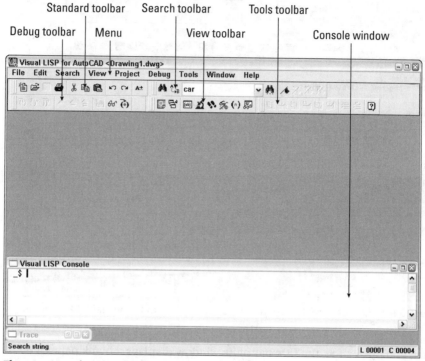

Figure 34-1: The Visual LISP window

Opening and loading an AutoLISP file with Visual LISP

As soon as you are in the Visual LISP environment, you can create a new AutoLISP file or open an existing file.

To edit or view a file in the Visual LISP text editor, follow these steps:

1. Choose File ➪ Open File from the Visual LISP menu.

2. In the Open File to Edit/View dialog box, locate and choose the file you want to open.

3. Click Open. Visual LISP opens the file in its own window, as shown in Figure 34-2.

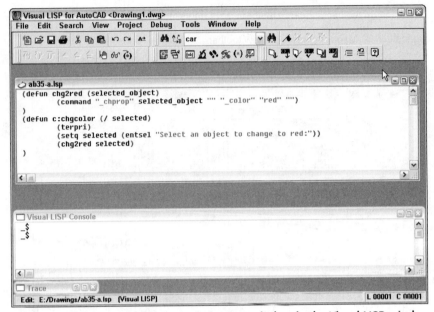

Figure 34-2: An AutoLISP file open in its own window in the Visual LISP window

When you open a file, the title bar of its window displays a blank paper icon to show that the file has not been changed. If you make any changes to the file, Visual LISP adds a pencil to the image to show that you have edited the file.

You can open as many files as you want.

Loading an AutoLISP file

To use the AutoLISP program in AutoCAD, you must load it. You can load it from within Visual LISP or from within AutoCAD.

If you have a file open in Visual LISP, choose Tools ➪ Load Text in Editor or choose Load Active Edit Window from the Tools toolbar.

If you are in AutoCAD, you can load AutoLISP files into AutoCAD in two ways. One method is on the command line. To load 3DARRAY from the command line, type **(load "3darray")** ↵. The parentheses are required, and they indicate that you are entering an AutoLISP expression. AutoLISP requires the quotation marks because you are specifying a file name. AutoCAD responds with 3DARRAY loaded.

When you enter the command to load 3DARRAY, AutoCAD searches all support paths for a file called 3darray.lsp. At installation time, AutoCAD automatically configures the support file search path to include the path of \AutoCAD 2004\Support. For a full list of folders in the support file search path, choose Tools ➪ Options and click the Files tab. Double-click the Support File Search Path item.

Note AutoLISP files have the extension of `.lsp`. However, for security and speed, you can compile AutoLISP routines as `.fas` or `.vlx` project application files. AutoCAD loads `.vlx` first, then `.fas`, and `.lsp` files last. For example, if you have both a `redline.vlx` and a `redline.lsp`, AutoCAD loads the `redline.vlx` file. If, however, the `.lsp` file is newer than the `.fas` file, AutoCAD will load the `.lsp` file. If an AutoLISP routine is associated with a menu, it has an `.mnl` extension. For more information, see Chapter 33.

If your file is not in a folder in AutoCAD's support file search path, you must specify the full path name. To specify the full path to the routine type, you would enter:

```
(load "c:/Program Files/AutoCAD 2004/Support/3darray") /↵
```

or

```
(load "c:\\Program Files\\AutoCAD 2004\\Support\\3darray") ↵
```

The backslash (\) has special meaning in AutoLISP, and you therefore need to use two of them or a regular slash (/) when specifying a path. (The backslash character tells AutoLISP to interpret the following character as a special control code. To use a double quote in an AutoLISP expression, for example, precede it with a backslash.)

You can also load AutoLISP routines with the APPLOAD command by choosing Tools ➪ Load Application or by typing **appload** ↵ at the command line. AutoCAD opens the Load/Unload Applications dialog box, shown in Figure 34-3.

Figure 34-3: The Load/Unload Applications dialog box

Use this dialog box to load .fax, .vlx, and .lsp files. (You can also load other types of programming files in this dialog box—ARX, DVB, and DBX files.) If you check Add to History, AutoCAD lists previously loaded applications in the dialog box—just click the History List tab. Locate and choose the file you want to load and click Load.

Using an AutoLISP routine in AutoCAD

After you load an AutoLISP routine, you can use it. How you use the routine depends on the routine. If the program creates a function, you can type the function's name on the command line like any other AutoCAD command. Most routines contain prompts to guide you in their use.

On the CD-ROM The AutoLISP file used in the following Step-by-Step exercise on loading and using an AutoLISP routine, circle3.lsp, is in the Drawings folder of the *AutoCAD 2004 Bible* CD-ROM.

Step-by-Step: Loading and Using an AutoLISP Routine

1. Use Windows Explorer to copy circle3.lsp from the CD-ROM to your \AutoCAD 2004\Support\ folder or to a folder you added to the support file search path.

2. Create a new drawing using any template.

3. Choose Tools ➪ AutoLISP ➪ Visual LISP Editor. The Visual LISP IDE opens.

4. If any AutoLISP files are displayed in the main area, click their Close boxes.

5. Choose Open on the Standard Visual LISP toolbar. In the Open dialog box, navigate to the folder where you saved circle3.lsp and double-click it. It appears in the Visual LISP window.

6. Choose Load Active Edit Window from the Visual LISP Tools toolbar. The Visual LISP Console window confirms that circle3.lsp has been loaded.

7. Choose Activate AutoCAD from the Visual LISP View toolbar. Visual LISP returns you to AutoCAD.

8. Now that circle3 has been loaded, at the command prompt, type **circle3** ⏎.

9. At the Please click a point: prompt, pick any point on-screen. You see a 3-unit radius circle with its center at the point you picked, as shown in Figure 34-4.

10. Save your drawing in your AutoCAD Bible folder as ab34-01.dwg.

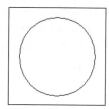

Figure 34-4: The circle drawn using the `circle3` AutoLISP routine

Looking at an AutoLISP routine

To examine the contents of the `circle3.lsp` file, open it in the Visual LISP editor. Figure 34-5 shows the `circle3` routine. At this point, ignore the color formatting, which is discussed later in this chapter.

```
circle3.lsp
(defun c:circle3 (/ pt) ;Creates a circle of radius 3
  (princ "Please click a point: ")
  (setq pt (getpoint))
  (command "_circle" pt "3")
)
```

Figure 34-5: The `circle3` AutoLISP routine

This figure illustrates several general characteristics of AutoLISP routines:

✦ As in many programming languages, indentation is used in AutoLISP to make it easier to read the code. It has no effect on the operation of the routine.

✦ The returns at the end of each line also make it easier to read and understand the code. All five lines could be placed on a single line, and the program would work exactly the same way.

✦ All AutoLISP statements are placed in parentheses. Therefore, whenever you open a parenthesis you must close it. Every AutoLISP routine must have the same number of left and right parentheses. The physical location of a right parenthesis is not relevant — it can be placed on a new line or positioned several spaces away from the left parenthesis. In both cases, the pair is interpreted the same way.

✦ AutoLISP is interpreted from the innermost parenthetical elements first. On line three of the code shown in Figure 34-5, for instance, `(getpoint)` is done first, and then the result is used for the `(setq pt (getpoint))` expression. This is analogous to mathematics, as in the expression $(3 + (5 \times 4))$, where 5×4 is computed first and the result is added to 3.

✦ At the end of the first line is a comment, ;Creates a circle of radius 3. The program ignores any text preceded by a semicolon. Use this technique to place explanations in your routines to help you and others understand what the routine is doing.

The following explains the routine in Figure 34-5 line by line:

✦ Line 1 begins with an open parenthesis that is balanced with the one on line 5. This pair of parentheses delineates the body of the function. The line begins with defun, which means *DEFine FUNction*, and the function is called c:circle3. When you prefix the function with c:, you can use it in AutoCAD by just entering **circle3** at the command line like any other AutoCAD command. (The c: stands for command and has no relation to your hard drive, which is also usually called c:.) You could use just circle3, but you would have to type **(circle3)** at the command line to use the routine. The last item on Line 1 is (/ pt). The pt after the slash means that pt is a *local variable*. A variable stores a value for later use in the routine. A local variable is used only in its own routine and is not retained for use in other routines. If you replaced (/ pt) with simply () the pt variable would be available to other AutoLISP routines as well.

✦ Line 2 is the simplest line in this routine — it simply prints the statement Please click a point: at the command line. Anything in the quotes after princ will be printed on the AutoCAD command line. In this case, the statement is used as a prompt to tell the user to pick a point.

✦ Line 3 is typical of AutoLISP routines in which nested parentheses can drive the reader crazy. Remember to read from the innermost parenthetical element outward. So reading from the innermost parenthetical element, you have first (getpoint). This means to simply get a point. Any of the AutoCAD input methods work — clicking the screen, typing coordinates for a point, or using object snaps. Reading outward you have (setq pt (getpoint)). The statement setq means that the variable pt is set to whatever comes back from getpoint. So if you enter the coordinates 2,2 by typing them or selecting them on the screen, the variable pt equals 2,2.

✦ Line 4 reads (command "_circle" pt "3"). The command function in AutoLISP is one of the easier functions to understand. It simply executes whatever AutoCAD command is specified in the quotes that follow, using all subsequent arguments. When the CIRCLE command is invoked in AutoCAD, it asks for the center point first and then the radius. Line 4 starts the CIRCLE command, uses for the center point whatever is assigned to the variable pt, and sets the radius to 3 units.

Note An underscore precedes the CIRCLE command so that it can be translated into other language versions of AutoCAD.

Using the Visual LISP interface

The Visual LISP window contains a number of tools that make your programming life simpler. These tools represent the difference between the old way of writing AutoLISP code — creating text files in a text editor — and the new visual way, with tools that help you format and complete your code. Some of the most useful tools include:

✦ **Format Edit Window:** Choose Format Edit Window on the Tools toolbar (or choose Tools ⇨ Format Code in Editor) to indent code (and comments) so that it is more readable. Indenting code helps you understand levels of nested parentheses more clearly. Of course, you can indent your code manually, but automatic indenting is a boon to all AutoLISP programmers.

✦ **Format Selection:** Select the code you want to format. Then choose Format Selection on the Tools toolbar (or choose Tools ⇨ Format Code in Selection) to indent only the selected code.

✦ **Check Edit Window:** Choose Check Edit Window from the Tools toolbar (or choose Tools ⇨ Check Text in Editor) to perform a preliminary evaluation prior to loading the file. This evaluation checks the code for unbalanced parentheses, invalid function definition formatting (an attempt to redefine a built-in or protected function), and many other common errors. Visual LISP opens the Build Output window to show you the results.

✦ **Check Selection:** Select the code you want to check. Choose Check Selection from the Tools toolbar (or choose Tools ⇨ Check Selection) to perform a preliminary evaluation on selected code. Visual LISP opens the Build Output window to show you the results.

✦ **Parentheses Matching:** The most common error for an AutoLISP programmer is incorrect parentheses matching. Visual LISP enables you to jump between matching parentheses and quickly check your current nesting level as you develop your application. While you can use the menu items (choose Edit ⇨ Parentheses Matching ⇨ Match Forward and Match Backward), you will find the keyboard shortcuts distract you less from the code you are looking at. To find a matching right parenthesis, press Ctrl+]. To find a left matching parenthesis, press Ctrl+[.

Tip

You can highlight all the code between matching parentheses. To highlight from left to right, place the cursor in front of a left parenthesis and press Ctrl+Shift+] or simply double-click. To highlight from right to left (backwards), place the cursor after a right parenthesis and press Ctrl+Shift+[or double-click.

✦ **Load Selection:** You have already seen how to load the code in the active window. You can also load selected code. Select the code you want to load and choose Load Selection from the Tools toolbar or choose Tools ⇨ Load Selection.

✦ ▤ **Comment Block:** In Figure 34-5, you see an example of a comment. Visual LISP supports several comment styles, which Chapter 35 covers. Visual LISP simplifies the addition of a 3-semicolon comment. To place a 3-semicolon comment, highlight the text you wish to change into a comment and click Comment Block on the Tools toolbar. See Chapter 35 for more information on creating comments.

✦ ▤ **Uncomment Block:** To remove a 3-semicolon comment, click Uncomment Block on the Tools toolbar.

Another feature of Visual LISP is the Console window. The Console window usually resides at the bottom of the Visual LISP window. The Console window is similar to the AutoCAD command line. Just as you can enter AutoLISP expressions on the AutoCAD command line, as explained later in this chapter, you can also enter AutoLISP expressions in the Console window and see the results. Each line uses a _$ prompt.

A nice feature of the Console window is that Visual LISP remembers everything you enter. You can retrieve it by pressing Tab for a forward history or Shift+Tab for a backward history.

Closing a file and Visual LISP

To close a file within Visual LISP, click its Close button. (You can also press Ctrl+F4.) To exit Visual LISP, click its Close button or press Alt+F4. As with AutoCAD, Visual LISP warns you about saving your changes.

On the CD-ROM The file used in the following Step-by-Step exercise on using the Visual LISP interface, ab34-a.lsp, is in the Drawings folder of the *AutoCAD 2004 Bible* CD-ROM.

Step-by-Step: Using the Visual LISP Interface

1. From AutoCAD, choose Tools ➪ AutoLISP ➪ Visual LISP Editor to open Visual LISP.

2. Choose Open File on the Visual LISP Standard toolbar and open ab34-a.lsp from the CD-ROM. Save the file as ab34-1.lsp in your AutoCAD Bible folder.

3. ▣ Choose Format Edit Window on the Tools toolbar. AutoCAD automatically formats the code.

4. Select the line of the code that reads:

```
(command "_circle" pt "3")
```

5. ▤ Choose Comment Block. AutoCAD places three semicolons before the text and shades it. Choose Uncomment Block. AutoCAD returns the code to its previous state.

6. ▽ Choose Check Edit Window on the toolbar. AutoCAD opens the Build Output window and issues the Check done message.

7. Click anywhere in the edit window to activate it. Choose Load Active Edit Window on the toolbar. AutoCAD loads the routine.

8. In the Visual LISP Console window, type **(c:circle3)** and press Enter. Visual LISP returns you to AutoCAD and starts the program. Pick a point. When you are done, you are automatically returned to the Visual LISP window.

9. Click the text editor window and choose Save File. Click the Close button at the top-right corner of the text editor window to close the routine.

10. Click the Close button at the top-right corner of your screen to close Visual LISP.

Getting Help in Visual LISP

Visual LISP offers two ways for you to get help while writing AutoLISP code — context-sensitive help on any term you select and the overall help system.

To get help on any AutoLISP function in your code, select the function (either in the edit window or in the Console window) and choose Help on the Visual LISP Tools toolbar. Figure 34-6 shows the screen that appears when you select setq and choose Help.

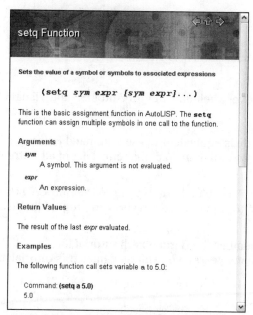

Figure 34-6: When you select any AutoLISP function in your code and choose Help, Visual LISP opens the help page for that function.

To open the entire Visual LISP and ActiveX Help system, choose Help ➪ Visual LISP
Help Topics on the Visual LISP menu or Press F1. Visual LISP displays the screen
shown in Figure 34-7.

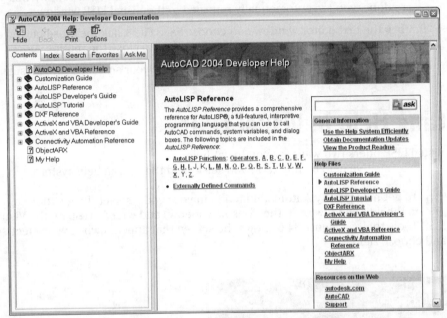

Figure 34-7: The main help page of Visual LISP's help system

All these help features can be a bit overwhelming, but for AutoLISP and Visual LISP
you basically have three choices:

- ✦ **AutoLISP Reference:** This guide is equivalent to the Command Reference in
 AutoCAD's help system. Here you will find an alphabetical list of all AutoLISP
 functions.

- ✦ **AutoLISP Developer's Guide:** This guide is equivalent to the AutoCAD User's
 Guide. It contains all the basic topics you need to know to program in Visual
 LISP.

- ✦ **AutoLISP Tutorial:** If you remember the Garden Path tutorial for AutoLISP
 (which has been around for many years), you will recognize this tutorial, now
 rewritten for Visual LISP.

Working with AutoLISP Expressions

As with any programming language, AutoLISP has its own functions and syntax.
This section explains how to start writing AutoLISP code. One big advantage to

AutoLISP is that you can test your code immediately, unlike the case of compiled languages for which extra steps are required. For compiled languages, every time a code change is made, the code must be recompiled and re-linked before you can see the changes in AutoCAD. This is the case with ObjectARX, for example.

Understanding AutoLISP syntax

All programming languages have syntax—such as the grammar and syntax of any language. In AutoLISP, an operator always comes first, followed by a number of operands. An operator can be thought of as a function that does something, and the operands are what the function operates on. Place a space between each component of the statement.

Another way to describe the syntax of AutoLISP is that within each set of parentheses the first item is a function, and what follows are parameters or arguments to that function.

Working with numbers and text

Table 34-1 lists the basic arithmetic functions. You can use these functions on anything that has a value. For example, if you create a variable with a value of 2, you can use that variable with the arithmetic functions.

<table>
<tr><th colspan="2">Table 34-1
Basic Arithmetic Functions</th></tr>
<tr><th>Function</th><th>Description</th></tr>
<tr><td>+</td><td>Addition</td></tr>
<tr><td>-</td><td>Subtraction</td></tr>
<tr><td>*</td><td>Multiplication</td></tr>
<tr><td>/</td><td>Division</td></tr>
<tr><td>sqrt</td><td>Square root</td></tr>
</table>

Table 34-1 lists only a few fundamental arithmetic operators (or functions). Many operators are available to the AutoLISP programmer; you can find them in the AutoLISP Function Synopsis Appendix of the AutoLISP Developer's Guide, under Basic Functions ⇨ Arithmetic Functions.

Some fundamental arithmetic operations can provide a feel for the fundamentals. If you type the following on the AutoCAD command line (being careful to put a blank space after the + and the 2),

```
(+ 2 3) ↵
```

AutoLISP responds with 5. This syntax of having the operator (the plus sign) come before the operands (2 and 3) is very different from that of many languages, but is important to understand in AutoLISP.

To nest expressions, simply add another set of parentheses to enclose the nested expression. For example, when you enter **(* 5 (+ 2 3))**, AutoCAD responds with 25.

The nested expression is evaluated from the innermost parenthesis pair out; first two and three are added, and then that sum is multiplied by five. This is the bread and butter of AutoLISP.

Working with floating point numbers (numbers with decimal points) is as easy as working with integers. If you type **(/ 7.3 5.84)** ↵ AutoLISP responds with 1.25.

Note If you are using a number less than 1, you must include the leading zero, as in (+ 2.5 0.5).

Working with text is as easy as working with numbers, but operations such as addition, subtraction, multiplication, and division have no meaning when operating on text. In AutoLISP, a *string* is simply some text. Table 34-2 lists some common string functions.

<table>
<tr><td colspan="2">Table 34-2
Basic String Functions</td></tr>
<tr><td>*Function*</td><td>*Description*</td></tr>
<tr><td>STRCAT</td><td>Concatenates (attaches) strings to one another.</td></tr>
<tr><td>SUBSTR</td><td>Returns (provides you with) a substring (a portion) of a string. The first argument is the string, the second is an integer that specifies the position of the first character you want, and the third (optional) is the number of characters you want.</td></tr>
<tr><td>STRLEN</td><td>Calculates string length; returns the number of characters including spaces in the string.</td></tr>
</table>

Here are two examples:

```
(strcat "Today is " "a good day" ".")
"Today is a good day."
(substr "Today is a good day." 12 4)
"good"
```

STRCAT stands for *STRing conCATenate* and appends one string with another. Any number of strings can come after the STRCAT function. (There are three strings enclosed in quotes in the STRCAT example.)

SUBSTR stands for *SUBSTRing,* and in this example, it returns the four characters starting at position 12 as shown in the example.

Note The first character of the string for SUBSTR is number 1. However, other functions that process elements of a list (such as NTH) count the first element as 0.

Table 34-3 offers you a few more functions that work with numbers and strings.

Table 34-3
AutoLISP Functions for Numbers and Strings

Function	Description
ABS	Returns the absolute value of the argument. (abs -76) returns 76.
ASCII	Returns the ASCII code of a character. (ASCII "B") returns 66.
CHR	Returns the text string for an ASCII code. (CHR 66) returns "B". (Stands for character.)
ATOI	Converts a string to an integer. (ATOI "2.7") returns 2. (Stands for ASCII to integer.)
ATOF	Converts a string to a real number. (ATOF "7.6") returns 7.6. (Stands for ASCII to float, as in floating point, that is, a real number.)
ITOA	Converts an integer to a text string. (ITOA 76) returns "76". (Stands for integer to ASCII.)
RTOS	Converts a real number to a text string, enclosed in quotes. You can add a mode (1=scientific, 2=decimal, 3=engineering, 4=architectural, 5=fractional) and a precision. Otherwise, RTOS uses the current settings. (RTOS 87.3 2 2) returns "87.30". (Stands for real to string.)
=	Equal to. Returns T for true if all arguments are numerically equal. (= 3 3.0) returns T. If the arguments are not equal, it returns nil.
/=	Not equal to. Returns T if all arguments are not numerically equal. (/= 5 6) returns T. If they are equal, it returns nil.
<	Less than. Returns T if each argument is numerically less than the next argument. Otherwise returns nil.
>	Greater than. Returns T if each argument is numerically greater than the next argument. Otherwise returns nil.
>=	Greater than or equal to. Returns T if each argument is numerically greater than or equal to the next argument. Otherwise returns nil.
<=	Less than or equal to. Returns T if each argument is numerically less than or equal to the next argument. Otherwise returns nil.

Using AutoLISP on the Command Line

AutoLISP can be used on the fly in AutoCAD because it is *interpreted*. By typing an expression on the command line, you get the result immediately. An interpreted language is one in which a single source statement is translated to machine language, executed, and then each subsequent source statement is operated on in the same way. This enables interactive entry of AutoLISP code into AutoCAD.

The output of an AutoLISP expression can be used in response to AutoCAD prompts as well. For example, you can type **(+ 1 7)** at the `Diameter/<Radius>:` prompt of the CIRCLE command for a circle with a radius of 8 units.

This capability to place AutoLISP expressions into AutoCAD commands is a very powerful tool.

AutoCAD enables you to edit the command line, which is very useful when experimenting with AutoLISP expressions. You can use the left and right arrow keys, as well as the Delete and Backspace keys. You can also open the Text Window (press F2), select any previous line, right-click, and choose Paste to CmdLine. This action copies the line to the current command line where you can press Enter to execute it or edit it first. Also, any previously used line can be placed on the command line by pressing the up-arrow key several times.

If you leave out a closing parenthesis, AutoCAD returns (_> when you press Enter. This tells you that one open parenthesis has not been closed. If two open parentheses remain to be closed, AutoCAD responds with ((_>. Just type the correct number of closing parentheses at the command line and press Enter. AutoCAD accepts the expression.

Step-by-Step: Working with Numbers and Text on the Command Line

1. Open a new drawing using the `acad.dwt` template.

2. Type **circle** ↵. Follow the prompts:

   ```
   Specify center point for circle or [3P/2P/Ttr (tan tan
   radius)]: Pick any point.
   Specify radius of circle or [Diameter]: (- 5 3) ↵
   ```

 AutoCAD draws a circle with a radius of 2.

3. Type **(strcat "This is an example of " "regular text.")** ↵. Don't forget the space between "of" and the quotation mark. When the two phrases are put together, this creates the space between "of" and "regular." AutoCAD returns `"This is an example of regular text."`

4. Press the up-arrow key. AutoCAD repeats the last line. Press the left-arrow key to move to the right of the last *r* in "regular" and press Backspace to delete the word "regular." Type **italic** ↵. AutoCAD returns the new string concatenation.

5. Save the drawing in your AutoCAD Bible folder as ab34-02.dwg.

Note When you create AutoLISP expressions on the command line or in the Console window, they are not saved with the drawing. They have the same status as any input you type at the command line.

Creating AutoLISP Files

If you want to use your AutoLISP expressions more than a couple of times, you should save them in a file. Create the routine in Visual LISP and choose Save File.

Tip A common practice is to consolidate all AutoLISP routines in one folder for ease of use. To do this, you can create a folder called LISP in any drive or folder where you keep files that you create and then choose Tools ⇨ Options. On the Files tab, expand the Support File Search Path and click Add. Add the path by typing it directly in the edit box or clicking Browse and navigating to it.

Because AutoCAD can open multiple drawings (called *Multiple Drawing Interface*, or MDI), you need to organize your AutoLISP routines based on whether you want them to apply to all drawings or just the first drawing you open.

AutoCAD offers two .lsp files that you can use for your AutoLISP routines:

✦ **Acad.lsp:** Use this file for routines that customize the initialization of AutoCAD. Acad.lsp is not automatically loaded for every consecutive drawing. For example, if you want to load a special menu for only a specific drawing, you could put the routine in acad.lsp. (You can choose to load acad.lsp with every drawing. Choose Tools ⇨ Options and click on the System tab. In the General Options section, check the Load Acad.lsp with Every Drawing check box.)

✦ **Acaddoc.lsp:** Use this file for routines that customize the initialization of individual drawings. This file is loaded every time a drawing is opened. If you have a menu that contains AutoLISP macros that include variables you want available for all your drawings, put the AutoLISP routines used by the menu in acaddoc.lsp.

Because of the AutoCAD Multiple Document Interface (MDI), each drawing contains its own AutoLISP environment. AutoLISP files you load in one drawing — and their variables — will not be accessible to another drawing. To share functions, use (vl-load-all "filename") instead of (load "filename"), where filename is the name of the AutoLISP file, to "populate" every current drawing, as well as any new drawing you may create. The VL-LOAD-ALL function is equivalent to placing an AutoLISP routine in acaddoc.lsp.

To create a new Visual LISP file, open the Visual LISP Editor (chooseTools ⇨ AutoLISP ⇨ Visual LISP Editor) and choose File ⇨ New File or choose New File on the Standard toolbar. Visual LISP opens an untitled document, as shown in Figure 34-8. You can now start typing code in the new document. When you start typing, you immediately notice that your code looks different than it would if you had typed it in a text editor — it's in color! Visual LISP has the capability to distinguish certain features in your code and colors it accordingly. Table 34-4 lists the colors and their meanings.

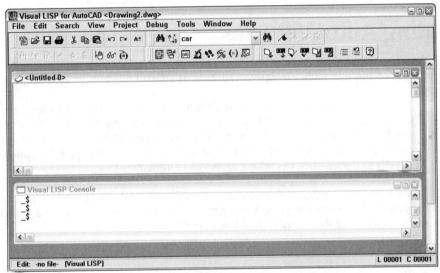

Figure 34-8: A new AutoLISP document in the Visual LISP editor

Table 34-4
Visual LISP Editor Coloring System

Color	AutoLISP Syntax Element
Blue	Built-in functions and protected symbols
Magenta	Text strings
Green	Integers
Teal	Real numbers
Purple on gray background	Comments
Red	Parentheses
Black	Unrecognized items such as variables you have created

If you want, you can customize these colors. From the Visual LISP menu, choose Tools ⇨ Window Attributes ⇨ Configure Current. In the Window Attributes dialog box, choose an element from the drop-down box and pick a color from the color swatches. You can also change the left margin and the tab width in this dialog box.

Step-by-Step: Creating a New Visual LISP File

1. Start a new drawing using any template. You shouldn't have any other drawings open.

2. Choose Tools ⇨ AutoLISP ⇨ Visual LISP Editor.

3. ▨ Choose New File from the Visual LISP Standard toolbar.

4. Type the following:

```
draws a horizontal line 3 units long
(defun c:line3 (/ pt)
(princ "Please pick a point: ")
(setq pt (getpoint))
(command "_line" pt "@3,0" "")
)
```

5. Select the first line of text and choose Comment Block from the Tools toolbar.

6. Choose Format Edit Window from the Tools toolbar to format the code.

7. Choose Check Edit Window and look at the result in the Build Output window.

8. Click the Visual LISP Editor to activate it again.

9. Choose Load Active Edit Window to load the routine.

10. Choose Activate AutoCAD from the View toolbar.

11. On the command line, type **line3** ↵.

12. At the `Please pick a point:` prompt, use any method to specify a point. AutoCAD draws a horizontal line 3 units long.

13. Use the Windows task bar to return to the Visual LISP window.

14. Click the Visual LISP Editor to activate it. Choose Save file on the Visual LISP Standard toolbar. Save the routine as `ab34-02.lsp` in your `AutoCAD Bible` folder.

15. Close the Visual LISP window by clicking its Close button. Do not save your drawing.

Summary

This chapter covers the fundamentals of AutoLISP programming and the Visual LISP environment. You read:

✦ How to open the Visual LISP interface and load and use AutoLISP files.

✦ How to use AutoLISP on the command line

✦ What AutoLISP routines look like

✦ How to get help in Visual LISP

✦ The basic structure of AutoLISP syntax as well as how to work with numbers and text

In the next chapter, you examine how to create variables, work with AutoCAD commands and system variables, modify AutoCAD objects (or entities, as they are often still called in AutoLISP), and work with the fundamental units of AutoLISP, known as lists.

✦ ✦ ✦

Exploring AutoLISP Further

AutoLISP offers many features that enable you to create sophisticated programs. These include variables, function, and conditional structures. You can easily work with drawing coordinates. You can retrieve information about drawing objects and then modify them. Getting input from the user makes your programs interactive.

Creating Variables

A very useful item in most programming languages is the variable. A *variable* is a symbolic name that can be operated on in a given program. An important part of using variables is that you can assign values to them.

The following example sets the value of 3 for a variable named radius.

```
(setq radius 3)
3
```

You can try this example out in Visual LISP in the Console window. If you want to use this variable on the AutoCAD command line, precede it with an exclamation point (!). For example,

```
Command: !radius
3
```

The exclamation point before a variable evaluates the value stored in the variable and returns it to the command line. When you use a variable in the Console window that you have already set, you don't need the exclamation point. The Console knows to assume that everything you type there is an AutoLISP expression.

Assigning strings to a variable is as easy as assigning numerals to a variable:

```
(setq name "Robin")
"Robin"
```

You can also nest AutoLISP expressions — place one inside the other.

```
(setq radius (+ 2 1))
3
```

As explained in the previous chapter, AutoLISP evaluates LISP expressions from the innermost set of parentheses outward. AutoLISP evaluates (+ 2 1) first, and then assigns the result to the variable radius.

Step-by-Step: Using AutoLISP Variables from within AutoCAD

1. Open a drawing using the acad.dwt template.

2. Type **(setq radius (+ 2 1))** ↵. AutoLISP returns 3.

3. Start the CIRCLE command. Specify any center point. At the Specify radius of circle or [Diameter]: prompt, type **!radius** ↵. AutoCAD draws a circle with a radius of 3 units.

4. Type **(setq color "green")** ↵. AutoLISP returns "green".

5. Type **-color** ↵. At the Enter default object color [Truecolor/Colorbook] <BYLAYER>: prompt, type **!color** ↵.

6. Draw a circle. The circle is green because the current color is now green.

7. Save your drawing in your AutoCAD Bible folder as ab35-01.dwg.

Working with AutoCAD Commands

Accessing AutoCAD commands from within AutoLISP is a powerful way to automate commonly used functions. By combining access to commands from AutoLISP with variables as described in the previous section, you gain a great deal of flexibility.

Accessing AutoCAD commands

In the previous chapter when you looked at an AutoLISP routine (see Figure 34-5), you saw an example of the COMMAND function. You use the COMMAND function in AutoLISP to execute AutoCAD commands. This function treats all subsequent operands as if they were typed at the command line interactively. When programming COMMAND functions in AutoLISP, exactly duplicate what you would do at the command line. For example, to draw a line, you follow the steps shown in the following table. The second column shows how you would accomplish the same action in an AutoLISP routine.

Enter **line** at the command line	"line" (or "_line")
Specify the start point for the line	Use a variable, actual coordinates, or pause for user input.
Specify the endpoint	Use a variable, actual coordinates, or pause for user input.
Press Enter to end the LINE command	Use an empty set of two quotation marks to represent pressing Enter either within a command or to end a command.

For example, if you are using the variables startpt and endpt for the start point and endpoint of a line, here's how you would access the LINE command in an AutoLISP expression:

```
(command "_line" startpt endpt "")
```

Creating functions

Functions always begin with the operator DEFUN. You can define three principal types of functions:

✦ The type you have been using thus far precedes the command name defined by DEFUN with c:, which is interpreted by AutoCAD as a command and enables you to use the function by name at the AutoCAD command line. The function becomes usable like any other AutoCAD command.

✦ You can also create a function definition without preceding the name with c:. This type is most valuable when it is called by other AutoLISP operations. If you need to execute it at the command line, you must enclose the function name in parentheses. Similarly, you can execute functions prefixed with a c: as an AutoLISP expression by enclosing the functions in parentheses, such as (c:circle3).

✦ The third type is S::STARTUP. By defining a function (usually in acaddoc.lsp, which is loaded into every drawing) with the name S::STARTUP, every AutoLISP function in the routine will automatically execute after the drawing has fully initialized. The reason for the S::STARTUP function is to ensure that AutoLISP routines that use the COMMAND function run only after AutoCAD fully initializes the components that can execute commands.

When you create an S::STARTUP function, you need to decide where to put it. Chapter 34 briefly explained the difference between acad.lsp and acaddoc.lsp. The need for two files arose because AutoCAD includes MDI, which enables you to open more than one drawing at a time. For more information, see the sidebar "Automatically loading .lsp files." S::STARTUP is a great tool for enhancing productivity. In this way, you can automate whatever general setup operations you normally do at the beginning of a drawing session or for every drawing you open.

Automatically loading .lsp files

AutoCAD automatically loads four AutoLISP files. Two files, `acad2004.lsp` and `acad2004doc.lsp`, are specific to AutoCAD 2004. Autodesk recommends that you reserve these files for AutoCAD use. `Acad2004.lsp` is loaded only once per AutoCAD session when you first load AutoCAD, while `acad2004doc.lsp` is loaded in the initial session and then each time a drawing is opened.

The other two automatically loaded AutoLISP files are reserved for you, the user. These files are `acad.lsp`, which is loaded once per AutoCAD session, and `acaddoc.lsp`, which is loaded every time a drawing is opened. What this means to you is that you can place different initialization routines in each file—one for AutoCAD initialization (`acad.lsp`) and the other for the initial drawing as well as future drawings. You can place an s::STARTUP function in both `acad.lsp` and `acaddoc.lsp`. However, be aware that placing different s::STARTUP functions in both files effectively disables the s::STARTUP function defined in `acad.lsp`.

You must create both `acad.lsp` and `acaddoc.lsp`. However, after you create any AutoLISP routine and save it under either name, you can add additional routines to the same file. AutoCAD 2004 knows to automatically load these files, as long as they exist.

The load order of these initialization files is:

1. `Acad2004.lsp`: Loaded by AutoCAD 2004

2. `Acad.lsp`: User-defined initialization file loaded once upon loading AutoCAD 2004

3. `Acad2004doc.lsp`: Document-level initialization file loaded by AutoCAD 2004

4. `Acaddoc.lsp`: User-defined document-level initialization file

Here's an AutoLISP routine that uses both DEFUN and COMMAND:

```
(defun c:redline (/ startpt endpt)
  (terpri)
  (setq startpt (getpoint "Select the redline start point:"))
  (terpri)
  (setq endpt (getpoint "Select the redline end point:"))
  (command "_line" startpt endpt "")
  (command "_chprop" "_last" "" "_color" "red" "")
  )
```

Here's an explanation of this routine:

✦ The first line of this routine defines a function called `redline`. Because `redline` is preceded by `c:`, you can type **redline** at the command line when using it within AutoCAD. As you may remember from the discussion of the circle3 routine, the expression (`/ startpt endpt`) means that redline has two local variables that are available only to this routine. These variables are used in the next two lines.

✦ The new instruction, `terpri`, on the second and fourth lines tells AutoCAD to print a blank line at the command line. You can use this to improve readability of the prompts. Otherwise, two or more prompts run together on one line.

✦ Reading the third line from the innermost parenthesis pair outward, AutoCAD obtains the redline's start point from the user with the prompt `Select the redline start point:` and sets the variable `startpt` equal to that start point's value. Similarly, the fifth line obtains the redline's endpoint and sets the variable `endpt` to that value.

✦ Line 6 uses the AutoLISP COMMAND function. It issues the LINE command, specifies the start and endpoints, and uses a set of empty quotation marks to replicate pressing Enter to end the LINE command.

✦ Line seven analogously uses the same syntax for the CHPROP command. It issues the CHPROP command, selects the line you just used by using the Last selection option, ends object selection by using the empty set of quotation marks, specifies the Color option, and sets the color to red. Another empty set of quotation marks ends the command.

✦ Line 8 ends the `redline` routine with a closing parenthesis.

To use this routine, you would follow these steps:

1. Open Visual LISP and start a new file.

2. Type the routine.

3. Save the routine as `redline.lsp` and place it in AutoCAD's `Support` folder or any other folder you may have created for AutoLISP routines and added to AutoCAD's support file search path.

4. Load the routine.

5. Switch to AutoCAD.

6. At the command prompt, type **redline** ↵.

7. In response to the prompts for the start point and endpoint of the redline, choose any two points onscreen. AutoCAD draws a red line between the two points selected.

On the CD-ROM The file `redline.lsp` is on your *AutoCAD 2004 Bible* CD-ROM. Feel free to copy it to your system and play around with it. For example, using your knowledge of the circle3 routine discussed in Chapter 34, you could create a red circle.

Here is another example of an AutoLISP routine that creates an S::STARTUP function. It uses several of the features I have been discussing in this chapter.

```
(defun s::startup ()
 (command "_rectang" "_width" "0.1" "0,0" "10,10")
 (command "_text" "8,1" "0.2" "0" "name")
 (command "_text" "8,0.7" "0.2" "0" "date")
 (command "_text" "8, 0.4" "0.2" "0" "revision")
 (command "_zoom" "_extents")
)
```

This routine creates a simple title block and border each time you open a new drawing, as shown in Figure 35-1.

Y

X

name
date
revision

Figure 35-1: The result of the S::STARTUP routine

In order to use this routine—or one of your own—add this to the end of acad-doc.lsp. AutoCAD 2004 does not come with this file, so the first time you want to use it, you must create it.

Caution Before using the s::STARTUP function, be sure an s::STARTUP function does not already exist in the file. Other applications you may have purchased or downloaded may include an s::STARTUP file. Adding a second s::STARTUP could possibly interfere with the operation of these other applications. In Notepad, choose Search ➪ Find and type **s::startup** in the Find what text box. Click Find Next. If an s::STARTUP routine already exists, then add the body of your s::STARTUP function (minus the first line, which already exists) to the end of the existing s::STARTUP routine and save the file.

Creating functions with arguments

You can create functions that accept arguments, sometimes called parameters. An *argument* is a value that must be supplied with the function. The function then uses the value of that argument in its operation.

Earlier in this chapter, I explained that local variables are placed in parentheses after a slash. Arguments go in the same set of parentheses but before the slash. If there are no local variables, you don't need the slash. Here is an example of a function with one argument:

```
(defun chg2red (selected_object)
...
)
```

To actually use this routine in AutoCAD or within another AutoLISP routine, use the format (chg2red selected_object). The argument is sent to the chg2red routine by adding the argument after the function name, all enclosed in parentheses.

Whenever you use the chg2red function within a routine, you must follow it by its argument. You can obtain the argument by using a variable whose value you have set in the routine, by obtaining a value through user input, or by typing in a specific value when you use the function.

The following exercise uses a function that is called from within the routine.

On the CD-ROM

The file used in the following Step-by-Step exercise, ab35-a.lsp, is in the Drawings folder of the *AutoCAD 2004 Bible* CD-ROM. If you haven't already done so, place the CD-ROM in your CD-ROM drive.

Step-by-Step: Using AutoLISP Functions and Commands

1. Start a new drawing using the acad.dwt template.

2. Use Windows Explorer to copy ab35-a.lsp from the CD-ROM to AutoCAD's Support folder or any folder you have created for AutoLISP routines and added to AutoCAD's support file search path. This file is shown in Figure 35-2.

```
(defun chg2red (selected_object)
        (command "_chprop" selected_object "" "_color" "red" "")
)
(defun c:chgcolor (/ selected)
        (terpri)
        (setq selected (entsel "Select an object to change to red:"))
        (chg2red selected)
)
```

Figure 35-2: An AutoLISP routine to change an object's color to red

3. Choose Tools ➪ AutoLISP ➪ Visual LISP Editor. In Visual LISP, open ab35-a.lsp. The routine appears in the Edit window.

4. Choose Load active edit window.

5. Choose Activate AutoCAD.

6. Draw any object.

7. At the command line, type **chgcolor** ↵.

8. At the Select an object to change to red: prompt, select the object you drew in Step 6. Watch its color change to red.

Do not save the routine or your drawing.

Here's how the routine works:

✦ This routine defines a function, chg2red, which is not preceded by c:. It has one argument, selected_object.

✦ What AutoLISP actually ran when you typed **chgcolor** in Step 7 is the function c:chgcolor on the fourth line of the routine. In the last AutoLISP statement in that function — (chg2red selected) — the variable selected is derived from the previous step as a result of the operation entsel (ENTity SELect).

✦ The variable selected is the argument passed to the function chg2red. The function chg2red now knows what object to operate on.

✦ The function chg2red then uses the CHPROP command to change the object's color to red.

Note To actually call this function at the command line, you would need to type **(chg2red arg)**, where arg is an argument (in this case, it must be an entity name). Entity names are discussed later in this chapter.

Working with system variables

AutoCAD has a wide variety of system variables to control the drawing environment. Thankfully, the creators of AutoLISP enabled the AutoLISP programmer to automate setting and retrieve AutoCAD system variables.

Don't get the terms *variable* and *system variable* confused. A variable is a value that is stored for use in a routine. A system variable is an AutoCAD setting that changes how AutoCAD works.

To set or retrieve AutoCAD system variables, you use two operators, SETVAR and GET-VAR, which can be used on AutoCAD system variables. (You can use SETVAR only on system variables that are not read-only.) Here's how they work:

✦ SETVAR stands for *SET VARiable*. You use SETVAR to change a system variable. Place the system variable in quotes, followed by the new value, as in (setvar "cmdecho" 0).

✦ GETVAR stands for *GET VARiable*. It enables you to obtain the value of any system variable. As soon as you have the value, you can set it to a variable. This is often done so that you can return a system variable to its previous value if you have changed it during a routine. Place the system variable in quotes after using GETVAR, as in (getvar "cmdecho").

While you can use SETVAR and GETVAR on many system variables, here are two system variables that are often changed in an AutoLISP routine:

✦ In all the AutoLISP routines created thus far, AutoCAD's command responses could be seen scrolling off the command-line window. The CMDECHO system variable determines whether you see prompts and input during the functioning of AutoLISP's COMMAND function. By default, echoing is on (set to 1). If you set it to zero, you do not see prompts and input, and the functioning of the AutoLISP routine looks cleaner and runs slightly faster.

✦ The FILEDIA system variable turns on and off the display of dialog boxes that enable you to choose files. Turning off this system variable enables you to work with files on the command line in AutoLISP routines.

On the CD-ROM

The file used in the following Step-by-Step exercise, ab35-a.lsp, is in the Drawings folder of the *AutoCAD 2004 Bible* CD-ROM.

Step-by-Step: Using AutoLISP to Work with System Variables

1. If you did the previous exercise and copied ab35-a.lsp to AutoCAD's \Support folder (or another folder you created for AutoLISP routines and added to AutoCAD's support file search path), open it from that folder. If you did not do the previous exercise, copy ab35-a.lsp from the CD-ROM to AutoCAD's \Support folder or another folder in AutoCAD's support file search path.

2. Open a new drawing using the acad.dwt template. Choose Tools ⇨ AutoLISP ⇨ Visual LISP Editor to open Visual LISP. Click Open and open ab35-a.lsp. Edit it to read as follows:

```
(defun chg2red (selected_object)
 (command "_chprop" selected_object "" "_color" "red" "")
 )
(defun c:chgcolor (/ selected old_cmdecho)
 (setq old_cmdecho (getvar "cmdecho"))
 (setvar "cmdecho" 0)
 (terpri)
 (setq selected (entsel "Select an object to change to
red:"))
 (chg2red selected)
 (setvar "cmdecho" old_cmdecho)
 )
```

3. Save the file as ab35-01.lsp in the same location.

4. Choose Load active edit window to load the routine.

5. Draw any object.

6. At the command line, type **chgcolor** ↵.

7. At the Select an object to change to red: prompt, select the object you drew in Step 5. You no longer see the prompts scrolling by. The object you select turns red, and AutoCAD immediately displays the command prompt.

Do not save your drawing.

Here's how this routine works. This discussion assumes you have already read the discussion of the previous routine, which was very similar.

✦ First, you added a new variable, old_cmdecho, to the chgcolor function.

✦ In the following line, you set this variable to the current value of the CMDECHO system variable. You obtained this current value using GETVAR.

✦ You then used SETVAR to set the AutoCAD system variable CMDECHO to zero.

✦ You may need to see the commands echoed for debugging purposes, so it would prove best to return CMDECHO to the value it was set to before running the routine. Therefore, in the last line you use SETVAR again to reset CMDECHO to the variable old_cmdecho, which stored the original value of CMDECHO.

As a result of these changes, the chgcolor program always sets the CMDECHO system variable back to the value it had before being run.

Working with Lists

Lists are the primary structures you work with while programming in AutoLISP. As you work with this chapter you will begin to understand the use of lists to modify objects (also called entities) in the AutoCAD database, and in a variety of other contexts with AutoLISP. AutoCAD represents all object data in a list that contains many smaller lists, but the lists are simple to use and manipulate.

Using lists for coordinates

A list is always enclosed in parentheses with spaces between the elements of the list. One common use for lists is for coordinates, as shown in the following example:

```
(1.0 3.5 2.0)
```

This list represents the X,Y,Z coordinates 1.0,3.5,2.0. You often need to extract one or more of the elements in a list. Table 35-1 shows the common list extraction functions using the example list (1.0 3.5 2.0).

Table 35-1
Basic List Extraction Functions

Function	Pronunciation	Example Output	Description
CAR	car	1.0	Returns the first element in a list
CDR	could-er	(3.5 2.0)	Removes the first element from a list
CADR	cad-er	3.5	Returns the second element in a list
caddr	ca-did-der	2.0	Returns the third element in a list

For more flexibility, you can use the NTH function. Use the NTH function to access any element in a list by passing two arguments that specify the number of the element (items are numbered starting from zero) and the list that you want.

The name of the list is usually a variable set with SETQ:

```
(setq corner (list 1.0 3.5 2.0))
```

In this example, (nth 0 corner) returns 1.0 because 1.0 is the first item in the list corner.

The LIST function creates a list. If all the items in a list are constant values (not variables), you can use the QUOTE function to create a list. You can use a single quote (the same as an apostrophe on the keyboard) as a shortcut for the QUOTE function. The following two functions are equivalent:

```
(setq corner (list 1.0 3.5 2.0))
(setq corner '(1.0 3.5 2.0))
```

Many more AutoLISP list extraction functions are detailed in the AutoLISP Function Synopsis Appendix of the Visual LISP Developer's Guide. Look under Basic Functions, then List Manipulation Functions. You can go a long way by remembering the functions listed here.

Creating dotted pairs

A *dotted pair* is a special type of list that contains only two elements. Some AutoLISP functions do not accept dotted pairs as an argument, but they are used to represent AutoCAD database objects. To construct a dotted pair, use the CONS function:

```
(cons 2.1 4.5)
```

This example returns (2.1 . 4.5). This list type is known as a *dotted pair* because it contains exactly two elements, and the elements are separated by a period or dot.

Step-by-Step: Working with AutoLISP Lists

1. Start a new drawing using the acad.dwt template.

2. Choose Tools ➪ AutoLISP ➪ Visual LISP Editor to open Visual LISP.

3. In the Visual LISP Console window, type **(setq endpt '(3.5 2.0 1.4))** ↵. AutoLISP returns (3.5 2.0 1.4).

4. Continue in the Visual LISP Console. Type **(car endpt)** ↵. AutoLISP returns 3.5.

5. Type **(cadr endpt)** ↵. AutoLISP returns 2.0.

6. Type **(cdr endpt)** ⏎. AutoLISP returns (2.0 1.4).

7. Type **(nth 1 endpt)** ⏎. AutoLISP returns 2.0.

Do not save your drawing.

Setting Conditions

Often you want to execute a procedure based on a certain condition. One way of doing this is with the ɪғ statement, which does one thing if a statement is true and another thing if it is false. In other words, the operation is conditioned on the truth of a certain statement.

Looping is an important part of programming. Frequently you want to execute a procedure over and over until the routine has finished operating on all the target objects or items. Looping sets up the condition that determines when the operation starts, the number of objects upon which the routine operates, and when the operation ends.

Conditional structures

Conditional structures enable program flow to be determined based on the outcome of a given decision. These decisions result in the return of either T, meaning true, or nil, meaning false. To try out the following statements, type them in the Visual LISP Console window. For instance, for the statement

```
(< 3 5)
T
```

AutoLISP returns T for true, having determined that 3 is less than 5. For the statement

```
(> 3 5)
nil
```

AutoLISP returns nil for false, having determined that 3 is not greater than 5. For the statement

```
(= 3 5)
nil
```

AutoLISP returns nil. Here we have determined that 3 is not equal to 5. Because these statements return either T or nil, you can use the ɪғ statement. The general syntax of the ɪғ statement is (if conditional-test if-true if-false).

Say you want to find circles whose radius is less than 0.25. Here's a sample ɪғ statement. In this example, radius is a variable that has been previously set.

```
(if (< radius .25)
 (princ "The radius is less than .25")
 (princ "The radius is not less than .25")
  )
```

The conditional test is `(< radius .25)`. The if-true statement is `(princ "The radius is less than .25")`. The if-false statement is `(princ "The radius is not less than .25")`. This IF statement is equivalent to saying, "If the radius is less than .25, print 'The radius is less than .25' but if not, print 'The radius is not less than .25.'"

You can leave out the if-false statement. Then AutoLISP executes the if-true statement if the conditional statement is true and does nothing if it is false, and continues to the rest of the program. In the following exercise, you see both types of IF statements, one nested inside the other.

Step-by-Step: Using the IF Statement

1. Start a new drawing in AutoCAD using the `acad.dwt` template.

2. Open Visual LISP, start a new file, and type the following:

```
(defun c:compare2three (/ entered_num)
 (setq entered_num (getint "\nEnter an integer: "))
 (if (< entered_num 3)
   (princ "\nThe entered number is less than 3.")
   (if   (= entered_num 3)
     (princ "\nThe entered number is equal to 3.")
     (princ "\nThe entered number is greater than 3.")
    )
  )
 (princ)
  )
```

The GETINT function gets an integer from the user and is covered later in this chapter. The \n before the Enter an integer: prompt starts a new line; it is similar to using (terpri). Using (princ) at the end of a routine is also covered later in this chapter.

3. Choose Check Edit Window. If you see any error message in the Build Output window, check your typing, make any necessary correction, and try again.

4. Save the file as ab35-02.lsp in a folder that is in the support file search path, or in AutoCAD 2004\Support\.

5. Choose Load active edit window and then choose Activate AutoCAD.

6. To try out the IF statement, type **compare2three** ↵. At the Enter an integer: prompt, type **5** ↵. AutoCAD displays: The entered number is greater than 3.

7. Repeat the COMPARE2THREE command. At the `Enter an integer:` prompt, type **3** ↵. AutoCAD displays: `The entered number is equal to 3`.

8. Repeat the COMPARE2THREE command. At the `Enter an integer:` command, type **2** ↵. AutoCAD displays: `The entered number is less than 3`.

Do not save your drawing.

Loop structures

Looping provides the capability to execute a step or a number of steps a given number of times based on an evaluation you make in your application. One way to do this is with the WHILE function.

The format of the WHILE function is:

```
(while conditional-test-if-true
        then-perform-the-following-code-until-the condition-is-
false)
```

One method that can be useful with a WHILE conditional-test-if-true is to include a *counter* for the WHILE expression. A counter counts how many times an operation is executed. You can then end the operation when the counter reaches a certain number. To create a counter, set a variable (perhaps named "counter") to the number at which you want to start. Then write the code for one pass through the operation. Then set the counter to the next higher number using an expression, such as the following:

```
(setq counter (+ 1 counter))
```

The routine then loops back over the operation until the counter reaches the value you set.

Here's a simple example:

```
(defun c:process (/ counter)
  (setq counter 1)
  (while (< counter 6)
    (princ "Processing number ")
    (princ counter)
    (terpri)
    (setq counter (+ 1 counter))
  )
)
```

In this example, the process function starts by setting the variable counter to 1. Then you start the WHILE statement and specify that the counter must be less than 6. Within the WHILE statement, you print the text string "Processing number" and

then the value of the `counter` variable. You use (`terpri`) so that each text string starts on a new line. Then you set the counter to the next higher number. Each time through the WHILE loop, the value of the counter is incremented by 1. Without the increment statement, line 3 would always evaluate to true and the WHILE loop would never exit because the counter would always be 1.

If you accidentally program an infinite loop like this, you can stop the execution of your AutoLISP routine by pressing Esc, Ctrl+Break, or from the Visual LISP menu, choose Debug ➪ Abort Evaluation.

In the preceding example, the WHILE loop continues as long as the counter is less than 6. When the counter reaches 6, the routine stops. The WHILE statement returns the last value of the routine, so AutoCAD prints 6 on the last line. Figure 35-3 shows the result.

```
Command: process
Processing number 1
Processing number 2
Processing number 3
Processing number 4
Processing number 5
6
```

Figure 35-3: The result of the process function

When using WHILE, you may want to combine several operations under the condition. The IF function normally evaluates one `then` expression if the test expression is true. Suppose you want an IF expression that processes various tasks if the test condition is true. An IF expression, as previously mentioned, processes a "do-if-true" and "do-if-false." Therefore, to process more than one "do-if true" expression, you need to separate the "do-if-true" processes from the "do-if-false" processes. To accomplish this, use PROGN (PROGram Nest) to include (or nest) all items you want executed when the test is true. In general, PROGN evaluates all the statements within its parentheses and returns the last evaluation as if it were one statement, as the following example demonstrates.

In the next example, you see the same IF statements used in an earlier example. However, after the second IF statement, you want your routine to print two lines if the entered number equals 3. You can do this by enclosing the two lines of code (plus a `terpri`) within a PROGN statement:

```
(defun c:compare2three (/ entered_num)
  (setq entered_num (getint "\nEnter an integer: "))
  (if (< entered_num 3)
    (princ "\nThe entered number is less than 3.")
    (if (= entered_num 3)
      (progn
(princ "\nThe entered number is equal to 3.")
(terpri)
```

```
(princ "\nThis is the one we are looking for.")
    )
    (princ "\nThe entered number is greater than 3.")
  )
)
(princ)
)
```

On the CD-ROM

The file used in the following Step-by-Step exercise on using WHILE, IF, PROGN, and a counter, ab35-b.lsp, is in the Drawings folder of the *AutoCAD 2004 Bible* CD-ROM.

Step-by-Step: Using WHILE, IF, PROGN, and a Counter

1. Open AutoCAD with any new drawing.

2. Open Visual LISP.

3. Click Open File on the Visual LISP Standard toolbar and open ab35-b.lsp from the *AutoCAD 2004 Bible* CD-ROM.

4. Save the file as ab35-03.lsp in \AutoCAD 2004\Support or any folder in the support file search path. Figure 35-4 shows this routine.

```
(defun c:print0to10 (/ counter halfway)
  (setq counter 0                          ; initial value of counter
        halfway 5                          ; initial value of halfway
      )
  (terpri)
  (while (< counter 11)                    ; as long as counter is less than 11
    (if (= counter halfway)
        (progn                             ; process this if the variable halfway is 5
               (princ "Hey The halfway mark is: ")
               (princ halfway)
               (terpri)
        )
        (progn                             ; otherwise just show the present counter value
               (princ "The Counter value is: ")
               (princ counter)
               (terpri)
        )
    )
    (setq counter (+ counter 1))           ; Increment the value of counter
  )
)
```

Figure 35-4: The print0to10 routine

5. Load ab35-03.lsp. Return to AutoCAD.

6. Type **print0to10** ↵. Press F2 to open the AutoCAD Text Window and see the result, shown in Figure 35-5.

Do not save your drawing.

```
Command: print0to10

The Counter value is: 0
The Counter value is: 1
The Counter value is: 2
The Counter value is: 3
The Counter value is: 4
Hey The halfway mark is: 5
The Counter value is: 6
The Counter value is: 7
The Counter value is: 8
The Counter value is: 9
The Counter value is: 10
11
```

Figure 35-5: The result of the print0to10 function

Managing Drawing Objects

The real power of AutoLISP is in manipulating drawing objects. This section reveals how many of the AutoLISP routines perform their magic. You can get information about an object and then use that information to change the object. You can also create selection sets of objects.

Getting information about an object

Every object in the AutoCAD database has an entity name. This name enables you to reference that object anywhere in your AutoLISP application. To see an example of an entity name, type the following after starting a new drawing:

```
(command "_line" "3,3" "5,5" "")
(entlast)
```

AutoLISP responds with an Entity name such as `<Entity name: 2ed0520>`.

The numbers will probably differ on your system, but using the information returned from ENTLAST enables you to programmatically get or set a variety of options on any given database object by referencing its entity name.

The ENTGET (ENTity GET) function is the key to making modifications to the drawing database. The ENTGET function takes an entity name as its one and only argument. After drawing the line in the preceding steps, type the following:

```
(setq myline (entget (entlast)))
```

AutoLISP responds with:

```
((-1 . <Entity name: 15ac558>) (0 . "LINE") (330 . <Entity
name: 15ac4f8>)(5 . "2B") (100 . "AcDbEntity") (67 . 0)
(410 . "Model") (8 . "0")(100 . "AcDbLine") (10 3.0 3.0 0.0)
(11 5.0 5.0 0.0) (210 0.0 0.0 1.0))
```

This is a representation of how the line is stored in the AutoCAD drawing database. AutoLISP returned one large list that contains 12 smaller lists. Each of the smaller lists is referred to as a group indexed by the first element. The entity name is in group –1. Each of the initial numbers in the small lists represents a different quality of the line. These numbers are called *object group codes*. The object group codes used most often are listed in Table 35-2.

Table 35-2
Commonly Used AutoCAD Object Group Codes

Group Code	Description
−1	Entity name
0	Entity type
1	Text value
8	Layer
10	Start point (or center)
11	Endpoint (or alignment point)
38	Elevation
39	Thickness
40	Radius (or height of text)
62	Color
67	Paper space flag

Note As you can see from the 10, 11, and 40 codes, the meaning of the group codes can change depending on the type of object it is used for.

You can also use Visual LISP to examine an AutoCAD object. Begin by choosing View ➪ Browse Drawing Database ➪ Browse Selection. At this point, Visual LISP will display a pickbox in your drawing so that you can select an object.

After you end object selection, you are returned to Visual LISP where you see the Inspect dialog box. Select the name of the entity and, while the cursor is over the selected text, right-click. Choose Inspect to see information about the object. Figure 35-6 shows information about an arc.

Figure 35-6: Getting information about a drawing object from Visual LISP

Not all these group codes are present in the line you drew. For instance, group 62 (color) is absent in the list returned by AutoLISP. Every time you draw a line, you do not explicitly set its color. As a result, it defaults to the current color. In the same way, AutoLISP does not explicitly set every attribute of every group. In this case, the color is ByLayer and the current layer is 0. AutoLISP returned (8. "0") in the preceding list to signify the line is on layer 0.

There are many other group codes than the ones listed in Table 35-2, and they can be found in the Visual LISP Help system. From Visual LISP, choose Help ⇨ Visual LISP Help Topics. From the Contents tab, double-click DXF Reference. (Because the group codes are also used for DXF files, they are found in the DXF Reference.) Double-click ENTITIES Section. You can then either choose Common Group Codes for Entities or choose the specific entity you want to look up. In many cases, one group code can have different meanings depending on the entity in which it appears. For example, in the list representing the line you drew, group 10 is represented by (10 3.0 3.0 0.0), which means the start point of the line is at X=3.0, Y=3.0, Z=0.0. If group 0 were a circle instead, the coordinates of group 10 would specify the center point of the circle.

To manipulate a given attribute of an object, two important functions are ASSOC and SUBST:

✦ ASSOC returns a list that finds the entry associated with an item in a list. It takes two arguments, the item in the list and the list itself. For example, if you specify the group code (such as 10) as the first argument, it returns the code's value (which would be the start point of a line). If a list named myobject contains three groups, as in ((0 . "group 0") (1 1.0 2.0) (3 4.2 1.5 6.75)), then (assoc 1 myobject) would return (1 1.0 2.0).

✦ SUBST substitutes a value for every occurrence in a list. The SUBST function takes three arguments. To make the substitution, the first argument specifies what to substitute with, the second argument specifies what to substitute for, and the third argument specifies on what list to perform this operation.

To manipulate the start point of your line, first get the start point:

```
(setq startpt (assoc 10 myline))
```

AutoLISP responds:

```
(10 3.0 3.0 0.0)
```

To modify the start point of your line, use:

```
(setq new_startpt '(10 6.5 1.0 0.0))
(setq myline (subst new_startpt startpt myline))
```

AutoLISP responds:

```
((-1 . <Entity name: 15ac558>) (0 . "LINE") (330 . <Entity
name: 15ac4f8>)(5 . "2B") (100 . "AcDbEntity") (67 . 0)
(410 . "Model") (8 . "0")(100 . "AcDbLine") (10 6.5 1.0 0.0)
(11 5.0 5.0 0.0) (?10 0.0 0.0 1.0))
```

In this case, the new_startpt is substituted for the existing startpt in the object myline. No changes to the line are yet apparent. To commit the change, you need the ENTMOD function.

Modifying objects

The key to modifying objects is the ENTMOD (ENTity MODify) function. The list returned by AutoLISP can be modified and then passed to ENTMOD as an argument to update the AutoCAD database. Continuing with the example, if you enter:

```
(entmod myline)
```

AutoLISP responds:

```
((-1 . <Entity name: 15ac558>) (0 . "LINE") (330 . <Entity
name: 15ac4f8>) (5 ."2B") (100 . "AcDbEntity") (67 . 0)
(410 . "Model") (8 . "0") (100."AcDbLine") (10 6.5 1.0 0.0)
(11 5.0 5.0 0.0) (210 0.0 0.0 1.0))
```

The AutoCAD database is changed as well, and the start point of your line is now at X=6.5, Y=1.0, Z=0.0.

Creating selection sets

A selection set is created with the SSGET (Selection Set GET) function. This prompts the user with the familiar Select objects: prompt. Table 35-3 shows the commonly used selection set functions.

<table>
<tr><td colspan="2" align="center">Table 35-3
Common AutoCAD Selection Set Functions</td></tr>
</table>

Function	Description
SSGET	Obtains a selection set from the user.
SSLENGTH	Returns the number of objects in a selection set. It takes one argument, the selection set.
ssname	Returns the entity name of a given object in a selection set. It takes two arguments: the selection set and the number of the object in the selection set. The first item number is 0, the second is 1, and so on.

You can use a maximum of 256 selection sets at any given time. To release a selection set back to AutoLISP so that it can be used again, set the selection set to nil — for example, (setq ss nil).

For example, you can enter the following in a new drawing:

```
(command "_circle" "3,3" "2")
nil
(command "_circle" "4,4" "3")
nil
(command "_line" "7,2" "6,6" "3,4" "5,5" "")
nil
(setq mysset (ssget))
Select objects: all ↵
5 found
Select objects: ↵
<Selection set 1>
```

Now mysset is set to the selection set specified by all, which includes the three lines segments and the two circles. To see what you have in your selection set, type the following either on the command line or in the Visual LISP Console:

```
(sslength mysset)
5
```

You now know that you have five objects in your selection set. The first object is number 0, and the fifth object is number 4. To see what the first object is, enter the following:

```
(ssname mysset 0)
<Entity name: 3fc0550>
```

To get the database data on the object, enter:

```
(entget (ssname mysset 0))
```

Visual LISP responds:

```
((-1 . <Entity name: 1601580>) (0 . "LINE") (330 . <Entity
name: 16014f8>)(5 . "30") (100 . "AcDbEntity") (67 . 0) (410 .
"Model") (8 . "0")(100 . "AcDbLine") (10 3.0 4.0 0.0) (11 5.0
5.0 0.0) (210 0.0 0.0 1.0))
```

By stepping through each of the entity names returned by SSNAME from 0 to 4, you can manipulate each of the objects in the selection set.

Step-by-Step: Creating Selection Sets

1. Start a new drawing using the acad.dwt template and type the following in a new file in the Visual LISP edit window. Save it as ab35-04.lsp in your \AutoCAD 2004\Support folder or any folder in the support file search path.

```
(defun c:listsset (/ mysset counter)
(setq mysset (ssget))
(setq counter 0)
(while (< counter (sslength mysset))
  (terpri)
  (princ (cdr (assoc 0 (entget (ssname mysset counter)))))
  (setq counter (+ counter 1))
  )
(princ)
)
```

2. Load ab35-04.lsp.

3. Activate AutoCAD and draw any number of objects on-screen — at least two different types of objects.

4. Type **listsset** ↵. AutoCAD prompts you to select objects (because of the ssget function).

5. Select all the objects in your drawing. The routine prints the type of each object you selected. (Press F2 to open the AutoCAD Text window to see the entire results.) Figure 35-7 shows the result. Of course, your result will be different because you probably drew different types of objects.

```
Command: listsset

Select objects: all
5 found

Select objects:

LWPOLYLINE
CIRCLE
TEXT
LINE
LINE
```

Figure 35-7: One possible result of the listsset routine

Here's how this routine works:

✦ **Line 1** creates a function and declares two variables, mysset and counter.

✦ **Line 2** sets the mysset variable equal to the selection set that the user provides using SSGET.

✦ **Line 3** sets the counter variable to zero, because selection sets work on a zero-based index (the first item is zero).

✦ **Line 4** starts a WHILE loop. Working from the innermost set of parentheses, first you obtain the number of objects in the mysset selection set, using SSLENGTH. Then you specify that the WHILE loop will continue as long as the counter is less than the number of objects in the mysset selection set. In other words, when the routine has cycled through all the objects in the selection set, it stops.

✦ **Line 5** uses TERPRI to start a new line before printing out the list of objects.

✦ **Line 6** prints the list. Working from the innermost set of parentheses, first the routine obtains the name of the object in the mysset selection set whose number is equal to the variable counter. Then the routine gets that object using ENTGET. Then the routine gets the name of that object using ASSOC with the 0 group code. The result is a dotted pair list whose second item is the name of the object. The CDR function eliminates the first item in the dotted pair list, leaving just the name of the object, which is what you want. The routine then prints the result.

✦ **Line 7** sets the counter up one to repeat the WHILE loop for the next object.

✦ **Line 8** closes the WHILE loop.

✦ **Line 9** exits the routine quietly. I discuss exiting quietly later in the chapter.

✦ **Line 10** closes the entire function.

Getting Input from the User

The course of your AutoLISP routines may often depend on user input. To satisfy this need, AutoCAD has a family of functions prefaced with the word "GET." You have seen GETVAR for obtaining system variable information. Table 35-4 shows some other useful GET functions.

Table 35-4
Basic User Input Functions

Function	Description
GETDIST	Returns the distance between two points
GETINT	Returns an integer
GETREAL	Returns a real number (which can be a non-integer, negative, and so on)
GETSTRING	Returns a text string

Within the COMMAND function, you can use the PAUSE function to pause the operation of the routine and enable user input, such as picking a point or typing a value. For example, the expression (command "circle" pause "3") pauses to let the user specify a center point and then creates a circle with a radius of 3.

Notice the function ENTSEL in the next exercise. This is a type of shorthand for SSGET. Use it when you want to limit the user to selecting a single object. ENTSEL returns an entity name and the coordinates of your pick point in a dotted-pair list. Therefore, you can use CAR before ENTSEL to get the entity name for ENTGET.

There is also a new argument for getstring, T. If you use this argument and it is not nil, users can place spaces in the input. Using this argument enables users to type a text value that includes more than one word. Without the "T", AutoLISP would interpret a space as equivalent to pressing Enter.

Step-by-Step: Getting User Input

1. Start a new drawing using the acad.dwt template.

2. Start Visual LISP, open a new file, and enter the following routine. Save it as ab35-05.lsp in AutoCAD2004\Support or a folder that you have added to the support file search path.

```
(defun c:chgmytext (/ src_object new_ht new_str)
(setq src_object (entget (car (entsel))))
(setq new_ht (getreal "\nWhat is the new height? "))
(setq new_str (getstring T "\nWhat is the new text value? "))
(setq src_object
(subst  (cons 40 new_ht)  (assoc 40 src_object ) src_object)
)
(setq src_object
(subst  (cons 1 new_str)  (assoc 1 src_object) src_object)
)
(entmod src_object)
(princ)
)
```

3. Choose Format Edit Window from the Tools toolbar.

4. Load `ab35-05.1sp`.

5. Create some text using either the DTEXT or the TEXT command and run `chgmytext` on it. AutoCAD changes the text object's height and content to the values you input in response to the prompts.

Do not save your drawing.

Here's how the routine works:

✦ **Line 1** defines the function and declares the three variables.

✦ **Line 2** uses ENTSEL to let the user select one object. As explained earlier, CAR enables you to get just the entity name. ENTGET gets this entity name so that you can modify it. Finally, this line sets the resulting entity name equal to the variable `src_object`.

✦ **Line 3** prompts the user for a new height for the text and sets the entered number equal to the `new_ht` variable.

✦ **Line 4** prompts the user for a new text value (a new string) and sets the entered text value equal to the `new_str` variable.

✦ **Line 5** starts the process of substituting the new values for the old values. Here the routine starts to set the new value for `src_object`.

✦ **Line 6** uses SUBST to substitute the new text height for the old text height for the object `src_object`. (Group code 40 represents text height.)

✦ **Line 7** closes the SETQ function.

✦ **Line 8** is the same as line 5. You will be repeating the process of lines 5 through 7 for the new text (string) value.

✦ **Line 9** uses SUBST to substitute the new text value for the old text value. (Group code 1 represents the text value.)

✦ **Line 10** closes the SETQ function.

✦ **Line 11** uses ENTMOD on `src_object` to make the change in the drawing database.

✦ **Line 12** exits quietly.

✦ **Line 13** closes the entire function.

Putting on the Finishing Touches

You have a number of finishing touches that you should add to a routine before you can call it complete. All AutoLISP expressions return a value and the last expression returns its value on the command line. You have noticed the PRINC function at the end of several routines. PRINC returns a blank line and therefore ensures that no

extraneous evaluation return values are echoed on the command line. Using the PRINC function in this way is called *exiting cleanly* or *quietly*.

Most of the AutoLISP applications covered thus far do not include much in the way of error handling. A new function called EQUAL is used on line 4 of the final routine in the next Step-by-Step exercise. EQUAL is different than = in that EQUAL returns true only if two expressions are equal (each of the two objects tested for equality are evaluated before checking if they are equal). A simple rule of thumb is to use EQUAL for list comparisons and = for numeric comparisons.

In the routine in the next Step-by-Step exercise, if you select an object that is not a text object, the program jumps to line 18 and prints the error message You must select a text object.

A similar type of error handling is to enclose the selection of objects in an IF function. The IF function's test condition has to exist for the IF function to work. Therefore, if your user doesn't select an object, the test evaluates as false. You can place an error message as the if-false part of the IF function to catch this type of error.

This type of error handling is crucial to making your AutoLISP programs look finished and function properly.

Another way to finish off your routine is to add comments. Start with a comment at the beginning that states the purpose and function of the routine. This helps others understand what the routine does and can help you as well when you look at the routine again a few months later! Comments are prefaced with a semicolon.

Then continue to make comments throughout your code. A lack of comments can make even the most useful code useless. Most professional programmers fully comment and document a function's purpose and behavior by placing comments within the code.

Visual LISP supports several commenting styles. When you click Format Edit Window on the Tools toolbar, Visual LISP uses these styles to automatically format your code. Here's how they work:

- ✦ **;;; Triple semicolon:** When you type a comment with three semicolons, Visual LISP places the comment at the left margin. A triple semicolon comment is good for the beginning of your routine to describe its overall purpose and what it does.

- ✦ **;; Double semicolon:** Visual LISP indents a comment with two semicolons at the current nesting level, flush with the next level of parentheses. Use this type of comment to explain the next line or lines of code.

- ✦ **; Single semicolon:** Visual LISP indents a comment with one semicolon by 40 spaces, by default. Choose Tools ➪ Environment Options ➪ Visual LISP Format

Options to open the Format options dialog box, shown in Figure 35-8 and change this value if you want. Use this type of comment for running comments at the right side of your code. Because they are indented, they stand out from the body of your code.

✦ **;| |; Inline comment:** Place an inline comment within any line of code so that it has code both before and after it. An inline comment is formatted as shown here: ;|This is a comment|;. You use the pipe symbol (usually over the backslash) along with the semicolon. Use an inline comment to explain a small section of code within a line or to span comments over several lines without adding a semicolon before each line.

✦ **;_ End-of-line comment:** Place an end-of-line comment at the end of any line of code. An end of line comment is formatted as shown here: ;_ This is an end of line comment. You use the underscore symbol along with the semicolon. Use an end-of-line comment to explain which function to which the closing parenthesis is matched. This is especially useful for conditional functions, such as one closing parenthesis can be several lines from the opening parenthesis.

Figure 35-8: Use the Format options dialog box to format margins and indentation in the Visual LISP editor.

See the sidebar "Using AutoLISP to match properties" for several examples of comment styles.

Using AutoLISP to match properties

This routine modifies the layer of objects to match the layer of one other object. This powerful routine was a mainstay of many AutoCAD users before the advent of the MATCHPROP command introduced in AutoCAD R14. The general method used here for matching layers can be used to change any properties you wish on any AutoCAD object.

```
;;;Matches the layer of one selected source object in any number
of destination objects.
(defun c:matchlayer (/ src_object mysset counter
cur_ent ent_layer)
  (princ "\n*** Select Source object to match ***")  ; prompt the
user
  (if (setq src_object (car (entsel)))     ; select the object
    (progn
      (setq src_layer (assoc 8 (entget src_object)))  ; get the
object's layer
      ;; prompt the user
      (princ "\n*** Select Destination objects to match layer
***")
      ;; collect some objects using ssget
(if (setq mysset (ssget))     ; verify the user selected
something
      (progn     ; if the user selected some items do the
following
      (setq counter 0)
      (while (< counter (sslength mysset))

        (setq cur_ent (entget (ssname mysset counter)))
        (setq ent_layer (assoc 8 cur_ent))
        (entmod (subst src_layer ent_layer cur_ent))
        (setq counter (+ counter 1))
        )
      )
    (princ "\nYou did not select any items")  ; prompt the user
    )      ;_end of if verification
    )       ;_end of progn for the selection of object to match
  ;; prompt the user they did not select a source object
  (princ "\nSorry you did not select an Object")
  )         ;_end of if
(princ)
  )         ;_end of function c:matchlayer
```

This routine first gets the name of the selected object with (car (entsel)). It determines its layer by using ENTGET on the object name and using ASSOC with the 8 group code. Then it gets a selection set of the Destination objects. It creates a loop that cycles through these objects, gets their layers (the ent_layer variable), and uses ENTMOD and SUBST to change the object's current layer to the source object's layer.

Each selection of objects (the source object and the destination objects) is enclosed in an IF function whose if-false statement prints an error message telling users that they did not select an object (or objects).

Step-by-Step: Putting on the Finishing Touches

1. Load the application completed in the previous Step-by-Step exercise. If you didn't do the previous exercise, enter it from that exercise in Visual LISP's edit window and save it as ab35-05.lsp in \AutoCAD 2004\Support or a folder that you have added to the support file search path. Then load it with any drawing open in AutoCAD.

2. Now run chgmytext and choose an object that is not a text object (such as a circle) in response to the Select object: prompt. Answer the prompts for new height and new text value.

 If you have done this to a circle, you see its radius change to match the value you specified to be the new text height. This is definitely not what you intended when writing this program.

3. Modify the program so that it reads this way and save it as ab35-06.lsp:

```
;;;modifies text height and content (value)
 (defun c:chgmytext (/ src_object new_ht new_str)
     (terpri)
     (setq src_object (entget (car (entsel))))
     (if (equal (assoc 0 src_object) '(0 . "TEXT"))
         (progn
             (princ "What is the new height for the text?
")
             (setq new_ht (getreal))
             (princ "What is the new text value? ")
             (setq new_str (getstring))
             (setq src_object
                 (subst (cons 40 new_ht) (assoc 40
src_object) src_object)
             )
             (setq src_object
                 (subst (cons 1 new_str) (assoc 1
src_object)src_object)
             )
             (entmod src_object)
         )
         (princ "You must select a text object.")
     )
     (princ)
 )
```

4. Load ab35-06.lsp. Start chgmytext and try out the routine again with a circle or other non-text object.

Do not save your drawing.

Summary

In this chapter, you read how to create variables, create AutoLISP functions, and work with AutoCAD commands and system variables. You extended AutoLISP's power by using lists and looping. This chapter explained how to modify and get information about drawing objects. You also read how to create selection sets. Using these techniques, along with user input, you can automate the modification of objects in your drawing to suit your needs.

You should always finish off your AutoLISP routines by adding some error handling, making sure the routine exits quietly, and adding helpful comments about the routine's function.

In the next chapter, you read some of the more advanced features of Visual LISP.

✦ ✦ ✦

Exploring Advanced AutoLISP Topics

This chapter introduces you to a few helpful advanced AutoLISP topics, including local and global variables, ActiveX, and debugging.

Understanding Local and Global Variables

In this section, you read how local and global variables are accessed within a function, as well as some common syntax. You also discover what can happen when global variables are not properly documented.

Chapter 35 explained that a *variable* is a symbolic name that can be operated on in a given program. An important part of using variables is being able to assign values to them. There are two types of variables — global and local.

A *global* variable is exposed, or available, to all AutoLISP functions that you have loaded into your drawing. A global variable retains its value after the program that defined it is finished. You use a global variable when you want its value to be available across an entire project as opposed to just one function within a project, to retain a fixed value that might be used and assigned by different functions, or for debugging. Any variable you do not specifically define as a local variable is a global variable.

A *local* variable is temporarily assigned a value during a function's execution. After the function completes executing, the local variable value is discarded. AutoLISP can now use the memory that was taken up by that local variable. You use a local variable when you want to be sure you don't have variable values floating around interfering with other functions. Local variables are also easier to debug because they only affect the code within their function. In general, most of your variables should be local. You create a local variable and declare it in the DEFUN statement after the slash and a space, as in this example:

```
(defun list-objects ( / counter sset)...
```

Caution

Global variables can be tricky. They can easily cause bugs: Their values persist and can be hard to debug because the values are hard to find. A common syntax for global variables is to prefix and suffix the variable with an asterisk as in *aGlobal*. In this way, you can easily identify global variables in your code. Keep your use of global variables to a minimum and carefully document those you do use. Failure to follow these simple rules could result in undesirable and difficult-to-trace bugs.

Step-by-Step: Using Local and Global Variables

1. Start a new drawing using the acad.dwt template. You should not have any other drawing open.

2. Open the Visual LISP Editor.

3. In the Console window, type the following line and then press Ctrl+Enter. You use Ctrl+Enter in the Console window to enter in code of more than one line. This line declares one local variable:

```
(defun local-variable (/ var1)
```

4. Type the second line of code in the Console window as follows:

```
(setq var1 "I'm local")) ↵
```

This sets the local variable to the string you typed. The Console returns the name of the function.

```
LOCAL-VARIABLE
```

5. Before you test this function, you can check out the current value of the local variable: var1. Type the following in the Visual LISP Console:

```
var1 ↵
```

The Console returns

```
nil
```

As you can see, the value is nil.

6. Test the local-variable function to check the value it sets to the var1 variable. In the Console, type **(local-variable)** ↵. The Console returns:

```
"I'm local"
```

You now know that the local-variable function definitely assigns the value of "I'm local" to the variable var1.

7. To create a global variable, type the following in the Console.

```
(setq var1 "I'm global") ↵
```

The Console returns "I'm global" so you know that the value of var1 is now "I'm global".

8. Test the local variable again by typing **(local-variable)** in the Console. The Console returns "I'm local" because it executes the local-variable function.

9. Test the variable var1 to see what its value is now. In the Console, type **var1** ↵. The Console returns "I'm global". The local variable was not retained when the function used the variable because the variable was local to the function. However, the global variable's value persisted.

Working with Visual LISP ActiveX Functions

ActiveX is an interface that exposes objects to the user, a programmer, or an application. AutoLISP supports ActiveX, giving you more information and flexibility in working with your drawings. You can also use ActiveX to work with objects in other Windows applications that support ActiveX. ActiveX is a *programming interface* that is used within a programming language that supports it. For example, you can also use ActiveX with Visual Basic for Applications (see the next chapter) and C++.

Cross-Reference In ActiveX, objects are structured in a hierarchy. You need to understand this structure before working extensively with ActiveX. Chapter 37, on Visual Basic for Applications (VBA), covers this hierarchical structure in more detail.

ActiveX enables you to get information about objects (called *get functions*) and modify them (called *put functions*). The next section first reviews how you create these two functions in AutoLISP.

Reviewing AutoLISP retrieval and modification

In this section, you look at developing a small routine, written in AutoLISP, that mimics ActiveX properties and methods. This will help you compare how AutoLISP works compared to ActiveX.

To understand Visual LISP's ActiveX features, you need to know how AutoCAD exposes an object's properties in AutoLISP. The following examples work with a line 10 units long created using the following AutoLISP function:

```
;;; This function creates a line using the AutoLISP
;;; command function and returns nil.
(defun make-aLine ()
 (command "_line" "5,5" "15,5" "")
  )
```

Note The uppercase letter (in the function name) is used for readability, but you can type all lowercase letters if that is easier for you.

After loading it, you can use this function (that is, draw the line) by typing the following at the Visual LISP Console:

```
(make-aLine)
```

As explained in Chapter 35, to retrieve the last object created (the line), you use ENTLAST as shown in the following code fragment. The next expression places the value of the last created entity, as an entity name, to the variable LineEntity. To try this out, type the following code in the Console.

```
(setq LineEntity (entlast)) ↵
```

Visual LISP responds with the entity name. As soon as you receive the entity name, you can use ENTGET to retrieve the object property list of the line entity name. The following code fragment places the property list value in the variable LinePropertyList. If you type the following in the Console and press Enter, Visual LISP responds with the property list:

```
(setq LinePropertyList (entget LineEntity)) ↵
```

Here is an example of a property list, formatted for readability.

```
((-1 . <Entity name: 1456d60>)
 (0 . "LINE")
 (330 . <Enlity name: 1456cf8>)
 (5 . "2C")
 (100 . "AcDbEntity")
 (67 . 0)
 (410 . "Model")
 (8 . "0")
 (100 . "AcDbLine")
 (10 5.0 5.0 0.0)
 (11 15.0 5.0 0.0)
 (210 0.0 0.0 1.0))
```

As you can see, ENTGET returns an entity's properties as a collection of lists, all of which have a distinctive number at their first position. These group codes (also commonly known as DXF fields because you can also find them in DXF files) were listed in Chapter 35. For this exercise, you just need to remember that the 10 group code is associated with the start point of a line.

Having the entity list and knowing which values to retrieve, you can use the AutoLISP function ASSOC, which returns an associated item from a property list.

To retrieve the start point of the line, you would use the following code, which you can type in the Console:

```
(setq StartofLineList (assoc 10 LinePropertyList)) ↵
```

The Console returns the list associated with the 10 group code, including the group code and the coordinates:

```
(10 5.0 5.0 0.0)
```

Because the only value you require is the start point of the line object, use the function CDR to remove the first element of the list, as shown in the following code.

```
(setq StartofLine (cdr (assoc 10 LinePropertyList))) ↵
```

This code returns only the start point coordinate:

```
(5.0 5.0 0.0)
```

Now that you have reviewed how to retrieve a value from an AutoCAD object, you can see that retrieving information from an associated list is somewhat straightforward. But how about retrieving more than one property at a time? As you can see from the preceding example, you would have to repeat the same body of code many times over to retrieve any information. Knowing this, you could write a simple interface function, putting together all the steps just explained, to retrieve any group code, not just the 10 group code, from an object.

Note An interface function is a function that hides a complex behavior to the user. The user need provide only basic information, but the function uses the information in several steps to obtain the desired result.

An example of an interface function is shown in the following lines:

```
;;; returns any group code value if it is present in the entity
;;; the required parameters are an entity name and a group
code.
 (defun Get-A-Group-Code (EntityName GroupCode)
(cdr (assoc GroupCode (entget EntityName)))
)
```

After you create this function and load it, you can test it out in the Console as follows, using the `LineEntity` variable previously defined:

```
(Get-A-Group-Code LineEntity 10) ↵
(5.0 5.0 0.0)
```

As you can see, the function returns only the value of the 10 group code.

You can refine this small interface by defining a separate 10 group 10 function, such as the following. The only required parameter is an entity name. The group code is included in the call to Get-A-Group-Code. You could do the same for an 11 group code, if you want.

```
(defun Get-Group-10-Code (anEntityName)
  (Get-A-Group-Code anEntityName 10)
)
```

After loading, test the function, as follows:

```
(Get-Group-10-Code LineEntity) ↵
```

Visual LISP returns the start point of the line:

```
(5.0 5.0 0.0)
```

These examples summarize how you would create a simple function to get the start point of a line using AutoLISP. What if you need to change an object's property? You can do this by using the functions CONS, SUBST, and ENTMOD, which Chapter 35 covers.

CONS constructs a list. Use it when you want to create new values for a group code within an entity list, as in the following example, which you can type in the Console window:

```
(setq NewStartPoint (cons 10 '( 0 0 0 ))) ↵
```

Visual LISP returns the following:

```
(10 0 0 0)
```

Using the variables `NewStartPoint` and `LinePropertyList`, you can now substitute the newly created group 10 code. You do this using the SUBST function explained in Chapter 35. The following code substitutes the new group 10 code represented by the variable `NewStartPoint` for the 10 association in `LinePropertyList` in the list called LinePropertyList.

```
(Setq LinePropertyList
      (subst NewStartPoint (assoc 10 LinePropertyList)
LinePropertyList)
  )
```

To test this out, type the preceding code in the Console window. To see the new start point, you need to scroll all the way to the right. The list (nicely formatted) now has a new group 10 value (the start point), shown on the third-to-last line that follows:

```
((-1 . <Entity name: 1456d60>)
  (0 . "LINE")
  (330 . <Entity name: 1456cf8>)
  (5 . "2C")
  (100 . "AcDbEntity")
  (67 . 0)
  (410 . "Model")
  (8 . "0")
  (100 . "AcDbLine")
  (10 0 0 0)
  (11 15.0 5.0 0.0)
  (210 0.0 0.0 1.0))
```

To reflect the modification of this line in AutoCAD, as explained in Chapter 35, you can now use the function ENTMOD, as follows, by typing it in the Console. This code actually changes the start point of the line. (You can return to AutoCAD to check it out.)

```
(entmod LinePropertyList) ↵
```

As you can see from this example, getting object properties and modifying them can be a tedious and time-consuming process. For the next example, you write an interface function that modifies any group code contained in any object.

```
(defun put-group-code-value (Entityname Groupcode Value /
PropertyList)
  (setq PropertyList (entget EntityName))
  (setq PropertyList
    (subst
      (cons GroupCode Value)
      (assoc GroupCode PropertyList)
      PropertyList
    )
  )
  (entmod PropertyList)
)
```

This function combines all the preceding steps into one function. Here's how it works:

✦ **Line 1** defines the function with three arguments: the entity name, a group code, and a new value for the group code. It also declares a local variable, PropertyList, which is the property list of the object.

✦ **Line 2** sets the property list equal to the ENTGET of the entity name.

✦ **Line 3** starts the process of setting the same property list to the new value.

✦ **Lines 4 through 7** execute the substitution. They substitute the new group, created by (cons GroupCode Value), for the current group value, created with the ASSOC function, in the property list named PropertyList.

✦ **Line 8** closes the SUBST function.

✦ **Line 9** closes the second SETQ function.

✦ **Line 10** modifies the drawing database using ENTMOD.

✦ **Line 11** closes the DEFUN function.

Using the preceding function, you now have a much simpler interface for modifying any group code. Next, you use the function Put-a-Group-Code-Value to modify the 10 group code of the line object.

After entering and loading the preceding function, you can test the function by typing the following in Visual LISP:

```
(Put-Group-Code-Value LineEntity 10 '(5 5 0)) ↵
```

This function changes the start point of the line to 5,5,0.

Using the same logic to write the get functions, you can now define a separate 10 group code modifier function. You can do the same for any group code.

```
(defun Put-Group-10-Code (EntityName Value)
  (Put-Group-Code-Value EntityName 10 Value)
  )
```

After entering and loading this function, type the following at the Console to change the start point of the line to 15,–5,0.

```
(Put-Group-10-Code LineEntity '( 15 -5 0 )) ↵
```

Activate AutoCAD to check that the line has been changed.

Using ActiveX with Visual LISP

You have just seen how to retrieve and modify object information by writing small get and put interface functions using AutoLISP. ActiveX provides a similar way to retrieve and modify objects but it requires some preparation. In the following section, you read about using some ActiveX functions to create, retrieve, and modify an object.

Retrieving and modifying object information with ActiveX

Visual LISP enables you to retrieve and modify any AutoCAD object using AutoCAD's ActiveX interface. That is to say, AutoCAD exposes all of its objects to ActiveX-enabled applications. This includes Visual LISP as ActiveX objects, all of which expose their properties, including put (modify) and get (retrieve) functions.

Using Visual LISP to communicate with AutoCAD 2004 is very straightforward. You must first load all of the ActiveX functions using the VL-LOAD-COM function within Visual LISP. This exposes all of the ActiveX interface functions. You need to load the VL-LOAD-COM function only once each time you open AutoCAD because VL-LOAD-COM loads the ActiveX functions for the entire drawing session. (Using VL-LOAD-COM more than once, however, doesn't cause any harm.)

```
(vl-load-com) ↵
```

After the ActiveX interface is loaded, you can interrogate the line you created previously, but first you need to convert the entity name into a vla-object. A vla-object is no different from an entity name, except that the ActiveX object exposes certain properties that its AutoLISP counterpart does not. To convert the entity name into a vla-object, you use the function VLAX-ENAME->VLA-OBJECT, as demonstrated here:

```
(setq vla-line (vlax-ename->vla-object (entlast))) ↵
```

Visual LISP returns the following:

```
#<VLA-OBJECT IAcadLine 03612b14>
```

As you can see by the return value of vlax-ename->vla-object, the value of the variable vla-line contains a VLA-OBJECT. At this point, you can visually inspect the variable by selecting it and choosing View ➪ Inspect. Although you see the line's property in a dialog box, you can also "dump" its property and values to the Console by using the VLAX-DUMP-OBJECT Visual LISP function as follows:

```
(vlax-dump-object vla-line) ↵
```

This causes Visual LISP to display the following:

```
;  IAcadLine: AutoCAD Line Interface
;  Property values:
;    Angle (RO) = 1.5708
;    Application (RO) = #<VLA-OBJECT IAcadApplication 00af9594>
;    Delta (RO) = (0.0 10.0 0.0)
;    Document (RO) = #<VLA-OBJECT IAcadDocument 038be900>
;    EndPoint = (15.0 5.0 0.0)
;    Handle (RO) = "89"
;    HasExtensionDictionary (RO) = 0
;    Hyperlinks (RO) = #<VLA-OBJECT IAcadHyperlinks 01011d44>
;    Layer = "0"
;    Length (RO) = 10.0
;    Linetype = "ByLayer"
;    LinetypeScale = 1.0
;    Lineweight = -1
;    Normal = (0.0 0.0 1.0)
;    ObjectID (RO) = 2130009736
;    ObjectName (RO) = "AcDbLine"
;    OwnerID (RO) = 2130009336
;    PlotStyleName = "ByLayer"
```

```
;    StartPoint = (15.0 -5.0 0.0)
;    Thickness = 0.0
;    TrueColor = #<VLA-OBJECT IAcadAcCmColor 01015170>
;    Visible = -1
T
```

You'll probably have to resize the window to see all these properties. Notice the similarities between the "named" properties shown here, such as EndPoint and StartPoint, and the line's group codes that you retrieve using AutoLISP. As you can see, one of the advantages of using an ActiveX-enabled object is that ActiveX exposes more information to the programmer than standard AutoLISP. One of the benefits of using ActiveX is its interface. Previously, you queried and modified a line object's start point and endpoint by using the 10 and 11 group codes. Using ActiveX to query the start point and endpoint is very straightforward. However, ActiveX returns these points in a data type called a *variant* that you need to convert to the familiar coordinate format.

To get the start point of an object, you use the VLA-GET-STARTPOINT function. In the current example, the line has been set to vla-line, so you would type the following expression:

```
(setq Starting (vla-get-startpoint vla-line)) ⏎
```

Visual LISP responds as follows:

```
#<variant 8197 ...>
```

To convert the start point from the variant data type to a usable coordinate format, you would type the following line:

```
(safearray-value (vlax-variant-value Starting)) ⏎
```

Visual LISP responds with a coordinate:

```
(15.0 -5.0 0.0)
```

To modify the StartPoint property of a line to (0,0,0) you would use the following expression:

```
(vla-put-startpoint vla-line (vlax-3d-point '(0 0 0 ))) ⏎
```

You can return to AutoCAD to check out the line. To verify the new StartPoint you can also use the VLA-GET-STARTPOINT function:

```
(safearray-value (vlax-variant-value (vla-get-StartPoint vla-
line))) ⏎
```

Visual LISP returns the start point of the line:

```
(0.0 0.0 0.0)
```

As you can see, this is very similar to the small routine developed in AutoLISP earlier in this chapter.

Step-by-Step: Retrieving and Modifying Objects with ActiveX

1. To start a new drawing session, close AutoCAD if it is open. Open AutoCAD.

2. Start a new drawing using the `acad.dwt` template.

3. Draw any line. Neither the start point nor the endpoint should be 0,0,0.

4. Choose Tools ➪ AutoLISP ➪ Visual LISP Editor.

5. In the Console window, type **(vl-load-com)** ↵ to load the ActiveX functions.

6. To convert the entity name into a vla-object, type **(setq vla-line (vlax-ename->vla-object (entlast)))** ↵.

7. To view the line's properties, type **(vlax-dump-object vla-line)** ↵.

8. To get the start point of the line, type **(setq Starting (vla-get-startpoint vla-line))** ↵.

9. To convert the start point from the variant data type to coordinate format, type **(safearray-value (vlax-variant-value Starting))** ↵.

10. To change the line's start point to 0,0,0, type **(vla-put-startpoint vla-line (vlax-3d-point '(0 0 0)))** ↵.

11. Choose Activate AutoCAD on the Visual LISP View toolbar to check out the line. Its start point is now 0,0,0.

Creating objects with ActiveX

This section looks at object creation functions. When you work with ActiveX you need to retrieve objects in their hierarchical order. This hierarchy concept is discussed in more detail in the next chapter. For this chapter, you need to know that before you can retrieve an object, you need to retrieve the following:

✦ **Acad-object:** Represents the AutoCAD application.

✦ **ActiveDocument:** Represents your drawing.

✦ **ModelSpace/PaperSpace:** Represents the type of space you want to use within the AutoCAD application.

In AutoLISP, you first retrieve the space (model or paper), then your drawing, and finally the AutoCAD application. Here you take the simple line command used earlier in this chapter and convert it using ActiveX:

```
;;; This function creates a line using Visual LISP
;;; ActiveX and returns the line object as a vla-object.
(defun ax-make-aLine ()
  (vla-AddLine
    (vla-get-ModelSpace              ; retrieve the model
```

```
                                        ; space object
     (vla-get-ActiveDocument           ; get the current
                                        ; active document
   (vlax-get-acad-object)              ; get the acad object
   )
     )
   (vlax-3d-point '(5 5 0))            ; starting point
   (vlax-3d-point '(15 5 0))           ; ending point
   )
 )
```

You can type this in the Visual LISP Editor and load it. To try it out, type the following in the Console:

```
(ax-make-aLine) ↵
```

Visual LISP responds with the following:

```
#<VLA-OBJECT IAcadLine 03614934>
```

This might seem a little cumbersome—as if it might be a lot of work to create a line—but quite honestly, it isn't. It's actually quite flexible.

To locate other ActiveX functions that create objects, you need to look in the AutoCAD ActiveX and VBA Reference. In Visual LISP, choose Help, Visual LISP Help Topics. From the Contents tab, double-click ActiveX and VBA Reference, and then Methods. You immediately see an alphabetical list with the A's displayed. Here are all the VBA methods that add drawing objects. To create a Visual LISP function, add VLA- before the method. For example, to add a circle, you would use VLA-AddCircle.

Tip　You immediately know if the function is correct, because it turns from black to blue as you enter it.

Debugging Code

Because few people can write perfect code at first try, there's always a need to debug code. Debugging is simply the process of trying to locate and correct mistakes. In this section, you look at some simple examples, using some of the debugging tools Visual LISP has to offer.

In the first example, you define a function that is guaranteed to fail. You can type this in the Visual LISP editor and load it:

```
;;; The function below will produce an error
;;; because strcat concatenates strings.
(defun Error-Prone-Code ()
(strcat "This is will never print the number: " 1)
   )
```

Before you continue you need to choose Debug ➪ Break on Error. By selecting this menu option, Visual LISP enables you to jump to the error in your source code automatically.

Using the function error-prone code produces an error because `strcat` concatenates strings, as the following demonstrates. You can type this at the console:

```
(Error-Prone-Code) ↵
```

Visual LISP responds with the following:

```
; error: bad argument type: stringp 1
```

After you receive the error, choose Last Break on the Debug toolbar. Visual LISP places you in the line in the code where the error occurred.

How can you find the source of the problem in a routine? To answer this question, you often need to perform some detective work. Visual LISP provides a wealth of debugging tools, which you can leverage when you encounter an unplanned "enhancement" or bug.

Step-by-Step: Finding the Last Break

1. Open a drawing in AutoCAD using the `acad.dwt` template.

2. Start Visual LISP and start a new file.

3. In the Visual LISP Editor, type the following:

```
;;; The function add-3-numbers will not produce
;;; an error if all of its arguments are numbers.
(defun add-3-numbers (num1 num2 num3)
  (+ num1 num2 num3)
  )
```

4. Choose Load Active Edit Window on the Tools toolbar.

5. In the Console window, type the following:

```
(add-3-numbers 1 2 3) ↵
```

Visual LISP returns 6.

6. However, if you substitute a string for one of its arguments, an error occurs. Type the following in the Console window:

```
(add-3-numbers 1 "a" 3) ↵
```

Visual LISP returns the following:

```
error: bad argument type: numberp: "a"
```

7. Choose Debug ➪ Break on Error. Look again to confirm Break on Error is checked.

8. Choose Last Break on the Debug toolbar. Visual LISP places you in the function add-3-numbers, with (+ num1 num2 num3) as the cause of the error.

To continue after turning on Break on Error, click Reset on the Debug toolbar.

Using the Error trace window

Any time an error occurs, you can use the last break along with the Visual LISP Error trace window. To display the Error trace window, choose View ➪ Error Trace to see an error list, as shown in Figure 36-1.

Figure 36-1: To help you debug your code, the Error trace window displays every function call before the error as well as where the error occurred.

The item numbered <5> in Figure 36-1 is what you entered in the Console. The item labeled [2] (+ 1 "a" 3) is where the error occurred, while <1> :ERROR-BREAK signaled the function's termination because of the error.

Visual LISP enables you to find the source *position* (the line of code that produced the error) and the *call source point* (the position in your code where the function was called) for the error. To find them, right-click the third item in the Error trace window. From the shortcut menu you can choose either Source Position or Call Source Point. Jumping to the position in your code where the function was called is extremely handy when debugging a large application.

Working with break points

Sometimes when you choose Last Break to highlight an error, you find that a great deal of code is highlighted, which is not very helpful for finding the error. This is where break points come in handy. *Break points* are locations in your code, specified by you, that are used to signal Visual LISP to stop and wait until you are ready to continue processing the code. Visual LISP executes your code and stops at each break point and waits for your instructions. Break points enable you to break down your code into smaller pieces and watch what is going on piece by piece so you can more easily find the error.

To place a break point, position your cursor to the left of an opening parenthesis or the right of a closing parenthesis and press F9. Visual LISP places a temporary red mark in your code.

After creating your break points, you need to reload your code to tell Visual LISP about your break points. Then try to execute the function again. Notice that the Debug toolbar buttons become available. Visual LISP executes your code up to the first break point.

You can now use the Debug toolbar to help find your error. The first three buttons offer three different ways to move through your code:

✦ **Step Into:** Use this button to "step in" one expression from the innermost nested expression (from opening to closing parentheses) to the outer-most, one at a time.

✦ **Step Over:** Use this button to ignore the nested expressions; that is, step over the highlighted expression.

✦ **Step Out:** Use this button to move to the end of the function. You can ignore the entire function being debugged.

To remove break points, choose View ➪ Breakpoints Window to open the Breakpoints dialog box, shown in Figure 36-2.

Figure 36-2: Use the Breakpoints dialog box to remove, show, or disable break points.

In the Breakpoints dialog box, you can do the following:

✦ Delete all break points by clicking Delete all.

✦ Delete individual break points by choosing a break point and clicking Delete.

✦ Jump to a break point by choosing a break point and clicking Show. Visual LISP places a blinking cursor at the break point.

✦ Edit a break point by choosing a break point and clicking Edit. Visual LISP then lets you disable (or delete or show) the break point.

The file used in the following Step-by-Step exercise on working with break points, ab36-a.lsp, is in the Drawings folder of the *AutoCAD 2004 Bible* CD-ROM.

Step-by-Step: Working with Break Points

1. Open AutoCAD and start a drawing using any template.

2. Start the Visual LISP Editor. Open ab36-a.lsp from the *AutoCAD 2004 Bible* CD-ROM. Choose File ➪ Save As and save it as ab36-01.lsp in the \AutoCAD 2004\Support folder or in another folder you have added to the support file search path.

3. Choose Load Active Edit Window from the Tools toolbar.

4. Read through the code. This routine creates a vertical list of numbers. The new FOREACH function steps through each item in a list. The comments explain why it contains a bug.

5. If you didn't do the previous exercise, choose Debug ➪ Break on Error. (Don't do anything if the Break on Error item is already checked.)

6. Type the following in the Console window:

```
(list-beautify-with-bug '(1 2 3 4 5 ))
```

The Console returns the following:

```
(1
; error: bad argument type: FILE 1
```

7. Choose Last Break on the Debug toolbar to jump to the error in the source code.

8. To place a break point in the code, place the cursor after (princ (chr 40)). Press F9. Visual LISP marks the break with a red box.

9. Place another break point after (princ (car aList)). Finally, place a third break point after the closing parenthesis on the line that follows (princ item 1). Your code should look like Figure 36-3.

10. After the code produces an error, you need to reset. Click Reset on the Debug toolbar.

11. Click the Visual LISP Editor window and reload the function into Visual LISP. (Choose Load Active Edit Window on the Tools toolbar.)

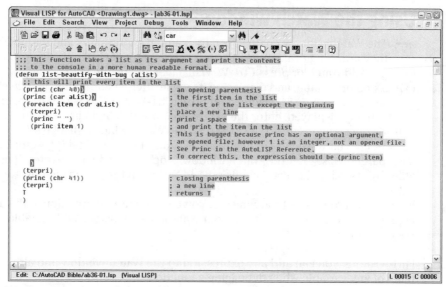

Figure 36-3: Your code after placing three break points

12. Type the same expression that produced the error in the Console:

```
(list-beautify-with-bug '(1 2 3 4 5 )) ↵
```

13. Visual LISP highlights the expression (princ (chr 40)). Choose Step Into on the Debug toolbar. Visual LISP highlights (princ (car aList)).

14. Choose Step Into. Now only (car aList)) is highlighted.

15. Choose Step Into until you reach the error, (princ item 1).

16. Edit (princ item 1) so that it reads (princ item).

17. Click Reset again.

18. Choose Debug ➪ Clear All Breakpoints. Click Yes to confirm.

19. Activate the Editor window and reload the function.

20. In the Console, type **(list-beautify-with-bug '(1 2 3 4 5))** ↵.

21. Activate the Editor window and save the file.

On the CD-ROM

If you have difficulty in fixing this bug, you can find the "repaired" version in the Results folder of the *AutoCAD 2004 Bible* CD-ROM with the file name list-beautify-without-bug.lsp.

Using the Watch window

 The Watch window enables you to examine expressions and variable values as they are being evaluated. To watch a variable, select it in the code and choose Debug ⇨ Add Watch or press Ctrl+W. Visual LISP opens the Watch window listing the expression or variable and displaying its value after an equal sign. If you select an expression or nothing is selected and press Ctrl+W, the Add Watch dialog box opens. If not already displayed, enter the expression to watch and click OK. For example, if you add a watch for (princ (chr 40)), the Watch window displays (PRINC (CHR 40)) = "(" because (princ (chr 40)) is another way of telling AutoLISP to print a left parenthesis. After the Watch window is open you can add expressions or variables by selecting them and choosing Add Watch on the Watch window toolbar.

If you have a routine with arguments, you can execute the function with various arguments and see the results on your watched expressions and variables in the Watch window.

Furthermore, you can add any expression to the Watch window and alter the contents of any variable while debugging a function.

On the CD-ROM The file used in the following Step-by-Step exercise on using the Watch window, ab36-01.lsp, is in the Results folder of the *AutoCAD 2004 Bible* CD-ROM.

Step-by-Step: Using the Watch Window

1. Open AutoCAD and start a drawing using the acad.dwt template.

2. Start the Visual LISP Editor. Open ab36-01.lsp from the Results folder of the *AutoCAD 2004 Bible* CD-ROM. If you did the previous exercise, you can open it from your AutoCAD Bible folder.

3. Select the expression (princ (chr 40)). Choose Debug ⇨ Add Watch. Click OK in the Add Watch dialog box. Visual LISP opens the Watch window and displays the expression as well as its value.

4. To add a variable to the Watch window, select item to the right of the foreach function and choose Add Watch in the Watch window. The Watch window should look like Figure 36-4.

Figure 36-4: The Watch window shows an expression and a variable and displays their values.

5. Add a break point after `(princ item)` by placing the cursor there and pressing F9.

6. Choose Load Active Edit Window from the Tools toolbar.

7. To examine the Watch window display as the function `list-beautify-with-bug` is evaluated, type the following in the Visual LISP Console:

 `(list-beautify-with-bug '(1 2 3 4 5 ))` ↵

8. The `(princ item)` expression should be highlighted. Choose Step Into on the Debug toolbar. The `item` variable in the Watch window should now display its current value. Continue to click Step Into, watching the value of `item` increase in the Watch window each time you step through the cycle.

9. In the Visual LISP console, type **aList** ↵ after the last prompt. This is a variable argument used in the function list-beautify-with-bug. The Console returns:

 `(1 2 3 4 5)`

 As you can see, you can interrogate any variable while debugging the function.

10. To add a new expression to the Watch window, select the variable `aList` and press Ctrl+W.

11. To change the value of `aList`, return to the Console window and type the following:

 `(setq aList (list 6 7 8 9 10))`

 The Console responds as follows:

 `(6 7 8 9 10)`

 Notice the change in the Watch window.

12. To remove the break point, choose View ⇨ Breakpoints Window to open the Breakpoints dialog box. Click Delete All to delete the break point. Visual LISP automatically closes the dialog box.

13. Click Reset on the Debug toolbar.

14. Close the Visual LISP IDE without saving the file.

As you can see, Visual LISP is not just an editor; it's a full-featured, integrated development environment for AutoLISP.

Summary

In this chapter, you examined some of the advanced features of AutoLISP and Visual LISP. You read:

✦ About some of the features of ActiveX

✦ How to use some of Visual LISP's debugging features, including the Error trace window, break points, and the Watch window

In the next chapter, you read the basics of Visual Basic for Applications, another programming language you can use with AutoCAD.

✦　　✦　　✦

Programming with Visual Basic for Applications

◆ ◆ ◆ ◆

In This Chapter

Understanding VBA and AutoCAD

Writing VBA code

Getting user input

Creating dialog boxes

Modifying objects

Creating loops and conditions

Debugging and trapping errors

◆ ◆ ◆ ◆

Visual Basic for Applications (VBA) is a programming language and environment included with many Microsoft applications, such as Word, Excel, PowerPoint, and Access. Since Release 14, VBA has been available with AutoCAD as well. VBA is ideally suited for situations in which you need to work with more than one application at a time. ActiveX, discussed in the last chapter in relation to Visual LISP, enables you to access objects in other applications. However, you can also use VBA to program AutoCAD alone. This chapter introduces you to VBA and shows how you can start to use this powerful language to customize AutoCAD.

Visual Basic for Applications is a variation of Visual Basic. Visual Basic is not related to any specific application. Visual Basic code is compiled into an executable file that stands alone, unrelated to any specific document. VBA, on the other hand, is connected to its application and the document in which you created the code. VBA provides a simple way to customize AutoCAD, automate tasks, and program applications from within the application.

VBA in AutoCAD works slightly differently from VBA in most other applications in that VBA projects are stored in a separate file, with the extension .dvb, but can also be stored within the drawing file.

Starting to Work with VBA

After you decide to program AutoCAD, the first step is to select a programming language to use.

VBA has the following advantages:

✦ It is faster than AutoLISP, even when AutoLISP is compiled.

✦ VBA is common to many other applications. If you have used VBA before, you can easily transfer your knowledge to using VBA in AutoCAD. You are also more likely to find other programmers who know VBA compared to AutoLISP.

✦ VBA is generally easier to learn than AutoLISP because of its syntax.

On the other hand, AutoLISP has the advantage of backward compatibility with prior releases of AutoCAD. Of course, if you are familiar with AutoLISP but not VBA, it's hard to beat the ease of working with a language that you already know and use.

VBA programs are saved in *projects*. A project contains all the parts needed to execute the function of the program. You can use the VBA Manager to view your VBA projects. The VBA Manager also enables you to load, unload, save, and create VBA projects. To open the VBA Manager, choose Tools ➪ Macro ➪ VBA Manager.

Opening the VBA environment

To start working with VBA, you must open the VBA environment. VBA has its own interface, just like Visual LISP. To open VBA in AutoCAD, choose Tools ➪ Macro ➪ Visual Basic Editor (or type **vbaide** ↵). Like Visual LISP, VBA has its own interface, called an IDE, for *integrated development environment*. AutoCAD displays the VBA environment window.

VBA projects can contain *modules*. A module is a self-contained piece of programming code. A VBA project can have one or more modules.

To add a module, choose Insert ➪ Module or click the drop-down arrow to the right of the second button on the VBA IDE Standard toolbar; then choose Module. AutoCAD opens a module text editor window so you can start typing code. In the Project window, VBA adds a new module to the list of modules. By default, the first module is called Module1. Figure 37-1 shows the VBA IDE including the text editor. If you don't see the Project Explorer or the Properties window, use the View menu of the VBA IDE and choose Project Explorer or Properties Window.

Tip You can resize the module text editor as you would any window. As you start adding code to the text editor, you will find it easier to work with a larger window. Click the Maximize button to enlarge the text editor to its maximum size.

Figure 37-1: The VBA environment window

 AutoCAD is still running in the background. You can return to it at any time by clicking its button on the Windows task bar or by clicking View AutoCAD on the VBA IDE Standard toolbar.

Getting acquainted with VBA

VBA enables you to easily retrieve, create, and manipulate objects. To get a list of objects, open the Object Browser by clicking Object Browser on the toolbar or choosing View ➪ Object Browser. Objects are organized into libraries. All the objects you work with in AutoCAD are in the AutoCAD library.

To see the list of AutoCAD objects, click the <All Libraries> drop-down list and choose AutoCAD. You can see the result in Figure 37-2.

Tip You can resize the panes in the VBA window. Place the mouse cursor on the bar between the panes until you see the double-headed arrow and drag it either left or right.

Objects and collections of objects

In the left pane, labeled Classes, you see the list of objects. In VBA, you can have both individual objects and collections of objects. For example, AcadLayer would be the layer object and AcadLayers would be the collection of layers. The purpose of collections is to enable you to work with a group of objects. For example, to add a layer, you add it to the collection of layers because the new layer is not related to any existing layer.

Figure 37-2: You can use the Object Browser to see the AutoCAD library of objects.

Methods and properties

What can you do with objects in VBA? First, objects can have properties. For example, you can set an ellipse to the color red because one of the properties of the ellipse object is color. (Of course, all drawing objects have color as one of their properties.)

Second, objects have methods. A *method* is an action you can take on the object. For example, you can erase an ellipse because erase is a method of the ellipse object (as well as of all drawing objects).

In the Object Browser, the right pane, Members, lists the properties and methods of any object you choose in the Classes pane.

Investigating the Hierarchy Model

Although you might first think that an object in VBA is the same as an object in an AutoCAD drawing, there is more to the story. In VBA, *everything* is an object. For example, AutoCAD as an application is an object. Your current drawing is also an object. Model space and paper space are also objects. Therefore, to specify an object in your drawing, you need to specify the application, the drawing, and finally the object in the drawing. To do this, VBA works with a hierarchy of objects. The hierarchy makes it possible to distinguish between an object in your drawing and an object in an Excel spreadsheet, for example.

Objects are specified from the most general to the most specific with a period between each part of the definition. You then add the desired method or properties after another period. For example, you can use the following VBA code to add a circle:

```
Application.ActiveDocument.ModelSpace.AddCircle(center, radius)
```

A shortcut for `Application.ActiveDocument` is `ThisDrawing`, so you can also use:

```
ThisDrawing.ModelSpace.AddCircle(center, radius)
```

In order to work with any object, you need to know where it fits in the hierarchy. The quickest way to see the hierarchical structure from the VBA IDE is to choose any method or property in the Object Browser and choose Help on the Object Browser's toolbar. On the Contents tab, choose Object Model to see the listing in Figure 37-3.

Figure 37-3: The object model shows you the hierarchy of all the VBA objects so that you can work with them.

Note Within AutoCAD, choose Help ➪ Developer Help. You are now in a new help system. On the Contents tab, double-click ActiveX and VBA Reference. Click Object Model to see the hierarchical model shown in Figure 37-3 or double-click Objects to see the alphabetical object list.

Step-by-Step: Getting Acquainted with the VBA Environment

1. With any drawing open in AutoCAD, choose Tools ➪ Macro ➪ Visual Basic Editor. AutoCAD opens the VBA IDE.

2. Choose Insert ➪ Module from the menu. The VBA IDE opens the module text editor window.

3. Move down to the Windows task bar and click the AutoCAD button to return to AutoCAD. Now click the Microsoft Visual Basic button to return to the VBA IDE.

4. Click Object Browser on the VBA IDE Standard toolbar. Click the <All Libraries> drop-down list and choose AutoCAD. If necessary, maximize the window by clicking the maximize button at the top-right corner of the window.

5. In the Classes pane, click AcadLine. You see the associated properties and methods in the right pane.

6. In the right pane (Members of AcadLine), click Delete. You see the following at the bottom of the window:

```
Sub Delete()
    Member of AutoCAD.AcadLine
    Deletes a specified object.
```

Sub indicates the start of a VBA subroutine. Methods are listed in this way.

7. In the right pane, click Layer. At the bottom of the window, you see the following:

```
Property Layer As String
    Member of AutoCAD.AcadLine
    Specifies the current layer of the object.
```

This indicates that Layer is a property of AcadLine. String refers to the data type, discussed later in this chapter.

8. Click Help in the Object Browser window. You see the Help page for the Layer property.

9. On the Contents tab, double-click Objects and then click Line object. Scroll down to see all the properties and methods that belong to the Line object.

10. In the second paragraph of the description, the word AddLine is underlined with a hypertext line. Click it to see the description of the AddLine Method.

11. At the top of the page, click Example (also with a hypertext underline). You see an example of VBA code for creating a line.

12. Close Help by clicking the Close button at the top-right corner of each window. Leave the VBA IDE window open if you are continuing on to the next Step-by-Step exercise.

Getting help

VBA offers several help features. You have already seen the Object Browser, which provides you with a list of objects as well as their properties and methods.

To get help on an object, choose it in Object Browser and click Help. You can do the same for a method or property, as shown in Figure 37-4.

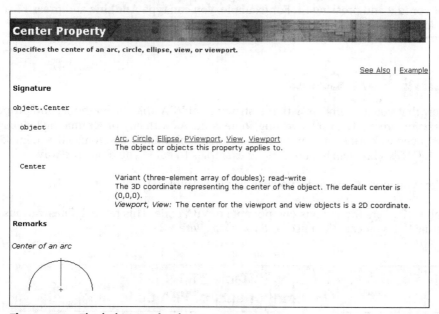

Figure 37-4: The help page for the Center Property

After you open a help page, click Example to see an example. These examples are a great way to learn VBA. You can copy a snippet of VBA code and paste it into your own routine and then edit it as you want.

For more general help, AutoCAD offers two systems:

✦ The ActiveX and VBA Reference is an alphabetical listing of objects, methods, properties, and events.

✦ The ActiveX and VBA Developer's Guide explains ActiveX automation concepts and techniques.

To access these reference guides, switch to AutoCAD and choose Help ➪ Developer Help.

The Microsoft Visual Basic for Applications Help provides information on the general VBA environment. Click Help on the VBA IDE Menu Bar toolbar or choose Help ➪ Microsoft Visual Basic Help. Here you see help for other VBA-enabled applications you may have. Use this when you are ready to write VBA code that integrates more than one application.

After you start programming, you can get help on any expression by placing the cursor in it and pressing F1. For example, you can type **AddLine** and press F1 to get help on how to create a line.

Writing VBA Code

Now that you are familiar with the structure of VBA objects, methods, and properties, you are ready to start writing some code. As with any programming language, you need to learn syntax and understand variables and when to use them. Luckily, AutoCAD's VBA Help includes many examples to guide you along the way.

After you write some code, you can use it in AutoCAD.

Table 37-1 lists the various components of VBA code. This table defines various terms that you can often use when working with VBA.

Table 37-1
Components of VBA Code

Term	Definition
Procedure	Code that does something and has a name. A procedure can be a subroutine, a function, or a property.
Project	A set of forms and modules.
Module	A set of subroutines, functions, and declarations that are usually related and comprise a distinct component in a project. A module can contain zero (0) or more procedures (subroutines and functions).

Term	Definition
Form	A container for the visual components, such as buttons and text boxes, of a dialog box that you create for your VBA project.
Subroutine	A procedure, written in VBA code, that does not return a value.
Function	A procedure, written in VBA code, that returns a value.
Property	A procedure, written in VBA code that specifies a value (the property of an object).
Declaration	One or more nonexecutable statements that name constants or variables and define their attributes (such as data type).
Macro	A public subroutine that a user can directly execute.

When you start to create code, VBA can create the basic structure for each procedure for you. Choose Insert ➪ Procedure (the Object Browser must be closed) to open the Add Procedure dialog box shown in Figure 37-5.

In the Name text box, type in a name for the new procedure, and then choose the type of procedure you want to create. Choose whether you want the scope to be Public or Private and then click OK. If a subroutine (called *sub* for short) is declared Public it is visible (can be called) from other modules or from the AutoCAD vbarun dialog box. A sub that is declared Private is only visible within that module.

Figure 37-5: The Add Procedure dialog box

Note If you check All Local variables as Statics in the Add Procedure dialog box, your variables retain their values between the times they are used.

Looking at VBA syntax

To start programming, you need an idea of how a VBA routine is put together. Here is a complete VBA routine that draws a 3D box.

```
 'Insert a 3D Solid Box
Sub Box()
'declare input variables to AddBox()
     Dim dOrigin(0 To 2) As Double 'origin is array of doubles
'(x,y,z)
     Dim dLength As Double         'length
     Dim dWidth As Double          'width
     Dim dHeight As Double         'height
     Dim myBox As Acad3DSolid      'holds return from AddBox()

     dOrigin(0) = 0#              'set origin to (0,0,0)
     dOrigin(1) = 0#
     dOrigin(2) = 0#

     dLength = 5#                 'make a cube 5 by 5 by 5
     dWidth = 5#
     dHeight = 5#

     'create the box in modelspace of the current drawing
     Set myBox = ThisDrawing.ModelSpace.AddBox(dOrigin,
dLength, dWidth, dHeight)
     'change the viewpoint to better see the box
ThisDrawing.SendCommand ("VPOINT 1,1,1 ")

End Sub
```

Here's what the code means:

✦ **Line 1:** Any text starting with an apostrophe (') is a comment. Placing comments in your routines helps you and others understand what you are doing.

✦ **Line 2:** Sub indicates the start of a procedure—a named, unified piece of code. You can have several subroutines in a VBA project. A project is the file you save, and it has a *.dvb* file name extension. Each project contains the components of your subroutines, dialog boxes, and so on. The next word is the name of the subroutine. Within the parentheses, you can add arguments, if any. Use an empty set of parentheses if there are no arguments. Declaring variables is discussed later in this chapter.

✦ **Line 3:** Another comment describing the next few lines of code. It is always a good idea to comment your code, indicate what is happening, and even write notes to yourself to remind you of your intent.

✦ **Line 4:** You can also declare variables using the Dim statement. Here dOrigin is used as the variable for the center of the box. (0 To 2) means that the

origin will have three parts to it, for the X, Y, and Z coordinates. Double is a type of variable suitable for most coordinates. More about variable types later.

✦ **Lines 5–7:** Here you declare the dLength, dWidth, and dHeight variables, which will be used as the length, width, and height of the box. These are declared as type Double, which is also indicated by the "d" prefix on the variable names. This is not required but it is a good idea to use a naming scheme for variables to help remind you of its type, especially as you get deeper into programming or have to come back to some code after not seeing it for a while.

✦ **Line 8:** Here you declare a variable called myBox as an Acad3DSolid to refer to the new box that will be created. Acad3DSolid is a data type specific to AutoCAD, suitable for (you guessed it) referencing a 3D solid in your drawing. You can find other AutoCAD data types by looking in the Object Browser or looking at the Object Model as explained earlier in this chapter.

✦ **Lines 9–11:** Here you specify the X, Y, and Z coordinates of the origin of the box. The values are assigned to the dOrigin variable. The pound sign (#) is used to indicate a double-precision floating-point value. Use of the # sign is not required here but is more accurate and more clearly indicates your intentions. In some situations rounding errors can occur when assigning numbers of one type to variables of another type, such as assigning integers to doubles and doubles to integers.

✦ **Lines 12–14:** Set the length, width, and height of the box to 5.

✦ **Line 15:** Another comment.

✦ **Line 16:** Finally, you're ready to actually do something. The Set statement is used to set a variable to an object. Here you set the variable myBox to an Acad3DSolid defined by AddBox(dOrigin, dLength, dWidth, dHeight). The AddBox method creates a new 3D Box. You need to define its origin, length, width, and height by using the variables you have previously defined. The AddBox method is a member of ModelSpace, which is a member of ThisDrawing. You use ThisDrawing in VBA to access the current drawing. Because VBA within AutoCAD is automatically connected to AutoCAD, you don't need to specify the application (that is, AutoCAD).

✦ **Line 17:** Not another comment! Ask yourself these questions: If I look at this code without the comments would I have a harder time understanding it? What if there is a bug and I ask another programmer to find it? What if I am that programmer?

✦ **Line 18:** Here we send the VPOINT command to change the viewpoint. Otherwise the box we just created will simply look like a square viewed from the top. The space after the numbers 1,1,1 and before the quotation mark is important. It signifies the end of the command. It's like pressing the Enter key for this command.

✦ **Line 19:** End Sub ends the subroutine.

To find the syntax for a statement you want to use, look in VBA Help, as explained in the section "Getting help" earlier in this chapter. In the preceding VBA routine, you might want to click AddBox and press F1 to find the syntax and elements required for creating a box. Then click Example to see an actual example of code for that statement.

Saving a VBA routine

As I mention earlier, the AutoCAD version of VBA saves VBA projects as separate files with a .dvb extension. However, when you run a routine, AutoCAD lists it in the format ModuleName:Procedure Name. If your project has only one module, you can give the module and the procedure the same name. However, most VBA routines have more than one module, with one module controlling the rest. By running the controlling module, you run the whole project.

To name a module, look in the Properties window. Once you have created a module, the VBA IDE lists its name property as Module1 by default. Double-click Module1 and type a new name. Notice that the module name in the Project window also changes accordingly.

Note A module name (as well as the names of other forms and controls) must start with a letter and can be up to 40 characters. Only letters, numbers, and the underscore character are allowed.

 To save a project as a separate file, which includes all the modules, click Save on the VBA IDE Standard toolbar. VBA returns you to AutoCAD and opens the Save As dialog box. Type a name for your project, choose a location, and click Save.

You can save your project in the \Sample\VBA subfolder in the AutoCAD 2004 folder or use another folder that is in AutoCAD's support file search path.

Loading a VBA routine

Before running a VBA routine, it must be loaded. If you are working on the routine and want to run it to check how it works — which you will do often — you do not need to load the routine. However, if you want to run a routine that has not been opened, you need to use the VBALOAD command. Choose Tools ➪ Macro ➪ Load Project (or type **vbaload** ↵) and AutoCAD opens the Open VBA Project dialog box. Navigate to your project, choose it, and click Open. (AutoCAD asks you to confirm that you want to enable macros.) The project is now loaded.

Running a VBA routine

After you complete a subroutine, you can run it in AutoCAD. After all, that's the reason for writing VBA code in the first place. To run a VBA routine, choose

Tools ➪ Macro ➪ Macros (or type **vbarun** ↵). In the Macros dialog box, shown in Figure 37-6, choose the module you want to run and click Run. AutoCAD runs the module, including other modules that may be controlled by the module you run.

Figure 37-6: Use the Macros dialog box to run a VBA routine.

Using the Visual Basic Editor

When you type code from scratch in the Visual Basic Editor, you immediately notice that Visual Basic color-codes your text as you go. The most common colors are:

Normal text	Black
Syntax error text	Red
Comments	Green
Keyword text	Blue

Keywords include variable types and other words that Visual Basic knows, such as Dim and Sub.

Tip You can customize these colors by choosing Tools ➪ Options from the Visual Basic menu and then choosing the Editor Format tab. Choose a type of text and then choose the desired color. Click OK.

When you start to type a keyword that Visual Basic knows, you will often see a box pop up that enables you to choose from a list or helps you complete the word. The editor also adds or removes spaces and capitalizes certain words for you to

improve your syntax. If you make a syntax mistake, a small error message often appears as you work. In these ways, the Visual Basic Editor helps you type accurate code.

Step-by-Step: Creating, Saving, and Running a VBA Program

1. Open a new drawing using the `acad.dwt` template. Choose Tools ⇨ Macro ⇨ Visual Basic Editor.

2. Choose Insert ⇨ Module. VBA opens the module text editor. (If you have previously opened a module, Visual Basic may open with a blank module already open. In that case, skip this step.)

3. Choose Insert ⇨ Procedure. In the Name text box, type **DrawTorus**. The type should be Sub and the scope should be public. Click OK.

4. Type the following code. (Note that the second and last lines are already there for you.)

```
'insert a Torus
Public Sub DrawTorus()
    'declare variables
    Dim dCenter(0 To 2) As Double
    Dim dRadius1 As Double
    Dim dRadius2 As Double
    Dim myTorus As Acad3DSolid

    'set center of torus to 0,0,0
    dCenter(0) = 0#
    dCenter(1) = 0#
    dCenter(2) = 0#

    dRadius1 = 10#      ' torus radius
    dRadius2 = 2#       ' tube radius

    'insert the torus
    Set myTorus = ThisDrawing.ModelSpace.AddTorus(dCenter,
dRadius1, dRadius2)

    'set the viewpoint and shade it
    ThisDrawing.SendCommand ("VPOINT 1,1,1 SHADEMODE GOURAUD
")
End Sub
```

5. In the Properties window, change the name of the module to **DrawTorus**.

6. Because this routine is active, you don't need to load it. Choose Save on the VBA IDE Standard toolbar. Save the project as `ab37-01.dvb` in your AutoCAD Bible folder.

7. Use the Windows task bar to return to your drawing. Choose Tools ⇨ Macro ⇨ Macros. In the Macro dialog box, choose DrawTorus and click Run. VBA draws and shades the torus.

Do not save your drawing.

Here's an explanation of the routine you just wrote and used. Note that blank lines are ignored.

✦ **Line 1:** This is a public subroutine named DrawTorus with no parameters.

✦ **Line 2:** Comment describing routine.

✦ **Line 3:** Comment indicating which variable declarations are next.

✦ **Line 4:** Declare the array to hold the X, Y, and Z coordinates for the center of the torus.

✦ **Line 5:** Declare the variable to hold the radius of the torus.

✦ **Line 6:** Declare the variable to hold the radius of the tube.

✦ **Line 7:** Declare the variable to hold the created 3D object.

✦ **Line 8:** Comment.

✦ **Lines 9–11:** Set the center to 0,0,0.

✦ **Line 12:** Set the torus radius to 10.0.

✦ **Line 13:** Set the tube radius to 2.0.

✦ **Line 14:** Comment.

✦ **Line 15:** Create the torus.

✦ **Line 16:** Comment.

✦ **Line 17:** Send commands to AutoCAD to set the viewpoint and shade the torus for better viewing.

✦ **Line 18:** End of subroutine.

Understanding variables

As I explained earlier, a variable holds a value for later use in your program. (See Chapter 35 for a discussion of variables in Visual LISP.)

In VBA, you do not need to explicitly declare your variables in advance (as long as you do not include Option Explicit, explained later). You can use the Set statement to set a variable to an object, as in the example here. This statement creates a variable, cir, and sets its value equal to the circle that the AddCircle method creates.

```
Set cir = ThisDrawing.ModelSpace.AddCircle(cen, radius)
```

When you create a variable in this way, VBA assigns the default *variant* type to it. The variant type of variable can contain numbers, dates, or strings (of text).

However, declaring variables explicitly in advance has two advantages:

✦ You can specify the type of variable, which usually uses less memory than the default variant type.

✦ As you continue to enter code, VBA checks the variable's spelling for you, reducing the chance for errors.

You declare variables using the Dim statement. Here's an example:

```
Dim radius As Double
```

You can create three different levels of variables:

✦ A public variable is available to all procedures in the project. It is shown as follows:

```
Public dRadius As Double
```

✦ A module-level variable is available to all the procedures in the module. You create a module-level variable by placing the declaration (with the Dim statement) at the top of a module, in a Declarations section. Another way to create a module-level variable is to use the Private statement. Examples are shown here:

```
Dim dNum3 as Double
Private dNum2 as Double
```

✦ A procedure-level variable is used only within a procedure. You can place the variable anywhere within the procedure as long as you declare the variable before you use it.

Placing the statement Option Explicit in a Declarations section requires all variables to be declared. Using Option Explicit is a way to force yourself to write your code more carefully. Declared variables are easier to debug because they are easier to find.

Table 37-2 describes the kinds of variables you can declare.

Table 37-2
VBA Variable Types

Variable	Description
Boolean	For variables that can have only two values—True or False.
Byte	Positive integers from 0 to 255.
Integer	Integers from −32,768 to +32,768.

Variable	Description
Long	Integers from −2,147,483,648 to +2,147,483,648.
Currency	Values from −922,337,203,685,477.5808 to +922,337,203,685,477.5808. Use this variable for currency or for other values that need accuracy to several decimals.
Single	Single-precision floating-point values. Single variables use less memory than double variables but their values are limited.
Double	Double-precision floating-point values. Double variables offer much greater precision than single variables. Most coordinates use this variable type. Three double variables create the X, Y, and Z values.
Date	Holds dates and times stored as real numbers. The number to the left of the decimal is the date and the number to the right of the decimal is the time.
String	Fixed or variable-length text strings, including letters, numbers, spaces, and punctuation characters.
Object	Objects such as an application, a drawing, or a drawing object.
Variant	Contains numbers, dates, or strings. When you do not declare a type for a variable, VBA uses this type by default.

Here's an example that uses the date variable type and displays it in a message box:

```
Sub DateDemo()
Dim dt As Date
Dim dbl As Double
    dt = Now        ' set the dt to the current date and time
    dbl = dt        ' assign this date value to a double
MsgBox "Normal date version: " & dt & "  Double version: " &
dbl
End Sub
```

Running DateDemo (by pressing F5) would show something similar to:

```
Normal date version: 1/25/2003 10:16:27 AM
Double version: 37646.4280902778
```

Creating VBA statements

While a complete discussion of how to write VBA code is beyond the scope of this book, some general principles will be helpful.

A statement in VBA is the most basic unit of code. It contains a complete instruction. There are three kinds of statements:

✦ A declaration names a variable, constant, or procedure, as in this example:

```
Dim dOrigin as Double
```

✦ An assignment assigns a value to a variable or constant. For example:

```
dOrigin = 0#
```

✦ An executable creates an action. For example, it can execute a method or function or create a loop or branch that acts on a block of code, as shown here:

```
Set myBox = ThisDrawing.ModelSpace.AddBox(dOrigin, dLength,
dWidth, dHeight)
```

VBA has many keywords and functions and other components you use to create code. To find the basic components of the VBA language, choose Help ➪ Microsoft Visual Basic Help. From the Contents tab, double-click Visual Basic Language Reference, which lists terms that are part and parcel of VBA. Here are some examples:

✦ **Constants:** Constants can be used anywhere in your code to provide a named value. For example, VBA offers color and date constants you can use to specify colors and dates.

✦ **Functions:** VBA includes many functions you will find familiar if you have used AutoLISP. For example, the ABS function returns the absolute value (without a plus or minus sign) of any number. The DATE function returns the current system date.

✦ **Keywords:** Keywords are words that have a special meaning in VBA. They are often used as parts of VBA statements. For example `Else` is a keyword that is used in the `If. . .Then. . .Else` Statement. You are already familiar with the `Set` keyword, which is used in the `Set` statement.

✦ **Operators:** VBA includes all the usual arithmetic operations, such as +, –, *, /, and ^. You can also use & to concatenate text strings. There are several logical operators, such as `and`, `not`, and `or`.

✦ **Statements:** Statements help you create the flow of your code. You are already familiar with the `Set` statement. Other statements are `For Each. . .Next` and `If. . .Then. . .Else`. These provide looping capabilities in VBA.

Remember that you can also get a list of objects and their properties and methods from the Object Browser, as explained earlier in this chapter.

Getting User Input

The examples used in this chapter were not very useful, partly because the routines provided no way to get user input for the properties of the objects they drew. There are two main ways to get user input — on the command line and via a dialog box. In this section, I explain how to get user input on the command line.

In order to use the user-input methods, you need to first use something called the Utility object. The Utility object belongs to the Document object and controls the methods that get user input. You can also use ThisDrawing, as in the following example.

```
Dim iReturn as Integer
iReturn = ThisDrawing.Utility.GetInteger("Enter an integer: ")
```

Here you set a variable called iReturn equal to the integer that the user types on the command line. The prompt is Enter an integer:.

You can use this type of user input to get a pick point, a numeric value (such as the radius of a circle), a text string, or an object. Use this method when the input is short and sweet.

To avoid several prompts appearing on the same line, use vbCrLf, the carriage return/linefeed constant, at the beginning of a prompt, as in the following example:

```
prompt1 = vbCrLf & "Specify center point: "
```

Here's an example that illustrates how to get user input on the command line:

```
Sub AddCircle()
    Dim thePt As Variant
    Dim theRadius As Double
    Dim myCircle As AcadCircle

    thePt = ThisDrawing.Utility.GetPoint(, vbCrLf & "Enter
Center Point:")
    theRadius = ThisDrawing.Utility.GetReal("Enter radius: ")
    Set myCircle = ThisDrawing.ModelSpace.AddCircle(thePt,
theRadius)
End Sub
```

Table 37-3 lists some commonly used methods for getting user input. If you know the GET functions in AutoLISP, you'll be familiar with these methods.

Table 37-3
Common User Input Methods

Method	Syntax	Description
GetEntity	object.GetEntity Object, PickedPoint, Prompt	The user selects an object (entity) by picking it. Returns the object in the first parameter and the point picked in the second parameter. The prompt is optional. Example: `ThisDrawing. utility. GetEntity getObj, basePnt, "Select an object"` where getObj has been declared as an Object type variable.
GetInteger	RetVal = GetInteger (Prompt)	Any integer from −32,768 to +32,767 is valid. The prompt is optional. Example: `getInt = ThisDrawing.utility. GetInteger("Enter an integer: ")`
GetPoint	RetVal = GetPoint (Point, Prompt)	Returns a variant (which contains a three-element array of doubles). The user can pick a point or type in a coordinate. If the Point parameter (optional) is provided, AutoCAD draws a rubberband line from Point to the current crosshair position. The prompt is also optional. Example: `getPnt = ThisDrawing. utility.GetPoint (, "Specify a point: ")`
GetReal	RetVal = GetReal (Prompt)	Gets any real (positive or negative) number. The prompt is optional. Example: `getaReal = ThisDrawing.utility. GetReal("Enter a real number: ")`
GetString	RetVal = GetString (HasSpaces, Prompt)	The `HasSpaces` parameter specifies whether the string can contain spaces. If the `HasSpaces` parameter is TRUE, the string can contain blanks and the user must press Enter to end input. If `HasSpaces` is FALSE, entering either a blank or Enter ends input. The prompt is optional. Example: `getaString = This Drawing.utility. GetString (False, "Enter text (a space or <enter> terminates input):")`

Step-by-Step: Creating a VBA Routine That Gets User Input

1. Open a new AutoCAD drawing using the `acad.dwt` template.

2. To start a new project, choose Tools ➪ Macro ➪ VBA Manager. Click New and then click Visual Basic Editor.

3. Choose Insert ➪ Module and then choose Insert ➪ Procedure. Name it HappyFace and click OK.

4. At the cursor, type the following:

```
Dim prompt As String, prompt2 As String
Dim cen As Variant
Dim rad As Double
Dim cir As AcadCircle
Dim arc As AcadArc
Dim pi As Double
Dim dStart As Double    'start angle
Dim dEnd As Double     'end angle

    pi = 3.1415
    prompt = vbCrLf & "Specify center point: "
    prompt2 = vbCrLf & "Specify radius: "

    'get center point from user
    cen = ThisDrawing.Utility.GetPoint(, prompt)
    rad = ThisDrawing.Utility.GetDistance(cen, prompt2)

    'draw head
    Set cir = ThisDrawing.ModelSpace.AddCircle(cen, rad)
    'draw smile
dStart = 225 * pi / 180    'pi / 180 converts to radians
DEnd = 315 * pi / 180
Set arc = ThisDrawing.ModelSpace.AddArc(cen, rad / 2, dStart,
dEnd)
    'draw eyes
    cen(0) = cen(0) - rad / 4
    cen(1) = cen(1) + rad / 4
    Set cir = ThisDrawing.ModelSpace.AddCircle(cen, rad / 8)
    cen(0) = cen(0) + rad / 2
    Set cir = ThisDrawing.ModelSpace.AddCircle(cen, rad / 8)
```

5. Change the module name to HappyFace.

6. Choose Save from the VBA IDE Standard toolbar and save the VBA project as `ab37-02.dvb` in your `AutoCAD Bible` folder.

7. Return to your drawing and choose Tools ➪ Macro ➪ Macros. In the Macro dialog box, choose HappyFace and click Run.

8. Respond to the prompts. HappyFace draws the circle with the center point and radius you specify.

You don't need to save your drawing.

The previous example uses `GetDistance` rather than `GetReal` to enable the user to select the radius of the circle with the mouse. The center point you previously selected feeds into the `GetDistance` function. Also, there are calculations to convert degrees to radians. The location and size of the eyes and smile are relative to the center and radius.

Creating Dialog Boxes

One of the main characteristics of VBA is the ease with which you can create dialog boxes to get user input. Whenever you need input that is more complex than you can get using the Get methods, you should use a dialog box. You can also use a dialog box to create a more professional look or for ease of use.

When working with a dialog box, you generally create the dialog box first and then attach code to the dialog box buttons. You then use a second module to display the dialog box. Running the second module then controls the entire routine.

In VBA, a dialog box is called a *user form*. To create one, choose Insert ⇨ UserForm. VBA creates a blank user form that will become your dialog box. Simultaneously, the Toolbox toolbar appears. If this toolbar covers up some other part of your screen, drag it to one side. Your screen looks like Figure 37-7.

Figure 37-7: The VBA IDE with a blank user form and the Toolbox toolbar

Understanding the Toolbox toolbar

The Toolbox toolbar contains the tools you need to create a dialog box. These are the familiar controls you see in the dialog boxes you use all the time, such as text boxes, list boxes, check boxes, and so on. Figure 37-8 shows the buttons on the Toolbox toolbar, stretched out into one row.

Figure 37-8: Use the buttons on the Toolbox toolbar to create dialog boxes.

Table 37-4 explains the Toolbox toolbar buttons.

Table 37-4	
The Toolbox Toolbar Buttons	
Button	**Description**
Select Objects	Enables the user to select objects
Label	Creates a label on the dialog box
TextBox	Enables the user to type in text
ComboBox	Combines features of text and list boxes
ListBox	Enables the user to choose from a list
CheckBox	Creates a box that can be checked or unchecked
OptionButton	Enables the user to choose one option from several possibilities (also called a radio button)

Continued

Table 37-4 (continued)

Button	Description
ToggleButton	Creates an on/off switch
Frame	Creates a box around a section of the dialog box
CommandButton	Creates a button that executes a command, such as OK and Cancel buttons
TabStrip	Creates tabs along the top of the dialog box
MultiPage	Creates multiple pages
ScrollBar	Creates a scrollbar
SpinButton	Enables the user to specify a number
Image	Inserts an image

Tip If you think the Toolbox toolbar has lots of possibilities, right-click the Toolbox toolbar and choose Additional Controls. From the Additional Controls dialog box, you can choose from many more controls.

Changing dialog box properties

After you insert a user form, you should name it. Find the Name property in the Properties window and change it from UserForm1 (the default name) to any useful name you want. You might find it useful to use the word "form" in the name. For example, for a routine to draw a circle, you could call the user form formCircle.

Figure 37-9 shows the property box when you insert a user form. You can easily change the dialog box's properties in the property box.

One property you will want to change is the Caption property of the dialog box. The dialog box should have a caption that summarizes its purpose. When you type the new caption in the property box, the caption on the dialog box changes at the same time.

Adding dialog box controls

One of the most commonly used controls is the *command button*. A command button is a button you click in the dialog box to execute an action. The most familiar command buttons are the OK and Cancel buttons.

Figure 37-9: When you insert a user form (dialog box), the Properties window lists all its properties.

Add a command button

To add a command button, click CommandButton on the Toolbox toolbar. Move your cursor over the dialog box and drag to create a button. Figure 37-10 shows a dialog box with a new command button. The selection border and handles indicate that the button is a selected object. You can move the button by dragging it. You can resize the button by dragging one of the handles. Add all the command buttons you need. Don't forget to include at least a Cancel button. Many dialog boxes also have an OK button. If you know in advance all the controls you will need, you can add them all at once.

Figure 37-10: A dialog box with one selected command button

Tip There's an art to laying out a dialog box so that it is clear and easy to understand. After a while you'll get the hang of it. Pay more attention to the dialog boxes you use every day to pick up some design pointers.

Just as the dialog box has properties, each control on the dialog box has properties. When a control such as a command button is selected, you see its properties in the Properties window. You generally would change at least the caption and the name of a command button. It is a good idea to change the names to something meaningful rather than using the default name. For example, instead of CommandButton1, use something such as cmdDrawBox or cmdOk.

Write the VBA Code for a command button

After you create a command button, you can attach VBA code to it. To attach VBA code to a control, double-click the control. The text editor opens with the Sub and End Sub lines already entered for you. Type the code you want to attach to the button.

VBA dialog boxes are modal by default, which means that they must be closed before AutoCAD can do anything further. To close a dialog box once your VBA code has run, use Unload Me at the end of a routine.

To run VBA code attached to a dialog box, you need to show the dialog box so you can use it—click a command button, type in text, and so on. The VBA IDE creates private subroutines for each dialog box control. To show the dialog box, start a new module and create code that looks like the code in this example.

```
Sub DrawArc()
FormArc.Show
End Sub
```

Getting user input for a circle radius

Here's another example of a routine that draws a circle, but here you get user input for the radius using the VAL function. The VAL function returns a numerical value from a text string. Here you create a text box that enables users to type in a radius. The VAL function converts the string in the text box to a number and uses it as the circle's radius. Follow these steps:

1. Open AutoCAD with a new drawing using the `acad.dwt` template. Open the VBA IDE.

2. Choose Insert ⇨ UserForm.

3. In the Properties window, change the name of the form to `frmDrawCircle` and the caption to Draw a Circle Demo.

4. From the Toolbox toolbar, choose Label and drag a small rectangle on the left side of the form, around the middle.

5. Change the caption to Radius.

6. Choose Textbox on the Toolbox toolbar and drag a box on the form to the right of the label.

7. Change the name to `txtRadius`.

8. Choose CommandButton on the Toolbox toolbar and drag a larger box at the top center of the form.

9. Change the name to `cmdDrawCircle` and the caption to Draw Circle.

10. Double-click this command button to bring up the code editor in the `cmdDrawCircle_Click ()` subroutine.

11. Add the following lines:

```
Dim dCenter(0 To 2) As Double
Dim dRadius As Double
Dim myCircle as AcadCircle

dCenter(0) = 0#
dCenter(1) = 0#
dCenter(2) = 0#

dRadius = Val(txtRadius)
Set myCircle = ThisDrawing.ModelSpace.AddCircle(dCenter, dRadius)
myCircle.Update
```

12. Close the code window. Save the routine if you want. On the VBA IDE menu, choose Run ⇨ Run Sub/UserForm. Visual Basic returns you to your drawing and displays the dialog box. Enter a number for the radius and click the Draw Circle command button.

13. Add as many circles as you like. Click the Close box of the dialog box when you're done.

FormArc is the name of the user form in this example. Don't forget to name the user form in the Properties window. Also, remember to name the module because the module name is what appears in the Macro dialog box when you want to run the routine.

Add a label

A command button is quite simple. You just click it, and it performs. You can label its function right on the command button. However, most other controls require some more explanation. For example, if you want the user to type in text, you need a text box. However, a text box has no caption. Therefore, you need to add instructions to the user. A dialog box may also need other instructions to clarify the purpose of the controls, which responses are required, and so on.

You add instructions with the Label tool on the Toolbox toolbar. Click Label and drag a rectangle on your dialog box. Then type the label. You can resize or move the label as needed.

Add other dialog box controls

The code for some of the dialog box controls can be quite complex. For example, to create a list box that enables the user to choose from an existing list of options, you would probably create the list of options in advance. For help on creating dialog boxes, choose Help ➪ Microsoft Visual Basic Help. On the Contents tab, double-click Microsoft Forms Reference, then Microsoft Forms Object Model Reference. From there you may want to double-click Objects, Collections, and Controls. You can double-click a control, such as the ListBox control, and read more about it. The specific controls also offer hyperlinks to examples you can look at.

Step-by-Step: Creating a Dialog Box with a Command Button

1. Open a new drawing in AutoCAD using the acad.dwt template. Choose Tools ➪ Macro ➪ Visual Basic Editor.

2. Choose Insert ➪ UserForm. If the Toolbox toolbar covers the user form or project window, drag it to the right.

3. With the user form active (click its title bar to make it active), change the Name property of the user form to frmArc in the Properties window.

4. Change the Caption property of the user form to Draw an arc. Watch the caption of the user form change as you type.

5. Choose CommandButton on the Toolbox toolbar. (It's the last button in the second row. If you don't see the Toolbox toolbar, click in the user form on the right side of your screen.) Move the cursor over the user form and drag to create a wide button across the upper center of the user form.

6. Change the Caption property of the button to Draw the Arc! Change the name property to cmdDrawArc.

7. Again, choose CommandButton on the Toolbox toolbar. Create a smaller button below the first one near the right side of the user form.

8. Change the Caption property of the smaller button to Cancel. Change its name property to cmdCancel. Your dialog box should look like the one in Figure 37-11.

Figure 37-11: A simple dialog box created in VBA

9. Double-click the larger button. In the text editor, type the following code at the cursor's current location between the Private Sub and End Sub statements:

```
'declare variables
Dim startang As Double
Dim endang As Double
Dim ctr(0 To 2) As Double
Dim rad As Double
Dim newarc As Object
'specify arc parameters
startang = 0
'angles are in radians.
endang = 100
ctr(0) = 5
ctr(1) = 2
ctr(2) = 0
rad = 2
'draw arc
Set newarc = ThisDrawing.ModelSpace.AddArc(ctr, rad,
startang, endang)
'close dialog box
Unload Me
```

10. From the left (Object) drop-down list at the top of the text editor, choose cmdCancel to add the code for the second button. In the space below the start of the subroutine (Private Sub cmdCancel_Click()), type Unload Me.

11. Choose Insert ⇨ Module. In the new text editor, type the following to display the dialog box.

```
Sub DrawArc()
frmArc.Show
```

Visual Basic places the End Sub statement for you after the code.

12. In the Properties window, change the module's name to DrawArc.

13. Click Save on the toolbar and save the file in your AutoCAD Bible folder as ab37-03.dvb.

14. Return to your drawing, Choose Tools ⇨ Macro ⇨ Macros. In the Macro dialog box, choose DrawArc and click Run.

15. Click the large button. AutoCAD draws the arc.

Modifying Objects

Modifying objects is usually very easy. You need to know the name of the object. If you have created it, you set it equal to a variable and you can use that variable.

If you have created a circle named cir1, the following code changes its layer to "fixtures", assuming "fixtures" exists:

```
Cir1.layer = "fixtures"
```

To add a layer, use the Add method of the Layers collection of objects:

```
Set Newlayer1 = ThisDrawing.Layers.Add("fixtures")
```

To set the new layer's color, use the Color property. This code sets the color to red, using the red color constant. Constants are discussed in the next section.

```
Newlayer1.Color = acRed
```

The update command forces the changes to the current view. It updates the change to the screen so you can see it. For example, you can create a circle with the following code:

```
Set myCircle = ThisDrawing.ModelSpace.AddCircle(dCenter,
cRadius)
```

This adds the circle to the current drawing's database but has not yet updated the view. If you do this from a dialog box, the view will not be updated until you exit the dialog box *unless* you force an update with the following code.

```
myCircle.Update
```

Using constants

Constants are names given to commonly used values. For instance, AutoCAD defines constants for the seven standard colors: acRed, acYellow, acGreen, acCyan, acBlue, acMagenta, and acWhite. In the DrawCircle example, after creating the circle you could add the following to change its color to blue:

```
myCircle.Color = acBlue
```

Most functions or properties that have a standard set of values will have corresponding constants defined.

Using functions

Functions are a type of procedure (like subroutines) except they return a value. Here's an example for those of you who are counting the days until January 1, 2004. (If you're reading this after that date, you can change it to a later date.) Or it will tell you how many days ago January 1, 2004 occurred (indicated by a negative value).

```
Function DaysTil2004() As Integer  'notice "As Integer" tells
'the return type of                'the function
    Dim dtToday As Date            'holds todays date
    Dim dt2004 As Date             'holds Jan 1, 2004

    dtToday = Now()                'assign today's date
    dt2004 = CDate("1/1/2004")     'assign Jan 1, 2004
    DaysTil2004 = dt2004 - dtToday 'calculate difference,
'return value assigned             'to function name
End Function                       'same as End Sub
```

To use this function you must do something with the return value via an assignment or use it as a parameter to another procedure. For example:

```
Public Sub Test2004()
MsgBox "Days until year 2004: " & DaysTil2004()
End Sub
```

You can then run the Test2004 sub to open a message box that tells you how many days are left until the year 2004.

Accessing other applications

The true power of VBA comes when you can integrate other applications into your work. For the most part, accessing other applications is beyond the scope of this book, but here are a couple of simple examples you may find helpful to explain the process.

The technology enabling two applications or components to communicate with each other is called *automation*. Automation requires a client and a server. The *server* is the application or component that provides services to the client. The *client* is the application that makes use of these services. Many applications can perform as both Automation clients and Automation servers including AutoCAD, Access, Excel, and Word. Most ActiveX controls are Automation servers. Any application that supports VBA has the capability to be an Automation client.

In order for a client to properly communicate with a server, it must properly use the server's object model or hierarchy. (The AutoCAD object hierarchy was discussed earlier in this chapter.) You can view a server's object model or hierarchy using the Object Browser. Most components have a Type Library file (most have a .tlb or .olb file extension) that can be imported from the Tools ⇨ References menu in the VBA IDE. If the server is in the current list, make sure it is checked. If it is not in the list, click Browse, locate its .tlb file, and click Open. This will add it to the list of references and make it available to the Object Browser.

There are two approaches for creating instances of automation component objects—early binding and late binding. With early binding you use the VBA keyword *New* to reference the components type library at design time. With late binding you declare a variable using the Object data type and later use CreateObject or GetObject to create the specified type at runtime. Early binding offers several benefits over late binding, including speed, syntax checking in the VBA editor, and online help. Some automation components do not support early binding.

Here are two Excel examples, one using early binding and the other using late binding:

```
Sub XlsEarly()
    Dim objXls As New Excel.Application
    ' Note that the application is not launched until a property
or method is referenced
    MsgBox "Application: " & objXls.Name & "  Version: " &
objXls.Version
    objXls.Visible = True
    objXls.Quit
    Set objXls = Nothing
End Sub

Sub XlsLate()
    Dim objXls As Object

    ' CreateObject will launch the application
    Set objXls = CreateObject("Excel.Application")
    MsgBox "Application: " & objXls.Name & "  Version: " &
objXls.Version
```

```
        objXls.Visible = True
        objXls.Quit
        Set objXls = Nothing
End Sub
```

Debugging and Trapping Errors

As with all programming languages there are techniques to help you find the errors that inevitably crop up. Here is a simple debugging technique to get you started:

1. Go to the code editor and to the procedure where you suspect the error resides.

2. Place the cursor on the first executable statement in the procedure and choose Debug ⇨ Toggle Breakpoint (or press F9).

3. Begin stepping through each statement by pressing F8 (Step Into).

4. For simple variables (Integers, Doubles, and Strings) you can place the mouse cursor over the variable, and it will display the current contents. You can also add variables to the Watch window (choose View ⇨ Watch Window) or enter commands in the Immediate window (choose View ⇨ Immediate Window) to verify your logic.

5. When an error is located, choose Run ⇨ Reset and make the correction. You can also use Reset any time you want to halt the routine.

6. The next time you run the procedure your breakpoint is still set. At this point you can either step through again and verify if your changes are correct or press F9 to toggle the breakpoint off and choose Run ⇨ Run to run the routine normally.

Unexpected errors occur. A file you attempt to open doesn't exist, your system runs out of memory and can't insert that AutoCAD block into your drawing, or you unintentionally write a routine that divides by zero. Some of these errors you can and should plan for, others maybe not. VBA provides a mechanism for catching errors and handling them gracefully rather than burping all over your screen or locking up your system.

A simple framework to begin error trapping would be:

```
Sub MyRoutine()
    ' declare variables
    ...
    On Error GoTo ErrorHandler
    ' rest of procedure goes here
    Exit Sub       ' Tells subroutine to exit ignoring the
                   ' ErrorHandler statements
```

```
ErrorHandler:
MsgBox "Error " & Err.Number & " " & Err.Description
    Resume Next
End Sub
```

This simple error trapping will at least alert you to any errors that occur by providing an error number and description. This will give you the opportunity to begin handling specific errors appropriately as required.

Active X and VBA Developer's Guide has a good discussion on handling errors in the "Developing Applications with VBA" section.

Moving to Advanced Programming

The chapters in this part have reviewed the fundamentals of Visual LISP and VBA, and you have seen the power these languages provide for automating your work.

ObjectARX applications share the same memory space as AutoCAD and are many times faster than routines written in AutoLISP or VBA. ObjectARX is based on C++ and enables full *object-oriented* interfacing with AutoCAD. An object-oriented interface enables the programmer to create an object in memory (such as an arc), modify its attributes, and then modify the AutoCAD database.

You can create custom objects that inherit properties from AutoCAD objects; that is, your object can assume all the properties of a given object already in AutoCAD, and you can add to it. For example, you can inherit from a line so your custom object has everything the line does, and then you can add width to it if you want. A variety of tools unavailable to AutoLISP programmers are also available with ObjectARX. ObjectARX involves much greater development time than AutoLISP. ObjectARX also requires a Visual C++ 6.0 compiler for AutoCAD 2002 and earlier. AutoCAD 2004 requires the Visual C++ .NET compiler to compile and link applications for use with AutoCAD. ObjectARX can be obtained at the Autodesk Web site (www.autodesk.com).

A Final Word

AutoCAD offers almost unlimited potential for the design and drawing of real-world objects. I hope this book helps you understand the world of AutoCAD and makes it easier for you to create the professional drawings you need to redesign the world and make it a better place. Although I cannot provide technical support for my readers, I would be happy to hear your comments and suggestions at ellenfinkl@ bigfoot.com. Good luck and enjoy!

✦ ✦ ✦

Appendix

Part VIII explains in detail what is on the CD-ROM and how to use the files. On the CD-ROM, you will find four appendixes that provide additional information for AutoCAD users. These appendixes are especially useful when you first start to use AutoCAD 2004, but offer a great deal of information for ongoing use as well.

Appendix A runs you through the process of installing AutoCAD and configuring it to suit your personal needs. Appendix B displays and labels the menus and toolbars, which is very helpful for users who are upgrading. Appendix C lists all the new, changed, and discontinued commands and system variables, which are invaluable when you are upgrading. Also included is a list of often-used system variables that are helpful at any time. Appendix D is an overview of further AutoCAD resources, including discussion groups and Web sites.

What's on the CD-ROM

The *AutoCAD 2004 Bible* CD-ROM contains all the drawings and files you need to do the exercises as well as the results of those exercises. In addition, I've tried out as many useful shareware programs and AutoLISP routines as I could to see if they work with AutoCAD 2004 and selected those I felt would be most useful. You can also find the entire book in PDF format. I hope you find this CD-ROM a valuable addition to your AutoCAD arsenal. This appendix provides you with information on the contents of the CD that accompanies this book. For the latest and greatest information, please refer to the ReadMe file located at the root of the CD. Here is what you will find:

✦ System Requirements

✦ What's on the CD

✦ Troubleshooting

System Requirements

Make sure that your computer meets the minimum system requirements listed in this section. If your computer doesn't match up to most of these requirements, you may have a problem using the contents of the CD.

For Windows 9x, Windows 2000, Windows NT4 (with SP 4 or later), Windows Me, or Windows XP:

✦ PC with a Pentium processor running at 200 Mhz or faster

✦ At least 64 MB of total RAM installed on your computer; for best performance, we recommend at least 128 MB

✦ Ethernet network interface card (NIC) or modem with a speed of at least 28,800 bps

✦ A CD-ROM drive

For system requirements for AutoCAD 2004, see Appendix A on the CD-ROM.

What's on the CD

I have placed all the files you need for the exercises in the \Drawings folder of the CD-ROM. Almost all of these files are named as in the following examples — ab15-a.dwg, ab15-b.dwg, ab15-c.dwg, and so on. In these examples, the number 15 corresponds to the chapter number, whereas the letters correspond to the first, second, and third drawings you need to open.

A few files have other names, such as sky.gif and others. In each case, I give you the name of the file to open. You can easily find them with Explorer, because Explorer automatically alphabetizes the files. (If they are not alphabetized, click the Name column of the right-hand window. If Explorer alphabetizes them in reverse order, click Name one more time.)

The CD-ROM contains five other folders: Results, eBook, Links, and Software.

Using the Results folder

The Results folder offers you the results of all the exercises. You might want to check your work in the exercise. Also, sometimes you might use the result of one exercise as the basis for a second exercise (although I try not to require this very often). In this situation, if you haven't done the previous exercise, you can get the resulting file from the Results folder and use it for the next exercise. If you have any difficulty opening a drawing from the Results folder, copy it to your hard drive and remove its read-only attribute as described in the "Changing the Windows read-only attribute" sidebar.

Using the eBook folder

You can now have access to *AutoCAD 2004 Bible* without lugging around a heavy book. The entire book is on the CD-ROM in Adobe Acrobat PDF format. The PDF format displays a picture of the pages of the book. To read the book in this format, you need the Acrobat Reader for Windows, which is on the CD in the Reader folder.

You can put Acrobat Reader on your laptop and read while you travel. You can refer to the book when you are in the field or on-site.

Changing the Windows read-only attribute

You can use the exercise drawings directly from the CD-ROM, but you might get better results by copying them to your hard drive. In most cases, the exercises instruct you to do this.

To use the software from the CD-ROM, you should copy the files to a folder in AutoCAD's Support File Search Path.

You might run initially into the problem of not being able to access files on the CD-ROM after you copy the files to your computer. After you copy or move a file from the CD to your hard disk or another storage medium (such as a Zip drive), you may get the following error message when you attempt to open or save a file with its associated application:

```
[Application] is unable to open the [file].
Please make sure the drive and file are writable.
```

Windows sees all files on a CD-ROM drive as "read-only." This makes sense normally because a CD-ROM is a read-only medium—that is, you can't write data back to the disc. However, when you copy a file from a CD-ROM to your hard disk or to a Zip drive, Windows doesn't automatically change the file attribute from read-only to writable. Installation software normally takes care of this chore for you, but in the case in which the files are to be manually copied to your disk, you have to change the file attribute yourself. Luckily, this is easy:

1. Click the Start menu button.

2. Choose (All) Programs ⇨ Accessories ⇨ Windows Explorer.

3. Highlight the file name(s).

4. Right-click the highlighted file name(s) to display a pop-up menu.

5. Select Properties to display the Properties dialog box.

6. Click the Read-only option so that it is no longer checked.

7. Click OK.

You should now be able to use the file(s) with the specific application without getting the annoying error message.

Using Acrobat Reader folder

Adobe Acrobat Reader is included on the CD-ROM to enable you to read this book in its electronic form. Follow these steps to install the software:

1. Start Windows Explorer and open the Acrobat Reader folder on the CD-ROM.

2. In the Acrobat Reader folder, locate the .exe file and double-click it.

3. Follow the instructions on-screen to install the software.

4. To view this book in its electronic form, start Windows Explorer and open the eBook folder from the CD-ROM.

5. Double-click the book's .pdf file in the Book PDF folder.

Using the Links folder

Appendix D on the CD-ROM of this book contains numerous links of AutoCAD resources. The Links folder contains these resources as live links to make it easy for you to navigate to them with a single click.

Using the Software folder

I assembled what I think is an excellent collection of useful software that works with AutoCAD 2004. The Software folder is divided into subfolders by chapter. Not all chapters have software, so subfolders appear only for the chapters that have software. This makes it easy for you to find software by function. For example, you can find software for text objects by looking in the Chapter 13 subfolder because Chapter 13 covers text. Table 1 at the end of this appendix lists the software alphabetically so that you can review it at a glance. Within each chapter's subfolder, you'll find subfolders for each program or AutoLISP routine.

New Feature I am very excited to include a 30-day trial version of AutoCAD 2004 with this book. This trial version is in the \Software|AutoCAD folder. Run Setup.EXE to install.

To find out in detail what each software program or AutoLISP routine does, read the text (.txt) file if there is one. It provides details about what the software does and how to install it. Sometimes details are at the beginning of the .lsp file. You can open and read it.

Most of the software on the CD-ROM is *freeware* — you can use it at no cost. Most of these are AutoLISP routines. However, some of it is *shareware*. Here's the scoop on shareware — you try it out and if you like it, you buy it. It works on the honor system, so please be honorable and pay for the shareware you use. All shareware comes with a text file that explains how much to pay for it, what you get when you register, and where to send your payment. Often you get additional features when you register.

The CD-ROM also has one or two demo programs. Demos are not fully functional — usually they either shut down after a short time or they do not work to the fullest extent. Demos are not shareware — they demonstrate regular software programs that you must buy.

Using AutoLISP routines

AutoLISP routines are easy to install. Follow these steps:

1. Copy the .lsp file to AutoCAD's \Support folder or to a folder that you have placed in AutoCAD's Support File Search Path.

> **Note** To add a folder to AutoCAD's Support File Search Path, choose Tools ⇨ Options and click the plus sign (+) next to Support File Search Path on the Files tab. Choose Add. Type in a folder path or choose Browse to locate one.

2. In AutoCAD, type **(load "file name")** where **file name** is the name of the .lsp file. You don't need the .lsp, but don't forget the parentheses or the quotation marks. AutoCAD responds with the name of the last function defined in the routine.

3. Type the name of the function to use the AutoLISP routine.

You can also choose Tools ⇨ Load Application to load an AutoLISP or ARX program.

Most of the AutoLISP routines were written before AutoCAD 2004 came out. Sometimes the installation instructions are out of date and don't include the capability of adding the folder to the Support File Search Path.

If no text file explains how to use the program, brief instructions may be displayed on the command line. If not, type the name of the file, such as **atc**, and press Enter.

Using VBA programs

To load a VBA program, copy it to a folder in AutoCAD's Support File Search Path. Choose Tools ⇨ Macro ⇨ Load Project. Locate the VBA program (a .dvb file), select it, and click Open. AutoCAD displays a message telling you that the VBA program contains macros and enabling you to disable them. Of course, the VBA program doesn't work if you disable the macros. If you want, you can check the file with a virus-checker first. To enable the macros, choose Enable Macros. AutoCAD loads the VBA program.

To use a VBA program, choose Tools ⇨ Macro ⇨ Macros. Select the VBA program and click Run. For more information on VBA programs, see Chapter 37.

Using a setup or install file

If you see a setup or install file (such as setup.exe), use it to install the software. You might need to remove the read-only attribute first, as explained at the beginning of this appendix. Copy all the files to a folder in AutoCAD's Support File Search Path. In Windows Explorer, double-click the setup or install file and the process should start automatically.

A List of Software

Table 1 lists all the software on the *AutoCAD 2004 Bible* CD-ROM.

Table 1 The CD-ROM Software			
Name	**Description**	**Chapter**	**Type**
3dspiral.lsp	Constructs 2D and 3D spirals	21	Shareware
AccuRender	Rendering program	25	Evaluation
Adobe Acrobat Reader	View electronic content		Freeware
Ar1.exe	Creates a label of the area of an enclosed polyline	16	Freeware
AutoCAD 2004 Trial	30-Day Trial of AutoCAD 2004	–	Commercial Trial
Br	Draws a break symbol	10	Freeware
Flatten.lsp	Converts 3D plines to 2D; flattens everything except blocks	22	Shareware
GeomCurves	Creates mathematical curves	16	Freeware
Keypad.zip	Creates a keypad toolbar	33	Freeware
ldt.lsp	Lets you specify spacing between lines of dtext	13	Freeware
lt.lsp	Lets you specify spacing between lines of text	13	Freeware
Mend	Combines two lines into one	6	Freeware
Mmt	Merges two mtext objects	13	Freeware
Mpe-arch drawing	Mechanical and electrical components for architectural drawings	18	Freeware
Pend	Creates a pipe break symbol in a line	10	Freeware
Savea.lsp	Saves to a: drive	1	Freeware

Name	Description	Chapter	Type
Stmplot	Adds drawing information to plots	17	Freeware
Wb.exe	Creates a list of blocks in a folder and wblocks the blocks to that folder	18	Freeware
WinRAR	A compression and decompression program	—	Trial Version

Troubleshooting

If you have difficulty installing or using any of the materials on the companion CD, try the following solutions:

✦ **Turn off any anti-virus software that you may have running.** Installers sometimes mimic virus activity and can make your computer incorrectly believe that it is being infected by a virus. (Be sure to turn the anti-virus software back on later.)

✦ **Close all running programs.** The more programs you're running, the less memory is available to other programs. Installers also typically update files and programs; if you keep other programs running, installation may not work properly.

✦ **Reference the ReadMe:** Please refer to the ReadMe file located at the root of the CD-ROM for the latest product information at the time of publication.

✦ If you are trying to use an AutoCAD drawing, copy it to your local hard drive and remove its Read-Only attribute as described in the sidebar, "Changing the windows read-only attribute."

✦ There is no way to install the CD-ROM as a whole; you can only install individual software applications on the CD-ROM. For AutoLISP and VBA software, see information under the section, "Using the software folder."

If you still have trouble with the CD, please call the Customer Care phone number: (800) 762-2974. Outside the United States, call 1 (317) 572-3994. You can also contact Customer Service by e-mail at techsupdum@wiley.com. Wiley Publishing, Inc. will provide technical support only for installation and other general quality control items; for technical support on the applications themselves, consult the program's vendor or author.

✦ ✦ ✦

Index

Continued

Continued

Continued

Continued

Continued

Continued

Continued

Continued

Wiley Publishing, Inc.
End-User License Agreement

READ THIS. You should carefully read these terms and conditions before opening the software packet(s) included with this book "Book." This is a license agreement "Agreement" between you and Wiley Publishing, Inc. "WPI". By opening the accompanying software packet(s), you acknowledge that you have read and accept the following terms and conditions. If you do not agree and do not want to be bound by such terms and conditions, promptly return the Book and the unopened software packet(s) to the place you obtained them for a full refund.

1. **License Grant.** WPI grants to you (either an individual or entity) a nonexclusive license to use one copy of the enclosed software program(s) (collectively, the "Software," solely for your own personal or business purposes on a single computer (whether a standard computer or a workstation component of a multi-user network). The Software is in use on a computer when it is loaded into temporary memory (RAM) or installed into permanent memory (hard disk, CD-ROM, or other storage device). WPI reserves all rights not expressly granted herein.

2. **Ownership.** WPI is the owner of all right, title, and interest, including copyright, in and to the compilation of the Software recorded on the disk(s) or CD-ROM "Software Media." Copyright to the individual programs recorded on the Software Media is owned by the author or other authorized copyright owner of each program. Ownership of the Software and all proprietary rights relating thereto remain with WPI and its licensers.

3. **Restrictions on Use and Transfer.**

 (a) You may only (i) make one copy of the Software for backup or archival purposes, or (ii) transfer the Software to a single hard disk, provided that you keep the original for backup or archival purposes. You may not (i) rent or lease the Software, (ii) copy or reproduce the Software through a LAN or other network system or through any computer subscriber system or bulletin-board system, or (iii) modify, adapt, or create derivative works based on the Software.

 (b) You may not reverse engineer, decompile, or disassemble the Software. You may transfer the Software and user documentation on a permanent basis, provided that the transferee agrees to accept the terms and conditions of this Agreement and you retain no copies. If the Software is an update or has been updated, any transfer must include the most recent update and all prior versions.

4. **Restrictions on Use of Individual Programs.** You must follow the individual requirements and restrictions detailed for each individual program in the About the CD-ROM appendix of this Book. These limitations are also contained in the individual license agreements recorded on the Software Media. These limitations may include a requirement that after using the program for a specified period of time, the user must pay a registration fee or discontinue use. By opening the Software packet(s), you will be agreeing to abide by the licenses and restrictions for these individual programs that are detailed in the About the CD-ROM appendix and on the Software Media. None of the material on this Software Media or listed in this Book may ever be redistributed, in original or modified form, for commercial purposes.

5. Limited Warranty.

(a) WPI warrants that the Software and Software Media are free from defects in materials and workmanship under normal use for a period of sixty (60) days from the date of purchase of this Book. If WPI receives notification within the warranty period of defects in materials or workmanship, WPI will replace the defective Software Media.

(b) WPI AND THE AUTHOR OF THE BOOK DISCLAIM ALL OTHER WARRANTIES, EXPRESS OR IMPLIED, INCLUDING WITHOUT LIMITATION IMPLIED WARRANTIES OF MERCHANTABILITY AND FITNESS FOR A PARTICULAR PURPOSE, WITH RESPECT TO THE SOFTWARE, THE PROGRAMS, THE SOURCE CODE CONTAINED THEREIN, AND/OR THE TECHNIQUES DESCRIBED IN THIS BOOK. WPI DOES NOT WARRANT THAT THE FUNCTIONS CONTAINED IN THE SOFTWARE WILL MEET YOUR REQUIREMENTS OR THAT THE OPERATION OF THE SOFTWARE WILL BE ERROR-FREE.

(c) This limited warranty gives you specific legal rights, and you may have other rights that vary from jurisdiction to jurisdiction.

6. Remedies.

(a) WPI's entire liability and your exclusive remedy for defects in materials and workmanship shall be limited to replacement of the Software Media, which may be returned to WPI with a copy of your receipt at the following address: Software Media Fulfillment Department, Attn.: *AutoCAD 2004 Bible,* Wiley Publishing, Inc., 10475 Crosspoint Blvd., Indianapolis, IN 46256, or call 1-800-762-2974. Please allow four to six weeks for delivery. This Limited Warranty is void if failure of the Software Media has resulted from accident, abuse, or misapplication. Any replacement Software Media will be warranted for the remainder of the original warranty period or thirty (30) days, whichever is longer.

(b) In no event shall WPI or the author be liable for any damages whatsoever (including without limitation damages for loss of business profits, business interruption, loss of business information, or any other pecuniary loss) arising from the use of or inability to use the Book or the Software, even if WPI has been advised of the possibility of such damages.

(c) Because some jurisdictions do not allow the exclusion or limitation of liability for consequential or incidental damages, the above limitation or exclusion may not apply to you.

7. U.S. Government Restricted Rights.
Use, duplication, or disclosure of the Software for or on behalf of the United States of America, its agencies and/or instrumentalities "U.S. Government" is subject to restrictions as stated in paragraph (c)(1)(ii) of the Rights in Technical Data and Computer Software clause of DFARS 252.227-7013, or subparagraphs (c) (1) and (2) of the Commercial Computer Software - Restricted Rights clause at FAR 52.227-19, and in similar clauses in the NASA FAR supplement, as applicable.

8. General.
This Agreement constitutes the entire understanding of the parties and revokes and supersedes all prior agreements, oral or written, between them and may not be modified or amended except in a writing signed by both parties hereto that specifically refers to this Agreement. This Agreement shall take precedence over any other documents that may be in conflict herewith. If any one or more provisions contained in this Agreement are held by any court or tribunal to be invalid, illegal, or otherwise unenforceable, each and every other provision shall remain in full force and effect.